# THE
# OXFORD-DUDEN
# PICTORIAL
# SPANISH-ENGLISH
# DICTIONARY

# THE
# OXFORD-DUDEN
# PICTORIAL
# SPANISH-ENGLISH
# DICTIONARY

CLARENDON PRESS · OXFORD

1985

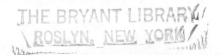

Oxford University Press, Walton Street, Oxford OX2 6DP
Oxford   New York   Toronto
Delhi   Bombay   Calcutta   Madras   Karachi
Kuala Lumpur   Singapore   Hong Kong   Tokyo
Nairobi   Dar es Salaam   Cape Town
Melbourne   Auckland
and associated companies in
Beirut   Berlin   Ibadan   Nicosia

Oxford is a trade mark of Oxford University Press

Published in the United States
by Oxford University Press, New York

British Library Cataloguing in Publication Data
The Oxford-Duden pictorial Spanish-English dictionary.
1.   Spanish language – Dictionaries – English
2.   English language – Dictionaries – Spanish
463'.21        PC4640
ISBN 0-19-864158-3

Library of Congress Cataloging-in-Publication Data
Main entry under title:
The Oxford-Duden pictorial Spanish-English dictionary.

Includes index.
1. Picture dictionaries, Spanish.
2. Picture dictionaries, English.
3. Spanish language – Glossaries, vocabularies, etc.
4. English language – Glossaries, vovabularies, etc.
PC4629.094 1986        463'.21        85-24365
ISBN 0-19-864158-3

Spanish text edited by Manuel Alvar Ezquerra, with
the assistance of María Aurora Miró Domínguez,
Marta C. Ayala Castro, María José Blanco Rodríguez,
Inmaculada Anaya Revuelta, Antonio Ruiz Noguera

English text edited by John Pheby, with the
assistance of Roland Breitsprecher, Michael Clark,
Judith Cunningham, Derek Jordan, and Werner
Scholze-Stubenrecht

Illustrations by Jochen Schmidt, Mannheim

Printed in Germany by Klambt-Druck GmbH, Speyer

# Prólogo

El diccionario en imágenes inglés y español se ha preparado a partir de la nueva versión del *Bildwörterbuch,* volumen tercero del diccionario Duden en diez tomos. La versión española es equivalente del original alemán, a pesar de las dificultades surgidas en más de una ocasión, pues el mundo que se nos presenta en las ilustraciones no es el español o hispanoamericano, sino el centroeuropeo: algunos objetos no existen en nuestro ámbito, o no hay otro semejante. Sin embargo, estos casos son los menos, y por ello mismo los diferenciadores; el resto es propio de nuestra cultura, de nuestra industria, de nuestras técnicas, esto es, común a todos nosotros, alemanes, ingleses e hispanohablantes. Por otra parte, hemos intentado dar cabida al mundo americano a través de la única vía posible, el léxico peculiar utilizado en ámbitos más o menos extensos de aquel continente y que se pudiera aplicar a imágenes surgidas en Alemania -ni siquiera en España.

La traducción se ha realizado bajo mi dirección por licenciados en filología hispánica y por especialistas con conocimientos sobrados para efectuar la tarea encomendada. El peso mayor del trabajo lo han soportado D. Antonio Ruiz Noguera (profesor agregado de Lengua Española de INB), Da. María José Blanco Rodríguez (becaria de investigación del Departamento de Lengua Española de la Universidad de Málaga), Da. María Aurora Miró Domínguez (profesora ayudante del Departamento de Historia del Arte de la Universidad de Málaga) y Da. Inmaculada Anaya Revuelta (becaria de investigación del Departamento de Geografía Lingüística del CSIC). Hemos tenido numerosos colaboradores e informantes ocasionales, comerciantes, artesanos, profesionales diversos que nos han facilitado valiosos datos, muchas veces sin saberlo ellos mismos; quienes más ayuda nos han prestado han sido D. Carlos Alvar (catedrático de Literaturas Románicas de la Universidad de Murcia), D. Conrado Salmerón Rodríguez (tecnólogo de automoción del Instituto de Formación Profesional de Tarifa, Cádiz), Da. María del Pilar Nuño Álvarez (profesora ayudante del Departamento de Lengua Española de la Universidad Complutense), Da. María del Pilar Palanco Aguado (profesora agregada de Lengua Española de INB), Da. Marta C. Ayala Castro (profesora ayudante del Departamento de Lengua Española de la Universidad de Málaga), y D. Jorge Denis Zambrana (librero). He de dejar constancia, también, de la generosa ayuda prestada en todo momento por el Departamento de Geografía Lingüística del Consejo Superior de Investigaciones Científicas, y por la Oficina de Información y Observación del Español del Instituto de Cooperación Iberoamericana.

Las imágenes proporcionan cierta información con mayor facilidad y rapidez que las explicaciones y descripciones. Una imagen permite a menudo identificar antes el objeto designado por una palabra que la definición de esa palabra; es bien sabido aquello de „una imagen vale más que mil palabras".

Cada doble página del diccionario tiene una lámina que ilustra el vocabulario de un dominio completo con los términos ingleses y sus correspondientes españoles. La organización temática evita la enojosa búsqueda de las distintas voces proporcionando en dos páginas enfrentadas toda la información concerniente a un dominio completo. La presentación del texto y el índice final permiten utilizar esta obra como si se tratara de un diccionario bilingüe de doble entrada. Pero que nadie se llame a engaño, éste no es un diccionario ideológico, sino temático, y por tanto más restringido, al serle imposible dar cuenta de aquellas palabras cuyo contenido no su puede expresar en forma de imágenes. La temática es, tal vez, la manera más antigua de organizar los saberes del hombre; arranca de los enciclopedistas medievales y llega hasta nuestros días, habiendo tenido entre nosotros cultivadores tan insignes como San Isidoro, Lorenzo Palmireno, Francisco Sobrino o el P. Esteban de Terreros.

La forma de presentar los materiales, y la modernidad de la obra, hacen que el vocabulario esté constituido en gran medida por términos especiales y técnicos, de modo que este diccionario se convierte, así, en el complemento indispensable de cualquier diccionario bilingüe español-inglés e inglés-español. Al mismo tiempo, la presencia del vocabulario científico y técnico impide la aparición de voces de ámbitos geográficos restringidos; es el precio que tiene que pagar la riqueza de la lengua en aras de la comprensión general.

Por último, si un diccionario debe ser un instrumento, una herramienta para conocer el mundo que nos rodea, éste lo es sobradamente. Y cumple con generosidad con la misión didáctica que encierra todo diccionario: no sólo nos presenta el mundo de una manera organizada, sino que nos enseña a nombrarlo en varias lenguas. Es una obra que no sólo aprovechará a los adultos, sino que, utilizada adecuadamente, servirá a los más jóvenes para conocer la realidad y para aprender idiomas, esto es, le permitirá entender y ser entendido por los demás, en su lengua y en otra. ¿Cabe esperar nada mejor de un diccionario?

Manuel Alvar Ezquerra

# Foreword

This Spanish-English pictorial dictionary is based on the third, completely revised edition of the German *Bildwörterbuch* published as Volume 3 of the ten-volume Duden series of monolingual German dictionaries. An attempt has been made to include American Spanish by giving also the vocabulary used in various parts of Latin America.

The Spanish translation has been prepared under the supervision of Professor Manuel Alvar Ezquerra by graduates in Spanish, with the assistance of various experts having the appropriate subject knowledge. The greater part of the work has been done by Don Antonio Ruiz Noguera (associate professor of Spanish language at INB), Doña María José Blanco Rodríguez (research fellow in the Spanish language department, University of Málaga), Doña María Aurora Miró Domínguez (assistant professor in the history of art department, University of Málaga), and Doña Inmaculada Anaya Revuelta (research fellow in the linguistic geography department, Conseja Superior de Investigaciones Científicas).

There have been many who assisted and gave occasional information – business people, craftsmen, professional people who provided valuable information, often unconsciously; the greatest amount of help has come from Don Carlos Alvar (professor of Romance literature, University of Murcia), Don Conrado Salmerón Rodríguez (automotive engineer, Instituto de Formación Profesional, Tarifa, Cádiz), Doña María del Pilar Nuño Álvarez (assistant professor in the Spanish language department, Universidad Complutense, Madrid), Doña María del Pilar Palanco Aguado (associate professor of Spanish language at INB), Doña Marta C. Ayala Castro (assistant professor in the Spanish language department, University of Málaga), and Don Jorge Denis Zambrana (bookseller). Generous help was also received at all times from the linguistic geography department of the Consejo Superior de Investigaciones Científicas, and from the Spanish language information and observation office of the Instituto de Cooperación Iberoamericana.

The English text was produced by the Oxford University Press Dictionary Department, with the assistance of numerous British companies, institutions and technical experts.

There are certain kinds of information which can be conveyed more readily and clearly by pictures than by descriptions and explanations, and an illustration will support the simple translation by helping the reader to visualize the object denoted by a given word. This applies both to technical vocabulary sought by the layman and to everyday objects foreign to the general user.

Each double page contains a plate illustrating the vocabulary of a whole subject, together with the exact Spanish names and their correct English equivalents. The arrangement of the text and the presence of alphabetical indexes in Spanish and English allow the dictionary to be used either way: as a Spanish-English or an English-Spanish dictionary. This, together with the wide range of vocabulary, which includes a large proportion of specialized words and technical terms, makes the Oxford-Duden Pictorial Dictionary an indispensable supplement to any Spanish-English or English-Spanish dictionary.

# Abreviaturas empleadas en el texto español

| | | | |
|---|---|---|---|
| *amb.* | ambivalente | *Hond.* | Honduras |
| *Amér.* | América | *m* | masculino |
| *Amér. Merid.* | América Meridional | *Mé.* | Méjico |
| *anál.* | análogo | *Nicar.* | Nicaragua |
| *angl.* | anglicismo | *Pan.* | Panamá |
| *ant.* | anticuado | *Par.* | Paraguay |
| *Arg.* | Argentina | *p. e.* | por ejemplo |
| *Bol.* | Bolivia | *pop.* | lenguaje popular |
| *col.* | lenguaje coloquial | *P. Rico* | Puerto Rico |
| *Col.* | Colombia | *Salv.* | El Salvador |
| *C. Rica* | Costa Rica | *S. Dgo.* | República Dominicana |
| *Ec.* | Ecuador | *sin.* | sinónimo |
| *f* | femenino | *Urug.* | Uruguay |
| *fam.* | lenguaje familiar | *var.* | variedades |
| *Filip.* | Filipinas | *Venez.* | Venezuela |
| *Guat.* | Guatemala | | |

# Abbreviations used in the English text

| | |
|---|---|
| Am. | *American usage* |
| c. | *castrated (animal)* |
| coll. | *colloquial* |
| f. | *female (animal)* |
| form. | *formerly* |
| joc. | *jocular* |
| m. | *male (animal)* |
| poet. | *poetic* |
| sg. | *singular* |
| sim. | *similar* |
| y. | *young (animal)* |

# Índice

*Los números arábigos son los de la lámina*

# Contents

*The arabic numerals are the numbers of the pictures*

# Índice

# Contents

# Índice                                                    *Contents*

# Índice

*Contents*

# Índice

# Contents

# Índice
# Contents

# Índice

# Contents

**1-8 modelos *m* atómicos**
- *atom models*
1 el modelo del átomo de hidrógeno *m* (H)
- *model of the hydrogen (H) atom*
2 el núcleo atómico, un protón
- *atomic nucleus, a proton*
3 el electrón
- *electron*
4 el espín del electrón (el giro del electrón)
- *electron spin*
5 el modelo del átomo de helio *m* (He)
- *model of the helium (He) atom*
6 la órbita del electrón
- *electron shell*
7 el principio de Pauli (principio *m* de exclusión *f* de Pauli)
- *Pauli exclusion principle (exclusion principle, Pauli principle)*
8 las órbitas estacionarias del electrón del átomo Na (átomo *m* de sodio *m*)
- *complete electron shell of the Na atom (sodium atom)*
**9-14 las estructuras moleculares** (las estructuras cristalinas)
- *molecular structures*
9 el cristal de cloruro *m* de sodio *m* (la sal común)
- *crystal of sodium chloride (of common salt)*
10 el ion de cloruro *m*
- *chlorine ion*
11 el ion de sodio *m*
- *sodium ion*
12 el cristal de cristobalita *f*
- *crystal of cristobalite*
13 el átomo de oxígeno *m*
- *oxygen atom*
14 el átomo de silicio *m*
- *silicon atom*
15 **los niveles de energía *f*** (los saltos *m* cuánticos posibles) del átomo de hidrógeno *m*
- *energy levels (possible quantum jumps) of the hydrogen atom*
16 el núcleo atómico (el protón)
- *atomic nucleus (proton)*
17 el electrón
- *electron*
18 el estado fundamental
- *ground state level*
19 el estado excitado
- *excited state*
**20-25 los saltos cuánticos**
- *quantum jumps (quantum transitions)*
20 la serie de Lyman
- *Lyman series*
21 la serie de Balmer
- *Balmer series*
22 la serie de Paschen
- *Paschen series*
23 la serie de Bracket
- *Brackett series*

24 la serie de Pfund
- *Pfund series*
25 el electrón libre
- *free electron*
26 el modelo atómico Bohr-Sommerfeld del átomo de H
- *Bohr-Sommerfeld model of the H atom*
27 los niveles enérgicos del electrón
- *energy levels of the electron*
28 **la desintegración espontánea** de una materia radioactiva
- *spontaneous decay of radioactive material*
29 el núcleo atómico
- *atomic nucleus*
**30-31 la partícula alfa (α, la radiación alfa, el núcleo de helio *m*)**
- *alpha (α) particle (alpha ray, helium nucleus)*
30 el neutrón
- *neutron*
31 el protón
- *proton*
32 la partícula beta (β, la radiación beta, el electrón)
- *beta (β) particle (beta ray, electron)*
33 la radiación gamma (γ, una radiación Roentgen dura)
- *gamma (γ) ray, a hard X-ray*
34 **la fisión nuclear**
- *nuclear fission*
35 el núcleo *m* atómico pesado
- *heavy atomic nucleus*
36 el bombardeo neutrónico
- *neutron bombardment*
**37-38 los fragmentos de fisión *f***
- *fission fragments*
39 el neutrón liberado
- *released neutron*
40 la radiación gamma (γ)
- *gamma (γ) ray*
41 **la reacción en cadena *f***
- *chain reaction*
42 el neutrón de incidencia *m* [el neutrón que desintegra el núcleo atómico]
- *incident neutron*
43 el núcleo antes de la fisión
- *nucleus prior to fission*
44 el fragmento de fisión *f*
- *fission fragment*
45 el neutrón liberado
- *released neutron*
46 la fisión repetida (la fisión nuclear nueva)
- *repeated fission*
47 el fragmento de fisión *f*
- *fission fragment*
48 **la reacción en cadena *f* controlada en un reactor atómico**
- *controlled chain reaction in a nuclear reactor*

49 el núcleo atómico de un elemento fisionable
- *atomic nucleus of a fissionable element*
50 el bombardeo por un neutrón
- *neutron bombardment*
51 el fragmento de fisión *f* (núcleo *m* atómico nuevo)
- *fission fragment, a new atomic nucleus*
52 el neutrón liberado
- *released neutron*
53 los neutrones absorbidos
- *absorbed neutrons*
54 el moderador, una capa amortiguadora de grafito *m*
- *moderator, a retarding layer of graphite*
55 la liberación de calor *m* (la producción de energía *f*)
- *extraction of heat (production of energy)*
56 la radiación Roentgen (los rayos X)
- *X-ray*
57 la cubierta del reactor de hormigón *m* y plomo *m*
- *concrete and lead shield*
58 **la cámara de burbujas *f*** para mostrar la trayectoria de las partículas ionizadas con alta energía *f*
- *bubble chamber for showing the tracks of high-energy ionizing particles*
59 la fuente de luz *f*
- *light source*
60 la cámara fotográfica
- *camera*
61 la línea de expansión *f*
- *expansion line*
62 la trayectoria de los rayos de luz *f*
- *path of light rays*
63 el imán
- *magnet*
64 el punto de entrada del rayo (de luz *f*)
- *beam entry point*
65 el reflector
- *reflector*
66 la cámara
- *chamber*

**1-23  los detectores de irradiación** f (los contadores de irradiación)
– *radiation detectors (radiation meters)*
1  el monitor de irradiación f
– *radiation monitor*
2  la cámara de ionización f
– *ionization chamber (ion chamber)*
3  el electrodo central
– *central electrode*
4  el selector de alcance m regulable
– *measurement range selector*
5  el alojamiento (la caja) de los instrumentos
– *instrument housing*
6  el medidor
– *meter*
7  el ajuste en cero m (el botón de puesta en cero m)
– *zero adjustment*
**8-23  los dosímetros**
– *dosimeter (dosemeter)*
8  el dosímetro de película f
– *film dosimeter*
9  el filtro
– *filter*
10  la película
– *film*
11  el dosímetro anular de película f
– *film-ring dosimeter*
12  el filtro
– *filter*
13  la película
– *film*
14  la cubierta con filtro m
– *cover with filter*
15  el medidor de bolsillo m (el medidor de pluma f, la cámara de bolsillo m)
– *pocket meter (pen meter, pocket chamber)*
16  el visor
– *window*
17  la cámara de ionización f
– *ionization chamber (ion chamber)*
18  el sujetador (el clip de la pluma)
– *clip (pen clip)*
19  el contador Geiger
– *Geiger counter (Geiger-Müller counter)*
20  la cubierta del tubo contador m
– *counter tube casing*
21  el tubo contador m
– *counter tube*
22  la caja de los instrumentos
– *instrument housing*
23  el selector de alcance m regulable
– *measurement range selector*

24  la cámara de niebla f de Wilson (la cámara de condensación f)
– *Wilson cloud chamber (Wilson chamber)*
25  la plancha de compresión f
– *compression plate*
26  la fotografía de la cámara de Wilson
– *cloud chamber photograph*
27  la estela en la cámara de Wilson (estela f de ionización f) de una partícula alfa
– *cloud chamber track of an alpha particle*
**28  el aparato de telerradiación** f de **cobalto** m *(col.* la bomba de cobalto m)
– *telecobalt unit ( coll. cobalt bomb)*
29  la columna de soporte m
– *pillar stand*
30  los cables de apoyo m
– *support cables*
31  el escudo protector de la radiación
– *radiation shield (radiation shielding)*
32  el escudo de corredera f
– *sliding shield*
33  el diafragma laminar
– *bladed diaphragm*
34  el visor luminoso
– *light-beam positioning device*
35  el dispositivo pendular (el péndulo)
– *pendulum device (pendulum)*
36  la mesa de irradiación f (la mesa de radioterapia f)
– *irradiation table*
37  la corredera
– *rail (track)*
**38  el manipulador de bolas** f (el manipulador)
– *manipulator with sphere unit*
39  el mango
– *handle*
40  el pestillo de seguridad f
– *safety catch (locking lever)*
41  la articulación de bolas f (la rótula)
– *wrist joint*
42  la barra de dirección f
– *master arm*
43  el dispositivo de sujeción f (la abrazadera)
– *clamping device (clamp)*
44  las tenazas
– *tongs*
45  el tablero de ranuras f
– *slotted board*
46  el escudo protector de la irradiación, una pared protectora de plomo m [sección]
– *radiation shield (protective shield, protective shielding), a lead shielding wall [section]*

47  el brazo de sujeción f de un manipulador gemelo (de un manipulador master-slave)
– *grasping arm of a pair of manipulators (of a master/slave manipulator)*
48  el protector del polvo
– *dust shield*
**49  el ciclotrón**
– *cyclotron*
50  la zona de peligro m
– *danger zone*
51  el imán
– *magnet*
52  las bombas para hacer el vacío en la cámara de vacío m
– *pumps for emptying the vacuum chamber*

**1-35 el mapa de las estrellas del cielo septentrional** (el hemisferio norte)
- *star map of the northern sky (northern hemisphere)*
**1-8** la división del cielo
- *divisions of the sky*
**1** el polo celeste con la Estrella Polar (la Polar, la Estrella del Norte)
- *celestial pole with the Pole Star (Polaris, the North Star)*
**2** la eclíptica (órbita *f* aparente anual del sol)
- *ecliptic (apparent annual path of the sun)*
**3** el ecuador celeste (la línea equinoccial)
- *celestial equator (equinoctial line)*
**4** el trópico de Cáncer
- *tropic of Cancer*
**5** el círculo límite de las estrellas circumpolares
- *circle enclosing circumpolar stars*
**6-7** los puntos equinocciales (los equinoccios)
- *equinoctial points (equinoxes)*
**6** el punto equinoccial de primavera *f* (primer punto *m* de Aries, punto *m* vernal, comienzo *m* de la primavera)
- *vernal equinoctial point (first point of Aries)*
**7** el punto equinoccial de otoño *m* (comienzo *m* del otoño, primer punto *m* de Libra)
- *autumnal equinoctial point*
**8** el solsticio de verano *m* (el solsticio)
- *summer solstice*
**9-48 Constelaciones** *f* (agrupaciones *f* de las estrellas fijas en figuras *f*) **y nombres** *m* **de estrellas** *f*
- *constellations (grouping of fixed stars into figures) and names of stars*
**9** Aquila (el Águila *f*) con la estrella principal Altaír (la estrella brillante)
- *Aquila (the Eagle) with Altair the principal star (the brightest star)*
**10** Pegaso (el Caballo Alado)
- *Pegasus (the Winged Horse)*
**11** Cetus (la Ballena) con Mira, una estrella variable
- *Cetus (the Whale) with Mira, a variable star*
**12** Erídano (el Río Celeste)
- *Eridamus (the Celestial River)*
**13** Orión (el Cazador) con Rigel, Betelgeuse y Bellatrix
- *Orion (the Hunter) with Rigel, Betelgeuse and Bellatrix*
,

**14** Canis Maior (el Can Mayor) con Sirio (la Estrella Perro), una estrella de primera magnitud *f*
- *Canis Major (the Great Dog, the Greater Dog) with Sirius (the Dog Star), a star of the first magnitude*
**15** Canis Minor (el Can Menor) con Porción
- *Canis Minor (the Little Dog, the Lesser Dog) with Procyon*
**16** Hydra (la Hidra, la Culebra de Agua *f*)
- *Hydra (the Water Snake, the Sea Serpent)*
**17** Leo (el León)
- *Leo (the Lion)*
**18** Virgo (la Virgen) con Spica (Espiga)
- *Virgo (the Virgin) with Spica*
**19** Libra (la Balanza)
- *Libra (the Balance, the Scales)*
**20** Serpens (la Serpiente)
- *Serpens (the Serpent)*
**21** Hércules
- *Hercules*
**22** Lyra (la Lira) con Vega
- *Lyra (the Lyre) with Vega*
**23** Cygnus (el Cisne, la Cruz del Norte) con Deneb
- *Cygnus (the Swan, the Northern Cross) with Deneb*
**24** Andrómeda
- *Andromeda*
**25** Taurus (el Toro) con Aldebarán
- *Taurus (the Bull) with Aldebaran*
**26** las Pléyades (las Siete Hermanas), un grupo abierto de estrellas *f*
- *The Pleiades (Pleiads, the Seven Sisters), an open cluster of stars*
**27** Auriga (el Cochero) con Capella (la Cabra)
- *Auriga (the Wagoner, the Charioteer) with Capella*
**28** Gemini (los Gemelos) con Cástor y Pólux
- *Gemini (the Twins) with Castor and Pollux*
**29** Ursa Maior (la Osa Mayor, el Gran Carro) con la estrella doble Mizar y Alcor
- *Ursa Major (the Great Bear, the Greater Bear, the Plough, Charles's Wain, Am. the Big Dipper) with the double star (binary star) Mizar and Alcor*
**30** Bootes (el Boyero) con Arturo
- *Boötes (the Herdsman)*
**31** Corona Boreal (la Corona del Norte)
- *Corona Borealis (the Northern Crown)*
**32** Draco (el Dragón)
- *Draco (the Dragon)*
**33** Casiopea
- *Cassiopeia*

**34** Ursa Minor (la Osa Menor, el Pequeño Carro) con la Estrella Polar
- *Ursa Minor (the Little Bear, Lesser Bear, Am. Little Dipper) with the Pole Star (Polaris, the North Star)*
**35** la Vía Láctea (la Galaxia, el Camino de Santiago)
- *the Milky Way (the Galaxy)*
**36-48 el cielo meridional** (el hemisferio sur *m*)
- *the southern sky*
**36** Capricornus (el Capricornio, la Cabra de Mar)
- *Capricorn (the Goat, the Sea Goat)*
**37** Sagittarius (el Sagitario, el Arquero)
- *Sagittarius (the Archer)*
**38** Scorpius (el Escorpión)
- *Scorpio (the Scorpion)*
**39** Centaurus (el Centauro)
- *Centaurus (the Centaur)*
**40** Triangulum Australe (el Triángulo Austral)
- *Triangulum Australe (the Southern Triangle)*
**41** Pavo (el Pavo Real)
- *Pavo (the Peacock)*
**42** Grus (la Grulla)
- *Grus (the Crane)*
**43** Octans (el Octante)
- *Octans (the Octant)*
**44** Crux (la Cruz del Sur, la Cruz)
- *Crux (the Southern Cross, the Cross)*
**45** Argo (el Navío Argos, el Navío Celeste)
- *Argo (the Celestial Ship)*
**46** Carina (la Quilla)
- *Carina (the Keel)*
**47** Pictor, Machina Pictoris (el Pintor, el Caballete)
- *Pictor (the Painter)*
**48** Reticulum (la Red)
- *Reticulum (the Net)*

**1-9** la Luna
- *the moon*
**1** la trayectoria de la Luna (la órbita de la Luna alrededor de la Tierra)
- *moon's path (moon's orbit round the earth)*
**2-7** las fases lunares (las fases de la Luna, lunación *f*)
- *lunar phases (moon's phases);* also: *lunation*
**2** la Luna nueva
- *new moon*
**3** la creciente de la Luna (la Luna creciente)
- *crescent (crescent moon, waxing moon)*
**4** el primer cuarto (cuarto *m* creciente)
- *half-moon [first quarter]*
**5** la Luna llena
- *full moon*
**6** el último cuarto (cuarto *m* menguante)
- *half-moon [last quarter, third quarter]*
**7** la menguante de la Luna (la Luna menguante)
- *crescent (crescent moon, waning moon)*
**8** la Tierra (el globo terráqueo)
- *the earth (terrestrial globe)*
**9** la dirección de los rayos del Sol
- *direction of the sun's rays*
**10-21** el curso aparente del Sol al comienzo de las estaciones
- *apparent path of the sun at the beginning of the seasons*
**10** el eje celeste
- *celestial axis*
**11** el cénit
- *zenith*
**12** el plano horizontal
- *horizontal plane*
**13** el nadir
- *nadir*
**14** el este
- *east point*
**15** el oeste
- *west point*
**16** el norte
- *north point*
**17** el sur
- *south point*
**18** el curso aparente del Sol el 21 de diciembre
- *apparent path of the sun on 21 December*
**19** el curso aparente del Sol el 21 de marzo y el 23 de septiembre *m*
- *apparent path of the sun on 21 March and 23 September*
**20** el curso aparente del Sol el 21 de junio *m*
- *apparent path of the sun on 21 June*
**21** la orla del área *f* crepuscular (la zona límite del crepúsculo)
- *border of the twilight area*
**22-28** los movimientos de rotación *f* del eje de la Tierra

- *rotary motions of the earth's axis*
**22** el eje de la eclíptica
- *axis of the ecliptic*
**23** la esfera celeste
- *celestial sphere*
**24** el curso del polo celeste (precesión *f* y nutación *f*)
- *path of the celestial pole [precession and nutation]*
**25** el eje instantáneo de rotación *f*
- *instantaneous axis of rotation*
**26** el polo celeste
- *celestial pole*
**27** el eje medio de rotación *f*
- *mean axis of rotation*
**28** la polodía
- *polhode*
**29-35** el eclipse solar y lunar [no precisado a escala]
- *solar and lunar eclipse [not to scale]*
**29** el Sol
- *the sun*
**30** la Tierra
- *the earth*
**31** la Luna
- *the moon*
**32** el eclipse solar
- *solar eclipse*
**33** el área *f* de la Tierra en que el eclipse aparece total
- *area of the earth in which the eclipse appears total*
**34-35** el eclipse lunar
- *lunar eclipse*
**34** la penumbra (la oscuridad parcial)
- *penumbra (partial shadow)*
**35** la sombra (la oscuridad total)
- *umbra (total shadow)*
**36-41** el Sol
- *the sun*
**36** el disco solar (la esfera solar)
- *solar disc (disk) (solar globe, solar sphere)*
**37** las manchas solares
- *sunspots*
**38** los torbellinos del área *f* de las manchas solares
- *cyclones in the area of sunspots*
**39** la corona (la corona solar) observable durante un eclipse total de Sol o por medio de instrumentos *m* especiales
- *corona (solar corona), observable during total solar eclipse or by means of special instruments*
**40** las protuberancias (protuberancias *f* solares)
- *prominences (solar prominences)*
**41** el borde lunar durante un eclipse total de Sol *m*
- *moon's limb during a total solar eclipse*
**42-52** los planetas (el sistema planetario, el sistema solar) [no precisado a escala] y los signos de los planetas (los símbolos de los planetas)

- *planets (planetary system, solar system) [not to scale] and planet symbols*
**42-45** los planetas (el sistema planetario, el sistema solar) [no precisado a escala] y los signos de los planetas (los símbolos de los planetas)
- *planets (planetary system, solar system) [not to scale] and planet symbols*
**42** el Sol
- *the sun*
**43** Mercurio
- *Mercury*
**44** Venus
- *Venus*
**45** la Tierra, con la Luna, un satélite
- *Earth, with the moon, a satellite*
**46** Marte con dos satélites *m*
- *Mars, with two moons (satellites)*
**47** los asteroides (planetas *m* menores)
- *asteroids (minor planets)*
**48** Júpiter con catorce satélites *m*
- *Jupiter, with 14 moons (satellites)*
**49** Saturno con diez satélites *m*
- *Saturn, with 10 moons (satellites)*
**50** Urano con cinco satélites *m*
- *Uranus, with five moons (satellites)*
**51** Neptuno con dos satélites *m*
- *Neptune, with two moons (satellites)*
**52** Plutón
- *Pluto*
**53-64** los signos del Zodiaco (los símbolos del Zodiaco)
- *signs of the zodiac (zodiacal signs)*
**53** Aries (el Carnero)
- *Aries (the Ram)*
**54** Tauro (el Toro)
- *Taurus (the Bull)*
**55** Gemini (los Gemelos)
- *Gemini (the Twins)*
**56** Cancer (el Cangrejo)
- *Cancer (the Crab)*
**57** Leo (el León)
- *Leo (the Lion)*
**58** Virgo (la Virgen)
- *Virgo (the Virgin)*
**59** Libra (la Balanza)
- *Libra (the Balance, the Scales)*
**60** Scorpio (el Escorpión)
- *Scorpio (the Scorpion)*
**61** Sagitario (el Arquero)
- *Sagittarius (the Archer)*
**62** Capricornio (la Cabra, la Cabra de Mar)
- *Capricorn (the Goat, the Sea Goat)*
**63** Acuario (el Aguador)
- *Aquarius (the Water Carrier, the Water Bearer)*
**64** Piscis (los Peces)
- *Pisces (the Fish)*

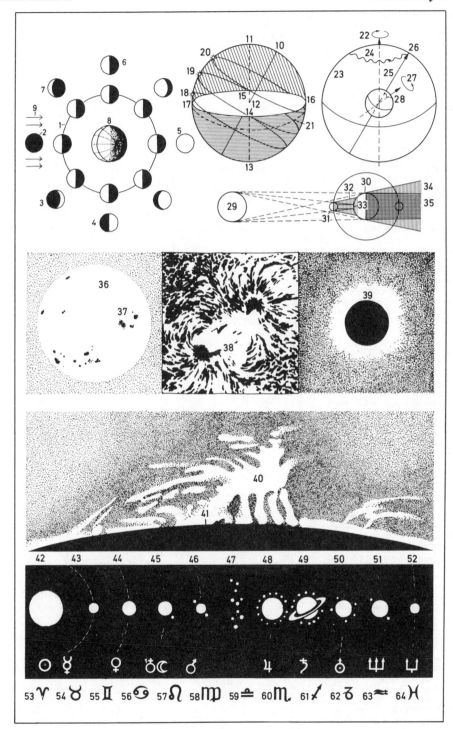

# 5 Astronomía III

1-16 el observatorio meridional europeo (ESO) de La Silla (Chile), un observatorio [sección]
- *the European Southern Observatory (ESO) on* Cerro la Silla, Chile, *an observatory [section]*
1 el espejo principal con un diámetro de 3,6 m
- *primary mirror (main mirror) with a diameter of 3.6 m (144 inches)*
2 el objetivo primario con montaje *m* para los espejos secundarios
- *prime focus cage with mounting for secondary mirrors*
3 el espejo plano para la observación de la trayectoria de los rayos coudé
- *flat mirror for the coudé ray path*
4 la cabina Cassegrain
- *Cassegrain cage*
5 el espectrógrafo de rejilla *f*
- *grating spectrograph*
6 la cámara espectrográfica
- *spectrographic camera*
7 el mecanismo de transmisión *f* del eje horario
- *hour axis drive*
8 el eje horario
- *hour axis*
9 el montaje de herradura *f*
- *horseshoe mounting*
10 el soporte hidráulico
- *hydrostatic bearing*
11 los dispositivos de enfoque *m* primario y secundario
- *primary and secondary focusing devices*
12 la cúpula del observatorio (la cúpula giratoria)
- *observatory dome, a revolving dome*
13 la abertura de observación *f*
- *observation opening*
14 la contraventana vertical de la cúpula movible
- *vertically movable dome shutter*
15 la pantalla enrollada (el biombo)
- *wind screen*
16 el sideroestato
- *siderostat*
17-28 el planetarium de Stuttgart [sección]
- *the* Stuttgart *Planetarium [section]*
17 la administración, los talleres y los almacenes
- *administration, workshop, and store area*
18 el andamio de acero *m*
- *steel scaffold*
19 la pirámide de vidrio *m*
- *glass pyramid*
20 la escalera giratoria abovedada
- *revolving arched ladder*

21 la cúpula de proyección *f*
- *projection dome*
22 el obturador de la luz (el diafragma)
- *light stop*
23 el proyector planetario
- *planetarium projector*
24 el pozo
- *well*
25 el vestíbulo
- *foyer*
26 la sala de proyección *f*
- *theatre* (Am. *theater)*
27 la cabina de proyección *f*
- *projection booth*
28 el pilar del cimiento
- *foundation pile*
29-33 el observatorio solar Kitt Peak de Tucson (Arizona) [sección]
- *the* Kitt Peak *solar observatory near* Tucson, Ariz. *[section]*
29 el helioestato
- *heliostat*
30 el pozo de observación *f* semisubterráneo
- *sunken observation shaft*
31 el escudo protector refrigerado por agua *f*
- *water-cooled windshield*
32 el espejo cóncavo
- *concave mirror*
33 la sala de observación *f*, alojamiento *m* del espectrógrafo
- *observation room housing the spectrograph*

1 la nave espacial Apolo
- *Apollo spacecraft*
2 el módulo de servicio *m* (Service Module SM)
- *service module (SM)*
3 la tobera del propulsor principal
- *nozzle of the main rocket engine*
4 la antena direccional
- *directional antenna*
5 los cohetes de maniobra *f* (de pilotaje *m*)
- *manoeuvring (Am. maneuvering) rockets*
6 los tanques de oxígeno *m* e hidrógeno *m* para el sistema de energía *f* de la nave espacial
- *oxygen and hydrogen tanks for the spacecraft's energy system*
7 el depósito de combustible *m*
- *fuel tank*
8 los radiadores del sistema de energía *f* de la nave espacial
- *radiators of the spacecraft's energy system*
9 el módulo de mando *m* (la cápsula espacial Apolo)
- *command module; here: Apollo space capsule*
10 la escotilla de entrada *f* a la cápsula espacial
- *entry hatch of the space capsule*
11 el astronauta
- *astronaut*
12 el módulo lunar
- *lunar module (LM)*
13 la superficie lunar, una superficie de polvo *m*
- *moon's surface (lunar surface), a dust-covered surface*
14 el polvo lunar
- *lunar dust*
15 el trozo de roca *f* (la roca lunar)
- *piece of rock*
16 el cráter de un meteorito
- *meteorite crater*
17 la Tierra
- *the earth*

18-27 el traje espacial
- *space suit (extra-vehicular suit)*
18 el aparato con el oxígeno de emergencia *f* (la reserva de oxígeno *m*)
- *emergency oxygen apparatus*
19 el bolsillo de las gafas de sol *m* de a bordo *m*
- *sunglass pocket [with sunglasses for use on board]*
20 el equipamiento autónomo de supervivencia *f*, un aparato portátil
- *life support system (life support pack), a backpack unit*
21 la válvula de acceso *m*
- *access flap*
22 el casco del traje espacial con filtros *m* solares
- *space suit helmet with sun filters*
23 la caja de control *m* del equipo de supervivencia *f*
- *control box of the life support pack*
24 el bolsillo para la linterna
- *penlight pocket*
25 la trampilla de acceso *m* a la válvula de limpieza *f*
- *access flap for the purge valve*
26 las conexiones de los cables para la radio y de los tubos de los sistemas de ventilación *f* y refrigeración *f*
- *tube and cable connections for the radio, ventilation, and water-cooling systems*
27 el bolsillo para los lápices, los utensilios, etc.
- *pocket for pens, tools, etc.*
28-36 el piso de bajada *f*
- *descent stage*
28 el conector
- *connector*
29 el depósito de combustible *m*
- *fuel tank*
30 el motor (el propulsor)
- *engine*
31 el mecanismo de despliegue *m* del sistema de alunizaje *m*
- *mechanism for unfolding the legs*
32 el amortiguador principal
- *main shock absorber*

33 la almohadilla de alunizaje *m*
- *landing pad*
34 la plataforma de acceso *m*
- *ingress/egress platform (hatch platform)*
35 la escalera de la plataforma y de la escotilla (la escalera de acceso *m*)
- *ladder to platform and hatch*
36 el cardán del propulsor
- *cardan mount for engine*
37-47 el piso de subida *f*
- *ascent stage*
37 el depósito de combustible *m*
- *fuel tank*
38 la escotilla de entrada *f* y de salida *f* (la escotilla de acceso *m*)
- *ingress/egress hatch (entry/exit hatch)*
39 los cohetes de maniobra *f* del módulo lunar (ML)
- *LM manoeuvring (Am. maneuvering) rockets*
40 la ventanilla
- *window*
41 la cabina de la tripulación
- *crew compartment*
42 la antena del radar de acoplamiento *m*
- *rendezvous radar antenna*
43 la unidad de medición *f* de la inercia (la central de la inercia)
- *inertial measurement unit*
44 la antena direccional para el control con la estación de tierra *f*
- *directional antenna for ground control*
45 la escotilla superior
- *upper hatch (docking hatch)*
46 la antena de vuelo *m*
- *inflight antenna*
47 el sistema activo de anclaje *m*
- *docking target recess*

**1 la troposfera**
- *the troposphere*
**2** los nubarrones
- *thunderclouds*
**3** la montaña más alta del mundo, el monte Everest [8 882 m.] *f*
- *the highest mountain,* Mount Everest *[8,882 m]*
**4** el arco iris
- *rainbow*
**5** la capa de las corrientes chorro (jets-stream *m*)
- *jet stream level*
**6** el nivel cero (la inversión de los movimientos verticales del aire)
- *zero level [inversion of vertical air movement]*
**7** la capa del suelo (la capa límite de la superficie exterior)
- *ground layer (surface boundary layer)*
**8 la estratosfera**
- *the stratosphere*
**9** la tropopausa
- *tropopause*
**10** la capa de separación *f* (la capa de movimientos *m* débiles del aire)
- *separating layer [layer of weaker air movement]*
**11** la explosión atómica
- *atomic explosion*
**12** la explosión de la bomba de hidrógeno *m*
- *hydrogen bomb explosion*
**13** la capa de ozono *m*
- *ozone layer*

**14** el radio de propagación *f* de las ondas sonoras
- *range of sound wave propagation*
**15** el avión estratosférico
- *stratosphere aircraft*
**16** el globo pilotado
- *manned balloon*
**17** el globo sonda
- *sounding balloon*
**18** el meteorito
- *meteor*
**19** el límite superior de la capa de ozono *m*
- *upper limit of ozone layer*
**20** el nivel cero
- *zero level*
**21** la explosión del Krakatoa
- *eruption of Krakatoa*
**22** las nubes luminosas (nubes *f* nocturnas luminosas)
- *luminous clouds (noctilucent clouds)*
**23 la ionosfera**
- *the ionosphere*
**24** el radio de exploración *f* de los cohetes
- *range of research rockets*
**25** la estrella fugaz
- *shooting star*
**26** la onda corta (alta frecuencia *f*)
- *short wave, a high frequency wave*
**27** la capa E
- *E-layer (Heaviside-Kennelly Layer)*
**28** la capa F₁
- *F₁-layer*
**29** la capa F₂
- *F₂-layer*

**30** la aurora boreal (la luz polar)
- *aurora (polar light)*
**31 la exosfera**
- *the exosphere*
**32** la capa atómica
- *atom layer*
**33** el radio de exploración de los satélites
- *range of satellite sounding*
**34** el margen de la zona (el paso hacia la zona interestelar)
- *fringe region*
**35** la escala de altitud *f*
- *altitude scale*
**36** la escala de las temperaturas
- *temperature scale (thermometric scale)*
**37** la gráfica de las temperaturas (curva *f* de las temperaturas)
- *temperature graph*

**1-19 las nubes** y el tiempo
- *clouds and weather*
**1-4 las nubes de masas *f* de aire *m*
homogéneas**
- *clouds found in homogeneous*
  *air masses*
**1** el cúmulo (cumulus, cumulus
humilis), una nube fluida
(conjunto *m* de nubes *f* bajas,
nubes *f* de buen tiempo *m*)
- *cumulus (woolpack cloud), a*
  *heap cloud;* here: *cumulus*
  *humilis (fair-weather cumulus),*
  *a flat-based heap cloud*
**2** el cumulus congestus, un
conjunto de nubes *f* muy
fluidas
- *cumulus congestus, a heap cloud*
  *with more marked vertical*
  *development*
**3** el estratocúmulo, una serie de
nubes *f* bajas y en capas *f*
- *stratocumulus, a layer cloud*
  *(sheet cloud) arranged in heavy*
  *masses*
**4** el estrato (la niebla alta) una
capa de nubes *f* espesas y
homogéneas
- *stratus (high fog), a thick,*
  *uniform layer cloud (sheet*
  *cloud)*
**5-12 las nubes da los frentes
cálidos**
- *clouds found at warm fronts*
**5** el frente cálido
- *warm front*
**6** el cirro (cirrus), una nube alta
o muy alta de cristales *f* de
hielo *m* delgados, con formas *f*
muy diversas
- *cirrus, a high to very high ice-*
  *crystal cloud, thin and assuming*
  *a wide variety of forms*
**7** el cirroestrato, una nube de
cristales *f* de hielo *m* en
forma *f* de velo *m*
- *cirrostratus, an ice-crystal cloud*
  *veil*
**8** el altoestrato, una capa de
nubes *f* de altura *f* media
- *altostratus, a layer cloud (sheet*
  *cloud) of medium height*
**9** el altoestrato precipitante, una
nube en capas *f* con precipitaciones *f* en la parte superior
- *altostratus praecipitans, a layer*
  *cloud (sheet cloud) with*
  *precipitation in its upper parts*
**10** el nimboestrato, una nube de
lluvia *f*, nube *f* de formación *f*
vertical muy marcada de la que
caen precipitaciones *f*, lluvia *f*
o nieve *f*
- *nimbostratus, a rain cloud, a*
  *layer cloud (sheet cloud) of very*
  *large vertical extent which*
  *produces precipitation (rain or*
  *snow)*

**11** el fractoestrato, jirones *m* de
nubes *f* que se encuentran
debajo del nimboestrato
- *fractostratus, a ragged cloud*
  *occurring beneath nimbostratus*
**12** el fractocúmulo, unos jirones
de nubes *f* como el ll pero con
formas *f* onduladas
- *fractocumulus, a ragged cloud*
  *like 11 but with billowing shapes*
**13-17 las nubes de los frentes fríos**
- *clouds at cold fronts*
**13** el frente frío
- *cold front*
**14** el cirrocúmulo, una nube
ligeramente aborregada
(enladrillada)
- *cirrocumulus, thin fleecy cloud*
  *in the form of globular masses;*
  *covering the sky: mackerel sky*
**15** el altocúmulo, una nube
voluminosamenta aborregada
- *altocumulus, a cloud in the form*
  *of large globular masses*
**16** el altocúmulo castellano y el
altocúmulo floccus, variantes *f*
del 15
- *altocumulus castellanus and*
  *altocumulus floccus, species of*
  *15*
**17** el cúmulonimbo, una nube
fluida vertical muy marcada,
asociada con las nubes de
tormenta *f* pertenecientes al
grupo *m* 1-4
- *cumulonimbus, a heap cloud of*
  *very large vertical extent, to be*
  *classified under 1-4 in the case*
  *of tropical storms*
**18-19 los tipos de precipitaciones *f***
- *types of precipitation*
**18** la lluvia constante o la nevada
cubierta, unas precipitaciones
de intensidad *f* uniforme (*Col.,
Guat. y Venez.:* la llovedera)
- *steady rain or snow covering a*
  *large area, precipitation of*
  *uniform intensity*
**19** el chubasco (aguacero *m*,
chaparrón *m*), una
precipitación irregular
(precipitaciones *f* locales) (*Col.
y P. Rico:* el aguaceral; *Amer.
Central, Cuba y Ec.:* el aguaje)
- *shower, scattered precipitation*

flecha *f* negra = aire *m* frío
- *black arrow = cold air*
flecha *f* blanca = aire *m*
caliente
- *white arrow = warm air*

1-39 **el mapa meteorológico**
- *weather chart (weather map, surface chart, surface synoptic chart)*
1 la isobara (línea *f* de igual presión *f* atmosférica al nivel del mar)
- *isobar (line of equal or constant atmospheric or barometric pressure at sea level)*
2 la pliobara (isobara *f* por encima de 1 000 mb)
- *pleiobar (isobar of over 1,000 mb)*
3 la miobara (isobara *f* de menos de 1 000 mb)
- *meiobar (isobar of under 1,000 mb)*
4 la presión atmosférica indicada en milibares *m*
- *atmospheric (barometric) pressure given in millibars*
5 el área *f* de (baja) presión *f* (el ciclón, la depresión)
- *low-pressure area (low, cyclone, depression)*
6 el área *f* de (alta) presión *f* (el anticiclón)
- *high-pressure area (high, anticyclone)*
7 una estación para la observación del tiempo (la estación meteorológica) o un barco meteorológico
- *observatory (meteorological watch office, weather station) or ocean station vessel (weather ship)*
8 la temperatura
- *temperature*
9-19 **la representación de la dirección y de la velocidad del viento** (los símbolos que representan el viento)
- *means of representing wind direction (wind-direction symbols)*
9 la flecha que indica la dirección del viento
- *wind-direction shaft (wind arrow)*
10 el trazo que indica la velocidad (la fuerza) del viento
- *wind-speed barb (wind-speed feather) indicating wind speed*
11 la calma
- *calm*
12 1-2 nudos *m*
- *1-2 knots (1 knot = 1.852 kph)*
13 3-7 nudos *m*
- *3-7 knots*
14 8-12 nudos *m*
- *8-12 knots*
15 13-17 nudos *m*
- *13-17 knots*
16 18-22 nudos *m*
- *18-22 knots*
17 23-27 nudos *m*
- *23-27 knots*
18 28-32 nudos *m*
- *28-32 knots*
19 58-62 nudos *m*
- *58-62 knots*
20-24 **el estado del cielo** (grado *m* de nubosidad *f*)
- *state of the sky (distribution of the cloud cover)*
20 despejado (sin nubes *f*)
- *clear (cloudless)*
21 casi despejado
- *fair*
22 poco nuboso (semicubierto)
- *partly cloudy*

23 nuboso
- *cloudy*
24 cubierto
- *overcast (sky mostly or completely covered)*
25-29 **frentes *m* y corrientes *f* de aire *m***
- *fronts and air currents*
25 la oclusión
- *occlusion (occluded front)*
26 el frente cálido
- *warm front*
27 el frente frío
- *cold front*
28 la corriente de aire *m* cálido
- *warm airstream (warm current)*
29 la corriente de aire *m* frío
- *cold airstream (cold current)*
30-39 **fenómenos *m* meteorológicos**
- *meteorological phenomena*
30 el área *f* de precipitaciones *f*
- *precipitation area*
31 la niebla (el nublado; Mé., Perú, Guat. y P. Rico: el nublazón; Ec.: la lancha)
- *fog*
32 la lluvia
- *rain*
33 la llovizna (el calabobos, la garúa, el mojabobos.)
- *drizzle*
34 la nieve (nevada *f*; Arg., Chile y Ec.: la nevazón)
- *snow*
35 la nieve granulada (nevisca *f*, cellisca *f*)
- *ice pellets (graupel, soft hail)*
36 el granizo (el pedrisco, la granizada; Col., Chile, Guat. y Mé.: el granizal)
- *hail*
37 el chubasco
- *shower*
38 la tormenta (la tempestad)
- *thunderstorm*
39 relámpago (Arg. y Urug.: el refocilo)
- *lightning*
40-58 **el mapa climático**
- *climatic map*
40 la isoterma (línea *f* que une los puntos que tienen igual temperatura *f* media)
- *isotherm (line connecting points having equal mean temperature)*
41 la isoterma cero (línea *f* que une los puntos que tienen una temperatura media anual de 0° C)
- *0 °C (zero) isotherm (line connecting points having a mean annual temperature of 0 °C)*
42 la isoquimena (línea *f* que une los puntos de igual temperatura *f* invernal)
- *isocheim (line connecting points having equal mean winter temperature)*
43 la isótera (línea *f* que une los puntos de igual temperatura *f* estival)
- *isothere (line connecting points having equal mean summer temperature)*
44 la isohelia (línea *f* que une los puntos de igual insolación *f*)
- *isohel (line connecting points having equal duration of sunshine)*

45 la isoyeta (línea *f* que une los puntos de igual cantidad *f* de lluvia *f*)
- *isohyet (line connecting points having equal amounts of precipitation)*
46-52 **los sistemas de vientos *m***
- *atmospheric circulation (wind systems)*
46-47 las zonas de calmas *f*
- *calm belts*
46 las zonas de calmas *f* ecuatoriales
- *equatorial trough (equatorial calms, doldrums)*
47 las zonas de calmas *f* subtropicales
- *subtropical high-pressure belts (horse latitudes)*
48 el alisio del Nordeste
- *north-east trade winds (north-east trades, tropical easterlies)*
49 el alisio del Sudeste
- *south-east trade winds (south-east trades, tropical easterlies)*
50 las zonas de los vientos variables del Oeste
- *zones of the variable westerlies*
51 las zonas de los vientos polares
- *polar wind zones*
52 el monzón de verano *m*
- *summer monsoon*
53-58 **los climas de la Tierra**
- *earth's climates*
53 el clima ecuatorial: la zona de lluvias *f* tropicales
- *equatorial climate: tropical zone (tropical rain zone)*
54 las zonas secas: las zonas desérticas y esteparias
- *the two arid zones (equatorial dry zones): desert and steppe zones*
55 las dos zonas lluviosas templadas
- *the two temperate rain zones*
56 el clima boreal (clima *m* de nieve y bosque *m*)
- *boreal climate; sim.: snow forest climate*
57-58 **los climas polares**
- *polar climates*
57 el clima de la tundra
- *tundra climate*
58 el clima del hielo eterno
- *perpetual frost climate*

# 10 Los instrumentos meteorológicos  *Meteorological Instruments*

1 el barómetro de mercurio *m*, un barómetro de sifón *m*, un barómetro de columna *f* líquida
– *mercury barometer, a siphon barometer, a liquid-column barometer*
2 la columna de mercurio *m*
– *mercury column*
3 la escala en milibares *m* (escala *f* en milímetros *m*)
– *millibar scale, a millimetre* (Am. *millimeter*) *scale*
4 el barógrafo, un barómetro aneroide registrador
– *barograph, a self-registering aneroid barometer*
5 el tambor (el cilindro)
– *drum (recording drum)*
6 la serie de cápsulas *f* aneroides (las cajas aneroides)
– *bank of aneroid capsules (aneroid boxes)*
7 el brazo (la palanca, la varilla) registrador (a)
– *recording arm*
8 el higrómetro
– *hygrograph*
9 el hilo higrométrico (el haz de cabellos *m*)
– *hygrometer element (hair element)*
10 el reglaje de lectura *f* (el tornillo de reglaje *m* de lectura *f*)
– *reading adjustment*
11 el reglaje de amplitud *f* del registro
– *amplitude adjustment*
12 el brazo (la palanca, la varilla) registrador (a)
– *recording arm*
13 la pluma registradora
– *recording pen*
14 las ruedas intercambiables del mecanismo de relojería *f*
– *change gears for the clockwork drive*
15 la palanca de desbloqueo *m* de la varilla registradora
– *off switch for the recording arm*
16 el tambor (el cilindro)
– *drum (recording drum)*
17 la escala de tiempos *m*
– *time scale*
18 la caja
– *case (housing)*
19 el termógrafo
– *thermograph*
20 el tambor (el cilindro)
– *drum (recording drum)*
21 el brazo (la palanca, la varilla) registrador(a)
– *recording arm*
22 el elemento de percepción *f* (el elemento sensitivo)
– *sensing element*
23 el pirheliómetro de disco *m* de plata *f*, un instrumento para medir la energía de los rayos del Sol

– *silver-disc (silver-disk) pyrheliometer, an instrument for measuring the sun's radiant energy*
24 el disco de plata *f*
– *silver disc (disk)*
25 el termómetro
– *thermometer*
26 el revestimiento aislante de madera *f*
– *wooden insulating casing*
27 el tubo con diafragma *m*
– *tube with diaphragm (diaphragmed tube)*
28 el aparato medidor del viento (el anemómetro)
– *wind gauge* (Am. *gage*) *(anemometer)*
29 el indicador de la velocidad del viento
– *wind-speed indicator (wind-speed meter)*
30 la cruz de paletillas *f* semiesféricas
– *cross arms with hemispherical cups*
31 el indicador de la dirección del viento
– *wind-direction indicator*
32 la veleta
– *wind vane*
33 el psicrómetro de aspiración *f*
– *aspiration psychrometer*
34 el termómetro "seco"
– *dry bulb thermometer*
35 el termómetro "húmedo"
– *wet bulb thermometer*
36 el protector de los rayos solares
– *solar radiation shielding*
37 el tubo de succión *f* (el tubo de aspiración *f*)
– *suction tube*
38 el pluviógrafo (pluviómetro *m* registrador)
– *recording rain gauge* (Am. *gage*)
39 la caja protectora
– *protective housing (protective casing)*
40 el recipiente colector (el colector de lluvia *f*)
– *collecting vessel*
41 la cubierta de protección *f* (el sombrerete para la lluvia)
– *rain cover*
42 el mecanismo registrador
– *recording mechanism*
43 el tubo sifón *m*
– *siphon tube*
44 el medidor de las precipita- ciones (el medidor de la lluvia: el pluviómetro)
– *precipitation gauge* (Am. *gage*) *(rain gauge)*
45 el recipiente colector (el colector de lluvia *f*)
– *collecting vessel*
46 la cuba
– *storage vessel*
47 la probeta graduada
– *measuring glass*

48 el instrumento para medir la nevada
– *insert for measuring snowfall*
49 la garita (la estación) meteorológica
– *thermometer screen (thermometer shelter)*
50 el higrógrafo
– *hygrograph*
51 el termógrafo
– *thermograph*
52 el psicrómetro
– *psychrometer (wet and dry bulb thermometer)*
53-54 los termómetros para medir las temperaturas extremas
– *thermometers for measuring extremes of temperature*
53 el termómetro de máxima *f*
– *maximum thermometer*
54 el termómetro de mínima *f*
– *minimum thermometer*
55 la radiosonda
– *radiosonde assembly*
56 el globo de hidrógeno *m*
– *hydrogen balloon*
57 el paracaídas
– *parachute*
58 el reflector radar *m* con líneas *f* de espaciamiento *m*
– *radar reflector with spacing lines*
59 la caja de instrumentos *m* con radiosonda *f* (un transmisor de onda *f* corta) y antena *f*
– *instrument housing with radiosonde [a short-wave transmitter] and antenna*
60 el transmisómetro, un instrumento para medir la visibilidad
– *transmissometer, an instrument for measuring visibility*
61 el instrumento registrador
– *recording instrument (recorder)*
62 el transmisor
– *transmitter*
63 el receptor
– *receiver*
64 el satélite meteorológico (ITOS)
– *weather satellite (ITOS satellite)*
65 las trampillas de regulación *f* de la temperatura
– *temperature regulation flaps*
66 el panel solar
– *solar panel*
67 la cámara de televisión *f*
– *television camera*
68 la antena
– *antenna*
69 el sensor solar
– *solar sensor (sun sensor)*
70 la antena telemétrica
– *telemetry antenna*
71 el radiómetro
– *radiometer*

# 11 Geografía general I

**1-5 la estructura en estratos** *m* **de la Tierra**
- *layered structure of the earth*
1 la corteza terrestre (litosfera *f*)
- *earth's crust (outer crust of the earth, lithosphere, oxysphere)*
2 la hidrosfera (la zona fluida)
- *hydrosphere*
3 el manto (la capa inferior)
- *mantle*
4 el sima (la capa intermedia)
- *sima (intermediate layer)*
5 el núcleo (el núcleo terrestre)
- *core (earth core, centrosphere, barysphere)*
**6-12 la curva hipsométrica de la superficie terrestre**
- *hypsographic curve of the earth's surface*
6 la cima (lo más alto)
- *peak*
7 la plataforma continental
- *continental mass*
8 la plataforma submarina superior (el "schelf")
- *continental shelf (continental platform, shelf)*
9 la vertiente continental
- *continental slope*
10 el fondo oceánico (la plataforma submarina inferior)
- *deep-sea floor (abyssal plane)*
11 el nivel del mar
- *sea level*
12 la fosa submarina
- *deep-sea trench*
**13-28 el volcanismo**
- *volcanism (vulcanicity)*
13 el volcán en escudo *m*
- *shield volcano*
14 la meseta de lava *f*
- *lava plateau*
15 el volcán activo, un estrato de volcán *m*, un volcán compuesto
- *active volcano, a stratovolcano (composite volcano)*
16 el cráter volcánico (el cráter)
- *volcanic crater (crater)*
17 la chimenea volcánica
- *volcanic vent*
18 el río de lava *f*
- *lava stream*
19 la toba (la masa de materia *f* volcánica)
- *tuff (fragmented volcanic material)*
20 el volcán subterráneo
- *subterranean volcano*
21 el géiser (el surtidor termal)
- *geyser*
22 el surtidor de agua *f* caliente y de vapor *m*
- *jet of hot water and steam*
23 las terrazas de geiserita *f*
- *sinter terraces (siliceous sinter terraces, fiorite terraces, pearl sinter terraces)*

24 el cono
- *cone*
25 el "maar" (el volcán apagado)
- *maar (extinct volcano)*
26 el depósito de toba *f*
- *tuff deposit*
27 la escoria (brecha *f*) de la chimenea
- *breccia*
28 la chimenea de un volcán apagado
- *vent of extinct volcano*
**29-31 el magmatismo plutónico** (el magma de las profundidades, el hipomagma)
- *plutonic magmatism*
29 el batolito (la roca de profundidad *f*)
- *batholite (massive protrusion)*
30 el lacolito, una intrusión
- *lacolith, an intrusion*
31 el yacimiento, un yacimiento de mena *f*
- *sill, an ore deposit*
**32-38 el terremoto** (el seísmo; *S. Dgo.*: el turrumote; *clases*: el terremoto tectónico, el terremoto volcánico, el terremoto por hundimiento; *Amér.*: el remezón) **y la sismología**
- *earthquake* (kinds: *tectonic quake, volcanic quake)* **and seismology**
32 el hipocentro
- *earthquake focus(seismic focus, hypocentre, Am. hypocenter)*
33 el epicentro (el punto de la superficie de la tierra situado encima del hipocentro)
- *epicentre (Am. epicenter), point on the earth's surface directly above the focus*
34 la profundidad del foco
- *depth of focus*
35 la propagación de la onda
- *shock wave*
36 las ondas superficiales (las ondas sísmicas)
- *seismic waves; here: surface waves*
37 la isosísmica (la línea que une los puntos de igual intensidad *f* sísmica)
- *isoseismal (line connecting points of equal intensity of earthquake shock)*
38 el área *f* epicentral (el área *f* de mayor vibración *f* sísmica)
- *epicentral area, an area of macroseismic vibration*
**39 el sismógrafo horizontal** (el sismómetro)
- *horizontal seismograph (seismometer)*
40 el amortiguador electromagnético
- *electromagnetic damper*

41 el botón de ajuste *m* para el periodo de oscilación *f* libre del péndulo
- *adjustment knob for the period of free oscillation of the pendulum*
42 el dispositivo del resorte para la suspensión del péndulo
- *spring attachment for the suspension of the pendulum*
43 la masa pendular (la masa estacionaria)
- *mass*
44 los carretes de inducción *f* para el voltaje del galvanómetro registrador
- *induction coils for recording the voltage of the galvanometer*
**45-54 los efectos de los terremotos**
- *effects of earthquakes*
45 la cascada (la catarata)
- *waterfall (cataract, falls)*
46 el desprendimiento de tierras *f* (el deslizamiento de tierras)
- *landslide (rockslide, rockslip, Am. rock slip)*
47 el talud (cascotes *m*, cantos *m* rodados)
- *talus (rubble, scree)*
48 la concavidad
- *scar (scaur, scaw)*
49 el hundimiento en forma *f* de embudo *m* (el cráter de hundimiento *m*)
- *sink (sinkhole, swallowhole)*
50 la dislocación (el corrimiento de tierras *f*, el desplazamiento de tierras *f*)
- *dislocation (displacement)*
51 el desbordamiento de fango *m* (el cono de fango *m*)
- *solifluction lobe (solifluction tongue)*
52 la fisura
- *fissure*
53 la ola sísmica producida por un maremoto (el "tsunami")
- *tsunami (seismic sea wave) produced by seaquake (submarine earthquake)*
54 la playa en realce *m* (terraza *f* de la playa)
- *raised beach*

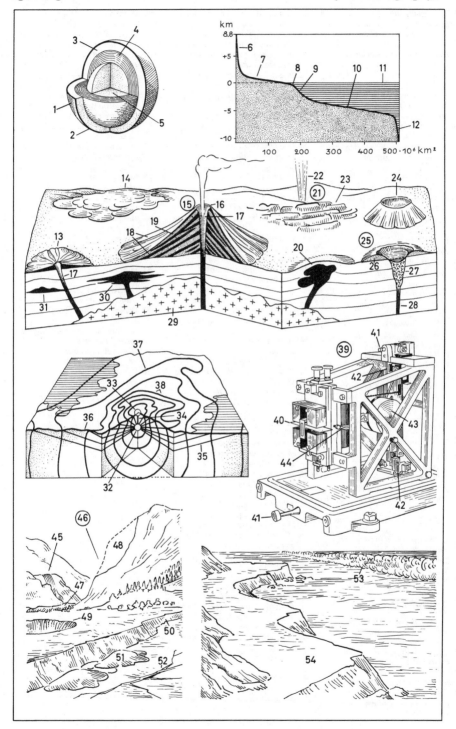

# 12  Geografía general II

**Physical Geography II**

**1-33 la geología**
- *geology*
1 la estratificación de las rocas sedimentarias
- *stratification of sedimentary rock*
2 la orientación
- *strike*
3 el buzamiento (el ángulo de inclinación *f*)
- *dip (angle of dip, true dip)*
**4-20 los movimientos orogénicos** (orogénesis *f*, tectogénesis *f*, deformación *f* de las rocas por pliegues *m* y fallas *f*)
- *orogeny (orogenis, tectogenis, deformation of rocks by folding and faulting)*
**4-11 las montañas de bloques *m* de fallas *f***
- *fault-block mountain (block mountain)*
4 la falla
- *fault*
5 el plano de falla *f*
- *fault line (fault trace)*
6 el salto de falla *f*
- *fault throw*
7 la falla normal (la falla de dislocación *f* normal: la falla oblicua inversa)
- *normal fault (gravity fault, normal slip fault, slump fault)*
**8-11 las fallas complejas**
- *complex faults*
8 la falla en escalera *f* (falla *f* distributiva, falla *f* múltiple)
- *step fault (distributive fault, multiple fault)*
9 el bloque de inclinación *f*
- *tilt block*
10 el horst
- *horst*
11 la fosa tectónica
- *graben*
**12-20 los pliegues orogénicos** (la montaña de pliegues *m*)
- *range of fold mountains (folded mountains)*
12 el pliegue simétrico (el pliegue derecho –vertical–)
- *symmetrical fold (normal fold)*
13 el pliegue asimétrico (el pliegue oblicuo)
- *asymmetrical fold*
14 el pliegue inclinado
- *overfold*
15 el pliegue recostado (el pliegue tendido)
- *recumbent fold (reclined fold)*
16 la cresta (el anticlinal)
- *saddle (anticline)*
17 el eje del anticlinal
- *anticlinal axis*
18 la hoya (el sinclinal)
- *trough (syncline)*
19 el eje del sinclinal
- *trough surface (trough plane, synclinal axis)*

20 la montaña plegada de fallas *f*
- *anticlinorium*
21 el agua *f* subterránea a presión *f* (el agua *f* artesiana)
- *groundwater under pressure (artesian water)*
22 la capa portadora de agua *f* (capa *f* freática)
- *water-bearing stratum (aquifer, aquafer)*
23 la roca impermeable
- *impervious rock (impermeable rock)*
24 la cuenca de drenaje *m* (la zona de captación *f*)
- *drainage basin (catchment area)*
25 el tubo del pozo
- *artesian well*
26 el surtidor de agua *f*, un pozo artesiano (*Amér.*: la casimba)
- *rising water, an artesian spring*
27 el depósito de petróleo *m* en un anticlinal
- *petroleum reservoir in an anticline*
28 el estrato impermeable
- *impervious stratum (impermeable stratum)*
29 la capa porosa como roca *f* depósito *m*
- *porous stratum acting as reservoir rock*
30 el gas natural, un casquete de gas *m*
- *natural gas, a gas cap*
31 el petróleo (aceite *m* mineral, el crudo)
- *petroleum (crude oil)*
32 el agua *f* subyacente
- *underlying water*
33 la torre de perforación *f*
- *derrick*
34 el área *f* montañosa (la montaña secundaria)
- *mountainous area*
35 la cima de la montaña
- *rounded mountain top*
36 la cresta de la montaña (*Amér. Merid.*: la cuchilla)
- *mountain ridge (ridge)*
37 la pendiente de la montaña (*Chile, Ec., Guat. y Perú*: la gradiente)
- *mountain slope*
38 la fuente de la ladera
- *hillside spring*
**39-47 la alta montaña**
- *high-mountain region*
39 la cordillera, un macizo (*Amér. Merid.*: la cerrillada)
- *mountain range, a massif*
40 la cima (la cumbre, el pico de la montaña)
- *summit (peak, top of the mountain)*
41 la espalda (la antecumbre) de la montaña (*Chile*: la placeta)
- *shoulder*

42 el collado
- *saddle*
43 la pendiente escarpada (el tajo)
- *rock face (steep face)*
44 el barranco (la quebrada)
- *gully*
45 el talud (cantos *m* rodados, talud *m* detrítico)
- *talus (scree, detritus)*
46 el camino de herradura *f* (*Amér. Central, Arg., Bol., Cuba, Urug.*: la picada)
- *bridle path*
47 el paso (paso *m* de montaña *f*, el puerto)
- *pass (col)*
**48-56 el glaciar**
- *glacial ice*
48 el circo de alimentación *f* (el banco de nieve *f*, el "névé")
- *firn field (firn basin, nevé)*
49 el glaciar del valle
- *valley glacier*
50 la grieta del glaciar
- *crevasse*
51 la boca del glaciar
- *glacier snout*
52 el arroyo del glaciar
- *subglacial stream*
53 la morena (morrena *f*) lateral
- *lateral moraine*
54 la morena (morrena *f*) media
- *medial moraine*
55 la morena (morrena *f*) final
- *end moraine*
56 la mesa del glaciar
- *glacier table*

**1-13 la topografía fluvial**
- *fluvial topography*
1 la desembocadura de un río, un delta (*Amér.:* la bocana)
- *river mouth, a delta*
2 el brazo de la desembocadura, ur brazo de río *m* (un brazo fluvial)
- *distributary (distributary channel), a river branch (river arm)*
3 el lago
- *lake*
4 la orilla (*Chile:* el ribo)
- *bank*
5 la península
- *peninsula (spit)*
6 la isla
- *island*
7 la bahía (la ensenada, el golfo)
- *bay (cove)*
8 el arroyo (*Amér. Merid.:* la acequia; *Amér. Central, Bol., Pan., Perú, P. Rico y Venez.:* la quebrada)
- *stream (brook, rivulet, creek)*
9 el dique
- *levee*
10 la zona aluvial (la zona de sedimentación *f*)
- *alluvial plain*
11 el meandro (un recodo del río)
- *meander, a river bend*
12 el monte contorneado (el monte causante del meandro)
- *meander core (rock island)*
13 la vega (*Chile, Guat., Mé. y Venez.:* el plan)
- *meadow*
**14-24 el pantano** (*Col.:* el pantanero)
- *bog (marsh)*
14 el páramo bajo del pantano (el pantano superficial)
- *low-moor bog*
15 las capas de material *m* vegetal podrido (las capas de fango *m*)
- *layers of decayed vegetable matter*
16 la bolsa de agua *f*
- *entrapped water*
17 la turba del pantano (la turba de juncos *m* y cañas *f*)
- *fen peat [consisting of rush and sedge]*
18 la turba de aliso *m*
- *alder-swamp peat*
19 el páramo alto del pantano (el pantano alto)
- *high-moor bog*
20 la bolsa reciente de turba *f* de musgo *m*
- *layer of recent sphagnum mosses*
21 el límite entre capas *f*
- *boundary between layers (horizons)*
22 la bolsa antigua de turba *f* de musgo *m*
- *layer of older sphagnum mosses*
23 la charca del pantano (*Col. y Ec.:* la chamba)
- *bog pool*
24 la ciénaga (la zona cubierta de agua *f*)
- *swamp*
**25-31 los acantilados**
- *cliffline (cliffs)*
25 la roca (el peñasco, el escollo; *Cuba:* el molejón)
- *rock*
26 el mar
- *sea (ocean)*

27 las olas (rompientes)
- *surf*
28 el acantilado (el farallón)
- *cliff (cliff face, steep rock face)*
29 los guijarros (la rocalla)
- *scree*
30 el hueco producido por la erosión del oleaje (el socavón)
- *[wave-cut] notch*
31 la planicie de erosión *f* (el llano del rompiente)
- *abrasion platform (wave-cut platform)*
32 el atolón (arrecife *m* coralino en forma *f* circular), un arrecife coralino
- *atoll, a ring-shaped coral reef*
33 la laguna (*Amér.:* el aguaje; *Bol., Ec. y Perú:* la cocha; *Cuba:* el itabo)
- *lagoon*
34 la brecha (el canal de la laguna)
- *breach (hole)*
**35-44 la playa**
- *beach*
35 la línea de la marea (el límite de la pleamar)
- *high-water line (high-water mark, tidemark)*
36 las olas rompiéndose en la orilla
- *waves breaking on the shore*
37 el malecón (la escollera)
- *groyne (Am. groin)*
38 la cabeza del malecón
- *groyne (Am. groin) head*
39 la duna movediza, una duna
- *wandering dune (migratory dune, travelling, Am. traveling, dune), a dune*
40 la duna en forma *f* de media luna *f*
- *barchan (barchane, barkhan, crescentic dune)*
41 las marcas rizadas (las marcas del viento)
- *ripple marks*
42 el morón (forma *f* de erosión *f* eólica)
- *hummock*
43 el árbol azotado por el viento
- *wind cripple*
44 el lago costero (la laguna de la playa)
- *coastal lake*
45 el cañón (*Amér.:* el cajón; *Arg., Cuba y Urug.:* el cañadón)
- *canyon (cañon, coulee)*
46 la meseta (*Amér.:* la sabana)
- *plateau (tableland)*
47 la terraza de roca *f*
- *rock terrace*
48 la roca sedimentaria (la roca estratificada)
- *sedimentary rock (stratified rock)*
49 el escalón estratificado (la terraza estratificada)
- *river terrace (bed)*
50 la grieta
- *joint*
51 el río del cañón
- *canyon river*
**52-56 formas *f* de valles *m* [corte transversal]**
- *types of valley [cross section]*
52 la garganta (el barranco)
- *gorge (ravine)*
53 el valle en forma *f* de V
- *V-shaped valley (V-valley)*

54 el valle en forma *f* de V abierta
- *widened V-shaped valley*
55 el valle en forma *f* de U (el valle de depresión *f*)
- *U-shaped valley (U-valley, trough valley)*
56 el valle sinclinal (el valle viejo)
- *synclinal valley*
**57-70 el valle fluvial**
- *river valley*
57 la pendiente escarpada (el acantilado)
- *scarp (escarpment)*
58 la pendiente suave (*Arg. y Chile:* el faldeo)
- *slip-off slope*
59 la meseta
- *mesa*
60 la sierra (la cordillera)
- *ridge*
61 el río
- *river*
62 la vega (la avenida)
- *flood plain*
63 la terraza de roca *f*
- *river terrace*
64 la terraza de grava *f*
- *terracette*
65 la pendiente (*Chile, Ec., Guat. y Perú:* la gradiente)
- *pediment*
66 la colina
- *hill*
67 el fondo del valle
- *valley floor (valley bottom)*
68 el lecho del río (*Chile:* la caja)
- *riverbed*
69 los depósitos sedimentarios
- *sediment*
70 el lecho de roca *f* (la roca sólida)
- *bedrock*
**71-83 las formaciones kársticas** en las rocas calcáreas
- *karst formation in limestone*
71 la dolina, el hundimiento en forma *f* de embudo *m*
- *dolina, a sink (sinkhole, swallowhole)*
72 el poljé (las depresiones)
- *polje*
73 la infiltración de un río
- *percolation of a river*
74 el manantial del karst
- *karst spring*
75 el valle seco
- *dry valley*
76 el sistema de grutas *f*
- *system of caverns (system of caves)*
77 el nivel del agua *f* del karst
- *water level (water table) in a karst formation*
78 la capa rocosa impermeable
- *impervious rock (impermeable rock)*
79 la cueva de estalactitas *f* (la cueva de karst *m*)
- *limestone cave (dripstone cave)*
**80-81 concreaciones *f* calcáreas**
- *speleothems (cave formations)*
80 la estalactita (*Chile y Mé.:* el achichicle)
- *stalactite (dripstone)*
81 la estalagmita
- *stalagmite*
82 la columna de concreaciones *f* calcáreas
- *linked-up stalagmite and stalactite*
83 el río subterráneo
- *subterranean river*

1-7 **las coordenadas geográficas**
(la red de meridianos *m* y
paralelos *m* de la superficie
terrestre)
- *graticule of the earth (network
of meridians and parallels on
the earth's surface)*
1 el ecuador
- *equator*
2 un paralelo
- *line of latitude (parallel of
latitude, parallel)*
3 el polo (el polo norte o el polo
sur), un polo terrestre
- *pole (North Pole or South Pole),
a terrestrial pole (geographical
pole)*
4 el meridiano
- *line of longitude (meridian of
longitude, meridian, terrestrial
meridian)*
5 el meridiano cero
(el meridiano de origen *m*,
el meridiano de Greenwich)
- *Standard meridian (Prime
meridian, Greenwich meridian,
meridian of Greenwich)*
6 la latitud (latitud *f* geográfica)
- *latitude*
7 la longitud (longitud *f*
geográfica)
- *longitude*
8-9 **proyecciones *f* cartográficas**
- *map projections*
8 la proyección cónica
- *conical (conic) projection*
9 la proyección cilíndrica
- *cylindrical projection (Mercator
projection, Mercator's
projection)*
10-45 **el mapamundi** (el mapa de
la Tierra)
- *map of the world*
10 los trópicos
- *tropics*
11 los círculos polares
- *polar circles*
12-18 **los continentes**
- *continents*
12-13 América *f*
- *America*
12 América del Norte
(Norteamérica *f*)
- *North America*
13 América del Sur (Sudamérica
*f*)
- *South America*
14 África *f*
- *Africa*
15-16 Eurasia *f*
- *Europe and Asia*
15 Europa *f*
- *Europe*
16 Asia *f*
- *Asia*
17 Australia *f*
- *Australia*
18 la Antártida (el continente
antártico)
- *Antarctica (Antarctic Continent)*
19-26 **el océano**
- *ocean (sea)*

19 el océano Pacífico
- *Pacific Ocean*
20 el océano Atlántico
- *Atlantic Ocean*
21 el océano Glacial Ártico
- *Arctic Ocean*
22 el océano Glacial Antártico
- *Antarctic Ocean (Southern
Ocean)*
23 el océano Índico
- *Indian Ocean*
24 el estrecho de Gibraltar,
un estrecho de mar *m*
- *Strait of Gibraltar, a sea strait*
25 el mar Mediterráneo
(el Mediterráneo)
- *Mediterranean (Mediterranean
Sea, European Mediterranean)*
26 el mar del Norte, un mar
marginal
- *North Sea, a marginal sea
(epeiric sea, epicontinental sea)*
27-29 **la leyenda (la explicación de
los símbolos)**
- **key (explanation of map
symbols)**
27 la corriente marina fría
- *cold ocean current*
28 la corriente marina cálida
- *warm ocean current*
29 la escala
- *scale*
30-45 **las corrientes marinas**
- *ocean (oceanic) currents (ocean
drifts)*
30 la corriente del Golfo (el Gulf
Stream)
- *Gulf Stream (North Atlantic
Drift)*
31 el Kuro-Sivo
- *Kuroshio (Kuro Siwo, Japan
Current)*
32 la corriente ecuatorial del
Norte
- *North Equatorial Current*
33 la contracorriente ecuatorial
- *Equatorial Countercurrent*
34 la corriente ecuatorial del Sur
- *South Equatorial Current*
35 la corriente del Brasil
- *Brazil Current*
36 la corriente de Somalia
- *Somali Current*
37 la corriente de las Agulhas
- *Agulhas Current*
38 la corriente australiana oriental
- *East Australian Current*
39 la corriente de California
- *California Current*
40 la corriente del Labrador
- *Labrador Current*
41 la corriente de las Canarias
- *Canary Current*
42 la corriente de Humboldt
(la corriente del Perú)
- *Peru Current*
43 la corriente de Benguela
- *Benguela (Benguella) Current*
44 la corriente de viento del Oeste
- *West Wind Drift (Antarctic
Circumpolar Drift)*

45 la corriente australiana
occidental
- *West Australian Current*
46-62 **la agrimensura** (topografía *f*,
geodesia *f*)
- *surveying;* here: *land surveying;*
also: *geodetic surveying
(geodesy)*
46 la nivelación (medición *f*
geométrica de la altura)
- *levelling* (Am. *leveling)
(geometrical measurement of
height)*
47 la mira (regla *f* de nivelación)
- *graduated measuring rod
(levelling, Am. leveling, staff)*
48 el nivel, un anteojo de
nivelación *f*
- *level (surveying level, surveyor's
level), a surveyor's telescope*
49 el punto trigonométrico
- *triangulation station
(triangulation point)*
50 la armazón
- *supporting scaffold*
51 la torre de señalización *f*
- *signal tower (signal mast)*
52-62 **el teodolito, un aparato para
medir ángulos *m***
- **theodolite, an instrument for
measuring angles**
52 el botón micrométrico
- *micrometer head*
53 el ocular del microscopio
- *micrometer eyepiece*
54 el tornillo del nonio de
inclinación *f*
- *vertical tangent screw*
55 la tuerca de inclinación *f*
- *vertical clamp*
56 el tornillo del nonio de
rotación *f*
- *tangent screw*
57 la tuerca de rotación *f*
- *horizontal clamp*
58 el botón de ajuste *m* para el
espejo de iluminación *f*
- *adjustment for the illuminating
mirror*
59 el espejo de iluminación *f*
- *illuminating mirror*
60 el telescopio
- *telescope*
61 el nivel de burbuja *f*
transversal
- *spirit level*
62 el ajuste circular
- *circular adjustment*
63-66 **la fotogrametría**
(la fototopografía)
- **photogrammetry** (*phototopo-
graphy*)
63 la cámara topográfica para la
producción de series *f*
coincidentes de imágenes *f*
- *air survey camera for producing
overlapping series of pictures*
64 el estereótopo
- *stereoscope*
65 el pantógrafo
- *pantograph*
66 el estereoplanígrafo
- *stereoplanigraph*

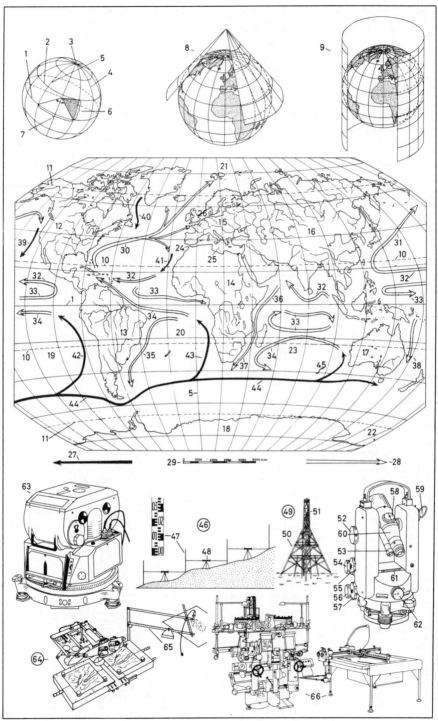

# 15  Mapa II

*Map II*

1-114 los signos convencionales de un
  mapa a escala 1:25 000
– *map signs (map symbols,
  conventional signs) on a 1:25 000 map*
1 el bosque de coníferas *f*
– *coniferous wood (coniferous trees)*
2 el claro
– *clearing*
3 la oficina forestal
– *forestry office*
4 el bosque de árboles *m* de hojas *f*
  caducas
– *deciduous wood (non-coniferous trees)*
5 el erial
– *heath, rough grassland, rough pasture,
  heath and moor, bracken*
6 la arena
– *sand or sand hills*
7 el elimo arenario
– *beach grass*
8 el faro
– *lighthouse*
9 el límite de los bajos
– *mean low water*
10 la boya
– *beacon*
11 las curvas de nivel *m* submarinas (las
  líneas isobáticas)
– *submarine contours*
12 el transbordador de trenes *m* (*Amér.:*
  el ferryboat)
– *train ferry*
13 el buque faro
– *lightship*
14 el bosque mixto
– *mixed wood (mixed trees)*
15 la maleza (el monte bajo)
– *brushwood*
16 la autopista con rampa *f* de acceso *m*
– *motorway with slip road* (Am.
  *freeway with on-ramp, freeway with
  acceleration lane)*
17 la carretera principal
– *trunk road*
18 la pradera
– *grassland*
19 la pradera pantanosa
– *marshy grassland*
20 la marisma
– *marsh*
21 la línea principal de ferrocarril *m*
– *main line railway* (Am. *trunk line)*
22 el paso bajo la carretera
– *road over railway*
23 el ramal (la línea secundaria de
  ferrocarril *m)*
– *branch line*
24 la estación de enclavamiento *m* (la
  casilla del guardavía)
– *signal box* (Am. *switch tower)*
25 la línea local de ferrocarril *m* (la vía
  estrecha)
– *local line*
26 el paso a nivel *m*
– *level crossing*
27 la estación (la parada)
– *halt*
28 el área *f* residencial
– *residential area*
29 el fluviómetro
– *water gauge* (Am. *gage)*
30 la carretera de tercer orden *m*
– *good, metalled road*
31 el molino de viento *m*
– *windmill*
32 la salina
– *thorn house (graduation house, salina,
  salt-works)* [no symbol]
33 la torre emisora de radio *f*
– *broadcasting station (wireless or
  television mast)*
34 la mina
– *mine*

35 la mina abandonada
– *disused mine*
36 la carretera secundaria
– *secondary road (B road)*
37 la fábrica
– *works*
38 la chimenea
– *chimney*
39 la cerca de alambre (la alambrada)
– *wire fence*
40 el paso elevado de la carretera
– *bridge over railway*
41 la estación de ferrocarril *m*
– *railway station* (Am. *railroad station)*
42 el paso elevado de la vía férrea
– *bridge under railway*
43 la senda
– *footpath*
44 el paso inferior de la senda
– *bridge for footpath under railway*
45 el río navegable
– *navigable river*
46 el puente de barcas *f* (el pontón de
  barcas *f)*
– *pontoon bridge*
47 el transbordador de vehículos *m*
– *vehicle ferry*
48 el espigón de piedra *f* (el malecón)
– *mole*
49 el fanal
– *beacon*
50 el puente de piedra *f*
– *stone bridge*
51 la ciudad
– *town or city*
52 la plaza del mercado
– *market place (market square)*
53 la iglesia mayor con dos torres *f*
– *large church*
54 el edificio público
– *public building*
55 el puente de la carretera
– *road bridge*
56 el puente de hierro *m*
– *iron bridge*
57 el canal
– *canal*
58 el dique de esclusas *f*
– *lock*
59 el embarcadero
– *jetty*
60 el transbordador de pasajeros *m*
– *foot ferry (foot passenger ferry)*
61 la capilla (la ermita)
– *chapel (church) without tower or spire*
62 las curvas de nivel *m* (las isohipsas)
– *contours*
63 el monasterio (el convento)
– *monastery or convent* [named]
64 la iglesia visible a larga distancia *f*
– *church landmark*
65 la viña
– *vineyard*
66 la presa
– *weir*
67 el funicular aéreo (el teleférico)
– *aerial ropeway*
68 la torre de observación *f*
– *view point*
69 la esclusa de retención *f*
– *dam*
70 el túnel
– *tunnel*
71 el punto trigonométrico (el punto
  geodésico)
– *triangulation station (triangulation
  point)*
72 la ruina
– *remains of a building*
73 el molinillo de viento *m*
– *wind pump*
74 el fuerte
– *fortress*

75 el meandro aislado
– *ox-bow lake*
76 el río
– *river*
77 el molino de agua *f*
– *watermill*
78 la pasadera
– *footbridge*
79 el estanque
– *pond*
80 el arroyo
– *stream (brook, rivulet, creek)*
81 la alcubilla (el arca *f*
  de agua *f)*
– *water tower*
82 la fuente (el manantial)
– *spring*
83 la carretera principal
– *main road (A road)*
84 el desmonte
– *cutting*
85 la cueva
– *cave*
86 el horno de cal *f*
– *lime kiln*
87 la cantera
– *quarry*
88 el hoyo de arcilla *f* (el gredal)
– *clay pit*
89 el tejar (*Col.:* el chircal)
– *brickworks*
90 el ferrocarril ligero de explotación *f*
– *narrow-gauge* (Am. *narrow gage)
  railway*
91 el cargadero
– *goods depot (freight depot)*
92 el monumento
– *monument*
93 el campo de batalla *f*
– *site of battle*
94 la hacienda, una finca rústica
– *country estate, a demesne*
95 el muro
– *wall*
96 el castillo
– *stately home*
97 el parque
– *park*
98 el seto
– *hedge*
99 el camino transitable regularmente
  cuidado (la carretera local)
– *poor or unmetalled road*
100 el pozo
– *well*
101 el caserío (el cortijo)
– *farm*
102 el camino forestal
– *unfenced path (unfenced track)*
103 el límite del término municipal
– *district boundary*
104 el terraplén
– *embankment*
105 el pueblo
– *village*
106 el cementerio
– *cemetery*
107 la iglesia del pueblo
– *church or chapel with spire*
108 el huerto (el vergel)
– *orchard*
109 el mojón kilométrico (el hito
  kilométrico)
– *milestone*
110 el poste indicador
– *guide post*
111 el plantel
– *tree nursery*
112 la vereda
– *ride (aisle, lane, section line)*
113 la línea de conducción *f* eléctrica (la
  línea de alta tensión *f)*
– *electricity transmission line*
114 la plantación de lúpulo *m*
– *hop garden*

en España:

**1-54 el cuerpo humano**
- *the human body*
**1-18 la cabeza** (*Chile y Río de la Plata:* el mate)
- *head*
1 la coronilla (el vértice)
- *vertex (crown of the head, top of the head)*
2 el occipucio (la parte posterior de la cabeza)
- *occiput (back of the head)*
3 el cabello (el pelo)
- *hair*
**4-17 la cara**
- *face*
**4-5 la frente**
- *forehead*
4 la eminencia frontal
- *frontal eminence (frontal protuberance)*
5 la protuberancia frontal
- *superciliary arch*
6 la sien (*Amér.:* el sentido)
- *temple*
7 el ojo
- *eye*
8 el pómulo
- *zygomatic bone (malar bone, jugal bone, cheekbone)*
9 la mejilla (el carrillo)
- *cheek*
10 la nariz (las narices; *Amér.:* las ñatas)
- *nose*
11 el surco nasolabial (el surco desde la nariz hasta la comisura de la boca)
- *nasolabial fold*
12 el philtrum (el surco subnasal)
- *philtrum*
13 la boca (*Chile:* la borotera)
- *mouth*
14 la comisura labial (el ángulo de la boca; *C. Rica:* el camanance)
- *angle of the mouth (labial commissure)*
15 la barbilla
- *chin*
16 el hoyuelo de la barbilla
- *dimple (fossette) in the chin*
17 la mandíbula
- *jaw*
18 la oreja
- *ear*
**19-21 el cuello**
- *neck*
19 la garganta
- *throat*
20 la fosa yugular (el hueco de la garganta, la hoyuela)
- *hollow of the throat*
21 la nuca
- *nape of the neck*
**22-41 el tronco**
- *trunk*

**22-25 la espalda**
- *back*
22 el hombro
- *shoulder*
23 el omóplato
- *shoulderblade (scapula)*
24 la región lumbar
- *loins*
25 la región del sacro
- *small of the back*
26 el hombro (el sobaco, la axila)
- *armpit*
27 el vello de la axila
- *armpit hair*
**28-30 el tórax** (el pecho)
- *thorax (chest)*
**28-29 los pechos** (*Amér.:* los chiches)
- *breasts (breast, mamma)*
28 el pezón
- *nipple*
29 la aréola
- *areola*
30 el pecho
- *bosom*
31 la cintura
- *waist*
32 el flanco (el costado)
- *flank (side)*
33 la cadera
- *hip*
34 el ombligo (*Amér.:* el pupo)
- *navel*
**35-37 el abdomen** (el vientre, *fam.:* la barriga)
- *abdomen (stomach)*
35 la parte superior del abdomen (el epigastrio)
- *upper abdomen*
36 el abdomen medio (el mesogastrio)
- *abdomen*
37 el bajo vientre (el hipogastrio)
- *lower abdomen*
38 la ingle
- *groin*
39 el pubis
- *pudenda (vulva)*
40 el trasero (las posaderas, las nalgas, los glúteos, *fam.:* el culo; *Arg., Bol., Chile y Perú:* el poto)
- *seat (backside,* coll. *bottom)*
41 el pliegue anal (*fam.:* la raja del culo)
- *anal groove (anal cleft)*
42 el pliegue glúteo (la arruga glútea)
- *gluteal fold (gluteal furrow)*
**43-54 las extremidades**
- *limbs*
**43-48 el brazo** (la extremidad superior)
- *arm*
43 el brazo
- *upper arm*
44 el pliegue del codo
- *crook of the arm*

45 el codo
- *elbow*
46 el antebrazo
- *forearm*
47 la mano
- *hand*
48 el puño (los puños; *Ecuad.:* los ñeques)
- *fist (clenched fist, clenched hand)*
**49-54 la pierna** (la extremidad inferior)
- *leg*
49 el muslo
- *thigh*
50 la rodilla
- *knee*
51 la corva (el hueco poplíteo; *Arg., Col., Guat. y Venez.:* el garrete)
- *popliteal space*
52 la caña (la pierna)
- *shank*
53 la pantorrilla (*Mé.:* el chamorro)
- *calf*
54 el pie
- *foot*

**1-29 el esqueleto** (la armazón
     ósea, la osamenta, los huesos)
– *skeleton (bones)*
1 el cráneo
– *skull*
**2-5 la columna vertebral**
– *vertebral column (spinal
     column, spine, backbone)*
2 las vértebras cervicales
– *cervical vertebra*
3 las vértebras dorsales
– *dorsal vertebra (thoracic
     vertebra)*
4 las vértebras lumbares
– *lumbar vertebra*
5 el cóccix (las vértebras
     coccígeas)
– *coccyx (coccygeal vertebra)*
**6-7** los huesos del hombro
     (la cintura escapular)
– *shoulder girdle*
6 la clavícula
– *collarbone (clavicle)*
7 el omóplato (la escápula)
– *shoulderblade (scapula)*
**8-11 el tórax** (la caja torácica)
– *thorax (chest)*
8 el esternón
– *breastbone (sternum)*
9 las costillas verdaderas
– *true ribs*
10 las costillas falsas
– *false ribs*
11 el cartílago costal
– *costal cartilage*
**12-14 el brazo** (la extremidad
     superior)
– *arm*
12 el húmero
– *humerus*
13 el radio
– *radius*
14 el cúbito
– *ulna*
**15-17 la mano**
– *hand*
15 los huesos del carpo (el carpo)
– *carpus*
16 los huesos del metacarpo
     (el metacarpo)
– *metacarpal bone (metacarpal)*
17 las falanges del dedo
– *phalanx (phalange)*
**18-21 la pelvis**
– *pelvis*
18 el ilion
– *ilium (hip bone)*
19 el isquion
– *ischium*
20 el pubis
– *pubis*
21 el sacro
– *sacrum*
**22-25 la pierna** (la extremidad
     inferior)
– *leg*
22 el fémur
– *femur (thigh bone, thigh)*
23 la rótula
– *patella (kneecap)*

24 el peroné
– *fibula (splint bone)*
25 la tibia
– *tibia (shinbone)*
**26-29 el pie**
– *foot*
26 los huesos del tarso (el tarso)
– *tarsal bones (tarsus)*
27 el calcáneo
– *calcaneum (heelbone)*
28 los huesos del metatarso
     (el metatarso)
– *metatarsus*
29 las falanges
– *phalanges*
**30-41 el cráneo**
– *skull*
30 el frontal
– *frontal bone*
31 el parietal izquierdo
– *left parietal bone*
32 el occipital
– *occipital bone*
33 el temporal
– *temporal bone*
34 el conducto auditivo
– *external auditory canal*
35 el maxilar inferior
– *lower jawbone (lower jaw,
     mandible)*
36 el maxilar superior
– *upper jawbone (upper jaw,
     maxilla)*
37 el hueso pómulo
– *zygomatic bone (cheekbone)*
38 el esfenoides
– *sphenoid bone (sphenoid)*
39 el etmoides
– *ethmoid bone (ethmoid)*
40 el unguis (el lacrimal)
– *lachrimal (lacrimal) bone*
41 el nasal
– *nasal bone*
**42-55 la cabeza** [corte]
– *head [section]*
42 el cerebro
– *cerebrum (great brain)*
43 la glándula pituitaria
     (la hipófisis cerebral)
– *pituitary gland (pituitary body,
     hypophysis cerebri)*
44 el cuerpo calloso
– *corpus callosum*
45 el cerebelo
– *cerebellum (little brain)*
46 el puente de Varolio
– *pons (pons cerebri, pons
     cerebelli)*
47 la médula oblonga
– *medulla oblongata (brain-stem)*
48 la médula espinal
– *spinal cord*
49 el esófago
– *oesophagus (esophagus, gullet)*
50 la tráquea
– *trachea (windpipe)*
51 la epiglotis
– *epiglottis*
52 la lengua
– *tongue*

53 la cavidad nasal
– *nasal cavity*
54 el seno esfenoidal
– *sphenoidal sinus*
55 el seno frontal
– *frontal sinus*
**56-65 el órgano del equilibrio y del
     oído**
– *organ of equilibrium and
     hearing*
**56-58 el oído externo**
– *external ear*
56 el pabellón auditivo (la oreja)
– *auricle*
57 el lóbulo de la oreja
– *ear lobe*
58 el conducto auditivo
– *external auditory canal*
**59-61 el oído medio**
– *middle ear*
59 la membrana del tímpano
– *tympanic membrane*
60 la caja del tímpano
– *tympanic cavity*
61 los huesecillos: el martillo,
     el yunque, el estribo
– *auditory ossicles: hammer,
     anvil, and stirrup (malleus,
     incus, and stapes)*
**62-64 el oído interno**
– *inner ear (internal ear)*
62 el laberinto
– *labyrinth*
63 el caracol
– *cochlea*
64 el nervio auditivo
– *auditory nerve*
65 la trompa de Eustaquio
– *eustachian tube*

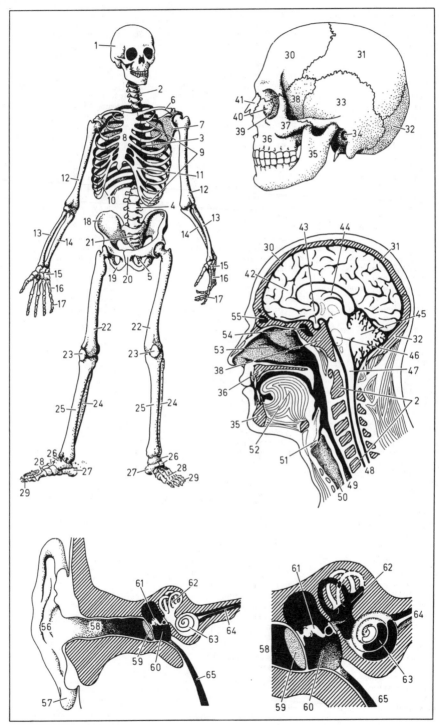

**1-21 la circulación sanguínea**
(el sistema circulatorio)
– *blood circulation (circulatory system)*
1 la carótida, una arteria
– *common carotid artery, an artery*
2 la yugular, una vena
– *jugular vein, a vein*
3 la arteria temporal
– *temporal artery*
4 la vena temporal
– *temporal vein*
5 la arteria frontal
– *frontal artery*
6 la vena frontal
– *frontal vein*
7 la arteria subclavia
– *subclavian artery*
8 la vena subclavia
– *subclavian vein*
9 la vena cava superior
– *superior vena cava*
10 el cayado de la aorta (la aorta)
– *arch of the aorta (aorta)*
11 la arteria pulmonar [con sangre *f* venosa]
– *pulmonary artery [with venous blood]*
12 la vena pulmonar [con sangre *f* arterial]
– *pulmonary vein [with arterial blood]*
13 los pulmones
– *lungs*
14 el corazón
– *heart*
15 la vena cava inferior
– *inferior vena cava*
16 la aorta abdominal (rama *f* descendente de la aorta)
– *abdominal aorta (descending portion of the aorta)*
17 la arteria ilíaca
– *iliac artery*
18 la vena ilíaca
– *iliac vein*
19 la arteria femoral
– *femoral artery*
20 la arteria tibial
– *tibial artery*
21 la arteria radial
– *radial artery*
**22-33 el sistema nervioso**
– *nervous system*
22 el cerebro
– *cerebrum (great brain)*
23 el cerebelo
– *cerebellum (little brain)*
24 la médula oblonga
– *medulla oblongata (brain-stem)*
25 la médula espinal
– *spinal cord*
26 los nervios torácicos
– *thoracic nerves*
27 el plexo branquial
– *brachial plexus*
28 el nervio radical
– *radial nerve*

29 el nervio cubital
– *ulnar nerve*
30 el nervio ciático mayor [en la parte posterior]
– *great sciatic nerve [lying posteriorly]*
31 el nervio femoral
– *femoral nerve (anterior crural nerve)*
32 el nervio tibial
– *tibial nerve*
33 el nervio peroneo
– *peroneal nerve*
**34-64 la musculatura** (el sistema muscular)
– *musculature (muscular system)*
34 el esternocleidomastoideo
– *sternocleidomastoid muscle (sternomastoid muscle)*
35 el músculo deltoide
– *deltoid muscle*
36 el pectoral mayor
– *pectoralis major (greater pectoralis muscle, greater pectoralis)*
37 el bíceps
– *biceps brachii (biceps of the arm)*
38 el tríceps
– *triceps brachii (triceps of the arm)*
39 el supinador largo
– *brachioradialis*
40 el radical anterior
– *flexor carpi radialis (radial flexor of the wrist)*
41 el flexor corto del pulgar
– *thenar muscle*
42 el serrato mayor
– *serratus anterior*
43 el oblicuo mayor
– *obliquus externus abdominis (external oblique)*
44 el recto del abdomen
– *rectus abdominis*
45 el sartorio
– *sartorius*
46 el vasto externo y el vasto interno
– *vastus lateralis and vastus medialis*
47 el tibial anterior
– *tibialis anterior*
48 el tendón de Aquiles
– *tendo calcanaeus (Achilles' tendon)*
49 el abductor del pie, un músculo del pie
– *abductor hallucis (abductor of the hallux), a foot muscle*
50 el músculo occipital
– *occipitalis*
51 el esplenio
– *splenius of the neck*
52 el trapecio
– *trapezius*
53 el infraespinoso
– *infraspinatus*
54 el redondo menor
– *teres minor (lesser teres)*

55 el redondo mayor
– *teres major (greater teres)*
56 el extensor largo del pulgar (el supinador largo)
– *extensor carpi radialis longus (long radial extensor of the wrist)*
57 el extensor común de los dedos de la mano
– *extensor communis digitorum (common extensor of the digits)*
58 el cubital posterior
– *flexor carpi ulnaris (ulnar flexor of the wrist)*
59 el dorsal ancho
– *latissimus dorsi*
60 el glúteo mayor
– *gluteus maximus*
61 el bíceps crural
– *biceps femoris (biceps of the thigh)*
62 los gemelos
– *gastrocnemius, medial and lateral heads*
63 el extensor común de los dedos del pie
– *extensor communis digitorum (common extensor of the digits)*
64 el peroneo largo
– *peroneus longus (long peroneus)*

**1-13 la cabeza y el cuello**
- *head and neck*
1 el esternocleidomastoideo
- *sternocleidomastoid muscle (sternomastoid muscle)*
2 el músculo occipital
- *occipitalis*
3 el músculo temporal
- *temporalis (temporal, temporal muscle)*
4 el músculo frontal
- *occipito frontalis (frontalis)*
5 el músculo orbicular de los párpados
- *orbicularis oculi*
6 los músculos de la expresión facial (músculos *m* faciales)
- *muscles of facial expression*
7 el masetero
- *masseter*
8 el músculo orbicular de los labios
- *orbicularis oris*
9 la glándula parótida
- *parotid gland*
10 el ganglio linfático; *mal llamado:* la glándula linfática
- *lymph node (submandibular lymph gland)*
11 la glándula submaxilar
- *submandibular gland (submaxillary gland)*
12 los músculos de cuello
- *muscles of the neck*
13 el bocado de Adán (la nuez) [más apreciable en los hombres]
- *Adam's apple (laryngeal prominence) [in men only]*
**14-37 la boca y la faringe**
- *mouth and throat*
14 el labio superior
- *upper lip*
15 la encía
- *gum*
**16-18 la dentadura**
- *teeth (set of teeth)*
16 los incisivos
- *incisors*
17 el colmillo
- *canine tooth (canine)*
18 los molares (la muelas)
- *premolar (bicuspid) and molar teeth (premolars and molars)*
19 la comisura de los labios
- *angle of the mouth (labial commissure)*
20 el paladar duro
- *hard palate*
21 el paladar blando (el velo del paladar)
- *soft palate (velum palati, velum)*
22 la úvula (la campanilla)
- *uvula*
23 la amígdala
- *palatine tonsil (tonsil)*
24 la cavidad faríngea (la faringe)
- *pharyngeal opening (pharynx, throat)*
25 la lengua
- *tongue*
26 el labio inferior
- *lower lip*

27 la mandíbula superior
- *upper jaw (maxilla)*
**28-37 el diente** (*Salv.:* el tuco)
- *tooth*
28 el periostio dental
- *periodontal membrane (periodontium, pericementum)*
29 el cemento
- *cement (dental cementum, crusta petrosa)*
30 el esmalte
- *enamel*
31 la dentina (el marfil)
- *dentine (dentin)*
32 la pulpa dental
- *dental pulp (tooth pulp, pulp)*
33 los nervios y los vasos sanguíneos
- *nerves and blood vessels*
34 el incisivo
- *incisor*
35 la muela (el molar)
- *molar tooth (molar)*
36 la raíz
- *root (fang)*
37 la corona
- *crown*
**38-51 el ojo**
- *eye*
38 la ceja
- *eyebrow (supercilium)*
39 el párpado superior
- *upper eyelid (upper palpebra)*
40 el párpado inferior
- *lower eyelid (lower palpebra)*
41 la pestaña
- *eyelash (cilium)*
42 el iris
- *iris*
43 la pupila
- *pupil*
44 los músculos del ojo
- *eye muscles (ocular muscles)*
45 el globo ocular
- *eyeball*
46 el humor (cuerpo *m*) vítreo
- *vitreous body*
47 la córnea
- *cornea*
48 el cristalino
- *lens*
49 la retina
- *retina*
50 el punto ciego (la mácula)
- *blind spot*
51 el nervio óptico
- *optic nerve*
**52-63 el pie**
- *foot*
52 el dedo gordo
- *big toe (great toe, first toe, hallux, digitus I)*
53 el segundo dedo
- *second toe (digitus II)*
54 el tercer dedo
- *third toe (digitus III)*
55 el cuarto dedo
- *fourth toe (digitus IV)*
56 el dedo chico
- *little toe (digitus minimus, digitus V)*

57 la uña del pie
- *toenail*
58 la parte lateral del pie (la región tenar, el pulpejo)
- *ball of the foot*
59 el maléolo externo
- *lateral malleolus (external malleolus, outer malleolus, malleolus fibulae)*
60 el maléolo interno
- *medial malleolus (internal malleolus, inner malleolus, malleolus tibulae, malleolus medialis)*
61 el empeine (el dorso del pie)
- *instep (medial longitudinal arch, dorsum of the foot, dorsum pedis)*
62 la planta del pie
- *sole of the foot*
63 el talón (el calcaño)
- *heel*
**64-83 la mano**
- *hand*
64 el pulgar
- *thumb (pollex, digitus I)*
65 el dedo índice
- *index finger (forefinger, second finger, digitus II)*
66 el dedo corazón (el cordial)
- *middle finger (third finger, digitus medius, digitus III)*
67 el dedo anular
- *ring finger (fourth finger, digitus anularis, digitus IV)*
68 el dedo meñique (el auricular)
- *little finger (fifth finger, digitus minimus, digitus V)*
69 el lado radial de la mano
- *radial side of the hand*
70 el lado cubital de la mano
- *ulnar side of the hand*
71 la palma de la mano
- *palm of the hand (palma manus)*
**72-74 las líneas de la mano**
- *lines of the hand*
72 la línea de la vida
- *life line (line of life)*
73 la línea de la cabeza
- *head line (line of the head)*
74 la línea del corazón
- *heart line (line of the heart)*
75 la región tenar (el pulpejo)
- *ball of the thumb (thenar eminence)*
76 la muñeca
- *wrist (carpus)*
77 la falange
- *phalanx (phalange)*
78 la yema del dedo
- *finger pad*
79 la punta del dedo
- *fingertip*
80 la uña del dedo
- *fingernail (nail)*
81 la lúnula
- *lunule (lunula) of the nail*
82 el nudillo
- *knuckle*
83 el dorso de la mano
- *back of the hand (dorsum of the hand, dorsum manus)*

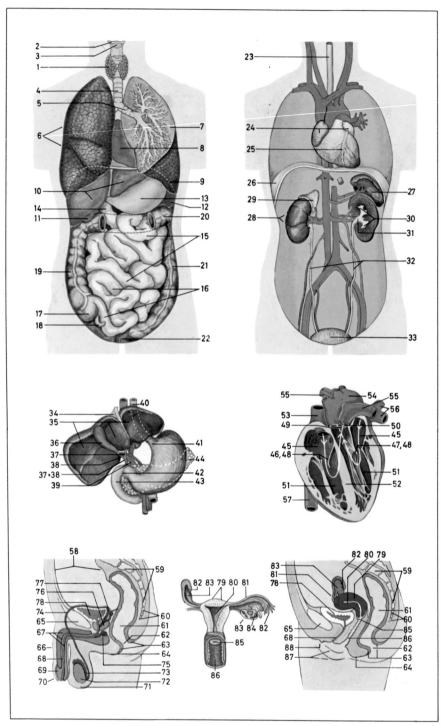

1-57 los órganos internos [vistos de frente]
– *internal organs [front view]*
1 la glándula tiroides
– *thyroid gland*
2-3 la laringe
– *larynx*
2 el hueso hioides
– *hyoid bone (hyoid)*
3 el cartílago tiroides
– *thyroid cartilage*
4 la tráquea
– *trachea (windpipe)*
5 los bronquios
– *bronchus*
6-7 los pulmones
– *lung*
6 el pulmón derecho
– *right lung*
7 el lóbulo pulmonar superior [corte]
– *upper pulmonary lobe (upper lobe of the lung) [section]*
8 el corazón
– *heart*
9 el diafragma
– *diaphragm*
10 el hígado
– *liver*
11 la vesícula biliar
– *gall bladder*
12 el bazo
– *spleen*
13 el estómago
– *stomach*
14-22 los intestinos
– *intestines (bowel)*
14-16 el intestino delgado
– *small intestine (intestinum tenue)*
14 el duodeno
– *duodenum*
15 el yeyuno
– *jejunum*
16 el íleon
– *ileum*
17-22 el intestino grueso
– *large intestine (intestinum crassum)*
17 el ciego
– *caecum (cecum)*
18 el apéndice
– *appendix (vermiform appendix)*
19 el colon ascendente
– *ascending colon*
20 el colon transverso
– *transverse colon*
21 el colon descendente
– *descending colon*
22 el recto
– *rectum*
23 el esófago
– *oesophagus (esophagus, gullet)*
24-25 el corazón
– *heart*
24 la aurícula
– *auricle*
25 el surco longitudinal anterior (el surco interventricular anterior)
– *anterior longitudinal cardiac sulcus*
26 el diafragma
– *diaphragm*
27 el bazo
– *spleen*
28 el riñón derecho
– *right kidney*
29 las glándulas suprarrenales
– *suprarenal gland*
30-31 el riñón izquierdo [corte longitudinal]
– *left kidney [longitudinal section]*

30 el cáliz renal
– *calyx (renal calyx)*
31 la pelvis renal
– *renal pelvis*
32 la uretra
– *ureter*
33 la vejiga
– *bladder*
34-35 el hígado [visto desde atrás]
– *liver [from behind]*
34 el ligamento suspensor del hígado
– *falciform ligament of the liver*
35 el lóbulo del hígado
– *lobe of the liver*
36 la vesícula biliar
– *gall bladder*
37-38 el conducto común de la bilis
– *common bile duct*
37 el conducto hepático
– *hepatic duct (common hepatic duct)*
38 el conducto cístico
– *cystic duct*
39 la vena porta
– *portal vein (hepatic portal vein)*
40 el esófago
– *oesophagus (esophagus, gullet)*
41-42 el estómago
– *stomach*
41 el cardias
– *cardiac orifice*
42 el píloro
– *pylorus*
43 el duodeno
– *duodenum*
44 el páncreas
– *pancreas*
45-57 el corazón [corte longitudinal]
– *heart [longitudinal section]*
45 la aurícula
– *atrium*
46-47 las válvulas del corazón
– *valves of the heart*
46 la válvula tricúspide
– *tricuspid valve (right atrioventricular valve)*
47 la válvula mitral
– *bicuspid valve (mitral valve, left atrioventricular valve)*
48 la válvula semilunar (válvula ƒ de Eustaquio)
– *cusp*
49 la válvula aórtica
– *aortic valve*
50 la válvula pulmonar
– *pulmonary valve*
51 el ventrículo
– *ventricle*
52 el tabique interventricular
– *ventricular septum (interventricular septum)*
53 la vena cava superior
– *superior vena cava*
54 la aorta
– *aorta*
55 la arteria pulmonar
– *pulmonary artery*
56 la vena pulmonar
– *pulmonary vein*
57 la vena cava inferior
– *inferior vena cava*
58 el peritoneo
– *peritoneum*
59 el sacro
– *sacrum*
60 el cóccix
– *coccyx (coccygeal vertebra)*
61 el recto
– *rectum*

62 el ano
– *anus*
63 el esfínter anal
– *anal sphincter*
64 el perineo
– *perineum*
65 la sínfisis del pubis
– *pubic symphysis (symphysis pubis)*
66-77 los órganos sexuales masculinos [corte longitudinal]
– *male sex organs [longitudinal section]*
66 el pene (*Cuba:* la virtud)
– *penis*
67 el cuerpo cavernoso
– *corpus cavernosum and spongiosum of the penis (erectile tissue of the penis)*
68 la uretra
– *urethra*
69 el glande (bálano *m*)
– *glans penis*
70 el prepucio
– *prepuce (foreskin)*
71 el escroto
– *scrotum*
72 el testículo derecho (*Mé.:* el tompeate)
– *right testicle (testis)*
73 el epidídimo
– *epididymis*
74 el conducto espermático
– *spermatic duct (vas deferens)*
75 la glándula de Cowper
– *Cowper's gland (bulbourethral gland)*
76 la próstata
– *prostate (prostate gland)*
77 la vesícula seminal
– *seminal vesicle*
78 la vejiga
– *bladder*
79-88 los órganos sexuales femeninos [corte longitudinal]
– *female sex organs [longitudinal section]*
79 el útero
– *uterus (matrix, womb)*
80 la cavidad uterina
– *cavity of the uterus*
81 la trompa de Falopio
– *fallopian tube (uterine tube, oviduct)*
82 la fimbria
– *fimbria (fimbriated extremity)*
83 el ovario
– *ovary*
84 el folículo con el óvulo
– *follicle with ovum (egg)*
85 el orificio uterino externo (el cuello del útero)
– *os uteri externum*
86 la vagina
– *vagina*
87 los labios de la vulva
– *lip of the pudendum (lip of the vulva)*
88 el clítoris
– *clitoris*

**1-13 vendajes** *m* **de urgencia** *f*
- *emergency bandages*
1 el vendaje de brazo *m*
- *arm bandage*
2 el pañuelo triangular usado como cabestrillo *m* (un brazo en cabestrillo *m*)
- *triangular cloth used as a sling (an arm sling)*
3 el vendaje de cabeza *f* (la capellina)
- *head bandage (capeline)*
4 el paquete de vendajes *m*
- *first aid kit*
5 el vendaje adhesivo (el vendaje plástico; una tirita)
- *first aid dressing*
6 la gasa esterilizada
- *sterile gauze dressing*
7 el esparadrapo
- *adhesive plaster (sticking plaster)*
8 la herida (*Amér. Central y Mé.:* el tajarrazo)
- *wound*
9 la venda de gasa *f*
- *bandage*
10 el entablillado de urgencia *f* para la fractura de un miembro
- *emergency splint for a broken limb (fractured limb)*
11 la pierna fracturada
- *fractured leg (broken leg)*
12 la tablilla
- *splint*
13 la almohadilla
- *headrest*
**14-17 medidas** *f* **para restañar la sangre (cuidados** *m* **en caso** *m* **de hemorragia** *f***) (la ligadura de un vaso sanguíneo)**
- *measures for stanching the blood flow;* here: *tying up (ligature) of a blood vessel*
14 los puntos de presión *f* de las arterias
- *pressure points of the arteries*
15 el torniquete de emergencia *f* en el muslo
- *emergency tourniquet on the thigh*
16 el bastón utilizado para apretar el torniquete
- *walking stick used as a screw*
17 el vendaje de compresión *f*
- *compression bandage*
**18-23 el rescate y el transporte de una persona herida**
- *rescue and transport of an injured person*
18 el asimiento Rautek (para el rescate de la víctima de un accidente de tráfico *m*)
- *Rautek grip [for rescue of a car accident victim]*
19 el asistente (el auxiliador)
- *helper*
20 el herido sin conocimiento *m* (la víctima de un accidente)
- *injured person (casualty)*

21 el agarre de silla *f* (la silla de la reina)
- *chair grip*
22 la silla de anilla *f* improvisada
- *carrying grip*
23 la camilla de emergencia *f* hecha con bastones *m* y una chaqueta
- *emergency stretcher of sticks and a jacket*
**24-27 la posición de una persona inconsciente y la respiración artificial**
- *positioning of an unconscious person and resuscitation,* e. g. *by artificial respiration*
24 la posición lateral de seguridad *f*
- *coma position*
25 la persona inconsciente
- *unconscious person*
26 la respiración boca *f* a boca *f* (*variante:* la respiración boca *f* a nariz *f*)
- *mouth-to-mouth resuscitation* (variation: *mouth-to-nose resuscitation*)
27 el reanimador eléctrico, un aparato de reanimación *f,* un aparato de respiración *f* artificial
- *resuscitator (respiratory apparatus, resuscitation apparatus), a respirator (artificial breathing device)*
**28-33 métodos** *m* **de rescate** *m* **en los accidentes sobre hielo** *m*
- *methods of rescue in ice accidents*
28 la persona hundida en el hielo
- *person who has fallen through the ice*
29 el socorrista
- *rescuer*
30 la cuerda (*Amér. Central y Merid.:* el peal)
- *rope*
31 la mesa (u otro medio de socorro *m*)
- *table (or similar device)*
32 la escalera
- *ladder*
33 el salvamento por uno mismo (el autosalvamento)
- *self-rescue*
**34-38 el rescate de los ahogados**
- *rescue of a drowning person*
34 la liberación del apretón
- *method of release (release grip, release) to free rescuer from the clutch of a drowning person*
35 el ahogado (la persona que se está ahogando)
- *drowning person*
36 el socorrista
- *lifesaver*
37 la presa axilar, una presa para el transporte del ahogado
- *chest grip, a towing grip*
38 la presa por las caderas
- *tired swimmer grip (hip grip)*

**1-74 el consultorio de medicina *f* general**
- *general practice* ( Am. *physician's office*)
1 **la sala de espera *f***
- *waiting room*
2 el paciente
- *patient*
3 los pacientes citados (para un reconocimiento de rutina *f* o para la renovación de recetas *f*)
- *patients with appointments, e.g. for a routine check-up or renewal of prescription*
4 las revistas de la sala de espera *f*
- *magazines [for waiting patients]*
5 la consulta (el despacho de la consulta)
- *reception*
6 el fichero de pacientes *m*
- *patients file*
7 las fichas médicas caducadas
- *eliminated index cards*
8 la ficha médica
- *medical record (medical card)*
9 el volante de asistencia *f* médica
- *health insurance certificate*
10 el almanaque de propaganda *f*
- *advertising calendar (publicity calendar)*
11 el libro de citas *f*
- *appointments book*
12 el archivador de correspondencia *f*
- *correspondence file*
13 el teléfono con contestador *m* y grabador *m* automáticos

- *automatic telephone answering and recording set (telephone answering device)*
14 el radioteléfono
- *radiophone*
15 el micrófono
- *microphone*
16 el panel de exhibición *f*
- *illustrated chart*
17 el almanaque de pared *f*
- *wall calendar*
18 el teléfono
- *telephone*
19 la enfermera
- *[doctor's] assistant*
20 la receta
- *prescription*
21 el listín telefónico
- *telephone index*
22 el diccionario médico
- *medical dictionary*
23 la farmacopea (el vademécum de los medicamentos registrados)
- *pharmacopoeia (list of registered medicines)*
24 la máquina de franquear (*Amér.:* el contador de franqueo)
- *franking machine* (Am. *postage meter)*
25 la grapadora (la cosegrapas)
- *stapler*
26 el fichero de diabéticos *m*
- *diabetics file*
27 el dictáfono
- *dictating machine*

28 la taladradora de papeles *m*
- *paper punch*
29 el sello (la estampilla) del médico
- *doctor's stamp*
30 el tampón (la almohadilla) de tinta *f*
- *ink pad*
31 el portalápices
- *pencil holder*

**32-74 la sala de curas** f
- *surgery*
**32** el cuadro de agudeza f visual
- *chart of eyegrounds*
**33** el maletín del médico
- *doctor's bag (doctor's case)*
**34** el interfono
- *intercom*
**35** el armario de las medicinas
- *medicine cupboard*
**36** el dispensador de algodón m
- *swab dispenser*
**37** el inhalador (el globo de Politzer)
- *inflator (Politzer bag)*
**38** el electrotomo
- *electrotome*
**39** el esterilizador de vapor m
- *steam sterilizer*
**40** el armario de pared f
- *cabinet*
**41** las muestras de medicamentos m
- *medicine samples (from the pharmaceutical industry)*
**42** el pesabebés
- *baby scales*
**43** la mesa de reconocimiento m
- *examination couch*
**44** la lámpara con el haz de luz f dirigible
- *directional lamp*
**45** la mesa de instrumentos m
- *instrument table*
**46** el portatubos
- *tube holder*
**47** el tubo de pomada f
- *tube of ointment*

**48-50 los instrumentos de cirugía** f **menor**
- *instruments for minor surgery*
**48** el abreboca
- *mouth gag*
**49** las pinzas Kocher
- *Kocher's forceps*
**50** el raspador
- *scoop (curette)*
**51** las tijeras curvas
- *angled scissors*
**52** las pinzas
- *forceps*
**53** la sonda de botón m
- *olive-pointed (bulb-headed) probe*
**54** la jeringa para irrigación f del oído o de la vejiga (*Hond., Mé., P. Rico, S. Dgo.:* la visitadora)
- *syringe for irrigations of the ear or bladder*
**55** el esparadrapo
- *adhesive plaster (sticking plaster)*
**56** el material quirúrgico de sutura f
- *surgical suture material*
**57** una aguja curva para suturas f
- *curved surgical needle*
**58** la gasa esterilizada
- *sterile gauze*
**59** el portaagujas
- *needle holder*
**60** el pulverizador para desinfectar la piel
- *spray for disinfecting the skin*
**61** el portahilos
- *thread container*

**62** el oftalmoscopio
- *ophthalmoscope*
**63** el aparato de congelación f para intervención f crioquirúrgica
- *freezer for cryosurgery*
**64** el dispensador de esparadrapo m y de elementos m pequeños
- *dispenser for plasters and small pieces of equipment*
**65** las agujas y las jeringas de un solo uso
- *disposable hypodermic needles and syringes*
**66** el peso, un peso de corredera f
- *scales, sliding-weight scales*
**67** la plataforma (el platillo) del peso
- *weighing platform*
**68** la corredera del peso
- *sliding weight (jockey)*
**69** la talla (el listón para tallar)
- *height gauge (Am. gage)*
**70** el cubo de la basura
- *waste bin (Am. trash bin)*
**71** el esterilizador de aire m caliente
- *hot-air sterilizer*
**72** la pipeta
- *pipette*
**73** el martillo de reflejos m (el martillo percusor)
- *percussor*
**74** el otoscopio (el espéculo auricular)
- *aural speculum (auriscope, aural syringe)*

# 23 Médico II

Doctor II

1 la consulta
– consulting room
2 el médico de medicina f general
– general practitioner
3-21 los instrumentos de reconocimiento m ginecológico y proctológico
– instruments for gynecological and proctological examinations
3 el calentador de los instrumentos a la temperatura del cuerpo
– warming the instruments up to body temperature
4 la mesa de reconocimiento m
– examination couch
5 el colposcopio
– colposcope
6 el binocular
– binocular eyepiece
7 la cámara miniatura (la cámara para fotos m de pequeño formato m)
– miniature camera
8 la fuente de luz f fría
– cold light source
9 el disparador
– cable release
10 el tubo para la fijación del pie
– bracket for the leg support
11 el soporte para la pierna
– leg support (leg holder)
12 las pinzas de asidero m (para coger los apósitos de algodón m)
– holding forceps (sponge holder)
13 el espéculo vaginal
– vaginal speculum

14 la paleta inferior del espéculo
– lower blade of the vaginal speculum
15 la corcheta de platino m (para los frotis)
– platinum loop [for smears]
16 el rectoscopio
– rectoscope
17 las pinzas de biopsia f para el rectoscopio
– biopsy forceps used with the rectoscope (proctoscope)
18 el insuflador de aire m para el rectoscopio
– insufflator for proctoscopy (rectoscopy)
19 el proctoscopio (el espéculo rectal)
– proctoscope (rectal speculum)
20 el fibroscopio urinario (el uretroscopio)
– urethroscope
21 la sonda guía para el proctoscopio
– guide for inserting the proctoscope
22 la unidad diatérmica (el aparato de ondas f cortas)
– diathermy unit (short-wave therapy apparatus)
23 el radiador
– radiator
24 el inhalador
– inhaling apparatus (inhalator)
25 la escupidera (el lavabo para los esputos; Arg., Chile y Urug.: la salivadera)
– basin [for sputum]

26-31 la ergometría
– ergometry
26 el cicloergómetro (el ergómetro de bicicleta f)
– bicycle ergometer
27 el monitor (la pantalla de visualización f del ECG y de la frecuencia cardíaca y respiratoria durante el esfuerzo)
– monitor [for visual display of the ECG and of pulse and respiratory rates when performing work]
28 el ECG (el electrocardiógrafo)
– ECG (electrocardiograph)
29 los electrodos de ventosa f
– suction electrodes
30 los electrodos de correa f para las extremidades
– strap-on electrodes for the limbs
31 el espirómetro (para medir las funciones respiratorias)
– spirometer [for measuring respiratory functions]
32 la toma de la presión sanguínea (de la tensión)
– measuring the blood pressure
33 el tensiómetro (el esfigmómetro)
– sphygmomanometer
34 la abrazadera hinchable
– inflatable cuff
35 el estetoscopio
– stethoscope
36 la unidad de tratamiento f por microondas f
– microwave treatment unit

**37** el aparato de faradización *f* (aplicación *f* de las corrientes de baja frecuencia *f* con diferentes formas *f* de impulsos *m*)
– *faradization unit [for applying low-frequency currents with different pulse shapes]*
**38** el aparato de sintonización *f* automática
– *automatic tuner*
**39** el aparato de terapia *f* con ondas *f* cortas
– *short-wave therapy apparatus*
**40** el microcronómetro
– *timer*
**41-59 el laboratorio**
– *laboratory*
**41** la ayudante técnica del laboratorio (la laborante)
– *medical laboratory technician*
**42** el soporte de los tubos capilares para la sedimentación de la sangre
– *capillary tube stand for blood sedimentation*
**43** la probeta para medir
– *measuring cylinder*
**44** la pipeta automática
– *automatic pipette*
**45** la cubeta de forma *f* arriñonada
– *kidney dish*
**46** el electrocardiógrafo portátil para urgencias *f*
– *portable ECG machine for emergency use*

**47** el aparato de pipeta *f* automático (el titrímetro automático)
– *automatic pipetting device*
**48** el baño de agua a temperatura *f* constante
– *constant temperature water bath*
**49** el grifo con trompa *f* de agua *f*
– *tap with water jet pump*
**50** la cubeta de coloración *f* (para la coloración de los frotis sanguíneos, los sedimentos y otros frotis *m*)
– *staining dish [for staining blood smears, sediments, and other smears]*
**51** el microscopio binocular de investigación *f*
– *binocular research microscope*
**52** el soporte de pipetas *f* para la fotometría
– *pipette stand for photometry*
**53** el calculador y analizador *m* de fotometría *f*
– *computer and analyser for photometry*
**54** el fotómetro
– *photometer*
**55** el contador potenciométrico
– *potentiometric recorder*
**56** la sección de transformación *f*
– *transforming section*
**57** el material de laboratorio *m*
– *laboratory apparatus (laboratory equipment)*

**58** el cuadro de sedimentos *m* de la orina
– *urine sediment chart*
**59** la centrifugadora
– *centrifuge*

1 el dentista (el odontólogo)
- *dentist (dental surgeon)*
2 el paciente
- *patient*
3 el sillón de dentista *m*
- *dentist's chair*
4 los instrumentos dentales
- *dental instruments*
5 la bandeja de los instrumentos
- *instrument tray*
6 las fresas con diferentes piezas *f* de mano *f*
- *drills with different handpieces*
7 la caja de las medicinas
- *medicine case*
8 la unidad (el armario) de almacenaje (para los instrumentos dentales)
- *storage unit [for dental instruments]*
9 la unidad de asistencia *f*
- *assistant's unit*
10 la jeringa multifuncional (para agua *f* fría y caliente, spray *m* o aire *m*)
- *multi-purpose syringe [for cold and warm water, spray, or air]*
11 el aparato de succión *f* de la saliva
- *suction apparatus*
12 la escudilla para escupir (la escupidera)
- *basin*
13 el vaso de agua con relleno automático
- *water glass, filled automatically*
14 el taburete del dentista
- *stool*

15 el lavamanos (*sin.:* la palangana. *Amér.:* el platón; *Chile:* la taza)
- *washbasin*
16 el mueble de los instrumentos
- *instrument cabinet*
17 el cajón de las fresas
- *drawer for drills*
18 la ayudante del dentista (la enfermera)
- *dentist's assistant*
19 la lámpara de dentista *m*
- *dentist's lamp*
20 la luz del techo
- *ceiling light*
21 el aparato de rayos *m* X para radiografías *f* panorámicas
- *X-ray apparatus for panoramic pictures*
22 el generador de rayos *m* X
- *X-ray generator*
23 el aparato de microondas *f,*un aparato de irradiación *f*
- *microwave treatment unit, a radiation unit*
24 el asiento
- *seat*

# Dentista

25 la prótesis dental (la dentadura postiza)
– *denture (set of false teeth)*
26 el puente dental
– *bridge (dental bridge)*
27 el raigón debidamente preparado
– *prepared stump of the tooth*
28 la corona (*clases*: la corona de oro *m*, la corona de pasta *f*)
– *crown*; kinds: *gold crown, jacket crown*
29 el diente de porcelana *f*
– *porcelain tooth (porcelain pontic)*
30 el empaste
– *filling*
31 el diente de pivote *m*
– *post crown*
32 el revestimiento
– *facing*
33 el anillo
– *diaphragm*
34 el pivote
– *post*
35 el disco de carborundo *m*
– *carborundum disc (disk)*
36 el disco de esmeril *m*
– *grinding wheel*
37 fresas *f* para cavidades *f*
– *burs*
38 la fresa en forma *f* de llama *f*
– *flame-shaped finishing bur*
39 fresas *f* de fisuras *f*
– *fissure burs*
40 la fresa diamantada
– *diamond point*
41 el espejo de boca *f*
– *mouth mirror*
42 la lámpara de boca *f*
– *mouth lamp*
43 el termocauterio (el cauterio)
– *cautery*
44 el electrodo de platino *m* iridiado
– *platinum-iridium electrode*
45 instrumentos *m* para limpiar los dientes
– *tooth scalers*
46 la sonda
– *probe*
47 las tenazas de extracción *f*
– *extraction forceps*
48 el elevador (el botador de pie *m* de cabra *f*)
– *tooth-root elevator*
49 el cincel de huesos *m*
– *bone chisel*
50 la espátula
– *spatula*
51 el mezclador del material de empaste *m*
– *mixer for filling material*
52 el sincronizador
– *synchronous timer*
53 la jeringa hipodérmica para la anestesia local (anestesia *f* del nervio)
– *hypodermic syringe for injection of local anaesthetic*
54 la aguja hipodérmica
– *hypodermic needle*
55 el portamatrices
– *matrix holder*
56 la cubeta para la impresión
– *impression tray*
57 la lamparilla de alcohol *m*
– *spirit lamp*

**1-30 la sala de cuidados _m_ intensivos (la unidad de vigilancia _f_ intensiva, UVI)**
- *intensive care unit*

**1-9 la sala de control _m_**
- *control room*

1 el pupitre (la consola) para vigilar el ritmo _m_ cardíaco y la presión sanguínea
- *central control unit for monitoring heart rhythm (cardiac rhythm) and blood pressure*

2 el monitor del electrocardiograma (ECG)
- *electrocardiogram monitor (ECG monitor)*

3 el aparato registrador
- *recorder*

4 el papel de registro _m_
- *recording paper*

5 la ficha del paciente
- *patient's card*

6 la lámpara indicadora (con una tecla de selección para cada enfermo _m_)
- *indicator lights [with call buttons for each patient]*

7 la espátula
- *spatula*

8 la pared transparente
- *window (observation window, glass partition)*

9 la persiana de separación
- *blind*

10 la cama del paciente
- *bed (hospital bed)*

11 el soporte para los dispositivos de infusión _f_
- *stand for infusion apparatus*

12 el frasco de infusión _f_
- *infusion bottle*

13 el tubo para el goteo intravenoso (el gotero)
- *tube for intravenous drips*

14 el dispositivo de infusión _f_ para los medicamentos hidrosolubles
- *infusion device for water-soluble medicaments*

15 el esfigmómetro (el tensiómetro)
- *sphygmomanometer*

16 la abrazadera hinchable
- *cuff*

17 la pera para inflar
- *inflating bulb*

18 el manómetro de mercurio _m_
- *mercury manometer*

19 el monitor de cama _f_
- *bed monitor*

20 los cables de conexión _f_ con la unidad de control _m_ central
- *connecting lead to the central control unit*

21 el monitor del electrocardiograma (ECG)
- *electrocardiogram monitor (ECG monitor)*

22 el manómetro de distribución _f_ de oxígeno _m_
- *manometer for the oxygen supply*

23 la conexión de pared _f_ para el tratamiento con oxígeno _m_
- *wall connection for oxygen treatment*

24 la unidad móvil de vigilancia _f_ del paciente
- *mobile monitoring unit*

25 el cable del electrodo del estimulador cardíaco temporal
- *electrode lead to the short-term pacemaker*

26 los electrodos para el tratamiento de un shock
- *electrodes for shock treatment*

27 el electrocardiógrafo
- *ECG recording unit*

28 el monitor del electrocardiograma (ECG)
- *electrocardiogram monitor (ECG monitor)*

29 los botones para regular el monitor
- *control switches and knobs (controls) for adjusting the monitor*

30 los botones de control _m_ del estimulador cardíaco
- *control buttons for the pacemaker unit .*

31 **el estimulador cardíaco (el marcapasos)**
 – *pacemaker (cardiac pacemaker)*
32 la pila de mercurio *m*
 – *mercury battery*
33 el generador de impulsos *m* programado
 – *programmed impulse generator*
34 la salida del electrodo
 – *electrode exit point*
35 el electrodo
 – *electrode*
36 la implantación del marcapasos
 – *implantation of the pacemaker*
37 el marcapasos interno
 – *internal cardiac pacemaker (internal pacemaker, pacemaker)*
38 el electrodo introducido a través de la vena
 – *electrode inserted through the vein*
39 la silueta cardíaca en rayos *m* X
 – *cardiac silhouette on the X-ray*
40 **la unidad de control del marcapasos**
 – *pacemaker control unit*
41 el electrocardiógrafo
 – *electrocardiograph (ECG recorder)*
42 el contador automático de impulsos *m*
 – *automatic impulse meter*
43 el cable de conexión *f* con el paciente (cable *m* ECG)
 – *ECG lead to the patient*
44 el monitor para el control visual de los impulsos del marcapasos
 – *monitor unit for visual monitoring of the pacemaker impulses*
45 el analizador del ECG de larga duración *f*
 – *long-term ECG analyser*

46 la cinta magnética para la grabación de los impulsos del ECG durante el análisis
 – *magnetic tape for recording the ECG impulses during analysis*
47 el monitor de control del ECG
 – *ECG monitor*
48 el análisis automático del ritmo del ECG sobre papel *m*
 – *automatic analysis on paper of the ECG rhythm*
49 el botón de ajuste *m* de amplitud *f* del ECG
 – *control knob for the ECG amplitude*
50 el teclado de selección *f* del programa de análisis *m* del ECG
 – *program selector switches for the ECG analysis*
51 el cargador de las pilas del marcapasos del paciente
 – *charger for the pacemaker batteries*
52 el comprobador de las pilas
 – *battery tester*
53 el manómetro del catéter cardíaco derecho
 – *pressure gauge* (Am. *gage) for the right cardiac catheter*
54 el monitor de control *m* de curvas *f*
 – *trace monitor*
55 el indicador de presión *f*
 – *pressure indicator*
56 el cable de conexión *f* con la impresora de papel *m*
 – *connecting lead to the paper recorder*
57 la impresora de papel *m* para las curvas de presión *f*
 – *paper recorder for pressure traces*

**1-54 la sección quirúrgica
(la clínica quirúrgica)**
- *surgical unit*
**1-33 el quirófano (la sala de
operaciones *f*)**
- *operating theatre* (Am. *theater*)
**1** el aparato de anestesia *f* y de
respiración *f*
- *anaesthesia and breathing
apparatus (respiratory machine)*
**2** el tubo de inhalación *f*
- *inhalers (inhaling tubes)*
**3** el indicador volumétrico del
óxido nitroso (protóxido *m* de
nitrógeno *m*)
- *flowmeter for nitrous oxide*
**4** el indicador volumétrico del
oxígeno
- *oxygen flow meter*
**5** la mesa de operaciones *f* sobre
pedestal *m*
- *pedestal operating table*
**6** el pedestal de la mesa de
operaciones *f*
- *table pedestal*
**7** el aparato de control *m*
- *control device (control unit)*
**8** la superficie (el tablero)
regulable de la mesa de
operaciones *f*
- *adjustable top of the operating
table*

**9** el soporte para el goteo
intravenoso
- *stand for intravenous drips*
**10** la lámpara de operaciones *f*
giratoria sin sombras *f*
- *swivel-mounted shadow-free
operating lamp*
**11** la lámpara
- *individual lamp*
**12** la agarradera
- *handle*
**13** el brazo orientable
- *swivel arm*
**14** el aparato móvil de radiología *f*
- *mobile fluoroscope*
**15** el monitor transformador de la
imagen
- *monitor of the image converter*
**16** el monitor [parte trasera]
- *monitor [back]*
**17** el tubo
- *tube*
**18** el transformador de la imagen
- *image converter*
**19** la armazón en forma *f* de C
- *C-shaped frame*
**20** el panel de control *m* del aire
acondicionado
- *control panel for the air-
conditioning*
**21** el material quirúrgico de
sutura *f*
- *surgical suture material*

**22** la batea para apósitos *m*
- *mobile waste tray*
**23** el bote de compresas *f* no
esterilizadas
- *containers for unsterile
(unsterilized) pads*
**24** el respirador artificial
- *anaesthesia and respiratory
apparatus*
**25** la bolsa de control *m* de la
respiración (el respirador)
- *respirator*
**26** el recipiente de fluotano *m*
(halotano *m*)
- *fluothane container (halothane
container)*
**27** el botón de regulación *f* de la
ventilación
- *ventilation control knob*
**28** el panel de registro *m* con
indicador *m* del volumen
respiratorio
- *indicator with pointer for
respiratory volume*
**29** el soporte con los tubos
inhaladores y el manómetro
- *stand with inhalers (inhaling
tubes) and pressure gauges* (Am.
*gages)*
**30** el portacatéter
- *catheter holder*
**31** el catéter en el envase estéril
- *catheter in sterile packing*

32 el esfigmógrafo (el registrador de los impulsos)
– *sphygmograph*
33 el monitor
– *monitor*
34-54 **la sala de preparación *f* y de esterilización *f***
– *preparation and sterilization room*
34 el material de vendaje *m*
– *dressing material*
35 el esterilizador pequeño
– *small sterilizer*
36 el carro de la mesa de operaciones *f*
– *carriage of the operating table*
37 la mesa de instrumentos *m* móvil
– *mobile instrument table*
38 el paño estéril
– *sterile cloth*
39 la cubeta de los instrumentos
– *instrument tray*
40-53 **los instrumentos quirúrgicos**
– *surgical instruments*
40 la sonda de botón *m*
– *olive-pointed (bulb-headed) probe*
41 la sonda acanalada
– *hollow probe*
42 las tijeras curvadas
– *curved scissors*

43 el bisturí
– *scalpel (surgical knife)*
44 las pinzas para ligaduras *f*
– *ligature-holding forceps*
45 las pinzas de secuestro *m*
– *sequestrum forceps*
46 la mandíbula de las pinzas
– *jaw*
47 el tubo de drenaje *m*
– *drainage tube*
48 el torniquete (el clamp arterial)
– *surgeon's tourniquet*
49 las pinzas para arterias *f*
– *artery forceps*
50 el separador de alambre *m*
– *blunt hook*
51 las cizallas para huesos *m*
– *bone nippers (bone-cutting forceps)*
52 la cucharilla (la cureta) para el raspado *m* (para el curetaje)
– *scoop (curette) for erasion (curettage)*
53 los fórceps
– *obstetrical forceps*
54 el rollo de esparadrapo *m*
– *roll of plaster*

**1-35 el servicio de radiología (la unidad de rayos *m* X)**
– *X-ray unit*
1 la mesa de reconocimiento *m* de rayos *m* X
– *X-ray examination table*
2 el soporte para las placas de rayos *m* X
– *support for X-ray cassettes*
3 el ajuste vertical del haz central para los clichés laterales
– *height adjustment of the central beam for lateral views*
4 la compresa para la radiografía de los riñones y de las vías biliares (urografía *f* y colecistografía *f*)
– *compress for pyelography and cholecystography*
5 la cubeta de los instrumentos
– *instrument basin*
6 el equipo de rayos *m* X para la urétero-pielografía
– *X-ray apparatus for pyelograms*
7 el tubo de rayos *m* X
– *X-ray tube*
8 el soporte telescópico del tubo de rayos *m* X
– *telescopic X-ray support*
9 la sala de control *m* central de rayos *m* X
– *central X-ray control unit*

10 el pupitre de control *m*
– *control panel (control desk)*
11 la enfermera radiógrafa
– *radiographer (X-ray technician)*
12 la ventana que da a la sala de angiografía *f*
– *window to the angiography room*
13 el oxímetro
– *oxymeter*
14 las placas para urografía *f*
– *pyelogram cassettes*
15 el aparato para inyección *f* de productos *m* de contraste *m*
– *contrast medium injector*
16 el amplificador de imagen *f* de rayos *m* X
– *X-ray image intensifier*
17 la armazón en forma *f* de C
– *C-shaped frame*
18 la cabeza de radiografía *f* con el tubo de rayos *m* X
– *X-ray head with X-ray tube*
19 el transformador de imagen *f* con el tubo transformador
– *image converter with converter tube*
20 la cámara de película *f*
– *film camera*
21 el interruptor de pedal *m*
– *foot switch*

22 el soporte móvil
– *mobile mounting*
23 el monitor
– *monitor*
24 el brazo giratorio del monitor
– *swivel-mounted monitor support*
25 la lámpara sin sombras *f*
– *operating lamp*
26 la mesa de reconocimientos *m* angiográficos
– *angiographic examination table*
27 la almohada
– *pillow*
28 el registrador de ocho canales *m*
– *eight-channel recorder*
29 el papel de registro *m*
– *recording paper*
30 la unidad de control *m* del catéter para la cateterización del corazón
– *catheter gauge (Am. gage) unit for catheterization of the heart*
31 el monitor de seis canales *m* para las curvas de tensión *f* y ECG *m*
– *six-channel monitor for pressure graphs and ECG*
32 las cajas transductoras de presión *f*
– *slide-in units of the pressure transducer*

33 la unidad del papel de
registro *m* con revelador *m*
para la reproducción
fotográfica
- *paper recorder unit with
developer for photographic
recording*
34 el papel de registro *m* (de
grabación *f*)
- *recording paper*
35 el cronómetro (el reloj)
- *timer*
**36-50 espirometría *f***
- *spirometry*
36 el espirógrafo para la
exploración del
funcionamiento respiratorio
- *spirograph for pulmonary
function tests*
37 el tubo respiratorio
- *breathing tube*
38 la boquilla
- *mouthpiece*
39 el absorbedor de cal *f* sosa
- *soda-lime absorber*
40 el papel de registro *m*
- *recording paper*
41 la regulación para el suministro
de gas *m*
- *control knobs for gas supply*

42 el estabilizador de O₂
- *Og2-stabilizer*
43 la válvula regualdora
- *throttle valve*
44 la conexión del absorbedor
- *absorber attachment*
45 la botella de oxígeno *m*
- *oxygen cylinder*
46 el suministro de agua *f*
- *water supply*
47 el soporte del tubo flexible
- *tube support*
48 la mascarilla
- *mask*
49 el contador del consumo de
CO₂
- *COg2 consumption meter*
50 el taburete del paciente
- *stool for the patient*

1 la cuna con ruedecillas *f*
– *collapsible cot*
2 el balancín de bebé *m*
– *bouncing cradle*
3 la bañera
– *baby bath*
4 el soporte para poner los pañales (el vestidor, el envolvedero)
– *changing top*
5 el recién nacido (el bebé; *Amér.:* la guagua; *Perú:* el ñaño)
– *baby (new-born baby)*
6 la madre
– *mother*
7 el cepillo del pelo
– *hairbrush*
8 el peine
– *comb*
9 la toalla de mano *m*
– *hand towel*
10 el juguete flotante
– *toy duck*
11 la cómoda de la ropita del niño
– *changing unit*
12 el anillo de dentición *f*
– *teething ring*
13 la caja de crema *f*
– *cream jar*
14 el bote de polvos *m* de talco *m*
– *box of baby powder*

15 el chupete (*Amér.:* el chupón)
– *dummy*
16 la pelota
– *ball*
17 el saco de dormir del bebé (*Guat.:* el jatico)
– *sleeping bag*
18 la caja de aseo *m*
– *layette box*
19 el biberón (*Amér.:* la mamadera; *Col. y Venez.:* el tetero; *Guat. y Hond.:* el pepe; *Col.:* el chupo)
– *feeding bottle*
20 la tetilla (la tetina)
– *teat*
21 el calientabiberones
– *bottle warmer*
22 las braguitas de plástico *m* para los pañales de usar y tirar (de un solo uso)
– *rubber baby pants for disposable nappies* (Am. *diapers)*
23 la camisita de niño *m*
– *vest*
24 las polainas
– *leggings*
25 la chaquetita del bebé
– *baby's jacket*
26 el gorro
– *hood*

27 la taza para niño *m*
– *baby's cup*
28 el plato para niño *m* (el plato para papillas *f*), un plato calentador
– *baby's plate, a stay-warm plate*
29 el termómetro
– *thermometer*

30 el moisés, un cochecito de
  niño *m*
– *bassinet, a wicker pram*
31 el juego de ropa de cama *f* del
  moisés
– *set of bassinet covers*
32 el baldaquín (el dosel)
– *canopy*
33 la silla alta de niño *m*, una silla
  plegable
– *baby's high chair, a folding chair*
34 el landó (cochecito *m* de niño
  *m*) con visión *f* panorámica
– *pram (baby-carriage) [with
  windows]*
35 la capota plegable
– *folding hood*
36 la ventana
– *window*
37 la silla con ruedas *f*
– *pushchair* (Am. *stroller*)
38 el folgo (bolsa *f* para abrigar
  los pies)
– *foot-muff* (Am. *foot-bag*)
39 el parque plegable (el corral
  plegable)
– *play pen*
40 el suelo del parque
– *floor of the play pen*
41 el juego de construcción *f*
– *building blocks (building bricks)*

42 el niño pequeño (*Amér.:* el
  pibe; *Arg. y Urug.:* el pabete)
– *small child*
43 el babero
– *bib*
44 el sonajero (*Chile:* la sonajera)
– *rattle (baby's rattle)*
45 las botitas de bebé *m*
– *bootees*
46 el osito de peluche *m*
– *teddy bear*
47 el orinal (*Chile:* la pava; *Cuba:*
  el tibor; *Mé.:* la cotorra)
– *potty (baby's pot)*
48 el capacho (el capazo)
  portabebés
– *carrycot*
49 la ventana
– *window*
50 las asas
– *handles*

# 29 Ropa de niños

**1-12 la ropa de niños *m* pequeños**
– *baby clothes*
1 el conjunto de calle *f*
– *pram suit*
2 el gorro (la capucha; *Antillas:* la escofieta)
– *hood*
3 la chaqueta
– *pram jacket (matinée coat)*
4 el pompón (la borla)
– *pompon (bobble)*
5 los patucos (los patines)
– *bootees*
6 la camiseta
– *sleeveless vest*
7 la camiseta de mangas *f* cortas
– *envelope-neck vest*
8 la camisita de bebé *m*
– *wrapover vest*
9 el jersey de bebé *m*
– *baby's jacket*
10 el bragapañal de plástico *m*
– *rubber baby pants*
11 el pelele entero (el pelele con pies *m*)
– *playsuit*
12 el traje de dos piezas *f* para el bebé
– *two-piece suit*
**13-30 los trajes de niños *m***
– *infants' wear*
13 el vestido de verano *m*, un vestido con tirantes *m*
– *child's sundress, a pinafore dress*
14 el tirante con volantes *m*
– *frilled shoulder strap*
15 el peto de pliegues *m* fruncidos y bordados
– *shirred top*
16 el sombrero de sol *m*
– *sun hat*
17 el traje de punto *m* de una pieza
– *one-piece jersey suit*
18 la cremallera delantera
– *front zip*
19 el mono
– *catsuit (playsuit)*
20 la aplicación (el bordado sobrepuesto)
– *motif (appliqué)*
21 el pantaloncito de jugar (el pelele)
– *romper*
22 el jubón (la ranita)
– *playsuit (romper suit)*
23 el pijama entero (el pijama de una pieza)
– *coverall (sleeper and strampler)*
24 el albornoz
– *dressing gown (bath robe)*
25 los pantalones cortos
– *children's shorts*
26 los tirantes
– *braces* (Am. *suspenders*)
27 la camiseta (el tee-shirt)
– *children's T-shirt*
28 el vestido de punto *m*
– *jersey dress, a knitted dress*

29 el bordado
– *embroidery*
30 los calcetines de niño *m* (*Chile:* los botines)
– *children's ankle socks*
**31-47 los trajes del escolar**
– *school children's wear*
31 el impermeable
– *raincoat*
32 los pantalones de piel *f* (los pantalones de cuero *m*)
– *leather shorts (lederhosen)*
33 el botón de asta *f*
– *staghorn button*
34 el tirante de cuero *m*
– *braces* (Am. *suspenders*)
35 la bragueta
– *flap*
36 el vestido tirolés infantil
– *girl's dirndl*
37 el cordón cruzado
– *cross lacing*
38 el traje entero de nieve *f* (el traje guateado)
– *snow suit, a quilted suit*
39 el pespunte (el enguatado)
– *quilt stitching (quilting)*
40 el pantalón con peto *m*
– *dungarees (bib and brace)*
41 la falda con peto *m*
– *bib skirt (bib top pinafore)*
42 los leotardos, los pantis (*ant.:* las calzas)
– *tights*
43 el suéter (el jersey)
– *sweater (jumper)*
44 la chaqueta de símil piel *f*
– *pile jacket*
45 los pantalones de trabillas *f*
– *leggings*
46 la falda (*Amér.:* la pollera)
– *girl's skirt*
47 el jersey (el niqui)
– *child's jumper*
**48-68 la ropa de jóvenes *m***
– *teenagers' clothes*
48 la marinera (el blusón de muchacha)
– *girl's overblouse (overtop)*
49 los pantalones de chica *f*
– *slacks*
50 el conjunto de dos piezas *f* (falda *f* y chaqueta *f*) de chica *f*
– *girl's skirt suit*
51 la chaqueta (*Amér.:* el saco)
– *jacket*
52 la falda (*Amér.:* la pollera)
– *skirt*
53 las medias-calcetín
– *knee-length socks*
54 el abrigo de chica *f*
– *girl's coat*
55 el cinturón
– *tie belt*
56 el bolso de chica *f*
– *girl's bag*
57 el sombrero de lana *f*
– *woollen (Am. woolen) hat*

58 la blusa de chica *f*
– *girl's blouse*
59 la falda-pantalón
– *culottes*
60 los pantalones
– *boy's trousers*
61 la camisa
– *boy's shirt*
62 el anorak
– *anorak*
63 los bolsillos sesgados
– *inset pockets*
64 el cordón de la capucha
– *hood drawstring (drawstring)*
65 los puños de punto *m*
– *knitted welt*
66 la cazadora
– *parka coat (parka)*
67 el cordón para atar
– *drawstring (draw cord)*
68 los bolsillos pegados (los bolsillos de parche *m*)
– *patch pockets*

1 la chaqueta de visón *m*
- *mink jacket*
2 el jersey de cuello *m* enrollado
- *cowl neck jumper*
3 el cuello enrollado (*variedades:* cuello vuelto, cuello de cisne)
- *cowl collar*
4 el gabán de punto *m*
- *knitted overtop*
5 el cuello marinero
- *turndown collar*
6 la manga vuelta
- *turn-up (turnover) sleeve*
7 el polo de cuello *m* alto
- *polo neck jumper*
8 la saya de vestir (*Cuba:* la sayuela)
- *pinafore dress*
9 la blusa (con el cuello de solapa *f*)
- *blouse with revers collar*
10 el vestido de blusa *f*, un vestido enteramente abotonado
- *shirt-waister dress, a button-through dress*
11 el cinturón (*Antillas y Perú:* la correa)
- *belt*
12 el vestido de invierno *m*
- *winter dress*
13 el ribete
- *piping*
14 el puño
- *cuff*
15 la manga larga
- *long sleeve*
16 el chaleco acolchado (enguatado)
- *quilted waistcoat*
17 el punto de colcha *f* (el pespunte)
- *quilt stitching (quilting)*
18 el adorno de cuero *m*
- *leather trimming*
19 el pantalón largo de invierno *m*
- *winter slacks*
20 el jersey a rayas *f*
- *striped polo jumper*
21 el mono
- *boiler suit (dungarees, bib and brace)*
22 el bolsillo de parche *m*
- *patch pocket*
23 el bolsillo del pecho
- *front pocket*
24 el peto
- *bib*
25 el vestido de cubrir por encima (el guardapolvo)
- *wrapover dress (wrap-around dress)*
26 la blusa de polo *m*
- *shirt*
27 el vestido de folklore *m*
- *peasant-style dress*
28 el ribete de flores *f*
- *floral braid*
29 la túnica (el vestido de túnica *f*)
- *tunic (tunic top)*

30 el puño
- *ribbed cuff*
31 los pespuntes decorativos
- *quilted design*
32 la falda plisada
- *pleated skirt*
33 el vestido de dos piezas *f* de punto *m*
- *two-piece knitted dress*
34 el escotado de barco *m*
- *boat neck, a neckline*
35 la vuelta de manga *f*
- *turn-up*
36 la manga de quimono *m*
- *kimono sleeve*
37 el dibujo de punto *m*
- *knitted design*
38 la cazadora (*Arg.:* la campera)
- *lumber-jacket*
39 el dibujo de trenza *f*
- *cable pattern*
40 la blusa (*Mé.:* el caracol; *Perú:* el polquin)
- *shirt-blouse*
41 la presilla
- *loop fastening*
42 el bordado
- *embroidery*
43 el cuello alto
- *stand-up collar*
44 el pantalón bombacho
- *cossack trousers*
45 el combinado de dos piezas *f* (el vestido de casaca *f*)
- *two-piece combination (shirt top and long skirt)*
46 el lazo
- *tie (bow)*
47 el canesú
- *decorative facing*
48 la raja de la manga
- *cuff slit*
49 la raja del costado
- *side slit*
50 la casulla
- *tabard*
51 la falda abierta por el costado
- *inverted pleat skirt*
52 el pliegue invertido
- *godet*
53 el vestido de noche *f*
- *evening gown*
54 la manga de campana *f* plisada
- *pleated bell sleeve*
55 la blusa de gala *f*
- *party blouse*
56 la falda de gala *f*
- *party skirt*
57 el traje pantalón *m*
- *trouser suit (slack suit)*
58 la chaqueta (*Amér.:* el saco) de ante *m*
- *suede jacket*
59 el adorno de piel *f*
- *fur trimming*
60 el abrigo de piel *f* (*variedades:* astracán, breitschwanz *m*, visón *m*, marta *f* cebellina)

- *fur coat;* kinds: *Persian lamb, broadtail, mink, sable*
61 el abrigo de invierno *m* (el abrigo de paño *m*) (*Arg., Chile y Salv.:* el tapado)
- *winter coat, a cloth coat*
62 el puño de piel *f*
- *fur cuff (fur-trimmed cuff)*
63 el cuello de piel *f*
- *fur collar (fur-trimmed collar)*
64 el abrigo de loden *m*
- *loden coat*
65 la esclavina (*Chile y Arg.:* el capingo)
- *cape*
66 los botones de palillo *m*
- *toggle fastenings*
67 la falda de loden *m*
- *loden skirt*
68 la capa-poncho
- *poncho-style coat*
69 la capucha
- *hood*

# 31 Ropa de señora II (ropa de verano)

# Ladies' Wear II (Summer Wear)

1 el traje sastre
 – skirt suit
2 la chaqueta (*Amér.*: el saco) del traje
 – jacket
3 la falda del traje
 – skirt
4 el bolsillo sesgado
 – inset pocket
5 el pespunte
 – decorative stitching
6 el traje chaqueta *f*
 – dress and jacket combination
7 el ribete
 – piping
8 el vestido de tirantes *m*
 – pinafore dress
9 el vestido de verano *m*
 – summer dress
10 el cinturón (*Antillas y Perú*: la correa)
 – belt
11 el vestido de dos piezas *f*
 – two-piece dress
12 la hebilla de cinturón *m*
 – belt buckle
13 la falda cruzada
 – wrapover (wrap-around) skirt
14 la línea tubo *m*
 – pencil silhouette
15 los botones de la hombrera *f*
 – shoulder buttons
16 la manga de murciélago *m*
 – batwing sleeve
17 el sobrevestido
 – overdress
18 el canesú quimono *m*
 – kimono yoke
19 el cinturón anudado
 – tie belt
20 el abrigo de verano *m*
 – summer coat
21 la capucha fija
 – detachable hood
22 la blusa de verano *m*
 – summer blouse
23 la solapa
 – lapel
24 la falda
 – skirt
25 el pliegue delantero
 – front pleat
26 el vestido tirolés (el vestido dirndl)
 – dirndl (dirndl dress)
27 la manga fofa (la manga abombada)
 – puffed sleeve
28 el collar tirolés (el collar de folklore *m)*
 – dirndl necklace
29 la blusa tirolesa
 – dirndl blouse
30 el corpiño
 – bodice
31 el delantal tirolés
 – dirndl apron

32 el adorno de encaje *m* (el encaje), un encaje de algodón *m*
 – lace trimming (lace), cotton lace
33 el delantal de volantes *m*
 – frilled apron
34 el volante (*Arg. y Venez.*: el colado)
 – frill
35 la casaca (*Col., C. Rica y Chile:* el palto)
 – smock overall
36 el vestido de casa *f*
 – house frock (house dress)
37 la chaqueta (*Amér.*: el saco) de popelina *f*
 – poplin jacket
38 la camiseta (el tee-shirt)
 – T-shirt
39 el pantalón corto de señora *f* (el short)
 – ladies' shorts
40 la vuelta del pantalón
 – trouser turn-up
41 el cinturón
 – waistband
42 la cazadora
 – bomber jacket
43 la cinturilla elástica
 – stretch welt
44 las bermudas
 – Bermuda shorts
45 el pespunte
 – saddle stitching
46 el cuello de volantes *m*
 – frill collar
47 el nudo
 – knot
48 la falda-pantalón
 – culotte
49 el conjunto
 – twin set
50 la chaqueta (*Amér.*: el saco) de punto *m*
 – cardigan
51 el suéter
 – sweater
52 el pantalón de verano *m*
 – summer (lightweight) slacks
53 el mono
 – jumpsuit
54 la vuelta de manga *f* (el puño vuelto)
 – turn-up
55 la cremallera
 – zip
56 el bolsillo de parche *m* (*Amér. Central, Mé., y Perú*: la bolsa)
 – patch pocket
57 el pañuelo de cuello *m*
 – scarf (neckerchief)
58 el conjunto de dos piezas *f* vaqueras
 – denim suit
59 la chaqueta vaquera
 – denim waistcoat
60 el pantalón vaquero (los jeans, blue jeans)
 – jeans (denims)

61 la sobreblusa (la túnica; *Ec. y Perú*: la polca)
 – overblouse
62 la manga remangada
 – turned-up sleeve
63 el cinturón elástico
 – stretch belt
64 la camiseta de espaldas *f* desnudas (el tee-shirt de espaldas *f* desnudas)
 – halter top
65 el jersey casaca *f*
 – knitted overtop
66 el cinturón de jareta *f*
 – drawstring waist
67 el suéter de verano *m*
 – short-sleeved jumper
68 el escote en forma *f* de V
 – V-neck (vee-neck)
69 el cuello camisero
 – turndown collar
70 la elástico de punto *m*
 – knitted welt
71 el chal (el chal tiangular; *Mé.*: el tápalo)
 – shawl

74

**1-15 la ropa interior de señora** *f*
(la lencería)
- *ladies' underwear (ladies'*
  *underclothes, lingerie)*
1 el sostén (el sujetador)
- *brassière (bra)*
2 la faja de braga *f*
- *pantie-girdle*
3 la faja corsé *m*
- *pantie-corselette*
4 el sostén de cuerpo *m* (el sostén
  largo)
- *longline brassière (longline bra)*
5 la faja elástica
- *stretch girdle*
6 la liga
- *suspender*
7 la camiseta de señora *f*
- *vest*
8 las bragas
- *pantie briefs*
9 la media corta (la calceta) de
  señora *f*
- *ladies' knee-high stocking*
10 la braga pantalón *m*
- *long-legged (long leg) panties*
11 los calzoncillos largos (los
  leotardos sin pie *m*)
- *long pants*
12 los leotardos (*ant.:* las calzas)
- *tights (pantie-hose)*
13 la combinación (*Amér.:* el
  fustán)
- *slip*
14 la media combinación (la
  enagua)
- *waist slip*
15 las bragas slip *m*
- *bikini briefs*
**16-21 ladies' nightwear**
16 el camisón (*Col. y P. Rico:* la
  camisola)
- *nightdress (nightgown, nightie)*
17 el pijama
- *pyjamas* (Am. *pajamas*)
18 la camiseta del pijama
- *pyjama top*
19 el pantalón del pijama
- *pyjama trousers*
20 la bata de casa *f* y de baño *m*
  (*Col.:* el chingue)
- *housecoat*
21 el juego de camiseta *f* y
  pantalón *m* corto (utilizado
  como pijama *m* o para los ratos
  de ocio *m*)
- *vest and shorts set [for leisure*
  *wear and as nightwear]*
**22-29 la ropa interior de**
  **caballero** *m*
- *men's underwear (men's*
  *underclothes)*
22 la camiseta de red *f* (de malla
  *f*)
- *string vest*
23 los calzoncillos de red *f*
- *string briefs*
24 la bragueta
- *front panel*

25 la camiseta sin mangas *f*
  (*P. Rico y Río de Plata:* la
  camisilla; *Cuba, P. Rico y*
  *Venez.:* la franela; *Col.:* el
  capisayo; *Cuba y Chile:* la
  paloma)
- *sleeveless vest*
26 los calzoncillos (el slip; *P. Rico:*
  los pantaloncillos)
- *briefs*
27 los calzoncillos largos
- *trunks*
28 la camiseta de mangas *f* cortas
- *short-sleeved vest*
29 los calzones
- *long johns*
30 los tirantes (*Arg., Bol. y Urug.:*
  los tiradores; *Col. y Mé.:* las
  tirantas; *Arg.:* los tiros; *Chile:*
  los suspensores; *Col.:* las
  cargaderas)
- *braces (Am. suspenders)*
31 el clip de los tirantes
- *braces clip*
**32-34 los calcetines de caballero** *m*
- *men's socks*
32 el calcetín de caña *f* larga
- *knee-length sock*
33 el elástico del calcetín
- *elasticated top*
34 el calcetín bajo (*Chile:* el botín)
- *long sock*
**35-37 la ropa de noche** *f* **de**
  **caballero** *m*
- *men's nightwear*
35 el batín (la bata)
- *dressing gown*
36 el pijama
- *pyjamas* (Am. *pajamas*)
37 la camisa de cama *f*
  (de caballero *m*)
- *nightshirt*
**38-47 las camisas de caballero** *m*
- *men's shirts*
38 la camisa de sport *m*
- *casual shirt*
39 el cinturón (la correa; *Amér.:* el
  fajo)
- *belt*
40 el pañuelo de cuello *m* (el
  fular)
- *cravat*
41 la corbata
- *tie*
42 el nudo de corbata
- *knot*
43 la camisa de smoking *m*
- *dress shirt*
44 la pechera plisada (el plastrón
  plisado)
- *frill (frill front)*
45 el puño
- *cuff*
46 los gemelos (*P. Rico, Urug. y*
  *Venez.:* las yuntas)
- *cuff link*
47 la pajarita (el lazo de
  smoking *m*, la palomita)
- *bow-tie*

**1-67** la moda masculina
– **men's fashion**
**1** el traje de chaqueta f, un traje de caballero m (Antillas, Arg. y Col.: el flus)
– single-breasted suit, a men's suit
**2** la chaqueta (la americana; Amér.: el saco)
– jacket
**3** el pantalón
– suit trousers
**4** el chaleco
– waistcoat (vest)
**5** la solapa
– lapel
**6** la pernera del pantalón con raya f
– trouser leg with crease
**7** el smoking, un traje de noche f (un traje de fiesta f)
– dinner dress, an evening suit
**8** la solapa de seda f
– silk lapel
**9** el bolsillo de pecho m
– breast pocket
**10** el pañuelo del traje (el pañuelo que se coloca en el bolsillo superior de la chaqueta)
– dress handkerchief
**11** la pajarita (el lazo de smoking m, la palomita)
– bow-tie
**12** el bolsillo exterior
– side pocket
**13** el frac, un traje de etiqueta f
– tailcoat (tails), evening dress
**14** el faldón
– coat-tail
**15** el chaleco blanco del frac
– white waistcoat (vest)
**16** la pajarita blanca
– white bow-tie
**17** el traje de sport m
– casual suit
**18** la solapa del bolsillo
– pocket flap
**19** el canesú delantero
– front yoke
**20** el traje vaquero
– denim suit
**21** la chaqueta (Amér.: el saco) vaquera
– denim jacket
**22** el pantalón vaquero (los jeans, blue jeans)
– jeans (denims)
**23** el cinturón (la correa; Amér.: el fajo)
– waistband
**24** el traje playero
– beach suit
**25** el pantalón corto (los shorts)
– shorts
**26** la chaqueta de mangas f cortas
– short-sleeved jacket
**27** el traje de deporte m (el chandal)
– tracksuit

**28** la chaqueta del chandal con cremallera f
– tracksuit top with zip
**29** el pantalón del chandal
– tracksuit bottoms
**30** la chaqueta de punto m
– cardigan
**31** el cuello de punto m
– knitted collar
**32** el jersey de verano m para hombres m
– men's short-sleeved pullover (men's short-sleeved sweater)
**33** la camisa de mangas f cortas
– short-sleeved shirt
**34** el botón de la camisa
– shirt button
**35** la vuelta de la manga
– turn-up
**36** la camisa de punto m (el polo)
– knitted shirt
**37** la camisa de sport m (Amér.: la guayabera; S. Dgo.: la guerrillera)
– casual shirt
**38** el bolsillo de parche m
– patch pocket
**39** la chaqueta de sport m (la cazadora; Arg.: la campera)
– casual jacket
**40** el pantalón de cinturilla en la rodilla (el pantalón de media pierna f)
– knee-breeches
**41** la cinturilla de la rodilla f
– knee strap
**42** el calcetín largo (la calceta)
– knee-length sock
**43** la chaqueta de cuero m
– leather jacket
**44** el mono de peto m y tirantes m
– bib and brace overalls
**45** los tirantes regulables
– adjustable braces (Am. suspenders)
**46** el bolsillo de pecho m
– front pocket
**47** el bolsillo del pantalón
– trouser pocket
**48** el bragueta
– fly
**49** el bolsillo para el metro
– rule pocket
**50** la camisa a cuadros m
– check shirt
**51** el jersey de hombre m
– men's pullover
**52** el jersey de esquí m
– heavy pullover
**53** el chaleco de punto m
– knitted waistcoat (vest)
**54** el blazer (la chaqueta ligera)
– blazer
**55** el botón de la chaqueta
– jacket button
**56** el guardapolvo de trabajo m (el guardapolvo blanco; la bata blanca)
– overall

**57** la trinchera de lluvia f, una trinchera
– trenchcoat
**58** el cuello de la trinchera
– coat collar
**59** el cinturón de la trinchera
– coat belt
**60** el abrigo (de entretiempo m) de popelina f
– poplin coat
**61** el bolsillo del abrigo
– coat pocket
**62** la hilera oculta de botones m
– fly front
**63** el chaquetón de paño m (el gabán, el sobretodo)
– car coat
**64** el botón del abrigo
– coat button
**65** el pañuelo de cuello m (el fular)
– scarf
**66** el abrigo de paño m
– cloth coat
**67** los guantes
– glove

1-25 cortes *m* de barba *f* y
peinados *m* de caballero *m*
- **men's beards and hairstyles
(haircuts)**
1 el cabello largo y suelto
- *long hair worn loose*
2 la peluca larga (la peluca de
Estado *m*, peluca *f* de
circunstancias *f*), una peluca;
*más corta y lisa:* la media
peluca (el bisoñé)
- *allonge periwig (full-bottomed
wig), a wig;* shorter and
smoother: *bob wig, toupet*
3 los rizos (*Amér.:* los churos;
*Bol.:* los quimachis; *Chile:* los
lulos; *Ec.:* los enganchabobos;
*Mé.:* los compromisos)
- *curls*
4 la peluca de bolsa *f* (la peluca a
lo Mozart)
- *bag wig (purse wig)*
5 la peluca de coleta *f*
- *pigtail wig*
6 la coleta
- *queue (pigtail)*
7 el lazo de la coleta (*Bol.:* el
jarichi)
- *bow (ribbon)*
8 el bigote
- *handlebars (handlebar
moustache,* Am. *mustache)*
9 la raya en medio *m*
- *centre* (Am. *center*) *parting*
10 la barba en punta *f* (la perilla)
- *goatee (goatee beard), chintuft*
11 el corte de pelo *m* al cepillo *m*
(cabellos *m* al cepillo *m*)
- *closely-cropped head of hair
(crew cut)*
12 las patillas (*Col. y Ec.:* las
balcarrotas)
- *whiskers*
13 la barba a lo Enrique IV, una
barba puntiaguda y bigote *m*
(la barba de chivo *m*)
- *Vandyke beard (stiletto beard,
bodkin beard), with waxed
moustache* (Am. *mustache)*
14 la raya al lado *m*
- *side parting*
15 la barba cerrada (la barba
corrida)
- *full beard (circular beard, round
beard)*
16 la barba cuadrada
- *tile beard*
17 la mosca [bajo el labio inferior]
(*Mé.:* la piocha; *Col.:* el
candado)
- *shadow*
18 el cabello ensortijado (la
cabeza de artista *m*)
- *head of curly hair*
19 el bigote estilo *m* inglés (el
bigote de cepillo *m*)
- *military moustache* (Am.
*mustache) (English-style
moustache)*

20 la cabeza calva (el calvo)
- *partly bald head*
21 la calva (la calvicie)
- *bald patch*
22 la calva total (el calvo; *Arg., Ec.
y Perú:* el mate)
- *bald head*
23 la barba de tres días *m* (la
barba hirsuta; los cañones de la
barba)
- *stubble beard (stubble, short
beard bristles)*
24 las patillas (*Col. y Ec.:* las
balcarrotas)
- *side-whiskers (sideboards,
sideburns)*
25 el afeitado completo (la cara
afeitada)
- *clean shave*
26 el peinado afro (para
hombres *m* y mujeres *f*)
- *Afro look [for men and women]*
27-38 peinados *m* de mujer *f*
(peinados *m* de señoras *f* y
señoritas *f*)
- **ladies' hairstyles (coiffures,
women's and girls' hairstyles)**
27 la cola de caballo *m*
- *ponytail*
28 el cabello tirante hacia atrás
- *swept-back hair (swept-up hair,
pinned-up hair)*
29 el moño (el rodete; *Amér.:* el
molote; *S. Dgo. y Venez.:* la
clineja)
- *bun (chignon)*
30 las trenzas (*Col. y Chile:* los
chapes; *Venez.:* las crinejas;
*Bol.:* las chanecas; *Col. y Ec.:*
las chimbas; *Ec.:* las jimbas;
*Bol.:* las pichicas; *Guat. y Mé.:*
las chongas)
- *plaits (bunches)*
31 el peinado estilo *m* guirnalda
(peinado *m* estilo *m* griego)
- *chaplet hairstyle (Gretchen style)*
32 la guirnalda (la corona) de
cabello
- *chaplet (coiled plaits)*
33 el pelo rizado
- *curled hair*
34 el corte a lo garçon (el pelo a lo
garçon)
- *shingle (shingled hair, bobbed
hair)*
35 el pelo a lo Colón (el peinado a
la romana; el peinado estilo *m*
paje)
- *pageboy style*
36 el flequillo (*Mé.:* el burrito)
- *fringe* (Am. *bangs)*
37 el peinado de caracoles *m*
(de rodetes *m*; *Col.:* la llovizna)
- *earphones*
38 el caracol (el rodete) de pelo *m*
- *earphone (coiled plait)*

**1-21 los sombreros y las gorras de señora** *f*
- *ladies' hats and caps*

**1** la sombrerera haciendo un sombrero
- *milliner making a hat*

**2** la capucha (la forma)
- *hood*

**3** la horma
- *block*

**4** los diferentes adornos (un adorno; *Arg., Mé., Perú y Urug.:* el cabuchón)
- *decorative pieces*

**5** el sombrero (*Col.:* la coterna)
- *sombrero*

**6** el sombrero de moer *m* con plumas *f*
- *mohair hat with feathers*

**7** el sombrero con encajes *m* de adorno *m*
- *model hat with fancy appliqué*

**8** la gorra de lino *m*
- *linen cap (jockey cap)*

**9** el gorro hecho con lana *f* gruesa
- *hat made of thick candlewick yarn*

**10** el gorro de punto *m*
- *woollen* (Am. *woolen*) *hat (knitted hat)*

**11** el gorro de tejido *m* de moer *m*
- *mohair hat*

**12** el sombrero con plumas *f*
- *cloche with feathers*

**13** el sombrero grande de hombre *m* hecho de fibra *f* de pita *f* con cinta *f* encordelada
- *large men's hat made of sisal with corded ribbon*

**14** el sombrero de hombre *m* con cinta *f* de adorno *m*
- *trilby-style hat with fancy ribbon*

**15** el sombrero blando de fieltro *m* (*Venez.:* el garrotín)
- *soft felt hat*

**16** el panamá (el sombrero de jipijapa *f*)
- *Panama hat with scarf*

**17** la gorra de visón *m*
- *peaked mink cap*

**18** el sombrero de visón *m*
- *mink hat*

**19** el gorro de zorro *m* con la parte alta de cuero *m*
- *fox hat with leather top*

**20** el gorro de visón *m*
- *mink cap*

**21** el sombrero florentino (una pamela)
- *slouch hat trimmed with flowers*

# Sombreros

**22-40 sombreros *m* y gorras *f* de caballero *m***
- **men's hats and caps**
22 el sombrero de fieltro *m* estilo *m* ciudad *f*
- *trilby hat (trilby)*
23 el sombrero de loden *m*
- *loden hat (Alpine hat)*
24 el sombrero de fieltro *m* con borlas *f*
- *felt hat with tassels (Tyrolean hat, Tyrolese hat)*
25 la gorra de terciopelo *m* (gorra *f* de pana *f*)
- *corduroy cap*
26 el gorro de lana *f*
- *woollen (Am. woolen) hat*
27 la boina
- *beret*
28 la gorra príncipe *m* Enrique, una gorra de marino *m*
- *German sailor's cap (Prinz Heinrich' cap)*
29 la gorra de visera *f* (la gorra de velero *m*)
- *peaked cap (yachting cap)*
30 el sueste
- *sou'wester (southwester)*
31 el gorro de piel *f* de zorro *m* con solapas *f* para las orejas
- *fox cap with earflaps*

32 la gorra de cuero *m* con solapas *f* de piel *f*
- *leather cap with fur flaps*
33 la gorra de piel *f* de almizclero *m*
- *musquash cap*
34 el gorro de piel *f*, un gorro de astracán *m*, un gorro de cosaco *m*
- *astrakhan cap, a real or imitation astrakhan cap*
35 el sombrero de paja *f* (el canotié; *Mé.:* el chilapeño; *Chile y Mé.:* la chupalla; *Col., Ec., P. Rico y Venez.:* la pava; *Arg.:* el rancho; *Perú:* la sarita)
- *boater*
36 el sombrero de copa *f* hecho de tafetán *m* de seda *f* (la chistera; *Amér. Central, Col., Pan. y Venez.:* el cubilete; *Amér. Central y Mé.:* el bolero; *Mé.:* la cubeta, el sorbete); *plegable:* el bicornio (el clac)
- *top hat made of silk taffeta; collapsible: crush hat (opera hat, claque)*
37 el sombrero de verano *m* de tela *f* con bolsillito *m*
- *sun hat (lightweight hat) made of cloth with small patch pocket*

38 el sombrero flexible de alas *f* anchas (el sombrero de artista *m; Bol., Chile y Perú:* el guarapón)
- *wide-brimmed hat*
39 el gorro con borla *f* (el gorro de esquí *m*)
- *toboggan cap (skiing cap, ski cap)*
40 la gorra
- *workman's cap*

**45** la talla rosa *f*
– *rose cut*
**46** la tabla llana
– *flat table*
**47** la tabla en cabujón *m*
– *table en cabochon*
**48** la talla ovalada normal
– *standard cut*
**49** la talla antigua (la talla inglesa)
– *standard antique cut*
**50** la talla escalonada rectangular
– *rectangular step-cut*
**51** la talla escalonada cuadrada
– *square step-cut*
**52** la talla escalonada octogonal
– *octagonal step-cut*
**53** la talla octogonal con caras *f*
cruzadas
– *octagonal cross-cut*
**54** la talla en forma *f* de pera *f*
– *standard pear-shape (pendeloque)*
**55** la naveta (la navette)
– *marquise (navette)*
**56** la talla en forma *f* de barril *m*
normal
– *standard barrel-shape*
**57** la talla escalonada de trapecio *m*
– *trapezium step-cut*
**58** la talla de trapecio *m* con caras *f*
cruzadas
– *trapezium cross-cut*
**59** la talla escalonada de rombo *m* (el
rombo en talla *f* escalonada)
– *rhombus step-cut*
**60-61** el triángulo en talla *f*
escalonada
– *triangular step-cut*

**62** la talla escalonada hexagonal
– *hexagonal step-cut*
**63** la talla hexagonal ovalada con
caras *f* cruzadas
– *oval hexagonal cross-cut*
**64** la talla escalonada hexagonal
redonda
– *round hexagonal step-cut*
**65** la talla hexagonal con caras *f*
cruzadas
– *round hexagonal cross-cut*
**66** la talla a cuadros *m*
– *chequer-board cut*
**67** la talla a triángulos *m*
– *triangle cut*
**68-71** tallas *f* de fantasía *f*
– *fancy cuts*
**72-77** piedras *f* preciosas para
anillos *m*
– *ring gemstones*
**72** la tabla llana ovalada
– *oval flat table*
**73** la tabla llana rectangular
– *rectangular flat table*
**74** la tabla llana rectangular con
ángulos *m* redondos
– *octagonal flat table*
**75** la forma de tonel *m*
– *barrel-shape*
**76** la tabla abombada antigua (con
ángulos *m* redondos)
– *antique table en cabochon*
**77** la tabla abombada rectangular con
ángulos *m* agudos
– *rectangular table en cabochon*

**78-81** los cabujones
– *cabochons*
**78** el cabujón redondo
– *round cabochon (simple cabochon)*
**79** el cono redondo
– *high dome (high cabochon)*
**80** el cabujón ovalado
– *oval cabochon*
**81** el cabujón octogonal
– *octagonal cabochon*
**82-86** esferas *f* y formas *f* de peras *f*
– *spheres and pear-shapes*
**82** la esfera lisa
– *plain sphere*
**83** la forma de pera *f* lisa
– *plain pear-shape*
**84** la forma de pera *f* con caras *f*
– *faceted pear-shape*
**85** la gota lisa
– *plain drop*
**86** el briolet con caras *f*
– *faceted briolette*

**1-53 la vivienda unifamiliar**
- *detached house*
**1** el sótano
- *basement*
**2** la planta baja
- *ground floor* (Am. *first floor*)
**3** el primer piso
- *upper floor (first floor, Am. second floor)*
**4** el desván (el sobrado; *Col.:* el zarzo)
- *loft*
**5** el tejado, un tejado a dos aguas *f*
- *roof, a gable roof (saddle roof, saddleback roof)*
**6** el canalón (el canelón, la canal del tejado)
- *gutter*
**7** el caballete
- *ridge*
**8** el cordón y el guardacabio
- *verge with bargeboards*
**9** el ristrel, un cornisamento de cabrio *m*
- *eaves, rafter-supported eaves*
**10** la chimenea (*Venez.:* el torreón; *Mé.:* la tronera)
- *chimney*
**11** la bajada de aguas *f*
- *gutter*
**12** el codo de la bajada de aguas *f*
- *swan's neck (swan-neck)*
**13** el tubo de la bajada de aguas *f*
- *rainwater pipe (downpipe, Am. downspout, leader)*
**14** el tubo de hierro *m* fundido
- *vertical pipe, a cast-iron pipe*
**15** la fachada lateral
- *gable (gable end)*
**16** la pared de cristal *m* (la mampara)
- *glass wall*
**17** el zócalo
- *base course (plinth)*
**18** la galería
- *balcony*
**19** la barandilla
- *parapet*
**20** la jardinera
- *flower box*
**21** la puerta de dos hojas *f* en la galería
- *French window (French windows) opening on to the balcony*
**22** la ventana de dos batientes *m* (*Col.:* la ventana de dos abras *f*)
- *double casement window*
**23** la ventana de un batiente
- *single casement window*
**24** el alféizar con antepecho *m*
- *window breast with window sill*
**25** el dintel de la ventana
- *lintel (window head)*
**26** la jamba de la ventana
- *reveal*
**27** el respiradero del sótano (el tragaluz)
- *cellar window*
**28** la persiana enrollable
- *rolling shutter*
**29** la guía de la persiana enrollable
- *rolling shutter frame*
**30** la contraventana (el postigo)
- *window shutter (folding shutter)*
**31** el pestillo de la contraventana
- *shutter catch*
**32** el garaje, con cuarto *m* de herramientas *f*
- *garage with tool shed*

**33** el espaldar
- *espalier*
**34** la puerta de tablas *f* de madera *f*
- *batten door (ledged door)*
**35** el montante con travesaños *m* en cruz *f*
- *fanlight with mullion and transom*
**36** la terraza
- *terrace*
**37** el muro del jardín con albardilla *f*
- *garden wall with coping stones*
**38** la lámpara del jardín
- *garden light*
**39** la escalera del jardín
- *steps*
**40** la rocalla (el jardín de rocas *f*)
- *rockery (rock garden)*
**41** el grifo de la manguera
- *outside tap (Am. faucet) for the hose*
**42** la manguera para regar
- *garden hose*
**43** la rociadera del césped (*Amér.:* de la grama)
- *lawn sprinkler*
**44** el estanque para chapotear
- *paddling pool*
**45** el camino de losas *f*
- *stepping stones*
**46** el césped (*Amér.:* la grama) para los baños de sol *m* (para tenderse al sol)
- *sunbathing area (lawn)*
**47** la tumbona
- *deck-chair*
**48** la sombrilla de jardín *m*
- *sunshade (garden parasol)*
**49** la silla de jardín *m*
- *garden chair*
**50** la mesa de jardín *m*
- *garden table*
**51** el colgadero (el bastidor) para sacudir alfombras *f*
- *frame for beating carpets*
**52** la entrada al garaje *m*
- *garage driveway*
**53** la cerca, una valla de madera *f*
- *fence, a wooden fence*
**54-57 la urbanización residencial**
- *housing estate (housing development)*
**54** la casa de la urbanización
- *house on a housing estate (on a housing development)*
**55** el tejado caedizo (*Amér.:* el caedizo)
- *pent roof (penthouse roof)*
**56** la buhardilla (*Col.:* el ventolín)
- *dormer (dormer window)*
**57** el jardín particular
- *garden*
**58-63 la serie de casas *f* escalonadas**
- *terraced house [one of a row of terraced houses], stepped*
**58** el jardín delantero
- *front garden*
**59** el seto
- *hedge*
**60** la acera (*Guat., Mé.:* la banqueta)
- *pavement (Am. sidewalk, walkway)*
**61** la calle
- *street (road)*
**62** la farola de la calle
- *street lamp (street light)*
**63** la papelera
- *litter bin (Am. litter basket)*

**64-68 la vivienda para dos familias *f***
- *house divided into two flats (Am. house divided into two apartments, duplex house)*
**64** el tejado a cuatro aguas *f*
- *hip (hipped) roof*
**65** la puerta de la casa (la puerta de entrada; *Col.:* la umbralada)
- *front door*
**66** la escalera de entrada *f*
- *front steps*
**67** la marquesina (el colgadizo)
- *canopy*
**68** la ventana para plantas *f* o para flores *f*
- *flower window (window for house plants)*
**69-71 la vivienda doble para cuatro familias *f***
- *pair of semi-detached houses divided into four flats (Am. apartments)*
**69** el balcón
- *balcony*
**70** la vidriera (la solana)
- *sun lounge (Am. sun parlor)*
**71** el toldo (la marquesina)
- *awning (sun blind, sunshade)*
**72-76 el bloque de galerías *f* cubiertas**
- *block of flats (Am. apartment building, apartment house) with access balconies*
**72** el cubo de la escalera
- *staircase*
**73** la galería cubierta
- *balcony*
**74** el estudio de artista *m* (taller *m* de artista *m*)
- *studio flat (Am. studio apartment)*
**75** la terraza, un solario
- *sun roof, a sun terrace*
**76** la superficie verde
- *open space*
**77-81 el bloque de pisos *m***
- *multi-storey block of flats (Am. multistory apartment building, multistory apartment house)*
**77** el tejado plano
- *flat roof*
**78** el tejado de pendiente *f*
- *pent roof (shed roof, lean-to roof)*
**79** el garaje
- *garage*
**80** la pérgola
- *pergola*
**81** la ventana de la caja de la escalera
- *staircase window*
**82** la torre de pisos *m*
- *high-rise block of flats (Am. high-rise apartment building, high-rise apartment house)*
**83** el ático (la vivienda de la azotea *f*)
- *penthouse*
**84-86 la residencia secundaria (la segunda vivienda *f*), una casa de madera *f***
- *weekend house, a timber house*
**84** el encofrado de tablas *f* horizontal (la tablazón horizontal)
- *horizontal boarding*
**85** el zócalo de piedra *f* natural (el basamento de piedra *f*)
- *natural stone base course (natural stone plinth)*
**86** el ventanal
- *strip windows (ribbon windows)*

**1-29  el desván,** (el sobrado; *Col.:* el zarzo)
– *attic*
1  el tejado
– *roof cladding (roof covering)*
2  el tragaluz
– *skylight*
3  la pasarela
– *gangway*
4  la escalera (la escala del tejado)
– *cat ladder (roof ladder)*
5  la chimenea (*Mé.:* la tronera; *Venez.:* el torreón)
– *chimney*
6  el gancho del tejado
– *roof hook*
7  el tragaluz (la lumbrera)
– *dormer window (dormer)*
8  el enrejado paranieves *m* (el guardanieves)
– *snow guard (roof guard)*
9  el canalón (el canelón, la canal del tejado)
– *gutter*
10  el tubo de bajada de aguas *f*
– *rainwater pipe (downpipe,* Am. *downspout, leader)*
11  la cornisa
– *eaves*
12  el desván superior
– *pitched roof*
13  la trampilla
– *trapdoor*
14  el hueco de la trampilla
– *hatch*
15  la escalera de mano *m* (la escala; *Cuba, Mé. y P. Rico:* el burro)
– *ladder*
16  el larguero
– *stile*
17  el peldaño
– *rung*
18  el desván (el sobrado; *Col.:* el zarzo)
– *loft (attic)*
19  el tabique de madera *f*
– *wooden partition*
20  la puerta de la buhardilla
– *lumber room door (boxroom door)*
21  el candado
– *padlock*
22  el gancho de la cuerda para tender la ropa
– *hook [for washing line]*
23  la cuerda para tender la ropa
– *clothes line (washing line)*
24  el depósito de expansión *f* de la calefacción
– *expansion tank for boiler*
25  la escalera de madera *f* y la barandilla
– *wooden steps and balustrade*
26  la zanca
– *string* (Am. *stringer)*
27  el peldaño
– *step*
28  el pasamano
– *handrail (guard rail)*
29  el pilar de la barandilla
– *baluster*
30  el pararrayos
– *lightning conductor (lightning rod)*
**31  el deshollinador**
– *chimney sweep* (Am. *chimney sweeper)*

32  el cepillo con el peso esférico para golpear
– *brush with weight*
33  el raspador
– *shoulder iron*
34  el saco para el hollín
– *sack for soot*
35  la escoba de la deshollinar
– *flue brush*
36  la escoba
– *broom (besom)*
37  el palo de escoba
– *broomstick (broom handle)*
**38-81  la calefacción por agua *f*
caliente,** una calefacción central
– *hot-water heating system, full central heating*
**38-43  el cuarto de la caldera**
– *boiler room*
38  el sistema de calefacción *f* de coque *m* (el quemador de coque *m*)
– *coke-fired central heating system*
39  la portezuela de la ceniza
– *ash box door* (Am. *cleanout door)*
40  el humero
– *flueblock*
41  el atizador
– *poker*
42  el hurgón
– *rake*
43  la pala de carbón *m*
– *coal shovel*
**44-60  la calefacción de fuel-oil *m***
– *oil-fired central heating system*
44  el depósito de fuel-oil *m*
– *oil tank*
45  el registro
– *manhole*
46  la tapa del registro
– *manhole cover*
47  el tubo de carga *f*
– *tank inlet*
48  la tapa abovedada
– *dome cover*
49  la válvula de fondo *m* del depósito
– *tank bottom valve*
50  el fuel-oil (el gasóleo)
– *fuel oil (heating oil)*
51  el conducto de evacuación *f* de aire *m*
– *air-bleed duct*
52  el casquete de ventilación *f*
– *air vent cap*
53  la tubería del nivel del fuel-oil
– *oil level pipe*
54  el indicador del fuel-oil
– *oil gauge* (Am. *gage)*
55  la tubería de succión *f*
– *suction pipe*
56  la tubería de retorno *m*
– *return pipe*
57  la caldera de la calefacción de fuel-oil *m*
– *central heating furnace;* here: *oil-heating furnace*
**58-60  el quemador de fuel-oil *m***
– *oil burner*
58  el inyector de aire *m,* (el ventilador)
– *fan*
59  el motor eléctrico
– *electric motor*
60  el fuego piloto (el quemador) revestido
– *covered pilot light*
61  la portezuela para cargar
– *charging door*

62  la mirilla de inspección *f*
– *inspection window*
63  el indicador del nivel del agua *f*
– *water gauge* (Am. *gage)*
64  el termómetro de la caldera
– *furnace thermometer*
65  el grifo de carga *f* y vaciado *m*
– *bleeder*
66  el asiento de la caldera
– *furnace bed*
67  el tablero de control *m*
– *control panel*
68  el calentador de agua *f* (el termosifón)
– *hot water tank (boiler)*
69  el rebosadero
– *overflow pipe (overflow)*
70  la válvula de seguridad *f*
– *safety valve*
71  el conducto principal de distribución *f*
– *main distribution pipe*
72  el aislamiento
– *lagging*
73  la válvula
– *valve*
74  el tubo de alimentación *f*
– *flow pipe*
75  la válvula de regulación *f*
– *regulating valve*
76  el radiador
– *radiator*
77  el elemento del radiador
– *radiator rib*
78  el termostato de la habitación
– *room thermostat*
79  el tubo de retorno *m*
– *return pipe (return)*
80  el conducto principal de retorno *m* (la línea colectora de retorno *m*)
– *return pipe [in two-pipe system]*
81  la salida de humo *m*
– *smoke outlet (smoke extract)*

1  el ama *f* de casa *f*
– *housewife*
2  el frigorífico (la nevera, el
refrigerador; *Argent.*: la heladera)
– *refrigerator (fridge,* Am. *icebox)*
3  la parrilla del frigorífico
– *refrigerator shelf*
4  la cubeta de la verdura
– *salad drawer*
5  el congelador incorporado
– *cooling aggregate*
6  el botellero de la puerta del
frigorífico
– *bottle rack (in storage door)*
7  el congelador
– *upright freezer*
8  el armario de pared *f*, un armario
para la vajilla
– *wall cupboard, a kitchen cupboard*
9  el módulo (el mueble) base
– *base unit*
10  el cajón de los cubiertos
– *cutlery drawer*
11  la encimera (el poyo)
– *working top*
**12-17  el mueble de cocina *f***
– *cooker unit*
12  la cocina eléctrica (*también*: la
cocina de gas *m*)
– *electric cooker (*also: *gas cooker)*
13  el horno
– *oven*
14  la ventanilla del horno
– *oven window*
15  la placa de cocina *f* (la placa
calentadora rápida automática)
– *hotplate, an automatic high-speed
plate*

16  el hervidor (el hervidor de
silbato *m*; *Amér.*: la pava)
– *kettle;* here: *whistling kettle*
17  la campana
– *cooker hood*
18  la manopla (el agarrador)
– *pot holder*
19  el cuelgamanoplas
– *pot holder rack*
20  el reloj de cocina *f*
– *kitchen clock*
21  el avisador
– *timer*
22  la batidora
– *hand mixer*
23  la varilla de batir
– *whisk*
24  el molinillo de café *m* eléctrico
– *electric coffee grinder [with rotating
blades]*
25  el cordón eléctrico (el cable de la
corriente)
– *lead*
26  el enchufe de pared *f*
– *wall socket*
27  el módulo (el mueble) de ángulo *m*
– *corner unit*
28  el anaquel giratorio
– *revolving shelf*
29  la olla (*Mé. y Guat.;* el apaste;
*Bol.*: la manca; *Arg. y. Col.*: la
cayana; *Hond.*: el platón)
– *pot (cooking pot)*
30  la jarra (la cafetera)
– *jug*
31  el estante de las especias (el
especiero)
– *spice rack*
32  el tarro de especia *f*
– *spice jar*

**33-36  el fregadero** (*Chile:* el
lavaplatos)
– **sink unit**
33  el escurridor de platos *m*
(escurreplatos *m*)
– *dish drainer*
34  el plato de desayuno *m*
– *tea plate*
35  el fregadero (la pila)
– *sink*
36  el grifo de agua *f*, el grifo
mezclador (*Col., P. Rico y Urug.*:
la pluma; *Amér. Central:* el
chorro; *Col., Guat. y Nicar.*: la
paja; *Mé. y Rio de la Plata:* el
bitoque)
– *water tap (*Am. *faucet); here: mixer
tap (*Am. *mixing faucet)*
37  la planta de maceta *f*, una planta
de follaje *m*
– *pot plant, a foliage plant*
38  la cafetera eléctrica (una cafetera
de filtro *m; Antillas, Col. y Venez.*:
la freca)
– *coffee maker*
39  la lámpara de la cocina
– *kitchen lamp*
40  el lavavajillas
– *dishwasher (dishwashing machine)*
41  la rejilla de los platos
– *dish rack*
42  el plato
– *dinner plate*
43  la silla de cocina *f*
– *kitchen chair*
44  la mesa de cocina *f*
– *kitchen table*

1 el distribuidor de papel *m* de cocina *f*
– *general-purpose roll holder with kitchen roll (paper towels)*
2 el juego de utensilios *m* de madera *f*
– *set of wooden spoons*
3 la cuchara de madera *f* (*Mé.:*- la jumaca; *Col.:* la panadora)
– *mixing spoon*
4 la sartén (*Cuba y Mé.:* la freidera)
– *frying pan*
5 el termo (la jarra termo *m*)
– *Thermos jug*
6 las fuentes de cocina *f*
– *set of bowls*
7 la quesera
– *cheese dish with glass cover*
8 el plato de entremeses *m* (el plato de compartimientos *m*)
– *three-compartment dish*
9 el exprimidor
– *lemon squeezer*
10 el hervidor de silbato *m* (el hervidor; *Amér.:* la pava)
– *whistling kettle*
11 el silbato de vapor *m*
– *whistle*
12-16 **el juego de cacerolas** *f* (la batería de cocina *f*)
– *pan set*
12 la olla (*Arg. y Col.:* la cayana; *Hond.:* el platón; *Mé. y Guat.:* el apaste; *Bol.:* la manca)
– *pot (cooking pot)*
13 la tapadera
– *lid*

14 la marmita
– *casserole dish*
15 el jarro de la leche
– *milk pot*
16 el cacillo (*Col. y Venez.:* la gacha; *Col. y Cuba:* el pailón)
– *saucepan*
17 el calentador de inmersión *f*
– *immersion heater*
18 el sacacorchos con brazos *m*
– *corkscrew [with levers]*
19 el extractor de jugos *m*
– *juice extractor*
20 la pinza del tubo
– *tube clamp (tube clip)*
21 la olla a presión *f* (la olla exprés)
– *pressure cooker*
22 la válvula de seguridad *f*
– *pressure valve*
23 el esterilizador
– *fruit preserver*
24 el portabotes
– *removable rack*
25 el bote de conserva *f*
– *preserving jar*
26 el aro de goma *f*
– *rubber ring*
27 el molde redondo con muelles *m*
– *spring form*
28 el molde rectangular
– *cake tin*
29 el molde de escudilla *f* (el molde alto)
– *cake tin*
30 el tostador de pan *m*
– *toaster*
31 la rejilla para el pan
– *rack for rolls*

32 el asador
– *rotisserie*
33 el espetón del asador
– *spit*
34 el barquillero eléctrico
– *electric waffle iron*
35 el peso de cocina *f* con pesa *f* corredera
– *sliding-weight scales*
36 la pesa corredera
– *sliding weight*
37 el platillo del peso
– *scale pan*
38 la máquina para cortar (para rebanar)
– *food slicer*
39 la máquina para picar carne (Am. *meat chopper*)
– *mincer* (Am. *meat chopper*)
40 las cuchillas
– *blades*
41 la freidora de patatas *f*
– *chip pan*
42 la canastilla (el escurridor del aceite)
– *basket*
43 la máquina de cortar patatas *f*
– *potato chipper*
44 la yogurtera
– *yoghurt maker*
45 el robot de cocina *f* (la máquina batidora y amasadora)
– *mixer*
46 la batidora
– *blender*
47 el aparato para cerrar herméticamente las bolsas
– *bag sealer*

**1-29 el vestíbulo** (el recibidor, la
entrada)
- *hall (entrance hall)*
**1** el perchero (*Chile, Guat. y
Hond.:* la capotera)
- *coat rack*
**2** el colgadero (el gancho)
- *coat hook*
**3** la percha
- *coat hanger*
**4** el impermeable (el
chubasquero)
- *rain cape*
**5** el bastón
- *walking stick*
**6** el espejo
- *hall mirror*
**7** el teléfono
- *telephone*
**8** la cómoda para los zapatos,
maletín *m*, etc.
- *chest of drawers for shoes, etc.*
**9** el cajón
- *drawer*
**10** el banco
- *seat*
**11** el sombrero de señora *f*
- *ladies' hat*
**12** el paraguas plegable
- *telescopic umbrella*
**13** las raquetas de tenis *m*
- *tennis rackets (tennis racquets)*

**14** el paragüero (*Col., Chile y
P. Rico:* la paragüera)
- *umbrella stand*
**15** el paraguas
- *umbrella*
**16** los zapatos
- *shoes*
**17** la cartera (el maletín)
- *briefcase*
**18** la moqueta
- *fitted carpet*
**19** la caja de fusibles *m*
- *fuse box*
**20** los fusibles automáticos
- *miniature circuit breaker*
**21** la silla metálica de tubo *m*
- *tubular steel chair*
**22** el aplique de luz *f* de la
escalera
- *stair light*
**23** el pasamano
- *handrail*
**24** el escalón
- *step*
**25** la puerta de entrada *f* (la
puerta principal)
- *front door*
**26** el marco de la puerta
- *door frame*
**27** la cerradura de la puerta
- *door lock*

**28** la manivela de la puerta
- *door handle*
**29** la mirilla
- *spyhole*

1 el mueble combinado (la estantería por módulos *m*, por elementos *m*)
– *wall units*
2 el panel lateral
– *side wall*
3 el estante (la balda, el anaquel)
– *bookshelf*
4 la hilera de libros *m*
– *row of books*
5 la vitrina
– *display cabinet unit*
6 el módulo de base *f*
– *cupboard base unit*
7 el módulo armario *m*
– *cupboard unit*
8 el televisor
– *television set (TV set)*
9 la cadena estereofónica
– *stereo system (stereo equipment)*
10 el altavoz (la pantalla)
– *speaker (loudspeaker)*
11 el portapipas (el pipario)
– *pipe rack*
12 la pipa (*Amér.:* la churumbela)
– *pipe*
13 el globo terráqueo
– *globe*
14 la tetera de cobre *m* (*Amér.:* la pava)
– *brass kettle*

15 el telescopio
– *telescope*
16 el reloj de mesa *f*
– *mantle clock*
17 el busto
– *bust*
18 la enciclopedia en varios volúmenes *m*
– *encyclopaedia [in several volumes]*
19 el separador de ambientes *m*
– *room divider*
20 el mueble bar *m*
– *drinks cupboard*
21-26 **el tresillo por módulos *m***
– **upholstered suite** (*seating group*)
21 el sillón (la butaca)
– *armchair*
22 el brazo
– *arm*
23 el cojín del asiento
– *seat cushion (cushion)*
24 el sofá
– *settee*
25 el respaldo
– *back cushion*
26 la rinconera (la esquinera)
– *[round] corner section*
27 el cojín
– *scatter cushion*
28 la mesa de centro *m*
– *coffee table*

29 el cenicero
– *ashtray*
30 la bandeja
– *tray*
31 la botella de güisqui *m* (de whisky *m*)
– *whisky (whiskey) bottle*
32 la botella de soda *f*
– *soda water bottle (soda bottle)*
33-34 **el comedor**
– **dining set**
33 la mesa de comedor *m*
– *dining table*
34 la silla (*Col., Chile, Perú y Venez.:* la silleta)
– *chair*
35 el visillo (la cortina)
– *net curtain*
36 las plantas de interior *m*
– *indoor plants (houseplants)*

1  el armario del dormitorio (el
   ropero; *Col., Cuba, Chile, Pan.
   y Venez.*: el escaparate)
–  *wardrobe (Am. clothes closet)*
2  el anaquel (el estante) de ropa *f*
   blanca
–  *linen shelf*
3  el sillón de mimbre *m*
–  *cane chair*
4-13  **la cama de matrimonio** *m*
–  ***double bed*** *(sim.: double divan)*
4-6  **la cuja** (la armazón de la
   cama)
–  ***bedstead***
4  los pies de la cama
–  *foot of the bed*
5  el larguero de la cama
–  *bed frame*
6  la cabecera
–  *headboard*
7  la colcha (*Amér. Central y
   Venez.*: la chamarra)
–  *bedspread*
8  la manta, una manta
   edredón *m* (*Ec.*: el cobijo; *Col.*:
   la coriana; *Amér. Central, Mé. y
   Chile*: el chamarro)
–  *duvet, a quilted duvet*
9  la sábana, una sábana de lino *m*
–  *sheet, a linen sheet*

10  el colchón, un colchón de
   espuma *f* con funda *f* de cutí *m*
–  *mattress, a foam mattress with
   drill tick*
11  el travesaño
–  *[wedge-shaped] bolster*
12-13  la almohada
–  *pillow*
12  la funda de la almohada
–  *pillowcase (pillowslip)*
13  la funda interior de la
   almohada
–  *tick*
14  el estante para libros *m*
–  *bookshelf [attached to the
   headboard]*
15  la lámpara de cabecera *f*
–  *reading lamp*
16  el despertador eléctrico
–  *electric alarm clock*
17  la consola de la cama (*Arg.,
   Perú y Venez.*: el velador)
–  *bedside cabinet*
18  el cajón
–  *drawer*
19  el aplique de iluminación *f* del
   dormitorio
–  *bedroom lamp*
20  el cuadro
–  *picture*

21  el marco del cuadro
–  *picture frame*
22  la alfombra de cama *f* (*Chile y
   Perú*: el piso)
–  *bedside rug*
23  la moqueta
–  *fitted carpet*
24  el taburete del tocador
–  *dressing stool*
25  el tocador (*Arg., Bol., Cuba y
   Chile*: el peinador; *Col.*: la
   peinadora)
–  *dressing table*
26  el pulverizador de perfume *m*
–  *perfume spray*
27  el frasco de perfume *m*
–  *perfume bottle*
28  la polvera (*Cuba*: la motera; *Ec.
   y Perú*: la polvorera; *P. Rico*: la
   polveta)
–  *powder box*
29  el espejo del tocador
–  *dressing-table mirror (mirror)*

**1-11 la sección (el rincón) de comer**
- *dining set*
**1** la mesa
- *dining table*
**2** la pata de la mesa
- *table leg*
**3** el tablero de la mesa
- *table top*
**4** el salvamantel (el posaplatos)
- *place mat*
**5** el cubierto
- *place (place setting, cover)*
**6** el plato sopero (el plato hondo)
- *soup plate (deep plate)*
**7** el plato llano
- *dinner plate*
**8** la sopera
- *soup tureen*
**9** el vaso de vino *m*
- *wineglass*
**10** la silla del comedor
- *dining chair*
**11** el asiento
- *seat*
**12** la lámpara, una lámpara colgante
- *lamp;* here: *pendant lamp*
**13** la cortina
- *curtains*

**14** el visillo
- *net curtain*
**15** el riel de la cortina
- *curtain rail*
**16** la alfombra (*Arg., Perú y Urug.*: el camino; *Perú:* la pisadera)
- *carpet*
**17** el mueble de pared *f* (*Mé.:* el trinchador)
- *wall unit*
**18** la puerta de cristal *m*
- *glass door*
**19** el estante
- *shelf*
**20** el aparador (*Col., P. Rico, S. Dgo. y Venez.:* el seibo)
- *sideboard*
**21** el cajón de los cubiertos
- *cutlery drawer*
**22** el cajón de la mantelería
- *linen drawer*
**23** la base (el zócalo)
- *base*
**24** la bandeja redonda
- *round tray*
**25** la planta de maceta *f*
- *pot plant*
**26** el armario de la vajilla (la vitrina)
- *china cabinet (display cabinet)*

**27** el juego de café *m* (el servicio de café *m*)
- *coffee set (coffee service)*
**28** la cafetera
- *coffee pot*
**29** la taza de café *m*
- *coffee cup*
**30** el platillo de la taza (*Guat.:* la porcelana)
- *saucer*
**31** el jarrito de la leche
- *milk jug*
**32** el azucarero
- *sugar bowl*
**33** el servicio de mesa *f*
- *dinner set (dinner service)*

1 la mesa de comedor *m*
- *dining table*
2 el mantel, un mantel adamascado
- *tablecloth, a damask cloth*
3-12  **el servicio de mesa** *f* (el cubierto)
- ***place** (place setting, cover)*
3 el posaplatos (el salvamantel)
- *bottom plate*
4 el plato llano
- *dinner plate*
5 el plato sopero (el plato hondo)
- *deep plate (soup plate)*
6 el plato de postre *m*
- *dessert plate (dessert bowl)*
7 el cubierto
- *knife and fork*
8 el cubierto de pescado *m*
- *fish knife and fork*
9 la servilleta
- *serviette (napkin, table napkin)*
10 el servilletero
- *serviette ring (napkin ring)*
11 el portacuchillo (el soporte de los cuchillos)
- *knife rest*
12 las copas de vino *m*
- *wineglasses*
13 la tarjeta de mesa *f*
- *place card*
14 el cucharón (el cazo) de la sopa
- *soup ladle*
15 la sopera
- *soup tureen (tureen)*

16 el candelabro de mesa *f* ( *Mé.:* el candil)
- *candelabra*
17 la salsera
- *sauceboat (gravy boat)*
18 la cuchara para la salsa
- *sauce ladle (gravy ladle)*
19 el adorno de la mesa
- *table decoration*
20 la canastilla del pan (la panera)
- *bread basket*
21 el panecillo
- *roll*
22 la rebanada de pan *m*
- *slice of bread*
23 la ensaladera
- *salad bowl*
24 el cubierto de la ensalada
- *salad servers*
25 el plato (la fuente) de legumbres *f*
- *vegetable dish*
26 el plato del asado
- *meat plate* (Am. *meat platter*)
27 el asado
- *roast meat (roast)*
28 el plato de compota *f* (la compotera)
- *fruit dish*
29 la escudilla de compota *f* (el cuenco de compota *f*)
- *fruit bowl*
30 la compota
- *fruit (stewed fruit)*
31 la fuente de las patatas
- *potato dish*

32 el carrito de servicio *m*
- *serving trolley*
33 la fuente de verdura *f*  ,
- *vegetable plate* (Am. *vegetable platter*)
34 la tostada
- *toast*
35 el plato de quesos *m*
- *cheeseboard*
36 la mantequera
- *butter dish*
37 la rebanada de pan *m*
- *open sandwich*
38 la guarnición de la rebanada
- *filling*
39 el sándwich (emparedado *m*)
- *sandwich*
40 el frutero
- *fruit bowl*
41 las almendras ( *también:* las patatas crujientes, los cacahuetes)
- *almonds; also: potato crisps, peanuts*
42 las vinagreras (el convoy)
- *oil and vinegar bottle*
43 la salsa de tomate *m* picante (el catchup)
- *ketchup (catchup, catsup)*
44 el aparador
- *sideboard*
45 el calientaplatos eléctrico
- *electric hotplate*
46 el sacacorchos
- *corkscrew*

47 el abridor de tapones *m* de
    corona *f* (un abrebotellas)
  – *crown cork bottle-opener (crown*
    *cork opener), a bottle-opener*
48 la garrafita para el licor
  – *liqueur decanter*
49 el cascanueces
  – *nutcrackers (nutcracker)*
50 el cuchillo (*Arg., Bol. y Urug.:* el
    alfajor)
  – *knife*
51 el mango
  – *handle*
52 la espiga
  – *tang (tongue)*
53 la virola
  – *ferrule*
54 la hoja
  – *blade*
55 el cabezal (el tope)
  – *bolster*
56 el lomo (el canto)
  – *back*
57 el filo (el filo cortante)
  – *edge (cutting edge)*
58 el tenedor (*Col., Chile, Ec., Mé.:* el
    trinche)
  – *fork*
59 el mango
  – *handle*
60 el diente (la púa)
  – *prong (tang, tine)*
61 la cuchara sopera
  – *spoon (dessert spoon, soup spoon)*
62 el mango
  – *handle*

63 el cuenco (la pala) de la cuchara
  – *bowl*
64 el cuchillo de pescado *m*
  – *fish knife*
65 la pala de pescado *m*
  – *fish fork*
66 la cucharilla de postre *m*
  – *dessert spoon (fruit spoon)*
67 la cuchara para servir la ensalada
  – *salad spoon*
68 el tenedor para servir la ensalada
  – *salad fork*
69-70 el juego de trinchantes *m* (el
    cubierto de trinchar)
  – *carving set (serving cutlery)*
69 el cuchillo de trinchar
  – *carving knife*
70 el tenedor de trinchar (el
    trinchante; *Col:* el trinchete)
  – *serving fork*
71 el cuchillo para la fruta
  – *fruit knife*
72 el cuchillo para el queso
  – *cheese knife*
73 el cuchillo para la mantequilla
  – *butter knife*
74 la cuchara para servir la verdura
  – *vegetable spoon, a serving spoon*
75 la cuchara para servir patatas *f*
  – *potato server (serving spoon for*
    *potatoes)*
76 el tenedor para sándwich *m*
  – *cocktail fork*
77 la pala para espárragos *m*
  – *asparagus server (asparagus slice)*
78 el tenedor para sardinas *f*
  – *sardine server*

79 el tenedor para las langostas
  – *lobster fork*
80 el tenedor para las ostras
  – *oyster fork*
81 el cuchillo para el caviar
  – *caviare knife*
82 la copa de vino *m* blanco
  – *white wine glass*
83 la copa de vino *m* tinto
  – *red wine glass*
84 la copa de vino *m* dulce (la copa
    de madeira)
  – *sherry glass (madeira glass)*
85-86 las copas de champaña *m*
  – *champagne glasses*
85 la copa alta
  – *tapered glass*
86 la copa llana
  – *champagne glass, a crystal glass*
87 la copa para vinos *m* del Rin
  – *rummer*
88 la copa de coñac *m*
  – *brandy glass*
89 la copa de licor *m*
  – *liqueur glass*
90 el vasito de aguardiente *m*
  – *spirit glass*
91 el vaso de cerveza *f*
  – *beer glass*

1 la pared del apartamento (los
  muebles de pared *f*, la estantería)
– *wall units (shelf units)*
2 el frente del armario (la puerta del
  armario)
– *wardrobe door* (Am. *clothes closet
  door)*
3 el cuerpo
– *body*
4 el panel lateral
– *side wall*
5 la cornisa
– *trim*
6 el módulo de dos puertas *f*
– *two-door cupboard unit*
7 el estante de los libros (el estante
  de vitrina *f; Mé.:* el librero)
– *bookshelf unit (bookcase unit) [with
  glass door]*
8 los libros
– *books*
9 la vitrina
– *display cabinet*
10 los ficheros
– *card index boxes*
11 el cajón
– *drawer*
12 la bombonera
– *decorative biscuit tin*
13 el animal de tela *f*
– *soft toy animal*
14 el televisor
– *television set (TV set)*
15 los discos
– *records (discs)*

16 la cama empotrable (la cama-
  mueble)
– *bed unit*
17 el cojín (el almohadón) del sofá
– *scatter cushion*
18 el cajón de la cama-mueble
– *bed unit drawer*
19 el estante de la cama-mueble
– *bed unit shelf*
20 las revistas
– *magazines*
21 el emplazamiento del escritorio
– *desk unit (writing unit)*
22 el escritorio (la mesa escritorio *m*)
– *desk*
23 la carpeta
– *desk mat (blotter)*
24 la lámpara de mesa *f*
– *table lamp*
25 el cesto de los papeles (la
  papelera)
– *wastepaper basket*
26 el cajón del escritorio
– *desk drawer*
27 el sillón del escritorio
– *desk chair*
28 el brazo del sillón
– *arm*
29 el mueble de la cocina (el módulo
  de la cocina)
– *kitchen unit*
30 el armario alto
– *wall cupboard*
31 la campana extractora de
  humos *m*
– *cooker hood*

32 la cocina eléctrica
– *electric cooker*
33 el frigorífico (la nevera, el
  refrigerador)
– *refrigerator (fridge,* Am. *icebox)*
34 la mesa de comedor *m*
– *dining table*
35 el tapete de la mesa
– *table runner*
36 la alfombra oriental
– *oriental carpet*
37 la lámpara de pie *m*
– *standard lamp*

1 la cama de los niños, una litera
– children's bed, a bunk-bed
2 el cajón de la cama
– storage box
3 el colchón
– mattress
4 la almohada
– pillow
5 la escala
– ladder
6 un elefante de tela f (de trapo m)
– soft toy elephant, a cuddly toy animal
7 el perro de tela f (de trapo)
– soft toy dog
8 el puf
– cushion
9 la muñeca-maniquí (la muñeca para vestir; Hond.: la pichinga)
– fashion doll
10 el cochecito de la muñeca
– doll's pram
11 la muñeca acostada
– sleeping doll
12 el baldaquín (el dosel)
– canopy
13 la pizarra
– blackboard
14 las bolas para contar (una bolita; Chile, Mé. y Perú: el tiro)
– counting beads
15 el caballo de peluche m con balancín y ruedecillas f
– toy horse for rocking and pulling

16 los patines-balancín
– rockers
17 el libro infantil
– children's book
18 la caja de juegos m
– compendium of games
19 el juego de los caballitos
– ludo
20 el tablero de ajedrez m (el damero)
– chessboard
21 el armario de la habitación de los niños
– children's cupboard
22 el cajón de la ropa blanca
– linen drawer
23 el escritorio
– drop-flap writing surface
24 el cuaderno (la libreta)
– notebook (exercise book)
25 los libros de clase f (de la escuela)
– school books
26 el lápiz (también: el lápiz de color m, el rotulador, el bolígrafo)
– pencil; also: crayon, felt tip pen, ballpoint pen
27 la tienda de ultramarinos m
– toy shop
28 el mostrador
– counter
29 el estante de especias f
– spice rack
30 el escaparate (Amér.: la vidriera)
– display

31 los caramelos surtidos
– assortment of sweets (Am. candies)
32 el cartucho para los caramelos
– bag of sweets (Am. candies)
33 la balanza (el peso)
– scales
34 la caja registradora
– cash register
35 el teléfono de juguete m
– toy telephone
36 la estantería de las mercancías (Amér.: de las mercaderías)
– shop shelves (goods shelves)
37 el tren de madera f
– wooden train set
38 el volquete, un camión de juguete m
– dump truck, a toy lorry (toy truck)
39 la grúa
– tower crane
40 la hormigonera
– concrete mixer
41 el perro de peluche m grande
– large soft toy dog
42 el cubilete de los dados
– dice cup

**1-20  la educación preescolar**
- *pre-school education (nursery education)*
1 la maestra del parvulario
- *nursery teacher*
2 el niño del parvulario (el párvulo)
- *nursery child*
3 los trabajos manuales
- *handicraft*
4 el pegamento
- *glue*
5 la acuarela
- *watercolour (Am. watercolor) painting*
6 la caja de pinturas *f*
- *paintbox*
7 el pincel
- *paintbrush*
8 el vaso de agua *f*
- *glass of water*
9 el rompecabezas (el puzzle)
- *jigsaw puzzle (puzzle)*
10 la pieza del rompecabezas (del puzzle)
- *jigsaw puzzle piece*
11 los lápices de colores *m* (lápices *m* de cera *f*)
- *coloured (Am. colored) pencils; also: wax crayons*
12 la pasta de modelar (la plastilina)
- *modelling (Am. modeling) clay; sim.: Plasticine*

13 las figuras modeladas (las figuras de plastilina *f*)
- *clay figures; sim.: Plasticine figures*
14 el tablero para modelar
- *modelling (Am. modeling) board*
15 la tiza (la barra de tiza *f*)
- *chalk (blackboard chalk)*
16 la pizarra
- *blackboard*
17 los cubos de contar
- *counting blocks*
18 el rotulador
- *felt pen (felt tip pen)*
19 el juego de las formas
- *shapes game*
20 el grupo de jugadores *m*
- *group of players*
**21-32  los juguetes**
- *toys*
21 el juego de los cubos
- *building and filling cubes*
22 la caja de construcciones *f*
- *construction set*
23 los libros infantiles
- *children's books*
24 el cochecito de la muñeca, un cochecito de mimbre *m*
- *doll's pram, a wicker pram*
25 la muñeca bebé *m*
- *baby doll*
26 el baldaquín (el dosel)
- *canopy*

27 los bloques de construcción *f*
- *building bricks (building blocks)*
28 la construcción de madera *f*
- *wooden model building*
29 el tren de madera *f*
- *wooden train set*
30 el oso de peluche *m* con balancín *m*
- *rocking teddy bear*
31 el cochecito de la muñeca
- *doll's pushchair*
32 la muñeca-maniquí (la muñeca para vestir)
- *fashion doll*
33 el niño en edad *f* preescolar
- *child of nursery school age*
34 el guardarropa (el vestuario)
- *cloakroom*

1  la bañera (*Amér.:* la bañadera)
–  *bath*
2  el grifo mezclador del agua *f* caliente y fría (*Col., P. Rico y Urug.:* la pluma; *Amér. Central:* el chorro; *Col., Guat. y Nicar.:* la paja; *Mé. y Río de la Plata:* el bitoque)
–  *mixer tap (Am. mixing faucet) for hot and cold water*
3  el baño de espuma *f*
–  *foam bath (bubble bath)*
4  el patito de caucho *m* (de goma *f*)
–  *toy duck*
5  las sales de baño *m*
–  *bath salts*
6  la esponja de baño *m*
–  *bath sponge (sponge)*
7  el bidé (*Antillas, Col., Perú, Mé., Urug. y Venez.:* el bidel)
–  *bidet*
8  el toallero
–  *towel rail*
9  la toalla de felpa *f*
–  *terry towel*
10 el portarrollo de papel *m* higiénico
–  *toilet roll holder (Am. bathroom tissue holder)*
11 el papel higiénico, un rollo de papel *m* crepé
–  *toilet paper (Am. bathroom tissue)*
12 el retrete (el excusado, el wáter, el inodoro)
–  *toilet (lavatory, W.C., coll. loo)*
13 la taza del retrete
–  *toilet pan (toilet bowl)*
14 la tapa del retrete con una cubierta de felpa *f*
–  *toilet lid with terry cover*
15 el asiento del retrete
–  *toilet seat*

16 la cisterna
–  *cistern*
17 la palanca de la cisterna
–  *flushing lever*
18 la esterilla de los pies
–  *pedestal mat*
19 los azulejos
–  *tile*
20 la ventilación (el respiradero)
–  *ventilator (extraction vent)*
21 la jabonera
–  *soap dish*
22 el jabón
–  *soap*
23 la toalla de mano *f* (*Guat. y Hond.:* los limpiamanos)
–  *hand towel*
24 el lavabo (*Arg., Chile, Ec., Perú, Urug. y Venez.:* el lavatorio; *Guat.:* el lavador)
–  *washbasin*
25 el rebosadero
–  *overflow*
26 el grifo de agua *f* fría y caliente
–  *hot and cold water tap*
27 el pedestal del lavabo con sifón *m*
–  *washbasin pedestal with trap (anti-syphon trap)*
28 el vaso para los dientes
–  *tooth glass (tooth mug)*
29 el cepillo de dientes *m* eléctrico
–  *electric toothbrush*
30 los cepillos de recambio *m*
–  *detachable brush heads*
31 el armario de tocador *m* con espejos *m*
–  *mirrored bathroom cabinet*
32 el tubo fluorescente
–  *fluorescent lamp*
33 el espejo
–  *mirror*

34 el cajón
–  *drawer*
35 la polvera (*Cuba:* la motera; *Ec. y Perú:* la polvorera; *P. Rico:* la polveta)
–  *powder box*
36 el elixir dentífrico
–  *mouthwash*
37 la máquina de afeitar eléctrica
–  *electric shaver*
38 la loción para después del afeitado (el after-shave)
–  *aftershave lotion*
39 el cuartito de la ducha
–  *shower cubicle*
40 la cortina de la ducha
–  *shower curtain*
41 la ducha regulable (la ducha de mano)
–  *adjustable shower head*
42 el pulverizador (la roseta) de la ducha
–  *shower nozzle*
43 el riel de regualción *f* de la altura
–  *shower adjustment rail*
44 el plato de ducha *f*
–  *shower base*
45 el rebosadero
–  *waste pipe*
46 las zapatillas de baño *m*
–  *bathroom mule*
47 la báscula de baño *m*
–  *bathroom scales*
48 la alfombra del baño
–  *bath mat*
49 el botiquín
–  *medicine cabinet*

**1-20  los aparatos para la plancha**
- *irons*
1  la plancha automática eléctrica
- *electric ironing machine*
2  el interruptor de pie *m* eléctrico
- *electric foot switch*
3  el rodillo con envoltura *f* de muletón *m*
- *roller covering*
4  la cabeza de planchado *m*
- *ironing head*
5  la sábana de cama *f*
- *sheet*
6  la plancha eléctrica (la plancha de viaje *m*)
- *electric iron, a lightweight iron*
7  la planta (el pie) de la plancha
- *sole-plate*
8  el selector de temperatura *f*
- *temperature selector*
9  el mango de la plancha
- *handle (iron handle)*
10  la luz piloto *m*
- *pilot light*
11  la plancha de vapor *m*, la plancha con pulverizador *m* y secado *m*
- *steam, spray, and dry iron*
12  el orificio de relleno *m*
- *filling inlet*
13  el pulverizador para humedecer la ropa
- *spray nozzle for damping the washing*
14  el agujero del vapor (el canal de vaporización *f*)
- *steam hole (steam slit)*
15  la mesa de planchar
- *ironing table*
16  la tabla de planchar
- *ironing board (ironing surface)*
17  la cubierta de la tabla de planchar
- *ironing-board cover*
18  el reposa plancha
- *iron well*
19  la armazón de aluminio *m*
- *aluminium (Am. aluminum) frame*
20  la tabla para (planchar) las mangas
- *sleeve board*
21  el cubo de la ropa blanca
- *linen bin*
22  la ropa blanca sucia
- *dirty linen*
**23-34  los aparatos de lavado *m* y secado *m***
- *washing machines and driers*
23  la lavadora (la lavadora automática, la automática)
- *automatic washing machine*
24  el tambor de lavado *m*
- *washing drum*
25  el pestillo de seguridad *f* (el dispositivo de seguridad *f*)
- *safety latch (safety catch)*
26  el selector de programas *m*
- *program selector control*
27  la cubeta delantera del detergente (con varios compartimientos *m*)
- *front soap dispenser [with several compartments]*
28  la secadora eléctrica con aire *m* de salida *f*
- *tumble drier*
29  el tambor de secado *m*
- *drum*
30  la puerta delantera con rajas *f* para la ventilación
- *front door with ventilation slits*

31  la encimera
- *work top*
32  el tendedero
- *airer*
33  la cuerda de la ropa (*Cuba y Guat.:* la tendedera; *Amér. Central, Chile y S. Dgo.:* el cáñamo)
- *clothes line (washing line)*
34  el tendedero de tijeras *f*
- *extending airer*
35  la escalera de tijeras *f*, una escalera matálica
- *stepladder (steps), an aluminium (Am. aluminum) ladder*
36  el montante
- *stile*
37  el apoyo
- *prop*
38  el peldaño
- *tread (rung)*
**39-43  los utensilios para el cuidado de (para limpiar) los zapatos**
- *shoe care utensils*
39  la lata de betún *m* (crema *f*)
- *tin of shoe polish*
40  el pulverizador de zapatos *m*, un pulverizador para impregnar
- *shoe spray an impregnating spray*
41  el cepillo para zapatos *m*
- *shoe brush*
42  el cepillo para aplicar el betún (la crema)
- *brush for applying polish*
43  el tubo de betún *m* (crema *f*)
- *tube of shoe polish*
44  el cepillo de la ropa
- *clothes brush*
45  el cepillo de la alfombra
- *carpet brush*
46  el cepillo de barrer (*Col.:* la pichanga)
- *broom*
47  las cerdas del cepillo (la pelambre)
- *bristles*
48  la armazón del cepillo
- *broom head*
49  el palo del cepillo
- *broomstick (broom handle)*
50  la rosca
- *screw thread*
51  el cepillo para la vajilla
- *washing-up brush*
52  el recogedor
- *pan (dust pan)*
**53-86  la limpieza del suelo**
- *floor and carpet cleaning*
53  el escobillón (la escoba de mano *f*)
- *brush*
54  el cubo (*Venez.:* el tobo)
- *bucket (pail)*
55  el trapo del suelo (el trapo de limpieza *f*, la bayeta; *Mé.:* el chapalolo)
- *floor cloth (cleaning rag)*
56  la bruza (la estregadera, un cepillo de cerdas *f* fuertes para fregar)
- *scrubbing brush*
57  el cepillo mecánico
- *carpet sweeper*
58  la aspiradora de mano *f*
- *upright vacuum cleaner*
59  el interruptor de cambio *m* (el selector de posición *f*)
- *changeover switch*
60  la cabeza de articulación *f*
- *swivel head*

61  el indicador del saco del polvo
- *bag-full indicator*
62  el depósito del saco del polvo
- *dust bag container*
63  el mango
- *handle*
64  el tubo
- *tubular handle*
65  el gancho del cordón
- *flex hook*
66  el cordón de la corriente enrollado
- *wound-up flex*
67  la boquilla chupadora para todo uso *m*
- *all-purpose nozzle*
68  la aspiradora rodante
- *cylinder vacuum cleaner*
69  la articulación giratoria
- *swivel coupling*
70  el tubo de prolongación *f*
- *extension tube*
71  la boquilla chupadora para el suelo (*sin.:* la boquilla para la alfombra)
- *floor nozzle;* sim.: *carpet beater nozzle*
72  el mando de succión *f*
- *suction control*
73  el indicador del saco del polvo
- *bag-full indicator*
74  el mando regulador de succión *f*
- *sliding fingertip suction control*
75  el tubo de succión *f* (la manguera)
- *hose (suction hose)*
76  el aparato para el cuidado (la limpieza) de la alfombra combinado
- *combined carpet sweeper and shampooer*
77  el cordón eléctrico
- *electric lead (flex)*
78  la toma de corriente *f*
- *plug socket*
79  la cabeza para sacudir la alfombra (*sin.:* la cabeza para limpiar en seco la alfombra, la cabeza para cepillar la alfombra)
- *carpet beater head;* sim.: *shampooing head, brush head*
80  la aspiradora para todo uso *m*
- *all-purpose vacuum cleaner [for wet and dry operation]*
81  la ruedecilla
- *castor*
82  el motor (el bloque del motor)
- *motor unit*
83  el cierre de la tapa
- *lid clip*
84  la manguera para la succión de la suciedad (basura *f*) gruesa
- *coarse dirt hose*
85  el accesorio especial para la suciedad gruesa
- *special accessory (special attachment) for coarse dirt*
86  el depósito del polvo
- *dust container*
87  el carrito de la compra
- *shopper (shopping trolley)*

**1-35 el jardín**
- *flower garden*

**1** la pérgola
- *pergola*

**2** la hamaca (la tumbona)
- *deck-chair*

**3** la escoba de césped *m* (la escoba de hojas *f*)
- *lawn rake, a wire-tooth rake*

**4** el rastrillo del césped
- *garden rake*

**5** la vid silvestre, una planta tepradora
- *Virginia creeper (American ivy, woodbine), a climbing plant (climber, creeper)*

**6** el jardín adornado con piedras *f* (la rocalla)
- *rockery (rock garden)*

**7** las plantas de rocalla *f* (las plantas alpestres); *variedades:* el telefio, la uña de gato *m* (la siempreviva menor), la dríada, la aubrietia
- *rock plants; varieties: stonecrop (wall pepper), houseleek, dryas, aubretia*

**8** la hierba de las pampas
- *pampas grass*

**9** el seto del jardín
- *garden hedge*

**10** el abeto azul (la epícea)
- *blue spruce*

**11** las hortensias
- *hydrangeas*

**12** el roble
- *oak (oak tree)*

**13** el abedul
- *birch (birch tree)*

**14** la senda (la vereda, el camino; *Amér.:* la picada) del jardín
- *garden path*

**15** el bordillo de la senda
- *edging*

**16** el estanque del jardín
- *garden pond*

**17** la rosa (la baldosa)
- *flagstone (stone slab)*

**18** el nenúfar (el lirio de agua *f*)
- *water lily*

**19** las begonias de tubérculos *m*
- *tuberous begonias*

**20** las dalias
- *dahlias*

**21** la regadera
- *watering can (Am. sprinkling can)*

**22** la azada de desherbar (escabuche *m*)
- *weeding hoe*

**23** el lupino noble
- *lupin*

**24** las margaritas
- *marguerites (oxeye daisies, white oxeye daisies)*

**25** la rosa de tallo *m* alto
- *standard rose*

**26** la gerbera
- *gerbera*

**27** el lirio
- *iris*

**28** los gladiolos
- *gladioli*

**29** los crisantemos
- *chrysanthemums*

**30** la amapola
- *poppy*

**31** la serrátula
- *blazing star*

**32** la boca de dragón *m*
- *snapdragon (antirrhinum)*

**33** el césped (*Amér.:* la grama)
- *lawn*

**34** el diente de león *m*
- *dandelion*

**35** el girasol
- *sunflower*

**1-32 el huerto familiar** (la plantación de hortalizas *f* y árboles *m* frutales; *P. Rico:* la tala)
- *allotment, a fruit and vegetable garden*

**1, 2, 16, 17, 29** árboles *m* frutales enanos (árboles *m* frutales de espaldera *f*, árboles frutales de forma *f* plana)
- *dwarf fruit trees (espaliers, espalier fruit trees)*

**1** la palmeta Verrier, un árbol de espaldera *f*
- *quadruple cordon, a wall espalier*

**2** el cordón vertical
- *vertical cordon*

**3** el cobertizo de las herramientas
- *tool shed (garden shed)*

**4** el bidón (barril *m*) para el agua *f* de lluvia *f* (*Arg., Cuba, Perú y Venez.:* la casimba)
- *water butt (water barrel)*

**5** la planta trepadora (la enredadera)
- *climbing plant (climber, creeper, rambler)*

**6** el montón de abono *m* compuesto
- *compost heap*

**7** el girasol
- *sunflower*

**8** la escala de huerto *m*
- *garden ladder (ladder)*

**9** la planta vivaz
- *flowering perennial*

**10** la valla del huerto (la valla de madera *f*, la empalizada, la cerca; *Amér. Central, Arg., Col., Chile, P. Rico y Urug.:* el cerco)
- *garden fence, a paling fence (paling)*

**11** las bayas de tronco *m* alto
- *standard berry tree*

**12** el rosal trepador, en la espaldera de arco *m*
- *climbing rose (rambling rose) on the trellis arch*

**13** el rosal arbusto (el rosal común)
- *bush rose (standard rose tree)*

**14** el cenador (la glorieta)
- *summerhouse (garden house)*

**15** el farolillo (farolillo *m* a la veneciana, el farol de papel *m*)
- *Chinese lantern (paper lantern)*

**16** el árbol piramidal, la pirámide, un árbol de espaldera *f* sin apoyo *m*
- *pyramid tree (pyramidal tree, pyramid), a free-standing espalier*

**17** el cordón horizontal de dos brazos *m*
- *double horizontal cordon*

**18** el arriate de flores *f*, un arriate
- *flower bed, a border*

**19** el arbusto de baya *f* (el arbusto de uva *f* espina, el grosellero negro)
- *berry bush;* here: *gooseberry bush; also: currant bush*

**20** el bordillo de losetas *f* de cemento *m*
- *concrete edging*

**21** el rosal de tallo *m* alto (rosal *m*, la rosa de tallo alto)
- *standard rose (standard rose tree)*

**22** el arriate con plantas *f* vivaces
- *border with perennials*

**23** el sendero (*Amér.:* la picada) del huerto
- *garden path*

**24** el hortelano aficionado
- *allotment holder*

**25** el arriate de espárragos *m*
- *asparagus patch (asparagus bed)*

**26** el arriate de verduras *f*
- *vegetable patch (vegetable plot)*

**27** el espantapájaros (el espantajo; *Chile y Perú:* el dominguejo)
- *scarecrow*

**28** las judías (rodrigadas con estacas *f*), una planta de judías *f* (*Amér.:* fríjoles *m*) con estaca (caña *f*) (las estacas de judías *f*)
- *runner bean (Am. scarlet runner), a bean plant on poles (bean poles)*

**29** el cordón horizontal simple, de un brazo
- *horizontal cordon*

**30** el árbol frutal de tronco *m* alto
- *standard fruit tree*

**31** el rodrigón
- *tree stake*

**32** el seto
- *hedge*

1 el geranio (el pelargonio), una geraniácea (*Chile:* el cardenal)
– *pelargonium (crane's bill), a geranium*
2 la pasionaria, una pasiflora, una de las parietales (*Ec., Perú:* el tumbo)
– *passion flower (Passiflora), a climbing plant (climber, creeper)*
3 la fucsia, una onagrácea
– *fuchsia, an anagraceous plant*
4 la capuchina (espuela *f* de galán *m*), un tropaeolum
– *nasturtium (Indian cress, tropaeolum)*
5 el ciclamen, una primulácea
– *cyclamen, a primulaceous herb*
6 la petunia, una solanácea
– *petunia, a solanaceous herb*
7 la gloxínea (siningia *f*), una gesneriácea
– *gloxinia (Sinningia), a gesneriaceous plant*
8 la clivia, una amarilidácea, una narcisácea
– *Clivia minata, an amaryllis (narcissus)*
9 el cáñamo africano, una sparmannia, una tiliea
– *African hemp (Sparmannia), a tiliaceous plant, a linden plant*

10 la begonia (*Mé.:* la tronadora)
– *begonia*
11 el mirto (el arrayán)
– *myrtle (common myrtle, Myrtus)*
12 la azalea, una ericácea
– *azalea, an ericaceous plant*
13 el áloe, una liliácea
– *aloe, a liliaceous plant*
14 el equinocacto (el asiento de la suegra)
– *globe thistle (Echinops)*
15 la estapelia (la flor de la carroña), una asclepiadácea
– *stapelia (carrion flower), an asclepiadaceous plant*
16 la araucaria excelsa
– *Norfolk Island Pine, an araucaria grown as an ornamental*
17 la juncia, una ciperácea
– *galingale, a cyperacious plant of the sedge family*

1 la siembra
– *seed sowing (sowing)*
2 la cubeta de la semilla (el semillero, la almáciga)
– *seed pan*
3 la semilla
– *seed*
4 la etiqueta con el nombre
– *label*
5 el trasplante
– *pricking out (pricking off, transplanting)*
6 la planta (el plantón)
– *seedling (seedling plant)*
7 el plantador
– *dibber (dibble)*
8 la maceta, el tiesto
– *flower pot (pot)*
9 la hoja de vidrio *m*
– *sheet of glass*
10 la propagación por acodo *m*
– *propagation by layering*
11 el acodo
– *layer*
12 el acodo enraizado (*Cuba y Venez.*: el margullo)
– *layer with roots*
13 la rama horquillada para la fijación
– *forked stick used for fastening*
14 la propagación por estolones *m*
– *propagation by runners*
15 la planta madre *f*
– *parent (parent plant)*

16 el estolón (el tallo rastrero, el vástago)
– *runner*
17 la plántula (el retoño) enraizada(o)
– *small rooted leaf cluster*
18 la acodadura en macetas *f*
– *setting in pots*
19 el desqueje en agua *f*
– *cutting in water*
20 el esqueje
– *cutting (slip, set)*
21 la raíz
– *root*
22 el desqueje de la viña por esquejes *m* de yema *f*
– *bud cutting on vine tendril*
23 la yema, un botón
– *scion bud, a bud*
24 la planta de esqueje *m* (el vástago)
– *sprouting (shooting) cutting*
25 el esqueje leñoso (la estaca de rama *f*)
– *stem cutting (hardwood cutting)*
26 el botón (la yema, el brote)
– *bud*
27 la propagación por bulbos *m*
– *propagation by bulbils (brood bud bulblets)*
28 el bulbo
– *old bulb*
29 el bulbo reproductor
– *bulbil (brood bud bulblet)*

30-39 el injerto
– *grafting (graftage)*
30 el injerto en escudete *m*
– *budding; here: shield budding*
31 la navaja
– *budding knife*
32 la incisión en forma *f* de T
– *T-cut*
33 el patrón (el masto)
– *support (stock, rootstock)*
34 la yema injertada
– *inserted scion bud*
35 la ligadura de rafia *f*
– *raffia layer (bast layer)*
36 el injerto de púa *f*
– *side grafting*
37 la púa con yema *f*
– *scion (shoot)*
38 el corte en forma de cuña *f*
– *wedge-shaped notch*
39 el injerto de cúpula *f* (el injerto de empalme *m*)
– *splice grafting*

29 el estanque de agua *f* (la pileta
   de agua *f*)
 – *water tank*
30 el tubo del agua *f*
 – *water pipe*
31 la bala de turba *f* (la paca de
   turba *f*)
 – *bale of peat*
32 el invernadero templado
 – *warm house (heated greenhouse)*
33 el invernadero frío
 – *cold house (unheated greenhouse)*
34 el generador eólico (el molino
   de viento *m*)
 – *wind generator*
35 la rueda de paletas *f* (de
   aletas *f*)
 – *wind wheel*
36 la paleta (la aleta)
 – *wind vane*
37 el arriate, un macizo de flores *f*
 – *shrub bed, a flower bed*
38 el reborde de anillos *m*
 – *hoop edging*
39 el arriate de verduras *f*
 – *vegetable plot*
40 el invernadero de abrigo *m* (el
   túnel de plástico *m*)
 – *plastic tunnel (polythene
   greenhouse)*
41 el tragaluz
 – *ventilation flap*

42 la calle central
 – *central path*
43 las cajas de verduras *f*
 – *vegetable crate*
44 la planta de tomates *m* (la
   tomatera)
 – *tomato plant*
45 el ayudante del hortelano (*Mé.:*
   el tecolero)
 – *nursery hand*
46 la ayudante del hortelano
 – *nursery hand*
47 la planta en tina *f*
 – *tub plant*
48 la tina
 – *tub*
49 el plantón de naranjo *m* (un
   naranjo pequeño)
 – *orange tree*
50 el cesto de alambre *m*
 – *wire basket*
51 la caja de las plantas de
   semilla *f*
 – *seedling box*

1 el plantador
- *dibber (dibble)*
2 la laya (pala *f* para remover la tierra)
- *spade*
3 la escoba para el césped
- *lawn rake, a wire-tooth rake*
4 el rastrillo
- *rake*
5 el aporcador
- *ridging hoe*
6 el desplantador
- *trowel*
7 el escardillo de mano *f* (el combinado de azada *f* y horquilla *f*; *Amér.:* el carpidor)
- *combined hoe and fork*
8 la hoz (*Arg. y Chile:* la echona)
- *sickle*
9 la navaja jardinera
- *gardener's knife (pruning knife, billhook)*
10 el cuchillo esparraguero (el cortaespárragos)
- *asparagus cutter (asparagus knife)*
11 las tijeras de podar (la podadera de mango *m* largo, podadera de varilla *f*)
- *tree pruner (long-handled pruner)*
12 la laya semiautomática
- *semi-automatic spade*
13 el cultivador de tres dientes *m*
- *three-pronged cultivator*
14 el raspador de árboles *m* (el raspador de corteza *f*)
- *tree scraper (bark scraper)*
15 el aireador del césped
- *lawn aerator (aerator)*
16 la sierra de poda *f* (la sierra para cortar ramas *f*)
- *pruning saw (saw for cutting branches)*
17 el cortasetos impulsado por batería *f*
- *battery-operated hedge trimmer*
18 el cultivador de motor *m*
- *motor cultivator*
19 la taladradora de mano *f*
- *electric drill*
20 la transmisión
- *gear*
21 los dos juegos de fresas *f*
- *cultivator attachment*
22 el cogedor de frutas *f*
- *fruit picker*
23 el cepillo de árboles *m* (el cepillo para la corteza)
- *tree brush (bark brush)*
24 el pulverizador para el insecticida
- *sprayer for pest control*
25 la varilla (la boquilla) de aspersión *f*
- *lance*

26 el enrollador móvil
- *hose reel (reel and carrying cart)*
27 la manguera de riego *m*
- *garden hose*
28 el cortacésped de motor *m*
- *motor lawn mower (motor mower)*
29 el recipiente para la hierba
- *grassbox*
30 el motor de dos tiempos *m*
- *two-stroke motor*
31 el cortacésped eléctrico
- *electric lawn mower (electric mower)*
32 el cable de la corriente
- *electric lead (electric cable)*
33 la superficie de corte *m*
- *cutting unit*
34 el cortacésped mecánico
- *hand mower*
35 el cilindro de corte *m*
- *cutting cylinder*
36 la cuchilla
- *blade*
37 el cortacésped autoportado
- *riding mower*
38 la palanca del freno (el freno de mano *f*)
- *brake lock*
39 el arranque eléctrico
- *electric starter*
40 el pedal del freno (el freno de pie *m*)
- *brake pedal*
41 el mecanismo de cortar
- *cutting unit*
42 el remolque volquete *m*
- *tip-up trailer*
43 el regador giratorio, un regador (la rociadera)
- *revolving sprinkler, a lawn sprinkler*
44 el torniquete
- *revolving nozzle*
45 el manguito de unión *f* del tubo
- *hose connector*
46 la regadora fija
- *oscillating sprinkler*
47 la carretilla
- *wheelbarrow*
48 la cizalla para el césped
- *grass shears*
49 la cizalla para los setos
- *hedge shears*
50 las tijeras de podar
- *secateurs (pruning shears)*

# 57 Hortalizas

Vegetables (Vegetable Plants)

**1-11 plantas ƒ leguminosas (legumbres ƒ)**
- *leguminous plants (Leguminosae)*
1 el guisante (la arveja), una planta papilionácea
- *pea, a plant with a papilionaceous corola*
2 la flor del guisante
- *pea flower*
3 la hoja pinada
- *pinnate leaf*
4 el zarcillo del guisante, un zarcillo foliáceo
- *pea tendril, a leaf tendril*
5 la estípula
- *stipule*
6 la vaina, la cápsula de la semilla
- *legume (pod), a seed vessel (pericarp, legume)*
7 el guisante [la semilla]
- *pea [seed]*
8 la judía (la alubia, la habichuela; *Amér.:* el poroto, el frijol, el fríjol, el fréjol), una planta trepadora; *clases:* la judía verde (*Amér. Central:* el ejote; *Amér. Merid.:* la chaucha), la judía de enrame *m*, la judía de España; *más pequeña:* la judía enana; *otras clases:* la judía de careta ƒ, la judía de panoja ƒ, la judía de grande estandarte *m*, la judía lunada, la judía purpúrea
- *bean plant (bean), a climbing plant (climber, creeper); varieties: broad bean (runner bean, Am. scarlet runner), climbing bean (climber, pole bean), scarlet runner bean; smaller: dwarf French bean (bush bean)*
9 la flor de la judía
- *bean flower*
10 el tallo voluble (el tallo trepador) de la judía
- *twining beanstalk*
11 la judía [la vaina con las semillas]
- *bean [pod with seeds]*
12 el tomate
- *tomato*
13 el pepino (el cohombro)
- *cucumber*
14 el espárrago
- *asparagus*
15 el rábano redondo
- *radish*
16 el rábano largo (el rábano negro)
- *white radish*
17 la zanahoria larga
- *carrot*
18 la zanahoria de cascabel *m*
- *stump-rooted carrot*
19 el perejil
- *parsley*
20 el rábano blanco
- *horse-radish*
21 el puerro
- *leeks*
22 la cebolleta
- *chives*
23 la calabaza; *anal.:* el melón
- *pumpkin (Am. squash);* sim.: *melon*
24 la cebolla
- *onion*
25 la binza (la cáscara de la cebolla)
- *onion skin*
26 el nabo
- *kohlrabi*
27 el apio (*Chile:* el panul)
- *celeriac*
**28-34 las verduras**
- *brassicas (leaf vegetables)*
28 la acelga
- *chard (Swiss chard, seakale beet)*
29 la espinaca
- *spinach*
30 la col de Bruselas
- *Brussels sprouts (sprouts)*
31 la coliflor
- *cauliflower*
32 la col, una berza; *clases:* el repollo, la lombarda; *otras clases:* la col arbórea, el brécol (el brócoli), la col de san Dionisio, la col de Estrasburgo, la col de York, el colinabo
- *cabbage, a brassica; cultivated races (cultivars): green cabbage, red cabbage*
33 la col de Milán (la lombarda blanca)
- *savoy (savoy cabbage)*
34 la col rizada
- *kale (curly kale, kail), a winter green*
35 la escorzonera (el salsifí negro)
- *scorzonera (black salsify)*
**36-40 verduras ƒ para ensalada ƒ**
- *salad plants*
36 la lechuga
- *lettuce;* here: *cabbage lettuce*
37 la hoja de lechuga
- *lettuce leaf*
38 la lechuga silvestre (la hierba de los canónigos, la valeriana de huerta ƒ, el rapónchigo, el ruiponce)
- *corn salad (lamb's lettuce)*
39 la escarola (la endibia)
- *endive*
40 la achicoria amarga (la achicoria silvestre)
- *chicory (succory, salad chicory)*
41 la alcachofa
- *globe artichoke*
42 el pimiento picante (la guindilla; *Amér.:* el ají, el chile)
- *pepper;* here: *Spanish paprika*

**1-30  frutas ƒ de bayas ƒ**
(arbustos *m* de baya ƒ)
– *soft fruit*
**1-15  plantas ƒ grosularieas**
– *Ribes*
1  la grosella espinosa (la uva
espina)
– *gooseberry bush*
2  la rama florecida de la grosella
espinosa
– *flowering gooseberry cane*
3  la hoja
– *leaf*
4  la flor
– *flower*
5  la oruga geómetra de la grosella
espinosa
– *magpie moth larva*
6  la flor de la grosella espinosa
– *gooseberry flower*
7  el ovario inferior
– *epigynous ovary*
8  el cáliz (los sépalos)
– *calyx (sepals)*
9  la grosella espinosa, una baya
– *gooseberry, a berry*
10  el grosellero de racimo *m*
– *currant bush*
11  el racimo de frutas ƒ
– *cluster of berries*
12  la grosella
– *currant*
13  el pedúnculo
– *stalk*
14  la rama en flor ƒ del grosellero
– *flowering cane of the currant*
15  el racimo de flores ƒ
– *raceme*
16  la fresa; *clases:* la fresa
silvestre, el fresón, la fresa
alpina
– *strawberry plant;* varieties: *wild
strawberry (woodland
strawberry), garden strawberry,
alpine strawberry*
17  la planta con flores ƒ y frutos *m*
– *flowering and fruit-bearing plant*
18  el rizoma
– *rhizome*
19  la hoja trifoliada
– *ternate leaf (trifoliate leaf)*
20  el estolón (el tallo rastrero, el
brote rastrero)
– *runner (prostrate stem)*
21  la fresa, una fruta compuesta
– *strawberry, a pseudocarp*
22  el calículo
– *epicalyx*
23  el aquenio (la semilla, la
pepita)
– *achene (seed)*
24  la carne (la pulpa)
– *flesh (pulp)*
25  el frambueso
– *raspberry bush*
26  la flor del frambueso
– *raspberry flower*
27  el capullo floral (el botón)
– *flower bud (bud)*

28  el fruto (la frambuesa), un fruto
compuesto
– *fruit (raspberry), an aggregate
fruit (compound fruit)*
29  la mora (la zarzamora)
– *blackberry*
30  la espina (la púa)
– *thorny tendril*
**31-61  frutos *m* de pepitas ƒ**
– *pomiferous plants*
31  el peral (*Arg., Bol.:* el pero);
*var.:* el peral silvestre
– *pear tree;* wild: *wild pear tree*
32  la rama en flor ƒ del peral
– *flowering branch of the pear tree*
33  la pera [corte longitudinal]
– *pear [longitudinal section]*
34  el pedúnculo (el rabillo de la
pera)
– *pear stalk (stalk)*
35  la carne (la pulpa)
– *flesh (pulp)*
36  el corazón, el lóculo (la cápsula
de las pepitas)
– *core (carpels)*
37  la pepita (la semilla)
– *pear pip (seed), a fruit pip*
38  la flor del peral
– *pear blossom*
39  el óvulo
– *ovules*
40  el ovario
– *ovary*
41  el estigma
– *stigma*
42  el estilo
– *style*
43  el pétalo
– *petal*
44  el sépalo
– *sepal*
45  el estambre (la antera)
– *stamen*
46  el membrillero (el membrillo)
– *quince tree*
47  la hoja del membrillo
– *quince leaf*
48  la estípula
– *stipule*
49  el membrillo en forma ƒ de
manzana ƒ [corte longitudinal]
– *apple-shaped quince
[longitudinal section]*
50  el membrillo en forma ƒ de
pera ƒ [corte longitudinal]
– *pear-shaped quince [longitudinal
section]*
51  el manzano; *var.:* el manzano
silvestre (el maguillo)
– *apple tree;* wild: *crab apple tree*
52  la rama en flor ƒ del manzano
– *flowering branch of the apple
tree*
53  la hoja
– *leaf*
54  la flor del manzano
– *apple blossom*
55  la flor marchita
– *withered flower*

56  la manzana [corte longitudinal]
– *apple [longitudinal section]*
57  la piel de la manzana
– *apple skin*
58  la carne (la pulpa)
– *flesh (pulp)*
59  el corazón, el lóculo (la cápsula
con las semillas)
– *core (apple core, carpels)*
60  la pepita (la semilla)
– *apple pip, a fruit pip*
61  el pedúnculo (el rabillo de la
manzana)
– *apple stalk (stalk)*
62  la mariposa de la manzana, un
lepidóptero
– *codling moth (codlin moth)*
63  la galería del gusano
– *burrow (tunnel)*
64  la larva (el gusano, la oruga de
la mariposa)
– *larva (grub, caterpillar) of a
small moth*
65  el agujero del gusano
– *wormhole*

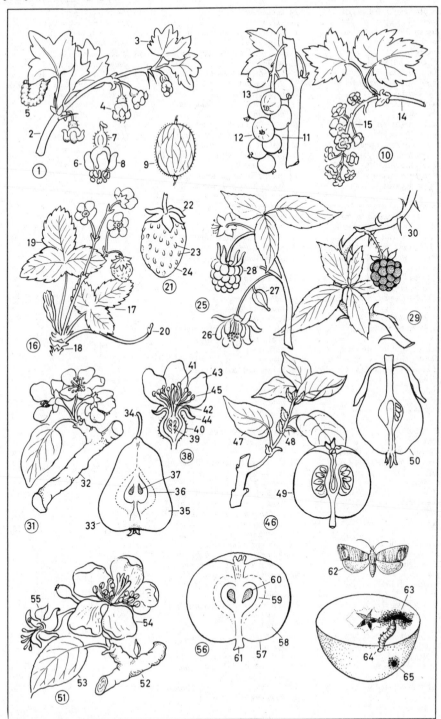

# 59 Frutas de hueso y de nuez

*Drupes and Nuts*

**1-36 plantas *f* de frutas *f* de hueso *m* (drupas *f*)**
- *drupes (drupaceous plants)*
**1-18 el cerezo**
- *cherry tree*
1 la rama en flor *f* del cerezo
- *flowering branch of the cherry tree (branch of the cherry tree in blossom)*
2 la hoja del cerezo
- *cherry leaf*
3 la flor del cerezo
- *cherry flower (cherry blossom)*
4 el tallo floral (el pedúnculo)
- *peduncle (pedicel, flower stalk)*
5 la cereza; *clases:* la cereza de corazón *m* negro, la cereza dulce, la cereza silvestre, la picota
- *cherry;* varieties: *sweet cherry (heart cherry), wild cherry (bird cherry), sour cherry, morello cherry (morello)*
**6-8 la cereza [corte longitudinal]**
- *cherry (cherry fruit) [cross section]*
6 la carne (la pulpa)
- *flesh (pulp)*
7 el hueso (*Amér.:* el carozo) de la cereza
- *cherry stone*
8 la almendra (la semilla)
- *seed*
9 la flor [corte longitudinal]
- *flower (blossom) [cross section]*
10 el estambre (la antera)
- *stamen*
11 el pétalo
- *corolla (petals)*
12 el sépalo
- *sepal*
13 el carpelo
- *pistil*
14 el óvulo en el ovario central
- *ovule enclosed in perigynous ovary*
15 el estilo
- *style*
16 el estigma
- *stigma*
17 la hoja
- *leaf*
18 el nectario peciolar
- *nectary (honey gland)*
**19-23 el ciruelo**
- *plum tree*
19 la rama con frutos *m* del ciruelo
- *fruit-bearing branch*
20 la ciruela damascena, una ciruela
- *oval, black-skinned plum*
21 la hoja del ciruelo
- *plum leaf*
22 la yema (el botón)
- *bud*
23 el hueso (*Amér.:* el carozo) de la ciruela
- *plum stone*

24 la ciruela claudia
- *greengage*
25 la mirabel (una ciruela pequeña y amarilla)
- *mirabelle (transparent gage), a plum*
**26-32 el melocotonero**
- *peach tree*
26 la rama florida
- *flowering branch (branch in blossom)*
27 la flor del melocotonero
- *peach flower (peach blossom)*
28 la inserción de la flor (el pimpollo de la flor)
- *flower shoot*
29 la hoja joven (la hoja naciente)
- *young leaf (sprouting leaf)*
30 la rama con frutos *m*
- *fruiting branch*
31 el melocotón
- *peach*
32 la hoja del melocotonero
- *peach leaf*
**33-36 el albaricoquero**
- *apricot tree*
33 la rama en flor *f* del albaricoquero
- *flowering apricot branch (apricot branch in blossom)*
34 la flor del albaricoquero
- *apricot flower (apricot blossom)*
35 el albaricoque (*Perú:* el aurimelo)
- *apricot*
36 la hoja del albaricoquero
- *apricot leaf*
**37-51 nueces *f***
- *nuts*
**37-43 el nogal**
- *walnut tree*
37 la rama en flor *f* del nogal
- *flowering branch of the walnut tree*
38 el amento femenino (flores *f* femeninas)
- *female flower*
39 el amento masculino (flores *f* masculinas con los estambres)
- *male inflorescence (male flower);* here: *catkins with stamens*
40 la hoja imparipinada plumada
- *alternate pinnate leaf*
41 la nuez, una drupa dehiscente
- *walnut, a drupe (stone fruit)*
42 el pericarpio (la cáscara, la cubierta exterior blanda)
- *cupule*
43 la nuez, una drupa dehiscente (un fruto de hueso *m*)
- *walnut, a drupe (stone fruit)*
**44-51 el avellano,** una planta anemófila
- *hazel tree (hazel bush), an anemophilous shrub (a wind-pollinating shrub)*
44 la rama en flor *f* del avellano
- *flowering hazel branch*
45 el amento masculino
- *male catkin*

46 el amento femenino
- *female inflorescence*
47 el brote de la hoja (la yema)
- *leaf bud*
48 la rama con frutos *m*
- *fruit-bearing branch*
49 la avellana, un fruto de hueso *m* (*Amér.:* de carozo *m*)
- *hazelnut (hazel, cobnut, cob), a drupe (stone fruit)*
50 la cúpula (el cáliz)
- *involucre (husk)*
51 la hoja del avellano
- *hazel leaf*

1 el narciso de las nieves (la campanilla de invierno *m*, el galanto de las nieves)
– *snowdrop (spring snowflake)*
2 el pensamiento, una violácea
– *garden pansy (heartsease pansy), a pansy*
3 el narciso atrompetado, un narciso
– *trumpet narcissus (trumpet daffodil, Lent lily), a narcissus*
4 el narciso de los poetas (el narciso blanco); *otros:* el narciso junquillo, el narciso oloroso
– *poet's narcissus (pheasant's eye, poet's daffodil);* sim.: *polyanthus narcissus*
5 la flor de corazón *m*, una dicentra, una fumariácea
– *bleeding heart (lyre flower), a fumariaceous flower*
6 la minutisa (el clavel de ramillete *m*, el clavel de los poetas), un clavel (una cariofilácea)
– *sweet william (bunch pink), a carnation*
7 el clavel de jardín *m*
– *gillyflower (gilliflower, clove pink, clove carnation)*
8 el lirio, el lirio de jardín *m* (lirio *m* de agua *f*), una iridácea (un iris)
– *yellow flag (yellow water flag, yellow iris), an iris*
9 el nardo
– *tuberose*
10 la aguileña común (pajarilla *f*, los pelícanos, el manto real, las campanillas)
– *columbine (aquilegia)*
11 el gladíolo (la espadaña, la hierba estoque *m*, la cresta de gallo *m*)
– *gladiolus (sword lily)*
12 el lirio blanco (la azucena), un lirio
– *Madonna lily (Annunciation lily, Lent lily), a lily*
13 la espuela de caballero *m* (la consuelda real), una consólida
– *larkspur (delphinium), a ranunculaceous plant*
14 el polemonio, un flox
– *moss pink (moss phlox), a phlox*
15 la rosa india (rosa *f* china)
– *garden rose*
16 el capullo de la rosa
– *rosebud, a bud*
17 la rosa doble
– *double rose*
18 la espina de la rosa
– *rose thorn, a thorn*
19 la gallardía
– *gaillardia*
20 el tagetes (el clavelón, la maravilla, la flamenquilla)
– *African marigold (tagetes)*
21 la carricera (la cola de zorra *f*), un amaranto *m*
– *love-lies-bleeding, an amaranthine flower*
22 la zinnia (el rascamoño)
– *zinnia*
23 la dalia borla, una dalia
– *pompon dahlia, a dahlia*

# 61 Malas hierbas

*Weeds*

1 el azulejo (el aciano), una
centáurea
- *corn flower (bluebottle), a
centaury*
2 la amapola, una papaverácea
- *corn poppy (field poppy), a poppy*
3 el capullo
- *bud*
4 la flor de la amapola
- *poppy flower*
5 la cápsula de la amapola con
las semillas
- *seed capsule containing poppy
seeds*
6 la neguilla (la arañuela)
- *corn cockle (corn campion,
crown-of-the-field)*
7 los ojos de los sembrados (la
margarita del trigo), un
crisantemo
- *corn marigold (field marigold), a
chrysanthemum*
8 la manzanilla bastarda (la
manzanilla hedionda)
- *corn camomile (field camomile,
camomile, chamomile)*
9 la bolsa de pastor *m*
- *shepherd's purse*
10 la flor
- *flower*
11 el fruto (la vaina) en forma *f* de
bolsa *f*
- *fruit, a pouch-shaped pod*
12 la hierba cana (el zuzón, el
senecio, la hierba de las
quemaduras, el lechocino)
- *common groundsel*
13 el diente de león *m*
- *dandelion*
14 la cabezuela
- *flower head (capitulum)*
15 la fructificación
- *infructescence*
16 el erísimo
- *hedge mustard, a mustard*
17 el aliso [una crucífera]
- *stonecrop*
18 la mostaza silvestre
- *wild mustard (charlock, runch)*
19 la flor
- *flower*
20 el fruto, una vaina
- *fruit, a siliqua (pod)*
21 el rabanillo
- *wild radish (jointed charlock)*
22 la flor
- *flower*
23 el fruto (la vaina)
- *fruit, a siliqua (pod)*
24 el armuelle silvestre
- *common orache (common orach)*
25 el cenizo
- *goosefoot*
26 la correhuela
- *field bindweed (wild morning
glory), a bindweed*
27 los murajes
- *scarlet pimpernel (shepherd's
weatherglass, poor man's
weatherglass, eye-bright)*

28 la cebada de las ratas (la
cebadilla)
- *wild barley (wall barley)*
29 la cizaña (el joyo)
- *wild oat*
30 la grama (la grama de olor *m*, la
grama canina, la grama de
playa *f*, el rabo de zorra *f*);
*anál.:* la agróstide (el carrizo).
- *common couch grass (couch,
quack grass, quick grass, quitch
grass, scutch grass, twitch grass,
witchgrass);* sim.: *bearded couch
grass, sea couch grass*
31 la galinsoga parviflora
- *gallant soldier*
32 el cardo borriquero (el cardo de
los campos, el cardo corredor,
el erigio; *Amér.:* el caraguatá),
un cardo
- *field eryngo (Watling Street
thistle), a thistle*
33 la ortiga
- *stinging nettle, a nettle*

1 la casa (la vivienda)
- *house*
2 la cuadra
- *stable*
3 el gato doméstico
- *house cat (cat)*
4 la granjera
- *farmer's wife*
5 la escoba
- *broom*
6 el granjero (el cultivador, el campesino) (*Amér.:* el paisano; *Arg.:* el afincado)
- *farmer*
7 el establo (la vaquería)
- *cowshed*
8 la pocilga (la corte)
- *pigsty (sty,* Am. *pigpen, hogpen)*
9 el comedero exterior (el pesebre)
- *outdoor trough*
10 el cerdo (el puerco, el marrano, el cochino, el guarro, el gorrino) (*Amér.:* el chancho)
- *pig*
11 el silo-torre o silo elevado (el silo para el forraje)
- *above-ground silo (fodder silo)*
12 la columna montante de abastecimiento *m* (de carga *f*) del silo
- *silo pipe (standpipe for filling the silo)*
13 el silo de abono *m* líquido
- *liquid manure silo*
14 el edificio colateral
- *outhouse*
15 el cobertizo de las máquinas (el garaje; *Amér.:* el galpón)
- *machinery shed*
16 la puerta corredera
- *sliding door*
17 la puerta de acceso *m* al taller
- *door to the workshop*
18 el volquete de tres bandas, un vehículo de transporte *m*
- *three-way tip-cart, a transport vehicle*
19 el cilindro basculante
- *tipping cylinder*
20 la lanza (el brazo de tiro *m,* la barra de tracción *f*)
- *shafts*
21 la esparcidora de estiércol *m* (el distribuidor de estiércol *m*)
- *manure spreader (fertilizer spreader, manure distributor)*
22 el grupo (el dispositivo) de esparcimiento *m* (de distribución *f*)
- *spreader unit (distributor unit)*
23 el cilindro distribuidor
- *spreader cylinder (distributor cylinder)*
24 la batea rascadora fija
- *movable scraper floor*
25 el panel lateral (el adral)
- *side planking (side board)*
26 el adral de reja *f*
- *wire mesh front*
27 el vehículo de riego *m*
- *sprinkler cart*
28 el soporte (el chasis, el armazón) de riego *m*
- *sprinkler stand*
29 el regador (el regador-devanadera de caudal *m* pequeño), un regador giratorio
- *sprinkler, a revolving sprinkler*
30 la goma flexible de riego *m* enrollada en la devanadera
- *sprinkler hoses*
31 el patio de la granja
- *farmyard*
32 el perro de la granja
- *watchdog*
33 el ternero
- *calf*
34 la vaca lechera
- *dairy cow (milch-cow, milker)*
35 el seto de la granja
- *farmyard hedge*
36 la gallina
- *chicken*
37 el gallo
- *cock* (Am. *rooster)*
38 el tractor
- *tractor*
39 el conductor del tractor
- *tractor driver*
40 el remolque de carga *f* universal
- *all-purpose trailer*
41 el dispositivo de recogida *f* (de carga) replegado (levantado)
- *[folded] pickup attachment*
42 el dispositivo de descarga *f* (el distribuidor)
- *unloading unit*
43 el silo de politileno *m,* un silo para el forraje
- *polythene silo, a fodder silo*
44 el pasto
- *meadow*
45 el ganado de pasto *m*
- *grazing cattle*
46 la cerca electrificada
- *electrified fence*

# 63 Agricultura

**1-41 labores *f* del campo** (las labores agrícolas)
- *work in the fields*
1 el barbecho (*Col. y Cuba:* el placer)
- *fallow (fallow field, fallow ground)*
2 el mojón
- *boundary stone*
3 la linde (lindero *m*, límite *m*)
- *boundary ridge, a balk (baulk)*
4 el campo (la tierra de labor *f*)
- *field*
5 el obrero agrícola (el bracero del campo)
- *farmworker (agricultural worker, farmhand, farm labourer, Am. laborer)*
6 el arado
- *plough (Am. plow)*
7 el terrón
- *clod*
8 el surco
- *furrow*
9 la piedra
- *stone*
10-12 la siembra (la sementera)
- *sowing*
10 el sembrador (*Amér. Central:* el tayacán)
- *sower*
11 el sementero
- *seedlip*
12 la simiente (la semilla)
- *seed corn (seed)*
13 el guarda de campo *m* (el meseguero)
- *field guard*
14 el abono artificial (el abono químico); *clases:* el abono potásico, el abono fosfático, el abono cálcico, el abono nitrogenado
- *chemical fertilizer (artificial fertilizer);* kinds: *potash fertilizer, phosphoric acid fertilizer, lime fertilizer, nitrogen fertilizer*
15 la carretada de estiércol *m*
- *cartload of manure (farmyard manure, dung)*
16 la yunta de bueyes *m*
- *oxteam (team of oxen, Am. span of oxen)*
17 la campiña
- *fields (farmland)*
18 el camino vecinal (*Col. y S. Dgo.:* la trilla; *Amér. Central, Antillas, Ec., Pan., Urug.:* el trillo)
- *farm track (farm road)*
**19-30 la siega del heno** (de la hierba)
- *hay harvest (haymaking)*
19 la segadora agavilladora
- *rotary mower with swather (swath reaper)*
20 la barra de enganche *m*
- *connecting shaft (connecting rod)*
21 la toma de fuerza *f*
- *power take-off (power take-off shaft)*
22 el prado
- *meadow*
23 el tajo de heno *m* (la ringlera de heno *m* segado)
- *swath (swathe)*
24 la henificadora giratoria
- *tedder (rotary tedder)*
25 el heno esparcido (la hierba esparcida)
- *tedded hay*
26 la agavilladora giratoria
- *rotary swather*
27 la recogedora-cargadora
- *trailer with pickup attachment*
28 el caballete sueco para el secado del heno, un secador de heno *m*
- *fence rack (rickstand), a drying rack for hay*
29 el colgadero de heno *m*
- *rickstand, a drying rack for hay*
30 el trípode para el secado del heno *m*
- *hay tripod*
**31-41 la cosecha (la recolección) y la preparación de la tierra** (*Col. y Venez.:* la cogienda)
- *grain harvest and seedbed preparation*
31 la segadora-trilladora (la cosechadora)
- *combine harvester*
32 la mies
- *cornfield*
33 la rastrojera
- *stubble field*
34 la bala (la paca) de paja *f* (una bala de paja *f* prensada)
- *bale of straw*
35 la empacadora de paja *f*, una empacadora de alta presión *f*
- *straw baler (straw press), a high-pressure baler*
36 el rastrojo
- *swath (swathe) of straw (windrow of straw)*
37 el cargador hidráulico de balas *f*
- *hydraulic bale loader*
38 el remolque de carga *f*
- *trailer*
39 el distribuidor de estiércol *m* (la esparcidora de estiércol *m*)
- *manure spreader*
40 el arado de cuatro rejas *f*
- *four-furrow plough (Am. plow)*
41 la sembradora a chorrillo *m*
- *combination seed-harrow*

**1-33  la cosechadora**
- *combine harvester (combine)*
1 el separador de cañas *f*
- *divider*
2 el elevador de espigas *f*
- *grain lifter*
3 la barra de cuchillas *f* (la barra de corte *m*)
- *cutter bar*
4 el tambor (el rodillo) de recolección *f* (el tambor con púas *f* de muelle *m*)
- *pickup reel, a spring-tine reel*
5 el mecanismo de regulación *f* del tambor
- *reel gearing*
6 el rodillo de entrada *f*
- *auger*
7 la cinta transportadora con cadenas *f*
- *chain and slat elevator*
8 el cilindro hidráulico para la regulación del sistema de energía *f*
- *hydraulic cylinder for adjusting the cutting unit*
9 el dispositivo de eliminación *f* de piedras *f*
- *stone catcher (stone trap)*
10 la desbarbadora (la desgranadora)
- *awner*
11 el cóncavo del tambor desgranador (la reja trilladora)
- *concave*
12 el tambor desgranador
- *threshing drum (drum)*
13 el tambor de conducción *f* de la paja
- *revolving beater [for freeing straw from the drum and preparing it for the shakers]*
14 el tamiz (la criba) de la paja
- *straw shaker (strawwalker)*
15 el aventador para la limpieza con aire *m* a presión *f*
- *fan for compressed-air winnowing*
16 la cinta de preparación *f*
- *preparation level*
17 el tamiz (la criba) de la paja corta
- *louvred-type sieve*
18 el alargamiento del tamiz
- *sieve extension*
19 la vuelta del tamiz
- *shoe sieve (reciprocating sieve)*
20 el tornillo sin fin *m* [para introducir el grano en la tolva]
- *grain auger*
21 el tornillo sin fin *m* hacia el desgranador
- *tailings auger*
22 la salida de la parte trasera (la salida de la rosca)
- *tailings outlet*
23 el depósito del grano
- *grain tank*
24 el tornillo sin fin *m* de alimentación *f* del depósito del grano
- *grain tank auger*
25 el tornillo sin fin *m* para el vaciado del depósito del grano
- *augers feeding to the grain tank unloader*
26 el conducto de vaciado *m* del depósito del grano
- *grain unloader spout*
27 la abertura para controlar el relleno del depósito
- *observation ports for checking tank contents*
28 el motor Diesel de seis cilindros *m*
- *six-cylinder diesel engine*
29 la bomba hidráulica con reserva *f* de aceite *m*
- *hydraulic pump with oil reservoir*
30 el árbol de transmisión *f*
- *driving axle gearing*
31 el neumático de una rueda motriz
- *driving wheel tyre (Am. tire)*
32 el neumático de una rueda direccional
- *rubber-tyred (Am. rubber-tired) wheel on the steering axle*
33 el puesto del conductor
- *driver's position*

**34-39  la recogedora picadora automotriz**
- *self-propelled forage harvester (self-propelled field chopper)*
34 el tambor de corte *m*
- *cutting drum (chopper drum)*
35 el pico (la dentadura) para el maíz
- *corn head*
36 la cabina del conductor
- *cab (driver's cab)*
37 el tubo de eyección *f*
- *swivel-mounted spout (discharge pipe)*
38 el escape
- *exhaust*
39 una rueda direccional trasera
- *rear-wheel steering system*
**40-45  la gavilladora de torbellino *m***
- *rotary swather*
40 el árbol de articulación *f*
- *cardan shaft*
41 la rueda
- *running wheel*
42 las púas de muelle *m*
- *double spring tine*
43 la manivela
- *crank*
44 el rastrillo
- *swath rake*
45 el acoplamiento (el soporte) de tres puntos *m*
- *three-point linkage*
**46-58  la henificadora giratoria**
- *rotary tedder*
46 el tractor
- *tractor*
47 la lanza de remolque *m*
- *draw bar*
48 el árbol de articulación *f*
- *cardan shaft*
49 la toma de fuerza *f*
- *power take-off (power take-off shaft)*
50 el mecanismo
- *gearing (gears)*
51 el tubo de soporte *m* (el chasis)
- *frame bar*
52 el platillo giratorio
- *rotating head*
53 el tubo de soporte *m* de las púas
- *tine bar*
54 las púas de muelle *m*
- *double spring tine*
55 la brida de protección *f*
- *guard rail*
56 la rueda
- *running wheel*
57 la manivela de regulación *f* de la altura
- *height adjustment crank*
58 la regulación de las ruedas
- *wheel adjustment*
**59-84  la arrancadora-recogedora de patatas *f***
- *potato harvester*
59 las palancas de mando *m*
- *control levers for the lifters of the digger and the hopper and for adjusting the shaft*
60 el gancho de tiro *m* para regular la altura
- *adjustable hitch*
61 la lanza de tiro *m* (de tracción *f*)
- *drawbar*
62 el soporte de la lanza
- *drawbar support*
63 el empalme de la toma de fuerza *f*
- *cardan shaft connection*
64 el cilindro compresor
- *press roller*
65 el mecanismo del motor hidráulico
- *gearing (gears) for the hydraulic system*
66 la cuchilla de disco *m* (la cuchilla circular)
- *disc (disk) coulter (Am. colter) (rolling coulter)*
67 la reja de tres láminas *f*
- *three-bladed share*
68 el mecanismo de mando *m* de la cuchilla de disco *m*
- *disc (disk) coulter (Am. colter) drive*

69 la cinta transportadora
- *open-web elevator*
70 el mecanismo de sacudida *f* de la cinta transportadora
- *agitator*
71 el desmultiplicador de varias velocidades *f*
- *multi-step reduction gearing*
72 el cargador
- *feeder*
73 el arrancador de hierbas *f* (el rotor de aletas *f*)
- *haulm stripper (flail rotor)*
74 la rueda elevadora
- *rotary elevating drum*
75 el separador oscilante
- *mechanical tumbling separator*
76 la cinta transportadora de hierbas *f* con arrancadores *m* flexibles
- *haulm conveyor with flexible haulm strippers*
77 el dispositivo de sacudida *f* de la cinta transportadora de hierbas *f*
- *haulm conveyor agitator*
78 el mecanismo de mando *m* con correa *f* trapezoidal
- *haulm conveyor drive with V-belt*
79 la correa de caucho *m* claveteada para la separación de los tallos, de los terrones de tierra *f* y de las piedras
- *studded rubber belt for sorting vines, clods and stones*
80 la cinta transportadora de las impurezas
- *trash conveyor*
81 la cinta de inspección *f* y clasificación *f*
- *sorting table*
82 los rodillos de discos *m* de caucho *m* para asegurar la primera selección *f*
- *rubber-disc (rubber-disk) rollers for presorting*
83 la cinta de descarga *f*
- *discharge conveyor*
84 la tolva con fondo *m* móvil
- *endless-floor hopper*
**85-96  la extractora de remolachas *f* (una arrancadora-cortadora-carga dora de remolachas *f*)**
- *beet harvester*
85 la cortadora
- *topper*
86 la rueda direccional
- *feeler*
87 la cuchilla de extracción *f*
- *topping knife*
88 la rueda de apoyo *m* con regulación *f* de profundidad *f*
- *feeler support wheel with depth adjustment*
89 el limpiador de remolachas *f*
- *beet cleaner*
90 el elevador de las hojas
- *haulm elevator*
91 la bomba hidráulica
- *hydraulic pump*
92 el depósito de aire *m* comprimido
- *compressed-air reservoir*
93 el depósito de aceite *m*
- *oil tank (oil reservoir)*
94 el dispositivo de regulación *f* de la tensión del elevador de remolachas *f*
- *tensioning device for the beet elevator*
95 la cinta elevadora de remolachas *f*
- *beet elevator belt*
96 la tolva de las remolachas
- *beet hopper*

1 el arado de vertedera *f*
- *wheel plough* ( Am. *plow*), *a single-bottom plough* [form.]
2 la empuñadura
- *handle*
3 la esteva (la mancera)
- *plough* (Am. *plow*) *stilt (plough handle)*
4-8 el cuerpo del arado
- *plough* (Am. *plow*) *bottom*
4 la vertedera
- *mouldboard* (Am. *moldboard)*
5 el montante vertical
- *landside*
6 la cabeza
- *sole (slade)*
7 la reja
- *ploughshare (share*, Am. *plowshare)*
8 el montante (el puntal)
- *frog (frame)*
9 la cama del arado
- *beam (plough beam*, Am. *plowbeam)*
10 la cuchilla (el punzón)
- *knife coulter* (Am. *colter), a coulter*
11 la reja anterior
- *skim coulter* (Am. *colter)*
12 el regulador para la dirección *f* automática por cadena *f*
- *guide-chain crossbar*
13 la cadena para la guía automática
- *guide chain*
14-19 el carro del arado (el carro, el antetrén; *Cuba:* el trinqueval)
- *forecarriage*
14 el yugo (el estribo)
- *adjustable yoke*
15 la rueda del caballón
- *land wheel*
16 la rueda del surco
- *furrow wheel*
17 la cadena de suspensión *f*
- *hake chain*
18 la lanza de tiro *m*
- *draught beam (drawbar)*
19 el gancho de tiro *m*
- *hake*
20 el tractor agrícola
- *tractor (general-purpose tractor)*
21 el bastidor de la cabina (el arco de seguridad *f*)
- *cab frame*
22 el asiento
- *seat*
23 el cambio de velocidad *f* de la toma de fuerza *f*
- *power take-off gear-change (gearshift)*
24-29 el sistema hidráulico de elevación *f*
- *power lift*
24 el pistón hidráulico
- *ram piston*
25 el regulador del puntal de elevación *f*
- *lifting rod adjustment*
26 el marco de unión *f*
- *drawbar frame*
27 la barra conductora superior
- *top link*
28 la barra conductora inferior
- *lower link*
29 el puntal (la varilla) de elevación *f*
- *lifting rod*
30 el engache (el acoplamiento de remolque *m*)
- *drawbar coupling*
31 la toma de fuerza *f* del motor (la toma de fuerza *f* independiente)
- *live power take-off (live power take-off shaft, take-off shaft)*
32 el engranaje diferencial (el diferencial)
- *differential gear (differential)*
33 el eje fijo
- *floating axle*
34 la palanca de cambio *m* del par motor
- *torque converter lever*

35 la palanca de velocidad *f*
- *gear-change (gearshift)*
36 la transmisión de velocidades *f* múltiples
- *multi-speed transmission*
37 el embrague hidráulico
- *fluid clutch (fluid drive)*
38 la transmisión de toma *f* de fuerza *f*
- *power take-off gear*
39 el embrague principal (el embrague)
- *main clutch*
40 el cambio de velocidad *f* de la toma de fuerza *f*, con embrague *m* de toma *f* de fuerza *f*
- *power take-off gear-change (gearshift) with power take-off clutch*
41 la dirección hidráulica con transmisión *f* reversible
- *hydraulic power steering and reversing gears*
42 el depósito de combustible *m*
- *fuel tank*
43 la palanca flotante
- *float lever*
44 el motor Diesel de cuatro cilindros *m*
- *four-cylinder diesel engine*
45 el cárter de aceite *m* con bomba *f* para la lubrificación por circulación *f* forzada
- *oil sump and pump for the pressure-feed lubrication system*
46 el depósito de aceite *m* fresco
- *fresh oil tank*
47 la barra de acoplamiento *m*
- *track rod* (Am. *tie rod)*
48 el soporte del eje delantero
- *front axle pivot pin*
49 la suspensión del eje delantero
- *front axle suspension*
50 el dispositivo de remolque *m* de la delantera
- *front coupling (front hitch)*
51 el radiador
- *radiator*
52 el ventilador
- *fan*
53 la batería
- *battery*
54 el filtro de aire *m* con baño *m* de aceite *m*
- *oil bath air cleaner (oil bath air filter)*
55 el cultivador
- *cultivator (grubber)*
56 el bastidor
- *sectional frame*
57 la púa de muelle *m*
- *spring tine*
58 la reja de arado *m*
- *share, a diamond-shaped share;* sim.: *chisel-shaped share*
59 la rueda de apoyo *m*
- *depth wheel*
60 el regulador de profundidad *f*
- *depth adjustment*
61 el dispositivo de remolque *m*
- *coupling (hitch)*
62 el arado reversible, un arado de cultivo *m*
- *reversible plough* ( Am. *plow), a mounted plough*
63 la rueda de apoyo *m*
- *depth wheel*
64-67 el cuerpo del arado, un cuerpo de arado *m* universal
- *plough* (Am. *plow) bottom, a general-purpose plough bottom*
64 la vertedera
- *mouldboard* (Am. *moldboard)*
65 la reja del arado
- *ploughshare (share*, Am. *plowshare), a pointed share*
66 la cabeza
- *sole (slade)*

67 el montante vertical
- *landside*
68 la cuchilla (el punzón)
- *skim coulter* (Am. *colter)*
69 la cuchilla de disco *m* (la cuchilla circular)
- *disc (disk) coulter* (Am. *colter) (rolling coulter)*
70 el bastidor del arado
- *plough* (Am. *plow) frame*
71 la cama del arado
- *beam (plough beam*, Am. *plowbeam)*
72 el enganche de tres puntos *m*
- *three-point linkage*
73 el mecanismo basculante (el mecanismo de báscula *f*)
- *swivel mechanism*
74 la sembradora a chorrillo *m*
- *drill*
75 la caja de la semilla
- *seed hopper*
76 la cuchilla de hacer surcos *m*
- *drill coulter* (Am. *colter)*
77 el tubo de llegada *f*, un tubo telescópico
- *delivery tube, a telescopic tube*
78 el aparato distribuidor
- *feed mechanism*
79 la caja de engranajes *m*
- *gearbox*
80 la rueda motriz
- *drive wheel*
81 el indicador del surco
- *track indicator*
82 el pulverizador de discos *m*
- *disc (disk) harrow, a semimounted implement*
83 la disposición de los discos en forma *f* de X
- *discs (disks) in X-configuration*
84 el disco redondo
- *plain disc (disk)*
85 el disco dentado
- *serrated-edge disc (disk)*
86 el enganche rápido
- *quick hitch*
87 la combinación grada-desterronador
- *combination seed-harrow*
88 la grada con dientes *m* de tres secciones *f*
- *three-section spike-tooth harrow*
89 el desterronador de tres secciones *f*
- *three-section rotary harrow*
90 el bastidor (la armazón) fijo(a)
- *frame*

1 la azada de arrastre *m* (*Arg., Bol., Ec. y Perú:* la lampa; *Col.:* la palendra)
 – *draw hoe (garden hoe)*
2 el mango de la azada
 – *hoe handle*
3 la horca de tres puntas *f* para el estiércol (la horca del estiércol, la horca)
 – *three-pronged (three-tined) hay fork (fork)*
4 la púa (la punta, el pincho, el gajo)
 – *prong (tine)*
5 la horca para las patatas (la bielda para las patatas, el trente, la pala de las patatas; *Col.:* la garlancha)
 – *potato fork*
6 la azada para las patatas (*Ec.:* el palancón)
 – *potato hook*
7 la horca de cuatro puntas *f* para el heno (la horca del heno, la horca)
 – *four-pronged (four-tined) manure fork (fork)*
8 la azada para el estiércol (*Perú, P. Rico, Guat., S. Dgo. y Venez.:* el desyerbo)
 – *manure hoe*
9 el martillo de la guadaña
 – *whetting hammer [for scythes]*
10 el corte del martillo
 – *peen (pane)*
11 el yunque de la guadaña
 – *whetting anvil [for scythes]*
12 la guadaña (el dalle, la dalla)
 – *scythe*
13 la hoja de la guadaña
 – *scythe blade*
14 el filo de la guadaña (el corte de la guadaña)
 – *cutting edge*
15 el talón de la guadaña (la culata de la guadaña)
 – *heel*
16 el mango de la guadaña (el asta *f* de la guadaña)
 – *snath (snathe, snead, sneath)*
17 la manija de la guadaña
 – *handle*
18 la guarda (el protector del filo de la guadaña)
 – *scythe sheath*
19 la piedra de afilar (la afiladera) [*se lleva en* la aliara]
 – *whetstone (scythestone)*
20 el rastro para las patatas
 – *potato rake*
21 el cesto (la sera) para patatas *f* de siembra *f* (*Mé.:* el quiligua)
 – *potato planter*
22 la laya
 – *digging fork (fork)*
23 el rastrillo para el heno (el rastrillo, el rastro para el heno)
 – *hayrake, a wooden rake*
24 el azadón de rozar (el azadón de patatas *f*; *Chile:* el gualato)
 – *potato hoe*
25 el cesto de las patatas, un cesto de alambre *m*
 – *potato basket, a wire basket*
26 la carretilla del trébol, una máquina sembradora de trébol *m*
 – *clover broadcaster*

1 el tubo oscilante con surtidores *m*
– *oscillating spray line*
2 el caballete de soporte *m*
– *stand (steel chair)*
3 el dispositivo móvil de riego *m*
– *portable irrigation system*
4 el regador giratorio
– *revolving sprinkler*
5 el empalme de tubo *m*
– *standpipe coupler*
6 el codo de cardán *m*
– *elbow with cardan joint (cardan coupling)*
7 el caballete de soporte *m*
– *pipe support (trestle)*
8 el codo de empalme *m* de la bomba
– *pump connection*
9 el empalme a presión *f*
– *delivery valve*
10 el manómetro
– *pressure gauge (Am. gage) (manometer)*
11 la bomba de evacuación *f*
– *centrifugal evacuating pump*
12 la alcachofa de aspiración *f*
– *basket strainer*
13 la zanja (el canal)
– *channel*
14 el chasis de la bomba accionada por la toma de fuerza *f* del tractor
– *chassis of the p.t.o.-driven pump (power take-off-driven pump)*

15 la bomba de tractor *m* (la bomba accionada por la toma de fuerza *f* del tractor)
– *p.t.o.-driven (power take-off-driven) pump*
16 el árbol de articulación *f*
– *cardan shaft*
17 el tractor
– *tractor*
18 el regador para grandes superficies *f*
– *long-range irrigation unit*
19 la tubuladura de propulsión *f*
– *drive connection*
20 la turbina
– *turbine*
21 el cambio de velocidades *f* (el reductor)
– *gearing (gears)*
22 el apoyo ajustable
– *adjustable support*
23 la bomba de evacuación *f*
– *centrifugal evacuating pump*
24 la rueda
– *wheel*
25 la guía del tubo
– *pipe support*
26 el tubo de poliéster *m*
– *polyester pipe*
27 la boquilla (la tobera) del regador
– *sprinkler nozzle*
28 el tubo de empalme *m* instantáneo con junta *f* de articulación *f* cardán *m*
– *quick-fitting pipe connection with cardan joint*

29 la pieza macho del cadán
– *M-cardan*
30 el acoplamiento
– *clamp*
31 la pieza hembra del cardán
– *V-cardan*
32 el regador giratorio
– *revolving sprinkler, a field sprinkler*
33 la boquilla
– *nozzle*
34 la palanca oscilante
– *breaker*
35 el muelle de la palanca oscilante
– *breaker spring*
36 el tapón
– *stopper*
37 el contrapeso
– *counterweight*
38 la rosca
– *thread*

**1-47 frutos** *m* **del campo**
(productos *m* agrícolas)
- *arable crops*
**1-37 clases** *f* **de cereales** *m*
(granos *m* panificables)
- *varieties of grain (of cereals, farinaceous plants)*
1 el centeno (*también:* el grano; "grano" significa a menudo el principal grano panificable, en España: el trigo, en el norte de Alemania: el centeno, en el sur de Alemania e Italia: el trigo, en Suecia y Noruega: la cebada, en Escocia: la avena, en Norteamérica: el maíz, en China: el arroz)
- *rye (also: corn, 'corn' often meaning the main cereal of a country or region; in Northern Germany: rye; in Southern Germany and Italy: wheat; in Sweden: barley; in Scotland: oats; in North America: maize; in China: rice)*
2 la espiga de centeno *m*, una espiga
- *ear of rye, a spike (head)*
3 la espiguilla
- *spikelet*
4 el cornezuelo, un grano deformado por un hongo
- *ergot, a grain deformed by fungus [shown with mycelium]*
5 la macolla de un cereal
- *corn stem after tillering*
6 la caña
- *culm (stalk)*
7 el nudo
- *node of the culm*
8 la hoja
- *leaf (grain leaf)*
9 la vaina de la hoja
- *leaf sheath (sheath)*
10 la espiguilla
- *spikelet*
11 el cascabillo
- *glume*
12 la arista (la barba)
- *awn (beard, arista)*
13 la semilla (el grano, la cariópside)
- *seed (grain, kernel, farinaceous grain)*
14 el germen de la planta (el grano germinado)
- *embryo plant*
15 la semilla
- *seed*
16 el brote
- *embryo*
17 la raíz
- *root*
18 los pelos absorbentes de la raíz
- *root hair*
19 la hoja del cereal
- *grain leaf*
20 el limbo
- *leaf blade (blade, lamina)*

21 la vaina de la hoja
- *leaf sheath*
22 la lígula
- *ligule (ligula)*
23 el trigo
- *wheat*
24 la espelta (la escanda común, escaña *f* mayor)
- *spelt*
25 la semilla; *no madurada:* la espelta verde, un grano verde para guisos *m*
- *seed; unripe: green spelt, a soup vegetable*
26 la cebada
- *barley*
27 la avena
- *oat panicle, a panicle*
28 el mijo
- *millet*
29 el arroz
- *rice*
30 el grano de arroz *m*
- *rice grain*
31 el maíz; *variedades:* maíz perlado, maíz de diente *m* de caballo *m*, maíz duro, maíz de vainas, maíz tierno, maíz dulce, maíz tostado (*Arg. y Chile:* el ancua), maíz morocho, maíz dental, maíz amarillo, maíz híbrido
- *maize (Indian corn, Am. corn); varieties: popcorn, dent corn, flint corn (flint maize, Am. Yankee corn), pod corn (Am. cow corn, husk corn), soft corn (Am. flour corn, squaw corn), sweet corn*
32 la inflorescencia femenina
- *female inflorescence*
33 la perfolla (la farfolla; *Arg., Bol., Chile, Mé., Perú y Urug.:* la chala)
- *husk (shuck)*
34 el pistilo
- *style*
35 la inflorescencia masculina en panícula *f*
- *male inflorescence (tassel)*
36 la mazorca (la panoja, la panocha; *Mé.:* el cenancle; *Arg. y Par.:* el abatí)
- *maize cob (Am. corn cob)*
37 el grano de maíz *m* (*Arg. y Par.:* el grano de abatí *m*)
- *maize kernel (grain of maize)*
**38-45 tubérculos** *m*
- *root crops*
38 la patata (*Amér.:* la papa), un tubérculo; *clases:* redonda, ovalada, alargada, arriñonada; *según el color:* blanca, amarilla, roja, rosa; *según la precocidad:* muy precoz, precoz, semitardía, tardía; *según la utilidad:* industrial, forrajera, de huerta

- *potato plant (potato), a tuberous plant;* varieties: *round, round-oval (pear-shaped), flat-oval, long, kidney-shaped potato;* according to colour: *white (Am. Irish), yellow, red, purple potato*
39 la patata de siembra *f* (el tubérculo madre *f*)
- *seed potato (seed tuber)*
40 la patata (el tubérculo) (*Amér.:* la papa, el bulbo)
- *potato tuber (potato, tuber)*
41 la hoja de la patata
- *potato top (potato haulm)*
42 la flor
- *flower*
43 la baya no comestible (la baya de la patata)
- *poisonous potato berry (potato apple)*
44 la remolacha azucarera, una remolacha
- *sugar beet, a beet*
45 la raíz (la remolacha)
- *root (beet)*
46 el cuello de la remolacha
- *beet top*
47 la hoja de la remolacha
- *beet leaf*

**1-28 plantas *f* forrajeras cultivadas**
- *fodder plants (forage plants) for tillage*
**1** el trébol del prado *m* (*Col.:-* el carretonero)
- *red clover (purple clover)*
**2** el trébol blanco
- *white clover (Dutch clover)*
**3** el trébol híbrido
- *alsike clover (alsike)*
**4** el trébol encarnado
- *crimson clover*
**5** el trébol de cuatro hojas *f* (*pop.:* el trébol de la suerte)
- *four-leaf (four-leaved) clover*
**6** la vulneraria
- *kidney vetch (lady's finger, lady-finger)*
**7** la flor del trébol
- *flower*
**8** la vaina
- *pod*
**9** la alfalfa
- *lucerne (lucern, purple medick)*
**10** la esparceta (el pipirigallo, la gallocresta)
- *sainfoin (cock's head, cockshead)*
**11** el trébol de pie de pájaro *m* (la serradella)
- *bird's foot (bird-foot, bird's foot trefoil)*
**12** la arenaria, una cariofilácea
- *corn spurrey (spurrey, spurry)*
**13** la consuelda (el sínfito mayor)
- *common comfrey, one of the borage family (Boraginaceae)*
**14** la flor
- *flower (blossom)*
**15** el haba *f* gruesa (el haba *f* panosa; *anál.:* el haba *f* común, la judía escarlata, el haba *f* del ganado, el haba *f* de los caballos)
- *field bean (broad bean, tick bean, horse bean)*
**16** la vaina
- *pod*
**17** el lupino amarillo (el altramuz amarillo)
- *yellow lupin*
**18** la arveja (la veza)
- *common vetch*
**19** la almorta (el garbanzo forrajero, la muela, la guija)
- *chick-pea*
**20** el girasol
- *sunflower*
**21** la remolacha forrajera
- *mangold (mangelwurzel, mangoldwurzel, field mangel)*
**22** la espiguilla
- *false oat (oat-grass)*
**23** la espiguilla
- *spikelet*
**24** la cañuela (la festuca de los prados), una festuca
- *meadow fescue grass, a fescue*
**25** la grama en jopillos *m*, un dáctilo
- *cock's foot (cocksfoot)*
**26** el ballico (el césped inglés, el raigrás italiano)
- *Italian ryegrass;* sim.: *perennial ryegrass (English ryegrass)*
**27** la cola de zorra *f* (el alopecuro), una graminácea
- *meadow foxtail, a paniculate grass*
**28** la pimpinela mayor (la sanguisorba)
- *greater burnet saxifrage*

1  el bulldog
–  *bulldog*
2  la oreja colgante
–  *ear, a rose-ear*
3  el hocico (la boca)
–  *muzzle*
4  las narices
–  *nose*
5  la pata delantera (el brazo)
–  *foreleg*
6  la mano
–  *forepaw*
7  la pata trasera
–  *hind leg*
8  el pie
–  *hind paw*
9  el doguino (el doguillo)
–  *pug (pug dog)*
10  el bóxer
–  *boxer*
11  la cruz
–  *withers*
12  la cola, una cola cortada
–  *tail, a docked tail*
13  el collar de perro *m*
–  *collar*
14  el gran danés (el dogo alemán)
–  *Great Dane*
15  el foxterrier
–  *wire-haired fox terrier*
16  el bullterrier
–  *bull terrier*

17  el terrier escocés
–  *Scottish terrier*
18  el terrier bedlington
–  *Bedlington terrier*
19  el perrito pequinés
–  *Pekinese (Pekingese, Pekinese dog, Pekingese dog)*
20  el lulú (el perro de Pomerania)
–  *spitz (Pomeranian)*
21  el chow-chow
–  *chow (chow-chow)*
22  el perro esquimal
–  *husky*
23  el afgano (el galgo afgano)
–  *Afghan (Afghan hound)*
24  el galgo
–  *greyhound (Am. grayhound), a courser*
25  el pastor alemán (un perro lobo *m*), un perro de ayuda *f*, un perro guardián y de compañía *f*
–  *Alsatian (German sheepdog, Am. German shepherd), a police dog, watch dog, and guide dog*
26  los belfos
–  *flews (chaps)*
27  el doberman
–  *Dobermann terrier*

**28-31  el equipo del perro**
- *dog's outfit*
**28**  el cepillo para perros *m*
- *dog brush*
**29**  el peine para perros *m*
- *dog comb; en cacerías:* la traílla
**30**  la correa; *en cacerías:* la traílla
- *lead (dog lead, leash);* for
  hunting: *leash*
**31**  el bozal (*Cuba y Perú:* la
  hociquera)
- *muzzle*
**32**  la escudilla de la comida (el
  comedero)
- *feeding bowl (dog bowl)*
**33**  el hueso
- *bone*
**34**  el perro de Terranova (el
  terranova)
- *Newfoundland dog*
**35**  el grifón
- *schnauzer*
**36**  el perro de lanas (el caniche);
  *más pequeño:* el perro de
  lanas *f* enano (el caniche
  enano; *Amér. Merid.:* el choco)
- *poodle;* sim. and smaller: *pygmy
  (pigmy) poodle*
**37**  el perro de san Bernardo (el san
  Bernardo)
- *St. Bernard (St. Bernard dog)*

**38**  el cócker
- *cocker spaniel*
**39**  el teckel de pelo *m* corto (el
  perro zarcero, el teckel, el
  basset, el perro tejonero)
- *dachshund, a terrier*
**40**  el perro de muestra *f* alemán
- *German pointer*
**41**  el setter (un perro de muestra *f*
  inglés)
- *English setter*
**42**  el perro perdiguero, un perro
  de muestra *f*
- *trackhound*
**43**  el pointer, un perro rastrero
- *pointer, a trackhound*

**1-6 equitación** *f* (el arte de montar a caballo *m*, la equitación de alta escuela *f*)
– *equitation (high school riding, haute école)*
**1** el piafe
– *piaffe*
**2** el paso (el paso corto, el paso de escuela *f*)
– *walk*
**3** el passage (el paso español)
– *passage*
**4** la levade (la pirueta)
– *levade (pesade)*
**5** la cabriola
– *capriole*
**6** la corveta
– *courbette (curvet)*
**7-25 los arreos** (los arneses; *Antillas, Chile, Guat. y Perú:* el aparejo; *Col. y Cuba:* los arretrancos; *P. Rico:* los ensillos)
– *harness*
**7-13** las guarniciones
– *bridle*
**7-11 la cabezada** (*Amér. Central:* el gamarrón; *Ec., Mé y Perú:* el bozalillo; *Mé. y Chile:* el cabeceador; *Col.:* la martingala; *Col. y Ec.:* la tapanca)
– *headstall (headpiece, halter)*
**7** la muserola
– *noseband*
**8** la quijera
– *cheek piece (cheek strap)*
**9** la frontalera
– *browband (front band)*
**10** la testera
– *crownpiece*
**11** el ahogadero
– *throatlatch (throatlash)*
**12** la cadenilla de barbada *f*
– *curb chain*
**13** el bocado con la barbada
– *curb bit*
**14** el gancho del tirante
– *hasp (hook) of the hame* (Am. *drag hook)*
**15** la collera (*Mé.:* el gargantón)
– *pointed collar, a collar*
**16** el adorno de la collera
– *trappings (side trappings)*
**17** el sillín
– *saddle-pad*
**18** la cincha (la barriguera; *Arg., Col., Chile, Urug. y Venez.:* el cinchón)
– *girth*
**19** la sufra (*Cuba:* la tiradera)
– *backband*
**20** la cadena de la vara
– *shaft chain (pole chain)*
**21** la vara (la lanza, la flecha)
– *pole*
**22** el tirante
– *trace*

**23** la cincha (la barriguera) auxiliar
– *second girth (emergency girth)*
**24** el tiro
– *trace*
**25** las riendas (las bridas)
– *reins* (Am. *lines)*
**26-36 los arreos de pecho** *m*
– *breast harness*
**26** las anteojeras (*Cuba y P. Rico:* la visera)
– *blinker (*Am. *blinder, winker)*
**27** la anilla del petral
– *breast collar ring*
**28** el petral
– *breast collar (Dutch collar)*
**29** la horquilla del sobrecuello
– *fork*
**30** el sobrecuello
– *neck strap*
**31** el sillín
– *saddle-pad*
**32** la correa del lomo
– *loin strap*
**33** las riendas (las bridas)
– *reins (rein,* Am. *line)*
**34** la baticola (la correa de la cola, el ataharre)
– *crupper (crupper-strap)*
**35** el tirante
– *trace*
**36** la cincha (la barriguera)
– *girth (belly-band)*
**37-49 sillas** *f* **de montar** [*la silla para mujer en Guat., Hond., S. Dgo. y Venez.:* el galápago; *en Ec. y Cuba:* el gancho]
– *saddles*
**37-44 la silla de paseo** *m*
– *stock saddle* (Am. *western saddle)*
**37** el sillín (el asiento)
– *saddle seat*
**38** el borrén delantero
– *pommel horn (horn)*
**39** el borrén trasero
– *cantle*
**40** la hoja (el faldón) lateral (*Arg. y Chile:* el mandil; *Arg. y Urug.:* el sobrepelo)
– *flap* (Am. *fender)*
**41** los refuerzos
– *bar*
**42** la ación (*Amér.:* la estribera)
– *stirrup leather*
**43** el estribo
– *stirrup (stirrup iron)*
**44** la manta de la silla (el sudadero; *Arg. y. Urug.:* el sobrepelo; *Col. y Venez.:* el sufridor; *S. Dgo.:* el panó; *Amér. Central y Chile:* el pelero; *Mé.:* el cuascle)
– *blanket*
**45-49 la silla inglesa**
– *English saddle (cavalry saddle)*
**45** el sillín (el asiento)
– *seat*

**46** el pomo
– *cantle*
**47** la hoja (el faldón) lateral
– *flap*
**48** la hoja falsa
– *roll (knee roll)*
**49** el baste
– *pad*
**50-51 las espuelas** (*Col. y Venez.:* las orejonas)
– *spurs*
**50** el espolín (la espuela fija, la espuela clavada)
– *box spur (screwed jack spur)*
**51** la espuela de correílla *f*
– *strapped jack spur*
**52** el bocado (*Antillas, C. Rica, Ec. y Mé.:* el basbiquejo)
– *curb bit*
**53** el freno de boca *f*
– *gag bit (gag)*
**54** la almohaza (*Amér. Merid.:* la rasqueta)
– *currycomb*
**55** la bruza
– *horse brush (body brush, dandy brush)*

**1-38 la forma exterior** del caballo
- **points** of the horse
**1-11 la cabeza** (la cabeza del caballo)
- **head** (horse's head)
1 la oreja
- ear
2 el copete (*Chile:* el moño; *Venez.:* la guaya)
- forelock
3 la frente
- forehead
4 el ojo
- eye
5 la cara (la mejilla)
- face
6 el testuz
- nose
7 el ollar
- nostril
8 el labio (belfo *m*) superior
- upper lip
9 la boca
- mouth
10 el labio (belfo *m*) inferior
- underlip (lower lip)
11 la quijada inferior
- lower jaw
12 la nuca
- crest (neck)
13 la crin
- mane (horse's mane)
14 la cerviz (las crines; *Chile:* la tusa)
- crest (horse's crest)
15 el cuello
- le cou
16 la garganta
- throat (Am. throatlatch, throatlash)
17 la cruz
- withers

**18-27 la mano delantera**
- **forehand**
18 la espaldilla (la paletilla)
- shoulder
19 el pecho
- breast
20 el codillo
- elbow
21 el brazuelo
- forearm
**22-26 la pata delantera**
- **forefoot**
22 la rodilla delantera
- knee (carpus, wrist)
23 la caña
- cannon
24 el menudillo
- fetlock
25 el espolón
- pastern
26 el casco
- hoof
27 el espejuelo (la castaña), una callosidad
- chestnut (castor), a callosity
28 la vena torácica larga (la vena de la espuela)
- spur vein
29 el lomo
- back
30 los riñones
- loins (lumbar region)
31 la grupa (*Venez.:* la tarraza; *Guat.:* la tenedora)
- croup (rump, crupper)
32 el anca *f*
- hip

**33-37 el cuarto trasero**
- **hind leg**
33 la babilla (el gordetillo)
- stifle (stifle joint)
34 el maslo de la cola
- root (dock) of the tail
35 el muslo
- haunch
36 la pierna
- gaskin
37 el corvejón
- hock
38 la cola
- tail
**39-44 los pasos** de los caballos (los aires del caballo)
- **gaits** of the horse
39 el paso (*Urug.:* el tranco)
- walk
40 el paso de andadura *f*
- pace
41 el trote (*Col. y Venez.:* la trocha; *Col.:* el troche)
- trot
42 el galope a la izquierda
- canter; sim.: hand gallop
**43-44 el galope tendido** (el galope de carrera *f*)
- full gallop
43 el galope en el momento de la caída sobre los remos anteriores
- full gallop at the moment of descent on to the two forefeet
44 el galope en el momento en que los cuatro pies están en el aire
- full gallop at the moment when all four feet are off the ground

Abreviaturas:
*m.* = macho; *c* = castrado;
*h* = hembra; *j* = joven
*Abbreviations:*
m. = *male;* c. = *castrated;*
f. = *female;* y. = *young*

1-2 ganado *m* mayor
– *cattle*
1 el ganado vacuno, un animal con
cuernos *m,* un rumiante; *m.* el toro; *c.*
el buey; *h.* la vaca; *j. m.* el ternero; *j.*
*h.* la ternera
– *cow, a bovine animal, a horned*
*animal, a ruminant;* m. *bull;* c. *ox;* f.
*cow;* y. *calf*
2 el caballo; *m.* el caballo padre (el
caballo semental; *Amér.:* el
garañón); *c.* el caballo castrado; *h.* la
yegua; *j.* el potro
– *horse;* m. *stallion;* c. *gelding;* f. *mare;*
y. *foal*
3 el asno (burro *m,* borrico m); *m.* el
garañón; *j.* el pollino
– *donkey*
4 la albarda
– *pack saddle (carrying saddle)*
5 la carga
– *pack (load)*
6 la cola empenachada
– *tufted tail*
7 la borla
– *tuft*
8 el mulo, un cruce de asno *m* y yegua *f*
(el muleto; el burdégano, un cruce de
caballo *m* y burro *f*)
– *mule, a cross between a male donkey*
*and a mare*
9 el cerdo (el puerco, el cochino, el
marrano, el guarro, el gorrino; *Amér.:*
el chancho; *Perú:* el cuchí), un animal

con cerdas *f,* un animal con pezuñas *f*
hendidas (artiodáctilo *m*); *m.* el cerdo
padre (el verraco); *h.* la perca; *j.* el
lechón, el cochinillo
– *pig, a cloven-hoofed animal;* m. *boar;*
f. *sow;* y. *piglet*
10 el hocico
– *pig's snout (snout)*
11 la oreja
– *pig's ear*
12 la cola ensortijada
– *curly tail*
13 la oveja; *m.* el morueco; *c.* el
carnero; *h.* la oveja; *j.* el cordero (el
borrego)
– *sheep;* m. *ram;* c. *wether;* f. *ewe;* y.
*lamb*
14 la cabra; *m.* el cabrón; *j.* el chivo
– *goat*
15 la barba de la cabra (*también tiene:* las
mamellas)
– *goat's beard*
16 el perro, un perro Leonberg; *h.* la
perra; *j.* el cachorro
– *dog, a Leonberger;* m. *dog;* f. *bitch;* y.
*pup (puppy, whelp)*
17 el gato, un gato de angora; *h.* la gata
– *cat, an Angora cat (Persian cat);* m.
*tom (tom cat)*
18-36 animales *m* de corral *f*
– *small domestic animals*
18 el conejo; *m.* el conejo macho; *h.* la
coneja; *j.* el gazapo
– *rabbit;* m. *buck;* f. *doe*
19-36 aves *f* de corral *m*
– *poultry (domestic fowl)*
19-26 la gallina y el gallo
– *chicken*
19 la gallina
– *hen*

20 el buche
– *crop (craw)*
21 el gallo; *c.* el capón; *j.* el pollo
– *cock (Am. rooster);* c. *capon*
22 la cresta (*Bol.:* la corota; *Pan.:* la
sierra)
– *cockscomb (comb, crest)*
23 la carúncula (el lóbulo de la oreja)
– *lap*
24 la barba
– *wattle (gill, dewlap)*
25 la cola en forma *f* de hoz *f*
– *falcate (falcated) tail*
26 el espolón (*Amér.:* la espuela)
– *spur*
27 la gallina de Guinea (la pintada)
– *guinea fowl*
28 el pavo; *h.* la pava
– *turkey;* m. *turkey cock (gobbler);* f.
*turkey hen*
29 la cola en abanico *m* (la rueda)
– *fan tail*
30 el pavo real
– *peacock*
31 la pluma del pavo real
– *peacock's feather*
32 el ocelo
– *eye (ocellus)*
33 la paloma; *m.* el palomo; *j.* el pichón
– *pigeon;* m. *cock pigeon*
34 el ganso; *h.* la gansa; *j.* el ansarino
– *goose;* m. *gander;* y. *gosling*
35 el pato; *h.* la pata; *j.* el patito
– *duck;* m. *drake;* y. *duckling*
36 la membrana interdigital [de las aves
palmípedas]
– *web (palmations) of webbed foot*
*(palmate foot)*

# 74 Postura de las gallinas, la producción de huevos

1-27 **la postura de huevos** *m* **(la postura intensiva)**
- *poultry farming (intensive poultry management)*

1-17 **la postura de suelo** *m* (la cría sobre la paja)
- *straw yard (strawed yard) system*

1 la pollera
- *fold unit for growing stock (chick unit)*

2 el pollito
- *chick*

3 la incubadora (la pollera) artificial
- *brooder (hover)*

4 el reguero móvil del alimento (el comedero móvil)
- *adjustable feeding trough*

5 el gallinero de los pollos
- *pullet fold unit*

6 el abrevadero, el bebedero
- *drinking trough*

7 el tubo del agua *f*
- *water pipe*

8 la pajaza
- *litter*

9 el pollo
- *pullet*

10 el ventilador
- *ventilator*

11-17 **la cría de pollos** *m*
- *broiler rearing (rearing of broiler chickens)*

11 el gallinero
- *chicken run ( Am. fowl run)*

12 el pollo
- *broiler chicken (broiler)*

13 el comedero automático
- *mechanical feeder (self-feeder, feed dispenser)*

14 la cadena de apoyo *m*
- *chain*

15 la reguera de alimentación *f*
- *feed supply pipe*

16 el abrevadero automático (el bebedero automático)
- *mechanical drinking bowl (mechanical drinker)*

17 el ventilador
- *ventilator*

18 la postura en batería *f*
- *battery system (cage system)*

19 la jaula superior
- *battery (laying battery)*

20 la jaula inferior (la jaula de escalones *m*, la jaula en batería *f*)
- *tiered cage (battery cage, stepped cage)*

21 el comedero
- *feeding trough*

22 la cinta recolectora de huevos *m*
- *egg collection by conveyor*

23-27 **el sistema automático de alimentación** *f* **y recogida** *f*
- *mechanical feeding and dunging (manure removal, droppings removal)*

23 el sistema rápido de alimentación *f* para la batería (la máquina de alimentación *f*)
- *rapid feeding system for battery feeding (mechanical feeder)*

24 el silo (la tolva)
- *feed hopper*

25 la cinta transportadora del alimento
- *endless-chain feed conveyor (chain feeder)*

26 la conducción del agua *f*
- *water pipe (liquid feed pipe)*

27 la cinta transportadora de excrementos *m*
- *dunging chain (dunging conveyor)*

28 el armario de incubación *f* y de nacimiento *m* (de salida del huevo)
- *setting and hatching machine*

29 el ventilador de la cámara de incubación *f*
- *ventilation drum [for the setting compartment]*

30 el departamento de la incubación
- *hatching compartment (hatcher)*

31 la carretilla metálica con los casilleros de huevos *m*
- *metal trolley for hatching trays*

32 el casillero de los huevos
- *hatching tray*

33 el motor del ventilador
- *ventilation drum motor*

34-53 **la producción de huevos** *m*
- *egg collection system*

34 el sistema de recogida *f* de los huevos
- *egg collection system*

35 la cinta transportadora
- *multi-tier transport*

36 la mesa de clasificación *f*
- *collection by pivoted fingers*

37 el motor de impulsión *f*
- *drive motor*

38 la clasificadora de huevos *m*
- *sorting machine*

39 el carrito de transporte *m*
- *conveyor trolley*

40 la pantalla para mirar los huevos al trasluz
- *fluorescent screen*

41 el mecanismo de succión *f* para el transporte de los huevos
- *suction apparatus (suction box) for transporting eggs*

42 el estante para las bandejas de los huevos llenos o vacíos
- *shelf for empty and full egg boxes*

43 el peso de los huevos
- *egg weighers*

44 la clasificación
- *grading*

45 la bandeja de los huevos
- *egg box*

46 la empaquetadora automática de huevos *m*
- *fully automatic egg-packing machine*

47 la cabina para mirar los huevos al trasluz
- *radioscope box*

48 la mesa de mirado *m*
- *radioscope table*

49-51 el sistema de alimentación *f*
- *feeder*

49 el transportador de depresión *f*
- *suction transporter*

50 el tubo flexible de vacío *m*
- *vacuum line*

51 la mesa de alimentación *f*
- *supply table*

52 la escogedora-clasificadora automática
- *automatic counting and grading*

53 el distribuidor de cajas *f*
- *packing box dispenser*

54 la anilla de la pata de la gallina
- *leg ring*

55 la placa de identificación *f* de las aves
- *wing tally (identification tally)*

56 la gallina americana (la gallina enana, la gallina bantam)
- *bantam*

57 la gallina ponedora
- *laying hen*

58 el huevo de gallina *f* (*Cuba:* el blanquín de gallina; *Mé.:* el blanquillo)
- *hen's egg (egg)*

59 la cáscara caliza, un integumento del huevo
- *eggshell, an egg integument*

60 la membrana de la cáscara
- *shell membrane*

61 la cámara de aire *m*
- *air space*

62 la clara del huevo
- *white [of the egg] (albumen)*

63 la chalaza
- *chalaza (Am. treadle)*

64 la membrana de la yema (la membrana vitelina)
- *vitelline membrane (yolk sac)*

65 el blastodisco (la marca del gallo; *Chile:* el migajón)
- *blastodisc (germinal disc, cock's tread, cock's treadle)*

66 la vesícula germinativa (la cicatrícula)
- *germinal vesicle*

67 la yema blanca
- *white*

68 la yema amarilla
- *yolk*

1  **la caballeriza** (la cuadra)
–  *stable*
2  el compartimiento de los
   caballos (el box)
–  *horse stall (stall, horse box, box)*
3  el pasillo de circulación *f*
–  *feeding passage*
4  el poney
–  *pony*
5  las barras
–  *bars*
6  la cama de paja *f* (la pajaza)
–  *litter*
7  la bala de paja *f*
–  *bale of straw*
8  la claraboya (la lumbrera)
–  *ceiling light*
9  **el aprisco** (la majada, la tenada)
–  ***sheep pen***
10  la oveja
–  *mother sheep (ewe)*
11  el cordero
–  *lamb*
12  el pesebre (el comedero) de
   heno *m*
–  *double hay rack*
13  el heno
–  *hay*
14  **el establo de las vacas lecheras**
   (la vaqueriza)
–  ***dairy cow shed***
15-16  el amarre
–  *tether*
15  la cadena
–  *chain*
16  la barra de fijación
–  *rail*
17  la vaca lechera
–  *dairy cow (milch-cow, milker)*
18  la ubre
–  *udder*
19  el pezón
–  *teat*
20  la reguera de los excrementos
–  *manure gutter*
21  las barras de evacuación *f* del
   estiércol
–  *manure removal by sliding bars*
22  el compartimiento pequeño
–  *short standing*
23  **la sala de ordeñar**
–  ***milking parlour*** *(Am. parlor), a
   herringbone parlour*
24  el pasillo de servicio *m*
–  *working passage*
25  el ordeñador
–  *milker (Am. milkman)*
26  el racimo de ventosas *f* de
   goma *f* de la ordeñadora
–  *teat cup cluster*
27  el tubo de la leche
–  *milk pipe*
28  el tubo del aire
–  *air line*
29  el tubo de vacío *m* (el tubo de
   pulsación *f*)
–  *vacuum line*
30  el cubilete del ordeñador
–  *teat cup*

31  el cristal de visión *f* (el visor, la
   mirilla)
–  *window*
32  el colector-pulsador de la leche
–  *pulsator*
33  la fase de reposo *m*
–  *release phase*
34  la fase de aspiración (la fase de
   succión *f*)
–  *squeeze phase*
35  **la porqueriza** (la pocilga)
–  ***pigsty*** *(Am. pigpen, hogpen)*
36  el compartimiento de los
   cochinillos
–  *pen for young pigs*
37  el comedero
–  *feeding trough*
38  el tabique de separación *f*
–  *partition*
39  el cochinillo
–  *pig, a young pig*
40  el compartimiento de parto *m*
   (el paridero)
–  *farrowing and store pen*
41  la cerda madre (*Amér.:* la
   verraca)
–  *sow*
42  el lechón (el lechoncillo, el
   cerdo de leche [hasta 8
   semanas])
–  *piglet* (Am. *shoat, shote) (sow
   pig [for first 8 weeks])*
43  la reja de cierre *m*
–  *farrowing rails*
44  la reguera del estiércol
–  *liquid manure channel*

**1-48 la central lechera**
- *dairy (dairy plant)*
1 la recepción de la leche
- *milk reception*
2 el camión cisterna f de leche f
- *milk tanker*
3 la bomba de la leche cruda
- *raw milk pump*
4 el indicador volumétrico (el contador de reloj m, el caudalímetro), un contador de rueda ovalada
- *flowmeter, an oval (elliptical) gear meter*
5 el tanque de la leche cruda
- *raw milk storage tank*
6 el indicador del nivel
- *gauge (Am. gage)*
7 **la sala de mandos** m
- *central control room*
8 el diagrama de la fábrica (el panel sinóptico)
- *chart of the dairy*
9 el esquema funcional de la fábrica
- *flow chart (flow diagram)*
10 los indicadores del nivel de los tanques
- *storage tank gauges (Am. gages)*
11 el pupitre de mando m (la consola de mando m)
- *control panel*
**12-48 la instalación de tratamiento m de la leche**
- *milk processing area*
12 el esterilizador (el homogeneizador)
- *sterilizer; also: homogenizer*
13 el pasteurizador
- *milk heater; sim.: cream heater*
14 la descremadora
- *cream separator*
15 los tanques de leche f fresca
- *fresh milk tanks*
16 el tanque de la leche esterilizada
- *tank for sterilized milk*
17 el tanque de la leche descremada
- *skim milk (skimmed milk) tank*
18 el tanque de suero m (para la mantequilla)
- *buttermilk tank*
19 el tanque de nata f (de crema f)
- *cream tank*
20 la instalación de acondicionamiento m y envase m de la leche fresca
- *fresh milk filling and packing plant*
21 la máquina de llenado m de los cartones de leche f
- *filling machine for milk cartons; sim.: milk tub filler*
22 el cartón de leche f (el tetrabrik)
- *milk carton*
23 la cinta transportadora
- *conveyor belt (conveyor)*

24 la máquina para empaquetar con hojas f de plástico m retractables
- *shrink-sealing machine*
25 el paquete de doce cartones m hecho con la hoja de plástico m retractable
- *pack of twelve in shrink foil*
26 la instalación de envase m en bolsas f de diez litros m
- *ten-litre filling machine*
27 la máquina de cierre m por calor m (Amér.: la tapadora)
- *heat-sealing machine*
28 la hoja de plástico m
- *plastic sheets*
29 la bolsa cerrada herméticamente
- *heat-sealed bag*
30 la caja de transporte m
- *crate*
31 el tanque de afinado m de la nata
- *cream maturing vat*
32 la instalación de moldeado m y envase m de la mantequilla
- *butter shaping and packing machine*
33 la mantequera, una máquina de hacer mantequilla f de funcionamiento m continuo
- *butter churn, a creamery butter machine for continuous butter making*
34 el tubo transporte m de la mantequilla
- *butter supply pipe*
35 la moldeadora (la máquina de dar forma f a la mantequilla)
- *shaping machine*
36 la máquina de embalaje m
- *packing machine*
37 la mantequilla de marca f en paquetes m de 250 gramos m
- *branded butter in 250 g packets*
38 la instalación de producción f de la cuajada
- *plant for producing curd cheese (curd cheese machine)*
39 la bomba de la cuajada
- *curd cheese pump*
40 la bomba dosificadora de la crema
- *cream supply pump*
41 el separador de la cuajada
- *curds separator*
42 el tanque de la leche agria (de la cuajada)
- *sour milk vat*
43 el batidor
- *stirrer*
44 la máquina de envase m de la cuajada
- *curd cheese packing machine*
45 el tarro de cuajada f
- *curd cheese packet (curd cheese; sim.: cottage cheese)*
46 la capsuladora de botellas f
- *bottle-capping machine (capper)*

47 la máquina de hacer queso m en lonchas f
- *cheese machine*
48 el tanque del cuajo
- *rennet vat*

1-25  **la abeja** (abeja melífica, abeja de colmena *f*)
–  *bee (honey-bee, hive-bee)*
1, 4, 5  **las castas** de las abejas
–  *castes (social classes) of bees*
1  la obrera (la abeja neutra)
–  *worker (worker bee)*
2  los tres ojos sencillos (tres ocelos *m*)
–  *three simple eyes (ocelli)*
3  la carga de polen *m* en la pata trasera
–  *load of pollen on the hind leg*
4  la abeja machiega (maesa, maestra, la reina)
–  *queen (queen bee)*
5  el zángano (la abeja macho)
–  *drone (male bee)*
6-9  **la pata trasera izquierda de una obrera**
–  *left hind leg of a worker*
6  el cestillo de polen *m*
–  *pollen basket*
7  el cepillo
–  *pollen comb (brush)*
8  el gancho bífido
–  *double claw*
9  la pinza suctoria
–  *suctorial pad*
10-19  **el abdomen de la obrera**
–  *abdomen of the worker*
10-14  el órgano de defensa *f*
–  *stinging organs*
10  el gancho
–  *barb*
11  el aguijón (el rejo; *Chile, Guat., Mé. y Perú:* la lanceta)
–  *sting*
12  la vaina del aguijón
–  *sting sheath*
13  la vejiga del veneno
–  *poison sac*
14  la glándula del veneno
–  *poison gland*
15-19  **el tubo digestivo**
–  *stomachic-intestinal canal*
15  el intestino
–  *intestine*
16  el estómago
–  *stomach*
17  el esfínter (el tejido contráctil)
–  *contractile muscle*
18  la bolsa de la miel
–  *honey bag (honey sac)*
19  el esófago
–  *oesophagus (esophagus, gullet)*
20-24  **el ojo afacetado** (ojo compuesto, ojo de insecto *m*)
–  *compound eye*
20  la faceta
–  *facet*
21  el cono cristalino
–  *crystal cone*
22  la parte sensitiva
–  *light-sensitive section*
23  la fibra del nervio óptico
–  *fibre (Am. fiber) of the optic nerve*
24  el nervio óptico
–  *optic nerve*
25  las laminillas (las escamas) de cera *f*
–  *wax scale*
26-30  **la celda**
–  *cell*
26  el huevo
–  *egg*

27  la celda con el huevo en su interior *m*
–  *cell with the egg in it*
28  la cresa
–  *young larva*
29  la larva
–  *larva (grub)*
30  la ninfa (la crisálida)
–  *chrysalis (pupa)*
31-43  **el panal de miel** *f*
–  *honeycomb*
31  la celda de incubación *f*
–  *brood cell*
32  la celda tapada con la ninfa
–  *sealed (capped) cell with chrysalis (pupa)*
33  la celda operculada llena de miel *f*
–  *sealed (capped) cell with honey (honey cell)*
34  las celdas de las obreras
–  *worker cells*
35  las celdas depósito de polen *m*
–  *storage cells, with pollen*
36  las celdas de los zánganos
–  *drone cells*
37  la celda real
–  *queen cell*
38  la reina (machiega, maesa, maestra) saliendo
–  *queen emerging from her cell*
39  el opérculo
–  *cap (capping)*
40  el bastidor (el marco)
–  *frame*
41  el asa *f* separadora
–  *distance piece*
42  el panal artificial
–  *[artificial] honeycomb*
43  la base de cera *f* prensada troquelada
–  *septum (foundation, comb foundation)*
44  la caja para transportar la reina
–  *queen's travelling (Am. traveling) box*
45-50  **la colmena de madera** *f* (*Col.:* la pegadilla)
–  *frame hive (movable-frame hive, movable-comb hive [into which frames are inserted from the rear], a beehive (hive))*
45  la colmena movilista (colmena *f* múltiple) con los panales
–  *super (honey super) with honeycombs*
46  la cámara de incubación *f* con los panales para la cresa
–  *brood chamber with breeding combs*
47  el separador (la rejilla que impide el paso de la reina)
–  *queen-excluder*
48  la piquera
–  *entrance*
49  la tablilla para el vuelo
–  *flight board (alighting board)*
50  la ventana
–  *window*
51  el colmenar antiguo
–  *old-fashioned bee shed*
52  la colmena
–  *straw hive (skep), a hive*
53  el enjambre de abejas *f*
–  *swarm (swarm cluster) of bees*
54  la red del enjambre
–  *swarming net (bag net)*
55  el gancho candente
–  *hooked pole*

56  el colmenar moderno
–  *apiary (bee house)*
57  el apicultor (el colmenero)
–  *beekeeper (apiarist, Am. beeman)*
58  el velo contra las abejas
–  *bee veil*
59  la pipa del apicultor (la pipa ahumadora)
–  *bee smoker*
60  el panal natural
–  *natural honeycomb*
61  el meloextractor
–  *honey extractor (honey separator)*
62-63  la miel colada
–  *strained honey (honey)*
62  la vasija para la miel
–  *honey pail*
63  el tarro de miel *f*
–  *honey jar*
64  la miel en panales *m*
–  *honey in the comb*
65  el torzal de cera *f* (la cerilla)
–  *wax taper*
66  la candela de cera *f* (el cirio)
–  *wax candle*
67  la cera de abejas *f*
–  *beeswax*
68  la pomada contra las picaduras de abejas *f*
–  *bee sting ointment*

**1-21 la región vitícola** (la región vinícola)
- *vineyard area*
1 el viñedo (la viña) con enrejado *m* de alambre *m* para cultivo *m* de la vid
- *vineyard using wire trellises for training vines*
**2-9 la vid**
- *vine* (Am. *grapevine*)
2 el sarmiento (el pámpano)
- *vine shoot*
3 el brote largo (el retoño, el zarcillo, la tijereta)
- *long shoot*
4 la pámpana (la hoja de la vid)
- *vine leaf*
5 el racimo de uvas *f*
- *bunch of grapes (cluster of grapes)*
6 la cepa
- *vine stem*
7 el rodrigón
- *post (stake)*
8 el amarre del enrejado de alambre *m*
- *guy (guy wire)*
9 el enrejado de alambre *m*
- *wire trellis*
10 el recipiente de recolección *f*
- *tub for grape gathering*
11 la vendimiadora
- *grape gatherer*

12 las tijeras de la vid (unas tijeras de podar)
- *secateurs for pruning vines*
13 el viñador (el viticultor)
- *wine grower (viniculturist, viticulturist)*
14 el portador de cuévanos *m*
- *dosser carrier*
15 el cuévano
- *dosser (pannier)*
16 el tanque cisterna *f* del mosto
- *crushed grape transporter*
17 la prensa de uva *f*
- *grape crusher*
18 la tolva
- *hopper*
19 la pared de quita y pon de tres lados *m*
- *three-sided flap extension*
20 la tarima
- *platform*
21 el tractor de viña *f*, un tractor de vía *f* estrecha
- *vineyard tractor, a narrow-track tractor*

1-22 la bodega (la cava)
- *wine cellar (wine vault)*
1 la bóveda
- *vault*
2 el tonel (el barril) de bodega *f*
- *wine cask*
3 el depósito del vino, un depósito de hormigón *m*
- *wine vat, a concrete vat*
4 el depósito de acero *m* fino (*también:* el tanque de materia *f* plástica)
- *stainless steel vat ( also: vat made of synthetic material)*
5 el agitador de hélice *f*
- *propeller-type high-speed mixer*
6 la hélice
- *propeller mixer*
7 la bomba centrífuga
- *centrifugal pump*
8 el filtro de capas *f* de acero *m* fino
- *stainless steel sediment filter*
9 el embotellador circular semiautomático
- *semi-automatic circular bottling machine*
10 la máquina semiautomática para taponar (las botellas) con corchos *m* naturales
- *semi-automatic corking machine*

11 la estantería de las botellas (el botellero)
- *bottle rack*
12 el ayudante de bodega *f*
- *cellarer's assistant*
13 la canastilla de las botellas
- *bottle basket*
14 la botella de vino *m*
- *wine bottle*
15 la jarra del vino
- *wine jug*
16 la cata del vino
- *wine tasting*
17 el maestro tonelero (el bodeguero)
- *head cellarman*
18 el tonelero (el catador de vino *m*)
- *cellarman*
19 el vaso de vino *m* (un catavinos)
- *wineglass*
20 el aparato de examen *m* rápido
- *inspection apparatus [for spot-checking samples]*
21 la prensa para uvas *f* horizontal
- *horizontal wine press*
22 el humectador
- *humidifier*

**1-19 parásitos de los frutos**
- *fruit pests*
1 la lagarta, un lepidóptero
- *gipsy (gypsy) moth*
2 la bolsa de huevos *m*
- *batch (cluster) of eggs*
3 la oruga
- *caterpillar*
4 la crisálida (el capullo)
- *chrysalis (pupa)*
5 la polilla del ciruelo, un hiponomeuta
- *small ermine moth, an ermine moth*
6 la larva
- *larva (grub)*
7 la red hilada
- *tent*
8 la oruga comiendo las partes blandas de la hoja
- *caterpillar skeletonizing a leaf*
9 la polilla del manzano, un tortrícido
- *fruit surface eating tortrix moth (summer fruit tortrix moth)*
10 el gorgojo de la flor del manzano (el gorgojo del manzano)
- *appleblossom weevil, a weevil*
11 la flor destruida
- *punctured, withered flower (blossom)*
12 la picadura
- *hole for laying eggs*
13 la mariposa de la oruga de librea *f,* la falsa lagarta
- *lackey moth*
14 la oruga
- *caterpillar*
15 los huevos
- *eggs*
16 la mariposa de la escarcha (la defoliadora invernal, el azote de los frutales)
- *winter moth, a geometrid*
17 la oruga
- *caterpillar*
18 la mosca del cerezo (la mosca del fruto del cerezo), una mosca taladradora
- *cherry fruit fly, a borer*
19 la larva (el gusano blanco; la cresa)
- *larva (grub, maggot)*
**20-27 parásitos *m* de la vid**
- *vine pests*
20 el mildiu, una enfermedad que causa la caída de las hojas
- *downy mildew, a mildew, a disease causing leaf drop*
21 la uva dañada
- *grape affected with downy mildew*
22 el piral de la vid
- *grape-berry moth*
23 la oruga de la 1ª generación
- *first-generation larva of the grape-berry moth (Am. grape worm)*
24 la oruga de la 2ª generación
- *second-generation larva of the grape-berry moth (Am. grape worm)*
25 la ninfa (la crisálida)
- *chrysalis (pupa)*
26 la filoxera
- *root louse, a grape phylloxera*
27 la excrecencia vesicular de la raíz (la agalla de la raíz)
- *root gall, a knotty swelling of the root (nodosity, tuberosity)*

28 la mariposa de cola *f* dorada
- *brown-tail moth*
29 la oruga
- *caterpillar*
30 la bolsa de huevos *m*
- *batch (cluster) of eggs*
31 el nido de invernación *f*
- *hibernation cocoon*
32 el pulgón lanígero
- *woolly apple aphid (American blight), an aphid*
33 la agalla del pulgón, una excrecencia
- *gall caused by the woolly apple aphid*
34 la colonia de pulgones *m*
- *woolly apple aphid colony*
35 la cochinilla de San José, un cocoideo
- *San-José scale, a scale insect (scale louse)*
36 las larvas [las masculinas, alargadas; las femeninas, redondas]
- *larvae (grubs) [male elongated, female round]*
**37-55 parásitos *m* del campo**
- *field pests*
37 el escarabajo elástico (el escarabajo de resorte, de muelle), un elaténido
- *click beetle, a snapping beetle (Am. snapping bug)*
38 el gusano de alambre *m,* una larva de elaténido
- *wireworm, larva of the click beetle*
39 el escarabajo pulga *f*
- *flea beetle*
40 la mosca de Hessen (el mosquito de Hessen), un mosquito de agalla *f*
- *Hessian fly, a gall midge (gall gnat)*
41 la larva
- *larva (grub)*
42 el agrotis de los sembrados, un noctuido
- *turnip moth, an earth moth*
43 la crisálida (la ninfa)
- *chrysalis (pupa)*
44 una larva de agrótido *m,* una oruga
- *cutworm, a caterpillar*
45 el escarabajo de la remolacha
- *beet carrion beetle*
46 la larva
- *larva (grub)*
47 la gran mariposa blanca de la col
- *large cabbage white butterfly*
48 la oruga de la pequeña mariposa blanca de la col
- *caterpillar of the small cabbage white butterfly*
49 el gorgojo, un curculiónido
- *brown leaf-eating weevil, a weevil*
50 la parte comida
- *feeding site*
51 la anguílula de la remolacha, un nematodo
- *sugar beet eelworm, a nematode (threadworm, hairworm)*
52 el escarabajo de la patata (el escarabajo de Colorado)
- *Colorado beetle (potato beetle)*
53 la larva adulta
- *mature larva (grub)*
54 la larva joven
- *young larva (grub)*
55 los huevos
- *eggs*

# 81 Insectos domésticos, dañinos y parásitos

**1-14 insectos** *m* **domésticos**
- *house insects*
1 la mosquita doméstica
- *lesser housefly*
2 la mosca doméstica común
- *common housefly*
3 la crisálida (la ninfa)
- *chrysalis (pupa), a coarctate pupa*
4 el tábano
- *stable fly (biting housefly)*
5 la antena tricótoma
- *trichotomous antenna*
6 la cochinilla de humedad *f*, un crustáceo segmentado
- *wood louse (slater, Am. sow bug)*
7 el grillo doméstico (*Bol.*: la siripita; *Arg.*: el chilicote)
- *house cricket*
8 el ala *f* con élitro *m* (órgano *m* que produce un sonido estridente)
- *wing with stridulating apparatus (stridulating mechanism)*
9 la araña doméstica
- *house spider*
10 la telaraña
- *spider's web*
11 la tijereta (el cortapicos)
- *earwig*
12 la pinza abdominal
- *caudal pincers*
13 la polilla de la ropa, una polilla
- *clothes moth, a moth*
14 el pececillo de plata (el lepisma saccharina), un tisanuro
- *silverfish ( Am. slicker), a bristletail*

**15-30 insectos** *m* **dañinos para los alimentos**
- *food pests (pests to stores)*
15 la mosca del queso (del gusanillo del queso)
- *cheesefly*
16 el gorgojo de los cereales
- *grain weevil (granary weevil)*
17 la cucaracha doméstica (la curiana; *Chile*: la barata)
- *cockroach (black beetle)*
18 el escarabajo molinero (el escarabajo del gusano de la harina), un tenebriónido
- *meal beetle (meal worm beetle, flour beetle)*
19 el gorgojo de las judías
- *spotted bruchus*
20 la larva
- *larva (grub)*
21 la crisálida (la ninfa)
- *chrysalis (pupa)*
22 el escarabajo del tocino (el dermesto), un derméstido
- *leather beetle (hide beetle)*
23 la carcoma del pan
- *yellow meal beetle*
24 la crisálida (la ninfa)
- *chrysalis (pupa)*
25 el cascarudo cigarrero (la lasioderma serricorne)
- *cigarette beetle (tobacco beetle)*

26 el gorgojo del maíz
- *maize billbug (corn weevil)*
27 un parásito de los cereales
- *one of the Cryptolestes, a grain pest*
28 la polilla de los frutos secos
- *Indian meal moth*
29 la polilla de los cereales
- *Angoumois grain moth (Angoumois moth)*
30 la oruga de la polilla de los cereales en el grano de trigo *m*
- *Angoumois grain moth caterpillar inside a grain kernel*

**31-42 parásitos** *m* **del hombre**
- *parasites of man*
31 la lombriz intestinal (la ascáride)
- *round worm (maw worm)*
32 la hembra
- *female*
33 la cabeza
- *head*
34 el macho
- *male*
35 la tenia (la solitaria), un platelminto
- *tapeworm, a flatworm*
36 la cabeza (el escólex), un órgano de adherencia *f*
- *head, a suctorial organ*
37 la ventosa
- *sucker*
38 la corona de ganchos *m*
- *crown of hooks*
39 la chinche (la chinche de las camas), un hemíptero heteróptero
- *bug (bed bug, Am. chinch)*
40 la ladilla
- *crab louse, a human louse*
41 el piojo de las ropas (el piojo del cuerpo; un piojo humano)
- *clothes louse (body louse), a human louse*
42 la pulga del hombre
- *flea (human flea, common flea)*
43 la mosca tsetsé (la mosca del sueño)
- *tsetse fly*
44 el mosquito del paludismo (de la malaria), el anofeles
- *malaria mosquito*

1 el escarabajo sanjuanero (el cochorro, el abejorro de San Juan), un coleóptero
 – *cockchafer (May bug), a lamellicorn*
2 la cabeza
 – *head*
3 la antena
 – *antenna (feeler)*
4 el protórax
 – *thoracic shield (prothorax)*
5 el escudete
 – *scutellum*
6-8 las patas
 – *legs*
6 la pata anterior
 – *front leg*
7 la pata media
 – *middle leg*
8 la pata trasera
 – *back leg*
9 el abdomen
 – *abdomen*
10 el élitro
 – *elytron (wing case)*
11 el ala *f* membranosa
 – *membranous wing*
12 la larva del abejorro sanjuanero (el gusano blanco), una larva
 – *cockchafer grub, a larva*
13 la crisálida (la ninfa)
 – *chrysalis (pupa)*
14 la procesionaria, una mariposa nocturna
 – *processionary moth, a nocturnal moth (night-flying moth)*
15 la mariposa
 – *moth*
16 las orugas marchando en procesión *f*
 – *caterpillars in procession*
17 la monja
 – *nun moth (black arches moth)*
18 la mariposa
 – *moth*
19 los huevos
 – *eggs*
20 la oruga
 – *caterpillar*
21 la crisálida (la ninfa)
 – *chrysalis (pupa) in its cocoon*
22 el escarabajo tipógrafo, un escarabajo de las cortezas (un barrenillo)
 – *typographer beetle, a bark beetle*
23-24 las galerías bajo la corteza
 – *galleries under the bark*
23 la galería de la madre
 – *egg gallery*
24 la galería de la larva
 – *gallery made by larva*
25 la larva
 – *larva (grub)*
26 el escarabajo
 – *beetle*
27 la esfinge del pino, un esfíngido
 – *pine hawkmoth, a hawkmoth*

28 la mariposa blanca orlada, un geómetra
 – *pine moth, a geometrid*
29 la mariposa macho
 – *male moth*
30 la mariposa hembra
 – *female moth*
31 la oruga
 – *caterpillar*
32 la crisálida (la ninfa)
 – *chrysalis (pupa)*
33 la avispa de las agallas del roble, un cinípedo
 – *oak-gall wasp, a gall wasp*
34 la agalla
 – *oak gall (oak apple), a gall*
35 la avispa
 – *wasp*
36 la larva en la cámara larval
 – *larva (grub) in its chamber*
37 la agalla de la hoja de roble *m*
 – *beech gall*
38 el pulgón de la agalla del abeto, un adélgido
 – *spruce-gall aphid*
39 el pulgón en la forma alada
 – *winged aphid*
40 la agalla de la piña
 – *pineapple gall*
41 el gorgojo del pino
 – *pine weevil*
42 el gorgojo (el escarabajo)
 – *beetle (weevil)*
43 la piral del roble, un tortrícido
 – *green oak roller moth (green oak tortrix), a leaf roller*
44 la oruga
 – *caterpillar*
45 la mariposa
 – *moth*
46 la esfinge del pino
 – *pine beauty*
47 la oruga
 – *caterpillar*
48 la mariposa
 – *moth*

1 la pulverización de superficie *f*
- *area spraying*
2 la armazón del pulverizador
- *tractor-mounted sprayer*
3 el bastidor de aspersión *f*
- *spray boom*
4 el surtidor de chorro *m* plano
- *fan nozzle*
5 el depósito del caldo de pulverización *f*
- *spray fluid tank*
6 el depósito de espuma *f* de plástico para hacer marcas *f* de espuma *f*
- *foam canister for blob marking*
7 la suspensión
- *spring suspension*
8 la pulverización de niebla *f*
- *spray*
9 el dispositivo de hacer marcas *f* con la espuma
- *blob marker*
10 la tubería de alimentación de espuma *f*
- *foam feed pipe*
11 la instalación de desinfectación *f* por vacío *m* en una fábrica de tabaco *m*
- *vacuum fumigator (vacuum fumigation plant) of a tobacco factory*
12 la cámara de vacío *m*
- *vacuum chamber*
13 las balas de tabaco *m* en rama *f*
- *bales of raw tobacco*
14 el tubo del gas
- *gas pipe*
15 la cámara móvil de fumigación *f* para tratar con cianhídrico *m* los planteles, los viñedos jóvenes, los depósitos de semillas *f* y los sacos vacíos
- *mobile fumigation chamber for fumigating nursery saplings, vine layers, seeds, and empty sacks with hydrocyanic (prussic) acid*
16 el dispositivo de circulación *f* del gas
- *gas circulation unit*
17 la batea
- *tray*
18 la pistola-pulverizadora
- *spray gun*
19 la empuñadura giratoria para la regulación del chorro
- *twist grip (control grip, handle) for regulating the jet*
20 el asa *f* de protección *f*
- *finger guard*
21 la palanca de accionamiento *m*
- *control lever (operating lever)*
22 el tubo (la lanza) del chorro
- *spray tube*
23 el pulverizador circular
- *cone nozzle*
24 el pulverizador de mano *m*
- *hand spray*
25 el depósito de plástico *m*
- *plastic container*

26 el gatillo (la bomba de mano *m*)
- *hand pump*
27 el varillaje de pulverización *f* de péndulo *m* para el cultivo del lúpulo
- *pendulum spray for hop growing on slopes*
28 la boquilla de aspersión *f*
- *pistol-type nozzle*
29 el tubo (la lanza) de aspersión *f*
- *spraying tube*
30 el manguito de tubo *m* flexible
- *hose connection*
31 el tubo para la diseminación de cebo *m* envenenado
- *tube for laying poisoned bait*
32 la pala matamoscas
- *fly swat*
33 el inyector de suelo *m* (el inyector de bisulfuro *m* de carbono *m*) para matar la filoxera
- *soil injector (carbon disulphide, Am. carbon disulfide, injector) for killing the vine root louse*
34 la válvula inyectora
- *foot lever (foot pedal, foot treadle)*
35 el tubo del gas (el tubo de inyección *f*, la boquilla)
- *gas tube*
36 la ratonera (*Perú:* la pericotera)
- *mousetrap*
37 la trampa para topos *m* y campañoles *m*
- *vole and mole trap*
38 el pulverizador móvil para los árboles frutales
- *mobile orchard sprayer, a wheelbarrow sprayer (carriage sprayer)*
39 el depósito de insecticida *m*
- *spray tank*
40 la tapa de rosca *f*
- *screw-on cover*
41 la motobomba con motor de gasolina *f*
- *direct-connected motor-driven pump with petrol motor*
42 el manómetro
- *pressure gauge (Am. gage) (manometer)*
43 el pulverizador portátil de pistón *m*
- *plunger-type knapsack sprayer*
44 el depósito del pulverizador con cámara *f* de aire *m* a presión
- *spray canister with pressure chamber*
45 la palanca de la bomba de pistón *m*
- *piston pump lever*
46 la lanza de pulverización *f* con boquilla *f*
- *hand lance with nozzle*
47 el pulverizador semitransportado
- *semi-mounted sprayer*

48 el tractor de viñedos *m*
- *vineyard tractor*
49 el ventilador
- *fan*
50 el depósito del insecticida
- *spray fluid tank*
51 la hilera (el liño) de cepas *f*
- *row of vines*
52 el aparato de desinfección *f* de semillas *f* secas
- *dressing machine (seed-dressing machine) for dry-seed dressing (seed dusting)*
53 el ventilador de desinfección *f* con motor *m* eléctrico
- *dedusting fan (dust removal fan) with electric motor*
54 el filtro tubular
- *bag filter*
55 la tubuladura de ensacado *m*
- *bagging nozzle*
56 el saco de desinfección *f*
- *dedusting screen (dust removal screen)*
57 el depósito de agua *f* de pulverización *f*
- *water canister [containing water for spraying]*
58 el dispositivo de pulverización *f*
- *spray unit*
59 el grupo de transporte *m* con tornillo *m* sin fin *m* mezclador
- *conveyor unit with mixing screw*
60 el depósito de polvos *m* desinfectantes con dispositivo *m* para dosificar
- *container for disinfectant powder with dosing mechanism*
61 la ruedecilla
- *castor*
62 la cámara de mezcla *f*
- *mixing chamber*

**1-34  el bosque**
- *forest, a wood*
1 la vereda del bosque (el camino abierto en el monte)
- *ride (aisle, lane, section line)*
2 la sección forestal
- *compartment (section)*
3 el arrastradero, un camino forestal (*Hond.*: el tiro)
- *wood haulage way, a forest track*
4-14 **el sistema de tala** *f* (de desmonte *m*; *Cuba y P. Rico*: la tumba)
- *clear-felling system*
4 el bosque viejo (el monte alto), un oquedal
- *standing timber*
5 el monte bajo
- *underwood (underbrush, undergrowth, brushwood, Am. brush)*
6 la almáciga, un semillero de árboles *m*
- *seedling nursery, a tree nursery*
7 el enrejado contra los animales monteses, un enrejado de alambre *m*
- *deer fence (fence), a wire netting fence, a protective fence for seedlings;* sim.: *rabbit fence*
8 el listón de protección *f* (la barrera)
- *guard rail*
9 los plantones
- *seedlings*

10-11 la plantación joven
- *young trees*
10 el plantel (el criadero, el cultivo después del trasplante, la plantación nueva)
- *tree nursery after transplanting*
11 la espesura de la plantación joven
- *young plantation*
12 la plantación joven (después de la poda)
- *young plantation after brashing*
13 el claro (el espacio talado)
- *clearing*
14 el tocón
- *tree stump (stump, stub)*

**15-37 la tala y recogida f de madera f**
- **wood cutting** (timber cutting, tree felling, Am. lumbering)
**15** los troncos apilados
- timber skidded to the stack (stacked timber, Am. yarded timber)
**16** el estéreo, un metro cúbico de madera f
- stack of logs, one cubic metre (Am. meter) of wood
**17** el poste (la estaca)
- post (stake)
**18** el obrero forestal dando la vuelta a un madero
- forest labourer (woodsman, Am. logger, lumberer, lumberjack, lumberman, timberjack) turning (Am. canting) timber
**19** el tronco (el madero)
- bole (tree trunk, trunk, stem)
**20** el capataz numerando
- feller numbering the logs
**21** el gran pie m de rey m (la terraja de medir) de acero m
- steel tree calliper (caliper)
**22** la motosierra (cortando un tronco)
- power saw (motor saw) cutting a bole
**23** el casco de protección f con visera f y protección f acústica
- safety helmet with visor and ear pieces
**24** los cercos (anillos m) anuales
- annual rings

**25** el gato hidráulico
- hydraulic felling wedge
**26** la vestimenta protectora [camisa f naranja, pantalón m verde]
- protective clothing [orange top, green trousers]
**27** el corte (el derribo, la tala) con motosierra f
- felling with a power saw (motor saw)
**28** el corte (la muesca, la entalladura)
- undercut (notch, throat, gullet, mouth, sink, kerf, birdsmouth)
**29** el corte de sierra f
- back cut
**30** el bolsillo con la cuña de tala f
- sheath holding felling wedge
**31** el trozo
- log
**32** la sierra para cortar los troncos bajos y las malas hierbas
- free-cutting saw for removing underwood and weeds
**33** la sierra circular (o cuchilla f circular) adaptable
- circular saw attachment; sim.: activated blade attachment
**34** el motor
- power unit (motor)
**35** el bidón de aceite m adherente para las cadenas de la sierra
- canister of viscous oil for the saw chain

**36** el bidón de gasolina f
- petrol canister (Am. gasoline canister)
**37** el derribo (la tala) del tronco menudo (el aclareo)
- felling of small timber (of small-sized thinnings) (thinning)

1 el hacha *f*
- *axe (Am. ax)*
2 el filo (el corte)
- *edge (cutting edge)*
3 el mango (el astil)
- *handle (helve)*
4 la cuña de tala *f* con
inserción *f* de madera *f* y
anilla *f*
- *felling wedge (falling wedge)
with wood insert and ring*
5 el martillo de hender (el
hacha *f* de rajar)
- *riving hammer (cleaving
hammer, splitting hammer)*
6 el gancho de palanca *f* (el pico
para dar la vuelta a los troncos)
- *lifting hook*
7 el gancho para dar la vuelta a
los troncos
- *cant hook*
8 el descortezador (el escoplo de
descortezar)
- *barking iron (bark spud)*
9 la cuña de fijación *f* con
gancho *m* para los troncos
- *peavy*
10 el calibrador
- *slide calliper (caliper) (calliper
square)*
11 el podón (el bodollo), un
machete
- *billhook, a knife for lopping*
12 el martillo numerador giratorio
- *revolving die hammer (marking
hammer, marking iron, Am.
marker)*
13 la motosierra
- *power saw (motor saw)*
14 la cadena de la sierra
- *saw chain*
15 el freno de seguridad *f* (para la
cadena de la sierra) con
protector *m* de manos *f*
- *safety brake for the saw chain,
with finger guard*
16 la guía (el raíl, la llanta) de la
cadena
- *saw guide*
17 el bloqueo del acelerador
- *accelerator lock*
18 la máquina de mondar (de
desramar)
- *snedding machine (trimming
machine, Am. knotting machine,
limbing machine)*
19 los cilindros de avance *m*
- *feed rolls*
20 la cuchilla articulada
- *flexible blade*
21 el gato hidráulico
- *hydraulic arm*
22 la herramienta para cortar las
puntas
- *trimming blade*
23 el descortezamiento de los
troncos
- *debarking (barking, bark
stripping) of boles*

24 el cilindro de avance *m*
- *feed roller*
25 el rotor de cuchillas *f*
- *cylinder trimmer*
26 la cuchilla rotativa
- *rotary cutter*
27 el tractor forestal (para el
transporte de la madera en el
bosque)
- *short-haul skidder*
28 la grúa de carga *f*
- *loading crane*
29 el gancho para la madera
- *log grips*
30 el telero de la caja
- *post*
31 la dirección de acodamiento *m*
(la dirección pivotante)
- *Ackermann steering system*
32 la pila de troncos *m*
- *log dump*
33 la numeración
- *number (identification number)*
34 el tractor de troncos *m* (el
skidder)
- *skidder*
35 la placa frontal
- *front blade (front plate)*
36 la cabina con arco *m* de
seguridad *f*
- *crush-proof safety bonnet (Am.
safety hood)*
37 la dirección de acodamiento *m*
(la dirección pivotante)
- *Ackermann steering system*
38 el torno de cable *m*
- *cable winch*
39 el rodillo guía del cable
- *cable drum*
40 la placa trasera
- *rear blade (rear plate)*
41 los troncos levantados
- *boles with butt ends held off the
ground*
42 el transporte por carretera *f* de
los troncos
- *haulage of timber by road*
43 el tractor
- *tractor (tractor unit)*
44 la grúa de carga *f*
- *loading crane*
45 el apoyo hidráulico
- *hydraulic jack*
46 el torno de cable *m*
- *cable winch*
47 el telero
- *post*
48 el banquillo de acoplamiento *m*
articulado
- *bolster plate*
49 el remolque (la base) trasero(a)
- *rear bed (rear bunk)*

**1-52 la caza** (las diferentes clases de cacería *f*)
- *kinds of hunting*

**1-8 la caza con perro** *m* (la caza en cotos *m* o vedados *m*)
- *stalking (deer stalking, Am. stillhunting) in the game preserve*

**1** el cazador (el tirador, el montero)
- *huntsman (hunter)*

**2** el traje de caza *f*
- *hunting clothes*

**3** el morral (la mochila)
- *knapsack*

**4** la escopeta de caza *f*
- *sporting gun (sporting rifle, hunting rifle)*

**5** el sombrero de caza *f* (el sombrero de cazador *m*)
- *huntsman's hat*

**6** los gemelos de campo *m*
- *field glasses (binoculars)*

**7** el perro de caza *f*
- *gun dog*

**8** el rastro (la huella de pisadas *f*)
- *track (trail, hoofprints)*

**9-12 la caza en época *f* de brama *f* y celo** *m*
- *hunting in the rutting season and the pairing season*

**9** la paranza
- *hunting screen (screen, Am. blind)*

**10** el bastón-taburete (el asiento de caza *f*)
- *shooting stick (shooting seat, seat stick)*

**11** el urogallo (el gallo silvestre) haciendo la rueda
- *blackcock, displaying*

**12** el ciervo en brama *f* (bramando)
- *rutting stag*

**13** la cierva pastando (paciendo)
- *hind, grazing*

**14-17 el puesto** (el aguardo, el tiradero)
- *hunting from a raised hide (raised stand)*

**14** el puesto en alto *m* (el mirador)
- *raised hide (raised stand, high seat)*

**15** la manada a tiro *m*
- *herd within range*

**16** el paso (el paso de los animales montaraces)
- *game path ( Am. runway)*

**17** el corzo, herido en una paletilla y rematado por un disparo final
- *roebuck, hit in the shoulder and killed by a finishing shot*

**18** el coche de caza *f*
- *phaeton*

**19-27 la caza con trampas** *f*
- *types of trapping*

**19** la caza de animales *m* de presa *f* con trampas *f*
- *trapping of small predators*

**20** la trampa de caja *f* (*Hond.:* la tapegua)
- *box trap, a trap for small predators*

**21** el cebo
- *bait*

**22** la marta, un animal carnicero (un depredador)
- *marten, a small predator*

**23** la caza con hurón *m* (la caza de conejos *m* sacados de sus madrigueras *f*)
- *ferreting (hunting rabbits out of their warrens)*

**24** el hurón (el bicho)
- *ferret*

**25** el huronero
- *ferreter*

**26** la madriguera (la conejera)
- *burrow (rabbit burrow, rabbit hole)*

**27** la bolsa de red *f* en la boca de la madriguera
- *net (rabbit net) over the burrow opening*

**28** el comedero de invierno *m*
– *feeding place for game (winter feeding place)*
**29** el cazador furtivo
– *poacher*
**30** la carabina, un rifle corto
– *carbine, a short rifle*
**31** la caza del jabalí
– *boar hunt*
**32** el jabalí
– *wild sow (sow, wild boar)*
**33** el perro de jabalí *m* (el mastín, el perro jabalinero; *varios:* la jauría, la muta)
– *boarhound, a hound (hunting dog; collectively: pack, pack of hounds)*
**34-39 la batida** (la caza de la liebre)
– *beating (driving, hare hunting)*
**34** la puntería (el encaro)
– *aiming position*
**35** la liebre, un animal de pelo *m*
– *hare, furred game (ground game)*
**36** la cobranza
– *retrieving*
**37** el batidor
– *beater*
**38** la caza (las piezas cobradas)
– *bag (kill)*
**39** la carreta para la caza
– *cart for carrying game*
**40** la caza acuática (la caza de patos *m*)
– *waterfowling (wildfowling, duck shooting,* Am. *duck hunting)*

**41** la bandada de patos *m* silvestres, la caza de pluma *f*
– *flight of wild ducks, winged game*
**42-46 la cetrería** (la halconería, la caza con halcones *m*, la caza con gerifaltes *m*)
– *falconry (hawking)*
**42** el halconero (el cetrero)
– *falconer*
**43** la gorga (la cortesía), un trozo de carne *f* (*C. Rica:* la tureca)
– *reward, a piece of meat*
**44** el capirote del halcón
– *falcon's hood*
**45** la pihuela
– *jess*
**46** un halcón macho (terzuelo *m*) abatiéndose sobre una garza real
– *falcon, a hawk, a male hawk (tiercel) swooping (stooping) on a heron*
**47-52 la caza con reclamo *m* desde un tollo**
– *shooting from a butt*
**47** el árbol al que acuden las aves
– *tree to which birds are lured*
**48** el búho, un pájaro reclamo (cimbel *m*)
– *eagle owl, a decoy bird (decoy)*
**49** la percha
– *perch*
**50** el ave *f* atraída, una corneja
– *decoyed bird, a crow*

**51** el tollo (el tiradero)
– *butt for shooting crows or eagle owls*
**52** la aspillera
– *gun slit*

**1-40 armas *f* deportivas (escopetas *f* de caza *f*)**
– *sporting guns (sporting rifles, hunting rifles)*
**1** la carabina
– *single-loader (single-loading rifle)*
**2** el rifle de repetición *f*, una arma de fuego *m* portátil, un rifle de caza *f* de repetición *f* automático (un rifle con depósito *m*)
– *repeating rifle, a small-arm (fire-arm), a repeater (magazine rifle, magazine repeater)*
**3, 4, 6, 13** la caja del rifle
– *stock*
**3** la culata
– *butt*
**4** la carrillera
– *cheek [on the left side]*
**5** la anilla de la correa
– *sling ring*
**6** el puño de pistola *f*
– *pistol grip*
**7** la garganta de la culata
– *small of the butt*
**8** la aleta del seguro (del fiador)
– *safety catch*
**9** el cierre
– *lock*
**10** el guardamonte
– *trigger guard*
**11** el punto del disparador
– *second set trigger (firing trigger)*
**12** el disparador (el gatillo)
– *hair trigger (set trigger)*

**13** la caña
– *foregrip*
**14** la cantonera
– *butt plate*
**15** la recámara
– *cartridge chamber*
**16** el cajón de los mecanismos
– *receiver*
**17** el cargador
– *magazine*
**18** el elevador
– *magazine spring*
**19** la munición
– *ammunition (cartridge)*
**20** el cerrojo
– *chamber*
**21** el percutor
– *firing pin (striker)*
**22** la bola del cerrojo
– *bolt handle (bolt lever)*
**23** la escopeta de tres cañones *m*, una escopeta que se monta automáticamente
– *triple-barrelled (triple-barreled) rifle, a self-cocking gun*
**24** el pasador de cambio *m*
– *reversing catch; in various guns: safety catch*
**25** la palanca (la llave) de cierre *m*
– *sliding safety catch*
**26** el cañón de rifle *m* (de bala *f*)
– *rifle barrel (rifled barrel)*
**27** el cañón de perdigones *m*
– *smooth-bore barrel*

**28** los grabados (las incrustaciones)
– *chasing*
**29** la mira telescópica
– *telescopic sight (riflescope, telescope sight)*
**30** el tornillo para el ajuste del retículo
– *graticule adjuster screws*
**31-32** el retículo visual
– *graticule (sight graticule)*
**31** diversos sistemas *m* de retículo *m*
– *various graticule systems*
**32** los hilos cruzados (la cruz reticular)
– *cross wires (Am. cross hairs)*
**33** el rifle de dos cañones *m* superpuestos (una escopeta de cañón *m* doble)
– *over-and-under shotgun*
**34** el cañón rayado (el cañón de ánima *f* rayada)
– *rifled gun barrel*
**35** la pared del cañón
– *barrel casing*
**36** la estría (la raya)
– *rifling*
**37** el calibre de estría *f*
– *rifling calibre (Am. caliber)*
**38** el eje del ánima *f*
– *bore axis*
**39** la pared del ánima *f*
– *land*
**40** el calibre del fusil
– *calibre (bore diameter, Am. caliber)*

**41-48** útiles *m* de caza *f*
- *hunting equipment*
**41** el cuchillo de caza *f* de doble filo *m*
- *double-edged hunting knife*
**42** el puñal, el cuchillo de monte *m*
- *single-edged hunting knife*
**43-47** reclamos *m* para atraer la caza
- *calls for luring game (for calling game)*
**43** el reclamo del corzo
- *roe call*
**44** el reclamo de la liebre
- *hare call*
**45** el reclamo de la codorniz
- *quail call*
**46** el reclamo del ciervo
- *stag call*
**47** el reclamo de la perdiz
- *partridge call*
**48** la trampa "cuello *m* de cisne *m*", una trampa de arco *m*
- *bow trap (bow gin), a jaw trap*
**49** el cartucho de perdigones *m*
- *small-shot cartridge*
**50** la vaina de cartón *m*
- *cardboard case*
**51** la carga de perdigones *m*
- *small-shot charge*
**52** el taco
- *felt wad*
**53** la pólvora sin humo *m* (la pólvora negra)
- *smokeless powder; also: black powder*
**54** el cartucho de bala *f*
- *cartridge*
**55** el proyectil (la bala con su envuelta *f; Arg. y Urug.:* el chumbo)
- *full-jacketed cartridge*
**56** el núcleo de plomo *m* blando
- *soft-lead core*
**57** la carga de pólvora *f*
- *powder charge*
**58** el culote
- *detonator cap*
**59** la cápsula fulminante (el pistón con el fulminante)
- *percussion cap*
**60** la trompa de caza *f* (el cuerno de caza *f*)
- *hunting horn*
**61-64** los avíos para la limpieza de las armas
- *rifle cleaning kit*
**61** el lavador (la baqueta)
- *cleaning rod*
**62** la escobilla para la limpieza de los cañones
- *cleaning brush*
**63** la estopa de limpieza *f*
- *cleaning tow*
**64** el cordel para la limpieza
- *pull-through (Am. pull-thru)*
**65** el alza *f* de mira *f*
- *sights*
**66** la muesca
- *notch (sighting notch)*
**67** la chapa del alza *f*
- *back sight leaf*
**68** la escala del pie del alza *f*
- *sight scale division*
**69** la corredera
- *back sight slide*
**70** la muesca para la fijación del muelle
- *notch [to hold the spring]*

**71** el punto de mira *f*
- *front sight (foresight)*
**72** la cúspide del punto de mira *f*
- *bead*
**73** balística *f*
- *ballistics*
**74** el horizonte
- *azimuth*
**75** el ángulo de proyección *f*
- *angle of departure*
**76** el ángulo de elevación *f*
- *angle of elevation*
**77** la sagita (la flecha)
- *apex (zenith)*
**78** el ángulo de caída *f*
- *angle of descent*
**79** la curva balística (la trayectoria)
- *ballistic curve*

**1-27 la caza de montería** (la caza mayor)
- *red deer*
1 el anime (la cierva, la hembra del ciervo), una madre o una hembra sin cubrir; *varias:* la manada; *el joven:* el cervatillo, el gabato
- *hind (red deer), a young hind or a dam;* collectively: *antlerless deer,* (y.) *calf*
2 la lengua
- *tongue*
3 el cuello
- *neck*
4 el ciervo en celo *m*
- *rutting stag*
**5-11 los cuernos** (la cornamenta, la cuerna)
- *antlers*
5 la roseta
- *burr (rose)*
6 el candil de ojo *m* (el candil basilar, la luchadera, la garceta)
- *brow antler (brow tine, brow point, brow snag)*
7 el candil de hierro *m*
- *bez antler (bay antler, bay, bez tine)*
8 el candil medio
- *royal antler (royal, tray)*
9 la paleta (la corona, la palma)
- *surroyal antlers (surroyals)*
10 las puntas (las hitas)
- *point (tine)*
11 el asta *f*
- *beam (main trunk)*
12 la cabeza
- *head*
13 la boca (el hocico)
- *mouth*
14 la fosa lacrimal
- *larmier (tear bag)*
15 el ojo
- *eye*
16 la oreja
- *ear*
17 el codillo
- *shoulder*
18 el lomo
- *loin*
19 la cola
- *scut (tail)*
20 el espejo (la mancha blanca)
- *rump*
21 el pernil
- *leg (haunch)*
22 la pata trasera (el cuarto trasero)
- *hind leg*
23 el espolón
- *dew claw*
24 la pezuña
- *hoof*
25 la pata delantera (el cuarto delantero)
- *foreleg*
26 el flanco
- *flank*
27 la melena de la brama
- *collar (rutting mane)*
**28-39 el corzo**
- *roe (roe deer)*
28 el corzo macho
- *roebuck (buck)*
**29-31 los cuernos** (la cornamenta, la cuerna)
- *antlers (horns)*
29 la roseta
- *burr (rose)*
30 el asta *f* con las perlas
- *beam with pearls*
31 la punta
- *point (tine)*
32 la oreja
- *ear*
33 el ojo
- *eye*

34 la corza, una hembra joven o una madre
- *doe (female roe), a female fawn or a barren doe*
35 el lomo
- *loin*
36 el espejo (la mancha blanca)
- *rump*
37 el pernil
- *leg (haunch)*
38 el codillo
- *shoulder*
39 el corcino, un corzo joven o una corza joven
- *fawn,* (m.) *young buck,* (f.) *young doe*
**40-41 el gamo**
- *fallow deer*
40 el gamo (el paleto); *hembra:* la gama
- *fallow buck, a buck with palmate (palmated) antlers,* (f.) *doe*
41 la palma
- *palm*
42 el zorro común (el zorro rojo); *hembra:* la zorra
- *red fox,* (m.) *dog,* (f.) *vixen,* (y.) *cub*
43 los ojos
- *eyes*
44 la oreja
- *ear*
45 el hocico
- *muzzle (mouth)*
46 las patas
- *pads (paws)*
47 el rabo (la cola, el hopo)
- *brush (tail)*
48 el tejón
- *badger,* (f.) *sow*
49 el rabo (la cola)
- *tail*
50 las garras
- *paws*
51 el jabalí; *hembra:* la jabalina; *joven:* el rayón, el jabato, el bermejo
- *wild boar,* (m.) *boar,* (f.) *wild sow (sow),* (y.) *young boar*
52 las cerdas
- *bristles*
53 el hocico (la jeta)
- *snout*
54 el colmillo (la navaja)
- *tusk*
55 el escudo (la cota, la piel especialmente dura en la espaldilla)
- *shield*
56 la corteza del tocino (la piel)
- *hide*
57 el espolón
- *dew claw*
58 la cola del jabalí (el rabo)
- *tail*
59 la liebre; *macho:* lebrón, el matacán; *joven:* el lebrato
- *hare,* (m.) *buck,* (f.) *doe*
60 el ojo
- *eye*
61 la oreja
- *ear*
62 el rabo (la cola)
- *scut (tail)*
63 la pata trasera
- *hind leg*
64 la pata delantera
- *foreleg*
65 el conejo; *hembra:* la coneja; *joven:* el gazapo
- *rabbit*
66 el grigallo (el gallo silvestre, el faisán de montaña *f*)
- *blackcock*
67 la cola (la lira)
- *tail*
68 las plumas de hoz *f*)
- *falcate (falcated) feathers*

69 la ortega (la corteza)
- *hazel grouse (hazel hen)*
70 la perdiz
- *partridge*
71 la mancha del pecho
- *horseshoe (horseshoe marking)*
72 el urogallo (el gallo de bosque *m;* el faisán de bosque *m*)
- *wood grouse (capercaillie)*
73 la barba de plumas *f*
- *beard*
74 el espejo (la mancha blanca)
- *axillary marking*
75 la cola (el abanico)
- *tail (fan)*
76 el ala *f*
- *wing (pinion)*
77 el faisán común, un faisán; *macho:* el faisán; *hembra:* la faisana
- *common pheasant, a pheasant,* (m.) *cock pheasant (pheasant cock),* (f.) *hen pheasant (pheasant hen)*
78 el moñito (el copete)
- *plumicorn (feathered ear, ear tuft, ear, horn)*
79 el ala *f*
- *wing*
80 la cola
- *tail*
81 la pata
- *leg*
82 el espolón
- *spur*
83 la chocha (la becada, la ardea sorda)
- *snipe*
84 el pico
- *bill (beak)*

# 89 Piscicultura y el deporte de la pesca con anzuelo

**1-19 la piscicultura**
– *fish farming (fish culture, pisciculture)*
1 la jaula en agua *f* corriente
– *cage in running water*
2 la sacadera (el salabre, la manga, la cuchara)
– *hand net (landing net)*
3 el tonelete de transporte *m* de los pescados
– *semi-oval barrel for transporting fish*
4 la tina
– *vat*
5 el enrejado del rebosadero
– *trellis in the overflow*
6 el vivero (la cría de truchas *f*); también: el estanque para carpas *f*, el estanque de cría *f*
– *trout pond; sim.: carp pond, a fry pond, fattening pond, or cleansing pond*
7 la llegada de agua *f*
– *water inlet (water supply pipe)*
8 el desagüe (la salida de agua *f*)
– *water outlet (outlet pipe)*
9 el dispositivo de vaciado *m*
– *monk*
10 la rejilla de retención *f* (el filtro)
– *screen*
**11-19 el criadero de peces *m***
– *hatchery*
11 la recolección de huevos *m* de lucio *m*
– *stripping the spawning pike (seed pike)*
12 los huevos del pez (la hueva, la desova, la freza)
– *fish spawn (spawn, roe, fish eggs)*
13 el pez hembra (el pez que tiene huevas *f*)
– *female fish (spawner, seed fish)*
14 la cría de truchas *f*
– *trout breeding (trout rearing)*
15 la incubadora californiana
– *Californian incubator*
16 los huevos de trucha *f*
– *trout fry*
17 la botella de cría *f* del esturión
– *hatching jar for pike*
18 la artesa de incubación *f* en la corriente de agua *f* continua
– *long incubation tank*
19 la rejilla para contar los huevos
– *Brandstetter egg-counting board*
**20-94 la pesca (la pesca con caña *f*)**
– *angling*
**20-31 la pesca de fondo *m***
– *coarse fishing*
20 la caña de lanzar
– *line shooting*
21 el rollo de hilo *m*
– *coils*
22 el trozo de trapo *m* o de papel *m*
– *cloth (rag) or paper*
23 el soporte de cañas *f*
– *rod rest*
24 la lata (caja *f*) del cebo (de los gusanos)
– *bait tin*
25 la cestilla de los pescadores (*Venez.:* el humare)
– *fish basket (creel)*
26 la pesca de la carpa en bote *m*
– *fishing for carp from a boat*
27 el bote de remos *m* (el bote de pesca *f*)
– *rowing boat (fishing boat)*
28 la nasa (el butrón; *Arg.:* el tilbe)
– *keep net*
29 la red cuadrada (la red de fondo *m*; *Col.:* el congolo, la charqueza)
– *drop net*
30 la pértiga (la vara)
– *pole (punt pole, quant pole)*
31 la red de lanzamiento *m*
– *casting net*
32 el lanzamiento de dos manos *m* con carrete *m* de instalación *f* fija
– *two-handed side cast with fixed-spool reel*
33 la posición inicial (la posición de partida)
– *initial position*
34 el punto de lanzamiento *m*
– *point of release*
35 la trayectoria del extremo de la caña
– *path of the rod tip*
36 la trayectoria de vuelo *m* de la plomada del cebo
– *trajectory of the baited weight*
**37-94 los útiles de pesca *f***
– *fishing tackle*
37 las tenazas de pescador *m*
– *fishing pliers*
38 el cuchillo de descuartizar
– *filleting knife*
39 el cuchillo de pescado *m* (el cuchillo para quitar las escamas; *Col.:* la pacora)
– *fish knife*
40 el desembuchador de gancho *m*
– *disgorger (hook disgorger)*
41 la aguja del cebo
– *bait needle*
42 la mordaza para lucios *m*
– *gag*
**43-48 flotadores *m* (corchos *m*)**
– *floats*
43 el corcho de caña *f* fusiforme
– *sliding cork float*
44 el flotador de materia *f* plástica
– *plastic float*
45 el flotador con pluma *f* (la pluma)
– *quill float*
46 el flotador de espuma *f* de plástico *m*
– *polystyrene float*
47 la bola de agua *f* ovalada
– *oval bubble float*
48 el flotador cargado de plomo *m*
– *lead-weighted sliding float*
**49-58 las cañas de pescar**
– *rods*
49 la caña de fibra *f* de vidrio *m*
– *solid glass rod*
50 la empuñadura de corcho *m* aglomerado
– *cork handle (cork butt)*
51 la anilla de acero *m* para resortes *m*
– *spring-steel ring*
52 la anilla del extremo
– *top ring (end ring)*
53 la caña telescópica
– *telescopic rod*
54 la varilla
– *rod section*
55 la parte de la empuñadura enfundada
– *bound handle (bound butt)*
56 la anilla de rodadura *f*
– *ring*
57 la caña de fibra *f* de carbono *m*; también: la caña de vidrio *m* hueco (vidrio *m* soplado)
– *carbon-fibre rod; sim.: hollow glass rod*
58 la anilla para un lanzamiento largo, una anilla de puente *m* metálico
– *all-round ring (butt ring for long cast), a steel bridge ring*
**59-64 los carretes (*Amér. Central, Mé. y Venez.:* las carruchas)**
– *reels*
59 el carrete multiplicador
– *multiplying reel (multiplier reel)*
60 la guía del hilo
– *line guide*
61 el carrete de instalación *f* fija
– *fixed-spool reel (stationary-drum reel)*
62 el asa *f* de recogida del hilo
– *bale arm*
63 el hilo de pescar
– *fishing line*
64 el control del lazamiento con el dedo índice
– *controlling the cast with the index finger*
**65-76 cebos *m***
– *baits*
65 la mosca
– *fly*
66 el cebo de ninfas *f* (la ninfa)
– *artificial nymph*
67 el cebo de lombriz *f* de tierra *f*
– *artificial earthworm*
68 el cebo de saltamontes *m*
– *artificial grasshopper*
69 el pez artificial de metal *m* de una sola parte
– *single-jointed plug (single-jointed wobbler)*
70 el pez artificial de metal *m* de dos partes *f*
– *double-jointed plug (double-jointed wobbler)*
71 el pez artificial de metal *m* esférico
– *round wobbler*
72 el pez cuchara *f* imitando a uno vivo
– *wiggler*
73 la cucharilla
– *spoon bait (spoon)*
74 la cucharilla moteada
– *spinner*
75 la cucharilla con anzuelo *m* oculto
– *spinner with concealed hook*
76 la guadañeta
– *long spinner*
77 el gancho
– *swivel*
78 la hijuela (la sotileza, el reinal)
– *cast (leader)*
**79-87 anzuelos *m***
– *hooks*
79 el anzuelo
– *fish hook*
80 la punta del anzuelo con púa *f*
– *point of the hook with barb*
81 la curva del anzuelo
– *bend of the hook*
82 la laminilla (el ojete)
– *spade (eye)*
83 el anzuelo doble
– *open double hook*
84 el anzuelo inglés derecho
– *limerick*
85 el anzuelo triple
– *closed treble hook (triangle)*
86 el anzuelo de carpa *f*
– *carp hook*
87 el anzuelo de anguila *f*
– *eel hook*
**88-92 pesas *f* de plomo *m***
– *leads (lead weights)*
88 la aceituna de plomo *m*
– *oval lead (oval sinker)*
89 las bolas de plomo *m*
– *lead shot*
90 el plomo piriforme
– *pear-shaped lead*
91 la plomada (la sonda)
– *plummet*
92 el plomo (para la pesca) de mar
– *sea lead*
93 el paso de los peces
– *fish ladder (fish pass, fish way)*
94 la red de estaca *f*
– *stake net*

**1-23 la pesca de altura**
- *deep-sea fishing*

**1-10 la pesca con red *f* de arrastre**
- *drift net fishing*

1 el lugre para la pesca de arenques *m*
- *herring lugger (fishing lugger, lugger)*

**2-10 la red de arrastre para la pesca de arenques *m***
- *herring drift net*

2 el boyarín
- *buoy*

3 la cuerda del boyarín
- *buoy rope*

4 la cuerda flotante (la guindaleza)
- *float line*

5 la atadura
- *seizing*

6 los flotadores de corcho *m*
- *wooden float*

7 la cuerda superior
- *headline*

8 la red (la red vertical)
- *net*

9 la cuerda de fondo *m* (la relinga)
- *footrope*

10 los pesos de fondo *m*
- *sinkers (weights)*

**11-23 la pesca con red *f* barredera**
- *trawl fishing (trawling)*

11 un buque factoría *f*
- *factory ship, a trawler*

12 la sirga (la malleta)
- *warp (trawl warp)*

13 el panel divergente
- *otter boards*

14 el cable de las sondas de la red
- *net sonar cable*

15 el calabrote de alambre *m*
- *wire warp*

16 la banda
- *wing*

17 la sonda de la red
- *net sonar device*

18 la relinga de fondo *m*
- *footrope*

19 las esferas de corcho *m*
- *spherical floats*

20 el vientre (la panza) de la red
- *belly*

21 el peso de hierro *m* de 1 800 kgs.
- *1,800 kg iron weight*

22 el copo
- *cod end (cod)*

23 la cuerda para cerrar el copo
- *cod line for closing the cod end*

**24-29 la pesca costera** (la pesca de bajura *f*)
- *inshore fishing*

24 el barco de pesca *f* (la trainera)
- *fishing boat*

25 la traíña, una red circular flotante (*Guat., Hond. y Mé.:* la billarda)
- *ring net cast in a circle*

26 el cable para cerrar la red, la jareta
- *cable for closing the ring net*

27 el dispositivo de cierre *m*
- *closing gear*

**28-29 la pesca con palangre *m***
- *long-line fishing (long-lining)*

28 el palangre (el cordel largo)
- *long line*

29 la pernada (el reinal, el pipio, la brazolada), un sedal de algodón *m*
- *suspended fishing tackle*

**1-34 el molino de viento** *m*
- *windmill*
**1** el aspa *f* del molino de viento *m*
- *windmill vane (windmill sail, windmill arm)*
**2** el alma *f* central del aspa *f*
- *stock (middling, back, radius)*
**3** el listón del borde
- *frame*
**4** la persiana (la compuerta del viento)
- *shutter*
**5** el árbol (el eje de giro *m*)
- *wind shaft (sail axle)*
**6** la cabeza del aspa *f*
- *sail top*
**7** la rueda dentada
- *brake wheel*
**8** el freno de la rueda
- *brake*
**9** el diente de madera *f* (el álabe)
- *wooden cog*
**10** el cojinete de soporte *m*
- *pivot bearing (step bearing)*
**11** el engranaje del molino de viento *m*
- *wallower*
**12** el eje del molino
- *mill spindle*
**13** la tolva
- *hopper*
**14** el vibrador (la caja oscilante)
- *shoe (trough, spout)*
**15** el molinero
- *miller*
**16** la muela
- *millstone*

**17** la estría de refrigeración *f* por aire *m*
- *furrow (flute)*
**18** la estría de molienda *f*
- *master furrow*
**19** el ojo de la muela (el foramen)
- *eye*
**20** la caja de las muelas
- *hurst (millstone casing)*
**21** el juego de muelas *f*
- *set of stones (millstones)*
**22** la volandera (la corredera, la voladora)
- *runner (upper millstone)*
**23** la solera (la muela fija)
- *bed stone (lower stone, bedder)*
**24** la pala de madera *f*
- *wooden shovel*
**25** el engranaje cónico
- *bevel gear (bevel gearing)*
**26** el cilindro cernedor
- *bolter (sifter)*
**27** el cubo de madera
- *wooden tub (wooden tun)*
**28** la harina
- *flour*
**29** el molino de viento *m* holandés
- *smock windmill (Dutch windmill)*
**30** el casquete giratorio del molino de viento *m*
- *rotating (revolving) windmill cap*
**31** el molino de caja *f* giratoria
- *post windmill (German windmill)*
**32** el timón (la cola, el gobierno)
- *tailpole (pole)*
**33** la armazón de soporte *m*
- *base*
**34** el árbol real (el poste de giro *m*)
- *post*

**35-44 el molino de agua** *f* (la aceña)
- *watermill*
**35** la rueda hidráulica de corriente *f* alta, una rueda de molino *m* de agua *f*, un rodezno
- *overshot mill wheel (high-breast mill wheel), a mill wheel (waterwheel)*
**36** el cangilón (el arcaduz)
- *bucket (cavity)*
**37** la rueda hidráulica de corriente *f* media
- *middleshot mill wheel (breast mill wheel)*
**38** la paleta curva
- *curved vane*
**39** la rueda hidráulica de corriente *f* baja
- *undershot mill wheel*
**40** la paleta recta
- *flat vane*
**41** el caz de traída *f*
- *headrace (discharge flume)*
**42** la presa del molino (el azud)
- *mill weir*
**43** la compuerta
- *overfall (water overfall)*
**44** el caz de salida *f* (el riachuelo) del molino
- *millstream (millrace, Am. raceway)*

**1-41 la preparación de la malta**
- *preparation of malt (malting)*
1 la torre de maltaje *m* (la instalación de producción *f* de malta *f*)
- *malting tower (maltings)*
2 la entrada de la cebada
- *barley hopper*
3 la planta de lavado *m* con aire *m* comprimido
- *washing floor with compressed-air washing unit*
4 el condensador de desagüe *m*
- *outflow condenser*
5 el depósito colector *m* de agua *f*
- *water-collecting tank*
6 el condensador para el agua *f* de remojo *m*
- *condenser for the steep liquor*
7 el recolector medio de refrigeración *f*
- *coolant-collecting plant*
8 la planta de remojo *m* y de germinación *f*
- *steeping floor*
9 el depósito de agua *f* fría
- *cold water tank*
10 el depósito de agua *f* caliente
- *hot water tank*
11 la sala de las bombas de agua *f*
- *pump room*
12 la instalación neumática
- *pneumatic plant*
13 la instalación hidráulica
- *hydraulic plant*
14 la chimenea de ventilación *f*
- *ventilation shaft (air inlet and outlet)*
15 el ventilador
- *exhaust fan*
**16-18 el secadero de la malta**
- *kilning floors*
16 la planta de secado *m*
- *drying floor*
17 el ventilador del quemador
- *burner ventilator*
18 la planta de desecación *f*
- *curing floor*
19 el conducto de evacuación *f* del secador
- *outlet duct from the kiln*
20 la tolva de la malta preparada
- *finished malt collecting hopper*
21 la instalación de los transformadores
- *transformer station*
22 los compresores frigoríficos
- *cooling compressors*
23 la malta verde (la cebada en germinación *f*)
- *green malt (germinated barley)*
24 la rejilla rotativa
- *turner (plough)*
25 la central de conexión *f* con diagrama sinóptico
- *central control room with flow diagram*

26 el tornillo sin fin *m* de alimentación *f*
- *screw conveyor*
27 la planta de lavado *m*
- *washing floor*
28 la planta de remojo *m* y de germinación *f*
- *steeping floor*
29 la planta de secado *m*
- *drying kiln*
30 la planta de desecación *f*
- *curing kiln*
31 el silo de cebada *f*
- *barley silo*
32 la balanza
- *weighing apparatus*
33 el elevador de cebada *f*
- *barley elevator*
34 el distribuidor de tres vías *f*
- *three-way chute (three-way tippler)*
35 el elevador de malta *f*
- *malt elevator*
36 el dispositivo de limpieza *f*
- *cleaning machine*
37 el silo de malta *f*
- *malt silo*
38 el dispositivo de aspiración *f* de los gérmenes
- *corn removal by suction*
39 la máquina de ensacado *m*
- *sacker*
40 el aspirador del polvo
- *dust extractor*
41 la recepción de cebada *f*
- *barley reception*
**42-53 el proceso de cocción *f* en la cámara de cocción *f***
- *mashing process in the mashhouse*
42 el macerador para la mezcla de harina *f* y de agua *f*
- *premasher (converter) for mixing grist and water*
43 la tina de mezcla *f* (la cuba de maceración *f*) para la maceración de la malta
- *mash tub (mash tun) for mashing the malt*
44 la caldera de sacarificación *f* (la caldera de la mezcla)
- *mash copper (mash tun*, Am. *mash kettle) for boiling the mash*
45 la tapadera (la cúpula) de la caldera
- *dome of the tun*
46 la batidora (el girador)
- *propeller (paddle)*
47 la puerta de corredera *f*
- *sliding door*
48 la tubería para la entrada de agua *f*
- *water (liquor) supply pipe*
49 el cervecero (el maestro cervecero)
- *brewer (master brewer, masher)*

50 la tina de clarificación *f* para asentar los residuos y filtrar el mosto
- *lauter tun for settling the draff (grains) and filtering off the wort*
51 la batería de clarificación *f* para la comprobación de la finura del mosto
- *lauter battery for testing the wort for quality*
52 la caldera para la cocción del mosto con el lúpulo (la tina de mosto *m*)
- *hop boiler (wort boiler) for boiling the wort*
53 el termómetro en forma *f* de cucharón *m*
- *ladle-type thermometer (scoop thermometer)*

**1-31  la cervecería** (la fábrica de
cerveza *f*)
– *brewery (brewhouse)*
**1-5  la refrigeración del mosto y la
separación de los residuos**
– *wort cooling and break removal
(trub removal)*
**1**  el pupitre de mando *m*
– *control desk (control panel)*
**2**  el separador de torbellino *m*
para la eliminación por calor *m*
de los residuos
– *whirlpool separator for removing
the hot break (hot trub)*
**3**  el recipiente dosificador del
kieselguhr
– *measuring vessel for the
kieselguhr*
**4**  el filtro para kieselguhr *f*
– *kieselguhr filter*
**5**  el refrigerador del mosto
lupulado
– *wort cooler*
**6**  el aparato de preparación *f* de
la levadura biológicamente
pura
– *pure culture plant for yeast
(yeast propagation plant)*
**7**  la bodega de fermentación *f*
– *fermenting cellar*
**8**  la cuba de fermentación *f*
– *fermentation vessel (fermenter)*
**9**  el termómetro de
fermentación *f* (el termómetro
de maceración *f*)
– *fermentation thermometer (mash
thermometer)*
**10**  el mosto
– *mash*
**11**  el sistema de serpentín *m*
refrigerador
– *refrigeration system*
**12**  la bodega (el depósito
subterráneo de conservación *f*)
– *lager cellar*
**13**  el orificio de acceso *m* al
depósito *m* de
almacenamiento *m*
– *manhole to the storage tank*
**14**  el grifo para sacar la cerveza
– *broaching tap*
**15**  el filtro de la cerveza
– *beer filter*
**16**  el almacenamiento en toneles *m*
– *barrel store*
**17**  el tonel (el barril) de cerveza *f*
de aluminio *m*
– *beer barrel, an aluminium (Am.
aluminum) barrel*
**18**  la instalación de lavado *m* de
las botellas
– *bottle-washing plant*
**19**  la máquina de lavar botellas *f*
– *bottle-washing machine (bottle
washer)*
**20**  la instalación de mando *m*
– *control panel*
**21**  las botellas limpias
– *cleaned bottles*

**22**  el llenado de las botellas (el
embotellado)
– *bottling*
**23**  la carretilla elevadora de
horquilla *f*
– *forklift truck (fork truck, forklift)*
**24**  la pila de cajas *f* de cerveza *f*
– *stack of beer crates*
**25**  la lata de cerveza *f*
– *beer can*
**26**  la botella de cerveza *f*, una
botella conforme a las normas
europeas; *clases de cerveza:*
cerveza dorada, cerveza negra,
cerveza estilo Pilsen, cerveza de
Munich, cerveza sin alcohol *m*,
cerveza malteada, cerveza
fuerte (cerveza bock), porter,
ale, stout, salvator, cerveza de
Goslar, cerveza de trigo *m*,
cerveza suave, cerveza sin
alcohol
– *beer bottle, a Eurobottle with
bottled beer; kinds of beer: light
beer (lager, light ale, pale ale or
bitter), dark beer (brown ale,
mild), Pilsener beer, Munich
beer, malt beer, strong beer
(bock beer), porter, ale, stout,
Salvator beer, wheat beer, small
beer*
**27**  la cápsula de la botella (la
chapa de la botella, el tapón de
la botella)
– *crown cork (crown cork closure)*
**28**  el paquete de un solo uso (el
envase perdido)
– *disposable pack (carry-home
pack)*
**29**  la botella de un solo uso (la
botella desechable, la botella
no retornable)
– *non-returnable bottle (single-trip
bottle)*
**30**  el vaso de cerveza *f*
– *beer glass*
**31**  la espuma
– *head*

1 el matarife (el carnicero, el jifero)
- *slaughterman (Am. slaughterer, killer)*
2 la res de matanza *f*, una vaca
- *animal for slaughter, an ox*
3 la pistola de perno *m* percutor, un aparato para atronar
- *captive-bolt pistol (pneumatic gun), a stunning device*
4 el perno percutor (el percutor)
- *bolt*
5 los cartuchos
- *cartridges*
6 el disparador (el gatillo)
- *release lever (trigger)*
7 el aparato de atronamiento *m* eléctrico
- *electric stunner*
8 el electrodo
- *electrode*
9 el cable de alimentación *f*
- *lead*
10 la protección de la mano (el aislamiento de protección *f*)
- *hand guard (insulation)*
11 el cerdo de matanza *f*
- *pig (Am. hog) for slaughter*
12 la vaina de cuchillos *m*
- *knife case*
13 el cuchillo de desollar
- *flaying knife*
14 el cuchillo de matar
- *sticking knife (sticker)*
15 el cuchillo de carnicero *m*
- *butcher's knife (butcher knife)*
16 el afilador de acero *m* (el afilón, la chaira)
- *steel*
17 el cuchillo-rajadera
- *splitter*
18 la cuchilla
- *cleaver (butcher's cleaver, meat axe (Am. meat ax))*
19 la sierra para cortar los huesos
- *bone saw (butcher's saw)*
20 la sierra para cortar la carne en trozos *m* (en porciones *f*, la sierra para despiezar)
- *meat saw for sawing meat into cuts*
21-24 **el frigorífico** (la cámara frigorífica)
- *cold store (cold room)*
21 la percha (el colgadero, el gancho)
- *gambrel (gambrel stick)*
22 el cuarto de vaca *f*
- *quarter of beef*
23 la mitad del cerdo (medio cerdo)
- *side of pork*
24 el sello de sanidad (de control) puesto por la inspección del matadero
- *meat inspector's stamp*

a la izquierda: parte de la carne;
a la derecha: parte del hueso
*left: meat side;*
*right: bone side*

**1-13 la ternera**
- animal: *calf;* meat: *veal*
1 la pierna con la culata
- *leg with hind knuckle*
2 la falda
- *flank*
3 la costilla (la costilla de ternera, la mediana)
- *loin and rib*
4 el pecho (el pecho de ternera, la aleta)
- *breast (breast of veal)*
5 la espalda con la pierna delantera (con el garrón)
- *shoulder with fore knuckle*
6 el cuello
- *neck with scrag (scrag end)*
7 la riñonada (*Mé.*: el diezmillo)
- *best end of loin (of loin of veal)*
8 el brazuelo (el morcillo) de la espalda
- *fore knuckle*
9 la espalda
- *shoulder*
10 el garrón (el jarrete de la pierna)
- *hind knuckle*
11 la babilla y la cadera
- *roasting round (oyster round)*
12 el fricandó (el tajo redondo)
- *cutlet for frying or braising*
13 la tapa y la contra
- *undercut (fillet)*
**14-37 la vaca**
- animal: *ox;* meat: *beef*
14 la pierna con el jarrete
- *round with rump and shank*
15-16 las faldas
- *flank*
15 la falda trasera
- *thick flank*
16 la punta de costillas *f* (ternillas *f*)
- *thin flank*

17 el lomo bajo
- *sirloin*
18 el lomo alto
- *prime rib (fore ribs, prime fore rib)*
19 la espaldilla
- *middle rib and chuck*
20 el cuello
- *neck*
21 el antepecho
- *flat rib*
22 la espalda con el jarrete delantero
- *leg of mutton piece (bladebone) with shin*
23 el pecho de la vaca
- *brisket (brisket of beef)*
24 el solomillo de vaca *f*
- *fillet (fillet of beef)*
25 la parte trasera del pecho
- *hind brisket*
26 la parte central del pecho
- *middle brisket*
27 el esternón
- *breastbone*
28 el morcillo delantero
- *shin*
29 la carne de la espaldilla
- *leg of mutton piece*
30 la carne de la paletilla
- *part of bladebone*
31 el tajo redondo de la espalda
- *part of top rib*
32 el revés de la paletilla
- *part of bladebone*
33 el morcillo trasero
- *shank*
34 la contra
- *silverside*
35 la cadera
- *rump*
36 la babilla
- *thick flank*
37 la tapa y el tajo redondo
- *top side*

**38-54 el cerdo**
- animal: *pig;* meat: *pork*
38 el jamón con la mano y el codillo
- *leg with knuckle and trotter*
39 la panza (el cuadro)
- *ventral part of the belly*
40 el tocino del lomo (la canal)
- *back fat*
41 la falda
- *belly*
42 la paletilla con la mano
- *bladebone with knuckle and trotter*
43 la cabeza de cerdo *m*
- *head (pig's head)*
44 el solomillo de cerdo *m*
- *fillet (fillet of pork)*
45 la grasa de riñón *m* de cerdo *m* (la manteca de cerdo *m*)
- *leaf fat (pork flare)*
46 la chuleta de cerdo *m* (la cinta)
- *loin (pork loin)*
47 la aguja de cerdo *m*
- *spare rib*
48 la mano de cerdo *m*
- *trotter*
49 el codillo (el brazuelo)
- *knuckle*
50 la carne magra de la espalda
- *butt*
51 la carne del jamón
- *fore end (ham)*
52 la nuez
- *round end for boiling*
53 el tocino del jamón (la culeta, la cadera)
- *fat end*
54 el codillo trasero
- *gammon steak*

**1-30 la carnicería** (la tablajería;
*Amér.:* la chanchería; *Col., C. Rica
y Venez.:* la pesa; *Ec.:* la tercena)
– *butcher's shop*
**1-4 los productos cárnicos**
– *meat*
**1** el jamón
– *ham on the bone*
**2** la hoja de tocino *m* (la panceta, el
bacon)
– *flitch of bacon*
**3** la carne seca (la carne ahumada;
la cecina)
– *smoked meat*
**4** el lomo (el solomillo)
– *piece of loin (piece of sirloin)*
**5** la manteca de cerdo *m*
– *lard*
**6-11 los embutidos** (la salchichería)
– *sausages*
**6** la etiqueta del precio
– *price label*
**7** la mortadela
– *mortadella*
**8** las salchichas cocidas; *clases:* la
salchicha de Viena, de Francfort
– *scalded sausage;* kinds: *Vienna
sausage (Wiener), Frankfurter
sausage (Frankfurter)*
**9** el queso de cerdo *m*
– *collared pork* (Am. *headcheese*)
**10** la longaniza
– *ring of [Lyoner] sausage*

**11** la salchicha (el chorizo; la
salchicha para asar)
– *bratwurst (sausage for frying or
grilling)*
**12** la vitrina frigorífica (el mostrador
frigorífico)
– *cold shelves*
**13** la ensalada de fiambres *m*
– *meat salad (diced meat salad)*
**14** las lonjas de carne *f*
– *cold meats* (Am. *cold cuts*)
**15** el pâté
– *pâté*
**16** la carne picada
– *mince (mincemeat, minced meat)*
**17** el jamón cocido
– *knuckle of pork*
**18** el cesto con las ofertas especiales
– *basket for special offers*
**19** el letrero con el precio especial
– *price list for special offers*
**20** el producto en oferta *f*
– *special offer*
**21** el congelador
– *freezer*
**22** el asado preempaquetado
– *pre-packed joints*
**23** el plato preparado congelado
– *deep-frozen ready-to-eat meal*
**24** el pollo
– *chicken*
**25** las conservas (las conservas de
larga duración *f;* con fecha límite
de venta: semiconservas *f*)
– *canned food*

**26** la caja de conserva *f*
– *can*
**27** las legumbres en conserva *f* (las
conservas vegetales)
– *canned vegetables*
**28** el pescado en conserva *f* (la
conserva de pescado *m*)
– *canned fish*
**29** la salsa mayonesa con mostaza *f*
– *salad cream*
**30** los refrescos
– *soft drinks*

**31-59 la cocina de la charcutería** (la sala de adobo *m*)

**31-59 la cocina de la charcutería** (la
  sala de adobo *m*)
– *kitchen for making sausages*
**31-37 cuchillos** *m* **de carnicero** *m*
– *butcher's knives*
**31** el cuchillo de corte *m*
– *slicer*
**32** la hoja del cuchillo
– *knife blade*
**33** el filo de sierra *f* (la sierra del
  cuchillo)
– *saw teeth*
**34** el mango del cuchillo
– *knife handle*
**35** el cuchillo para la carne (la
  rajadera)
– *carver (carving knife)*
**36** el cuchillo de desosar
– *boning knife*
**37** el cuchillo de carnicero *m*
– *butcher's knife (butcher knife)*
**38** el maestro carnicero (el carnicero;
  *Cuba:* el mataronero; *Col. y
  Venez.:* el pesador)
– *butcher (master butcher)*
**39** el delantal del carnicero
– *butcher's apron*
**40** la artesa de la carne (la cuba de
  amasar)
– *meat-mixing trough*
**41** el relleno de las salchichas (la
  masa de las salchichas)
– *sausage meat*
**42** el rascador
– *scraper*

**43** la espumadera (la rasera)
– *skimmer*
**44** el tenedor de las salchichas
– *sausage fork*
**45** el colador del caldo
– *scalding colander*
**46** el cubo de la basura
– *waste bin (Am. trash bin)*
**47** el armario de cocinar (el horno)
  con dispositivo *m* de producción *f*
  de vapor *m* o aire *m* caliente para
  estofar
– *cooker, for cooking with steam or
  hot air*
**48** el ahumadero (la cámara de
  ahumar)
– *smoke house*
**49** el embutidor de mano *m* (el
  embutidor de mesa *f*)
– *sausage filler (sausage stuffer)*
**50** el tubo de rellenar
– *feed pipe (supply pipe)*
**51** el recipiente de las verduras
– *containers for vegetables*
**52** la máquina para preparar la carne
  de las salchichas
– *mincing machine for sausage meat*
**53** la máquina de picar carne *f*
– *mincing machine (meat mincer,
  mincer, Am. meat grinder)*
**54** las rejillas con cuchilla *f* para
  picar
– *plates (steel plates)*
**55** el garabato (de cocinero *m*)
– *meathook (butcher's hook)*

**56** la sierra para huesos *m*
– *bone saw*
**57** la tabla de carnicero *m*
– *chopping board*
**58** el mozo de carnicero *m* cortando
  la carne
– *butcher, cutting meat*
**59** el trozo de carne *f*
– *piece of meat*

1-54 **el local de venta** *f* de la panadería
(la panadería, la confitería)
- *baker's shop*
1 la vendedora
- *shop assistant (Am. salesgirl,
saleslady)*
2 el pan
- *bread (loaf of bread, loaf)*
3 la miga
- *crumb*
4 la corteza
- *crust (bread crust)*
5 el cantero
- *crust (Am. heel)*
6-12 **clases** *f* **de pan** *m*
- *kinds of bread (breads)*
6 el pan redondo (el pan cateto, la
hogaza, un pan moreno)
- *round loaf, a wheat and rye bread*
7 el pan redondo pequeño
- *small round loaf*
8 el pan alargado, un pan de mezcla *f*
(un pan de trigo *m* y centeno *m*)
- *long loaf (bloomer), a wheat and rye
bread*
9 el pan blanco (el pan de Viena)
- *white loaf*
10 el pan inglés, un pan integral
- *pan loaf, a wholemeal rye bread*
11 el pan trenzado (el bollo de
Nochebuena, el bollo de Navidad)
- *yeast bread (Am. stollen)*
12 el pan blanco francés (la barra de
pan *m*)
- *French loaf (baguette, French stick)*
13-16 **panecillos** *m*
- *rolls*

13 el panecillo (blanco o de canela;
*Amér.:* el pancito)
- *roll*
14 los panecillos de canela *f* o trigo *m*
(panecillo blancos, el bollo de pan *m*;
*también:* panecillos salados,
panecillos con adormidera, panecillos
con comino *m; Amér.:* los besitos)
- *[white] roll*
15 el panecillo doble
- *double roll*
16 el panecillo de centeno *m*
- *rye-bread roll*
17-47 **dulces** *m* (confites *m*, pasteles *m*)
- *cakes (confectionery)*
17 el rollito de nata *f*
- *cream roll*
18 el hojaldre
- *vol-au-vent, a puff pastry (Am. puff
paste)*
19 el bizcocho enrollado
- *Swiss roll (Am. jelly roll)*
20 la tartita (*Amér.:* las masitas)
- *tartlet*
21 el merengue
- *cream slice*
22-24 **tartas** *f*
- *flans (Am. pies) and gateaux (torten)*
22 la tarta de frutas *f* (*var.:* tarta de
fresas *f*, tarta de cerezas *f*, tarta de
grosellas *f*, tarta de melocotón *m*, tarta
de ruibarbo *m*)
- *fruit flan;* kinds: *strawberry flan,
cherry flan, gooseberry flan, peach
flan, rhubarb flan*
23 la tarta de queso *m*
- *cheesecake*

24 la tarta de crema *f* (*también:-* la tarta
de nata *f; var.:* la tarta de crema *f* de
mantequilla *f*, la tarta de cerezas *f* de
la Selva Negra)
- *cream cake (Am. cream pie);* kinds:
*butter-cream cake, Black Forest gateau*
25 la bandeja de tarta *f*
- *cake plate*
26 el merengue
- *meringue*
27 la col de crema *f* (el suspiro de
monja *f*)
- *cream puff*
28 la nata batida (la crema chantillí)
- *whipped cream*
29 los bollos de Berlín (*Chile:* el queque)
- *doughnut (Am. bismarck)*
30 la palmera
- *Danish pastry*
31 la barrita salada (*también:* la barrita
con comino *m*)
- *saltstick, also: caraway roll, caraway
stick*
32 el cuernecito (el croissant; *Amér.:* la
media luna)
- *croissant (crescent roll, Am. crescent)*
33 el pastel de molde *m* (la torta
alemana; *también:* el bizcocho de
Saboya)
- *ring cake (gugelhupf)*
34 el dulce de molde *m* cubierto con una
capa de chocolate *m*
- *slab cake with chocolate icing*
35 la tortita espolvoreada
- *streusel cakes*
36 la cabeza de moro *m*
- *marshmallow*

**37** el macarrón (el mostachón, el
almendrado)
- *coconut macaroon*
**38** la rosca (la ensaimada)
- *schnecke*
**39** el dulce americano
- *[kind of] iced bun*
**40** el bizcocho tostado blando
- *sweet bread*
**41** la trenza
- *plaited bun (plait)*
**42** la corona de Francfort
- *Frankfurter garland cake*
**43** el dulce en trozos (*var.:* el dulce
espolvoreado con recortes *m* de
pasta *f*, el dulce cubierto de azúcar *f*
el dulce de ciruelas *f*)
- *slices (kinds: streusel slices, sugared
slices, plum slices)*
**44** la rosquilla
- *pretzel*
**45** el barquillo
- *wafer* (Am. *waffle*)
**46** el dulce de pisos *m*
- *tree cake (baumkuchen)*
**47** el suelo de masa *f* para las tartas
- *flan case*
**48-50 clases *f* de pan *m* empaquetado**
- ***wrapped bread***
**48** el pan integral (*también:* el pan de
germen *m* de trigo *m*)
- *wholemeal bread; also: wheatgerm
bread*
**49** el pan negro de Westfalia
- *pumpernickel (wholemeal rye bread)*
**50** el biscote
- *crispbread*
**51** el pan de especias *f* (el alajú)
- *gingerbread* (Am. *lebkuchen*)

**52** la harina (*var.:* la harina de trigo *m*, la
harina de centeno *m*)
- *flour;* kinds: *wheat flour, rye flour*
**53** la levadura
- *yeast (baker's yeast)*
**54** los bizcochos (los bizcochos tostados
para los niños; *C. Rica:* los tosteles)
- *rusks (French toast)*
**55-74 la tahona**
- ***bakery** (bakehouse)*
**55** la amasadora
- *kneading machine (dough mixer)*
**56-57 la unidad de fabricación *f* del pan**
- ***bread unit***
**56** la máquina de cortar la masa
- *divider*
**57** la unidad para dar la forma al pan
- *moulder* (Am. *molder*)
**58** el aparato para medir y mezclar el
agua *f*
- *premixer*
**59** el mezclador (la amasadera)
- *dough mixer*
**60** la mesa de trabajo *m*
- *workbench*
**61** la unidad de fabricación *f* de los
panecillos
- *roll unit*
**62** la mesa de trabajo *m*
- *workbench*
**63** la máquina de cortar y redondear la
masa
- *divider and rounder (rounding
machine)*
**64** la máquina para dar la forma a los
croissants
- *crescent-forming machine*
**65** el congelador
- *freezers*

**66** la freidora
- *oven [for baking with fat]*
**67-70 la confitería**
- ***confectionery unit***
**67** la mesa de enfriamiento *m*
- *cooling table*
**68** el fregadero
- *sink*
**69** el hornillo
- *boiler*
**70** la batidora-mezcladora
- *whipping unit [with beater]*
**71** el horno de pisos *m* (el horno de
panificación *f*)
- *reel oven (oven)*
**72** la cámara de fermentación *f*
- *fermentation room*
**73** la carretilla de la cámara de
fermentación *f*
- *fermentation trolley*
**74** el silo de harina *f*
- *flour silo*

**1-87 la tienda de comestibles** *m* (el almacén de ultramarinos *m*, el colmado; *Amér.:* la fiambrería, la pulpería), una tienda de venta *f* al por menor
– *grocer's shop (grocer's,* Am. *grocery store), a retail shop (Am. retail store);* sim.: *delicatessen*
1 el escaparate
– *window display*
2 el cartel de propaganda (el anuncio)
– *poster (advertisement)*
3 la vitrina frigorífica
– *cold shelves*
4 los embutidos (los fiambres)
– *sausages*
5 el queso
– *cheese*
6 el pollo asado
– *roasting chicken (broiler)*
7 la pularda, una gallina cebada
– *poulard, a fattened hen*
**8-11 los ingredientes de pastelería** *f*
– *baking ingredients*
8 las pasas; *anál.:* las pasas gorronas
– *raisins;* sim.: *sultanas*
9 las pasas de Corinto
– *currants*
10 la cidra confitada
– *candied lemon peel*
11 la naranja confitada
– *candied orange peel*
12 la balanza automática (el peso)
– *computing scale, a rapid scale*
13 el vendedor
– *shop assistant* (Am. *salesclerk)*

14 la estantería (el anaquel de los artículos)
– *goods shelves (shelves)*
**15-20 las conservas**
– *canned food*
15 la leche condensada (la leche en lata *f*)
– *canned milk*
16 las frutas en conserva *f*
– *canned fruit (cans of fruit)*
17 las verduras en conserva *f*
– *canned vegetables*
18 el zumo (el jugo de frutas *f*)
– *fruit juice*
19 las sardinas en aceite *m*, una conserva de pescado *m*
– *sardines in oil, a can of fish*
20 la carne en conserva *f*
– *canned meat (cans of meat)*
21 la margarina
– *margarine*
22 la mantequilla
– *butter*
23 la manteca de coco *m*, una grasa vegetal
– *coconut oil, a vegetable oil*
24 el aceite; *clases:* el aceite de mesa, el aceite de oliva *f*, el aceite de girasol *m*, el aceite de germen *m* de trigo *m*, el aceite de cacahuetes *m*, el aceite de maíz
– *oil; kinds: salad oil, olive oil, sunflower oil, wheatgerm oil, ground-nut oil*
25 el vinagre
– *vinegar*
26 el cubito (la pastilla) de sopa *f*
– *stock cube*

27 el cubito (la pastilla) de caldo *m*
– *bouillon cube*
28 la mostaza
– *mustard*
29 el pepinillo en vinagre *m*
– *pickled gherkin*
30 el condimento para sopas *f*
– *soup seasoning*
31 la vendedora
– *shop assistant* (Am. *salesgirl, saleslady)*
**32-34 las pastas alimenticias**
– *pastas*
32 los spaghetti
– *spaghetti*
33 los macarrones
– *macaroni*
34 los tallarines
– *noodles*
**35-39 Productos alimenticios** *f* (los cereales)
– *cereal products*
35 la cebada perlada
– *pearl barley*
36 la sémola
– *semolina*
37 los copos de avena *f*
– *rolled oats (porridge oats, oats)*
38 el arroz
– *rice*
39 la fécula de sagú *m* (la tapioca)
– *sago*
40 la sal
– *salt*
41 el comerciante, un comerciante al por menor
– *grocer* (Am. *groceryman), a shopkeeper (tradesman, retailer,* Am. *storekeeper)*

| | | |
|---|---|---|
| 42 las alcaparras | 56 el aguardiente (*P. Rico, S. Dgo. y* | 72 la paleta para probar el café |
| – *capers* | *Venez.:* el romo; *Arg., Bol., S. Dgo.* | – *sample scoop* |
| 43 la clienta | *y Urug.:* la tafia; *Perú:* el trinque) | 73 la lista de precios *m* |
| – *customer* | – *schnapps distilled from grain* | – *price list* |
| 44 el vale | *[usually wheat]* | 74 el mostrador frigorífico |
| – *receipt (sales check)* | 57 el ron | – *freezer* |
| 45 la bolsa para las compras | – *rum* | 75-86 los dulces (las golosinas) |
| – *shopping bag* | 58 el licor | – *confectionery* (Am. *candies*) |
| 46-49 el material para envolver | – *liqueur* | 75 el caramelo |
| – *wrapping material* | 59 el coñac | – *sweet* (Am. *candy*) |
| 46 el papel de envolver | – *brandy;* here: *cognac* | 76 los drops (los caramelos ácidos) |
| – *wrapping paper* | 60-64 vino embotellado *m* | – *drops* |
| 47 la cinta adhesiva | – *wine in bottles* (*bottled wine*) | 77 el caramelo |
| – *adhesive tape* | 60 el vino blanco | – *toffees* |
| 48 la bolsa de papel *m* (el cartucho) | – *white wine* | 78 la tableta de chocolate *m* |
| – *paper bag* | 61 el chianti | – *bar of chocolate* |
| 49 el cucurucho | – *Chianti* | 79 la caja de bombones *m* |
| – *cone-shaped paper bag* | 62 el vermut | – *chocolate box* |
| 50 los polvos para budines *m* | – *vermouth* | 80 el bombón, un artículo de |
| – *blancmange powder* | 63 el champaña (el vino espumoso) | confitería *f* |
| 51 la confitura | – *sparkling wine* | – *chocolate, a sweet* |
| – *whole-fruit jam (preserve)* | 64 el vino tinto | 81 el nuégado [un turrón de nueces *f*] |
| 52 la mermelada | – *red wine* | – *nougat* |
| – *jam* | 65-68 los estimulantes | 82 el mazapán |
| 53-55 azúcar *m* y *f* | – *tea, coffee, etc.* | – *marzipan* |
| – *sugar* | 65 el café (el café en grano *m*) | 83 el bombón de licor *m* |
| 53 el azúcar en terrones *m* | – *coffee (pure coffee)* | – *chocolate liqueur* |
| – *cube sugar* | 66 el cacao | 84 la lengua de gato *m* |
| 54 el azúcar en polvo *m* | – *cocoa* | – *cat's tongue* |
| – *icing sugar* (Am. *confectioner's* | 67 la variedad de café *m* | 85 el crocante (el guirlache) |
| *sugar)* | – *coffee* | – *croquant* |
| 55 el azúcar cristalizado (el azúcar | 68 el té en bolsitas *f* | 86 las trufas de chocolate *m* |
| refinado) | – *tea bag* | – *truffle* |
| – *refined sugar in crystals* | 69 el molinillo eléctrico de café *m* | 87 el agua *f* de mesa *f* (agua *f* de |
| 56-59 las bebidas alcohólicas (los | – *electric coffee grinder* | Seltz, agua *f* carbónica, agua |
| licores) | 70 la tostadora de café *m* | mineral) |
| – *spirits* | – *coffee roaster* | – *soda water* |
| | 71 el bombo para tostar el café | |
| | – *roasting drum* | |

186

1-95 **el supermercado,** una tienda de
alimentación *f* de autoservicio *m*
- **supermarket,** *a self-service food
store*
1 el carro para las compras
- *shopping trolley*
2 el cliente (el comprador)
- *customer*
3 la bolsa de la compra
- *shopping bag*
4 la entrada al local de venta *f*
- *entrance to the sales area*
5 la barrera
- *barrier*
6 la señal prohibiendo la entrada a
los perros
- *sign (notice) banning dogs*
7 los perros atados
- *dogs tied by their leads*
8 el cesto de ventas *f*
- *basket*
9 **la sección de los productos de
panadería** *f* **y confitería** *f*
- **bread and cake counter** *(bread
counter, cake counter)*
10 el expositor
- *display counter for bread and cakes*
11 las variedades de pan *m*
- *kinds of bread (breads)*
12 los panecillos (los bollos de
pan *m*)
- *rolls*
13 los cuernos (las medias lunas, los
croissants)
- *croissants (crescent rolls,* Am.
*crescents)*
14 el pan casero (el pan cateto, la
hogaza)
- *round loaf (strong rye bread)*

15 la tarta
- *gateau*
16 la rosquilla grande [desconocida
en España]
- *pretzel [made with yeast dough]*
17 la vendedora
- *shop assistant (*Am. *salesgirl,
saleslady)*
18 la clienta (la compradora)
- *customer*
19 el cartel de las ofertas
- *sign listing goods*
20 la tarta de frutas *f*
- *fruit flan*
21 el bizcocho
- *slab cake*
22 el pastel de molde *m*
- *ring cake*
23 **la góndola de los cosméticos,** una
góndola (una estantería)
- **cosmetics gondola,** *a gondola (sales
shelves)*
24 el baldaquín
- *canopy*
25 el estante de las medias
- *hosiery shelf*
26 la bolsa de medias *f*
- *stockings pack (nylons pack)*
27-35 **los productos para el aseo
personal** (los cosméticos)
- **toiletries** *(cosmetics)*
27 el tarro de crema *f* (la crema;
clases: crema *f* hidratante, crema *f*
de día *m*, crema *f* de noche *f*,
crema *f* para las manos)
- *jar of cream (kinds: moisturising
cream, day cream, night-care
cream, hand cream)*
28 el paquete de algodón *m* en rama *f*
- *packet of cotton wool*

29 la caja de polvos *m*
- *powder tin*
30 el paquete de tapones *m* de
algodón *m*
- *packet of cotton wool balls*
31 el tubo de pasta *f* dentífrica
- *toothpaste box*
32 el esmalte para las uñas
- *nail varnish (nail polish)*
33 el tubo de crema *f*
- *cream tube*
34 las sales de baño *m*
- *bath salts*
35 artículos *m* de higiene *f*
- *sanitary articles*
36-37 la comida para animales *m*
- *pet foods*
36 la comida completa para perros *m*
- *complete dog food*
37 el paquete de bizcochos *m* para
perros *m*
- *packet of dog biscuits*
38 el paquete de serrín *m* para
gatos *m*
- *bag of cat litter*
39 **la sección del queso** (la quesería)
- **cheese counter**
40 el pan (la rueda) de queso *m*
- *whole cheese*
41 el queso suizo (el queso
emmental) con agujeros *m*
- *Swiss cheese (Emmental cheese)
with holes*
42 el queso de bola *f* (el queso
holandés), un queso redondo
- *Edam cheese, a round cheese*
43 la góndola (la estantería) de
productos *m* lecheros
- *gondola for dairy products*

44 la leche (la leche de larga
   duración f, la leche pasteurizada y
   homogeneizada)
 – long-life milk (milk with good
   keeping properties, pasteurized and
   homogenized milk)
45 el cartón de leche f (el brik de
   leche f)
 – plastic milk bag
46 la crema (la nata)
 – cream
47 la mantequilla
 – butter
48 la margarina
 – margarine
49 la cajita de queso m
 – box of cheeses
50 el paquete (el cartón) de huevos m
 – box of eggs
51 la sección de la carne fresca
 – fresh meat counter (meat counter)
52 el jamón
 – ham on the bone
53 los productos cárnicos (la carne)
 – meat (meat products)
54 los embutidos
 – sausages
55 la salchicha (la longaniza)
 – ring of pork sausage
56 la morcilla (Col. y Mé.: la rellena)
 – ring of blood sausage
57 el congelador
 – freezer
58-61 los productos congelados
 – frozen food
58 la pularda (la gallina cebada)
 – poulard
59 el muslo de pavo m
 – turkey leg (drumstick)

60 la gallina para caldo m
 – boiling fowl
61 las verduras congeladas
 – frozen vegetables
62 la góndola de productos m de
   pastelería f y de alimentos m
 – gondola for baking ingredients and
   cereal products
63 la harina de trigo m
 – wheat flour
64 el pilón de azúcar m y f
 – sugar loaf
65 el paquete de pastas para sopas f
 – packet of noodles [for soup]
66 el aceite de mesa f
 – salad oil
67 el paquete de especias f
 – packet of spice
68-70 los estimulantes
 – tea, coffee, etc.
68 el café
 – coffee
69 el paquete de té m
 – packet of tea
70 el café soluble (el café
   instantáneo)
 – instant coffee
71 la góndola (la estantería) de las
   bebidas
 – drinks gondola
72 el paquete de cerveza f
 – beer crate (crate of beer)
73 la lata de cerveza f (la cerveza en
   lata f)
 – can of beer (canned beer)
74 la botella de zumo m de frutas f
 – bottle of fruit juice (bottled fruit
   juice)
75 la lata de zumo m de frutas f
 – can of fruit juice (canned fruit juice)

76 la botella de vino m
 – bottle of wine
77 la botella de chianti m
 – bottle of Chianti
78 la botella de vino m espumoso
 – bottle of champagne
79 la salida de urgencia f
 – emergency exit
80 la sección de verduras f y frutas f
 – fruit and vegetable counter
81 la caja de las verduras
 – vegetable basket
82 los tomates
 – tomatoes
83 los pepinos
 – cucumbers
84 la coliflor
 – cauliflower
85 la piña tropical
 – pineapple
86 las manzanas
 – apples
87 las peras
 – pears
88 la balanza (el peso)
 – scales for weighing fruit
89 las uvas
 – grapes (bunches of grapes)
90 los plátanos (las bananas)
 – bananas
91 las latas de conservas f
 – can
92 la caja
 – checkout
93 la caja registradora
 – cash register
94 la cajera
 – cashier
95 la cadena
 – chain

1-68  el taller de zapatero *m* (la zapatería)
–  *shoemaker's workshop (bootmaker's workshop)*
1  los zapatos arreglados
–  *finished (repaired) shoes*
2  la máquina de pespuntear
–  *auto-soling machine*
3  la máquina pulidora
–  *finishing machine*
4  la fresa para el tacón
–  *heel trimmer*
5  las fresas de recambio *m*
–  *sole trimmer*
6  la muela
–  *scouring wheel*
7  el disco de pulimentar
–  *naum keag*
8  la propulsión
–  *drive unit (drive wheel)*
9  el pulsador de corte *m*
–  *iron*
10  el disco de paño *m*
–  *buffing wheel*
11  el cepillo para pulir
–  *polishing brush*
12  el cepillo de cerdas *f*
–  *horsehair brush*
13  la rejilla de aspiración *f*
–  *extractor grid*
14  la prensa automática para las suelas
–  *automatic sole press*

15  las hormas
–  *press attachment*
16  la almohadilla de prensa *f*
–  *pad*
17  el arco de prueba *f*
–  *press bar*
18  el aparato para ensanchar (la máquina de ahormar, la horma)
–  *stretching machine*
19  el dispositivo para regular la anchura
–  *width adjustment*
20  el dispositivo para regular el largo
–  *length adjustment*
21  la máquina de coser
–  *stitching machine*
22  el dispositivo para regular la tensión del hilo
–  *power regulator (power control)*
23  la barra para la aguja
–  *foot*
24  el volante
–  *handwheel*
25  el pie prensatelas
–  *arm*
26  la máquina para montar las suelas
–  *sole stitcher (sole-stitching machine)*
27  la palanca del pie
–  *foot bar lever*
28  el reglaje de avance *m*
–  *feed adjustment (feed setting)*
29  la bobina de hilo *m*
–  *bobbin (cotton bobbin)*

30  el guiahilos
–  *thread guide (yarn guide)*
31  el cuero para las suelas
–  *sole leather*
32  la horma
–  *[wooden] last*
33  la mesa de trabajo *m*
–  *workbench*
34  la horma de hierro *m*
–  *last*
35  el pulverizador de tinte *m*
–  *dye spray*
36  el estante del material
–  *shelves for materials*

37 el martillo de zapatero *m*
– *shoemaker's hammer*
38 las tenazas para el cuero
– *shoemaker's pliers (welt pincers)*
39 las cizallas para el cuero de las
suelas
– *sole-leather shears*
40 las tenazas pequeñas
– *small pincers (nippers)*
41 las tenazas gruesas
– *large pincers (nippers)*
42 las tijeras para cortar el cuero
superior
– *upper-leather shears*
43 las tijeras para el hilo
– *scissors*
44 los alicates sacabocados
– *revolving punch (rotary punch)*
45 el sacabocados
– *punch*
46 el sacabocados de asa *f*
– *punch with handle*
47 el sacaclavos
– *nail puller*
48 el desvirador
– *welt cutter*
49 la lima de zapatero *m*
– *shoemaker's rasp*
50 el cuchillo de zapatero *m* (el
tranchete de zapatero *m*)
– *cobbler's knife (shoemaker's knife)*
51 el tranchete cortante
– *skiving knife (skife knife, paring
knife)*

52 las pinzas desmochadas (las
pinzas con las puntas cortadas)
– *toecap remover*
53 la máquina para colocar a
presión *f* ojetes *m*, corchetes *m* y
botones *m*
– *eyelet, hook, and press-stud setter*
54 la horma de trabajo *m*
– *stand with iron lasts*
55 la horma tensora
– *width-setting tree*
56 el puño con punzón *m*
– *nail grip*
57 la bota
– *boot*
58 la puntera
– *toecap*
59 el contrafuerte
– *counter*
60 la pala (la empella)
– *vamp*
61 la parte lateral (la caña)
– *quarter*
62 el corchete
– *hook*
63 el ojete
– *eyelet*
64 el cordón
– *lace (shoelace, bootlace)*
65 la lengüeta; *anál.:* la oreja del
zapato
– *tongue*
66 la suela (la planta)
– *sole*

67 el tacón
– *heel*
68 el arqueo (el enfranque)
– *shank (waist)*

1 la bota de invierno *m*
– *winter boot*
2 la suela de PVC (la suela de materia *f* plástica)
– *PVC sole;* sim.: *plastic sole*
3 el forro de peluche *m* (de felpa *f*)
– *high-pile lining*
4 el nylon
– *nylon*
5 el botín de caballero *m*
– *men's boot*
6 el cierre de cremallera *f* en el interior
– *inside zip*
7 la bota alta para caballeros *m*
– *men's high leg boot*
8 la suela de plataforma *f*
– *platform sole (platform)*
9 las botas vaqueras
– *Western boot (cowboy boot)*
10 la bota de piel *f* de potro *m*
– *pony-skin boot*
11 la suela moldeada sobre la piel
– *cemented sole*
12 la bota de señora *f*
– *ladies' boot*
13 la bota de calle *f* de caballero *m*
– *men's high leg boot*
14 la bota de PVC inyectado sin costuras *f* para la lluvia
– *seamless PVC waterproof wellington boot*
15 la suela translúcida
– *natural-colour* (Am. *natural-color*) *sole*
16 la puntera de la bota
– *toecap*
17 el forro de tejido *m* de punto *m*
– *tricot lining (knitwear lining)*
18 la bota de marcha *f* (para excursiones *f*)
– *hiking boot*
19 la suela perfilada
– *grip sole*
20 el alto de la caña relleno
– *padded collar*
21 los cordones
– *tie fastening (lace fastening)*
22 las zapatillas de baño *m*
– *open-toe mule*
23 la parte superior (la pala) de tejido *m* de rizo *m*
– *terry upper*
24 la suela corrida
– *polo outsole*
25 las babuchas (las pantuflas)
– *mule*
26 la pala de pana *f* de canutillo *m*
– *corduroy upper*
27 el zapato de tacón *m* alto con hebillas *f*
– *evening sandal (sandal court shoe)*
28 el tacón alto (el tacón aguja)
– *high heel (stiletto heel)*
29 el zapato de tacón *m*
– *court shoe* (Am. *pump*)
30 el mocasín
– *moccasin*
31 el zapato bajo (el zapato de cordones *m*)
– *shoe, a tie shoe (laced shoe, Oxford shoe,* Am. *Oxford)*
32 la lengüeta
– *tongue*
33 el zapato bajo con tacón *m* alto
– *high-heeled shoe (shoe with raised heel)*

34 el mocasín
– *casual*
35 la zapatilla de deporte *m*
– *trainer (training shoe)*
36 la zapatilla de tenis *m*
– *tennis shoe*
37 el contrafuerte
– *counter (stiffening)*
38 la suela de caucho *m* translúcido
– *natural-colour* (Am. *natural-color*) *rubber sole*
39 el calzado de trabajo *m*
– *heavy-duty boot* (Am. *stogy, stogie*)
40 la puntera reforzada
– *toecap*
41 la zapatilla de casa *f* (la pantufla)
– *slipper*
42 el patín de lana *f*
– *woollen* (Am. *woolen*) *slip sock*
43 el modelo de punto *m*
– *knit stitch (knit)*
44 el zueco
– *clog*
45 la suela de madera *f*
– *wooden sole*
46 la pala de cuero *m* flexible
– *soft-leather upper*
47 la suela de materia *f* plástica
– *sabot*
48 la sandalia de tirilla *f* (un calzado de playa *f*)
– *toe post sandal*
49 la sandalia
– *ladies' sandal*
50 la plantilla ortopédica
– *surgical footbed (sock)*
51 la sandalia frailuna
– *sandal*
52 la hebilla
– *shoe buckle (buckle)*
53 el zapato de tacón *m* alto con presilla *f*
– *sling-back court shoe (* Am. *sling pump)*
54 el zapato de tela *f* con tacón *m* alto
– *fabric court shoe*
55 el tacón de cuña *f*
– *wedge heel*
56 la bota de marcha *f* para niños *m*
– *baby's first walking boot*

1 el pespunte
- *backstitch seam*
2 el punto de cadeneta *f*
- *chain stitch*
3 el punto de adorno *m* (el punto de fantasía *f*)
- *ornamental stitch*
4 el punto de tallo *m*
- *stem stitch*
5 el punto de cruz *f*
- *cross stitch*
6 el punto de festón *m* (el festón de uña *f*)
- *buttonhole stitch (button stitch)*
7 el punto de espiga *f*
- *fishbone stitch*
8 el punto de cordón *m*
- *overcast stitch*
9 el punto de escapulario *m* (el punto de arista *f*)
- *herringbone stitch (Russian stitch, Russian cross stitch)*
10 el bordado plano
- *satin stitch (flat stitch)*
11 el bordado inglés
- *eyelet embroidery (broderie anglaise)*
12 el punzón para bordado *m* inglés
- *stiletto*
13 el punto de nudos *m*
- *French knot (French dot, knotted stitch, twisted knot stitch)*

14 la vainica (el calado)
- *hem stitch work*
15 el bordado de tul *m* (la puntilla de tul *m*)
- *tulle work (tulle lace)*
16 el fondo de tul *m*
- *tulle background (net background)*
17 el punto de zurcidura *f*
- *darning stitch*
18 el encaje de bolillos *m; especiali-dades:* puntillas *f* de Valenciennes y de Bruselas
- *pillow lace (bobbin lace, bone lace);* kinds: *Valenciennes, Brussels lace*
19 el trabajo con lanzadera *f* (el encaje con lanzadera *f*)
- *tatting*
20 la lanzadera
- *tatting shuttle (shuttle)*
21 el macramé
- *knotted work (macramé)*
22 la malla (la red)
- *filet (netting)*
23 el nudo de la malla
- *netting loop*
24 el hilo de la malla
- *netting thread*
25 la varilla de la malla
- *mesh pin (mesh gauge)*
26 la lanzadera para malla *f*
- *netting needle*
27 el deshilado (el calado)
- *open work*
28 el trabajo con horquillas *f*
- *gimping (hairpin work)*

29 la horquilla
- *gimping needle (hairpin)*
30 los encajes (las puntillas); *especialidades:* encajes *m* de Reticella, de Venecia, de Alençon; *anál.:* la filigrana (con hilo *m* de metal *m*)
- *needlepoint lace (point lace, needlepoint);* kinds: *reticella lace, Venetian lace, Alençon lace;* sim. with metal thread: *filigree work*
31 el bordado con cintas *f*
- *braid embroidery (braid work)*

**1-27 el taller de la modista**
- *dressmaker's workroom*
**1** la modista
- *dressmaker*
**2** la cinta métrica, un metro
- *tape measure (measuring tape),*
  *a metre* (Am. *meter) tape*
  *measure*
**3** las tijeras de corte *m*
- *cutting shears*
**4** la mesa de corte *m*
- *cutting table*
**5** el vestido modelo
- *model dress*
**6** el maniquí
- *dressmaker's model*
  *(dressmaker's dummy, dress*
  *form)*
**7** el abrigo modelo
- *model coat*
**8** la máquina de coser de
  modista *f*
- *sewing machine*
**9** el motor de impulsión *f*
- *drive motor*
**10** la correa de transmisión *f*
- *drive belt*
**11** el pedal
- *treadle*

**12** el hilo de la máquina de coser
  (una bobina de hilo *m*)
- *sewing machine cotton (sewing*
  *machine thread) (bobbin)*
**13** el patrón de corte *m*
- *cutting template*
**14** la cinta de costura *f* (la cinta
  para los extremos)
- *seam binding*
**15** la caja de los botones
- *button box*
**16** el resto (el retal) de tela *f*
- *remnant*
**17** el perchero de pie *m* móvil
- *movable clothes rack*
**18** la mesa (la superficie) de
  planchado *m*
- *hand-iron press*
**19** la planchadora
- *presser (ironer)*
**20** la plancha de vapor *m*
- *steam iron*
**21** el tubo de alimentación *f* del
  agua *f*
- *water feed pipe*
**22** el depósito del agua *f*
- *water container*
**23** la superficie de planchado *m*
  inclinable
- *adjustable-tilt ironing surface*

**24** el mecanismo de suspensión *f*
  de la plancha
- *lift device for the iron*
**25** el recipiente de aspiración *f*
  para el vapor
- *steam extractor*
**26** el pedal de aspiración *f*
- *foot switch controlling steam*
  *extraction*
**27** el tejido de lana *f* planchado
- *pressed non-woven woollen* (Am.
  *woolen) fabric*

**1-32 el taller del sastre**
- *tailor's workroom*
1 el espejo triple
- *triple mirror*
2 los cortes de tejido *m*
- *lengths of material*
3 el tejido para trajes *m*
- *suiting*
4 la revista de moda *f*
- *fashion journal (fashion magazine)*
5 el cenicero
- *ashtray*
6 el catálogo de moda *f*
- *fashion catalogue*
7 la mesa de trabajo *m*
- *workbench*
8 la estantería de pared *f*
- *wall shelves (wall shelf unit)*
9 la bobina (el carrete) de hilo *m* para coser
- *cotton reel*
10 la bobina de seda *f* para coser
- *small reels of sewing silk*
11 las tijeras de mano *m*
- *hand shears*
12 la máquina de coser combinada, eléctrica y de pedal *m*
- *combined electric and treadle sewing machine*

13 el pedal
- *treadle*
14 el guardafaldas (la pieza de protección *f*)
- *dress guard*
15 la rueda volante (el volante)
- *band wheel*
16 el rebobinador del hilo (el dispositivo para encanrillar)
- *bobbin thread*
17 la mesa de la máquina de coser
- *sewing machine table*
18 el cajón de la máquina de coser
- *sewing machine drawer*
19 la cinta para los extremos (la cinta de extrafort *m*)
- *seam binding*
20 la almohadilla para clavar los alfileres (el alfiletero, el acerico)
- *pincushion*
21 la acción de marcar
- *marking out*
22 el sastre
- *tailor*
23 el cojín de molde *m*
- *shaping pad*
24 la tiza de sastre *m* (el jaboncillo de sastre *m*)
- *tailor's chalk (French chalk)*

25 la pieza
- *workpiece*
26 la mesa de planchar al vapor
- *steam press (steam pressing unit)*
27 el brazo orientable
- *swivel arm*
28 la tabla para planchar las mangas
- *pressing cushion (pressing pad)*
29 la plancha
- *iron*
30 la manopla para planchar
- *hand-ironing pad*
31 el cepillo de la ropa
- *clothes brush*
32 el paño de planchar
- *pressing cloth*

**1-39 el salón de peluquería *f* de señoras *f* (el instituto de belleza *f*), un salón de cosmética *f***
– *ladies' hairdressing salon and beauty salon* (Am. *beauty parlor, beauty shop*)
**1-16 los utensilios de peluquería *f***
– *hairdresser's tools*
**1** la escudilla para el agente (el producto) de decoloración *f*
– *bowl containing bleach*
**2** el cepillo para desenredar los cabellos
– *detangling brush*
**3** el tubo del producto de decoloración *f* (el producto para teñir los cabellos)
– *bleach tube*
**4** el rizador (el bigudí) del tinte
– *curler [used in dyeing]*
**5** las tenacillas de rizar
– *curling tongs (curling iron)*
**6** la peineta
– *comb (back comb, side comb)*
**7** las tijeras para cortar el cabello
– *haircutting scissors*
**8** las tijeras de aclarar el cabello
– *thinning scissors* (Am. *thinning shears)*
**9** la cuchilla para aclarar (entresacar) el cabello
– *thinning razor*
**10** el cepillo para el cabello
– *hairbrush*
**11** la pinza para el cabello
– *hair clip*

**12** el rulo (el rizador, el bigudí)
– *roller*
**13** el cepillo para ondular los cabellos
– *curl brush*
**14** la pinza para rizar el cabello
– *curl clip*
**15** el peine de tocador *m*
– *dressing comb*
**16** el cepillo de púas *f*
– *stiff-bristle brush*
**17** el sillón de peluquería *f* regulable
– *adjustable hairdresser's chair*
**18** el reposapiés
– *footrest*
**19** el tocador
– *dressing table*
**20** el espejo de peluquería *f* (la luna)
– *salon mirror (mirror)*
**21** la máquina eléctrica para cortar el pelo
– *electric clippers*
**22** el peine secapelos eléctrico (el secador eléctrico)
– *warm-air comb*
**23** el espejo de mano *m*
– *hand mirror (hand glass)*
**24** el fijador para el cabello (la laca para el cabello)
– *hair spray (hair-fixing spray)*
**25** el casco secador, un casco de brazo *m* orientable
– *drier, a swivel-mounted drier*
**26** el brazo orientable del casco
– *swivel arm of the drier*

**27** el pie (el pedestal) de disco *m*
– *round base*
**28** la instalación de lavado *m*
– *shampoo unit*
**29** el lavabo para los cabellos
– *shampoo basin*
**30** la ducha de mano *m*
– *hand spray (shampoo spray)*
**31** la mesita de servicio *m*
– *service tray*
**32** la botella de champú *m*
– *shampoo bottle*
**33** el secador
– *hair drier, a hand-held hair drier (hand hair drier)*
**34** el peinador
– *cape (gown)*
**35** la peluquera
– *hairdresser*
**36** el frasco de perfume *m*
– *perfume bottle*
**37** el frasco con agua *f* de olor *m*
– *bottle of toilet water*
**38** la peluca
– *wig*
**39** la cabeza para la peluca (el portapelucas)
– *wig block*

**1-42 el salón de peluquería *f* de caballeros *m***
- *men's salon (men's hairdressing salon, barber's shop,* Am. *barbershop)*
1 el peluquero (el maestro peluquero)
- *hairdresser (barber)*
2 la bata (la blusa) de trabajo *m* (la blusa de peluquero *m*)
- *overalls (hairdresser's overalls)*
3 el peinado (el corte del cabello)
- *hairstyle (haircut)*
4 el peinador
- *cape (gown)*
5 el cuello de papel *m*
- *paper towel*
6 el espejo de peluquería *f* (la luna)
- *salon mirror (mirror)*
7 el espejo de mano *f*
- *hand mirror (hand glass)*
8 la lámpara de peluquería *f*
- *light*
9 el agua *f* de olor *m* (agua *f* de Colonia)
- *toilet water*
10 la loción capilar (el tónico capilar)
- *hair tonic*
11 la instalación para lavar el cabello (el lavabo)
- *shampoo unit*
12 el lavamanos
- *shampoo basin*
13 la ducha de mano *f*
- *hand spray (shampoo spray)*
14 la grifería mezcladora
- *mixer tap (Am. mixing faucet)*
15 la toma de corriente *f* para el enchufe del secador
- *sockets, e.g. for hair drier*

16 el sillón de peluquería *f* regulable
- *adjustable hairdresser's chair (barber's chair)*
17 la barra de regulación *f* (la barra de ajuste *m*)
- *height-adjuster bar (height adjuster)*
18 el brazo del sillón
- *armrest*
19 el descansapiés
- *footrest*
20 el champú
- *shampoo*
21 el pulverizador de perfume *m*
- *perfume spray*
22 el secador del pelo
- *hair drier, a hand-held hair drier (hand hair drier)*
23 el fijador para el pelo (la laca) en un bote pulverizador
- *setting lotion in a spray can*
24 la toallas para secar el pelo
- *hand towels for drying hair*
25 las toallas pequeñas para compresas *f* faciales
- *towels for face compresses*
26 el rizador para el pelo (la plancha para cardar el pelo)
- *crimping iron*
27 el cepillo para el cuello
- *neck brush*
28 el peine de peluquero *m*
- *dressing comb*
29 el peine de aire *m* caliente
- *warm-air comb*
30 el cepillo de aire *m* caliente
- *warm-air brush*
31 el rizador para el pelo (el moldeador)
- *curling tongs (hair curler, curling iron)*

32 la maquinilla eléctrica para cortar el pelo
- *electric clippers*
33 las tijeras de aclarar (entresacar) el pelo
- *thinning scissors (Am. thinning shears)*
34 las tijeras para cortar el pelo; *anál:* las tijeras de esculpir
- *haircutting scissors; sim.: styling scissors*
35 la hoja de las tijerras
- *scissor-blade*
36 el eje (el clavillo)
- *pivot*
37 el mango
- *handle*
38 la navaja de afeitar (la navaja barbera; *P. Rico y S. Dgo.:* la jusilla)
- *open razor (straight razor)*
39 el mango de la navaja
- *razor handle*
40 la hoja de afeitar (el filo de la navaja de afeitar
- *edge (cutting edge, razor's edge, razor's cutting edge)*
41 la navaja de aclarar (entresacar) el pelo
- *thinning razor*
42 el diploma de maestría (el diploma de maestro *m* peluquero)
- *diploma*

1 la caja de puros *m* (de cigarros *m* puros)
– *cigar box*
2 el puro (el cigarro puro); *clases:* el habano, el puro canario, el puro de Brasil, el puro de Sumatra
– *cigar; kinds: Havana cigar (Havana), Brazilian cigar, Sumatra cigar*
3 el entreacto (el bocadito)
– *cigarillo*
4 la señorita (un purito)
– *cheroot*
5 la capa
– *wrapper*
6 la sobretripa (el capillo)
– *binder*
7 la tripa
– *filler*
8 la cigarrera (la petaca de puros *m*)
– *cigar case*
9 el cortapuros (el cortacigarros)
– *cigar cutter*
10 la pitillera (*Amér.:* la petaca)
– *cigarette case*
11 el paquete (la cajetilla) de cigarros *m* (de cigarrillos *m*)
– *cigarette packet* (Am. *pack*)
12 el cigarro (el cigarrillo, el pitillo; *P. Rico y S. Dgo.:* el túbano), un cigarro con filtro *m* (un cigarro emboquillado)
– *cigarette, a filter-tipped cigarette*
13 el filtro (la boquilla); *clases:* dorado, de corcho *m*, blanco
– *cigarette tip;* kinds: *cork tip, gold tip*
14 el cigarrillo ruso
– *Russian cigarette*
15 la maquinilla para liar cigarros *m*
– *cigarette roller*
16 la boquilla
– *cigarette holder*
17 el librillo (el cuaderno) de papel *m* de fumar
– *packet of cigarette papers*
18 el andullo (la hoja larga de tabaco *m* arrollada)
– *pigtail (twist of tobacco)*

19 el tabaco para mascar; un pedazo de tabaco *m* para mascar, una mascada (una mascadura de tabaco *m*)
– *chewing tobacco;* a piece: *plug (quid, chew)*
20 la cajita (la tabaquera) con rapé (con tabaco *m* en polvo *m*)
– *snuff box, containing snuff*
21 la caja de cerillas *f* (de mixtos *m*, de fósforos *m*)
– *matchbox*
22 la cerilla (el mixto, el fósforo; *Bol.:* la pajuela)
– *match*
23 la cabeza de la cerilla
– *head (match head)*
24 el raspador (el frotador)
– *striking surface*
25 el paquete de tabaco *m; clases:* picadura *f* fina, picadura *f* entrefina
– *packet of tobacco;* kinds: *fine cut, shag, navy plug*
26 el sello (la precinta) de impuestos (el timbre fiscal) [*en España:* el sello (el timbre) de la Tabacalera]
– *revenue stamp*
27 el encendedor (el mechero) de gasolina *f* (*Amér.:* el quemador)
– *petrol cigarette lighter (petrol lighter)*
28 la piedra
– *flint*
29 la mecha
– *wick*
30 el encendedor (el mechero) de gas *m*, un encendedor no recargable
– *gas cigarette lighter (gas lighter),* a *disposable lighter*
31 el regulador de la llama
– *flame regulator*
32 el chibuqui
– *chibonk (chibonque)*
33 la pipa (la cachimba) corta (*Amér.:* la churumbela; *Hond.:* la faifa; *Arg., Bol., Chile y Urug.:* el pito)
– *short pipe*

34 la pipa de barro *m*
– *clay pipe (Dutch pipe)*
35 la pipa larga
– *long pipe*
36 la cazoleta
– *pipe bowl (bowl)*
37 la tapa de la cazoleta (la tapadera de la pipa)
– *bowl lid*
38 el tubo de la pipa
– *pipe stem (stem)*
39 la pipa de madera *f* de brezo *m*
– *briar pipe*
40 la boquilla de la pipa
– *mouthpiece*
41 el brezo veteado (abrillantado con arena *f* o pulido)
– *sand-blast finished or polished briar grain*
42 el narguile, una pipa de agua *f*
– *hookah (narghile, narghileh),* a *water pipe*
43 la bolsa tabaquera (la petaca)
– *tobacco pouch*
44 el equipo de fumador *m*
– *smoker's companion*
45 el raspador
– *pipe scraper*
46 el limpiador de la pipa (el mondapipas)
– *pipe cleaner*
47 el prensador
– *tobacco presser*
48 la escobilla para limpiar la pipa
– *pipe cleaner*

1 el laminador para alambre *m* y chapa *f*
– *wire and sheet roller*
2 el banco de estirar
– *drawbench (drawing bench)*
3 el alambre (alambre *m* de oro *m* o de plata *f*)
– *wire, e.g. gold or silver wire*
4 el berbiquí de vaivén *m*
– *archimedes drill (drill)*
5 la traviesa (la empuñadura)
– *crossbar*
6 la taladradora eléctrica
– *suspended (pendant) electric drilling machine*
7 la fresa esférica
– *spherical cutter (cherry)*
8 el hornillo de fusión *f*
– *melting pot*
9 la tapadera (el crisol)
– *fireclay top*
10 el crisol de grafito *m*
– *graphite crucible*
11 las tenazas para el crisol
– *crucible tongs*
12 la sierra de arco *m*
– *piercing saw (jig saw)*
13 la hoja de sierra *f* de marquetería *f*
– *piercing saw blade*
14 el soplete
– *soldering gun*
15 la terraja
– *thread tapper*
16 el soplete de cilindro *m*
– *blast burner (blast lamp) for soldering*
17 el orfebre
– *goldsmith*

18 el dado de embutir
– *swage block*
19 el punzón
– *punch*
20 el tablero de trabajo *m* (el obrador)
– *workbench (bench)*
21 el tapete de piel *m*
– *bench apron*
22 la astillera [un soporte de madera *f* para limar]
– *needle file*
23 las tijeras para chapa *f*
– *metal shears*
24 la máquina de alianzas *f*
– *wedding ring sizing machine*
25 la lastra de medidas *f*
– *ring gauge (Am. gage)*
26 la lastra de ajuste *m*
– *ring-rounding tool*
27 el sortijero (la anillera)
– *ring gauge (Am. gage)*
28 la escuadra de acero *m*
– *steel set-square*
29 la almohadilla de cuero *m*
– *leather pad*
30 la caja de punzones *m*
– *box of punches*
31 el punzón
– *punch*
32 el imán
– *magnet*
33 la escobilla de mesa *f*
– *bench brush*
34 la bola para grabar
– *engraving ball (joint vice, clamp)*
35 la balanza para el oro y la plata, una balanza de precisión *f*
– *gold and silver balance (assay balance), a precision balance*

36 el líquido para soldar
– *soldering flux (flux)*
37 la placa incandescente, de carbón *m* vegetal
– *charcoal block*
38 la varilla de soldar
– *stick of solder*
39 el bórax
– *soldering borax*
40 el martillo de modelar
– *shaping hammer*
41 el martillo para cincelar
– *chasing (enchasing) hammer*
42 la pulidora (la alisadora)
– *polishing and burnishing machine*
43 el ventilador de mesa *f* (el aspirador de polvo *m* de mesa *f*)
– *dust exhauster (vacuum cleaner)*
44 la brocha de pulir
– *polishing wheel*
45 la caja colectora del polvo
– *dust collector (dust catcher)*
46 la máquina para pulir en líquido *m*
– *buffing machine*
47 la lima redonda
– *round file*
48 la hematites roja (el bruñidor)
– *bloodstone (haematite, hematite)*
49 la lima plana
– *flat file*
50 el mango de la lima
– *file handle*
51 el pulidor
– *polishing iron (burnisher)*

1 el relojero
- *watchmaker;* also: *clockmaker*
2 la mesa de trabajo *m*
- *workbench*
3 el reposabrazo
- *armrest*
4 el distribuidor de aceite *m*
- *oiler*
5 la aceitera para relojes *m* pequeños
- *oil stand*
6 el juego de destornilladores *m*
- *set of screwdrivers*
7 el yunque para las agujas
- *clockmaker's anvil*
8 la lezna plana, un escariador
- *broach, a reamer*
9 el instrumento para colocar y quitar los resortes
- *spring pin tool*
10 la manecilla para el reloj de pulsera *m*
- *hand-removing tool*
11 el instrumento para abrir y cerrar la caja del reloj
- *watchglass-fitting tool*
12 la lámpara de trabajo *m*, una lámpara de varios usos *m*
- *workbench lamp, a multi-purpose lamp*
13 el motor de varios usos *m*
- *multi-purpose motor*
14 las pinzas
- *tweezers*

15 los accesorios de la máquina de pulir
- *polishing machine attachments*
16 el mandril de mano *m*
- *pin vice (pin holder)*
17 la máquina para enrollar, pulir, redondear y acortar los ejes
- *burnisher, for burnishing, polishing, and shortening of spindles*
18 el pincel para el polvo
- *dust brush*
19 el cortador para los brazaletes metálicos
- *cutter for metal watch straps*
20 el torno de relojero *m* (el torno para mecánica *f* de precisión *f*)
- *watchmaker's lathe, a precision bench lathe*
21 la contramarcha de la correa trapezoidal
- *drive-belt gear*
22 la mesita de taller *m* para las piezas de repuesto *m*
- *workshop trolley for spare parts*
23 la máquina de limpiar mediante vibraciones *f*
- *ultrasonic cleaner*
24 el aparato giratorio para comprobar los relojes automáticos
- *rotating watch-testing machine for automatic watches*
25 el pupitre de medida para comprobar los componentes electrónicos
- *watch-timing machine for electronic components*

26 el aparato para comprobar la impermeabilidad de los relojes
- *testing device for waterproof watches*
27 el cronocomparador
- *electronic timing machine*
28 el torno de banco *m*
- *vice (*Am. *vise)*
29 el dispositivo de ajuste *m* para armar (colocar) los cristales de los relojes
- *watchglass-fitting tool for armoured (*Am. *armored) glasses*
30 la máquina automática para la limpieza convencional
- *[automatic] cleaning machine for conventional cleaning*
31 el reloj de cuco *m* (reloj *m* de la Selva Negra)
- *cuckoo clock, a Black Forest clock*
32 el reloj de pared *f* (el regulador)
- *wall clock, a regulator*
33 el péndulo compensador
- *compensation pendulum*
34 el reloj de cocina *f*
- *kitchen clock*
35 el cuentaminutos (el avisador)
- *timer*

1 el reloj de pulsera *f* electrónico
– *electronic wristwatch*
2 el registro digital (numérico) (un
registro con diodos *m* luminosos;
*también:* el registro de cristal
líquido)
– *digital readout, a light-emitting
diode (LED) readout; also: liquid
crystal readout*
3 el pulsador para las horas y los
minutos
– *hour and minute button*
4 el pulsador para la fecha y los
segundos
– *date and second button*
5 la pulsera (el brazalete)
– *strap (watch strap)*
6 el principio del diapasón (el
principio del reloj de diapasón *m*)
– *tuning fork principle (principle of
the tuning fork watch)*
7 la fuente de impulsión *f* (una pila
de botón *m*)
– *power source (battery cell)*
8 el circuito electrónico
– *transformer*
9 el elemento del diapasón (el
elemento oscilante)
– *tuning fork element (oscillating
element)*
10 la rueda con trinquetes *m*
– *wheel ratchet*
11 el engranaje
– *wheels*
12 la aguja grande (la aguja de los
minutos, el minutero)
– *minute hand*
13 la aguja pequeña (la aguja de las
horas; *Bol. Ec. y Mé.:* el horero)
– *hour hand*
14 el principio del reloj de cuarzo *m*
electrónico
– *principle of the electronic quartz
watch*
15 el cuarzo (el cuarzo oscilante)
– *quartz*
16 la subdivisión de frecuencia *f*
(circuitos *m* integrados)
– *integrated circuit*
17 el motor paso a paso *m*
– *oscillation counter*
18 el descodificador
– *decoder*
19 el despertador (el reloj
despertador)
– *calendar clock (alarm clock)*
20 el registro (la lectura) digital
(numérico, -a) con cifras *f*
giratorias
– *digital display with flip-over
numerals*
21 el registro (la lectura) de los
segundos
– *second indicator*
22 el botón de parada *f*
– *stop button*
23 la rueda de ajuste *m*
– *forward and backward wind knob*
24 el reloj de antesala *f*
– *grandfather clock*
25 el cuadrante (la esfera; *Mé. y
Guat.:* la carátula)
– *face*
26 la caja del reloj
– *clock case*
27 el péndulo
– *pendulum*

28 la pesa de los toques (de las
campanadas)
– *striking weight*
29 la pesa de la marcha
– *time weight*
30 el reloj de sol *m*
– *sundial*
31 el reloj de arena *f* (la ampolleta)
– *hourglass (egg timer)*
32-43 **los componentes de salto *m* de
un reloj de pulsera *f* automático** (el
reloj con un mecanismo de
cuerda *f* automático)
– ***components of an automatic watch***
*(automatic wristwatch)*
32 la masa oscilante (el rotor)
– *weight (rotor)*
33 la piedra (la piedra de cojinete *m*),
un rubí sintético
– *stone (jewel, jewelled bearing), a
synthetic ruby*
34 el trinquete de ajuste *m* (de
sujeción *f*)
– *click*
35 la rueda de sujeción *f*
– *click wheel*
36 el mecanismo del reloj
– *clockwork (clockwork mechanism)*
37 la platina
– *bottom train plate*
38 el barrilete
– *spring barrel*
39 el volante
– *balance wheel*
40 la rueda de áncora *f*
– *escape wheel*
41 la rueda de la cuerda (la rueda de
corona *f*)
– *crown wheel*
42 la corona (la corona de la cuerda)
– *winding crown*
43 el mecanismo de impulsión *f*
– *drive mechanism*

1-19 **el local de venta** *f*
- *sales premises*
1-4 **la prueba de las gafas**
- *spectacle fitting*
1 el óptico
- *optician*
2 el cliente
- *customer*
3 la montura de prueba *f*
- *trial frame*
4 el espejo
- *mirror*
5 el estante de las monturas (la elección de montura *f*, la elección de gafas *f*)
- *stand with spectacle frames*
6 las gafas de sol *m*
- *sunglasses (sun spectacles)*
7 la montura metálica
- *metal frame*
8 la montura de carey *m* (la montura de pasta *f*)
- *tortoiseshell frame (shell frame)*
9 las gafas (*Amér.:* los anteojos)
- *spectacles (glasses)*
10-14 **la montura de las gafas**
- *spectacle frame*
10 la montura
- *fitting (mount) of the frame*
11 el puente
- *bridge*

12 la placa del puente
- *pad bridge*
13 la patilla
- *side*
14 la bisagra de la patilla
- *side joint*
15 el cristal de las gafas, un cristal bifocal (un cristal de doble foco *m*)
- *spectacle lens, a bifocal lens*
16 el espejo de mano *f*
- *hand mirror (hand glass)*
17 los gemelos (los prismáticos)
- *binoculars*
18 el tubo monocular (el anteojo, el catalejo)
- *monocular telescope (tube)*
19 el microscopio
- *microscope*

**20-47 el taller de óptico _m_**
- _optician's workshop_
**20** la mesa de trabajo _m_
- _workbench_
**21** el aparato para centrar
universal (el focómetro
universal)
- _universal centring (centering)_
_apparatus_
**22** el soporte de la ventosa de
centrado _m_
- _centring (centering) suction_
_holder_
**23** la ventosa de centrado _m_
-- _sucker_
**24** el aparato automático para
modelar los bordes de los
cristales de las gafas
- _edging machine_
**25** los cristales de molde _m_ para la
modelación automática de los
bordes (los cristales que se
utilizan como modelos _m_)
- _formers for the lens edging_
_machine_
**26** el cristal modelo _m_ colocado
en el aparato
- _inserted former_
**27** la copia de cristal a cristal _m_
- _rotating printer_
**28** el juego de piedras _f_ de afilar
(el conjunto de muelas _f_)
- _abrasive wheel combination_

**29** el aparato de mando _m_
- _control unit_
**30** la maquinaria (el mecanismo)
- _machine part_
**31** la llegada del agua _f_
refrigerante
- _cooling water pipe_
**32** el líquido de limpieza _f_
- _cleaning fluid_
**33** el focómetro de vértice _m_
- _focimeter (vertex refractiono-_
_meter)_
**34** el aparato de bloque _m_ de
metal _m_ para centrar y poner
ventosas _f_
- _metal-blocking device_
**35** el juego de muelas _f_ para dar
forma _f_ a los cristales
- _abrasive wheel combination and_
_forms of edging_
**36** la muela de desbaste _m_
- _roughing wheel for preliminary_
_surfacing_
**37** la muela de acabado _m_ para el
biselado de los cristales
positivos y negativos
- _fining lap for positive and_
_negative lens surfaces_
**38** la muela de acabado _m_ para el
biselado de los cristales
especiales y llanos
- _fining lap for special and flat_
_lenses_

**39** el cristal plano-cóncavo con
cara _f_ plana
- _plano-concave lens with a flat_
_surface_
**40** el cristal plano-cóncavo con
cara _f_ especial
- _plano-concave lens with a special_
_surface_
**41** el cristal cóncavo-convexo con
cara _f_ especial
- _concave and convex lens with a_
_special surface_
**42** el cristal cóncavo-convexo con
cara _f_ negativa
- _convex and concave lens with a_
_special surface_
**43** el sillón para el reconocimiento
oftalmológico
- _ophthalmic test stand_
**44** el foróptero con el oftalmómetro
y el refractómetro
- _phoropter with ophthalmometer_
_and optometer (refractometer)_
**45** la caja de los cristales de
prueba _f_
- _trial lens case_
**46** el soporte de proyección _f_ de
las letras
- _collimator_
**47** el proyector de la señal óptica
- _acuity projector_

1 el microscopio de laboratorio *m* e investigación *f*, sistema *m* Leitz [corte parcial]
– *laboratory and research microscope, Leitz system*
2 el soporte (la montura)
– *stand*
3 el pie
– *base*
4 el ajuste (el botón) grueso
– *coarse adjustment*
5 el ajuste (el botón) fino
– *fine adjustment*
6 la trayectoria de los rayos luminosos
– *illumination beam path (illumination path)*
7 la óptica de iluminación *f*
– *illumination optics*
8 el condensador
– *condenser*
9 el portaobjetos
– *microscope (microscopic, object) stage*
10 el portaobjetos cruzado
– *mechanical stage*
11 el revólver de objetivos *m* (el portaobjetivos)
– *objective turret (revolving nosepiece)*
12 el tubo binocular
– *binocular head*
13 los prismas de desviación *f*
– *beam-splitting prisms*
14 el microscopio de luz *f* transmitida con cámara *f* fotográfica y polarizador, sistema *m* Zeiss
– *transmitted-light microscope with camera and polarizer, Zeiss system*
15 la base del portaobjetos
– *stage base*
16 el cursor del diafragma de abertura *f*
– *aperture-stop slide*
17 el portaobjetos giratorio universal
– *universal stage*
18 el módulo portaobjetivos
– *lens panel*
19 el módulo de observación *f*
– *polarizing filter*
20 la parte de la cámara fotográfica
– *camera*
21 la pantalla de ajuste *m*
– *focusing screen*
22 la pieza de fijación *f* de los tubos de discusión *f*
– *discussion tube arrangement*
23 el microscopio de metalografía *f* de gran campo *m* visual, un microscopio de luz *f* reflejada
– *wide-field metallurgical microscope, a reflected-light microscope (microscope for reflected light)*
24 el cristal esmerilado de proyección *f*
– *matt screen (ground glass screen), projection screen)*
25 la cámara fotográfica de gran formato *m*
– *large-format camera*
26 la cámara fotográfica de pequeño formato *m*
– *miniature camera*
27 la plataforma de base *f* (el zócalo)
– *base plate*
28 la caja de la lámpara
– *lamphouse*
29 el portaobjetivos cruzado giratorio
– *mechanical stage*

30 el revólver de objetivos *m*
– *objective turret (revolving nosepiece)*
31 el microscopio quirúrgico
– *surgical microscope*
32 el soporte de columna *f*
– *pillar stand*
33 la iluminación del campo del objeto
– *field illumination*
34 el microscopio de microfoto-grafía *f*
– *photomicroscope*
35 el chasis de pequeño formato *m*
– *miniature film cassette*
36 la toma de foto *m* adicional para la cámara de gran formato *m* o de televisión *f*
– *photomicrographic camera attachment for large-format or television camera*
37 el comprobador de superficies *f*
– *surface-finish microscope*
38 el tubo de cortes *m* ópticos
– *light section tube*
39 el piñón (la rueda motriz)
– *rack and pinion*
40 el estereomicroscopio de gran campo *m* equipado con un zoom
– *zoom stereomicroscope*
41 el zoom
– *zoom lens*
42 el aparato para medir el polvo óptico
– *dust counter*
43 la cámara de medida *f*
– *measurement chamber*
44 la salida de los datos
– *data output*
45 la salida analógica
– *analogue (Am. analog) output*
46 el selector de la zona de medida *f*
– *measurement range selector*
47 el indicador de los datos numéricos (el indicador numérico)
– *digital display (digital readout)*
48 el refractómetro de inmersión *f*, para examen *m* de alimentos *m*
– *dipping refractometer for examining food*
49 el microscopio fotómetro
– *microscopic photometer*
50 la fuente de luz *f* del fotómetro
– *photometric light source*
51 el dispositivo de medida *f* (el fotomultiplicador)
– *measuring device, a photomultiplier (multiplier phototube)*
52 la fuente de luz *f* para la iluminación panorámica
– *light source for survey illumination*
53 el bloque electrónico
– *remote electronics*
54 el microscopio universal de gran campo *m*
– *universal wide-field microscope*
55 el adaptador para la cámara o para el accesorio de proyección *f*
– *adapter for camera or projector attachment*
56 el botón de ajuste *m* del ocular
– *eyepiece focusing knob*
57 el alojamiento del filtro
– *filter pick-up*
58 el soporte de apoyo *m*
– *handrest*
59 la lámpara para la luz reflejada
– *lamphouse for incident (vertical) illumination*

60 el enchufe de la lámpara para la luz transmitida
– *lamphouse connector for transillumination*
61 el estereomicroscopio de gran campo *m*
– *wide-field stereomicroscope*
62 los objetivos intercambiables
– *interchangeable lenses (objectives)*
63 la iluminación reflejada
– *incident (vertical) illumination (incident top lighting)*
64 la cámara de microscopio *m* completamente automática, una cámara fotográfica con adaptador *m*
– *fully automatic microscope camera, a camera with photomicro mount adapter*
65 la cajita de la película (del film) fotográfica(o)
– *film cassette*
66 el condensador universal del microscopio de investigación *f*
– *universal condenser for research microscope 1*
67 la cámara métrica universal para fotogrametría *f* (el fototeodolito)
– *universal-type measuring machine for photogrammetry (phototheodolite)*
68 la cámara de fotogrametría *f*
– *photogrammetric camera*
69 el nivelador de motor *m*, un nivelador compensador
– *motor-driven level, a compensator level*
70 el aparato electro-óptico para medir las distancias
– *electro-optical distance-measuring instrument*
71 la cámara de estereometría *f*
– *stereometric camera*
72 la base horizontal
– *horizontal base*
73 el teodolito universal
– *one-second theodolite*

1 el telescopio de espejo m de 2,2 m
- *2.2 m reflecting telescope (reflector)*
2 la estructura de soporte m (la armazón inferior)
- *pedestal (base)*
3 el soporte axial y radial
- *axial-radial bearing*
4 el mecanismo de declinación f
- *declination gear*
5 el eje de declinación f
- *declination axis*
6 el soporte de declinación f
- *declination bearing*
7 el anillo de frente m (el anillo superior)
- *front ring*
8 el tubo del telescopio
- *tube (body tube)*
9 la parte central del tubo
- *tube centre (Am. center) section*
10 el espejo principal
- *primary mirror (main mirror)*
11 el espejo de desviación f (el espejo secundario)
- *secondary mirror (deviation mirror, corrector plate)*
12 la horquilla (la montura en forma f de horquilla f)
- *fork mounting (fork)*
13 el recubrimiento
- *cover*
14 el cojinete guía f
- *guide bearing*
15 el mando principal del eje horario
- *main drive unit of the polar axis*
**16-25 monturas f de telescopio m**
- *telescope mountings (telescope mounts)*
16 el telescopio de lentes f (el refractor) sobre montura f alemana
- *refractor (refracting telescope) on a German-type mounting*

17 el eje de declinación f
- *declination axis*
18 el eje horario (el eje polar)
- *polar axis*
19 el contrapeso
- *counterweight (counterpoise)*
20 el ocular
- *eyepiece*
21 la montura con columna f de acodamiento m
- *knee mounting with a bent column*
22 la montura inglesa de eje m
- *English-type axis mounting (axis mount)*
23 la montura inglesa con soporte m
- *English-type yoke mounting (yoke mount)*
24 la montura de horquilla f
- *fork mounting (fork mount)*
25 la montura de herradura f
- *horseshoe mounting (horseshoe mount)*
26 el círculo meridiano
- *meridian circle*
27 el círculo graduado
- *divided circle (graduated circle)*
28 el microscopio de lectura f
- *reading microscope*
29 el telescopio meridiano
- *meridian telescope*
30 el microscopio electrónico
- *electron microscope*
**31-39 el tubo del microscopio**
- *microscope tube (microscope body, body tube)*
31 el sistema de producción de la radiación f (la cabeza de radiación f)
- *electron gun*
32 las lentes del condensador
- *condensers*
33 el orificio de introducción f del objeto
- *specimen insertion air lock*

34 el ajuste del portaobjetos del objetivo (el desplazamiento del objeto)
- *control for the specimen stage adjustment*
35 el botón de apertura f del diafragma
- *control for the objective apertures*
36 la lente del objetivo
- *objective lens*
37 el visor de la imagen intermedia
- *intermediate image screen*
38 el visor de observación f (la lente de aumento m)
- *telescope magnifier*
39 el visor de la imagen final (la pantalla fluorescente de la imagen final)
- *final image tube*
40 la cámara fotográfica para película f y para placas f
- *photographic chamber for film and plate magazines*

1 la cámara fotográfica de pequeño
   formato *m* (de paso *m* universal)
 – *miniature camera (35 mm camera)*
2 la ventana del visor
 – *viewfinder eyepiece*
3 el fotómetro (la ventanilla del fotómetro)
 – *meter cell*
4 la guía de accesorios *m*
 – *accessory shoe*
5 el objetivo
 – *flush lens*
6 la palanca de rebobinado *m*
 – *rewind handle (rewind, rewind crank)*
7 el carrete de pequeño formato *m* 135 (de
   paso *m* universal)
 – *miniature film cassette (135 film cassette,
   35 mm cassette)*
8 la canilla del carrete (el eje del carrete)
 – *film spool*
9 la lengüeta de la película (la película con
   la lengüeta de carga *f*)
 – *film with leader*
10 la ranura del chasis
 – *cassette slit (cassette exit slot)*
11 la cámara fotográfica de cartuchos *m* (una
   cámara instamatic)
 – *cartridge-loading camera*
12 el disparador
 – *shutter release (shutter release button)*
13 el contacto de cuboflash *m*
 – *flash cube contact*
14 el visor cuadrangular
 – *rectangular viewfinder*
15 el cartucho de película *f* 126 (el cartucho
   instamatic)
 – *126 cartridge (instamatic cartridge)*
16 la cámara fotográfica pocket
 – *pocket camera (subminiature camera)*
17 el cartucho de pequeño *m* 110
 – *110 cartridge (subminiature cartridge)*
18 la ventanilla de numeración *f* del carrete
 – *film window*
19 el rollo de película *f* de 120
 – *120 rollfilm*
20 la bobina del rollo de película *f*
 – *rollfilm spool*
21 el papel de protección *f*
 – *backing paper*
22 la cámara fotográfica réflex de doble
   lente *f*
 – *twin-lens reflex camera*
23 la tapa de la pantalla de enfoque *m*
 – *folding viewfinder hood (focusing hood)*
24 la ventanilla del fotómetro
 – *meter cell*
25 el objetivo de enfoque *m*
 – *viewing lens*

26 el objetivo de toma *f* de vista *f*
 – *object lens*
27 el botón de la bobina
 – *spool knob*
28 el botón para ajustar la distancia
 – *distance setting (focus setting)*
29 el mando del fotómetro acoplado
 – *exposure meter using needle-matching system*
30 el contacto de flash *m*
 – *flash contact*
31 el disparador
 – *shutter release*
32 la manivela de arrastre *m* de la película
 – *film transport (film advance, film wind)*
33 el conmutador del flash
 – *flash switch*
34 la rueda de graduación del diafragma
 – *aperture-setting control*
35 la rueda del tiempo de exposición *f*
 – *shutter speed control*
36 la cámara fotográfica de mano *m* de gran
   formato *m* (la cámara de prensa *f*)
 – *large-format hand camera (press camera)*
37 la empuñadura
 – *grip (handgrip)*
38 el cable disparador
 – *cable release*
39 el anillo grafilado para el enfoque de la
   distancia
 – *distance-setting ring (focusing ring)*
40 la ventana del telémetro
 – *rangefinder window*
41 el visor multiformato
 – *multiple-frame viewfinder (universal
   viewfinder)*
42 el pie tubular (el trípode)
 – *tripod*
43 la pata del trípode
 – *tripod leg*
44 el brazo de tubo *m*
 – *tubular leg*
45 el pie de caucho *m*
 – *rubber foot*
46 la columna central
 – *central column*
47 la cabeza de articulación *f* esférica
 – *ball and socket head*
48 la cabeza niveladora de cine *m*
 – *cine camera pan and tilt head*
49 la cámara de fuelle de gran formato *m*
 – *large-format folding camera*
50 el banco óptico
 – *optical bench*
51 el piñón de regulación *f* frontal
 – *standard adjustment*
52 la chapa del objetivo *m*
 – *lens standard*

53 el fuelle
 – *bellows*
54 el respaldo de la cámara
 – *camera back*
55 el piñón de regulación *f* trasera
 – *back standard adjustment*
56 el fotómetro
 – *hand-held exposure meter (exposure meter)*
57 el disco de cálculo *m*
 – *calculator dial*
58 la escala con aguja *f* indicadora
 – *scales (indicator scales) with indicator
   needle (pointer)*
59 el selector de escala *f* (el selector de
   banda *f* alta y baja)
 – *range switch (high/low range selector)*
60 el difusor para medir la luz incidente
 – *diffuser for incident light measurement*
61 el fotómetro para cámaras *f* de gran
   formato *m*
 – *probe exposure meter for large-format
   cameras*
62 el aparato de medida *f*
 – *meter*
63 la sonda
 – *probe*
64 la corredera del chasis
 – *dark slide*
65 el flash electrónico portátil de batería *f*
 – *battery-portable electronic flash (battery-
   portable electronic flash unit)*
66 el acumulador (la batería)
 – *powerpack unit (battery)*
67 la lámpara del flash (la antorcha del flash)
 – *flash head*
68 el flash electrónico de una sola pieza
 – *single-unit electronic flash (flashgun)*
69 el reflector orientable
 – *swivel-mounted reflector*
70 el fotodiodo
 – *photodiode*
71 la zapata
 – *foot*
72 el contacto central
 – *hot-shoe contact*
73 el cuboflash
 – *flash cube*
74 la lámpara del cuboflash
 – *flash cube*
75 la barra de flash *m* (AGFA)
 – *flash bar (AGFA)*
76 el proyector de diapositivas *f*
 – *slide projector*
77 el carro de diapositivas *f*
 – *rotary magazine*

**1-105 la cámara fotográfica con objetivos** *m* **intercambiables**
– *system camera*
1 la cámara fotográfica réflex de pequeño formato *m* con un solo objetivo
– *miniature single-lens reflex camera*
2 el cuerpo de la cámara fotográfica
– *camera body*
3-8 el objetivo, un objetivo normal
– *lens, a normal lens (standard lens)*
3 el tubo del objetivo *m*
– *lens barrel*
4 la escala de distancias *f* en metros *m* y pies *m*
– *distance scale in metres and feet*
5 el anillo del diafragma
– *aperture ring (aperture-setting ring, aperture control ring)*
6 la montura de la lente frontal con fijación *f* para filtros *m*
– *front element mount with filter mount*
7 la lente frontal
– *front element*
8 el anillo grafilado de enfoque *m*
– *focusing ring (distance-setting ring)*
9 el ojete de la correa portadora
– *ring for the carrying strap*
10 la cámara (el alojamiento) de la pila
– *battery chamber*
11 la tapa roscada
– *screw-in cover*
12 la manivela de rebobinaje *m*
– *rewind handle (rewind, rewind crank)*
13 el interruptor de la pila
– *battery switch*
14 la toma de flash *m* para F y X
– *flash socket for F and X contact*
15 la palanca de resorte *m* para el dispardor automático
– *self-time lever (setting lever for the self-timer, setting lever for the delayed-action release)*
16 la palanca de avance *m* de la película
– *single-stroke film advance lever*
17 el contador de las fotografías
– *exposure counter (frame counter)*
18 el disparador
– *shutter release (shutter release button)*
19 el botón de regulación *f* de los tiempos de exposición *f*
– *shutter speed setting knob (shutter speed control)*
20 la uña (la zapata) de los accesorios
– *accessory shoe*
21 el contacto central para flash *m*
– *hot-shoe flash contact*
22 la ventanilla (el ocular) del visor con lente *f* de corrección *f*
– *viewfinder eyepiece with correcting lens*
23 la tapa de la cámara fotográfica
– *camera back*
24 el prensapelícula
– *pressure plate*
25 el pitón (el tope de arrastre) de la película del sistema de carga *f* rápida
– *take-up spool of the rapid-loading system*
26 la ruedecilla dentada de arrastre *m* de la película
– *transport sprocket*
27 la rueda (el piñón) libre de rebobinaje *m*
– *rewind release button (reversing clutch)*
28 la ventana de la película (la ventana del negativo, la ventana de la fotografía)
– *film window*
29 el tope de arrastre *m* del rebobinaje
– *rewind cam*
30 la tuerca del pie
– *tripod socket (tripod bush)*
31 el sistema réflex
– *reflex system (mirror reflex system)*
32 el objetivo
– *lens*
33 el espejo réflex
– *reflex mirror*
34 la ventana de la imagen
– *film window*
35 la trayectoria luminosa de la imagen
– *path of the image beam*
36 la trayectoria luminosa de la medida
– *path of the sample beam*
37 la célula fotoeléctrica
– *meter cell*
38 el espejo auxiliar
– *auxiliary mirror*

39 el cristal de enfoque *m*
– *focusing screen*
40 la lente del campo de la imagen
– *field lens*
41 el pentaprisma de tejado *m*
– *pentaprism*
42 el ocular
– *eyepiece*
**43-105 los accesorios del sistema**
– *system of accessories*
43 el objetivo intercambiable
– *interchangeable lenses*
44 el objetivo ojo *m* de pez *m*
– *fisheye lens (fisheye)*
45 el objetivo gran angular (de distancia *f* focal corta)
– *wide-angle lens (short focal length lens)*
46 el objetivo normal
– *normal lens (standard lens)*
47 el objetivo de distancia *f* focal media
– *medium focal length lens*
48 el teleobjetivo (el objetivo de distancia *f* focal larga)
– *telephoto lens (long focal length lens)*
49 el objetivo para gran distancia *f* (la lente para imágenes *f* lejanas)
– *long-focus lens*
50 el objetivo de espejo *m*
– *mirror lens*
51 la imagen del visor
– *viewfinder image*
52 la señal para el reglaje manual
– *signal to switch to manual control*
53 el anillo de cristal *m* esmerilado
– *matt collar (ground glass collar)*
54 el retículo de microprismas *m*
– *microprism collar*
55 el estigmómetro (el prisma de medida *f*)
– *split-image rangefinder (focusing wedges)*
56 la escala de diafragmas *f*
– *aperture scale*
57 la aguja del fotómetro
– *exposure meter needle*
**58-66 los cristales de enfoque *m* intercambiables**
– *interchangeable focusing screens*
58 el cristal esmerilado con retículo *m* de microprismas *m*
– *all-matt screen (ground glass screen) with microprism spot*
59 el cristal esmerilado con retículo *m* de microprismas *m* y estigmómetro *m*
– *all-matt screen (ground glass screen) with microprism spot and split-image rangefinder*
60 el cristal esmerilado sin accesorios *m* de enfoque *m*
– *all-matt screen (ground glass screen) without focusing aids*
61 el cristal esmerilado con división *f* de reja *f* (el cristal esmerilado cuadriculado)
– *matt screen (ground glass screen) with reticle*
62 el retículo de microprismas *m* para objetivos *m* de gran abertura *f*
– *microprism spot for lenses with a large aperture*
63 el retículo de microprismas *m* para objetivos *m* de abertura *f* a partir de 1 : 3.5
– *microprism spot for lenses with an aperture of f = 1 : 3.5 or larger*
64 la lente de Fresnel con anillo *m* de cristal *m* esmerilado y estigmómetro *m*
– *Fresnel lens with matt collar (ground glass collar) and split-image rangefinder*
65 el cristal esmerilado con zona central de grano fino y retículo *m* graduado
– *all-matt screen (ground glass screen) with finely matted central spot and graduated markings*
66 el cristal esmerilado con zona *f* central clara y doble retículo *m*
– *matt screen (ground glass screen) with clear spot and double cross hairs*
67 la tapa especial para el registro de los datos de toma *f* de vistas *f*
– *data recording back for exposing data about shots*
68 el visor de capuchón *m*
– *viewfinder hood (focusing hood)*
69 el visor de prisma *m* intercambiable
– *interchangeable pentaprism viewfinder*

70 el pentaprisma de techo *m*
– *pentaprism*
71 el visor de ángulo *m*
– *right-angle viewfinder*
72 la lente de corección *f*
– *correction lens*
73 el borde del ocular
– *eyecup*
74 el ocular regulable (el telescopio de enfoque *m*)
– *focusing telescope*
75 el empalme con la batería
– *battery unit*
76 la empuñadura de la pila para el motor de la cámara
– *combined battery holder and control grip for the motor drive*
77 la cámara de disparo *m* rápido
– *rapid-sequence camera*
78 el motor de la cámara desmontable
– *attachable motor drive*
79 el suministro externo de corriente *f*
– *external (outside) power supply*
80 la carga de película *f* de diez metros *m*
– *ten meter film back (magazine back)*
**81-98 los dispositivos de macrofotografía *f***
– *close-up and macro equipment*
81 el tubo alargador
– *extension tube*
82 el anillo adaptador
– *adapter ring*
83 el anillo de inversión *f*
– *reversing ring*
84 el objetivo en posición *f* invertida
– *lens in retrofocus position*
85 el fuelle
– *bellows unit (extension bellows, close-up bellows attachment)*
86 el carro de regulación *f*
– *focusing stage*
87 el adaptador para reproducción *f* de diapositivas *f*
– *slide-copying attachment*
88 el portadiapositivas
– *slide-copying adapter*
89 el dispositivo de microfotografía *f*
– *micro attachment (photomicroscope adapter)*
90 el pie de reproducción *f*
– *copying stand (copy stand, copypod)*
91 la pata de araña *f*
– *spider legs*
92 el soporte de reproducción *f*
– *copying stand (copy stand)*
93 el brazo de reproducción *f*
– *arm of the copying stand (copy stand)*
94 el pie de macrofotografía *f*
– *macrophoto stand*
95 las platinas intercambiables para el pie de macrofotografía *f*
– *stage plates for the macrophoto stand*
96 el disco insertable
– *insertable disc (disk)*
97 el reflector Lieberkühn
– *Lieberkühn reflector*
98 el dispositivo para las coordenadas
– *mechanical stage*
99 el pie de mesa *f* (el trípode de mesa *f*)
– *table tripod (table-top tripod)*
100 el soporte de hombro *m*
– *rifle grip*
101 el disparador de cable *m*
– *cable release*
102 el disparador de doble cable *m*
– *double cable release*
103 la bolsa (la funda) de la cámara
– *camera case (ever-ready case)*
104 el estuche del objetivo
– *lens case*
105 la bolsa de cuero *m* flexible del objetivo
– *soft-leather lens pouch*

1-60  equipo *m* de laboratorio *m*
– *darkroom equipment*
1  la caja de revelado *m*
– *developing tank*
2  la espiral portapelícula
– *spiral (developing spiral, tank reel)*
3  la caja de revelado *m* de varias
unidades *f*
– *multi-unit developing tank*
4  la espiral de película *f* de varias
unidades *f*
– *multi-unit tank spiral*
5  la caja de carga *f* a plena luz *f*
– *daylight-loading tank*
6  el receptor de la película
– *loading chamber*
7  el botón de arrastre *m* de la
película
– *film transport handle*
8  el termómetro de revelado *m*
– *developing tank thermometer*
9  la botella plisada para el líquido
revelador
– *collapsible bottle for developing
solution*
10  las botellas con productos *m*
químicos para primer revelador *m*,
baño *m* de parada *f*, revelador *m*
de color *m*, baño *m* de
blanqueo *m*, estabilizador *m*
– *chemical bottles for first developer,
stop bath, colour developer, bleach-
hardener, stabilizer*
11  las probetas graduadas
– *measuring cylinders*
12  el embudo
– *funnel*
13  el termómetro de baño *m* (el
termómetro de cubeta *f*)
– *tray thermometer (dish
thermometer)*
14  la pinza para película *f* (el
sujetapelículas)
– *film clip*
15  la bañera (la cubeta) de lavado *m*
– *wash tank (washer)*
16  la llegada de agua *f*
– *water supply pipe*
17  el desagüe
– *water outlet pipe*
18  el reloj de laboratorio *m* (el reloj
de corta duración *f*)
– *laboratory timer (timer)*
19  el agitador de película *f*
– *automatic film agitator*
20  el tambor de revelado *m*
– *developing tank*
21  la lámpara de laboratorio *m*
(*también:* cuarto *m* oscuro)
– *darkroom lamp (safelight)*
22  el cristal de filtro *m*
– *filter screen*
23  el secador de películas *f*
– *film drier (drying cabinet)*
24  el interruptor horario de
exposición *f*
– *exposure timer*
25  la cubeta de revelado *m*
– *developing dish (developing tray)*
26  la ampliadora
– *enlarger*
27  la placa base (la platina)
– *baseboard*
28  la columna inclinada
– *angled column*

29  la cabeza de la lámpara (la caja de
la lámpara)
– *lamphouse (lamp housing)*
30  el portanegativo
– *negative carrier*
31  el fuelle
– *bellows*
32  el objetivo
– *lens*
33  la transmisión fina por fricción *f*
– *friction drive for fine adjustment*
34  la regulación de la altura
(regulación *f* en escala *f*)
– *height adjustment (scale
adjustment)*
35  el bastidor de ampliación *f*
– *masking frame (easel)*
36  el analizador del color
– *colour (Am. color) analyser*
37  la lámpara de control *m* del color
– *colour (Am. color) analyser lamp*
38  el cable de medida *f*
– *probe lead*
39  el botón de corrección *f* del
tiempo
– *exposure time balancing knob*
40  la ampliadora de color *m*
– *colour (Am. color) enlarger*
41  la cabeza del aparato
– *enlarger head*
42  la columna perfilada
– *column*
43-45  la cabeza mezcladora del color
– *colour-mixing (Am. color-mixing)
knob*
43  el regulador del filtro púrpura
– *magenta filter adjustment (minus
green filter adjustment)*
44  el regulador del filtro amarillo
– *yellow filter adjustment (minus blue
filter adjustment)*
45  el regulador del filtro gris azulado
– *cyan filter adjustment (minus red
filter adjustment)*
46  el filtro regulable
– *red swing filter*
47  las pinzas de revelado *m*
– *print tongs*
48  el tambor de revelado *m* de
papel *m*
– *processing drum*
49  el rodillo de secado *m*
– *squeegee*
50  el surtido de papel *m*
– *range (assortment) of papers*
51  el papel de ampliación *f* en
color *m*, un paquete de papel *m*
fotográfico
– *colour (Am. color) printing paper, a
packet of photographic printing
paper*
52  los productos químicos para el
revelado en color *m*
– *colour (Am. color) chemicals (colour
processing chemicals)*
53  el exposímetro del papel (el
exposímetro de ampliación *f*)
– *enlarging meter (enlarging
photometer)*
54  el botón de ajuste *m* con la
sensibilidad del papel
– *adjusting knob with paper speed
scale*
55  la célula (la sonda) de medida *f*
– *probe*

56  la cubeta semiautomática de
revelado *m* con termostato *m*
– *semi-automatic thermostatically
controlled developing dish*
57  la prensa de secado *m* rápido
– *rapid print drier (heated print drier)*
58  la hoja (la lámina) de brillo *m*
intenso
– *glazing sheet*
59  la tela de tensión *f* (de presión *f*)
– *pressure cloth*
60  la máquina de revelado *m* de
rodillos *m*
– *automatic processor (machine
processor)*

1 la cámara de película *f* estrecha, una
  cámara sonora de súper 8
- *cine camera, a Super-8 sound camera*
2 el objetivo zoom *m* intercambiable
- *interchangeable zoom lens (variable focus
  lens, varifocal lens)*
3 el enfoque de la distancia y la regulación
  manual de la distancia focal
- *distance setting (focus setting) and manual
  focal length setting*
4 el anillo de los diafragmas para regular
  manualmente la abertura
- *aperture ring (aperture-setting ring,
  aperture control ring) for manual aperture
  setting*
5 la empuñadura de batería *f*
- *handgrip with battery chamber*
6 el disparador con empalme *m* para el
  disparador de cable *m*
- *shutter release with cable release socket*
7 la toma de señal *f* de sincronización *o*
  del generador de impulsos *m* para el
  registro sonoro (para el procedimiento de
  doble banda *f*)
- *pilot tone or pulse generator socket for the
  sound recording equipment [with the dual
  film-tape system]*
8 el cable de conexión *f* del sonido para el
  micrófono o para la fuente sonora (para el
  procedimiento de banda *f* única)
- *sound connecting cord for microphone or
  external sound source [in single-system
  recording]*
9 la conexión del disparador a distancia *f*
- *remote control socket (remote control jack)*
10 la conexión de los auriculares
- *headphone socket; sim.: earphone socket*
11 el conmutador del sistema de regulación *f*
- *autofocus override switch*
12 el conmutador de la velocidad de la
  película
- *filming speed selector*
13 el selector de toma *f* de sonido *m* para el
  funcionamiento automático o manual
- *sound recording selector switch for
  automatic or manual operation*
14 el ocular con reborde *m* para el ojo
- *eyepiece with eyecup*
15 el regulador de las dioptrías
- *diopter control ring (dioptric adjustment
  ring)*
16 el regulador del nivel de la toma de
  sonido *m*
- *recording level control (audio level control,
  recording sensitivity selector)*
17 el fotómetro-selector
- *manual/automatic exposure control switch*
18 el selector de sensibilidad *f* de la película
- *film speed setting*
19 el mando del zoom automático
- *power zooming arrangement*
20 el sistema automático del diafragma
- *automatic aperture control*
21 **el sistema para la grabación sobre pista *f***
  **sonora**
- ***sound track system***
22 la cámara sonora
- *sound camera*
23 el brazo del micrófono telescópico
- *telescopic microphone boom*
24 el micrófono
- *microphone*
25 el cable del micrófono
- *microphone connecting lead (microphone
  connecting cord)*
26 **el estuche (la caja) de mezcla *f* (el**
  **mezclador)**
- ***mixing console (mixing desk, mixer)***
27 las entradas para las diferentes fuentes
  sonoras
- *inputs from various sound sources*
28 la salida hacia la cámara
- *output to camera*
29 el cartucho (el cassette) de película *f*
  sonora de súper 8
- ***Super-8 sound film cartridge***
30 la ventana del cartucho
- *film gate of the cartridge*
31 la bobina de alimentación *f*
- *feed spool*
32 la bobina receptora
- *take-up spool*

33 la cabeza de grabación *f* del sonido
- *recording head (sound head)*
34 el rodillo de transporte *m* (el cabrestante)
- *transport roller (capstan)*
35 el contarrodillo de goma *f*
- *rubber pinch roller (capstan idler)*
36 la ranura guía
- *guide step (guide notch)*
37 la ranura de sensibilidad *f* de la película *f*
- *exposure meter control step*
38 la ranura de inserción *f* de filtros *m*
- *conversion filter step (colour, Am. color,
  conversion filter step)*
39 **el cartucho (cassette) de película *f* 8 mm**
- ***single-8 cassette***
40 la ventana de exposición *f*
- *film gate opening*
41 la película sin impresionar
- *unexposed film*
42 la película impresionada
- *exposed film*
43 **la cámara de 16 mm**
- ***16 mm camera***
44 el visor réflex
- *reflex finder (through-the-lens reflex
  finder)*
45 la carga
- *magazine*
46-49 **la cabeza del objetivo**
- ***lens head***
46 el revólver del objetivo
- *lens turret (turret head)*
47 el teleobjetivo
- *telephoto lens*
48 el objetivo gran angular
- *wide-angle lens*
49 el objetivo normal
- *normal lens (standard lens)*
50 la manivela
- *winding handle*
51 **la cámara de súper 8 compacta**
- ***compact Super-8 camera***
52 el contador de la película
- *footage counter*
53 el objetivo macrozoom *m*
- *macro zoom lens*
54 la palanca del zoom
- *zooming lever*
55 la macrolente adicional (la lente
  suplementaria)
- *macro lens attachment (close-up lens)*
56 el macrorraíl (el dispositivo fijador para
  las muestras pequeñas)
- *macro frame (mount for small originals)*
57 **la caja (la cámara) submarina**
- ***underwater housing (underwater case)***
58 la dioptra
- *direct-vision frame finder*
59 el distanciador (el espaciador)
- *measuring rod*
60 la superficie de estabilización *f*
- *stabilizing wing*
61 la empuñadura
- *grip (handgrip)*
62 el cierre (el bloqueo)
- *locking bolt*
63 la palanca de mando *m*
- *control lever (operating lever)*
64 el cristal frontal
- *porthole*
65 **la sincronización**
- ***synchronization start (sync start)***
66 la cámara de reportaje *m* cinematográfico
- *professional press-type camera*
67 el operador (el cameraman)
- *cameraman*
68 el ayudante del operador (el ayudante del
  sonido)
- *camera assistant; also: sound assistant*
69 la palmada de sincronización *f*
- *handclap marking sync start*
70 **la toma de imagen *f* y la grabación de**
  **sonido *m* a doble pista *f***
- ***dual film-tape recording using a tape
  recorder***
71 la cámara generadora de impulsos *m*
- *pulse-generating camera*
72 el cable de impulsos *m*
- *pulse cable*
73 la grabadora de cassettes *f*
- *cassette recorder*

74 el micrófono
- *microphone*
75 **la proyección sonora de doble cinta *f***
- ***dual film-tape reproduction***
76 el cassette de la cinta del sonido
- *tape cassette*
77 el dispositivo de sincronización *f*
- *synchronization unit*
78 el proyector de película *f* estrecha
- *cine projector*
79 la bobina de la película original
- *film feed spool*
80 la bobina receptora, una bobina para
  enrollado *m* automático
- *take-up reel (take-up spool), an automatic
  take-up reel (take-up spool)*
81 **el proyector sonoro**
- ***sound projector***
82 la película sonora con banda *f* lateral
  magnética
- *sound film with magnetic stripe (sound
  track, track)*
83 el botón de grabación *f*
- *automatic-threading button*
84 el botón de trucaje *m*
- *trick button*
85 el regulador del nivel del sonido
- *volume control*
86 el botón de borrado *m*
- *reset button*
87 el conmutador de programa *m* de
  trucaje *m*
- *fast and slow motion switch*
88 el selector del modo de funcionamiento *m*
- *forward, reverse, and still projection switch*
89 el pegacintas
- *splicer for wet splices*
90 el sujetador de cinta *f* articulado
- *hinged clamping plate*
91 **el visor de películas *f*** (el visor de
  película *f* cinematográfica)
- *film viewer (animated viewer editor)*
92 el brazo portabobinas giratorio
- *foldaway reel arm*
93 la manivela de rebobinaje *m*
- *rewind handle (rewinder)*
94 el cristal opaco (el cristal esmerilado)
- *viewing screen*
95 la punzadora de la película
- *film perforator (film marker)*
96 **la mesa de montaje *m* sonoro de seis**
  **platos *m***
- *six-turntable film and sound cutting table
  (editing table, cutting bench, animated
  sound editor)*
97 el monitor
- *monitor*
98 las teclas de mando *m*
- *control buttons (control well)*
99 el plato de la película
- *film turntable*
100 el primer plato del sonido, para el sonido
  live (sonido *m* original)
- *first sound turntable, e.g. for live sound*
101 el segundo plato del sonido, para el sonido
  procurado (sonido *m* secundario)
- *second sound turntable for post-sync sound*
102 la cabeza unificada del sonido y de la
  imagen
- *film and tape synchronizing head*

# 118 Construcción I

**1-49 la obra** [la construcción de una casa]
- *carcase (carcass, fabric)*
1 el sótano de hormigón *m* apisonado
- *basement of tamped (rammed) concrete*
2 el zócalo de hormigón *m* (*Amér.:* de concreto *m*)
- *concrete base course*
3 la ventana del sótano (el respiradero)
- *cellar window (basement window)*
4 la escalera de acceso *m* al sótano por la parte exterior
- *outside cellar steps*
5 la ventana del lavadero
- *utility room window*
6 la puerta del lavadero
- *utility room door*
7 la planta baja
- *ground floor* (Am. *first floor*)
8 la pared de ladrillos *m*
- *brick wall*
9 el dintel de la ventana
- *lintel (window head)*
10 el marco exterior lateral de la ventana (el intradós de la ventana)
- *reveal*
11 el marco interior lateral de la ventana (el intradós interior de la ventana)
- *jamb*
12 el antepecho (*Bol.:* la patilla)
- *window ledge (window sill)*
13 el dintel de cemento *m* armado
- *reinforced concrete lintel*
14 la primera planta
- *upper floor (first floor,* Am. *second floor)*
15 la pared de ladrillos *m* huecos
- *hollow-block wall*
16 el suelo macizo
- *concrete floor*
17 el andamio de trabajo *m* (el andamio de caballete *m*)
- *work platform (working platform)*
18 el albañil
- *bricklayer* (Am. *brickmason)*
19 el peón
- *bricklayer's labourer* (Am. *laborer);* also: *builder's labourer*
20 el cuezo de argamasa *f*
- *mortar trough*
21 la chimenea
- *chimney*
22 la cubierta provisional de la caja de la escalera
- *cover (boards) for the staircase*
23 el pie del andamio (el arbotante del andamio)
- *scaffold pole (scaffold standard)*
24 la baranda de protección *f*
- *platform railing*
25 el puntal en diagonal *f* (la riostra)
- *angle brace (angle tie) in the scaffold*
26 la carrera
- *ledger*
27 la almojaya del andamio
- *putlog (putlock)*
28 la plataforma de tablones *m*
- *plank platform (board platform)*
29 la pasarela
- *guard board*
30 la ligadura del andamio, con cables *m* o cuerdas *f* de seguridad *f*
- *scaffolding joint with chain or lashing or whip or bond*

31 el montacargas
- *builder's hoist*
32 el operador de máquinas *f* (el maquinista)
- *mixer operator*
33 la mezcladora de hormigón *m*, una hormigonera
- *concrete mixer, a gravity mixer*
34 el tambor mezclador
- *mixing drum*
35 el cargador (la cuchara para llenar la hormigonera)
- *feeder skip*
36 las materias primas [arena *f* y gravilla *f*]
- *concrete aggregate [sand and gravel]*
37 la carretilla
- *wheelbarrow*
38 la manguera del agua *f*
- *hose (hosepipe)*
39 la amasadera del mortero (la balsa del mortero)
- *mortar pan (mortar trough, mortar tub)*
40 el montón de los bloques (la pila de ladrillos *m*)
- *stack of bricks*
41 la pila de madera *f* de construcción *f*
- *stacked shutter boards (lining boards)*
42 la escalera de mano *f* (las escalas)
- *ladder*
43 el saco de cemento *m* (*Chile y Ec.:* la concagua)
- *bag of cement*
44 la valla de protección *f*, una valla de madera *f*
- *site fence, a timber fence*
45 la superficie para la publicidad
- *signboard (billboard)*
46 la puerta de quita y pon (la puerta desmontable)
- *removable gate*
47 los letreros (los rótulos – de la empresa y técnicos *m* constructores–)
- *contractors' name plates*
48 la barraca de la obra
- *site hut (site office)*
49 el retrete de la obra
- *building site latrine*
**50-57 las herramientas del albañil**
- **bricklayer's** (Am. **brickmason's**) **tools**
50 la plomada
- *plumb bob (plummet)*
51 el lápiz de albañil *m*
- *thick lead pencil*
52 la paleta de albañil *m* (el palustre; *Bol., Mé., Perú y S. Dgo.:* la barreta)
- *trowel*
53 la piqueta (el martillo de albañil *m*, la alcotana)
- *bricklayer's* (Am. *brickmason's) hammer (brick hammer)*
54 la maceta (*Ec. y Perú:* la comba)
- *mallet*
55 el nivel de aire *m* (el nivel de burbuja *f*)
- *spirit level*
56 la llana (la trulla; *Amér.:* la cuchara; *Col.:* el babilejo)
- *laying-on trowel*
57 el fratás
- *float*
**58-68 aparejos *m* de construcción *f***
- **masonry bonds**

58 el ladrillo de dimensiones *f* normales (de forma *f* normal; *Mé.:* la solera)
- *brick (standard brick)*
59 las hiladas
- *stretching bond*
60 los aparejos de ladrillo *m*
- *heading bond*
61 el aparejo escalonado
- *racking (raking) back*
62 el aparejo de bloque *m*
- *English bond*
63 el ladrillo colocado a soga *f*
- *stretching course*
64 el ladrillo colocado a tizón *m*
- *heading course*
65 el aparejo en cruz *f*
- *English cross bond (Saint Andrew's cross bond)*
66 los aparejos de chimenea *f*
- *chimney bond*
67 la primera hilada
- *first course*
68 la segunda hilada
- *second course*
**69-82 la excavación de la obra**
- **excavation**
69 las camillas de replanteo *m*
- *profile* (Am. *batterboard) [fixed on edge at the corner]*
70 el punto de intersección *f* de las cuerdas
- *intersection of strings*
71 la plomada
- *plumb bob (plummet)*
72 el talud
- *excavation side*
73 la pasarela superior
- *upper edge board*
74 la pasarela inferior
- *lower edge board*
75 la zanja de cimentación *f*
- *foundation trench*
76 el peón zapador
- *navvy* (Am. *excavator)*
77 la cinta transportadora (de tierra *f*)
- *conveyor belt (conveyor)*
78 los escombros (la tierra excavada)
- *excavated earth*
79 la pasarela (el camino) de tablones *m*
- *plank roadway*
80 la jaula protectora del árbol
- *tree guard*
81 la pala excavadora
- *mechanical shovel (excavator)*
82 la cuchara de la excavadora
- *shovel bucket (bucket)*
**83-91 los trabajos de enlucimiento *m***
- **plastering**
83 el yesero (el estuquista)
- *plasterer*
84 el cuezo para el mortero
- *mortar trough*
85 la criba (*Chile:* el chayo)
- *screen*
**86-89 el andamio de escalera *f***
- **ladder scaffold**
86 la escalera (los montantes)
- *standard ladder*
87 la pasarela
- *boards (planks, platform)*
88 la riostra en forma *f* de cruz *f*
- *diagonal strut (diagonal brace)*
89 la baranda
- *railing*
90 la reja de protección *f*
- *guard netting*
91 la cuerda de la polea
- *rope-pulley hoist*

**1-89 la construcción de hormigón** *m*
**armado**
– *reinforced concrete (ferroconcrete)*
  *construction*
1 la estructura de hormigón *m*
  armado
– *reinforced concrete (ferroconcrete)*
  *skeleton construction*
2 el bastidor de hormigón *m* armado
– *reinforced concrete (ferroconcrete)*
  *frame*
3 la viga maestra
– *inferior purlin*
4 el cabio de hormigón *m*
– *concrete purlin*
5 la jácena
– *ceiling joist*
6 la cartela
– *arch (flank)*
7 la pared de hormigón *m* colado
– *rubble concrete wall*
8 el techo de hormigón *m* armado
– *reinforced concrete (ferroconcrete)*
  *floor*
9 el especialista en hormigón *m*,
  aplanando
– *concreter (concretor), flattening out*
10 el hierro (la varilla) de empalme *m*
– *projecting reinforcement (Am.*
  *connection rebars)*
11 el encofrado
– *column box*
12 el encofrado de las jácenas
– *joist shuttering*
13 los puntales del encofrado (los
  rollizos)
– *shuttering strut*
14 el puntal de arriostramiento *m*
– *diagonal bracing*
15 la cuña
– *wedge*
16 el madero (el tablón)
– *board*
17 la hilera de estacas (el
  tablestacado)
– *sheet pile wall (sheet pile, sheet*
  *piling)*
18 las tablas para encofrar
– *shutter boards (lining boards)*
19 la sierra circular
– *circular saw (buzz saw)*
20 el banco para el doblado (de
  varillas *f* de hierro *m*)
– *bending table*
21 el ferrallista
– *bar bender (steel bender)*
22 la cizalla de mano *f*
– *hand steel shears*
23 el hierro de armadura *f* (de
  refuerzo *m*)
– *reinforcing steel (reinforcement*
  *rods)*
24 el bloque hueco de piedra *f* pómez
– *pumice concrete hollow block*
25 la mampara para separación *f*, una
  mampara de madera *f*
– *partition wall, a timber wall*
26 las materias primas para el
  hormigón [arena *f* y gravilla *f* de
  distinto grueso *m*]
– *concrete aggregate [gravel and sand*
  *of various grades]*
27 el carril de la grúa
– *crane track*
28 la vagoneta basculante
– *tipping wagon (tipping truck)*

29 la hormigonera
– *concrete mixer*
30 el silo para el cemento
– *cement silo*
31 la grúa de torre *f* giratoria (la
  pluma)
– *tower crane (tower slewing crane)*
32 la plataforma (el carro de grúa *f*)
– *bogie (Am. truck)*
33 el contrapeso
– *counterweight*
34 la torre
– *tower*
35 la cabina del conductor de la grúa
– *crane driver's cabin (crane driver's*
  *cage)*
36 el aguilón (el pescante)
– *jib (boom)*
37 el cable portador
– *bearer cable*
38 el cubilote para el hormigón
– *concrete bucket*
39 las traviesas de madera *f*
– *sleepers (Am. ties)*
40 la zapata de freno *m*
– *chock*
41 la rampa
– *ramp*
42 la carretilla
– *wheelbarrow*
43 el pasamano (la barandilla)
– *safety rail*
44 la barraca de la obra
– *site hut*
45 la cantina
– *canteen*
46 el andamio hecho con tubos *m*
  de acero *m*
– *tubular steel scaffold (scaffolding)*
47 el pie derecho (el pilar)
– *standard*
48 el crucero (el tubo horizontal)
– *ledger tube*
49 la almojaya (el tubo perpendicular
  a la pared)
– *tie tube*
50 el plinto (la base)
– *shoe*
51 el puntal en diagonal *f* (la riostra)
– *diagonal brace*
52 la plataforma
– *planking (platform)*
53 la abrazadera de unión *f*
– *coupling (coupler)*
**54-76 los encofrados de hormigón** *m* **y**
  **el montaje del hierro**
– *formwork (shuttering) and*
  *reinforcement*
54 el suelo encofrado (el encofrado)
– *bottom shuttering (lining)*
55 el encofrado lateral de la jácena
– *side shutter of a purlin*
56 el encofrado inferior de la jácena
– *cut-in bottom*
57 el travesaño
– *cross beam*
58 la grapa de obra *f*
– *cramp iron (cramp, dog)*
59 el puntal del extremo, el puntal de
  encabezamiento *m*
– *upright member, a standard*
60 la pieza de unión *f*
– *strap*
61 el travesaño de apoyo *m*
– *cross piece*
62 el tablón de presión *f*
– *stop fillet*

63 la tabla de sujeción *f*
– *strut (brace, angle brace)*
64 el travesaño de refuerzo *m*
– *frame timber (yoke)*
65 el cubrejunta
– *strap*
66 la riostra de alambre *m*
– *reinforcement binding*
67 el tirante de tope *m*
– *cross strut (strut)*
68 la armadura
– *reinforcement*
69 las barras de repartición *f*
– *distribution steel*
70 el estribo
– *stirrup*
71 el hierro de empalme *m*
– *projecting reinforcement (Am.*
  *connection rebars)*
72 el hormigón (el hormigón seco;
  *Amér.:* el concreto; *Col.:* el
  gorgón)
– *heavy concrete*
73 el encofrado de puntales *m*
– *column box*
74 el marco de madera *f* atornillado
– *bolted frame timber (bolted yoke)*
75 el tornillo (el perno)
– *nut (thumb nut)*
76 el tablón para encofrados *m*
– *shutter board (shuttering board)*
**77-89 herramientas** *f*
– *tools*
77 la barra para doblar los hierros
– *bending iron*
78 el transportador móvil de
  encofrados *m*
– *adjustable service girder*
79 el tornillo de ajuste *m*
– *adjusting screw*
80 la barra de acero *m* (el redondo)
– *round bar reinforcement*
81 el distanciador (el fiel para cortar
  los hierros)
– *distance piece (separator, spacer)*
82 la barra de acero *m* grabado
– *Torsteel*
83 el pisón del hormigón
– *concrete tamper*
84 el molde para cubos *m* de
  muestra *f*
– *mould (Am. mold) for concrete test*
  *cubes*
85 las tenazas
– *concreter's tongs*
86 el puntal para encofrados *m*
– *sheeting support*
87 la cizalla de mano *f* (para cortar
  hierros *m*)
– *hand shears*
88 el vibrador para hormigón *m*
  armado
– *immersion vibrator (concrete*
  *vibrator)*
89 la aguja de vibrar
– *vibrating cylinder (vibrating head,*
  *vibrating poker)*

**1-59 la carpintería de armar**
- *carpenter's yard*
1 el acopio de tablones *m*
- *stack of boards (planks)*
2 los troncos largos (rollizos *m*, la madera de construcción *f*)
- *long timber* (Am. *lumber)*
3 el cobertizo de aserrado *m*
- *sawing shed*
4 el taller de carpintería *f*
- *carpenter's workshop*
5 la puerta del taller
- *workshop door*
6 el carro de mano *f*
- *handcart*
7 el entramado del tejado (la armazón para techar)
- *roof truss*
8 el árbol con la corona puesta (*en España*: la bandera al cubrir de aguas *f*)
- *tree [used for topping out ceremony], with wreath*
9 el entablado
- *timber wall*
10 los cuartones (la madera para construcciones *f*, la madera escuadrada)
- *squared timber (building timber, scantlings)*
11 el plano de montea *f*
- *drawing floor*
12 el carpintero
- *carpenter*
13 el sombrero del carpintero
- *carpenter's hat*
14 la sierra tronzadora, una sierra de cadena *f*
- *cross-cut saw, a chain saw*
15 el portacadena guía
- *chain guide*
16 la cadena de la sierra
- *saw chain*
17 la escopleadora (la fresadora de cadena *f* cortante)
- *mortiser (chain cutter)*
18 el caballete de soporte *m* (la asnilla)
- *trestle (horse)*
19 la viga en el caballete
- *beam mounted on a trestle*
20 la caja de las herramientas
- *set of carpenter's tools*
21 el taladrador eléctrico
- *electric drill*
22 el agujero para la espiga
- *dowel hole*
23 la señal para el agujero de la espiga
- *mark for the dowel hole*
24 el material listo para ensamblar
- *beams*
25 la columna (el pilar)
- *post (stile, stud, quarter)*
26 el pasador
- *corner brace*
27 el travesaño (el puntal)
- *brace (strut)*
28 el zócalo de la casa
- *base course (plinth)*
29 la pared de la casa
- *house wall (wall)*
30 el hueco de la ventana
- *window opening*
31 el intradós exterior (el marco exterior, el cerco exterior)
- *reveal*
32 el intradós interior (el marco interior, el cerco interior)
- *jamb*
33 la solera (el alféizar)
- *window ledge (window sill)*
34 el zuncho perimetral
- *cornice*
35 el rollizo
- *roundwood (round timber)*

36 la pasarela (el entablado, el entarimado)
- *floorboards*
37 la cuerda del montacargas
- *hoisting rope*
38 la viga del techo (la viga maestra)
- *ceiling joist (ceiling beam, main beam)*
39 la viga de la pared
- *wall joist*
40 la viga de retallo *m*
- *wall plate*
41 la traviesa (el brochal, la viga secundaria)
- *trimmer (trimmer joist,* Am. *header, header joist)*
42 el cabestrillo
- *dragon beam (dragon piece)*
43 el entrevigado (las piezas de relleno *m*)
- *false floor (inserted floor)*
44 el relleno entre vigas *f*, de bloques *m*, de coque *m*, o de arcilla *f*
- *floor filling of breeze, loam, etc.*
45 el listón
- *fillet (cleat)*
46 el hueco de la escalera
- *stair well (well)*
47 la chimenea
- *chimney*
48 el maderaje de la fachada (la pared entramada)
- *framed partition (framed wall)*
49 la viga solera (el durmiente)
- *wall plate*
50 el travesaño de solera *f*
- *girt*
51 la jamba de la ventana, el bastidor
- *window jamb*
52 el pie derecho de esquina *f* (el cornijal)
- *corner stile (corner strut, corner stud)*
53 el pie derecho de unión *f*
- *principal post*
54 la riostra
- *brace (strut) with skew notch*
55 el travesaño intermedio (el contrapuente)
- *nogging piece*
56 la barra de apoyo *m*
- *sill rail*
57 el dintel de la ventana (el cargadero)
- *window lintel (window head)*
58 el cabezal (la carrera)
- *head (head rail)*
59 el forjado del entramado
- *filled-in panel (bay, pan)*

**60-82 las herramientas de carpintero *m***
- *carpenter's tools*
60 el serrucho
- *hand saw*
61 la sierra de mano *f*
- *bucksaw*
62 la hoja de la sierra
- *saw blade*
63 el serrucho de calar (la sierra de punta *f*)
- *compass saw (keyhole saw)*
64 el cepillo de carpintero *m* (la garlopa)
- *plane*
65 la barrena de cola *f* (la broca)
- *auger (gimlet)*
66 el gato (la cárcel)
- *screw clamp (cramp, holdfast)*
67 el mazo
- *mallet*
68 el tronzador
- *two-handed saw*
69 el gramil
- *try square*
70 el hacha *f* de carpintero *m*
- *broad axe* (Am. *broadax)*
71 el formón
- *chisel*

72 el escoplo
- *mortice axe (mortice axe,* Am. *mortise ax)*
73 la azuela (el hacha *f*)
- *axe* (Am. *ax)*
74 el martillo de carpintero *m*
- *carpenter's hammer*
75 la boca sacaclavos
- *claw head (nail claw)*
76 el metro plegable
- *folding rule*
77 el lápiz de carpintero *m*
- *carpenter's pencil*
78 la escuadra de hierro *m*
- *iron square*
79 el rascador (el cuchillo de desbastar)
- *drawknife (drawshave, drawing knife)*
80 la viruta
- *shaving*
81 la falsa escuadra
- *bevel*
82 la escuadra a inglete *m*
- *mitre square* (Am. *miter square, miter angle)*
**83-96 maderas *f* de construcción *f***
- *building timber*
83 la troza (el tronco)
- *round trunk (undressed timber,* Am. *rough lumber)*
84 el núcleo (el corazón) del tronco (el duramen)
- *heartwood (duramen)*
85 el leñame (el sámago, la albura)
- *sapwood (sap, alburnum)*
86 la corteza
- *bark (rind)*
87 el corte para una sola pieza de sección *f* cuadrangular (el tronco de sección *f* entera)
- *baulk (balk)*
88 el corte para dos piezas en aristas *f* vivas (el tronco de sección *f* media)
- *halved timber*
89 el corte en aristas *f* truncadas (el tronco de media sección *f*)
- *wane (waney edge)*
90 el madero cortado en cruz *f* (el tronco de cuarto de sección *f*)
- *quarter baulk (balk)*
91 el tablón
- *plank (board)*
92 la madera de testa *f*
- *end-grained timber*
93 el tablón del núcleo (del corazón, del duramen)
- *heartwood plank (heart plank)*
94 la tabla no escuadrada
- *unsquared (untrimmed) plank (board)*
95 la tabla escuadrada
- *squared (trimmed) board*
96 el costero
- *slab (offcut)*

**1-26 estilos *m* y partes *f* del tejado**
- *styles and parts of roofs*
1 el tejado a dos vertientes *m*
- *gable roof (saddle roof, saddleback roof)*
2 el caballete del tejado
- *ridge*
3 el borde (el saliente del tejado)
- *verge*
4 el alero del tejado
- *eaves*
5 el frontón (la fachada)
- *gable*
6 la buhardilla rampante (*Arg., Chile y Urug.*: el entretecho)
- *dormer window (dormer)*
7 el tejado a una sola vertiente
- *pent roof (shed roof, lean-to roof)*
8 la claraboya (el tragaluz, la lumbrera; *Col:* la aojada)
- *skylight*
9 la pared cortafuegos *m*
- *fire gable*
10 el tejado de faldón *m* (el tejado a cuatro aguas *f*)
- *hip (hipped) roof*
11 la terminación *f* del tejado de copete *m* (el chaflán)
- *hip end*
12 la cresta del copete (la lima tesa)
- *hip (arris)*
13 la buhardilla de copete *m* (*Arg., Chile y Urug.*: el entretecho)
- *hip (hipped) dormer window*
14 el linternón
- *ridge turret*
15 la lima hoya
- *valley (roof valley)*
16 el tejado de semicopete *m*
- *hipped-gable roof (jerkin head roof)*
17 el chaflán (el faldoncillo)
- *partial-hip (partial-hipped) end*
18 el tejado a la Mansard (la cubierta quebrantada)
- *mansard roof (Am. gambrel roof)*
19 la ventana de mansarda *f*
- *mansard dormer window*
20 el tejado en diente *m* de sierra *f*
- *sawtooth roof*
21 el lucernario
- *north light*
22 el tejado de pabellón *m*
- *broach roof*
23 la buhardilla redondeada (*Arg., Chile y Urug.*: el entretecho)
- *eyebrow*
24 el tejado cónico
- *conical broach roof*
25 el tejado imperial (la cúpula en forma *f* de bulbo *m*)
- *imperial dome (imperial roof)*
26 la veleta
- *weather vane*
**27-83 la construcción de tejados *m* de madera *f***
- *roof structures of timber*
27 el tejado de cabrios *m*
- *rafter roof*
28 el cabrio
- *rafter*
29 la viga del tejado
- *roof beam*
30 la riostra
- *diagonal tie (cross tie, sprocket piece, cocking piece)*
31 el ristrel (el cabrio de quiebra *f*)
- *arris fillet (tilting fillet)*
32 la pared exterior
- *outer wall*
33 la cabeza de la viga
- *beam head*
34 el tejado con viga *f* de lima *f*
- *collar beam roof (trussed-rafter roof)*

35 la viga de lima *f* (el puente, el falso tirante)
- *collar beam (collar)*
36 el cabrio
- *rafter*
37 la cubierta de puentes *m* con doble apoyo *m* vertical (el tejado con buhardilla *f*)
- *strutted collar beam roof structure*
38 la viga de lima *f* (el falso tirante *m*)
- *collar beams*
39 el cabio lateral
- *purlin*
40 el poste (el pilar)
- *post (stile, stud)*
41 el codillo
- *brace*
42 la cubierta de una sola cámara
- *unstrutted (king pin) roof structure*
43 el cabio del caballete
- *ridge purlin*
44 el cabio inferior
- *inferior purlin*
45 la cabeza del cabrio
- *rafter head (rafter end)*
46 la armadura con buhardilla *f* y cámara *f* de aire *m*
- *purlin roof with queen post and pointing sill*
47 el jabalcón (la jamba)
- *pointing sill*
48 la viga del caballete (la viga cumbrera)
- *ridge beam (ridge board)*
49 la pinza sencilla
- *simple tie*
50 la pinza doble
- *double tie*
51 el cabio central
- *purlin*
52 la armadura de dos pisos *m* con cabios *m* (correas *f*) horizontales
- *purlin roof structure with queen post*
53 la viga de unión *f*
- *tie beam*
54 la viga del techo
- *joist (ceiling joist)*
55 el cabio principal (el cabrio de unión *f*)
- *principal rafter*
56 el cabio central
- *common rafter*
57 el codillo de ángulo *m*
- *angle brace (angle tie)*
58 el tornapunta
- *brace (strut)*
59 las pinzas
- *ties*
60 la cubierta holandesa con armadura *f* de copete *m*
- *hip (hipped) roof with purlin roof structure*
61 el cabio de unión *f* (de copete *m*)
- *jack rafter*
62 el cabio de lima tesa *f* (de la cresta)
- *hip rafter*
63 el cabrio del copete
- *jack rafter*
64 el cabrio de la lima hoya
- *valley rafter*
65 el techo de doble suspensión *f* (la armadura de doble espolón *m*)
- *queen truss*
66 la viga suspendida (la viga principal)
- *main beam*
67 la viga maestra (la jácena)
- *summer (summer beam)*
68 el pendolón
- *queen post (truss post)*
69 la tornapunta
- *brace (strut)*
70 la viga de trabazón *f*
- *collar beam (collar)*

71 el brochal
- *trimmer (Am. header)*
72 la armadura de cubierta *f* con huecos *m* macizados (la viga de alma *f* llena)
- *solid-web girder*
73 el tirante (la cabeza inferior)
- *lower chord*
74 el par (la cabeza superior)
- *upper chord*
75 el entablado
- *boarding*
76 el cabio (la correa)
- *purlin*
77 la pared exterior de soporte *m*
- *supporting outer wall*
78 la armadura de celosía *f*
- *roof truss*
79 el tirante (la cabeza inferior)
- *lower chord*
80 el par (la cabeza superior)
- *upper chord*
81 el poste (el pilar)
- *post*
82 la tornapunta
- *brace (strut)*
83 el soporte
- *support*
**84-98 las uniones de madera *f***
- *timber joints*
84 la mecha sencilla (unión *f* de caja *f* y espiga *f*)
- *mortise (mortice) and tenon joint*
85 la unión de espiga *f* de doble mecha *f*
- *forked mortise (mortice) and tenon joint*
86 la unión recta a media madera *f*
- *halving (halved) joint*
87 el ensamble con resalte *m*
- *simple scarf joint*
88 la unión oblicua con resalte *m* (el ensamble oblicuo con resalte *m*)
- *oblique scarf joint*
89 el ensamble a media madera *f* en cola *f* de milano *m*
- *dovetail halving*
90 el bisel con muesca *f* de encaje *m*
- *single skew notch*
91 el doble bisel de encaje *m*
- *double skew notch*
92 el clavo de madera *f*
- *wooden nail*
93 la clavija
- *pin*
94 el clavo de hierro *m* forjado
- *clout nail (clout)*
95 la punta de París (el clavo de cabeza *f* redonda)
- *wire nail*
96 la cuña de madera *f* dura
- *hardwood wedges*
97 la grapa
- *cramp iron (timber dog, dog)*
98 el perno roscado
- *bolt*

# 122 Tejado y tejador

1 el tejado (la cubierta) de tejas *f*
– *tiled roof*
2 la teja plana de doble falda *f*
– *plain-tile double-lap roofing*
3 la teja de caballete *m*
– *ridge tile*
4 la media teja terminal, junto al caballete
– *ridge course tile*
5 la teja de alero *m* (la bocateja)
– *under-ridge tile*
6 la teja plana
– *plain (plane) tile*
7 la teja de ventilación *f*
– *ventilating tile*
8 la teja de cresta *f* (de copete *m*)
– *ridge tile*
9 la teja de casquete *m* para tejado *m* holandés
– *hip tile*
10 el chaflán del tejado
– *hipped end*
11 la lima hoya
– *valley (roof valley)*
12 la claraboya (el tragaluz; *Col.:* la aojada)
– *skylight*
13 la chimenea
– *chimney*
14 el cerco metálico de la chimenea, de zinc *m*
– *chimney flashing, made of sheet zinc*
15 el gancho para las escalas
– *ladder hook*
16 el soporte del enrejado paranieve
– *snow guard bracket*
17 el listón
– *battens (slating and tiling battens)*
18 el medidor de distancia *f* entre listones *m*
– *batten gauge (Am. gage)*
19 el cabrio
– *rafter*
20 el martillo de tejador *m*
– *tile hammer*
21 el hacha *f* de enlistonar
– *lath axe (Am. ax)*
22 el cubo de tejador *m* (el cuezo)
– *hod*
23 el gancho del cubo
– *hod hook*
24 la salida
– *opening (hatch)*
25 la fachada (el frontispicio)
– *gable (gable end)*
26 el listón dentado
– *toothed lath*
27 el sofito
– *soffit*
28 el canalón del tejado
– *gutter*
29 el bajante (el tubo de desagüe *m*)
– *rainwater pipe (downpipe)*
30 el tubo de entrada *f* (la embocadura)
– *swan's neck (swan-neck)*
31 la abrazadera (la brida)
– *pipe clip*
32 el soporte del canalón
– *gutter bracket*
33 la máquina para agujerear tejas *f*
– *tile cutter*
34 el andamio de trabajo *m*
– *scaffold*
35 la pared de protección *f*
– *safety wall*
36 la cornisa del tejado
– *eaves*
37 la pared exterior
– *outer wall*
38 el revestimiento exterior
– *exterior rendering*
39 el ramate de obra *f*
– *frost-resistant brickwork*
40 el cabio inferior
– *inferior purlin*

41 la cabeza del cabrio
– *rafter head (rafter end)*
42 el encofrado de la cornisa
– *eaves fascia*
43 el doble listón
– *double lath (tiling lath)*
44 las placas de aislamiento *m*
– *insulating boards*
45-60 las tejas y las cubiertas (los tejados) de tejas *f*
– *tiles and tile roofings*
45 el tejado con eclisas *f*
– *split-tiled roof*
46 la teja plana
– *plain (plane) tile*
47 la teja de remate *m*
– *ridge course*
48 la eclisa
– *slip*
49 el remate del alero
– *eaves course*
50 el tejado real
– *plain-tiled roof*
51 la nariz
– *nib*
52 la teja de caballete *m*
– *ridge tile*
53 el tejado acanalado (el tejado italiano)
– *pantiled roof*
54 la teja acanalada
– *pantile*
55 el relleno con mortero *m*
– *pointing*
56 el tejado árabe (el tejado de teja *f* cóncava y teja *f* convexa)
– *Spanish-tiled roof (Am. mission-tiled roof)*
57 la teja de canal *m*
– *under tile*
58 la teja superior (la cobija)
– *over tile*
59 la teja de encaje *m*
– *interlocking tile*
60 la teja de tejado *m* plano
– *flat interlocking tile*
61-89 el tejado de pizarra *f*
– *slate roof*
61 el entarimado del tejado
– *roof boards (roof boarding, roof sheathing)*
62 la tela asfáltica (el cartón asfaltado)
– *roofing paper (sheathing paper); also: roofing felt (Am. rag felt)*
63 la escalera de tejado *m*
– *cat ladder (roof ladder)*
64 el gancho de conexión *f*
– *coupling hook*
65 el gancho de cumbrera *f*
– *ridge hook*
66 el caballete
– *roof trestle*
67 la cuerda de sujeción *f* del caballete
– *trestle rope*
68 el nudo
– *knot*
69 el gancho de la escalera
– *ladder hook*
70 el tablón del andamio (el tablón puente)
– *scaffold board*
71 el pizarrero
– *slater*
72 la cajita para los clavos
– *nail bag*
73 el martillo del pizarrero
– *slate hammer*
74 el clavo para colocar pizarra *f*, un clavo de alambre *m* galvanizado
– *slate nail, a galvanized wire nail*
75 el zapato de pizarrero *m*, una alpargata de cáñamo *m* o esparto *m*
– *slater's shoe, a bast or hemp shoe*
76 la pizarra del alero
– *eaves course (eaves joint)*
77 la pieza en ángulo *m*
– *corner bottom slate*

78 la pieza corriente (la pizarra de tejado *m*)
– *roof course*
79 la pizarra de caballete *m*
– *ridge course (ridge joint)*
80 la pizarra del copete (la pieza del faldón)
– *gable slate*
81 la línea límite (la línea a cubrir)
– *tail line*
82 la lima hoya
– *valley (roof valley)*
83 el canalón rectangular
– *box gutter (trough gutter, parallel gutter)*
84 las tijeras (la cizalla) para pizarra *f*
– *slater's iron*
85 la pizarra
– *slate*
86 la espalda
– *back*
87 la cabeza
– *head*
88 el borde frontal
– *front edge*
89 la cola
– *tail*
90-103 la cubierta de tela *f* asfáltica y la cubierta de fibrocemento *m* ondulado (la cubierta de uralita® *f*)
– *asphalt-impregnated paper roofing and corrugated asbestos cement roofing*
90 la cubierta de cartón *m* asfáltico (de tela *f* asfáltica)
– *asphalt-impregnated paper roof*
91 la tira [paralela al canalón]
– *width [parallel to the gutter]*
92 el canalón
– *gutter*
93 el caballete (la cumbrera)
– *ridge*
94 la unión
– *join*
95 la tira [perpendicular al canalón]
– *width [at right angles to the gutter]*
96 el clavo para el cartón
– *felt nail (clout nail)*
97 la cubierta (el techo) de fibrocemento *m* ondulado
– *corrugated asbestos cement roof*
98 la chapa ondulada (la uralita®)
– *corrugated sheet*
99 la cubierta del caballete (de la cumbrera)
– *ridge capping piece*
100 el recubrimiento (la pieza sobrepuesta, la solapa)
– *lap*
101 el tornillo para madera *f*
– *wood screw*
102 el sombrerete de zinc *m* para la lluvia
– *rust-proof zinc cup*
103 la arandela de plomo *m*
– *lead washer*

# 123 Construcción de suelos, techos, escaleras

1 la pared del sótano, una pared de
hormigón m
- basement wall, a concrete wall
2 la fundación (la faja del cimiento)
- footing (foundation)
3 el arranque del cimiento
- foundation base
4 la capa aislante horizontal
- damp course (damp-proof course)
5 la capa protectora (la capa
impermeable)
- waterproofing
6 la primera capa de revoque m
- rendering coat
7 la solería de ladrillos m
- brick paving
8 el lecho de arena f
- sand bed
9 la tierra
- ground
10 el tablón lateral
- shuttering
11 la estaquilla
- peg
12 el firme del suelo
- hardcore
13 el lecho de hormigón m
- oversite concrete
14 el pavimento de cemento m
- cement screed
15 el muro de ladrillos m
- brickwork base
16 la escalera del sótano, una
escalera maciza
- basement stairs, solid concrete
stairs
17 el peldaño macizo (el peldaño en
bloque m enterizo)
- block step
18 el primer peldaño (el peldaño de
arranque m)
- curtail step (bottom step)
19 el peldaño del descansillo
- top step
20 la protección del canto (la
moldura de protección f)
- nosing
21 el embaldosado del zócalo
- skirting (skirting board, Am.
mopboard, washboard, scrub board,
base)
22 el pasamano, la balaustrada
metálica
- balustrade of metal bars
23 el descansillo (la meseta)
- ground-floor (Am. first-floor)
landing
24 la puerta de entrada f de la casa
- front door
25 el limpiabarros de los pies
- foot scraper
26 el pavimento de losetas f
- flagstone paving
27 la capa de mortero m
- mortar bed
28 el techo macizo, un techo de
hormigón m armado
- concrete ceiling, a reinforced
concrete slab
29 la pared de ladrillos m de la
planta baja
- ground-floor (Am. first-floor) brick
wall
30 la rampa
- ramp
31 el escalón de cuña f
- wedge-shaped step

32 el escalón (la huella)
- tread
33 la contrahuella (la altura)
- riser
34-41 el descansillo (la meseta)
- landing
34 la viga del descansillo
- landing beam
35 el techo nervado de hormigón m
armado
- ribbed reinforced concrete floor
36 la nervadura (la viga)
- rib
37 la armadura de acero m
- steel-bar reinforcement
38 la placa prensada
- subfloor (blind floor)
39 la capa de nivel m
- level layer
40 la capa de acabado m
- finishing layer
41 el revestimiento del suelo (el piso)
- top layer (screed)
42-44 la escalera truncada, una
escalera con descansillo m
- dog-legged staircase, a staircase
without a well
42 el primer peldaño (el peldaño de
arranque m)
- curtail step (bottom step)
43 el pilar (el poste) de arranque m
- newel post (newel)
44 la zanca libre
- outer string (Am. outer stringer)
45 la zanca (el alma f) de la pared
- wall string (Am. wall stringer)
46 el tornillo de escalera f
- staircase bolt
47 el escalón (la huella)
- tread
48 la contrahuella
- riser
49 la pieza de ángulo m
- wreath piece (wreathed string)
50 la barandilla de la escalera
- balustrade
51 el balaustre
- baluster
52-62 el descansillo intermedio
- intermediate landing
52 la corvadura de la barandilla
- wreath
53 el pasamano (el barandal)
- handrail (guard rail)
54 el pilar (el poste) de llegada f
- head post
55 la viga del descansillo
- landing beam
56 la tabla de revestimiento m
- lining board
57 la varilla de recubrimiento m
- fillet
58 la plancha aislante ligera
- lightweight building board
59 el enlucido del techo
- ceiling plaster
60 el enlucido de la pared
- wall plaster
61 el techo intermedio (el forjado del
techo)
- false ceiling
62 el suelo de tiras f (el suelo de
tabletas f)
- strip flooring (overlay flooring,
parquet strip)
63 el listón del zócalo
- skirting board (Am. mopboard,
washboard, scrub board, base)

64 la varilla de recubrimiento m (el
junquillo, el tapajuntas)
- beading
65 la ventana de la caja de la escalera
- staircase window
66 la viga principal (la viga maestra)
del descansillo
- main landing beam
67 el listón de soporte m
- fillet (cleat)
68-69 el techo intermedio
- false ceiling
68 el suelo intermedio
- false floor (inserted floor)
69 el relleno del suelo intermedio
- floor filling (plugging, pug)
70 los listones
- laths
71 el soporte del enlucido (el cañizo)
- lathing
72 el enlucido del techo
- ceiling plaster
73 el suelo falso
- subfloor (blind floor)
74 el entarimado (el machiembrado)
de ranuras f y lengüetas f
- parquet floor with tongued-and-
grooved blocks
75 la escalera de cuarto de
conversión f
- quarter-newelled (Am. quarter-
newelled) staircase
76 la escalera circular de abanico m
(la escalera de caracol m), con
eje m (con árbol m) abierto
- winding staircase (spiral staircase)
with open newels (open-newel
staircase)
77 la escalera de caracol m de eje m
cerrado
- winding staircase (spiral staircase)
with solid newels (solid-newel
staircase)
78 el eje (el árbol)
- newel (solid newel)
79 el pasamano (el barandal)
- handrail

1 la vidriería (la cristalería)
- *glazier's workshop*
2 las muestras de molduras *f* (las muestras de marcos *m*)
- *frame wood samples (frame samples)*
3 la moldura (el marco)
- *frame wood*
4 el inglete (la ensambladura)
- *mitre joint (mitre, Am. miter joint, miter)*
5 el vidrio plano; *clases:* vidrio de ventana *f*, vidrio mate (vidrio esmerilado), vidrio muselina, vidrio luna, vidrio grueso, vidrio opalino, vidrio compuesto, vidrio inastillable (cristal *m* de seguridad *f*)
- *sheet glass; kinds: window glass, frosted glass, patterned glass, crystal plate glass, thick glass, milk glass, laminated glass (safety glass, shatterproof glass)*
6 el vidrio de fundición *f*; *clases:* vidrio de catedral (vidrio de colores *m*), vidrio ornamental, vidrio basto, vidrio de ojo *m* de buey *m*, vidrio armado, cristal hilado
- *cast glass; kinds: stained glass, ornamental glass, raw glass, bull's-eye glass, wired glass, line glass (lined glass)*
7 el montador de ingletes *m*
- *mitring (Am. mitering) machine*

8 el vidriero; *categorías:* vidriero de construcción *f*, vidriero de marcos *m*, vidriero artístico
- *glassworker, e.g. glazier, building glazier, decorative glass worker*
9 el portacristales
- *glass holder*
10 los pedazos de cristal *m* (los añicos de vidrio *m*)
- *piece of broken glass*
11 el martillo de plomo *m*
- *lead hammer*
12 el cuchillo de plomo *m* (el tingle)
- *lead knife*
13 la varilla de plomo *m*
- *came (lead came)*
14 la ventana de cristal *m* emplomado
- *leaded light*
15 la mesa de trabajo *m*
- *workbench*
16 la hoja de vidrio *m*
- *pane of glass*
17 la masilla
- *putty*
18 el martillo de pico *m* (el martillo de vidriero *m*)
- *glazier's hammer*
19 las tenazas de vidriero *m*
- *glass pliers*
20 la escuadra de vidriero *m* para cortar
- *glazier's square*
21 la regla para cortar
- *glazier's rule*

22 el cortador del vidrio en círculo *m* (el compás cortador)
- *glazier's beam compass*
23 la corcheta
- *eyelet*
24 la punta (el ángulo) de vidrio *m*
- *glazing sprig*
25-26 cortadores *m* de cristal *m*
- *glass cutters*
25 el diamante de cristalero *m*, un cortador de diamante *m*
- *diamond glass cutter*
26 el cortavidrios de disco *m* de acero *m*
- *steel-wheel (steel) glass cutter*
27 la espátula para la masilla
- *putty knife*
28 el alambre de espiga *f*
- *pin wire*
29 el alfiler de espiga *f*
- *panel pin*
30 la sierra para cortar en ingletes *m*
- *mitre (Am. miter) block (mitre box) [with saw]*
31 el ensamblador de ingletes *m*
- *mitre (Am. miter) shoot (mitre board)*

1 las tijeras para chapa *f*
  – *metal shears (tinner's snips,* Am.
    *tinner's shears)*
2 las tijeras angulares
  – *elbow snips (angle shears)*
3 la placa para enderezar
  – *gib*
4 la placa para alisar
  – *lapping plate*
5-7 los aparatos para soldar de
    gas *m* propano
  – *propane soldering apparatus*
5 el soldador (el soplete de gas *m*
    propano, un soldador tipo
    martillo *m*)
  – *propane soldering iron, a hatchet
    iron*
6 la piedra para soldar, una
    piedra de amoníaco *m*
  – *soldering stone, a sal-ammoniac
    block*
7 el ácido para soldar
  – *soldering fluid (flux)*
8 la bigornia, para formar
    bordes *m*
  – *beading iron for forming
    reinforcement beading*
9 el escariador de ángulo *m*, un
    rayador
  – *angled reamer*
10 el banco de trabajo *m*
  – *workbench (bench)*

11 el compás de varas *f*
  – *beam compass (trammel,* Am.
    *beam trammel)*
12 la terraja eléctrica de
    cojinetes *m*
  – *electric hand die*
13 el sacabocados
  – *hollow punch*
14 el martillo de embutir (de
    rebordear)
  – *chamfering hammer*
15 el martillo de orlar
  – *beading swage (beading
    hammer)*
16 la máquina para afilar y cortar
  – *abrasive-wheel cutting-off
    machine*
17 el hojalatero (el lampista;
    *Venez.:* el perolero)
  – *plumber*
18 el mazo
  – *mallet*
19 el cuerno
  – *mandrel*
20 la trancha
  – *socket (tinner's socket)*
21 el tronco (el cepo)
  – *block*
22 el yunque
  – *anvil*
23 el tas
  – *stake*

24 la sierra mecánica circular
  – *circular saw (buzz saw)*
25 la máquina para enchapar,
    acanalar y rebordear
  – *flanging, swaging, and wiring
    machine*
26 la cizalla para plancha *f*
  – *sheet shears (guillotine)*
27 la máquina de filetear
    (aterrajar)
  – *screw-cutting machine (thread-
    cutting machine, die stocks)*
28 la máquina para doblar los
    tubos
  – *pipe-bending machine (bending
    machine, pipe bender)*
29 el transformador de soldadura *f*
  – *welding transformer*
30 la máquina para doblar
    dándole a la chapa la forma de
    embudo *m*
  – *bending machine (rounding
    machine) for shaping funnels*

# 126 Fontanero

Plumber, Gas Fitter, Heating Engineer

1 el instalador del agua *f* y del gas
(el fontanero; *Venez.:* el perolero)
 – *gas fitter and plumber*
2 la escalera de tijeras *f* ( *Cuba, Mé. y
P. Rico:* el burro)
 – *stepladder*
3 la cadena de seguridad *f*
 – *safety chain*
4 la llave de paso *m*
 – *stop valve*
5 el contador de gas *m*
 – *gas meter*
6 el soporte (la repisa)
 – *bracket*
7 la tubería de subida *f*
 – *service riser*
8 la tubería de ramificación *f*(el
ramal)
 – *distributing pipe*
9 la tubería de distribución *f*
 – *supply pipe*
10 la sierra mecánica para tubos *m*
 – *pipe-cutting machine*
11 el burro para sujetar el tubo
 – *pipe repair stand*
12-25 aparatos *m* de gas *m* y de agua *f*
 – *gas and water appliances*
12-13 el calentador continuo de
agua *f*, un calentador de agua *f*
 – *geyser, an instantaneous water
heater*
12 el calentador de gas *m*
 – *gas water heater*
13 el calentador eléctrico
 – *electric water heater*
14 el depósito del retrete (WC) (la
cisterna)
 – *toilet cistern*
15 el flotador (el nivel)
 – *float*
16 la válvula de desagüe *m*
 – *bell*
17 el tubo de vaciado *m*
 – *flush pipe*
18 la entrada de agua *f*
 – *water inlet*
19 la palanca de servicio *m* (la
manivela)
 – *flushing lever (lever)*
20 el radiador
 – *radiator*
21 la nervadura del radiador
 – *radiator rib*
22 el sistema de dos tuberías *f*
 – *two-pipe system*
23 la tubería de salida *f*
 – *flow pipe*
24 la tubería de vuelta *f*
 – *return pipe*
25 la estufa (el radiador) de gas *m*
 – *gas heater*
26-37 grifería *f*
 – *plumbing fixtures*
26 el sifón inodoro
 – *trap (anti-syphon trap)*
27 la batería mezcladora para el
lavamanos
 – *mixer tap* (Am. *mixing faucet) for
washbasins*
28 el grifo de agua *f* caliente
 – *hot tap*
29 el grifo de agua *f* fría
 – *cold tap*
30 la ducha de tubo *m* flexible
 – *extendible shower attachment*
31 el grifo de lavabo *m*
 – *water tap (pillar tap) for washbasins*

32 el huso
 – *spindle top*
33 la capa protectora
 – *shield*
34 el grifo de agua *f* (el grifo, el grifo
codillo, la canilla; *Mé.:* el bitoque)
 – *draw-off tap* (Am. *faucet)*
35 el grifo de doble cierre *m*, con
junta *f* especial
 – *supatap*
36 el grifo giratorio
 – *swivel tap*
37 el pulsador a presión *f*
 – *flushing valve*
38-52 accesorios *m* de tubo *m*
 – *fittings*
38 la juntura con rosca *f* macho *m*
 – *joint with male thread*
39 la reducción macho-hembra
 – *reducing socket (reducing coupler)*
40 la atornilladura de ángulo *m*
 – *elbow screw joint (elbow coupling)*
41 la reducción macho-hembra con
rosca *f* interior
 – *reducing socket (reducing coupler)
with female thread*
42 la atornilladura
 – *screw joint*
43 el manguito
 – *coupler (socket)*
44 la pieza en forma *f* de T (la te)
 – *T-joint (T-junction joint, tee)*
45 la atornilladura de ángulo *m* con
rosca *f* interior
 – *elbow screw joint with female
thread*
46 el recodo
 – *bend*
47 la pieza en forma *f* de T con
rosca *f* interior hembra *f*
 – *T-joint (T-junction joint, tee) with
female taper thread*
48 la juntura de techo *m*
 – *ceiling joint*
49 el codo reductor
 – *reducing elbow*
50 la cruz
 – *cross*
51 la juntura de codo *m* con rosca *f*
macho
 – *elbow joint with male thread*
52 el codo
 – *elbow joint*
53-57 fijación *f* de tubos *m*
 – *pipe supports*
53 la abrazadera de tubo *m*
 – *saddle clip*
54 la abrazadera de espaciamiento *m*
 – *spacing bracket*
55 la espiga
 – *plug*
56 las abrazaderas de tubo *m* simples
 – *pipe clips*
57 la abrazaderas de distancia-
miento *m* de dos piezas *f* (el
puente)
 – *two-piece spacing clip*
58-86 herramientas *f* de instalación *f*
(herramientas *f* de fontanero *m*)
 – *plumber's tools, gas fitter's tools*
58 las tenazas de gasista *m*
 – *gas pliers*
59 la llave para tubos *m*
 – *footprints*
60 los alicates universales
 – *combination cutting pliers*

61 la llave corrediza (el cocodrilo, el
sargento)
 – *pipe wrench*
62 los alicates de boca *f* plana
 – *flat-nose pliers*
63 la chaveta de boquilla *f* roscada
 – *nipple key*
64 las tenazas de puntas *f* redondas
 – *round-nose pliers*
65 las tenazas
 – *pincers*
66 la llave ajustable [forma sueca]
 – *adjustable S-wrench*
67 la llave francesa, una llave de
tuercas *f*
 – *screw wrench*
68 la llave inglesa
 – *shifting spanner*
69 el destornillador
 – *screwdriver*
70 el serrucho de calar o de punta *f*
 – *compass saw (keyhole saw)*
71 el arco de sierra *f* de metal *m*
 – *hacksaw frame*
72 el serrucho
 – *hand saw*
73 el soldador
 – *soldering iron*
74 la lámpara de soldar (el soplete;
*Amér.:* la antorcha)
 – *blowlamp (blowtorch) [for soldering]*
75 la cinta aislante
 – *sealing tape*
76 el estaño para soldar
 – *tin-lead solder*
77 el martillo de porra *f* (la maza)
 – *club hammer*
78 el martillo de mano *f*
 – *hammer*
79 el nivel de agua *f* (el nivel de
burbuja *f*)
 – *spirit level*
80 el tornillo de banco *m* de
cerrajero *m*
 – *steel-leg vice* (Am. *vise)*
81 el tornillo de banco *m* para
tubos *m* (el sujetatubos)
 – *pipe vice* (Am. *vise)*
82 la curvadora de tubos *m*
 – *pipe-bending machine*
83 la forma curvada (la cimbra)
 – *former (template)*
84 el cortatubos
 – *pipe cutter*
85 la terraja de cojinetes *m*
 – *hand die*
86 la máquina de terrajar
 – *screw-cutting machine (thread-
cutting machine)*

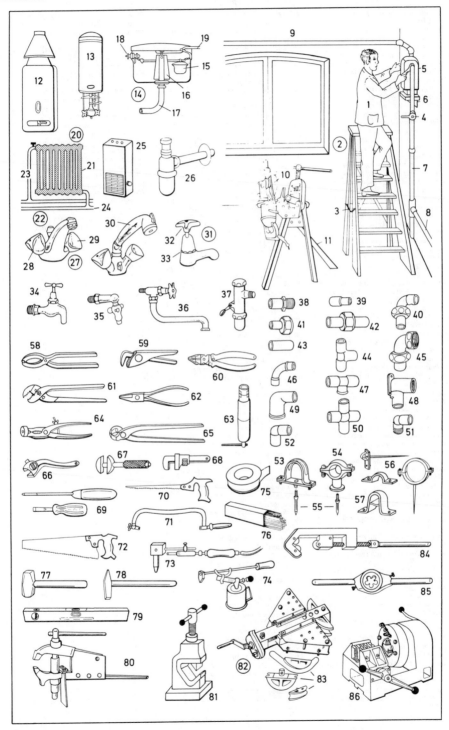

# 127 Electricista

1 el instalador-electricista (el electricista)
- *electrician (electrical fitter, wireman)*
2 el pulsador del timbre para bajo voltaje *m*
- *bell push (doorbell) for low-voltage safety current*
3 el interfono con botón *m* de llamada *f*
- *house telephone with call button*
4 el interruptor con mando *m* basculante empotrable
- *[flush-mounted] rocker switch*
5 la caja de enchufe *m* empotrable
- *[flush-mounted] earthed socket (wall socket, plug point, Am. wall outlet, convenience outlet, outlet)*
6 la caja de enchufe *m* doble empotrable
- *[surface-mounted] earthed double socket (double wall socket, double plug point, Am. double wall outlet, double convenience outlet, double outlet)*
7 la caja combinada (un interruptor y un enchufe)
- *switched socket (switch and socket)*
8 la caja (el adaptador) de cuatro enchufes *m*
- *four-socket (four-way) adapter*
9 la clavija macho (la clavija de contacto *m*; Amér.: la ficha)
- *earthed plug*
10 la alargadera (el cordón prolongador)
- *extension lead (Am. extension cord)*
11 la clavija macho (Amér.: la ficha) de la alargadera
- *extension plug*
12 la clavija hembra (el enchufe) de la alargadera
- *extension socket*
13 el enchufe de superficie *f* tripolar [para circuito *m* trifásico] con toma *f* de tierra *f*
- *surface-mounted three-pole earthed socket [for three-phase circuit] with neutral conductor*
14 la clavija trifásica
- *three-phase plug*
15 el timbre eléctrico
- *electric bell (electric buzzer)*
16 el interruptor con cordón *m*
- *pull-switch (cord-operated wall switch)*
17 el interruptor con regulador *m* de voltaje *m* [para ajustar con progresión *f* continua la intensidad de luz *f* de una lámpara]
- *dimmer switch [for smooth adjustment of lamp brightness]*
18 el interruptor giratorio con caja *f* de hierro *m* fundido
- *drill-cast rotary switch*
19 el automático de seguridad *f* de tornillo *m*
- *miniature circuit breaker (screw-in circuit breaker, fuse)*
20 el pulsador automático (el chivato)
- *resetting button*
21 el tornillo calibrado [para fusibles *m* e interruptores *m* automáticos]
- *set screw [for fuses and miniature circuit breakers]*
22 la caja de enchufe *m* empotrable en el suelo
- *underfloor mounting (underfloor sockets)*
23 el enchufe de bisagra *f* de suelo *m* para corriente *f* y líneas *f* de comunicación *f*
- *hinged floor socket for power lines and communication lines*
24 el enchufe empotrable en el suelo con tapadera *f* de bisagra *f*
- *sunken floor socket with hinged lid (snap lid)*

25 el enchufe de superficie *f* con caja *f* de toma *f*
- *surface-mounted socket outlet (plug point) box*
26 la lámpara de bosillo *m*, una lámpara de pilas *f* (la linterna)
- *pocket torch, a torch (Am. flashlight)*
27 la pila seca (la pila de linterna *f*)
- *dry cell battery*
28 el muelle de contacto *m*
- *contact spring*
29 la regleta (la clema)
- *strip of thermoplastic connectors*
30 el alambre de acero *m* para pasar el conductor
- *steel draw-in wire (draw wire) with threading key, and ring attached*
31 el cajetín del contador
- *electricity meter cupboard*
32 el contador de la electricidad
- *electricity meter*
33 el interruptor automático
- *miniature circuit breakers (miniature circuit breaker consumer unit)*
34 la cinta aislante
- *insulating tape (Am. friction tape)*
35 el portafusibles
- *fuse holder*
36 el fusible, un cartucho con pieza *f* fusible
- *circuit breaker (fuse), a fuse cartridge with fusible element*
37 el indicador de color *m* (que señala el paso de corriente *f*)
- *colour (Am. color) indicator [showing current rating]*
38-39 el contacto
- *contact maker*
40 la grapa de plástico *m*
- *cable clip*
41 el voltímetro
- *universal test meter (multiple meter for measuring current and voltage)*
42 el cable termoplástico resistente a la humedad
- *thermoplastic moisture-proof cable*
43 el conductor de cobre *m*
- *copper conductor*
44 el cable de tres polos *m*
- *three-core cable*
45 el soldador eléctrico
- *electric soldering iron*
46 el destornillador
- *screwdriver*
47 la llave corrediza (el cocodrilo, el sargento)
- *pipe wrench*
48 el casco de seguridad *f* de plástico *m* antigolpes
- *shock-resisting safety helmet*
49 el maletín (la caja) de herramientas *f*
- *tool case*
50 los alicates redondos (los alicates de puntas *f* redondas)
- *round-nose pliers*
51 los alicates para cortar
- *cutting pliers*
52 la sierra pequeña
- *junior hacksaw*
53 los alicates universales
- *combination cutting pliers*
54 la funda protectora
- *insulated handle*
55 el comprobador (el detector) de electricidad *f* (de tensión *f*)
- *continuity tester*
56 la bombilla incandescente (la bombilla; Amér. Central, Col., Pan., P. Rico y S. Dgo.: el bombillo)
- *electric light bulb (general service lamp, filament lamp)*
57 la ampolla de vidrio *m*
- *glass bulb (bulb)*

58 el filamento luminoso incandescente
- *coiled-coil filament*
59 la rosca de la bombilla
- *screw base*
60 el casquillo portabombillas (portalámparas *m*)
- *lampholder*
61 el tubo fluorescente
- *fluorescent tube*
62 el portatubos fluorescentes
- *bracket for fluorescent tubes*
63 la navaja de usos múltiples
- *electrician's knife*
64 los alicates pelacables
- *wire strippers*
65 el portalámparas de bayoneta *f*
- *bayonet fitting*
66 el enchufe tripolar con interruptor *m*
- *three-pin socket with switch*
67 la clavija tripolar
- *three-pin plug*
68 el portafusibles con fusible *m* de cable *m*
- *fuse carrier with fuse wire*
69 la bombilla de bayoneta *f*
- *light bulb with bayonet fitting*

**1-17 la preparación de superficies** *f*
- *preparation of surfaces*
1 el producto para despegar el papel pintado
- *wallpaper-stripping liquid (stripper)*
2 el yeso
- *plaster (plaster of Paris)*
3 la masilla tapaporos
- *filler*
4 el engrudo para el papel pintado
- *glue size (size)*
5 los rollos de papel *m* de desecho *m* (el papel de apresto *m*), el tejido de base *f*
- *lining paper, a backing paper*
6 el aparejo
- *primer*
7 la vasija de fluoruro *m*
- *fluate*
8 el papel de desecho *m* fino
- *shredded lining paper*
9 la máquina para despegar los papeles pintados
- *wallpaper-stripping machine (stripper)*
10 la espátula japonesa
- *scraper*
11 el alisador
- *smoother*
12 el perforador de papeles *m* pintados
- *perforator*
13 el bloque para lijar
- *sandpaper block*
14 el papel de lija *f*
- *sandpaper*
15 el raspador de papeles *m* pintados
- *stripping knife*
16 el papel indicador
- *masking tape*
17 el calicó (la base de tela *f* de algodón *m*)
- *strip of sheet metal [on which wallpaper is laid for cutting]*
**18-53 el empapelado**
- *wallpapering (paper hanging)*

18 el papel pintado (*clases:* papel *m* de fibra *f* gruesa, de tejido, de plástico, metálico, de material *m* natural, el papel pintado con dibujos *m*)
- *wallpaper; kinds: wood pulp paper, wood chip paper, fabric wallhangings, synthetic wallpaper, metallic paper, natural (e.g. wood or cork) paper, tapestry wallpaper*
19 la tira de papel *m* pintado
- *length of wallpaper*
20 la costura de papel *m* pintado, por encima de la juntura
- *butted paper edges*
21 la unión recta
- *matching edge*
22 la unión en aspa *f*
- *non-matching edge*
23 el engrudo para el papel pintado
- *wallpaper paste*
24 el engrudo para el papel pintado especial
- *heavy-duty paste*
25 la máquina de encolar (el papel pintado)
- *pasting machine*
26 el engrudo (para la máquina de encolar)
- *paste [for the pasting machine]*
27 la brocha de encolar (la brocha del engrudo)
- *paste brush*
28 el gluten de dispersión *f*
- *emulsion paste*
29 la varilla para papel *m* pintado
- *picture rail*
30 los clavos para las varillas
- *beading pins*
31 la mesa de encolar
- *pasteboard (paperhanger's bench)*
32 el barniz protector para papel *m* pintado
- *gloss finish*
33 el maletín de empapelador *m*
- *paperhanging kit*

34 las tijeras de empapelador *m*
- *shears (bull-nosed scissors)*
35 la espátula
- *filling knife*
36 el rodillo de empapelador *m* (el rodillo para las junturas)
- *seam roller*
37 el machete
- *hacking knife*
38 el cuchillo de recortar
- *knife (trimming knife)*
39 la regla de empapelador *m* (la regla de borde *m* recto)
- *straightedge*
40 la brocha de empapelador *m*
- *paperhanging brush*
41 la paleta para cortar el papel de la pared
- *wallpaper-cutting board*
42 el cortador
- *cutter*
43 el cuchillo para las junturas
- *trimmer*
44 la espátula de plástico *m*
- *plastic spatula*
45 el cordel para marcar
- *chalked string*
46 la espátula de dientes *m*
- *spreader*
47 el rodillo para el papel pintado
- *paper roller*
48 el tejido de franela *f*
- *flannel cloth*
49 el escobillón de empapelador *m*
- *dry brush*
50 el aparato para empapelar el techo
- *ceiling paperhanger*
51 el ángulo en punta *f* del rincón
- *overlap angle*
52 la escalera doble (la escalera de empapelador *m*)
- *paperhanger's trestles*
53 el papel pintado del techo
- *ceiling paper*

1 la pintura
- *painting*
2 el pintor
- *painter*
3 la brocha de recubrir
- *paintbrush*
4 la pintura de dispersión *f*
- *emulsion paint (emulsion)*
5 la escalera plegable (la escalera doble)
- *stepladder*
6 el bote de pintura *f*
- *can (tin) of paint*
7-8 las latas de pintura *f*
- *cans (tins) of paint*
7 la lata con mango *m* (con empuñadura *f*)
- *can (tin) with fixed handle*
8 la lata con asa *f*
- *paint kettle*
9 el barril de pintura *f*
- *drum of paint*
10 el cubo de pintura *f*
- *paint bucket*
11 el rodillo de pintar
- *paint roller*
12 la rejilla raspadora
- *grill [for removing excess paint from the roller]*
13 el rodillo para granear
- *stippling roller*
14 **el barnizado**
- *varnishing*
15 el zócalo pintado con óleo *m*
- *oil-painted dado*
16 el bidón de disolvente *m*
- *canister for thinner*
17 la brocha plana (para superficies *f*)
- *flat brush for larger surfaces (flat wall brush)*
18 la brocha de motear
- *stippler*
19 el pincel redondo
- *fitch*
20 el pincel para resaltar los contornos
- *cutting-in brush*

21 el pincel para los radiadores
- *radiator brush (flay brush)*
22 la espátula de pintor *m*
- *paint scraper*
23 la espátula japonesa (el raspador)
- *scraper*
24 el cuchillo para la masilla
- *putty knife*
25 el papel de lija *f*
- *sandpaper*
26 el bloque para lijar
- *sandpaper block*
27 el cepillo para el suelo
- *floor brush*
28 **el pulimento y la pintura con pistola *f***
(el pulverizado)
- **sanding and spraying**
29 la lijadora
- *grinder*
30 la lijadora orbital
- *sander*
31 el depósito del aire
- *pressure pot*
32 la pistola de pulverización *f*
- *spray gun*
33 el compresor
- *compressor (air compressor)*
34 el aparato para rellenar de agua *f* los radiadores
- *flow coating machine for flow coating radiators, etc.*
35 la pistola pulverizadora de mano *f*
- *hand spray*
36 el equipo de pulverizar sin aire *m*
- *airless spray unit*
37 la pistola pulverizadora sin aire *m*
- *airless spray gun*
38 el cubilete de salida *f* para medir la viscosidad
- *efflux viscometer*
39 el cuentasegundos
- *seconds timer*

40 **la inscripción y el dorado**
- **lettering and gilding**
41 el pincel para las letras
- *lettering brush (signwriting brush, pencil)*
42 la ruleta para calcar
- *tracing wheel*
43 el cuchillo para plantillas *f*
- *stencil knife*
44 el aceite de aplique *m*
- *oil gold size*
45 el oro de aplique *m* (el oro en hojas *f*, la hoja de oro *m*)
- *gold leaf*
46 el trazado de los contornos
- *outline drawing*
47 el bastón de pintura *f*
- *mahlstick*
48 el pulimento del dibujo
- *pouncing*
49 la bolsa de calco *m*
- *pounce bag*
50 la almohadilla para el oro
- *gilder's cushion*
51 el cuchillo para el oro
- *gilder's knife*
52 el cepillo para coger las hojas de oro *m*
- *sizing gold leaf*
53 el relleno de las letras con pintura *f* granulada
- *filling in the letters with stipple paint*
54 el pincel de dorador (el pincel de motear)
- *gilder's mop*

**1-33 la tonelería y la construcción de depósitos** *m*
- *cooper's and tank construction engineer's workshops*
1 la cuba
- *tank*
2 la circunferencia hecha de duelas *f*
- *circumference made of staves (staved circumference)*
3 el aro metálico (el cincho)
- *iron rod*
4 el tensor
- *turnbuckle*
5 el tonel (el barril)
- *barrel (cask)*
6 el cuerpo del barril
- *body of barrel (of cask)*
7 el agujero del barril (el canillero)
- *bunghole*
8 el aro del barril (el cincho)
- *band (hoop) of barrel*
9 la duela
- *barrel stave*
10 el témpano
- *barrelhead (heading)*
11 el tonelero
- *cooper*
12 el gato de armar
- *trusser*
13 el bidón metálico
- *drum*
14 el soplete de soldar autógeno
- *gas welding torch*

15 la cuba de pintura *f* de materia *f* termoplástica
- *staining vat made of thermoplastics*
16 el cerco de refuerzo *m* perfilado
- *iron reinforcing bands*
17 el depósito de bodega *f*, hecho de resina *f* de poliéster *m* reforzada con fibra *f* de vidrio *m*
- *storage container, made of glass fibre (Am. glass fiber) reinforced polyester resin*
18 el agujero de entrada *f*
- *manhole*
19 la tapadera del agujero de entrada *f* con *f* rueda de rosca *f*
- *manhole cover with handwheel*
20 el soporte para brida *f*
- *flange mount*
21 el obturador
- *flange-type stopcock*
22 el depósito graduado
- *measuring tank*
23 la envoltura (la pared)
- *shell (circumference)*
24 la virola
- *shrink ring*
25 la pistola de aire *m* caliente
- *hot-air gun*
26 el tubo de resina *f* sintética reforzada con fibra *f* de vidrio *m*
- *roller made of glass fibre (Am. glass fiber) reinforced synthetic resin*

27 el cilindro
- *cylinder*
28 el disco de soporte *m* del cilindro
- *flange*
29 el tejido de fibra *f* de vidrio *m*
- *glass cloth*
30 el cilindro acanalado
- *grooved roller*
31 el rodillo de piel *f* de cordero *m*
- *lambskin roller*
32 el cazo para medir la viscosidad
- *ladle for testing viscosity*
33 el dosificador del endurecedor
- *measuring vessel for hardener*

**1-25 el taller de peletero** *m*
– *furrier's workroom*
**1** el peletero
– *furrier*
**2** la pistola pulverizadora de vapor *m*
– *steam spray gun*
**3** la plancha de vapor *m*
– *steam iron*
**4** la máquina de sacudir
– *beating machine*
**5** la máquina de cortar para alargar las pieles
– *cutting machine for letting out furskins*
**6** la piel no cortada
– *uncut furskin*
**7** la piel cortada en tiras *f*
– *let-out strips (let-out sections)*
**8** la trabajadora de la piel (la peletera; la costurera de piel *f*)
– *fur worker*
**9** la máquina de coser las pieles
– *fur-sewing machine*
**10** el ventilador
– *blower for letting out*
**11-21 pieles** *m*
– *furskins*
**11** la piel de visón *m*
– *mink skin*

**12** la flor del cuero (la cara del pelo, el lado del pelo)
– *fur side*
**13** el lado del cuero
– *leather side*
**14** la piel cortada
– *cut furskin*
**15** la piel de lince *m* antes de ser alargada
– *lynx skin before letting out*
**16** la piel de lince *m* alargada
– *let-out lynx skin*
**17** la flor del cuero (la cara del pelo, el lado del pelo)
– *fur side*
**18** el lado del cuero
– *leather side*
**19** la piel de visón *m* alargada
– *let-out mink skin*
**20** la piel de lince *m* empalmada
– *lynx fur, sewn together (sewn)*
**21** la piel de astracán *m* (de breitschwanz *m*)
– *broadtail*
**22** la puntilla para la piel
– *fur marker*
**23** la trabajadora de la piel (la cortadora de la piel; la peletera)
– *fur worker*

**24** el abrigo de visón *m*
– *mink coat*
**25** el abrigo de ocelote *m*
– *ocelot coat*

1-73 **el taller de carpintero** *m* (la carpintería)
- *joiner's workshop*
1-28 **las herramientas de carpintero** *m*
- *joiner's tools*
1 la escofina de madera *f*
- *wood rasp*
2 la escofina de media caña *f*
- *wood file*
3 el serrucho de calar (el serrucho de punta *f*)
- *compass saw (keyhole saw)*
4 la manija del serrucho
- *saw handle*
5 el mazo de madera *f* cuadrado
- *[square-headed] mallet*
6 la escuadra de carpintero *m*
- *try square*
7-11 **formón** *m* **de carpintero** *m*
- *chisels*
7 el escoplo de alfajía *f*
- *bevelled-edge chisel (chisel)*
8 el escoplo para agujeros *m* (el escoplo de fijas *f*)
- *mortise (mortice) chisel*
9 la gubia
- *gouge*
10 el mango
- *handle*
11 el escoplo en bisel *m*
- *framing chisel (cant chisel)*
12 el pote para hacer la cola al baño de María
- *glue pot in water bath*
13 el bote con cola *f*, un bote con cola *f* de carpintero *m* (*Col. y Mé.:* un bote con aguacola *f*)
- *glue pot (glue well), an insert for joiner's glue*
14 la prensa de tornillo *m* (el sargento)
- *handscrew*
15-28 **cepillos** *m* **de carpintero** *m*
- *planes*
15 el cepillo de alisar (*Chile:* el rodón)
- *smoothing plane*
16 el cepillo de desbastar
- *jack plane*
17 el cepillo dentado
- *toothing plane*
18 la empuñadura
- *handle (toat)*
19 la cuña
- *wedge*
20 el hierro (la cuchilla del cepillo)
- *plane iron (cutter)*
21 el hueco de la cuña
- *mouth*
22 la suela (el talón)
- *sole*
23 la parte lateral
- *side*
24 el zoquete (la caja)
- *stock (body)*
25 el cepillo de molduras *f* (el cepillo bocel)
- *rebate (rabbet) plane*
26 la guimbarda
- *router plane (old woman's tooth)*
27 la raedera
- *spokeshave*
28 el cepillo combado (el cepillo en forma *f* de barco *m*)
- *compass plane*

29-37 **el banco de carpintero** *m*
- *woodworker's bench*
29 el pie
- *foot*
30 el torno frontal
- *front vice (Am. vise)*
31 el tornillo del torno con mango *m*
- *vice (Am. vise) handle*
32 el husillo
- *vice (Am. vise) screw*
33 la mandíbula del torno
- *jaw*
34 la plataforma del banco
- *bench top*
35 el herramental
- *well*
36 el gancho (la uña) del banco (el hierro del banco)
- *bench stop (bench holdfast)*
37 el torno trasero
- *tail vice (Am. vise)*
38 el carpintero
- *cabinet maker (joiner)*
39 la garlopa
- *trying plane*
40 las virutas (*Amér. Central:* los colochos)
- *shavings*
41 el tornillo para madera *f*
- *wood screw*
42 el triscador
- *saw set*
43 la caja para cortar en inglete *m*
- *mitre (Am. miter) box*
44 el serrucho, un serrucho de costilla *f*
- *tenon saw*
45 la cepilladora de regrosar (de poner a grueso *m*) las maderas
- *thicknesser (thicknessing machine)*
46 la mesa de cepillado *m*, la mesa con los rodillos
- *thicknessing table with rollers*
47 la defensa contra el retroceso
- *kick-back guard*
48 el colector de virutas *f* con aspirador *m*
- *chip-extractor opening*
49 la fresadora de cadena *f*
- *chain mortising machine (chain mortiser)*
50 la cadena fresadora sin fin *m*
- *endless mortising chain*
51 el dispositivo de fijación *f* de la madera (la abrazadera)
- *clamp (work clamp)*
52 la máquina fresadora de nudo *m*
- *knot hole moulding (Am. molding) machine*
53 la fresa de nudo *m*
- *knot hole cutter*
54 el mandril de sujeción *f* rápido
- *quick-action chuck*
55 la palanca de mano *f*
- *hand lever*
56 la palanca de cambio *m*
- *change-gear handle*
57 la sierra circular para cantear y dar la forma
- *sizing and edging machine*
58 el interruptor principal (el botón de mando *m*)
- *main switch*
59 la hoja de la sierra circular
- *circular-saw (buzz saw) blade*

60 el volante de regulación *f* de la altura
- *height (rise and fall) adjustment wheel*
61 la guía prismática
- *V-way*
62 la mesa para encuadrar la madera
- *framing table*
63 el brazo de extensión *f*
- *extension arm (arm)*
64 la mesa de cantear
- *trimming table*
65 la guía de ingletes *m*
- *fence*
66 el volante para regular la guía
- *fence adjustment handle*
67 la palanca de sujeción *f*
- *clamp lever*
68 la sierra circular para tableros *m*
- *board-sawing machine*
69 el motor móvil (el motor basculante)
- *swivel motor*
70 el dispositivo fijador de los tableros
- *board support*
71 el carro de la sierra
- *saw carriage*
72 el pedal para levantar los rodillos transportadores
- *pedal for raising the transport rollers*
73 el tablero de carpintería *f*
- *block board*

1 la máquina para desenrollar chapas *f* de madera *f*
- *veneer-peeling machine (peeling machine, peeler)*
2 la chapa de madera *f*
- *veneer*
3 la máquina para pegar (con cola *f*) la chapa de madera *f*
- *veneer-splicing machine*
4 la canilla de hilo *m* de nylon *m*
- *nylon-thread cop*
5 el dispositivo de costura *f*
- *sewing mechanism*
6 la taladradora de espiga *f*
- *dowel hole boring machine (dowel hole borer)*
7 el motor de taladrar con broca *f* de eje *m* hueco
- *boring motor with hollow-shaft boring bit*
8 el volante de sujeción *f*
- *clamp handle*
9 el estribo de sujeción *f*
- *clamp*
10 la uña de sujeción *f*
- *clamping shoe*
11 el tope (el riel de tope *m*)
- *stop bar*
12 la máquina afiladora de los cantos
- *edge sander (edge-sanding machine)*
13 el rodillo tensor con brazo *m* de extensión *f*
- *tension roller with extension arm*
14 el tornillo para regular la cinta abrasiva
- *sanding belt regulator (regulating handle)*
15 la cinta abrasiva sin fin *m*
- *endless sanding belt (sand belt)*
16 la palanca de sujeción de la cinta
- *belt-tensioning lever*
17 la mesa de apoyo *m* inclinable
- *canting table (tilting table)*
18 el rodillo de la cinta
- *belt roller*
19 la regla de ángulo *m* para ingletes *m* (la guía para ingletes *m*)
- *angling fence for mitres* (Am. *miters*)
20 el colector del polvo articulado
- *opening dust hood*
21 el dispositivo para regular la profundidad de la mesa de apoyo *m*
- *rise adjustment of the table*
22 el volante para regular la altura de la mesa
- *rise adjustment wheel for the table*
23 el tornillo prisionero para regular la altura de la mesa
- *clamping screw for the table rise adjustment*
24 la repisa de la mesa
- *console*

25 el pie de la máquina
- *foot of the machine*
26 la máquina para pegar los cantos
- *edge-veneering machine*
27 el disco abrasivo
- *sanding wheel*
28 el dispositivo de aspiración *f* del polvo de esmerilado *m*
- *sanding dust extractor*
29 el dispositivo de pegar
- *splicing head*
30 la máquina lijadora de cinta *f* simple (de una sola cinta)
- *single-belt sanding machine (single-belt sander)*
31 el recubrimiento de la cinta
- *belt guard*
32 el recubrimiento circular de la cinta
- *bandwheel cover*
33 el extractor
- *extractor fan (exhaust fan)*
34 el patín lijador del bastidor
- *frame-sanding pad*
35 la mesa de lijar
- *sanding table*
36 el ajuste de precisión *f*
- *fine adjustment*
37 la máquina de precisión *f* para cortar y ensamblar
- *fine cutter and jointer*
38 el carro de la sierra (la combinación de sierra *f* y cepillo *m*) con transmisión *f* por cadena *f*
- *saw carriage with chain drive*
39 el soporte del cable colgado
- *trailing cable hanger (trailing cable support)*
40 el tubo extractor del aire
- *air extractor pipe*
41 el riel (la guía) transportador(a)
- *rail*
42 la prensa de bastidor *m* (la prensa de encuadrar)
- *frame-cramping (frame-clamping) machine*
43 el soporte del bastidor
- *frame stand*
44 la pieza de trabajo *m*, un bastidor de ventana *f*
- *workpiece, a window frame*
45 el conducto de llegada *f* del aire comprimido
- *compressed-air line*
46 el cilindro de presión *f*
- *pressure cylinder*
47 el émbolo (el patín de presión *f*)
- *pressure foot*
48 la sujeción del bastidor
- *frame-mounting device*
49 la máquina para chapear rápidamente
- *rapid-veneer press*
50 el suelo (el lecho) de la prensa
- *bed*

51 el techo de la prensa (la prensa)
- *press*
52 el pistón de la prensa
- *pressure piston*

**1-34** el armario de herramientas *f* para bricolaje *m* (para chapuzas *f*)
– *tool cupboard (tool cabinet) for do-it-yourself work*
**1** el cepillo de alisar
– *smoothing plane*
**2** el juego de llaves *f* de boca *f*
– *set of fork spanners (fork wrenches, open-end wrenches)*
**3** la sierra de arco *m*
– *hacksaw*
**4** el destornillador
– *screwdriver*
**5** el destornillador de estrella *f* (americano)
– *cross-point screwdriver*
**6** el raspador de sierra *f* (la escofina)
– *saw rasp*
**7** el martillo (*Chile y Perú:* el combo)
– *hammer*
**8** la escofina de madera *f*
– *wood rasp*
**9** la lima gruesa
– *roughing file*
**10** el tornillo (el torno) de banco *m* pequeño (*C. Rica, Chile y Ec.:* la taquilla)
– *small vice (Am. vise)*
**11** la llave de tubo *m* (la llave corrediza, el sargento, el cocodrilo)
– *pipe wrench*
**12** la llave para apretar los tubos *m*
– *multiple pliers*
**13** las tenazas
– *pincers*
**14** los alicates universales
– *all-purpose wrench*
**15** los alicates pelacables
– *wire stripper and cutter*
**16** la taladradora eléctrica
– *electric drill*
**17** la sierra para metales *m*
– *hacksaw*
**18** el cubo para el yeso (el cuezo)
– *plaster cup*
**19** el soldador
– *soldering iron*
**20** el hilo de estaño *m* para soldar
– *tin-lead solder wire*
**21** el disco de piel *f* de cordero *m* (el bonete de pulir)
– *lamb's wool polishing bonnet*
**22** el disco de pulir (el disco de goma *f*) para la taladradora
– *rubber backing disc (disk)*
**23** la muela abrasiva (el disco abrasivo)
– *grinding wheel*
**24** el cepillo metálico (con forma *f* de disco *m*)
– *wire wheel brush*
**25** el papel de lija *f* (con forma *f*) de disco *m* (el disco lija *f*)
– *sanding discs (disks)*

**26** la escuadra con espaldón *m*
– *try square*
**27** el serrucho
– *hand saw*
**28** el cortador universal
– *universal cutter*
**29** el nivel de agua *f* (el nivel de burbuja *f*)
– *spirit level*
**30** el formón de carpintero *m*
– *firmer chisel*
**31** el punzón (el granete)
– *centre* (Am. *center) punch*
**32** el punzón de mano *f* (el sacaclavos)
– *nail punch*
**33** el metro plegable
– *folding rule (rule)*
**34** la caja para las piezas pequeñas
– *storage box for small parts*
**35** la caja de las herramientas
– *tool box*
**36** la cola blanca (la cola de carpintero; *Col. y Mé.:* la aguacola)
– *woodworking adhesive*
**37** la espátula
– *stripping knife*
**38** la cinta adhesiva
– *adhesive tape*
**39** la caja con compartimientos para clavos *m*, tornillos *m* y espigas *f*
– *storage box with compartments for nails, screws, and plugs*
**40** el martillo de cerrajero *m*
– *machinist's hammer*
**41** el banco de trabajo *m* plegable
– *collapsible workbench (collapsible bench)*
**42** el dispositivo de sujeción *f*
– *jig*
**43** la taladradora *f* eléctrica con percutor *m*
– *electric percussion drill (electric hammer drill)*
**44** la empuñadura de pistola *f* (la empuñadura de revólver *m*)
– *pistol grip*
**45** la empuñadura adicional
– *side grip*
**46** el pulsador para el cambio de velocidad *f*
– *gearshift switch*
**47** la empuñadura con distanciador *m*
– *handle with depth gauge* (Am. *gage)*
**48** el cabezal portabrocas
– *chuck*
**49** la broca espiral
– *twist bit (twist drill)*
**50-55** accesorios *m* y suplementos *m* para taladradora *f* eléctrica
– *attachments for an electric drill*
**50** la sierra mixta (circular y de vaivén *m*)
– *combined circular saw (buzz saw) and bandsaw*

**51** el torno para madera *f*
– *wood-turning lathe*
**52** el protector de la sierra circular
– *circular saw attachment*
**53** la lijadora orbital
– *orbital sanding attachment (orbital sander)*
**54** el soporte para la taladradora
– *drill stand*
**55** el recortasetos
– *hedge-trimming attachment (hedge trimmer)*
**56** la pistola de soldar
– *soldering gun*
**57** el soldador
– *soldering iron*
**58** el soldador instantáneo
– *high-speed soldering iron*
**59** la tapicería, el tapizado de un sillón
– *upholstery, upholstering an armchair*
**60** la tela del forro
– *fabric (material) for upholstery*
**61** el chapucero (el trabajador que hace toda clase de oficios, el manitas)
– *do-it-yourself enthusiast*

**1-26 la tornería** (el taller de tornero *m*)
– *turnery (turner's workshop)*
**1** el torno al aire (el torno para madera *f*)
– *wood-turning lathe*
**2** el banco del torno de punta *f*
– *lathe bed*
**3** el reóstato de puesta *f* en marcha *f*
– *starting resistance (starting resistor)*
**4** la caja de engranajes *m*
– *gearbox*
**5** el soporte de la herramienta de mano *f*
– *tool rest*
**6** el mandril de agujero *m* simple
– *chuck*
**7** el cabezal móvil
– *tailstock*
**8** la punta fija
– *centre (Am. center)*
**9** la polea, una garrucha con perno *m* de arrastre *m*
– *driving plate with pin*
**10** el mandril de dos mordazas *f*
– *two-jaw chuck*
**11** la broca de centrar de tres puntas *f* (la broca de madera *f*)
– *live centre (Am. center)*
**12** la sierra de calar (la sierra de contornear)
– *fretsaw*

**13** la hoja de la sierra de contornear
– *fretsaw blade*
**14, 15, 24** herramientas *f* de tornero *m*
– *turning tools*
**14** el peine para roscado *m* interior de madera *f*
– *thread chaser, for cutting threads in wood*
**15** el punzón, para practicar el agujero preparatorio del centrado
– *gouge, for rough turning*
**16** la broca de cuchara *f*
– *spoon bit (shell bit)*
**17** el gancho circular
– *hollowing tool*
**18** el calibrador exterior
– *outside calliper (caliper)*
**19** la pieza de madera *f* torneada
– *turned work (turned wood)*
**20** el maestro tornero (el tornero)
– *master turner (turner)*
**21** la madera en bruto *m*
– *[piece of] rough wood*
**22** el berbiquí de carrete *m* (*Amér. Central, Ec. y. Perú:* el biriquí)
– *drill*
**23** el calibrador interior
– *inside calliper (caliper)*
**24** el escoplo de acanalar
– *parting tool*
**25** el papel de lija *f*
– *glass paper; sim.: sandpaper, emery paper*
**26** las virutas
– *shavings*

1-40 la cestería
- *basket making (basketry, basketwork)*
1-4 clases *f* de trenzado *m*
- *weaves (strokes)*
1 el enrejado
- *randing*
2 el cruzadillo
- *rib randing*
3 el trenzado en series *f* diagonales
- *oblique randing*
4 el trenzado simple, un enrejado de mimbre *m*
- *randing, a piece of wickerwork (screen work)*
5 la trama horizontal
- *weaver*
6 la armazón (el montante)
- *stake*
7 el tablero de trabajo *m*
- *workboard;* also: *lapboard*
8 el listón transversal
- *screw block*
9 el agujero para fijar el listón
- *hole for holding the block*
10 el caballete
- *stand*
11 el cesto hecho con virutas *f*
- *chip basket (spale basket)*
12 la viruta
- *chip (spale)*
13 la tina de remojo *m*
- *soaking tub*
14 las varillas de mimbre *m*
- *willow stakes (osier stakes)*

15 los palos de mimbre *m*
- *willow rods (osier rods)*
16 el cesto (*Bol., Col., Cuba, Chile y Perú:* el balay), un trabajo trenzado
- *basket, a piece of wickerwork (basketwork)*
17 el ribete
- *border*
18 el trenzado lateral
- *woven side*
19 el fondo
- *round base*
20 el trenzado del fondo
- *woven base*
21 la cruz del fondo
- *slath*
22-24 el trabajo de bastidor *m* (de armazón *f*)
- *covering a frame*
22 la armazón (el bastidor)
- *frame*
23 el cabo
- *end*
24 la varilla guía
- *rib*
25 el varillaje
- *upsett*
26 las gramíneas; *clases:* esparto *m*, alfa *f*
- *grass;* kinds: *esparto grass, alfalfa grass*
27 la caña
- *rush,* e.g. *bulrush, reed mace*

28 el junco (cordón *m* de junco *m* de la China)
- *reed (China reed, string)*
29 la rafia
- *raffia;* sim.: *bast*
30 la paja
- *straw*
31 la caña de bambú *m*
- *bamboo cane*
32 la rota (el bejuco)
- *rattan (ratan) chair cane*
33 el cestero
- *basket maker*
34 el curvador
- *bending tool*
35 el rajador
- *cutting point (bodkin)*
36 el batidor
- *rapping iron*
37 las tenazas
- *pincers*
38 la raedera
- *picking knife*
39 el cepillo para las varillas guías
- *shave*
40 la sierra de arco *m*
- *hacksaw*

**1-8  la fragua con el fuego de fragua** *f*
- *hearth (forge) with blacksmith's fire*
**1** la fragua
- *hearth (forge)*
**2** el badil (la pala para mover el fuego)
- *shovel (slice)*
**3** el escobillón para la extinción
- *swab*
**4** el hurgón
- *rake*
**5** el atizador
- *poker*
**6** la llegada del aire
- *blast pipe (tue iron)*
**7** la campana de la chimenea
- *chimney (cowl, hood)*
**8** la pila para el remojo
- *water trough (quenching trough, bosh)*
**9** el martillo neumático (el martillo pilón) de herrería *f*
- *power hammer*
**10** la maza
- *ram (tup)*
**11-16  el yunque**
- *anvil*
**11** el yunque
- *anvil*
**12** el cuerno cuadrado
- *flat beak (beck, bick)*
**13** el cuerno redondo
- *round beak (beck, bick)*
**14** la tabla auxiliar del yunque
- *auxiliary table*

**15** el pie del yunque
- *foot*
**16** el tronco para golpear (el bloque para remachar)
- *upsetting block*
**17** la placa matriz de agujeros *m*
- *swage block*
**18** la máquina para afilar las herramientas (la afiladora)
- *tool-grinding machine (tool grinder)*
**19** la muela abrasiva
- *grinding wheel*
**20** el aparejo (el polipasto)
- *block and tackle*
**21** el banco de trabajo *m*
- *workbench (bench)*
**22-39  herramientas** *f* **de herrería** *f*
- *blacksmith's tools*
**22** el martillo a dos manos *f* (el macho de fragua *f*; Amér.: el marrón)
- *sledge hammer*
**23** el martillo de mano *f*
- *blacksmith's hand hammer*
**24** las tenazas de boca *f* plana
- *flat tongs*
**25** las tenazas de pico *m* redondo
- *round tongs*
**26** las partes de los martillos
- *parts of the hammer*
**27** el corte (la pala, la peña)
- *peen (pane, pein)*
**28** el plano (el cotillo)
- *face*
**29** el ojo
- *eye*

**30** el mango (el astil)
- *haft*
**31** la cuña
- *cotter punch*
**32** la tajadera
- *hardy (hardie)*
**33** el martillo plano
- *set hammer*
**34** el martillo de calderero *m*
- *sett (set, sate)*
**35** la aplanadora de forja (el martillo de allanar)
- *flat-face hammer (flatter)*
**36** el martillo para agujerear
- *round punch*
**37** las tenazas angulares
- *angle tongs*
**38** el cincel tajador (el cortafrío)
- *blacksmith's chisel (scaling hammer, chipping hammer)*
**39** el hierro para curvar
- *moving iron (bending iron)*

1 la instalación de aire *m* comprimido
– *compressed-air system*
2 el motor eléctrico
– *electric motor*
3 el compresor
– *compressor*
4 el depósito de aire *m* comprimido
– *compressed-air tank*
5 la canalización (la tubería) del aire comprimido
– *compressed-air line*
6 el destornillador de percusión *f* de aire *m* comprimido
– *percussion screwdriver*
7 el aparato para afilar (la máquina afiladora de taller *m*)
– *pedestal grinding machine (floor grinding machine)*
8 la muela
– *grinding wheel*
9 la cubierta de protección *f*
– *guard*
10 el remolque
– *trailer*
11 el tambor del freno
– *brake drum*
12 las zapatas del freno
– *brake shoe*
13 el forro del freno
– *brake lining*
14 la caja de prueba *f*
– *testing kit*

15 el aparato para medir el aire comprimido (el manómetro)
– *pressure gauge (Am. gage)*
16 el banco de prueba *f* de los frenos, un banco de prueba *f* de los frenos de rodillos *m*
– *brake-testing equipment, a rolling road*
17 el foso
– *pit*
18 el rodillo de frenada *f*
– *braking roller*
19 el aparato de registro *m* (el registrador)
– *meter (recording meter)*
20 el torno de precisión *f* para el tambor del freno
– *precision lathe for brake drums*
21 la rueda de camión *m*
– *lorry wheel*
22 el mecanismo de perforación *f*
– *boring mill*
23 la sierra rápida, una sierra de arco *m*
– *power hacksaw, a power saw*
24 el tornillo de banco *m*
– *vice (Am. vise)*
25 el arco de la sierra *f*
– *saw frame*
26 la canalización de refrigerante *m*
– *coolant supply pipe*
27 la remachadora
– *riveting machine*

28 el chasis de remolque *m* en construcción *f*
– *trailer frame (chassis) under construction*
29 el aparato para soldar en atmósfera *f* controlada (con gas *m* inerte)
– *inert-gas welding equipment*
30 el rectificador de corriente *f*
– *rectifier*
31 la unidad de control (el aparato de mando *m*)
– *control unit*
32 la botella de $CO_2$
– *$CO_2$ cylinder*
33 el yunque
– *anvil*
34 la fragua con el fuego de fragua *f*
– *hearth (forge) with blacksmith's fire*
35 el carrito de soldadura *f* autógena
– *trolley for gas cylinders*
36 el vehículo en reparación *f*, un tractor
– *vehicle under repair, a tractor*

# 139 Taller de forja libre y en estampa (Forja industrial)

1 el horno de empuje m
(impulsión f) continuo(a) con
solera f de rejilla f para
calentar los materiales
redondos (redondeles m)
– continuous furnace with grid
hearth for annealing of round
stock
2 la puerta (la boca) de descarga f
– discharge opening (discharge
door)
3 el quemador de gas m
– gas burners
4 la puerta de carga f
– charging door
5 el martillo pilón de
contragolpe m
– counterblow hammer
6 la maza superior
– upper ram
7 la maza inferior
– lower ram
8 la guía de la masa
– ram guide
9 la impulsión (el empuje)
hidráulica(o)
– hydraulic drive
10 el pilar (el montante)
– column
11 el martillo estampador de corta
elevación f
– short-stroke drop hammer
12 la maza del martillo pilón (la
maza, el martillo pilón)
– ram (tup)
13 la matriz superior (de forjar en
estampa f)
– upper die block
14 la matriz inferior (de forjar en
estampa f)
– lower die block
15 la impulsión (el empuje)
hidráulica(o)
– hydraulic drive
16 el montante (la armazón) del
martillo pilón
– fiame
17 el yunque
– anvil
18 la prensa de forjar en estampa f
y de calibrar
– forging and sizing press
19 el pilar (el montante) de la
máquina
– standard
20 el tablero de la mesa
– table
21 el embrague de fricción f de
láminas f
– disc (disk) clutch
22 la tubería del aire comprimido
– compressed-air pipe
23 la electroválvula
– solenoid valve
24 el martillo pilón neumático
– air-lift gravity hammer (air-lift
drop hammer)
25 el motor de impulsión f
– drive motor

26 la maza
– hammer (tup)
27 el pedal
. – foot control (foot pedal)
28 la pieza forjada en estampa f
– preshaped (blocked) workpiece
29 la cabeza guía de la maza
– hammer guide
30 el cilindro de la maza
– hammer cylinder
31 el yunque (el macho de
estampa f)
– anvil
32 el manipulador para mover la
pieza en la forja libre
– mechanical manipulator to move
the workpiece in hammer forging
33 las tenazas (la quijada)
– dogs
34 el contrapeso
– counterweight
35 la prensa de forja f hidráulica
– hydraulic forging press
36 el sistema hidráulico
– crown
37 la cruceta de cabeza f
– cross head
38 la matriz superior (de forjar en
estampa f)
– upper die block
39 la matriz inferior (de forjar en
estampa f)
– lower die block
40 el tajo del yunque (la chabota)
– anvil
41 el pistón hidráulico
– hydraulic piston
42 la columna guía
– pillar guide
43 el mecanismo de vuelta f
– rollover device
44 la cadena grúa
– burden chain (chain sling)
45 el gancho de la grúa
– crane hook
46 la pieza de forja f
– workpiece
47 el horno de forja f de gas m
– gas furnace (gas-fired furnace)
48 el quemador (el mechero) de
gas m
– gas burner
49 la boca de carga f
– charging opening
50 la cortina de cadenas f
– chain curtain
51 la puerta levadiza
– vertical-lift door
52 la tubería de aire m caliente
– hot-air duct
53 el precalentador de aire m
– air preheater
54 la tubería de conducción f del
gas
– gas pipe
55 el dispositivo de elevación f de
la puerta
– electric door-lifting mechanism
56 la cortina de aire m
– air blast

22

1-22 **el taller de cerrajero** *m* (la cerrajería)
- *metalwork shop*, e.g. *mechanic's workshop, fitter's workshop, locksmith's workshop*
1 el cerrajero (*ejemplos:* el cerrajero mecánico, el cerrajero de taller *m*, el cerrajero de taller *m* de acero *m*)
- *metalworker*, e.g. *mechanic, fitter, locksmith, wrought-iron craftsman*
2 el tornillo paralelo
- *parallel-jaw vice (Am. vise)*
3 la mandíbula
- *jaw*
4 la barra de rosca *f*
- *screw*
5 la palanca
- *handle*
6 la pieza de trabajo *m*
- *workpiece*
7 el banco de trabajo *m*
- *workbench (bench)*
8 la lima (*clases:* lima *f* bastarda, lima *f* dulce, lima *f* de precisión *f*)
- *files; kinds: rough file, smooth file, precision file*
9 la sierra de arco *m*
- *hacksaw*
10 el tornillo de banco *m* plano, el tornillo de mordaza *f*
- *leg vice (Am. vise), a spring vice*
11 la mufla, un horno de banco *m* (horno *m* de forja *f* de gas *m*, horno *m* para templar)
- *muffle furnace, a gas-fired furnace*

12 la entrada del gas
- *gas pipe*
13 la taladradora de mano *f*
- *hand brace (hand drill)*
14 el tas (la estampa) de banco *m*, para curvar, enderezar y estampar
- *swage block*
15 la máquina de limar (la limadora)
- *filing machine*
16 la lima de cinta *f*
- *file*
17 el tubo quitalimaduras
- *compressed-air pipe*
18 la máquina de afilar (la afiladora)
- *grinding machine (grinder)*
19 la muela
- *grinding wheel*
20 la cubierta protectora
- *guard*
21 las gafas de protección *f*
- *goggles (safety glasses)*
22 el casco de protección *f*
- *safety helmet*
23 el martillo de cerrajero *m* (el martillo de remachar)
- *machinist's hammer*
24 el tornillo de mano *f* (las entenallas)
- *hand vice (Am. vise)*
25 el cincel cruciforme (el cincel puntiagudo)
- *cape chisel (cross-cut chisel)*
26 el cincel plano
- *flat chisel*
27 la lima plana
- *flat file*

28 la picadura de la lima
- *file cut (cut)*
29 la lima redonda (la lima de media caña *f*)
- *round file;* also: *half-round file*
30 el giramachos
- *tap wrench*
31 el escariador
- *reamer*
32 la terraja de cojinetes *m*
- *die (die and stock)*
33-35 **la llave**
- *key*
33 la tija
- *stem (shank)*
34 el ojo (el anillo)
- *bow*
35 el paletón
- *bit*
36-43 **la cerradura de puerta** *f*, una cerradura empotrable
- *door lock, a mortise (mortice) lock*
36 el palastro
- *back plate*
37 el pestillo
- *spring bolt (latch bolt)*
38 el fiador (la gacheta)
- *tumbler*
39 el cerrojo (el pestillo)
- *bolt*
40 el ojo de la cerradura (la bocallave)
- *keyhole*
41 la espiga guía del pestillo
- *bolt guide pin*

**42** el muelle *m* de la gacheta (del fiador)
 - *tumbler spring*
**43** la nuez, con agujero *m* cuadrangular
 - *follower, with square hole*
**44** la cerradura cilíndrica (cerradura *f* de seguridad *f*)
 - *cylinder lock (safety lock)*
**45** el cilindro
 - *cylinder (plug)*
**46** el muelle
 - *spring*
**47** la clavija de tope *m*
 - *pin*
**48** la llave de seguridad *f*, una llave plana
 - *safety key, a flat key*
**49** el gozne
 - *lift-off hinge*
**50** la bisagra acodada
 - *hook-and-ride band*
**51** la bisagra de ramal *m* (el pernio)
 - *strap hinge*
**52** el calibre para medir gruesos *m* (el pie de rey *m*)
 - *vernier calliper (caliper) gauge* (Am. *gage)*
**53** la galga de espesores *m*
 - *feeler gauge* (Am. *gage)*
**54** el calibre para huecos *m* (para alturas *f*, para profundidades *f*)
 - *vernier depth gauge* (Am. *gage)*
**55** el nonio
 - *vernier*
**56** la regla de filo *m*
 - *straightedge*
**57** la escuadra de medida *f*
 - *square*
**58** el taladro de pecho *m*
 - *breast drill*
**59** la broca espiral
 - *twist bit (twist drill)*
**60** el macho de roscar
 - *screw tap (tap)*
**61** los cojinetes de rosca *f*
 - *halves of a screw die*
**62** el destornillador
 - *screwdriver*
**63** el rascador (*igual:* el rascador triangular)
 - *scraper; also: pointed triangle scraper*
**64** el granete (el punzón) de marcar
 - *centre* (Am. *center) punch*
**65** el taladro
 - *round punch*
**66** los alicates planos
 - *flat-nose pliers*
**67** las tenazas articuladas de corte *m*
 - *detachable-jaw cut nippers*
**68** las mordazas para tubos *m* (mordazas *f* de gas *m*)
 - *gas pliers*
**69** las tenazas
 - *pincers*

1 la batería de botellas *f*
- *gas cylinder manifold*
2 la botella de acetileno *m*
- *acetylene cylinder*
3 la botella de oxígeno *m*
- *oxygen cylinder*
4 el manómetro de alta presión *f*
- *high-pressure manometer*
5 la válvula reductora de la presión
- *pressure-reducing valve (reducing valve, pressure regulator)*
6 el manómetro de baja presión *f*
- *low-pressure manometer*
7 la válvula de cierre *m*
- *stop valve*
8 la válvula hidráulica de baja presión *f*
- *hydraulic back-pressure valve for low-pressure installations*
9 el tubo (de goma *f*) del gas
- *gas hose*
10 el tubo (de goma *f*) del oxígeno
- *oxygen hose*
11 el soplete de soldar (*Amér.*: la antorcha)
- *welding torch (blowpipe)*
12 la varilla de aportación *f* (la varilla de fusión *f*)
- *welding rod (filler rod)*
13 la mesa de soldar
- *welding bench*
14 el enrejado de corte *m*
- *grating*
15 la caja de hierro *m* de desecho *m*
- *scrap box*

16 la cubierta de la mesa, de ladrillo *m* refractario
- *bench covering of chamotte slabs*
17 el depósito de agua *f*
- *water tank*
18 la pasta de soldar
- *welding paste (flux)*
19 el soplete de soldar, equipado con boquilla *f* de corte *m* y carrito *m* guía de la llama
- *welding torch (blowpipe) with cutting attachment and guide tractor*
20 la pieza de trabajo (la pieza para soldar)
- *workpiece*
21 la botella de oxígeno *m*
- *oxygen cylinder*
22 la botella de acetileno *m*
- *acetylene cylinder*
23 la carretilla de las botellas
- *cylinder trolley*
24 las gafas de soldador *m*
- *welding goggles*
25 el martillo de desbastar
- *chipping hammer*
26 el cepillo de alambre *m*
- *wire brush*
27 el encendedor del soplete
- *torch lighter (blowpipe lighter)*
28 el soplete de soldar (*Amér.*: la antorcha)
- *welding torch (blowpipe)*
29 la válvula del oxígeno
- *oxygen control*

30 la conexión del oxígeno
- *oxygen connection*
31 la conexión del gas combustible
- *gas connection (acetylene connection)*
32 la válvula del gas combustible
- *gas control (acetylene control)*
33 la boquilla de soldar
- *welding nozzle*
34 la máquina de corte *m* autógeno (la máquina de oxicorte *m*)
- *cutting machine*
35 la plantilla (el modelo) circular
- *circular template*
36 la máquina de corte *m* autógeno universal
- *universal cutting machine*
37 la cabeza de mando *m*
- *tracing head*
38 la boquilla del soplete
- *cutting nozzle*

1 el transformador de soldadura *f*
– *welding transformer*
2 el soldador eléctrico
– *arc welder*
3 la capucha de soldar
– *arc welding helmet*
4 el vidrio protector abatible
– *flip-up window*
5 la protección de los hombros
– *shoulder guard*
6 la manga de protección *f*
– *protective sleeve*
7 el carcaj de los electrodos
– *electrode case*
8 el guante de soldador de tres
dedos *m*
– *three-fingered welding glove*
9 el portaelectrodos
– *electrode holder*
10 el electrodo
– *electrode*
11 el mandil (el delantal de cuero *m*)
– *leather apron*
12 la protección de las espinillas (las
polainas de protección *f*, la
espinillera)
– *shin guard*
13 la mesa de soldar por aspiración *f*
– *welding table with fume extraction
equipment*
14 el tablero (la superficie) de la
mesa de aspiración *f*
– *table top*
15 la trompa (el tubo) de aspiración *f*
orientable
– *movable extractor duct*

16 la tubuladura del aire de escape *m*
– *extractor support*
17 el martillo de desbastar
– *chipping hammer*
18 el cepillo de alambre *m* de
acero *m*
– *wire brush*
19 el cable de soldar
– *welding lead*
20 el portaelectrodos
– *electrode holder*
21 la mesa de soldar
– *welding bench*
22 la soldadura por puntos *m*
– *spot welding*
23 las pinzas para soldar por
puntos *m*
– *spot welding electrode holder*
24 el brazo portaelectrodos
– *electrode arm*
25 la llegada de corriente *f* (el cable
de conexión *f*)
– *lead*
26 el cilindro de presión *f* del
electrodo
– *electrode-pressure cylinder*
27 el transformador de soldadura *f*
– *welding transformer*
28 la pieza de trabajo *m* (la pieza
para soldar)
– *workpiece*
29 la máquina de soldar por
puntos *m* accionada por pedal *m*
– *foot-operated spot welder*
30 los brazos de soldar
– *welder electrode arms*

31 el pedal para regular la presión *f*
del electrodo
– *foot pedal for welding pressure
adjustment*
32 el guante de soldador *m* de cinco
dedos *m*
– *five-fingered welding glove*
33 el soplete (*Amér.*: la antorcha) de
soldadura *f* en atmósfera *f*
controlada (la soldadura con
gas *m* inerte)
– *inert-gas torch for inert-gas welding
(gas-shielded arc welding)*
34 la llegada del gas inerte
– *inert-gas (shielding-gas) supply*
35 el borne de tierra *f* (la pinza de
masa *f*)
– *work clamp, an earthing clamp*
36 el calibre de soldadura *f* de
ángulo *m*
– *fillet gauge* (Am. *gage*) *(weld
gauge) [for measuring throat
thickness]*
37 el tornillo micrométrico
– *micrometer*
38 el brazo de medida *f*
– *measuring arm*
39 el escudo (el casco) de
protección *f* para soldar
– *arc welding helmet*
40 el cristal del casco de soldar
– *filter lens*
41 la mesa giratoria pequeña
– *small turntable*

# 143 Perfiles, tornillos y piezas de máquinas

1 el ángulo (el hierro de ángulo, la rinconera)
– angle iron (angle)
2 el ala f (el lado)
– leg (flange)
3-7 **viguetas f de hierro** m (vigas f de acero m de construcción f)
– **steel girders**
3 el hierro en T (la T)
– T-iron (tee-iron)
4 el alma f
– vertical leg
5 el ala f
– flange
6 el hierro en doble T
– H-girder (H-beam)
7 el hierro en U (la U)
– E-channel (channel iron)
8 el hierro cilíndrico (el hierro redondo)
– round bar
9 el hierro cuadrado
– square iron (Am. square stock)
10 el hierro plano
– flat bar
11 el fleje de hierro m
– strip steel
12 el alambre
– iron wire
13-50 **tornillos** m
– **screws and bolts**
13 el tornillo de cabeza f hexagonal
– hexagonal-head bolt
14 la cabeza
– head
15 el vástago (el tallo, la varilla)
– shank
16 el filete (la rosca)
– thread
17 la arandela
– washer
18 la tuerca hexagonal
– hexagonal nut
19 la chaveta (el pasador)
– split pin
20 el extremo redondo
– rounded end
21 la abertura de la llave
– width of head (of flats)
22 el espárrago
– stud
23 la punta (el extremo)
– point (end)
24 la tuerca hexagonal con entalladuras f (la tuerca corona)
– castle nut (castellated nut)
25 el orificio para la chaveta
– hole for the split pin
26 el tornillo de cabeza f cruciforme (un tornillo para chapa f)
– cross-head screw, a sheet-metal screw (self-tapping screw)
27 el tornillo de cabeza f cilíndrica con seis lados m en el interior
– hexagonal socket head screw
28 el tornillo de cabeza f avellanada (el tornillo embutido)
– countersunk-head bolt
29 el fiador (la uña)
– catch
30 la contratuerca
– locknut (locking nut)
31 la espiga
– bolt (pin)
32 el tornillo con collar m
– collar-head bolt
33 el collar
– set collar (integral collar)
34 la arandela de muelle m
– spring washer (washer)
35 la tuerca redonda con agujero m, una tuerca de ajuste m
– round nut, an adjusting nut
36 el tornillo de cabeza f cilíndrica, un tornillo de cabeza f ranurada
– cheese-head screw, a slotted screw

37 el pasador cónico
– tapered pin
38 la ranura (la muesca) del tornillo
– screw slit (screw slit, screw groove)
39 el tornillo de cabeza f cuadrada
– square-head bolt
40 el pasador con muesca f, un pasador cilíndrico
– grooved pin, a cylindrical pin
41 el tornillo de cabeza f de martillo m (de cabeza f en T)
– T-head bolt
42 la tuerca de orejas f
– wing nut (fly nut, butterfly nut)
43 el tornillo para piedra f (el perno de anclaje m)
– rag bolt
44 el garfio
– barb
45 el tornillo para madera f
– wood screw
46 la cabeza avellanada
– countersunk head
47 la rosca de madera f (la rosca golosa)
– wood screw thread
48 el tornillo prisionero (la punta con filete m)
– grub screw
49 la ranura (la muesca)
– pin slot (pin slit, pin groove)
50 la punta esférica
– round end
51 el clavo (la punta de París)
– wire nail
52 la cabeza
– head
53 la espiga
– shank
54 la punta
– point
55 la punta para cartón m asfaltado (el clavo de techar, la tachuela)
– roofing nail
56 el remachado (la roblonadura)
– riveting; here: lap riveting
57-60 **el remache** (el roblón)
– **rivet**
57 la cabeza de la matriz, una cabeza de roblón m
– set head (swage head, die head), a rivet head
58 la espiga del remache
– rivet shank
59 la cabeza de cierre m
– closing head
60 la distancia entre los remaches
– pitch of rivets
61 el eje (el árbol)
– shaft
62 el chaflán (el bisel)
– chamfer (bevel)
63 el gorrón (el muñón)
– journal
64 el cuello
– neck
65 el asiento
– seat
66 el encaje del pasador (la ranura para la chaveta)
– keyway
67 el asiento cónico (el cono)
– conical seat (cone)
68 la rosca
– thread
69 el rodamiento de bolas f, un rodamiento (cojinete m de bolas f)
– ball bearing, an antifriction bearing
70 la bola de acero m
– steel ball (ball)
71 el anillo exterior
– outer race
72 el anillo interior
– inner race

73-74 **las chavetas**
– **keys**
73 la chaveta embutida (la chaveta de resorte m)
– sunk key (feather)
74 la chaveta con talón m (la contraclavija)
– gib (gib-headed key)
75-76 **el rodamiento de agujas f**
– **needle roller bearing**
75 la jaula de las agujas f
– needle cage
76 la aguja
– needle
77 la tuerca hexagonal con entalladuras f
– castle nut (castellated nut)
78 la chaveta (el pasador)
– split pin
79 la caja
– casing
80 la cubierta de la caja
– casing cover
81 la boquilla roscada para el engrase a presión f
– grease nipple (lubricating nipple)
82-96 **ruedas f dentadas** (engranajes m)
– **gear wheels, cog wheels**
82 el engranaje escalonado
– stepped gear wheel
83 el diente
– cog (tooth)
84 el fondo del diente
– space between teeth
85 la ranura para la chaveta
– keyway (key seat, key slot)
86 el calibre
– bore
87 la rueda dentada cilíndrica doble helicoidal (rueda f de dientes m en ángulo m)
– herringbone gear wheel
88 el rayo (la rueda f)
– spokes (arms)
89 el engranaje helicoidal
– helical gearing (helical spur wheel)
90 la corona dentada
– sprocket
91 la rueda dentada cónica
– bevel gear wheel (bevel wheel)
92-93 **el engranaje en espiral** f
– **spiral toothing**
92 el piñón
– pinion
93 la corona dentada
– crown wheel
94 el engranaje (el tren) planetario
– epicyclic gear (planetary gear)
95 el engranaje interior
– internal toothing
96 el engranaje exterior
– external toothing
97-107 **frenos** m **dinamométricos**
– **absorption dynamometer**
97 el freno de zapatas f
– shoe brake (check brake, block brake)
98 el disco de freno m
– brake pulley
99 el árbol del freno
– brake shaft (brake axle)
100 la zapata (almohadilla f) de freno m
– brake block (brake shoe)
101 el tirante
– pull rod
102 la magneto del freno
– brake magnet
103 el contrapeso del freno
– brake weight
104 el freno de cinta f
– band brake
105 la cinta del freno
– brake band
106 la cubierta del freno
– brake lining
107 el tornillo de ajuste m, para asegurar una aplicación uniforme del freno
– adjusting screw, for even application of the brake

**1-51 la mina de carbón *m* de piedra *f*** (la mina de hulla *f*, la mina)
- **coal mine** *(colliery, pit)*
1 el castillete de extracción *f*
- *pithead gear (headgear)*
2 la sala de máquinas *f*
- *winding engine house*
3 la torre de extracción *f*
- *pithead frame (head frame)*
4 el edificio del pozo (de la mina)
- *pithead building*
5 la planta de preparación *f*
- *processing plant*
6 el aserradero
- *sawmill*
**7-11 la coquería**
- **coking plant**
7 la batería de horno *m* de coque *m*
- *battery of coke ovens*
8 el vagón de carga *f*
- *larry car (larry, charging car)*
9 la torre de carbón *m* de coque *m*
- *coking coal tower*
10 la torre de extinción *f* del coque
- *coke-quenching tower*
11 el vagón de extinción *f* del coque
- *coke-quenching car*
12 el gasómetro
- *gasometer*
13 la central eléctrica
- *power plant (power station)*
14 la torre de agua *f*
- *water tower*
15 la torre de refrigeración *f*
- *cooling tower*
16 el ventilador de la mina
- *mine fan*
17 el emplazamiento (*Amér.:* la ubicación) del almacén de material *m*
- *depot*
18 el edificio de la administración
- *administration building (office building, offices)*
19 el escorial
- *tip heap (spoil heap)*
20 la estación de depuración *f* (de aguas *f* residuales)
- *cleaning plant*
**21-51 la explotación subterránea**
- **underground workings**
21 el pozo de ventilación *f*
- *ventilation shaft*
22 el canal de tiro *m* del ventilador
- *fan drift*
23 el montacargas con jaulas de extracción *f* [transporte de productos]
- *cage-winding system with cages*
24 el pozo principal
- *main shaft*
25 la instalación de extracción *f* por montacargas *m*
- *skip-winding system*

26 el cargadero
- *winding inset*
27 el pozo interior (el pozo ciego)
- *staple shaft*
28 el resbaladero en espiral *f*
- *spiral chute*
29 la galería del yacimiento
- *gallery along seam*
30 la galería recta
- *lateral*
31 la galería (el corte) transversal
- *cross-cut*
32 la máquina de propulsión *f* para los trazados (la máquina para hacer túneles *m*)
- *tunnelling (Am. tunneling) machine*
**33-37 cortes *m***
- **longwall faces**
33 el corte horizontal a cepillo *m*
- *horizontal ploughed longwall face*
34 el corte horizontal por capas *f* paralelas a la estratificación
- *horizontal cut longwall face*
35 el corte vertical a martillo *m* neumático
- *vertical pneumatic pick longwall face*
36 el corte vertical a martillo *m* pilón
- *diagonal ram longwall face*
37 los desechos (*Bol., Chile, Hond. y Perú:* el desmonte)
- *goaf (gob, waste)*
38 la esclusa de aire *m* (la esclusa de ventilación *f*)
- *air lock*
39 el traslado del personal en vagonetas *f*
- *transportation of men by cars*
40 la cinta transportadora
- *belt conveying*
41 la carbonera de hulla *f* en bruto *m*
- *raw coal bunker*
42 la cinta de carga *f*
- *charging conveyor*
43 el transporte de las mercancías en monocarril *m* aéreo
- *transportation of supplies by monorail car*
44 el traslado del personal en monocarril *m* aéreo
- *transportation of men by monorail car*
45 el transporte de materiales *m* en vagonetas *f*
- *transportation of supplies by mine car*
46 el drenaje de agua *f*
- *drainage*
47 el sumidero del pozo
- *sump (sink)*
48 el terreno de recubrimiento *m*
- *capping*
49 el terreno de carbón *m* de piedra *f* (de hulla *f*)
- *coal-bearing rock*

50 el filón de hulla *f*
- *coal seam*
51 la falla
- *fault*

**1-21 el sondeo petrolífero**
- *oil drilling*
1 la torre de perforación *f*
- *drilling rig*
2 la subestructura (el cimiento)
- *substructure*
3 la plataforma de trabajo *m*
- *crown safety platform*
4 las poleas de la torre
- *crown blocks*
5 la plataforma de celosías *f*, una plataforma intermedia
- *working platform, an intermediate platform*
6 los tubos de perforación *f*
- *drill pipes*
7 el cable de perforación *f*
- *drilling cable (drilling line)*
8 el polipasto (el grupo móvil de poleas *f*)
- *travelling (Am. traveling) block*
9 el gancho de tracción *f*
- *hook*
10 el eslabón giratorio (la unión giratoria)
- *swivel*
11 el mecanismo elevador, un torno (*Amér. Merid.:* el guinche)
- *draw works, a hoist*
12 la máquina motriz (el motor)
- *engine*
13 el tubo de extracción *f* del fango
- *standpipe and rotary hose*
14 la varilla de arrastre *m*
- *kelly*
15 el platillo giratorio
- *rotary table*

16 la bomba de extracción *f* del fango
- *slush pump (mud pump)*
17 el pozo de sondeo *m* (el taladro)
- *well*
18 el tubo vertical de revestimiento *m*
- *casing*
19 la varilla de perforación *f*
- *drilling pipe*
20 el entubado
- *tubing*
21 el punzón (el taladro, la broca, la barrena); *clases:* barrena *f* de cola *f* de pescado *m*, taladro *m* de ballesta *f*, barrena *f* sacamuestras
- *drilling bit;* kinds: *fishtail (blade) bit, rock (Am. roller) bit, core bit*
**22-27 la extracción de petróleo *m***
- *oil (crude oil) production*
22 el grupo impulsor de bombeo *m*
- *pumping unit (pump)*
23 el émbolo buzo
- *plunger*
24 los tubos elevadores
- *tubing*
25 la varilla de la bomba
- *sucker rods (pumping rods)*
26 el prensaestopas
- *stuffing box*
27 la varilla pulimentada
- *polish (polished) rod*
**28-35 el refino del petróleo crudo** [esquema]
- *treatment of crude oil [diagram]*
28 el separador de gas *m*
- *gas separator*
29 la tubería (la conducción) de gas *m*
- *gas pipe (gas outlet)*

30 el depósito del petróleo líquido
- *wet oil tank (wash tank)*
31 el precalentador
- *water heater*
32 la unidad de drenaje *m* y de desmineralización *f*
- *water and brine separator*
33 la canalización del agua *f* salada
- *salt water pipe (salt water outlet)*
34 el depósito del petróleo refinado
- *oil tank*
35 la canalización de transporte *m* del petróleo refinado [para la refinería o para transpote *m* por camión *m* cisterna *f*, petrolero *m*, oleoducto *m*]
- *trunk pipeline for oil [to the refinery or transport by tanker lorry (Am. tank truck), oil tanker, or pipeline]*
**36-64 la transformación del petróleo crudo** [esquema]
- *processing of crude oil [diagram]*
36 el calentador del petróleo (el horno tubular)
- *oil furnace (pipe still)*
37 la columna de destilación *f* (la torre fraccionadora) con plataformas *f* superpuestas
- *fractionating column (distillation column) with trays*
38 los gases ligeros (acumulados en la cima de la columna)
- *top gases (tops)*
39 la fracción de bencina *f* ligera
- *light distillation products*
40 la fracción de bencina *f* pesada
- *heavy distillation products*

# Petróleo

41 el petróleo lampante
- *petroleum*
42 la fracción de gasoil *m*
- *gas oil component*
43 los residuos
- *residue*
44 el refrigerador
- *condenser (cooler)*
45 el compresor
- *compressor*
46 la unidad de desulfuración *f*
- *desulphurizing (desulphurization, Am. desulfurizing, desulfurization) plant*
47 la unidad de reforma *f*
- *reformer (hydroformer, platformer)*
48 la instalación de craqueo *m* catalítico
- *catalytic cracker (cat cracker)*
49 la columna de destilación *f*
- *distillation column*
50 la separación de la parafina
- *de-waxing (wax separation)*
51 la instalación de vacío *m* (el canal de aspiración *f*)
- *vacuum equipment*
**52-64 los productos derivados del petróleo**
- *oil products*
52 el gas de combustión *f*
- *fuel gas*
53 el gas líquido
- *liquefied petroleum gas (liquid gas)*
54 la gasolina normal (la gasolina para automóvil; *Amér.:* la nafta)
- *regular grade petrol (Am. gasoline)*

55 la gasolina súper
- *super grade petrol (Am. gasoline)*
56 el carburante diesel (el combustible para motores *m* diesel)
- *diesel oil*
57 la gasolina de aviación *f* (el carburante para reactores *m*)
- *aviation fuel*
58 el fuel-oil ligero (el aceite combustible ligero)
- *light fuel oil*
59 el fuel-oil pesado
- *heavy fuel oil*
60 la parafina
- *paraffin (paraffin oil, kerosene)*
61 el lubrificante para ejes *m*
- *spindle oil*
62 el aceite lubrificante
- *lubricating oil*
63 el lubrificante para cilindros *m*
- *cylinder oil*
64 el betún
- *bitumen*
**65-74 la refinería de petróleo *m***
- *oil refinery*
65 el oleoducto
- *pipeline (oil pipeline)*
66 las instalaciones de destilación *f*
- *distillation plants*
67 la refinería del aceite lubrificante
- *lubricating oil refinery*
68 la recuperación del azufre
- *desulphurizing (desulphurization, Am. desulfurizing, desulfurization) plant*

69 la instalación de separación *f* del gas
- *gas-separating plant*
70 el fraccionador (craqueador *m*) catalítico
- *catalytic cracking plant*
71 el reformador catalítico (el hidroformador)
- *catalytic reformer*
72 el tanque de almacenamiento *m*
- *storage tank*
73 el tanque esférico
- *spherical tank*
74 el puerto petrolero
- *tanker terminal*

# 146 Perforación a poca distancia de la costa (Perforación off-shore)

**1-39 la plataforma de perforación** *f* (la plataforma de extracción *f*)
– *drilling rig (oil rig)*
**1-37 la plataforma del castillete de perforación** *f*
– *drilling platform*
**1** la instalación de abastecimiento *m* de energía *f*
– *power station*
**2** las chimeneas para los gases quemados (los tubos de escape *m*) de los generadores
– *generator exhausts*
**3** la grúa giratoria
– *revolving crane (pedestal crane)*
**4** el almacén de los tubos
– *piperack*
**5** los tubos de escape *m* de las turbinas
– *turbine exhausts*
**6** el almacén de los materiales
– *materials store*
**7** la cubierta (el puente) para helicópteros *m*
– *helicopter deck (heliport deck, heliport)*
**8** el montacargas
– *elevator*
**9** el dispositivo para separar el gas y el petróleo
– *production oil and gas separator*
**10** el separador de muestras *f*
– *test oil and gas separators (test separators)*
**11** la antorcha de emergencia *f*
– *emergency flare stack*
**12** la torre de perforación *f*
– *derrick*
**13** el tanque de gasóleo *m*
– *diesel tank*
**14** las oficinas
– *office building*
**15** los tanques para el almacenamiento de cemento *m*
– *cement storage tanks*
**16** el tanque para el agua *f* potable
– *drinking water tank*
**17** el tanque de reserva para el agua *f* salada
– *salt water tank*
**18** los tanques de carburante *m* para helicópteros *m*
– *jet fuel tanks*
**19** el bote salvavidas
– *lifeboats*
**20** la caja del ascensor
– *elevator shaft*
**21** el depósito del aire comprimido
– *compressed-air reservoir*
**22** la estación de bombeo *m*
– *pumping station*
**23** el compresor del aire
– *air compressor*
**24** la instalación de climatización *f*
– *air lock*
**25** la instalación de desmineralización *f* del agua *f* del mar
– *seawater desalination plant*

**26** la instalación para filtrar el gasóleo
– *inlet filters for diesel fuel*
**27** el refrigerador de gas *m*
– *gas cooler*
**28** el pupitre de mando *m* (el panel de control *m*) para los separadores
– *control panel for the separators*
**29** los servicios (los aseos, los lavabos)
– *toilets (lavatories)*
**30** el taller
– *workshop*
**31** la esclusa del tritón [el "tritón" se utiliza para limpiar el oleoducto]
– *pig trap [the 'pig' is used to clean the oil pipeline]*
**32** la sala de control *m*
– *control room*
**33** las habitaciones
– *accommodation modules (accommodation)*
**34** las bombas de cimentación *f* a alta presión *f*
– *high-pressure cementing pumps*
**35** la cubierta inferior
– *lower deck*
**36** la cubierta intermedia
– *middle deck*
**37** la cubierta superior
– *top deck (main deck)*
**38** la construcción de soporte *m* (la infraestructura)
– *substructure*
**39** el nivel del mar
– *mean sea level*

# 147 Planta siderúrgica                                    *Iron and Steel Works*

**1-20 la instalación de los altos hornos**
- *blast furnace plant*
1 el alto horno, un horno de cubilote *m*
- *blast furnace, a shaft furnace*
2 el montacargas inclinado, para el mineral y fundentes *m* o coque *m*
- *furnace incline (lift) for ore and flux or coke*
3 el carro corredizo
- *skip hoist*
4 la plataforma del tragante (de carga *f*)
- *charging platform*
5 la cuba de la tolva
- *receiving hopper*
6 el cono de cierre *m* (la campana del tragante)
- *bell*
7 la cuba del alto horno
- *blast furnace shaft*
8 la zona de reducción *f*
- *smelting section*
9 el caño de la escoria
- *slag escape*
10 la cuba de la escoria
- *slag ladle*
11 el caño del hierro crudo
- *pig iron (crude iron, iron) runout*
12 el caldero del hierro crudo
- *pig iron (crude iron, iron) ladle*
13 el tubo de salida *f* del gas del tragante
- *downtake*
14 el colector de polvo *m*
- *dust catcher, a dust-collecting machine*
15 el calentador del aire
- *hot-blast stove*
16 el pozo externo de combustión *f*
- *external combustion chamber*
17 la entrada de aire *m* frío
- *blast main*
18 el conducto del gas
- *gas pipe*
19 el conducto del aire caliente
- *hot-blast pipe*
20 la tobera
- *tuyère*
**21-69 la fábrica de acero *m***
- *steelworks*
**21-30 el horno Martin-Siemens**
- *Siemens-Martin open-hearth furnace*
21 el caldero (el crisol) del hierro crudo
- *pig iron (crude iron, iron) ladle*
22 la reguera del bebedero (el canal de alimentación *f*)
- *feed runner*
23 el horno fijo
- *stationary furnace*
24 el hogar
- *hearth*
25 la máquina de carga *f*
- *charging machine*
26 el molde (la lingotera) para chatarra *f*
- *scrap iron charging box*
27 el conducto del gas
- *gas pipe*
28 la cámara para calentar el gas
- *gas regenerator chamber*
29 la tubería de alimentación *f* de aire *m*
- *air feed pipe*
30 la cámara para calentar el aire
- *air regenerator chamber*

31 el caldero del acero fundido, con cierre *m* tapón *m* [descarga por el fondo]
- *[bottom-pouring] steel-casting ladle with stopper*
32 la lingotera
- *ingot mould* (Am. *mold*)
33 el lingote de acero *m* (el tocho)
- *steel ingot*
**34-44 la máquina de colar lingotes *m***
- *pig-casting machine*
34 el recogedor de colada *f*
- *pouring end*
35 el canal del hierro
- *metal runner*
36 la cinta de lingoteras *f* [la serie de moldes *m* de tochos *m*]
- *series (strand) of moulds* (Am. *molds*)
37 la lingotera
- *mould* (Am. *mold*)
38 la pasarela
- *catwalk*
39 el dispositivo de caída *f*
- *discharging chute*
40 el lingote (el hierro crudo)
- *pig*
41 la grúa de corredera *f*
- *travelling* (Am. *traveling*) *crane*
42 el caldero de hierro *m* crudo con descarga *f* por arriba
- *top-pouring pig iron (crude iron, iron) ladle*
43 el pico del caldero de colada *f*
- *pouring ladle lip*
44 el dispositivo basculante
- *tilting device (tipping device,* Am. *dumping device)*
**45-50 el convertidor soplado por oxígeno *m* (el convertidor L-D, el convertidor Linz-Donawitz)**
- *oxygen-blowing converter;* here: *Linz-Donawitz (L-D) converter*
45 el sombrerete del convertidor
- *conical converter top*
46 el anillo portador
- *mantle*
47 el fondo del convertidor
- *solid converter bottom*
48 la mampostería refractaria
- *fireproof lining (refractory lining)*
49 la lanza para oxígeno *m*
- *oxygen lance*
50 la piquera de colada *f*
- *tapping hole (tap hole)*
**51-54 el horno eléctrico de arco *m* Siemens, un horno de cubilote *m* bajo**
- *Siemens electric low-shaft furnace*
51 la boca de carga *f*
- *feed*
52 los electrodos [dispuestos en círculo]
- *electrodes [arranged in a circle]*
53 la tubería circular, para expulsar los gases del horno
- *bustle pipe*
54 la colada
- *runout*
**55-69 el convertidor Thomas**
- *Thomas converter (basic Bessemer converter)*
55 la posición de carga *f* para el hierro crudo líquido
- *charging position for molten pig iron*
56 la posición de carga *f* para la cal
- *charging position for lime*

57 la posición para el soplado
- *blow position*
58 la posición de descarga *f*
- *discharging position*
59 el dispositivo volcador
- *tilting device (tipping device,* Am. *dumping device)*
60 el caldero movido por grúa *f*
- *crane-operated ladle*
61 la cabria auxiliar de la grúa
- *auxiliary crane hoist*
62 la tolva de la cal
- *lime bunker*
63 el tubo de caída *f*
- *downpipe*
64 la vagoneta con chatarra *f* ligera de hierro *m*
- *tipping car* (Am. *dump truck)*
65 la alimentación de chatarra *f* de hierro *m*
- *scrap iron feed*
66 la mesa de control *m*
- *control desk*
67 la chimenea del convertidor
- *converter chimney*
68 el tubo de inyección *f* de aire *m*
- *blast main*
69 el fondo de convertidor *m*
- *wind box*

258

**1-45 el taller de fundición** (*Ec. y Perú:* la factoría)
– *iron foundry*
**1-12 la fusión**
– *melting plant*
**1** el cubilote, un horno de fusión *f*
– *cupola furnace (cupola), a melting furnace*
**2** el conducto de aire *m* (la tubería de aire *m*)
– *blast main (blast inlet, blast pipe)*
**3** el canal de la colada
– *tapping spout*
**4** el agujero de observación *f* (la mirilla)
– *spyhole*
**5** el antecrisol basculante
– *tilting-type hot-metal receiver*
**6** el caldero de tambor *m* móvil
– *mobile drum-type ladle*
**7** el fundidor
– *melter*
**8** el vaciador
– *founder (caster)*
**9** la varilla de colada *f*
– *tap bar (tapping bar)*
**10** la varilla tapón *m*
– *bott stick (Am. bot stick)*
**11** el hierro líquido
– *molten iron*
**12** el canal de la escoria
– *slag spout*
**13** la cuadrilla de vaciadores *m*
– *casting team*
**14** el caldero para horquilla *f* (el caldero portátil)
– *hand shank*
**15** la horquilla portacaldero
– *double handle (crutch)*

**16** la barra de transporte *m*
– *carrying bar*
**17** la varilla de la escoria
– *skimmer rod*
**18** la caja cerrada de moldeo *m*
– *closed moulding* (Am. *molding*) *box*
**19** la caja superior
– *upper frame (cope)*
**20** la caja inferior
– *lower frame (drag)*
**21** el bebedero (la piquera)
– *runner (runner gate, down-gate)*
**22** el respiradero
– *riser (riser gate)*
**23** el caldero de mano *f* (la cuchara de colada *f*)
– *hand ladle*
**24-29 la colada continua**
– *continuous casting*
**24** la mesa de colada descendente
– *sinking pouring floor*
**25** el lingote de metal *m* solidific- ándose
– *solidifying pig*
**26** la fase sólida
– *solid stage*
**27** la fase líquida
– *liquid stage*
**28** la refrigeración por agua *f*
– *water-cooling system*
**29** la pared de la lingotera
– *mould (Am. mold) wall*
**30-37 el moldeo**
– *moulding* (Am. *molding*) *department (moulding shop)*
**30** el moldeador
– *moulder* (Am. *molder*)
**31** el atacador de aire *m* comprimido
– *pneumatic rammer*

**32** el atacador de mano *f*
– *hand rammer*
**33** la caja abierta de moldeado *m*
– *open moulding* (Am. *molding*) *box*
**34** el molde (la impresión del molde)
– *pattern*
**35** la arena de moldear
– *moulding* (Am. *molding*) *sand*
**36** el macho
– *core*
**37** la portada de macho *m*
– *core print*
**38-45 el taller de rebarbado *m***
– *cleaning shop (fettling shop)*
**38** el tubo de alimentación *f* de gravilla *f* de acero *m* o de arena *f*
– *steel grit or sand delivery pipe*
**39** el soplete automático de mesa *m* giratoria
– *rotary-table shot-blasting machine*
**40** la defensa de la piedra arenisca
– *grit guard*
**41** la mesa giratoria
– *revolving table*
**42** la pieza de fundición *f*
– *casting*
**43** el rebarbador
– *fettler*
**44** la máquina afiladora de aire *m* comprimido
– *pneumatic grinder*
**45** el cincel de aire *m* comprimido
– *pneumatic chisel*

**46-75 el laminador**
- *rolling mill*
**46** el horno de foso *m*
- *soaking pit*
**47** la grúa para el horno de foso *m*,
una grúa de tenazas *f*
- *soaking pit crane*
**48** el lingote en bruto (el lingote de
acero *m* bruto moldeado)
- *ingot*
**49** la vagoneta volquete *m* para los
lingotes
- *ingot tipper*
**50** el tren blooming
- *blooming train (roller path)*
**51** el material laminado
- *workpiece*
**52** las tijeras para lingotes *m*
- *bloom shears*
**53** el laminador dúo
- *two-high mill*
**54-55 el juego de cilindros *m***
- *set of rolls (set of rollers)*
**54** el cilindro superior
- *upper roll (upper roller)*
**55** el cilindro inferior
- *lower roll (lower roller)*
**56-60 la caja de laminado *m***
- *roll stand*
**56** la plataforma base
- *base plate*
**57** el montante de cilindros *m*
- *housing (frame)*
**58** el árbol de acoplamiento *m*
- *coupling spindle*
**59** el calibre
- *groove*
**60** el cojinete del cilindro
- *roll bearing*

**61-65 el dispositivo de ajuste *m***
- *adjusting equipment*
**61** la guarnición del bastidor
- *chock*
**62** el tornillo de presión *f*
- *main screw*
**63** el engranaje
- *gear*
**64** el motor
- *motor*
**65** el indicador, para el ajuste grueso
o fino
- *indicator for rough and fine
adjustment*
**66-75 el tren de laminado *m* continuo
para manufacturar flejes *m* de
acero *m* (el tren de bandas *f*)
[esquema]**
- *continuous rolling mill train for the
manufacture of strip [diagram]*
**66-68** el acabado del producto
semimanufacturado
- *processing of semi-finished product*
**66** el producto semimanufacturado
- *semi-finished product*
**67** la instalación de corte *m* autógeno
- *gas cutting installation*
**68** la pila de láminas *f* acabadas
- *stack of finished steel sheets*
**69** el horno de empuje *m*
- *continuous reheating furnaces*
**70** el tren desbastador
- *blooming train*
**71** el tren de acabado
- *finishing train*
**72** el rodillo (la bobina para enrollar)
- *coiler*

**73** el almacén de flejes (coronas *f*)
para la venta
- *collar bearing for marketing*
**74** el tren de corte *m* de 5 mm
- *5 mm shearing train*
**75** el tren de corte *m* de 10 mm
- *10 mm shearing train*

# 149 Máquinas-herramientas I        *Machine Tools I*

1 el torno para cilindrar y roscar (filetear)
- centre *(Am. center) lathe*
2 el cabezal fijo con el cambio de velocidades *f*
- *headstock with gear control (geared headstock)*
3 la palanca de mando *m* del reductor
- *reduction drive lever*
4 la palanca para roscas *f* normales y de paso *m* empinado
- *lever for normal and coarse threads*
5 el reglaje de la velocidad
- *speed change lever*
6 la palanca para el mecanismo de viraje *m* del husillo patrón
- *leadscrew reverse-gear lever*
7 la caja de engranajes *m* para cambiar
- *change-gear box*
8 la caja de avances *m* (el dispositivo Norton, la caja Norton)
- *feed gearbox; here: Norton tumbler gear*
9 las palancas para los cambios de avance *m* y de pasos *m* de rosca *f*
- *levers for changing the feed and thread pitch*
10 la palanca del mecanismo de avance *m*
- *feed gear lever (tumbler lever)*
11 la palanca de maniobra *f* para la marcha a la derecha o a la izquierda del husillo principal
- *switch lever for right or left hand action of main spindle*
12 el pie (la base) del torno
- *lathe foot (footpiece)*
13 el volante para el movimiento longitudinal del carro
- *leadscrew handwheel for traversing of saddle (longitudinal movement of saddle)*
14 la palanca para el mecanismo inversor del sentido del avance
- *tumbler reverse lever*
15 el husillo de regulación *f*
- *feed screw*
16 el tablero del carro
- *apron (saddle apron, carriage apron)*
17 la palanca para el movimiento longitudinal y transversal
- *lever for longitudinal and transverse motion*
18 el tornillo sin fin *m* de caída *f* para embragar los avances
- *drop (dropping) worm (feed trip, feed tripping device) for engaging feed mechanisms*
19 la palanca para la tuerca partida del husillo principal
- *lever for engaging half nut of leadscrew (lever for clasp nut engagement)*
20 el husillo giratorio (el husillo de trabajo *m*, el portabrocas)
- *lathe spindle*
21 el portaherramientas
- *tool post*
22 el carro superior (el carrito longitudinal)
- *top slide (tool slide, tool rest)*
23 el carrito transversal
- *cross slide*

24 el carro de la bancada
- *bed slide*
25 el tubo para el refrigerante
- *coolant supply pipe*
26 la contrapunta del cabezal móvil
- *tailstock centre (Am. center)*
27 el casquillo (el cañón)
- *barrel (tailstock barrel)*
28 la palanca para el bloqueo del casquillo
- *tailstock barrel clamp lever*
29 el cabezal móvil
- *tailstock*
30 el volante para el ajuste del casquillo
- *tailstock barrel adjusting handwheel*
31 la bancada del torno
- *lathe bed*
32 el husillo principal (la barra de roscar)
- *leadscrew*
33 el husillo de tracción *f* (la barra de cilindrar, el árbol de guía *f*)
- *feed shaft*
34 el árbol de cambio *m* de marcha *f* para movimiento *m* a la derecha e izquierda *f*
- *reverse shaft for right and left hand motion and engaging and disengaging*
35 el mandril (el plato) de cuatro mordazas *f* (garras *f*)
- *four-jaw chuck (four-jaw independent chuck)*
36 la mordaza de sujeción *f*
- *gripping jaw*
37 el mandril (el plato) de tres mordazas *f* (garras *f*)
- *three-jaw chuck (three-jaw self-centring, self-centering, chuck)*
38 el torno (de) revólver *m*
- *turret lathe*
39 el carrito transversal
- *cross slide*
40 el cabezal revólver
- *turret*
41 el portapunteros (el portacuchillas) múltiple
- *combination toolholder (multiple turning head)*
42 el carrito lingitudinal
- *top slide*
43 la palanca cruciforme
- *star wheel*
44 la cubeta para las virutas y para refrigerar la sustancia (el aceite) lubricante
- *coolant tray for collecting coolant and swarf*

45-53 herramientas (cuchillas *f*) de torno *m*
- *lathe tools*
45 la herramienta con placas *f* giratorias para cortar
- *tool bit holder (clamp tip tool) for adjustable cutting tips*
46 la placa cortante de metal *m* duro o de cerámica *f* de óxidos *m*
- *adjustable cutting tip (clamp tip) of cemented carbide or oxide ceramic*
47 las formas de las placas ajustables de cerámica *f* de óxidos *m*
- *shapes of adjustable oxide ceramic tips*

48 la cuchilla de torno con corte *m* de metal *m* duro
- *lathe tool with cemented carbide cutting edge*
49 el mango de la cuchilla
- *tool shank*
50 la placa de metal *m* duro (la cuchilla de metal *m* duro) soldada
- *brazed cemented carbide cutting tip (cutting edge)*
51 la herramienta para los ángulos interiores
- *internal facing tool (boring tool) for corner work*
52 la cuchilla de torno *m* encorvada
- *general-purpose lathe tool*
53 la cuchilla de torno *m* para punzar
- *parting (parting-off) tool*
54 el perro de arrastre *m*
- *lathe carrier*
55 el tope de arrastre *m*
- *driving (driver) plate*
56-72 instrumental *m* de medida *f*
- *measuring instruments*
56 el calibre de interiores *m* para agujeros *m* (calibre *m* macho)
- *plug gauge (Am. gage)*
57 el tapón "bueno" (o de aceptación *f*)
- *'GO' gauging (Am. gaging) member (end)*
58 el tapón "malo" (o de rechazo *m*)
- *'NOT GO' gauging (Am. gaging) member (end)*
59 el calibrador de exteriores *m* (calibrador *m* de mordazas *f*)
- *calliper (caliper, snap) gauge (Am. gage)*
60 el lado pasa (la abertura máxima)
- *'GO' side*
61 el lado no pasa (la abertura mínima)
- *'NOT GO' side*
62 el tornillo micrométrico (el palmer)
- *micrometer*
63 la escala graduada
- *measuring scale*
64 el tambor graduado
- *graduated thimble*
65 el arco de medida *f*
- *frame*
66 el husillo de medida *f* (la punta de contacto *m*)
- *spindle (screwed spindle)*
67 el pie de rey *m*
- *vernier calliper (caliper) gauge (Am. gage)*
68 la medida de profundidad *f*
- *depth gauge (Am. gage) attachment rule*
69 la escala de nonio *m*
- *vernier scale*
70 los picos de medida *f* exterior
- *outside jaws*
71 los picos de medida *f* interior
- *inside jaws*
72 el calibrador de profundidades *f*
- *vernier depth gauge (Am. gage)*

1 la máquina rectificadora
cilíndrica universal
– *universal grinding machine*
2 el cabezal fijo
– *headstock*
3 el carrito de rectificación *f*
– *wheelhead slide*
4 la muela
– *grinding wheel*
5 el cabezal móvil
– *tailstock*
6 el banco de la rectificadora
– *grinding machine bed*
7 la mesa de la rectificadora
– *grinding machine table*
8 la cepilladora de dos
montantes *m*
– *two-column planing machine
(two-column planer)*
9 el motor de accionamiento *m*,
un motor de corriente *f*
continua con velocidad *f*
regulable
– *drive motor, a direct current
motor*
10 el montante
– *column*
11 la mesa de cepillado *m*
– *planer table*
12 el travesaño
– *cross slide (rail)*
13 el carrito portaherramientas
– *tool box*
14 la sierra de arco *m*
– *hacksaw*
15 el dispositivo de fijación *f*
– *clamping device*
16 la hoja de sierra *f*
– *saw blade*
17 el arco de sierra *f*
– *saw frame*
18 la taladradora giratoria o
(taladradora) radial
– *radial (radial-arm) drilling
machine*
19 el plinto (*sin.:* el pie, la base, el
zócalo)
– *bed (base plate)*
20 la mesa para guardar las piezas
de trabajo *m*
– *block for workpiece*
21 la columna
– *pillar*
22 el motor elevador
– *lifting motor*
23 el husillo portabrocas
– *drill spindle*
24 el brazo radial
– *arm*
25 la mandriladora-fresadora *f*
horizontal (una taladradora de
mesa *f*)
– *horizontal boring and milling
machine*
26 la caja portabrocas
– *movable headstock*
27 la broca (el husillo)
– *spindle*

28 la mesa de cruz *f* (la mesa de
movimientos *m* cruzados)
– *auxiliary table*
29 el banco
– *bed*
30 la columna de la luneta
– *fixed steady*
31 el montante de la mandriladora
– *boring mill column*
32 la fresadora universal
– *universal milling machine*
33 la mesa de fresar
– *milling machine table*
34 el accionamiento del avance de
la mesa
– *table feed drive*
35 la palanca de cambio *m* de
velocidad *f* de rotación *f* de la
broca de fresado *m*
– *switch lever for spindle rotation
speed*
36 la caja de velocidades *f*
– *control box (control unit)*
37 la broca de fresado *m* vertical
– *vertical milling spindle*
38 la cabeza de accionamiento *m*
vertical
– *vertical drive head*
39 la broca de fresado *m*
horizontal
– *horizontal milling spindle*
40 el cojinete delantero para
estabilizar la broca horizontal
– *end support for steadying
horizontal spindle*
41 el centro de mecanizado *m*, una
máquina de mesa *f* circular
– *machining centre (Am. center), a
rotary-table machine*
42 la mesa de mando *m* circular
– *rotary (circular) indexing table*
43 la fresa para agujeros *m*
oblongos (la fresa para ranuras
*f*)
– *end mill*
44 el macho de roscar a máquina *f*
– *machine tap*
45 la limadora (máquina
limadora) de gran velocidad *f*
– *shaping machine (shaper)*

# 151 Oficina de proyectos (oficina de dibujo) *Drawing Office*

1 el tablero de dibujo *m*
- *drawing board*
2 la máquina de dibujar con guía *f*
- *drafting machine with parallel motion*
3 la cabeza de dibujar regulable
- *adjustable knob*
4 la regla de escuadra *f*
- *drawing head (adjustable set square)*
5 la regulación del tablero de dibujo *m*
- *drawing board adjustment*
6 la mesa de dibujar
- *drawing table*
7 la escuadra de dibujar (la escuadra de delineante *m*)
- *set square (triangle)*
8 la escuadra equilátera
- *triangle*
9 la regla en forma *f* de T
- *T-square (tee-square)*
10 el rollo de plano *m*
- *rolled drawing*
11 la representación gráfica (el diagrama)
- *diagram*
12 el panel para el plano terminado (el planning mural)
- *time schedule*
13 el soporte para el papel
- *paper stand*
14 el rollo de papel *m*
- *roll of paper*
15 el dispositivo de corte *m* (la cuchilla)
- *cutter*
16 el plano industrial
- *technical drawing (drawing, design)*
17 la vista de frente *m* (la vista frontal)
- *front view (front elevation)*
18 la vista lateral (la vista de lado *m*)
- *side view (side elevation)*
19 la vista superior
- *plan*
20 la superficie no trabajada
- *surface not to be machined*
21 la superficie pulida, una superficie trabajada
- *surface to be machined*
22 la superficie alisada en fino
- *surface to be superfinished*
23 el borde visible
- *visible edge*
24 el borde no visible
- *hidden edge*
25 la línea de cota *f*
- *dimension line*
26 la flecha de cota *f*
- *arrow head*
27 la indicación (la dirección) de corte *m*
- *section line*
28 el corte A-B
- *section A-B*

29 la superficie rayada
- *hatched surface*
30 la mediana (el eje)
- *centre (Am. center) line*
31 el cuadrito de los caracteres
- *title panel (title block)*
32 la nomenclatura (los datos técnicos)
- *technical data*
33 la regla plana graduada
- *ruler (rule)*
34 la escala de reducción *f* triangular
- *triangular scale*
35 la plantilla para grabar
- *erasing shield*
36 el tintero de tinta *f* china
- *drawing ink cartridge*
37 el soporte para las plumas de tinta *f* china
- *holders for tubular drawing pens*
38 el juego de plumas *f* de tinta *f* china
- *set of tubular drawing pens*
39 el higrómetro
- *hygrometer*
40 el capuchón con indicación *f* del espesor del trazo (del punto)
- *cap with indication of nib size*
41 el lápiz de borrar
- *pencil-type eraser*
42 la goma de borrar (*Amér.*: el borrador)
- *eraser*
43 el (cuchillo) raspador
- *erasing knife*
44 la cuchilla de raspar
- *erasing knife blade*
45 el lapicero de presión *f* (el portaminas)
- *clutch-type pencil*
46 la mina de grafito *m*
- *pencil lead (refill lead, refill, spare lead)*
47 el pincel de borrar (el borrador de fibra *f* de vidrio *m*)
- *glass eraser*
48 las fibras de vidrio *m*
- *glass fibres (Am. fibers)*
49 el tiralíneas
- *ruling pen*
50 la bisagra de cruz *f*
- *cross joint*
51 el disco graduado
- *index plate*
52 el compás de puntas *f* recambiables
- *compass with interchangeable attachments*
53 la guía (la corredera)
- *compass head*
54 la unión de las puntas
- *needle point attachment*
55 la mina de plomo *m*
- *pencil point attachment*
56 la aguja (la punta)
- *needle*

57 la alargadera
- *lengthening arm (extension bar)*
58 el recambio del tiralíneas
- *ruling pen attachment*
59 la bigotera de bomba *f*
- *pump compass (drop compass)*
60 la punta corrediza
- *piston*
61 el tiralíneas del compás
- *ruling pen attachment*
62 el suplemento de mina *f* de plomo *m*
- *pencil attachment*
63 el frasco de tinta *f* china
- *drawing ink container*
64 el compás de ajuste *m* rápido (el compás de precisión *f*)
- *spring bow (rapid adjustment, ratchet-type) compass*
65 la arandela de muelle
- *spring ring hinge*
66 el arco de ajuste *m* micrométrico con muelle *m*
- *spring-loaded fine adjustment for arcs*
67 la aguja desviada
- *right-angle needle*
68 el suplemento tubular de tinta *f* china
- *tubular ink unit*
69 la plantilla de letras *f*
- *stencil lettering guide (lettering stencil)*
70 la plantilla de círculos *m* (el trazacírculos)
- *circle template*
71 la plantilla de elipses *f* (el trazaelipses)
- *ellipse template*

**1-28 la central termoeléctrica,** una
central eléctrica
- *steam-generating station, an
  electric power plant*
**1-21 el edificio (la sala) de
calderas** *f*
- *boiler house*
**1** la cinta transportadora de
carbón *m*
- *coal conveyor*
**2** el depósito del carbón
- *coal bunker*
**3** la cinta de evacuación *f* del
carbón
- *travelling-grate (Am. traveling-
  grate) stoker*
**4** la trituradora del carbón
- *coal mill*
**5** la caldera de vapor *m*, una
caldera tubular (caldera *f* de
radiación *f*)
- *steam boiler, a water-tube boiler
  (radiant-type boiler)*
**6** la cámara de combustión *f*
- *burners*
**7** los tubos del agua *f*
- *water pipes*
**8** el cenicero
- *ash pit (clinker pit)*
**9** el recalentador
- *superheater*

**10** el precalentador de agua *f*
- *water preheater*
**11** el precalentador de aire *m*
- *air preheater*
**12** el canal del gas
- *gas flue*
**13** el filtro de los gases de
combustión *f*, un filtro eléctrico
- *electrostatic precipitator*
**14** el aspirador
- *induced-draught (Am. induced-
  draft) fan*
**15** la chimenea
- *chimney (smokestack)*
**16** el desgasificador
- *de-aerator*
**17** el depósito de agua *f*
- *feedwater tank*
**18** la bomba de alimentación *f* de
la caldera
- *boiler feed pump*
**19** la instalación de mando *m*
- *control room*
**20** el túnel de los cables
- *cable tunnel*
**21** el sótano de los cables
- *cable vault*
**22** la sala de máquinas *f* (la sala
de las turbinas)
- *turbine house*

**23** la turbina de vapor *m*, con
alternador
- *steam turbine with alternator*
**24** el condensador de superficie *f*
- *surface condenser*
**25** el precalentador de baja
presión *f*
- *low-pressure preheater*
**26** el precalentador de alta
presión *f*
- *high-pressure preheater
  (economizer)*
**27** la tubería de agua *f* refrigerante
- *cooling water pipe*
**28** la sala de control *m*
- *control room*
**29-35 la instalación al aire libre,**
una instalación distribuidora
de alta tensión *f*
- *outdoor substation, a substation*
**29** las barras colectoras
- *busbars*
**30** el transformador de potencia *f*,
un transformador transportable
- *power transformer, a mobile
  (transportable) transformer*
**31** el caballete de distensión *f*
- *stay poles (guy poles)*
**32** el cable conductor de alta
tensión *f*
- *high-voltage transmission line*

33 el cable de alta tensión *f*
– *high-voltage conductor*
34 el conmutador rápido de aire *m*
comprimido (un disyuntor)
– *air-blast circuit breaker (circuit breaker)*
35 el desviador de sobretensión *f*
– *surge diverter (Am. lightning arrester, arrester)*
36 el poste de alta tensión *f*, una torre reticular (poste *m* de celosía *f*)
– *overhead line support, a lattice steel tower*
37 la traviesa (el travesaño)
– *cross arm (traverse)*
38 el aislador de amarre *m* (el aislador de suspensión *f*)
– *strain insulator*
39 **el transformador transportable** (el transformador de energía *f*, el transformador)
– ***mobile (transportable) transformer,*** *a power transformer (transformer)*
40 la caja (la caldera) del transformador
– *transformer tank*
41 el bastidor de ruedas *f*
– *bogie (Am. truck)*

42 el conservador del aceite
– *oil conservator*
43 el terminal de alta tensión *f*
– *primary voltage terminal (primary voltage bushing)*
44 los terminales de baja tensión *f*
– *low-voltage terminals (low-voltage bushings)*
45 la bomba de circulación *f* del aceite
– *oil-circulating pump*
46 el refrigerador de agua *f* para el aceite
– *oil cooler*
47 el brazo para el arco voltaico (para las chispas)
– *arcing horn*
48 la corcheta para el transporte
– *transport lug*

1-8 la sala de control *m*
- *control room*
1-6 el pupitre de control *m*
- *control console (control desk)*
1 los controles para los generadores
trifásicos
- *control board (control panel) for the
alternators*
2 el interruptor de control *m*
- *master switch*
3 el avisador luminoso (la lámpara
de señalización *f*)
- *signal light*
4 el tablero de control *m* de los
circuitos de alta tensión *f*
- *feeder panel*
5 el aparato supervisor, para el
control de los conmutadores
- *monitoring controls for the
switching systems*
6 los botones de control *m*
- *controls*
7 el panel, con los instrumentos de
medición *f* del control de
ejecución *f*
- *revertive signal panel*
8 el diagrama luminoso, para
indicar el estado de la red
- *matrix mimic board*
9-18 el transformador
- *transformer*
9 el depósito de dilatación *f* del
aceite
- *oil conservator*
10 la ventilación (el respiradero)
- *breather*
11 el indicador del nivel del aceite
- *oil gauge* (Am. *gage)*
12 el aislador de verificación *f*
(terminal)
- *feed-through terminal (feed-through
insulator)*
13 el interruptor de toma *f* de alta
tensión *f*
- *on-load tap changer*
14 la culata
- *yoke*
15 el enrollamiento primario
(enrollamiento *m* de alta
tensión *f*)
- *primary winding (primary)*
16 el enrollamiento secundario
(enrollamiento *m* de baja
tensión *f*)
- *secondary winding (secondary, low-
voltage winding)*
17 el núcleo
- *core*
18 el conductor de toma *f*
- *tap (tapping)*
19 la conexión del transformador
- *transformer connection*
20 la conexión en estrella *f*
- *star connection (star network,
Y-connection)*
21 la conexión en triángulo *m* (la
conexión delta)
- *delta connection (mesh connection)*
22 el punto neutro
- *neutral point*
23-30 la turbina de vapor *m*, un grupo
turboalternador a vapor *m*
- *steam turbine,* a turbogenerator
unit
23 el cilindro de alta presión *f*
- *high-pressure cylinder*

24 el cilindro de presión *f* media
- *medium-pressure cylinder*
25 el cilindro de baja presión *f*
- *low-pressure cylinder*
26 el alternador (el generador)
trifásico
- *three-phase generator*
27 el enfriador de hidrógeno *m*
- *hydrogen cooler*
28 el codo conductor de vapor *m*
- *leakage steam path*
29 la válvula reguladora
- *jet nozzle*
30 la mesa de control *m* de la turbina
con los instrumentos de
medición *f*
- *turbine monitoring panel with
measuring instruments*
31 el regulador de la tensión
- *automatic voltage regulator*
32 el dispositivo de sincronización *f*
(el sincronizador)
- *synchro*
33 la caja terminal de cables *m*
- *cable box*
34 el conductor
- *conductor*
35 el aislador (terminal)
- *feed-through terminal (feed-through
insulator)*
36 el cono de refuerzo *m*
- *core*
37 la caja
- *casing*
38 la pasta de relleno *m*
- *filling compound (filler)*
39 la envoltura de plomo *m*
- *lead sheath*
40 la cápsula de entrada *f*
- *lead-in tube*
41 el cable
- *cable*
42 el cable de alta tensión *f*, para
corriente trifásica *f*
- *high voltage cable, for three-phase
43 el conductor
- *conductor*
44 el papel metálico
- *metallic paper (metallized paper)*
45 el aislamiento del conductor
- *tracer (tracer element)*
46 la cinta de batista *f*
- *varnished-cambric tape*
47 la envoltura de plomo *m*
- *lead sheath*
48 el papel asfalto
- *asphalted paper*
49 la envoltura de yute *m*
- *jute serving*
50 la armadura de cinta *f* de acero *m*
o de alambre *m* de acero *m*
- *steel tape or steel wire armour* (Am.
*armor)*
51-62 el conmutador rápido de aire *m*
comprimido, un disyuntor
- *air-blast circuit breaker, a circuit
breaker*
51 el depósito de aire *m* comprimido
- *compressed-air tank*
52 la válvula de control *m*
- *control valve (main operating valve)*
53 la conexión del aire comprimido
- *compressed-air inlet*
54 el aislador de aguja *f* hueca, un
aislador en cadena *f*, un aislador
tipo casquete *m*
- *support insulator,* a hollow
porcelain supporting insulator

55 la cámara de conexión *f* (la
cámara de extinción *f*)
- *interrupter*
56 la resistencia
- *resistor*
57 los contactos auxiliares
- *auxiliary contacts*
58 el transformador de corriente *f*
- *current transformer*
59 el transformador de la tensión
- *voltage transformer (potential
transformer)*
60 la caja de bornes *m* (de
terminales *m*)
- *operating mechanism housing*
61 el cuerno de chispas *f*
- *arcing horn*
62 el descargador de chispas *f*
- *spark gap*

1 el reactor superregenerador rápido [esquema]
- *fast-breeder reactor (fast breeder) [diagram]*
2 el circuito primario de enfriamiento *m* (el circuito primario de sodio *m*)
- *primary circuit (primary loop, primary sodium system)*
3 el reactor
- *reactor*
4 los ensamblajes de elementos *m* combustibles (el combustible nuclear)
- *fuel rods (fuel pins)*
5 la bomba de circulación *f* primaria
- *primary sodium pump*
6 el intercambiador de calor *m*
- *heat exchanger*
7 el circuito secundario de enfriamiento *m* (el circuito secundario de sodio *m*)
- *secondary circuit (secondary loop, secondary sodium system)*
8 la bomba de circulación *f* secundaria
- *secondary sodium pump*
9 el generador de vapor *m*
- *steam generator*
10 el circuito terciario (el circuito de agua *f* de refrigeración *f*)
- *cooling water flow circuit*
11 la tubería de vapor *m*
- *steam line*
12 la tubería del agua *f* de alimentación *f*
- *feedwater line*
13 la bomba del agua *f* de alimentación *f*
- *feed pump*
14 la turbina de vapor *m*
- *steam turbine*
15 el generador
- *generator*
16 la alimentación de la red (eléctrica) (la línea de transmisión *f*)
- *transmission line*
17 el condensador
- *condenser*
18 el agua *f* de refrigeración *f*
- *cooling water*
19 **el reactor nuclear,** un reactor de agua *f* a presión *f* (la central nuclear; *fam.*: la central atómica)
- *nuclear reactor, a pressurized-water reactor (nuclear power plant, atomic power plant)*
20 la cubierta de hormigón *m* (el edificio del reactor)
- *concrete shield (reactor building)*
21 el recinto de seguridad *f* de acero *m* con hendidura *f* para la aspiración de aire *m*
- *steel containment (steel shell) with air extraction vent*
22 el recipiente a presión *f* del reactor
- *reactor pressure vessel*
23 el mecanismo de impulsión *f* de los reactores
- *control rod drive*
24 las barras absorbentes (las barras de mando)
- *control rods*
25 la bomba del refrigerante principal
- *primary coolant pump*

26 el generador de vapor *m*
- *steam generator*
27 la máquina de carga *f* para los elementos combustibles
- *fuel-handling hoists*
28 el depósito para los elementos combustibles
- *fuel storage*
29 la tubería del refrigerante del reactor
- *coolant flow passage*
30 la tubería del agua *f* de alimentación *f*
- *feedwater line*
31 la tubería del vapor vivo
- *prime steam line*
32 la esclusa personal
- *manway*
33 el juego de turbinas *f*
- *turbogenerator set*
34 el generador trifásico
- *turbogenerator*
35 el condensador
- *condenser*
36 el edificio contiguo
- *service building*
37 la chimenea de evacuación *f*
- *exhaust gas stack*
38 el puente grúa *f* circular
- *polar crane*
39 la torre refrigerante, una torre refrigerante seca
- *cooling tower, a dry cooling tower*
40 el sistema (el principio) de agua *f* a presión *f*
- *pressurized-water system*
41 el reactor
- *reactor*
42 el circuito primario
- *primary circuit (primary loop)*
43 la bomba de circulación *f*
- *circulation pump (recirculation pump)*
44 el intercambiador de calor *m* (el generador de vapor *m*)
- *heat exchanger (steam generator)*
45 el circuito secundario (el circuito de vapor *m* y del agua *f* de alimentación *f*)
- *secondary circuit (secondary loop, feedwater steam circuit)*
46 la turbina de vapor *m*
- *steam turbine*
47 el generador
- *generator*
48 el sistema de refrigeración *f*
- *cooling system*
49 el sistema (el principio) de agua *f* en ebullición *f* [esquema]
- *boiling water system [diagram]*
50 el reactor
- *reactor*
51 el circuito de vapor *m* condensado (de vapor *m* de agua *f*)
- *steam and recirculation water flow paths*
52 la turbina de vapor *m*
- *steam turbine*
53 el generador
- *generator*
54 la bomba de circulación *f*
- *circulation pump (recirculation pump)*
55 el sistema de agua *f* de refrigeración *f* (la refrigeración con agua *f* corriente)
- *coolant system*

56 el almacenamiento de desechos *m* atómicos en una mina de sal *f*
- *radioactive waste storage in salt mine*
57-68 las condiciones geológicas de una mina de sal *f* acondicionada para el almacenamiento de residuos *m* radiactivos (desechos *m* atómicos)
- *geological structure of abandoned salt mine converted for disposal of radioactive waste (nuclear waste)*
57 el keuper inferior (el triásico inferior, las margas abigarradas)
- *Lower Keuper*
58 la caliza de conchas *f* superior
- *Upper Muschelkalk*
59 la caliza de conchas *f* media
- *Middle Muschelkalk*
60 la caliza de conchas *f* inferior
- *Lower Muschelkalk*
61 el zócalo de arenisca *f* roja
- *Bunter downthrow*
62 los residuos de lixiviación *f* de la piedra calcárea
- *residue of leached (lixiviated) Zechstein (Upper Permian)*
63 la sal gema de Aller
- *Aller rock salt*
64 la sal gema de Leine
- *Leine rock salt*
65 la vena de Stassfurt (la vena – el filón – de sal *f* potásica)
- *Stassfurt seam, a potash salt seam (bed)*
66 la sal gema de Stassfurt
- *Stassfurt salt*
67 la anhidrita límite
- *grenzanhydrite*
68 la arcilla de piedra *f* calcárea
- *Zechstein shale*
69 el pozo
- *shaft*
70 la explotación a cielo *m* abierto
- *minehead buildings*
71 la cámara de almacenamiento *m*
- *storage chamber*
72 el almacenamiento de desechos *m* de actividad *f* media en una mina de sal *f*
- *storage of medium-active waste in salt mine*
73 la planta (el fondo) a 511 m
- *511 m level*
74 la pared de protección *f* contra las radiaciones
- *protective screen (anti-radiation screen)*
75 la ventanilla de cristal *m* de plomo *m*
- *lead glass window*
76 la cámara de almacenamiento *m*
- *storage chamber*
77 el barril enarcado con desechos *m* radiactivos
- *drum containing radioactive waste*
78 la cámara de televisión *f*
- *television camera*
79 la cámara de alimentación *f*
- *charging chamber*
80 el pupitre de control *m*
- *control desk (control panel)*
81 la instalación para evacuar el aire
- *upward ventilator*
82 el depósito blindado
- *shielded container*
83 la planta (el fondo) a 490 m
- *490 m level*

1 **el sistema de bomba *f* de calor *m***
– **heat pump system**
2 la entrada de agua *f* subterránea
– *source water inlet*
3 el intercambiador de calor *m* del agua *f* de refrigeración *f*
– *cooling water heat exchanger*
4 el compresor
– *compressor*
5 el motor Diesel o de gas *m* natural
– *natural-gas or diesel engine*
6 el evaporizador
– *evaporator*
7 la válvula reductora
– *pressure release valve*
8 el condensador
– *condenser*
9 el intercambiador de calor *m* para gas *m* de escape *m*
– *waste-gas heat exchanger*
10 el tubo de alimentación *f*
– *flow pipe*
11 la tubería del aire de escape *m*
– *vent pipe*
12 la chimenea
– *chimney*
13 la caldera de la calefacción
– *boiler*
14 el soplante (el fuelle)
– *fan*
15 el aparato de calefacción *f* (el radiador)
– *radiator*
16 el pozo de filtración *f* (el sumidero)
– *sink*
**17-36 el aprovechamiento de la energía solar**
– *utilization of solar energy*
17 la casa calentada por la energía solar

– *solar (solar-heated) house*
18 la admisión del calor irradiado por el sol
– *solar radiation (sunlight, insolation)*
19 el colector (la placa solar)
– *collector*
20 el acumulador de calor *m*
– *hot reservoir (heat reservoir)*
21 la alimentación eléctrica
– *power supply*
22 la bomba de calor *m*
– *heat pump*
23 la tubería de evacuación *f* del agua *f*
– *water outlet*
24 la entrada de aire *m*
– *air supply*
25 la chimenea del aire de escape *m*
– *flue*
26 el aprovisionamiento de agua *f* caliente
– *hot water supply*
27 la calefacción por radiador *m*
– *radiator heating*
28 el elemento (el colector) de central *f* (*Amér.:* usina *f*) solar
– *flat plate solar collector*
29 el colector negro (con lámina *f* de aluminio *m* recubierta de asfalto *m*)
– *blackened receiver surface with asphalted aluminium* (Am. *aluminum) foil*
30 el tubo de acero *m*
– *steel tube*
31 el medio de transporte *m* del calor
– *heat transfer fluid*
32 el colector solar (la placa solar, el ladrillo solar, la teja solar)
– *flat plate solar collector, containing solar cell*

33 el recubrimiento de cristal *m*
– *glass cover*
34 la célula solar
– *solar cell*
35 el canal de aire *m*
– *air ducts*
36 el aislamiento
– *insulation*
37 **la central** (*Amér.:* la usina) **maremotriz**
– *tidal power plant [section]*
38 el dique de contención *f*
– *dam*
39 la turbina reversible
– *reversible turbine*
40 el canal de la turbina al lado del mar (el canal de traída *f* del agua *f*)
– *turbine inlet for water from the sea*
41 el canal de la turbina al lado de la cuenca (el canal de evacuación *f* del agua *f*)
– *turbine inlet for water from the basin*
42 **la central eólica**
– **wind power plant** *(wind generator, aerogenerator)*
43 la torre de tubos *m*
– *truss tower*
44 la retención (el soporte) de cable *m* metálico
– *guy wire*
45 el rotor
– *rotor blades (propeller)*
46 el generador y el servomotor de orientación *f* (mecanismo *m* de autoorientación *f*)
– *generator with variable pitch for power regulation*

**1-15 la coquería**
- *coking plant*
1 la descarga del carbón de coque *m*
- *dumping of coking coal*
2 la cinta transportadora
- *belt conveyor*
3 el silo de los componentes de carbón *m* de coque *m*
- *service bunker*
4 la cinta transportadora de la torre de carbón *m*
- *coal tower conveyor*
5 la torre de carbón *m*
- *coal tower*
6 el vagón (el carrito) de carga *f*
- *larry car (larry, charging car)*
7 la (máquina) deshornadora de coque *m*
- *pusher ram*
8 la batería del horno de coque *m*
- *battery of coke ovens*
9 el carro guía de la torta de coque *m*
- *coke guide*
10 el carro de extinción *f* con locomotora *f*
- *quenching car, with engine*
11 la torre de extinción *f*
- *quenching tower*
12 la rampa del coque
- *coke loading bay (coke wharf)*
13 la cinta de la rampa del coque
- *coke side bench*
14 la instalación de cribado *m* del coque fino y grueso
- *screening of lump coal and culm*
15 el cargamento de coque *m*
- *coke loading*
**16-45 el tratamiento del gas de coquería *f***
- *coke-oven gas processing*

16 la salida del gas de los hornos de coque *m*
- *discharge (release) of gas from the coke ovens*
17 la canalización principal del gas
- *gas-collecting main*
18 la extracción del alquitrán mineral
- *coal tar extraction*
19 el refrigerador de gas *m*
- *gas cooler*
20 el electrofiltro
- *electrostatic precipitator*
21 el extractor de gas *m*
- *gas extractor*
22 el lavador de ácido *m* sulfhídrico
- *hydrogen sulphide (Am. hydrogen sulfide) scrubber (hydrogen sulphide wet collector)*
23 el lavador de amoníaco *m*
- *ammonia scrubber (ammonia wet collector)*
24 el lavador de benceno *m*
- *benzene (benzol) scrubber*
25 el depósito colector de gas *m*
- *gas holder*
26 el compresor de gas *m*
- *gas compressor*
27 el desbenzolaje por refrigerador *m* e intercambiador *m* de calor *m*
- *debenzoling by cooler and heat exchanger*
28 la desulfuración del gas a presión *f*
- *desulphurization (Am. desulfurization) of pressure gas*
29 la refrigeración del gas
- *gas cooling*
30 el secado del gas
- *gas drying*
31 el contador de gas *m*
- *gas meter*
32 el depósito de alquitrán *m* bruto
- *crude tar tank*

33 la entrada de ácido *m* sulfúrico
- *sulphuric acid (Am. sulfuric acid) supply*
34 la producción de ácido *m* sulfúrico
- *production of sulphuric acid (Am. sulfuric acid)*
35 la producción de sulfato *m* de amonio *m*
- *production of ammonium sulphate (Am. ammonium sulfate)*
36 el sulfato de amonio *m*
- *ammonium sulphate (Am. ammonium sulfate)*
37 la instalación de regeneración *f* de los productos de lavado *m*
- *recovery plant for recovering the scrubbing agents*
38 la evacuación de las aguas residuales
- *waste water discharge*
39 la extracción del fenol de las aguas gaseosas
- *phenol extraction from the gas water*
40 el depósito de fenol *m* crudo
- *crude phenol tank*
41 la producción de benceno *m* crudo
- *production of crude benzol (crude benzene)*
42 el depósito de benceno *m* crudo
- *crude benzol (crude benzene) tank*
43 el depósito de aceite *m* de lavado *m*
- *scrubbing oil tank*
44 la tubería de gas *m* de baja presión *f*
- *low-pressure gas main*
45 la tubería de gas *m* de alta presión *f*
- *high-pressure gas main*

# 157 Aserradero — Sawmill

1 el aserradero (la serrería; *Col. y Ec.*: el aserrío)
- *sawmill*
2 la sierra alternativa de hojas *f* múltiples
- *vertical frame saw* (Am. *gang mill*)
3 las hojas de sierra *f*
- *saw blades*
4 el cilindro de entrada *f*
- *feed roller*
5 el cilindro trepador (el rodillo guía)
- *guide roller*
6 la acanaladura
- *fluting (grooving, grooves)*
7 el manómetro de presión *f* del aceite (el indicador de la presión del aceite)
- *oil pressure gauge* (Am. *gage*)
8 el bastidor de la sierra
- *saw frame*
9 el indicador de avance *m*
- *feed indicator*
10 la escala para la altura del corte
- *log capacity scale*
11 el carrito auxiliar
- *auxiliary carriage*
12 el carro de presa *f*
- *carriage*
13 las pinzas de sujeción *f*
- *log grips*
14 el mando a distancia *f* (el telemando)
- *remote control panel*

15 (el sistema) de accionamiento *m* del carro de presa *f*
- *carriage motor*
16 el carro para las astillas (las tablillas)
- *truck for splinters (splints)*
17 el transportador de trozas *f* (la cadena sin fin *m* para troncos *m*)
- *endless log chain* (Am. *jack chain*)
18 el tablero de tope *m*
- *stop plate*
19 el eyector de troncos *m*
- *log-kicker arms*
20 el transportador transversal
- *cross conveyor*
21 la instalación de lavado *m*
- *washer (washing machine)*
22 el transportador de cadenas *f* para la madera cortada
- *cross chain conveyor for sawn timber*
23 la mesa de rodillos *m*
- *roller table*
24 la sierra oscilante bajo la mesa
- *undercut swing saw*
25 la pila
- *piling*
26 el soporte de rodillo *m*
- *roller trestles*
27 la grúa de pórtico *m*
- *gantry crane*
28 el motor de la grúa
- *crane motor*
29 las pinzas (la garra) orientables
- *pivoted log grips*

30 el rollo (de madera *f*) (el rollizo)
- *roundwood (round timber)*
31 el montón de rollizos *m* (el montón de rollizos *m* seleccionados)
- *log dump*
32 el emplazamiento (*Amér.*: la ubicación) de la madera cortada
- *squared timber store*
33 la troza serrada
- *sawn logs*
34 los maderos
- *planks*
35 las planchas (de madera *f*)
- *boards (planks)*
36 la madera escuadrada
- *squared timber*
37 la cuña (de hormigón *m*) de la pila
- *stack bearer*

276

38 la tronzadora de cadenas *f*
   automática
 – *automatic cross-cut chain saw*
39 la sujeción del tronco de madera *f*
 – *log grips*
40 el cilindro de avance *m*
 – *feed roller*
41 el dispositivo de sujeción *f* de
   cadenas *f*
 – *chain-tensioning device*
42 la máquina de afilar y aserrar
   automática
 – *saw-sharpening machine*
43 la muela
 – *grinding wheel (teeth grinder)*
44 el trinquete de avance *m*
 – *feed pawl*
45 el regulador de profundidad *f* para
   la muela
 – *depth adjustment for the teeth
   grinder*
46 la palanca para la cabeza de
   afilado *m*
 – *lifter (lever) for the grinder chuck*
47 el dispositivo fijador de la hoja de
   la sierra
 – *holding device for the saw blade*
48 la sierra de cinta *f* horizontal
 – *horizontal bandsaw for sawing logs*
49 la regulación de la altura
 – *height adjustment*
50 el frotador de virutas *f*
 – *chip remover*
51 el aspirador de virutas *f*
 – *chip extractor*

52 el carro transportador
 – *carriage*
53 la hoja de la sierra de cinta *f*
 – *bandsaw blade*
54 la sierra automática para la leña
 – *automatic blocking saw*
55 el canal de alimentación *f* (de
   entrada)
 – *feed channel*
56 la abertura de eyección *f*
 – *discharge opening*
57 la sierra de cantear doble
 – *twin edger (double edger)*
58 la escala de la anchura
 – *breadth scale (width scale)*
59 la pantalla de protección *f* (el
   dispositivo de seguridad *f*, las
   láminas de protección *f*)
 – *kick-back guard*
60 la escala de la altura
 – *height scale*
61 la escala de avance *m*
 – *in-feed scale*
62 los indicadores luminosos
 – *indicator lamps*
63 la mesa de carga *f*
 – *feed table*
64 la sierra oscilante (la sierra con
   movimineto *m* de vaivén *m*)
 – *undercut swing saw*
65 el prensador automático (con
   cubierta protectora *f*)
 – *automatic hold-down with
   protective hood*

66 el interruptor de pie *m* (el
   conmutador de pedal *m*)
 – *foot switch*
67 la instalación de distribución *f*
 – *distribution board (panelboard)*
68 el tope longitudinal
 – *length stop*

1 **la cantera,** una explotación a
  cielo *m* abierto
– *quarry, an open-cast working*
2 la tierra de recubrimiento *m* (los
  escombros)
– *overburden*
3 el frente de arranque *m*
– *working face*
4 el montón de piedras *f* sueltas (de
  piedras *f* arrancadas)
– *loose rock pile*
5 el picapedrero, un trabajador de la
  cantera
– *quarryman (quarrier), a quarry
  worker*
6 el mazo (la almádena, el martillo
  de cuña *f*)
– *sledge hammer*
7 la cuña
– *wedge*
8 el bloque de roca *f*
– *block of stone*
9 el barrenero
– *driller*
10 el casco protector
– *safety helmet*
11 la perforadora de percursión *f* (el
  martillo perforador, la
  perforadora de roca *f*)
– *hammer drill (hard-rock drill)*
12 el taladro
– *borehole*
13 la excavadora universal
– *universal excavator*

14 la vagoneta de gran capacidad *f*
– *large-capacity truck*
15 la pared de roca *f*
– *rock face*
16 el montacargas inclinado
– *inclined hoist*
17 la trituradora previa
– *primary crusher*
18 la instalación productora de
  grava *f*
– *stone-crushing plant*
19 la trituradora giratoria en grueso
  (*anál.:* la trituradora giratoria en
  fino; *Chile:* la chancadora)
– *coarse rotary (gyratory) crusher;
  sim.: fine rotary (gyratory) crusher*
20 la machacadora (la trituradora de
  mordazas *f*)
– *hammer crusher (impact crusher)*
21 la criba vibradora
– *vibrating screen*
22 la piedra pulverizada
– *screenings (fine dust)*
23 la gravilla
– *stone chippings*
24 la grava
– *crushed stone*
25 el maestro en explosivos *m* (el
  artificiero)
– *shot firer*
26 el jalón
– *measuring rod*
27 el cartucho explosivo
– *blasting cartridge*

28 la mecha
– *fuse (blasting fuse)*
29 el cubo con arena *f* de relleno *m*
– *plugging sand (stemming sand)
  bucket*
30 el sillar (la piedra de sillería *f*)
– *dressed stone*
31 el pico
– *pick*
32 la palanca
– *crowbar (pinch bar)*
33 la horca de rocas *f*
– *fork*
34 el picapedrero (el cantero)
– *stonemason*
35-38 **las herramientas de cantero** *m*
– *stonemason's tools*
35 el martillo de mano *f*
– *stonemason's hammer*
36 el mazo
– *mallet*
37 el cincel de raspar
– *drove chisel (drove, boaster, broad
  chisel)*
38 la trincheta (la escoda)
– *dressing axe* (Am. *ax*)

# Fábrica de tejas y ladrillos (obra de ladrillo)

## Brickworks (Brickyard, Brickfield) 159

1 la barrera (el pozo de barro *m*)
– *clay pit*
2 el barro, una arcilla impura
 (arcilla *f* bruta)
– *loam, an impure clay (raw clay)*
3 la excavadora del terreno de
 cobertura *f*, una excavadora de
 gran capacidad *f*
– *overburden excavator, a large-scale
 excavator*
4 el ferrocarril de vía *f* estrecha
– *narrow-gauge* (Am. *narrow-gage)
 track system*
5 el montacargas inclinado
– *inclined hoist*
6 el pudridero del barro
– *souring chambers*
7 el alimentador
– *box feeder (feeder)*
8 el triturador de muelas *f* verticales
– *edge runner mill (edge mill, pan
 grinding mill)*
9 la laminadora
– *rolling plant*
10 la mezcladora de árbol *m* doble
– *double-shaft trough mixer (mixer)*
11 la prensa de extrusión *f* (una
 prensa de ladrillos *m*)
– *extrusion press (brick-pressing
 machine)*
12 la cámara de vacío *m*
– *vacuum chamber*

13 la boca de salida *f*
– *die*
14 la columna de arcilla *f*
– *clay column*
15 la cortadora (la cortadora de
 ladrillos *m*)
– *cutter (brick cutter)*
16 el ladrillo crudo (el ladrillo sin
 cocer)
– *unfired brick (green brick)*
17 el secadero (la cámara secadora)
– *drying shed*
18 la carretilla elevadora de
 horquilla *f* (la carretilla apiladora)
– *mechanical finger car (stacker
 truck)*
19 el horno circular (horno *m* para
 ladrillos *m*)
– *circular kiln, a brick kiln*
20 el ladrillo macizo (ladrillo *m*)
– *solid brick*
21-22 ladrillos *m* perforados
– *perforated bricks and hollow blocks*
21 el ladrillo con perforaciones *f*
 verticales
– *perforated brick with vertical
 perforations*
22 el ladrillo hueco con canales *m*
 horizontales
– *hollow clay block with horizontal
 perforations*
23 el ladrillo de rejilla *f*
– *hollow clay block with vertical
 perforations*

24 el ladrillo de techar (la bovedilla)
– *floor brick*
25 el ladrillo de chimenea *f*
 (ladrillo *m* radial)
– *compass brick (radial brick,
 radiating brick)*
26 el ladrillo hueco plano (el ladrillo
 hueco para bóvedas *f*)
– *hollow flooring block*
27 el ladrillo aplanillado de establo *m*
– *paving brick*
28 el ladrillo perfilado de chimenea *f*
– *chimney brick*

1 las materias primas (caliza *f*,
arcilla *f* y marga *f* arcillosa)
– *raw materials (limestone, clay
and, marl)*
2 la trituradora de martillos *m*
– *hammer crusher (hammer mill)*
3 el almacén de las materias
primas
– *raw material store*
4 el molino para la molienda y el
secado simultáneos de las
materias primas mediante el
gas de escape *m* de la
instalación intercambiadora de
calor *m*
– *raw mill for simultaneously
grinding and drying the raw
materials with exhaust gas from
the heat exchanger*
5 los silos para las materias
primas pulverizadas (los silos
de homogeneización *f*)
– *raw meal silos*
6 la instalación intercambiadora
de calor *m* (el intercambiador
de calor *m* de ciclón *m*)
– *heat exchanger, a cyclone heat
exchanger*
7 la instalación de desempolva-
miento (un electrofiltro) para el
gas de escape *m* del
intercambiador de calor *m* del
molino de materia *f* cruda

– *dust collector [an electrostatic
precipitator for the heat
exchanger exhaust from the raw
mill]*
8 el horno rotatorio (horno *m*
giratorio)
– *rotary kiln*
9 el refrigerador de clinker *m*
– *clinker cooler*
10 el almacén de clinker *m*
– *clinker store*
11 el soplante (el fuelle) de aire *m*
primario
– *primary air blower*
12 la instalación trituradora de
cemento *m*
– *cement-grinding mill*
13 el almacén (el depósito) de
yeso *m*
– *gypsum store*
14 la trituradora (*sin.:* la
quebrantadora, la
machacadora) de yeso *m*
– *gypsum crusher*
15 el silo para el cemento
– *cement silo*
16 las máquinas envasadoras de
cemento *m* en sacos *m* de
papel *m*
– *cement-packing plant for paper
sacks*

1 el molino de tambor *m* (molino *m* de bolas *f*), para la preparación por vía *f* húmeda de la mezcla de materias *f* primas
– *grinding cylinder (ball mill) for the preparation of the raw material in water*
2 la cápsula refractaria, con abertura *f* para la observación del proceso de cocción *f*
– *sample sagger (saggar, seggar), with aperture for observing the firing process*
3 el horno redondo (horno *m* discontinuo) [esquema]
– *bottle kiln (beehive kiln) [diagram]*
4 el molde de cocción *f*
– *firing mould* (Am. *mold*)
5 el horno de túnel *m*
– *tunnel kiln*
6 el cono Seger, para medir altas temperaturas *f*
– *Seger cone (pyrometric cone, Am. Orton cone) for measuring high temperatures*
7 la prensa de vacío *m*, una prensa de extrusión *f*
– *de-airing pug mill (de-airing pug press), an extrusion press*

8 la barra de material *m* (de masa *f*)
– *clay column*
9 el tornero, torneando una pieza en bruto
– *thrower throwing a ball (bat) of clay*
10 la masa de arcilla *f* (la pieza en bruto)
– *slug of clay*
11 el plato giratorio; *anál.:* el torno de alfarero *m*
– *turntable;* sim.: *potter's wheel*
12 el filtro-prensa
– *filter press*
13 la torta de masa *f* (la torta del filtro-prensa)
– *filter cake*
14 el torneado, con plantilla *f* de tornear
– *jiggering, with a profiling tool;* sim.: *jollying*
15 el molde, para echar barro *m* (para el colado)
– *plaster mould* (Am. *mold) for slip casting*
16 la máquina de vidriar de mesa *f* circular
– *turntable glazing machine*
17 el pintor (el esmaltador) de porcelana *f*
– *porcelain painter (china painter)*

18 el jarrón pintado a mano *f*
– *hand-painted vase*
19 el modelador (retocador *m*)
– *repairer*
20 la varilla (la espátula) de modelar
– *pallet, a modelling* (Am. *modeling) tool*
21 los añicos de porcelana *f* (los trozos)
– *shards (sherds, potsherds)*

**38-47 la fabricación de vidrio** *m*
(soplado *m* con la boca, el trabajo
de dar forma *f*)
– **glassmaking;** here: *glassblowing by
hand*
**38** el vidriero (el soplador de
vidrio *m*)
– *glassmaker (glassblower)*
**39** el tubo de vidriero *m* (la caña de
soplador *m*)
– *blowing iron*
**40** la masa de vidrio *m*
– *gob*
**41** la copa (en forma *f* de cáliz *m*)
soplada con la boca
– *hand-blown goblet*
**42** la tablilla, para dar forma *f* al pie
de la copa
– *clappers for shaping the base (foot)
of the goblet*
**43** el calibre de forma *f*
– *trimming tool*
**44** las tenazas de soplador *m* (las
pinzas cortantes)
– *tongs*
**45** el banco de vidriero *m*
– *glassmaker's chair (gaffer's chair)*
**46** el crisol de vidriería *f* cubierto
– *covered glasshouse pot*
**47** el molde, para acabar de soplar la
masa soplada previamente
– *mould* (Am. *mold), into which the
parison is blown*

**48-55 la producción de vidrio** *m* **textil**
– **production of glass fibre** (Am.
*glass fiber)*
**48** el procedimiento de filamento *m*
continuo
– *continuous filament process*
**49** el horno de fusión *f* del vidrio
– *glass furnace*
**50** la cuba con la fusión de vidrio *m*
(la cubeta con vidrio *m* fundido)
– *bushing containing molten glass*
**51** la boquilla agujereada
– *bushing tips*
**52** los hilos elementales del vidrio
textil
– *glass filaments*
**53** el encolado (el ensimaje)
– *sizing*
**54** el hilado
– *strand (thread)*
**55** la cabeza de la bobina
– *spool*
**56-58 los productos de vidrio** *m* **textil**
– **glass fibre** (Am. *glass fiber)
products*
**56** el hilo de vidrio *m* textil
– *glass yarn (glass thread)*
**57** el hilo de vidrio *m* en bobina *f*
– *sleeved glass yarn (glass thread)*
**58** el fieltro de vidrio *m*
– *glass wool*

**1-13  el aprovisionamiento de algodón** *m*
– *supply of cotton*
1  el copo de algodón *m* maduro
– *ripe cotton boll*
2  la husada de hilo *m* (la husada, la bobina)
– *full cop (cop wound with weft yarn)*
3  la bala de algodón *m* prensado
– *compressed cotton bale*
4  el embalaje (la arpillera) de yute *m*
– *jute wrapping*
5  el fleje de hierro *m*
– *steel band*
6  los números de la partida de la bala
– *identification mark of the bale*
7  la abridora abrebalas (el limpiador de algodón *m*)
– *bale opener (bale breaker)*
8  la telera sin fin *m* de alimentación *f*
– *cotton-feeding brattice*
9  el depósito de alimentación *f*
– *cotton feed*
10  la tolva aspiradora del polvo
– *dust extraction fan*
11  el conducto de la cámara de polvo *m*
– *duct to the dust-collecting chamber*
12  el motor impulsor
– *drive motor*
13  la telera sin fin *m* reunidora
– *conveyor brattice*
14  **el batán doble**
– **double scutcher** *(machine with two scutchers)*
15  el dispositivo de enrollamiento *m* (el soporte para las telas)
– *lap cradle*
16  la guía de compresión *f* (el corchete compresor)
– *rack head*
17  la palanca de puesta *f* en marcha *f*
– *starting handle*
18  el volante, para subir o bajar la guía de presión *f*
– *handwheel, for raising and lowering the rack head*
19  la tabla móvil de la tela de batán *m*
– *movable lap-turner*
20  los cilindros de presión *f*
– *calender rollers*
21  la cubierta, para el par de cilindros *m* de aspiración *f*
– *cover for the perforated cylinders*
22  el canal de polvo *m*
– *dust escape flue (dust discharge flue)*
23  los motores impulsores
– *drive motors (beater drive motors)*
24  el eje, para el movimiento de las alas batidoras
– *beater driving shaft*
25  la devanadera triplecardante
– *three-blade beater (Kirschner beater)*
26  la rejilla
– *grid [for impurities to drop]*
27  el cilindro de alimentación *f*
– *pedal roller (pedal cylinder)*
28  la palanca reguladora de alimentación *f*, una palanca de pedal *m*
– *control lever for the pedal roller, a pedal lever*

29  el variador de velocidad *f*
– *variable change-speed gear*
30  la caja de conos *m*
– *cone drum box*
31  el sistema de palancas *f*, para la regulación de la alimentación
– *stop and start levers for the hopper*
32  el cilindro de presión *f* de madera *f*
– *wooden hopper delivery roller*
33  la cargadora automática
– *hopper feeder*
34  **la carda de chapones** *m* (carda *f*, percha *f*)
– *carding machine (card, carding engine)*
35  el bote de la carda, para el depósito de la mecha de carda *f*
– *card can (carding can), for receiving the coiled sliver*
36  el soporte giratorio del bote
– *can holder*
37  los cilindros de calandria *f* (los cilindros compresores)
– *calender rollers*
38  la cinta de carda *f*
– *carded sliver (card sliver)*
39  el peine descargador
– *vibrating doffer comb*
40  la palanca para parar
– *start-stop lever*
41  el soporte del esmerilador
– *grinding-roller bearing*
42  el cardador (el rastrillador)
– *doffer*
43  la bota (el gran tambor)
– *cylinder*
44  el mecanismo para limpiar los chapones
– *flat clearer*
45  la cadena de los chapones
– *flats*
46  las poleas tensoras, para la cadena de los chapones
– *supporting pulleys for the flats*
47  el rollo de tela *f* del batán
– *scutcher lap (carded lap)*
48  el soporte del rollo
– *scutcher lap holder*
49  el motor impulsor, con correa *f* plana
– *drive motor with flat belt*
50  la polea principal de accionamiento *m*
– *main drive pulley (fast-and-loose drive pulley)*
51  el esquema de la carda
– *principle of the card (of the carding engine)*
52  el cilindro de alimentación *f*
– *fluted feed roller*
53  el cilindro tomador (el cilindro abridor)
– *licker-in (taker-in, licker-in roller)*
54  la rejilla del tomador
– *licker-in undercasing*
55  la rejilla del gran tambor
– *cylinder undercasing*
56  **la peinadora**
– **combing machine** *(comber)*
57  la caja de engranajes *m*
– *drive gearbox (driving gear)*
58  la napa
– *laps ready for combing*
59  el condensador de la mecha
– *calender rollers*

60  el cabezal (el banco) de estiraje *m*
– *comber draw box*
61  el contador
– *counter*
62  el dispositivo de plegado *m* de la cinta
– *coiler top*
63  el esquema de la peinadora
– *principle of the comber*
64  la cinta de carda *f*
– *lap*
65  la mordaza inferior
– *bottom nipper*
66  la mordaza superior
– *top nipper*
67  el peine fijo
– *top comb*
68  el peine circular
– *combing cylinder*
69  el segmento de cuero *m*
– *plain part of the cylinder*
70  el segmento de agujas *f*
– *needled part of the cylinder*
71  los cilindros de arranque *m* (los cilindros condensadores)
– *detaching rollers*
72  el peinado (la cinta peinada)
– *carded and combed sliver*

# Hilatura de algodón II

# *Cotton Spinning II*

1 **el estirado** (el manuar)
– *draw frame*
2 la caja de engranajes *m*, con motor *m* incorporado
– *gearbox with built-in motor*
3 los botes de la carda
– *sliver cans*
4 el cilindro de contacto *m*, para el paro automático de la máquina en caso de rotura *f* de la mecha
– *broken thread detector roller*
5 el doblado de las mechas de carda *f*
– *doubling of the slivers*
6 la palanca de paro *m* de la máquina
– *stopping handle*
7 el recubrimiento de los cilindros (del banco) de estiraje *m*
– *draw frame cover*
8 las lámparas de control *m*
– *indicator lamps (signal lights)*
9 el banco de estiraje *m* sencillo de cuatro cilindros *m* [esquema]
– *simple four-roller draw frame [diagram]*
10 los cilindros inferiores (los cilindros de acero *m* ranurado)
– *bottom rollers (lower rollers), fluted steel rollers*
11 los cilindros superiores con recubrimiento *m* de plástico *m*
– *top rollers (upper rollers) covered with synthetic rubber*
12 la cinta gruesa (la napa), antes del estiraje
– *doubled slivers before drafting*
13 la cinta adelgazada mediante los cilindros de estiraje *m*
– *thin sliver after drafting*
14 el tren de gran estiraje *m* [esquema]
– *high-draft system (high-draft draw frame) [diagram]*
15 el embudo de entrada (el embudo guía *f*) de las mechas
– *feeding-in of the sliver*
16 la correa de cuero *m* (*Antillas y Amér. Merid.:* la guasca)
– *leather apron (composition apron)*
17 el raíl de viraje *m*
– *guide bar*
18 el cilindro de presión *f* (el cilindro de retención *f*)
– *light top roller (guide roller)*
19 la mechera en grueso
– *high-draft speed frame (fly frame, slubbing frame)*
20 los botes de estiraje *m* (los botes del manuar)
– *sliver cans*
21 la entrada de las cintas en el banco de estiraje *m*
– *feeding of the slivers to the drafting rollers*
22 el estiraje de la mechera, con chapón *m* de limpieza *f* (limpiador *m*)
– *drafting rollers with top clearers*
23 las bobinas de la mechera
– *roving bobbins*
24 la operaria mechera
– *fly frame operator (operative)*
25 la aleta de la mechera
– *flyer*
26 la bancada extrema de la máquina
– *frame end plate*

27 la mechera intermedia
– *intermediate yarn-forming frame*
28 la fileta de las bobinas
– *bobbin creel (creel)*
29 la mecha saliendo del banco de estiraje *m*
– *roving emerging from the drafting rollers*
30 la bancada portabobinas
– *lifter rail (separating rail)*
31 el mando de los husos
– *spindle drive*
32 la palanca de paro *m* de la máquina
– *stopping handle*
33 la caja de engranajes *m*, con motor incorporado
– *gearbox, with built-on motor*
34 **la continua de hilar** (continua de aros *m*, continua de anillos *m*)
– *ring frame (ring spinning frame)*
35 el motor colector trifásico
– *three-phase motor*
36 la placa-base del motor
– *motor base plate (bedplate)*
37 la anilla para el transporte del motor
– *lifting bolt [for motor removal]*
38 el regulador de hilado *m*
– *control gear for spindle speed*
39 la caja de engranajes *m*
– *gearbox*
40 el piñón de cambio *m*, para la variación del número de finura *f* del hilo
– *change wheels for varying the spindle speed [to change the yarn count]*
41 la fileta llena de bobinas *f*
– *full creel*
42 los ejes y los soportes para impulsar el banco de anillas *f*
– *shafts and levers for raising and lowering the ring rail*
43 los husos, con los separadores de hilo *m*
– *spindles with separators*
44 la caja colectora de los hilos aspirados
– *suction box connected to the front roller underclearers*
45 **el huso modelo** de la continua de aros *m*
– *standard ring spindle*
46 la caña del huso
– *spindle shaft*
47 el cojinete de rodillos *m*
– *roller bearing*
48 el piñón (la poleíta de accionamiento *m*)
– *wharve (pulley)*
49 el gancho del huso
– *spindle catch*
50 el portahúsos (la regla portahúsos)
– *spindle rail*
51 el órgano hilador
– *ring and traveller* (Am. *traveler*)
52 el huso desnudo (vacío)
– *top of the ring tube (of the bobbin)*
53 el hilado (el hilo)
– *yarn (thread)*
54 el aro fijo del banco portaaros
– *ring fitted into the ring rail*
55 el corredor
– *traveller* (Am. *traveler*)
56 el hilado (el hilo) enrollado
– *yarn wound onto the bobbin*

57 **la máquina retorcedora**
– *doubling frame*
58 la fileta, con bobinas *f* cruzadas
– *creel, with cross-wound cheeses*
59 el dispositivo alimentador
– *delivery rollers*
60 la husada de hilo *m* retorcido
– *bobbins of doubled yarn*

**1-57 la preparación del tejido**
- *processes preparatory to weaving*
1 la bobinadora (la encarretadora) de cruzado *m*
- *cone-winding frame*
2 el soplante móvil
- *travelling (Am. traveling) blower*
3 el carril guía *f*, para el soplante móvil
- *guide rail, for the travelling (Am. traveling) blower*
4 el soplante (el fuelle) del ventilador
- *blowing assembly*
5 la boquilla de soplado *m*
- *blower aperture*
6 las barras soporte del carril del ventilador
- *superstructure for the blower rail*
7 el indicador del diámetro de la bobina cruzada
- *full-cone indicator*
8 la bobina cónica (la bobina cruzada) de plegado cruzado
- *cross-wound cone*
9 el portabobinas
- *cone creel*
10 el cilindro ranurado (tambor *m* con muescas *f*)
- *grooved cylinder*
11 la ranura en zigzag *m*, para el cruzado del hilo
- *guiding slot for cross-winding the threads*
12 la testera enrolladora, con motor *m*
- *side frame, housing the motor*
13 la palanca reguladora, para retirar la bobina cruzada
- *tension and slub-catching device*
14 la bancada extrema, con filtro *m*
- *off-end framing with filter*
15 la husada
- *yarn package, a ring tube or mule cop*
16 el depósito de husadas *f*
- *yarn package container*
17 el mando de embrague *m* y desembrague *m*
- *starting and stopping lever*
18 el arco, para enhilar automáticamente
- *self-threading guide*
19 el mecanismo de paro *m* automático en caso *m* de rotura *f* de hilo *m*
- *broken thread stop motion*
20 la rendija purgadora para el hilo
- *thread clearer*
21 el disco frotador, para tensar el hilo
- *weighting disc (disk) for tensioning the thread*
22 el urdidor mecánico
- *warping machine*
23 el ventilador
- *fan*

24 la bobina cruzada
- *cross-wound cone*
25 la fileta
- *creel*
26 el peine ajustable (el peine de expansión *f*)
- *adjustable comb*
27 el bastidor (la bancada) del urdidor
- *warping machine frame*
28 el contador métrico de hilado *m* (de urdimbre *f*)
- *yarn length recorder*
29 el plegador de urdimbre *f*
- *warp beam*
30 el disco (la arandela) del plegador
- *beam flange*
31 el listón de protección *f*
- *guard rail*
32 el cilindro de contacto *m* (el tambor impulsor)
- *driving drum (driving cylinder)*
33 la transmisión por correa *f*
- *belt drive*
34 el motor
- *motor*
35 el pedal de puesta *f* en marcha *f*
- *release for starting the driving drum*
36 el tornillo, para regular (ajustar) la anchura del peine
- *screw for adjusting the comb setting*
37 las agujas, para parar en caso *m* de rotura *f* del hilo
- *drop pins, for stopping the machine when a thread breaks*
38 la barra guía *f*
- *guide bar*
39 el par de cilindros *m* de sujeción *f*
- *drop pin rollers*
40 la máquina de encolado *m* y de teñir con índigo *m*
- *indigo dying and sizing machine*
41 el bastidor de desenrollar
- *take-off stand*
42 el plegador de urdimbre *f*
- *warp beam*
43 la urdimbre (el hilado)
- *warp*
44 el depósito reticular (el depósito de mojado *m*)
- *wetting trough*
45 el cilindro de inmersión *f*
- *immersion roller*
46 el cilindro escurridor
- *squeeze roller (mangle)*
47 el depósito (la cuba) de la pintura
- *dye liquor padding trough*
48 la cámara de aire *m*
- *air oxidation passage*
49 la cuba de aclarado *m*
- *washing trough*
50 el secador de cilindros *m* para el presecado
- *drying cylinders for pre-drying*

51 el compensador acumulador
- *tension compensator (tension equalizer)*
52 la máquina encoladora
- *sizing machine*
53 el secador de cilindros *m*
- *drying cylinders*
54 el trozo seco
- *for cotton: stenter; for wool: tenter*
55 la máquina plegadora
- *beaming machine*
56 el plegador de urdimbre *f* encolado
- *sized warp beam*
57 los cilindros prensadores
- *rollers*

1 el telar automático
- *weaving machine (automatic loom)*
2 el contador de vueltas *f* (de pasadas *f*)
- *pick counter (tachometer)*
3 el carril guía *f* de los lizos
- *shaft (heald shaft, heald frame) guide*
4 los lizos
- *shafts (heald shafts, heald frames)*
5 el tambor de revólver *m*, para el cambio automático de las canillas
- *rotary battery for weft replenishment*
6 la tapa del batán
- *sley (slay) cap*
7 la canilla
- *weft pirn*
8 la palanca de embrague *m* y desembrague *m*
- *starting and stopping handle*
9 la caja de las lanzaderas, con lanzaderas *f* de tejer
- *shuttle box, with shuttles*
10 el peine de telar *m*
- *reed*
11 el orillo del tejido
- *selvedge (selvage)*
12 el tejido (la tela terminada)
- *cloth (woven fabric)*
13 el templazo (templén *m*)
- *temple (cloth temple)*
14 el pulsador eléctrico del hilo (de la trama)
- *electric weft feeler*
15 el volante
- *flywheel*
16 la tabla del antepecho
- *breast beam board*
17 la espada (el brazo) de batir
- *picking stick (pick stick)*
18 el motor eléctrico
- *electric motor*
19 los piñones de cambio *m*
- *cloth take-up motion*
20 el plegador del tejido
- *cloth roller (fabric roller)*
21 la caja de las bobinas, para las canillas vacías
- *can for empty pirns*
22 la correa, para la impulsión de la espada
- *lug strap, for moving the picking stick*
23 la caja de fusibles *m*
- *fuse box*
24 el bastidor (la bancada) del telar
- *loom framing*
25 la punta metálica
- *metal shuttle tip*
26 la lanzadera
- *shuttle*
27 el lizo (el lizo de alambre *m*)
- *heald (heddle, wire heald, wire heddle)*

28 el ojal para el hilo (el ojal del lizo)
- *eye (eyelet, heald eyelet, heddle eyelet)*
29 el ojal de la lanzadera
- *eye (shuttle eye)*
30 la canilla
- *pirn*
31 la banda metálica, para el contacto del pulsador
- *metal contact sleeve for the weft feeler*
32 la ranura para el pulsador
- *slot for the feeler*
33 el muelle de sujeción *f* de la canilla
- *spring-clip pirn holder*
34 el caballero (la laminilla) para el hilo de urdimbre *f*
- *drop wire*
35 el telar [corte transversal esquemático]
- *weaving machine (automatic loom) [side elevation]*
36 las poleas de los lizos
- *heald shaft guiding wheels*
37 el guiahílos móvil
- *backrest*
38 la cruz
- *lease rods*
39 la urdimbre (el hilo de urdimbre *m*)
- *warp (warp thread)*
40 la calada
- *shed*
41 el peine en el batán
- *sley (slay)*
42 las tablas (el zócalo) del batán
- *race board*
43 la uña para el dispositivo de paro *m*
- *stop rod blade for the stop motion*
44 el encaje del tope
- *bumper steel*
45 el vástago del tope del paro
- *bumper steel stop rod*
46 el antepecho (el plegador delantero)
- *breast beam*
47 el cilindro estriado
- *cloth take-up roller*
48 el plegador de urdimbre *f*
- *warp beam*
49 el disco (la arandela) del plegador
- *beam flange*
50 el árbol (el eje) principal
- *crankshaft*
51 el piñón (la rueda dentada) del eje cigüeñal
- *crankshaft wheel*
52 la biela ajustable
- *connector*
53 el soporte del batán
- *sley (slay)*
54 el tensor de los lizos
- *lam rods*

55 el piñón del árbol de excéntrica *f*
- *camshaft wheel*
56 el árbol de excéntrica *f*
- *camshaft (tappet shaft)*
57 la excéntrica
- *tappet (shedding tappet)*
58 la palanca de accionamiento *m* de la excéntrica
- *treadle lever*
59 el freno del plegador de urdimbre *f*
- *let-off motion*
60 el disco del freno
- *beam motion control*
61 el cable del freno
- *rope of the warp let-off motion*
62 la palanca del freno
- *let-off weight lever*
63 el contrapeso del freno
- *control weight [for the treadle]*
64 el taco con almohadilla *f* de cuero *m* o de resina *f* sintética
- *picker with leather or bakelite pad*
65 el amortiguador de la espada
- *picking stick buffer*
66 la excéntrica de gatillo *m* de la espada (la excéntrica de golpeo *m*)
- *picking cam*
67 el rodillo de excéntrica *f*
- *picking bowl*
68 el muelle recuperador de la espada
- *picking stick return spring*

## 167 Fabricación de géneros de punto, tricotaje

*Knitting*

**1-66 la fábrica de medias** *f*
- *hosiery mill*
1 el telar (la tricotosa) circular, para la elaboración de tejido *m* de punto *m* tubular
- *circular knitting machine for the manufacture of tubular fabric*
2 la pértiga soporte *m* del guiahílos
- *yarn guide support post (thread guide support post)*
3 el guiahílos
- *yarn guide (thread guide)*
4 la bobina botella *f*
- *bottle bobbin*
5 el tensor del hilo
- *yarn-tensioning device*
6 el cerrojo
- *yarn feeder*
7 el volante, para la colocación del hilo detrás de las agujas
- *handwheel for rotating the machine by hand*
8 el cilindro de agujas *f*
- *needle cylinder (cylindrical needle holder)*
9 el tejido tubular
- *tubular fabric*
10 el depósito del tejido
- *fabric drum (fabric box, fabric container)*
11 el cilindro de agujas *f* [sección]
- *needle cylinder (cylindrical needle holder) [section]*
12 las agujas de lengüeta *f* dispuestas radialmente
- *latch needles arranged in a circle*
13 la cubierta de la leva
- *cam housing*
14 la leva de aguja *f*
- *needle cams*
15 la ranura (el canal) de la aguja
- *needle trick*
16 el diámetro del cilindro; al mismo tiempo: anchura *f* del tejido tubular
- *cylinder diameter and diameter of tubular fabric*
17 el hilo
- *thread (yarn)*
18 la máquina Cotton, para la fabricación de medias *f* de señora *f*
- *Cotton's patent flat knitting machine for ladies' fully-fashioned hose*
19 la cadena patrón *m* (la cadena modelo *m*)
- *pattern control chain*
20 la bancada lateral
- *side frame*
21 la fontura (la zona de trabajo *m*); varias fonturas: producción *f* simultánea de varias medias *f*
- *knitting head; with several knitting heads: simultaneous production of several stockings*

22 la barra de puesta *f* en marcha *f* y paro *m*
- *starting rod*
23 la máquina Raschel (un telar de urdimbre *f* de dos fonturas *f*)
- *Raschel warp-knitting machine*
24 la urdimbre (el plegador de urdimbre *f*)
- *warp on warp beam*
25 el plegador de distribución *f*
- *yarn-distributing (yarn-dividing) beam*
26 la arandela del plegador de distribución *f*
- *beam flange*
27 la fontura de agujas *f* (la serie de agujas *f* de lengüeta *f*)
- *row of needles*
28 la barra de agujas *f*
- *needle bar*
29 el tejido (el tejido de Raschel) [cortinas *f* y géneros *m* de malla *f*] en el plegador del tejido
- *Raschel fabric [for curtain lace and net] on the fabric roll*
30 el volante para la impulsión a mano *f*
- *handwheel*
31 las ruedas impulsoras y el motor
- *motor drive gear*
32 el dispositivo tensor (el peso)
- *take-down weight*
33 el bastidor
- *frame*
34 la placa de base *f*
- *base plate*
35 la tricotosa rectilínea (máquina *f* manual de hacer punto *m*)
- *hand flat (flat-bed) knitting machine*
36 el hilo
- *thread (yarn)*
37 el resorte de retorno *m* (el muelle recuperador)
- *return spring*
38 el soporte, para los resortes
- *support for springs*
39 el carro deslizante
- *carriage*
40 el cerrojo (las levas)
- *feeder-selecting device*
41 la empuñadura para el deslizamiento del carro
- *carriage handles*
42 la escala para regular el tamaño de los puntos
- *scale for regulating size of stitches*
43 el contador de pasadas *f*
- *course counter (tachometer)*
44 la palanca conmutadora
- *machine control lever*
45 el riel guía *f*
- *carriage rail*
46 la hilera superior de agujas *f*
- *back row of needles*

47 la hilera inferior de agujas *f*
- *front row of needles*
48 el tejido de punto *m*
- *knitted fabric*
49 la barra tensora
- *tension bar*
50 el peso tensor
- *tension weight*
51 la fontura dispuesta para hacer punto *m*
- *needle bed showing knitting action*
52 los dientes del peine de desprendimiento *m*
- *teeth of knock-over bit*
53 las agujas dispuestas en orden *m* paralelo
- *needles in parallel rows*
54 el guiahílos
- *yarn guide (thread guide)*
55 el lecho de agujas *f*
- *needle bed*
56 el raíl de recubrimiento *m*, sobre las agujas *f* de lengüeta *f*
- *retaining plate for latch needles*
57 la leva de acoplamiento *m* de las agujas
- *guard cam*
58 la leva de descenso *m* de las agujas
- *sinker*
59 la leva de ascenso *m* de las agujas
- *needle-raising cam*
60 el talón de aguja *f*
- *needle butt*
61 la aguja de lengüeta *f*
- *latch needle*
62 la malla
- *loop*
63 el empuje de la aguja a través de la malla
- *pushing the needle through the fabric*
64 la colocación del hilo sobre el gancho de la aguja mediante el guiahílos
- *yarn guide (thread guide) placing yarn in the needle hook*
65 la confección (la formación) de la malla
- *loop formation*
66 la retención de la malla
- *casting off of loop*

9y0

**1-65 el procedimiento de acabado** *m* **de los tejidos**
- *finishing*
**1** el batán de cilindros *m*, para el enfurtido de los géneros de lana *f* (de los tejidos de lana *f*)
- *rotary milling (fulling) machine for felting the woollen (Am. woollen) fabric*
**2** la carga de pesos *m*
- *pressure weights*
**3** el cilindro de arrastre *m* superior
- *top milling roller (top fulling roller)*
**4** la polea de impulsión *f* del cilindro de arrastre *m* inferior
- *drive wheel of bottom milling roller (bottom fulling roller)*
**5** el rodillo guía del tejido
- *fabric guide roller*
**6** el cilindro de arrastre *m* inferior
- *bottom milling roller (bottom fulling roller)*
**7** la tabla de tracción *f* (el seleccionador)
- *draft board*
**8** la máquina de lavar al ancho, para tejidos *m* delicados
- *open-width scouring machine for finer fabrics*
**9** la entrada del tejido
- *fabric being drawn off the machine*
**10** la caja de mecanismos *m* (la caja de engranajes *m*)
- *drive gearbox*
**11** la tubería del agua *f*
- *water inlet pipe*
**12** el rodillo guía *f*
- *drawing-in roller*
**13** el travesaño tensor
- *scroll-opening roller*
**14** la centrífuga pendular, para el secado (el escurrido) de los tejidos
- *pendulum-type hydro-extractor (centrifuge), for extracting liquors from the fabric*
**15** el bastidor base
- *machine base*
**16** la columna
- *casing over suspension*
**17** la caja, con el tambor interior giratorio
- *outer casing containing rotating cage (rotating basket)*
**18** la tapa de la centrífuga
- *hydro-extractor (centrifuge) lid*
**19** el dispositivo de paro *m* de seguridad *f*
- *stop-motion device (stopping device)*
**20** el dispositivo de arranque *m* y de freno *m* automático
- *automatic starting and braking device*
**21** la máquina de secar tejidos *m*
- *for cotton: stenter; for wool: tenter*

**22** el tejido húmedo
- *air-dry fabric*
**23** la plataforma de servicio *m*
- *operator's (operative's) platform*
**24** la fijación del tejido, mediante cadenas *f* de agujas *f* o de pinzas *f*
- *feeding of fabric by guides onto stenter (tenter) pins or clips*
**25** la caja del control eléctrico (la caja de los electroconmutadores)
- *electric control panel*
**26** la entrada en pliegues *m* del tejido, para facilitar el proceso de contracción *f* longitudinal en el secado
- *initial overfeed to produce shrink-resistant fabric when dried*
**27** el termómetro
- *thermometer*
**28** la cámara de secado *m*
- *drying section*
**29** la tubería de salida *f* del aire
- *air outlet*
**30** la salida del secador
- *plaiter (fabric-plaiting device)*
**31** la máquina perchadora para cardar el derecho del tejido con cardas *f* para afelpar
- *wire-roller fabric-raising machine for producing raised or nap surface*
**32** la caja de engranajes *m*
- *drive gearbox*
**33** el tejido sin cardar
- *unraised cloth*
**34** los cilindros rugosos
- *wire-covered rollers*
**35** el dispositivo plegador del tejido (el abanico)
- *plaiter (cuttling device)*
**36** el tejido cardado
- *raised fabric*
**37** el banco para el género
- *plaiting-down platform*
**38** la prensa continua, para el planchado del tejido
- *rotary press (calendering machine), for press finishing*
**39** el paño
- *fabric*
**40** los pulsadores y el volante de control *m*
- *control buttons and control wheels*
**41** el cilindro de presión *f* calentado
- *heated press bowl*
**42** la máquina tundidora del tejido
- *rotary cloth-shearing machine*
**43** el aspirador del tamo
- *suction slot, for removing loose fibres (Am. fibers)*
**44** la cuchilla de tundir (el cilindro tundidor)
- *doctor blade (cutting cylinder)*
**45** la rejilla de protección *f*
- *protective guard*

**46** el cepillo giratorio
- *rotating brush*
**47** el deslizamiento del tejido
- *curved scray entry*
**48** el pedal de mando *m*
- *treadle control*
**49** la máquina decatizadora, para la obtención de tejidos *m* inencogibles
- *[non-shrinking] decatizing (decating) fabric-finishing machine*
**50** el cilindro decatizador
- *perforated decatizing (decating) cylinder*
**51** la pieza de tejido *m*
- *piece of fabric*
**52** la manivela
- *cranked control handle*
**53** la máquina de rodillos *m* para estampar diez colores *m* (la máquina de estampar tejidos *m*)
- *ten-colour (Am. ten-color) roller printing machine*
**54** el bastidor base de la máquina
- *base of the machine*
**55** el motor
- *drive motor*
**56** la almohadilla (la blanqueta)
- *blanket [of rubber or felt]*
**57** el género estampado
- *fabric after printing (printed fabric)*
**58** el dispositivo electroconmutador
- *electric control panel (control unit)*
**59** la estampación del tejido a la lionesa
- *screen printing*
**60** el carro móvil para plantillas *f*
- *mobile screen frame*
**61** la raedera (el limpiador)
- *squeegee*
**62** la plantilla estampadora
- *pattern stencil*
**63** la mesa de estampación *f*
- *screen table*
**64** el tejido fijado con goma *f* para ser estampado
- *fabric gummed down on table ready for printing*
**65** el estampador textil (el operario estampador)
- *screen printing operator (operative)*

# 169 Fibras artificiales y sintéticas I

**1-34** la fabricación del **rayón** (de seda artificial) y de **fibras textiles** por elaboración *f* de la viscosa
- *manufacture of **continuous filament and staple fibre*** (Am. *fiber*) ***viscose rayon yarns*** *by means of the viscose process*

**1-12** de la materia prima a la viscosa
- *from raw material to viscose rayon*

**1** la materia base [hojas *f* de celulosa *f* de haya *f* y de pino *m*, láminas *f* de celulosa *f*]
- *basic material [beech and spruce cellulose in form of sheets]*

**2** la mezcla de las láminas de celulosa *f*
- *mixing cellulose sheets*

**3** la sosa cáustica
- *caustic soda*

**4** la impregnación de las láminas de celulosa *f* en sosa *f* cáustica
- *steeping cellulose sheets in caustic soda*

**5** el prensado para (el escurrido de) la sosa cáustica sobrante
- *pressing out excess caustic soda*

**6** el desfibrado de las láminas de celulosa *f*
- *shredding the cellulose sheets*

**7** la maduración de la álcalicelulosa
- *maturing (controlled oxidation) of the alkali-cellulose crumbs*

**8** el sulfuro de carbón *m*
- *carbon disulphide (Am. carbon disulfide)*

**9** la sulfuración (transformación *f* de la álcalicelulosa en xantogenato *m* de celulosa *f*)
- *conversion of alkali-cellulose into cellulose xanthate*

**10** la disolución del xantogenato en sosa *f* cáustica, para la obtención de la solución hilable de viscosa *f*
- *dissolving the xanthate in caustic soda for the preparation of the viscose spinning solution*

**11** la caldera-depósito al vacío
- *vacuum ripening tanks*

**12** el filtro-prensa
- *filter press*

**13-27** de la viscosa al hilo de rayón *m*
- *from viscose to viscose rayon thread*

**13** la bomba de hilatura *f*
- *metering pump*

**14** la hilera (tobera *f* de hilar)
- *multi-holed spinneret (spinning jet)*

**15** el baño de coagulación *f*, para la transformación de la viscosa viscosa (pegajosa) en hilos *m* de celulosa *f* coagulada
- *coagulating (spinning) bath for converting (coagulating) viscose (viscous solution) into solid filaments*

**16** el cristalero, una polea de cristal *m*
- *Godet wheel, a glass pulley*

**17** la centrífuga de hilar, para la unión de los filamentos
- *Topham centrifugal pot (box) for twisting the filaments into yarn*

**18** la corona de rayón *m*
- *viscose rayon cake*

**19-27** el tratamiento de la corona de rayón *m*
- *processing of the cake*

**19** la desacidificación
- *washing*

**20** la desulfuración
- *desulphurizing (desulphurization, Am. desulfurizing, desulfurization)*

**21** el blanqueo
- *bleaching*

**22** el acabado de la corona (para dar blancura *f* y ductilidad *f* a la materia)
- *treating of cake to give filaments softness and suppleness*

**23** la centrifugación, para la separación del exceso de líquido *m*
- *hydro-extraction to remove surplus moisture*

**24** el secado, en la cámara de secado
- *drying in heated room*

**25** el bobinado
- *winding yarn from cake into cone form*

**26** la máquina de bobinar
- *cone-winding machine*

**27** el hilo de rayón *m* sobre bobina *f* cónica de plegado *m* para la manipulación textil
- *viscose rayon yarn on cone ready for use*

**28-34** de la solución hilable de viscosa *f* a la fibra textil
- *from viscose spinning solution to viscose rayon staple fibre* (Am. *fiber*)

**28** el cable (la cuerda de hilos *m*)
- *filament tow*

**29** la instalación de lavado *m* por aspersión *f*
- *overhead spray washing plant*

**30** el dispositivo cortador, para cortar los hilos a una longitud determinada
- *cutting machine for cutting filament tow to desired length*

**31** la máquina secadora múltiple para las fibras
- *multiple drying machine for cut-up staple fibre (Am. fiber) layer (lap)*

**32** la correa transportadora
- *conveyor belt (conveyor)*

**33** la prensa de balas *f*
- *baling press*

**34** las balas de fibras *f* de viscosa *f* listas para el envío
- *bale of viscose rayon ready for dispatch (despatch)*

# 170 Fibras artificiales y sintéticas II

**1-62 la fabricación del perlón**
- *manufacture of polyamide (nylon 6, perlon) fibres (Am. fibers)*
1 la hulla [la materia prima para la producción del perlón]
- *coal [raw material for manufacture of polyamide (nylon 6, perlon) fibres (Am. fibers)]*
2 la coquería, para la destilación seca de la hulla
- *coking plant for dry coal distillation*
3 la extracción del alquitrán y del fenol
- *extraction of coal tar and phenol*
4 la destilación gradual del alquitrán
- *gradual distillation of tar*
5 el condensador
- *condenser*
6 la extracción y el transporte del benzol
- *benzene extraction and dispatch (despatch)*
7 el cloro
- *chlorine*
8 la cloración del benzol
- *benzene chlorination*
9 el clorobenzol
- *monochlorobenzene (chlorobenzene)*
10 la sosa cáustica
- *caustic soda solution*
11 la evaporación del clorobenzol y de la sosa cáustica
- *evaporation of chlorobenzene and caustic soda*
12 el depósito de reacción *f* (el autoclave)
- *autoclave*
13 el cloruro de sodio *m* (la sal común), un subproducto
- *sodium chloride (common salt), a by-product*
14 el fenol
- *phenol (carbolic acid)*
15 la alimentación de hidrógeno *m*
- *hydrogen inlet*
16 la hidrogenación del fenol, para la obtención del ciclohexano bruto
- *hydrogenation of phenol to produce raw cyclohexanol*
17 la destilación
- *distillation*
18 el ciclohexano puro
- *pure cyclohexanol*
19 la deshidrogenación
- *oxidation (dehydrogenation)*
20 la formación de la ciclohexanona
- *formation of cyclohexanone (pimehinketone)*
21 la tubería de la hidroxilamina
- *hydroxylamine inlet*
22 la formación de la ciclohexanona-oxima
- *formation of cyclohexanoxime*
23 la adición del ácido sulfúrico, para la poliadición molecular
- *addition of sulphuric acid (Am. sulfuric acid) to effect molecular rearrangement*
24 el amoníaco, para la neutralización del ácido sulfúrico
- *ammonia to neutralize sulphuric acid (Am. sulfuric acid)*
25 la formación de la lactama
- *formation of caprolactam oil*

26 la solución de sulfato *m* de amonio *m*
- *ammonium sulphate (Am. ammonium sulfate) solution*
27 el cilindro refrigerador
- *cooling cylinder*
28 la caprolactama
- *caprolactam*
29 la báscula
- *weighing apparatus*
30 la caldera de fusión *f*
- *melting pot*
31 la bomba
- *pump*
32 el filtro
- *filter*
33 la polimerización en el autoclave (recipiente *m* a presión *f*)
- *polymerization in the autoclave*
34 la refrigeración de la poliamida
- *cooling of the polyamide*
35 la fusión de la poliamida
- *solidification of the polyamide*
36 el elevador de rosario *m*
- *vertical lift (Am. elevator)*
37 el extractor, para separar de la poliamida la lactama restante
- *extractor for separating the polyamide from the remaining lactam oil*
38 el secador
- *drier*
39 la escama seca de la poliamida
- *dry polyamide chips*
40 el depósito de escamas *f*
- *chip container*
41 la cámara de hilatura *f* para la fusión de la poliamida y para el prensado a través de las hileras
- *top of spinneret for melting the polyamide and forcing it through spinneret holes (spinning jets)*
42 las hileras
- *spinneret holes (spinning jets)*
43 la solidificación de los hilos de poliamida *f* (de perlón *m*) en la columna refrigerante
- *solidification of polyamide filaments in the cooling tower*
44 el enrollado del hilo
- *collection of extruded filaments into thread form*
45 la torsión preliminar
- *preliminary stretching (preliminary drawing)*
46 el estiraje, para la obtención de gran resistencia *f* y flexibilidad *f* del hilo de poliamida *f*
- *stretching (cold-drawing) of the polyamide thread to achieve high tensile strength*
47 la torsión final
- *final stretching (final drawing)*
48 el lavado de las bobinas
- *washing of yarn packages*
49 la cámara de secado *m*
- *drying chamber*
50 el rebobinado
- *rewinding*
51 la bobina de arrollado *m* cruzado
- *polyamide cone*
52 la bobina de arrollado *m* cruzado lista para enviar
- *polyamide cone ready for dispatch (despatch)*

53 la caldera de mezcla *f*
- *mixer*
54 la polimerización, en la caldera de vacío *m*
- *polymerization under vacua*
55 el estiraje
- *stretching (drawing)*
56 el lavado
- *washing*
57 la preparación, para dejar el hilo en condiciones de ser hilado
- *finishing of tow for spinning*
58 el secado del cable (el secado del hilo)
- *drying of tow*
59 el ondulado del hilo
- *crimping of tow*
60 el cortado del hilo con la longitud de fibra *f* normal
- *cutting of tow into normal staple lengths*
61 la fibra de poliamida *f* (de perlón *m*)
- *polyamide staple*
62 la bala de fibra *f* de poliamida *f* (de perlón *m*)
- *bale of polyamide staple*

**1-29 ligamentos *m* de tejidos *m***
[cuadros negros: hilo *m* de
urdimbre *f* por encima, hilo de
trama *f* por debajo; cuadros
blancos: hilo de trama por
encima, hilo de urdimbre por
debajo]
– *weaves [black squares: warp
thread raised, weft thread
lowered; white squares: weft
thread raised, warp thread
lowered]*
**1** el ligamento tafetán (el
ligamento a la plana) [la vista
superior del tejido]
– *plain weave (tabby weave)
[weave viewed from above]*
**2** el hilo de urdimbre *f*
– *warp thread*
**3** el hilo de trama *f*
– *weft thread*
**4** la carta del ligamento para el
tafetán [el proyecto para el
tejedor]
– *draft (point paper design) for
plain weave*
**5** el remetido en los lizos
– *threading draft*
**6** el remetido del peine
– *denting draft (reed-threading
draft)*
**7** el hilo de urdimbre *f* por
encima
– *raised warp thread*
**8** el hilo de urdimbre *f* por
debajo
– *lowered warp thread*
**9** la armadura
– *tie-up of shafts in pairs*
**10** el picado (el dibujo)
– *treadling diagram*
**11** la carta (el patrón) para el
ligamento panameño (el
ligamento regular, el ligamento
inglés)
– *draft for basket weave (hopsack
weave, matt weave)*
**12** el curso (la parte del ligamento
que continúa y se repite)
– *pattern repeat*
**13** el patrón (la carta) para el reps
por trama *f*
– *draft for warp rib weave*
**14** corte *m* de tejido *m* del reps
por trama *f*, un corte de
urdimbre *f*
– *section of warp rib fabric, a
section through the warp*
**15** el hilo de *f* trama por debajo
– *lowered weft thread*
**16** el hilo de trama *f* por encima
– *raised weft thread*
**17** el primer hilo y el segundo hilo
de urdimbre *f* [levantados]
– *first and second warp threads
[raised]*
**18** el tercer hilo y el cuarto hilo de
urdimbre *f* [bajados]
– *third and fourth warp threads
[lowered]*

**19** el patrón del reps acanalado
irregular
– *draft for combined rib weave*
**20** el remetido de los hilos en los
licetes (los lizos adicionales
para el orillo del tejido)
– *selvedge (selvage) thread draft*
**21** el remetido de los hilos en los
lizos del tejido
– *draft for the fabric shafts*
**22** la armadura de los licetes
– *tie-up of selvedge (selvage) shafts*
**23** la armadura de los lizos del
tejido
– *tie-up of fabric shafts*
**24** el orillo en ligamento *m* de
tela *f*
– *selvedge (selvage) in plain weave*
**25** el corte de tejido *m* del reps
acanalado irregular
– *section through combination rib
weave*
**26** el ligamento del tejido de
punto *m* longitudinal
– *thread interlacing of reversible
warp-faced cord*
**27** el patrón para el ligamento del
tejido de punto *m* longitudinal
– *draft (point paper design) for
reversible warp-faced cord*
**28** los puntos de ligadura *f*
– *interlacing points*
**29** el ligamento de barquillo *m*
para el patrón de barquillo *m*
en el tejido (el ligamento
"nido *m* de abeja *f*" o
"punto *m* de tripa *f*")
– *weaving draft for honeycomb
weave in the fabric*
**30-48 ligamentos *m* fundamentales
de tejidos *m* y cuerdas *f***
– *basic knits*
**30** la malla, una malla abierta
– *loop, an open loop*
**31** la cabeza
– *head*
**32** la rama (el lado)
– *side*
**33** el pie
– *neck*
**34** el punto de ligamento *m* de
cabeza *f*
– *head interlocking point*
**35** el punto de ligamento *m* de
pie *m*
– *neck interlocking point*
**36** la malla cerrada
– *closed loop*
**37** la red
– *mesh [with inlaid yarn]*
**38** la trayectoria diagonal del hilo
– *diagonal floating yarn (diagonal
floating thread)*
**39** el nudo con ligamento *m* de
cabeza *f*
– *loop interlocking at the head*
**40** el flotador
– *float*

**41** la trayectoria libre (vertical) del
hilo
– *loose floating yarn (loose
floating thread)*
**42** la vuelta de malla *f*
– *course*
**43** la trama
– *inlaid yarn*
**44** la puntada izquierda-derecha
– *tuck and miss stitch*
**45** el cruzado izquierda-derecha
– *pulled-up tuck stitch*
**46** la puntada cruzada izquierda-
derecha (la puntada al sesgo)
– *staggered tuck stitch*
**47** la puntada doble
izquierda-derecha
– *2 x 2 tuck and miss stitch*
**48** el cruzado doble
izquierda-derecha
– *double pulled-up tuck stitch*

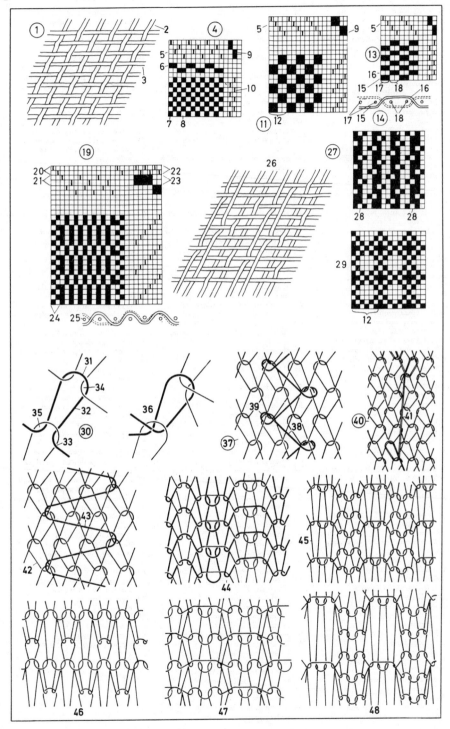

**1-52** la fábrica de celulosa *f* al sulfato [esquema]
– *sulphate* (Am. *sulfate) pulp mill (kraft pulp mill) [in diagram form]*
**1** la máquina cortadora con separador *m* de polvo *m*
– *chippers with dust extractor*
**2** el tamiz giratorio
– *rotary screen (riffler)*
**3** el aparato distribuidor de la celulosa (de la pasta)
– *chip packer (chip distributor)*
**4** el soplante
– *blower*
**5** el molino centrífugo
– *disintegrator (crusher, chip crusher)*
**6** la cámara colectora del polvo
– *dust-settling chamber*
**7** el digestor de celulosa *f*
– *digester*
**8** el precalentador de lejía *f*
– *liquor preheater*
**9** el grifo de control *m*
– *control tap*
**10** el tubo giratorio
– *swing pipe*
**11** el difusor
– *blow tank (diffuser)*
**12** la válvula de pulverización *f*
– *blow valve*
**13** la caja del difusor
– *blow pit (diffuser)*
**14** el separador de la trementina
– *turpentine separator*
**15** el separador central
– *centralized separator*
**16** el condensador de inyección *f*
– *jet condenser (injection condenser)*
**17** el depósito de condensado *m*
– *storage tank for condensate*
**18** el depósito de agua *f* caliente
– *hot water tank*
**19** el intercambiador de calor *m*
– *heat exchanger*
**20** el filtro
– *filter*
**21** el preclasificador
– *presorter*
**22** la centrífuga depuradora
– *centrifugal screen*
**23** la máquina clasificadora rotativa
– *rotary sorter (rotary strainer)*
**24** el cilindro de drenaje *m*
– *concentrator (thickener, decker)*
**25** la cuba
– *vat (chest)*
**26** el depósito colector, para el agua *f* de vuelta *f*
– *collecting tank for backwater (low box)*
**27** el refinador cónico
– *conical refiner (cone refiner, Jordan, Jordan refiner)*
**28** el filtro para lejía *f* negra
– *black liquor filter*
**29** el depósito de lejía *f* negra
– *black liquor storage tank*
**30** el condensador
– *condenser*
**31** los separadores
– *separators*
**32** el calorífero (el aparato de calefacción *f*)
– *heaters (heating elements)*
**33** la bomba de la lejía
– *liquor pump*
**34** la bomba de la lejía espesa
– *heavy liquor pump*

**35** el depósito de mezcla *f*
– *mixing tank*
**36** el depósito de sulfato *m*
– *salt cake storage tank (sodium sulphate storage tank)*
**37** el tanque para disolver (el disolvedor)
– *dissolving tank (dissolver)*
**38** la caldera de vapor *m*
– *steam heater*
**39** el electrofiltro
– *electrostatic precipitator*
**40** la bomba de aire *m*
– *air pump*
**41** el depósito para la lejía verde poco clara
– *storage tank for the uncleared green liquor*
**42** el condensador
– *concentrator (thickener, decker)*
**43** el precalentador de lejía *f* verde
– *green liquor preheater*
**44** el condensador (el espesador) de lavado *m*
– *concentrator (thickener, decker) for the weak wash liquor (wash water)*
**45** el depósito parta la lejía floja
– *storage tank for the weak liquor*
**46** el depósito de lejía *f* de cocción *f*
– *storage tank for the cooking liquor*
**47** el agitador
– *agitator (stirrer)*
**48** el condensador (el espesador)
– *concentrator (thickener, decker)*
**49** los agitadores caustificadores
– *causticizing agitators (causticizing stirrers)*
**50** el clasificador
– *classifier*
**51** el tambor para apagar la cal
– *lime slaker*
**52** la cal cocida (calcinada)
– *reconverted lime*
**53-65** la instalación para refinar la madera [esquema]
– *groundwood mill (mechanical pulp mill) [diagram]*
**53** la trituradora continua
– *continuous grinder (continuous chain grinder)*
**54** el colador para las astillas (para los nudos de la madera)
– *strainer (knotter)*
**55** la bomba para el agua *f* de la pasta
– *pulp water pump*
**56** la centrífuga depuradora
– *centrifugal screen*
**57** el clasificador
– *screen (sorter)*
**58** el segundo clasificador
– *secondary screen (secondary sorter)*
**59** la cuba para la pasta gruesa
– *rejects chest*
**60** el refinador cónico
– *conical refiner (cone refiner, Jordan, Jordan refiner)*
**61** la máquina de drenaje *m*
– *pulp-drying machine (pulp machine)*
**62** la cuba de espesar
– *concentrator (thickener, decker)*
**63** la bomba de las aguas residuales
– *waste water pump (white water pump, pulp water pump)*
**64** la tubería de vapores *m*
– *steam pipe*
**65** la tubería de agua *f*
– *water pipe*

**66** la trituradora continua
– *continuous grinder (continuous grinder (continuous chain grinder)*
**67** la cadena de avance *m*
– *feed chain*
**68** la madera molida
– *groundwood*
**69** la reducción para la impulsión de la cadena de avance *m*
– *reduction gear for the feed chain drive*
**70** el dispositivo cortante de la piedra (de la muela)
– *stone-dressing device*
**71** la piedra moledora (la muela)
– *grinding stone (grindstone, pulpstone)*
**72** el tubo pulverizador
– *spray pipe*
**73** el refinador cónico
– *conical refiner (cone refiner, Jordan, Jordan refiner)*
**74** el volante para regular la distancia de las cuchillas
– *handwheel for adjusting the clearance between the knives (blades)*
**75** el cono giratorio de las cuchillas
– *rotating bladed cone (rotating bladed plug)*
**76** el cono fijo de las cuchillas
– *stationary bladed shell*
**77** la entrada para la celulosa (*también*: pasta *f* de madera *f* no refinada)
– *inlet for unrefined cellulose (chemical wood pulp, chemical pulp) or groundwood pulp (mechanical pulp)*
**78** la salida para la celulosa (*también*: pasta *f* de madera *f* refinada)
– *outlet for refined cellulose (chemical wood pulp, chemical pulp) or groundwood pulp (mechanical pulp)*
**79-86** la instalación para preparar (tratar) la pasta
– *stuff (stock) preparation plant [diagram]*
**79** la cinta transportadora para levantar la celulosa *o* pasta de madera
– *conveyor belt (conveyor) for loading cellulose (chemical wood pulp, chemical pulp) or groundwood pulp (mechanical pulp)*
**80** el disociador de celulosa *f*
– *pulper*
**81** la cuba de vaciado *m*
– *dump chest*
**82** el desintegrador cónico
– *cone breaker*
**83** el molino cónico
– *conical refiner (cone refiner, Jordan, Jordan refiner)*
**84** el refinador
– *refiner*
**85** la cuba de pasta acabada
– *stuff chest (stock chest)*
**86** la cuba de máquina *f*
– *machine chest (stuff chest)*

**1** la cubeta agitadora, una cubeta mezcladora de la pasta de papel *m*
– *stuff chest (stock chest, machine chest), a mixing chest for stuff (stock)*
**2-10** los instrumentos de laboratorio *m* para la pasta de papel *m* y para el examen del papel
– *laboratory apparatus (laboratory equipment) for analysing stuff (stock) and paper*
**2** el frasco (de) Erlenmeyer
– *Erlenmeyer flask*
**3** el matraz de mezcla *f*
– *volumetric flask*
**4** la probeta de medida *f*
– *measuring cylinder*
**5** el quemador Bunsen
– *Bunsen burner*
**6** las trébedes
– *tripod*
**7** el plato de laboratorio *m*
– *petri dish*
**8** el soporte de los tubos de ensayo *m*
– *test tube rack*
**9** la balanza para el peso bruto
– *balance for measuring basis weight*
**10** el micrómetro de espesores *m*
– *micrometer*
**11** los depuradores centrífugos delante de la caja de entrada *f* de una máquina de papel *m*
– *centrifugal cleaners ahead of the breastbox (headbox, stuff box) of a paper machine*
**12** el tubo vertical
– *standpipe*
**13-28** la máquina de papel *m* [esquema]
– *paper machine (production line) [diagram]*
**13** la tubería de alimentación *f* para la cubeta de la máquina con purgador de nudos *m* y arena *f*
– *feed-in from the machine chest (stuff chest) with sand table (sand trap, riffler) and knotter*
**14** el tamiz (la tela metálica)
– *wire (machine wire)*
**15** el aspirador del tamiz
– *vacuum box (suction box)*
**16** el rodillo aspirador del tamiz
– *suction roll*
**17** el primer fieltro húmedo
– *first wet felt*
**18** el segundo fieltro húmedo
– *second wet felt*
**19** la primera prensa húmeda
– *first press*
**20** la segunda prensa húmeda
– *second press*
**21** la prensa offset
– *offset press*

**22** el cilindro secador
– *drying cylinder (drier)*
**23** el fieltro secador (*también:* el tamiz secador)
– *dry felt (drier felt)*
**24** la prensa encoladora
– *size press*
**25** el cilindro refrigerador
– *cooling roll*
**26** los rodillos de calandrar
– *calender rolls*
**27** el casco secador
– *machine hood*
**28** la enrolladora
– *delivery reel*
**29-35** la máquina de recubrir por extensión *f* de rasqueta *f*
– *blade coating machine (blade coater)*
**29** el papel bruto
– *raw paper (body paper)*
**30** el rollo continuo de papel *m*
– *web*
**31** la instalación para extender la parte delantera
– *coater for the top side*
**32** la estufa infrarroja
– *infrared drier*
**33** el tambor secador calentado
– *heated drying cylinder*
**34** el dispositivo para extender la parte trasera
– *coater for the underside (wire side)*
**35** el rollo de papel *m* acabado de extender
– *reel of coated paper*
**36** la calandria
– *calender (Super-calender)*
**37** el sistema de comprimir hidráulico
– *hydraulic system for the press rolls*
**38** el rodillo de la calandria
– *calender roll*
**39** el mecanismo de desenrollar
– *unwind station*
**40** la plataforma de elevación *f*
– *lift platform*
**41** el mecanismo de enrollar
– *rewind station (rewinder, re-reeler, reeling machine, re-reeling machine)*
**42** el cortador de rollos *m*
– *roll cutter*
**43** el tablero de mandos *m*
– *control panel*
**44** el aparato de corte (la cuchilla)
– *cutter*
**45** el rollo continuo de papel *m*
– *web*
**46-51** la fabricación del papel a mano *f*
– *papermaking by hand*
**46** el laurente
– *vatman*
**47** la tina
– *vat*

**48** la forma de mano *f*
– *mould (Am. mold)*
**49** el lavador
– *coucher (couchman)*
**50** la pila de papel *m* preparado para la prensa *f*
– *post ready for pressing*
**51** el fieltro
– *felt*

# 174 Taller de composición I

**174 Taller de composición I** — *Composing Room (Case Room) I*

1 la composición a mano *f* (la sección de cajas *f* a mano *f*)
- **hand-setting room (hand-composing room)**
2 el chibalete
- *composing frame*
3 la caja tipográfica
- *case (typecase)*
4 la caja colocada en el chibalete
- *case cabinet (case rack)*
5 el cajista (el tipógrafo)
- *hand compositor (compositor, typesetter); also: maker-up*
6 el manuscrito (el original)
- *manuscript (typescript)*
7 los caracteres (los tipos)
- *sorts (types, type characters, characters)*
8 la estantería, para lingotes *m* y blancos *m* (material *m* de relleno *m*)
- *rack (case) for furniture (spacing material)*
9 el estante de composición *f*
- *standing type rack (standing matter rack)*
10 el tablero de los moldes
- *storage shelf (shelf for storing formes, Am. forms)*
11 la composición conservada
- *standing type (standing matter)*
12 la galera
- *galley*
13 el componedor
- *composing stick (setting stick)*
14 la regleta (el filete sacalíneas)
- *composing rule (setting rule)*
15 la composición
- *type (type matter, matter)*
16 el cordel para la columna
- *page cord*
17 la punta (el punzón)
- *bodkin*
18 las pinzas
- *tweezers*
19 **la linotipia**, una máquina de almacén *m* múltiple
- **Linotype line-composing (line-casting, slug-composing, slug-casting) machine,** a multi-magazine machine
20 el mecanismo de distribución *f*
- *distributing mechanism (distributor)*
21 el almacén con las matrices
- *type magazines with matrices (matrixes)*
22 el elevador, para transportar las matrices al distribuidor
- *elevator carrier for distributing the matrices (matrixes)*
23 el componedor
- *assembler*
24 los espacios cuneiformes (espacios *m* de cuñas *f*)
- *spacebands*
25 el crisol (el dispositivo fundidor)
- *casting mechanism*

26 el alimentador automático de metal *m*
- *metal feeder*
27 la composición mecánica (las líneas fundidas)
- *machine-set matter (cast lines, slugs)*
28 las matrices de mano *f*
- *matrices (matrixes) for hand-setting (sorts)*
29 la matriz de linotipia *f*
- *Linotype matrix*
30 el dentado, para el mecanismo de distribución *f*
- *teeth for the distributing mechanism (distributor)*
31 el ojo de caracteres *m* (la matriz)
- *face (type face, matrix)*
32-45 **la monotipo**, una máquina para componer y fundir en tipo *m* suelto (tipo *m* individual)
- **monotype single-unit composing (typesetting) and casting machine (monotype single-unit composition caster)**
32 la máquina componedora monotipo normal (el teclado)
- *monotype standard composing (typesetting) machine [keyboard]*
33 el carrete (la torre) de papel *m*
- *paper tower*
34 la tira de papel *m* de composición *f*
- *paper ribbon*
35 el tambor
- *justifying scale*
36 el indicador de unidades *f*
- *unit indicator*
37 el teclado
- *keyboard*
38 el tubo de aire *m* a presión *f*
- *compressed-air hose*
39 la máquina fundidora monotipo
- *monotype casting machine (monotype caster)*
40 el alimentador automático de metal *m*
- *automatic metal feeder*
41 el muelle de compresión *f* de la bomba
- *pump compression spring (pump pressure spring)*
42 el bastidor portamatrices
- *matrix case (die case)*
43 el carrete de papel *m*
- *paper tower*
44 la galera, con el tipo suelto (tipo *m* individual)
- *galley with types (letters, characters, cast single types, cast single letters)*
45 la calefacción eléctrica
- *electric heater (electric heating unit)*
46 el bastidor portamatrices
- *matrix case (die case)*

47 las matrices de los tipos
- *type matrices (matrixes) (letter matrices)*
48 la entalla, para encajar en la guía de corredera *f* cruzada
- *guide block for engaging with the cross-slide guide*

**1-17 la composición**
- *composition (type matter, type)*
1 la letra inicial
- *initial (initial letter)*
2 la letra seminegra
- *bold type (bold, boldfaced type, heavy type, boldface)*
3 la letra negrita
- *semibold type (semibold)*
4 la línea
- *line*
5 el espacio entre dos renglones *m* (el interlineado)
- *space*
6 la ligadura
- *ligature (double letter)*
7 la letra cursiva (la letra itálica)
- *italic type (italics)*
8 la letra fina
- *light face type (light face)*
9 la letra gruesa (la letra supernegra)
- *extra bold type (extra bold)*
10 la letra negra estrecha
- *bold condensed type (bold condensed)*
11 la letra mayúscula (la letra versal, la letra capital)
- *majuscule (capital letter, capital, upper case letter)*
12 la letra minúscula
- *minuscule (small letter, lower case letter)*
13 la seperación (la palabra espaciada)
- *letter spacing (interspacing)*
14 la letra versalita
- *small capitals*
15 el punto y aparte
- *break*
16 la sangría (el principio de párrafo *m*)
- *indention*
17 el espacio
- *space*
18 **los cuerpos de las letras de imprenta** *f* [un punto tipográfico = 0,376 mm.]
- *type sizes [one typographic point = 0.376 mm (Didot system), 0.351 mm (Pica system)*
19 el non plus ultra (2 puntos *m*)
- *six-to-pica (2 points)*
20 el brillante (3 puntos *m*)
- *half nonpareil (four-to-pica) (3 points)*
21 el diamante (4 puntos *m*)
- *brilliant (4 points); sim.: diamond (4½ points)*
22 la perla (5 puntos *m*)
- *pearl (5 points); sim.: ruby (Am. agate) (5½ points)*
23 el nomparell (6 puntos *m*)
- *nonpareil (6 points); sim.: minionette (6½ points)*
24 la miñona (7 puntos *m*)
- *minion (7 points)*
25 la gallarda (8 puntos *m*)
- *brevier (8 points)*

26 el breviario (9 puntos *m*)
- *bourgeois (9 points)*
27 el garamón (10 puntos *m*)
- *long primer (10 points)*
28 la lectura (12 puntos *m*)
- *pica (12 points)*
29 el texto (14 puntos *m*)
- *english (14 points)*
30 la atanasia (16 puntos *m*)
- *great primer (two-line brevier, Am. Columbian) (16 points)*
31 el pequeño parangón (20 puntos *m*)
- *paragon (two-line primer) (20 points)*
**32-37 la fabricación de caracteres** (tipos *m*, letras *f*)
- *typefounding (type casting)*
32 el grabador de punzones *m*
- *punch cutter*
33 el buril de acero *m*
- *graver (burin, cutter)*
34 la lupa
- *magnifying glass (magnifier)*
35 el cuño (el punzón)
- *punch blank (die blank)*
36 el punzón de acero *m* acabado
- *finished steel punch (finished steel die)*
37 la matriz punzonada
- *punched matrix (stamped matrix, strike, drive)*
38 **la letra** (el tipo)
- *type (type character, character)*
39 la cabeza
- *head*
40 el hombro
- *shoulder*
41 el punzón
- *counter*
42 el ojo
- *face (type face)*
43 la línea de la letra
- *type line (bodyline)*
44 la altura del tipo
- *height to paper (type height)*
45 la altura del hombro
- *height of shank (height of shoulder)*
46 el cuerpo
- *body size (type size, point size)*
47 el cran
- *nick*
48 el grueso
- *set (width)*
49 **la taladradora de matrices** *f*, una taladradora especial
- *matrix-boring machine (matrix-engraving machine), a special-purpose boring machine*
50 el soporte
- *stand*
51 la fresa
- *cutter (cutting head)*
52 la mesa de fresar
- *cutting table*
53 el soporte del pantógrafo
- *pantograph carriage*

54 la guía prismática
- *V-way*
55 la plantilla
- *pattern*
56 la mesa portaplantillas
- *pattern table*
57 el punzón copiador
- *follower*
58 el pantógrafo
- *pantograph*
59 el portamatrices
- *matrix clamp*
60 el portafresas
- *cutter spindle*
61 el motor de impulsión *f*
- *drive motor*

Alfred **John Dodsley,** essayist and journalist, was born in Wenlock on the 5th August 1841 and died on the 4th October 1920 in Birmingham. His father was a journeyman thatcher and as a boy Dodsley was sent to work in the fields as a bird-scarer. Having taught himself to read and write fluently – for many years the only books he possessed were a Bible and a volume of Tillotson's sermons – he went to Shrewsbury to study. Living in extreme poverty he began to write for the EAST HEREFORDSHIRE GAZETTE and a collection of his essays together with some poems on country life was published in 1868 under the title *"Rural Thoughts".* Among his most popular works were *"The Diary of a Derbyshire Shepherd"* (1872), *"Rural Verses"* (1879), *"Leaves from a Countryman's Notebook"* (1893) and *"Memoirs of Nineteenth Century Shropshire",* published posthumously. Dodsley also contributed many articles on country life to London papers and championed the cause of the agricultural worker during the depression of the 1880's. The latter years of his life were embittered by controversy raised by his protests against the unemployment caused by mechanised farming.

He was for many years president of the **Society for the Protection of the Liberties of the Farm-worker.**

. 19

■ 20   (18)

■ 21   N n

■ 22   N n

■ 23   N n

■ 24   N n

■ 25   N n

■ 26   **N n**

■ 27   **N n**

■ 28   **N n**

■ 29   **N n**

■ 30   **N n**

■ 31   **N n**

# 176 Taller de composición III (Fotocomposición)

1 la unidad de teclado *m* para la fotocomposición
- *keyboard console (keyboard unit) for phototypesetting*
2 el teclado
- *keyboard*
3 el manuscrito (el original)
- *manuscript (copy)*
4 el tecleador (el operador del teclado)
- *keyboard operator*
5 el perforador de cinta *f*
- *tape punch (perforator)*
6 la cinta perforada
- *punched tape (punch tape)*
7 la unidad fotográfica
- *filmsetter*
8 la cinta perforada
- *punched tape (punch tape)*
9 la instalación de mando *m* de la exposición
- *exposure control device*
10 la computadora de composición *f*
- *typesetting computer*
11 la unidad de memoria *f* (la unidad de almacenamiento *m*)
- *memory unit (storage unit)*
12 la cinta perforada
- *punched tape (punch tape)*
13 la lectora de la cinta perforada
- *punched tape (punch tape) reader*
14 la unidad de fotocomposición *f* automática controlada por computadora *f*
- *photo-unit (photographic unit) for computer-controlled typesetting (composition)*
15 la lectura (la exploración) de la cinta perforada
- *punched tape (punch tape) reader*
16 las matrices de caracteres *m*
- *type matrices (matrixes) (letter matrices)*
17 el bastidor portamatrices
- *matrix case (film matrix case)*
18 la entalla (la ranura) guía *f*
- *guide block*
19 el motor sincrónico
- *synchronous motor*
20 el disco de caracteres *m*
- *type disc (disk) (matrix disc)*
21 el grupo de espejos *m*
- *mirror assembly*
22 la cuña óptica
- *optical wedge*
23 el objetivo
- *lens*
24 el sistema de espejos *m*
- *mirror system*
25 la película
- *film*
26 los tubos de luz *f* relámpago (los tubos de flash *m*)
- *flash tubes*
27 el almacén de diapositivas *f*
- *matrix drum*
28 la copiadora automática de películas *f*
- *automatic film copier*

29 la unidad central de fotocomposición *f* de periódicos *m*
- *central processing unit of a photocomposition system (photosetting system) for newspaper typesetting*
30 la unidad de entrada *f* de la cinta perforada
- *punched tape (punch tape) input (input unit)*
31 la teleimpresora de hoja *f* de servicio *m*
- *keyboard send-receive teleprinter (Teletype)*
32 la memoria de discos *m* del sistema
- *on-line disc (disk) storage unit*
33 la memoria de discos *m* del texto
- *alphanumeric (alphameric) disc (disk) store (alphanumeric disc file)*
34 la pila de discos *m* (el disc pack)
- *disc (disk) stack (disc pack)*

1 la cámara de reproducción *f* construida a manera *f* de puente *m*
- *overhead process camera (overhead copying camera)*
2 el cristal esmerilado
- *focusing screen (ground glass screen)*
3 el marco orientable del cristal esmerilado
- *hinged screen holder*
4 la cruz del eje (el retículo)
- *graticule*
5 el puesto de manejo *m* (de control *m*)
- *control console*
6 el pupitre de maniobra *f* suspendido y orientable
- *hinged bracket-mounted control panel*
7 las escalas de porcentajes *m*
- *percentage focusing charts*
8 el portapelículas vacío
- *vacuum film holder*
9 el depósito (el almacén) del retículo
- *screen magazine*
10 el fuelle
- *bellows*
11 el estandarte (el bastidor portaobjetivos)
- *standard*
12 el dispositivo indicador
- *register device*
13 el soporte (el caballete) del puente
- *overhead gantry*
14 el portaoriginales
- *copyboard*
15 el bastidor del portaoriginales
- *copyholder*
16 el brazo articulado portalámparas *f*
- *lamp bracket*
17 la lámpara de xenón *m*
- *xenon lamp*
18 el original
- *copy (original)*
19 la mesa de retoque *m* y montaje *m*
- *retouching and stripping desk*
20 la superficie luminosa
- *illuminated screen*
21 la regulación de la altura y de la inclinación
- *height and angle adjustment*
22 el portamodelos
- *copyboard*
23 el cuentahílos plegable, una lupa (un cristal de aumento *m*)
- *linen tester, a magnifying glass*
24 la cámara de reprodución *f* universal
- *universal process and reproduction camera*
25 la caja de la cámara
- *camera body*
26 el fuelle
- *bellows*

27 el portalentes
- *lens carrier*
28 el espejo de ángulo *m*
- *angled mirror*
29 el soporte en forma *f* de T
- *stand*
30 el portamodelos
- *copyboard*
31 la lámpara de halógeno *m*
- *halogen lamp*
32 la cámara de reproducción *f* vertical, una cámara compacta
- *vertical process camera, a compact camera*
33 la caja de la cámara
- *camera body*
34 el cristal esmerilado
- *focusing screen (ground glass screen)*
35 la tapa de vacío *m*
- *vacuum back*
36 el panel de mandos *m*
- *control panel*
37 la lámpara de exposición *f* (la lámpara del flash)
- *flash lamp*
38 el espejo para la entrada correcta de las imágenes
- *mirror for right-reading images*
39 el scanner (el aparato corrector del color)
- *scanner (colour, Am. color, correction unit)*
40 la armazón inferior
- *base frame*
41 el compartimiento de la lámpara
- *lamp compartment*
42 la caja de la lámpara de xenón *m*
- *xenon lamp housing*
43 los motores de avance *m*
- *feed motors*
44 el brazo portadiapositivas
- *transparency arm*
45 el cilindro de exploración *f*
- *scanning drum*
46 la cabeza de exploración *f*
- *scanning head*
47 la cabeza de exploración *f* de máscara *f*
- *mask-scanning head*
48 el cilindro de máscara *f*
- *mask drum*
49 el espacio de registro *m*
- *recording space*
50 el estuche (la cassette) para la luz de día *m*
- *daylight cassette*
51 el calculador de color *m* con unidad *f* de mando *m* y corrector *m* selectivo de color *m*
- *colour (Am. color) computer with control unit and selective colour correction*
52 el aparato de clisar
- *engraving machine*
53 la regulación (el regulador) de grabado *m* continuo
- *seamless engraving adjustment*

54 el embrague de impulsión *f*
- *drive clutch*
55 la brida del embrague
- *clutch flange*
56 la torre de impulsión *f* (la unidad motriz)
- *drive unit*
57 el banco de la máquina
- *machine bed*
58 el portaherramientas
- *equipment carrier*
59 el carro de la bancada
- *bed slide*
60 el panel de control *m*
- *control panel*
61 el soporte del cojinete
- *bearing block*
62 el cabezal móvil
- *tailstock*
63 la cabeza de exploración *f*
- *scanning head*
64 el cilindro del modelo
- *copy cylinder*
65 el cojinete central
- *centre* (Am. *center*) *bearing*
66 el sistema de grabado *m*
- *engraving system*
67 el cilindro impresor
- *printing cylinder*
68 el brazo del cilindro
- *cylinder arm*
69 el armario adosado
- *electronics (electronic) cabinet*
70 las unidades de cálculo *m*
- *computers*
71 la entrada (el empuje) del programa
- *program input*
72 el revelador de películas *f* automático para las películas de scanner *m*
- *automatic film processor for scanner films*

**1-6 la instalación galvánica**
- *electrotyping plant*
1 la cubeta de lavado *m*
- *cleaning tank*
2 el rectificador de corriente *f*
- *rectifier*
3 el aparato de medida *f* y de regulación *f*
- *measuring and control unit*
4 la pila de galvanizar
- *electroplating tank (electroplating bath, electroplating vat)*
5 la barra del ánodo (con ánodos *m* de cobre *m*)
- *anode rod [with copper anodes]*
6 la barra de moldes *m* (el cátodo)
- *plate rod (cathode)*
7 **la prensa hidráulica para hacer (acuñar) matrices *f***
- *hydraulic moulding* (Am. *molding*) *press*
8 el manómetro
- *pressure gauge* (Am. *gage*) *(manometer)*
9 la mesa para hacer las matrices
- *apron*
10 el pie cilíndrico
- *round base*
11 la bomba hidráulica de presión *f*
- *hydraulic pressure pump*
12 el motor de impulsión *f*
- *drive motor*
13 **la fundidora de plato *m* curvado**
- *curved plate casting machine (curved electrotype casting machine)*
14 el motor
- *motor*
15 los botones (los pulsadores) de control *m*
- *control knobs*
16 el pirómetro
- *pyrometer*

17 la boca de inyección *f* del metal
- *mouth piece*
18 la cámara de fundición *f*
- *core*
19 el horno de fusión *f*
- *melting furnace*
20 el conmutador
- *starting lever*
21 la plancha curvada fundida (la teja), para la impresión rotativa
- *cast curved plate (cast curved electrotype) for rotary printing*
22 el molde fijo de fundición *f*
- *fixed mould (Am. mold)*
23 **la máquina de grabar clisés *m* al agua *f* fuerte**
- *etching machine*
24 la cubeta de grabado *m* con el líquido corrosivo y el producto para la protección de los lados
- *etching tank with etching solution (etchant, mordant) and filming agent (film former)*
25 los cilindros de paleta *f*
- *paddles*
26 el plato rotor
- *turntable*
27 el dispositivo fijador de la placa
- *plate clamp*
28 el motor de impulsión *f*
- *drive motor*
29 el grupo (la unidad) de control *m*
- *control unit*
30 **la máquina gemela de grabados *m* al agua *f* fuerte**
- *twin etching machine*
31 el baño para el agua *f* fuerte [sección]
- *etching tank (etching bath) [in section]*
32 la plancha de cinc *m* para copiar
- *photoprinted zinc plate*

33 la rueda de paletas *f*
- *paddle*
34 el grifo de desagüe *m*
- *outlet cock (drain cock*, Am. *faucet)*
35 el soporte de la plancha
- *plate rack*
36 el conmutador
- *control switches*
37 la tapa del baño
- *lid*
38 **la autotipia, un clisé**
- **halftone photoengraving *(halftone block, halftone plate), a block (plate, printing plate)***
39 el punto de trama *f*, un elemento impreso
- *dot (halftone dot), a printing element*
40 la placa de cinc *m* grabada al agua *f* fuerte
- *etched zinc plate*
41 el pie del clisé (la madera del clisé)
- *block mount (block mounting, plate mount, plate mounting)*
42 **el grabado de trazo *m***
- *line block (line engraving, line etching, line plate, line cut)*
43 la parte corroída no impresora
- *non-printing, deep-etched areas*
44 el biselado del clisé
- *flange (bevel edge)*
45 el costado (el borde) del grabado al agua *f* fuerte
- *sidewall*

1 la centrífuga de planchas *f*, para emulsionar las planchas de offset *m*
– *plate whirler (whirler, plate-coating machine) for coating offset plates*
2 la tapa deslizante
– *sliding lid*
3 la calefacción eléctrica
– *electric heater*
4 el termómetro
– *temperature gauge* (Am. *gage*)
5 la conexión del agua *f* de aclarado *m*
– *water connection for the spray unit*
6 el lavado por circulación *f*
– *spray unit*
7 la ducha de mano *f*
– *hand spray*
8 las barras de fijación *f* de la plancha
– *plate clamps*
9 la plancha de cinc *m (también:* plancha de magnesio *m*, plancha de cobre *m)*
– *zinc plate;* also: *magnesium plate, copper plate*
10 el pupitre de control *m*
– *control panel*
11 el motor de impulsión *f*
– *drive motor*
12 el pedal de freno *m*
– *brake pedal*
13 el marco neumático para copiar
– *vacuum printing frame (vacuum frame, printing-down frame)*
14 la armazón inferior del marco para copiar
– *base of the vacuum printing frame (vacuum frame, printing-down frame)*

15 la parte superior del marco con cristal *m* de espejo *m*
– *plate glass frame*
16 la plancha de offset *m* recubierta
– *coated offset plate*
17 el tablero de mando *m*
– *control panel*
18 el regulador del tiempo de exposición *f*
– *exposure timer*
19 el interruptor para la producción del vacío
– *vacuum pump switches*
20 las varillas-guía (el soporte)
– *support*
21 la lámpara para copiar con luz *f* de punto *m*, una lámpara de halógeno *m* de metal *m*
– *point light exposure lamp, a quartz-halogen lamp*
22 el soplante de la lámpara
– *fan blower*
23 la mesa de montaje *m*, para el montaje de películas *f*
– *stripping table (make-up table) for stripping films*
24 la pantalla de vidrio *m* de cristal *m*
– *crystal glass screen*
25 la caja de la luz
– *light box*
26 el dispositivo deslizable de trazado *m*
– *straightedge rules*
27 la secadora centrífuga vertical
– *vertical plate-drying cabinet*
28 el higrómetro
– *hygrometer*
29 la regulación de la velocidad
– *speed control*

30 el pedal del freno
– *brake pedal*
31 la máquina de tratamiento *m* para las planchas presensibilizadas
– *processing machine for presensitized plates*
32 el horno de calcinación *f* para las planchas de esmalte *m* caliente (planchas *f* diazo)
– *burning-in oven for glue-enamel or diazo plates*
33 la caja de mandos *m*
– *control box (control unit)*
34 la plancha diazo
– *diazo plate*

1 la máquina offset *m* de bobinas *f* de cuatro colores *m*
- *four-colour (Am. four-color) rotary offset press (rotary offset machine, web-offset press)*
2 la bobina de papel *m* no impreso
- *roll of unprinted paper (blank paper)*
3 el portabobinas (dispositivo *m* para colocar la bobina de papel *m* no impreso)
- *reel stand (carrier for the roll of unprinted paper)*
4 los rodillos transportadores del papel
- *forwarding rolls*
5 el regulador lateral de la bobina
- *side margin control (margin control, side control, side lay control)*
6-13 los mecanismos entintadores
- *inking units (inker units)*
6, 8, 10, 12 los mecanismos entintadores del mecanismo impresor superior
- *inking units (inker units) in the upper printing unit*
6-7 el mecanismo de retiración *f* del amarillo
- *perfecting unit (double unit) for yellow*
7, 9, 11, 13 los mecanismos entintadores del mecanismo impresor inferior
- *inking units (inker units) in the lower printing unit*
8-9 el mecanismo de retiración *f* del cyan (azul-verde)
- *perfecting unit (double unit) for cyan*
10-11 el mecanismo de retiración *f* del magenta
- *perfecting unit (double unit) for magenta*
12-13 el mecanismo de retiración *f* del negro
- *perfecting unit (double unit) for black*
14 el horno secador
- *drier*
15 la plegadora
- *folder (folder unit)*
16 el pupitre de mando *m*
- *control desk*
17 el pliego impreso
- *sheet*
18 la máquina offset *m* de bobinas *f* de cuatro colores *m* [esquema]
- *four-colour (Am. four-color) rotary offset press (rotary offset machine, web-offset press) [diagram]*
19 el portabobinas
- *reel stand*
20 el regulador lateral de la bobina
- *side margin control (margin control, side control, side lay control)*
21 el rodillo entintador
- *inking rollers (ink rollers, inkers)*
22 la caja de tinta *f*
- *ink duct (ink fountain)*
23 los rodillos mojadores
- *damping rollers (dampening rollers, dampers, dampeners)*
24 el cilindro de caucho *m*
- *blanket cylinder*
25 el cilindro de plancha *f*
- *plate cylinder*
26 la tira de papel *m*
- *route of the paper (of the web)*

27 el horno secador
- *drier*
28 los cilindros de refrigeración *f*
- *chilling rolls (cooling rollers, chill rollers)*
29 la plegadora
- *folder (folder unit)*
30 la máquina offset *m* de hojas *f* de cuatro colores *m* [esquema]
- *four-colour (Am. four-color) sheet-fed offset machine (offset press) [diagram]*
31 el alimentador de hojas *f*
- *sheet feeder (feeder)*
32 la mesa de alimentación *f*
- *feed table (feed board)*
33 el balancín transmitiendo la hoja al tambor alimentador
- *route of the sheets through swing-grippers to the feed drum*
34 el tambor alimentador
- *feed drum*
35 el cilindro impresor
- *impression cylinder*
36 los tambores de transmisión *f*
- *transfer drums (transfer cylinders)*
37 el cilindro de caucho *m*
- *blanket cylinder*
38 el cilindro de plancha *f*
- *plate cylinder*
39 el mecanismo humedecedor
- *damping unit (dampening unit)*
40 el mecanismo entintador
- *inking unit (inker units)*
41 el mecanismo impresor
- *printing unit*
42 el tambor expositor (tambor *m* de salida *f*)
- *delivery cylinder*
43 la salida de cadenas *f*
- *chain delivery*
44 la pila de hojas *f*
- *delivery pile*
45 el expositor (la salida) de hojas *f*
- *delivery unit (delivery mechanism)*
46 la máquina offset *m* de un color
- *single-colour (Am. single-color) offset press (offset machine)*
47 la pila de hojas *f* de papel *m* (el papel para imprimir)
- *pile of paper (sheets, printing paper)*
48 el alimentador de hojas *f* (un alimentador automático)
- *sheet feeder (feeder), an automatic pile feeder*
49 la mesa de alimentación *f*
- *feed table (feed board)*
50 los rodillos entintadores
- *inking rollers (ink rollers, inkers)*
51 el mecanismo entintador
- *inking units (inker units)*
52 los rodillos mojadores
- *damping rollers (dampening rollers, dampers, dampeners)*
53 el cilindro de la plancha, una plancha de zinc *m*
- *plate cylinder, a zinc plate*
54 el cilindro de caucho *m*, un cilindro de acero *m* recubierto de caucho *m*
- *blanket cylinder, a steel cylinder with rubber blanket*
55 la plataforma de salida *f* de las hojas impresas
- *pile delivery unit for the printed sheets*
56 las pinzas prensoras, un dispositivo prensor de cadenas *f*
- *gripper bar, a chain gripper*

57 la pila de papel *m* (impreso)
- *pile of printed paper (printed sheets)*
58 la chapa de protección *f* de la correa de transmisión *f*
- *guard for the V-belt (vee-belt) drive*
59 la máquina offset *m* de un color [esquema]
- *single-colour (Am. single-color) offset press (offset machine) [diagram]*
60 el mecanismo entintador con los rodillos entintadores
- *inking unit (inker unit) with inking rollers (ink rollers, inkers)*
61 el mecanismo mojador con los rodillos mojadores
- *damping unit (dampening unit) with damping rollers (dampening rollers, dampers, dampeners)*
62 el cilindro de la plancha
- *plate cylinder*
63 el cilindro de caucho *m*
- *blanket cylinder*
64 el cilindro impresor
- *impression cylinder*
65 el tambor de salida *f*, con el sistema de agarre *m*
- *delivery cylinders with grippers*
66 el piñón de impulsión *f*
- *drive wheel*
67 la mesa de alimentación *f* de hojas *f*
- *feed table (feed board)*
68 el alimentador de hojas *f*
- *sheet feeder (feeder)*
69 la pila de papel *m* (con papel *m* para imprimir)
- *pile of unprinted paper (blank paper, unprinted sheets, blank sheets)*
70 la máquina de imprimir en offset *m* tamaño *m* pequeño
- *small sheet-fed offset press*
71 el mecanismo entintador
- *inking unit (inker unit)*
72 el alimentador por succión *f*
- *suction feeder*
73 la pila de alimentación *f*
- *pile feeder*
74 el cuadro de mandos *m* con contador *m*, manómetro *m*, regulador *m* de aire *m* y conmutador *m* para la alimentación de papel *m*
- *instrument panel (control panel) with counter, pressure gauge (Am. gage), air regulator, and control switch for the sheet feeder (feeder)*
75 la máquina offset *m* plana (prensa *f* para sacar pruebas *f* Mailänder)
- *flat-bed offset press (offset machine)*
76 el mecanismo entintador
- *inking unit (inker unit)*
77 los rodillos entintadores
- *inking rollers (ink rollers, inkers)*
78 el lecho (el carro) de impresión *f*
- *bed (press bed, type bed, forme bed, Am. form bed)*
79 el cilindro de caucho *m*
- *cylinder with rubber blanket*
80 la palanca de arranque *m* y parada *f* de los mecanismos de impresión *f*
- *starting and stopping lever for the printing unit*
81 el volante para regular la presión
- *impression-setting wheel (impression-adjusting wheel)*

1-65 máquinas *f* tipográficas
- *presses (machines) for letterpress printing (letterpress printing machines)*
1 la rotativa de doble revolución *f*
- *two-revolution flat-bed cylinder press*
2 el cilindro impresor
- *impression cylinder*
3 la palanca de elevación *f* y descenso *m* del cilindro
- *lever for raising or lowering the cylinder*
4 la mesa de alimentación *f*
- *feed table (feed board)*
5 el alimentador automático de hojas *f* [accionado por succión *f* y aire *m* comprimido]
- *automatic sheet feeder (feeder) [operated by vacuum and air blasts]*
6 la bomba de aire *m*, para el mecanismo de alimentación *f* y expulsión *f* de hojas *f*
- *air pump for the feeder and delivery*
7 el mecanismo entintador cilíndrico, con rodillos *m* extendedores y rodillos *m* dadores
- *inking unit (inker unit) with distributing rollers (distributor rollers, distributors) and forme rollers (Am. form rollers)*
8 el mecanismo entintador de mesa *f*
- *ink slab (ink plate) inking unit (inker unit)*
9 la pila de papel *m*, papel *m* para imprimir
- *delivery pile for printed paper*
10 el aparato pulverizador antimácula
- *sprayer (anti set-off apparatus, anti set-off spray) for dusting the printed sheets*
11 el dispositivo de intercalar
- *interleaving device*
12 el pedal, para interrumpir la presión
- *foot pedal for starting and stopping the press*
13 la minerva [corte]
- *platen press (platen machine, platen) [in section]*
14 la alimentación y suelta *f* del papel
- *paper feed and delivery (paper feeding and delivery unit)*
15 la platina de impresión *f*
- *platen*
16 la impulsión de la palanca acodada
- *toggle action (toggle-joint action)*
17 el plato de impresión *f*
- *bed (type bed, press bed, forme bed, Am. form bed)*
18 los rodillos entintadores
- *forme rollers (Am. form rollers) (forme-inking, Am. form-inking, rollers)*
19 el mecanismo entintador, para distribuir la tinta de imprenta *f*
- *inking unit (inker unit) for distributing the ink (printing ink)*
20 la prensa de parada *f* de cilindro *m*
- *stop-cylinder press (stop-cylinder machine)*
21 la mesa de alimentación *f*
- *feed table (feed board)*
22 el alimentador mecánico
- *feeder mechanism (feeding apparatus, feeder)*

23 la pila de papel *m* (con papel *m* para ser impreso)
- *pile of unprinted paper (blank paper, unprinted sheets, blank sheets)*
24 la rejilla de protección *f* del extractor del papel
- *guard for the sheet feeder (feeder)*
25 la pila de papel *m* (con papel *m* impreso)
- *pile of printed paper (printed sheets)*
26 el mecanismo de mando *m*
- *control mechanism*
27 los rodillos entintadores
- *forme rollers (Am. form rollers) (forme-inking, Am. form-inking, rollers)*
28 el mecanismo entintador
- *inking unit (inker unit)*
29 la minerva (la gato) [Heidelberg]
- *[Heidelberg] platen press (platen machine, platen)*
30 la mesa de alimentación *f* con la pila de papel *m* para ser impreso
- *feed table (feed board) with pile of unprinted paper (blank paper, unprinted sheets, blank sheets)*
31 la mesa de distribución *f*
- *delivery table*
32 la palanca de arranque *m* y parada *f*
- *starting and stopping lever*
33 el pulverizador automático
- *delivery blower*
34 la pistola pulverizadora
- *spray gun (sprayer)*
35 la bomba de aire *m*, para succión *f* y soplado *m*
- *air pump for vacuum and air blasts*
36 la forma cerrada (forma *f* de composición *f*)
- *locked-up forme (Am. form)*
37 la composición
- *type (type matter, matter)*
38 el bastidor de cierre *f*
- *chase*
39 la cuña de fijación *f*
- *quoin*
40 la regleta
- *length of furniture*
41 la rotativa tipográfica para periódicos *m*, de hasta 16 páginas *f*
- *rotary letterpress press (rotary letterpress machine, web-fed letterpress machine) for newspapers of up to 16 pages*
42 los cilindros cortadores, para cortar longitudinalmente la banda de papel *m*
- *slitters for dividing the width of the web*
43 la banda de papel *m*
- *web*
44 el cilindro de impresión *f*
- *impression cylinder*
45 el cilindro tensor (el cilindro compensador)
- *jockey roller (compensating roller, compensator, tension roller)*
46 la bobina de papel *m*
- *roll of paper*
47 el freno automático de la bobina de papel *m*
- *automatic brake*
48 el mecanismo para la impresión de una cara
- *first printing unit*

49 el mecanismo para la impresión de la segunda cara (retiración *f*)
- *perfecting unit*
50 el mecanismo entintador
- *inking unit (inker unit)*
51 el cilindro portaplanchas (cilindro *m* estereotipo)
- *plate cylinder*
52 el mecanismo de impresión *f* en colores *m*
- *second printing unit*
53 el enderezador del plegado
- *former*
54 el tacómetro, con cuentapliegos *m*
- *tachometer with sheet counter*
55 el plegador
- *folder (folder unit)*
56 el periódico plegado
- *folded newspaper*
57 el mecanismo entintador, de la máquina rotativa [corte]
- *inking unit (inker unit) for the rotary press (web-fed press) [in section]*
58 la banda de papel *m*
- *web*
59 el cilindro impresor
- *impression cylinder*
60 el cilindro portaplanchas (el cilindro estereotipo)
- *plate cylinder*
61 los cilindros entintadores
- *forme rollers (Am. form rollers) (forme-inking, Am. form-inking, rollers)*
62 el cilindro distribuidor del color
- *distributing rollers (distributor rollers, distributors)*
63 el cilindro tomador del color
- *lifter roller (ductor, ductor roller)*
64 el cilindro del tintero
- *duct roller (fountain roller, ink fountain roller)*
65 la caja de tinta *f* (el tintero)
- *ink duct (ink fountain)*

1 la insolación del papel
  carbón *m*
– *exposure of the carbon tissue*
  *(pigment paper)*
2 el chasis neumático
– *vacuum frame*
3 la lámpara de insolación *f*, una
  hilera de lámparas *f* halógenas
– *exposing lamp, a bank of quartz-*
  *halogen lamps*
4 la lámpara con la luz
  concentrada en un punto
– *point source lamp*
5 la campana de evacuación *f* del
  calor
– *heat extractor*
6 la máquina de reporte *m* del
  papel carbón *m*
– *carbon tissue transfer machine*
  *(laydown machine, laying*
  *machine)*
7 el cilindro de cobre *m* pulido
– *polished copper cylinder*
8 el rodillo de caucho *m* para
  comprimir el papel carbón *m*
  insolado
– *rubber roller for pressing on the*
  *printed carbon tissue (pigment*
  *paper)*
9 la máquina de revelado *m* del
  rodillo
– *cylinder-processing machine*
10 el rodillo huecograbado
  recubierto de papel *m*
  carbón *m*
– *gravure cylinder coated with*
  *carbon tissue (pigment paper)*
11 la cuba de revelado *m*
– *developing tank*
12 el retoque del rodillo
– *staging*
13 el rodillo revelado
– *developed cylinder*
14 el retocador efectuando un
  recubrimiento
– *retoucher painting out (stopping*
  *out)*
15 la máquina de grabar al agua *f*
  fuerte
– *etching machine*
16 la cuba de grabar con el líquido
  corrosivo
– *etching tank with etching*
  *solution (etchant, mordant)*
17 el rodillo de huecograbado *m*
  copiado
– *printed gravure cylinder*
18 el huecograbador
– *gravure etcher*
19 el disco de cálculo *m*
– *calculator dial*
20 el reloj de control *m*
– *timer*
21 la corrección del grabado
– *revising (correcting) the cylinder*
22 el cilindro huecograbado
– *etched gravure cylinder*
23 el pupitre de corrección *f*
– *ledge*

24 la rotativa de huecograbado *m*
  multicolor
– *multicolour* (Am. *multicolor*)
  *rotogravure press*
25 la canalización de evacuación *f*
  de vapores *m* del disolvente
– *exhaust pipe for solvent fumes*
26 el mecanismo impresor de
  doble cara *f*
– *reversible printing unit*
27 el plegador
– *folder (folder unit)*
28 la mesa de control *m* y
  manejo *m*
– *control desk*
29 el mecanismo de salida *f* de
  periódicos *m*
– *newspaper delivery unit*
30 la cinta transportadora
– *conveyor belt (conveyor)*
31 la pila de periódicos *m*
  empaquetados
– *bundled stack of newspapers*

1-23 **máquinas** *f* **de**
  **encuadernación** *f*
- *bookbinding machines*
1 **la encuadernadora sin costura** *f*
  (la máquina de pegar) para
  tiradas *f* pequeñas
- *adhesive binder (perfect binder)*
  *for short runs*
2 el dispositivo para la
  introducción manual
- *manual feed station*
3 el dispositivo de refilado *m*
- *cutoff knife and roughing station*
4 el mecanismo de encolado *m*
- *gluing mechanism*
5 la salida de libros *m*
- *delivery (book delivery)*
6 **la máquina de hacer tapas** *f*
- *case maker (case-making*
  *machine)*
7 el almacén para las tapas de
  cartón *m*
- *board feed hopper*
8 los sacadores del cartón
- *pickup sucker*
9 el depósito (la caja) de cola *f*
- *glue tank*
10 el rodillo para empastar
- *cover cylinder*
11 el brazo succionador
- *picker head*

12 la bandeja depósito *m* de los
   materiales [tela *f*, papel *m*,
   piel *f*]
- *feed table for covering materials*
  *[linen, paper, leather]*
13 el mecanismo de prensa
- *pressing mechanism*
14 la mesa de distribución *f*
- *delivery table*
15 **la máquina de coser con**
   **alambre** *m*
- *gang stitcher; sim.: gathering*
  *and wire-stitching machine*
  *(gatherer and wire stitcher)*
16 el alimentador de hojas *f*
- *sheet feeder (sheet-feeding*
  *station)*
17 el plegador
- *folder-feeding station*
18 el mecanismo para desbobinar
   el alambre de coser
- *stitching wire feed mechanism*
19 el mecanismo (la mesa) de
   entrega *f*
- *delivery table*
20 la cizalla circular para cartón *m*
- *rotary board cutter (rotary*
  *board-cutting machine)*
21 el tablero de introducción del
   material, con entalladura *f*
- *feed table with cut-out section*

22 la cuchilla circular
- *rotary cutter*
23 la regla de entrada *f* (la regla
   guía)
- *feed guide*

**1-35 máquinas *f* de encuadernación *f***
- *bookbinding machines*
1 la guillotina, una máquina automática para cortar papel *m*
- *guillotine (guillotine cutter, automatic guillotine cutter)*
2 el pupitre de mando *m*
- *control panel*
3 el travesaño de presión *f*
- *clamp*
4 el travesaño de avance *m*
- *back gauge (Am. gage)*
5 le escala de presión *f* de la prensa
- *calibrated pressure adjustment [to clamp]*
6 el indicador óptico de medida *f*
- *illuminated cutting scale*
7 el mando manual para el travesaño
- *single-hand control for the back gauge (Am. gage)*
8 la máquina de plegar con cuchillas *f* y bolsas *f*
- *combined buckle and knife folding machine (combined buckle and knife folder)*
9 la mesa de alimentación *f* de papel *m*
- *feed table (feed board)*
10 las bolsas del plegado
- *fold plates*
11 la escala reguladora de medida *f* del primer pliego
- *stop for making the buckle fold*
12 las cuchillas dobladoras del segundo pliego
- *cross fold knives*
13 la salida de la cinta, para el pliego paralelo
- *belt delivery for parallel-folded signatures*
14 el mecanismo del tercer pliego
- *third cross fold unit*
15 la salida después del tercer pliego
- *delivery tray for cross-folded signatures*
16 la máquina encuadernadora de hilo *m*
- *sewing machine (book-sewing machine)*
17 el portabobinas
- *spool holder*
18 la bobina de hilo *m*
- *thread cop (thread spool)*
19 el portarollo (el tambor) de gasa *f* (de tarlatana *f*)
- *gauze roll holder (mull roll holder, scrim roll holder)*
20 la gasa (la tarlatana)
- *gauze (mull, scrim)*
21 el cuerpo con las agujas de encuadernar
- *needle cylinder with sewing needles*
22 el libro cosido
- *sewn book*
23 la salida
- *delivery*
24 el carro portaagujas
- *reciprocating saddle*
25 el alimentador de hojas *f*
- *sheet feeder (feeder)*
26 el depósito de alimentación *f*
- *feed hopper*
27 la máquina de encartonar libros *m*
- *casing-in machine*
28 la encoladora de pliegue *m*
- *joint and side pasting attachment*

29 la cuchilla
- *blade*
30 el precalentamiento
- *preheater unit*
31 la máquina engomadora, para el encolado a pleno, de lomo *m*, de canto *m* y en tiras *f*
- *gluing machine for whole-surface, stencil, edge, and strip gluing*
32 el depósito para la cola
- *glue tank*
33 el rodillo engomador
- *glue roller*
34 la mesa de alimentación *f*
- *feed table*
35 el depósito de evacuación *f*
- *delivery*
36 **el libro**
- *book*
37 la sobrecubierta (la camisa), una cubierta publicitaria
- *dust jacket (dust cover, bookjacket, wrapper), a publisher's wrapper*
38 la solapa de la sobrecubierta
- *jacket flap*
39 el texto de la solapa
- *blurb*
**40-42 la encuadernación del libro**
- *binding*
40 la tapa
- *cover (book cover, case)*
41 el lomo
- *spine (backbone, back)*
42 la cabezada
- *tailband (footband)*
**43-47 las hojas del título (la portada y la portadilla)**
- *preliminary matter (prelims, front matter)*
43 la portadilla (la anteportada o falsa portada *m*)
- *half-title*
44 el título de la obra
- *half-title (bastard title, fly title)*
45 la portada (*Amér.*: la carátula)
- *title page*
46 autor *m* y título *m* de la obra
- *full title (main title)*
47 el subtítulo
- *subtitle*
48 el pie editorial
- *publisher's imprint (imprint)*
49 las guardas
- *fly leaf (endpaper, endleaf)*
50 la dedicatoria manuscrita
- *handwritten dedication*
51 el ex libris
- *bookplate (ex libris)*
52 el libro abierto
- *open book*
53 la página del libro
- *page*
54 el pliegue
- *fold*
**55-58 los márgenes**
- *margin*
55 el margen del lomo
- *back margin (inside margin, gutter)*
56 el margen superior (el margen de la cabeza)
- *head margin (upper margin)*
57 el margen exterior (el margen de delante)
- *fore edge margin (outside margin, fore edge)*

58 el margen inferior (el margen del pie)
- *tail margin (foot margin, tail, foot)*
59 la justificación (la caja de impresión *f*)
- *type area*
60 el título del capítulo
- *chapter heading*
61 el asterisco
- *asterisk*
62 la nota a pie *m* de página *f*, una anotación
- *footnote, a note*
63 el número de la página
- *page number*
64 el texto a dos columnas *f*
- *double-column page*
65 la columna
- *column*
66 el titulillo
- *running title (running head)*
67 el subtítulo del capítulo
- *caption*
68 la nota marginal (el registro lateral)
- *marginal note (side note)*
69 la signatura
- *signature (signature code)*
70 el registro fijo (la señal fija)
- *attached bookmark (attached bookmarker)*
71 el registro suelto (la señal suelta)
- *loose bookmark (loose bookmarker)*

**1-54** coches *m* (vehículos *m*)
 – *carriages (horse-drawn vehicles)*
**1-3, 26-39, 45, 51-54** coches *m*
 (carruajes)
 – *carriages and coaches (coach
 wagons)*
**1** la berlina
 – *berlin*
**2** el break
 – *wagonette*; larger: *brake
 (break)*
**3** el cupé
 – *coupé*; sim.: *brougham*
**4** la rueda delantera
 – *front wheel*
**5** la caja
 – *coach body*
**6** el guardabarros
 – *dashboard (splashboard)*
**7** el apoyo para los pies
 – *footboard*
**8** el pescante (el asiento del
 conductor)
 – *coach box (box, coachman's
 seat, driver's seat)*
**9** el farol
 – *lamp (lantern)*
**10** la ventanilla
 – *window*
**11** la portezuela (la puerta del
 coche)
 – *door (coach door)*
**12** el tirador
 – *door handle (handle)*
**13** el estribo
 – *footboard (carriage step, coach
 step, step, footpiece)*
**14** la capota fija
 – *fixed top*
**15** la ballesta
 – *spring*
**16** el freno (la almohadilla –la
 zapata– del freno)
 – *brake (brake block)*
**17** la rueda trasera
 – *back wheel (rear wheel)*
**18** el dogcart, un vehículo de un
 caballo
 – *dogcart, a one-horse carriage*
**19** la lanza
 – *shafts (thills, poles)*
**20** el lacayo (*Chile:* el librea)
 – *lackey (lacquey, footman)*
**21** la librea, el uniforme del lacayo
 – *livery*
**22** el cuello galoneado
 – *braided (gallooned) collar*
**23** la chaqueta galoneada
 – *braided (gallooned) coat*
**24** la manga galoneada
 – *braided (gallooned) sleeve*
**25** el sombrero de copa *f*
 – *top hat*
**26** el coche de alquiler *m* (el coche
 de punto *m*, el simón, el fiacre;
 *Chile:* el postino)
 – *hackney carriage (hackney
 coach, cab, growler, Am. hack)*

**27** el mozo de establo *m* (el mozo
 de caballos *m*, el mozo de
 cuadras *f*)
 – *stableman (groom)*
**28** el caballo (el caballo de tiro *m*)
 – *coach horse (carriage horse, cab
 horse, thill horse, thiller)*
**29** el cabriolé con pescante *m*
 elevado por detrás, un coche de
 un caballo
 – *hansom cab (hansom), a
 cabriolet, a one-horse chaise
 (one-horse carriage)*
**30** las varas
 – *shafts (thills, poles)*
**31** las riendas
 – *reins (rein, Am. line)*
**32** el cochero, con macferlán *m*
 – *coachman (driver) with inverness*
**33** el carabán cubierto (la
 jardinera), un coche de
 excursión *f*
 – *covered char-a-banc (brake,
 break), a pleasure vehicle*
**34** el cabriolé
 – *gig (chaise)*
**35** la calesa
 – *barouche*
**36** el landó, un coche de dos
 caballos *m*; *anál.:* el landó
 pequeño
 – *landau, a two-horse carriage;
 sim.: landaulet, landaulette*
**37** el ómnibus (el ómnibus con
 imperial *m*)
 – *omnibus (horse-drawn omnibus)*
**38** el faetón
 – *phaeton*
**39** la diligencia (*Chile:* la
 carretela); *al mismo tiempo:* el
 coche de viaje *m*
 – *Continental stagecoach
 (mailcoach, diligence); also:
 road coach*
**40** el mayoral (el postillón, el
 cochero de la diligencia)
 – *mailcoach driver*
**41** la corneta del postillón
 – *posthorn*
**42** la capota del coche
 – *hood*
**43** los caballos de posta *f* (los
 caballos de relevo *m*)
 – *post horses (relay horses, relays)*
**44** el tílburi
 – *tilbury*
**45** la troica (el coche ruso de tres
 caballos *m*)
 – *troika (Russian three-horse
 carriage)*
**46** el caballo de varas *f* (el central)
 – *leader*
**47** el caballo lateral
 – *wheeler (wheelhorse, pole horse)*
**48** el buggy inglés
 – *English buggy*
**49** el buggy americano
 – *American buggy*
**50** el tiro en tándem *m*
 – *tandem*

**51** la victoria
 – *vis-à-vis*
**52** la capota plegable
 – *collapsible hood (collapsible top)*
**53** el mail-coach (la berlina
 inglesa)
 – *mailcoach (English stagecoach)*
**54** la silla de posta *f* (el calesín)
 – *covered (closed) chaise*

# 187 Bicicleta

*Bicycle*

1 la bicicleta (el velocípedo; *pop.:* la
  bici), una bicicleta de hombre *m*,
  una bicicleta de paseo *m*
- bicycle (cycle, coll. bike, Am.
  wheel), a gent's bicycle, a touring
  bicycle (touring cycle, roadster)
2 el manillar (*Amér.:* el manubrio),
  un manillar de paseo *m*
- handlebar (handlebars), a touring
  cycle handlebar
3 el puño
- handlebar grip (handgrip, grip)
4 el timbre de la bicicleta
- bicycle bell
5 el freno de mano *f* (el freno
  delantero, un freno sobre la llanta)
- hand brake (front brake), a rim
  brake
6 el soporte del faro
- lamp bracket
7 el faro
- headlamp, a bicycle lamp
8 la dinamo
- dynamo
9 el rodillo de transmisión *f*
- pulley
10-12 la horquilla de la rueda
  delantera
- front forks
10 la tija de la horquilla
- handlebar stem
11 la cabeza de la horquilla
- steering head
12 los tirantes de la horquilla
- fork blades (fork ends)
13 el guardabarros delantero (*Ec.,
  Guat., Perú:* el guardafango)
- front mudguard (Am. front fender)
14-20 el cuadro de la bicicleta
- bicycle frame
14 la barra de dirección *f* (la cabeza
  de la barra de dirección *f*)
- steering tube (fork column)
15 el escudo de la marca
- head badge

16 el tubo superior del cuadro (el
  tubo superior)
- crossbar (top tube)
17 el tubo inferior del cuadro (el tubo
  inferior)
- down tube
18 el tubo soporte del sillín (el tubo
  del sillín)
- seat tube
19 la horquilla superior de la rueda
  trasera
- seat stays
20 la horquilla inferior de la rueda
  trasera
- chain stays
21 el sillín para niños *m*
- child's seat (child carrier seat)
22 el sillín (el sillín de muelles *m*) de
  la bicicleta
- bicycle saddle
23 el muelle del sillín
- saddle springs
24 el soporte (la tija) del sillín
- seat pillar
25 la cartera de las herramientas
- tool bag
26-32 la rueda (la rueda delantera)
- front wheel
26 el cubo (el buje)
- hub
27 el radio
- spoke
28 la llanta
- rim (wheel rim)
29 el tensor de radios *m*
- spoke nipple (spoke flange, spoke
  end)
30 el neumático (el neumático de alta
  presión *f*); *dentro:* la cámara de
  aire *m; fuera:* la cubierta
- tyres (Am. tires) types: pneumatic
  tyre, high-pressure tyre; inside:
  tube (inner tube); outside: tyre
  (outer case, cover)

31 la válvula, una válvula de
  neumático *m* con tubo *m*, o un
  obturador a presión *f* con bola *f*
- valve, a tube valve with valve tube
  or a patent valve with ball
32 el capuchón de la válvula
- valve sealing cap
33 el tacómetro de bicicleta *f*, con
  cuentakilómetros *m*
- bicycle speedometer with milometer
34 la patilla de apoyo de la bicicleta
- kick stand (prop stand)
35-42 la transmisión de la bicicleta
  (la transmisión de cadena *f*)
- bicycle drive
35-39 la propulsión por cadena *f*
- chain transmission
35 el plato (la rueda dentada
  delantera de la cadena)
- chain wheel
36 la cadena, una cadena de
  rodillos *m*
- chain, a roller chain
37 el cubrecadena
- chain guard
38 el piñón (la rueda dentada trasera
  de la cadena)
- sprocket wheel (sprocket)
39 la tuerca de palometa *f*
- wing nut (fly nut, butterfly nut)
40 el pedal
- pedal
41 la biela (la manivela de pedal *m*)
- crank
42 el eje "pedalier" (el eje de los
  pedales)
- bottom bracket bearing
43 el guardabarros trasero
- rear mudguard (Am. rear fender)
44 el portaequipajes
- luggage carrier (carrier)
45 el catafaro (el reflectante)
- reflector
46 la luz trasera (el piloto)
- rear light (rear lamp)

47 el descansapiés
 – *footrest*
48 la bomba de bicicleta *f* (la bomba
 de aire *m; Amér.:* el inflador)
 – *bicycle pump*
49 la cerradura de la bicicleta, una
 cerradura de radios *m*
 – *bicycle lock, a wheel lock*
50 la llave antirrobo
 – *patent key*
51 el número de la bicicleta (el
 número de fabricación *f*)
 – *cycle serial number (factory
 number, frame number)*
52 el cubo de la rueda delantera
 – *front hub (front hub assembly)*
53 la tuerca
 – *wheel nut*
54 la contratuerca estrellada
 – *locknut (locking nut)*
55 las arandelas suplementarias
 – *washer (slotted cone adjusting
 washer)*
56 la bola
 – *ball bearing*
57 la tapa guardapolvo
 – *dust cap*
58 el cono
 – *cone (adjusting cone)*
59 las cazoletas
 – *centre* (Am. *center*) *hub*
60 el caño (el tubo)
 – *spindle*
61 el eje
 – *axle*
62 el engrasador
 – *clip covering lubrication hole
 (lubricator)*
63 el piñón libre, con freno *m*
 contrapedal [inexistente en las
 bicicletas españolas]
 – *free-wheel hub with back-pedal
 brake (with coaster brake)*

64 la tuerca de seguridad *f*
 – *safety nut*
65 el orificio de engrase *m* (el
 lubrificador)
 – *lubricator*
66 la palanca del freno
 – *brake arm*
67 el cono de la palanca del freno
 – *brake arm cone*
68 el anillo interior de bolas *f,* con
 bolas en el cojinete
 – *bearing cup with ball bearings in
 ball race*
69 la caja del piñón
 – *hub shell (hub body, hub barrel)*
70 la cubierta del freno
 – *brake casing*
71 el cono del freno
 – *brake cone*
72 el tambor de enrollamiento *m*
 – *driver*
73 el rodillo de impulsión *f*
 – *driving barrel*
74 la corona dentada
 – *sprocket*
75 la cabeza de rosca *f*
 – *thread head*
76 el eje
 – *axle*
77 el bandaje
 – *bracket*
78 el pedal de bicicleta *f* (el pedal, un
 pedal de bloque *m*)
 – *bicycle pedal (pedal, reflector pedal)*
79 la arandela
 – *cup*
80 la caña del pedal
 – *spindle*
81 el eje del pedal
 – *axle*
82 la tapa guardapolvo
 – *dust cap*
83 el bastidor del pedal
 – *pedal frame*

84 el tornillo de sujeción *f* del taco de
 goma *f*
 – *rubber stud*
85 el taco de goma *f*
 – *rubber block (rubber tread)*
86 el cristal reflectante
 – *glass reflector*

1 la bicicleta plegable
– *folding bicycle*
2 la articulación *f* de bisagra *f*
(también: la palanca de ajuste
*m*)
– *hinge; also: locking lever*
3 el manillar regulable
– *adjustable handlebar*
*(handlebars)*
4 el sillín regulable
– *adjustable saddle*
5 las ruedas de apoyo *m* para
aprender (las ruedas auxiliares)
– *stabilizers*
6 el ciclomotor
– *motor-assisted bicycle*
7 el motor de dos tiempos *m*
refrigerado por aire *m*
– *air-cooled two-stroke engine*
8 la horquilla telehidráulica
– *telescopic forks*
9 el cuadro tabular
– *tubular frame*
10 el depósito de combustible *m*
– *fuel tank (petrol tank,* Am.
*gasoline tank)*
11 el manillar elevado
– *semi-rise handlebars*
12 la palanca de embrague *m* de
dos velocidades *f*
– *two-speed gear-change*
*(gearshift)*
13 el sillín moldeado
– *high-back polo saddle*
14 el brazo oscilante de la rueda
trasera
– *swinging-arm rear fork*
15 el tubo de escape elevado
– *upswept exhaust*
16 la rejilla de protección *f* contra
el calor
– *heat shield*
17 la cadena de transmisión *f*
– *drive chain*
18 el arco de protección *f*
– *crash bar (roll bar)*
19 el tacómetro (el cuentakilómetros)
– *speedometer* (coll. *speedo)*
20 la bicicleta de acumuladores *m*
(la bicicleta eléctrica, la city-
bike)
– *battery-powered moped, an*
*electrically-powered vehicle*
21 el sillín móvil
– *swivel saddle*
22 el compartimiento de los
acumuladores
– *battery compartment*
23 el cesto de alambre *m* (el
portaequipajes)
– *wire basket*
24 el ciclomotor
– *touring moped (moped)*
25 el pedal
– *pedal crank (pedal drive, starter*
*pedal)*
26 el motor monocilíndrico de dos
tiempos *m*
– *single-cylinder two-stroke engine*

27 la clavija de la bujía
– *spark-plug cap*
28 el depósito de combustible *m*
(el depósito de mezcla *f*)
– *fuel tank (petrol tank,* Am.
*gasoline tank)*
29 el faro del ciclomotor
– *moped headlamp (front lamp)*
30-35 los accesorios del manillar
– *handlebar fittings*
30 el puño giratorio del gas
– *twist grip throttle control*
*(throttle twist grip)*
31 el puño giratorio para el
cambio de velocidades *f*
– *twist grip (gear-change,*
*gearshift)*
32 la palanca de embrague *m*
– *clutch lever*
33 el freno de mano *f*
– *hand brake lever*
34 el velocímetro (el tacómetro, el
cuentakilómetros)
– *speedometer* (coll. *speedo)*
35 el espejo retrovisor
– *rear-view mirror (mirror)*
36 el freno de tambor *m* delantero
– *front wheel drum brake (drum*
*brake)*
37 los cables Bowden
– *Bowden cables (brake cables)*
38 la luz trasera, la luz de freno *m*
– *stop and tail light unit*
39 el velomotor
– *light motorcycle with kickstarter*
40 el tablero de mando *m* con
cuentakilómetros *m* y
cuentarrevoluciones *m*
electrónico
– *housing for instruments with*
*speedometer and electronic rev*
*counter (revolution counter)*
41 la horquilla telehidráulica con
goma *f* de protección *f*
– *telescopic shock absorber*
42 el sillín biplaza (de dos
asientos *m*)
– *twin seat*
43 el pedal de arranque *m*
– *kickstarter*
44 el descansapiés del pasajero
– *pillion footrest, a footrest*
45 el manillar deportivo
– *handlebar (handlebars)*
46 el guardacadena cerrado
herméticamente
– *chain guard*
47 el scooter, el escúter
– *motor scooter (scooter)*
48 el panel lateral fijo
– *removable side panel*
49 el cuadro tubular
– *tubular frame*
50 el revestimiento de chapa *f*
– *metal fairings*
51 el patín de apoyo *m* (la patilla)
– *prop stand (stand)*
52 el pedal de freno *m*
– *foot brake*

53 la bocina (el claxon)
– *horn (hooter)*
54 el gancho para el maletín o la
cartera
– *hook for handbag or briefcase*
55 el pedal selector de
velocidades *f*
– *foot gear-change control (foot*
*gearshift control)*
56 la motoreta; con una rueda
mayor que otra: el chopper
– *high-riser; sim.: Chopper*
57 el manillar bifurcado
– *high-rise handlebar (handlebars)*
58 la horquilla imitando a la de la
moto
– *imitation motorcycle fork*
59 el sillín
– *banana saddle*
60 el arco cromado
– *chrome bracket*

1 el velomotor (la motocicleta) [50 cm³]
- *lightweight motorcycle (light motorcycle) [50 cc]*
2 el depósito de combustible *m*
- *fuel tank (petrol tank, Am. gasoline tank)*
3 el motor monocilíndrico de cuatro tiempos *m* refrigerado por aire *m*
- *air-cooled single-cylinder four-stroke engine with overhead camshaft*
4 el carburador
- *carburettor (Am. carburetor)*
5 el tubo de admisión *f*
- *intake pipe*
6 el cambio de cinco marchas *f*
- *five-speed gearbox*
7 la biela oscilante de la rueda trasera
- *swinging-arm rear fork*
8 la placa de la matrícula
- *number plate (Am. license plate)*
9 la luz trasera (el piloto)
- *stop and tail light (rear light)*
10 el faro
- *headlight (headlamp)*
11 el tambor del freno delantero
- *front drum brake*
12 el cable del freno, una transmisión Bowden
- *brake cable (brake line), a Bowden cable*
13 el tambor del freno trasero
- *rear drum brake*
14 el sillín
- *racing-style twin seat*
15 el tubo de escape *m* elevado
- *upswept exhaust*
16 la motocicleta todo terreno *m* [125 cm³] (una moto campera)
- *scrambling motorcycle (cross-country motorcycle) [125 cc], a light motorcycle*
17 el cuadro de doble soporte *m*
- *lightweight cradle frame*
18 la placa para el número de competición *f*
- *number disc (disk)*
19 el sillín monoplaza (de un solo asiento)
- *solo seat*
20 las aletas de refrigeración *f*
- *cooling ribs*
21 el soporte (la patilla) de la motocicleta
- *motorcycle stand*
22 la cadena
- *motorcycle chain*
23 la horquilla telehidráulica
- *telescopic shock absorber*
24 los radios (los rayos)
- *spokes*
25 la llanta
- *rim (wheel rim)*
26 el neumático
- *motorcycle tyre (Am. tire)*

27 el perfil del neumático
- *tyre (Am. tire) tread*
28 la palanca del embrague
- *gear-change lever (gearshift lever)*
29 el puño giratorio del gas
- *twist grip throttle control (throttle twist grip)*
30 el retrovisor
- *rear-view mirror (mirror)*
31-58 motocicletas *f* de gran cilindrada *f*
- *heavy (heavyweight, large-capacity) motorcycles*
31 una moto grande (una moto de carretera *f*) con motor refrigerado por agua *f*
- *heavyweight motorcycle with water-cooled engine*
32 el freno de disco *m* delantero
- *front disc (disk) brake*
33 la pinza del freno de disco *m*
- *disc (disk) brake calliper (caliper)*
34 el eje delantero
- *floating axle*
35 el radiador del agua *f*
- *water cooler*
36 el depósito de aceite *m*
- *oil tank*
37 el intermitente (el indicador de cambio *m* de dirección *f*)
- *indicator (indicator light, turn indicator light)*
38 el pedal de arranque
- *kickstarter*
39 el motor refrigerado por agua *f*
- *water-cooled engine*
40 el tacómetro (el cuentakiló-metros)
- *speedometer*
41 el cuentarrevoluciones
- *rev counter (revolution counter)*
42 el intermitente trasero
- *rear indicator (indicator light)*
43 la moto pesada con carenado *m* integral [1 000 cm³]
- *heavy (heavyweight, high-performance) machine with fairing [1000 cc]*
44 el carenado integral
- *integrated streamlining, an integrated fairing*
45 la luz intermitente (el intermitente)
- *indicator (indicator light, turn indicator light)*
46 el cristal transparente
- *anti-mist windscreen (Am. windshield)*
47 el motor de dos cilindros *m* con transmisión *f* cardán
- *horizontally-opposed twin engine with cardan transmission*
48 la rueda de aleación *f* de metal ligero
- *light alloy wheel*
49 la moto de cuatro cilindros *m* [400 cm³]
- *four-cylinder machine [400 cc]*

50 el motor de cuatro tiempos *m* con cuatro cilindros *m* refrigerados por aire *m*
- *air-cooled four-cylinder four-stroke engine*
51 el tubo de escape *m* cuatro en uno
- *four-pipe megaphone exhaust pipe*
52 el dispositivo de arranque *m* (el arrancador) eléctrico
- *electric starter button*
53 la motocicleta con sidecar *m*
- *sidecar machine*
54 el sidecar
- *sidecar body*
55 el parachoques del sidecar
- *sidecar crash bar*
56 la luz (el piloto) de posición *f*
- *sidelight (Am. sidemarker lamp)*
57 la rueda del sidecar
- *sidecar wheel*
58 el parabrisas del sidecar
- *sidecar windscreen (Am. windshield)*

1 el motor de explosión *f* (Otto) de ocho cilindros *m* en V con inyección *f* de gasolina *f* [corte longitudinal]
– *eight-cylinder V (vee) fuel-injection spark-ignition engine (Otto-cycle engine)*
2 el motor de explosión *f* (Otto) [corte transversal]
– *cross-section of spark-ignition engine (Otto-cycle internal combustion engine)*
3 el motor Diesel de cinco cilindros *m* en línea *f* [corte longitudinal]
– *sectional view of five-cylinder in-line diesel engine*
4 el motor Diesel [corte transversal]
– *cross-section of diesel engine*
5 el motor rotativo de dos rotores *m* (el motor Wankel)
– *two-rotor Wankel engine (rotary engine)*
6 el motor de explosión *f* (Otto) monocilíndrico de dos tiempos *m*
– *single-cylinder two-stroke internal combustion engine*
7 el ventilador
– *fan*
8 el embrague del ventilador
– *fan clutch for viscous drive*
9 el distribuidor de encendido *m* con avance al encendido por depresión *f*
– *ignition distributor (distributor) with vacuum timing control*
10 la cadena doble de rodillos *m*
– *double roller chain*
11 el árbol de levas *f* (de camones *m*)
– *camshaft bearing*
12 el conducto de ventilación *f*
– *air-bleed duct*
13 el engrase del árbol de levas *f*
– *oil pipe for camshaft lubrication*
14 el árbol de levas *f*, un árbol de levas *f* en cabeza *f*
– *camshaft, an overhead camshaft*
15 el colector de admisión *f* con mariposa *f*
– *venturi throat*
16 el silencioso de admisión *f*
– *intake silencer (absorption silencer, Am. absorption muffler)*
17 el regulador de la presión del combustible
– *fuel pressure regulator*
18 el conducto (el tubo) de admisión *f*
– *inlet manifold*
19 el bloque del motor
– *cylinder crankcase*
20 el volante
– *flywheel*
21 la biela
– *connecting rod (piston rod)*
22 el sombrerete del apoyo del cigüeñal
– *cover of crankshaft bearing*
23 el cigüeñal
– *crankshaft*
24 el tapón de vaciado *m* del aceite
– *oil bleeder screw (oil drain plug)*
25 la cadena de rodillos *m* de mando *m* de la bomba de aceite *m*
– *roller chain of oil pump drive*
26 el amortiguador de oscilaciones *f*
– *vibration damper*
27 el árbol de mando *m* del distribuidor de encendido *m*
– *distributor shaft for the ignition distributor (distributor)*
28 el orificio para echar el aceite
– *oil filler neck*
29 el cartucho del filtro de aire *m*
– *diaphragm spring*
30 las varillas reguladoras
– *control linkage*

31 los tubos de alimentación *f* del combustible
– *fuel supply pipe* (Am. *fuel line*)
32 el inyector
– *fuel injector (injection nozzle)*
33 el balancín
– *rocker arm*
34 el asiento del balancín
– *rocker arm mounting*
35 la bujía con capuchón *m* antiparasitario
– *spark plug (sparking plug) with suppressor*
36 el colector de escape *m*
– *exhaust manifold*
37 el pistón con segmentos *m* de comprensión *f* y segmento *m* rascador de aceite *m*
– *piston with piston rings and oil scraper ring*
38 el soporte-motor
– *engine mounting*
39 la brida intermediaria
– *dog flange (dog)*
40 el cárter superior del aceite
– *crankcase*
41 el cárter inferior del aceite
– *oil sump (sump)*
42 la bomba de aceite *m*
– *oil pump*
43 el filtro de aceite *m*
– *oil filter*
44 el motor de arranque *m*
– *starter motor (starting motor)*
45 la culata
– *cylinder head*
46 la válvula de escape *m*
– *exhaust valve*
47 la varilla del nivel de aceite *m*
– *dipstick*
48 la tapa de balancines *m*
– *cylinder head cover*
49 la cadena remachada doble
– *double bushing chain*
50 la sonda de temperatura *f*
– *warm-up regulator*
51 el cable para el ajuste del ralentí
– *tapered needle for idling adjustment*
52 la canalización de gas-oil *m* a presión *f*
– *fuel pressure pipe (fuel feed line)*
53 la canalización para fugas *f* de gas-oil *m*
– *fuel leak line (drip fuel line)*
54 el inyector
– *injection nozzle (spray nozzle)*
55 la fijación de la bujía de precalentamiento *m*
– *heater plug*
56 el disco de equilibrado *m*
– *thrust washer*
57 el árbol de piñón *m* intermediario para el accionamiento de la bomba de inyección *f*
– *intermediate gear shaft for the injection pump drive*
58 el mecanismo de avance de la inyección
– *injection timer unit*
59 la bomba de vacío *m*
– *vacuum pump (low-pressure regulator)*
60 el disco de leva *f* para el accionamiento de la bomba de vacío *m*
– *cam for vacuum pump*
61 la bomba de agua *f*
– *water pump (coolant pump)*
62 el termostato del agua *f* de refrigeración *f*
– *cooling water thermostat*
63 el termocontacto
– *thermo time switch*
64 la bomba manual para el gas-oil
– *fuel hand pump*

65 la bomba de inyección *f*
– *injection pump*
66 la bujía de precalentamiento *m*
– *glow plug*
67 la válvula de descarga *f* del aceite
– *oil pressure limiting valve*
68 el rotor del motor rotativo (el émbolo del motor Wankel)
– *rotor*
69 la lámina de estanquidad *f*
– *seal*
70 el convertidor de par *m*
– *torque converter*
71 el embrague monodisco
– *single-plate clutch*
72 la caja de cambio *m*
– *multi-speed gearing (multi-step gearing)*
73 los filtros para purificar los gases del colector de escape *m*
– *port liners in the exhaust manifold for emission control*
74 el freno de disco *m*
– *disc (disk) brake*
75 el diferencial
– *differential gear (differential)*
76 el generador de corriente *f* (la dinamo, el alternador)
– *generator*
77 el pedal de cambio *m* de velocidades *f*
– *foot gear-change control (foot gearshift control)*
78 el embrague de disco *m* en seco
– *dry multi-plate clutch*
79 el carburador horizontal
– *cross-draught (Am. cross-draft) carburettor (Am. carburetor)*
80 las aletas de refrigeración *f*
– *cooling ribs*

1-56 el coche (el automóvil, el auto;
  *Amér.:* el carro), un turismo
- *motor car (car, Am. automobile,*
  *auto), a passenger vehicle*
1 la carrocería autoportante
- *monocoque body (unitary body)*
2 el chasis (*Amér.:* el chasis; la
  carrocería)
- *chassis, the understructure of the body*
3 la aleta delantera
- *front wing (Am. front fender)*
4 la puerta del coche
- *car door*
5 el tirador de la puerta
- *door handle*
6 la cerradura de la puerta
- *door lock*
7 la puerta del maletero
- *boot lid (Am. trunk lid)*
8 el capó (*Col., C. Rica, Chile y Mé.:* la
  tapa del motor)
- *bonnet (Am. hood)*
9 el radiador
- *radiator*
10 la canalización del agua *f* de
  refrigeración *f*
- *cooling water pipe*
11 la calandra (la rejilla del radiador;
  *Amér.:* la parrilla)
- *radiator grill*
12 el emblema (la marca del auto)
- *badging*
13 el parachoques delantero con
  escudo *m* de caucho (*C. Rica,*
  *Guat. y S. Dgo.:* el bomper)
- *rubber-covered front bumper (Am.*
  *front fender)*
14 la rueda de automóvil *m*, una rueda
  de disco *m*
- *car wheel, a disc (disk) wheel*
15 el neumático
- *car tyre (Am. automobile tire)*
16 la llanta
- *rim (wheel rim)*
17-18 el freno de disco *m*
- *disc (disk) brake*
17 el disco del freno
- *brake disc (disk) (braking disc)*

18 la pinza del freno
- *calliper (caliper)*
19 el intermitente delantero (*Amér.:* la
  luz direccional)
- *front indicator light (front turn*
  *indicator light)*
20 el faro (*Chile y Pan.:* el foco; *Guat.,*
  *Mé. y. P. Rico:* la luz) con luz *f* larga
  (luz *f* de carretera; *Amér.:* luz *f* alta),
  luz *f* de cruce *m* (luz *f* corta; *Amér.:*
  luz *f* baja) y luz *f* de posición *f*
  (*Chile:* luz *f* de estacionamiento *m*)
- *headlight (headlamp) with main beam*
  *(high beam), dipped beam (low beam),*
  *sidelight (side lamp, Am. sidemarker*
  *lamp)*
21 el parabrisas (*Pan. y P. Rico:* el
  guinchil), un parabrisas panorámico
- *windscreen (Am. windshield), a*
  *panoramic windscreen*
22 la ventanilla de la puerta, con
  manivela *f*
- *crank-operated car window*
23 la ventanilla trasera giratoria (la
  ventanilla oscilante)
- *quarter light (quarter vent)*
24 el maletero (*Amér.:* el baúl)
- *boot (Am. trunk)*
25 la rueda de repuesto *m*
- *spare wheel*
26 el amortiguador
- *damper (shock absorber)*
27 el brazo oscilante longitudinal
- *trailing arm*
28 el muelle helicoidal
- *coil spring*
29 el silencioso (el silenciador)
- *silencer (Am. muffler)*
30 la ventilación por circulación *f*
  forzada
- *automatic ventilation system*
31 el asiento trasero
- *rear seats*
32 el cristal trasero
- *rear window*
33 el cabezal (el reposacabezas) regulable
- *adjustable headrest (head restraint)*
34 el asiento del conductor, un asiento
  reclinable
- *driver's seat, a reclining seat*

35 el respaldo reclinable
- *reclining backrest*
36 el asiento del acompañante; *pop.:* el
  asiento de la muerte
- *passenger seat*
37 el volante (*Amér.:* el timón; *Col. y P.*
  *Rico:* la volanta)
- *steering wheel*
38 el tablero de mandos *m* (el
  salpicadero) con tacómetro *m*, el
  cuentarrevoluciones, el reloj, el
  indicador del nivel de gasolina *f*, el
  indicador de la temperatura de
  refrigeración *f* (el termómetro del
  agua *f*) y el reloj de la presión del
  aceite
- *centre (Am. center) console containing*
  *speedometer (coll. speedo), revolution*
  *counter (rev counter, tachometer),*
  *clock, fuel gauge (Am. gage), water*
  *temperature gauge, oil temperature*
  *gauge*
39 el espejo retrovisor interior
- *inside rear-view mirror*
40 el espejo retrovisor exterior del lado
  izquierdo
- *left-hand wing mirror*
41 el limpiaparabrisas
- *windscreen wiper (Am. windshield*
  *wiper)*
42 la abertura de ventilación *f*
- *defroster vents*
43 la moqueta del suelo; *encima:* la
  alfombrilla
- *carpeting*
44 el pedal del embrague (el embrague)
- *clutch pedal (coll. clutch)*
45 el pedal del freno (el freno)
- *brake pedal (coll. brake)*
46 el pedal del acelerador (el acelerador,
  el pedal del gas)
- *accelerator pedal (coll. accelerator)*
47 la toma de aire *m*
- *inlet vent*
48 el ventilador para la aireación
- *blower fan*
49 el depósito del líquido *m* de freno *m*
- *brake fluid reservoir*
50 la batería
- *battery*

51 el tubo de escape *m*
– *exhaust pipe*
52 el tren delantero con tracción *f* delantera
– *front running gear with front wheel drive*
53 el soporte del motor
– *engine mounting*
54 el silencioso de admisión *f*
– *intake silencer (Am. intake muffler)*
55 el filtro del aire
– *air filter (air cleaner)*
56 el espejo retrovisor exterior del lado derecho
– *right-hand wing mirror*
57-90 el tablero de mandos *m* (el salpicadero)
– *dashboard (fascia panel)*
57 el centro del volante con protector *m* antichoque
– *controlled-collapse steering column*
58 el radio del volante
– *steering wheel spoke*
59 el conmutador de luces *f* y del intermitente
– *indicator and dimming switch*
60 el conmutador del limpiaparabrisas con avisador *m* sonoro
– *wiper/washer switch and horn*
61 la aireación lateral
– *side window blower*
62 el interruptor de la luz de posición *f*
– *sidelight, headlight, and parking light switch*
63 el indicador de la luz antiniebla
– *fog lamp warning light*
64 el interruptor de las luces antiniebla delantera y trasera
– *fog headlamp and rear lamp switch*
65 el indicador del nivel de la gasolina
– *fuel gauge (Am. gage)*
66 el termómetro del agua *f* de refrigeración *f*
– *water temperature gauge (Am. gage)*
67 el indicador de la luz antiniebla trasera
– *warning light for rear fog lamp*

68 el interruptor del warning
– *hazard flasher switch*
69 el indicador de la luz larga
– *main beam warning light*
70 el cuentarrevoluciones eléctrico
– *electric rev counter (revolution counter)*
71 el chivato del nivel de la gasolina
– *fuel warning light*
72 el chivato del freno de mano *f* y del sistema de frenado *m* de los dos circuitos independientes
– *warning light for the hand brake and dual-circuit brake system*
73 el chivato de la presión del aceite
– *oil pressure warning light*
74 el tacómetro (el velocímetro) con cuentakilómetros *m*
– *speedometer (coll. speedo) with trip mileage recorder*
75 la cerradura antirrobo y de contacto *m*
– *starter and steering lock*
76 el chivato de las luces intermitentes y del warning
– *warning lights for turn indicators and hazard flashers*
77 el potenciómetro de la iluminación interior con puesta *f* a cero del cuentakilómetros parcial
– *switch for the courtesy light and reset button for the trip mileage recorder*
78 el chivato de carga *f*
– *ammeter*
79 el reloj eléctrico
– *electric clock*
80 el chivato de desempañado *m* de la luneta trasera
– *warning light for heated rear window*
81 el interruptor para la ventilación de la parte baja
– *switch for the leg space ventilation*
82 el interruptor para desempañar la luneta trasera
– *rear window heating switch*
83 la palanca para graduar la ventilación
– *ventilation switch*
84 la palanca para regular la temperatura
– *temperature regulator*

85 la aireación regulable
– *fresh-air inlet and control*
86 la palanca para distribuir el aire frío
– *fresh-air regulator*
87 la palanca para distribuir el aire caliente
– *warm-air regulator*
88 el encendedor
– *cigar lighter*
89 la cerradura de la guantera
– *glove compartment (glove box) lock*
90 la radio
– *car radio*
91 la palanca de cambio *m* de velocidades *f*
– *gear lever (gearshift lever), a floor-type gear-change*
92 la guarnición (el manguito) de piel *f*
– *leather gaiter*
93 la palanca del freno de mano *f* (*C. Rica y Pan.*: el freno de emergencia *f*)
– *hand brake lever*
94 el pedal del acelerador (el acelerador, el pedal del gas)
– *accelerator pedal*
95 el pedal del freno (el freno)
– *brake pedal*
96 el pedal del embrague (el embrague)
– *clutch pedal*

**1-15 el carburador,** un carburador
descendente
- *carburettor (Am. carburetor), a*
*down-draught (Am. down-draft)*
*carburettor*
1 el chiclé del ralentí
- *idling jet (slow-running jet)*
2 el chiclé del aire del ralentí
- *idling air jet (idle air bleed)*
3 el chiclé de corrección f de aire m
- *air correction jet*
4 el aire de compensación f
- *compensating airstream*
5 el aire principal
- *main airstream*
6 la palomilla de arranque m en frío
(el starter)
- *choke flap*
7 el pico de salida f
- *plunger*
8 el difusor (el venturi)
- *venturi*
9 la palomilla de gases m
- *throttle valve (butterfly valve)*
10 el tubo emulsionante
- *emulsion tube*
11 el tornillo de reglaje de la
velocidad del ralentí
- *idle mixture adjustment screw*
12 el surtidor principal (*sin.*: el
calibre, el chiclé)
- *main jet*
13 la llegada de gasolina f
- *fuel inlet (Am. gasoline inlet) (inlet
manifold)*
14 la cuba de nivel m constante
- *float chamber*
15 el flotador
- *float*
**16-27 el engrase bajo presión f**
- *pressure-feed lubricating system*
16 la bomba de aceite m
- *oil pump*
17 el cárter del aceite
- *oil sump*
18 la alcachofa de aspiración f
- *sump filter*
19 el refrigerador de aceite m (el
radiador de aceite m)
- *oil cooler*
20 el filtro del aceite
- *oil filter*
21 el canal principal de engrase m
- *main oil gallery (drilled gallery)*
22 el canal secundario
- *crankshaft drilling (crankshaft
tributary, crankshaft bleed)*
23 el cigüeñal
- *crankshaft bearing (main bearing)*
24 el árbol de levas f (camones m)
- *camshaft bearing*
25 la muñequilla del cigüeñal
- *connecting-rod bearing*
26 el calibre para el eje del pistón
- *gudgeon pin (piston pin)*
27 la canalización superior
- *bleed*
**28-47 la caja de cambios m**
**sincronizada de cuatro velocidades f**
- *four-speed synchromesh gearbox*
28 el pedal de embrague m
- *clutch pedal*
29 el cigüeñal
- *crankshaft*
30 el árbol motor
- *drive shaft (propeller shaft)*

31 la corona de arranque m
- *starting gear ring*
32 el anillo sincronizador para la 3ª y
4ª velocidades
- *sliding sleeve for 3rd and 4th gear*
33 el cono de sincronización f
- *synchronizing cone*
34 el piñón helicoidal para la 3ª
velocidad
- *helical gear wheel for 3rd gear*
35 el anillo sincronizador de la 1ª y la
2ª velocidades
- *sliding sleeve for 1st and 2nd gear*
36 el piñón helicoidal de la 1ª
velocidad
- *helical gear wheel for 1st gear*
37 el árbol intermediario (de
reenvío m)
- *lay shaft*
38 el accionamiento del tacómetro
(del marcador de velocidad)
- *speedometer drive*
39 el piñón para el accionamiento del
tacómetro
- *helical gear wheel for speedometer
drive*
40 el árbol primario
- *main shaft*
41 los ejes de mando de la horquilla
- *gearshift rods*
42 la horquilla de la 1ª y la 2ª
velocidades
- *selector fork for 1st and 2nd gear*
43 el piñón helicoidal de la 2ª
velocidad
- *helical gear wheel for 2nd gear*
44 la horquilla de marcha f atrás
- *selector head with reverse gear*
45 la horquilla para la 3ª y la 4ª
velocidades
- *selector fork for 3rd and 4th gear*
46 la palanca de cambio m
- *gear lever (gearshift lever)*
47 la palanca selectora
- *gear-change pattern (gearshift
pattern, shift pattern)*
**48-55 el freno de disco m**
- *disc (disk) brake [assembly]*
48 el disco del freno
- *brake disc (disk) (braking disc)*
49 la pinza del freno, una pinza fija
con las pastillas del freno
- *calliper (caliper), a fixed calliper
with friction pads*
50 el tambor del freno de mano f
- *servo cylinder (servo unit)*
51 las zapatas del freno
- *brake shoes*
52 el forro del freno
- *brake lining*
53 el racor de la canalización del
freno
- *outlet to brake line*
54 el bombín del freno
- *wheel cylinder*
55 el muelle recuperador
- *return spring*
**56-59 el mecanismo de dirección f** (la
dirección de tornillo m sin fin m
globoide)
- *steering gear (worm-and-nut
steering gear)*
56 el árbol de dirección f (la columna
de dirección f)
- *steering column*
57 el soporte de rodillo m
- *worm gear sector*

58 la palanca de mando m de
dirección f
- *steering drop arm*
59 el tornillo sin fin m (la espiral)
- *worm*
**60-64 el sistema de calefacción f**
**regulado por agua f**
- *water-controlled heater*
60 la entrada de aire m frío
- *air intake*
61 el transformador de calor m
- *heat exchanger (heater box)*
62 el ventilador de calefacción f
- *blower fan*
63 la válvula reguladora
- *flap valve*
64 la abertura para el deshielo
- *defroster vent*
**65-71 el eje rígido**
- *live axle (rigid axle)*
65 el tubo de reacción f (el árbol de
transmisión f)
- *propeller shaft*
66 el brazo oscilante longitudinal
- *trailing arm*
67 el cojinete de caucho m
- *rubber bush*
68 el muelle helicoidal
- *coil spring*
69 el amortiguador
- *damper (shock absorber)*
70 la barra de torsión f
- *Panhard rod*
71 la barra estabilizadora
- *stabilizer bar*
**72-84 la suspensión MacPherson**
- *MacPherson strut unit*
72 la placa de fijación f sobre la
carrocería
- *body-fixing plate*
73 el soporte de fijación f superior
- *upper bearing*
74 el muelle helicoidal
- *suspension spring*
75 el eje (caña f) del pistón
- *piston rod*
76 el amortiguador (*P. Rico:* el
shockabsorver)
- *suspension damper*
77 la llanta
- *rim (wheel rim)*
78 el gorrón (el muñón, la mangueta)
- *stub axle*
79 el pivote de mangueta f
- *steering arm*
80 la rótula del pivote de mangueta f
- *track-rod ball-joint*
81 el brazo trasero de triángulo m (la
horquilla trasera)
- *trailing link arm*
82 el cojinete de caucho m
- *bump rubber (rubber bonding)*
83 la caja del eje (el cubo de rueda f)
- *lower bearing*
84 el travesaño principal
- *lower suspension arm*

# 193 Automóvil III

Motor Car (Am. Automobile)III

**1-36 tipos _m_ de coches _m_**
(coches _m_ de turismo _m_)
– _car models_ (Am. _automobile models_)
**1** el pullman de ocho plazas _f_ (la limusina; _Col. y Pan.:_ la camioneta)
– _eight-cylinder limousine with three rows of three-abreast seating_
**2** la puerta del conductor
– _driver's door_
**3** la puerta trasera
– _rear door_
**4** el turismo (el sedán) de cuatro puertas _f_
– _four-door saloon car_ (Am. _four-door sedan_)
**5** la puerta delantera (_Col. y Mé._: la portezuela delantera)
– _front door_
**6** la puerta trasera (_Col. y Mé.:_ la portezuela trasera)
– _rear door_
**7** el reposacabezas fijo delantero
– _front seat headrest (front seat head restraint)_
**8** el reposacabezas fijo trasero
– _rear seat headrest (rear seat head restraint)_
**9** el coche descapotable (_Amér._: el convertible)
– _convertible_
**10** la capota replegable
– _convertible (collapsible) hood (top)_
**11** el asiento envolvente (el asiento anatómico)
– _bucket seat_
**12** el buggy
– _buggy (dune buggy)_
**13** el arco de tubo _m_
– _roll bar_
**14** la carrocería de plástico _m_
– _fibre glass body_
**15** el break
– _estate car (shooting brake, estate, Am. station wagon)_
**16** la puerta posterior (el portón trasero, la quinta puerta)
– _tailgate_
**17** el portaequipajes (el maletero; _Amér._: el baúl)
– _boot space (luggage compartment)_
**18** el turismo de tres puertas
– _three-door hatchback_
**19** el coche pequeño de tres puertas _f_
– _small three-door car_
**20** la puerta posterior (el portón trasero, la quinta puerta)
– _rear door (tailgate)_
**21** el faldón trasero
– _sill_
**22** el asiento trasero abatible
– _folding back seat_

**23** el portaequipajes (el maletero; _Amér._: el baúl)
– _boot (luggage compartment, Am. trunk)_
**24** el techo corredizo (el techo corredizo de acero _m_)
– _sliding roof (sunroof, steel sunroof)_
**25** el turismo (el sedán) de dos puertas _f_
– _two-door saloon car_ (Am. _two-door sedan_)
**26** el coche de dos plazas _f_ (el cabriolé sport, el deportivo, el cupé)
– _roadster (hard-top), a two-seater_
**27** el techo duro (la capota desmontable dura)
– _hard top_
**28** el coche deportivo de cuatro asientos _m_ (con dos asientos _m_ de transportines _m_)
– _sporting coupé, a two-plus-two coupé (two-seater with removable back seats)_
**29** la parte trasera aerodinámica
– _fastback (liftback)_
**30** el borde del spoiler
– _spoiler rim_
**31** el reposacabezas incorporado
– _integral headrest (integral head restraint)_
**32** el coche deportivo GT (el coche deportivo de gran turismo _m_)
– _GT car (gran turismo car)_
**33** el parachoques incorporado
– _integral bumper (Am. integral fender)_
**34** el spoiler trasero
– _rear spoiler_
**35** la parte trasera
– _back_
**36** el spoiler delantero
– _front spoiler_

1 el pequeño camión todo
terreno *m* con cuatro ruedas *f*
motrices
– *light cross-country lorry (light
truck, pickup truck) with all-
wheel drive (four-wheel drive)*
2 la cabina
– *cab (driver's cab)*
3 la plataforma de carga *f* (la
caja)
– *loading platform (body)*
4 el neumático de recambio *m* (la
rueda de repuesto), un
neumático todo terreno *m*
– *spare tyre (Am. spare tire), a
cross-country tyre*
5 la camioneta (*C. Rica, Guat. y
Pan.:* el pick up; *Amér. Central:*
la cazadora)
– *light lorry (light truck, pickup
truck)*
6 la camioneta con plataforma *f*
(con caja *f*)
– *platform truck*
7 el furgón (la camioneta
cerrada)
– *medium van*
8 la puerta lateral corredera (la
puerta de carga *f*)
– *sliding side door [for loading and
unloading]*
9 el microbús (*Arg.:* el colectivo;
*Ec. y Par.:* el micro; *Pan.:* el
busito; *S. Dgo.:* el minibús)
– *minibus*
10 la capota (el techo plegable)
– *folding top (sliding roof)*
11 la puerta posterior
– *rear door*
12 la puerta lateral pivotante
– *hinged side door*
13 el maletero (el portaequipajes)
– *luggage compartment*
14 el asiento del viajero
– *passenger seat*
15 la cabina
– *cab (driver's cab)*
16 la rejilla de aireación *f* (la
ranura del aire)
– *air inlet*
17 el autobús (el autocar;
*Canarias, Cuba y P. Rico:* la
guagua)
– *motor coach (coach, bus)*
18 la bodega del autobús (el
compartimiento del equipaje)
– *luggage locker*
19 el equipaje de mano *f* (una
maleta)
– *hand luggage (suitcase, case)*
20 el camión pesado (el camión de
gran tonelaje *m*, el convoy)
– *heavy lorry (heavy truck, heavy
motor truck)*
21 el tractor (el vehículo de tiro *m*)
– *tractive unit (tractor, towing
vehicle)*
22 el remolque (el trailer)
– *trailer (drawbar trailer)*

23 la plataforma fija (la caja)
– *swop platform (body)*
24 el camión basculante de tres
bandas *m*
– *three-way tipper (three-way
dump truck)*
25 la plataforma basculante
– *tipping body (dump body)*
26 el gato hidráulico
– *hydraulic cylinder*
27 el container descargado
– *supported container platform*
28 el camión articulado, un
camión cisterna *f* (*Col.:* el
carrotanque; *Par. y P. Rico:* el
camión tanque; *Venez.:* la
gandola)
– *articulated vehicle, a vehicle
tanker*
29 el tractor del semirremolque
– *tractive unit (tractor, towing
vehicle)*
30-33 la cisterna remolcada
– *semi-trailer (skeletal)*
30 la cisterna (el depósito)
– *tank*
31 la articulación giratoria
– *turntable*
32 los patines de ruedas *f*
– *undercarriage*
33 la rueda de repuesto *m*
– *spare wheel*
34 el autobús pequeño en
versión *f* urbana (*Col.:* el bus
intermunicipal)
– *midi bus [for short-route town
operations]*
35 la puerta exterior basculante
– *outward-opening doors*
36 el autobús de dos pisos *m*
– *double-deck bus (double-decker
bus)*
37 el primer piso (el piso bajo)
– *lower deck (lower saloon)*
38 el piso superior
– *upper deck (upper saloon)*
39 la subida
– *boarding platform*
40 el trolebús
– *trolley bus*
41 la pértiga del trole
– *current collector*
42 el trole de contacto *m*
– *trolley (trolley shoe)*
43 el tendido aéreo con dos
cables *m* para el doble contacto
– *overhead wires*
44 el remolque del trolebús
– *trolley bus trailer*
45 el acoplamiento con fuelles de
caucho *m*
– *pneumatically sprung rubber
connection*

1-55  el taller especializado
– **agent's garage** *(distributor's garage,*
  Am. *specialty shop)*
1-23  la sección de diagnóstico *m*
– *diagnostic test bay*
1  el aparato de diagnóstico *m*
– *computer*
2  la clavija de diagnóstico *m*
– *main computer socket*
3  el cable de diagnóstico *m*
– *computer harness (computer cable)*
4  el inversor para la medida
  automática o manual
– *switch from automatic to manual*
5  la ranura para introducir *f* las
  fichas del programa
– *slot for program cards*
6  la impresora
– *print-out machine (printer)*
7  el informe del diagnóstico (el
  diagnóstico)
– *condition report, a data print-out*
8  el mando manual
– *master selector (hand control)*
9  las lámparas de valoración *f*
  [verde: bueno; rojo: malo]
– *light read-out [green: OK; red: not
  OK]*
10  el fichero para las fichas del
  programa
– *rack for program cards*
11  el interruptor de red *f*
– *mains button*
12  la tecla de programa *m* rápido
– *switch for fast readout*

13  el distribuidor de secuencia *f* de
  encendido *m*
– *firing sequence insert*
14  la caja de almacenamiento *m* (el
  archivador)
– *shelf for used cards*
15  la horca portacables
– *cable boom*
16  el cable para medir la temperatura
  del aceite
– *oil temperature sensor*
17  el comprobador de la
  convergencia y la inclinación de la
  rueda hacia la derecha (el
  alineador de dirección *f*)
– *test equipment for wheel and
  steering alignment*
18  la placa óptica derecha
– *right-hand optic plate*
19  los transistores de disparo *m*
– *actuating transistors*
20  el conmutador del proyector *m*
– *projector switch*
21  la línea fotorreceptora para medir
  el ángulo de inclinación *f*
– *check light for wheel alignment. a
  row of photocells*
22  la línea fotorreceptora para medir
  la convergencia
– *check light for steering alignment, a
  row of photocells*
23  el destornillador eléctrico
– *power screwdriver*

24  el comprobador de reglaje *m* de
  los faros
– *beam setter*
25  la plataforma de elevación *f*
  hidráulica
– *hydraulic lift*
26  el brazo ajustable de la plataforma
  de elevación *f*
– *adjustable arm of hydraulic lift*
27  la almohadilla de la plataforma de
  elevación *f*
– *hydraulic lift pad*
28  la cavidad de la rueda
– *excavation*
29  el manómetro (para medir la
  presión del aire)
– *pressure gauge (Am. gage)*
30  el engrasador a presión *f*
– *grease gun*
31  la caja de las piezas pequeñas
– *odds-and-ends box*
32  el catálogo de las piezas de
  recambio *m*
– *wall chart [of spare parts]*

33 el diagnóstico automático
- *automatic computer test*
34 el automóvil (el auto, el coche), un turismo
- *motor car (car, Am. automobile, auto), a passenger vehicle*
35 el compartimiento motor
- *engine compartment*
36 el capó
- *bonnet (Am. hood)*
37 la varilla del capó
- *bonnet support (Am. hood support)*
38 el cable de diagnosis *f*
- *computer harness (computer cable)*
39 el conector hembra (el manguito) de diagnosis *f*
- *main computer socket; also: multi-outlet socket*
40 el cable de sonda *f* de la temperatura del aceite
- *oil temperature sensor*
41 el espejo de rueda *f* para medir ópticamente la convergencia y la inclinación
- *wheel mirror for visual wheel and steering alignment*
42 el carrito de las herramientas
- *tool trolley*
43 las herramientas
- *tools*
44 la llave para tuercas *f*
- *impact wrench*
45 la llave dinamométrica
- *torque wrench*

46 el martillo de alisar (aplanar)
- *body hammer (roughing-out hammer)*
47 el vehiculo en reparación, un microbús
- *vehicle under repair, a minibus*
48 el número de reparación *f*
- *car location number*
49 el motor trasero
- *rear engine*
50 la tapa del motor trasero
- *tailgate*
51 el escape
- *exhaust system*
52 la reparación del escape
- *exhaust repair*
53 el mecánico de automóviles *m*
- *motor car mechanic (motor vehicle mechanic, Am. automotive mechanic)*
54 la goma del aire comprimido
- *air hose*
55 el interfono
- *intercom*

1-29 la estación de servicio *m* (la
gasolinera; *Mé. y P. Rico:* la
gasolinería; *S. Dgo.:* el puesto
de gasolina*f*), una estación de
autoservicio *m*
– *service station (petrol station,
filling station, Am. gasoline
station, gas station), a self-
service station*
1 el distribuidor (el surtidor) de
gasolina *f* súper o normal
(*anál.:* gasóleo *m*); la bomba de
gasolina *f*
– *petrol* (Am. *gasoline) pump, a
blending pump for regular and
premium grade petrol;* sim.: *for
derv*
2 la goma del surtidor
– *hose (petrol pump,* Am. *gasoline
pump, hose)*
3 la pistola del surtidor
– *nozzle*
4 la suma (la cantidad) de
dinero *m* a pagar
– *cash readout*
5 el volumen suministrado
– *volume readout*
6 el precio del litro
– *price display*
7 la señal luminosa
– *indicator light*
8 el automovilista utilizando el
surtidor de autoservicio *m*
– *driver using self-service petrol
pump* (Am. *gasoline pump)*

9 el extintor
– *fire extinguisher*
10 el distribuidor de servilletas *f*
de papel *m*
– *paper-towel dispenser*
11 la servilleta de papel *m*
– *paper towel*
12 el cubo de la basura
– *litter receptacle*
13 el depósito de mezcla *f* de dos
tiempos
– *two-stroke blending pump*
14 el cristal (el tubo) de medida *f*
– *meter*
15 el aceite para motores *m*
– *engine oil*
16 la aceitera de motores *m*
– *oil can*
17 el comprobador de la presión
de inflado *m*
– *tyre pressure gauge* (Am. *tire
pressure gage)*
18 la tubería del aire comprimido
– *air hose*
19 el depósito de aire *m*
– *static air tank*
20 el manómetro (el comprobador
de inflado *m*)
– *pressure gauge* (Am. *gage)
(manometer)*
21 la tubuladura de inflado *m*
– *air filler neck*
22 el hangar (el box) de
reparación *f*
– *repair bay (repair shop)*

23 la manguera de lavado *m*, una
manguera de agua *f*
– *car-wash hose, a hose (hosepipe)*
24 la tienda de la estación de
servicio *m*
– *accessory shop*
25 el bidón de gasolina *f*
– *petrol can* (Am. *gasoline can)*
26 el capote para la lluvia (el
impermeable)
– *rain cape*
27 los neumáticos
– *car tyres* (Am. *automobile tires)*
28 los accesorios para
automóviles *m*
– *car accessories*
29 la caja
– *cash desk (console)*

1 el ferrobús articulado de doce ejes *m*
  para la red interurbana
– *twelve-axle articulated railcar for*
  *interurban rail service*
2 el pantógrafo (colector *m* de
  corriente *f*)
– *current collector*
3 la cabeza (la delantera) del tren
– *head of the railcar*
4 la cola (la trasera) del tren
– *rear of the railcar*
5 el vagón A con motor *m* de tracción *f*
– *carriage A containing the motor*
6 el vagón B (*igual:* vagón C o D)
– *carriage B; also: carriages C and D*
7 el vagón E con motor *m* de tracción *f*
– *carriage E containing the motor*
8 el despacho de billetes *m* trasero
  (*Amér.:* la boletería)
– *rear controller*
9 el bogie de impulsión *f*
– *bogie*
10 el bogie portador
– *carrying bogie*
11 el protector de rueda *f* (el
  quitapiedras)
– *wheel guard*
12 el tope
– *bumper* (Am. *fender*)
13 el ferrobús articulado *m* urbano e
  interurbano de seis ejes *m* tipo
  "Mannheim"
– *six-axle articulated*
  *railcar ('Mannheim' type) for tram*
  *(Am. streetcar, trolley) and urban rail*
  *services*
14 la puerta de entrada *f* y salida *f*, una
  puerta plegable
– *entrance and exit door, a double*
  *folding door*

15 el estribo
– *step*
16 el fechador de billetes *m* (el
  cancelador de billetes *m*)
– *ticket-cancelling machine*
17 el asiento individual
– *single seat*
18 la plaza sin asiento (el sitio para estar
  de pie *m*, el pasillo)
– *standing room portion*
19 el asiento doble
– *double seat*
20 la placa indicadora de la línea y del
  destino
– *route (number) and destination sign*
21 la placa indicadora de la línea
– *route sign (number sign)*
22 el indicador de dirección *f* (el
  intermitente)
– *indicator (indicator light)*
23 el pantógrafo
– *pantograph (current collector)*
24 las zapatas de arco *m* del pantógrafo
  de carbono *m* o de aleación *f* de
  aluminio *m*
– *carbon or aluminium* (Am. *aluminum)*
  *alloy trolley shoes*
25 la cabina del conductor
– *driver's position*
26 el micrófono
– *microphone*
27 el despacho de billetes *m* (*Amér.:* la
  boletería); el indicador del valor
  teórico)
– *controller*
28 el aparato de radio *f*
– *radio equipment (radio*
  *communication set)*
29 el cuadro (el tablero) de mandos *m*
– *dashboard*

30 la iluminación del cuadro de
  mandos *m*
– *dashboard lighting*
31 el indicador de velocidad *f* (el
  velocímetro)
– *speedometer*
32 los botones de mando *m* para abrir las
  puertas, para los limpiaparabrisas y
  para la luz interior y exterior
– *buttons controlling doors, windscreen*
  *wipers, internal and external lighting*
33 el distribuidor de billetes *m* con
  cambiador *m* de moneda *f*
– *ticket counter with change machine*
34 la antena radio *f*
– *radio antenna*
35 la estación (la parada)
– *tram stop (Am. streetcar stop, trolley*
  *stop)*
36 la placa del punto de parada *f*
– *tram stop sign (Am. streetcar stop sign,*
  *trolley stop sign)*
37 la posición de las agujas eléctricas
– *electric change points*
38 la señal de cambio *m* de vía *f*
– *points signal (switch signal)*
39 el transmisor de la señal de cambio *m*
  de vía *f* (el indicador de dirección *f)*
– *points change indicator*
40 el contacto de catenaria *f*
– *trolley wire contact point*
41 la catenaria
– *trolley wire (overhead contact wire)*
42 el arriostramiento transversal de la
  línea de toma *f*
– *overhead cross wire*
43 el mecanismo de mando *m* de
  agujas *f* electromagnético (*también:*
  electromotor)
– *electric points mechanism; sim.:*
  *electrohydraulic points mechanism,*
  *electromechanical points mechanism*

1-5  las capas de la calzada
- *road layers*
1 la capa de protección *f* contra las heladas
- *anti-frost layer*
2 la capa de base *f* bituminosa
- *bituminous sub-base course*
3 la capa adhesiva inferior
- *base course*
4 la capa adhesiva superior
- *binder course*
5 la capa bituminosa de circulación *f* (el revestimiento de la calzada)
- *bituminous surface*
6 el borde de la acera (el bordillo; *Chile:* la solera; *P. Rico:* el cintillo)
- *kerb (curb)*
7 el encintado (la piedra del bordillo)
- *kerbstone (curbstone)*
8 el empedrado de la acera
- *paving (pavement)*
9 la acera (*Guat. y Mé.:* la banqueta; *Amér. Merid.:* la vereda)
- *pavement (Am. sidewalk, walkway)*
10 el arroyo (la reguera)
- *gutter*
11 el paso de peatones *m* (el paso de cebra *f*)
- *pedestrian crossing (zebra crossing, Am. crosswalk)*
12 la esquina de la calle
- *street corner*
13 la calzada
- *street*
14 los cables de suministro *m* de corriente *f*
- *electricity cables*

15 los cables telefónicos
- *telephone cables*
16 la línea telefónica de tránsito *m*
- *telephone cable pipeline*
17 el pozo de cables *m* con recubrimiento *m*
- *cable manhole with cover (with manhole cover)*
18 la farola con luz *f*
- *lamp post with lamp*
19 los cables eléctricos para instalaciones *f* técnicas
- *electricity cables for technical installations*
20 la línea telefónica para el empalme de las casas
- *subscribers' (Am. customers') telephone lines*
21 la canalización de gas *m*
- *gas main*
22 la canalización de agua *f* potable
- *water main*
23 la alcantarilla con colector *m* de cieno *m* (*Amér.:* el resumidero)
- *drain*
24 la rejilla del sumidero
- *drain cover*
25 la acometida de la alcantarilla
- *drain pipe*
26 la acometida de las casas para las aguas fecales
- *waste pipe*
27 la cloaca mixta (para las aguas fecales y llovedizas; *Mé.:* la coladera)
- *combined sewer*
28 el conducto de calefacción *f* urbana
- *district heating main*
29 el túnel del metro
- *underground tunnel*

1 el camión de recogida f de basuras f, un vehículo que prensa la basura
– refuse collection vehicle (Am. garbage truck)
2 el dispositivo basculante para los cubos de la basura, un sistema de vaciado m estanco
– dustbin-tipping device (Am. garbage can dumping device), a dust-free emptying system
3 el cubo de la basura
– dustbin (Am. garbage can, trash can)
4 el contenedor de basura f
– refuse container (Am. garbage container)
5 el barrendero
– road sweeper (Am. street sweeper)
6 la escoba
– broom
7 el brazalete (con franjas f reflectantes)
– fluorescent armband
8 la gorra (con franjas f reflectantes)
– cap with fluorescent band
9 la carretilla del barrendero
– road sweeper's (Am. street sweeper's) barrow
10 la descarga controlada (el depósito de basuras f; un basurero)
– controlled tip (Am. sanitary landfill, sanitary fill)
11 la línea de árboles m (para que no se vea el depósito de basuras f)
– screen
12 el control de entrada f
– weigh office
13 el vallado para los animales salvajes
– fence
14 la pared del foso
– embankment

15 la rampa de acceso m
– access ramp
16 el bulldozer
– bulldozer
17 la basura reciente
– refuse (Am. garbage)
18 el compresor para depositar (la basura)
– bulldozer for dumping and compacting
19 el pozo de bomba f
– pump shaft
20 la bomba para las aguas fecales
– waste water pump
21 el recubrimiento poroso
– porous cover
22 la basura comprimida y en descomposición f
– compacted and decomposed refuse
23 la capa filtrante de grava f
– gravel filter layer
24 la capa filtrante de morena f
– morainic filter layer
25 la capa de drenaje m
– drainage layer
26 la tubería para las aguas residuales
– drain pipe
27 el depósito colector de las aguas residuales
– water tank
28 la fábrica de incineración f de basura f
– refuse (Am. garbage) incineration unit
29 la caldera
– furnace
30 el hogar de fuel-oil m
– oil-firing system
31 el separador de polvo m
– separation plant
32 el ventilador de tracción f por aspiración f
– extraction fan

33 el ventilador de aire m bajo para la rejilla
– low-pressure fan for the grate
34 la rejilla móvil
– continuous feed grate
35 el soplante del hogar de fuel-oil m
– fan for the oil-firing system
36 el transportador de desechos m incinerados por separado
– conveyor for separately incinerated material
37 la instalación de alimentación f (carga f) de carbón m
– coal feed conveyor
38 el carrito transportador de tierra f de batán m
– truck for carrying fuller's earth
39 la barredera
– mechanical sweeper
40 el cepillo circular
– circular broom
41 el vehículo barredor
– road-sweeping lorry (street-cleaning lorry, street cleaner)
42 el cilindro escoba
– cylinder broom
43 la boca (el tubo) de aspiración f
– suction port
44 la escoba de alimentación f
– feeder broom
45 la circulación de aire m
– air flow
46 el ventilador
– fan
47 el depósito (el colector) de barro m
– dust collector

**1-54 máquinas _f_ para la construcción de carreteras _f_**
- _road-building machinery_
1 la excavadora de pala _f_ alta
- _shovel (power shovel, excavator)_
2 la caja de la maquinaria
- _machine housing_
3 la oruga
- _caterpillar mounting_ (Am. _caterpillar tractor)_
4 el brazo de la excavadora
- _digging bucket arm (dipper stick)_
5 la pala (el cucharón) de la excavadora
- _digging bucket (bucket)_
6 los dientes de la pala (los dientes rompedores)
- _digging bucket (bucket) teeth_
7 el volquete, un camión de carga _f_
- _tipper (dump truck), a heavy lorry_ (Am. _truck)_
8 la caja basculante de chapa _f_ de acero _m_
- _tipping body_ (Am. _dump body)_
9 el nervado de refuerzo _m_
- _reinforcing rib_
10 el salvacabina
- _extended front_
11 la cabina del conductor
- _cab (driver's cab)_
12 los escombros
- _bulk material_
13 el mecanismo de tráilla _f_
- _concrete scraper, an aggregate scraper_
14 la caja montacargas
- _skip hoist_
15 la hormigonera
- _mixing drum (mixer drum), a mixing machine_
16 la oruga excavadora con cubeta _f_ de arrastre _m_
- _caterpillar hauling scraper_
17 la cubeta de arrastre _m_
- _scraper blade_
18 la hoja niveladora
- _levelling_ (Am. _leveling) blade (smoothing blade)_
19 la escarificadora (la niveladora)
- _grader (motor grader)_
20 el escarificador (los arrancadores)
- _scarifier (ripper, road ripper, rooter)_
21 la reja niveladora
- _grader levelling_ (Am. _leveling) blade (grader ploughshare,_ Am. _plowshare)_
22 la corona giratoria de la reja
- _blade-slewing gear (slew turntable)_
23 el ferrocarril de vía _f_ estrecha (un ferrocaril de obras _f_)
- _light railway (narrow-gauge,_ Am. _narrow-gage, railway)_

24 la locomotora Diesel ligera, una locomotora de vía _f_ estrecha
- _light railway (narrow-gauge,_ Am. _narrow-gage) diesel locomotive_
25 la vagoneta de remolque _m_
- _trailer wagon (wagon truck, skip)_
26 el pisón de explosión _f_ (el pisón de combustión _f_ interna), una apisonadora; _más pesado:_ el pisón de explosión _f_ tipo rana _f_
- _tamper (rammer) [with internal combustion engine];_ heavier: _frog (frog-type jumping rammer)_
27 las varillas de guía _f_ y de control _m_
- _guide rods_
28 la oruga aplanadora (bulldozer _m_)
- _bulldozer_
29 la aplanadera
- _bulldozer blade_
30 el bastidor de empuje _m_
- _pushing frame_
31 la máquina distribuidora de grava _f_
- _road-metal spreading machine (macadam spreader, stone spreader)_
32 la viga apisonadora
- _tamping beam_
33 los patines
- _sole-plate_
34 la chapa de limitación _f_ lateral
- _side stop_
35 la pared lateral del depósito de almacenamiento _m_
- _side of storage bin_
36 la apisonadora a motor _m_ de tres rulos _m_ (cilindros _m_), una apisonadora para obras _f_ viales
- _three-wheeled roller, a road roller_
37 el rulo (el cilindro)
- _roller_
38 el tejadillo para todo tiempo _m_
- _all-weather roof_
39 el tractor compresor Diesel
- _mobile diesel-powered air compressor_
40 la botella de oxígeno _m_
- _oxygen cylinder_
41 la esparcidora automotriz de gravilla _f_
- _self-propelled gritter_
42 la aleta esparcidora
- _spreading flap_
43 la acabadora para el recubrimiento de negro (la bituminadora)
- _surface finisher_
44 la chapa de limitación _f_ lateral
- _side stop_
45 el depósito de material _m_
- _bin_

46 la bituminadora alquitranadora, con caldera _f_ para el alquitrán y el betún
- _tar-spraying machine (bituminous distributor) with tar and bitumen heater_
47 la caldera de alquitrán _m_
- _tar storage tank_
48 la instalación para la mezcla, secado _m_ y apisonado _m_ del asfalto
- _fully automatic asphalt drying and mixing plant_
49 el elevador de cangilones _m_
- _bucket elevator (elevating conveyor)_
50 el tambor para la mezcla del asfalto
- _asphalt-mixing drum (asphalt mixer drum)_
51 el montacargas llenador
- _filler hoist_
52 la abertura de alimentación _f_
- _filler opening_
53 el inyector de sustancia _f_ aglutinante
- _binder injector_
54 la salida del asfalto mezclado
- _mixed asphalt outlet_
55 la sección transversal normal de una carretera
- _typical cross-section of a bituminous road_
56 el arcén de hierba _f_
- _grass verge_
57 la inclinación transversal
- _crossfall_
58 la capa de asfalto _m_
- _asphalt surface (bituminous layer, bituminous coating)_
59 la infraestructura
- _base (base course)_
60 el firme o la capa de grava _f_, una capa de protección _f_ contra las heladas
- _hardcore sub-base course (Telford base), an anti-frost layer;_ sim.: _gravel sub-base course_
61 el drenaje del subsuelo
- _sub-drainage_
62 el tubo de drenaje _m_ de cemento _m_
- _perforated cement pipe_
63 el canal de drenaje _m_
- _drainage ditch_
64 la cubierta de humus _m_ (la capa de mantillo _m_)
- _soil covering_

### Road Construction II (Road Building, Road Making)

**1-24 construcción *f* de carreteras *f* de hormigón *m*** (construcción *f* de autopistas *f*)
– **concrete road construction**
1 la niveladora del subsuelo, una máquina para la construcción de carreteras *f*
– subgrade grader
2 la viga apisonadora
– tamping beam (consolidating beam)
3 la viga niveladora
– levelling (Am. leveling) beam
4 los rodillos guía *f* para la viga niveladora
– roller guides for the levelling (Am. leveling) beam
5 la distribuidora de hormigón *m*
– concrete spreader
6 la cubeta distribuidora de hormigón *m*
– concrete spreader box
7 la guía de cables *m*
– cable guides
8 la palanca de mando *m*
– control levers
9 el volante (la rueda de mano *f*) para el vaciado de las cubetas
– handwheel for emptying the boxes
10 el vibrador de superficie *f*
– concrete-vibrating compactor
11 el engranaje
– gearing (gears)
12 las palancas de maniobra *f*
– control levers (operating levers)

13 el árbol de impulsión *f* para los vibradores de la viga vibradora
– axle drive shaft to vibrators (tampers) of vibrating beam
14 la viga alisadora
– screeding board (screeding beam)
15 el soporte de los carriles guía *f*
– road form
16 la máquina de cortar juntas *f* (el cortador de juntas *f*)
– joint cutter
17 la cuchilla cortadora de juntas *f*
– joint-cutting blade
18 la manivela de avance *m*
– crank for propelling machine
19 la instalación para la mezcla de hormigón *m*, una estación central de mezcla *f*, una instalación de peso *m* y mezcla *f* automáticos
– concrete-mixing plant, a stationary central mixing plant, an automatic batching and mixing plant
20 la artesa colectora
– collecting bin
21 el elevador de cangilones *m*
– bucket elevator
22 el silo del cemento
– cement store
23 la hormigonera de mezcla *f* forzada
– concrete mixer
24 la cuba del hormigón
– concrete pump hopper

1-38 la vía
- *line (track)*
1 el carril (el raíl)
- *rail*
2 la cabeza del raíl
- *rail head*
3 el alma *f* del raíl
- *web (rail web)*
4 el patín del raíl
- *rail foot (rail bottom)*
5 la placa de asiento *m*
- *sole-plate (base plate)*
6 la plantilla
- *cushion*
7 el tirafondo
- *coach screw (coach bolt)*
8 las arandelas de muelle *m* (las arandelas elásticas)
- *lock washers (spring washers)*
9 la placa de sujeción *f*
- *rail clip (clip)*
10 el tornillo de sujeción *f*
- *T-head bolt*
11 la junta de los raíles
- *rail joint (joint)*
12 la eclisa (la mordaza del carril)
- *fishplate*
13 el tornillo de eclisa *f*
- *fishbolt*
14 la traviesa de junta *f* acoplada
- *coupled sleeper* (Am. *coupled tie, coupled crosstie)*
15 el tornillo de acoplamiento *m*
- *coupling bolt*
16 las agujas movidas a mano *f*
- *manually-operated points (switch)*
17 el aparato de maniobra *f* de las agujas movidas a mano *f*
- *switch stand*
18 el contrapeso
- *weight*
19 la señal de agujas *f* (el farol indicando la posición de las agujas)
- *points signal (switch signal, points signal lamp, switch signal lamp)*

20 el tirante de ajuste *m*
- *pull rod*
21 la lengüeta de la aguja
- *switch blade (switch tongue)*
22 el patín de deslizamiento *m*
- *slide chair*
23 el contracarril
- *check rail (guard rail)*
24 el cruzamiento (la punta de corazón *m* de las agujas)
- *frog*
25 la pata de liebre *f*
- *wing rail*
26 el raíl del cambio
- *closure rail*
27 el cambio de agujas *f* a distancia *f*
- *remote-controlled points (switch)*
28 el cerrojo del aparato de cambio *m*
- *point lock (switch lock)*
29 el tirante de unión *f* (del cerrojo con las agujas)
- *stretcher bar*
30 el alambre de transmisión *f*
- *point wire*
31 el tensor
- *turnbuckle*
32 el canal
- *channel*
33 la señal de cambio *m* con alumbrado *m* eléctrico
- *electrically illuminated points signal (switch signal)*
34 el foso del cambio
- *trough*
35 la caja protectora de la transmisión del cambio
- *points motor with protective casing*
36 la traviesa de acero *m*
- *steel sleeper* (Am. *steel tie, steel crosstie)*
37 la traviesa de hormigón *m*
- *concrete sleeper* (Am. *concrete tie, concrete crosstie)*
38 la traviesa de junta *f* acoplada
- *coupled sleeper* (Am. *coupled tie, coupled crosstie)*

39-50 pasos *m* a nivel *m*
- *level crossings* (Am. *grade crossings)*
39 el paso a nivel *m*, con barrera *f* (P. Rico: el paso-nivel)
- *protected level crossing* (Am. *protected grade crossing)*
40 la barrera
- *barrier (gate)*
41 la cruz de aviso *m* (la cruz de San Andrés)
- *warning cross* (Am. *crossbuck)*
42 el guardabarrera
- *crossing keeper* (Am. *gateman)*
43 la caseta del guardabarrera
- *crossing keeper's box* (Am. *gateman's box)*
44 el vigilante de la vía
- *linesman* (Am. *trackwalker)*
45 el paso de media barrera *f*
- *half-barrier crossing*
46 la luz intermitente
- *warning light*
47 la barrera accionada por micrófono *m*
- *intercom-controlled crossing; sim.: telephone-controlled crossing*
48 el interfono
- *intercom system*
49 el paso a nivel *m* sin guarda *f*
- *unprotected level crossing* (Am. *unprotected grade crossing)*
50 la luz intermitente
- *warning light*

# 203 Vía férrea II (señalización)

**1-6 los semáforos**
- *stop signals (main signals)*
1 el semáforo, una señal en posición *f* de "parada" *f*
- *stop signal (main signal), a semaphore signal in 'stop' position*
2 el brazo de la señal
- *signal arm (semaphore arm)*
3 el semáforo eléctrico (la señal eléctrica) en posición *f* de "parada" *f*
- *electric stop signal (colour light, Am. color light, signal) at 'stop'*
4 la posición de la señal de "disminución *f* de velocidad *f*"
- *signal position: 'proceed at low speed'*
5 la posición de la señal de "vía *f* libre"
- *signal position: 'proceed'*
6 la señal de sustitución *f*
- *substitute signal*
**7-24 señales *f* de aviso *m***
- *distant signals*
7 la señal en posición *f* de "parada *f* próxima"
- *semaphore signal at 'be prepared to stop at next signal'*
8 el brazo adicional
- *supplementary semaphore arm*
9 la señal luminosa de aviso *m* de "parada *f* próxima"
- *colour light (Am. color light) distant signal at 'be prepared to stop at next signal'*
10 la posición de la señal de "disminución *f* de velocidad *f* próxima"
- *signal position: 'be prepared to proceed at low speed'*
11 la posición de la señal de "vía *f* libre próxima"
- *signal position: 'proceed main signal ahead'*
12 la señal de aviso *m* con panel *m* adicional para reducción *f* de la distancia de frenado *m* de más de 5%
- *semaphore signal with indicator plate showing a reduction in braking distance of more than 5%*
13 el panel triangular
- *triangle (triangle sign)*
14 la señal luminosa de aviso *m* con luz *f* adicional para reducción *f* de la distancia de frenado *m*
- *colour light (Am. color light) distant signal with indicator light for showing reduced braking distance*
15 la luz blanca adicional
- *supplementary white light*
16 la señal de aviso *m* de "parada *f* próxima" (luz *f* amarilla)
- *distant signal indicating 'be prepared to stop at next signal' (yellow light)*
17 la señal de aviso *m* repetida (la señal de aviso *m* con luz *f* adicional, sin panel *m*)
- *second distant signal [distant signal with supplementary light, without indicator plate]*
18 la señal de aviso *m* con indicación *f* de velocidad *f*
- *distant signal with speed indicator*

19 el indicador de la velocidad (la pancarta de limitación *f* de velocidad *f*)
- *distant speed indicator*
20 la señal de aviso *m* con indicador *m* de dirección *f*
- *distant signal with route indicator*
21 el indicador de dirección *f* (*Cuba y P. Rico:* el abanico)
- *route indicator*
22 la señal de aviso *m* sin brazo *m* adicional en posición *f* de "parada próxima"
- *distant signal without supplementary arm in position: 'be prepared to stop at next signal'*
23 la señal de aviso *m* sin brazo *m* adicional en posición *f* de "vía *f* libre próxima"
- *distant signal without supplementary arm in 'be prepared to proceed' position*
24 el panel de la señal de aviso *m*
- *distant signal identification plate*
**25-44 señales *f* suplementarias**
- *supplementary signals*
25 la placa trapezoidal para marcar el punto de parada *f* en la estación
- *stop board for indicating the stopping point at a control point*
**26-29 las señales de aviso *m* de balizas *f***
- *approach signs*
26 la señal de aviso *m* de baliza *f* a 100 m de distancia *f* de la señal
- *approach sign 100 m from distant signal*
27 la señal de aviso *m* de baliza *f* a 175 m de distancia *f*
- *approach sign 175 m from distant signal*
28 la señal de aviso *m* de baliza *f* a 250 m de distancia *f*
- *approach sign 250 m from distant signal*
29 la señal de aviso *m* de baliza *f* a menos de un 5% de distancia *f* de la vía de parada *f* de la sección
- *approach sign at a distance of 5% less than the braking distance on the section*
30 la señal a cuadros *m* indicando señales *f* de parada *f* no situadas inmediatamente a la derecha o sobre el rail de parada *f*
- *chequered sign indicating stop signals (main signals) not positioned immediately to the right of or over the line (track)*
**31-32 las placas de parada *f* para indicar el punto de parada *f* frente al tren**
- *stop boards to indicate the stopping point of the front of the train*
33 la placa del punto de parada *f* (prepararse para parar)
- *stop board indicating 'be prepared to stop'*
**34-35 las placas quitanieves *m***
- *snow plough (Am. snowplow) signs*
34 la placa quitanieves *m* levantada
- *'raise snow plough (Am. snowplow)' sign*
35 la placa quitanieves *m* bajada
- *'lower snow plough (Am. snowplow)' sign*

**36-44 señales *f* de limitación *f* de velocidad *f***
- *speed restriction signs*
**36-38 disco *m* de limitación *f* de velocidad *f* [velocidad máxima 3 × 10 = 30 km/h]**
- *speed restriction sign [maximum speed 3 x 10 = 30 kph]*
36 la señal diurna
- *sign for day running*
37 el número de velocidad *f*
- *speed code number*
38 la señal nocturna
- *illuminated sign for night running*
39 el comienzo de la limitación de velocidad *f* provisional
- *commencement of temporary speed restriction*
40 el final de la limitación de velocidad *f* provisional
- *termination of temporary speed restriction*
41 la señal de limitación *f* de velocidad *f* para una sección con limitación *f* de velocidad *f* permanente [velocidad máxima 5 × 10 = 50 km/h]
- *speed restriction sign for a section with a permanent speed restriction [maximum speed 5 x 10 = 50 kph]*
42 el comienzo de la limitación de velocidad *f* permanente
- *commencement of permanent speed restriction*
43 la placa de advertencia de limitación *f* de velocidad *f* [sólo en vías *f* principales]
- *speed restriction warning sign [only on main lines]*
44 la señal de limitación *f* de velocidad *f* [sólo en vías *f* principales]
- *speed restriction sign [only on main lines]*
**45-52 señales *f* de cambio *m* de vía *f***
- *point signals (switch signals)*
**45-48 agujas *f* simples**
- *single points (single switches)*
45 la ramificación recta
- *route straight ahead (main line)*
46 la ramificación doblada [a derecha]
- *[right] branch*
47 la ramificación doblada [a izquierda]
- *[left] branch*
48 la ramificación curva [vista desde el cruce (punta *f* de corazón *m*)]
- *branch [seen from the frog]*
**49-52 cruces *m* de vías *f* dobles**
- *double crossover*
49 el cruce rectilíneo de izquierda a derecha
- *route straight ahead from left to right*
50 el cruce rectilíneo de derecha a izquierda
- *route straight ahead from right to left*
51 la curva a la izquierda
- *turnout to the left from the left*
52 la curva a la derecha
- *turnout to the right from the right*
**53 el puesto de agujas *f* (*Amér.:* el chucho) mecánico**
- *manually-operated signal box (Am. signal tower, switch tower)*

**54** el juego de palancas *f*
– *lever mechanism*
**55** la palanca de cambio *m* [azul], una palanca de cerrojo *m*
– *points lever (switch lever) [blue], a lock lever*
**56** la palanca de señales *f* [rojo]
– *signal lever [red]*
**57** el gatillo (el pestillo) de mano *f*
– *catch*
**58** la palanca de vía *f* libre
– *route lever*
**59** el bloqueo de tramos *m* (de secciones *f*)
– *block instruments*

**60** el tablero del bloque
– *block section panel*
**61** el cuadro de agujas *f* eléctrico
– *electrically-operated signal box* (Am. *signal tower, switch tower*)
**62** la palanca de agujas *f* y de señales *f*
– *points (switch) and signal knobs*
**63** el registro de cierre *m*
– *lock indicator panel*
**64** el tablero de control *m*
– *track and signal indicator*

**65** el cuadro luminoso de agujas *f*
– *track diagram control layout*
**66** el pupitre del diagrama de vías *f*
– *track diagram control panel (domino panel)*
**67** los pulsadores
– *push buttons*
**68** los itinerarios (las vías)
– *routes*
**69** el interfono
– *intercom system*

1  el despacho de expedición *f* y
   recepción *f* de paquetes *m* por
   expreso *m*
–  *parcels office*
2  la carga por expreso *m* (el
   paquete por expreso *m*)
–  *parcels*
3  la canasta con candado *m*
–  *basket [with lock]*
4  el despacho de facturación *f* y
   recepción *f* de equipaje *m*
–  *luggage counter*
5  la báscula automática
–  *platform scale with dial*
6  la maleta (*Amér.:* la valija)
–  *suitcase (case)*
7  la etiqueta (con la dirección)
   del equipaje
–  *luggage sticker*
8  el resguardo de consigna *f*
–  *luggage receipt*
9  el empleado del despacho
–  *luggage clerk*
10 el cartel publicitario
–  *poster (advertisement)*
11 el buzón de la estación
–  *station post box (*Am. *station
   mailbox)*
12 la pizarra para anunciar los
   retrasos de trenes *m*
–  *notice board indicating train
   delays*

13 el restaurante de la estación
–  *station restaurant*
14 la sala de espera *f*
–  *waiting room*
15 el plano de la ciudad
–  *map of the town (street map)*
16 el panel guía de ferrocarriles *m*
–  *timetable (*Am. *schedule)*
17 el mozo de hotel *m* (el botones)
–  *hotel porter*
18 el horario de trenes *m* de
   pared *f* (el indicador mural)
–  *arrivals and departures board
   (timetable)*
19 el tablero de las horas de
   llegada *f*
–  *arrival timetable (*Am. *arrival
   schedule)*
20 el tablero de las horas de
   salida *f*
–  *departure timetable (*Am.
   *departure schedule)*

**21** la consigna automática
– *left luggage lockers*
**22** la máquina automática para cambiar monedas *f*
– *change machine*
**23** el túnel de acceso *m* al andén
– *tunnel to the platforms*
**24** los pasajeros (viajeros *m*)
– *passengers*
**25** la escalera del andén
– *steps to the platforms*
**26** la librería de la estación
– *station bookstall (*Am. *station bookstand)*
**27** la consigna para las maletas (*Amér.:* las valijas)
– *left luggage office (left luggage)*
**28** la agencia de viajes *m; también:* la oficina de información *f* de hoteles *m*, la oficina de turismo *m*
– *travel centre (*Am. *center); also: accommodation bureau*
**29** información *f*
– *information office (*Am. *information bureau)*
**30** el reloj de la estación
– *station clock*
**31** la sucursal bancaria, con oficina *f* de cambio *m*
– *bank branch with foreign exchange counter*

**32** la lista de cambio *m*
– *indicator board showing exchange rates*
**33** el plano de la red ferroviaria
– *railway map (*Am. *railroad map)*
**34** el despacho de billetes *m*
– *ticket office*
**35** la taquilla de venta *f* de billetes *m*
– *ticket counter*
**36** el billete
– *ticket (railway ticket,* Am. *railroad ticket)*
**37** el platillo giratorio
– *revolving tray*
**38** el higiafón
– *grill*
**39** el taquillero (expendedor *m* de billetes *m*)
– *ticket clerk (*Am. *ticket agent)*
**40** la máquina de imprimir billetes *m*
– *ticket-printing machine (ticket-stamping machine)*
**41** el aparato impresor manual
– *hand-operated ticket printer*
**42** la guía de bolsillo *m*
– *pocket timetable (*Am. *pocket train schedule)*
**43** el banco para el equipaje
– *luggage rest*

**44** el puesto de socorro *m*
– *first aid station*
**45** la misión de la estación
– *Travellers' (*Am. *Travelers') Aid*
**46** la cabina telefónica pública
– *telephone box (telephone booth, telephone kiosk, call box)*
**47** el estanco (*Amér.:* la cigarrería; el quiosco de tabaco *m*)
– *cigarettes and tobacco kiosk*
**48** la floristería (el quiosco de flores *f*)
– *flower stand*
**49** el agente de información *f*
– *railway information clerk*
**50** la guía oficial de ferrocarriles *m*
– *official timetable (official railway guide,* Am. *train schedule)*

1 el andén
– *platform*
2 la escalera del andén
– *steps to the platform*
3 el paso superior del andén
– *bridge to the platforms*
4 el número de andén *m*
– *platform number*
5 el techo del andén
– *platform roofing*
6 los viajeros
– *passengers*
7-12 **el equipaje**
– *luggage*
7 la maleta (*Amér.*: la valija)
– *suitcase (case)*
8 la etiqueta de la maleta
– *luggage label*
9 la etiqueta del hotel
– *hotel sticker*
10 el saco de mano *f* (el bolso de
viaje *m; Amér.*: el carriel; *Mé.*:
el veliz)
– *travelling (Am. traveling) bag*
11 la sombrerera
– *hat box*
12 el paraguas, un bastón
paraguas *m*
– *umbrella, a walking-stick
umbrella*
13 el edificio de recepción *f*
– *main building; also: offices*

14 el andén número 1
– *platform*
15 el paso a nivel *m*
– *crossing*
16 el quiosco rodante de
periódicos *m*
– *news trolley*
17 el vendedor de periódicos *m*
– *news vendor (Am. news dealer)*
18 la lectura para el viaje
– *reading matter for the journey*
19 el bordillo del andén
– *edge of the platform*
20 la policía de ferrocarriles *m*
– *railway policeman (Am. railroad
policeman)*
21 el indicador de dirección *f*
– *destination board*
22 la casilla para anunciar la
estación *f* de destino *m*
– *destination indicator*
23 la casilla para anunciar la hora
de salida *f*
– *departure time indicator*
24 la casilla para anunciar el
retraso del tren
– *delay indicator*
25 el tren de ferrocarril *m*
interurbano, un tren automotor
– *suburban train, a railcar*
26 el compartimiento reservado
– *special compartment*

27 el altavoz (*Amér.*: el
altoparlante) del andén
– *platform loudspeaker*
28 el letrero de la estación
– *station sign*
29 el carro eléctrico
– *electric trolley (electric truck)*
30 el encargado del equipaje
– *loading foreman*
31 el mozo de estación *f* (el mozo
de cuerda *f; Arg.*: el changador;
*Col.*: el altozanero)
– *porter (Am. redcap)*
32 el carrito del equipaje
– *barrow*
33 la fuente de agua *f* potable
– *drinking fountain*
34 el Trans-Europa-Exprés
eléctrico (el T.E.E.); *también:* el
tren rápido interurbano
– *electric Trans-Europe Express;
also: Intercity train*
35 la locomotora eléctrica, una
locomotora exprés eléctrica
– *electric locomotive, an express
locomotive*
36 el arco de toma *f* de corriente *f*
(el pantógrafo)
– *collector bow (sliding bow)*
37 el compartimiento secretaría *f*
– *secretarial compartment*
38 la placa de ruta *f* y destino *m*
– *destination board*

**39** el inspector del material
rodante y vagones *m*
– *wheel tapper*
**40** el martillo comprobador de
ruedas *f*
– *wheel-tapping hammer*
**41** el inspector
– *station foreman*
**42** el bastón de mando *m* (el
bastón de señales *f*)
– *signal*
**43** la gorra roja
– *red cap*
**44** el agente de información *f*
– *inspector*
**45** el horario de bolsillo *m*
– *pocket timetable* (Am. *pocket
train schedule*)
**46** el reloj del andén
– *platform clock*
**47** la señal de partida *f*
– *starting signal*
**48** el alumbrado del andén
– *platform lighting*
**49** el quiosco (del andén) de
refrescos *m* y comidas *f* para el
viaje
– *refreshment kiosk*
**50** la botella de cerveza *f*
– *beer bottle*
**51** el periódico
– *newspaper*

**52** el beso de despedida *f* (*Guat.:* el
pico)
– *parting kiss*
**53** el abrazo
– *embrace*
**54** el banco del andén
– *platform seat*
**55** la papelera para los
desperdicios
– *litter bin* (Am. *litter basket*)
**56** el buzón del andén
– *platform post box* (Am. *platform
mailbox*)
**57** la cabina telefónica del andén
– *platform telephone*
**58** el hilo de contacto *m* (el cable
de contacto *m*)
– *trolley wire (overhead contact
wire)*
**59-61** la vía
– *track*
**59** el rail
– *rail*
**60** la traviesa (*Amér.:* el
durmiente)
– *sleeper* (Am. *tie, crosstie*)
**61** los cascajos (el lecho de
cascajos *m*, los balastos)
– *ballast (bed)*

1 la rampa de acceso *m* (la rampa de vehiculos *m*); *anál:* la rampa del ganado
– *ramp (vehicle ramp); sim.: livestock ramp*
2 el tractor eléctrico
– *electric truck*
3 la vagoneta (el remolque transportador)
– *trailer*
4 los bultos (los bultos sueltos, fardos *m*, la mercancía en fardos *m*); *en transportes colectivos:* carga *f* colectiva
– *part loads (Am. package freight, less-than-carload freight); in general traffic: general goods in general consignments (in mixed consignments)*
5 el cajón (la caja)
– *crate*
6 el vagón para la mercancía en fardos *m*
– *goods van (Am. freight car)*
7 el cobertizo de mercancías *f* (el almacén de mercancías *f*)
– *goods shed (Am. freight house)*
8 la calle de carga *f*
– *loading strip*
9 la rampa del cobertizo (la rampa de carga *f*)
– *loading dock*
10 la cesta de mimbre *m*
– *bale of peat*
11 la bala de lienzo *m*
– *bale of linen (of linen cloth)*
12 la atadura
– *fastening (cord)*
13 la damajuana (la botella, la garrafa) forrada de paja *f*
– *wicker bottle (wickered bottle, demijohn)*
14 la carretilla para los sacos
– *trolley*
15 el camión para la mercancía en fardos *m*
– *goods lorry (Am. freight truck)*
16 la carretilla elevadora de horquilla *f*
– *forklift truck (fork truck, forklift)*
17 la vía de carga *f*
– *loading siding*
18 las mercancías voluminosas
– *bulky goods*
19 el contenedor pequeño propiedad del ferrocarril
– *small railway-owned (Am. railroad-owned) container*
20 el vagón de feriantes *m* ( *anál.:* el vagón de circo *m*)
– *showman's caravan; sim.: circus caravan*
21 el vagón plano (la batea)
– *flat wagon (Am. flat freight car)*
22 el gálibo
– *loading gauge (Am. gage)*
23 la bala de paja *f*
– *bale of straw*
24 el vagón plataforma con teleros *m* (la batea con teleros *m*)

– *flat wagon (Am. flatcar) with side stakes*
25 el parque de coches *m* y de vagones *m*
– *fleet of lorries (Am. trucks)*
26-39 el tinglado (el cobertizo) de las mercancías
– *goods shed (Am. freight house)*
26 la recepción de mercancías *f* (el despacho de mercancías *f*)
– *goods office (forwarding office, Am. freight office)*
27 las mercancías
– *part-load goods (Am. package freight)*
28 el contratista de mercancías *f*
– *forwarding agent (Am. freight agent, shipper)*
29 el jefe de carga *f*
– *loading foreman*
30 la carta de porte *m* (el talón de expedición *f; Amér.:* la boleta de expedición *f*)
– *consignment note (waybill)*
31 las báscula de los bultos sueltos
– *weighing machine*
32 la paleta
– *pallet*
33 el obrero del cobertizo de mercancías *f*
– *porter*
34 la carretilla eléctrica
– *electric cart (electric truck)*
35 el remolque de la carretilla
– *trailer*
36 el empleado de la oficina de consignación *f* (la inspección de carga *f*)
– *loading supervisor*
37 la puerta del cobertizo
– *goods shed door (Am. freight house door)*
38 el riel guía *f*
– *rail (slide rail)*
39 la polea (la rueda de corredera *f*)
– *roller*
40 la caseta para pesar
– *weighbridge office*
41 la báscula para vagones *m*
– *weighbridge*
42 la estación de maniobras *f*
– *marshalling yard (Am. classification yard, switch yard)*
43 la locomotora de maniobras *f*
– *shunting engine (shunting locomotive, shunter, Am. switch engine, switcher)*
44 el puesto de control de maniobras *f*
– *marshalling yard signal box (Am. classification yard switch tower)*
45 el jefe de maniobras *f*
– *yardmaster*
46 la albardilla
– *hump*
47 la vía de maniobras *f*
– *sorting siding (classification siding, classification track)*

48 el freno de vía *f* (el freno de raíl *m*)
– *rail brake (retarder)*
49 la calza (la zapata de freno *m*)
– *slipper brake (slipper)*
50 la vía de maniobras *f* (el apartadero)
– *storage siding (siding)*
51 el tope fijo (el tope hidráulico)
– *buffer (buffers, Am. bumper)*
52 el vagón completo (*Amér.:* el carro completo)
– *wagon load (Am. carload)*
53 el almacén
– *warehouse*
54 la estación de contenedores *m*
– *container station*
55 la grúa de pórtico *m*
– *gantry crane*
56 el mecanismo de elevación *f*
– *lifting gear (hoisting gear)*
57 el contenedor
– *container*
58 el vagón portacontenedores *m*
– *container wagon (Am. container car)*
59 el semirremolque
– *semi-trailer*

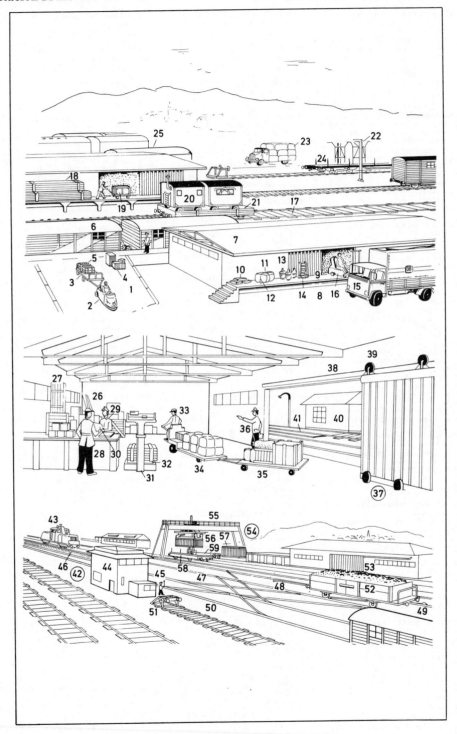

1-21 **el vagón de tren** *m* **expreso,** un vagón (*Amér.:* un carro)
- *express train coach (express train carriage, express train car, corridor compartment coach), a passenger coach*
1 la vista lateral (el perfil)
- *side elevation (side view)*
2 la caja del vagón
- *coach body*
3 el chasis
- *underframe (frame)*
4 el bogie (el carretón) con suspensión *f* de muelles *m* de acero *m* y amortiguadores *m*
- *bogie (truck) with steel and rubber suspension and shock absorbers*
5 el compartimiento de las baterías
- *battery containers (battery boxes)*
6 el intercambiador de calor *m* para la calefacción a vapor *m* o eléctrica
- *steam and electric heat exchanger for the heating system*
7 la ventanilla de corredera *f*
- *sliding window*
8 la junta con almohadilla *f* de caucho *m*
- *rubber connecting seal*
9 el ventilador estático
- *ventilator*
10-21 **el plano**
- *plan*
10 el compartimiento de 2ª clase *f*
- *second-class section*
11 el pasillo lateral
- *corridor*
12 el asiento plegable (el traspuntín, el trasportín)
- *folding seat (tip-up seat)*
13 el compartimiento de los pasajeros
- *passenger compartment (compartment)*
14 la puerta del compartimiento
- *compartment door*
15 el lavabo (*Amér.:* el lavatorio)
- *washroom*
16 el retrete (el excusado, el water-closet, el W.C.)
- *toilet (lavatory, WC)*
17 el compartimiento de 1ª clase
- *first-class section*
18 la puerta de vaivén *m*
- *swing door*
19 la puerta corrediza de la pared frontal
- *sliding connecting door*
20 la puerta de entrada *f*
- *door*
21 el vestíbulo
- *vestibule*
22-32 **el coche-restaurante** (*Amér.:* el vagón-restaurante)
- *dining car (restaurant car, diner)*
22-25 **vista lateral** (el perfil)
- *side elevation (side view)*
22 la puerta de entrada *f*
- *door*
23 la puerta de carga *f*
- *loading door*
24 la toma de corriente *f* para el abastecimento de energía *f* durante la parada
- *current collector for supplying power during stops*
25 los compartimientos de las baterías
- *battery boxes (battery containers)*
26-32 **el plano**
- *plan*
26 el lavabo del personal
- *staff washroom*
27 el armario de las provisiones
- *storage cupboard*
28 el fregadero
- *washing-up area*
29 la cocina
- *kitchen*

30 la cocina eléctrica con 8 placas *f*
- *electric oven with eight hotplates*
31 la barra (el bar)
- *counter*
32 el comedor
- *dining compartment*
33 la cocina del coche-restaurante
- *dining car kitchen*
34 el jefe de cocina *f*
- *chef (head cook)*
35 la despensa (la alacena)
- *kitchen cabinet*
36 el coche-cama
- *sleeping car (sleeper)*
37 la vista lateral (el perfil)
- *side elevation (side view)*
38-42 **el plano**
- *plan*
38 el compartimiento de dos camas *f*
- *two-seat twin-berth compartment (two-seat two-berth compartment,* Am. *bedroom)*
39 la puerta plegable y giratoria
- *folding doors*
40 el lavabo (*Amér.:* el lavatorio)
- *washstand*
41 la habitación de servicio *m*
- *office*
42 el retrete (el excusado, el water-closet, el W.C.)
- *toilet (lavatory, WC)*
43 el compartimiento del tren expreso
- *express train compartment*
44 el asiento acolchado reclinable
- *upholstered reclining seat*
45 el brazo del asiento
- *armrest*
46 el cenicero del brazo del asiento
- *ashtray in the armrest*
47 el reposacabezas ajustable
- *adjustable headrest*
48 la funda de tela *f*
- *antimacassar*
49 el espejo
- *mirror*
50 la percha (el cuelgacapas)
- *coat hook*
51 el portaequipajes
- *luggage rack*
52 la ventanilla del compartimiento
- *compartment window*
53 la mesita plegable
- *fold-away table (pull-down table)*
54 el botón para regular la calefacción
- *heating regulator*
55 la papelera
- *litter receptacle*
56 la cortina de cordón *m*
- *curtain*
57 el reposapiés (el apoyapiés)
- *footrest*
58 el asiento de ventanilla *f*
- *corner seat*
59 el coche de gran capacidad *f*
- *open car*
60 la vista lateral (el perfil)
- *side elevation (side view)*
61-72 **el plano**
- *plan*
61 el compartimiento de gran capacidad *f*
- *open carriage*
62 la fila de asientos *m* individuales
- *row of single seats*
63 la fila de asientos *m* dobles
- *row of double seats*
64 el asiento reclinable
- *reclining seat*
65 el cojín
- *seat upholstery*
66 el respaldo
- *backrest*
67 la cabecera
- *headrest*

68 la almohadilla de plumas *f* con funda *f* de nylón *m*
- *down-filled headrest cushion with nylon cover*
69 el brazo del asiento con cenicero *m*
- *armrest with ashtray*
70 el guardarropa
- *cloakroom*
71 el guardamaletas
- *luggage compartment*
72 los lavabos
- *toilet (lavatory, WC)*
73 el coche-bar, un coche-restaurante de autoservicio *m*
- *buffet car (quick-service buffet car), a self-service restaurant car*
74 la vista lateral (el perfil)
- *side elevation (side view)*
75 la toma de corriente *f* para el abastecimiento eléctrico durante la parada
- *current collector for supplying power*
76 el plano
- *plan*
77 el comedor
- *dining compartment*
78-79 **la barra** (el bar)
- *buffet (buffet compartment)*
78 el lado de los clientes
- *customer area*
79 el lado del personal del servicio
- *serving area*
80 la cocina
- *kitchen*
81 el compartimiento del personal
- *staff compartment*
82 los lavabos (los retretes, los W.C.) del personal
- *staff toilet (staff lavatory, staff WC)*
83 los casilleros de comidas *f*
- *food compartments*
84 los platos
- *plates*
85 el cubierto
- *cutlery*
86 la caja
- *till (cash register)*

1-30 **el servicio local**
– *local train service*
1-12 **el tren del servicio local**
– *local train (short-distance train)*
1 la locomotora Diesel monomotor
– *single-engine diesel locomotive*
2 el maquinista
– *engine driver* (Am. *engineer*)
3 el vagón del servicio local de cuatro ejes *m*, un vagón de viajeros *m*
– *four-axled coach (four-axled car) for short-distance routes, a passenger coach (passenger car)*
4 el bogie (el carretón) [con freno *m* de discos *m*]
– *bogie (truck) [with disc (disk) brakes]*
5 el chasis
– *underframe (frame)*
6 la caja del vagón con paneles *m* de chapa *f*
– *coach body with metal panelling (Am. paneling)*
7 la puerta doble plegable y giratoria
– *double folding doors*
8 la ventanilla del compartimiento
– *compartment window*
9 el compartimiento de gran capacidad *f*
– *open carriage*
10 la puerta de entrada *f*
– *entrance*
11 el paso [de un vagón a otro]
– *connecting corridor*

12 la junta con almohadilla *f* de caucho *m*
– *rubber connecting seal*
13 el automotor ligero, un automotor de servicio *m* local, un automotor Diesel
– *light railcar, a short-distance railcar, a diesel railcar*
14 la cabina del maquinista del automotor
– *cab (driver's cab, Am. engineer's cab)*
15 el compartimiento del equipaje
– *luggage compartment*
16 la conexión de tubos *m* y enganche *m* de vagones *m*
– *connecting hoses and coupling*
17 el eslabón de enganche *m*
– *coupling link*
18 el tensor (el tornillo de acoplamiento *m* con palanca *f* tensora)
– *tensioning device, a coupling screw with tensioning lever*
19 el acoplamiento suelto
– *unlinked coupling*
20 la manga de acoplamiento *m* del conducto de calefacción *f*
– *heating coupling hose (steam coupling hose)*
21 la manga de acoplamiento *m* de la conducción del freno
– *coupling hose (connecting hose) for the compressed-air braking system*

22 el compartimiento de 2ª clase
– *second-class section*
23 el pasillo central
– *central gangway*
24 el compartimiento
– *compartment*
25 el banco (el asiento) acolchado
– *upholstered seat*
26 el brazo del asiento
– *armrest*
27 el portaequipajes (la rejilla para el equipaje)
– *luggage rack*
28 la rejilla para el sombrero y para el equipaje pequeño
– *hat and light luggage rack*
29 el cenicero giratorio
– *ashtray*
30 el viajero
– *passenger*

**1-22 el tren T.E.E. (I.C.)** (el tren Trans-Europa-Exprés interurbano)
- **Trans-Europe Express** *(Intercity train)*
1 el coche automotor de los Ferrocarriles Federales Alemanes (DB), un coche automotor Diesel o un coche automotor de turbina *f* de gas *m*
- *German Federal Railway trainset, a diesel trainset or gas turbine trainset*
2 la cabeza motriz
- *driving unit*
3 el eje de ruedas *f* provisto de motor *m* (las ruedas motrices)
- *drive wheel unit*
4 la instalación de propulsión *f*(el motor Diesel de tracción *f*)
- *main engine*
5 el generador Diesel
- *diesel generator unit*
6 la cabina del maquinista
- *cab (driver's cab*, Am. *engineer's cab)*
7 el vagón intermediario
- *second coach*
8 la cabeza motriz de turbina *f* de gas *m* [en corte]
- *gas turbine driving unit [diagram]*
9 la turbina de gas *m*
- *gas turbine*
10 la transmisión de turbina *f*
- *turbine transmission*
11 el conducto de admisión *f* de aire *m*
- *air intake*
12 el tubo de escape de gas *m* con silencioso *m*
- *exhaust with silencers* (Am. *mufflers)*
13 el arranque eléctrico
- *dynastarter*

14 la transmisión Voith
- *Voith transmission*
15 el intercambiador de calor *m* para el aceite de transmisión *f*
- *heat exchanger for the transmission oil*
16 el armario de mando *m* de la turbina ' de gas *m*
- *gas turbine controller*
17 el depósito de combustible *m* para la turbina de gas *m*
- *gas turbine fuel tank*
18 la instalación de refrigeración *f* por aire del aceite de la transmisión y de la turbina
- *oil-to-air cooling unit for transmission and turbine*
19 el motor Diesel auxiliar
- *auxiliary diesel engine*
20 el depósito de combustible *m*
- *fuel tank*
21 la instalación de refrigeración *f*
- *cooling unit*
22 la tubería de escape *m*, con silencioso *m*
- *exhaust with silencers* (Am. *mufflers)*
23 **el coche automotor experimental** de la Sociedad Nacional de los Ferrocarriles Franceses (S.N.C.F.) con un motor Diesel de 6 cilindros *m* bajo el piso y una turbina de gas *m* con dos árboles *m*
- *experimental trainset of the Société Nationale des Chemins de Fer Français (SNCF) with six-cylinder underfloor diesel engine and twin-shaft gas turbine*

24 la instalación de turbina *f*(el turbogrupo) con silencioso *m*
- *turbine unit with silencers (Am. mufflers)*
25 la secretaría del tren
- *secretarial compartment*
26 el compartimiento de mecanografía *f*
- *typing compartment*
27 la secretaria del tren
- *secretary*
28 la máquina de escribir
- *typewriter*
29 el agente de comercio *m* (el hombre de negocios *m* –el ejecutivo– de viaje *m*)
- *travelling* (Am. *traveling) salesman (businessman on business trip)*
30 el dictáfono
- *dictating machine*
31 el micrófono
- *microphone*

**1-69  la locomotora de vapor** *m*
– *steam locomotives*
**2-37  la caldera de la locomotora y el mecanismo de propulsión** *f* **de la locomotora**
– *locomotive boiler and driving gear*
**2** la chapa de ténder *m*, con enganche *m*
– *tender platform with coupling*
**3** la válvula de seguridad *f*, para la sobrepresión de vapor *m*
– *safety valve for excess boiler pressure*
**4** la caja de fuego *m* (el hogar)
– *firebox*
**5** el emparrillado basculante
– *drop grate*
**6** el cenicero, con ventilación *f*
– *ashpan with damper doors*
**7** la compuerta de fondo *m* (la trampilla) del cenicero
– *bottom door of the ashpan*
**8** los tubos del humo
– *smoke tubes (flue tubes)*
**9** la bomba de alimentación *f* de agua *f*
– *feed pump*
**10** el cojinete del eje
– *axle bearing*
**11** la biela de acoplamiento *m*
– *connecting rod*
**12** la cúpula de caldera *f* (el domo de vapor *m*)
– *steam dome*

**13** la válvula reguladora (del vapor)
– *regulator valve (regulator main valve)*
**14** el domo de arena *f* (el depósito de arena *f*)
– *sand dome*
**15** los tubos de bajada *f* de la arena
– *sand pipes (sand tubes)*
**16** la caldera horizontal
– *boiler (boiler barrel)*
**17** los tubos del recalentador
– *fire tubes or steam tubes*
**18** el cambio de marcha *f*
– *reversing gear (steam reversing gear)*
**19** los tubos para echar la arena
– *sand pipes*
**20** la válvula de alimentación *f*
– *feed valve*
**21** la caja colectora del vapor (el colector de vapor *m*)
– *steam collector*
**22** la chimenea (salida *f* de humo *m* y de vapor *m* de escape *m*)
– *chimney (smokestack, smoke outlet and waste steam exhaust)*
**23** el precalentador del agua *f* de alimentación *f* (el precalentador de superficie *f*)
– *feedwater preheater (feedwater heater, economizer)*
**24** la rejilla parachispas
– *spark arrester*
**25** el tubo de escape *m*
– *blast pipe*

**26** la puerta de la caja de humos *m*
– *smokebox door*
**27** la cruceta
– *cross head*
**28** el colector de lodos *m*
– *mud drum*
**29** la rejilla separadora de lodos *m* del alimentador del agua *f*
– *top feedwater tray*
**30** la vara (el vástago) del distribuidor
– *combination lever*
**31** la caja del distribuidor
– *steam chest*
**32** el cilindro de vapor *m*
– *cylinder*
**33** el vástago del pistón (la biela) con prensaestopa *m*
– *piston rod with stuffing box (packing box)*
**34** el quitapiedras (*Arg.*: el miriñaque; *Chile*: la trompa; *P. Rico*: el botavaca)
– *guard iron (rail guard, Am. pilot, cowcatcher)*
**35** el eje portante
– *carrying axle (running axle, dead axle)*
**36** el eje acoplado
– *coupled axle*
**37** el eje motor
– *driving axle*
**38** la locomotora con ténder *m* para tren *m* expreso
– *express locomotive with tender*

# 211 Vehículos de ferrocarril V

1 la locomotora eléctrica
- *electric locomotive*
2 el pantógrafo de toma *f* de corriente *f*
- *current collector*
3 el interruptor principal
- *main switch*
4 el transformador de alta tensión f
- *high-tension transformer*
5 el cable del techo
- *roof cable*
6 el motor de tracción *f*
- *traction motor*
7 el sistema inductivo de control *m* de la marcha del tren
- *inductive train control system*
8 el depósito principal de aire *m*
- *main air reservoir*
9 el silbato
- *whistle*
10-18 el plano de la locomotora
- *plan of locomotive*
10 el transformador con cambio *m* de conexión *f*
- *transformer with tap changer*
11 el refrigerador de aceite *m* con ventilador *m*
- *oil cooler with blower*
12 la bomba de circulación *f* del aire
- *oil-circulating pump*
13 el mecanismo del cambio de conexión *f*
- *tap changer driving mechanism*
14 el compresor del aire
- *air compressor*
15 el ventilador del motor de tracción *f*
- *traction motor blower*
16 la caja de bornes *m*
- *terminal box*
17 los condensadores para los motores auxiliares
- *capacitors for auxiliary motors*
18 la tapa del conmutador
- *commutator cover*
19 la cabina del maquinista
- *cab (driver's cab, Am. engineer's cab)*
20 el volante del conductor
- *controller handwheel*
21 el interruptor de seguridad *f* del conductor
- *dead man's handle*
22 la válvula de freno del maquinista
- *driver's brake valve (Am. engineer's brake valve)*
23 la válvula del freno suplementario
- *ancillary brake valve (auxiliary brake valve)*
24 el manómetro del aire comprimido
- *pressure gauge (Am. gage)*
25 el interruptor de sobrepresión *f* del dispositivo de seguridad *f*
- *bypass switch for the dead man's handle*
26 el indicador de la tracción (el amperímetro de los motores de tracción *f*)
- *tractive effort indicator*
27 el voltímetro para la tensión de la calefacción
- *train heating voltage indicator*
28 el voltímetro de tensión *f* del hilo de contacto *m*
- *contact wire voltage indicator (overhead wire voltage indicator)*

29 el voltímetro de alta tensión *f*
- *high-tension voltage indicator*
30 el interruptor de mando *m* del pantógrafo
- *on/off switch for the current collector*
31 el interruptor principal
- *main switch*
32 el interruptor del arenero
- *sander switch (sander control)*
33 el interruptor para el freno de centrífuga *f*
- *anti-skid brake switch*
34 el indicador óptico de funcionamiento *m* de los motores auxiliares
- *visual display for the ancillary systems*
35 el velocímetro (el indicador de la velocidad)
- *speedometer*
36 el indicador del grado *m* de marcha *f*
- *running step indicator*
37 el reloj
- *clock*
38 los botones de mando *m* del sistema inductivo
- *controls for the inductive train control system*
39 el interruptor para la calefacción de la cabina del maquinista
- *cab heating switch*
40 la palanca para el silbato
- *whistle lever*
41 el coche automotor de mantenimiento de catenarias *f* (el coche automotor de plataforma *f* regulable), un coche automotor Diesel
- *contact wire maintenance vehicle (overhead wire maintenance vehicle), a diesel railcar*
42 la plataforma de trabajo *m*
- *work platform (working platform)*
43 la escala
- *ladder*
44-54 la instalación de maquinaria *f* del automotor de mantenimiento *m* de catenarias *f*
- *mechanical equipment of the contact wire maintenance vehicle*
44 el compresor de aire *m*
- *air compressor*
45 la bomba de aceite *m* del ventilador
- *blower oil pump*
46 la dinamo
- *generator*
47 el motor Diesel
- *diesel engine*
48 la bomba de inyección *f*
- *injection pump*
49 el silencioso
- *silencer (Am. muffler)*
50 el cambio de velocidades *f*
- *change-speed gear*
51 el árbol de transmisión *f* (el árbol de cardán *m*)
- *cardan shaft*
52 el engrase de la pestaña
- *wheel flange lubricator*
53 el engranaje de inversión *f* de marcha *f*
- *reversing gear*
54 el soporte del momento de torsión *f*
- *torque converter bearing*

55 el automotor de acumuladores *m*
- *accumulator railcar (battery railcar)*
56 la caja de la batería
- *battery box (battery container)*
57 la cabina del maquinista
- *cab (driver's cab, Am. engineer's cab)*
58 la disposición de los asientos de 2ª clase *f*
- *second-class seating arrangement*
59 el retrete (el excusado, el water-closet, el W. C.)
- *toilet (lavatory, WC)*
60 el automotor eléctrico rápido
- *fast electric multiple-unit train*
61 el coche automotor final
- *front railcar*
62 la coche automotor intermedio
- *driving trailer car*

# 212 Vehículos de ferrocarril VI

**1-84 la locomotora Diesel**
- *diesel locomotives*
1 **la locomotora Diesel hidráulica,** una locomotora Diesel de línea *f* para trenes *m* semipesados de viajeros *m* y mercancías *f*
- *diesel-hydraulic locomotive, a mainline locomotive for medium passenger and goods service (freight service)*
2 el bogie (el carretón)
- *bogie (truck)*
3 el juego de ruedas *f*
- *wheel and axle set*
4 el depósito principal de combustible *m*
- *main fuel tank*
5 la cabina del maquinista de una locomotora Diesel
- *cab (driver's cab, Am. engineer's cab) of a diesel locomotive*
6 el manómetro del conducto de aire *m* principal
- *main air pressure gauge (Am. gage)*
7 el manómetro del cilindro de freno *m*
- *brake cylinder pressure gauge (Am. gage)*
8 el manómetro del depósito de aire *m* principal
- *main air reservoir pressure gauge (Am. gage)*
9 el tacómetro (el velocímetro, el indicador de la velocidad *f*)
- *speedometer*
10 el freno de emergencia *f*
- *auxiliary brake*
11 la válvula de freno *m* del maquinista
- *driver's brake valve (Am. engineer's brake valve)*
12 el volante del combinador
- *controller handwheel*
13 el dispositivo de seguridad *f* (de hombre *m* muerto)
- *dead man's handle*
14 el sistema inductivo de control *m* de la marcha del tren
- *inductive train control system*
15 el avisador luminoso
- *signal lights*
16 el reloj
- *clock*
17 el voltímetro de la calefacción
- *voltage meter for the train heating system*
18 el amperímetro de la calefacción
- *current meter for the train heating system*
19 el termómetro del aceite del motor
- *engine oil temperature gauge (Am. gage)*
20 el termómetro del aceite de la transmisión
- *transmission oil temperature gauge (Am. gage)*
21 el termómetro del agua *f* de refrigeración *f*
- *cooling water temperature gauge (Am. gage)*
22 el cuentarrevoluciones del motor
- *revolution counter (rev counter, tachometer)*
23 el aparato de radio *f* del tren
- *radio telephone*
24 la locomotora Diesel hidráulica [en alzado y en plano]
- *diesel-hydraulic locomotive [plan and elevation]*
25 el motor Diesel
- *diesel engine*
26 la instalación de refrigeración *f*
- *cooling unit*
27 la transmisión hidráulica
- *fluid transmission*

28 la transmisión del juego de ruedas *f*
- *wheel and axle drive*
29 el árbol de transmisión *f* (el árbol cardán *m*)
- *cardan shaft*
30 el motor de arranque *m* eléctrico
- *starter motor*
31 la mesa de los instrumentos
- *instrument panel*
32 el pupitre del maquinista
- *driver's control desk (Am. engineer's control desk)*
33 el freno de mano *f*
- *hand brake*
34 el compresor de aire *m* con motor *m* eléctrico (electromotor *m*)
- *air compressor with electric motor*
35 el armario de los aparatos
- *equipment locker*
36 el intercambiador de calor *m* para el aceite de transmisión *f*
- *heat exchanger for transmission oil*
37 el ventilador del recinto de la máquina
- *engine room ventilator*
38 el electroimán inductivo del vehículo
- *magnet for the inductive train control system*
39 el generador de calefacción *f*
- *train heating generator*
40 el armario convertidor de calefacción *f*
- *casing of the train heating system transformer*
41 el precalentador
- *preheater*
42 el silencioso de escape *m*
- *exhaust silencer (Am. exhaust muffler)*
43 el intercambiador de calor *m* auxiliar para el aceite de transmisión *f*
- *auxiliary heat exchanger for the transmission oil*
44 el freno hidráulico
- *hydraulic brake*
45 la caja de las herramientas
- *tool box*
46 la batería de arranque *m*
- *starter battery*
47 **la locomotora Diesel hidráulica** para el servicio de maniobras *f* ligero o medio
- *diesel-hydraulic locomotive for light and medium shunting service*
48 el silencioso de escape *m*
- *exhaust silencer (Am. exhaust muffler)*
49 la campana y el silbato
- *bell and whistle*
50 la radio de maniobras *f*
- *yard radio*
**51-67 el alzado de la locomotora**
- *elevation of locomotive*
51 el motor Diesel con turbocompresor *m*
- *diesel engine with supercharged turbine*
52 la transmisión hidráulica
- *fluid transmission*
53 la transmisión secundaria
- *output gear box*
54 el radiador
- *radiator*
55 el intercambiador de calor *m* para el aceite de engrase *m* del motor
- *heat exchanger for the engine lubricating oil*
56 el depósito del combustible
- *fuel tank*
57 el depósito de aire *m* principal
- *main air reservoir*
58 el compresor de aire *m*
- *air compressor*
59 las cajas de arena *f*
- *sand boxes*

60 el depósito de reserva de combustible *m*
- *reserve fuel tank*
61 el depósito de combustible *m* auxiliar
- *auxiliary air reservoir*
62 la impulsión del ventilador hidrostático
- *hydrostatic fan drive*
63 el asiento con cofre *m* guardarropa
- *seat with clothes compartment*
64 el volante del freno de mano *f*
- *hand brake wheel*
65 el depósito de igualación *f* (de compensación *f*) del agua *f* de refrigeración *f*
- *cooling water*
66 el balasto de compensación *f*
- *ballast*
67 el volante de mando *m* del motor y de la transmisión
- *engine and transmission control wheel*
68 **la locomotora Diesel pequeña** para el servicio de maniobras *f*
- *small diesel locomotive for shunting service*
69 el silencioso
- *exhaust casing*
70 la bocina
- *horn*
71 el depósito de aire *m* principal
- *main air reservoir*
72 el compresor de aire *m*
- *air compressor*
73 el motor Diesel de ocho cilindros *m*
- *eight-cylinder diesel engine*
74 la transmisión Voith con mecanismo de inversión *f* de marcha *f*
- *Voith transmission with reversing gear*
75 el depósito de fuel-oil *m*
- *heating oil tank (fuel oil tank)*
76 la caja de arena *f*
- *sand box*
77 la instalación de refrigeración *f*
- *cooling unit*
78 el depósito de igualación *f* (de compensación *f*) del agua *f* de refrigeración *f*
- *header tank for the cooling water*
79 el filtro de aire *m* con baño *m* de aceite *m*
- *oil bath air cleaner (oil bath air filter)*
80 el volante del freno de mano *f*
- *hand brake wheel*
81 el volante de mando *m*
- *control wheel*
82 el embrague
- *coupling*
83 el árbol de transmisión *f* (el árbol cardán *m*)
- *cardan shaft*
84 la persiana
- *louvred shutter*

**213 Vehículos de ferrocarril VII**

1 la locomotora Diesel hidráulica
- *diesel-hydraulic locomotive*
2 la cabina del maquinista
- *cab (driver's cab, Am. engineer's cab)*
3 el juego de ruedas *f*
- *wheel and axle set*
4 la antena para la radio de las maniobras
- *aerial for the yard radio*
5 el vagón plataforma normal
- *standard flat wagon (Am. standard flatcar)*
6 el telero articulado de acero *m*
- *hinged steel stanchion (stanchion)*
7 el tope
- *buffers*
8 el vagón de mercancías *f* abierto normal (la batea; Amér.: la zorra)
- *standard open goods wagon (Am. standard open freight car)*
9 las puertas giratorias de la pared lateral
- *revolving side doors*
10 la pared frontal articulada
- *hinged front*
11 el vagón plataforma de bogies *m* normal
- *standard flat wagon (Am. standard flatcar) with bogies*

12 el tirante de refuerzo *m* de bastidor *m*
- *sole bar reinforcement*
13 el bogie (el carretón)
- *bogie (truck)*
14 el vagón de mercancías *f* cubierto
- *covered goods van (covered goods wagon, Am. boxcar)*
15 la puerta de corredera *f*
- *sliding door*
16 la ventana de aireación *f*
- *ventilation flap*
17 el quitanieves rotativo, una máquina limpiavías
- *snow blower (rotary snow plough, Am. snowplow), a track-clearing vehicle*
18 el vagón para descarga *f* neumática
- *wagon (Am. car) with pneumatic discharge*
19 la boca de carga *f* (la abertura de relleno *m*)
- *filler hole*
20 el empalme de aire *m* comprimido
- *compressed-air supply*
21 el empalme de descarga *f*
- *discharge connection valve*

22 el vagón de techo *m* de corredera *f*
- *goods van (Am. boxcar) with sliding roof*
23 la abertura del techo
- *roof opening*
24 el vagón abierto de bogies *m* de descarga *f* automática
- *bogie open self-discharge wagon (Am. bogie open self-discharge freight car)*
25 el lateral de descarga *f*
- *discharge flap (discharge door)*

26 el **vagón de bogies de techo** *m*
   pivotante
 – *bogie wagon with swivelling
   (Am. swiveling) roof*
27 el techo pivotante
 – *swivelling (Am. swiveling) roof*
28 al vagón de enrejado *m* de
   listones *m* de gran capacidad *f*
   para el transporte de
   animales *m* pequeños
 – *large-capacity wagon (Am.
   large-capacity car) for small
   livestock*
29 la pared lateral permeable al
   aire
 – *sidewall with ventilation flaps
   (slatted wall)*
30 la ventana de aireación *f*
 – *ventilation flap*
31 el vagón cisterna *f*
 – *tank wagon (Am. tank car)*
32 el automóvil de rail *m* (la
   vagoneta automóvil)
 – *track inspection railcar*
33 los vagones de plataforma *f*
   especial
 – *open special wagons (Am. open
   special freight cars)*
34 el camión con remolque *m*
 – *lorry (Am. truck) with trailer*

35 el vagón de dos pisos *m* para el
   transporte de automóviles *m*
 – *two-tier car carrier (double-deck
   car carrier)*
36 la rampa de acceso *m*
 – *hinged upper deck*
37 el vagón con vagonetas *f*
   basculantes
 – *tipper wagon (Am. dump car)
   with skips*
38 la vagoneta basculante
 – *skip*
39 el vagón frigorífico universal
 – *general-purpose refrigerator
   wagon (refrigerator van, Am.
   refrigerator car)*
40 la estructura superior
   intercambiable para el vagón
   plataforma
 – *interchangeable bodies for flat
   wagons (Am. flatcars)*

**1-14 ferrocarriles** *m* **de montaña** *f* **de riel** *m*
- *mountain railways* (Am. *mountain railroads*)

**1** el automotor, con adherencia *f* forzada
- *adhesion railcar*

**2** la tracción
- *drive*

**3** el freno de emergencia *f*
- *emergency brake*

**4-5** el ferrocarril de montaña *f* de cremallera *f*
- *rack mountain railway (rack-and-pinion railway, cog railway,* Am. *cog railroad, rack railroad)*

**4** la locomotora eléctrica de cremallera *f*
- *electric rack railway locomotive (*Am. *electric rack railroad locomotive)*

**5** el coche (el vagón) del ferrocarril de cremallera *f*
- *rack railway coach (rack railway trailer,* Am. *rack railroad car)*

**6** el túnel
- *tunnel*

**7-11 ferrocarriles** *m* **de cremallera** *f* **[sistema]**
- *rack railways (rack-and-pinion railways,* Am. *rack railroads) [systems]*

**7** la rueda de adherencia *f*
- *running wheel (carrying wheel)*

**8** la rueda dentada de tracción *f* (el piñón de tracción *f*)
- *driving pinion*

**9** la cremallera
- *rack [with teeth machined on top edge]*

**10** el riel
- *rail*

**11** la cremallera horizontal doble
- *rack [with teeth on both outer edges]*

**12** el funicular
- *funicular railway (funicular, cable railway)*

**13** el coche del funicular
- *funicular railway car*

**14** el cable de tracción *f*
- *haulage cable*

**15-38 funiculares** *m* **aéros de viajeros** *m* **(teleféricos** *m***)**
- *cableways (ropeways, cable suspension lines)*

**15-24 teleféricos** *m* **monocables, teleférico** *m* **de cable** *m* **sin fin** *m*
- *single-cable ropeways (single-cable suspension lines, endless cableways, endless ropeways)*

**15** el telesquí
- *drag lift*

**16-18** el telesilla
- *chair lift*

**16** la telesilla ligera, una telesilla individual
- *lift chair, a single chair*

**17** la telesilla doble, una telesilla de dos plazas *f*
- *double lift chair, a two-seater chair*

**18** la telesilla doble cubierta
- *double chair (two-seater chair) with coupling*

**19** el telecabina, un teleférico de cable *m* sin fin *m*
- *gondola cableway, an endless cableway*

**20** la cabina
- *gondola (cabin)*

**21** el cable sin fin *m*, un cable portante y de tracción *f*
- *endless cable, a suspension (supporting) and haulage cable*

**22** el riel de maniobra *f* (el riel de rodeo *m*)
- *U-rail*

**23** el pilón soporte *m*
- *single-pylon support*

**24** el castillete soporte *m*
- *gantry support*

**25** el teleférico bicable, un teleférico de lanzadera *f*
- *double-cable ropeway (double-cable suspension line), a suspension line with balancing cabins*

**26** el cable de tracción *f*
- *haulage cable*

**27** el cable portante
- *suspension cable (supporting cable)*

**28** la cabina para viajeros *m*
- *cabin*

**29** el pilón intermedio
- *intermediate support*

**30** el teleférico, un teleférico bicable
- *cableway (ropeway, suspension line), a double-cable ropeway (double-cable suspension line)*

**31** el castillete con estructura *f* de celosía *f*
- *pylon*

32 la polea del cable de tracción *f*
– *haulage cable roller*
33 el soporte del cable portante
– *cable guide rail (suspension cable bearing)*
34 la caja de la vagoneta, una caja basculante
– *skip, a tipping bucket* (Am. *dumping bucket*)
35 la palanca para descargar el volquete
– *stop*
36 el tren de poleas *f* de rodadura *f*
– *pulley cradle*
37 el cable de tracción *f*
– *haulage cable*
38 el cable portante
– *suspension cable (supporting cable)*
39 **la estación del valle**
– *valley station (lower station)*
40 el foso para el tensor (para el contrapeso)
– *tension weight shaft*
41 el tensor (el contrapeso) del cable portante
– *tension weight for the suspension cable (supporting cable)*
42 el tensor del cable tractor
– *tension weight for the haulage cable*
43 la polea del cable de tensión *f*
– *tension cable pulley*
44 el cable portante
– *suspension cable (supporting cable)*
45 el cable tractor (el cable de tracción *f*)
– *haulage cable*
46 el contracable (el cable inferior)
– *balance cable (lower cable)*
47 el cable auxiliar
– *auxiliary cable (emergency cable)*
48 el dispositivo de tensión *f* del cable auxiliar
– *auxiliary-cable tensioning mechanism (emergency-cable tensioning mechanism)*
49 los rodillos de apoyo *m* del cable tractor
– *haulage cable rollers*
50 el amortiguador de muelle *m*
– *spring buffer* (Am. *spring bumper*)
51 el andén de la estación del valle
– *valley station platform (lower station platform)*
52 la cabina de viajeros *m* (la góndola del teleférico), una cabina de gran capacidad *f*
– *cabin (cableway gondola, ropeway gondola, suspension line gondola), a large-capacity cabin*
53 el tren de poleas *f* de rodadura *f*
– *pulley cradle*
54 el sistema de suspensión *f*
– *suspension gear*
55 el amortiguador del balanceo
– *stabilizer*
56 el tope (la viga de tope *m*)
– *guide rail*
57 **la estación de montaña** *f*
– *top station (upper station)*
58 el soporte del cable portante
– *suspension cable guide (supporting cable guide)*
59 el anclaje del cable portante
– *suspension cable anchorage (supporting cable anchorage)*

60 la batería de rodillos *m* del cable tractor
– *haulage cable rollers*
61 la polea de vuelta *f* del cable tractor
– *haulage cable guide wheel*
62 la polea motriz del cable tractor
– *haulage cable driving pulley*
63 la propulsión (el motor) principal
– *main drive*
64 la propulsión (el motor) de reserva *f*
– *standby drive*
65 la cabina del maquinista
– *control room*
66 **el tren de poleas *f* de rodadura *f* de la cabina**
– *cabin pulley cradle*
67 el travesaño (la viga principal) del tren de poleas *f*
– *main pulley cradle*
68 la cuna doble
– *double cradle*
69 la cuna de dos ruedas *f*
– *two-wheel cradle*
70 los rodillos del tren de poleas *f*
– *running wheels*
71 el freno del cable portante, un freno de emergencia *f* en caso *m* de rotura *f* del cable tractor
– *suspension cable brake (supporting cable brake), an emergency brake in case of haulage cable failure*
72 la articulación (el eje, el bulón) de la suspensión
– *suspension gear bolt*
73 el manguito del cable tractor
– *haulage cable sleeve*
74 el manguito del contracable
– *balance cable sleeve (lower cable sleeve)*
75 la protección para evitar los descarrilamientos
– *derailment guard*
76 **pilones *m* de teleférico *m*** (pilones *m* intermedios)
– *cable supports (ropeway supports, suspension line supports, intermediate supports)*
77 el castillete de acero *m* con estructura *f* de celosía *f*, un castillete armado
– *pylon, a framework support*
78 el castillete (el pilón) de tubos *m* de acero *m*, un apoyo tubular de acero *m*
– *tubular steel pylon, a tubular steel support*
79 el soporte del cable portante (el soporte de apoyo *m*)
– *suspension cable guide rail (supporting cable guide rail, support guide rail)*
80 el andamio (las horcas) del pilón, un montaje para los trabajos en los cables
– *support truss, a frame for work on the cable*
81 los cimientos del pilón
– *base of the support*

1 el corte transversal de un puente
- *cross-section of a bridge*
2 la plataforma del tablero ortogonal anisótropo
- *orthotropic roadway (orthotropic deck)*
3 la armadura sobre puntales *m*
- *truss (bracing)*
4 el apuntalamiento (el arriostramiento)
- *diagonal brace (diagonal strut)*
5 el cajón hueco
- *hollow tubular section*
6 la chapa del tablero
- *deck slab*
7 el puente de vigas *f*
- *solid-web girder bridge (beam bridge)*
8 el borde superior del tablero
- *road surface*
9 el larguero (arco *m*) superior
- *top flange*
10 el larguero (arco *m*) inferior
- *bottom flange*
11 el soporte (el apoyo) fijo
- *fixed bearing*
12 el soporte (el apoyo) móvil
- *movable bearing*
13 el tramo de puente *m*
- *clear span*
14 la abertura (la luz)
- *span*
15 el puente de cuerdas *f* (el puente colgante primitivo)
- *rope bridge (primitive suspension bridge)*
16 el cable portador
- *carrying rope*
17 el cable colgante
- *suspension rope*
18 la pasarela trenzada
- *woven deck (woven decking)*
19 el puente de arcos *m* de piedra *f* (un puente de piedra *f*), un puente macizo
- *stone arch bridge, a solid bridge*
20 el arco del puente
- *arch*
21 el pilar del puente
- *pier*
22 la figura (la estatua) del puente
- *statue of saint on bridge*
23 el puente de arco *m* de entramado *m*
- *trussed arch bridge*
24 el elemento de entramado *m*
- *truss element*
25 el arco de entramado *m*
- *trussed arch*
26 la abertura del arco
- *arch span*
27 el pilar de tierra *f*
- *abutment (end pier)*
28 el puente de arco *m* sobre pilares *m*
- *spandrel-braced arch bridge*
29 el arranque del arco (el espolón)
- *abutment (abutment pier)*
30 el pilar del puente
- *bridge strut*
31 el vértice del arco
- *crown*
32 el puente de casas *f* medieval (el Puente Vecchio de Florencia)
- *covered bridge of the Middle Ages; here: the* Ponte Vecchio *in Florence*

33 el comercio de orfebre *m*
- *goldsmiths' shops*
34 el puente de entramado *m* metálico
- *steel lattice bridge*
35 la diagonal (puntal *m*)
- *counterbrace (crossbrace, diagonal member)*
36 el pilar del puente (la vertical)
- *vertical member*
37 el nudo del entramado
- *truss joint*
38 el pórtico del extremo
- *portal frame*
39 el puente colgante
- *suspension bridge*
40 el cable portador
- *suspension cable*
41 el colgante
- *suspender (hanger)*
42 el pilón (pórtico *m* de puente *m*)
- *tower*
43 el amarre del cable portador
- *suspension cable anchorage*
44 el tirante
- *tied beam [with roadway]*
45 el espolón
- *abutment*
46 el puente de cables *m* oblicuos
- *cable-stayed bridge*
47 el cable de enganche *m* (el cable oblicuo)
- *inclined tension cable*
48 el amarre del cable oblicuo
- *inclined cable anchorage*
49 el puente de hormigón *m* armado
- *reinforced concrete bridge*
50 el arco de hormigón *m* armado
- *reinforced concrete arch*
51 el sistema de cables *m* oblicuos
- *inclined cable system, a multiple cable system*
52 el puente llano, un puente sin pared *f*
- *flat bridge, a plate girder bridge*
53 el tensor transversal
- *stiffener*
54 el pilar
- *pier*
55 el apoyo (apoyo *m* de puente *m*)
- *bridge bearing*
56 el rompehielos
- *cutwater*
57 el puente de elementos *m* prefabricados
- *straits bridge, a bridge built of precast elements*
58 el elemento prefabricado
- *precast construction unit*
59 el viaducto
- *viaduct*
60 la vaguada
- *valley bottom*
61 el pilar de hormigón *m* armado
- *reinforced concrete pier*
62 el andamiaje
- *scaffolding*
63 el puente metálico de celosía *f* giratorio
- *lattice swing bridge*
64 la corona de rotación *f* (la corona giratoria)
- *turntable*
65 el pilar de rotación *f* (el pilar giratorio)
- *pivot pier*

66 la mitad giratoria del puente (el medio puente)
- *pivoting half (pivoting section, pivoting span, movable half) of bridge*
67 el puente giratorio llano
- *flat swing bridge*
68 la pared central
- *middle section*
69 la espiga de giro *m*
- *pivot*
70 el parapeto (la barandilla del puente)
- *parapet (handrailing)*

1 la balsa de cuerda *f* (*con propulsión
f propia:* balsa *f* con motor *m;
también:* balsa *f* de cadena *f;
Cuba:* el andarivel); una balsa
para pasajeros *m*
– *cable ferry, a passenger ferry;* also:
*chain ferry*
2 el cable (la cuerda) de la balsa
– *ferry rope (ferry cable)*
3 el brazo de río *m*
– *river branch (river arm)*
4 el islote fluvial
– *river island (river islet)*
5 la parte desplomada de la orilla
del río, efecto *m* de una
inundación
– *collapsed section of riverbank, flood
damage*
6 el transbordador con motor *m*
– *motor ferry*
7 el embarcadero de los barcos de
motor *m*
– *ferry landing stage (motorboat
landing stage)*
8 la cimentación sobre pilotes *m*
– *pile foundations*
9 la corriente (el curso del río)
– *current*
10 la balsa volante (el puente volante,
la balsa de río *m*), un
transbordador de coches *m*
– *flying ferry (river ferry), a car ferry*
11 el transbordador
– *ferry boat*
12 el flotador
– *buoy (float)*
13 el anclaje
– *anchorage*
14 el lugar de anclaje *m* (el puerto de
protección *f*, el puerto de
invierno *m*)
– *harbour* (Am. *harbor) for laying up
river craft*
15 la barca de botador *m*, una barca
de pértiga *f* (*Bol. y Ec.:* la
montería)
– *ferry boat (punt)*
16 la pértiga (*Ec.:* el guare; *Perú:* la
tangona)
– *pole (punt pole, quant pole)*
17 el barquero (*Col.:* el pasero)
– *ferryman*
18 el brazo muerto del río
– *blind river branch (blind river arm)*
19 el malecón (*Amér. Central y Chile:*
el tajamar)
– *groyne* (Am. *groin)*
20 el espigón (la cabeza del malecón)
– *groyne* (Am. *groin) head*
21 el canal de navegación *f* (parte *m*
del cauce)
– *fairway (navigable part of river)*
22 la flotilla de remolque *m*
– *train of barges*
23 el remolcador fluvial de vapor *m*
– *river tug*
24 el cable de remolque *m*
– *tow rope (tow line, towing hawser)*
25 la lancha de remolque *m* (la
lancha de carga *f*, la gabarra)
– *barge (freight barge, cargo barge,
lighter)*
26 el gabarrero
– *bargeman (bargee, lighterman)*
27 la navegación al la sirga
– *towing (hauling, haulage)*

28 el mástil de sirga *f*
– *towing mast*
29 el motor de sirga *f*
– *towing engine*
30 la vía de sirga *f*
– *towing track;* form.: *tow path
(towing path)*
31 el río, después de la regulación del
río
– *river after river training*
32 el dique contra la inundación (el
dique de invierno *m*)
– *dike (dyke, main dike, flood wall), a
winter dike*
33 el canal de desagüe *m*
– *drainage ditch*
34 la esclusa del dique (*Col., Chile,
Guat. y Perú:* la toma)
– *dike (dyke) drainage sluice*
35 el muro de ala *f*
– *wing wall*
36 el desagüe, una zanja de drenaje *m*
– *outfall*
37 la zanja lateral (la evacuación del
agua *f* de infiltración *f*)
– *drain, an infiltration drain*
38 la berma del dique
– *berm (berme)*
39 la coronación del dique
– *top of dike (dyke)*
40 el declive (la escarpa) del dique
– *dike (dyke) batter (dike slope)*
41 el lecho de inundación *f*
– *flood bed (inundation area)*
42 la zona de inundación *f*
– *flood containment area*
43 el indicador de la corriente
– *current meter*
44 el tablero kilométrico
– *kilometre* (Am. *kilometer) sign*
45 la casa del guarda del dique;
*también:* la casa del balsero
– *dikereeve's (dykereeve's) house
(dikereeve's cottage);* also:
*ferryman's house (cottage)*
46 el guarda del dique
– *dikereeve (dykereeve)*
47 la rampa del dique
– *dike (dyke) ramp*
48 el dique de verano *m*
– *summer dike (dyke)*
49 la presa (el dique) de río *m* (*Col.:*
la tupia)
– *levee (embankment)*
50 los sacos de arena *f*
– *sandbags*
51-55 la consolidación de la orilla
– *bank protection (bank stabilization,
revetment)*
51 la capa (el relleno) de piedras *f*
– *riprap*
52 el depósito aluvial (el depósito de
arena *f*)
– *alluvial deposit (sand deposit)*
53 la fajina (el haz de ramas *f*)
– *fascine (bundle of wooden sticks)*
54 la cerca trenzada
– *wicker fences*
55 el revestimiento de piedras *f* (el
muro de contención *f*)
– *stone pitching*
56 la draga flotante, una draga con
cadena *f* de cangilones *m*
– *floating dredging machine
(dredger), a multi-bucket ladder
dredge*

57 la cadena de cangilones *m*
– *bucket elevator chain*
58 el cangilón de extracción *f*
– *dredging bucket*
59 la draga de succión *f*, con tubo *m*
descendente de aspiración *f* o
aspirador *m* de gabarras *f*
– *suction dredger (hydraulic dredger)
with trailing suction pipe or barge
sucker*
60 la bomba de agua *f* a presión *f*
– *centrifugal pump*
61 la válvula de limpiado *m* de
retroacción *f*
– *back scouring valve*
62 la bomba de succión *f*, una bomba
de manga *f* con boquillas *f*
– *suction pump, a jet pump with
scouring nozzles*

1-14 **el muro de muelle** *m*
– *quay wall*
1 el pavimento
– *road surface*
2 el cuerpo del muro
– *body of wall*
3 la viga de acero *m*
– *steel sleeper*
4 el pilote de acero *m*
– *steel pile*
5 la hilera de estacas *f* (el tablestacado)
– *sheet pile wall (sheet pile bulkhead, sheet piling)*
6 la tablestaca (la chapa de hierro *m*)
– *box pile*
7 el terraplén (el relleno)
– *backfilling (filling)*
8 la escala
– *ladder*
9 la defensa (pilote *m* de defensa *f*)
– *fender (fender pile)*
10 el nicho bolardo (la cruz de amarre *m*)
– *recessed bollard*
11 el noray (el bolardo) doble
– *double bollard*
12 el noray (el bolardo)
– *bollard*
13 el noray en forma *f* de cruz *f*
– *cross-shaped bollard (cross-shaped mooring bitt)*
14 el noray de doble cruz *f*
– *double cross-shaped bollard (double cross-shaped mooring bitt)*
15-28 **el canal**
– *canal*
15-16 la entrada del canal
– *canal entrance*

15 el malecón (*Amér. Central y Chile:* el tajamar)
– *mole*
16 el rompeolas
– *breakwater*
17-25 la escalera de esclusas *f*
– *staircase of locks*
17 la testa de abajo (el morro inferior)
– *lower level*
18 la compuerta de esclusa *f*, una puerta de corredera *f*
– *lock gate, a sliding gate*
19 la puerta de esclusa *f*
– *mitre (Am. miter) gate*
20 la esclusa (la cámara de la esclusa; *Col., Chile, Guat., y Perú:* la toma)
– *lock (lock chamber)*
21 la sala de máquina *f*
– *power house*
22 el cabrestante de arrastre *m*, un cabrestante
– *warping capstan (hauling capstan), a capstan*
23 el cable de arrastre *m*, un cable (un cabo)
– *warp*
24 el edificio de administración *f* (*ejemplo:* la administración del canal, el servicio de protección *f* de las aguas, la aduana)
– *offices, e.g. river police, customs*
25 la testa de arriba (el morro superior)
– *upper level (head)*
26 el antepuerto de la esclusa, un antepuerto
– *lock approach*
27 el flanco del canal (el apartadero)
– *lay-by*

28 el talud de orilla *f*
– *bank slope*
29-38 **el elevador de barcos** *m*
– *boat lift (Am. boat elevator)*
29 el tramo inferior del canal
– *lower pound (lower reach)*
30 el fondo del canal
– *canal bed*
31 la puerta del tramo final, una puerta elevadora
– *pound lock gate, a vertical gate*
32 la puerta de cierre *m* de la cámara
– *lock gate*
33 el depósito del barco
– *boat tank (caisson)*
34 el flotador, un cuerpo ascensional
– *float*
35 el pozo del flotador
– *float shaft*
36 el husillo (el tornillo) de elevación *f*
– *lifting spindle*
37 el tramo superior
– *upper pound (upper reach)*
38 la puerta levadiza
– *vertical gate*
39-46 **la central hidráulica de bombeo** *m*
– *pumping plant and reservoir*
39 el embalse artificial
– *forebay*
40 el depósito de distribución *f* (la cámara de carga *f*)
– *surge tank*
41 la tubería bajo presión *f*
– *pressure pipeline*
42 la sala de válvulas *f* de compuertas *f*
– *valve house (valve control house)*
43 la sala de turbinas *f* (la sala de bombeo *m*)
– *turbine house (pumping station)*

44 la construcción de salida *f*
 – *discharge structure (outlet structure)*
45 la sala de mandos *m*
 – *control station*
46 la instalación del transformador
 – *transformer station*
47-52 **la bomba de rueda *f* de paletas *f*** (la bomba de hélice *f*)
 – *axial-flow pump (propeller pump)*
47 el motor de impulsión *f*
 – *drive motor*
48 la transmisión
 – *gear*
49 el árbol motor
 – *drive shaft*
50 el tubo de presión *f*
 – *pressure pipe*
51 el embudo de aspiración *f*
 – *suction head*
52 la rueda de paletas *f* (la hélice)
 – *impeller wheel*
53-56 **la corredera** (la válvula compuerta *f* de paso *m* o de cierre *m*)
 – *sluice valve (sluice gate)*
53 la impulsión (el mando) de manivela *f*
 – *crank drive*
54 el cuerpo de la válvula
 – *valve housing*
55 la válvula
 – *sliding valve (sliding gate)*
56 la abertura de descarga *f*
 – *discharge opening*
57-64 **la presa** (*Col.:* la tupia)
 – *dam (barrage)*
57 el pantano (*Col.:* el pantanero)
 – *reservoir (storage reservoir, impounding reservoir, impounded reservoir)*

58 el muro de contención *f*
 – *masonry dam*
59 la coronación del muro
 – *crest of dam*
60 el rebosadero (aliviadero *m*)
 – *spillway (overflow spillway)*
61 la zona de caída *f*
 – *stilling basin (stilling box, stilling pool)*
62 la descarga del fondo
 – *scouring tunnel (outlet tunnel, waste water outlet)*
63 la sala de válvulas *f* de compuertas *f*
 – *valve house (valve control house)*
64 la sala de turbinas *f*
 – *power station*
65-72 **el dique de cilindros** *m* (la presa cilíndrica), una represa; *otro sistema:* el dique basculante
 – *rolling dam, a barrage;* also: *shutter weir*
65 el cilindro, el cuerpo de contención *f*
 – *roller, a barrier*
66 el coronamiento del cilindro
 – *roller top*
67 la chapa lateral
 – *flange*
68 el cilindro sumergible
 – *submersible roller*
69 la cremallera
 – *rack track*
70 el nicho
 – *recess*
71 la cabina del mecanismo de elevación *f*
 – *hoisting gear cabin*
72 la pasarela de servicio *m*
 – *service bridge (walkway)*

73-80 **la presa de compuertas** *f*
 – *sluice dam*
73 el puente del mecanismo de elevación *f* por enrollamiento *m*
 – *hoisting gear bridge*
74 el mecanismo de enrollamiento *m*
 – *hoisting gear (winding gear)*
75 el canal guía *f*
 – *guide groove*
76 el contrapeso
 – *counterweight (counterpoise)*
77 la compuerta
 – *sluice gate (floodgate)*
78 el nervio de refuerzo *m*
 – *reinforcing rib*
79 el fondo de la presa
 – *dam sill (weir sill)*
80 el muro de la parte lateral (el contrafuerte)
 – *wing wall*

**1-6 el barco de remos** *m* **germánico**
[aproximadamente 400 d. J. C.] el
barco Nydam
- *Germanic rowing boat [ca. AD*
*400], the Nydam boat*
**1** el codaste
- *stern post*
**2** el timonel
- *steersman*
**3** los remeros
- *oarsman*
**4** la roda
- *stem post (stem)*
**5** el remo para bogar
- *oar, for rowing*
**6** el timo (el remo timón), un timón
lateral para gobernar
- *rudder (steering oar), a side rudder,*
*for steering*
**7 la canoa** (*Col.:* el bote; *Ec.:* el
guampo), un tronco de árbol *m*
vaciado
- *dugout, a hollowed-out tree trunk*
**8** la pagaya
- *paddle*
**9-12 la trirreme,** un barco de
guerra *f* romano
- *trireme, a Roman warship*
**9** el espolón
- *ram*
**10** el castillo
- *forecastle (fo'c'sle)*
**11** el garabato, un gancho para
sujetar el barco enemigo
- *grapple (grapnel, grappling iron),*
*for fastening the enemy ship*
*alongside*
**12** las tres líneas de remos *m*
- *three banks (tiers) of oars*
**13-17 el barco vikingo** (dragón *m*
vikingo, barco *m* dragón, el
dragón marino, el caballo del mar)
[nórdico antiguo]
- *Viking longship, a dragon ship*
*[Norse]*
**13** la caña del timón (la barra)
- *helm (tiller)*
**14** la horquilla del toldo, con
cabezas *f* de caballos *m* esculpidas
- *awning crutch with carved horses'*
*heads*
**15** el toldo
- *awning*
**16** la cabeza de dragón *m*
- *dragon figurehead*
**17** el escudo de protección *f*
- *shield*
**18-26 la kogge** (la kogge anseática)
- *cog, a Hansa cog (Hansa ship)*
**18** el cable del ancla *f* (la marona del
ancla *f*)
- *anchor cable (anchor rope, anchor*
*hawser)*
**19** el castillo de proa *f* (el castillo
delantero)
- *forecastle (fo'c'sle)*
**20** el bauprés
- *bowsprit*
**21** la vela cuadrada aferrada
- *furled (brailed-up) square sail*
**22** el pendón de la ciudad
- *town banner (city banner)*
**23** el castillo de popa *f* (el castillo
trasero)
- *aftercastle (sterncastle)*
**24** el timón, un timón de codaste *m*
- *rudder, a stem rudder*

**25** la popa redonda
- *elliptical stern (round stern)*
**26** la defensa de madera *f*
- *wooden fender*
**27-43 la carabela** [Santa María 1492]
- *caravel (carvel) ['Santa María'*
*1492]*
**27** el camarote del almirante
- *admiral's cabin*
**28** la verga de popa *f*
- *spanker boom*
**29** la mesana, una vela latina
- *mizzen (mizen, mutton spanker,*
*lateen spanker), a lateen sail*
**30** la verga de mesana *f* (la verga
latina)
- *lateen yard*
**31** el palo de mesana *f*
- *mizzen (mizen) mast*
**32** la ligada
- *lashing*
**33** la vela mayor, una vela cuadrada
- *mainsail (main course), a square*
*sail*
**34** la boneta, una vela desmontable
- *bonnet, a removable strip of canvas*
**35** la bolina
- *bowline*
**36** el briol
- *bunt line (martinet)*
**37** la verga mayor
- *main yard*
**38** la gavia mayor
- *main topsail*
**39** la verga de la gavia mayor
- *main topsail yard*
**40** el palo mayor
- *mainmast*
**41** la vela de trinquete *m*
- *foresail (fore course)*
**42** el palo de trinquete *m*
- *foremast*
**43** la cebadera
- *spritsail*
**44-50 la galera** [siglos XV a XVIII],
una galera de esclavos *m*
- *galley [15th to 18th century], a*
*slave galley*
**44** el fanal (el farol de popa *f*)
- *lantern*
**45** el camarote
- *cabin*
**46** la crujía
- *central gangway*
**47** el vigilante de los esclavos (el
cómitre), con látigo *m*
- *slave driver with whip*
**48** los esclavos de la galera (los
esclavos remeros, los galeotes)
- *galley slaves*
**49** la "rambata", una plataforma
cubierta de proa *f*
- *covered platform in the forepart of*
*the ship*
**50** el cañón
- *gun*
**51-60 el barco de línea** *f* [siglos
XVIII–XIX], un navío de tres
puentes *m*
- *ship of the line (line-of-battle ship)*
*[18th to 19th century], a three-*
*decker*
**51** el botalón de foque *m*
- *jib boom*
**52** la vela de juanete *m* de proa *f*
- *fore topgallant sail*

**53** la vela de juanete *m* del palo
mayor
- *main topgallant sail*
**54** la vela de juanete *m* de mesana *f*
- *mizzen (mizen) topgallant sail*
**55-57** la popa ornamentada
- *gilded stern*
**55** el espejo de popa *f*
- *upper stern*
**56** la galería (el corredor) de popa *f*
- *stern gallery*
**57** el mirador, una estructura con
ventanas *f* laterales ornamentadas
- *quarter gallery, a projecting balcony*
*with ornamental portholes*
**58** la bovedilla
- *lower stern*
**59** las troneras (las portas), para el
fuego de andanada *f*
- *gunports for broadside fire*
**60** el cierre de la porta
- *gunport shutter*

**1-72 el aparejo y el velamen de una corbeta de tres palos** *m*
- *rigging (rig, tackle) and sails of a bark (barque)*

**1-9 los palos**
- *masts*

**1 el bauprés con botalón** *m*
- *bowsprit with jib boom*

**2-4 el palo de trinquete** *m*
- *foremast*

**2 el macho del trinquete**
- *lower foremast*

**3 el mastelero de velacho** *m*
- *fore topmast*

**4 el mastelero del juanete de proa** *f*
- *fore topgallant mast*

**5-7 el palo mayor**
- *mainmast*

**5 el macho del palo mayor**
- *lower mainmast*

**6 el mastelero de gavia** *f*
- *main topmast*

**7 el mastelero de juanete** *m* **mayor**
- *main topgallant mast*

**8-9 el palo de mesana** *f*
- *mizzen (mizen) mast*

**8 el macho de mesana** *f*
- *lower mizzen (lower mizen)*

**9 el mastelero de mesana** *f*
- *mizzen (mizen) topmast*

**10-19 la jarcia muerta**
- *standing rigging*

**10 el estay**
- *forestay, mizzen (mizen) stay, mainstay*

**11 el estay del mastelero de trinquete** *m*
- *fore topmast stay, main topmast stay, mizzen (mizen) topmast stay*

**12 el estay mastelerillo de trinquete** *m*
- *fore topgallant stay, mizzen (mizen) topgallant stay, main topgallant stay*

**13 el estay mastelerillo sobrejuanete**
- *fore royal stay (main royal stay)*

**14 el estay de foque** *m*
- *jib stay*

**15 el barbiquejo**
- *bobstay*

**16 los obenques**
- *shrouds*

**17 los obenques de mastelero** *m*
- *fore topmast rigging (main topmast rigging, mizzen (mizen) topmast rigging)*

**18 los obenques de mastelerillo** *m* **de trinquete** *m*
- *fore topgallant rigging (main topgallant rigging)*

**19 los brandales**
- *backstays*

**20-31 las velas de cuchillo** *m*
- *fore-and-aft sails*

**20 el contrafoque**
- *fore topmast staysail*

**21 el fofoque (el foque de dentro)**
- *inner jib*

**22 el foque**
- *outer jib*

**23 el petifoque**
- *flying jib*

**24 la vela del estay de gavia** *f*
- *main topmast staysail*

**25 la vela del estay de juanete** *m*
- *main topgallant staysail*

**26 la vela del estay de sobrejuanete** *m*
- *main royal staysail*

**27 la vela del estay de mesana** *f*
- *mizzen (mizen) staysail*

**28 la vela del estay de sobremesana** *f*
- *mizzen (mizen) topmast staysail*

**29 la vela del estay de perico** *m*
- *mizzen (mizen) topgallant staysail*

**30 la vela cangreja (la mesana)**
- *mizzen (mizen, spanker, driver)*

**31 la escandalosa**
- *gaff topsail*

**32-45 las vergas**
- *spars*

**32 la verga de trinquete** *m*
- *foreyard*

**33 la verga de velacho** *m* **bajo**
- *lower fore topsail yard*

**34 la verga de velacho** *m* **alto**
- *upper fore topsail yard*

**35 la verga de juanete** *m* **bajo de proa** *f*
- *lower fore topgallant yard*

**36 la verga de juanete** *m* **alto de proa** *f*
- *upper fore topgallant yard*

**37 la verga de sobrejuanete** *m* **de proa** *f*
- *fore royal yard*

**38 la verga mayor**
- *main yard*

**39 la verga de gavia** *f* **baja**
- *lower main topsail yard*

**40 la verga de gavia** *f* **alta**
- *upper main topsail yard*

**41 la verga de juanete** *m* **mayor bajo**
- *lower main topgallant yard*

**42 la verga de juanete** *m* **mayor alto**
- *upper main topgallant yard*

**43 la verga de sobrejuanete** *m* **mayor**
- *main royal yard*

**44 la botavara**
- *spanker boom*

**45 el pico de la cangreja**
- *spanker gaff*

**46 el marchapié y estribos** *m*
- *footrope*

**47 los amantillos**
- *lifts*

**48 el amantillo de la botavara**
- *spanker boom topping lift*

**49 el amantillo del pico de la cangreja**
- *spanker peak halyard*

**50 la cofa de trinquete** *m*
- *foretop*

**51 la cruceta del mastelero de trinquete** *m*
- *fore topmast crosstrees*

**52 la cofa mayor (la cofa de gavia** *f*)
- *maintop*

**53 la cruceta del mastelero mayor (del mastelero de gavia** *f*)
- *main topmast crosstrees*

**54 la cofa de mesana** *f*
- *mizzen (mizen) top*

**55-66 las velas cuadradas**
- *square sails*

**55 la vela de trinquete** *m*
- *foresail (fore course)*

**56 el velacho bajo**
- *lower fore topsail*

**57 el velacho alto**
- *upper fore topsail*

**58 el juanete bajo**
- *lower fore topgallant sail*

**59 el juanete alto**
- *upper fore topgallant sail*

**60 el sobrejuanete**
- *fore royal*

**61 la vela mayor (la mayor)**
- *mainsail (main course)*

**62 la gavia baja**
- *lower main topsail*

**63 la gavia alta**
- *upper main topsail*

**64 el juanete mayor bajo**
- *lower main topgallant sail*

**65 el juanete mayor alto**
- *upper main topgallant sail*

**66 el sobrejuanete mayor**
- *main royal sail*

**67-71 las jarcias de labor** *f*
- *running rigging*

**67 las brazas**
- *braces*

**68 las escotas**
- *sheets*

**69 la escota de botavara** *f*
- *spanker sheet*

**70 la osta de la cangreja**
- *spanker vangs*

**71 los brioles**
- *bunt line*

**72 los rizos**
- *reef*

**1-5 formas f de velas f**
- *sail shapes*
1 la vela cangreja
- *gaffsail;* sim.: *trysail, spencer*
2 el foque (la vela de estay *m*)
- *jib*
3 la vela latina
- *lateen sail*
4 la vela al tercio
- *lugsail*
5 la vela de abanico *m*
- *spritsail*
**6-8 veleros *m* de un solo palo**
- *single-masted sailing boats (Am. sailboats)*
6 la balandra holandesa
- *tjalk*
7 la orza de deriva f
- *leeboard*
8 el cúter
- *cutter*
**9-10 veleros *m* con un palo de mesana f**
- *mizzen (mizen) masted sailing boats (Am. sailboats)*
9 el queche
- *ketch-rigged sailing barge*
10 el quechemarín
- *yawl*
**11-17 veleros *m* de dos palos *m***
- *two-masted sailing boats (Am. sailboats)*
11-13 la goleta de gavias f
- *topsail schooner*
11 la vela mayor
- *mainsail*
12 la cangreja del trinquete
- *boom foresail*
13 la redonda del trinquete (la cuadra)
- *square foresail*
14 el bergantín-goleta f
- *brigantine*
15 el palo de goleta f (el palo mayor) con velas f de cuchillo *m*
- *half-rigged mast with fore-and-aft sails*
16 el trinquete con velas f cuadras (redondas)
- *full-rigged mast with square sails*
17 el bergantín redondo
- *brig*
**18-27 veleros *m* de tres palos *m***
- *three-masted sailing vessels (three-masters)*
18 la goleta de tres palos *m* con velas f cangrejas
- *three-masted schooner*
19 la goleta de tres palos *m* con gavias f en el trinquete
- *three-masted topsail schooner*
20 la goleta de gavias f de tres palos *m*
- *bark (barque) schooner*

21-23 el bricbarca (la corbeta) de tres palos *m* [compárese aparejo y velamen con la lámina 219]
- *bark (barque) [cf. illustration of rigging and sails in plate 219]*
21 el trinquete
- *foremast*
22 el palo mayor
- *mainmast*
23 el palo de mesana f
- *mizzen (mizen) mast*
24-27 el barco completamente aparejado
- *full-rigged ship*
24 el palo de mesana f
- *mizzen (mizen) mast*
25 la verga de cruz f
- *crossjack yard (crojack yard)*
26 la vela de cruz f (la vela redonda)
- *crossjack (crojack)*
27 la fila de portas f
- *ports*
**28-31 veleros *m* de cuatro palos *m***
- *four-masted sailing ships (four-masters)*
28 la goleta de cuatro palos *m*
- *four-masted schooner*
29 la corbeta (el bricbarca) de cuatro palos *m*
- *four-masted bark (barque)*
30 el palo mayor popel
- *mizzen (mizen) mast*
31 el barco de cuatro palos *m* completamente aparejado
- *four-masted full-rigged ship*
**32-34 la corbeta (el bricbarca) de cinco palos *m***
- *five-masted bark (barque)*
32 el sosobre
- *skysail*
33 el palo mayor
- *middle mast*
34 el palo mayor popel
- *mizzen (mizen) mast*
**35-37 evolución f de los barcos de vela f en 400 años *m***
- *development of sailing ships over 400 years*
35 el barco de cinco palos *m* completamente aparejado "Preussen", 1902–1910
- *five-masted full-rigged ship 'Preussen' 1902–1910*
36 el clíper inglés "Spindrift", 1867
- *English clipper ship 'Spindrift' 1867*
37 la carabela "Santa María", 1492
- *caravel (carvel) 'Santa Maria' 1492*

# 221 Tipos de barcos

*Types of Ship*

1 **el superpetrolero** (ULCC, ultra large crudeoil carrier) del tipo de puente *m* de mando *m* en la popa
– *ULCC (ultra large crude carrier) of the 'all-aft' type*
2 el trinquete
– *foremast*
3 la pasarela con las tuberías
– *catwalk with the pipes*
4 la boca de incendio *m*
– *fire gun (fire nozzle)*
5 la grúa del puente
– *deck crane*
6 el castillo de popa *f* con el puente de mando *m*
– *deckhouse with the bridge*
7 el mástil de señales *f* y la antena del radar
– *aft signal (signalling) and radar mast*
8 la chimenea
– *funnel*
9 **un buque experimental a propulsión *f* nuclear,** el carguero a granel *m* "Otto Hahn"
– *nuclear research ship 'Otto Hahn', a bulk carrier*
10 las superestructuras de popa *f* (la sala de máquinas *f*)
– *aft superstructure; here: engine room*
11 la escotilla de carga *f*
– *cargo hatchway for bulk goods (bulk cargoes)*
12 el puente de mando *m*
– *bridge*
13 el castillo de proa *f*
– *forecastle (fo'c'sle)*
14 la roda
– *stem*
15 **el barco de recreo *m***
– *seaside pleasure boat*
16 la chimenea falsa
– *dummy funnel*
17 el conducto para el escape de gases *m*
– *exhaust mast*
18 **el buque de salvamento *m***
– *rescue cruiser*
19 la plataforma de aterrizaje *m* para los helicópteros (el puente de maniobras *f*)
– *helicopter platform; also: working deck*
20 el helicóptero de salvamento *m*
– *rescue helicopter*

21 **el buque portacontenedores**
– *all-container ship*
22 los contenedores estibados en la cubierta
– *containers stowed on deck*
23 **el carguero**
– *cargo ship*
24-29 la instalación para la manipulación de las mercancías
– *cargo gear (cargo-handling gear)*
24 el mástil bípodo
– *bipod mast*
25 el mástil de carga *f* de gran capacidad *f*
– *jumbo derrick boom (heavy-lift derrick boom)*
26 la botavara (la flecha)
– *derrick boom (cargo boom)*
27 la candaliza (sistema *m* de poleas *f*; polispasto *m*)
– *tackle*
28 la polea
– *block*
29 el cojinete de aguante *m*
– *thrust bearing*
30 la porta de la roda
– *bow doors*
31 la porta de carga *f* de popa *f*
– *stern loading door*
32 **el revituallador de las perforaciones offshore** (perforación *f* en el mar)
– *offshore drilling rig supply vessel*
33 las superestructuras
– *compact superstructure*
34 el puente de carga *f* (el puente de maniobras *f*)
– *loading deck; also: working deck*
35 **el buque cisterna *f* para gas *m* líquido**
– *liquefied-gas tanker*
36 el tanque esférico
– *spherical tank*
37 el mástil (la antena) de televisión *f* para la navegación
– *navigational television receiver mast*
38 el conducto para la salida del gas
– *vent mast*
39 el puente de mando *m*
– *deckhouse*
40 la chimenea
– *funnel*
41 el ventilador
– *ventilator*

42 el espejo de popa *f*
– *transom stern (transom)*
43 la pala del timón
– *rudder blade (rudder)*
44 la hélice
– *ship's propeller (ship's screw)*
45 el bulbo de la roda
– *bulbous bow*
46 el buque de pesca *f* de arrastre *m*
– *steam trawler*
47 **el buque faro *m*** (faro *m* flotante)
– *lightship (light vessel)*
48 el farol (el fanal)
– *lantern (characteristic light)*
49 el barco de pesca *f*
– *smack*
50 **el buque rompehielos**
– *ice breaker*
51 la luz de navegación *f*
– *steaming light mast*
52 el hangar de los helicópteros
– *helicopter hangar*
53 el punto de fijación *f* a la popa para remolcar a un barco por la proa
– *stern towing point, for gripping the bow of ships in tow*
54 **el transbordador de mercancías *f*** (el barco de carga *f* horizontal)
– *roll-on-roll-off (ro-ro) trailer ferry*
55 la porta de popa *f* con rampa *f* de acceso *m*
– *stern port (stern opening) with ramp*
56 el montacargas para vehículos *m* pesados
– *heavy vehicle lifts* (Am. *heavy vehicle elevators*)
57 **el carguero multifuncional**
– *multi-purpose freighter*
58 el mástil de carga *f* y ventilador *m*
– *ventilator-type samson (sampson) post (ventilator-type king post)*
59 la botavara (la flecha)
– *cargo gear (cargo handling gear), a derrick boom (cargo boom)*
60 el mástil de carga *f*
– *derrick mast*
61 la grúa del puente
– *deck crane*
62 el mástil de carga *f* de gran capacidad *f*
– *jumbo derrick boom (heavy-lift derrick boom)*

388

| | | |
|---|---|---|
| 63 la escotilla de carga *f* | – *flag dressing (rainbow dressing, string of* | 104 el aparejo |
| – *cargo hatchway* | *flags extending over mastheads, e.g., on* | – *tackle* |
| 64 **la plataforma de perforación *f* semisumer-** | *the maiden voyage)* | 105 el motón |
| **gible** | 86 **el pesquero de arrastre *m*, un buque** | – *block* |
| – *semisubmersible drilling vessel* | factoría *f* | 106 la beta del aparejo |
| 65 el flotador con la maquinaria | – *trawler, a factory ship* | – *fall* |
| – *floating vessel with machinery* | 87 la horca | 107 el bote salvavidas con su lona *f* |
| 66 la plataforma de perforación *f* | – *gallows* | impermeable |
| – *drilling platform* | 88 la rampa de popa *f* | – *ship's lifeboat covered with tarpaulin* |
| 67 la torre de perforación *f* (de extracción *f*) | – *stern ramp* | 108 la roda |
| – *derrick* | 89 **el carguero portacontenedores** | – *stem* |
| 68 el buque de transporte *m* de ganado *m* | – *container ship* | 109 el pasajero |
| – *cattleship (cattle vessel)* | 90 la carga sobre la cubierta | – *passenger* |
| 69 las superestructuras para el transporte de | – *loading bridge (loading platform)* | 110 el camarero (de buque *m*) |
| ganado *m* | 91 la escala de gato *m* | – *steward* |
| – *superstructure for transporting livestock* | – *sea ladder (jacob's ladder, rope ladder)* | 111 la tumbona de cubierta *f* |
| 70 los tanques de agua *f* dulce | 92 **el remolcador de empuje *m* y la gabarra** | – *deck-chair* |
| – *fresh water tanks* | (chalana *f*; barcaza *f*), dos | 112 el grumete |
| 71 el tanque de combustible *m* | embarcaciones *f* de interior | – *deck hand* |
| – *fuel tank* | – *barge and push tug assembly* | 113 el balde |
| 72 el tanque del estiércol | 93 el remolcador de empuje *m* (*Amér.* | – *deck bucket* |
| – *dung tank* | *Central y Ven.*: el bombote; *Bol., Col., Ec.* | 114 el contramaestre |
| 73 los tanques de forraje *m* | *y Perú*: el batelón) | – *boatswain (bo's'n, bo'sun, bosun)* |
| – *fodder tanks* | – *push tug* | 115 la marinera |
| 74 **el transbordador de trenes *m*** (el buque | 94 la gabarra (la chalana) sin motor *m* | – *tunic* |
| portatrenes, el ferry) [sección transversal] | (*Amér.*: el bongo) | 116 el toldo |
| – *train ferry [cross section]* | – *tug-pushed dumb barge (tug-pushed* | – *awning* |
| 75 la chimenea | *lighter)* | 117 el puntal del toldo |
| – *funnel* | 95 el barco del práctico | – *stanchion* |
| 76 las tuberías para el escape de gases *m* | – *pilot boat* | 118 el listón del toldo |
| – *exhaust pipes* | 96 **el buque mixto de carga *f* y pasajeros *m*** | – *ridge rope (jackstay)* |
| 77 el mástil | – *combined cargo and passenger liner* | 119 la trinca |
| – *mast* | 97 el desembarco de pasajeros *m* por medio | – *lashing* |
| 78 el bote salvavidas (*Amér. Central y Pan.*: | de botes *m* | 120 la amurada |
| la panga) en su pescante *m* (en la serviola) | – *passengers disembarking by boat* | – *bulwark* |
| – *ship's lifeboat hanging at the davit* | 98 la escala real | 121 la barandilla |
| 79 la cubierta para automóviles *m* | – *accommodation ladder* | – *guard rail* |
| – *car deck* | 99 el buque de cabotaje *m* | 122 el pasamano |
| 80 la cubierta para trenes *m* | – *coaster (coasting vessel)* | – *handrail (top rail)* |
| – *main deck (train deck)* | 100 la lancha aduanera | 123 la escalera de cámara *f* |
| 81 las máquinas principales | – *customs* or *police launch* | – *companion ladder (companionway)* |
| – *main engines* | 101-128 **el vapor de recreo *m*** (el vapor para | 124 la guindola |
| 82 **el transatlántico** (buque *m* de pasajeros *m*; | hacer cruceros *m*) | – *lifebelt (lifebuoy)* |
| un barco de línea *f*) | – *excursion steamer (pleasure steamer)* | 125 el farol de la guindola |
| – *passenger liner (liner, ocean liner)* | 101-106 la instalación para la botadura del | – *lifebuoy light (lifebelt light, signal light)* |
| 83 la roda | bote salvavidas | 126 el oficial de guardia *f* |
| – *stem* | – *lifeboat launching gear* | – *officer of the watch (watchkeeper)* |
| 84 la chimenea con revestimiento *m* de | 101 el pescante (la serviola) | 127 la guerrera de marinero *m* |
| rejilla *f* | – *davit* | – *reefer* (Am. *pea jacket*) |
| – *funnel with lattice casing* | 102 el brazalete intermedio | 128 los gemelos (los anteojos, los prismáticos) |
| 85 el empavesado (conjunto *m* de banderas *f* | – *wire rope span* | – *binoculars* |
| izadas de proa *f* a popa *f* para las fiestas o | 103 el guardamancebo | |
| el primer viaje) | – *lifeline* | |

**1-43 el astillero** (el arsenal; la atarazana)
- *shipyard (shipbuilding yard, dockyard,* Am. *navy yard)*
**1** el edificio de la administración
- *administrative offices*
**2** la oficina de dibujo *m* y proyectos *m* de barcos *m*
- *ship-drawing office*
**3-4** los cobertizos de construcción *f*
- *shipbuilding sheds*
**3** la sala de trazado *m* y gálibos *m*
- *mould (*Am. *mold) loft*
**4** el taller de montaje *m*
- *erection shop*
**5-9** el muelle de armamento *m*
- *fitting-out quay*
**5** el muelle
- *quay*
**6** la grúa de trípode *m*
- *tripod crane*
**7** la grúa de cabeza *f* de martillo *m*
- *hammer-headed crane*
**8** el taller de maquinaria *f*
- *engineering workshop*
**9** el taller de calderería *f*
- *boiler shop*
**10** el dique de reparaciones *f*
- *repair quay*
**11-26** las instalaciónes de la grada de construcción *f*
- *slipways (slips, building berths, building slips, stocks)*
**11-18** la grada de grúa *f* de cable *m* (la grada de pórtico *m*), una grada de construcción *f*
- *cable crane berth, a slipway (building berth)*
**11** el pórtico de la grada
- *slipway portal*

**12** el pilar del pórtico
- *bridge support*
**13** el cable de la grúa
- *crane cable*
**14** el carro corredizo
- *crab (jenny)*
**15** el travesaño
- *cross piece*
**16** la cabina del conductor de la grúa
- *crane driver's cabin (crane driver's cage)*
**17** el suelo de la grada
- *slipway floor*
**18** el andamiaje, un andamio
- *staging, a scaffold*
**19-21** la grada de andamiaje *m*
- *frame slipway*
**19** el andamiaje de la grada
- *slipway frame*
**20** la grúa móvil de techo *m* (la grúa de caballete *m*)
- *overhead travelling (*Am. *traveling) crane (gantry crane)*
**21** el carro corredizo giratorio
- *slewing crab*
**22** la quilla en su posición *f*
- *keel in position*
**23** la grúa giratoria de brazo *m* oscilante
- *luffing jib crane, a slipway crane*
**24** el carril (la vía) de la grúa
- *crane rails (crane track)*
**25** la grúa de pórtico *m* móvil (la grúa-puente)
- *gantry crane*
**26** el puente
- *gantry (bridge)*
**27** las vigas (los pilares) del puente
- *trestles (supports)*
**28** el carro corredizo (la grúa móvil)
- *crab (jenny)*

**29** las cuadernas del buque en su posición *f*
- *hull frames in position*
**30** el buque en construcción *f*
- *ship under construction*
**31-33** el dique seco (la dársena de carenaje *m*)
- *dry dock*
**31** el suelo del dique (el fondo del dique)
- *dock floor (dock bottom)*
**32** la puerta del dique
- *dock gates (caisson)*
**33** la casa de bombas *f* (el puesto de máquinas *f*)
- *pumping station; also: power house*
**34-43** el dique flotante
- *floating dock (pontoon dock)*
**34** la grúa del dique, una grúa de brazo *m* oscilante
- *dock crane (dockside crane), a jib crane*
**35** los pilotes de defensa *f* (los duques de alba)
- *fender pile*
**36-43** la disposición del dique
- *working of docks*
**36** la fosa del dique
- *dock basin*
**37-38** la estructura del dique
- *dock structure*
**37** el tanque lateral (el cajón vertical)
- *side tank (side wall)*
**38** el tanque del fondo (el cajón horizontal)
- *bottom tank (bottom pontoon)*
**39** los picaderos de la quilla
- *keel block*
**40** los picaderos del pantoque
- *bilge block (bilge shore, side support)*

**41-43** la entrada de un buque en el
dique
– *docking a ship*
**41** el dique flotante inundado
– *flooded floating dock*
**42** el remolcador atoando (llevando a
remolque *m;* espiando) el buque
– *tug towing the ship*
**43** el dique vaciado, después del
bombeo del agua *f*
– *emptied (pumped-out) dock*
**44-61 los elementos estructurales del
buque**
– *structural parts of the ship*
**44-56** los refuerzos longitudinales
– *longitudinal structure*
**44-49** el forro exterior
– *shell (shell plating, skin)*
**44** la traca (la hilada) de cinta *f*
– *sheer strake*
**45** la traca lateral
– *side strake*
**46** la traca de pantoque *m*
– *bilge strake*
**47** la quilla de balance *m* (la quilla de
pantoque *m*)
– *bilge keel*
**48** la traca de fondo *m* (la aparadura)
– *bottom plating*
**49** la quilla plana
– *flat plate keel (keel plate)*
**50** el trancanil
– *stringer (side stringer)*
**51** la plancha marginal del tanque
– *tank margin plate*
**52** la sobrequilla lateral
– *longitudinal side girder*

**53** la sobrequilla
– *centre (Am. center) plate girder
(centre girder, kelson, keelson,
vertical keel)*
**54** la cubierta del tanque
– *tank top plating (tank top, inner
bottom plating)*
**55** la traca central
– *centre (Am. center) strake*
**56** las planchas de cubierta *f*
– *deck plating*
**57** los baos
– *deck beam*
**58** la cuaderna
– *frame (rib)*
**59** la varenga
– *floor plate*
**60** el doble fondo
– *cellular double bottom*
**61** el puntal de la bodega
– *hold pillar (pillar)*
**62-63** las tablas de estiba *f*
– *dunnage*
**62** el forro lateral interior de la
bodega (las serretas)
– *side battens (side ceiling, spar
ceiling)*
**63** el forro interior del suelo de la
bodega
– *ceiling (floor ceiling)*
**64-65** la escotilla
– *hatchway*
**64** la brazola de la escotilla
– *hatch coaming*
**65** el cuartel (la tapa) de la escotilla
– *hatch cover (hatchboard)*
**66-72** la popa
– *stern*

**66** la barandilla (la batayola)
– *guard rail*
**67** la amurada
– *bulwark*
**68** la caña del timón
– *rudder stock*
**69-70** el timón Oertz
– *Oertz rudder*
**69** la pala del timón (el azafrán)
– *rudder blade (rudder)*
**70-71** el codaste
– *stern frame*
**70** el codaste del timón
– *rudder post*
**71** el codaste de la hélice
– *propeller post (screw post)*
**72** la hélice del buque
– *ship's propeller (ship's screw)*
**73** las marcas de calado *m*
– *draught (draft) marks*
**74-79** la proa
– *bow*
**74** la roda, una roda de bulbo *m* (la
proa bulbosa)
– *stem, a bulbous stem (bulbous bow)*
**75** el escobén del ancla
– *hawse*
**76** el tubo del escobén
– *hawse pipe*
**77** la cadena del ancla *f*
– *anchor cable, a chain cable*
**78** el ancla *f* de patente *f* (el ancla *f*
sin cepo *m*)
– *stockless anchor (patent anchor)*
**79** el ancla *f* con cepo *m*
– *stocked anchor*

**1-71 el barco mixto de carga *f* y
pasaje *m*** [de tipo antiguo]
- ***combined cargo and passenger ship***
  *[of the older type]*
**1** la chimenea
- *funnel*
**2** la contraseña de la chimenea
- *funnel marking*
**3** la sirena (la señal usada cuando
hay niebla *f*)
- *siren (fog horn)*
**4-11 la cubierta de marcación *f***
(cubierta *f* goniométrica)
- ***compass platform** (compass bridge,
  compass flat, monkey bridge)*
**4** las antenas
- *antenna lead-in (antenna down-
  lead)*
**5** la antena de cuadro *m* radiogoniométrica
- *radio direction finder (RDF)
  antenna, a rotatable antenna; also:
  aural null loop antenna*
**6** el compás magnético (la brújula)
- *magnetic compass (mariner's
  compass)*
**7** la lámpara morse *m*
- *morse lamp (signalling, Am.
  signaling, lamp)*
**8** la antena de radar *m*
- *radar antenna (radar scanner)*
**9** las banderas de señales *f*
- *code flag signal*
**10** la driza de las banderas de
señales *f*
- *code flag halyards*
**11** el estay de señales *f*
- *triatic stay (signal stay)*

**12-18 el puente de mando *m*** (el
puente)
- ***bridge deck** (bridge)*
**12** la cabina de radio *f*
- *radio room*
**13** el camarote del capitán
- *captain's cabin*
**14** el cuarto de derrota *f* (la cámara
de los instrumentos)
- *navigating bridge*
**15** la luz de navegación *f* de
estribor *m* [verde; la luz de
navegación *f* de babor *m* es roja]
- *starboard sidelight [green; port
  sidelight red]*
**16** el ala *f* del puente de mando *m*
- *wing of bridge*
**17** la cenefa (la tira de lona *f* que
resguarda del viento)
- *shelter (weather cloth, dodger)*
**18** la caseta del timón
- *wheelhouse*
**19-21 la cubierta de botes *m***
- *boat deck*
**19** el bote salvavidas
- *ship's lifeboat*
**20** el pescante (la serviola)
- *davit*
**21** el camarote de oficial *m*
- *officer's cabin*
**22-27 la cubierta de paseo *m***
- ***promenade deck***
**22** la cubierta de sol *m*
- *sun deck (lido deck)*
**23** la piscina
- *swimming pool*
**24** la escalera de cámara *f*
- *companion ladder (companionway)*
**25** la biblioteca
- *library (ship's library)*

**26** el salón de tertulia *f*
- *lounge*
**27** la galería de paseo *m*
- *promenade*
**28-30 la cubierta A** (la cubierta
superior)
- ***A-deck***
**28** la cubierta semicerrada
- *semi-enclosed deck space*
**29** el camarote doble (el camarote de
dos camas *f*), un camarote (*Bol. y
Río de la Plata:* una cucheta)
- *double-berth cabin, a cabin*
**30** el camarote de lujo *m*
- *de luxe cabin*
**31** el asta *f* de la bandera
- *ensign staff*
**32-42 la cubierta B** (la cubierta
principal)
- ***B-deck** (main deck)*
**32** la cubierta de popa *f*
- *after deck*
**33** la toldilla
- *poop*
**34** la chupeta (camareta *f* junto al
coronamiento de popa *f*; la
cámara alta)
- *deckhouse*
**35** el poste de carga *f*
- *samson (sampson) post (king post)*
**36** el botalón (la botavara)
- *derrick boom (cargo boom)*
**37** la cruceta
- *crosstrees (spreader)*
**38** la cofa
- *crow's nest*
**39** el mastelero
- *topmast*

**40** la luz de navegación f de proa f
- *forward steaming light*

**41** la cabeza del ventilador
- *ventilator lead*

**42** la cocina
- *galley (caboose, cookroom, ship's kitchen)*

**43** la despensa
- *ship's pantry*

**44** el comedor
- *dining room*

**45** la oficina del sobrecargo
- *purser's office*

**46** el camarote individual
- *single-berth cabin*

**47** la cubierta de proa f
- *foredeck*

**48** el castillo de proa f
- *forecastle (fo'c'sle)*

**49-51 el mecanismo de anclaje** m
- ***ground tackle***

**49** la maquinilla (el chigre del ancla f; *Arg.:* el guinche)
- *windlass*

**50** la cadena del ancla f
- *anchor cable, a chain cable*

**51** el estopor
- *compressor (chain compressor)*

**52** el ancla f
- *anchor*

**53** el asta f (el mástil) de la bandera de proa f
- *jackstaff*

**54** la bandera de proa f
- *jack*

**55** las bodegas de popa f
- *after holds*

**56** la cámara frigorífica
- *cold storage room (insulated hold)*

**57** el pañol
- *store room*

**58** la estela
- *wake*

**59** la chumacera de la hélice
- *shell bossing (shaft bossing)*

**60** la cola del árbol (la parte de atrás del eje)
- *tail shaft (tail end shaft)*

**61** el soporte del árbol
- *shaft strut (strut, spectacle frame, propeller strut, propeller bracket)*

**62** la hélice de tres paletas f
- *three-blade ship's propeller (ship's screw)*

**63** la pala del timón
- *rudder blade (rudder)*

**64** el prensaestopas (la caja de estopas f)
- *stuffing box*

**65** el árbol de la hélice (el eje de la hélice)
- *propeller shaft*

**66** el túnel de árbol de la hélice
- *shaft alley (shaft tunnel)*

**67** el tope de empuje m
- *thrust block*

**68-74 la propulsión Diesel eléctrica**
- ***diesel-electric drive***

**68** la sala de máquinas f eléctricas
- *electric engine room*

**69** el motor eléctrico
- *electric motor*

**70** la sala de máquinas f auxiliares
- *auxiliary engine room*

**71** las máquinas auxiliares
- *auxiliary engines*

**72** la sala de máquinas f principales
- *main engine room*

**73** el motor principal, un motor Diesel
- *main engine, a diesel engine*

**74** el generador
- *generator*

**75** las bodegas de proa f
- *forward holds*

**76** el entrepuente
- *tween deck*

**77** la carga
- *cargo*

**78** los tanques de lastre m de agua f (depósitos m de doble fondo m)
- *ballast tank (deep tank) for water ballast*

**79** el tanque de agua f dulce
- *fresh water tank*

**80** el tanque de combustible m
- *fuel tank*

**81** la ola levantada por la proa
- *bow wave*

**1 el sextante**
**– *sextant***
**2** el arco graduado (el limbo)
– *graduated arc*
**3** la alidada
– *index bar (index arm)*
**4** el tambor micrométrico
– *decimal micrometer*
**5** el nonio
– *vernier*
**6** el espejo grande
– *index mirror*
**7** el espejo pequeño
– *horizon glass (horizon mirror)*
**8** el telescopio
– *telescope*
**9** la empuñadura
– *grip (handgrip)*
**10-13 el aparato de radar *m***
– ***radar equipment** (radar apparatus)*
**10** el mástil del radar
– *radar pedestal*
**11** la antena reflectora giratoria
– *revolving radar reflector*
**12** la pantalla de radar *m*
– *radar display unit (radar screen)*
**13** la imagen del radar
– *radar image (radar picture)*
**14-38 la caseta del timón**
– ***wheelhouse***
**14** el puesto de mando *m* y navegación *f*
– *steering and control position*
**15** la rueda del timón
– *ship's wheel for controlling the rudder mechanism*
**16** el timonel
– *helmsman* (Am. *wheelsman*)
**17** el indicador del ángulo del timón
– *rudder angle indicator*
**18** el piloto automático
– *automatic pilot (autopilot)*
**19** el alzaprima de activación *f* de la hélice de paso *m* variable
– *control lever for the variable-pitch propeller (reversible propeller, feathering propeller, feathering screw)*
**20** el indicador de paso *m* de la hélice
– *propeller pitch indicator*

**21** el indicador de revoluciones *f* del motor principal
– *main engine revolution indicator*
**22** el indicador de la velocidad del barco
– *ship's speedometer (log)*
**23** el conmutador del timón de proa *f*
– *control switch for bow thruster (bow-manoeuvring, Am. maneuvering, propeller)*
**24** el ecógrafo
– *echo recorder (depth recorder, echograph)*
**25** el telégrafo transmisor de órdenes *f* a las máquinas
– *engine telegraph (engine order telegraph)*
**26** el aparato de control *m* de los amortiguadores del balanceo
– *controls for the anti-rolling system (for the stabilizers)*
**27** el teléfono interior a batería *f*
– *local-battery telephone*
**28** el aparato de radiotelefonía *f* entre barcos *m*
– *shipping traffic radio telephone*
**29** el panel indicador de las luces de navegación *f*
– *navigation light indicator panel (running light indicator panel)*
**30** el micrófono del sistema de difusión *f* general (para órdenes *f* y llamadas *f*)
– *microphone for ship's address system*
**31** el girocompás (la brújula giroscópica), un compás repetidor
– *gyro compass (gyroscopic compass), a compass repeater*
**32** el botón de activación *f* de la sirena del barco
– *control button for the ship's siren (ship's fog horn)*
**33** el control de la sobrecarga del motor principal
– *main engine overload indicator*
**34** el aparato Decca para la determinación de la posición del barco
– *detector indicator unit for fixing the ship's position*
**35** el indicador de sintonización *f* aproximada
– *rough focusing indicator*
**36** el indicador de sintonización *f* nítida
– *fine focusing indicator*

**37** el oficial de navegación *f*
– *navigating officer*
**38** el capitán
– *captain*
**39 el sistema de navegación *f* Decca**
– ***Decca navigation system***
**40** la estación principal
– *master station*
**41** la estación secundaria
– *slave station*
**42** la hipérbola cero
– *null hyperbola*
**43** la hipérbola de posición *f* 1
– *hyperbolic position line 1*
**44** la hipérbola de posición *f* 2
– *hyperbolic position line 2*
**45** la posición [del barco]
– *position (fix, ship fix)*
**46-53 compases *m***
– *compasses*
**46** el compás líquido, una brújula magnética
– *liquid compass (fluid compass, spirit compass, wet compass), a magnetic compass*
**47** la rosa náutica (la rosa de los vientos)
– *compass card*
**48** la línea de fe *f*
– *lubber's line (lubber's mark, lubber's point)*
**49** la caja de compás *m*
– *compass bowl*
**50** la suspensión cardán
– *gimbal ring*
**51-53** la brújula giroscópica (la instalación del girocompás)
– *gyro compass (gyroscopic compass, gyro compass unit)*
**51** la brújula maestra (el compás matriz)
– *master compass (master gyro compass)*
**52** el compás repetidor
– *compass repeater (gyro repeater)*
**53** el compás repetidor con alidada *f*
– *compass repeater with pelorus*
**54 la corredera perfeccionada,** una corredera
– ***patent log** (screw log, mechanical log, towing log, taffrail log, speedometer), a log*
**55** la hélice de la corredera
– *rotator*

**56** el regulador de volante *m*
 – *governor*
**57** el contador de la corredera
 – *log clock*
**58-67 sondas** *f*
 – *leads*
**58** la sonda de mano *m*
 – *hand lead*
**59** el escandallo
 – *lead (lead sinker)*
**60** la sondaleza
 – *leadline*
**61-67** la sonda acústica (la ecosonda)
 – *echo sounder (echo sounding machine)*
**61** el emisor de sonido *m*
 – *sound transmitter*
**62** el impulso de la onda sonora
 – *sound wave (sound impulse)*
**63** el eco
 – *echo (sound echo, echo signal)*
**64** el receptor del eco
 – *echo receiver (hydrophone)*
**65** el ecógrafo
 – *echograph (echo sounding machine recorder)*
**66** la escala de profundidad *f*
 – *depth scale*
**67** la imagen del eco
 – *echogram (depth recording, depth reading)*
**68-108 señales** *f* **marítimas, de balizaje** *m* **y alumbrado** *m*
 – *sea marks (floating navigational marks) for buoyage and lighting systems*
**68-83** señales *f* en aguas *f* navegables
 – *fairway marks (channel marks)*
**68** la boya luminosa con silbato *m*
 – *light and whistle buoy*
**69** el fanal
 – *light (warning light)*
**70** el silbato
 – *whistle*
**71** el flotador
 – *buoy*
**72** la cadena del ancla
 – *mooring chain*
**73** la piedra de la boya (el ancla *f* de piedra *f*)
 – *sinker (mooring sinker)*
**74** la boya luminosa de campana *f*
 – *light and bell buoy*

**75** la campana
 – *bell*
**76** la boya cónica (de punta *f*)
 – *conical buoy*
**77** la boya achaflanada
 – *can buoy*
**78** la señal de tope *m*
 – *topmark*
**79** la boya con asta *f* (con punta *f*; la boya de espegue *m*)
 – *spar buoy*
**80** la boya baliza
 – *topmark buoy*
**81** el barco faro
 – *lightship (light vessel)*
**82** el haz de luz *f*
 – *lantern mast (lantern tower)*
**83** el haz de luz *f*
 – *beam of light*
**84-102** las señales de un canal navegable
 – *fairway markings (channel markings) [German type]*
**84** naufragio *m* [baliza *f* verde]
 – *wreck [green buoys]*
**85** naufragio *m* a estribor *m* del canal de navegación *f*
 – *wreck to starboard*
**86** naufragio *m* a babor del canal
 – *wreck to port*
**87** bajo *m*
 – *shoals (shallows, shallow water,* Am. *flats)*
**88** bajo *m* a babor *m* del canal de navegación *f* principal
 – *middle ground to port*
**89** bifurcación *f* [el comienzo del bajo; señales *f* de tope *m*: cilindro *m* rojo sobre globo *m* rojo]
 – *division (bifurcation) [beginning of the middle ground; topmark: red cylinder above red ball]*
**90** confluencia *f* [el final del bajo; señales *f* de tope *m*: cruz *f* de San Antonio roja sobre globo *m* rojo]
 – *convergence (confluence) [end of the middle ground; topmark: red St. Antony's cross above red ball]*
**91** bajo *m*
 – *middle ground*

**92** el canal principal
 – *main fairway (main navigable channel)*
**93** el canal secundario
 – *secondary fairway (secondary navigable channel)*
**94** la boya de barril *m*
 – *can buoy*
**95** boyas *f* de babor *m* [rojas]
 – *port hand buoys (port hand marks) [red]*
**96** boyas *f* de estribor *m* [negras]
 – *starboard hand buoys (starboard hand marks) [black]*
**97** bajo *m* fuera del canal de navegación *f*
 – *shoals (shallows, shallow water,* Am. *flats) outside the fairway*
**98** el centro del canal [señales *f* de tope *m*: cruz *f* doble]
 – *middle of the fairway (mid-channel)*
**99** postes *m* de estribor *m* [escobas *f* invertidas]
 – *starboard markers [inverted broom]*
**100** postes *m* de babor *m* [escobas *f* hacia arriba]
 – *port markers [upward-pointing broom]*
**101-102** alineación *f* luminosa (dirección *f* de luces *f*)
 – *range lights (leading lights)*
**101** la luz de dirección *f* inferior
 – *lower range light (lower leading light)*
**102** la luz de dirección *f* superior
 – *higher range light (higher leading light)*
**103** el faro
 – *lighthouse*
**104** la antena de radar *m*
 – *radar antenna (radar scanner)*
**105** el fanal
 – *lantern (characteristic light)*
**106** la antena direccional de radio *f* (la antena radiogoniométrica)
 – *radio direction finder (RDF) antenna*
**107** el puente (la plataforma) de observación *f* y de máquinas *f*
 – *machinery and observation platform (machinery and observation deck)*
**108** la vivienda del guardián
 – *living quarters*

1  el barrio del puerto
–  *dock area*
2  el puerto franco
–  *free port (foreign trade zone)*
3  la frontera de la zona franca (la
   verja aduanera)
–  *free zone frontier (free zone
   enclosure)*
4  la barrera aduanera
–  *customs barrier*
5  el paso de aduanas *f*
–  *customs entrance*
6  el edificio de aduanas *f* del puerto
–  *port custom house*
7  el almacén
–  *entrepôt*
8  la gabarra (la chalana)
–  *barge (dumb barge, lighter)*
9  el almacén de tránsito *m* de
   mercancías *f* a granel *m*
–  *break-bulk cargo transit shed
   (general cargo transit shed, package
   cargo transit shed)*
10  la grúa flotante
–  *floating crane*
11  el transbordador del puerto
–  *harbour* (Am. *harbor) ferry
   (ferryboat)*
12  los duques de alba
–  *fender (dolphin)*
13  la lancha carbonera
–  *bunkering boat*

14  el carguero de mercancías *f* a
   granel *m*
–  *break-bulk carrier (general cargo
   ship)*
15  el remolcador
–  *tug*
16  el dique flotante
–  *floating dock (pontoon dock)*
17  el dique seco
–  *dry dock*
18  el muelle de carbón *m*
–  *coal wharf*
19  el depósito de carbón *m*
–  *coal bunker*
20  el puente grúa *f* de carga *f*
–  *transporter loading bridge*
21  la vía del puerto
–  *quayside railway*
22  la tolva del carbón
–  *weighing bunker*
23  el cobertizo del astillero (del
   arsenal)
–  *warehouse*
24  la grúa del arsenal
–  *quayside crane*
25  la barcaza con la gabarra
–  *launch and lighter*
26  el hospital del puerto
–  *port hospital*
27  el lazareto (el pabellón de
   cuarentena *f*)
–  *quarantine wing*

28  el instituto para enfermedades *f*
   tropicales (para medicina *f*
   tropical)
–  *Institute of Tropical Medicine*
29  el vapor de recreo *m* (el vapor de
   excursión *f*)
–  *excursion steamer (pleasure
   steamer)*
30  el embarcadero
–  *jetty*
31  el muelle de pasajeros *m*
–  *passenger terminal*
32  el transatlántico (un buque de
   línea *f*)
–  *liner (passenger liner, ocean liner)*
33  la oficina meteorológica, un
   observatorio del tiempo
–  *meteorological office, a weather
   station*
34  el mástil de señales *f*
–  *signal mast (signalling mast)*
35  la bola (la señal) de tempestad *f*
   (de temporal *m;* de tormenta *f*)
–  *storm signal*
36  la oficina del puerto
–  *port administration offices*
37  el indicador del nivel del agua *f*
–  *tide level indicator*
38  la carretera del muelle
–  *quayside road (quayside roadway)*
39  el sistema de carga *f* rodante (un
   transbordador de vehículos *m*, en
   el que estos entran por sí mismos
   mediante una rampa o
   puente *m*)

- roll-on roll-off (ro-ro) system
  (roll-on roll-off operation)
- **40** el puente elevador
  - *gantry*
- **41** el sistema de carga *f* por medio de
  carretillas *f*
  - *truck-to-truck system (truck-to-truck operation)*
- **42** el lote de la carga embalada con
  chapas *f* de metal *m*
  - *foil-wrapped unit loads*
- **43** las paletas
  - *pallets*
- **44** la carretilla elevadora
  - *forklift truck (fork truck, forklift)*
- **45** el carguero portacontenedores
  - *container ship*
- **46** la grúa de puente *m* rodante sobre
  dos vías *f* para la carga de
  contenedores *m*
  - *transporter container-loading
    bridge*
- **47** el camión portacontenedores
  - *container carrier truck*
- **48** el almacén portacontenedores
  (terminal *m* de contenedores *m*)
  - *container terminal (container berth)*
- **49** el lote de carga *f*
  - *unit load*
- **50** la cámara frigorífica
  - *cold store*
- **51** la cinta transportadora
  - *conveyor belt (conveyor)*

- **52** el cobertizo de la fruta
  - *fruit storage shed (fruit warehouse)*
- **53** el edificio de oficinas *f*
  - *office building*
- **54** la autopista urbana
  - *urban motorway (Am. freeway)*
- **55** los túneles por debajo del puerto
  - *harbour (Am. harbor) tunnels*
- **56** el puerto pesquero
  - *fish dock*
- **57** el mercado de pescado *m*
  - *fish market*
- **58** la lonja de pescado *m*
  - *auction room*
- **59** la fábrica de conservas *f* de
  pescado *m*
  - *fish-canning factory*
- **60** el remolcador de empuje *m*
  - *push tow*
- **61** el depósito de tanques *m* de
  petróleo *m* (el puerto petrolero)
  - *tank farm*
- **62** el ramal ferroviario
  - *railway siding*
- **63** el pontón de abordaje *m* (de
  atraque *m*)
  - *landing pontoon (landing stage)*
- **64** el muelle
  - *quay*
- **65** el rompeolas
  - *breakwater (mole)*
- **66** el embarcadero, una prolongación
  del muelle
  - *pier (jetty), a quay extension*

- **67** el carguero a granel *m*
  - *bulk carrier*
- **68** el silo
  - *silo*
- **69** la cuba del silo
  - *silo cylinder*
- **70** el puente elevador
  - *lift bridge*
- **71** la zona industrial del puerto
  - *industrial plant*
- **72** los tanques de almacenamiento *m*
  - *storage tanks*
- **73** el petrolero
  - *tanker*

1 la terminal de contenedores *m*,
una instalación moderna para
el transbordo de mercancías *f*
– *container terminal (container
berth), a modern cargo-handling
berth*
2 el puente de contenedores *m* (el
puente de transbordo *m*)
– *transporter container-loading
bridge (loading bridge);* sim.:
*transtainer crane (transtainer)*
3 el contenedor
– *container*
4 el carro transportador
– *truck (carrier)*
5 el buque portacontenedores
– *all-container ship*
6 los contenedores cargados en
cubierta *f*
– *containers stowed on deck*
7 el transbordo horizontal de los
contenedores por carretilla *f*
elevadora de horquilla *f*
– *truck-to-truck handling
(horizontal cargo handling with
pallets)*
8 la carretilla elevadora de
horquilla *f*
– *forklift truck (fork truck, forklift)*

9 la carga unitaria embalada en
hojas *f* de plástico *m*
– *unitized foil-wrapped load (unit
load)*
10 la paleta plana, una paleta
normal
– *flat pallet, a standard pallet*
11 la mercancía en fardos *m*
unitarios
– *unitized break-bulk cargo*
12 la máquina para embalar en
hojas *f* de plástico *m*
– *heat sealing machine*
13 el carguero de mercancía *f* en
fardos *m*
– *break-bulk carrier (general cargo
ship)*
14 la abertura de carga *f*
– *cargo hatchway*
15 la carretilla a bordo *m* del
buque
– *receiving truck on board ship*
16 la terminal de usos *m* múltiples
– *multi-purpose terminal*
17 el buque de transporte roll-on
roll-off (el buque de
transbordo *m* horizontal)
– *roll-on roll-off ship (ro-ro-ship)*
18 la puerta trasera
– *stern port (stern opening)*

19 la carga automotriz, un camión
de carga *f*
– *driven load, a lorry* (Am. *truck)*
20 la instalación de expedición *f*
de mercancías *f* Ro-ro (la
instalación especial Ro-ro)
– *ro-ro depot*
21 la carga unitaria
– *unitized load (unitized package)*
22 la terminal bananera [corte]
– *banana-handling terminal
[section]*
23 el elevador de cala *f*
– *seaward tumbler*
24 el brazo saledizo
– *jib*
25 el puente elevador
– *elevator bridge*
26 la eslinga de cadena *f*
– *chain sling*
27 el puesto de claridad *f*
– *lighting station*
28 el sistema de carga *f* de
camiones *m* y vagones *m*
– *shore-side tumbler for loading
trains and lorries* (Am. *trucks)*
29 el puesto de carga *f* a granel *m*
– *bulk cargo handling*
30 el carguero de mercancía *f* a
granel *m*
– *bulk carrier*

**31** el puente grúa *f* de carga *f*
– *floating bulk-cargo elevator*
**32** los tubos de aspiración *f*
– *suction pipes*
**33** el receptor
– *receiver*
**34** el tubo de embarque *m*
– *delivery pipe*
**35** la barcaza de transporte *m* a granel *m*
– *bulk transporter barge*
**36** el martinete
– *floating pile driver*
**37** la armazón del martinete
– *pile driver frame*
**38** el mazo
– *pile hammer*
**39** la guía
– *driving guide rail*
**40** el apoyo del martinete basculante
– *pile*
**41** la draga de cangilones *m*, una draga
– *bucket dredger, a dredger*
**42** la cadena de cangilones *m*
– *bucket chain*
**43** el transportador de cangilones *m*
– *bucket ladder*

**44** el cangilón de la draga
– *dredger bucket*
**45** el vertedor
– *chute*
**46** el lanchón de la draga
– *hopper barge*
**47** el material dragado
– *spoil*
**48** la grúa flotante
– *floating crane*
**49** el pescante (el brazo de la grúa)
– *jib (boom)*
**50** el contrapeso
– *counterweight (counterpoise)*
**51** el eje ajustable
– *adjusting spindle*
**52** la cabina del conductor
– *crane driver's cabin (crane driver's cage)*
**53** la armazón (el chasis) de la grúa
– *crane framework*
**54** la cabina del torno
– *winch house*
**55** el puente de mando *m*
– *control platform*
**56** la plataforma giratoria
– *turntable*
**57** el pontón, una gabarra (*Amér.*: chata *f*)
– *pontoon, a pram*

**58** la superestructura de los motores
– *engine superstructure (engine mounting)*

1 el salvamento de buques *m*
  encallados
– *salvaging (salving) of a ship run
  aground*
2 el buque encallado
– *ship run aground (damaged
  vessel)*
3 el banco de arena *f*
– *sandbank; also: quicksand*
4 el alta mar
– *open sea*
5 el remolcador
– *tug (salvage tug)*
6-15 la instalación de remolque *m*
– *towing gear*
6 el material para el remolque
  marítimo
– *towing gear for towing at sea*
7 el torno de remolque *m*
– *towing winch (towing machine,
  towing engine)*
8 el cable de remolque *m*
– *tow rope (tow line, towing
  hawser)*
9 la guía de remolque *m*
– *tow rope guide*
10 la pasteca
– *cross-shaped bollard*
11 el escobén
– *hawse hole*

12 la cadena del ancla *f*
– *anchor cable, a chain cable*
13 el material para el remolque en
  el puerto
– *towing gear for work in harbours
  (Am. harbors)*
14 la retenida
– *guest rope*
15 la dirección del cable en
  ausencia *f* de retenida *f*
– *position of the tow rope (tow line,
  towing hawser)*
16 el remolcador [proyección
  vertical]
– *tug (salvage tug) [vertical
  elevation]*
17 la defensa de estrave *m*
– *bow fender (pudding fender)*
18 el parapeto delantero
– *forepeak*
19 las habitaciones
– *living quarters*
20 la hélice carenada
– *Schottel propeller*
21 la tobera de la hélice
– *Kort vent*
22 la sala de máquinas *f*
– *engine and propeller room*
23 el sistema de acoplamiento (el
  embrague)
– *clutch coupling*

24 la cubierta radiogoniométrica
– *compass platform (compass
  bridge, compass flat, monkey
  bridge)*
25 la instalación para la extinción
  de incendios *m*
– *fire-fighting equipment*
26 el pañol (la bodega)
– *stowage*
27 el gancho de remolque *m*
– *tow hook*
28 el parapeto trasero
– *afterpeak*
29 la defensa de popa *f*
– *stern fender*
30 la quilla de maniobras *f*
– *main manoeuvring (Am.
  maneuvering) keel*

1 el cohete lanzacabos (el lanzacabos)
– *rocket apparatus (rocket gun, line-throwing gun)*
2 el cohete
– *life rocket (rocket)*
3 el cabo de salvamento *m*
– *rocket line (whip line)*
4 el traje de encerado *m* [traje *m* de hule *m;* un traje impermeabilizado]
– *oilskins*
5 el sueste (el sombreo de hule *m*)
– *sou'wester (southwester)*
6 la chaqueta de encerado *m*
– *oilskin jacket*
7 el abrigo de encerado *m*
– *oilskin coat*
8 el chaleco salvavidas hinchable
– *inflatable life jacket*
9 el chaleco salvavidas de corcho *m*
– *cork life jacket (cork life preserver)*
10 el buque encallado (averiado)
– *stranded ship;* also: *damaged vessel*

11 los sacos de aceite *m,* para dejar caer gota a gota el aceite en la superficie del agua *f*
– *oil bag, for trickling oil on the water surface*
12 la cuerda de salvamento *m*
– *lifeline*
13 la boya pantalón *m* (el pantalón de salvamento *m*)
– *breeches buoy*
14 la lancha de salvamento *m*
– *rescue cruiser*
15 la cubierta de aterrizaje *m* para helicópteros *m*
– *helicopter landing deck*
16 el helicóptero de salvamento *m*
– *rescue helicopter*
17 el bote anejo (*Amér. Central y Panamá:* la panga)
– *daughter boat*
18 la lancha de goma *f*
– *inflatable boat (inflatable dinghy)*
19 el refugio (la balsa de salvamento *m*)
– *life raft*
20 la instalación de extinción *f* de incendios *m*
– *fire-fighting equipment for fires at sea*

21 la enfermería con camarote *m* (sala *f*)de operaciones *f* y unidad *f* de reanimación *f*
– *hospital unit with operating cabin and exposure bath*
22 el cuarto de los instrumentos
– *navigating bridge*
23 el puente de mando *m* superior
– *upper tier of navigating bridge*
24 el puente de mando *m* inferior
– *lower tier of navigating bridge*
25 el cámara (mesa *f* de oficiales *m*)
– *messroom*
26 la hélice y el timón
– *rudders and propeller (screw)*
27 el pañol (la bodega)
– *stowage*
28 el depósito de espuma *f* para la extinción de incendios *m*
– *foam can*
29 los motores laterales
– *side engines*
30 las duchas
– *shower*
31 la cabina del patrón
– *coxswain's cabin*
32 la cabina de un miembro de la tripulación
– *crew member's single-berth cabin*
33 la hélice de estrave *m*
– *bow propeller*

**1-14  la disposición de las alas**
- *wing configurations*
**1** el monoplano de ala *f* alta
- *high-wing monoplane (high-wing plane)*
**2** la envergadura
- *span (wing span)*
**3** el avión de ala *f* alta
- *shoulder-wing monoplane (shoulder-wing plane)*
**4** el avión de ala *f* semialzada
- *midwing monoplane (midwing plane)*
**5** el avión de ala *f* baja
- *low-wing monoplane (low-wing plane)*
**6** el triplano
- *triplane*
**7** el ala *f* alta
- *upper wing*
**8** el ala *f* central
- *middle wing (central wing)*
**9** el ala *f* baja
- *lower wing*
**10** el biplano
- *biplane*
**11** el montante, un refuerzo
- *strut*
**12** el arriostramiento
- *cross bracing wires*
**13** el sesquiplano
- *sesquiplane*
**14** el avión de ala *f* baja con ala *f* de pliegue *m*
- *low-wing monoplane (low-wing plane) with cranked wings (inverted gull wings)*
**15-22  las formas de las alas**
- *wing shapes*
**15** el ala *f* elíptica
- *elliptical wing*
**16** el ala *f* rectangular
- *rectangular wing*
**17** el ala *f* trapezoidal
- *tapered wing*
**18** el ala *f* en media luna *f*
- *crescent wing*
**19** el ala *f* delta
- *delta wing*
**20** el ala *f* en flecha *f* positiva débil
- *swept-back wing with semi-positive sweepback*
**21** el ala *f* en flecha *f* positiva fuerte
- *swept-back wing with positive sweepback*
**22** el ala *f* ojival
- *ogival wing (ogee wing)*
**23-36  las formas de las alas guías**
- *tail shapes (tail unit shapes, empennage shapes)*
**23** el ala *f* guía normal
- *normal tail (normal tail unit)*
**24-25** el timón de dirección *f*
- *vertical tail (vertical stabilizer and rudder)*
**24** la aleta de dirección *f*
- *vertical stabilizer (vertical fin, tail fin)*

**25** el timón de mando *m*
- *rudder*
**26-27** el estabilizador de elevación *f*
- *horizontal tail*
**26** el plano fijo horizontal
- *tailplane (horizontal stabilizer)*
**27** el timón de profundidad
- *elevator*
**28** las alas guías cruciformes
- *cruciform tail (cruciform tail unit)*
**29** las alas guías en T
- *T-tail (T-tail unit)*
**30** el cuerpo expulsor
- *lobe*
**31** las alas guías en V
- *V-tail (vee-tail, butterfly tail)*
**32** las alas guías dobles
- *double tail unit (twin tail unit)*
**33** el disco lateral
- *end plate*
**34** las alas guías dobles de un avión de doble fuselaje *m*
- *double tail unit (twin tail unit) of a twin-boom aircraft*
**35** el fuselaje doble con alas *f* guías horizontales elevadas
- *raised horizontal tail with double booms*
**36** el ala *f* guía triple
- *triple tail unit*
**37** el sistema de alerones *m*
- *system of flaps*
**38** el pico de seguridad *f* móvil
- *extensible slat*
**39** el spoiler
- *spoiler*
**40** el alerón de doble curvatura *f*
- *double-slotted Fowler flap*
**41** el alerón exterior
- *outer aileron (low-speed aileron)*
**42** los aerofrenos internos
- *inner spoiler (landing flap, lift dump)*
**43** el alerón interior
- *inner aileron (all-speed aileron)*
**44** los aerofrenos externos
- *brake flap (air brake)*
**45** el perfil de base *f*
- *basic profile*
**46-48** los alerones de curvatura *f*
- *plain flaps (simple flaps)*
**46** el alerón normal
- *normal flap*
**47** el alerón de hendidura *f*
- *slotted flap*
**48** el alerón de hendidura *f* doble
- *double-slotted flap*
**49-50** los alerones de intradós *m*
- *split flaps*
**49** el alerón de intradós *m* sencillo
- *plain split flap (simple split flap)*
**50** el alerón Zap
- *zap flap*
**51** el ala *f* doble
- *extending flap*
**52** el alerón Fowler
- *Fowler flap*
**53** el pico de seguridad *f*
- *slat*

**54** el alerón de pico *m* perfilado
- *profiled leading-edge flap (droop flap)*
**55** el alerón Krüger
- *Krüger flap*

**1-31 la cabina de pilotaje** *m* de un monomotor de viaje *m* y de turismo *m*
- *cockpit of a single-engine (single-engined) racing and passenger aircraft (racing and passenger plane)*
**1** el tablero de instrumentos *m* (el tablero de a bordo *m*)
- *instrument panel*
**2** el velocímetro (el tacómetro)
- *air-speed* (Am. *airspeed) indicator*
**3** el horizonte artificial
- *artificial horizon (gyro horizon)*
**4** el altímetro
- *altimeter*
**5** el radiocompás (la brújula automática)
- *radio compass (automatic direction finder)*
**6** el compás magnético
- *magnetic compass*
**7** el manómetro de presión *f* de admisión *f*
- *boost gauge* (Am. *gage)*
**8** el contador del número de revoluciones *f* (el cuentarrevoluciones)
- *tachometer (rev counter, revolution counter)*
**9** el indicador de la temperatura de los cilindros
- *cylinder temperature gauge* (Am. *gage)*
**10** el acelerómetro
- *accelerometer*
**11** el reloj de a bordo *m*
- *chronometer*
**12** el indicador de viraje *m* con nivelación *f* de bola *f*
- *turn indicator with ball*
**13** el giroscopio del rumbo
- *directional gyro*
**14** el variómetro
- *vertical speed indicator (rate-of-climb indicator, variometer)*
**15** el indicador VOR [VOR: Very high frequency omnidirectional range]
- *VOR radio direction finder* [VOR: very high frequency omnidirectional range]
**16** el indicador de combustible *m* del depósito izquierdo
- *left tank fuel gauge* (Am. *gage)*
**17** el indicador de combustible *m* del depósito derecho
- *right tank fuel gauge* (Am. *gage)*
**18** el amperímetro
- *ammeter*
**19** el indicador de presión *f* (el manómetro) del combustible
- *fuel pressure gauge* (Am. *gage)*
**20** el indicador de presión *f* (el manómetro) del aceite
- *oil pressure gauge* (Am. *gage)*
**21** el indicador de temperatura *f* del aceite
- *oil temperature gauge* (Am. *gage)*
**22** el aparato de radiotelefonía *f* y de radionavegación *f*
- *radio and radio navigation equipment*
**23** la lámpara para iluminar la carta
- *map light*
**24** el volante (la palanca de mando *m*) para el accionamiento del alerón y del timón de profundidad *f*

- *wheel (control column, control stick) for operating the ailerons and elevators*
**25** el volante para el copiloto
- *co-pilot's wheel*
**26** los interruptores
- *switches*
**27** los pedales del timón de mando *m*
- *rudder pedals*
**28** los pedales del timón de mando *m* del copiloto
- *co-pilot's rudder pedals*
**29** el micrófono para el servicio de radiofonía *f*
- *microphone for the radio*
**30** la palanca del gas
- *throttle lever (throttle control)*
**31** el regulador de mezcla *f* (la palanca de mezcla *f*)
- *mixture control*
**32-66 la avioneta de viaje** *m* y de deporte *m* (el monomotor)
- *single-engine (single-engined) racing and passenger aircraft (racing and passenger plane)*
**32** la hélice
- *propeller (airscrew)*
**33** el casquete de la hélice
- *spinner*
**34** el motor de cuatro cilindros *m*
- *flat four engine*
**35** la cabina del piloto (la cabina de pilotaje *m*, la carlinga)
- *cockpit*
**36** el asiento del piloto
- *pilot's seat*
**37** el asiento del copiloto
- *co-pilot's seat*
**38** los asientos de los pasajeros
- *passenger seats*
**39** la cubierta
- *hood (canopy, cockpit hood, cockpit canopy)*
**40** la rueda de morro *m* dirigible
- *steerable nose wheel*
**41** el tren de aterrizaje *m* principal
- *main undercarriage unit (main landing gear unit)*
**42** el escalón de subida *f*
- *step*
**43** el plano de sustentación *f* (el ala *f*)
- *wing*
**44** la luz de posición *f* derecha
- *right navigation light (right position light)*
**45** el larguero
- *spar*
**46** la nervadura
- *rib*
**47** el puntal longitudinal
- *stringer (longitudinal reinforcing member)*
**48** el depósito de combustible *m*
- *fuel tank*
**49** el faro de aterrizaje *m*
- *landing light*
**50** la luz de posición *f* izquierda
- *left navigation light (left position light)*
**51** el pararrayos estático
- *electrostatic conductor*
**52** el alerón
- *aileron*
**53** la aleta de aterrizaje *m*
- *landing flap*
**54** el fuselaje
- *fuselage (body)*

**55** la costilla
- *frame (former)*
**56** la correa
- *chord*
**57** el puntal longitudinal
- *stringer (longitudinal reinforcing member)*
**58** el timón de dirección *f*
- *vertical tail (vertical stabilizer and rudder)*
**59** el estabilizador de dirección *f*
- *vertical stabilizer (vertical fin, tail fin)*
**60** el timón de mando *m*
- *rudder*
**61** el estabilizador de elevación *f*
- *horizontal tail*
**62** el plano fijo horizontal
- *tailplane (horizontal stabilizer)*
**63** el timón de profundidad *f*
- *elevator*
**64** la luz intermitente
- *warning light (anticollision light)*
**65** la antena dipolo
- *dipole antenna*
**66** la antena de alambre *m* largo
- *long-wire antenna (long-conductor antenna)*
**67-72 los movimientos principales del avión**
- *principal manoeuvres* (Am. *maneuvers) of the aircraft (aeroplane, plane, Am. airplane)*
**67** la inclinación de cabeza *f*
- *pitching*
**68** el eje transversal
- *lateral axis*
**69** el tambaleo
- *yawing*
**70** el eje vertical
- *vertical axis (normal axis)*
**71** la rotación (el movimiento giratorio)
- *rolling*
**72** el eje longitudinal
- *longitudinal axis*

**1-33 tipos** *m* **de aviones** *m*
- *types of aircraft (aeroplanes, planes,* Am. *airplanes)*
**1-6 aviones** *m* **de hélice** *f*
- *propeller-driven aircraft (aeroplanes, planes,* Am. *airplanes)*
**1** el (avión) monomotor de viaje *m* y de deporte *m* de ala *f* baja
- *single-engine (single-engined) racing and passenger aircraft (racing and passenger plane), a low-wing monoplane (low-wing plane)*
**2** el (avión) monomotor de viaje *m* de ala *f* alta
- *single-engine (single-engined) passenger aircraft, a high-wing monoplane (high-wing plane)*
**3** el (avión) bimotor comercial y de viaje *m*
- *twin-engine (twin-engined) business and passenger aircraft (business and passenger plane)*
**4** el avión de pasajeros *m* para trayectos cortos y medios, un avión turbopropulsado
- *short/medium haul airliner, a turboprop plane (turbopropeller plane, propeller-turbine plane)*
**5** el turbopropulsor
- *turboprop engine (turbopropeller engine)*
**6** el estabilizador de dirección *f*
- *vertical stabilizer (vertical fin, tail fin)*
**7-33 aviones** *m* **a reacción** *f*
- *jet planes (jet aeroplanes, jets,* Am. *jet airplanes)*
**7** el (avión) birreactor comercial y de turismo *m*
- *twin-jet business and passenger aircraft (business and passenger plane)*
**8** el control para la capa límite
- *fence*
**9** el depósito del extremo del ala *f*
- *wing-tip tank (tip tank)*
**10** el mecanismo propulsor trasero
- *rear engine*
**11** el (avión) birreactor de pasajeros *m* para trayectos cortos y medios
- *twin-jet short/medium haul airliner*
**12** el (avión) trirreactor para trayectos *m* medios
- *tri-jet medium haul airliner*
**13** el (avión) cuatrirreactor para trayectos *m* largos
- *four-jet long haul airliner*
**14** el avión de gran capacidad *f* para trayectos *m* largos (el Jumbo)
- *wide-body long haul airliner (jumbo jet)*
**15** el avión de pasajeros *m* supersónico [tipo Concorde]
- *supersonic airliner [Concorde]*

**16** el pico del fuselaje basculante
- *droop nose*
**17** el avión birreactor de gran capacidad *f* para trayectos cortos y medios (el Aerobús)
- *twin-jet wide-body airliner for short/medium haul routes (airbus)*
**18** el morro radar, con la antena del radar meteorológico
- *radar nose (radome, radar dome) with weather radar antenna*
**19** la cabina de pilotaje *m*
- *cockpit*
**20** la cocina de a bordo *m*
- *galley*
**21** el espacio de carga *f* (la bodega)
- *underfloor cargo hold (hold)*
**22** la cabina de los pasajeros con asientos *m* para los pasajeros
- *passenger cabin with passenger seats*
**23** el tren de aterrizaje *m* escamotable del morro
- *retractable nose undercarriage unit (retractable nose landing gear unit)*
**24** la puerta del tren de aterrizaje *m*
- *nose undercarriage flap (nose gear flap)*
**25** la puerta de pasajeros *m* central
- *centre (*Am. *center) passenger door*
**26** el motor turboreactor con el mecanismo propulsor
- *engine pod with engine (turbojet engine, jet turbine engine, jet engine, jet turbine)*
**27** el pararrayos estático
- *electrostatic conductors*
**28** el tren de aterrizaje *m* principal escamotable
- *retractable main undercarriage unit (retractable main landing gear unit)*
**29** la ventana lateral (la ventanilla lateral)
- *side window*
**30** la puerta de pasajeros *m* trasera
- *rear passenger door*
**31** los servicios
- *toilet (lavatory, WC)*
**32** el mamparo estanco de presión *f*
- *pressure bulkhead*
**33** el mecanismo propulsor auxiliar (la turbina de gas *m* auxiliar) para la alimentación de corriente *f*
- *auxiliary engine (auxiliary gas turbine) for the generator unit*

1 el hidroavión
- *flying boat, a seaplane*
2 el casco (el fuselaje) del hidroavión
- *hull*
3 el flotador de ala *f* de estabilización *f*
- *stub wing (sea wing)*
4 el arriostramiento del timón y estabilizador *m* de cola *f*
- *tail bracing wires*
5 el avión flotador, un hidroavión
- *floatplane (float seaplane), a seaplane*
6 el flotador (*Mé.:* la llanta)
- *float*
7 el estabilizador de cola *f*
- *vertical stabilizer (vertical fin, tail fin)*
8 **el avión anfibio**
- **amphibian** *(amphibian flying boat)*
9 el casco (el fuselaje) del avión
- *hull*
10 el tren de aterrizaje *m* escamoteable
- *retractable undercarriage (retractable landing gear)*
11-25 **el helicóptero**
- **helicopters**
11 el helicóptero universal ligero
- *light multirole helicopter*
12-13 el rotor principal
- *main rotor*
12 el ala *f* giratoria
- *rotary wing (rotor blade)*
13 la cabeza del rotor
- *rotor head*
14 el rotor de cola *f*
- *tail rotor (anti-torque rotor)*
15 los patines de aterrizaje *m*
- *landing skids*
16 el helicóptero grúa *f*
- *flying crane*
17 las turbinas del mecanismo propulsor (el turborreactor)
- *turbine engines*
18 el tren de aterrizaje *m* de pórtico *m*
- *lifting undercarriage*
19 la plataforma de carga *f* (la plataforma elevadora)
- *lifting platform*
20 el depósito auxiliar
- *reserve tank*
21 el helicóptero de transporte *m*
- *transport helicopter*
22 los rotores en tándem *m*
- *rotors in tandem*
23 el pilón del rotor
- *rotor pylon*
24 el turborreactor
- *turbine engine*
25 la puerta de carga *f* de la cola
- *tail loading gate*
26-32 **los aviones de despegue *m* y aterrizaje *m* verticales cortos**
- **V/STOL aircraft** *(vertical/short take-off and landing aircraft)*

26 el avión de ala *f* pivotante, un avión de despegue *m* y aterrizaje *m* verticales
- *tilt-wing aircraft, a VTOL aircraft (vertical take-off and landing aircraft)*
27 el ala *f* pivotante en posición *f* vertical
- *tilt wing in vertical position*
28 el propulsor de cola *f* de marcha *f* atrás
- *contrarotating tail propellers*
29 el girodino
- *gyrodyne*
30 el turbopropulsor
- *turboprop engine (turbopropeller engine)*
31 el avión de rotor *m* pivotante
- *convertiplane*
32 el rotor pivotante en posición *f* vertical
- *tilting rotor in vertical position*
33-60 **los mecanismos propulsores de avión *m***
- **aircraft engines** *(aero engines)*
33-50 los estatorreactores (los turborreactores)
- *jet engines (turbojet engines, jet turbine engines, jet turbines)*
33 el reactor soplante delantero
- *front fan-jet*
34 el soplante
- *fan*
35 el compresor de baja presión *f*
- *low-pressure compressor*
36 el compresor de alta presión *f*
- *high-pressure compressor*
37 la cámara de combustión *f*
- *combustion chamber*
38 la turbina motor soplante
- *fan-jet turbine*
39 la tobera (la tobera de empuje *m*)
- *nozzle (propelling nozzle, propulsion nozzle)*
40 las turbinas
- *turbines*
41 el canal de la corriente secundaria
- *bypass duct*
42 el reactor soplante trasero (el reactor soplante de cola *f*)
- *aft fan-jet*
43 el soplante
- *fan*
44 el canal de la corriente secundaria
- *bypass duct*
45 la tobera (la tobera de empuje *m*)
- *nozzle (propelling nozzle, propulsion nozzle)*
46 el reactor de doble flujo *m*
- *bypass engine*
47 las turbinas
- *turbines*
48 el mezclador
- *mixer*

49 la tobera (la tobera de empuje *m*)
- *nozzle (propelling nozzle, propulsion nozzle)*
50 la corriente (el flujo) secundaria (-o)
- *secondary air flow (bypass air flow)*
51 el turbopropulsor, un propulsor de dos árboles *m*
- *turboprop engine (turbopropeller engine), a twin-shaft engine*
52 la entrada de aire *m* en forma *f* de anillo *m*
- *annular air intake*
53 la turbina de alta presión *f*
- *high-pressure turbine*
54 la turbina de baja presión *f*
- *low-pressure turbine*
55 la tobera (la tobera de empuje *m*)
- *nozzle (propelling nozzle, propulsion nozzle)*
56 el árbol del embrague
- *shaft*
57 el árbol intermedio
- *intermediate shaft*
58 el árbol de entrada *f* de la transmisión
- *gear shaft*
59 el reductor
- *reduction gear*
60 el árbol de la hélice
- *propeller shaft*

1 la pista f de aterrizaje m y despegue m
– runway
2 la pista f de rodaje m
– taxiway
3 la pista f de estacionamiento m
– apron
4 la pista f de maniobras f
– apron taxiway
5 la terminal f de equipajes m
– baggage terminal
6 el túnel m de entrada a la terminal de equipajes m
– tunnel entrance to the baggage terminal
7 el servicio de bomberos m del aeropuerto m
– airport fire service
8 el edificio m de los enseres m de bomberos m
– fire appliance building
9 la terminal f postal y de carga f
– mail and cargo terminal
10 el depósito m de mercancías f
– cargo warehouse
11 el punto de encuentros m
– assembly point
12 el muelle de embarque m
– pier
13 la cabecera f del muelle
– pierhead
14 la pasarela f (el puente aéreo, el dique) de embarque m
– passenger loading bridge
15 el edificio m terminal de viajeros m (la terminal f de salida f)
– departure building (terminal)
16 el edificio m de administración f
– administration building
17 la torre de control m
– control tower (tower)
18 la sala de espera f
– waiting room (lounge)
19 el restaurante m del aeropuerto m
– airport restaurant

20 la terraza f de visitantes m (del público)
– spectators' terrace
21 el avión m en posición f de carga f
– aircraft in loading position (nosed in)
22 los vehículos m de servicio m; p. e.: el remolque de equipajes m, el tanque m (la cisterna) de agua f, el remolque de provisiones f, el vehículo de limpieza f de los aseos, el generador de energía f de tierra f, el camión cisterna f
– service vehicles, e.g. baggage loaders, water tankers, galley loaders, toilet-cleaning vehicles, ground power units, tankers
23 el tractor (el remolcador) de aviones m
– aircraft tractor (aircraft tug)
24-53 las señales de información f del aeropuerto
– airport information symbols [pictographs]
24 aeropuerto m
– 'airport'
25 salidas f
– 'departures'
26 llegadas f
– 'arrivals'
27 pasajeros m en tránsito m
– 'transit passengers'
28 sala de espera f
– 'waiting room' ('lounge')
29 punto de encuentros m
– 'assembly point' ('meeting point', 'rendezvous point')
30 terraza f de visitantes m
– 'spectators' terrace'
31 información f
– 'information'
32 taxis m
– 'taxis'

33 coches m de alquiler m (autos m de alquiler m)
– 'car hire'
34 tren m
– 'trains'
35 autobús m
– 'buses'
36 entrada f
– 'entrance'
37 salida f
– 'exit'
38 entrega f de equipajes m (recogida f de equipajes m)
– 'baggage retrieval'
39 consigna f de equipajes m
– 'luggage lockers'
40 teléfono m de urgencias f
– telephone - 'emergency calls only'
41 salida f de urgencia f
– 'emergency exit'
42 control m de pasaportes m
– 'passport check'
43 sala f de prensa f
– 'press facilities'
44 médico m (Amér.: doctor m)
– 'doctor'
45 farmacia f
– 'chemist' (Am. druggist')
46 ducha f
– 'showers'
47 servicios m de caballeros m
– 'gentlemen's toilet' ('gentlemen')
48 servicios m de señoras f
– 'ladies toilet' ('ladies')
49 capilla f
– 'chapel'
50 restaurante m (Amér.: restaurant m)
– 'restaurant'
51 cambio m
– 'change'
52 tienda f libre de impuestos m
– 'duty free shop'
53 peluquería f
– 'hairdresser'

1 el cohete portador Saturno V del
  "Apolo" [vista f de conjunto m]
- Saturn V 'Apollo' booster (booster
  rocket) [overall view]
2 el cohete portador Saturno V del
  "Apolo" [corte m general]
- Saturn V 'Apollo' booster (booster
  rocket) [overall sectional view]
3 la primera etapa del cohete S-IC
  (la etapa de despegue m)
- first rocket stage (S-IC)
4 los propulsores F-1
- F-1 engines
5 el escudo antitérmico (el protector
  del calor)
- heat shield (thermal protection
  shield)
6 el revestimiento aerodinámico del
  propulsor
- aerodynamic engine fairings
7 la aleta aerodinámica de estabilización f
- aerodynamic stabilizing fins
8 los retrocohetes separados por
  etapas f, 8 cohetes m para
  4 pares m
- stage separation retro-rockets, 8
  rockets arranged in 4 pairs
9 el depósito de queroseno m
  (Amér.: querosén) (RP-1)
  [811 000 l]
- kerosene (RP-1) tank [capacity:
  811,000 litres]
10 los conductos de alimentación f
  del oxígeno líquido
- liquid oxygen (LOX, LO₂) supply
  lines
11 el sistema antivortex
  (dispositivo m permanente para
  evitar la formación de
  torbellinos m en el carburante)
- anti-vortex system [device for
  preventing the formation of vortices
  in the fuel]
12 el depósito de oxígeno m líquido
  [1 315 000 l]
- liquid oxygen (LOX, LO₂) tank
  [capacity: 1,315,000 litres]
13 la amortiguación (la
  estabilización) del traqueteo
- anti-slosh baffles
14 las botellas de presión f para el
  helio
- compressed-helium bottles (helium
  pressure bottles)
15 el difusor para el oxígeno gaseoso
- diffuser for gaseous oxygen
16 la pieza intermedia del depósito
- inter-tank connector (inter-tank
  section)
17 los instrumentos para el control
  del sistema
- instruments and system-monitoring
  devices
18 la segunda etapa S-II
- second rocket stage (S-II)
19 los propulsores J-2
- J-2 engines
20 el escudo antitérmico (el protector
  del calor)
- heat shield (thermal protection
  shield)
21 el soporte del propulsor y la
  armazón del empuje
- engine mounts and thrust structure

22 los cohetes de aceleración f para
  la acumulación del carburante
- acceleration rockets for fuel
  acquisition
23 el conducto de admisión f de
  hidrógeno m líquido
- liquid hydrogen (LH₂) suction line
24 el depósito de oxígeno m líquido
  [1 315 000 l]
- liquid oxygen (LOX, LO²) tank
  [capacity: 1,315,000 litres]
25 el tubo vertical
- standpipe
26 el depósito de hidrógeno m
  líquido [1 020 000 l]
- liquid hydrogen (LH₂) tank
  [capacity: 1,020,000 litres]
27 el sensor vertical del nivel del
  combustible
- fuel level sensor
28 la plataforma de trabajo m
- work platform (working platform)
29 la canalización de cables m
- cable duct
30 el orificio de acceso m
- manhole
31 el compartimiento intermedio
  S-IC/S-II
- S-IC/S-II inter-stage connector
  (inter-stage section)
32 el depósito de gas m comprimido
- compressed-gas container (gas
  pressure vessel)
33 la tercera etapa del cohete S-IV B
- third rocket stage (S-IVB)
34 el propulsor J-2
- J-2 engine
35 el cono de empuje m
- nozzle (thrust nozzle)
36 el compartimiento intermedio
  S-II/S-IV B
- S-II/S-IVB inter-stage connector
  (inter-stage section)
37 los retrocohetes separados por
  etapas f para S-II, 4 cohetes m
- four second-stage (S-II) separation
  retro-rockets
38 los cohetes para regular la
  posición
- attitude control rockets
39 el depósito de oxígeno m líquido
  [77 200 l]
- liquid oxygen (LOX, LO₂) tank
  [capacity: 77,200 litres]
40 la tubería (el entramado de
  tubos m)
- fuel line duct
41 el depósito de hidrógeno m
  líquido [253 000 l]
- liquid hydrogen (LH₂) tank
  [capacity: 253,000 litres]
42 las sondas de medida f
- measuring probes
43 los depósitos de gas m
  comprimido y de helio m
- compressed-helium tanks (helium
  pressure vessels)
44 la ventilación del depósito
- tank vent
45 el anillo de la cabina superior
- forward frame section
46 la plataforma de trabajo m
- work platform (working platform)
47 la canalización de cables m
- cable duct

48 los cohetes de aceleración f para
  la acumulación del carburante
- acceleration rockets for fuel
  acquisition
49 el anillo de la cabina inferior
- aft frame section
50 el depósito de gas m comprimido
  y de helio m
- compressed-helium tanks (helium
  pressure vessels)
51 el conducto del hidrógeno líquido
- liquid hydrogen (LH₂) line
52 el conducto de oxígeno m líquido
- liquid oxygen (LOX, LO₂) line
53 el conjunto de instrumentos m con
  24 paneles m solares
- 24-panel instrument unit
54 el hangar LM
- LM hangar (lunar module hangar)
55 el LM (lunar Module, el módulo
  lunar)
- LM (lunar module)
56 el módulo de servicio Apolo
  (Servicio Module), un
  compartimiento para
  abastecimiento m y herramientas f
- Apollo SM (service module),
  containing supplies and equipment
57 el propulsor principal del módulo
  de servicio m
- SM (service module) main engine
58 el depósito de carburante m
- fuel tank
59 el depósito de tetraóxido m de
  nitrógeno m
- nitrogen tetroxide tank
60 el sistema de alimentación f de
  gas m comprimido
- pressurized gas delivery system
61 los depósitos de oxígeno m
- oxygen tanks
62 las cabinas de combustible m
- fuel cells
63 los grupos de cohetes m de
  control m
- manoeuvring (Am. maneuvering)
  rocket assembly
64 el grupo de antenas f dirigidas
- directional antenna assembly
65 la cápsula espacial (el módulo de
  mando m)
- space capsule (command section)
66 la torre de salvamento m para la
  fase de despegue m
- launch phase escape tower

**1-45 la nave espacial Orbiter**
- *Space Shuttle-Orbiter*
1 la aleta vertical de dos largueros *m*
- *twin-spar (two-spar, double-spar) vertical fin*
2 la estructura del propulsor
- *engine compartment structure*
3 el larguero lateral
- *fin post*
4 la chapa de unión *f* del fuselaje
- *fuselage attachment [of payload bay doors]*
5 la armazón soporte del empuje superior
- *upper thrust mount*
6 la armazón soporte del empuje inferior
- *lower thrust mount*
7 el soporte de la quilla
- *keel*
8 el escudo protector del calor
- *heat shield*
9 el larguero central del fuselaje
- *waist longeron*
10 la cuaderna maestra (la cuaderna principal) fresada integralmente
- *integrally machined (integrally milled) main rib*
11 el borde (el revestimiento) de aleación *f* ligera enteramente reforzado
- *integrally stiffened light alloy skin*
12 el soporte de reja *f*
- *lattice girder*
13 el revestimiento para el aislamiento del compartimiento de carga *f* útil
- *payload bay insulation*
14 la escotilla del compartimiento de carga *f* útil
- *payload bay door*
15 el revestimiento protector del frío
- *low-temperature surface insulation*
16 el compartimiento de la tripulación (la cabina de pilotaje *m*)
- *flight deck (crew compartment)*
17 el asiento (el puesto) del comandante
- *captain's seat (commander's seat)*
18 el asiento del piloto
- *pilot's seat (co-pilot's seat)*
19 la cuaderna de compresión *f* delantera
- *forward pressure bulkhead*
20 la punta (el pico) del fuselaje, una carena curva armada de fibras *f* de carbono *m*
- *nose-section fairings, carbon fibre reinforced nose cone*
21 los depósitos delanteros de carburante *m*
- *forward fuel tanks*
22 las consolas del equipo electrónico de la nave
- *avionics consoles*
23 el tablero de mando *m* para el pilotaje automático
- *automatic flight control panel*
24 la ventanilla de observación *f* superior
- *upward observation windows*
25 la ventanilla de observación *f* delantera
- *forward observation windows*
26 la escotilla de acceso *m* al compartimiento *m* de carga *f* útil
- *entry hatch to payload bay*
27 la esclusa de aire *m*
- *air lock*
28 la escala de acceso *m* al primer puente *m*
- *ladder to lower deck*
29 el brazo manipulador controlado a distancia *f*
- *payload manipulator arm*
30 el tren de aterrizaje *m* delantero con accionamiento *m* hidráulico
- *hydraulically steerable nose wheel*

31 el tren de aterrizaje *m* principal con accionamiento *m* hidráulico
- *hydraulically operated main landing gear*
32 el revestimiento de ataque *m* móvil, armado de fibras *f* de carbono *m*
- *removable (reusable) carbon fibre reinforced leading edge [of wing]*
33 las partes móviles del elevón *m* (alerón)
- *movable elevon sections*
34 la estructura resistente al calor *m* del elevón (alerón)
- *heat-resistant elevon structure*
35 el conducto (la llegada) principal de hidrógeno *m*
- *main liquid hydrogen (LH₂) supply*
36 el motor principal de combustibles líquidos
- *main liquid-fuelled rocket engine*
37 la tobera de empuje *m*
- *nozzle (thrust nozzle)*
38 el conducto de refrigeración *f*
- *coolant feed line*
39 las herramientas de mando *m* del motor
- *engine control system*
40 el escudo protector del calor *m*
- *heat shield*
41 la bomba de hidrógeno *m* a alta presión *f*
- *high-pressure liquid hydrogen (LH₂) pump*
42 la bomba de oxígeno *m* a alta presión *f*
- *high-pressure liquid oxygen (LOX, LO₂) pump*
43 el sistema de mando *m* del empuje
- *thrust vector control system*
44 el propulsor principal de maniobra *f* espacial de mando *m* electromecánico
- *electromechanically controlled orbital manoeuvring (Am. maneuvering) main engine*
45 los depósitos de carburante *m* de las toberas de empuje *m*
- *nozzle fuel tanks (thrust nozzle fuel tanks)*
**46 los depósitos de hidrógeno *m* y de oxígeno *m* eyectables**
- *jettisonable liquid hydrogen and liquid oxygen tank (fuel tank)*
47 la cuaderna circular reforzada integralmente
- *integrally stiffened annular rib (annular frame)*
48 la cuaderna de extremidad *f* hemisférica
- *hemispherical end rib (end frame)*
49 la pasarela trasera de acceso *m* al Orbiter
- *aft attachment to Orbiter*
50 la tubería del hidrógeno
- *liquid hydrogen (LH₂) line*
51 la tubería del oxígeno
- *liquid oxygen (LOX, LO₂) line*
52 el orificio de acceso *m*
- *manhole*
53 el sistema de amortiguación *f*
- *surge baffle system (slosh baffle system)*
54 la tubería bajo presión *f* para el depósito de hidrógeno *m*
- *pressure line to liquid hydrogen tank*
55 la canalización principal de electricidad *f*
- *electrical system bus*
56 la tubería de distribución *f* del oxígeno
- *liquid oxygen (LOX, LO₂) line*
57 la tubería bajo presión *f* para el depósito de oxígeno *m*
- *pressure line to liquid oxygen tank*

**58 el propulsor de combustible *m* sólido recuperable**
- *recoverable solid-fuel rocket (solid rocket booster)*
59 el compartimiento de los paracaídas auxiliares
- *auxiliary parachute bay*
60 el compartimiento de los paracaídas de salvamento *m* y de los motores-cohetes de separación *f* delantera
- *compartment housing the recovery parachutes and the forward separation rocket motors*
61 la caja (el compartimiento) de cables *m*
- *cable duct*
62 los motores-cohetes de separación *f* trasera
- *aft separation rocket motors*
63 el cono de revestimiento *m* trasero
- *aft skirt*
64 la tobera de empuje *m* (eyección *f*) orientable
- *swivel nozzle (swivelling, Am. swiveling, nozzle)*
**65 el Spacelab (el laboratorio espacial, la estación espacial)**
- *Spacelab (space laboratory, space station)*
66 el laboratorio de uso *m* múltiple
- *multi-purpose laboratory (orbital workshop)*
67 el astronauta
- *astronaut*
68 el telescopio de suspensión *f* cardán
- *gimbal-mounted telescope*
69 la plataforma de los instrumentos de medida *f*
- *measuring instrument platform*
70 el módulo espacial
- *spaceflight module*
71 el túnel de esclusas *f* (la esclusa de comunicación *f*)
- *crew entry tunnel*

**1-30  la sala de ventanillas** *f*
– *main hall*
**1**  la ventanilla de los paquetes
– *parcels counter*
**2**  la balanza para los paquetes
– *parcels scales*
**3**  el paquete (el paquete postal;
*Arg., Col., Chile y Perú:* la
encomienda; *Col. y Mé.:* el
recomendado)
– *parcel*
**4**  la dirección pegada, con la
etiqueta del número del
paquete
– *stick-on address label with parcel
registration slip*
**5**  el bote de engrudo *m*
– *glue pot*
**6**  el pequeño paquete
– *small parcel*
**7**  la máquina de franquear
(*Amér.:* la máquina de
estampillar) de los boletines de
expedición *f*
– *franking machine* (Am. *postage
meter) for parcel registration
cards*
**8**  la cabina telefónica
– *telephone box (telephone booth,
telephone kiosk, call box)*
**9**  el teléfono automático de
monedas *f*
– *coin-box telephone (pay phone,
public telephone)*
**10**  el soporte de las guías
telefónicas
– *telephone directory rack*
**11**  el portaguías basculante
– *directory holder*
**12**  la guía telefónica
– *telephone directory (telephone
book)*
**13**  los apartados de correos (*Chile
y Perú:* la casilla)
– *post office boxes*
**14**  la caja del apartado de correos
(la caja postal, la casilla postal)
– *post office box*
**15**  la ventanilla de venta *f* de los
sellos de correos (*Amér.:* de
estampillas *f*)
– *stamp counter*
**16**  el empleado de ventanilla *f*
– *counter clerk (counter officer)*
**17**  el recadero (el muchacho de los
recados)
– *company messenger*
**18**  el registro del correo (el
registro de envíos *m*)
– *record of posting book*
**19**  el distribuidor de sellos *m*
(*Amér.:* estampillas *f*)
– *counter stamp machine*
**20**  la carpeta de sellos *m* (*Amér.:*
estampillas *f*)
– *stamp book*
**21**  la hoja de sellos *m*
– *sheet of stamps*

**22**  el cajón de valores *m*
– *security drawer*
**23**  la caja de cambio *m*
– *change rack*
**24**  el pesacartas
– *letter scales*
**25**  la ventanilla de las operaciones
financieras (la ventanilla de los
giros y la caja postal)
– *paying-in* (Am. *deposit), post
office savings, and pensions
counter*
**26**  la máquina de contabilidad *f*
– *accounting machine*
**27**  la máquina de timbrar para los
giros postales
– *franking machine for money
orders and paying-in slips* (Am.
*deposit slips)*
**28**  el distribuidor de monedas *f*
– *change machine* (Am.
*changemaker)*
**29**  el sello de recibo *m*
– *receipt stamp*
**30**  la ventanilla
– *hatch*
**31-44**  la instalación de
clasificación *f* de la correspondencia (*fam.:* la sala de
batalla *f*)
– *letter-sorting installation*
**31**  la introducción de la
correspondencia
– *letter feed*
**32**  las cestas de la correspondencia
amontonada
– *stacked letter containers*
**33**  el transportador mecánico de
alimentación *f*
– *feed conveyor*
**34**  la máquina ordenadora
– *intermediate stacker*
**35**  la sección de codificación *f*
– *coding station*
**36**  la máquina de primera
clasificación *f*
– *pre-distributor channel*
**37**  la calculadora de procesos *m*
– *process control computer*
**38**  la máquina de clasificación de
cartas *f*
– *distributing machine*
**39**  la sección de videocodificación *f*
– *video coding station*
**40**  la pantalla
– *screen*
**41**  la imagen de la dirección
– *address display*
**42**  la dirección
– *address*
**43**  el código postal
– *post code (postal code,* Am. *zip
code)*
**44**  el teclado
– *keyboard*
**45**  el matasellos de puño *m*
– *handstamp*

**46**  el matasellos de rodillo *m*
– *roller stamp*
**47**  la máquina de timbrar (la
máquina de matasellar)
– *franking machine*
**48**  el dispositivo de introducción *f*
– *feed mechanism*
**49**  el dispositivo de distribución *f*
– *delivery mechanism*
**50-55**  la recogida de la correspondencia y el reparto de la
correspondencia
– *postal collection and and
delivery*
**50**  el buzón
– *postbox* (Am. *mailbox)*
**51**  la bolsa colectora de la
correspondencia
– *collection bag*
**52**  el coche de correos *m*
– *post office van (mail van)*
**53**  el repartidor (el cartero)
– *postman* (Am. *mail carrier, letter
carrier, mailman)*
**54**  la bolsa del cartero
– *delivery pouch (postman's bag,
mailbag)*
**55**  la remesa de correspondencia *f*
– *letter-rate item*
**56-60**  los sellados
– *postmarks*
**56**  el matasellos publicitario
– *postmark advertisement*
**57**  el matasellos con la fecha
– *date stamp postmark*
**58**  el sello de sobretasa *f*
– *charge postmark*
**59**  el matasellos especial
– *special postmark*
**60**  el matasellos de rodillo *m*
manual
– *roller postmark*
**61**  el sello postal (*Amér.:* la
estampilla)
– *stamp (postage stamp)*
**62**  el dentado del sello
– *perforations*

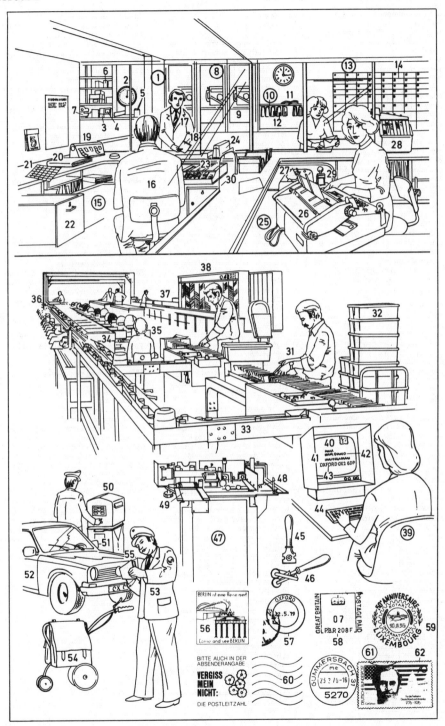

# 237 Correos II (Teléfono y telégrafo)

1 **la cabina telefónica**, un teléfono público
- *telephone box (telephone booth, telephone kiosk, call box), a public telephone*
2 el usuario del teléfono (*con conexión individual*: el abonado al teléfono)
- *telephone user;* with own telephone: *telephone subscriber (telephone customer)*
3 el teléfono público automático de monedas *f* para conferencias *f* urbanas e interurbanas
- *coin-box telephone (pay phone, public telephone) for local and long-distance calls (trunk calls)*
4 el dispositivo de llamada *f* de alarma *f*
- *emergency telephone*
5 la guía de teléfonos *m*
- *telephone directory (telephone book)*
6-26 **el teléfono** (el aparato telefónico)
- *telephone instruments (telephones)*
6 el teléfono de mesa *f* estándar (*en España*: modelo Heraldo)
- *standard table telephone*
7 el auricular (el microteléfono)
- *telephone receiver (handset)*
8 el receptor
- *earpiece*
9 el micrófono
- *mouthpiece (microphone)*
10 el disco selector (para los números)
- *dial;* sim.: *push-button keyboard*
11 la corona de orificios *m* (el disco de orificios *m* para el dedo)
- *finger plate (dial finger plate, dial wind-up plate)*
12 el tope
- *finger stop (dial finger stop)*
13 la horquilla (el conmutador de horquilla, el gancho conmutador)
- *cradle (handset cradle, cradle switch)*
14 el cable del auricular
- *receiver cord (handset cord)*
15 la caja del aparato telefónico
- *telephone casing (telephone cover)*
16 el indicador de la tasa
- *subscriber's (customer's) private meter*
17 el aparato de conexión *f* principal para un aparato telefónico secundario (supletorio *m*) (la centralita para supletorios; *en España*: un SATAI)
- *switchboard (exchange) for a system of extensions*
18 el botón para la línea de conexión *f* principal
- *push button for connecting main exchange lines*
19 los botones de selección *f* de los aparatos telefónicos secundarios (de los supletorios)
- *push buttons for calling extensions*
20 el teléfono de teclas *f*
- *push-button telephone*
21 el botón de tierra *f* para los aparatos telefónicos secundarios (los supletorios)
- *earthing button for the extensions*
22-26 la instalación para la elección de los supletorios
- *switchboard with extensions*

22 la centralita
- *exchange*
23 el aparato
- *switchboard operator's set*
24 la línea (la conexión) principal
- *main exchange line*
25 el armario de los conmutadores (la central)
- *switching box (automatic switching system, automatic connecting system, switching centre, Am. center)*
26 el aparato telefónico secundario (el supletorio)
- *extension*
27-41 **la central telefónica**
- *telephone exchange*
27 el servicio para medir las perturbaciones de radiodifusión *f* (los parásitos)
- *radio interference service*
28 la técnica de desparasitaje *m*
- *maintenance technician*
29 la posición de revisión *f*
- *testing board (testing desk)*
30 la telegrafía
- *telegraphy*
31 el aparato telegráfico (el telégrafo, la teleimpresora)
- *teleprinter (teletypewriter)*
32 el papel perforado (la cinta perforada)
- *paper tape*
33 el servicio de información telefónica
- *directory enquiries*
34 el puesto de información *f*
- *information position (operator's position)*
35 la telefonista (la operadora)
- *operator*
36 el lector de microfilmes *m*
- *microfilm reader*
37 el archivador de microfilmes *m*
- *microfilm file*
38 la proyección sobre la pantalla del microfilm de los números de llamada *f*
- *microfilm card with telephone numbers*
39 la indicación de la fecha
- *date indicator display*
40 el lugar de medida *f* y prueba *f*
- *testing and control station*
41 los equipos de autocomunicación *f* para el teléfono, el télex y la transmisión de datos *m*
- *switching centre (Am. center) for telephone, telex, and data transmission services*
42 **el selector** (el conmutador giratorio con motor *m* de metal *m* precioso; *en el futuro*: el dispositivo de conmutación *f* electrónica)
- *selector (motor uniselector made of noble metals;* in the future: *electronic selector)*
43 el anillo de contacto *m*
- *contact arc (bank)*
44 el brazo de contacto *m*
- *contact arm (wiper)*
45 el campo de contacto *m*
- *contact field*
46 el elemento de contacto *m*
- *contact arm tag*
47 el electroimán
- *electromagnet*

48 el motor selector
- *selector motor*
49 el elemento de ajuste *m*
- *restoring spring (resetting spring)*
50 **Radiocomunicaciones** *f*
- *communication links*
51-52 la transmisión vía *f* satélite *m*
- *satellite radio link*
51 la estación terrestre con antena *f* dirigida
- *earth station with directional antenna*
52 el satélite de telecomunicaciones *f* con antena *f* dirigida
- *communications satellite with directional antenna*
53 la estación costera
- *coastal station*
54-55 la transmisión intercontinental
- *intercontinental radio link*
54 la estación de ondas *f* cortas
- *short-wave station*
55 la ionosfera
- *ionosphere*
56 el cable submarino
- *submarine cable (deep-sea cable)*
57 el amplificador submarino
- *underwater amplifier*
58 **la transmisión de datos** *m* (datos *m* a distancia, la telemática; *servicios telemáticos en España*: teletex, telefax, datafono, videotex)
- *data transmission*
59 el aparato de entrada *f* y salida *f* para los datos
- *input/output device for data carriers*
60 el aparato de transmisión *f* de los datos
- *data processor*
61 la impresora de datos *m*
- *teleprinter*
62-64 los soportes de datos *m*
- *data carriers*
62 la cinta perforada
- *punched tape (punch tape)*
63 la cinta magnética
- *magnetic tape*
64 la ficha perforada
- *punched card (punch card)*
65 la comunicación por télex *m*
- *telex link*
66 la teleimpresora
- *teleprinter (page printer)*
67 el apaprato de conexión *f*
- *dialling (Am. dialing) unit*
68 la cinta perforada télex para la transmisión del télex a la máxima velocidad *f*
- *telex tape [punched tape (punch tape) for transmitting the text at maximum speed]*
69 el télex
- *telex message*
70 el teclado
- *keyboard*

# 238 Radiodifusión (radio y televisión) I

1-6 la cabina central de la toma del sonido de la radio (el estudio de grabación *f* radiofónica)
- *central recording channel of a radio station*
1 la mesa de control *m* y de mando *m*
- *monitoring and control panel*
2 la consola de visualización *f* del programa de radio *f* informatizado (el monitor vídeo)
- *data display terminal (video data terminal, video monitor) for visual display of computer-controlled programmes* (Am. *programs*)
3 el soporte del aparato de amplificación *f* y de alimentación *f*
- *amplifier and mains power unit*
4 el magnetófono de grabación *f* y reproducción *f* de cintas *f* magnéticas de un cuarto de pulgada *f* o 6,35 mm de anchura
- *magnetic sound recording and playback deck for ¹/₄" magnetic tape*
5 la cinta magnética, la cinta de un cuarto de pulgada
- *magnetic tape, a ¹/₄" tape*
6 el estuche de bobina de la película
- *film spool holder*
7-15 el estudio de explotación *f* del centro nacional de radio *f*
- *radio switching centre* (Am. *center*) *control room*
7 la mesa de control *m* y mando *m*
- *monitoring and control panel*
8 el altavoz de órdenes *f*
- *talkback speaker*
9 el teléfono de batería *f* local
- *local-battery telephone*
10 el teléfono de órdenes *f*
- *talkback microphone*
11 el aparato de visualización *f* de los datos
- *data display terminal (video data terminal)*
12 el teleimpresor
- *teleprinter*
13 el teclado para introducir los datos en la computadora
- *input keyboard for computer data*
14 el teclado para la instalación telefónica de servicio *m*
- *telephone switchboard panel*
15 el altavoz de escucha *f*
- *monitoring speaker (control speaker)*
16-26 el complejo de emisión *f* radiofónica
- *broadcasting centre* (Am. *center*)
16 el estudio de grabación *f* radiofónica
- *recording room*
17 la cabina de control *m* (la cabina de mezcla *f* de sonidos *m*)
- *production control room (control room)*
18 la cabina del locutor
- *studio*
19 el ingeniero de sonido *m*
- *sound engineer (sound control engineer)*
20 el pupitre de mezcla *f* (de control *m*) de sonido *m*
- *sound control desk (sound control console)*
21 el locutor (*Amér.:* el espíquer)
- *newsreader (newscaster)*

22 el director de la emisión
- *duty presentation officer*
23 el teléfono de reportaje *m*
- *telephone for phoned reports*
24 el tocadiscos (*Col., Venez. y Pan.:* el picá)
- *record turntable*
25 el pupitre de mezcla *f* de la cabina de grabación *f* radiofónica
- *recording room mixing console (mixing desk, mixer)*
26 el técnico de sonido *m*
- *sound technician (sound mixer, sound recordist)*
27-53 el estudio de postsincronización *f* de televisión *f*
- *television post-sync studio*
27 la cabina de mezcla *f* (de control *m*) del sonido
- *sound production control room (sound control room)*
28 el estudio de sincronización *f*
- *dubbing studio (dubbing theatre,* Am. *theater)*
29 la mesa del presentador
- *studio table*
30 la señal de indicación *f* óptica (la señal luminosa)
- *visual signal*
31 el cronómetro electrónico
- *electronic stopclock*
32 la pantalla de proyección *f*
- *projection screen*
33 el monitor de la imagen
- *monitor*
34 el micrófono del presentador
- *studio microphone*
35 el organillo de efectos *m* sonoros
- *sound effects box*
36 el panel de conexión *f* del micrófono
- *microphone socket panel*
37 el altavoz de sonorización *f*
- *recording speaker (recording loudspeaker)*
38 la ventana de control *m*
- *control room window (studio window)*
39 el micrófono de órdenes *f* para los productores
- *producer's talkback microphone*
40 el teléfono de batería *f* local
- *local-battery telephone*
41 el pupitre de mezcla *f* (de control *m*) del sonido
- *sound control desk (sound control console)*
42 el conmutador de grupos *m*
- *group selector switch*
43 el indicador luminoso
- *visual display*
44 el limitador
- *limiter display (clipper display)*
45 las cajitas (los módulos) de ajuste *m* de conexión *f*
- *control modules*
46 las teclas de preescucha *f* (las teclas de la escucha de prueba *f*)
- *pre-listening buttons*
47 el regulador de corredera *f* plano
- *slide control*
48 el corrector universal
- *universal equalizer (universal corrector)*
49 el selector de entrada *f*
- *input selector switch*
50 el altavoz de preescucha *f* (de audición *f* de prueba *f*)
- *pre-listening speaker*

51 el generador del sonido de referencia *f*
- *tone generator*
52 el altavoz de órdenes *f*
- *talkback speaker*
53 el micrófono de órdenes *f*
- *talkback microphone*
54-59 el estudio de premezcla *f* para el doblado y la mezcla de cintas *f* magnéticas perforadas de 16 mm, 17,5 mm, 35 mm
- *pre-mixing room for transferring and mixing 16 mm, 17.5 mm, 35 mm perforated magnetic film*
54 el pupitre de control *m* (de mezcla *f*) del sonido·
- *sound control desk (sound control console)*
55 el bloque compacto de grabación *f* y de reproducción *f* magnéticas
- *compact magnetic tape recording and playback equipment*
56 el desenrollador unicelular para la transmisión
- *single playback deck*
57 el aparato central de impulsión *f*
- *central drive unit*
58 el desenrollador unicelular para la grabación *f* y la transmisión
- *single recording and playback deck*
59 la mesa de rebobinado *m*
- *rewind bench*
60-65 la cabina de control *m* de las imágenes
- *final picture quality checking room*
60 el monitor de previsión *f*
- *preview monitor*
61 el monitor de programa *m*
- *programme* (Am. *program*) *monitor*
62 el cronómetro
- *stopclock*
63 el pupitre de mezcla *f* (de control *m*) de la imagen
- *vision mixer (vision-mixing console, vision-mixing desk)*
64 la instalación de órdenes *f*
- *talkback system (talkback equipment)*
65 el monitor de cámara *f*
- *camera monitor (picture monitor)*

1-15  **el coche de reportaje** *m* (la unidad móvil)
– *outside broadcast (OB) vehicle,* e.g. *television OB van, sound OB van (radio OB van)*
1  **el equipo trasero del coche de reportaje** *m*
– *rear equipment section of the OB vehicle*
2  el cable de cámara *f*
– *camera cable*
3  el panel de conexión *f* de los cables
– *cable connection panel*
4  la antena de televisión *f* portátil para la primera cadena
– *television (TV) reception aerial (receiving aerial) for Channel I*
5  la antena de televisión para la segunda cadena
– *television (TV) reception aerial (receiving aerial) for Channel II*
6  **el equipo interior del coche de reportaje** *m*
– *interior equipment (on-board equipment) of the OB vehicle*
7  la cabina de control *m* del sonido
– *sound production control room (sound control room)*

8  el pupitre de control *m* del sonido
– *sound control desk (sound control console)*
9  el altavoz de control *m*
– *monitoring loudspeaker*
10  la cabina de control *m* de la imagen
– *vision control room (video control room)*
11  el técnico de vídeo *m*
– *video controller (vision controller)*
12  el monitor de cámara *f*
– *camera monitor (picture monitor)*
13  el teléfono de a bordo *m*
– *on-board telephone (intercommunication telephone)*
14  el cable del micrófono
– *microphone cable*
15  la instalación de climatización *f*
– *air-conditioning equipment*

1 **el receptor de televisión $f$ en color** $m$ (televisión $f$ en color $m$; el aparato de televisión $f$ en color $m$) en un diseño por módulos $m$
– *colour (Am. **color) television (TV)** receiver (colour television set) of modular design*
2 la caja de la televisión (del televisor)
– *television cabinet*
3 el tubo de televisión $f$ (el tubo de imágenes $f$)
– *television tube (picture tube)*
4 el módulo amplificador de frecuencia $f$ intermedia (F. I.)
– *IF (intermediate frequency) amplifier module*
5 el módulo de descodificación $f$ del color
– *colour (Am. color) decoder module*
6 el selector VHF y UHF
– *VHF and UHF tuner*
7 el módulo de sincronización $f$ horizontal
– *horizontal synchronizing module*
8 el módulo de deflexión $f$ vertical
– *vertical deflection module*
9 el módulo de encuadre $m$
– *horizontal linearity control module*
10 el módulo de deflexión $f$ horizontal
– *horizontal deflection module*
11 el módulo de regulación $f$
– *control module*

12 el módulo de convergencia $f$
– *convergence module*
13 el módulo de la fase final de color $m$
– *colour (Am. color) output stage module*
14 el módulo de sonido $m$
– *sound module*
15 el filtro cromático blindado
– *colour (Am. color) picture tube*
16 los haces de electrones $m$
– *electron beams*
17 la máscara perforada con ranuras $f$
– *shadow mask with elongated holes*
18 las tiras de material $m$ fluorescente (luminiscente)
– *strip of fluorescent (luminescent, phosphorescent) material*
19 el revestimiento de material $m$ fluorescente
– *coating (film) of fluorescent material*
20 el blindaje interior magnético
– *inner magnetic screen (screening)*
21 el vacío
– *vacuum*
22 la suspensión de la máscara compensada térmicamente
– *temperature-compensated shadow mask mount*
23 el anillo de centrado $m$ del sistema de deflexión $f$
– *centring (centering) ring for the deflection system*

24 el sistema de cañones $m$ de electrones $m$
– *electron gun assembly*
25 el cátodo de calentamiento $m$ rápido
– *rapid heat-up cathode*
26 **la cámara de televisión** $f$
– *television (TV) camera*
27 la cabeza de la cámara
– *camera head*
28 el monitor de la cámara
– *camera monitor*
29 la palanca para dirigir la cámara
– *control arm (control lever)*
30 el ajuste del enfoque
– *focusing adjustment*
31 el panel de manejo $m$ de la cámara
– *control panel*
32 la regulación del contraste
– *contrast control*
33 la regulación de luminosidad $f$
– *brightness control*
34 el zoom
– *zoom lens*
35 el prisma de división $f$ de rayos $m$ (el separador de rayos $m$)
– *beam-splitting prism (beam splitter)*
36 el módulo de recepción $f$ (el tubo de color $m$)
– *pickup unit (colour, Am. color, pickup tube)*

1 **el radiocassette**
- *radio cassette recorder*
2 el asa *f* para el transporte
- *carrying handle*
3 los pulsadores (las teclas) de la sección cassette
- *push buttons for the cassette recorder unit*
4 las teclas de selección *f* de emisoras *f*
- *station selector buttons (station preset buttons)*
5 el micrófono incorporado
- *built-in microphone*
6 el compartimiento de la cassette
- *cassette compartment*
7 el dial de sintonización *f* (la escala de frecuencias *f*)
- *tuning dial*
8 el regulador de corredera *f* [para el volumen o el tono]
- *slide control [for volume or tone]*
9 el selector de frecuencias *f* (el botón de sintonización *f*)
- *tuning knob (tuning control, tuner)*
10 **la cassette**
- *compact cassette*
11 la caja de la cassette
- *cassette box (cassette holder, cassette cabinet)*
12 la cinta de la cassette
- *cassette tape*
13-48 **el sistema estereofónico** (sistema *m* cuadrafónico) de componentes *m* de alta fidelidad *f* (Hi-Fi)
- *stereo system made up of Hi-Fi components; also: quadrophonic system*
13-14 **los altavoces estereofónicos (los baffles)**
- *stereo speakers*
14 el altavoz de caja *f*, un baffle de tres altavoces *m* con agujas *f* de frecuencia *f* (una pantalla acústica)
- *speaker (loudspeaker), a three-way speaker with crossover (crossover network)*
15 el altavoz de sonidos *m* agudos
- *tweeter*
16 el altavoz de sonidos *m* medios
- *mid-range speaker*
17 el altavoz de sonidos *m* graves (de tonos *m* bajos)
- *woofer*
18 **el tocadiscos** (el plato, la pletina giradiscos)
- *record player*
19 el chasis (el bastidor) del tocadiscos
- *record player housing (record player base)*
20 el plato giratorio
- *turntable*
21 el brazo acústico (el pick-up, el brazo de tocadiscos *m*, el portaagujas)
- *tone arm*
22 el contrapeso
- *counterbalance (counterweight)*
23 la suspensión cardán
- *gimbal suspension*
24 la regulación de la presión de la cabeza
- *stylus pressure control (stylus force control)*
25 el dispositivo anti-skating
- *anti-skate control*
26 el sistema de brazo *m* acústico magnético con la aguja (cónica o esférica), un diamante
- *magnetic cartridge with (conical or elliptical) stylus, a diamond*
27 el inmovilizador (el mecanismo de parada *f*) del brazo acústico
- *tone arm lock*

28 el mecanismo elevador del brazo acústico
- *tone arm lift*
29 el selector de la velocidad de rotación *f* (del número de rotaciones *f*)
- *speed selector (speed changer)*
30 el interruptor de arranque *m*
- *starter switch*
31 el regulador del tono
- *treble control*
32 la tapadera
- *dust cover*
33 **el cassette estereofónico** (la pletina de cassette *f* estéreo)
- *stereo cassette deck*
34 el compartimiento de la cassette
- *cassette compartment*
35-36 los indicadores del nivel de grabación *f*
- *recording level meters (volume unit meters, VU meters)*
35 el indicador del nivel de grabación *f* del canal izquierdo
- *left-channel recording level meter*
36 el indicador del nivel de grabación *f* del canal derecho
- *right-channel recording level meter*
37 **el sintonizador**
- *tuner*
38 las teclas de selección *f* de emisoras *f* de frecuencia *f* modulada (FM)
- *VHF (FM) station selector buttons*
39 el indicador luminoso (el ojo mágico) de sintonía *f*
- *tuning meter*
40 **el amplificador**
- *amplifier;* tuner and amplifier together: *receiver (control unit)*
41 el control de volumen *m*
- *volume control*
42 el balance cuadrafónico
- *four-channel balance control (level control)*
43 la regulación de sonidos *m* agudos y graves
- *treble and bass tuning*
44 el selector de entradas *f*
- *input selector*
45 **el demodulador cuadrafónico** para discos *m* CD4
- *four-channel demodulator for CD4 records*
46 el conmutador estéreo-cuadrafónico
- *quadra/stereo converter*
47 el portacassettes
- *cassette box (cassette holder, cassette cabinet)*
48 el casillero de los discos
- *record storage slots (record storage compartments)*
49 **el micrófono**
- *microphone*
50 la rejilla del micrófono
- *microphone screen*
51 el pie (el soporte) del micrófono
- *microphone base (microphone stand)*
52 **el compacto triple** (radio *f*, cassette *m*, tocadiscos *m*)
- *three-in-one stereo component system [automatic record changer, cassette deck, and stereo receiver]*
53 el sistema de equilibrado *m* del brazo acústico
- *tone arm balance*
54 el control de sintonización *f*
- *tuning meters*
55 el indicador luminoso de conmutación *f* automática de óxido *m* de hierro *m*/óxido *m* de cromo *m*
- *indicator light for automatic FeO/CrO$_2$ tape switch-over*

56 **el magnetófono**, un aparato de bobinas *f* de dos o cuatro pistas *f*
- *open-reel-type recorder, a two or four-track unit*
57 la bobina de cinta *f* magnetofónica
- *tape reel (open tape reel)*
58 la cinta magnetofónica (la cinta para la grabación del sonido, una cinta de 1/4 de pulgada *f*)
- *open-reel tape (recording tape, 1/4" tape)*
59 el estuche de cabezas *f* de sonido *m* con cabeza *f* de borrado *m*, cabeza *f* de grabación *f* y cabeza *f* de reproducción *f* (o cabeza *f* combinada)
- *sound head housing with erasing head (erase head), recording head, and reproducing head; also: combined head*
60 la polea con interruptor *m* de fin *m* de cinta *f*
- *tape deflector roller and end switch (limit switch)*
61 el control del nivel de grabación *f*
- *recording level meter (VU meter)*
62 el selector de velocidades *f* de la cinta
- *tape speed selector*
63 el interruptor de encendido *m*/apagado *m*
- *on/off switch*
64 el contador de cinta *f*
- *tape counter*
65 las entradas del micrófono estéreo
- *stereo microphone sockets (stereo microphone jacks)*
66 **los auriculares de casco** *m* (el casco auricular, el juego de auriculares *m* con casco *m*)
- *headphones (headset)*
67 el muelle acolchado del casco
- *padded headband (padded headpiece)*
68 la membrana
- *membrane*
69 el auricular
- *earcups (earphones)*
70 la clavija de enchufe *m* del casco auricular, una clavija normalizada
- *headphone cable plug, a standard multi-pin plug (not the same as a phono plug)*
71 el cable de conexión *f*
- *headphone cable (headphone cord)*

# 242 Técnicas de enseñanza e información

1 la enseñanza en grupo *m* con una **máquina para instruir**
- *group instruction using a teaching machine*
2 la mesa del profesor con la unidad central de mandos *m*
- *instructor's desk with central control unit*
3 el panel indicador del nivel de la clase con indicadores *m* individuales y contadores *m* del total, situados diagonalmente
- *master control panel with individual diplays and cross total counters*
4 el dispositivo de entrada *f* del alumno en las manos de los alumnos (el dispositivo de respuesta *f* del estudiante)
- *student input device (student response device) in the hand of a student*
5 el contador del progreso de la enseñanza
- *study step counter (progress counter)*
6 el retroproyector
- *overhead projector*
7 la instalación para la elaboración de programas *m* audiovisuales de enseñanza *f*
- *apparatus for producing audio-visual learning programmes* (Am. *programs*)
8-10 la instalación de codificación *f* de imágenes *f*
- *frame coding device*
8 la pantalla para examinar la película
- *film viewer*
9 la unidad de memoria *f*
- *memory unit (storage unit)*
10 la instalación de perforación *f* de la película
- *film perforator*
11-14 la instalación de codificación *f* del sonido
- *audio coding equipment (sound coding equipment)*
11 el teclado de codificación *f*
- *coding keyboard*
12 el magnetófono de dos pistas *f*
- *two-track tape recorder*
13 el magnetófono de cuatro pistas *f*
- *four-track tape recorder*
14 el control del nivel de grabación *f*
- *recording level meter*
15 el sistema P.I.P. [P.I.P.: presentación *f* individual programada]
- *PIP (programmed individual presentation) system*
16 el proyector audiovisual para la enseñanza programada
- *AV (audio-visual) projector for programmed instruction*
17 la cassette de audio *m* (la audiocassette)
- *audio cassette*
18 la cassette de vídeo *m* (la videocassette)
- *video cassette*
19 el terminal de datos *m*
- *data terminal*
20 la conexión telefónica con la central de concentración *f* de datos *m* (el acoplador acústico)
- *telephone connection with the central data collection station*
21 **el videoteléfono** (el teléfono de imágenes *f*)
- **video telephone**
22 el conmutador de conferencias *f*
- *conference circuit (conference hook-up, conference connection)*
23 la tecla para transmitir la propia imagen
- *camera tube switch (switch for transmitting speaker's picture)*

24 la tecla de conversación *f*
- *talk button (talk key, speaking key)*
25 el dial (el teclado selector)
- *touch-tone buttons (touch-tone pad)*
26 la pantalla del videoteléfono
- *video telephone screen*
27 la transmisión infrarroja del sonido de televisión *f*
- *infrared transmission of television sound*
28 el receptor de televisión *f* (el televisor)
- *television receiver (television set, TV set)*
29 el transmisor de sonidos *m* por infrarrojos *m*
- *infrared sound transmitter*
30 los auriculares de casco *m* sin hilo *m*, un receptor de infrarrojos *m* y alimentación *f* autónoma
- *cordless battery-powered infrared sound headphones (headset)*
31 **el microfilmador** [en esquema *m*]
- **microfilming system** [diagram]
32 la estación de cinta *f* magnética (la unidad de almacenamiento *m* de datos *m*)
- *magnetic tape station, a data storage unit*
33 el depósito tapón *m*
- *buffer storage*
34 la unidad de adaptación *f*
- *adapter unit*
35 el control digital
- *digital control*
36 el control de la cámara
- *camera control*
37 el depósito de caracteres *m* (de tipos *m* de letra *f*; la memoria de texto *m*)
- *character storage*
38 el control analógico
- *analogue* (Am. *analog*) *control*
39 la corrección de la geometría del tubo de imágenes *f*
- *correction (adjustment) of picture tube geometry*
40 el tubo de rayos *m* catódicos
- *cathode ray tube (CRT)*
41 el sistema óptico
- *optical system*
42 la diapositiva de un formulario para la inserción de formularios *m*
- *slide (transparency) of a form for mixing-in images of forms*
43 el flash (la lámpara de destellos *m*, de fogonazos *m*)
- *flash lamp*
44 las cajas normalizadas para películas *f*
- *universal film cassettes*
45-84 **aparatos *m* de demostración *f* y enseñanza *f*** (material *m* didáctico)
- **demonstration and teaching equipment**
45 el modelo de demostración *f* de un motor de cuatro tiempos *m*
- *demonstration model of a four-stroke engine*
46 el pistón
- *piston*
47 la culata
- *cylinder head*
48 la bujía
- *spark plug (sparking plug)*
49 el ruptor de encendido *m*
- *contact breaker*
50 el cigüeñal
- *crankshaft with balance weights (counterbalance weights) (counterbalanced crankshaft)*
51 el cárter del cigüeñal
- *crankcase*
52 la válvula de admisión *f*
- *inlet valve*
53 la válvula de escape *m*
- *exhaust valve*

54 las cámaras de agua *f* de refrigeración *f*
- *coolant bores (cooling water bores)*
55 el modelo de demostración *f* de un motor de dos tiempos *m*
- *demonstration model of a two-stroke engine*
56 el pistón con deflector *m*
- *deflector piston*
57 la abertura de admisión *f*
- *transfer port*
58 la abertura de escape *m*
- *exhaust port*
59 el baño de aceite *m* del cárter del cigüeñal
- *crankcase scavenging*
60 las aletas de enfriamiento *m*
- *cooling ribs*
61-67 modelos *m* de moléculas *f*
- *models of molecules*
61 la molécula de etileno *m*
- *ethylene molecule*
62 el átomo de hidrógeno *m*
- *hydrogen atom*
63 el átomo de carbono *m*
- *carbon atom*
64 la mólecula de formaldehido *m*
- *formaldehyde atom*
65 el átomo de oxígeno *m*
- *oxygen molecule*
66 el anillo bencénico
- *benzene ring*
67 la molécula de agua *f*
- *water molecule*
68-72 circuitos *m* de elementos *m* modulares
- *electronic circuits made up of modular elements*
68 el elemento (el módulo) lógico, un circuito integrado
- *logic element (logic module), an integrated circuit*
69 el panel de enchufes *m* para los módulos electrónicos
- *plugboard for electronic elements (electronic modules)*
70 la conexión de los módulos
- *linking (link-up, joining, connection) of modules*
71 el contacto magnético
- *magnetic contact*
72 la construcción de un circuito con módulos *m* magnéticos
- *assembly (construction) of a circuit, using magnetic modules*
73 el multímetro para la medida de corriente *f*, voltaje *m* (tensión *f*) y resistencia *f*
- *multiple meter for measuring current, voltage and resistance*
74 el selector del tipo de medida *f*
- *measurement range selector*
75 la escala de medida *f*
- *measurement scale (measurement dial)*
76 la aguja indicadora
- *indicator needle (pointer)*
77 el voltiamperímetro (el contador de corriente *f* y voltaje *m*)
- *current/voltage meter*
78 el tornillo de reglaje *m* del cero
- *adjusting screw*
79 el banco óptico
- *optical bench*
80 el carril triangular
- *triangular rail*
81 el láser (el láser de enseñanza *f*)
- *laser, a teaching laser (instruction laser)*
82 el diafragma
- *diaphragm*
83 el sistema de lentes *f*
- *lens system*
84 la pantalla
- *target (screen)*

**1-4 la cámara de vídeo *m* con grabadora *f***
- *AV (audio-visual) camera with recorder*
1 la cámara
- *camera*
2 el objetivo
- *lens*
3 el micrófono incorporado
- *built-in microphone*
4 la grabadora portátil de vídeo *m* (para cinta *f* magnética de 1/4 de pulgada *f*)
- *portable video (videotape) recorder (for ¼" open-reel magnetic tape)*
**5-36 el sistema de grabación *f* de videocassettes *f* (VCR)**
- *VCR (video cassette recorder) system*
5 la videocassette (para cinta *f* magnética de 1/2 pulgada *f*)
- *VCR cassette for ½" magnetic tape*
6 el receptor de televisión *f* doméstico (*también:* el monitor)
- *monitor*
7 la grabadora de videocassettes *m* (el magnetoscopio)
- *video cassette recorder*
8 el compartimiento de la cassette
- *cassette compartment*
9 el contador de cinta *f*
- *tape counter*
10 el control de enfoque *m* de la imagen
- *centring (centering) control*
11 el control del nivel de grabación *f* del sonido
- *sound (audio) recording level control*
12 el indicador del nivel de grabación *f*
- *recording level indicator*
13 las teclas de control *m* (de mando *m*)
- *control buttons (operating keys)*
14 el indicador luminoso de engarce *m* de la cinta
- *tape threading indicator light*
15 el conmutador del indicador del nivel de grabación *f* sonido *m*/imagen *f*
- *changeover switch for selecting audio or video recording level display*
16 el interruptor de encendido *m*/apagado *m*
- *on/off switch*
17 las teclas de selección *f* del canal
- *station selector buttons (station preset buttons)*
18 el interruptor de reloj *m* incorporado (el programador)
- *built-in timer switch*
19 el tambor (el cabezal) de grabación *f* de videocassettes *f*
- *VCR (video cassette recorder) head drum*
20 la cabeza de borrado *m*
- *erasing head (erase head)*
21 la clavija guía
- *stationary guide (guide pin)*
22 la guía de la cinta
- *tape guide*
23 el cilindro de sonido *m*
- *capstan*

24 la cabeza de audiosincronización *f*
- *audio sync head*
25 el rodillo de presión *f*
- *pinch roller*
26 la cabeza vídeo *m*
- *video head*
27 las ranuras de la pared del tambor para la formación del cojín de aire *m*
- *grooves in the wall of the head drum to promote air cushion formation*
28 el esquema de pistas *f* de la grabación de videocassettes *f* (de VCR)
- *VCR (video cassette recorder) track format*
29 la dirección de avance *m* de la cinta
- *tape feed*
30 la dirección del movimiento de la cabeza vídeo
- *direction of video head movement*
31 la pista vídeo, una pista en diagonal *f*
- *video track, a slant track*
32 la pista sonora
- *sound track (audio track)*
33 la pista de sincronización *f*
- *sync track*
34 la cabeza de sincronización *f*
- *sync head*
35 la cabeza de sonido *m*
- *sound head (audio head)*
36 la cabeza vídeo *m*
- *video head*
**37-45 el sistema de videodisco *m***
- *TED (television disc) system*
37 el giradiscos vídeo *m*
- *video disc player*
38 la ranura de introducción *f* del disco con el videodisco incorporado
- *disc slot with inserted video disc*
39 el selector de programas *m*
- *programme (Am. program) selector*
40 la escala de programas *m*
- *programme (Am. program) scale (programme dial)*
41 la tecla de puesta *f* en marcha *f* ("Play")
- *operating key ['play']*
42 la tecla de repetición *f* de escena *f* ("Select")
- *scene-repeat key ['select']*
43 la tecla de parada *f*
- *stop key*
44 el videodisco
- *video disc*
45 la funda del videodisco
- *video disc jacket*
**46-60 el sistema de videodisco *m* de larga duración *f***
- *VLP (video long play) video disc system*
46 el giradiscos vídeo *m*
- *video disc player*
47 la tapa de proyección *f* (*debajo:* la zona de exploración *f*)
- *cover projection; below it: scanning zone*
48 las teclas de control *m* (de mando *m*)
- *operating keys*
49 el regulador del movimiento ralentizado
- *slow motion control*

50 el sistema óptico [esquema *m*]
- *optical system [diagram]*
51 el videodisco de larga duración *f*
- *VLP video disc*
52 el objetivo
- *lens*
53 el haz de láser *m*
- *laser beam*
54 el espejo giratorio
- *rotating mirror*
55 el espejo semitransparente
- *semi-reflecting mirror*
56 el fotodiodo
- *photodiode*
57 el láser de helio *m* – neón *m*
- *helium-neon laser*
58 la grabación vídeo *m* en la superficie del disco
- *video signals on the surface of the video disc*
59 la pista señal *f*
- *signal track*
60 el elemento de imagen *f* ("Pitt")
- *individual signal element ('pit')*

1 la unidad de disco *m* magnético
  (el disco magnético, la memoria
  de disco *m* magnético)
– *disc (disk) store (magnetic disc
  store)*
2 la cinta magnética
– *magnetic tape*
3 el operador de consola *f*
– *console operator*
4 la máquina de escribir (la
  impresora) de consola *f*
– *console typewriter*
5 el intercomunicador (el
  interfono)
– *intercom (intercom system)*
6 la unidad central con la
  memoria principal y la unidad
  aritmética
– *central processor with main
  memory and arithmetic unit*
7 los indicadores de
  operaciones *f* y errores *m*
– *operation and error indicators*
8 la unidad de disquetes *m* (de
  discos *m* flexibles)
– *floppy disc (disk) reader*
9 la unidad de cinta *f* magnética
– *magnetic tape unit*
10 la bobina de cinta *f* magnética
– *magnetic tape reel*

11 los indicadores de
   funcionamiento *m*
– *operating indicators*
12 la lectora-perforadora de fichas
– *punched card (punch card)
  reader and punch*
13 el archivador de fichas *f*
   perforadas (la gaveta de
   fichas *f* perforadas)
– *card stacker*
14 el operador
– *operator*
15 las instrucciones de servicio *m*
   (el manual)
– *operating instructions*

**1-33 la oficina de recepción** *f* (la oficina de las secretarias)
- *secretary's office*
1 el sistema telecopiador (el emisor-receptor de facsímiles *m*)
- *facsimile telegraph*
2 la telecopia (la copia recibida)
- *transmitted or received copy*
3 el calendario (el almanaque) de pared *f*
- *wall calendar*
4 el archivo
- *filing cabinet*
5 la puerta de persiana *f* a corredera *f*
- *tambour door (roll-up door)*
6 el archivador
- *file (document file)*
7 la máquina de imprimir direcciones *f*
- *transfer-type addressing machine*
8 el depósito vertical de recepción *f* de estarcidos *m*
- *vertical stencil magazine*
9 el depósito de estarcidos *m*
- *stencil ejection*
10 la gaveta de almacenaje *m* de estarcidos *m*
- *stencil storage drawer*
11 el dispositivo de alimentación *f* de papel *m*
- *paper feed*
12 las existencias de papel *m* de cartas *f*
- *stock of notepaper*

13 la centralita telefónica interior
- *switchboard (internal telephone exchange)*
14 el teclado de pulsadores *m* para las comunicaciones interiores
- *push-button keyboard for internal connections*
15 el auricular
- *handset*
16 el dial
- *dial*
17 el listín del teléfono interior
- *internal telephone list*
18 el reloj de control *m*
- *master clock (main clock)*
19 el portafirmas
- *folder containing documents, correspondence, etc. for signing (to be signed)*
20 el interfono
- *intercom (office intercom)*
21 la pluma
- *pen*
22 la bandeja portaplumas (*Amér.*: el canuero)
- *pen and pencil tray*
23 el fichero
- *card index*
24 la pila de formularios *m*
- *stack (set) of forms*
25 la mesa de la máquina de escribir
- *typing desk*
26 la máquina de escribir con memoria *f*
- *memory typewriter*

27 el teclado de la máquina de escribir
- *keyboard*
28 el interruptor giratorio de la memoria de trabajo *m* y del bucle de la cinta magnética
- *rotary switch for the main memory and the magnetic tape loop*
29 el bloc de taquigrafía *f*
- *shorthand pad* (Am. *steno pad*)
30 la bandeja de la correspondencia
- *letter tray*
31 la calculadora de oficina *f*
- *office calculator*
32 la impresora
- *printer*
33 la carta comercial
- *business letter*

**1-36 la oficina (el despacho) del jefe**
- *executive's office*
1 el sillón de la mesa de despacho *m* (del escritorio)
- *swivel chair*
2 la mesa de despacho *m* (el escritorio; *Perú:* la carpeta)
- *desk*
3 el tablero de la mesa de despacho *m*
- *desk top*
4 el cajón de la mesa de despacho *m*
- *desk drawer*
5 el armario de puerta *f* abatible
- *cupboard (storage area) with door*
6 el cartapacio (el vade)
- *desk mat (blotter)*
7 la carta comercial
- *business letter*
8 la agenda
- *appointments diary*
9 la bandeja portaplumas (*Amér.:* el canutero)
- *desk set*
10 el interfono
- *intercom (office intercom)*
11 la lámpara de escritorio *m* (de mesa *f* de despacho *m*)
- *desk lamp*
12 la calculadora de bolsillo *m* (la calculadora electrónica)
- *pocket calculator (electronic calculator)*

13 el teléfono, un dispositivo secretaria-jefe
- *telephone, an executive-secretary system*
14 el dial, *también:* el teclado de pulsadores *m*
- *dial; also: push-button keyboard*
15 las teclas de llamada *f*
- *call buttons*
16 el auricular (el auricular de teléfono *m*, el microteléfono)
- *receiver (telephone receiver)*
17 el dictáfono
- *dictating machine*
18 el indicador de la longitud del dictado
- *position indicator*
19 las teclas de manejo *m*
- *control buttons (operating keys)*
20 el armario
- *cabinet*
21 el sillón de la visita
- *visitor's chair*
22 la caja fuerte (la caja de caudales *m*)
- *safe*
23 el pasador de la cerradura
- *bolts (locking mechanism)*
24 el alojamiento blindado de la cerradura
- *armour (Am. armor) plating*
25 los documentos confidenciales
- *confidential documents*

26 la patente
- *patent*
27 el dinero en metálico *m* (el dinero efectivo; *P. Rico y S. Dgo.:* el cascajo; *Amér. Central:* el pisto; *Arg., Col., Cuba, Guat. y P. Rico:* el moni; *C. Rica:* el zacatillo)
- *petty cash*
28 el cuadro
- *picture*
29 el mueble bar
- *bar (drinks cabinet)*
30 el servicio del bar
- *bar set*
31-36 el conjunto para las reuniones
- *conference grouping*
31 la mesa de reuniones *f*
- *conference table*
32 el dictáfono de bolsillo *m*
- *pocket-sized dictating machine, a micro-cassette recorder*
33 el cenicero
- *ashtray*
34 la rinconera (la mesa auxiliar; *Amér.:* la esquinera)
- *corner table*
35 la lámpara de mesa *f*
- *table lamp*
36 el sofá de reuniones *f*
- *two-seater sofa [part of the conference grouping]*

**1-44 el material de oficina** *f*
- *office equipment (office supplies, office materials)*
1 el clip (*Chile:* el broche) pequeño (*Amér. Central y P. Rico:* el atache)
- *[small] paper clip*
2 el clip grande
- *[large] paper clip*
3 la taladradora
- *punch*
4 la grapadora (*Amér.:* el abrochador)
- *l'agrafeuse* f *de bureau* m
5 la matriz
- *anvil*
6 el tirador de carga *f*
- *spring-loaded magazine*
7 el cepillo de limpieza *f* de los tipos de la máquina de escribir
- *type-cleaning brush for typewriters*
8 el limpiador de los tipos
- *type cleaner (type-cleaning kit)*
9 el recipiente de líquido *m* disolvente
- *fluid container (fluid reservoir)*
10 la escobilla de limpieza *f*
- *cleaning brush*
11 el rotulador
- *felt tip pen*
12 la hoja de papel *m* correctora de los errores de máquina *f*
- *correcting paper [for typing errors]*
13 el líquido corrector de los errores de máquina *f*
- *correcting fluid [for typing errors]*
14 la calculadora electrónica de bolsillo *m*
- *electronic pocket calculator*

15 la información luminosa de ocho dígitos *m*
- *eight-digit fluorescent display*
16 el interruptor de encendido *m*/apagado *m*
- *on/off switch*
17 las teclas de función *f*
- *function keys*
18 las teclas de cifras *f*
- *number keys*
19 la tecla de coma *f*
- *decimal key*
20 la tecla de resultado *m* (de totalización *m*)
- *equals' key*
21 las teclas de operaciones *f* aritméticas
- *instruction keys (command keys)*
22 las teclas de la memoria
- *memory keys*
23 la tecla de cálculo *m* del porcentaje
- *percent key (percentage key)*
24 la tecla de π para el cálculo de las longitudes de las circunferencias
- *π-key (pi-key) for mensuration of circles*
25 el sacapuntas
- *pencil sharpener*
26 la goma de borrar de máquina *f* de escribir
- *typewriter rubber*
27 el aparato distribuidor de cinta *f* adhesiva
- *adhesive tape dispenser*
28 el soporte de mesa *f* de la cinta adhesiva
- *adhesive tape holder (roller-type adhesive tape dispenser)*

29 el rollo de cinta *f* adhesiva
- *roll of adhesive tape*
30 la arista (el borde) cortante
- *tear-off edge*
31 la esponjilla humedecedora
- *moistener*
32 la agenda de mesa *f*
- *desk diary*
33 la hoja con la fecha (la hoja de calendario *m*)
- *date sheet (calendar sheet)*
34 la hoja de anotaciones *f* (de notas *f*)
- *memo sheet*
35 la regla
- *ruler*
36 la graduación en centímetros *m* y milímetros *m*
- *centimetre and millimetre* (Am. *centimeter and millimeter) graduations*
37 el archivador
- *file (document file)*
38 el rótulo del lomo
- *spine label (spine tag)*
39 el orificio para la manipulación
- *finger hole*
40 el clasificador
- *arch board file*
41 el mecanismo del clasificador
- *arch unit*
42 la palanca de abrir o cerrar
- *release lever (locking lever, release/lock lever)*
43 la abrazadera
- *compressor*
44 la relación del estado de cuentas *f*
- *bank statement (statement of account)*

**1-48 la oficina colectiva**
- *open plan office*
1 el tabique (la mampara de separación *f*)
- *partition wall (partition screen)*
2 el cajón clasificador con un sistema de suspensión *f* de los archivadores
- *filing drawer with suspension file system*
3 el archivador (el clasificador) suspendido
- *suspension file*
4 la lengüeta guía
- *file tab*
5 el archivador
- *file (document file)*
6 la archivera
- *filing clerk*
7 el empleado de oficina *f* (el oficinista)
- *clerical assistant*
8 las apuntes para el archivador
- *note for the files*
9 el teléfono
- *telephone*
10 la estantería de los archivadores
- *filing shelves*
11 la mesa del empleado
- *clerical assistant's desk*
12 el armario de oficina *f*
- *office cupboard*

13 la jardinera con plantas *f*
- *plant stand (planter)*
14 la planta de interior *m*
- *indoor plants (houseplants)*
15 la programadora
- *programmer*
16 la pantalla terminal de datos *m*
- *data display terminal (visual display unit)*
17 el empleado del servicio al cliente
- *customer service representative*
18 el cliente
- *customer*
19 el dibujo realizado por computadora *f*
- *computer-generated design*
20 el tabique de absorción *f* del sonido (de insonorización *f*)
- *sound-absorbing partition*
21 la mecanógrafa
- *typist*
22 la máquina de escribir
- *typewriter*
23 el cajón fichero
- *filing drawer*
24 el fichero de los clientes
- *customer card index*
25 la silla de oficina *f*, una silla giratoria
- *office chair, a swivel chair*

26 la mesa de la máquina de escribir
- *typing desk*
27 el fichero
- *card index box*
28 la estantería de múltiples usos *m*
- *multi-purpose shelving*
29 el jefe
- *proprietor*
30 la carta comercial
- *business letter*
31 la secretaria del jefe (la secretaria de dirección *f*)
- *proprietor's secretary*
32 el bloc de taquigrafía *f*
- *shorthand pad (Am. steno pad)*
33 la audiomecanógrafa
- *audio typist*
34 el dictáfono
- *dictating machine*
35 el auricular en el pabellón de la oreja
- *earphone*
36 la gráfica (el diagrama) estadística (la estadística)
- *statistics chart*
37 el armario de debajo de la mesa de despacho *m*
- *pedestal containing a cupboard or drawers*

**38** el armario de puertas *f* de
   corredera *f*
 – *sliding-door cupboard*
**39** los elementos dispuestos en
   forma *f* de ángulo *m*
 – *office furniture arranged in an
   angular configuration*
**40** la estantería colgante
   (suspendida)
 – *wall-mounted shelf*
**41** la bandeja de correspondencia *f*
 – *letter tray*
**42** el calendario (el almanaque) de
   pared *f*
 – *wall calendar*
**43** la central de datos *m* (la central
   de transmisión *f* de datos *m*, el
   banco de datos *m*)
 – *data centre (Am. center)*
**44** la petición de información *f*
   inscrita en la pantalla terminal
   de datos *m*
 – *calling up information on the
   data display terminal (visual
   display unit)*
**45** la papelera
 – *waste paper basket*
**46** la estadística de ventas *f*
 – *sales statistics*

**47** el listado de ordenador *m* (de
   tratamiento *m* electrónico de la
   información) un impreso
   plegado en acordeón *m*
 – *EDP print-out, a continuous
   fan-fold sheet*
**48** el elemento de ensamblaje *m*
 – *connecting element*

1 la máquina de escribir eléctrica, una máquina de escribir de cabeza *f* esférica
- *electric typewriter, a golf ball typewriter*
2-6 el teclado
- *keyboard*
2 la barra espaciadora
- *space bar*
3 la tecla de las mayúsculas
- *shift key*
4 la tecla de interlineado *m*
- *line space and carrier return key*
5 la tecla fijamayúsculas
- *shift lock*
6 la tecla de margen *m* (el liberador del margen)
- *margin release key*
7 la tecla del tabulador
- *tabulator key*
8 la tecla de anulación *f* del tabulador
- *tabulator clear key*
9 el interruptor de encendido *m*/apagado *m*
- *on/off switch*
10 la palanca selectora de la intesidad de la impresión
- *striking force control (impression control)*
11 el selector de la cinta
- *ribbon selector*
12 la escala del margen (la escala de marginales *m*)
- *margin scale*
13 el margen izquierdo
- *left margin stop*
14 el margen derecho
- *right margin stop*
15 la cabeza esférica (la cabeza de imprimir, de escribir) con los tipos
- *golf ball (spherical typing element) bearing the types*
16 la cajita de la cinta
- *ribbon cassette*
17 la barra pisapapeles con los rodillos guía
- *paper bail with rollers*
18 el rodillo
- *platen*
19 el tarjetero
- *typing opening (typing window)*
20 la palanca de introducción *f* del papel
- *paper release lever*
21 la palanca de retorno *m* (de marcha *f* atrás) del carro
- *carrier return lever*
22 el botón giratorio del rodillo
- *platen knob*
23 el selector de interlineado *m*
- *line space adjuster*
24 la palanca liberadora del rodillo
- *variable platen action lever*
25 el botón de embrague *m* del rodillo
- *push-in platen variable*
26 la tablilla de apoyo *m* para borrar
- *erasing table*
27 la tapa transparente
- *transparent cover*
28 la cabeza esférica de repuesto *m*
- *exchange golf ball (exchange typing element)*
29 el tipo
- *type*
30 el casquete (la tapa) de la cabeza de imprimir
- *golf ball cap (cap of typing element)*

31 los segmentos dentados
- *teeth*
32 la copiadora (fotocopiadora *f*) automática con rollos *m* de papel *m*
- *web-fed automatic copier*
33 el depósito del rollo de papel *m*
- *magazine for paper roll*
34 la selección del formato (de la dimensión) del papel
- *paper size selection (format selection)*
35 la preselección del número de copias *f*
- *print quantity selection*
36 el regulador del contraste
- *contrast control*
37 el interruptor principal (el interruptor de encendido *m*/apagado *m*)
- *main switch (on/off switch)*
38 el interruptor de mando *m* (el botón de inicio *m* de la copia)
- *start print button*
39 el cristal portaoriginales
- *document glass*
40 la banda transportadora
- *transfer blanket*
41 el rodillo de tintaje *m*
- *toner roll*
42 el sistema de exposición *f*
- *exposure system*
43 la salida de copias *f* (de fotocopias *f*)
- *print delivery (copy delivery)*
44 la máquina de plegar cartas *f*
- *letter-folding machine*
45 el dispositivo de alimentación *f* de papel *m*
- *paper feed*
46 el mecanismo de plegado *m*
- *folding mechanism*
47 la bandeja recogedora
- *receiving tray*
48 la máquina de imprimir (la prensa) en offset de tamaño *m* pequeño
- *small offset press*
49 el dispositivo de alimentación *f* de papel *m*
- *paper feed*
50 la palanca de tintaje *m* de las placas de imprimir
- *lever for inking the plate cylinder*
51-52 la bateria de tintaje *m*
- *inking unit (inker unit)*
51 el rodillo distribuidor
- *distributing roller (distributor)*
52 el rodillo entintador
- *ink roller (inking roller, fountain roller)*
53 el botón de regulación *f* de la presión
- *pressure adjustment*
54 la salida del papel impreso
- *sheet delivery (receiving table)*
55 el botón de regulación *f* de la velocidad de impresión *f*
- *printing speed adjustment*
56 el vibrador para alinear los papeles impresos en pilas *f*
- *jogger for aligning the piles of sheets*
57 la pila de papel *m* impreso
- *pile of paper (pile of sheets)*
58 la máquina de plegar (la plegadora)
- *folding machine*

59 la máquina de alzado *m* para tiradas *f* cortas
- *gathering machine (collating machine, assembling machine) for short runs*
60 la estación de alzado *m*
- *gathering station (collating station, assembling station)*
61 la encuadernadora automática para la encuadernación térmica son cosido *m*
- *adhesive binder (perfect binder) for hot adhesives*
62 el dictáfono de cinta *f* magnética
- *magnetic tape dictating machine*
63 los auriculares de casco *m* (el casco auricular, el juego de auriculares *m* con casco *m*)
- *headphones (headset, earphones)*
64 el interruptor de encendido *m*/apagado *m*
- *on/off switch*
65 el mango del micrófono
- *microphone cradle*
66 el enchufe para el interruptor a pedal *m* de la mecanógrafa
- *foot control socket*
67 el enchufe para el teléfono
- *telephone adapter socket*
68 el enchufe para los auriculares de casco *m*
- *headphone socket (earphone socket, headset socket)*
69 el enchufe para el micrófono
- *microphone socket*
70 el altavoz incorporado
- *built-in loudspeaker*
71 la lámpara indicadora (la luz de control *m*)
- *indicator lamp (indicator light)*
72 el compartimiento de la cassette
- *cassette compartment*
73 las teclas de marcha *f* adelante, de marcha *f* atrás y de parada *f*
- *forward wind, rewind, and stop buttons*
74 la escala de tiempo *m* (el contador horario) con rayas *f* indicadoras
- *time scale with indexing marks*
75 el cursor de parada *f* de la escala de tiempo *m*
- *time scale stop*

**1-11 el vestíbulo de servicio *m* a los clientes**
– *main hall*
1 la caja
– *cashier's desk (cashier's counter)*
2 el cajero
– *teller (cashier)*
3 el cristal antibalas
– *bullet-proof glass*
4 el grupo de empleados *m* de servicio *m* (asistencia *f* y consejos *m* para cuentas *f* de ahorro *m*, cuentas *f* privadas y de empresas *f*, créditos *m* personales)
– *service counters [for service and advice on savings accounts, private and company accounts, personal loans, etc.]*
5 la empleada de banco *m*
– *bank clerk*
6 la clienta del banco
– *customer*
7 los folletos publicitarios
– *brochures*
8 el cartel con las cotizaciones
– *stock list (price list, list of quotations)*
9 el mostrador de información *f*
– *information counter*
10 la ventanilla de cambio *m* de moneda *f*
– *foreign exchange counter*
11 la entrada a la cámara acorazada
– *entrance to strong room*
12 **la letra de cambio** *m; en este caso:* una letra girada (giro *m*), una letra aceptada

en España:

– *bill of exchange (bill), e.g. draft, acceptance (bank acceptance)*
13 el lugar de libramiento *m* (la localidad de expedición *f*)
– *place of issue*
14 la fecha de libramiento *m* (de expedición *f*)
– *date of issue*
15 el lugar de pago *m*
– *place of payment*
16 el día del vencimiento
– *date of maturity (due date)*
17 la cláusula de "letra *f* de cambio *m*" (la designación del documento como letra *f* de cambio *m*)
– *bill clause (draft clause)*
18 la cuantía de la letra (el importe de la letra)
– *value*
19 la orden (el tomador)
– *payee (remittee)*

20 el librado (el girado)
– *drawee (payer)*
21 el librador (el girador)
– *drawer*
22 la domiciliación (el lugar de pago *m*)
– *domicilation (paying agent)*
23 la aceptación
– *acceptance*
24 el sello de la letra (*Chile, Guat. y Mé.:* el fechador)
– *stamp*
25 el endoso (la anotación de transferencia *f*)
– *endorsement (indorsement, transfer entry)*
26 el endosatario
– *endorsee (indorsee)*
27 el endosante
– *endorser (indorser)*

**1-10 la Bolsa** (la Bolsa de valores *m*
y fondos *m* públicos)
- *stock exchange*
**1** la sala de la Bolsa
- *exchange hall (exchange floor)*
**2** el mercado de valores *m*
- *market for securities*
**3** el mostrador para los corredores
- *broker's post*
**4** el agente de cambio *m* colegiado,
un corredor de comercio *m*
- *sworn stockbroker (exchange
broker, stockbroker,* Am. *specialist),
an inside broker*
**5** el corredor de comercio *m* (el
agente de cambio *m*) libre, para
las transacciones del mercado
libre
- *kerbstone broker (kerbstoner,
curbstone broker, curbstoner,
outside broker), a commercial
broker dealing in unlisted securities*
**6** el miembro de la Bolsa, un
particular admitido para las
transacciones de Bolsa *f*
- *member of the stock exchange
(stockjobber,* Am. *floor trader,
room trader)*
**7** el agente de Bolsa *f*, un empleado
de banco *m*
- *stock exchange agent (boardman),
a bank employee*
**8** el tablón con las cotizaciones
bursátiles
- *quotation board*
**9** el ujier de la Bolsa
- *stock exchange attendant (waiter)*

**10** la cabina telefónica
- *telephone box (telephone booth,
telephone kiosk, call box)*
**11-19 valores** *m* (efectos *m*): *clases:*
acción *f*, valor *m* de renta *f* fija,
título *m* de la deuda, cédula *f*
(título *m*) hipotecaria, obligación *f*
municipal, obligación *f* industrial,
obligación *f* convertible
- *securities; kinds: share (*Am.
stock), fixed-income security,
annuity, bond, debenture bond,
municipal bond (corporation
stock), industrial bond, convertible
bond*
**11** la acción (el título); *en este caso:* la
acción al portador
- *share certificate (*Am. *stock
certificate);* here: *bearer share
(share warrant)*
**12** el valor nominal de la acción
- *par (par value, nominal par, face
par) of the share*
**13** el número de orden *m*
- *serial number*
**14** el número de folio *m* del libro de
registro *m* de acciones *f* del banco
- *page number of entry in bank's
share register (bank's stock ledger)*
**15** la firma del presidente del
Consejo de Inspección *f*
- *signature of the chairman of the
board of governors*
**16** la firma del presidente del
Consejo de Administración *f*
- *signature of the chairman of the
board of directors*

**17** la hoja de cupones *m*
- *sheet of coupons (coupon sheet,
dividend coupon sheet)*
**18** el cupón de dividendos *m*
- *dividend warrant (dividend coupon)*
**19** el talón de renovación *f*
- *talon*

# 252 Dinero (monedas y billetes)

1-28 **monedas** *f (clases:* monedas de oro *m,* de plata *f,* de níquel *m,* de cobre *m* o de aluminio *m)*
- *coins (coin, coinage, metal money, specie,* Am. *hard money);* kinds: *gold, silver, nickel, copper, or aluminium,* Am. *aluminum, coins*
1 Atenas: tetradracma *m* en forma *f* de pepita *f*
- *Athens: nugget-shaped tetradrachm (tetradrachmon, tetradrachma)*
2 el búho (el ave *f* cívica de Atenas)
- *the owl, emblem of the city of Athens*
3 áureo *m* (aureus) de Constantino el Grande
- *aureus of Constantine the Great*
4 bracteada *f* del emperador Federico I Barbarroja
- *bracteate of Emperor Frederick I Barbarossa*
5 Francia: luis *m* de oro *m* de Luis XIV
- *Louis XIV louis-d'or*
6 Prusia: 1 tálero *m* de Federico el Grande
- *Prussia: 1 reichstaler (speciestaler) of Frederick the Great*
7 República Federal Alemana: moneda *f* de 5 marcos *m* alemanes (DM); 1 DM = 100 pfennigs *m*
- *Federal Republic of Germany: 5 Deutschmarks (DM); 1 DM = 100 pfennigs*
8 el anverso (la cara)
- *obverse*
9 el reverso (la cruz)
- *reverse (subordinate side)*
10 la marca de la ceca
- *mint mark (mintage, exergue)*
11 el cordoncillo
- *legend (inscription on the edge of a coin)*
12 el dibujo de la moneda, un escudo de armas *f* nacional
- *device (type), a provincial coat of arms*
13 Austria: moneda *f* de 25 chelines *m* (schillings); 1 sch. = 100 groschen *m*
- *Austria: 25 schillings; 1 sch = 100 groschen*
14 los escudos de armas *f* de las provincias (de los estados)
- *provincial coats of arms*
15 Suiza: moneda *f* de 5 francos *m;* 1 franco = 100 rappens *m* (céntimos *m)*
- *Switzerland: 5 francs; 1 franc = 100 centimes*
16 Francia: moneda *f* de 1 franco *m* = 100 céntimos *m*
- *France: 1 franc = 100 centimes*

17 Bélgica: moneda *f* de 100 francos *m*
- *Belgium: 100 francs*
18 Luxemburgo: moneda *f* de 1 franco *m*
- *Luxembourg (Luxemburg): 1 franc*
19 Holanda: moneda *f* de 2½ florines *m;* 1 florín (gulden *m)* = 100 centavos *m*
- *Netherlands: 2 1/2 guilders; 1 guilder (florin, gulden) = 100 cents*
20 Italia: moneda *f* de 10 liras *f;* 1 lira = 100 centésimos *m*
- *Italy: 10 lire (sg. lira)*
21 Estado del Vaticano: moneda *f* de 10 liras *f*
- *Vatican City: 10 lire (sg. lira)*
22 España: moneda *f* de 1 peseta *f* = 100 céntimos *m*
- *Spain: 1 peseta = 100 céntimos*
23 Portugal: moneda *f* de 1 escudo *m* = 100 centavos *m*
- *Portugal: 1 escudo = 100 centavos*
24 Dinamarca: moneda *f* de 1 corona *f* = 100 ores *m*
- *Denmark: 1 krone = 100 öre*
25 Suecia: moneda *f* de 1 corona *f* = 100 ores *m*
- *Sweden: 1 krona = 100 öre*
26 Noruega: moneda *f* de 1 corona *f* = 100 ores *m*
- *Norway: 1 krone = 100 öre*
27 Checoslovaquia: moneda *f* de 1 corona *f* = 100 halèru *m*
- *Czechoslovakia: 1 koruna = 100 heller*
28 Yugoslavia: moneda *f* de 1 dinar *m* = 100 paras *m*
- *Yugoslavia: 1 dinar = 100 paras*
29-39 **billetes** *m* **de banco** *m* (papel *m* moneda, billetes *m,* moneda *f* fiduciaria)
- *banknotes* (Am. *bills) (paper money, notes, treasury notes)*
29 República Federal Alemana: billete *m* de 20 marcos *m* alemanes (DM)
- *Federal Republic of Germany: 20 DM*
30 el banco emisor
- *bank of issue (bank of circulation)*
31 la filigrana (un retrato)
- *watermark [a portrait]*
32 el valor nominal
- *denomination*
33 Estados Unidos de América: billete *m* de 1 dólar *m* = 100 centavos *m* (*P. Rico: y S. Dgo.:* 1 pavo *m,* 1 tranca *f)*
- *USA: 1 dollar ($) = 100 cents*
34 las firmas facsímiles
- *facsimile signatures*
35 el sello de control *m*
- *impressed stamp*

36 la designación de la serie (el número de serie *f)*
- *serial number*
37 Gran Bretaña e Irlanda del Norte: billete *m* de 1 libra *f* esterlina (£) = 100 peniques *m* nuevos
- *United Kingdom of Great Britain and Northern Ireland: 1 pound sterling (£1) = 100 new pence (100p.),* sg. *new penny (new p.)*
38 el guilloque
- *guilloched pattern*
39 Grecia: billete *m* de 1 000 dracmas *m;* 1 dracma = 100 leptas *m*
- *Greece: 1,000 drachmas (drachmae); 1 drachma = 100 lepta (sg. lepton)*
40-44 **la acuñación de moneda** *f*
- *striking of coins (coinage, mintage)*
40-41 los troqueles (los cuños)
- *coining dies (minting dies)*
40 el cuño superior
- *upper die*
41 el cuño inferior
- *lower die*
42 el anillo de acuñación *f*
- *collar*
43 el cospel (el flan)
- *coin disc (disk) (flan, planchet, blank)*
44 la prensa de acuñación *f*
- *coining press (minting press)*

1-3 la bandera de las Naciones
Unidas (de la ONU)
– flag of the United Nations
1 el asta f de la bandera rematada
por un sombrerete
– flagpole (flagstaff) with truck
2 la driza
– halyard (halliard, haulyard)
3 la lanilla
– bunting
4 la bandera del Consejo de Europa
(la bandera de Europa)
– flag of the Council of Europe
5 la bandera olímpica
– Olympic flag
6 la bandera a media asta f[en
señal f de duelo m]
– flag at half-mast (Am. at half-staff)
[as a token of mourning]
7-11 el estandarte
– flag
7 el asta f (el mastil)
– flagpole (flagstaff)
8 el bollón (el tachón) de la bandera
– ornamental stud
9 la corbata
– streamer
10 la moharra
– pointed tip of the flagpole
11 la lanilla
– bunting
12 el pendón
– banner (gonfalon)
13 el estandarte de caballería f(el
banderín de la caballería)
– cavalry standard (flag of the
cavalry)
14 el estandarte del Presidente de la
República Federal Alemana [la
insignia de Jefe m del Estado]
– standard of the German Federal
President [ensign of head of state]

15-21 banderas f nacionales
(pabellones m)
– national flags
15 la Unión Jack (Gran Bretaña)
– the Union Jack [Great Britain]
16 la bandera tricolor (Francia)
– the Tricolour (Am. Tricolor)
[France]
17 la Danebrog (Dinamarca)
– the Danebrog (Dannebrog)
[Denmark]
18 la bandera estrellada (Estados
Unidos de América, EEUU)
– the Stars and Stripes (Star-
Spangled Banner) [USA]
19 la Media Luna (Turquía)
– the Crescent [Turkey]
20 la bandera del sol naciente
(Japón)
– the Rising Sun [Japan]
21 la hoz y el martillo (Unión de
Repúblicas Socialistas Soviéticas,
URSS)
– the Hammer and Sickle [USSR]
22-34 banderas f de señales f, un
juego de banderas
– signal flags, a hoist
22-28 banderas f de letras f
– letter flags
22 letra f A, una corneta (bandera f
de dos puntas f, de dos farpas f)
– letter A, a burgee (swallow-tailed
flag)
23 letra f G, la señal de llamada f del
práctico
– G, pilot flag
24 H ("práctico m a bordo m")
– H ['pilot on board']
25 L ("señal f de parada f para
comunicación f importante")
– L ['you should stop, I have
something important to
communicate']

26 P, "a punto m de zarpar", una
señal de salida f
– P, the Blue Peter ['about to set sail']
27 W ("requerimiento m de
aistencia f médica")
– W ['I require medical assistance']
28 Z, una cuadra (bandera f
rectangular)
– Z, an oblong pennant (oblong
pendant)
29 el gallardete del código de
señales f, un gallardete del Código
internacional de señales
– code pennant (code pendant), used
in the International Signals Code
30-32 gallardetes m auxiliares,
banderas f triangulares
– substitute flags (repeaters),
triangular flags (pennants,
pendants)
33-34 gallardetes m de números m
– numeral pennants (numeral
pendants)
33 el número 1
– number 1
34 el número 0
– number 0
35-38 banderasf de Aduana f
– customs flags
35 la bandera de Aduana f de las
lanchas aduaneras
– customs boat pennant (customs boat
pendant)
36 "barco m despachado por
Aduanas f"
– 'ship cleared through customs'
37 la señal pidiendo despacho m de
Aduanas f
– customs signal flag
38 la bandera de pólvora f ["carga f
inflamable"]
– powder flag ['inflammable
(flammable) cargo']

**1-36** heráldica *f* (blasón *m*)
- *heraldry (blazonry)*
**1, 11, 30-36** cimeras *f*
- *crests*
**1-6** el escudo de armas *f* (el blasón)
- *coat-of-arms (achievement of arms, hatchment, achievement)*
**1** la cimera
- *crest*
**2** el tortillo
- *wreath of the colours* (Am. *colors*)
**3** el lambrequín
- *mantle (mantling)*
**4, 7-9** yelmos *m* (celadas *f*)
- *helmets (helms)*
**4** la celada (el yelmo)
- *tilting helmet (jousting helmet)*
**5** el escudo
- *shield*
**6** la banda ondeada siniestra
- *bend sinister wavy*
**7** el yelmo en forma *f* de cubo *m* (el yelmo cerrado)
- *pot-helmet (pot-helm, heaume)*
**8** la celada (el yelmo) de grilleta *f*
- *barred helmet (grilled helmet)*
**9** el yelmo abierto (el yelmo con la visera levantada)
- *helmet affronty with visor open*
**10-13** el escudo de armas *f* matrimonial (el escudo de alianza *f*, el escudo doble)
- *marital achievement (marshalled,* Am. *marshaled, coat-of-arms)*
**10** el escudo de armas *f* del hombre (del marido)
- *arms of the baron (of the husband)*
**11-13** el escudo de armas *f* de la mujer (de la esposa)
- *arms of the family of the femme (of the wife)*
**11** el busto humano
- *demi-man;* also: *demi-woman*
**12** la corona de hojas *f*
- *crest coronet*
**13** la flor de lis *f*
- *fleur-de-lis*

**14** el pabellón heráldico
- *heraldic tent (mantling)*
**15-16** tenantes *m*, animales *m* heráldicos
- *supporters; here: heraldic beasts*
**15** el toro
- *bull*
**16** el unicornio
- *unicorn*
**17-23** la descripción del escudo de armas *f* (blasón *m;* arte *amb.* de explicar los escudos de armas; la ordenación de los cuarteles (campos *m*) del escudo)
- *blazon*
**17** el centro del escudo (el corazón)
- *inescutcheon (heart-shield)*
**18-23** los seis cuarteles del escudo
- *quarterings one to six*
**18, 20, 22** el flanco diestro
- *dexter (right)*
**18-19** el jefe
- *chief*
**19, 21, 23** el flanco siniestro
- *sinister (left)*
**22-23** la punta
- *base*
**24-29** los esmaltes
- *tinctures*
**24-25** los metales
- *metals*
**24** oro *m* [amarillo]
- *or (gold)*
**25** plata *f* [blanco]
- *argent (silver)*
**26** sable *m* (negro)
- *sable*
**27** gules *m* (rojo)
- *gules*
**28** azur *m* (azul)
- *azure*
**29** sinople *m* (sinoble; verde)
- *vert*
**30** las plumas de avestruz *f*
- *ostrich feathers (treble plume)*
**31** los garrotes de torneo *m*
- *truncheon*
**32** la cabra naciente
- *demi-goat*

**33** los pendoncillos de torneo *m*
- *tournament pennons*
**34** los cuernos de búfalo *m*
- *buffalo horns*
**35** la arpía
- *harpy*
**36** el penacho de pavo *m* real
- *plume of peacock's feathers*
**37, 38, 42-46** coronas *f*
- *crowns and coronets [continental type]*
**37** la tiara papal
- *tiara (papal tiara)*
**38** la corona imperial [alemana, hasta 1806]
- *Imperial Crown [German, until 1806]*
**39** la corona ducal
- *ducal coronet (duke's coronet)*
**40** la corona de príncipe *m*
- *prince's coronet*
**41** la corona de príncipe *m* elector (de elector *m*)
- *elector's coronet*
**42** la corona real inglesa
- *English Royal Crown*
**43-45** coronas *f* de títulos *m* nobiliarios
- *coronets of rank*
**43** la corona nobiliaria [de Alemania]
- *baronet's coronet*
**44** la corona de barón *m*
- *baron's coronet (baronial coronet)*
**45** la corona de conde *m*
- *count's coronet*
**46** la corona mural del escudo de armas *f* de una ciudad
- *mauerkrone (mural crown) of a city crest*

**1-98** el armamento del ejército de tierra *f*
- *army weaponry*

**1-39** armas *f* de fuego *m* portátiles
- *hand weapons*

**1** la pistola P 1
- *P1 pistol*

**2** el cañón
- *barrel*

**3** la mira (el punto de mira *f*)
- *front sight (foresight)*

**4** el percutor
- *hammer*

**5** el gatillo (el disparador)
- *trigger*

**6** la culata
- *pistol grip*

**7** el almacén del cargador
- *magazine holder*

**8** la metralleta MP 2 (el subfusil)
- *MP 2 sub-machine gun*

**9** la culata de apoyo *m* en el hombro
- *shoulder rest (butt)*

**10** la caja
- *casing (mechanism casing)*

**11** la boquilla (la abrazadera)
- *barrel clamp (barrel-clamping nut)*

**12** la palanca para cargar el arma *f*
- *cocking lever (cocking handle)*

**13** la caña
- *palm rest*

**14** el seguro
- *safety catch*

**15** el cargador
- *magazine*

**16** el fusil ametrallador G3-A3
- *G3-A3 self-loading rifle*

**17** el cañón
- *barrel*

**18** el tapafuegos
- *flash hider (flash eliminator)*

**19** la caña
- *palm rest*

**20** el dispositivo de disparo *m* (el disparador y el guardamonte)
- *trigger mechanism*

**21** el cargador
- *magazine*

**22** el alza *f*
- *notch (sighting notch, rearsight)*

**23** el soporte (la montura) de la mira
- *front sight block (foresight block) with front sight (foresight)*

**24** la culata del fusil
- *rifle butt (butt)*

**25** el lanzagranadas de 44 mm anticarro
- *44 mm anti-tank rocket launcher*

**26** la granada
- *rocket (projectile)*

**27** el tubo amortiguador del culatazo (del retroceso)
- *buffer*

**28** el alza *f* telescópica
- *telescopic sight (telescope sight)*

**29** el mecanismo de disparo *m*
- *firing mechanism*

**30** la pieza protectora de la mejilla
- *cheek rest*

**31** la culata de apoyo *m* en el hombro
- *shoulder rest (butt)*

**32** la ametralladora MG3
- *MG3 machine gun (Spandau)*

**33** la caja (la caña)
- *barrel casing*

**34** el amortiguador del retroceso (del culatazo)
- *gas regulator*

**35** la pestaña para el cambio de cañón *m*
- *belt-changing flap*

**36** el alza *f*
- *rearsight*

**37** el soporte (la montura) de la mira
- *front sight block (foresight block) with front sight (foresight)*

**38** la empuñadura de pistola *f* (la culata)
- *pistol grip*

**39** la culata de apoyo *m* en el hombro
- *shoulder rest (butt)*

**40-95** armamento *m* pesado
- *heavy weapons*

**40** el mortero AM 50 de 120 mm
- *120 mm AM 50 mortar*

**41** el tubo (el cañón)
- *barrel*

**42** el bípode (el caballete de puntería *f*)
- *bipod*

**43** el afuste del cañón
- *gun carriage*

**44** el amortiguador del retroceso (del culatazo)
- *buffer (buffer ring)*

**45** la mira (el mecanismo de puntería *f*)
- *sight (sighting mechanism)*

**46** la placa de base *m* (el espolón)
- *base plate*

**47** el cojinete esférico
- *striker pad*

**48** la manivela de dirección *f*
- *traversing handle*

**49-74** piezas *f* de artillería *f* autopropulsada
- *artillery weapons mounted on self-propelled gun carriages*

**49** el cañón SF M 107 de 175 mm
- *175 mm SFM 107 cannon*

**50** la rueda motriz
- *drive wheel*

**51** el cilindro elevador
- *elevating piston*

**52** el freno del cañón
- *buffer (buffer recuperator)*

**53** el sistema hidráulico
- *hydraulic system*

**54** la culata
- *breech ring*

**55** el espolón
- *spade*

**56** el cilindro del espolón
- *spade piston*

**57** el obús autopropulsado blindado M 109 G de 155 mm
- *155 mm M 109 G self-propelled gun*

**58** el freno de la boca de fuego *m*
- *muzzle*

**59** el extractor de humo *m*
- *fume extractor*

**60** la cuna del cañón
- *barrel cradle*

**61** el recuperador
- *barrel recuperator*

**62** la abrazadera soporte del cañón
- *barrel clamp*

**63** la ametralladora antiaérea (DCA)
- *light anti-aircraft (AA) machine gun*

**64** el lanzamisiles Honest John M 386
- *Honest John M 386 rocket launcher*

**65** el misil de cabeza *f* (ojiva *f*) explosiva (nuclear)
- *rocket with warhead*

**66** la rampa de lanzamiento *m*
- *launching ramp*

**67** el mecanismo de elevación *f*
- *elevating gear*

**68** el apoyo del vehículo
- *jack*

**69** el torno para el cable
- *cable winch*

**70** el lanzacohetes 110 SF
- *110 SF rocket launcher*

**71** los cañones (los tubos)
- *disposable rocket tubes*

**72** el blindaje del cañón
- *tube bins*

**73** la cureña giratoria
- *turntable*

**74** el sistema regulador del tiro
- *fire control system*

**75** el vehículo de trabajos *m* en el campo de 2,5 t
- *2.5 tonne construction vehicle*

**76** el mecanismo de elevación *f*
- *lifting arms (lifting device)*

**77** la pala de explanación *f*
- *shovel*

**78** el contrapeso
- *counterweight (counterpoise)*

**79-95** vehículos *m* blindados
- *armoured* (Am. *armored*) *vehicles*

**79** la ambulancia blindada M 113
- *M113 armoured* (Am. *armored*) *ambulance*

**80** el carro de combate *m* Leopard 1 A 3
- *Leopard 1 A 3 tank*

**81** el blindaje
- *protection device*

**82** el telémetro láser e infrarrojo
- *infrared laser rangefinder*

**83** los botes fumígenos
- *smoke canisters (smoke dispensers)*

**84** la torre blindada
- *armoured* (Am. *armored*) *turret*

**85** el blindaje de la cadena
- *skirt*

**86** la rueda de corredera *f*
- *road wheel*

**87** la cadena
- *track*

**88** el carro anticarro
- *anti-tank tank*

**89** el extractor de humo *m*
- *fume extractor*

**90** el blindaje del cañón
- *protection device*

**91** el vehículo blindado Marder de transporte *m* de personal *m*
- *Marder armoured* (Am. *armored*) *personnel carrier*

**92** el cañón automático
- *cannon*

**93** el vehículo blindado para terraplenes *m*
- *Standard armoured* (Am. *armored*) *recovery vehicle*

**94** la pala de explanación *f* y de apoyo *m*
- *levelling* (Am. *leveling*) *and support shovel*

**95** el brazo de la grúa
- *jib*

**96** el vehículo de usos *m* múltiples de 0,25 t (el jeep)
- *.25 tonne all-purpose vehicle*

**97** el parabrisas abatible
- *drop windscreen* (Am. *drop windshield*)

**98** la capota de lona *f*
- *canvascover*

1 **el cazabombardero e interceptor** McDonnell-Douglas F-4F Phantom II
– McDonnell-Douglas F-4F Phantom II *interceptor and fighter-bomber*
2 la insignia del escuadrón
– *squadron marking*
3 el cañón de 20 mm
– *aircraft cannon*
4 el tanque del ala *f* (debajo del ala *f*)
– *wing tank (underwing tank)*
5 la toma de aire *m*
– *air intake*
6 la trampilla de control *m* para la capa límite
– *boundary layer control flap*
7 la sonda para el reabastecimiento de combustible *m* en vuelo *m*
– *in-flight refuelling (Am. refueling) probe (flight refuelling probe, air refuelling probe)*
8 **el avión de combate *m* polivalente** (MRCA, Multirole Combat Aircraft) Panavia 200 Tornado
– Panavia 2000 Tornado *multirole combat aircraft (MRCA)*
9 el plano de sustentación *f* giratorio (el ala *f* de geometría *f* variable)
– *swing wing*
10 el radomo (la cúpula del radar)
– *radar nose (radome, radar dome)*
11 la percha anemométrica (el tubo de Pitot)
– *pitot-static tube (pitot tube)*
12 la trampilla del freno (el freno aerodinámico)
– *brake flap (air brake)*

13 las toberas de postcombustión *f* de los reactores
– *afterburner exhaust nozzles of the engines*
14 **el avión de transporte *m* de alcance *m* medio** C 160 Transall
– C160 Transall *medium-range transport aircraft*
15 la góndola del tren de aterrizaje *m*
– *undercarriage housing (landing gear housing)*
16 el turbopropulsor (la turbohélice)
– *propeller-turbine engine (turboprop engine)*
17 la antena
– *antenna*
18 **el helicóptero ligero de transporte *m* y rescate *m*** Bell UH-1D Iroquois
– Bell UH-ID Iroquois *light transport and rescue helicopter*
19 el rotor principal (la hélice de propulsión *f*)
– *main rotor*
20 el rotor antipar trasero (la hélice de dirección *f*)
– *tail rotor*
21 los patines de aterrizaje *m* (los esquíes de aterrizaje *m*)
– *landing skids*
22 los planos fijos de estabilización *f*
– *stabilizing fins (stabilizing surfaces, stabilizers)*
23 el patín de cola *f*
– *tail skid*
24 **el avión de transporte *m* y de enlace *m*** (de despegue *m* y aterrizaje *m* corto) Dornier DO 28 D-2 Skyservant

– Dornier DO 28 D-2 Skyservant *transport and communications aircraft*
25 la góndola del motor
– *engine pod*
26 el tren de aterrizaje *m* principal
– *main undercarriage unit (main landing gear unit)*
27 la rueda de cola *f*
– *tail wheel*
28 la antena ensiforme (xifoide)
– *sword antenna*
29 **el cazabombardero** F-104 G Starfighter
– F-104 G Starfighter *fighter-bomber*
30 el tanque en el extremo del ala
– *wing-tip tank (tip tank)*
31-32 el grupo de cola *f* en T
– *T-tail (T-tail unit)*
31 el plano fijo de cola *f* (el estabilizador)
– *tailplane (horizontal stabilizer, stabilizer)*
32 el plano fijo de deriva *f*
– *vertical stabilizer (vertical fin, tail fin)*

**1-41** el avión a reacción *f* franco-alemán de adiestramiento *m* Dornier-Dassault-Breguet Alpha Jet
– *Dornier-Dassault-Breguet Alpha Jet Franco-German jet trainer*
**1** la percha anemométrica (el tubo de Pitot)
– *pitot-static tube (pitot tube)*
**2** el depósito de oxígeno *m*
– *oxygen tank*
**3** el tren de aterrizaje *m* delantero replegable hacia delante
– *forward-retracting nose wheel*
**4** la cúpula de la cabina (de la carlinga)
– *cockpit canopy (cockpit hood)*
**5** el gato de la cúpula
– *canopy jack*
**6** el asiento del piloto (el asiento del piloto alumno), un asiento de eyección *f*
– *pilot's seat (student pilot's seat), an ejector seat (ejection seat)*
**7** el asiento del observador (el asiento del instructor de vuelo *m*), un asiento de eyección *f*
– *observer's seat (instructor's seat), an ejector seat (ejection seat)*
**8** la palanca de mando *m*
– *control column (control stick)*
**9** la palanca de potencia *f* (el mando de gases *m*)
– *thrust lever*
**10** los pedales del timón de dirección *f* con frenos *m*
– *rudder pedals with brakes*
**11** el compartimiento de proa *f* del equipo electrónico
– *front avionics bay*
**12** la entrada de aire *m* (la toma de aire *m* del reactor)
– *air intake to the engine*
**13** el tabique de control *m* para la capa límite
– *boundary layer control flap*

**14** el conducto de entrada *f* del aire
– *air intake duct*
**15** el turborreactor
– *turbine engine*
**16** el depósito de alimentación *f* del sistema hidráulico
– *reservoir for the hydraulic system*
**17** el compartimiento de las baterías
– *battery housing*
**18** el compartimiento de cola *f* del equipo electrónico
– *rear avionics bay*
**19** el compartimiento de equipajes *m*
– *baggage compartment*
**20** el plano fijo de deriva *f* de triple larguero *m*
– *triple-spar tail construction*
**21** el timón de profundidad *f*
– *horizontal tail*
**22** el servomando del timón de profundidad *f*
– *servo-actuating mechanism for the elevator*
**23** el servomando del timón de dirección *f*
– *servo-actuating mechanism for the rudder*
**24** la caja del paracaídas de frenado *m*
– *brake chute housing (drag chute housing)*
**25** la antena perfilada VHF [VHF: Very high frequency]
– *VHF (very high frequency) antenna (UHF antenna)*
**26** la antena de altísima frecuencia *f* multidireccional [VOR: Very high frequency omnidirectional range]
– *VOR (very high frequency omnidirectional range) antenna*
**27** la superficie de sustentación *f* de doble larguero *m*
– *twin-spar wing construction*
**28** la armazón formada por largueros *m*
– *former with integral spars*

**29** el tanque integrado en el ala *f*
– *integral wing tanks*
**30** el tanque central del fuselaje
– *centre-section (Am. center-section) fuel tank*
**31** los tanques del fuselaje
– *fuselage tanks*
**32** la sonda de llenado *m* de combustible *m* por gravedad *f*
– *gravity fuelling (Am. fueling) point*
**33** la toma de combustible *m* bajo presión *f*
– *pressure fuelling (Am. fueling) point*
**34** la suspensión interior del ala *f*
– *inner wing suspension*
**35** la suspensión exterior del ala *f*
– *outer wing suspension*
**36** las luces de navegación *f* (de posición *f*)
– *navigation lights (position lights)*
**37** los faros de aterrizaje *m*
– *landing lights*
**38** los alerones de profundidad *f*
– *landing flap*
**39** el servomando del alerón
– *aileron actuator*
**40** el tren de aterrizaje *m* principal replegable hacia delante
– *forward-retracting main undercarriage unit (main landing gear unit)*
**41** el gato hidráulico de levantamiento *m* (el dispositivo retráct: il hidromecánico) del tren de aterrizaje *m*
– *undercarriage hydraulic cylinder (landing gear hydraulic cylinder)*

**447**

**1-63 buques** *m* **de guerra** *f* **ligeros**
(barcos *m* de guerra *f*)
– *light battleships*
**1 el destructor lanzamisiles**
– *destroyer*
2 el casco de cubierta *f* corrida
– *hull of flush-deck vessel*
3 la proa (la roda)
– *bow (stem)*
4 el asta (el mástil) de la bandera
– *flagstaff (jackstaff)*
5 el ancla *f*, una ancla de patente *f* (sin cepo *m*)
– *anchor, a stockless anchor (patent anchor)*
6 el cabrestante del ancla *f*
– *anchor capstan (windlass)*
7 el rompeolas
– *breakwater* (Am. *manger board)*
8 la cuaderna de curvatura *f*
– *chine strake*
9 la cubierta principal
– *main deck*
**10-28** superestructuras *f*
– *superstructures*
10 la cubierta superior
– *superstructure deck*
11 la balsa salvavidas
– *life rafts*
12 el esquife (la lancha de a bordo *m*)
– *cutter (ship's boat)*
13 la serviola (el pescante)
– *davit (boat-launching crane)*
14 el puente de mando *m* (el puente)
– *bridge (bridge superstructure)*
15 la luz lateral de posición *f* (de situación *f*)
– *side navigation light (side running light)*
16 la antena
– *antenna*
17 el cuadro radiogoniométrico (el radiogoniómetro)
– *radio direction finder (RDF) frame*
18 el palo de celosía *f* (la torre metálica)
– *lattice mast*
19 la chimenea de proa *f*
– *forward funnel*
20 la chimenea de popa *f*
– *aft funnel*
21 la caperuza de la chimenea (el sombrerete de la chimenea)
– *cowl*
22 la toldilla (el castillo de popa *f*)
– *aft superstructure (poop)*
23 el cabrestante
– *capstan*
24 la escalera de cámara *f* (la escotilla de cámara *f*)
– *companion ladder (companionway, companion hatch)*
25 el asta de la bandera de popa *f*
– *ensign staff*
26 la popa, una popa cuadra (popa *f* de espejo *m*)
– *stern, a transom stern*
27 la línea de flotación *f*
– *waterline*
28 el reflector
– *searchlight*
**29-37** el armamento
– *armament*
29 la torreta con un cañón de 100 mm
– *100 mm gun turret*
30 el lanzamisiles de defensa *f* antisubmarina, un lanzamisiles cuádruple
– *four-barrel anti-submarine rocket launcher (missile launcher)*
31 el afuste de dos cañones *m* antiaéreos de 40 mm
– *40 mm twin anti-aircraft (AA) gun*
32 el lanzamisiles de defensa *f* antiaérea MM 38, en su contenedor *m* de lanzamiento *m*

– *MM 38 anti-aircraft (AA) rocket launcher (missile launcher) in launching container*
33 el tubo lanzatorpedos de defensa *f* antisubmarina
– *anti-submarine torpedo tube*
34 la plataforma de lanzamiento *m* de cargas *f* de profundidad *f*
– *depth-charge thrower*
35 el radar de telepuntería *f*
– *weapon system radar*
36 la antena de radar *m*
– *radar antenna (radar scanner)*
37 el telémetro óptico
– *optical rangefinder*
**38 el destructor lanzamisiles**
– *destroyer*
39 el ancla de proa *f*
– *bower anchor*
40 el guardahélice (la protección de la hélice)
– *propeller guard*
41 el palo trípode de celosía *f*
– *tripod lattice mast*
42 el palo de una sola pieza
– *pole mast*
43 los orificios de ventilación *f* (la rejilla de ventilación *f*)
– *ventilator openings (ventilator grill)*
44 el conducto de salida *f* del humo
– *exhaust pipe*
45 el esquife (la lancha de a bordo *m*)
– *ship's boat*
46 la antena
– *antenna*
47 el cañón multiusos de 127 mm dirigido por radar *m* en su torreta *f*
– *radar-controlled 127 mm all-purpose gun in turret*
48 el cañón multiusos de 127 mm
– *127 mm all-purpose gun*
49 la rampa de lanzamiento *m* de misiles *m* Tartar
– *launcher for Tartar missiles*
50 el lanzamisiles de defensa *f* antisubmarina
– *anti-submarine rocket (ASROC) launcher (missile launcher)*
51 las antenas de radar *m* para el control del tiro
– *fire control radar antennas*
52 el radomo
– *radome (radar dome)*
**53 la fragata**
– *frigate*
54 el tubo del escobén
– *hawse pipe*
55 la luz de navegación *f*
– *steaming light*
56 la luz de posición *f* (de situación *f*)
– *navigation light (running light)*
57 la boca de aspiración *f* de aire *m*
– *air extractor duct*
58 la chimenea
– *funnel*
59 la caperuza de la chimenea (el sombrerete de la chimenea)
– *cowl*
60 la antena de látigo *m*
– *whip antenna (fishpole antenna)*
61 el esquife (la lancha de a bordo *m*)
– *cutter*
62 la luz de popa *f*
– *stern light*
63 el anillo guardahélice (el protector de la hélice)
– *propeller guard boss*
**64-91 buques** *m* **de guerra** *f*
– *fighting ships*
**64 el submarino**
– *submarine*
65 el castillo de proa *f* sumergible
– *flooded foredeck*
66 el casco de presión *f*
– *pressure hull*

67 la torreta
– *turret*
68 los instrumentos retráctiles (escamoteables)
– *retractable instruments*
69 la lancha rápida lanzamisiles
– *E-boat (torpedo boat)*
70 el cañón *f* multiusos de 76 mm con torreta *f*
– *76 mm all-purpose gun with turret6 mm all-purpose gun with turret*
71 el contenedor de lanzamiento *m* de misiles *m*
– *missile-launching housing*
72 la chupeta (camareta *f* junto al coronamiento de popa *f*, cámara *f* alta)
– *deckhouse*
73 el cañón antiaéreo (DCA) de 40 mm
– *40 mm anti-aircraft (AA) gun*
74 el listón guardahélice (el protector de la hélice)
– *propeller guard moulding* (Am. *molding)*
75 la lancha rápida lanzamisiles
– *143 class E-boat (143 class torpedo boat)*
76 el rompeolas
– *breakwater* (Am. *manger board)*
77 el radomo
– *radome (radar dome)*
78 el tubo lanzatorpedos
– *torpedo tube*
79 el conducto de salida *f* de los gases de escape *m*
– *exhaust escape flue*
**80 el cazador de minas** *f*
– *mine hunter*
81 el cintón reforzado
– *reinforced rubbing strake*
82 el bote neumático
– *inflatable boat (inflatable dinghy)*
83 la serviola (el pescante) del bote
– *davit*
**84 el dragaminas** (el buque barreminas, el buque buscaminas)
– *minesweeper*
85 el torno de tambor *m* para el cable
– *cable winch*
86 el torno de remolque *m*
– *towing winch (towing machine, towing engine)*
87 la draga (el mecanismo para barrer minas *f*)
– *mine-sweeping gear;* here; *paravanes*
88 la grúa
– *crane (davit)*
**89 el buque de desembarco** *m*
– *landing craft*
90 la rampa de proa *f*
– *bow ramp*
91 la rampa de popa *f*
– *stern ramp*
**92-97 barcos** *m* **auxiliares**
– *auxiliaries*
92 el ténder (el barco avituallador)
– *tender*
93 el buque de mantenimiento *m*, versión *f* taller *m* de reparación *f*
– *servicing craft*
94 el buque fondeador de minas *f* (el buque minador, el buque portaminas)
– *minelayer*
95 el buque escuela
– *training ship*
96 el remolcador de salvamento *m* en alta mar *amb.*
– *deep-sea salvage tug*
97 el buque cisterna (el petrolero de reabastecimiento *m* de combustible *m*)
– *fuel tanker (replenishing ship)*

# 259 Buques de guerra II (buques de guerra modernos)

1 el portaaviones a propulsión *f* nuclear "Nimitz ICVN 68" (EEUU)
– *nuclear-powered aircraft carrier Nimitz ICVN68' (USA)*
2-11 el plano lateral
– *body plan*
2 la cubierta de vuelo *m*
– *flight deck*
3 la superestructura (el puente de mando *m*)
– *island (bridge)*
4 el ascensor de aviones *m*
– *aircraft lift (Am. aircraft elevator)*
5 el lanzamisiles óctuplo de defensa *f* antiaérea
– *eight-barrel anti-aircraft (AA) rocket launcher (missile launcher)*
6 el palo de una sola pieza (el poste de antenas *f*)
– *pole mast (antenna mast)*
7 la antena
– *antenna*
8 la antena de radar *m*
– *radar antenna (radar scanner)*
9 la proa blindada
– *fully enclosed bow*
10 la grúa de a bordo *m*
– *deck crane*
11 la popa cuadra (la popa de espejo *m*)
– *transom stern*
12-20 el plano de cubierta *f*
– *deck plan*
12 la cubierta de vuelo *m* (la cubierta en ángulo *m*)
– *angle deck (flight deck)*
13 el ascensor de aviones *m*
– *aircraft lift (Am. aircraft elevator)*
14 la catapulta de lanzamiento *m* doble
– *twin launching catapult*
15 la pantalla plegable (móvil) protectora contra las llamaradas
– *hinged (movable) baffle board*
16 el cable de retención *f* (el cable de freno *m*)
– *arrester wire*
17 la red (la barrera) de emergencia *f* para amortiguar el choque
– *emergency crash barrier*
18 el andarivel
– *safety net*
19 el camello
– *caisson (cofferdam)*
20 el lanzamisiles óctuplo de defensa *f* antiaérea
– *eight-barrel anti-aircraft (AA) rocket launcher (missile launcher)*
21 el crucero lanzamisiles "Kara" (URSS)
– *'Kara' class rocket cruiser (missile cruiser) (USSR)*
22 el casco de cubierta *f* corrida
– *hull of flush-deck vessel*
23 la arrufadura (el arrufo)
– *sheer*
24 el lanzamisiles de doce tubos *m* de defensa *f* antisubmarina
– *twelve-barrel underwater salvo rocket launcher (missile launcher)*
25 el lanzamisiles doble de defensa *f* antiaérea
– *twin anti-aircraft (AA) rocket launcher (missile launcher)*
26 la batería de lanzamiento *m* de 4 misiles *m* de corto recorrido *m*
– *launching housing for 4 short-range rockets (missiles)*
27 la pantalla protectora contra las llamaradas
– *baffle board*
28 el puente de mando *m* (el puente)
– *bridge*
29 la antena de radar *m*
– *radar antenna (radar scanner)*
30 la torreta con dos cañones *m* antiaéreos de 76 mm

– *twin 76 mm anti-aircraft (AA) gun turret*
31 la torre de combate *m*
– *turret*
32 la chimenea
– *funnel*
33 el lanzamisiles doble de defensa *f* antiaérea
– *twin anti-aircraft (AA) rocket launcher (missile launcher)*
34 el cañón automático antiaéreo (de defensa antiaérea, DCA)
– *automatic anti-aircraft (AA) gun*
35 el esquife (la lancha de a bordo *m*)
– *ship's boat*
36 la batería de cinco tubos *m* lanzatorpedos de defensa *f* antisubmarina
– *underwater 5-torpedo housing*
37 el lanzamisiles séxtuplo de defensa *f* antisubmarina
– *underwater 6-salvo rocket launcher (missile launcher)*
38 el hangar de helicópteros *m*
– *helicopter hangar*
39 la plataforma de aterrizaje *m* de los helicópteros
– *helicopter landing platform*
40 el sonar de profundidad *f* variable
– *variable depth sonar (VDS)*
41 el crucero lanzamisiles a propulsión *f* nuclear "California" (EEUU)
– *'California' class rocket cruiser (missile cruiser) (USA)*
42 el casco
– *hull*
43 la torre de combate *m* de proa *f*
– *forward turret*
44 la torre de combate *m* de popa *f*
– *aft turret*
45 la superestructura de proa *f*
– *forward superstructure*
46 las lanchas de desembarco *m*
– *landing craft*
47 la antena
– *antenna*
48 la antena de radar *m*
– *radar antenna (radar scanner)*
49 el radomo
– *radome (radar dome)*
50 el lanzamisiles contra objetivos *m* aéreos
– *surface-to-air rocket launcher (missile launcher)*
51 el lanzatorpedos de defensa *f* antisubmarina
– *underwater rocket launcher (missile launcher)*
52 el cañón de 127 mm con torreta *f*
– *127 mm gun with turret*
53 la plataforma de aterrizaje *m* de los helicópteros
– *helicopter landing platform*
54 el submarino atómico antisubmarino
– *nuclear-powered fleet submarine*
55-74 la sección central del submarino [esquema]
– *middle section [diagram]*
55 el casco de presión *f*
– *pressure hull*
56 la sala de máquinas *f* auxiliares
– *auxiliary engine room*
57 la bomba de la turbina centrífuga
– *rotary turbine pump*
58 el generador de la turbina a vapor *m* (el turboalternador)
– *steam turbine generator*
59 el árbol (el eje) de la hélice
– *propeller shaft*
60 el cojinete de empuje *m*
– *thrust block*
61 el reductor (el demultiplicador)
– *reduction gear*
62 la turbina de alta o baja presión *f*
– *high and low pressure turbine*

63 el conducto de vapor *m* de alta presión *f* del circuito secundario
– *high-pressure steam pipe for the secondary water circuit (auxiliary water circuit)*
64 el condensador
– *condenser*
65 el circuito primario
– *primary water circuit*
66 el cambiador de calor *m*
– *heat exchanger*
67 la cuba del reactor nuclear
– *nuclear reactor casing (atomic pile casing)*
68 el núcleo del reactor
– *reactor core*
69 los elementos de control *m*
– *control rods*
70 la pantalla de plomo *m* (el blindaje aislante contra las radiaciones)
– *lead screen*
71 la torreta
– *turret*
72 el tubo snorkel
– *snorkel (schnorkel)*
73 el inyector de aire *m* fresco
– *air inlet*
74 los instrumentos retráctiles (escamoteables)
– *retractable instruments*
75 el submarino guardacostas de propulsión *f* convencional (Diesel-eléctrica)
– *patrol submarine with conventional (diesel-electric) drive*
76 el casco de presión *f*
– *pressure hull*
77 el castillo de proa *f* sumergible
– *flooded foredeck*
78 la trampilla exterior [del tubo lanzatorpedos]
– *outer flap (outer doors) [for torpedoes]*
79 el tubo lanzatorpedos
– *torpedo tube*
80 la sentina (el pantoque) de proa *f*
– *bow bilge*
81 el ancla *f*
– *anchor*
82 el cabrestante (el torno) del ancla *f*
– *anchor winch*
83 la batería de acumuladores *m*
– *battery*
84 los camarotes con literas *f* plegables
– *living quarters with folding bunks*
85 el camarote del comandante
– *commanding officer's cabin*
86 la escotilla principal
– *main hatchway*
87 el asta *f* (el mástil) de la bandera
– *flagstaff*
88-91 los instrumentos retráctiles (escamoteables)
– *retractable instruments*
88 el periscopio de ataque *m*
– *attack periscope*
89 la antena
– *antenna*
90 el tubo snorkel
– *snorkel (schnorkel)*
91 la antena de radar *m*
– *radar antenna (radar scanner)*
92 la válvula de evacuación *f* de gases *m* de escape *m*
– *exhaust outlet*
93 el compartimento del tubo de calefacción *f*
– *heat space (hot-pipe space)*
94 el grupo Diesel
– *diesel generators*
95 el timón de profundidad *f* y el timón de dirección *f* de popa *f*
– *aft diving plane and vertical rudder*
96 el timón de profundidad *f* de proa *f*
– *forward vertical rudder*

# 260 Colegio I (Preescolar y enseñanza primaria)

1-85 el colegio de preescolar y
enseñanza f primaria
- *primary school*
1-45 la clase (el aula f)
- *classroom*
1 los pupitres puestos en forma f de
herradura f
- *arrangement of desks in a
horseshoe*
2 el pupitre doble (*Perú*: la carpeta)
- *double desk*
3 los alumnos (los escolares; *Perú*:
los escoleros; *Col., Mé. y Venez.*:
los escuelantes; *Bol.*: los
escolinos) sentados en grupos m
- *pupils (children) in a group (sitting
in a group)*
4 el cuaderno de ejercicios m
- *exercise book*
5 el lápiz (el lapicero)
- *pencil*
6 la barrita de cera f
- *wax crayon*
7 la cartera (para llevar en la mano;
*Amér.*: el bulto)
- *school bag*
8 el asa f
- *handle*
9 la cartera (para llevar a la espalda)
- *school satchel (satchel)*
10 el bolsillo delantero
- *front pocket*
11 la correa del hombro
- *strap (shoulder strap)*
12 el plumier (el estuche de
lápices; m; *Arg. y Chile*: la
lapicera)
- *pen and pencil case*
13 el cierre de cremallera f
- *zip*
14 la pluma estilográfica
- *fountain pen (pen)*
15 la carpeta de anillas f (el
archivador)
- *loose-leaf file (ring file)*
16 el libro de lectura f
- *reader*
17 el libro de ortografía f
- *spelling book*
18 el cuaderno de escritura f
- *exercise book*; sim.: *notebook*
19 el rotulador
- *felt tip pen*
20 el dedo levantado
- *raising the hand*
21 el profesor (*Amér. Central, Chile,
Mé., Perú, Urug. y Venez.*: el
esculero)
- *teacher*
22 la mesa del profesor
- *teacher's desk*
23 el libro de clase f
- *register*
24 la bandeja portaplumas
- *pen and pencil tray*
25 el cartapacio
- *desk mat (blotter)*
26 el cristal de la ventana pintado a
mano f
- *window painting with finger paints
(finger painting)*
27 las acuarelas pintadas por los
alumnos
- *pupils' (children's) paintings
(watercolours)*
28 la cruz (el crucifijo)
- *cross*

29 la pizarra de tres paneles m
(*Antillas y Río de la Plata*: el
pizarrón)
- *three-part blackboard*
30 la pinza para sostener los mapas
- *bracket for holding charts*
31 la ranura para las tizas
- *chalk ledge*
32 la tiza (blanca; *Amér. Central y
Mé.*: el tizate)
- *chalk*
33 el dibujo de la pizarra
- *blackboard drawing*
34 el diagrama (el esquema)
- *diagram*
35 el panel lateral reversible
- *reversible side blackboard*
36 el plano de proyección f (la
pantalla de proyección f)
- *projection screen*
37 la escuadra
- *triangle*
38 el transportador
- *protractor*
39 la división en grados m
- *divisions*
40 el compás de pizarra f (el compás
de tiza f)
- *blackboard compass*
41 la bandeja de la esponja
- *sponge tray*
42 la esponja
- *blackboard sponge (sponge)*
43 el armario de la clase
- *classroom cupboard*
44 el mapa (el mapa mural)
- *map (wall map)*
45 el muro (la pared) de ladrillos m
- *brick wall*
46-85 la clase de trabajos m manuales
(el taller)
- *craft room*
46 el banco de carpintero m
- *workbench*
47 el tornillo de banco m (la
mordaza)
- *vice* (Am. *vise*)
48 la manivela de sujeción f
- *vice* (Am. *vise*) *bar*
49 las tijeras
- *scissors*
50-52 el trabajo con pegamento m
- *working with glue (sticking paper,
cardboard, etc.)*
50 la superficie para pegar
- *surface to be glued*
51 el tubo de pegamento m
- *tube of glue*
52 el tapón del tubo
- *tube cap*
53 la sierra de marquetería f (la
serreta)
- *fretsaw*
54 la cuchilla de la serreta
- *fretsaw blade (saw blade)*
55 la escofina de madera f
- *wood rasp (rasp)*
56 el trozo de madera f aserrado
asido por el tornillo de banco m
- *piece of wood held in the vice* (Am.
*vise)*
57 el bote de cola f
- *glue pot*
58 el taburete
- *stool*
59 la escobilla
- *brush*

60 el recogedor
- *pan (dust pan)*
61 las virutas
- *broken china*
62 el esmalte (el trabajo de
esmaltado m)
- *enamelling* (Am. *enameling)*
63 el horno eléctrico para esmaltar
- *electric enamelling* (Am. *enameling)
stove*
64 el cobre en bruto
- *unworked copper*
65 el polvo para esmaltar
- *enamel powder*
66 el colador de hilos m finos de
alambre m
- *hair sieve*
67-80 los trabajos escolares
- *pupils' (children's) work*
67 las esculturas de arcilla f (los
trabajos de modelado m)
- *clay models (models)*
68 la decoración de la ventana en
vidrio m coloreado
- *window decoration of coloured
(Am. colored) glass*
69 el mosaico de vidrio m
- *glass mosaic picture (glass mosaic)*
70 el móvil
- *mobile*
71 la cometa (la birlocha, la milocha,
la pandorga, el pájaro bitango, la
pájara, el pandero; *Amér.*: el
volantín)
- *paper kite (kite)*
72 la construcción de madera f
- *wooden construction*
73 el poliedro
- *polyhedron*
74 las marionetas
- *hand puppets*
75 las máscaras de arcilla f
- *clay masks*
76 las velas de cera f
- *cast candles (wax candles)*
77 la talla de madera f
- *wood carving*
78 el jarro de arcilla f (de barro m)
- *clay jug*
79 las formas geométricas de arcilla f
(de barro m)
- *geometrical shapes made of clay*
80 el juguete de madera f
- *wooden toys*
81 los materiales de trabajo m
- *materials*
82 la provisión de madera f
- *stock of wood*
83 las tintas de imprenta f para el
grabado en madera f (para la
xilografía)
- *inks for wood cuts*
84 los pinceles
- *paintbrushes*
85 el saco de yeso m
- *bag of plaster of Paris*

water cycle.
condensation

beaker
ice cubes
drops of
water

steam
water

# 261 Colegio II (enseñanza media; enseñanza secundaria)

1-45 **el instituto;** *anál.:* el colegio de
enseñanza *f* media
- *grammar school;* also: *upper band
of a comprehensive school* (Am.
*alternative school)*
1-13 **la clase de química** *f*
- *chemistry*
1 el laboratorio de química *f* con los
bancos dispuestos en gradas *f*
- *chemistry lab (chemistry laboratory)
with tiered rows of seats*
2 el profesor de química *f*
- *chemistry teacher*
3 la mesa de experimentación *f*
- *demonstration bench (teacher's
bench)*
4 la toma de agua *f*
- *water pipe*
5 la superficie de la mesa de
trabajo *m* embaldosada
(alicatada)
- *tiled working surface*
6 el fregadero (la pila)
- *sink*
7 el monitor de vídeo *m*, una
pantalla para la difusión de
programas *m* pedagógicos
- *television monitor, a screen for
educational programmes* (Am.
*programs)*
8 el retroproyector
- *overhead projector*
9 el plano de proyección *f* para el
papel transparente
- *projector top for skins*
10 la lente de proyección *f* con el
espejo inclinado
- *projection lens with right-angle
mirror*
11 la mesa de los alumnos equipada
para los experimentos
- *pupils' (Am. students') bench with
experimental apparatus*
12 el enchufe hembra *f* (la toma de
corriente *f*)
- *electrical point (socket)*
13 la mesa de proyección *f*
- *projection table*
14-34 **el laboratorio de biología** *f*
- *biology preparation room (biology
prep room)*
14 el esqueleto
- *skeleton*
15 la colección de cráneos *m*, las
reproducciones de cráneos *m*
- *collection of skulls, models (casts) of
sculls*
16 la bóveda craneal del
Pithecantropus erectus
- *calvarium of Pithecanthropus
Erectus*
17 el cráneo del Homo
steinheimensis
- *skull of Steinheim man*
18 la bóveda craneal del hombre de
Pekín (del Sinanthropus)
- *calvarium of Peking man (of
Sinanthropus)*
19 el cráneo del hombre de
Neanderthal, un cráneo de
homínido *m*
- *skull of Neanderthal man, a skull of
primitive man*
20 el cráneo del Australopithecus
- *Australopithecine skull (skull of
Australopithecus)*

21 el cráneo del Homo sapiens (del
hombre actual)
- *skull of present-day man*
22 la mesa de disección *f*
- *dissecting bench*
23 los frascos de productos *m*
químicos
- *chemical bottles*
24 la espita del gas
- *gas tap*
25 la cápsula de Petri
- *petri dish*
26 la probeta graduada
- *measuring cylinder*
27 las fichas de trabajo *m* (el material
pedagógico)
- *work folder containing teaching
material*
28 el libro de texto *m* (el manual)
- *textbook*
29 los cultivos bacteriológicos
- *bacteriological cultures*
30 la estufa de incubación *f*
microbiana (la estufa de
cultivos *m*; la estufa
bacteriológica)
- *incubator*
31 el escurridor de probetas *f*
- *test tube rack*
32 el frasco lavador de gases *m*
- *washing bottle*
33 la cubeta
- *water tank*
34 el fregadero
- *sink*
35 **el laboratorio de idiomas** *m*
- *language laboratory*
36 la pizarra (*Antillas y Río de la
Plata:* el pizarrón)
- *blackboard*
37 la consola central
- *console*
38 el casco auricular
- *headphones (headset)*
39 el micrófono
- *microphone*
40 el auricular
- *earcups*
41 el muelle acolchado del casco
- *padded headband (padded
headpiece)*
42 la grabadora de programas *m*
pedagógicos (la grabadora de
cintas *f* magnetofónicas, de
cassettes *f*; un magnetófono)
- *programme* (Am. *program)
recorder, a cassette recorder*
43 el control de volumen *m* de la voz
de los alumnos
- *pupil's (Am. student's) volume
control*
44 el control de volumen *m* del
programa
- *master volume control*
45 el teclado de mandos *m*
- *control buttons (operating keys)*

**1-25 la Universidad**
- *university (college)*
1 la clase (la lección)
- *lecture*
2 el anfiteatro (el aula *f;* el auditorio)
- *lecture room (lecture theatre,* Am. *theater)*
3 el catedrático de Universidad *f,* un profesor de Universidad *f* o un lector
- *lecturer (university lecturer, college lecturer,* Am. *assistant professor), a university professor or assistant lecturer*
4 la cátedra
- *lectern*
5 el manuscrito (el guión)
- *lecture notes*
6 el ayudante
- *demonstrator*
7 el laborante
- *assistant*
8 el cuadro didáctico
- *diagram*
9 el estudiante
- *student*
10 la estudiante
- *student*
**11-25 la biblioteca universitaria** (*anál.:* biblioteca nacional, biblioteca municipal, biblioteca de Academia)
- *university library;* sim.: *national library, regional or municipal scientific library*

11 el depósito de los libros
- *stack (book stack) with the stock of books*
12 la librería, una estantería de acero *m*
- *bookshelf, a steel shelf*
13 la sala de lectura *f*
- *reading room*
14 la celadora, una bibliotecaria
- *member of the reading room staff, a librarian*
15 la estantería de las revistas, con revistas *f*
- *periodicals rack with periodicals*
16 la estantería de los periódicos (de los diarios)
- *newspaper shelf*
17 la biblioteca de los libros de consulta *f* (manuales *m;* diccionarios *m;* enciclopedias *f*)
- *reference library with reference books, e.g. handbooks, encyclopedias, dictionaries*
18 el servicio de préstamo *m* (la sala de préstamo *m*) y la sala de ficheros *m*
- *lending library and catalogue (*Am. *catalog) room*
19 el bibliotecario
- *librarian*
20 la mesa de préstamo *m*
- *issue desk*
21 el fichero principal
- *main catalogue (*Am. *catalog)*
22 la estantería de ficheros *m*
- *card catalogue (*Am. *catalog)*

23 el cajón de fichas *f* (el fichero, la gaveta de fichas *f*)
- *card catalogue (*Am. *catalog) drawer*
24 el lector (el usuario de la biblioteca)
- *library user*
25 la ficha de préstamo *m*
- *borrower's ticket (library ticket)*

**1-15** el mitin electoral
– *election meeting, a public meeting*
**1-2** la presidencia
– *committee*
**1** el presidente
– *chairman*
**2** el vocal
– *committee member*
**3** la mesa presidencial
– *committee table*
**4** la campanilla
– *bell*
**5** el orador
– *election speaker (speaker)*
**6** la tribuna
– *rostrum*
**7** el micrófono
– *microphone*
**8** el público (el auditorio)
– *meeting (audience)*
**9** el distribuidor de octavillas *f* de propaganda *f* (de folletos *m* de propaganda *f*)
– *man distributing leaflets*
**10** el servicio de orden *m*
– *stewards*
**11** el brazalete
– *armband (armlet)*
**12** el cartelón electoral
– *banner*
**13** la pancarta electoral
– *placard*
**14** el cartel con la consigna electoral
– *proclamation*

**15** el interpelador (*si es intencionadamente:* el reventador)
– *heckler*
**16-30** la elección
– *election*
**16** el colegio electoral
– *polling station (polling place)*
**17** el funcionario del censo
– *election officer*
**18** el censo electoral
– *electoral register*
**19** la tarjeta de elector *m*, con el número de registro *m*
– *polling card with registration number (polling number)*
**20** la papeleta de voto *m*, con los nombres de los partidos y de los candidatos
– *ballot paper with the names of the parties and candidates*
**21** el sobre para la papeleta de voto *m*
– *ballot envelope*
**22** la electora
– *voter*
**23** la cabina electoral
– *polling booth*
**24** el elector con derecho *m* a voto *m*
– *elector (qualified voter)*
**25** el reglamento electoral
– *election regulations*
**26** el secretario
– *clerk*

**27** el adjunto con la lista duplicada
– *clerk with the duplicate list*
**28** el presidente de la mesa electoral
– *election supervisor*
**29** la urna (*Mé.:* ánfora *f*)
– *ballot box*
**30** la ranura de la urna
– *slot*

1-33 el servicio de intervención *f* de la policía
- *police duties*
1 el helicóptero de policía *f* (el helicóptero de tráfico *m*) para el control del tráfico desde el aire
- *police helicopter, e.g. traffic helicopter for controlling traffic from the air*
2 la cabina del piloto
- *cockpit*
3 el rotor (el rotor principal)
- *rotor (main rotor)*
4 el rotor de cola *f*
- *tail rotor*
5 el servicio de los perros policías
- *use of police dogs*
6 el perro policía
- *police dog*
7 el uniforme
- *uniform*
8 la gorra de servicio *m*, una gorra de visera *f* con escarapela *f* (con cucarda *f*)
- *uniform cap, a peaked cap with cockade*
9 el control de la circulación por una patrulla motorizada de tráfico *m*
- *traffic control by a mobile traffic patrol*
10 el coche patrulla
- *patrol car*
11 la luz azul (el faro giratorio, la luz con destellos *m*)
- *blue light*

12 el altavoz
- *loud hailer (loudspeaker)*
13 el policía (el agente) de patrulla *f* (*Amér. Central, Col., Chile, Ec., Pan. y Venez.:* el policial; *Arg.:* el policiano; *Ec. y Col.:* el chapa)
- *patrolman (police patrolman)*
14 el disco de señalización *f* de la policía
- *police signalling* (Am. *signaling*) *disc (disk)*
15 la policía antidisturbios
- *riot duty*
16 el coche especial blindado
- *special armoured* (Am. *armored*) *car*
17 la barricada
- *barricade*
18 el agente de policía *f* con el equipo antidisturbios
- *policeman (police officer) in riot gear*
19 la porra de goma *f*
- *truncheon (baton)*
20 el escudo de protección *f*
- *riot shield*
21 el casco de protección *f*
- *protective helmet (helmet)*
22 la pistola reglamentaria
- *service pistol*
23 la empuñadura (el puño) de la pistola
- *pistol grip*
24 la pistolera (la funda de la pistola)
- *quick-draw holster*

25 el cargador de la pistola
- *magazine*
26 la insignia de la policía judicial
- *police identification disc (disk)*
27 la estrella de la policía
- *police badge*
28 la dactiloscopia (la identificación por comparación *f* de las huellas digitales)
- *fingerprint identification (dactyloscopy)*
29 la huella digital
- *fingerprint*
30 el panel luminoso
- *illuminated screen*
31 el cacheo
- *search*
32 el sospechoso
- *suspect*
33 el agente de policía *f* judicial de paisano *m*
- *detective (plainclothes policeman)*
34 el policía inglés (el bobby)
- *English policeman*
35 el casco
- *helmet*
36 el cuaderno de notas *f*
- *pocket book*
37 la mujer policía
- *policewoman*
38 el coche celular (el furgón celular)
- *police van*

**1-26 el café** (la cafetería); *anál.:* el
salón de té *m*
- *café,* sim.: *espresso bar, tea room*
**1** el mostrador (la barra)
- *counter (cake counter)*
**2** la cafetera (la máquina de hacer
café *m*) a presión *f*
- *coffee urn*
**3** el platillo del dinero
- *tray for the money*
**4** la tarta
- *gateau*
**5** el merengue (*Hond. y Guat.:* la
espumilla) con nata *f* batida
- *meringue with whipped cream*
**6** el aprendiz de repostero *m*
- *trainee pastry cook*
**7** la señorita del mostrador
- *girl (lady) at the counter*
**8** el estante de los periódicos (el
revistero)
- *newspaper shelves (newspaper rack)*
**9** el aplique
- *wall lamp*
**10** el sofá de rinconera *f*
- *corner seat, an upholstered seat*
**11** la mesa del café (*Amér.:* la zofra)
- *café table*
**12** el tablero de mármol *m*
- *marble top*
**13** la camarera (*Col.:* la prendedera)
- *waitress*
**14** la bandeja (*Amér.:* la charola)
- *tray*

**15** la botella de limonada *f*
- *bottle of lemonade*
**16** el vaso de limonada *f*
- *lemonade glass*
**17** los jugadores de ajedrez *m*
durante una partida
- *chess players playing a game of
chess*
**18** el servicio de café *m*
- *coffee set*
**19** la taza de café *m*
- *cup of coffee*
**20** el platillo con azúcar *amb.*
- *small sugar bowl*
**21** el jarrito de crema *f*
- *cream jug (*Am. *creamer)*
**22-24** los clientes del café
- *café customers*
**22** el señor (el caballero; *Amér.
Central:* el jalón)
- *gentleman*
**23** la señora (la señorita, la dama)
- *lady*
**24** el lector de periódicos *m*
- *man reading a newspaper*
**25** el periódico
- *newspaper*
**26** el portaperiódicos
- *newspaper holder*

1-29 **el restaurante** (*menos lujoso:* la casa de comidas *f*)
- *restaurant*
1-11 la barra
- *bar (counter)*
1 el grifo de la cerveza (el aparato para servir la cerveza a presión *f*)
- *beer pump (beerpull)*
2 la bandeja escurridora
- *drip tray*
3 el vaso de cerveza *f*, un bock
- *beer glass, a tumbler*
4 la espuma de la cerveza
- *froth (head)*
5 el cenicero esférico con soporte *m*
- *spherical ashtray for cigarette and cigar ash*
6 la jarra de cerveza *f*
- *beer glass (beer mug)*
7 el calentador (el calientacerveza)
- *beer warmer*
8 el barman (el camarero)
- *bartender (barman, Am. barkeeper, barkeep)*
9 el estante de los vasos
- *shelf for glasses*
10 el estante de las botellas
- *shelf for bottles*
11 la pila de platos *m* (el montón de loza *f*)
- *stack of plates*
12 el perchero (la percha de pie *m*; el cuelgacapas)
- *coat stand*

13 el gancho para colgar sombreros *m*
- *hat peg*
14 el gancho para colgar abrigos *m* u ostras prendas *f*
- *coat hook*
15 el ventilador de pared *f*
- *wall ventilator*
16 la botella
- *bottle*
17 el plato de comida *f*
- *complete meal*
18 la camarera (*Col.:* la prendedera)
- *waitress*
19 la bandeja (*Amér.:* la charola)
- *tray*
20 el vendedor de billetes *m* de lotería *f* (*Perú:* el suertero)
- *lottery ticket seller*
21 la carta (el menú del día)
- *menu (menu card)*
22 las vinagreras (las angarillas; el convoy; el taller)
- *cruet stand*
23 el palillero
- *toothpick holder*
24 la cerillera (la fosforera; *Amér.:* el cerillero)
- *matchbox holder*
25 el cliente, la clienta
- *customer*
26 el posavasos
- *beer mat*

27 el cubierto
- *meal of the day*
28 la florista (la vendedora de flores *f*)
- *flower seller (flower girl)*
29 la cesta (el canastillo; el azafate) de flores *f*
- *flower basket*
30-44 **el bar**
- *wine restaurant (wine bar)*
30 el camarero, un jefe de camareros *m*
- *wine waiter, a head waiter*
31 la carta (la lista) de vinos *m*
- *wine list*
32 la jarra de vino *m*
- *wine carafe*
33 la copa de vino *m*
- *wineglass*
34 la estufa de azulejos *m* (de loza *f*)
- *tiled stove*
35 el azulejo de estufa *f*
- *stove tile*
36 al banco de la estufa
- *stove bench*
37 el panel de madera *f*
- *wooden panelling (Am. paneling)*
38 el sofá de rinconera *f*
- *corner seat*
39 la mesa de la tertulia (la mesa reservada a los clientes habituales)
- *table reserved for regular customers*
40 el tertuliano (el contertulio; el cliente habitual)
- *regular customer*

41 el aparador (*Col., P. Rico, S. Dgo.
y Venez.*: el seibó)
– *cutlery chest*
42 el cubo de hielo *m* para refrescar
el vino
– *wine cooler*
43 la botella de vino *m*
– *bottle of wine*
44 los cubitos de hielo *m*
– *ice cubes (ice, lumps of ice)*
45-78 **el restaurante autoservicio** *m* (el
self-service)
– *self-service restaurant*
45 la pila (el montón) de bandejas *f*
– *stack of trays*
46 las pajitas para beber
– *drinking straws (straws)*
47 las servilletas
– *serviettes (napkins)*
48 las casillas de los cubiertos
– *cutlery holders*
49 la vitrina refrigeradora para
platos *m* fríos
– *cool shelf*
50 la raja de melón rociada con miel *f*
– *slice of honeydew melon*
51 el plato de ensalada *f*
– *plate of salad*
52 el plato de queso *m*
– *plate of cheeses*
53 el plato de pescado *m*
– *fish dish*
54 el emparedado (el sandwich)
– *filled roll*

55 el plato de carne *f* con
guarnición *f*
– *meat dish with trimmings*
56 el medio pollo
– *half chicken*
57 la cesta de frutas *f*
– *basket of fruit*
58 el zumo de fruta *f*
– *fruit juice*
59 el anaquel de las bebidas
– *drinks shelf*
60 la botella de leche *f*
– *bottle of milk*
61 la botella de agua *f* mineral
– *bottle of mineral water*
62 el menú de dieta *f* cruda (el menú
dietético)
– *vegetarian meal (diet meal)*
63 la bandeja (*Amér.*: la charola)
– *tray*
64 el deslizadero para las bandejas
– *tray counter*
65 los carteles anunciadores de los
platos
– *food price list*
66 la ventana de la cocina para servir
los platos
– *serving hatch*
67 el plato caliente
– *hot meal*
68 el aparato para servir la cerveza
– *beer pump (beerpull)*
69 la caja
– *cash desk*

70 la cajera
– *cashier*
71 el propietario (el jefe)
– *proprietor*
72 la barrera
– *rail*
73 el comedor
– *dining area*
74 la mesa del comedor (*Chile, Ec. y
Mé.*: el trinche)
– *table*
75 el sandwich de queso *m*
– *open sandwich*
76 la copa de helado *m*
– *ice-cream sundae*
77 el salero y el pimentero
– *salt cellar and pepper pot*
78 la decoración de la mesa (el
adorno floral)
– *table decoration*

461

**1-26 la recepción** (el vestíbulo)
- *vestibule (foyer, reception hall)*
1 el portero
- *doorman (commissionaire)*
2 el casillero del correo, con los cajetines para las cartas
- *letter rack with pigeon holes*
3 el tablero de las llaves
- *key rack*
4 el globo de luz *f*, un globo de cristal *m* blanco
- *globe lamp, a frosted glass globe*
5 el tablero de los números (el indicador de llamadas *f*)
- *indicator board*
6 la señal luminosa de llamada *f*
- *indicator light*
7 el recepcionista
- *chief receptionist*
8 el libro de registro *m*
- *register (hotel register)*
9 la llave de la habitación
- *room key*
10 la chapa numerada, con el número de la habitación
- *number tag (number tab) showing room number*
11 la factura del hotel
- *hotel bill*
12 el bloque de formularios *m* de inscripción *f*
- *block of registration forms*
13 el pasaporte
- *passport*

14 el huésped del hotel
- *hotel guest*
15 la maleta de avión *m*, una maleta ligera (*Amér. Central, Col., Ec. y Venez.*: el carriel; *Col. y Venez.*: la maletera) para viajes en avión *m*
- *lightweight suitcase*
16 el pupitre de pared *f*
- *wall desk*
17 el mozo del hotel
- *porter (Am. baggage man)*
18-26 el vestíbulo (el hall)
- *lobby (hotel lobby)*
18 el botones
- *page (pageboy, Am. bell boy)*
19 el gerente (el director) del hotel
- *hotel manager*
20 el comedor (el restaurante del hotel)
- *dining room (hotel restaurant)*
21 la araña, una lámpara de varios brazos *m*
- *chandelier*
22 el rincón de la chimenea
- *fireside*
23 la chimenea
- *fireplace*
24 la repisa de la chimenea
- *mantelpiece (mantelshelf)*
25 la lumbre (el fuego encendido)
- *fire*
26 el sillón
- *armchair*

27-38 **la habitación del hotel,** una habitación doble con baño *m*
- ***hotel room, a double room with bath***
27 la puerta doble
- *double door*
28 el tablero de timbres *m*
- *service bell panel*
29 el baúl armario
- *wardrobe trunk*
30 el departamento de los trajes
- *clothes compartment*
31 el departamento de la ropa blanca
- *linen compartment*
32 el lavabo doble
- *double washbasin*
33 el camarero de habitación *f*
- *room waiter*
34 el teléfono de habitación *f*
- *room telephone*
35 la alfombra de terciopelo *m* (*Chile y Perú:* el piso)
- *velour (velours) carpet*
36 la mesita de las flores
- *flower stand*
37 el ramo de flores *f* (el ramillete artísticamente dispuesto)
- *flower arrangement*
38 la cama doble
- *double bed*
39 **el salón de banquetes** *m* (el salón de fiestas *f*)
- ***banquet room***

**40-43** los convidados de un banquete privado
- *party (private party) at table (at a banquet)*
**40** el orador proponiendo un brindis
- *speaker proposing a toast*
**41** el vecino de mesa *f* del 42
- *42's neighbour (Am. neighbor)*
**42** el caballero compañero de mesa *f* de la convidada 43
- *43's partner*
**43** la señora compañera de mesa *f* del 42
- *42's partner*
**44-46 el té de las cinco,** en el bar del hotel
- *thé dansant (tea dance) in the foyer*
**44** el trío del bar
- *bar trio*
**45** el violonista de pie *m*
- *violinist*
**46** la pareja bailando
- *couple dancing (dancing couple)*
**47** el camarero
- *waiter*
**48** la servilleta
- *napkin*
**49** el cerillero
- *cigar and cigarette boy*
**50** la batea
- *cigarette tray*
**51 el bar del hotel**
- *hotel bar*

**52** la barra para apoyar los pies
- *foot rail*
**53** el taburete de bar *m*
- *bar stool*
**54** la barra (el mostrador) del bar
- *bar*
**55** el cliente del bar
- *bar customer*
**56** la copa de cóctel *m*
- *cocktail glass (Am. highball glass)*
**57** el vaso de whisky *m* (de güisqui *m*)
- *whisky (whiskey) glass*
**58** el corcho de la botella de champaña *m*
- *champagne cork*
**59** el cubo del champaña (el cubo de hielo *m* para refrescar el champaña)
- *champagne bucket (champagne cooler)*
**60** el vaso de medidas *f*
- *measuring beaker (measure)*
**61** la coctelera
- *cocktail shaker*
**62** el barman
- *bartender (barman, Am. barkeeper, barkeep)*
**63** la camarera del bar (*Col.:* la prendedera)
- *barmaid*
**64** el anaquel de las botellas
- *shelf for bottles*

**65** el anaquel de las copas
- *shelf for glasses*
**66** el revestimiento de espejos *m*
- *mirrored panel*
**67** el recipiente de hielo
- *ice bucket*

1  el parquímetro
– *parking meter*
2  el plano de la ciudad
– *map of the town (street map)*
3  el tablero luminoso
– *illuminated board*
4  la leyenda
– *key*
5  la papelera
– *litter bin (Am. litter basket)*
6  la farola
– *street lamp (street light)*
7  la placa con el nombre de la calle
– *street sign showing the name of the street*
8  el sumidero
– *drain*
9  la tienda de ropa f (la tienda de modas f; la boutique)
– *clothes shop; also: fashion house*
10  el escaparate (*Amér.:* la vidriera)
– *shop window*
11  la exhibición de los géneros en el escaparate
– *window display (shop window display)*
12  la decoración del escaparate
– *window decoration (shop window decoration)*
13  la entrada
– *entrance*
14  la ventana
– *window*
15  la jardinera
– *window box*

16  el anuncio luminoso
– *neon sign*
17  el taller de sastre (la sastrería)
– *tailor's workroom*
18  el transeúnte (*Bol., Chile, Perú y Río de la Plata:* el chasque)
– *pedestrian*
19  la bolsa de la compra
– *shopping bag*
20  el barrendero
– *road sweeper (Am. street sweeper)*
21  la escoba (el escobón)
– *broom*
22  la basura de las calles
– *rubbish (litter)*
23  los raíles del tranvía
– *tramlines (Am. streetcar tracks)*
24  el paso de peatones m (el paso de cebra f)
– *pedestrian crossing (zebra crossing, Am. crosswalk)*
25  la parada del tranvía
– *tram stop (Am. streetcar stop, trolley stop)*
26  la señal de la parada
– *tram stop sign (Am. streetcar stop sign, trolley stop sign)*
27  el horario del tranvía
– *tram timetable (Am. streetcar schedule)*
28  el distribuidor automático de billetes m (la máquina de tiques m)
– *ticket machine*

29  la señal de advertencia f de "paso m de peatones" m
– *'pedestrian crossing' sign*
30  el policía urbano, dirigiendo la circulación (el guardia de la circulación)
– *traffic policeman on traffic duty (point duty)*
31  la manopla reflectante
– *traffic control cuff*
32  la gorra reflectante
– *white cap*
33  la señal de la mano
– *hand signal*
34  el motorista (motociclista m)
– *motorcyclist*
35  la motocicleta (moto f)
– *motorcycle*
36  la pasajera de la moto (el paquete)
– *pillion passenger (pillion rider)*
37  la librería
– *bookshop*
38  la sombrerería
– *hat shop (hatter's shop); for ladies' hats: milliner's shop*
39  el cartel anunciador del comercio (el rótulo de la tienda)
– *shop sign*
40  la oficina de seguros m (de la compañía aseguradora)
– *insurance company office*
41  los grandes almacenes
– *department store*
42  el frente del escaparate
– *shop front*

**43** el panel de anuncios *m*
– *advertisement*
**44** las banderas
– *flags*
**45** el anuncio del tejado en letras *f* luminosas (el luminoso)
– *illuminated letters*
**46** el tranvía (*P. Rico:* el trole)
– *tram (Am. streetcar, trolley)*
**47** el camión de mudanzas *f*
– *furniture lorry (Am. furniture truck)*
**48** el paso elevado (el viaducto)
– *flyover*
**49** la iluminación de la calle, un farol suspendido en el centro de la calle
– *suspended street lamp*
**50** la raya de parada *f*
– *stop line*
**51** la señalización del paso de peatones *m*
– *pedestrian crossing (Am. crosswalk)*
**52** el semáforo
– *traffic lights*
**53** el poste del semáforo
– *traffic light post*
**54** el dispositivo de señales *f* luminosas (el juego de luces *f*)
– *set of lights*
**55** las señales luminosas para los peatones
– *pedestrian lights*
**56** la cabina telefónica
– *telephone box (telephone booth, telephone kiosk, call box)*

**57** la cartelera de cine *m* (el cartel anunciador de la película)
– *cinema advertisement (film poster)*
**58** la zona peatonal
– *pedestrian precinct (paved zone)*
**59** el café
– *street café*
**60** un grupo de gente *f* sentado en la terraza del café
– *group seated (sitting) at a table*
**61** la sombrilla (el parasol)
– *sunshade*
**62** la escalera de descenso *m* a los servicios públicos
– *steps to the public lavatories (public conveniences)*
**63** la parada de taxis *m*
– *taxi rank (taxi stand)*
**64** el taxi (*S. Dgo.:* el concho)
– *taxi (taxicab, cab)*
**65** el distintivo del taxi
– *taxi sign*
**66** la señal de tráfico *m* "parada *f* de taxis" *m*
– *'taxi rank' ('taxi stand') sign*
**67** el teléfono de taxis *m*
– *taxi telephone*
**68** la oficina de correos *m*
– *post office*
**69** la máquina de cigarrillos *m*
– *cigarette machine*
**70** la columna anunciadora
– *advertising pillar*
**71** el cartel de publicidad *f*
– *poster (advertisement)*

**72** la raya blanca
– *white line*
**73** la flecha obligatoria de giro *m* a la izquierda
– *lane arrow for turning left*
**74** la flecha obligatoria de seguir en línea *f* recta
– *lane arrow for going straight ahead*
**75** el vendedor de periódicos *m* (*Col. y Ec.:* el voceador; *Arg., Perú y Urug.:* el canillita; *Mé.:* el papelero; *Chile:* el suplementero)
– *news vendor (Am. news dealer)*

465

# 269  Abastecimiento de aguas                     Water Supply

1-66 el abastecimiento de agua *f*
  **potable**
  – *drinking water supply*
 1 el nivel de agua *f* freática (de
   agua *f* subterránea)
  – *water table (groundwater level)*
 2 la capa conductora del agua *f*
   freática
  – *water-bearing stratum (aquifer,
   aquafer)*
 3 la corriente de agua *f* subterránea
   (de agua *f* freática)
  – *groundwater stream (underground
   stream)*
 4 el pozo colector del agua *f* natural
  – *collector well for raw water*
 5 el tubo de aspiración *f*
  – *suction pipe*
 6 la alcachofa con válvula *f* de
   fondo *m*
  – *pump strainer (with foot valve)*
 7 la bomba aspirante con motor *m*
  – *bucket pump with motor*
 8 la bomba de vacío *m* con motor *m*
  – *vacuum pump with motor*
 9 la instalación de filtraje *m* rápido
  – *rapid-filter plant*
10 la grava (el guijo) filtradora
  – *filter gravel (filter bed)*
11 el fondo del filtro, una rejilla
  – *filter bottom, a grid*
12 el tubo de desagüe *m* del agua *f*
   filtrada
  – *filtered water outlet*

13 el depósito de agua *f* limpia
  – *purified water tank*
14 el tubo de aspiración *f* con
   alcachofa *f* y válvula *f* de fondo *m*
  – *suction pipe with pump strainer and
   foot valve*
15 la bomba principal con motor *m*
  – *main pump with motor*
16 la tubería a presión *f*
  – *delivery pipe*
17 la caldera de aire *m*
  – *compressed-air vessel (air vessel, air
   receiver)*
18 el depósito elevado de agua *f*
  – *water tower*
19 la tubería de subida *f* del agua *f*
  – *riser pipe (riser)*
20 la tubería de desagüe *m* del agua *f*
   sobrante (el rebosadero)
  – *overflow pipe*
21 la tubería de bajada *f* del agua *f*
  – *outlet*
22 la tubería de la red de
   distribución *f*
  – *distribution main*
23 la alcantarilla del agua *f* residual
   (el canal para el exceso de agua *f*)
  – *excess water conduit*
24-39 el alumbramiento de una
   fuente
  – *tapping a spring*
24 la cámara de la fuente
  – *chamber*

25 el muro de arena *f*
  – *chamber wall*
26 el pozo de acceso *m*
  – *manhole*
27 la chimenea de aireación *f*
  – *ventilator*
28 los peldaños de hierro *m*
  – *step irons*
29 el terraplén
  – *filling (backing)*
30 la válvula de cierre *m* (la llave de
   paso *m*)
  – *outlet control valve*
31 la válvula de vaciado *m*
  – *outlet valve*
32 el colador (el filtro)
  – *strainer*
33 el tubo de desagüe *m* del agua *f*
   sobrante (el rebosadero)
  – *overflow pipe (overflow)*
34 el desagüe subterráneo
  – *bottom outlet*
35 los tubos de terracota *f*
  – *earthenware pipes*
36 la capa impermeable
  – *impervious stratum (impermeable
   stratum)*
37 la capa de guijarros *m*
  – *rough rubble*
38 la capa conductora de agua *f*
  – *water-bearing stratum (aquifer,
   aquafer)*
39 la capa de arcilla *f* apisonada
  – *loam seal (clay seal)*

**40-52** el abastecimiento individual de agua *f*
- *individual water supply*
**40** el pozo
- *well*
**41** el tubo de aspiración *f*
- *suction pipe*
**42** el nivel de agua *f* subterránea
- *water table (groundwater level)*
**43** la alcachofa con válvula *f* de fondo *m*
- *pump strainer with foot valve*
**44** la bomba centrífuga
- *centrifugal pump*
**45** el motor
- *motor*
**46** el interruptor de protección *f* del motor
- *motor safety switch*
**47** el controlador de la presión, un conmutador
- *manostat, a switching device*
**48** la válvula de cierre *m* (la llave de paso *m*)
- *stop valve*
**49** la tubería a presión *f*
- *delivery pipe*
**50** la caldera de aire *m*
- *compressed-air vessel (air vessel, air receiver)*
**51** el agujero de hombre *m* (el orificio de limpieza *f*)
- *manhole*

**52** la tubería de distribución *f* al consumidor
- *delivery pipe*
**53** el contador de agua *f (Amér.:* el medidor de agua *f)*, un contador de turbina *f*
- *water meter, a rotary meter*
**54** la entrada del agua *f*
- *water inlet*
**55** el mecanismo contador
- *counter gear assembly*
**56** la tapa de cristal *m*
- *cover with glass lid*
**57** la salida del agua *f*
- *water outlet*
**58** la esfera (el cuadrante) del contador de agua *f*
- *water-meter dial*
**59** el mecanismo contador
- *counters*
**60** el pozo alumbrado por un pisón
- *driven well (tube well, drive well)*
**61** la punta del pisón (la punta de penetración *f*)
- *pile shoe*
**62** el filtro
- *filter*
**63** el nivel del agua *f* subterránea
- *water table (groundwater level)*
**64** el tubo envolvente
- *well casing*
**65** los bordes del pozo
- *well head*
**66** la bomba de mano *f*
- *hand pump*

**1-46 los ejercicios del servicio de incendios** m (los ejercicios de los bomberos; los ejercicios de extinción f, trepa f, escalera f, salvamento m)
- *fire service drill (extinguishing, climbing, ladder, and rescue work)*
**1-3 el cuartel de bomberos** m
- *fire station*
1 la cochera (el garaje) y el cuarto de herramientas f
- *engine and appliance room*
2 el alojamiento del personal
- *firemen's quarters*
3 la torre de prácticas f
- *drill tower*
4 la sirena de incendios m (la sirena de alarma f)
- *fire alarm (fire alarm siren, fire siren)*
5 el camión de bomberos m
- *fire engine*
6 la luz azul [en España: la luz roja] (la luz de advertencia f), una luz intermitente (una luz con destellos m)
- *blue light (warning light), a flashing light (Am. flashlight)*
7 la sirena
- *horn (hooter)*
8 la bomba a motor m (la motobomba), una bomba centrífuga
- *motor pump, a centrifugal pump*

9 la escalera giratoria a motor m
- *motor turntable ladder (Am. aerial ladder)*
10 la escalera extensible, una escalera de acero m (una escalera mecánica)
- *automatic extending ladder, a steel ladder*
11 el mecanismo de la escalera
- *ladder mechanism*
12 el puntal
- *jack*
13 el maquinista
- *ladder operator*
14 la escala de corredera f
- *extension ladder*
15 el gancho de derribo m
- *ceiling hook (Am. preventer)*
16 la escala de ganchos m
- *hook ladder (Am. pompier ladder)*
17 el personal de bomberos m sujetando la lona de salvamento m
- *holding squad*
18 la lona de bomberos m (de salto m)
- *jumping sheet (sheet)*
19 la ambulancia (el coche ambulancia f)
- *ambulance car (ambulance)*
20 el aparato de reanimación f, un aparato de inhalación f de oxígeno m
- *resuscitator (resuscitation equipment), oxygen apparatus*

21 el sanitario
- *ambulance attendant (ambulance man)*
22 el brazalete
- *armband (armlet, brassard)*
23 las parihuelas (la camilla)
- *stretcher*
24 el hombre inconsciente
- *unconscious man*
25 la boca de riego m subterránea
- *pit hydrant*
26 el tubo vertical
- *standpipe (riser, vertical pipe)*
27 la llave de la boca de riego m
- *hydrant key*
28 el carrete móvil para la manguera (para la manga)
- *hose reel (Am. hose cart, hose wagon, hose truck, hose carriage)*
29 el acoplamiento de la manguera
- *hose coupling*
30 el conducto de aspiración f, una manga (un tubo flexible)
- *soft suction hose*
31 el conducto a presión f
- *delivery hose*
32 la pieza de distribución f
- *dividing breeching*
33 la boquilla de la manga
- *branch*
34 el equipo de extinción f
- *branchmen*
35 la boca de riego m de superficie f
- *surface hydrant (fire plug)*

36 el jefe de bomberos *m*
– *officer in charge*
37 el bombero
– *fireman (Am. firefighter)*
38 el casco protector contra incendios *m*, con el cubrenuca
– *helmet (fireman's helmet, Am. fire hat) with neck guard (neck flap)*
39 el aparato de oxígeno *m* (de respiración *f*)
– *breathing apparatus*
40 la máscara antigás (la careta contra gases *m*)
– *face mask*
41 el aparato de radio *f* portátil (el transmisor-receptor portátil)
– *walkie-talkie set*
42 el reflector portátil (de mano *f*)
– *hand lamp*
43 el hacha *f* de bombero *m*
– *small axe (Am. ax, pompier hatchet)*
44 el cinturón de ganchos *m*
– *hook belt*
45 la cuerda (la cuerda de salvamento *m*)
– *beltline*
46 el traje protector contra el calor de amianto *m* o de tejido *m* metálico
– *protective clothing of asbestos (asbestos suit) or of metallic fabric*
47 el camión grúa *f*
– *breakdown lorry (Am. crane truck, wrecking crane)*

48 la grúa de salvamento *m*
– *lifting crane*
49 el gancho de tracción *f*
– *load hook (draw hook, Am. drag hook)*
50 la roldana de apoyo *m*
– *support roll*
51 el camión cisterna (el camión-tanque de extinción *f*)
– *water tender*
52 la bomba a motor *m* portátil
– *portable pump*
53 el camión de las mangueras y herramientas *f*
– *hose layer*
54 los rollos de las mangueras
– *flaked lengths of hose*
55 el tambor del cable
– *cable drum*
56 el cabrestante
– *winch*
57 el filtro de la máscara antigás
– *face mask filter*
58 el carbón activo
– *active carbon (activated carbon, activated charcoal)*
59 el filtro del polvo
– *dust filter*
60 la abertura de entrada *f* del aire
– *air inlet*
61 el extintor de mano *f*
– *portable fire extinguisher*
62 la válvula de pistola *f*
– *trigger valve*

63 el extintor transportable
– *large mobile extinguisher (wheeled fire extinguisher)*
64 el proyector de agua *f* y espuma *f*
– *foam-making branch (Am. foam gun)*
65 el barco de extinción *f* de incendios *m*
– *fireboat*
66 el cañón de agua *f*
– *monitor (water cannon)*
67 la manga de aspiración *f*
– *suction hose*

1 la cajera
- *cashier*
2 la caja registradora eléctrica
- *electric cash register (till)*
3 las teclas de números *m*
- *number keys*
4 el botón de anulación *f*
- *cancellation button*
5 el cajón del dinero
- *cash drawer (till)*
6 los departamentos del cajón, para monedas *f* de metal *m* y billetes *m* de banco *m*
- *compartments (money compartments) for coins and notes (Am. bills)*
7 el recibo de pago *m* (el tique de caja *f*)
- *receipt (sales check)*
8 el total a pagar
- *amount [to be paid]*
9 el mecanismo de suma *f*
- *adding mechanism*
10 la mercancía
- *goods*
11 el patio de luz *f* (techado con una claraboya)
- *glass-roofed well*
12 el departamento de artículos *m* de caballero *m*
- *men's wear department*
13 la vitrina de exposición *f* (el escaparate interior)
- *showcase (display case, indoor display window)*

14 el mostrador de entrega *f* de los artículos
- *wrapping counter*
15 la canastilla con los artículos a empaquetar
- *tray for purchases*
16 la clienta (la compradora)
- *customer*
17 el departamento de medias *f* (la sección de mercería *f*)
- *hosiery department*
18 la dependienta (la vendedora)
- *shop assistant (Am. salesgirl, saleslady)*
19 el cartel con los precios
- *price card*
20 el soporte para probarse los guantes
- *glove stand*
21 el abrigo tres cuartos
- *duffle coat, a three-quarter length coat*
22 la escalera mecánica
- *escalator*
23 el tubo de luz *f* fluorescente (el tubo de neón *m*)
- *fluorescent light (fluorescent lamp)*
24 la oficina (*por ej.*: la oficina de ventas *f* a crédito *m*; la agencia de viajes *m*; la oficina de la dirección)
- *office, e.g. customer accounts office, travel agency, manager's office*

25 el cartel publicitario (el anuncio publicitario)
- *poster (advertisement)*
26 el despacho de localidades *f* para teatro *m* y conciertos *m* (el despacho de venta *f* por adelantado)
- *theatre (Am. theater) and concert booking office (advance booking office)*
27 la estantería (*Amér.*: el armazón)
- *shelves*
28 el departamento (la sección) de vestidos *m* de señora *f*
- *ladies' wear department*
29 el vestido confeccionado
- *ready-made dress (ready-to-wear dress, coll. off-the-peg dress)*
30 el guardapolvo
- *dust cover*
31 la percha de los vestidos *m*
- *clothes rack*
32 el probador
- *changing booth (fitting booth)*
33 el encargado de la planta
- *shop walker (Am. floorwalker, floor manager)*
34 el maniquí
- *dummy*
35 la butaca
- *seat (chair)*
36 la revista de modas *f*
- *fashion journal (fashion magazine)*

37 el modista tomando medidas *f*
– *tailor marking a hemline*
38 la cinta métrica
– *measuring tape (tape measure)*
39 el jaboncillo de sastre *m*
– *tailor's chalk (French chalk)*
40 el medidor del largo de falda *f*
– *hemline marker*
41 el abrigo suelto
– *loose-fitting coat*
42 el mostrador de venta *f*
– *sales counter*
43 la cortina de aire *m* caliente
– *warm-air curtain*
44 el portero
– *doorman (commissionaire)*
45 el ascensor
– *lift (Am. elevator)*
46 la caja del ascensor
– *lift cage (lift car, Am. elevator car)*
47 el ascensorista
– *lift operator (Am. elevator operator)*
48 los botones de mando *m*
– *controls (lift controls, Am. elevator controls)*
49 el indicador del piso (de la planta)
– *floor indicator*
50 la puerta de corredera *f*
– *sliding door*
51 el hueco del ascensor
– *lift shaft (Am. elevator shaft)*
52 el cable de tracción *f*
– *bearer cable*
53 el cable de control *m*
– *control cable*

54 los raíles de deslizamiento *m*
– *guide rail*
55 el cliente (el comprador)
– *customer*
56 los géneros de punto *m*
– *hosiery*
57 los artículos de lencería *f* (mantelerías *f* y ropas *f* de cama *f*)
– *linen goods (table linen and bed linen)*
58 el departamento (la sección) de telas *f*
– *fabric department*
59 la pieza de tela *f* (de paño *m*)
– *roll of fabric (roll of material, roll of cloth)*
60 el encargado del departamento (el jefe de sección *f*)
– *head of department (department manager)*
61 el mostrador de venta *f*
– *sales counter*
62 el departamento de bisutería *f*
– *jewellery (Am. jewelry) department*
63 la vendedora de novedades *f*
– *assistant (Am. salesgirl, saleslady), selling new lines (new products)*
64 la mesa de las ofertas especiales (las gangas)
– *special counter (extra counter)*
65 el cartel con los precios de las ofertas especiales (las gangas)
– *placard advertising special offers*

66 el departamento (la sección) de cortinas *f*
– *curtain department*
67 la decoración de los techos de las estanterías
– *display on top of the shelves*

**1-40 el parque francés** (parque *m* barroco), un parque palaciego
- *formal garden (French Baroque garden), palace gardens*
1 la gruta
- *grotto (cavern)*
2 la estatua de piedra *f*, una ninfa
- *stone statue, a river nymph*
3 el invernadero de naranjos *m*
- *orangery (orangerie)*
4 el bosquecillo
- *boscage (boskage)*
5 el laberinto de setos *m*
- *maze (labyrinth of paths and hedges)*
6 el teatro al aire libre
- *open-air theatre (Am. theater)*
7 el palacio barroco (un palacio de estilo *m* Luis XIV)
- *Baroque palace*
8 los juegos de agua *f*
- *fountains*
9 la cascada artificial
- *cascade (broken artificial waterfall, artificial falls)*
10 la estatua, un monumento
- *statue, a monument*
11 el pedestal
- *pedestal*
12 el árbol modelado en forma *f* esférica
- *globe-shaped tree*
13 el árbol modelado en forma *f* cónica
- *conical tree*

14 el arbusto ornamental
- *ornamental shrub*
15 la fuente mural
- *wall fountain*
16 el banco del parque
- *park bench*
17 la pérgola
- *pergola (bower, arbour, Am. arbor)*
18 el sendero cubierto de braba *f*
- *gravel path (gravel walk)*
19 el árbol modelado en forma *f* piramidal
- *pyramid tree (pyramidal tree)*
20 el amorcillo
- *cupid (cherub, amoretto, amorino)*
21 la fuente (*Amér.:* el puquio)
- *fountain*
22 el surtidor
- *fountain (jet of water)*
23 la taza (pilón *m*) superior de la fuente
- *overflow basin*
24 la taza inferior de la fuente
- *basin*
25 el borde de la fuente
- *kerb (curb)*
26 el paseante
- *man out for a walk*
27 la guía turística
- *tourist guide*
28 el grupo de turistas *m*
- *group of tourists*
29 el reglamento del parque
- *park by-laws (bye-laws)*

30 el guarda del parque
- *park keeper*
31 la puerta del parque (la verja), una verja de hierro *m* forjado
- *garden gates made of wrought iron*
32 la entrada del parque
- *park entrance*
33 la verja del parque (el enrejado que sirve de muro *m*)
- *park railings*
34 el barrote de la verja
- *railing (bar)*
35 el jarrón de piedra *f*
- *stone vase*
36 el césped
- *lawn*
37 el borde del sendero, un seto vivo recortado
- *border, a trimmed (clipped) hedge*
38 el sendero del parque
- *park path*
39 el parterre
- *parterre*
40 el abedul
- *birch (birch tree)*
**41-72 el parque inglés** (el jardín inglés)
- *landscaped park (jardin anglais)*
41 el arriate
- *flower bed*
42 el banco del parque
- *park bench (garden seat)*
43 la papelera
- *litter bin (Am. litter basket)*

**44** el césped de juegos *m*
– *play area*
**45** el río
– *stream*
**46** el embarcadero
– *jetty*
**47** el puente
– *bridge*
**48** la silla del parque
– *park chair*
**49** el cercado de los animales
– *animal enclosure*
**50** el estanque
– *pond*
**51-54** las aves acuáticas
– *waterfowl*
**51** el pato salvaje con sus patitos *m*
– *wild duck with young*
**52** la oca salvaje
– *goose*
**53** el flamenco
– *flamingo*
**54** el cisne
– *swan*
**55** la isla
– *island*
**56** el nenúfar
– *water lily*
**57** el café con terraza *f*
– *open-air café*
**58** la sombrilla
– *sunshade*
**59** el árbol
– *park tree (tree)*

**60** la copa del árbol
– *treetop (crown)*
**61** el bosquecillo
– *group of trees*
**62** el surtidor
– *fountain*
**63** el sauce llorón
– *weeping willow*
**64** la escultura moderna
– *modern sculpture*
**65** el invernadero
– *hothouse*
**66** el jardinero
– *park gardener*
**67** el escobón para barrer la hojarasca
– *broom*
**68** el campo de minigolf *m*
– *minigolf course*
**69** el jugador de minigolf *m*
– *minigolf player*
**70** el recorrido del minigolf
– *minigolf hole*
**71** la madre con el cochecito de niño *m*
– *mother with pram (baby carriage)*
**72** la pareja de novios *m*
– *courting couple*

1 el tenis de mesa *f* (el ping-pong)
– *table tennis game*
2 la mesa de ping-pong *m*
– *table*
3 la red de ping-pong *m*
– *table tennis net*
4 la raqueta de ping-pong *m*
– *table tennis racket (raquet) (table tennis bat)*
5 la pelota de ping-pong *m*
– *table tennis ball*
6 el volante (el bádminton)
– *badminton game (shuttlecock game)*
7 el volante (el rehilete)
– *shuttlecock*
8 los pasos de gigantes *m*
– *maypole swing*
9 la bicicleta de niño *m*
– *child's bicycle*
10 el fútbol
– *football game (soccer game)*
11 la portería (la meta)
– *goal (goalposts)*
12 el balón de fútbol *m*
– *football*
13 el delantero (el ariete)
– *goal scorer*
14 el portero (el guardameta)
– *goalkeeper*

15 el juego de la comba (*Amér. Central y Cuba:* la suiza; *Chile:* el cordel)
– *skipping (Am. jumping rope)*
16 la cuerda (la comba)
– *skipping rope (Am. skip rope, jump rope, jumping rope)*
17 la torre para escalar
– *climbing tower*
18 el columpio de neumático *m*
– *rubber tyre (Am. tire) swing*
19 el neumático de camión *m*
– *lorry tyre (Am. truck tire)*
20 el balón de rebotes *m*
– *bouncing ball*
21 la construcción para juegos *m* de aventura *f*
– *adventure playground*
22 la escalera de palos *m*
– *log ladder*
23 la vigía (el mirador, la atalaya)
– *lookout platform*
24 el tobogán
– *slide*
25 la papelera
– *litter bin (Am. litter basket)*
26 el oso de peluche *m*
– *teddy bear*
27 el tren de madera *f* de juguete *m*
– *wooden train set*

28 el estanque para chapotear los niños
– *paddling pool*
29 el velero de juguete *m*
– *sailing boat (yacht, Am. sailboat)*
30 el pato de juguete *m*
– *toy duck*
31 el cochecito de niño *m*
– *pram (baby carriage)*
32 la barra fija
– *high bar (bar)*
33 el coche de carreras *f* de niño *m* (el kart)
– *go-cart (soap box)*
34 la bandera de salida *f*
– *starter's flag*
35 el subibaja (*Mé.:* el bimbalete)
– *seesaw*
36 el robot (el autómata)
– *robot*
37 el aeromodelismo
– *flying model aeroplanes (Am. airplanes)*
38 el avión de aeromodelismo *m*
– *model aeroplane (Am. airplane)*
39 el columpio doble
– *double swing*
40 la tabla (el asiento) del columpio
– *swing seat*

# El parque de juegos infantiles

Children's Playground 273

**41** el remonte de la cometa
– *flying kites*
**42** la cometa (la birlocha, la milocha, la pandorga, el pájaro bitango, la pájara, el pandero; *Amér.:* el volantín)
– *kite*
**43** la cola de la cometa
– *tail of the kite*
**44** la cuerda (el bramante) de la cometa
– *kite string*
**45** el cilindro rotativo
– *revolving drum*
**46** la telaraña
– *spider's web*
**47** el pórtico de escalada *f*
– *climbing frame*
**48** la cuerda
– *climbing rope*
**49** la escala de cuerda *f*
– *rope ladder*
**50** la red para trepar
– *climbing net*
**51** el monopatín
– *skateboard*
**52** el tobogán de montaña *f* rusa
– *up-and-down slide*
**53** el funicular de neumático *m*
– *rubber tyre (Am. tire) cable car*

**54** el neumático (que sirve de asiento *m*)
– *rubber tyre (Am. tire)*
**55** el tractor, un vehículo de pedales *m*
– *tractor, a pedal car*
**56** la casa de miniatura *f* de elementos *m* de construcción *f* intercambiables
– *den*
**57** la plancha de ensamblaje *m*
– *presawn boards*
**58** el banco
– *seat (bench)*
**59** la tienda (la cabaña) india
– *Indian hut*
**60** el tejado para escalar
– *climbing roof*
**61** el asta de la bandera
– *flagpole (flagstaff)*
**62** el camión de juguete *m*
– *toy lorry (Am. toy truck)*
**63** la muñeca que anda
– *walking doll*
**64** el cajón de arena *f*
– *sandpit (Am. sandbox)*
**65** la excavadora de juguete *m*
– *toy excavator (toy digger)*
**66** el montón de arena *f*
– *sandhill*

1-21 el parque del balneario
- *spa gardens*
1-7 la salina
- *salina (salt works)*
1 la torre de graduación *f* salinera
- *thorn house (graduation house)*
2 las brozas de zarzas *f*
- *thorns (brushwood)*
3 el canal de distribución *f* del agua *f* salobre
- *brine channels*
4 el tubo de agua *f* salobre de la estación de bombeo *m*
- *brine pipe from the pumping station*
5 el guardián de la torre de graduación *f* salinera
- *salt works attendant*
6-7 la cura (la terapia) por inhalación *f*
- *inhalational therapy*
6 el inhalatorio al aire libre
- *open-air inhalatorium (outdoor inhalatorium)*
7 el enfermo, durante la inhalación
- *patient inhaling (taking an inhalation)*
8 el pabellón de hidroterapia *f*, con el casino
- *hydropathic (pump room) with kursaal (casino)*

9 el pórtico (los soportales; la arcada)
- *colonnade*
10 el paseo del balneario
- *spa promenade*
11 la avenida de fuentes *f*
- *avenue leading to the mineral spring*
12-14 la cura de reposo *m*
- *rest cure*
12 el césped para el reposo *m*
- *sunbathing area (lawn)*
13 la tumbona
- *deck-chair*
14 el toldo
- *sun canopy*
15 el pabellón de la fuente
- *pump room*
16 la estantería de los vasos
- *rack for glasses*
17 el grifo
- *tap*
18 el paciente del balneario
- *patient taking the waters*
19 el quiosco de música *f*
- *bandstand*
20 la orquesta del balneario, dando un concierto
- *spa orchestra giving a concert*
21 el director de orquesta *f*
- *conductor*

**1-33 la ruleta** (*P. Rico:* la pica;
  *Amér.:* la rolata), un juego de
  suerte *f* (un juego de azar *m*)
- *roulette, a game of chance
  (gambling game)*
**1** la sala de la ruleta (la sala de
  juego *m*) en el casino
- *gaming room in the casino (in the
  gambling casino)*
**2** la caja
- *cash desk*
**3** el director del juego
- *tourneur (dealer)*
**4** el crupié (el auxiliar del banquero;
  *Perú, P. Rico y S. Dgo.:* el gurupié)
- *croupier*
**5** la raqueta
- *rake*
**6** el crupié de cabecera *f*
- *head croupier*
**7** el jefe de la sala
- *hall manager*
**8** la mesa de la ruleta (la mesa de
  juego *m*)
- *roulette table (gaming table,
  gambling table)*
**9** el tapete de juego *m* (el tapete
  verde)
- *roulette layout*
**10** la ruleta
- *roulette wheel*
**11** la caja de la mesa (la banca)
- *bank*
**12** la ficha
- *chip (check, plaque)*

**13** la apuesta (la postura)
- *stake*
**14** el carné de socio *m* del casino
- *membership card*
**15** el jugador de ruleta *f*
- *roulette player*
**16** el detective privado (el detective
  de la casa)
- *private detective (house detective)*
**17** el tapete del juego de la ruleta (el
  tapete verde)
- *roulette layout*
**18** el cero
- *zero (nought, O)*
**19** paso *m* (números *m* altos)
  [números del 19 al 36]
- *passe (high) [numbers 19 to 36]*
**20** par [números *m* pares]
- *pair (even numbers)*
**21** negro
- *noir (black)*
**22** falta *f* (números *m* bajos)
  [números del 1 al 18]
- *manque (low) [numbers 1 to 18]*
**23** impar [números *m* impares]
- *impair [odd numbers]*
**24** rojo
- *rouge (red)*
**25** primera docena *f* [números *m* del
  1 al 12]
- *douze premier (first dozen)
  [numbers 1 to 12]*
**26** segunda docena *f* (docena
  intermedia) [números *m* del 13 al
  24]

- *douze milieu (second dozen)
  [numbers 13 to 24]*
**27** última docena *f* [números *m* del 25
  al 36]
- *douze dernier (third dozen)
  [numbers 25 to 36]*
**28** la ruleta
- *roulette wheel (roulette)*
**29** el canal de la ruleta
- *roulette bowl*
**30** el obstáculo
- *fret (separator)*
**31** el disco giratorio, con los números
  del 0 al 36
- *revolving disc (disk) showing
  numbers 0 to 36*
**32** el aspa *f* giratoria
- *spin*
**33** la bola de la ruleta
- *roulette ball*

1-16  **el juego del ajedrez** (el
ajedrez, el juego real), un juego
de combinación *f* de
movimientos *m* o posiciones *f*
- **chess,** *a game involving*
  *combinations of moves, a*
  *positional game*
1  el tablero de ajedrez *m*, con las
figuras en posición *f* de salida *f*
- *chessboard (board) with the men*
  *(chessmen) in position*
2  el escaque blanco (la casilla del
tablero de ajedrez *m*)
- *white square, a chessboard*
  *square*
3  el escaque negro
- *black square*
4  las figuras blancas (los trebejos
blancos, las blancas) en forma *f*
simbólica [blancas = B]
- *white chessmen (white pieces)*
  *[white = W]*
5  las figuras negras (los trebejos
negros, las negras) en forma *f*
simbólica [negras = N]
- *black chessmen (black pieces)*
  *[black = B]*
6  las letras y números *m* para
designar los escaques en las
transcripciones de partidas *f*
(jugadas *f*) de ajedrez *m* y
problemas *m* de ajedrez
- *letters and numbers for*
  *designating chess squares in the*
  *notation of chess moves and*
  *chess problems*
7  las diferentes figuras del
ajedrez
- *individual chessmen (individual*
  *pieces)*
8  el rey
- *king*
9  la reina (la dama)
- *queen*
10  el alfil
- *bishop*
11  el caballo
- *knight*
12  la torre
- *rook (castle)*
13  el peón
- *pawn*
14  los movimientos (jugadas *f*) de
cada una de las figuras
(trebejos *m*)
- *moves of the individual pieces*
15  el mate (el jaque mate), un
mate de caballo *m*
- *mate (checkmate), a mate by*
  *knight*
16  el reloj de ajedrez *m*, un reloj
doble para los torneos
(campeonatos) de ajedrez *m*
- *chess clock, a double clock for*
  *chess matches (chess*
  *championships)*
17-19  **el juego de damas** *f* (las
damas)
- *draughts* (Am. *checkers*)

17  el damero (el tablero de las
damas)
- *draughtboard (*Am.
  *checkerboard)*
18  la dama blanca (la ficha de
damas blanca); *también:* la
ficha para el juego del chaquete
y del tres en raya *f*
- *white draughtsman (*Am.
  *checker, checkerman); also:*
  *piece for backgammon and nine*
  *men's morris*
19  la dama negra (la ficha de
damas negra)
- *black draughtsman (*Am.
  *checker, checkerman)*
20  **el juego de salta** *m* (el salta)
- *salta*
21  la ficha del salta
- *salta piece*
22  el damero (el tablero) para el
juego del chaquete
- *backgammon board*
23-25  **el juego de tres en raya** *f*
(*Arg.:* el tatetí)
- *nine men's morris*
23  el tablero de tres en raya *f*
- *nine men's morris board*
24  el tres en raya *f*
- *mill*
25  el tres en raya *f* doble
- *double mill*
26-28  **el juego del halma**
- *halma*
26  el damero (el tablero) para el
juego del halma
- *halma board*
27  el corral
- *yard (camp, corner)*
28  las figuras (las fichas) del
halma en diferentes colores *m*
- *halma pieces (halma men) of*
  *various colours (*Am. *colors)*
29  **el juego de los dados** (los dados)
- *dice (dicing)*
30  el cubilete (*Bol., Col., Chile, Ec.*
y *Perú:* el cacho; *Venez.:* el
tacuro; *Amér. Central:* el
churuco)
- *dice cup*
31  los dados
- *dice*
32  los puntos
- *spots (pips)*
33  **el juego de dominó** *m* (el
dominó)
- *dominoes*
34  la ficha de dominó *m*
- *domino (tile)*
35  el doble (*Chile:* el chancho)
- *double*
36  **los naipes** (las cartas)
- *playing cards*
37  el naipe (la carta) francés (de
póquer)
- *French playing card (card)*
38-45  los palos
- *suits*

38  trébol *m*
- *clubs*
39  pica *f*
- *spades*
40  corazón *m*
- *hearts*
41  diamante *m*
- *diamonds*
42-45  los palos alemanes
- *German suits*
42  la bellota [en las cartas
españolas: bastos *m*]
- *acorns*
43  el verde (la hoja) [en las cartas
españolas: espadas *f*]
- *leaves*
44  el rojo (el corazón) [en las
cartas españolas: copas *f*]
- *hearts*
45  el cascabel [en las cartas
españolas: oros *m*]
- *bells (hawkbells)*

1-19 el billar (el juego del billar)
- billiards
1 la bola de billar *m*, una bola de
   marfil *m* o de materia *f* plástica
- billiard ball, an ivory or plastic
   ball
2-6 tacadas *f* de billar *m*
- billiard strokes
2 la tacada en el centro (la tacada
   horizontal)
- plain stroke [hitting the cue ball
   dead centre (Am. center)]
3 la tacada alta [consigue un
   carambola]
- top stroke [promotes extra
   forward rotation]
4 la tacada baja [consigue un
   retroceso]
- screw-back [imparts a direct
   recoil or backward motion]
5 la tacada con efecto *m*
- side (running side, Am. English)
6 la tacada con efecto *m*
   contrario
- check side
7-19 la sala de billar *m*
- billiard room (Am. billiard
   parlor, billiard saloon, poolroom)
7 el billar francés (el billar de
   carambolas *f*); *anál.:* el billar
   alemán o inglés (el billar de
   troneras *f*)
- French billiards (carom billiards,
   carrom billiards); sim.: German
   or English billiards (pocket
   billiards, Am. poolbilliards)

8 el jugador de billar *m*
- billiard player
9 el taco
- cue (billiard cue, billiard stick)
10 la suela, una arandela de
   cuero *m*
- leather cue tip
11 la bola blanca (la bola con que
   se juega)
- white cue ball
12 la bola roja (el mingo)
- red object ball
13 la bola blanca del tanto (para
   anotarse puntos *m*)
- white spot ball (white dot ball)
14 la mesa de billar *m*
- billiard table
15 la superficie de juego *m*
   cubierta con un paño verde
- table bed with green cloth
   (billiard cloth, green baize
   covering)
16 la banda (la banda de goma *f*)
- cushions (rubber cushions,
   cushioned ledge)
17 el contador del billar, un reloj
   controlador
- billiard clock, a timer
18 la pizarra de anotaciones *f*
- billiard marker
19 el portatacos (estante de los
   tacos)
- cue rack

**1-59 el camping** (el emplazamiento del camping)
- *camp site (camping site,* Am. *campground)*
1 la recepción (la oficina)
- *reception (office)*
2 el guardián del camping
- *camp site attendant*
3 el remolque plegable (la roulotte, la caravana plegable)
- *folding trailer (collapsible caravan, collapsible trailer)*
4 la hamaca (*Venez.:* la campechana)
- *hammock*
5-6 las instalaciones sanitarias
- *washing and toilet facilities*
5 los aseos y lavaderos *m*
- *toilets and washrooms* (Am. *lavatories)*
6 los lavabos y fregaderos *m*
- *washbasins and sinks*
7 el bungalow (el chalé)
- *bungalow (chalet)*
8-11 **el campamento de los exploradores** (de los boys-scouts, el jamboree)
- *scout camp*
8 la tienda de campaña *f* redonda
- *bell tent*
9 el gallardete (la banderola)
- *pennon*
10 el fuego de campamento *m* (*Pan.:* la fogatada; *Amér. Central, Arg. y Chile:* el fogón)
- *camp fire*
11 el explorador (el boy-scout)
- *boy scout (scout)*
12 el barco de vela *f* (el velero; *Col. y Venez.:* la curiana)
- *sailing boat (yacht,* Am. *sailboat)*
13 el embarcadero (el desembarcadero, el muelle)
- *landing stage (jetty)*
14 el bote neumático
- *inflatable boat (inflatable dinghy)*
15 el motor fuera borda *f*
- *outboard motor (outboard)*
16 el trimarán
- *trimaran*
17 la bancada (el banco de los remeros)
- *thwart (oarsman's bench)*

18 la chumacera
- *rowlock (oarlock)*
19 el remo (*Perú:* la tangana)
- *oar*
20 el remolque del barco
- *boat trailer (boat carriage)*
21 **la tienda de campaña *f* de caballete *m***
(*Amér.:* la carpa; *Amér. Central y Mé.:* el manteado)
- *ridge tent*
22 el tejado doble
- *flysheet*
23 el viento (una cuerda tensora)
- *guy line (guy)*
24 la estaquilla de la tienda (la estaquilla)
- *tent peg (peg)*
25 el mazo
- *mallet*
26 la arandela para sujetar el suelo de la tienda
- *groundsheet ring*
27 el ábside
- *bell end*
28 la marquesina levantada
- *erected awning*
29 la lámpara de camping *m*
- *storm lantern, a paraffin lamp*
30 el saco de dormir
- *sleeping bag*
31 el colchón hinchable (el colchón neumático)
- *air mattress (inflatable air-bed)*
32 el saco de agua *f* para beber
- *water carrier (drinking water carrier)*
33 la hornilla (la cocina) de dos fuegos *m* de gas *m* propano *m* o de butano *m*
- *double-burner gas cooker for propane gas or butane gas*
34 la botella de gas *m* propano *m* (de butano *m*)
- *propane or butane gas bottle*
35 la olla a presión *f* (la olla exprés)
- *pressure cooker*
36 **la tienda bungalow** (una tienda de paredes *f* verticales)
- *frame tent*
37 la marquesina
- *awning*
38 el palo de la tienda
- *tent pole*

39 la entrada en arco *m*
- *wheelarch doorway*
40 la ventana de ventilación *f*
- *mesh ventilator*
41 la ventana transparente
- *transparent window*
42 el número del emplazamiento de la tienda
- *pitch number*
43 la silla de camping *m*, una silla de tijera *f* (extensible, plegable)
- *folding camp chair*
44 la mesa de camping *m*, una mesa de tijera *f* (extensible, plegable)
- *folding camp table*
45 la vajilla de camping *m*
- *camping eating utensils*
46 el acampador
- *camper*
47 la barbacoa (las parrillas de carbón *m* de leña *f*)
- *charcoal grill (barbecue)*
48 el carbón de leña *f*
- *charcoal*
49 el fuelle
- *bellows*
50 la baca
- *roof rack*
51 los pulpos
- *roof lashing*
52 **el remolque de camping** *m* (la caravana, la roulotte)
- *caravan* (Am. *trailer)*
53 el cajón para las botellas de gas *m*
- *box for gas bottle*
54 la rueda delantera de guía *f* (de timón *m*)
- *jockey wheel*
55 el acoplamiento (el enganche) del remolque
- *drawbar coupling*
56 la trampilla de ventilación *f* del techo
- *roof ventilator*
57 la marquesina de la caravana
- *caravan awning*
58 la tienda iglú *m* hinchable
- *inflatable igloo tent*
59 la tumbona
- *camp bed* (Am. *camp cot)*

**1-6** el surf
- *surf riding (surfing)*
**1** la tabla de surf *m* vista por abajo
- *plan view of surfboard*
**2** la tabla de surf *m*, una sección
- *section of surfboard*
**3** la orza (la aleta estabilizadora)
- *skeg (stabilizing fin)*
**4** el deslizamiento al punto de
rompimiento *m* de la ola
- *big wave riding*
**5** el surfista
- *surfboarder (surfer)*
**6** la ola que rompe (el chachón)
- *breaker*
**7-27** el buceo (el submarinismo)
- *skin diving (underwater swimming)*
**7** el buzo (el hombre rana, el
submarinista)
- *skin diver (underwater swimmer)*
**8-22** el equipo de buceo *m*
- *underwater swimming set*
**8** el cuchillo de buzo *m*
- *knife*
**9** el traje de buzo *m* de neopreno *m*,
un traje protector contra el frío
- *neoprene wetsuit*
**10** las gafas de buceo *m*, unas gafas
de presión *f* equilibrada
- *diving mask (face mask, mask), a
pressure-equalizing mask*
**11** el tubo respiratorio
- *snorkel (schnorkel)*
**12** las correas de los aparatos de
buceo *m* de aire *m* comprimido
- *harness of diving apparatus*

**13** el manómetro para control *m* del
contenido (del volumen de aire *m*)
de las botellas
- *compressed-air pressure gauge
(Am. gage)*
**14** el cinturón de plomo *m*
- *weight belt*
**15** el batímetro (el batómetro)
- *depth gauge (Am. gage)*
**16** el reloj impermeable para el
control del tiempo de
permanencia *f* bajo el agua
- *waterproof watch for checking
duration of dive*
**17** el descompresímetro para el
control de las etapas de
ascensión *f* (las etapas de
descompresión *f*)
- *decometer for measuring stages of
ascent*
**18** la aleta de buceo *m*
- *fin (flipper)*
**19** el aparato para la respiración
debajo de agua *f* (el pulmón
acuático), un aparato de dos
botellas *f*
- *diving apparatus (aqualung, scuba)
with two cylinders (bottles)*
**20** los dos tubos flexibles de la
máquina pulmonar
- *two-tube demand regulator*
**21** la botella de aire *m* comprimido
- *compressed-air cylinder
(compressed-air bottle)*
**22** la válvula de las botellas
- *on/off valve*

**23** la fotografía submarina
- *underwater photography*
**24** la máquina fotográfica submarina
(*anál.*: la cámara submarina)
- *underwater camera housing
(underwater camera case);* sim.:
*underwater camera*
**25** el flash submarino (la antorcha)
- *underwater flashlight*
**26** las burbujas de aire *m* espirado
- *exhaust bubbles*
**27** el bote neumático
- *inflatable boat (inflatable dinghy)*

1 el socorrista
– *lifesaver (lifeguard)*
2 la cuerda de salvamento *m*
– *lifeline*
3 el salvavidas
– *lifebelt (lifebuoy)*
4 el globo de tempestad *f* (la señal de tempestad *f*)
– *storm signal*
5 el globo horario (la señal indicadora de las horas de baño *m*)
– *time ball*
6 el cartel de advertencias *f*
– *warning sign*
7 el cartel de las mareas, un cartel indicador de las horas de flujo *m* y reflujo *m* (de la marea alta y la marea baja)
– *tide table, a notice board showing times of low tide and high tide*
8 el cartel, con los datos de temperatura *f* del agua y del aire
– *board showing water and air temperature*
9 el embarcadero (el desembarcadero, el muelle)
– *bathing platform*
10 el mástil de los gallardetes
– *pennon staff*
11 el gallardete (la banderola)
– *pennon*
12 el hidropedal
– *paddle boat (peddle boat)*
13 el acuaplano, tirado por una motora (el surf con motora)
– *surf riding (surfing) behind motorboat*
14 el surfista
– *surfboarder (surfer)*

15 la plancha de acuaplano *m* (de surf *m*)
– *surfboard*
16 el esquí acuático
– *water ski*
17 el colchón neumático (el colchón hinchable para la playa)
– *inflatable beach mattress*
18 el balón de playa *f* (para jugar en el agua)
– *beach ball*
19-23 la indumentaria de playa *f*
– *beachwear*
19 el traje playero (el conjunto playero)
– *beach suit*
20 el sombrero playero
– *beach hat*
21 la chaqueta playera
– *beach jacket*
22 los pantalones playeros
– *beach trousers*
23 las playeras
– *beach shoe (bathing shoe)*
24 la bolsa playera
– *beach bag*
25 el albornoz
– *bathing gown (bathing wrap)*
26 el biquini (el bañador de señora *f* de dos piezas *f*)
– *bikini (ladies' two-piece bathing suit)*
27 la braguita (la parte inferior del bikini)
– *bikini bottom*
28 el sujetador (la parte superior del biquini)
– *bikini top*
29 el gorro de baño *m*
– *bathing cap (swimming cap)*
30 el bañista
– *bather*

31 el tenis de anillas *f*
– *deck tennis (quoits)*
32 la anilla de goma *f*
– *rubber ring (quoit)*
33 el flotador de figura *f* de animal *m* inflable
– *inflatable rubber animal*
34 el vigilante de la playa
– *beach attendant*
35 el castillo de arena *f*
– *sand den [built as a wind-break]*
36 el sillón de playa *f* de mimbre *m*
– *roofed wicker beach chair*
37 el pescador subacuático (el buceador de pesca *f* submarina)
– *underwater swimmer*
38 las gafas de buceo *m*
– *diving goggles*
39 el tubo respiratorio
– *snorkel (schnorkel)*
40 el arpón de mano *f* (el dardo para pescar)
– *hand harpoon (fish spear, fish lance)*
41 la aleta de buceo *m*, para la práctica del submarinismo
– *fin (flipper) for diving (for underwater swimming)*
42 la indumentaria de baño *m*
– *bathing suit (swimsuit)*
43 el bañador
– *bathing trunks (swimming trunks)*
44 el gorro de baño *m*
– *bathing cap (swimming cap)*
45 la tienda de campaña *f* de playa *f*, una tienda de campaña *f* de caballete *m*
– *beach tent, a ridge tent*
46 el puesto de socorro *m*
– *lifeguard station*

# 281 El establecimiento de baños (centro para el ocio, para el tiempo libre)

1-9 la piscina de olas *f*
artificiales, una piscina
cubierta
– *swimming pool with artificial*
*waves, an indoor pool*
1 el oleaje artificial
– *artificial waves*
2 la playa
– *beach area*
3 el borde de la piscina
– *edge of the pool*
4 el vigilante de piscina *f*
– *swimming pool attendant (pool*
*attendant, swimming bath*
*attendant)*
5 la tumbona (*Venez.:* la
campechana)
– *sun bed*
6 el flotador
– *lifebelt*
7 los manguitos de natación *f* (los
flotadores)
– *water wings*
8 el gorro de baño
– *bathing cap*
9 el canal de acceso *m* a los
baños de aguas *f* minerales al
aire libre
– *channel to outdoor mineral bath*
10 el solario (baño *m* de sol *m*
artificial)
– *solarium*
11 la zona para tenderse a tomar el
sol
– *sunbathing area*
12 la bañista tomando un baño de
sol *m*
– *sun bather*
13 el sol artificial (las lámparas de
rayos *m* ultravioletas)
– *sun ray lamp*
14 la toalla de baño *m*
– *bathing towel*
15 el área *f* nudista (el terreno
naturista, desnudista)
– *nudist sunbathing area*
16 el nudista (el adepto al
nudismo, a la vida al aire libre
en estado *m* de desnudez *f*
total)
– *nudist (naturist)*
17 el recinto protegido de las
miradas por un muro
– *screen (fence)*
18 la sauna (la sauna finlandesa, el
baño de vapor *m* finlandés)
– *mixed sauna*
19 el revestimiento de las paredes
en madera *f*
– *wood panelling* (Am. *paneling*)
20 las gradas para sentarse o
tenderse
– *tiered benches*
21 la estufa de la sauna
– *sauna stove*
22 los guijarros
– *stones*
23 el higrómetro
– *hygrometer*

24 el termómetro
– *thermometer*
25 la toalla
– *towel*
26 la herrada de agua *f* para la
humidificación de los guijarros
de la estufa
– *water tub for moistening the*
*stones in the stove*
27 las ramas de abedul *m* para
azotar la piel
– *birch rods (birches) for beating*
*the skin*
28 el recinto de enfriamiento *m*,
para refrescarse después de la
sauna
– *cooling room for cooling off*
*(cooling down) after the sauna*
29 la ducha tibia (templada)
– *lukewarm shower*
30 la piscina de agua *f* fría
– *cold bath*
31 la bañera de remolinos *m* de
agua *f* caliente (el baño de
masaje *m* subacuático)
– *hot whirlpool (underwater*
*massage bath)*
32 el escalón de acceso *m*
– *step into the bath*
33 el baño de masaje *m*
– *massage bath*
34 el ventilador de inyección *f*
– *jet blower*
35 la bañera de remolinos *m* de
agua *f* caliente [esquema]
– *hot whirlpool [diagram]*
36 la sección transversal de la
bañera
– *section of the bath*
37 la entrada (el escalón de
acceso *m*)
– *step*
38 el banco circular
– *circular seat*
39 el extractor de agua *f*
– *water extractor*
40 el tubo (la cañería) de
inyección *f* de agua *f*
– *water jet pipe*
41 el tubo (la cañería) de
inyección *f* de aire *m*
– *air jet pipe*

282 Deporte de la natación · · · · · · · · · · · · · · · · · · · · · · · · · · · · · · · · · · · · · · · · · · · · · · · · · · · · · · · · · · · · · · · · · · · · · · · · · · · · · · · · · · · · · · · · · · · · · · · · · · · · · · · · · · · · · · · · · · · · · · · · · · · · · · · · · · · · · · · · · · · · · · · · · · · · · · · · · · · · · · · · · · · · · · · · · · · · · · · · · · · · · · · · · · · · · · · · · · · · · · · · · · · · · · · · · · · · · · · · · · · · · · · · · · · · · · · · · · · · · · · · · · · · · · · · · · · · · · · · · · · · · · · · · · · · · · · · · · · · · · · · · · · · · · · · · · · · · · · · · · · · · · · · · · · · · · · · · · · · · · · · · · · · · · · · · · · · · · · · · · · · · · · · · · · · · · · · · · · · · · · · · ·

*Swimming*

1-32 la piscina (las instalaciones para el deporte de la natación), una piscina al aire libre
- *swimming pool, an open-air swimming pool*
1 la caseta de baño *m*
- *changing cubicle*
2 la ducha
- *shower (shower bath)*
3 el vestuario (*Ec.:* el vestidero)
- *changing room*
4 el área *f* para los baños de sol *m* o tomar el aire
- *sunbathing area*
5-10 la instalación para saltos *m* (el trampolín)
- *diving boards (diving apparatus)*
5 el saltador de la torre
- *diver (highboard diver)*
6 la torre de saltos *m*
- *diving platform*
7 la palanca de diez metros *m*
- *ten-metre (Am. ten-meter) platform*
8 la palanca de cinco metros *m*
- *five-metre (Am. five-meter) platform*
9 el trampolín de tres metros *m*
- *three-metre (Am. three-meter) springboard (diving board)*
10 el trampolín de un metro
- *one-metre (Am. one-meter) springboard*
11 la piscina para saltos *m*
- *diving pool*
12 el salto de cabeza *f* con el cuerpo extendido (el salto del ángel)
- *straight header*
13 el salto de pie *m*
- *feet-first jump*
14 el salto con el cuerpo encogido (la bomba)
- *tuck jump (haunch jump)*
15 el vigilante de piscina *f*
- *swimming pool attendant (pool attendant, swimming bath attendant)*
16-20 la enseñanza de la natación
- *swimming instruction*
16 el profesor de natación *f* (el monitor de natación *f*)
- *swimming instructor (swimming teacher)*
17 el alumno de natación *f*, nadando
- *learner-swimmer*
18 la almohadilla flotadora para principiantes *m*
- *float;* sim.: *water wings*
19 el cinturón de corcho *m*
- *swimming belt;* here: *cork jacket*
20 el aprendizaje en seco
- *land drill*
21 la piscina de los no nadadores
- *non-swimmers' pool*
22 el reguero
- *footbath*
23 la piscina de los nadadores
- *swimmers' pool*

24-32 la competición de natación *f* en estilo *m* libre de relevos *m*
- *freestyle relay race*
24 el cronometrador
- *timekeeper (lane timekeeper)*
25 el juez de llegada *f*
- *placing judge*
26 el juez de viraje *m*
- *turning judge*
27 el podio de salida *f*
- *starting block (starting place)*
28 el toque en la línea de llegada *f* de un nadador de competición *f*
- *competitor touching the finishing line*
29 el salto de salida *f*
- *starting dive (racing dive)*
30 el juez de salida *f*
- *starter*
31 la calle
-↓ *swimming lane*
32 la corchera
- *rope with cork floats*
33-39 los estilos de natación *f*
- *swimming strokes*
33 la natación a braza *f* (la braza)
- *breaststroke*
34 el estilo mariposa (la mariposa)
- *butterfly stroke*
35 el estilo delfín
- *dolphin butterfly stroke*
36 la marinera (el over)
- *side stroke*
37 el crol
- *crawl stroke (crawl);* sim.: *trudgen stroke (trudgen, double overarm stroke)*
38 el buceo (la natación bajo el agua)
- *diving (underwater swimming)*
39 la bicicleta (la sustentación en el agua)
- *treading water*
40-45 los saltos (saltos de torre *f*, saltos de trampolín *m*)
- *diving,* e.g. *acrobatic diving, fancy diving, competitive diving, highboard diving*
40 el salto de la carpa
- *standing take-off pike dive*
41 el salto hacia delante con media vuelta *f* inversa [la patada a la luna]
- *one-half twist isander (reverse dive)*
42 el salto mortal hacia atrás (el doble salto mortal)
- *backward somersault (double backward somersault)*
43 el tirabuzón con impulso *m*
- *running take-off twist dive*
44 la barrena
- *screw dive*
45 el salto en equilibrio *m* sobre las manos
- *armstand dive (handstand dive)*

46-50 el juego de waterpolo *m*
- *water polo*
46 la portería de waterpolo *m*
- *goal*
47 el portero
- *goalkeeper*
48 el balón de waterpolo *m*
- *water polo ball*
49 el defensa
- *back*
50 el delantero
- *forward*

**1-18** la toma de posiciones *f* para la regata (para la regata de remos *m*)
– *taking up positions for the regatta*
**1** la batea impulsada a percha *f*, una barca de recreo *m*
– *punt, a pleasure boat*
**2** la motora (la lancha de motor *m*)
– *motorboat*
**3** la canoa canadiense
– *Canadian canoe*
**4** el kayak (el kayak groenlandés; *Col.*: el jámparo), una canoa
– *kayak (Alaskan canoe, slalom canoe), a canoe*
**5** el kayak biplaza
– *tandem kayak*
**6** el fuera borda (la canoa automóvil con motor *m* fuera borda *f*)
– *outboard motorboat (outboard speedboat, outboard)*
**7** el motor fuera borda *f*
– *outboard motor (outboard)*
**8** la cabina del piloto
– *cockpit*
**9-16** botes *m* de carreras *f* (botes deportivos, outriggers, botes de regatas *f*; *Amér. Central y Pan.*: la panga)
– *racing boats (sportsboats, outriggers)*
**9-15** botes *m* de remos *m* (*Bol. y Ec.*: la montería)
– *shells (rowing boats, Am. rowboats)*
**9** el bote de a cuatro sin timonel *m*, un bote de obra *f* cerrada (de construcción *f* lisa)
– *coxless four, a carvel-built boat*

**10** el bote de a ocho (el ocho de carrera *f*)
– *eight (eight-oared racing shell)*
**11** el timonel
– *cox*
**12** el cabo, un remero
– *stroke, an oarsman*
**13** el proel (el "número uno")
– *bow ('number one')*
**14** el remo
– *oar*
**15** el dos (el bote de remos *m* de a dos)
– *coxless pair*
**16** el bote de carreras *f* unipersonal (el skif)
– *single sculler (single skuller, racing sculler, racing skuller, skiff)*
**17** la espadilla
– *scull (skull)*
**18** el bote de un remero con timonel *m*, un bote de tingladillo *m*
– *coxed single, a clinker-built single*
**19** el embarcadero (el desembarcadero)
– *jetty (landing stage); also: mooring*
**20** el entrenador de remo *m*
– *rowing coach*
**21** el megáfono (la bocina)
– *megaphone*
**22** la escalera del muelle
– *quayside steps*
**23** el edificio del club (el club)
– *clubhouse (club)*
**24** el cobertizo de los botes
– *boathouse*

**25** la bandera del club
– *club's flag*
**26-33** la yola de a cuatro, una yola (bote *m* de chumaceras *f*, bote de recreo *m*)
– *four-oared gig, a touring boat*
**26** el timón
– *oar*
**27** el asiento del timonel
– *cox's seat*
**28** la bancada (el banco del remero)
– *thwart (seat)*
**29** la chumacera
– *rowlock (oarlock)*
**30** la regala
– *gunwale (gunnel)*
**31** el durmiente de las bancadas
– *rising*
**32** la quilla (la quilla exterior)
– *keel*
**33** el forro exterior [en tingladillo *m*]
– *skin (shell, outer skin) [clinker-built]*
**34** el canalete de una sola pala (*Filip.*: la pagaya; *Venez.*: el jarete)
– *single-bladed paddle (paddle)*
**35-38** el remo (la espadilla)
– *oar (scull, skull)*
**35** el guión
– *grip*
**36** el luchadero
– *leather sheath*
**37** el cuello del remo
– *shaft (neck)*
**38** la pala (la pala del remo)
– *blade*

**39** el canalete doble
– *double-bladed paddle (double-ended paddle)*
**40** el anillo engrasador
– *drip ring*
**41-50** el asiento de corredera *f*
– *sliding seat*
**41** la chumacera (la chumacera giratoria)
– *rowlock (oarlock)*
**42** el arbotante
– *outrigger*
**43** la falca
– *saxboard*
**44** el asiento de corredera *f*
– *sliding seat*
**45** la corredera (el raíl de deslizamiento *m*)
– *runner*
**46** el refuerzo
– *strut*
**47** el apoyo
– *stretcher*
**48** el forro exterior
– *skin (shell, outer skin)*
**49** la cuaderna
– *frame (rib)*
**50** la sobrequilla
– *kelson (keelson)*
**51-53** el timón (el gobernalle)
– *rudder (steering rudder)*
**51** la caña del timón
– *yoke*
**52** el guardín
– *lines (steering lines)*
**53** la pala (la pala del timón)
– *blade (rudder blade, rudder)*

**54-66** canoas *f* plegables
– *folding boats (foldboats, canoes)*
**54** la canoa plegable monoplaza, un bote deportivo individual
– *one-man kayak*
**55** el canoero (el piragüista)
– *canoeist*
**56** la cubierta protectora contra las salpicaduras
– *spraydeck*
**57** la cubierta
– *deck*
**58** el forro de lona *f* impermeabilizada (el forro exterior)
– *rubber-covered canvas hull*
**59** la brazola
– *cockpit coaming (coaming)*
**60** el canal construido a lo largo de una presa
– *channel for rafts alongside weir*
**61** la canoa plegable biplaza, un bote de recreo *m* con dos asientos *m*
– *two-seater folding kayak, a touring kayak*
**62** la vela de una canoa plegable
– *sail of folding kayak*
**63** la orza de deriva *f*
– *leeboard*
**64** el saco para la armazón
– *bag for the rods*
**65** la mochila para el casco (para el forro)
– *rucksack*
**66** el remolque para transportar el bote
– *boat trailer (boat carriage)*

**67** la armazón (el costillaje) de la canoa plegable
– *frame of folding kayak*
**68-70** kayaks *m* (canoas *f*)
– *kayaks*
**68** el kayak (la canoa) esquimal
– *Eskimo kayak*
**69** el kayak (la canoa) de regatas *f* en aguas *f* turbulentas (*Col. y Venez.*: la curiana)
– *wild-water racing kayak*
**70** el kayak (la canoa) de recreo *m*
– *touring kayak*

# 284 Navegación a vela I

Sailing (Yachting) I

1-9 **el windsurfing** (la tabla a vela
vela *f*)
- *windsurfing*
1 el windsurfista (el deportista de
windsurfing *m*)
- *windsurfer*
2 la vela
- *sail*
3 la ventana transparente
- *transparent window (window)*
4 el mástil
- *mast*
5 la tabla de surf *m*
- *surfboard*
6 el cojinete móvil para la
inclinación del mástil y el
gobierno de la tabla
- *universal joint (movable bearing)
for adjusting the angle of the
mast and for steering*
7 el botalón (la botavara)
- *boom*
8 la orza de quilla *f*
(desmontable)
- *retractable centreboard* (Am.
*centerboard)*
9 la orza auxiliar
- *rudder*
10-48 **el velero** (el barco de vela *f*)
- *yacht (sailing boat*, Am.
*sailboat)*
10 la cubierta de proa *f*
- *foredeck*
11 el mástil
- *mast*
12 el trapecio
- *trapeze*
13 la cruceta
- *crosstrees (spreader)*
14 la encapilladura
- *hound*
15 el estay de proa *f*
- *forestay*
16 el foque (el foque genovés,
Génova)
- *jib (Genoa jib)*
17 el aparejo para reclamar
- *jib downhaul*
18 el obenque
- *side stay (shroud)*
19 el acollador
- *lanyard (bottlescrew)*
20 el pie del mástil (la carlinga)
- *foot of the mast*
21 la trapa
- *kicking strap (vang)*
22 la escotera
- *jam cleat*
23 la escota del foque
- *foresheet (jib sheet)*
24 la caja de la orza de quilla *f*
- *centreboard* (Am. *centerboard)
case*
25 el perno de la orza de quilla *f*
- *bitt*
26 la orza de quilla *f*
- *centreboard* (Am. *centerboard)*

27 el escotero
- *traveller* (Am. *traveler)*
28 la escota mayor
- *mainsheet*
29 la guía (el pasacabo) de la
escota de foque *m*
- *fairlead*
30 la trapa
- *toestraps (hiking straps)*
31 el brazo de la caña del timón
- *tiller extension (hiking stick)*
32 la caña del timón (la barra)
- *tiller*
33 la cabeza del timón
- *rudderhead (rudder stock)*
34 la pala del timón
- *rudder blade (rudder)*
35 el espejo (la popa de espejo *m*,
la popa cuadra)
- *transom*
36 el espiche del orificio de
desagüe *m*
- *drain plug*
37 el puño de amura *f* de la vela
mayor
- *gooseneck*
38 la ventana de la vela
- *window*
39 la botavara
- *boom*
40 el pujamen
- *foot*
41 el puño de escota *f*
- *clew*
42 el caída de proa *f* (el grátil)
- *luff (leading edge)*
43 la funda del sable
- *leech pocket (batten cleat, batten
pocket)*
44 el sable
- *batten*
45 la caída de popa *f* (la baluma)
- *leech (trailing edge)*
46 la vela mayor
- *mainsail*
47 la tabla de grátil *m*
- *headboard*
48 la veleta (la grímpola)
- *racing flag (burgee)*
49-65 **clases *f* de yates *m*** (clases de
monotipos *m*)
- *yacht classes*
49 el Flying Dutchman
- *Flying Dutchman*
50 la yola 0
- *O-Joller*
51 el dingui Finn
- *Finn dinghy (Finn)*
52 el Pirata
- *pirate*
53 el Sharpie de 12 m²
- *12.00 m² sharpie*
54 el Tempest
- *tempest*
55 el Star
- *star*
56 el Soling
- *soling*

57 el Dragón
- *dragon*
58 el monotipo clase *f* 5,5 m
- *5.5-metre* (Am. *5.5-meter) class*
59 el monotipo clase *f* R de 6 m
- *6-metre* (Am. *6-meter) R-class*
60 el yate de crucero *m* de 30 m²
- *30.00 m² cruising yacht (coastal
cruiser)*
61 la yola de 30 m², un velero de
crucero *m*
- *30.00 m² dinghy cruiser*
62 el monotipo de 25 m² con
quilla *f*
- *25.00 m² one-design keelboat*
63 el monotipo clase *f* KR
- *KR-class*
64 el catamarán
- *catamaran*
65 el doble casco
- *twin hull*

**1-13  disposiciones *f* de las velas y direcciones *f* del viento**
- **points of sailing and wind directions**
1  la navegación a vela *f* viento *m* en popa *f*
- *sailing downwind*
2  la vela mayor
- *mainsail*
3  el foque
- *jib*
4  la disposición de las velas en forma *f* de tijeras *f*
- *ballooning sails*
5  el eje del barco
- *centre (Am. center) line*
6  la dirección del viento
- *wind direction*
7  el barco con el viento contrario (sin viento favorable)
- *yacht tacking*
8  la vela flameante
- *sail, shivering*
9  la orza (la orzada)
- *luffing*
10  la bolina
- *sailing close-hauled*
11  la navegación con viento *m* a la cuadra (con viento de través)
- *sailing with wind abeam*
12  la navegación con viento *m* a un largo
- *sailing with free wind*
13  la brisa en los estayes de proa *f*
- *quartering wind (quarter wind)*
**14-24  el recorrido de la regata**
- **regatta course**
14  la boya de salida *f* y de llegada *f*
- *starting and finishing buoy*
15  el barco del jurado
- *committee boat*
16  el recorrido triangular (el recorrido de la regata)
- *triangular course (regatta course)*
17  la boya de virada *f* (la baliza de virada)
- *buoy (mark) to be rounded*
18  la boya de señalización *f* del recorrido
- *buoy to be passed*
19  la primera bordada
- *first leg*
20  la segunda bordada
- *second leg*
21  la tercera bordada
- *third leg*
22  la bordada ciñendo el viento
- *windward leg*
23  la bordada con viento *m* en popa *f*
- *downwind leg*
24  la bordada con viento *m* a un largo
- *reaching leg*
**25-28  la virada de bordo *m***
- **tacking**

25  la bordada ciñendo el viento
- *tack*
26  el trasluche (la virada por redondo)
- *gybing (jibing)*
27  la virada (cambiada *f* del rumbo)
- *going about*
28  la pérdida de altura *f* durante el trasluche
- *loss of distance during the gybe (jibe)*
**29-41  formas *f* del casco de las embarcaciones de vela *f***
- **types of yacht hull**
29-34  el yate de crucero *m* con quilla *f*
- *cruiser keelboat*
29  la popa
- *stern*
30  la proa lanzada (la proa de cuchara *f*)
- *spoon bow*
31  la línea de flotación *f*
- *waterline*
32  la quilla (la quilla con lastre *m*)
- *keel (ballast keel)*
33  el lastre
- *ballast*
34  el timón
- *rudder*
35  el yate de regatas *f* con quilla *f*
- *racing keelboat*
36  la quilla de plomo *m*
- *lead keel*
37-41  el velero
- *keel-centreboard (Am. centerboard) yawl*
37  el timón izable
- *retractable rudder*
38  la bañera
- *cockpit*
39  la superestructura de la caseta
- *cabin superstructure (cabin)*
40  la roda recta (la roda vertical)
- *straight stem*
41  la orza de quilla *f* desmontable
- *retractable centreboard (Am. centerboard)*
**42-49  formas *f* de popas *f* de las embarcaciones de vela *f***
- **types of yacht stern**
42  la popa de yate *m* (la popa de bovedilla *f*)
- *yacht stern*
43  la popa cuadra de yate *m* (la popa de espejo *m*)
- *square stern*
44  la popa de canoa *f*
- *canoe stern*
45  la popa de crucero *m*
- *cruiser stern*
46  la placa con el nombre
- *name plate*
47  el dormido
- *deadwood*
48  la popa cuadra (la popa de espejo *m*)
- *transom stern*

49  el espejo
- *transom*
**50-57  el forro de las embarcaciones de madera *f***
- **timber planking**
50-52  el forro en tingladillo *m*
- *clinker planking (clench planking)*
50  la traca (la hilada) exterior
- *outside strake*
51  la cuaderna, una cuaderna transversal
- *frame (rib)*
52  el roblón
- *clenched nail (riveted nail)*
53  el forro a tope *m*
- *carvel planking*
54  la construcción de cuadernas *f* de costura *f*
- *close-seamed construction*
55  la cuaderna de costura *f*, una cuaderna longitudinal
- *stringer*
56  el forro a tope *m* en diagonal *f*
- *diagonal carvel planking*
57  el forro interior
- *inner planking*

1-5 barcos *m* a motor *m* (barcos *m* deportivos)
- *motorboats and powerboats (sportsboats)*
1 el bote neumático deportivo con motor *m* fuera borda *f* (el fuera borda *f* neumático)
- *inflatable sportsboat with outboard motor (outboard inflatable)*
2 el bote de motor *m* interior con transmisión *f* en Z
- *Z-drive motorboat (outdrive motorboat)*
3 la lancha motora con camarotes *m*
- *cabin cruiser*
4 el yate de crucero *m* a motor *m*
- *motor cruiser*
5 el yate de crucero *m* en alta mar *amb.*, de 30 m de eslora *f*
- *30-metre (Am. 30-meter) ocean-going cruiser*
6 la bandera del club
- *association flag*
7 el nombre del barco (*o:* el número de matrícula *f*)
- *name of craft or registration number*
8 el nombre del club y del puerto de matrícula *f*
- *club membership and port of registry (Am. home port)*
9 la bandera del club en la cruceta de estribor *m*
- *association flag on the starboard crosstrees*
10-14 el régimen de luces *f* de los barcos deportivos en aguas *f* costeras y de lagos *m* (las luces de situación *f*)
- *navigation lights of sportsboats in coastal and inshore waters*
10 la luz de tope *m* blanca
- *white top light*
11 la luz de estribor *m* verde
- *green starboard sidelight*
12 la luz de babor *m* roja
- *red port sidelight*
13 la luz de proa *f* roja y verde
- *green and red bow light (combined lantern)*
14 la luz de popa *f* blanca
- *white stern light*
15-18 anclas *f*
- *anchors*
15 el ancla *f* con cepo *m* (el ancla *f* almirantazgo), una ancla pesada
- *stocked anchor (Admiralty anchor), a bower anchor*
16-18 anclas *f* ligeras
- *lightweight anchor*
16 el ancla de reja *f* de arado *m*
- *CQR anchor (plough, Am. plow, anchor)*
17 el ancla *f* de patente *m* (el ancla *f* sin cepo *m*)
- *stockless anchor (patent anchor)*
18 el ancla *f* Danforth (el ancla *f* para embarcaciones *f* pequeñas de recreo *m*)
- *Danforth anchor*
19 la balsa de salvamento *m*
- *life raft*
20 el chaleco salvavidas
- *life jacket*
21-44 la carrera de motoras *f*
- *powerboat racing*

21 el catamarán con motor *m* fuera borda *f*
- *catamaran with outboard motor*
22 el hidroplano
- *hydroplane*
23 el motor fuera borda *f* de carreras *f*
- *racing outboard motor*
24 la caña del timón
- *tiller*
25 el conducto de la gasolina
- *fuel pipe*
26 el espejo de popa *f*
- *transom*
27 el flotador (*Mé., Col.:* la llanta)
- *buoyancy tube*
28 salida *f* y llegada *f*
- *start and finish*
29 la zona de salida *f*
- *start*
30 la línea de salida *f* y de llegada *f*
- *starting and finishing line*
31 la boya de viraje *m*
- *buoy to be rounded*
32-37 botes *m* con menor desplazamiento *m*
- *displacement boats*
32-34 el bote de cuaderna *f* redonda
- *round-bilge boat*
32 la vista del fondo del casco
- *view of hull bottom*
33 la sección transversal de la proa
- *section of fore ship*
34 la sección transversal de la popa
- *section of aft ship*
35-37 el bote con el fondo del casco en V
- *V-bottom boat (vee-bottom boat)*
35 la vista del fondo del casco
- *view of hull bottom*
36 la sección transversal de la proa
- *section of fore ship*
37 la sección transversal de la popa
- *section of aft ship*
38-44 hidroplanos *m*
- *planing boats (surface skimmers, skimmers)*
38-41 el hidroplano con redientes *m*
- *stepped hydroplane (stepped skimmer)*
38 el perfil
- *side view*
39 la vista del fondo del casco
- *view of hull bottom*
40 la sección transversal de la proa
- *section of fore ship*
41 la sección transversal de la popa
- *section of aft ship*
42 el hidroplano de tres puntos *m* de apoyo *m*
- *three-point hydroplane*
43 la aleta
- *fin*
44 el flotador (*Mé. y Col.:* la llanta)
- *float*
45-62 esquí *m* acuático
- *water skiing*
45 la esquiadora
- *water skier*
46 la salida en aguas *f* profundas
- *deep-water start*
47 el cable (el cable de arrastre *m*)
- *tow line (towing line)*
48 la empuñadura
- *handle*

49-55 el lenguaje de los esquiadores (el código de los esquiadores de señales *f* con la mano)
- *water-ski signalling (code of hand signals from skier to boat driver)*
49 la señal de "más deprisa"
- *signal for 'faster'*
50 la señal de "ralentizar" (de aminorar la velocidad)
- *signal for 'slower' ('slow down')*
51 la señal de "velocidad *f* en orden *m*" (velocidad, de acuerdo)
- *signal for 'speed OK'*
52 la señal de "viraje *m*"
- *signal for 'turn'*
53 la señal de "alto *m*"
- *signal for 'stop'*
54 la señal de "parar el motor"
- *signal for 'cut motor'*
55 la señal de "regreso al embarcadero"
- *signal for 'return to jetty' ('back to dock')*
56-62 tipos *m* de esquíes *m* acuáticos
- *types of water ski*
56 el esquí de figuras *f*, un monoesquí
- *trick ski (figure ski), a monoski*
57-58 la fijación de goma *f*
- *rubber binding*
57 la pieza de goma *f* del pie delantero
- *front foot binding*
58 la goma de sujeción *f* del talón
- *heel flap*
59 el estribo del segundo pie
- *strap support for second foot*
60 el esquí de slalon *m*
- *slalom ski*
61 la quilla (la aleta)
- *skeg (fixed fin, fin)*
62 el esquí de saltos *m*
- *jump ski*
63 el hovercraft (el barco sobre un cojín neumático)
- *hovercraft (air-cushion vehicle)*
64 la hélice
- *propeller*
65 el timón
- *rudder*
66 el cojín neumático (el cojín de aire *m*)
- *skirt enclosing air cushion*

1 el despegue a remolque *m* de
   un avión
–  *aeroplane* (Am. *airplane) tow
   launch (aerotowing)*
2 el avión remolcador, un avión a
   motor *m*
–  *tug (towing plane)*
3 el velero (el planeador)
   remolcado
–  *towed glider (towed sailplane)*
4 el cable de remolque *m*
–  *tow rope*
5 el despegue por torno *m*
–  *winched launch*
6 el torno de motor *m*
–  *motor winch*
7 el paracaídas del cable
–  *cable parachute*
8 el motovelero, un planeador
   con motor *m* auxiliar
–  *motorized glider (powered glider)*
9 el planeador (el velero) de altas
   prestaciones *f*
–  *high-performance glider (high-
   performance sailplane)*
10 el grupo de cola *f* (los
   estabilizadores) en T
–  *T-tail (T-tail unit)*
11 la manga veleta
–  *wind sock (wind cone)*
12 la torre de control *m*
–  *control tower (tower)*
13 el aeródromo de vuelo *m* sin
   motor *m*
–  *glider field*
14 el hangar
–  *hangar*
15 la pista de despegue *m* y
   aterrizaje *m* para los aviones
–  *runway for aeroplanes (Am.
   airplanes)*
16 el vuelo en ondas *f*
–  *wave soaring*
17 las ondas a sotavento *m* (las
   ondas del viento cálido del Sur)
–  *lee waves (waves, wave system)*
18 el rotor
–  *rotor*
19 las nubes de forma *f* lenticular
–  *lenticular clouds (lenticulars)*
20 el vuelo en la térmica
–  *thermal soaring*
21 la manga de aire *m* ascendente
   (la manga térmica, la corriente
   de aire *m* ascendente)
–  *thermal*
22 el cúmulo
–  *cumulus cloud (cumulus,
   woolpack cloud), a heap cloud*
23 el vuelo en frente *m* tormentoso
–  *storm-front soaring*
24 el frente tormentoso
–  *storm front*
25 la corriente ascendente del
   frente
–  *frontal upcurrent*
26 el cúmulo-nimbo
–  *cumulonimbus cloud
   (cumulonimbus)*

27 el vuelo por la ladera
–  *slope soaring*
28 el viento ascendente de la
   ladera
–  *hill upcurrent (orographic lift)*
29 el ala *f* de largueros *m*, un
   plano de sustentación *f*
–  *multispar wing, a wing*
30 el larguero principal, un
   larguero cajón
–  *main spar, a box spar*
31 el herraje de conexión *f*
–  *connector fitting*
32 la costilla de sujeción *f*
–  *anchor rib*
33 el larguero oblicuo
–  *diagonal spar*
34 el borde de ataque *m*
–  *leading edge*
35 la costilla principal
–  *main rib*
36 la costilla auxiliar (la falsa
   costilla)
–  *nose rib (false rib)*
37 el borde de salida *f*
–  *trailing edge*
38 la trampilla del freno (el freno
   para vuelo *m* en picado, el
   aerofreno)
–  *brake flap (spoiler)*
39 el alerón de curvatura *f* (el flap
   estabilizador)
–  *torsional clamp*
40 el revestimiento
–  *covering (skin)*
41 el alerón
–  *aileron*
42 los bordes marginales
–  *wing tip*
43 el vuelo con ala *f* delta
–  *hang gliding*
44 el ala *f* delta
–  *hang glider*
45 el piloto de ala *f* delta
–  *hang glider pilot*
46 la barra de apoyo *m*
–  *control frame*

**1-9 el vuelo acrobático** (las figuras del vuelo acrobático)
– *aerobatics, aerobatic manoeuvres (Am. maneuvers)*
1 el rizo (el looping)
– *loop*
2 el ocho horizontal
– *horizontal eight*
3 la rueda con cuatro toneles *m* sucesivos
– *rolling circle*
4 la torre
– *stall turn (hammer head)*
5 la campana (el deslizamiento de cola *f*)
– *tail slide (whip stall)*
6 la barrena vertical
– *vertical flick spin*
7 el picado en barrena *f*
– *spin*
8 la barrena horizontal
– *horizontal slow roll*
9 el vuelo invertido
– *inverted flight (negative flight)*
10 **la cabina del piloto** (la carlinga)
– *cockpit*
11 el tablero (el cuadro) de instrumentos *m*
– *instrument panel*
12 el compás
– *compass*
13 el aparato de radionavegación *f*
– *radio and navigation equipment*
14 la palanca de mando *m*
– *control column (control stick)*
15 la manija de los gases
– *throttle lever (throttle control)*
16 la palanca reguladora de la mezcla
– *mixture control*
17 el radioteléfono
– *radio equipment*
18 **el avión biplaza acrobático y deportivo**
– *two-seater plane for racing and aerobatics*
19 la cabina del piloto (la carlinga)
– *cabin*
20 la antena
– *antenna*
21 el plano fijo de deriva *f*
– *vertical stabilizer (vertical fin, tail fin)*
22 el timón de dirección *f*
– *rudder*
23 el plano de profundidad *f* (el plano de cola *f*, el estabilizador horizontal)
– *tailplane (horizontal stabilizer)*
24 el timón de profundidad *f*
– *elevator*
25 el flap estabilizador (el compensador del balanceo)
– *trim tab (trimming tab)*
26 el fuselaje
– *fuselage (body)*
27 el ala *f* (el plano de sustentación *f*)
– *wing*
28 el alerón
– *aileron*
29 el flap (el alerón) de aterrizaje *m* (para reducir la velocidad de aterrizaje *m*)
– *landing flap*
30 el flap estabilizador (el compensador del balanceo)
– *trim tab (trimming tab)*
31 la luz de situación *f* (la luz de posición *f*) [roja]
– *navigation light (position light) [red]*
32 el faro de aterrizaje *m*
– *landing light*
33 el tren de aterrizaje *m* principal
– *main undercarriage unit (main landing gear unit)*
34 la rueda del morro
– *nose wheel*

35 el motor (el propulsor)
– *engine*
36 la hélice
– *propeller (airscrew)*
**37-62 el paracaidismo**
– *parachuting*
37 el paracaídas
– *parachute*
38 el casquete
– *canopy*
39 el paracaídas auxiliar
– *pilot chute*
40 las cuerdas de suspensión *f*
– *suspension lines*
41 la cuerda de mando *m*
– *steering line*
42 la correa principal de sustentación *f*
– *riser*
43 el arnés
– *harness*
44 el saco envoltura del paracaídas
– *pack*
45 el sistema de aberturas *f* del paracaídas deportivo
– *system of slots of the sports parachute*
46 las aberturas de dirección *f*
– *turn slots*
47 la chimenea
– *apex*
48 el borde de ataque *m* del casquete
– *skirt*
49 el alerón estabilizador
– *stabilizing panel*
**50-51** el salto de estilo *m* (las figuras acrobáticas)
– *style jump*
50 el salto hacia atrás
– *back loop*
51 la espiral (el giro)
– *spiral*
**52-54** las señales visuales trazadas en el suelo
– *ground signals*
52 la señal de "autorización *f* de salto" *m* (la cruz del blanco)
– *signal for 'permission to jump' ('conditions are safe') (target cross)*
53 la señal de "prohibición *f* del salto *m* – reemprender el vuelo"
– *signal for 'parachuting suspended - repeat flight'*
54 la señal de "prohibición *f* de salto *m* – aterrizar inmediatamente"
– *signal for 'parachuting suspended - aircraft must land'*
55 el salto de precisión *f*
– *accuracy jump*
56 la cruz del blanco (el centro del blanco)
– *target cross*
57 el círculo interior del blanco [radio *m* 25 m]
– *inner circle [radius 25 m]*
58 el círculo medio del blanco [radio *m* 50 m]
– *middle circle [radius 50 m]*
59 el círculo exterior del blanco [radio *m* 100 m]
– *outer circle [radius 100 m]*
**60-62** posiciones *f* en caída *f* libre
– *free-fall positions*
60 la posición en X, piernas *f* y brazos *m* separados
– *full spread position*
61 la posición de la rana, piernas *f* ligeramente separadas y brazos *m* plegados
– *frog position*
62 la posición en T, piernas *f* unidas y brazos *m* en cruz *f*
– *T position*
**63-84 el vuelo en globo *m* libre** (la aeroestación)
– *ballooning*

63 el globo de gas *m*
– *gas balloon*
64 la barquilla (la cestilla)
– *gondola (balloon basket)*
65 el lastre (los sacos de arena *f*)
– *ballast [sandbags]*
66 la cuerda de amarre *m*
– *mooring line*
67 el anillo de la barquilla
– *hoop*
68 los instrumentos de vuelo *m* (los instrumentos de a bordo *m*)
– *flight instruments (instruments)*
69 la cuerda de arrastre *m* (la cuerda guía)
– *trail rope*
70 el manguito de llenado *m* (el apéndice de llenado)
– *mouth (neck)*
71 las cuerdas del manguito de llenado *m*
– *neck line*
72 la banda de desgarre *m* de emergencia *f*
– *emergency rip panel*
73 la cuerda de desgarre *m* de emergencia *f*
– *emergency ripping line*
74 las patas de ganso *m*
– *network (net)*
75 la banda de desgarre *m*
– *rip panel*
76 la cuerda de desgarre *m* (la cuerda de apertura *f* de la banda de desgarre *m*)
– *ripping line*
77 la válvula
– *valve*
78 la cuerda de la válvula
– *valve line*
79 el globo de aire *m* caliente (la montgolfiera, el montgolfier)
– *hot-air balloon*
80 la plataforma del quemador
– *burner platform*
81 el manguito de llenado *m* (el apéndice de llenado *m*)
– *mouth*
82 la válvula
– *vent*
83 la banda de desgarre *m*
– *rip panel*
84 la ascensión del globo (la salida del globo)
– *balloon take-off*
**85-91 el deporte del aeromodelismo**
– *flying model aeroplanes (Am. airplanes)*
85 el vuelo teledirigido por radio *m* de un aeromodelo
– *radio-controlled model flight*
86 el aeromodelo en vuelo *m* libre teledirigido
– *remote-controlled free flight model*
87 la teledirección por radio *m* (el aparato de radio de telecontrol *m*, la radio de control *m* a distancia *f*)
– *remote control radio*
88 la antena (la antena emisora)
– *antenna (transmitting antenna)*
89 el aeromodelo dirigido por cable *m*
– *control line model*
90 el sistema de control *m* por un único cable
– *mono-line control system*
91 la perrera volante, un aeromodelo estrafalario
– *flying kennel, a K9-class model*

**1-7  la doma de caballos** *m*
- *dressage*
1 el picadero
- *arena (dressage arena)*
2 la barrera
- *rail*
3 el caballo de doma *f*
- *school horse*
4 la chaqueta de montar negra
- *dark coat (black coat)*
5 los pantalones de montar blancos
- *white breeches*
6 la chistera (el sombrero de copa *f* alta)
- *top hat*
7 el paso (la figura de escuela *f*)
- *gait;* also: *school figure*
**8-14  el concurso de saltos** *m* de obstáculos *m* (el concurso hípico)
- *show jumping*
8 el obstáculo (la barrera), un obstáculo semifijo; *anál.:* la empalizada, la doble valla con seto *m* (el oxer), la valla, el muro, el foso, el seto
- *obstacle (fence), an almost-fixed obstacle;* sim.: *gate, gate and rails, palisade, oxer, mound, wall*
9 el caballo de saltos *m*
- *jumper*
10 la silla de saltos *m*
- *jumping saddle*
11 la barriguera
- *girth*
12 el bridón
- *snaffle*
13 la chaqueta de montar roja
- *red coat (hunting pink, pink);* also: *dark coat*
14 la gorra de montar
- *hunting cap (riding cap)*
15 el vendaje
- *bandage*
**16-19  el concurso completo de equitación** *f*
- *three-day event*
16 la prueba de fondo *m*
- *endurance competition*
17 el recorrido de campo *m* a través (el recorrido de cross *m*, de cross-country *m*)
- *cross-country*
18 el casco protector contra caídas *f*
- *helmet;* also: *hard hat (hard hunting cap)*
19 la señalización del recorrido
- *course markings*
**20-22  la carrera de obstáculos** *m* (la carrera de vallas *f*)
- *steeplechase*
20 la ría (precedida de un seto), un obstáculo fijo
- *water jump, a fixed obstacle*
21 el salto
- *jump*

22 la fusta
- *riding switch*
**23-40  la carrera al trote**
- *harness racing (harness horse racing)*
23 la pista de carreras *f* al trote
- *harness racing track (track)*
24 el sulky
- *sulky*
25 la rueda de rayos *m* con disco *m* protector de plástico *m*
- *spoke wheel (spoked wheel) with plastic wheel disc (disk)*
26 el conductor, con traje *m* de carreras *f* al trote
- *driver in trotting silks*
27 la rienda
- *rein*
28 el caballo trotador (el trotador)
- *trotter*
29 el caballo pío (el caballo picazo)
- *piebald horse*
30 la pantalla para impedir la vista del suelo
- *shadow roll*
31 la rodillera
- *elbow boot*
32 la polaina de goma *f* (la protección de goma)
- *rubber boot*
33 el número de salida *f*
- *number*
34 la tribuna acristalada con ventanillas *f* (taquillas *f*) de apuestas *f*
- *glass-covered grandstand with totalizator windows (tote windows) inside*
35 el marcador
- *totalizator (tote)*
36 el número de salida *f*
- *number*
37 la cotización
- *odds (price, starting price, price offered)*
38 el ganador
- *winners' table*
39 la cotización del ganador
- *winner's price*
40 el tiempo invertido en la carrera
- *time indicator*
**41-49  la caza a caballo** *m* (la montería), **una caza de rastreo** *m; anál.:* la caza del zorro, la caza con papelillos *m*
- *hunt, a drag hunt;* sim.: *fox hunt, paper chase (paper hunt, hare-and-hounds)*
41 el grupo de cazadores *m*
- *field*
42 la chaqueta de caza *f* roja
- *hunting pink*
43 el perrero de caza *f* (el criado encargado de los perros)
- *whipper-in (whip)*
44 la trompa de caza *f*
- *hunting horn*

45 el cazador mayor
- *Master (Master of foxhounds, MFH)*
46 la jauría
- *pack of hounds (pack)*
47 el perro de caza *f*
- *staghound*
48 el "zorro"
- *drag*
49 el rastro (las huellas artificiales)
- *scented trail (artificial scent)*
50 **la carrera al galope** (la carrera de velocidad *f*)
- *horse racing (racing)*
51 el grupo en carrera *f* (los caballos de carreras *f; Arg., Bol., Col. y Urug.:* los fletes)
- *field*
52 el favorito
- *favourite (Am. favorite)*
53 el caballo no favorito (el outsider)
- *outsider*

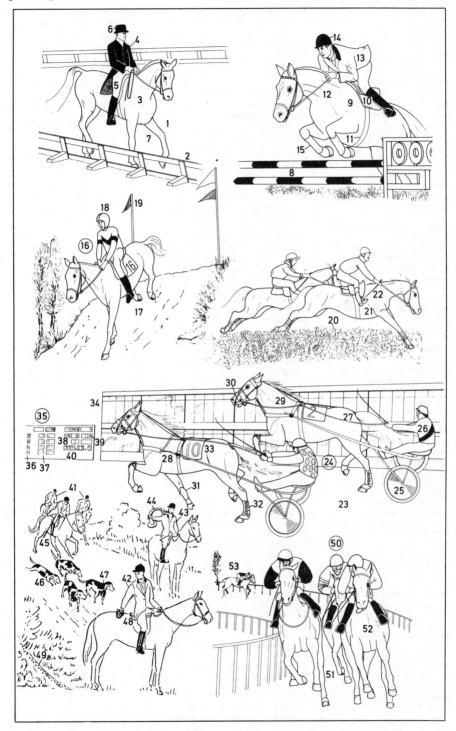

**1-23 ciclismo**
- *cycle racing*
1 el velódromo (la pista de carreras *f*); *en este caso:* el velódromo cubierto
- *cycling track (cycle track);* here: *indoor track*
**2-7** la carrera de los seis días
- *six-day race*
2 el corredor de los seis días, un corredor sobre pista *f* en equipo *m*
- *six-day racer, a track racer (track rider) on the track*
3 el casco protector
- *crash hat*
4 la dirección de la carrera
- *stewards*
5 el juez de meta *f* (el juez de llegada *f*)
- *judge*
6 el juez contador de las vueltas
- *lap scorer*
7 el vestuario de los corredores
- *rider's box (racer's box)*
**8-10** la carrera por carretera *f*
- *road race*
8 el corredor por carretera *f*(el rutista), un corredor ciclista
- *road racer, a racing cyclist*
9 la camiseta (el maillot) de ciclista *m*
- *racing jersey*
10 la botella para beber
- *water bottle*
**11-15** la carrera de persecución *f* tras moto *f* (la carrera de resistencia *f*)
- *long-distance racing,* e.g. *motor-paced racing*
11 el guía, un motorista
- *pacer, a motorcyclist*
12 la moto (la motocicleta) del guía
- *pacer's motorcycle*
13 el rodillo, un dispositivo de protección *f*
- *roller, a safety device*
14 el corredor de fondo *m*, un corredor ciclista tras moto *f*
- *stayer (motor-paced track rider)*
15 la bicicleta de carreras *f*tras moto *f*, una bicicleta de carreras *f*
- *motor-paced cycle, a racing cycle*
16 la bicicleta de carreras *f*por carretera *f*
- *racing cycle (racing bicycle) for road racing (road race bicycle)*
17 el sillín de carreras *f*, un sillín sin muelles *m*
- *racing saddle, an unsprung saddle*
18 el manillar de carreras *f*
- *racing handlebars (racing handlebar)*
19 el neumático (el neumático de carreras *f*)
- *racing tyre* (Am. *tire), a tubular tyre*

20 la cadena con cambio *m* de velocidades *f*
- *chain*
21 el calzapié (el calzapié de carreras *f*)
- *toe clip (racing toe clip)*
22 la correa
- *strap*
23 el neumático de repuesto *m*
- *spare tubular tyre* (Am. *tire)*
**24-38 el motorismo**
- *motorsports*
**24-28** la carrera de motos *f* (motocicletas *f*); *disciplinas:* carreras sobre hierba *f*, por carretera *f*, sobre pista *f* de arena *f*, sobre pista de cemento *m*, sobre pista de ceniza *f*, carrera en cuesta *f*, carrera sobre hielo *m*, trial *m*, carrera campo *m* a través, motocross *m*
- *motorcycle racing;* disciplines: *grasstrack racing, road racing, sand track racing, cement track racing, speedway [on ash or shale tracks], mountain racing, ice racing (ice speedway), scramble racing, trial, moto cross*
24 la pista de arena *f*
- *sand track*
25 el corredor de motos *f*
- *racing motorcyclist (rider)*
26 el traje (el mono) protector de cuero *m*
- *leather overalls (leathers)*
27 la motocicleta de carreras *f*, una máquina individual
- *racing motorcycle, a solo machine*
28 el número de salida *f*
- *number (number plate)*
29 la moto con sidecar *m*, en un viraje
- *sidecar combination on the bend*
30 el sidecar
- *sidecar*
31 la moto de carreras *f* de línea *f* aerodinámica [500 cm³]
- *streamlined racing motorcycle [500 cc.]*
32 el gymkhana, una competición de habilidad *f; en este caso:* el motorista caminando en zigzag *m*
- *gymkhana, a competition of skill;* here: *motorcyclist performing a jump*
33 la carrera de campo *m* a través (el cross), una prueba de resistencia *f*
- *cross-country race, a test in performance*
**34-38** coches *m* de carreras *f* (bólidos *m*)
- *racing cars*
34 el coche de carreras *f* de Fórmula 1 (un monoplaza)
- *Formula One racing car, a mono posto*

35 el spoiler
- *rear spoiler (aerofoil,* Am. *airfoil)*
36 el coche de carreras *f* de Fórmula 2
- *Formula Two racing car (a racing car)*
37 el coche de carreras *f* super-V
- *Super-Vee racing car*
38 el prototipo, un coche de carreras *f*
- *prototype, a racing car*

# 291 Juegos de pelota I (fútbol)

1-16 el campo de fútbol *m* (*Arg. y Urug.*: la cancha)
- *football pitch*
1 el terreno de juego *m*
- *field (park)*
2 el círculo central
- *centre* (Am. *center*) *circle*
3 la línea de medio campo *m*
- *half-way line*
4 el área *f* de penalty *m* (el área *f* de castigo *m*, de dieciséis metros *m*)
- *penalty area*
5 el área *f* de meta *f*
- *goal area*
6 el punto de ejecución *f* del penalty (el punto de penalty *m*)
- *penalty spot*
7 la línea de meta *f*
- *goal line (by-line)*
8 la bandera de esquina *f* (de córner *m*)
- *corner flag*
9 la línea de banda *f*
- *touch line*
10 el guardameta (el portero; *Amér.*: el arquero)
- *goalkeeper*
11 el líbero (el jugador libre)
- *spare man*
12 el defensa central
- *inside defender*
13 el defensa lateral (lateral *m* izquierdo, lateral *m* derecho)
- *outside defender*
14 el medio (el centrocampista)
- *midfield players*
15 el interior
- *inside forward (striker)*
16 el extremo (el ala)
- *outside forward (winger)*
17 el balón de fútbol *m*
- *football*
18 la válvula
- *valve*
19 los guantes del portero (del guardameta)
- *goalkeeper's gloves*
20 el acolchado de goma espuma *f*
- *foam rubber padding*
21 la bota de fútbol *m*
- *football boot*
22 el revestimiento de cuero *m*
- *leather lining*
23 el contrafuerte
- *counter*
24 la lengüeta enguatada
- *foam rubber tongue*
25 las franjas laterales
- *bands*
26 la pala (la empella)
- *shaft*
27 la plantilla
- *insole*
28 el taco de rosca *f*
- *screw-in stud*
29 la ranura
- *groove*
30 la suela de nailón *m*
- *nylon sole*

31 la palmilla
 – *inner sole*
32 el cordón
 – *lace (bootlace)*
33 la espinillera (la canillera) con
 tobillera *f*
 – *football pad with ankle guard*
34 la espinillera
 – *shin guard*
35 la portería (la meta; *Amér.:* el
 arco)
 – *goal*
36 el larguero
 – *crossbar*
37 el poste
 – *post (goalpost)*
38 el saque (el saque de puerta *f*)
 – *goal kick*
39 el despeje de puños *m*
 – *save with the fists*
40 el penalty
 – *penalty (penalty kick)*
41 el saque de esquina *f* (el
 córner)
 – *corner (corner kick)*
42 el fuera de juego *m*
 – *offside*
43 el tiro libre
 – *free kick*
44 la barrera
 – *wall*

45 el tiro hacia atrás (la contra)
 – *bicycle kick (overhead bicycle
 kick)*
46 el tiro de cabeza *f*
 – *header*
47 el pase
 – *pass (passing the ball)*
48 la recogida del balón
 – *receiving the ball (taking a pass)*
49 el pase corto (la pared)
 – *short pass (one-two)*
50 la falta (la jugada antirregla-
 mentaria)
 – *foul (infringement)*
51 la obstrucción
 – *obstruction*
52 el regate (el dribling)
 – *dribble*
53 el saque de banda *f*
 – *throw-in*
54 el reserva (el jugador suplente)
 – *substitute*
55 el entrenador
 – *coach*
56 la camiseta
 – *shirt (jersey)*
57 el pantalón de deporte *m* (el
 pantalón corto)
 – *shorts*
58 la media (la media de fútbol *m*)
 – *sock (football sock)*

59 el juez de línea *f* (el linier)
 – *linesman*
60 la bandera del juez de línea *f*
 – *linesman's flag*
61 la expulsión
 – *sending-off*
62 el árbitro
 – *referee*
63 la tarjeta de expulsión *f* (tarjeta
 roja; *como amonestación:* la
 tarjeta amarilla)
 – *red card; as a caution also:
 yellow card*
64 la bandera de la raya de medio
 campo *m*
 – *centre (Am. center) flag*

1 **el balonmano** (el balonmano sala; el balonmano reducido)
- *handball;* here: *indoor handball*
2 el jugador de balonmano *m*, un jugador de equipo *m*
- *handball player, a field player*
3 el delantero, efectuando un lanzamiento con salto *m*
- *attacker, making a jump throw*
4 el defensa
- *defender*
5 la línea de golpe *m* franco (de tiro *m* libre)
- *penalty line*
6 **el hockey**
- *hockey*
7 la portería de hockey *m*
- *goal*
8 el portero (el guardameta; *Amér.:* el arquero)
- *goalkeeper*
9 la protección de la pierna (la espinillera, la rodillera)
- *pad (shin pad, knee pad)*
10 la bota de hockey *m*
- *kicker*
11 la máscara protectora de la cara
- *face guard*
12 el guante
- *glove*
13 el palo de hockey *m* (el stick)
- *hockey stick*
14 la pelota de hockey *m*
- *hockey ball*
15 el jugador de hockey *m*
- *hockey player*
16 el círculo de tiro *m*
- *striking circle*
17 la línea de banda *f*
- *sideline*
18 la esquina
- *corner*
19 **el rugby** (el rugby europeo)
- *rugby (rugby football)*
20 la melée
- *scrum (scrummage)*
21 el balón de rugby *m*
- *rugby ball*
22 **el rugby americano** (el fútbol americano)
- *American football (Am. football)*
23 el jugador llevando el balón, un jugador de rugby *m* americano
- *player carrying the ball, a football player*
24 el casco
- *helmet*
25 la protección de la cara
- *face guard*
26 la camiseta con hombreras *f*
- *padded jersey*
27 el balón
- *ball (pigskin)*
28 **el baloncesto** (el basket-ball)
- *basketball*
29 el balón de baloncesto *m*
- *basketball*
30 el tablero de la canasta
- *backboard*
31 el poste de la canasta
- *basket posts*
32 la canasta (el cesto)
- *basket*
33 el aro de la canasta (del cesto)
- *basket ring*
34 el rectángulo de encuadre *m*
- *target rectangle*

35 el encestador, un jugador de baloncesto *m*
- *basketball player shooting*
36 la línea de fondo *m*
- *end line*
37 el área de tiro *m* libre
- *restricted area*
38 la línea de tiro *m* libre
- *free-throw line*
39 el jugador suplente
- *substitute*
40-69 **el béisbol** (la pelota base, el base-ball)
- *baseball*
40-58 el campo de juego *m*
- *field (park)*
40 la barrera para los espectadores
- *spectator barrier*
41 el exterior
- *outfielder*
42 el medio (el short-stop)
- *short stop*
43 la segunda base *m*
- *second base*
44 el jugador de base *m*
- *baseman*
45 el corredor
- *runner*
46 la primera base *m*
- *first base*
47 la tercera base *m*
- *third base*
48 la línea de penalización *f* (de falta *f*)
- *foul line (base line)*
49 la plataforma (la base) de lanzamiento *m*
- *pitcher's mound*
50 el pitcher (el lanzador)
- *pitcher*
51 la base meta (la base del cuadro)
- *batter's position*
52 el bateador
- *batter*
53 la base del bateador
- *home base (home plate)*
54 el catcher (el receptor)
- *catcher*
55 el árbitro
- *umpire*
56 el puesto del preparador (del entrenador)
- *coach's box*
57 el preparador (el entrenador)
- *coach*
58 los bateadores suplentes
- *batting order*
59-60 los guantes de béisbol *m*
- *baseball gloves (baseball mitts)*
59 los guantes de los "fielders" (jugadores *m* que paran la pelota)
- *fielder's glove (fielder's mitt)*
60 los guantes del catcher (del receptor)
- *catcher's glove (catcher's mitt)*
61 la pelota de béisbol *m*
- *baseball*
62 el bate
- *bat*
63 el bateador intentando un batazo
- *batter at bat*
64 el catcher (el receptor)
- *catcher*
65 el árbitro
- *umpire*
66 el corredor
- *runner*

67 la almohadilla de la base
- *base plate*
68 el pitcher (el lanzador)
- *pitcher*
69 la plataforma del pitcher (del lanzador)
- *pitcher's mound*
70-76 **el criquet**
- *cricket*
70 el rastrillo con el travesaño
- *wicket with bails*
71 la línea de tiro *m*
- *back crease (bowling crease)*
72 la línea del bateador
- *crease (batting crease)*
73 el guardián del rastrillo del equipo receptor (del equipo atacante)
- *wicket keeper of the fielding side*
74 el bateador (del equipo defensor)
- *batsman*
75 el bate
- *bat (cricket bat)*
76 el lanzador
- *fielder;* here: *bowler*
77-82 **el croquet**
- *croquet*
77 el poste de llegada *f*
- *winning peg*
78 el arco de croquet *m*
- *hoop*
79 el poste de viraje *m*
- *corner peg*
80 el jugador de croquet *m*
- *croquet player*
81 el mazo de croquet *m*
- *croquet mallet*
82 la bola (la pelota) de croquet *m*
- *croquet ball*

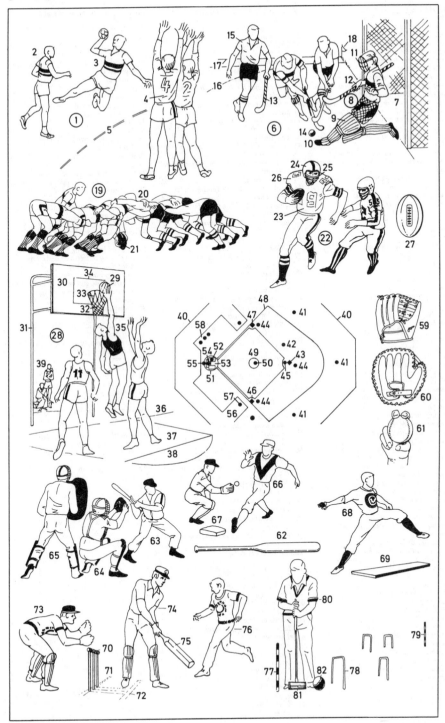

**1-42 el tenis**
- *tennis*
1 la pista de tenis *m*
- *tennis court*
2 *hasta* 3 la línea de banda *f* para el juego de dobles *m* (dobles; dobles de caballeros *m*, dobles de damas *f*, dobles mixtos)
- *sideline for doubles match (doubles; men's doubles, women's doubles, mixed doubles) (doubles sideline)*
3 *hasta* 10 la línea de fondo *m*
- *base line*
4 *hasta* 5 la línea de banda *f* para el juego individual (individual *m*; individual de caballeros *m*, individual de damas *f*)
- *sideline for singles match (singles; men's singles, women's singles) (singles sideline)*
6 *hasta* 7 la línea de saque *m*
- *service line*
8 *hasta* 9 la línea central de saque *m*
- *centre (Am. center) line*
11 la marca central
- *centre (Am. center) mark*
12 el cuadro de saque *m*
- *service court*
13 la red (la red de tenis *m*)
- *net (tennis net)*
14 la cinta de la red
- *net strap*
15 el poste de la red
- *net post*
16 el jugador de tenis *m* (el tenista)
- *tennis player*
17 el smash
- *smash*
18 el contrario (el adversario)
- *opponent*
19 el árbitro (el juez de silla)
- *umpire*
20 la silla del árbitro
- *umpire's chair*
21 el micrófono del árbitro
- *umpire's microphone*
22 el recogepelotas
- *ball boy*
23 el juez de red *f*
- *net-cord judge*
24 el juez de línea *f* de banda *f*
- *foot-fault judge*
25 el juez de línea *f* central de saque *m*
- *centre (Am. center) line judge*
26 el juez de línea *f* de fondo *m*
- *base line judge*
27 el juez de línea *f* de saque *m*
- *service line judge*
28 la pelota de tenis *m*
- *tennis ball*
29 la raqueta de tenis *m*
- *tennis racket (tennis racquet, racket, racquet)*
30 el mango de la raqueta
- *racket handle (racquet handle)*
31 el cordaje de la raqueta (la superficie para golpear la pelota)
- *strings (striking surface)*
32 el tensor
- *press (racket press, racquet press)*
33 la clavija tensora
- *tightening screw*
34 el marcador
- *scoreboard*
35 los resultados de los sets
- *results of sets*
36 el nombre del jugador
- *player's name*
37 el número de sets *m* [ganados por un jugador]
- *number of sets*

38 el número de juegos *m* [ganados por un jugador]
- *state of play*
39 el revés
- *backhand stroke*
40 el derecho
- *forehand stroke*
41 la volea (la volea con golpe *m* derecho a altura *f* normal)
- *volley; here: forehand volley at normal height*
42 el saque (el servicio)
- *service*
**43-44 el juego de volante *m* (el bádminton)**
- *badminton*
43 la raqueta del juego de volante *m* (del bádminton)
- *badminton racket (badminton racquet)*
44 el volante
- *shuttle (shuttlecock)*
**45-55 el tenis de mesa *f* (el ping-pong)**
- *table tennis*
45 la paleta del tenis de mesa *f* (de ping-pong *m*)
- *table tennis racket (racquet) (table tennis bat)*
46 el mango de la paleta
- *racket (racquet) handle (bat handle)*
47 el revestimiento de la paleta
- *blade covering*
48 la pelota del tenis de mesa *f* (de ping-pong *m*)
- *table tennis ball*
49 los jugadores de tenis *m* de mesa *f* (jugadores de ping-pong *m*); *en este caso:* dobles *m* mixtos
- *table tennis players; here: mixed doubles*
50 el resto
- *receiver*
51 el sacador (el saque)
- *server*
52 la mesa de ping-pong *m*
- *table tennis table*
53 la red del tenis de mesa *f* (de ping-pong *m*)
- *table tennis net*
54 la línea de centro *m*
- *centre (Am. center) line*
55 la línea de banda *f*
- *sideline*
**56-71 el balonvolea (el voleibol)**
- *volleyball*
56-57 la colocación correcta de las manos
- *correct placing of the hands*
58 el balón (la pelota) de balonvolea *m*
- *volleyball*
59 el servicio de balonvolea *m*
- *serving the volleyball*
60 el defensa (el zaguero)
- *blocker*
61 la zona de servicio *m* (de saque *m*)
- *service area*
62 el sacador (el saque)
- *server*
63 el delantero (el jugador de la red)
- *front-line player*
64 la zona de ataque *m*
- *attack area*
65 la línea de ataque *m*
- *attack line*
66 la zona de defensa *f*
- *defence (Am. defense) area*
67 el primer árbitro
- *referee*
68 el segundo árbitro
- *umpire*
69 el juez de línea *f*
- *linesman*
70 el marcador
- *scoreboard*
71 el tanteador
- *scorer*

**72-78 el juego de balón *m* a puños *m***
- *faustball*
72 la línea de fondo *m*
- *base line*
73 la cuerda
- *tape*
74 el balón (la pelota) del juego de balón a puños *m*
- *faustball*
75 el delantero
- *forward*
76 el medio (el jugador de centro *m*)
- *centre (Am. center)*
77 el zaguero
- *back*
78 el golpe de martillo *m* (el remate)
- *hammer blow*
**79-93 el golf**
- *golf*
79-82 el campo de golf *m* (los hoyos)
- *course (golf course, holes)*
79 la salida (el sitio de salida, el "tee")
- *teeing ground*
80 el obstáculo natural (el rough, el terreno escabroso)
- *rough*
81 el búnker (el hoyo de arena *f*)
- *bunker (Am. sand trap)*
82 el green (el putting green, el terreno nivelado y cubierto de césped *m* alrededor del hoyo)
- *green (putting green)*
83 el jugador de golf *m* (el golfista), en el golpe de salida *f* (en el drive)
- *golfer, driving*
84 el impulso
- *follow-through*
85 el carrito de golf *m*
- *golf trolley*
86 el tiro al hoyo (el put), con un putter
- *putting (holing out)*
87 el hoyo
- *hole*
88 la banderola
- *flagstick*
89 la pelota de golf *m*
- *golf ball*
90 el tee (la pieza para colocar la pelota)
- *tee*
91 el bastón (el club) de madera *f*, un driver; *anál.*: el brassy
- *wood, a driver; sim.: brassie (brassy, brassey)*
92 el bastón (el club) de hierro *m*; el iron
- *iron*
93 el putter
- *putter*

**1-33 la esgrima deportiva**
- *fencing (modern fencing)*
**1-18** la esgrima de florete *m* (el florete)
- *foil*
**1** el maestro de esgrima *f* (el maestro de armas *f*)
- *fencing master (fencing instructor)*
**2** la pista de esgrima *f*
- *piste*
**3** la línea de puesta *f* en guardia *f* (la línea de salida *f*)
- *on guard line*
**4** la línea del centro
- *centre (Am. center) line*
**5-6** los esgrimidores (*Amér.:* los esgrimistas; los floretistas, tiradores *m* de florete *m*) en un asalto
- *fencers (foil fencers, foilsmen, foilists) in a bout*
**5** el atacante en una entrada a fondo *m*
- *attacker (attacking fencer) in lunging position (lunging)*
**6** el atacado en una parada
- *defender (defending fencer), parrying*
**7** el golpe recto (el coup droit), una acción de esgrima *f*
- *straight thrust, a fencing movement*
**8** la parada en tercera *f* o en sexta *f*
- *parry of the tierce*
**9** la línea de esgrima *f*
- *line of fencing*
**10** las tres distancias entre los adversarios en esgrima *f* (larga, media, corta distancia)
- *the three fencing measures (short, medium, and long measure)*
**11** el florete, una arma de estocada *f*
- *foil, a thrust weapon*
**12** el guante de esgrima *f*
- *fencing glove*
**13** la careta de esgrima *f*
- *fencing mask (foil mask)*
**14** el peto (la protección del cuello) de la careta de esgrima *f*
- *neck flap (neck guard) on the fencing mask*
**15** el chaleco metálico
- *metallic jacket*
**16** la chaquetilla de esgrima *f*
- *fencing jacket*
**17** las zapatillas de esgrima *f* sin tacón *m*
- *heelless fencing shoes*
**18** la posición inicial para el saludo antes del asalto
- *first position for fencer's salute (initial position, on guard position)*

**19-24** la esgrima de sable *m*
- *sabre (Am. saber) fencing*
**19** el tirador de sable *m*
- *sabreurs (sabre fencers, Am. saber fencers)*
**20** el sable ligero (*Bol., Col. y Mé.:* el latón)
- *(light) sabre (Am. saber)*
**21** el guante de sable *m*
- *sabre (Am. saber) glove (sabre gauntlet)*
**22** la careta de sable *m*
- *sabre (Am. saber) mask*
**23** el ataque a la cabeza (el tajo a la cabeza)
- *cut at head*
**24** la parada en quinta *f*
- *parry of the fifth (quinte)*
**25-33** la esgrima de espada *f* con un marcador de tocados *m* eléctrico
- *épée, with electrical scoring equipment*
**25** el tirador de espada *f*
- *épéeist*
**26** la espada eléctrica; *anál.:* el florete eléctrico
- *electric épée; also: electric foil*
**27** la punta de la espada
- *épée point*
**28** el marcador luminoso de tocados *m*
- *scoring lights*
**29** la roldana (el carrete del cable)
- *spring-loaded wire spool*
**30** la lámpara indicadora de tocado *m*
- *indicator light*
**31** el cable
- *wire*
**32** el equipo marcador eléctronico
- *electronic scoring equipment*
**33** la posición de guardia *f*
- *on guard position*
**34-45 las armas de esgrima *f***
- *fencing weapons*
**34** el sable ligero (el sable de deporte *m*), una arma de tajos *m* y estocadas *f* (una arma de filo *m* y de punta *f*)
- *light sabre (Am. saber), a cut and thrust weapon*
**35** la guarnición (el guardamano)
- *guard*
**36** la espada, una arma de estocada *f*
- *épée, a thrust weapon*
**37** el florete francés, una arma de estocada *f*
- *French foil, a thrust weapon*
**38** la guarnición (la cazoleta)
- *guard (coquille)*
**39** el florete italiano
- *Italian foil*
**40** el pomo del florete
- *foil pommel*
**41** el puño
- *handle*

**42** el gavilán
- *cross piece (quillons)*
**43** la guarnición (la cazoleta)
- *guard (coquille)*
**44** la hoja
- *blade*
**45** el botón
- *button*
**46** los envolvimientos (las ligaduras)
- *engagements*
**47** el envolvimiento en cuarta *f*
- *quarte (carte) engagement*
**48** el envolvimiento en tercera *f* (o en sexta *f*)
- *tierce engagement; also: sixte engagement*
**49** el envolvimiento en círculo *m*
- *circling engagement*
**50** el envolvimiento en segunda *f* (o en octava *f*)
- *seconde engagement; also: octave engagement*
**51-53** las áreas válidas de tocado *m*
- *target areas*
**51** todo el cuerpo en la esgrima de espada *f*
- *the whole body in épée fencing [men]*
**52** la cabeza y la parte del cuerpo situada por encima de las ingles en la esgrima de sable *m* (caballeros *m*)
- *head and upper body down to the groin in sabre (Am. saber) fencing [men]*
**53** el tronco desde el cuello hasta las ingles en la esgrima de florete *m* (damas *f* y caballeros *m*)
- *trunk from the neck to the groin in foil fencing [ladies and men]*

# 295 Ejercicios gimnásticos sin aparatos

1 la posición de frente *f*
- *basic position (starting position)*
2 la iniciación de carrera *f*
- *running posture*
3 la iniciación de marcha *f*
- *side straddle*
4 la posición de piernas *f* abiertas
- *straddle (forward straddle)*
5 el elevación de talones *m* (la elevación de puntillas *f*)
- *toe stand*
6 la flexión completa de piernas *f*
- *crouch*
7 la posición de rodillas *f*
- *upright kneeling position*
8 la posición sentada sobre los talones, brazos *m* apoyados en la rodilla
- *kneeling position, seat on heels*
9 la posición sentada con flexión *f* completa de piernas *f* y brazos *m* atrás
- *squat*
10 la posición sentada en escuadra *f*
- *L seat (long sitting)*
11 la posición yoga *m*
- *tailor seat (sitting tailor-style)*
12 la flexión *f* pierna *f* izquierda y extensión *f* derecha
- *hurdle (hurdle position)*
13 la V
- *V-seat*
14 el spagat de perfil *m*
- *side split*
15 el spagat de frente
- *forward split*
16 la escuadra *f*, elevación *f* del cuerpo
- *L-support*
17 la V, elevación *f* del cuerpo
- *V-support*
18 la escuadra *f* con piernas *f* separadas, elevación *f* del cuerpo con apoyo *m* sobre las manos
- *straddle seat*
19 el puente
- *bridge*
20 la posición de rodillas *f* con apoyo *m* frontal
- *kneeling front support*
21 el tendido supino con extensión *f* de brazos *m* y flexión *f*
- *front support*
22 el tendido prono, extensión *f* y flexión *f* de brazos *m*
- *back support*
23 la posición en cuclillas con apoyo *m* frontal
- *crouch with front support*
24 la elevación de caderas *f* y extensión *f* de piernas *f*, con apoyo *m* frontal
- *arched front support*
25 el tendido lateral, extensión *f* de brazos *m* y equilibrio *m*
- *side support*

26 el pino con flexión *f* de brazos *m*
- *forearm stand (forearm balance)*
27 el pino
- *handstand*
28 el puntal
- *headstand*
29 el clavo (la vela)
- *shoulder stand (shoulder balance)*
30 la balanza frontal
- *forward horizontal stand (arabesque)*
31 la balanza lateral
- *rearward horizontal stand*
32 la flexión lateral del tronco
- *trunk-bending sideways*
33 la flexión del tronco hacia delante
- *trunk-bending forwards*
34 la flexión del tronco hacia atrás
- *arch*
35 el salto en extensión *f*
- *astride jump (butterfly)*
36 el salto en cuclillas *f*
- *tuck jump*
37 el salto esparrancado (con las piernas abiertas)
- *astride jump*
38 el salto de la carpa
- *pike*
39 el salto de tijera *f* (iniciación *f* de salto *m* de barra *f* de altura *f*)
- *scissor jump*
40 el salto de corzo *m*
- *stag jump (stag leap)*
41 el paso gimnástico (el paso de carrera *f*)
- *running step*
42 el paso con entrada *f* a fondo *m*
- *lunge*
43 la marcha
- *forward pace*
44 el tendido cúbito prono
- *lying on back*
45 el tendido cúbito supino
- *prone position*
46 el tendido lateral
- *lying on side*
47 la posición de brazos *m* hacia abajo
- *holding arms downwards*
48 los brazos en cruz *f*
- *holding (extending) arms sideways*
49 los brazos arriba
- *holding arms raised upward*
50 los brazos al frente
- *holding (extending) arms forward*
51 los brazos oblicuos atrás
- *arms held (extended) backward*
52 las manos en la nuca
- *hands clasped behind the head*

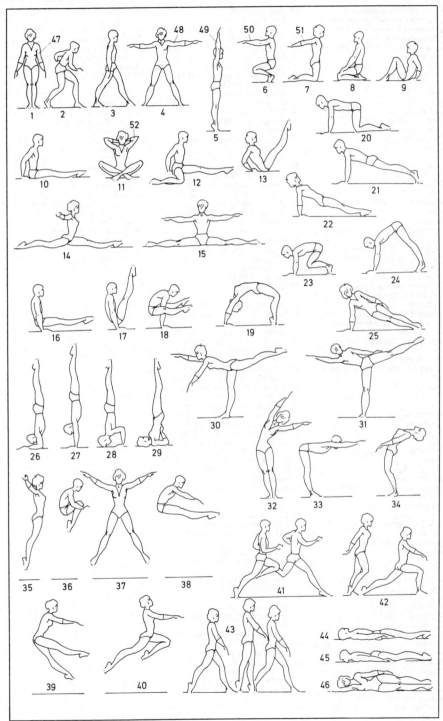

**1-11 los aparatos gimnásticos en gimnasia *f* olímpica masculina**
- *gymnastics apparatus in men's Olympic gymnastics*
**1** el caballo sin arco *m* (el caballo de saltos *m*)
- *long horse (horse, vaulting horse)*
**2** las paralelas
- *parallel bars*
**3** la barra
- *bar*
**4** las anillas
- *rings (stationary rings)*
**5** el caballo con arcos *m*
- *pommel horse (side horse)*
**6** el arco
- *pommel*
**7** la barra fija
- *horizontal bar (high bar)*
**8** la barra
- *bar*
**9** el poste (el soporte) de la barra fija
- *upright*
**10** el viento (el tirante) de fijación *f*
- *stay wires*
**11** la pista para la gimnasia en el suelo (la gimnasia de manos *m* libres, una superficie de 12 × 12 m)
- *floor [12 m × 12 m floor area]*
**12-21 aparatos *m* auxiliares y aparatos *m* de gimnasia *f* escolar y de club *m***
- *auxiliary apparatus and apparatus for school and club gymnastics*
**12** el trampolín
- *springboard (Reuther board)*
**13** la colchoneta dura
- *landing mat*
**14** la barra de equilibrio *m* (la barra sueca)
- *bench*
**15** el plinton (*Amér.:* el cajón)
- *box*
**16** el elemento del plinton
- *small box*
**17** el potro
- *buck*
**18** la colchoneta blanda
- *mattress*
**19** la cuerda fija
- *climbing rope (rope)*
**20** el espaldar sueco (la espaldera)
- *wall bars*
**21** la escalera de pared *f*
- *window ladder*
**22-39 la posición en relación *f* al aparato**
- *positions in relation to the apparatus*
**22** la posición facial lateral
- *side, facing*
**23** la posición dorsal lateral
- *side, facing away*
**24** la posición facial transversal
- *end, facing*
**25** la posición dorsal transversal
- *end, facing away*
**26** la posición facial lateral fuera del aparato
- *outside, facing*
**27** la posición transversal dentro del aparato (el el extremo de las barras)
- *inside, facing*
**28** el apoyo facial
- *front support*

**29** el apoyo dorsal
- *back support*
**30** la posición sentada a horcajadas *f*
- *straddle position*
**31** la posición sentada lateral fuera del aparato
- *seated position outside*
**32** la posición sentada transversal fuera del aparato
- *riding seat outside*
**33** la suspensión facial
- *hang*
**34** la suspensión dorsal
- *reverse hang*
**35** la suspensión con los brazos flexionados
- *hang with elbows bent*
**36** la suspensión invertida
- *piked reverse hang*
**37** la suspensión invertida con el cuerpo en extensión *f* (estirado)
- *straight inverted hang*
**38** el apoyo con el cuerpo en extensión *f* (estirado)
- *straight hang*
**39** el apoyo flexionado (con los brazos flexionados)
- *bent hang*
**40-46 las presas**
- *grasps (kinds of grasp)*
**40** la presa por encima de la barra fija (la presa facial)
- *overgrasp on the horizontal bar*
**41** la presa por debajo de la barra fija
- *undergrasp on the horizontal bar*
**42** la presa mixta en la barra fija
- *combined grasp on the horizontal bar*
**43** la presa en cruz *f* en la barra fija
- *cross grasp on the horizontal bar*
**44** la presa cubital en la barra fija
- *rotated grasp on the horizontal bar*
**45** la presa radial en las paralelas
- *outside grip on the parallel bars*
**46** la presa cubital en las paralelas
- *rotated grasp on the parallel bars*
**47** la correa de cuero *m* para la sujeción a la barra
- *leather handstrap*
**48-60 ejercicios *m* con los aparatos**
- *exercises*
**48** el salto en plancha en el caballo de saltos *m*
- *long-fly on the horse*
**49** la elevación con las piernas abiertas en las paralelas
- *rise to straddle on the parallel bars*
**50** el cristo en las anillas
- *crucifix on the rings*
**51** las tijeras en el caballo con arcos *m*
- *scissors (scissors movement) on the pommel horse*
**52** la elevación de las piernas en el pino sobre el suelo
- *legs raising into a handstand on the floor*
**53** el salto en cuclillas en el caballo de saltos *m*
- *squat vault on the horse*
**54** el círculo por los flancos en el caballo de arcos *m*
- *double leg circle on the pommel horse*

**55** el lanzamiento (la caída de pie *m* hacia atrás en las anillas)
- *hip circle backwards on the rings*
**56** la báscula facial en las anillas
- *lever hang on the rings*
**57** el giro hacia atrás en las paralelas
- *rearward swing on the parallel bars*
**58** la báscula con suspensión *f* del brazo
- *forward kip into upper arm hang on the parallel bars*
**59** el giro por debajo de la barra fija
- *backward underswing on the horizontal bar*
**60** el gran molinete
- *backward grand circle on the horizontal bar*
**61-63 el equipo (la indumentaria) de gimnasia *f***
- *gymnastics kit*
**61** la camiseta de gimnasia *f*
- *singlet (vest, Am. undershirt)*
**62** el pantalón de gimnasia *f*
- *gym trousers*
**63** las zapatillas de gimnasia *f*
- *gym shoes*
**64** la muñequera
- *wristband*

# 297 Ejercicios gimnásticos con aparatos II (Gimnasia femenina)

**1-6 los aparatos gimnásticos en gimnasia *f* olímpica femenina**
- *gymnastics apparatus in women's Olympic gymnastics*
1 el caballo sin arcos (el caballo de saltos *m*)
- *horse (vaulting horse)*
2 la barra de equilibrio *m* (la barra sueca)
- *beam*
3 las paralelas asimétricas
- *asymmetric bars (uneven bars)*
4 la barra inferior
- *bar*
5 el tirante (el viento) de fijación *f*
- *stay wires*
6 el suelo (la superficie del suelo de 12 × 12 m)
- *floor [12 m × 12 m floor area]*
**7-14 aparatos *m* auxiliares y aparatos de gimnasia *f* escolar y de club *m***
- *auxiliary apparatus and apparatus for school and club gymnastics*
7 la colchoneta dura
- *landing mat*
8 el trampolín
- *springboard (Reuther board)*
9 el elemento del plinton
- *small box*
10 la cama elástica
- *trampoline*
11 la lona de saltos *m*
- *sheet (web)*
12 el bastidor (el marco)
- *frame*
13 los tensores de goma *f*
- *rubber springs*
14 la minicama elástica para tomar impulso *m*
- *springboard trampoline*
**15-32 ejercicios *m* en los aparatos**
- *apparatus exercises*
15 el salto mortal hacia atrás con el cuerpo encogido
- *backward somersault*
16 la posición de ayuda *f* de una gimnasta
- *spotting position (standing-in position)*
17 el salto mortal hacia atrás con el cuerpo en extensión *f* en la cama elástica
- *vertical backward somersault on the trampoline*
18 el salto mortal hacia delante con el cuerpo encogido en la minicama elástica
- *forward somersault on the springboard trampoline*
19 la voltereta hacia delante en el suelo
- *forward roll on the floor*
20 la voltereta con salto *m* de carpa *f* en el suelo
- *long-fly to forward roll on the floor*

21 la rueda en la barra de equilibrio *m*
- *cartwheel on the beam*
22 la voltereta sobre las manos hacia delante en el caballo de saltos *m*
- *handspring on the horse*
23 el arco hacia atrás en el suelo
- *backward walkover*
24 la voltereta sobre las manos hacia atrás en el suelo
- *back flip (flik-flak) on the floor*
25 la mariposa (la voltereta libre hacia delante) en el suelo
- *free walkover forward on the floor*
26 la voltereta con paso *m* hacia delante en el suelo
- *forward walkover on the floor*
27 la voltereta de cabeza *f* en el suelo
- *headspring on the floor*
28 el balanceo de elevación *f* en las paralelas asimétricas
- *upstart on the asymmetric bars*
29 el molinete libre en las paralelas asimétricas
- *free backward circle on the asymmetric bars*
30 la vuelta en el caballo de saltos *m*
- *face vault over the horse*
31 el volteo en el caballo de saltos *m*
- *flank vault over the horse*
32 la tuerca (el salto y vuelta *f*)
- *back vault (rear vault) over the horse*
**33-50 gimnasia *f* con aparatos *m* de mano *f* (gimnasia *f* rítmica)**
- *gymnastics with hand apparatus*
33 el lanzamiento en arco *m*
- *hand-to-hand throw*
34 la pelota de gimnasia *f*
- *gymnastic ball*
35 el lanzamiento hacia arriba
- *high toss*
36 el rebote
- *bounce*
37 los círculos con dos mazas *f*
- *hand circling with two clubs*
38 la maza de gimnasia *f*
- *gymnastic club*
39 la oscilación
- *swing*
40 el salto final con el cuerpo encogido
- *tuck jump*
41 el bastón gimnástico
- *bar*
42 el salto
- *skip*
43 la cuerda de saltar
- *rope (skipping rope)*
44 el salto cruzado
- *criss-cross skip*
45 el salto a través del aro
- *skip through the hoop*

46 el aro gimnástico
- *gymnastic hoop*
47 el círculo frontal
- *hand circle*
48 la serpiente
- *serpent*
49 la cinta gimnástica
- *gymnastic ribbon*
50 la espiral
- *spiral*
**51-52 el equipo de gimnasia *f***
- *gymnastics kit*
51 las mallas (la ropa de gimnasia *f*)
- *leotard*
52 las zapatillas de gimnasia *f*
- *gym shoes*

**1-8 la carrera**
- *running*
**1-6** la salida
- *start*
**1** el bloque de salida *f*
- *starting block*
**2** el soporte del pie
- *adjustable block (pedal)*
**3** la posición de salida *f*
- *start*
**4** la salida en cuclillas *f*
- *crouch start*
**5** el corredor, un sprinter (un velocista); *también:* el corredor de medio fondo *m*, el corredor de fondo *m*
- *runner, a sprinter; also: middle-distance runner, long-distance runner*
**6** la pista de carreras *f*, una pista de ceniza *f* o de material *m* sintético
- *running track (track), a cinder track or synthetic track*
**7-8** la carrera de vallas *f; anál.:* la carrera de obstáculos *m* variados (el steeple-chase)
- *hurdles (hurdle racing); sim.: steeplechase*
**7** el salto de la valla
- *clearing the hurdle*
**8** la valla
- *hurdle*
**9-41 los saltos**
- *jumping and vaulting*
**9-27** el salto de altura *f*
- *high jump*
**9** el salto Fosbury
- *Fosbury flop (Fosbury, flop)*
**10** el saltador de altura *f*
- *high jumper*
**11** la rotación alrededor del eje longitudinal y transversal del cuerpo
- *body rotation (rotation on the body's longitudinal and latitudinal axes)*
**12** la caída de espaldas
- *shoulder landing*
**13** el saltómetro
- *upright*
**14** el listón (la barra)
- *bar (crossbar)*
**15** el Barrel Roll
- *Eastern roll*
**16** el Western Roll (el rodillo californiano)
- *Western roll*
**17** el rodillo
- *roll*
**18** la técnica de rodillo *m*
- *rotation*
**19** la caída
- *landing*
**20** la escala de altura *f*
- *height scale*
**21** la técnica de salto *m* de tijera *f* con giro *m*
- *Eastern cut-off*

**22** el salto de tijera *f*
- *scissors (scissor jump)*
**23** el salto de rodillo *m*
- *straddle (straddle jump)*
**24** la técnica de rodillo *m*
- *turn*
**25** la posición de las seis en el reloj (la pierna libre en posición *f* vertical)
- *vertical free leg*
**26** el salto
- *take-off*
**27** la pierna en extensión *f*
- *free leg*
**28-36** el salto con pértiga *f*
- *pole vault*
**28** la pértiga
- *pole (vaulting pole)*
**29** el saltador de pértiga *f* en la fase de elevación *f*
- *pole vaulter (vaulter) in the pull-up phase*
**30** la técnica del impulso
- *swing*
**31** el franqueamiento de la barra (el saltador salvando el listón)
- *crossing the bar*
**32** el aparato de salto *m* de altura *f*
- *high jump apparatus (high jump equipment)*
**33** el saltómetro
- *upright*
**34** el listón (la barra)
- *bar (crossbar)*
**35** el cajón de batir
- *box*
**36** la colchoneta para la caída
- *landing area (landing pad)*
**37-41** el salto de longitud *f*
- *long jump*
**37** el salto
- *take-off*
**38** la tabla de batir (la tabla de salto *m*)
- *take-off board*
**39** el foso
- *landing area*
**40** el salto con golpe *m* de tijera *f*
- *hitch-kick*
**41** la proyección del cuerpo hacia delante
- *hang*
**42-47** el lanzamiento de martillo *m*
- *hammer throw*
**42** el martillo
- *hammer*
**43** la cabeza del martillo
- *hammer head*
**44** el cable de acero *m*
- *handle*
**45** el puño del martillo
- *grip*
**46** la presa del martillo
- *holding the grip*
**47** el guante
- *glove*
**48** el lanzamiento de peso *m*
- *shot put*
**49** el peso
- *shot (weight)*

**50** la técnica O'Brien
- *O'Brien technique*
**51-53** el lanzamiento de jabalina *f*
- *javelin throw*
**51** la presa con el dedo índice y pulgar *m*
- *grip with thumb and index finger*
**52** la presa con el índice y el dedo medio (dedo corazón)
- *grip with thumb and middle finger*
**53** la presa en forma *f* de tenazas *f*
- *horseshoe grip*
**54** la ligadura
- *binding*

**1-5 la halterofilia** (el lavantamiento de pesos *m*)
- *weightlifting*
**1** el levantamiento con arranque *m*
- *squat-style snatch*
**2** el levantador de pesos *m*
- *weightlifter*
**3** la barra de discos *m*
- *disc (disk) barbell*
**4** el levantamiento con impulso *m* (el impulso con paso *m* al frente)
- *jerk with split*
**5** el peso inmovilizado
- *maintained lift*
**6-12 la lucha**
- *wrestling*
**6-9** la lucha grecorromana
- *Greco-Roman wrestling*
**6** la lucha de pie *m*
- *standing wrestling (wrestling in standing position)*
**7** el luchador
- *wrestler*
**8** la lucha en el suelo (*en este caso:* el inicio de un movimiento de desasimiento *m*)
- *on-the-ground wrestling; here: the referee's position*
**9** el puente
- *bridge*
**10-12** la lucha libre
- *freestyle wrestling*
**10** la llave de brazo *m* lateral con presa *f* de pierna *f*
- *bar arm (arm bar) with grapevine*
**11** la doble llave de pierna *f*
- *double leg lock*
**12** la colchoneta de lucha *f*
- *wrestling mat (mat)*
**13-17 el judo** (*anál.:* el jiu-jitsu)
- *judo;* sim.: *ju-jitsu (jiu-jitsu)*
**13** el derribo del oponente adelante y hacia la derecha
- *drawing the opponent off balance to the right and forward*
**14** el judoka
- *judoka (judoist)*
**15** el cinturón de colores *m* indicando el grado
- *coloured (Am. colored) belt, as a symbol of Dan grade*
**16** el judoka neutral
- *referee*
**17** el lanzamiento de judo *m*
- *judo throw*
**18-19 el karate**
- *karate*
**18** el karateka
- *karateka*
**19** la patada lateral, una técnica de pierna *f*
- *side thrust kick, a kicking technique*
**20-50 el boxeo** (el pugilato, el combate de boxeo)
- *boxing (boxing match)*

**20-24** los aparatos de entrenamiento *m*
- *training apparatus (training equipment)*
**20** la pelota súspendida por los dos extremos (el boxing-ball)
- *spring-supported punch ball*
**21** el saco de arena *f*
- *punch bag (Am. punching bag)*
**22** la pelota suspendida en un solo punto (el point-ball)
- *speed ball*
**23** la pera de maíz *m* (la pera de boxeo *m*)
- *suspended punch ball*
**24** el balón con plataforma *f* (el balón piriforme, el balón para pegar puñetazos *m*)
- *punch ball*
**25** el boxeador (el púgil), un boxeador amateur (el combate con camiseta *f*), o un boxeador profesional (el combate sin camiseta)
- *boxer;* here: *professional boxer [boxes without a singlet];* also: *amateur boxer [boxes in a singlet]*
**26** el guante de boxeo *m*
- *boxing glove*
**27** el compañero de entrenamiento *m* (el sparring)
- *sparring partner*
**28** el directo
- *straight punch (straight blow)*
**29** la flexión y la esquiva lateral
- *ducking and sidestepping*
**30** la protección de la cabeza
- *headguard*
**31** el cuerpo a cuerpo; *en este caso:* el clinch
- *infighting;* here: *clinch*
**32** el gancho hacia arriba (el uppercut)
- *uppercut*
**33** el gancho a la cabeza (el gancho hacia un lado)
- *hook to the head (hook, left hook or right hook)*
**34** el golpe bajo, un golpe prohibido
- *punch below the belt, a foul punch (illegal punch, foul)*
**35-50** el combate de boxeo *m*, un campeonato
- *boxing match (boxing contest), a title fight (title bout)*
**35** el ring (el cuadrilátero de boxeo *m*)
- *boxing ring (ring)*
**36** las cuerdas
- *ropes*
**37** los tirantes de fijación *f* del ring
- *stay wire (stay rope)*
**38** el rincón neutral
- *neutral corner*
**39** el vencedor
- *winner*

**40** el boxeador vencido por fuera de combate *m* (por knock-out, por K.O.)
- *loser by a knockout*
**41** el árbitro
- *referee*
**42** la cuenta de los segundos
- *counting out*
**43** el juez que adjudica los puntos
- *judge*
**44** el segundo (el asistente)
- *second*
**45** el representante (el mánager, el organizador)
- *manager*
**46** el gong (la campana)
- *gong*
**47** el cronometrador
- *timekeeper*
**48** el levantador del acta *f*
- *record keeper*
**49** el fotógrafo de prensa *f*
- *press photographer*
**50** el reportero de deportes *m*
- *sports reporter (reporter)*

1-57  **el alpinismo** (el montañismo, la ascensión a las altas montañas)
- *mountaineering (mountain climbing, Alpinism)*
1  el refugio (el albergue alpino, la cabaña de montaña *f*)
- *hut, e.g. Alpine Club hut, mountain hut*
2-13  **la escalada** (la escalada en roca *f*) [técnicas *f* de escalada *f* en roca]
- *climbing (rock climbing) [rock climbing technique]*
2  la pared rocosa (la roca, la pared cortada a pico *m*)
- *rock face (rock wall)*
3  la quiebra (la quiebra longitudinal, transversal u oblicua)
- *fissure, e.g. vertical fissure, horizontal fissure, diagonal fissure*
4  la cornisa (la cornisa rocosa, de hierba *f*, pedregosa, cornisa de nieve *f*, o de hielo *m*)
- *ledge, e.g. rock ledge, grass ledge, scree ledge, snow ledge, ice ledge*
5  el alpinista (el escalador)
- *mountaineer (climber, mountain climber, Alpinist)*
6  el anorak (la chaqueta enguatada para la nieve)
- *anorak; here: a high-altitude anorak; also: snowshirt, padded jacket*
7  los pantalones de escalada *f*
- *breeches (climbing breeches)*
8  la chimenea
- *chimney*
9  el pitón de roca *f* (la punta rocosa)
- *belay (spike, rock spike)*
10  el amarre de seguridad*f*
- *belay*
11  el nudo corredizo
- *rope sling (sling)*
12  la cuerda de escalada *f*
- *rope*
13  la cornisa
- *spur*
14-21  **la escalada en hielo** *m* [técnica *f* de escalada en hielo]
- *snow and ice climbing [snow and ice climbing technique]*
14  la pared de hielo *m* (la ladera de nieve *f* helada)
- *ice slope; also: firn slope*
15  el escalador de hielo *m*
- *snow and ice climber*
16  el piolet (la piqueta)
- *ice axe (Am. ax)*
17  el escalón (el escalón tallado en el hielo)
- *step (ice step)*
18  las gafas de nieve *f*
- *snow goggles*
19  la capucha (la capucha del anorak)
- *hood (anorak hood)*
20  la cornisa (la cornisa de hielo *m*, de nieve *f* helada)
- *cornice (snow cornice)*
21  el picacho (el picacho de hielo *m*, de nieve *f* helada)
- *ridge (ice ridge)*
22-27  **la cordada** [la marcha en cordada]
- *rope (roped party) [roped trek]*
22  el glaciar
- *glacier*

23  la grieta del glaciar
- *crevasse*
24  el puente de nieve *f* (el puente de nieve helada)
- *snow bridge*
25  el primero de la cordada (el jefe de la cordada)
- *leader*
26  el segundo de la cordada
- *second man (belayer)*
27  el tercero de la cordada (el último hombre)
- *third man (non-belayer)*
28-30  **el descenso en rapel** *m*
- *roping down (abseiling, rapelling)*
28  el nudo corredizo del descenso en rapel *m*
- *abseil sling*
29  el descenso con mosquetón *m*
- *sling seat*
30  el descenso "Dülfer"
- *Dülfer seat*
31-57  **el equipo de alpinismo** *m* (el equipo de montañismo *m*, el equipo de escalada *f* en roca *f* o hielo *m*)
- *mountaineering equipment (climbing equipment, snow and ice climbing equipment)*
31  el piolet (la piqueta)
- *ice axe (Am. ax)*
32  la correa de la muñeca
- *wrist sling*
33  el pico
- *pick*
34  la pala
- *adze (Am. adz)*
35  el ojo del piolet
- *karabiner hole*
36  el piolet para el hielo
- *short-shafted ice axe (Am. ax)*
37  el martillo para el hielo (el martillo mixto para hielo *m* y roca *f*)
- *hammer axe (Am. ax)*
38  el pitón universal (el pitón para usos *m* múltiples)
- *general-purpose piton*
39  el pitón para el descenso en rapel *m* (el pitón de anillo *m*)
- *abseil piton, a ringed piton*
40  el pitón de rosca *f* para hielo *m* (el pitón en forma *f* de sacacorchos *m*)
- *ice piton, a semi-tubular screw ice piton (corkscrew piton)*
41  el pitón de muescas *f* para hielo *m*
- *drive-in ice piton*
42  la bota de alpinismo *m*
- *mountaineering boot*
43  la suela estriada (la suela con muescas *f*, perfilada)
- *corrugated sole*
44  la bota de escalada *f*
- *climbing boot*
45  el borde rugoso de ebonita *f*
- *roughened stiff rubber upper*
46  el mosquetón
- *karabiner*
47  el cierre de rosca *f*
- *screwgate*
48  el crampón (el crampón ligero, el crampón de doce o diez puntas *f*)
- *crampons, e.g. lightweight crampons, twelve-point crampons, ten-point crampons*
49  las puntas delanteras
- *front points*

50  la protección de la punta
- *point guards*
51  la correa del crampón
- *crampon strap*
52  la fijación del crampón por cable *m*
- *crampon cable fastener*
53  el casco protector contra los golpes de las piedras
- *safety helmet (protective helmet)*
54  la lámpara del casco
- *helmet lamp*
55  las polainas para la nieve
- *snow gaiters*
56  el cinturón de escalada *f*
- *climbing harness*
57  el cinturón de asiento *m*
- *sit harness*

**1-72 el esquí**
- *skiing*
1 el esquí compacto
- *compact ski*
2 la fijación de seguridad *f* del esquí
- *safety binding (release binding)*
3 la correa de sujeción *f*
- *strap*
4 el canto de acero *m*
- *steel edge*
5 el bastón de esquí *m*
- *ski stick (ski pole)*
6 el puño del bastón
- *grip*
7 la correa para la mano
- *loop*
8 la arandela
- *basket*
9 el traje de esquí de una sola pieza (el mono) para mujeres *f*
- *ladies' one-piece ski suit*
10 el gorro de esquí *m*
- *skiing cap (ski cap)*
11 las gafas de esquí *m*
- *skiing goggles*
12 la bota de esquí de suela *f* reforzada
- *cemented sole skiing boot*
13 el casco de esquí *m*
- *crash helmet*
**14-20 el equipo de esquí *m* de fondo *m***
- *cross-country equipment*
14 el esquí de fondo *m*
- *cross-country ski*
15 la fijación de ratonera *f* para esquí *m* de fondo *m*
- *cross-country rat trap binding*
16 la bota de esquí *m* de fondo *m*
- *cross-country boot*
17 el traje de esquí *m* de fondo *m*
- *cross-country gear*
18 la gorra de visera *f*
- *peaked cap*
19 las gafas de sol *m*
- *sunglasses*
20 los bastones de esquí *m* de fondo *m*, de bambú *m*
- *cross-country poles made of bamboo*
**21-24 utensilios *m* de encerar los esquíes**
- *ski-waxing equipment*
21 la cera para esquí *m*
- *ski wax*
22 la plancha de encerar (la lámpara de soldar)
- *waxing iron, a blowlamp (blowtorch)*
23 el aplicador de cera *f* de corcho *m*
- *waxing cork*
24 el rascador (el raspador de cera *f*)
- *wax scraper*
25 el bastón de carrera f
- *downhill racing pole*
26 el paso en forma *f* de espina *f* de pescado *m*, para escalar una pendiente
- *herringbone, for climbing a slope*
27 el paso en escalera *f*, para escalar una pendiente
- *sidestep, for climbing a slope*
28 la bolsa de cadera *f*
- *ski bag*
29 el slálom
- *slalom*

30 el poste de la puerta
- *gate pole*
31 el traje de carrera *f*
- *racing suit*
32 la carrera de descenso *m* (el descenso)
- *downhill racing*
33 el "huevo", la posición ideal en el descenso
- *'egg' position, the ideal downhill racing position*
34 el esquí de descenso *m*
- *downhill ski*
35 el salto con esquíes *m*
- *ski jumping*
36 el "pez", la posición en vuelo *m*
- *lean forward*
37 el dorsal (el número de salida *f*)
- *number*
38 el esquí de salto *m*
- *ski jumping ski*
39 las ranuras guías (3 a 5 ranuras)
- *grooves (3 to 5 grooves)*
40 la fijación de cable *m*
- *cable binding*
41 la bota de salto *m*
- *ski jumping boots*
42 la carrera de fondo *m*
- *cross-country*
43 el mono de carrera *f*
- *cross-country stretch-suit*
44 el recorrido
- *course*
45 las banderolas de señalización *f* (la señalización del recorrido)
- *course-marking flag*
46 las diferentes capas de unos esquíes modernos
- *layers of a modern ski*
47 el núcleo especial
- *special core*
48 las láminas
- *laminates*
49 la lámina de amortiguación *f*
- *stabilizing layer (stabilizer)*
50 el canto de acero *m*
- *steel edge*
51 el canto superior de aluminio *m*
- *aluminium (Am. aluminum) upper edge*
52 la superficie de deslizamiento *m* de material *m* sintético
- *synthetic bottom (artificial bottom)*
53 el estribo de seguridad *f*
- *safety jet*
**54-56 los elementos de fijación *f***
- *parts of the binding*
54 la pieza automática del talón
- *automatic heel unit*
55 la pieza de sujeción *f* de la punta del pie
- *toe unit*
56 el freno del esquí
- *ski stop*
**57-63 los remontes de esquí *m***
- *ski lift*
57 el telesilla biplaza
- *double chair lift*
58 la barra de seguridad *f*, con reposapiés *m*
- *safety bar with footrest*
59 el telesquí
- *ski lift*
60 el rastro
- *track*
61 el gancho de suspensión *f*
- *hook*

62 la garrucha automática para el cable
- *automatic cable pulley*
63 el cable de tracción *f*
- *haulage cable*
64 el slálom
- *slalom*
65 la puerta abierta
- *open gate*
66 la puerta vertical ciega (cerrada)
- *closed vertical gate*
67 la puerta vertical abierta
- *open vertical gate*
68 la doble puerta en diagonal *m*
- *transversal chicane*
69 la horquilla
- *hairpin*
70 la doble puerta vertical desplazada
- *elbow*
71 el corredor
- *corridor*
72 la chicana Allais (el paso en zigzag *m* Allais)
- *Allais chicane*

**1-26 el patinaje sobre hielo** *m*
- *ice skating*
1 la patinadora sobre hielo *m*
(una patinadora individual)
- *ice skater, a solo skater*
2 la pierna de apoyo *m*
- *tracing leg*
3 la pierna libre
- *free leg*
4 los patinadores por parejas *f*
- *pair skaters*
5 la espiral de la muerte
- *death spiral*
6 el paso del arco
- *pivot*
7 el salto de corzo *m*
- *stag jump (stag leap)*
8 la pirueta sentada con salto *m*
- *jump-sit-spin*
9 la pirueta con el cuerpo
derecho (la pirueta de pie *m*)
- *upright spin*
10 el pie asido
- *holding the foot*
**11-19 las figuras obligatorias del**
patinaje sobre hielo *m*
- *compulsory figures*
11 el ocho
- *curve eight*
12 la serpiente
- *change*
13 el tres
- *three*
14 el tres doble
- *double-three*
15 el lazo
- *loop*
16 el lazo de serpiente *m*
- *change-loop*
17 el contratrés
- *bracket*
18 la contravuelta
- *counter*
19 la vuelta
- *rocker*
**20-25 patines** *m* (patines para el
patinaje sobre hielo *m*)
- *ice skates*
20 el patín para patinaje *m* de
velocidad *f*
- *speed skating set (speed skate)*
21 el canto
- *edge*
22 la hoja (la cuchilla) cóncava
- *hollow grinding (hollow ridge,
concave ridge)*
23 el patín de hockey *m* sobre
hielo *m*
- *ice hockey set (ice hockey skate)*
24 la bota para patinaje *m* sobre
hielo *m*
- *ice skating boot*
25 la funda protectora
- *skate guard*
26 el patinador de volocidad *f*
- *speed skater*

**27-28 el patinaje a vela** *f*
- *skate sailing*
27 el patinador a vela *f*
- *skate sailor*
28 la vela de mano *m*
- *hand sail*
**29-37 el hockey sobre hielo** *m*
- *ice hockey*
29 el jugador de hockey *m* sobre
hielo *m*
- *ice hockey player*
30 el stick de hockey *m* sobre
hielo *m*
- *ice hockey stick*
31 el mango del stick
- *stick handle*
32 la pala del stick
- *stick blade*
33 la espinillera
- *shin pad*
34 el casco protector
- *headgear (protective helmet)*
35 el puck (un disco de ebonita *f*)
- *puck, a vulcanized rubber disc
(disk)*
36 el portero (el guardameta)
- *goalkeeper*
37 la portería (la meta)
- *goal*
**38-40 el curling alemán** (el tiro del
palo sobre hielo *m*)
- *ice-stick shooting (Bavarian
curling)*
38 el jugador de curling *m* alemán
(el tirador del palo sobre hielo
*m*)
- *ice-stick shooter (Bavarian
curler)*
39 el palo
- *ice stick*
40 el cubo de madera *f* (la meta)
- *block*
**41-43 el curling**
- *curling*
41 el jugador de curling *m*
- *curler*
42 la piedra del curling
- *curling stone (granite)*
43 la escoba del curling
- *curling brush (curling broom,
besom)*
**44-46 la navegación a vela** *f* sobre
hielo *m*
- *ice yachting (iceboating, ice
sailing)*
44 el velero sobre hielo *m*
- *ice yacht (iceboat)*
45 el patín
- *steering runner*
46 el balancín (la batanga)
- *outrigged runner*

1 el trineo rígido (el luge)
– *toboggan (sledge, Am. sled)*
2 el luge con asiento *m* de
correas *f* trenzadas
– *toboggan (sledge, Am. sled) with
seat of plaid straps*
3 el luge modelo *m* júnior
– *junior luge toboggan (junior
luge, junior toboggan)*
4 los tirantes de conducción *f*
– *rein*
5 el larguero
– *bar (strut)*
6 el asiento
– *seat*
7 la plancha de ensamblaje *m* del
patín
– *bracket*
8 el puntal delantero
– *front prop*
9 el puntal trasero
– *rear prop*
10 el patín móvil
– *movable runner*
11 el carril
– *metal face*
12 el corredor de luge *m*
– *luge tobogganer*
13 el luge de carreras *f* (el luge de
competición *f*)
– *luge toboggan (luge, toboggan)*

14 el casco protector
– *crash helmet*
15 las gafas de carreras *f*
– *goggles*
16 el protector del codo
– *elbow pad*
17 la rodillera
– *knee pad*
18 el trineo Nansen, un trineo
polar
– *Nansen sledge, a polar sledge*
19-21 el bobsleigh
– *bobsleigh (bobsledding)*
19 el bob (el bobsleigh), un bob de
dos
– *bobsleigh (bobsled), a two-man
bobsleigh (a boblet)*
20 el capitán (el conductor del
bob)
– *steersman*
21 el encargado del freno
– *brakeman*
22-24 el deslizamiento en
skeleton *m*
– *skeleton tobogganing (Cresta
tobogganing)*
22 el skeleton
– *skeleton (skeleton toboggan)*
23 el conductor de skeleton *m*
– *skeleton rider*

24 las garras de hierro *m* (el
crampón), para conducir y
frenar
– *rake, for braking and steering*

1 el alud (la avalancha); *clases:* alud de nieve *f* en polvo *m*, alud de de témpanos *m*
– *avalanche (snow avalanche,* Am. *snowslide);* kinds: *wind avalanche, ground avalanche*
2 el rompealudes, un muro de disviación *f; anál.:* la cuña de aludes *m*
– *avalanche wall, a deflecting wall (diverting wall);* sim.: *avalanche wedge*
3 la galería de protección *f* contra aludes *m*
– *avalanche gallery*
4 la nevada
– *snowfall*
5 el ventisquero (la nieve amontonada)
– *snowdrift*
6 la empalizada contra la nieve
– *snow fence*
7 el bosque de protección *f* contra aludes *m*
– *avalanche forest [planted as protection against avalanches]*
8 el camión del servicio municipal de limpieza *f*
– *street-cleaning lorry (street cleaner)*
9 la pala quitanieves
– *snow plough (Am. snowplow) attachment*

10 la cadena antideslizante
– *snow chain (skid chain, tyre chain,* Am. *tire chain)*
11 el capó (la cubierta) del radiador
– *radiator bonnet (Am. radiator hood)*
12 la ventana del radiador y el enrejado (la pantalla) de la ventana
– *radiator shutter and shutter opening*
13 el muñeco de nieve *f*
– *snowman*
14 la batalla con bolas *f* de nieve *f*
– *snowball fight*
15 la bola de nieve *f*
– *snowball*
16 el trineo
– *ski bob*
17 el resbaladero
– *slide*
18 el joven resbalando sobre el hielo
– *boy, sliding*
19 el hielo resbaladizo
– *icy surface (icy ground)*
20 la capa de nieve *f* sobre el tejado
– *covering of snow, on the roof*
21 el carámbano
– *icicle*
22 el paleador, amontonando nieve *f*
– *man clearing snow*
23 la pala para la nieve
– *snow push (snow shovel)*
24 el montón de nieve *f*
– *heap of snow*

25 el trineo de caballos *m*
– *horse-drawn sleigh (horse sleigh)*
26 los cascabeles (las campanillas) del trineo
– *sleigh bells (bells, set of bells)*
27 el folgo
– *foot muff (Am. foot bag)*
28 las orejeras
– *earmuff*
29 el trineo de silla *f* (el trineo impulsado por el pie; *anál.:* el trineo de empuje *m*)
– *handsledge (tread sledge);* sim.: *push sledge*
30 la nieve fangosa (la nieve fundida, el lodo)
– *slush*

1-13 **el juego de los bolos** (el boliche;
  *Amér.*: el balero)
 – **skittles**
1-11 la disposición de los bolos (el
  cuadro de los bolos)
 – *skittle frame*
1 el bolo de la esquina anterior (el
  primero)
 – *front pin (front)*
2 el bolo de la calle anterior izquierda,
  una dama
 – *left front second pin (left front second)*
3 la calle anterior izquierda
 – *running three [left]*
4 el bolo de la calle anterior derecha,
  una dama
 – *right front second pin (right front
  second)*
5 la calle anterior derecha
 – *running three [right]*
6 el bolo de la esqina izquierda, un peón
  (copper)
7 el rey (el birlón)
 – *landlord*
8 el bolo de la esquina derecha, un peón
  (copper)
 – *right corner pin (right corner), a corner
  (copper)*
9 el bolo de la calle posterior izquierda,
  una dama
 – *back left second pin (back left second)*
10 el bolo de la calle posterior derecha,
  una dama
 – *back right second pin (back right
  second)*
11 el bolo de la esquina posterior (el
  último)
 – *back pin (back)*
12 el bolo
 – *pin*
13 el rey (el birlón)
 – *landlord*
14-20 **la bolera**
 – **tenpin bowling**
14 la disposición de los bolos
 – *frame*
15 la bola con agujeros *m* para los dedos
 – *bowling ball (ball with finger holes)*
16 el agujero para asir la bola
 – *finger hole*
17-20 las clases de lanzamientos *m*
 – *deliveries*
17 el lanzamiento en línea *f* recta
 – *straight ball*
18 el lanzamiento en gancho *m*
 – *hook ball (hook)*
19 el lanzamiento en arco *m*
 – *curve*
20 el lanzamiento en arco *m* inverso al
  de arriba
 – *back-up ball (back-up)*
21 **las bochas** (el juego de bochas, la
  petanca); *anál.*: el juego italiano de
  boccia, el juego inglés de bowls
 – *boules;* sim.: *Italian game of boccie,
  green bowls (bowls)*
22 el jugador de bochas *f*
 – *boules player*
23 el boliche (el bolín)
 – *jack (target jack)*
24 la bocha (la bola de lanzamiento *m*)
  estriada
 – *grooved boule*
25 el grupo de jugadores *m*
 – *group of players*
26 **el tiro con fusil** *m*
 – **rifle shooting**
27-29 posiciones *f* de tiro *m*
 – *shooting positions*
27 la posición de pie *m*
 – *standing position*
28 la posición de rodillas *f*
 – *kneeling position*

29 la posición tendida
 – *prone position*
30-33 blancos *m*
 – *targets*
30 el blanco para el tiro con fusil *m*
  a 50 m de distancia *f*
 – *target for 50 m events (50 m target)*
31 el círculo
 – *circle*
32 el blanco para el tiro con fusil *m*
  a 100 m de distancia *f*
 – *target for 100 m events (100 m target)*
33 el blanco móvil (el jabalí corriendo)
 – *running-boar target*
34-39 las municiones deportivas
 – *ammunition*
34 el balín (el diábolo) para escopeta *f* de
  aire *m* comprimido
 – *air rifle cartridge*
35 el cartucho con fulminante *m* en la
  base para carabina *f* de pequeño
  calibre *m*
 – *rimfire cartridge for zimmerstutzen
  (indoor target rifle), a smallbore
  German single-shot rifle*
36 la cápsula
 – *case head*
37 la bala en el extremo
 – *caseless round*
38 el cartucho calibre *m* 22 de rifle *m*
  largo
 – *.22 long rifle cartridge*
39 el cartucho calibre *m* 222 del
  Remington
 – *.222 Remington cartridge*
40-49 fusiles *m* deportivos
 – *sporting rifles*
40 el fusil de aire *m* comprimido
 – *air rifle*
41 la dioptra (la pínula)
 – *optical sight*
42 la mira
 – *front sight (foresight)*
43 el fusil estándar de pequeño calibre *m*
 – *smallbore standard rifle*
44 el arma *f* de pequeño calibre *m* para
  tiro *m* libre internacional
 – *international smallbore free rifle*
45 la pieza de apoyo *m* en la mano para
  la posición de pie *m*
 – *palm rest for standing position*
46 la cantonera con gancho *m*
 – *butt plate with hook*
47 la culata con orificio *m* para el pulgar
 – *butt with thumb hole*
48 el fusil de pequeño calibre *m* para el
  blanco móvil (para el jabalí
  corriendo)
 – *smallbore rifle for bobbing target
  (turning target)*
49 la mira telescópica
 – *telescopic sight (riflescope, telescope
  sight)*
50 la dioptra de puntería *f* con mira *f*
  redonda
 – *optical ring sight*
51 la dioptra de puntería *f* con mira *f* de
  lámina *f*
 – *optical ring and bead sight*
52-66 **el tiro con arco** *m*
 – *archery (target archery)*
52 el tiro
 – *shot*
53 el arquero
 – *archer*
54 el arco de competición *f*
 – *competition bow*
55 el brazo elástico
 – *riser*
56 el alza
 – *point-of-aim mark*

57 la empuñadura
 – *grip (handle)*
58 el estabilizador
 – *stabilizer*
59 la cuerda del arco
 – *bow string (string)*
60 la flecha
 – *arrow*
61 la punta de la flecha
 – *pile (point) of the arrow*
62 las plumas de dirección *f* (las plumas
  de pavo *m*)
 – *fletching*
63 la muesca
 – *nock*
64 el astil de la flecha
 – *shaft*
65 las marcas del tirador
 – *cresting*
66 el blanco
 – *target*
67 **el juego de pelota** *f* vasca (*vasco:* jai
  alai)
 – *Basque game of pelota (jai alai)*
68 el pelotari
 – *pelota player*
69 la cesta (la chistera)
 – *wicker basket (cesta)*
70-78 **el skeet**, una clase de tiro *m* al
  plato
 – **skeet** *(skeet shooting), a kind of clay
  pigeon shooting*
70 la escopeta de dos cañones *m* de
  skeet *m* (de tiro *m* al plato)
 – *skeet over-and-under shotgun*
71 la boca del cañón con calibre *m*
  especial para tiro *m* al plato
 – *muzzle with skeet choke*
72 la posición de "listo" reclamando
  plato *m*
 – *ready position on call*
73 la posición de disparo *m* (de fuego *m*)
 – *firing position*
74 el campo de tiro *m* al plato (el campo
  de skeet *m*)
 – *shooting range*
75 la cabina alta
 – *high house*
76 la cabina baja
 – *low house*
77 la trayectoria del plato
 – *target's path*
78 el puesto de tiro *m*
 – *shooting station (shooting box)*
79 **la rueda gigante**
 – **aero wheel**
80 el asidero
 – *handle*
81 el reposapiés
 – *footrest*
82 **el karting** (la carrera de karts *m*)
 – **go-karting** *(karting)*
83 el kart
 – *go-kart (kart)*
84 el número de salida *f*
 – *number plate (number)*
85 los pedales
 – *pedals*
86 el neumático sin perfil *m*
 – *pneumatic tyre (Am. tire)*
87 el tanque (el depósito) de gasolina *f*
 – *petrol tank (Am. gasoline tank)*
88 el chasis
 – *frame*
89 el volante
 – *steering wheel*
90 el asiento en forma *f* de concha *f*
 – *bucket seat*
91 el tabique protector contra el fuego
 – *protective bulkhead*
92 el motor de dos tiempos *m*
 – *two-stroke engine*
93 el silenciador
 – *silencer* (Am. *muffler*)

**1-48 el baile de máscaras** f (el baile de disfraces m, la mascarada)
- **masked ball** (masquerade, fancy-dress ball)
**1** la sala de baile m
- *ballroom*
**2** la orquesta de música f pop (la banda de música f pop), una orquesta de baile m
- *pop group, a dance band*
**3** el músico pop
- *pop musician*
**4** el farolillo veneciano
- *paper lantern*
**5** la cadeneta de papel m
- *festoon (string of decorations)*
**6-48** los disfraces de la mascarada
- *fancy dress at the masquerade*
**6** la bruja
- *witch*
**7** la máscara (la careta)
- *mask*
**8** el trampero (el cazador de pieles f)
- *fur trapper (trapper)*
**9** la muchacha apache
- *Apache girl*
**10** la media de malla f
- *net stocking*
**11** el primer premio de la tómbola, una cesta surtida
- *first prize in the tombola (raffle), a hamper*
**12** la pierrette
- *pierrette*

**13** el antifaz
- *half mask (domino)*
**14** el demonio (el diablo)
- *devil*
**15** el dominó
- *domino*
**16** la hawaiana
- *hula-hula girl (Hawaii girl)*
**17** la guirnalda (el collar de flores f)
- *garland*
**18** la falda de rafia f
- *grass skirt (hula skirt)*
**19** el pierrot
- *pierrot*
**20** la gola
- *ruff*
**21** la midinette
- *midinette*
**22** el vestido a lo Biedermeier (el vestido Luis Felipe)
- *Biedermeier dress*
**23** la papalina
- *poke bonnet*
**24** el escote con los lunares
- *décolletage with beauty spot*
**25** la bayadera (la danzarina hindú)
- *bayadère (Hindu dancing girl)*
**26** el Grande de España
- *grandee*
**27** la colombina
- *Columbine*
**28** el maharajá
- *maharaja (maharajah)*
**29** el mandarín, un dignatario chino
- *mandarin, a Chinese dignitary*

**30** la mujer exótica
- *exotic girl (exotic)*
**31** el vaquero (el cowboy)
- *cowboy; sim.: gaucho (vaquero)*
**32** la vampiresa, con vestido m de fantasía f
- *vamp, in fancy dress*
**33** el petimetre (el dandi, el pisaverde, el lechuguino, el gomoso, el niño gótico; Mé.: el catrín), un disfraz de carácter m
- *dandy (fop, beau), a disguise*
**34** la escarapela (el distintivo del baile de máscaras f)
- *rosette*
**35** el arlequín
- *harlequin*
**36** la zíngara (la gitana)
- *gipsy (gypsy) girl*
**37** la cocote (la mujer de costumbres f ligeras, la cortesana, la dama galante)
- *cocotte (demi-monde, demi-mondaine, demi-rep)*
**38** el bufón (el truhán)
- *owl-glass, a fool (jester, buffoon)*
**39** el gorro del bufón (el gorro de cascabeles m)
- *foolscap (jester's cap and bells)*
**40** el cascabelero (el sonajero)
- *rattle*
**41** la odalisca, una esclava oriental del harén
- *odalisque, Eastern female slave in Sultan's seraglio*

**42** el pantalón bombacho
– *chalwar (pantaloons)*
**43** el pirata (el corsario)
– *pirate (buccaneer)*
**44** el tatuaje
– *tattoo*
**45** el gorro de papel *m*
– *paper hat*
**46** la nariz de cartón *m*
– *false nose*
**47** la matraca (la carraca)
– *clapper (rattle)*
**48** la palmeta de bufón *m*
– *slapstick*
**49-54 artificios *m* pirotécnicos**
– *fireworks*
**49** el fulminante (el pistón)
– *percussion cap*
**50** el bombón explosivo
– *cracker*
**51** la bombita fulminante
– *banger*
**52** el buscapiés (*C. Rica:* el cachiflín)
– *jumping jack*
**53** el petardo
– *cannon cracker (maroon, marroon)*
**54** el cohete (el volador; *Ec.:* el
volatero)
– *rocket*
**55** la bola de confeti *m*
– *paper ball*
**56** la caja de sorpresa *f*
– *jack-in-the-box, a joke*

**57-70 el desfile** (la cabalgata) **de**
**carnaval** *m*
– *carnival procession*
**57** la carroza de carnaval *m*
– *carnival float (carnival truck)*
**58** el príncipe Carnaval
– *King Carnival*
**59** el cascabelero (la insignia del
bufón; de la locura, el cetro de
bufón *m*)
– *bauble (fool's sceptre, Am. scepter)*
**60** la orden de bufón *m* (la orden de
carnaval *m*)
– *fool's badge*
**61** la princesa Carnaval
– *Queen Carnival*
**62** el confeti (*Guat.:* los retacitos *pl.*)
– *confetti*
**63** el gigantón, una figura burlesca
– *giant figure, a satirical figure*
**64** la reina de la belleza
– *beauty queen*
**65** la figura de cuento *m* de hadas *f*
– *fairy-tale figure*
**66** la serpentina
– *paper streamer*
**67** la cantinera de la guardia del
príncipe
– *majorette*
**68** la guardia del príncipe
– *king's guard*
**69** el polichinela, un payaso
– *buffoon, a clown*
**70** el tambor de lansquenete *m*
– *lansquenet's drum*

1-63 el circo ambulante
- *travelling (Am. traveling) circus*
1 la carpa del circo (la tienda del circo), una carpa de cuatro mástiles
- *circus tent (big top), a four-pole tent*
2 el mástil de la carpa
- *tent pole*
3 el reflector
- *spotlight*
4 el técnico de iluminación *f*
- *lighting technician*
5 la plataforma para el artista
- *trapeze platform*
6 el trapecio
- *trapeze*
7 el trapecista
- *trapeze artist*
8 la escalera de cuerda *f*
- *rope ladder*
9 la tribuna de la banda de música *f*
- *bandstand*
10 la banda del circo
- *circus band*
11 la entrada a la pista
- *ring entrance (arena entrance)*
12 el túnel de espera *f* de los artistas
- *wings*

13 el puntal de la tienda
- *tent prop (prop)*
14 la red de protección *f* (la red de seguridad *f*)
- *safety net*
15 la gradería de los espectadores
- *seats for the spectators*
16 el palco del circo
- *circus box*
17 el director del circo
- *circus manager*
18 el representante (el agente) de los artistas
- *artiste agent (agent)*
19 la entrada y salida *f*
- *entrance and exit*
20 el pasillo de acceso *m* a la gradería
- *steps*
21 la pista
- *ring (arena)*
22 la barrera
- *ring fence*
23 el payaso músico (*Pan.*: el parrampán; *Chile*: el catimbao)
- *musical clown (clown)*
24 el payaso (el payaso "cara *f* blanca"; el clown; *Chile*: el catimbao)
- *clown*

25 el "número cómico", un número de circo *m*
- *comic turn (clown act), a circus act*
26 los caballistas (los artistas ecuestres)
- *circus riders (bareback riders)*
27 el mozo de pista *f*, un mozo de circo *m*
- *ring attendant, a circus attendant*
28 la torre humana (el castillo)
- *pyramid*
29 el hombre base
- *support*
30-31 la doma libre
- *performance by liberty horses*
30 el caballo de circo *m*, en una levade (encabritado)
- *circus horse, performing the levade (pesade)*
31 el domador, un caballista (*Amér.*: el chalán, el amansador)
- *ringmaster, a trainer*
32 el volteador a caballo *m*
- *vaulter*
33 la salida de emergencia *f*
- *emergency exit*

**34** la caravana (el remolque, la rulotte)
– *caravan (circus caravan,* Am. *trailer)*
**35** el acróbata de trampolín *m* (*Amér.:* el maromero)
– *springboard acrobat (springboard artist)*
**36** el trampolín
– *springboard*
**37** el lanzador de cuchillos *m*
– *knife thrower*
**38** el tirador de pistola *f*
– *circus marksman*
**39** la ayudante
– *assistant*
**40** la volatinera (la funámbula; *Cuba:* la caballitera)
– *tightrope dancer*
**41** el alambre
– *tightrope*
**42** el balancín (*Amér.:* la balanza)
– *balancing pole*
**43** el número de lanzamiento *m*
– *throwing act*
**44** el número de equilibrio *m*
– *balancing act*
**45** el hombre base
– *support*

**46** la pértiga (la vara de bambú *m*)
– *pole (bamboo pole)*
**47** el acróbata
– *acrobat*
**48** el equilibrista
– *equilibrist (balancer)*
**49** la jaula de fieras *f*, una jaula circular
– *wild animal cage, a round cage*
**50** el enrejado de la jaula
– *bars of the cage*
**51** el túnel de la jaula de fieras *f* (el pasillo enrejado para las fieras)
– *passage (barred passage, passage for the wild animals)*
**52** el domador (el domador de fieras *f*)
– *tamer (wild animal tamer)*
**53** el látigo (el fuete; *Amer.:* el enero, el chicote, el chirrión, el rejo; *Amér. Central y Ec.:* el acial, la coyunda)
– *whip*
**54** la horquilla protectora
– *fork*
**55** el pedestal
– *pedestal*
**56** la fiera (el tigre, el león)
– *wild animal, e.g. lion, tiger*

**57** el taburete para los animales
– *stand*
**58** el aro para saltar
– *hoop (jumping hoop)*
**59** el subibaja
– *seesaw*
**60** la pelota
– *ball*
**61** el campamento de tiendas *f*
– *camp*
**62** el remolque (la caravana) jaula *f*
– *cage caravan*
**63** la exhibición de animales *m*
– *menagerie*

1-69  la feria (la feria anual, la fiesta mayor, la fiesta del pueblo)
– *fair (annual fair)*
1  el real de la feria
– *fairground*
2  el tiovivo (los caballitos, el carrusel; *P. Rico:* la machina)
– *children's merry-go-round, (whirligig), a roundabout (Am. carousel)*
3  el puesto de refrescos *m* y bebidas *f* (*Chile:* la venta)
– *refreshment stall (drinks stall)*
4  las voladoras
– *chairoplane*
5  el tren del infierno, un tren fantasma
– *up-and-down roundabout, a ghost train*
6  la barraca de feria *f*
– *show booth (booth)*
7  la caja (el despacho de billetes *m*)
– *box (box office)*
8  el pregonero
– *barker*
9  la medium
– *medium*
10  el feriante
– *showman*
11  la máquina de medir la fuerza (el dinamómetro)
– *try-your-strength machine*
12  el vendedor ambulante
– *hawker*
13  el globo (*Bol.:* el tucucho)
– *balloon*
14  el matasuegras
– *paper serpent*
15  el molinete (la voladera)
– *windmill*

16  el carterista (el ladrón, el ratero; *Chile:* el arpista)
– *pickpocket, a thief*
17  el vendedor
– *vendor*
18  la miel turca
– *Turkish delight*
19  el barracón de los fenómenos
– *freak show*
20  el gigante
– *giant*
21  la mujer gorda
– *fat lady*
22  los enanos (los liliputienses)
– *dwarfs (midgets)*
23  la cervecería de feria *f*
– *beer marquee*
24  el barracón de las atracciones
– *sideshow*
25-28  los artistas ambulantes
– *travelling (Am. traveling) artistes (travelling show people)*
25  el tragafuegos (el pirófago)
– *fire eater*
26  el tragasables
– *sword swallower*
27  el forzudo (el hércules)
– *strong man*
28  el especialista en desatarse
– *escapologist*
29  los espectadores
– *spectators*
30  el vendedor de helados *m*
– *ice-cream vendor (ice-cream man)*
31  el cucurucho de helado *m*
– *ice-cream cornet, with ice cream*

32  el puesto de salchichas *f* asadas
– *sausage stand*
33  la parrilla
– *grill (Am. broiler)*
34  la salchicha asada
– *bratwurst (grilled sausage, Am. broiled sausage)*
35  las tenacillas para coger las salchichas
– *sausage tongs*
36  la echadora de cartas *f*, una adivina
– *fortune teller*
37  la noria gigante
– *big wheel (Ferris wheel)*
38  el orquestión (el órgano automático), un instrumento de música *f*
– *orchestrion (automatic organ), an automatic musical instrument*

# La feria (el parque de atracciones)

**39** la montaña rusa
– *scenic railway (switchback)*
**40** el tobogán
– *toboggan slide (chute)*
**41** el columpio de barcos *m*
– *swing boats*
**42** el columpio volteador
– *swing boat, turning full circle*
**43** el volteo (la voltereta)
– *full circle*
**44** la tómbola (*Amér. Central:* el turno)
– *lottery booth (tombola booth)*
**45** la rueda de la fortuna
– *wheel of fortune*
**46** la rueda del diablo (la rueda del tifón)
– *devil's wheel (typhoon wheel)*
**47** la anilla para lanzar
– *throwing ring (quoit)*
**48** los premios
– *prizes*
**49** el hombre anuncio (el hombre "sandwich") con zancos *m*
– *sandwich man on stilts*
**50** el cartel de anuncio *m*
– *sandwich board (placard)*
**51** el vendedor de cigarrillos *m*, un vendedor ambulante
– *cigarette seller, an itinerant trader (a hawker)*
**52** la batea
– *tray*
**53** el puesto de frutas *f*
– *fruit stall*
**54** el motorista del muro de la muerte
– *wall-of-death rider*
**55** el barracón de la risa (el barracón de espejos *m*)
– *hall of mirrors*
**56** el espejo cóncavo
– *concave mirror*
**57** el espejo convexo
– *convex mirror*
**58** la barraca de tiro *m* al blanco
– *shooting gallery*
**59** el hipódromo
– *hippodrome*
**60** el rastro (el mercado de viejo)
– *junk stalls (second-hand stalls)*
**61** el puesto de socorro *m*
– *first aid tent (first aid post)*
**62** la pista de los coches de choque *m*
– *dodgems (bumper cars)*
**63** el coche de choque *m*
– *dodgem car (bumper car)*
**64-66** la cacharrería
– *pottery stand*
**64** el pregonero
– *barker*
**65** la vendedora
– *market woman*
**66** los cacharros de loza *f*
– *pottery*
**67** los visitantes de la feria
– *visitors to the fair*
**68** la barraca de figuras *f* de cera *f*
– *waxworks*
**69** la figura de cera *f*
– *wax figure*

1 la máquina de coser de pedal *m*
– *treadle sewing machine*
2 el florero
– *flower vase*
3 el espejo de pared *f*
– *wall mirror*
4 la estufa
– *cylindrical stove*
5 el tubo de la estufa
– *stovepipe*
6 el codo del tubo de la estufa
– *stovepipe elbow*
7 la puerta de la estufa
– *stove door*
8 la pantalla de la estufa
– *stove screen*
9 el cubo del carbón
– *coal scuttle*
10 la cesta para las astillas
– *firewood basket*
11 la muñeca
– *doll*
12 el oso de peluche *m*
– *teddy bear*
13 el organillo (*Mé.:* el cilindro)
– *barrel organ*
14 el orquestrión (un instrumento de música *f* automático)
– *orchestrion*
15 el disco metálico perforado (el disco de las notas)
– *metal disc (disk)*
16 el receptor de radio *f* (el aparato de radio *f*, la radio, el receptor)
– *radio (radio set, joc.: 'steam radio'), a superheterodyne (superhet)*
17 la pantalla acústica (el baffle)
– *baffle board*

18 el ojo mágico, un tubo indicador de la sintonización
– *'magic eye', a tuning indicator valve*
19 la abertura del altavoz
– *loudspeaker aperture*
20 los pulsadores para la selección de las emisoras
– *station selector buttons (station preset buttons)*
21 el botón de sintonización *f*
– *tuning knob*
22 las escalas de campos *m* de frecuencia *f*
– *frequency bands*
23 el detector (el receptor de galena *f*)
– *crystal detector (crystal set)*
24 los auriculares de casco *m*
– *headphones (headset)*
25 la cámara plegable (la cámara de fuelle *m*)
– *folding camera*
26 el fuelle
– *bellows*
27 la chapa base de la corredera
– *hinged cover*
28 los extensores
– *spring extension*
29 el vendedor
– *salesman*
30 la cámara de cajón *m*
– *box camera*
31 el gramófono (un fonógrafo)
– *gramophone*
32 el disco de gramófono *m*
– *record (gramophone record)*
33 el pick-up (el brazo de toma *f* de sonido *m*, el portaagujas) con la aguja del gramófono
– *needle head with gramophone needle*

34 el altavoz
– *horn*
35 la caja del gramófono
– *gramophone box*
36 el portadiscos
– *record rack*
37 el magnetófono
– *tape recorder, a portable tape recorder*
38 el flash
– *flashgun*
39 la bombilla de flash *m*
– *flash bulb*
40-41 el flash electrónico
– *electronic flash (electronic flashgun)*
40 la antorcha
– *flash head*
41 el acumulador
– *accumulator*
42 el proyector de diapositivas *f*
– *slide projector*
43 el portadiapositivas
– *slide holder*
44 la caja de la lámpara
– *lamphouse*
45 el candelero
– *candlestick*
46 la concha de Santiago (la concha de peregrino *m*)
– *scallop shell*
47 los cubiertos
– *cutlery*
48 el plato de recuerdo *m*
– *souvenir plate*
49 el caballete para el secado de las placas fotográficas
– *drying rack for photographic plates*
50 la placa fotográfica
– *photographic plate*

**51** el disparador automático
– *delayed-action release*
**52** los soldaditos de plomo *m* (*anál.:* los soldaditos de estaño *m*)
– *tin soldiers; sim.: lead soldiers*
**53** el jarro de cerveza *f*
– *beer mug (stein)*
**54** la trompeta
– *bugle*
**55** los libros antiguos
– *second-hand books*
**56** el reloj de pesas *f*
– *grandfather clock*
**57** el mueble del reloj
– *clock case*
**58** la péndola (el péndulo del reloj)
– *·pendulum*
**59** la pesa de la marcha
– *time weight*
**60** la pesa de los toques
– *striking weight*
**61** la mecedora
– *rocking chair*
**62** el traje de marinero *m*
– *sailor suit*
**63** la gorra de marinero *m*
– *sailor's hat*
**64** el palanganero
– *washing set*
**65** la palangana
– *washing basin*
**66** el jarro de agua *f*
– *water jug*
**67** el soporte de la palangana
– *washstand*
**68** el removedor de la ropa
– *dolly*

**69** la tina de lavar
– *washtub*
**70** la tabla de lavar
– *washboard*
**71** el trompo de música *f* (*Col.:* el zambiloco; *Venez.:* la zaranda)
– *humming top*
**72** la pizarra (*Antillas y Río de la Plata:* el pizarrón)
– *slate*
**73** el plumier (el plumero, la cajita de plumas *f* o lápices *m; Arg. y Chile:* la lapicera)
– *pencil box*
**74** la máquina sumadora-calculadora, una máquina para sumar, restar y multiplicar
– *adding and subtracting machine*
**75** el rollo de papel *m*
– *paper roll*
**76** las teclas de números *m*
– *number keys*
**77** el ábaco
– *abacus*
**78** el tintero, un tintero con tapadera *f*
– *inkwell, with lid*
**79** la máquina de escribir
– *typewriter*
**80** la máquina calculadora
– *[hand-operated] calculating machine (calculator)*
**81** la manivela de accionamiento *m*
– *operating handle*
**82** el registro de resultado *m*
– *result register (product register)*
**83** el mecanismo contador rotativo
– *rotary counting mechanism (rotary counter)*

**84** la balanza de cocina *f* (el peso de cocina *f*)
– *kitchen scales*
**85** las enaguas (*Col.:* las hormadoras)
– *waist slip (underskirt)*
**86** el carro de adrales *m*
– *wooden handcart*
**87** el reloj de pared *f*
– *wall clock*
**88** la botella metálica de agua *f* caliente
– *bed warmer*
**89** la lechera (la vasija para leche *f*)
– *milk churn*

**1-13  los estudios cinematográficos**
- *film studios (studio complex*, Am.
  *movie studios)*
**1** el escenario exterior (el terreno
  para el rodaje de exteriores *m*)
- *lot (studio lot)*
**2** los laboratorios de copia *f*
- *processing laboratories (film
  laboratories, motion picture
  laboratories)*
**3** las salas de montaje *m* (de
  corte *m*)
- *cutting rooms*
**4** el edificio de la administración
- *administration building (office
  building, offices)*
**5** el depósito de películas *f* (el
  archivo de películas, la
  cinemateca)
- *film (motion picture) storage vault
  (film library, motion picture library)*
**6** los talleres
- *workshop*
**7** el decorado (el escenario de
  exteriores *m*)
- *film set* (Am. *movie set)*
**8** la estación eléctrica
- *power house*
**9** los laboratorios técnicos y de
  investigación *f*
- *technical and research laboratories*
**10** el grupo de estudios *m*
- *groups of stages*
**11** el estanque de hormigón *m* para
  escenas *f* acuáticas
- *concrete tank for marine sequences*

**12** el ciclorama
- *cyclorama*
**13** la colina del ciclorama
- *hill*
**14-60  filmaciones *f***
- *shooting (filming)*
**14** el estudio de música (el auditorio)
- *music recording studio (music
  recording theatre*, Am. *theater)*
**15** el revestimiento "acústico" de la
  pared
- *'acoustic' wall lining*
**16** la pantalla
- *screen (projection screen)*
**17** la orquesta cinematográfica
- *film orchestra*
**18** el rodaje en exteriores *m*
- *exterior shooting (outdoor shooting,
  exterior filming, outdoor filming)*
**19** la cámara sincrónica controlada
  por cristal *m* de cuarzo *m*
- *camera with crystal-controlled drive*
**20** el operador (el cameraman)
- *cameraman*
**21** la ayudante de dirección *f*
- *assistant director*
**22** el ayudante del micrófono
- *boom operator (boom swinger)*
**23** el jefe (el operador) de sonido *m*
- *recording engineer (sound recordist)*
**24** el magnetófono portátil
  controlado por cristal *m* de
  cuarzo *m*
- *portable sound recorder with
  crystal-controlled drive*
**25** la jirafa del micrófono
- *microphone boom*

**26-60** la filmación de interiores *m* en
  el plató (en el escenario sonoro)
- *shooting (filming) in the studio (on
  the sound stage)*
**26** el jefe de producción *f*
- *production manager*
**27** la estrella principal (la actriz de
  cine *m*)
- *leading lady;* also: *film actress, film
  star, star*
**28** el actor principal
- *leading man;* also: *film actor, film
  star, star*
**29** el extra (el comparsa, el actor
  secundario)
- *film extra (extra)*
**30** el dispositivo de micrófonos *m*
  para la grabación estereofónica y
  los efectos sonoros
- *arrangement of microphones for
  stereo and sound effects*
**31** el micrófono de estudio *m*
- *studio microphone*
**32** el cable del micrófono
- *microphone cable*
**33** el bastidor y el telón de fondo *m*
- *side flats and background*
**34** el claquista
- *clapper boy*
**35** la claqueta sincrónica, con
  tabilla *f* con el título de la
  película, el número de la escena y
  el número de la toma
- *clapper board (clapper) with slates
  (boards) for the film title, shot
  number (scene number), and take
  number*

36 el maquillador (el peluquero
cinematógrafo)
– *make-up artist and hairstylist*
37 el electricista
– *lighting electrician (studio
electrician, lighting man, Am.
gaffer)*
38 el reflector con filtro *m* de color *m*
– *diffusing screen*
39 la script-girl (la secretaria del
estudio)
– *continuity girl (script girl)*
40 el director cinematográfico
– *film director (director)*
41 el operador (el cameraman)
– *cameraman (first cameraman)*
42 el ayudante del operador
– *camera operator, an assistant
cameraman (camera assistant)*
43 el arquitecto cinematográfico
– *set designer (art director)*
44 el director de fotografía *f* y de
sonido *m* (el director general)
– *director of photography*
45 el guión cinematográfico
– *filmscript (script, shooting script,
Am. movie script)*
46 el ayudante de dirección *f*
– *assistant director*
47 la cámara cinematográfica
insonorizada (la cámara de
televisión), una cámara de
imagen *f* ancha (una cámara *f*
Cinemascope)

– *soundproof film camera
(soundproof motion picture
camera), a wide screen camera
(cinemascope camera)*
48 la cubierta de la cámara a
prueba *f* de sonidos *m*
– *soundproof housing (soundproof
cover, blimp)*
49 la grúa de la cámara
– *camera crane (dolly)*
50 el trípode ajustable
– *hydraulic stand*
51 la pantalla negra (la pantalla
absorbente), para eliminar los
reflejos
– *mask (screen) for protection from
spill light (gobo, nigger)*
52 el foco supletorio sobre trípode *m*
– *tripod spotlight (fill-in light, filler
light, fill light, filler)*
53 la pasarela de focos *m*
– *spotlight catwalk*
54 la cabina de toma *f* de sonido *m*
– *recording room*
55 el ingeniero de sonido *m*
– *recording engineer (sound recordist)*
56 el pupitre de mezcla *f*
– *mixing console (mixing desk)*
57 el ayudante del ingeniero de
sonido *m*
– *sound assistant (assistant sound
engineer)*

58 el equipo de registro *m* magnético
del sonido
– *magnetic sound recording
equipment (magnetic sound
recorder)*
59 el equipo de amplificación *f* y
trucaje *m*, para la reverberación y
los efectos sonoros
– *amplifier and special effects
equipment, e.g. for echo and sound
effects*
60 la cámara sonora (la cámara de
fotosonido *m*)
– *sound recording camera (optical
sound recorder)*

**1-46 grabación *f* y copia *f* del sonido**
- *sound recording and re-recording (dubbing)*
1 el equipo de grabación *f* magnética del sonido
- *magnetic sound recording equipment (magnetic sound recorder)*
2 la bobina de la película magnética
- *magnetic film spool*
3 el portacabezas magnético
- *magnetic head support assembly*
4 el tablero de mando *m*
- *control panel*
5 el amplificador de registro *m* y de lectura *f* del sonido magnético
- *magnetic sound recording and playback amplifier*
6 la cámara de fotosonido *m* (la cámara de sonido, la cámara cinematográfica de fotosonido *m*)
- *optical sound recorder (sound recording camera, optical sound recording equipment)*
7 la cassette de película *f* de luz *f* diurna
- *daylight film magazine*

8 el panel de mando *m* y de control *m*
- *control and monitoring panel*
9 el ocular para el control *m* óptico del registro de fotosonido *m*
- *eyepiece for visual control of optical sound recording*
10 el desenrollador
- *deck*
11 el amplificador de registro *m* y la alimentación de la red
- *recording amplifier and mains power unit*
12 el pupitre de mando *m*
- *control desk (control console)*
13 el altavoz de control *m*
- *monitoring loudspeaker (control loudspeaker)*
14 los indicadores del nivel de registro *m*
- *recording level indicators*
15 los dispositivos de control *m*
- *monitoring instruments*
16 el panel de conjuntores *m*
- *jack panel*
17 el panel de mando *m*
- *control panel*
18 el regulador de corredera *f*
- *sliding control*

19 el corrector
- *equalizer*
20 el plato de sonido *m* magnético
- *magnetic sound deck*
21 el equipo de mezcla *f* para películas *f* magnéticas
- *mixer for magnetic film*
22 el proyector de película *f*
- *film projector*
23 el equipo de registro *m* y de lectura *f*
- *recording and playback equipment*
24 la bobina de película *f*
- *film reel (film spool)*
25 el portacabezas con la cabeza de registro *m*, la cabeza de lectura *f* y la cabeza supresora
- *head support assembly for the recording head, playback head, and erasing head (erase head)*
26 el mecanismo de impulsión de la película
- *film transport mechanism*
27 el filtro de sincronización *f*
- *synchronizing filter*
28 el amplificador del sonido magnético
- *magnetic sound amplifier*

29 el panel de mando *m*
– *control panel*
30 la máquina para revelar
películas *f* en el laboratorio de
copiado *m*
– *film-processing machines (film-developing machines) in the
processing laboratory (film
laboratory, motion picture
laboratory)*
31 el estudio de resonancia *f*
– *echo chamber*
32 el altavoz del estudio de
resonancia *f*
– *echo chamber loudspeaker*
33 el micrófono del estudio de
resonancia *f*
– *echo chamber microphone*
34-36 la mezcla de sonido *m* (la
mezcla de varias bandas de
sonido *m*)
– *sound mixing (sound dubbing,
mixing of several sound tracks)*
34 el estudio de mezcla *f*
– *mixing room (dubbing room)*
35 el pupitre de mezcla *f*, para el
sonido monocanal o
estereofónico
– *mixing console (mixing desk) for
mono or stereo sound*

36 los ingenieros de mezcla *f* de
sonido *m*, en el trabajo de
mezcla *f*
– *dubbing mixers (recording
engineers, sound recordists)
dubbing (mixing)*
37-41 la sincronización (la
postsincronización, el doblaje)
– *synchronization (syncing,
dubbing, post-synchronization,
post-syncing)*
37 el estudio de sincronización *f*
(de doblaje *m*)
– *dubbing studio (dubbing theatre,
Am. theater)*
38 el director de doblaje *m*
– *dubbing director*
39 la locutora de doblaje *m*
– *dubbing speaker (dubbing
actress)*
40 el micrófono de jirafa *f*
– *boom microphone*
41 el cable del sonido
– *microphone cable*
42-46 el montaje
– *cutting (editing)*
42 la mesa de montaje *m*
– *cutting table (editing table,
cutting bench)*
43 el jefe de montaje *m*
– *film editor (cutter)*

44 los platos para las bandas de
imágenes *f* y sonidos *m*
– *film turntable, for picture and
sound tracks*
45 la proyección de imágenes *f*
– *projection of the picture*
46 el altavoz
– *loudspeaker*

**1-23  la proyección cinematográfica**
– *film projection (motion picture projection)*
**1** el cinema (el cine, la sala de cine)
– *cinema (picture house,* Am. *movie theater, movie house)*
**2** la taquilla del cine (*Amér.:* la boletería)
– *cinema box office (Am. movie theater box office)*
**3** la entrada de cine m (*Amér.:*- el boleto)
– *cinema ticket (Am. movie theater ticket)*
**4** la acomodadora
– *usherette*
**5** los espectadores del cine (el público del cine)
– *cinemagoers (filmgoers, cinema audience,* Am. *moviegoers, movie audience)*
**6** el alumbrado de seguridad f (el alumbrado de emergencia f)
– *safety lighting (emergency lighting)*
**7** la salida de urgencia f (de emergencia f)
– *emergency exit*
**8** el escenario
– *stage*
**9** las filas de butacas f
– *rows of seats (rows)*
**10** el telón (la cortina de la pantalla)
– *stage curtain (screen curtain)*
**11** la pantalla (la pantalla de proyección f)
– *screen (projection screen)*

**12** la cabina de proyección f
– *projection room (projection booth)*
**13** el proyector (la máquina) de la izquierda
– *lefthand projector*
**14** el proyector de la derecha
– *righthand projector*
**15** la ventanilla de la cabina, con aberturas para la proyección y la observación
– *projection room window with projection window and observation port*
**16** el tambor de película f
– *reel drum (spool box)*
**17** el panel de interruptores m para la iluminación de la sala
– *house light dimmers (auditorium lighting control)*
**18** el rectificador de corriente f, un rectificador de selenio m o de vapor de mercurio m para las lámparas de proyección f
– *rectifier, a selenium or mercury vapour rectifier for the projection lamps*
**19** el amplificador
– *amplifier*
**20** el operador de proyección f
– *projectionist*
**21** la mesa rebobinadora, para el rebobinado de la película
– *rewind bench for rewinding the film*
**22** la cola para película f
– *film cement (splicing cement)*

**23** el proyector de diapositivas, para diapositivas de publicidad f
– *slide projector for advertisements*
**24-52  proyectores** m **de películas** f
– *film projectors*
**24** el proyector de películas f sonoras
– *sound projector, a film projector, a cinema projector (theatre projector,* Am. *movie projector)*
**25-38** el mecanismo para el paso de la película
– *projector mechanism*
**25** los tambores protegidos contra incendios m, con refrigeración f por una corriente de aceite m
– *fireproof reel drums (spool boxes) with circulating oil cooling system*
**26** el tambor dentado para desenrollar la película
– *feed sprocket (supply sprocket)*
**27** el tambor dentado para enrollar la película
– *take-up sprocket*
**28** el lector del sonido magnético
– *magnetic head cluster*
**29** el rodillo de cambio m, con dispositivo m de encuadre m
– *guide roller (guiding roller) with framing control*
**30** la rueda tensora, para la preestabilización de la película; *también:* el contacto de rotura f de la película
– *loop former for smoothing out the intermittent movement; also: film break detector*

**31** el deslizador de la película
– *film path*
**32** la bobina de la película (el carrete)
– *film reel (film spool)*
**33** el rollo de la película
– *reel of film*
**34** la ventanilla de proyección *f,* con turbosoplador *f* refrigerador de la película
– *film gate (picture gate, projector gate) with cooling fan*
**35** el objetivo de proyección *f*
– *projection lens (projector lens)*
**36** el eje de desbobinado *m*
– *feed spindle*
**37** el eje de fricción *f* del bobinado
– *take-up spindle with friction drive*
**38** el mecanismo Cruz de Malta
– *maltese cross mechanism (maltese cross movement, Geneva movement)*
**39-44** la cámara de lámparas *f*
– *lamphouse*
**39** la lámpara reflectora de arco *m,* con espejo *m* hueco no esférico y magneto *f* sopladora para la estabilización del arco voltaico (*también:* la lámpara de xenón *m* de alta presión *f*)
– *mirror arc lamp, with aspherical (non-spherical) concave mirror and blowout magnet for stabilizing the arc; also: high-pressure xenon arc lamp*
**40** el carbón positivo
– *positive carbon (positive carbon rod)*

**41** el carbón negativo
– *negative carbon (negative carbon rod)*
**42** el arco luminoso (el arco voltaico, el arco eléctrico)
– *arc*
**43** el portacarbón
– *carbon rod holder*
**44** el cráter del carbón
– *crater (carbon crater)*
**45** el grupo fotoeléctrico de producción *f* del sonido [previsto también para la reproducción estereofónica por muchos canales *m* de tonos *m* de luz *f* y para el sistema de contrafase *f*]
– *optical sound unit [also designed for multi-channel optical stereophonic sound and for push-pull sound tracks]*
**46** la óptica de lectura del sonido
– *sound optics*
**47** la cabeza sonora (la cabeza de lectura del sonido)
– *sound head*
**48** la lámpara de sonido *m,* en su alojamiento *m*
– *exciter lamp in housing*
**49** la célula fotoeléctrica (en el eje hueco)
– *photocell in hollow drum*
**50** el aparato accesorio del sonido magnético de cuatro canales *m*
– *attachable four-track magnetic sound unit (penthouse head, magnetic sound head)*

**51** la cabeza magnética de cuatro pistas *f*
– *four-track magnetic head*
**52** el proyector de películas *f* estrechas, para cine *m* ambulante
– *narrow-gauge (Am. narrow-gage) cinema projector for mobile cinema*

**1-39 las cámaras cinematográficas**
- *motion picture cameras (film cameras)*
1 la cámara para película f normal (la cámara para película f de 35 mm)
- *standard-gauge (Am. standard-gage) motion picture camera (standard-gauge, Am. standard-gage, 35 mm camera)*
2 el objetivo (la óptica de toma f de vistas f)
- *lens (object lens, taking lens)*
3 el compendio (el parasol), con portafiltros m y portaocultadores
- *lens hood (sunshade) with matte box*
4 el ocultador
- *matte (mask)*
5 el tubo contra luz f
- *lens hood barrel*
6 el ocular del visor
- *viewfinder eyepiece*
7 el reglaje del ocular
- *eyepiece control ring*
8 el regulador de abertura f para el diafragma de sectores m
- *opening control for the segment disc (disk) shutter*
9 la caja del cassette de la película
- *magazine housing*
10 el riel del parasol
- *slide bar for the lens hood*
11 la palanca de mano f
- *control arm (control lever)*
12 la plataforma de panorámica f horizontal y vertical
- *pan and tilt head*
13 el trípode de madera f
- *wooden tripod*
14 la graduación
- *degree scale*

15 la cámara aislada contra el ruido
- *soundproof (blimped) motion picture camera (film camera)*
16-18 la caja protectora del ruido
- *soundproof housing (blimp)*
16 la parte superior protectora del ruido
- *upper section of the soundproof housing*
17 la parte inferior protectora del ruido
- *lower section of the soundproof housing*
18 la pared lateral protectora del ruido
- *open sidewall of the soundproof housing*
19 el objetivo de la cámara
- *camera lens*
20 la cámara ligera
- *lightweight professional motion picture camera*
21 la empuñadura
- *grip (handgrip)*
22 la palanca para regular el zoom
- *zooming lever*
23 el objetivo del zoom con distancia f focal continuamente variable
- *zoom lens (variable focus lens, varifocal lens) with infinitely variable focus*
24 la empuñadura para disparar
- *handgrip with shutter release*
25 la puerta de la cámara
- *camera door*
26 la cámara sonora (la cámara de reportaje m) para registro m simultáneo de la imagen y del sonido
- *sound camera (newsreel camera) for recording sound and picture*
27 la caja protectora de los ruidos
- *soundproof housing (blimp)*

28 la ventana de observación del contador de imágenes f y de los indicadores
- *window for the frame counters and indicator scales*
29 el cable de sincronización (el cable del sonido piloto)
- *pilot tone cable (sync pulse cable)*
30 el generador del sonido piloto
- *pilot tone generator (signal generator, pulse generator)*
31 la cámara de película f estrecha, una cámara de 16 mm
- *professional narrow-gauge (Am. narrow-gage) motion picture camera, a 16 mm camera*
32 el revólver de objetivos (el portaobjetivos)
- *lens turret (turret head)*
33 el bloqueo de la caja
- *housing lock*
34 el borde del ocular
- *eyecup*
35 la cámara de gran velocidad f, una cámara especial para película f estrecha
- *high-speed camera, a special narrow-gauge (Am. narrow-gage) camera*
36 la palanca del zoom
- *zooming lever*
37 el soporte de hombro m
- *rifle grip*
38 la empuñadura de disparo m (el disparador)
- *handgrip with shutter release*
39 el fuelle del parasol
- *lens hood bellows*

1-6 las cinco posiciones
- *the five positions (ballet positions)*
1 la primera posición
- *first position*
2 la segunda posición
- *second position*
3 la tercera posición
- *third position*
4 la cuarta posición [avanzada]
- *fourth position [open]*
5 la cuarta posición [cruzada; la quinta posición abierta]
- *fourth position [crossed; extended fifth position]*
6 la quinta posición
- *fifth position*
7-10 les ports de bras (la posición de los brazos)
- *ports de bras (arm positions)*
7 le port de bras à coté (la posición de brazo *m* al lado)
- *port de bras à coté*
8 le port de bras en bas (la posición de brazo *m* en bajo)
- *port de bras en bas*
9 le port de bras en avant (la posición de brazo *m* adelante)
- *port de bras en avant*
10 le port de bras en haut (la posición de brazo *m* en alto)
- *port de bras en haut*
11 le degagé à la quatrième devant (la salida de la cuarta por delante)
- *dégagé à la quatrième devant*

12 le degagé à la quatrième derrière (la salida de la cuarta por detrás)
- *dégagé à la quatrième derrière*
13 el effacé
- *effacé*
14 el sur le cou-de-pied
- *sur le cou-de-pied*
15 el écarté
- *écarté*
16 el croisé (el cruzado)
- *croisé*
17 la attitude (la posición)
- *attitude*
18 el arabesco
- *arabesque*
19 la punta
- *à pointe (on full point)*
20 el spagat (la caída con piernas *f* abiertas)
- *splits*
21 la cabriole (la cabriola, el salto en el aire)
- *cabriole (capriole)*
22 el entrechat (el entrechat quatre, el cruce con cuatro cambios *m*)
- *entrechat (entrechat quatre)*
23 la preparación [para la pirueta, por ejemplo]
- *préparation [e.g. for a pirouette]*
24 la pirouette (la pirueta, la vuelta)
- *pirouette*
25 le corps de ballet (el cuerpo de ballet *m*)
- *corps de ballet*

26 la bailarina de ballet *m*
- *ballerina (ballet dancer)*
27-28 le pas de trois (el paso de tres)
- *pas de trois*
27 la primera bailarina
- *prima ballerina*
28 el primer bailarín
- *principal male dancer (leading soloist)*
29 el tutú (la falda corta de bailarina *f*)
- *tutu*
30 la zapatilla de punta *f*, una zapatilla de ballet *m*
- *point shoe, a ballet shoe (ballet slipper)*
31 el vestido de bailarina *f*
- *ballet skirt*

**1-4 las aberturas de telón**
- *types of curtain operation*
**1** la abertura a la griega
- *draw curtain [side parting]*
**2** la abertura a la italiana
- *tableau curtain [bunching up sideways]*
**3** la abertura a la alemana
- *fly curtain [vertical ascent]*
**4** la abertura combinada a la griega-alemana
- *combined fly and draw curtain*
**5-11 el vestíbulo del guardarropa**
- *cloakroom hall (Am. checkroom hall)*
**5** el guardarropa
- *cloakroom (Am. checkroom)*
**6** la encargada del guardarropa
- *cloakroom attendant (Am. checkroom attendant)*
**7** la contraseña del guardarropa (el número del guardarropa)
- *cloakroom ticket (Am. check)*
**8** el espectador
- *playgoer (theatregoer, Am. theatergoer)*
**9** los gemelos de teatro *m*
- *opera glass (opera glasses)*
**10** el revisor
- *commissionaire*
**11** la entrada de teatro *m* (*Amér.*: el boleto), un billete de admisión *f*
- *theatre (Am. theater) ticket, an admission ticket*
**12-13 el foyer** (la sala *f* de descanso *m*)
- *foyer (lobby, crush room)*
**12** el acomodador
- *usher; form.: box attendant*
**13** el programa
- *programme (Am. program)*
**14-27 la sala de teatro *m***
- *auditorium and stage*
**14** el escenario
- *stage*
**15** el proscenio
- *proscenium*
**16-20 la sala de espectadores *m*** (la sala del auditorio)
- *auditorium*
**16** la galería (el gallinero, el paraíso; *Mé.:* la chilla)
- *gallery (balcony)*
**17** el segundo palco (el anfiteatro)
- *upper circle*
**18** el primer palco (el principal)
- *dress circle (Am. balcony, mezzanine)*
**19** el patio de butacas *f* (la platea; *Mé.:* el mosquete)
- *front stalls*
**20** la butaca (la butaca de espectador *m*, la butaca de teatro *m*)
- *seat (theatre seat, Am. theater seat)*

**21-27 el ensayo**
- *rehearsal (stage rehearsal)*
**21** el coro del teatro
- *chorus*
**22** el cantante
- *singer*
**23** la cantante
- *singer*
**24** el foso de la orquesta
- *orchestra pit*
**25** la orquesta
- *orchestra*
**26** el director
- *conductor*
**27** la batuta (del director de orquesta *f*)
- *baton (conductor's baton)*
**28-42 la sala de pintura *f*,** un taller de teatro *m*
- *paint room, a workshop*
**28** el tramoyista
- *stagehand (scene shifter)*
**29** el puente de trabajo *m*
- *catwalk (bridge)*
**30** la pieza de quitaipón (las decoraciones *f* movibles)
- *set piece*
**31** el refuerzo
- *reinforcing struts*
**32** el aplique (el forrado)
- *built piece (built unit)*
**33** el telón de fondo *m*
- *backcloth (backdrop)*
**34** la caja de pinturas *f* portátil
- *portable box for paint containers*
**35** el pintor de escenarios *m*, un pintor de decorados *m*
- *scene painter, a scenic artist*
**36** la paleta móvil
- *paint trolley*
**37** el escenógrafo
- *stage designer (set designer)*
**38** el encargado del vestuario
- *costume designer*
**39** el diseño de un traje
- *design for a costume*
**40** el figurín
- *sketch for a costume*
**41** la maqueta de escenario *m*
- *model stage*
**42** la maqueta de decoración *f*
- *model of the set*
**43-52 el vestuario de los artistas**
- *dressing room*
**43** el espejo para el maquillaje
- *dressing room mirror*
**44** el peinador de maquillaje *m*
- *make-up gown*
**45** la mesa de maquillaje *m*
- *make-up table*
**46** la barrita (el lápiz de maquillaje *m*)
- *greasepaint stick*
**47** el maestro maquillador
- *chief make-up artist (chief make-up man)*
**48** el maquillador (el peluquero de teatro *m*)
- *make-up artist and hairstylist*

**49** la peluca
- *wig*
**50** los accesorios
- *props (properties)*
**51** el vestido teatral
- *theatrical costume*
**52** la lámpara de llamada *f* a escena *f*
- *call light*

**1-60 la caja de escena con la maquinaria** (la maquinaria superior – bambalina *f* – y la maquinaria inferior – fosos *m* –)
– *stagehouse [showing machinery in the flies and below stage]*
1 el puesto de control *m*
– *control room*
2 el pupitre de control *m* con dispositivos *m* de memoria *f* para los efectos luminosos
– *control console (lighting console, lighting control console) with preset control for presetting lighting effects*
3 el plano del puesto de control *m*
– *lighting plot (light plot)*
4 el telar
– *grid (gridiron)*
5 la galería de trabajo *m*
– *fly floor (fly gallery)*
6 el sistema de rociadura *f*, para la protección de incendios *m*
– *sprinkler system for fire prevention (for fire protection)*
7 el maestro (el encargado) del telar
– *fly man*
8 las cuerdas (del telón) del foro
– *fly lines (lines)*
9 el horizonte redondo (el ciclorama)
– *cyclorama*
10 el telón de fondo *m*
– *backcloth (backdrop, background)*
11 el arco, una pieza colgada intermedia
– *arch, a drop cloth*
12 la bambalina
– *border*
13 la caja del alumbrado superior
– *compartment (compartment-type, compartmentalized) batten (Am. border light)*
14 el cuerpo de alumbrado *m* de escena *f*
– *stage lighting units (stage lights)*
15 el alumbrado horizontal (el alumbrado (del telón) de fondo *m*)
– *horizon lights (backdrop lights)*
16 los reflectores de escena *f* móviles
– *adjustable acting area lights (acting area spotlights)*
17 los aparatos proyectores de imágenes *f*
– *scenery projectors (projectors)*
18 el cañón de agua *f* (un dispositivo de seguridad *f*)
– *monitor (water cannon), a piece of safety equipment*

19 el puente de iluminación *f* móvil
– *travelling (Am. traveling) lighting bridge (travelling lighting gallery)*
20 el electricista
– *lighting operator (lighting man)*
21 el reflector de proscenio *m*
– *portal spotlight (tower spotlight)*
22 el telón de boca *f*
– *adjustable proscenium*
23 la cortina de escena *f*
– *curtain (theatrical curtain)*
24 el telón de hierro *m* (el telón metálico)
– *iron curtain (safety curtain, fire curtain)*
25 el proscenio
– *forestage (apron)*
26 las candilejas
– *footlight (footlights, floats)*
27 la concha del apuntador
– *prompt box*
28 el apuntador (*Ec. y Guat.*: el soplador; *Amér. Central*: el soplón)
– *prompter*
29 el pupitre de transpunte *m*
– *stage manager's desk*
30 el transpunte (el registrador de escena *f*)
– *stage director (stage manager)*
31 el escenario giratorio
– *revolving stage*
32 el escotillón
– *trap opening*
33 la tapa del escotillón
– *lift (Am. elevator)*
34 el tablado del escotillón, un tablado escalonado
– *bridge (Am. elevator), a rostrum*
35 los elementos de decoración *f*
– *pieces of scenery*
36 la escena
– *scene*
37 el actor (el comediante)
– *actor*
38 la actriz (la comedianta)
– *actress*
39 los figurantes (los comparsas)
– *extras (supers, supernumeraries)*
40 el director artístico (el director de escena *f*)
– *director (producer)*
41 el guión (el texto)
– *prompt book (prompt script)*
42 la mesa del director de escena *f*
– *director's table (producer's table)*
43 el ayudante del director de escena *f*
– *assistant director (assistant producer)*
44 el libro de escena *f*
– *director's script (producer's script)*
45 el jefe de escenografía *f*
– *stage carpenter*
46 el tramoyista
– *stagehand (scene shifter)*

47 la pieza de quitaipón *m*
– *set piece*
48 el reflector de lente *f* de espejo *m*
– *mirror spot (mirror spotlight)*
49 el panel giratorio de filtros *m* coloreados (con disco *m* de color *m*)
– *automatic filter change [with colour filters (colour mediums, gelatines)]*
50 la instalación de prensa *f* hidráulica
– *hydraulic plant room*
51 el depósito de agua *f*
– *water tank*
52 el tubo de succión *f*
– *suction pipe*
53 la bomba de presión *f* hidráulica
– *hydraulic pump*
54 la tubería bajo presión *f*
– *pressure pipe*
55 la cámara (el acumulador) de presión *f*
– *pressure tank (accumulator)*
56 el manómetro de contacto *m*
– *pressure gauge (Am. gage)*
57 el indicador del nivel del agua *f*
– *level indicator (liquid level indicator)*
58 la palanca de control *m*
– *control lever*
59 el maquinista (el mecánico, el jefe de máquinas)
– *operator*
60 los pistones hidráulicos (los émbolos)
– *rams*

1 el bar
– *bar*
2 la camarera del bar (*Col.:* la prendedera)
– *barmaid*
3 el taburete de bar *m*
– *bar stool*
4 el estante de botellas *f*
– *shelf for bottles*
5 el estante de vasos *m*
– *shelf for glasses*
6 el vaso para cerveza
– *beer glass*
7 el vaso para vino *m* y para licor *m*
– *wine and liqueur glasses*
8 el grifo distribuidor de cerveza *f*
– *beer tap (tap)*
9 el mostrador del bar (la barra)
– *bar*
10 el frigorífico
– *refrigerator (fridge,* Am. *icebox)*
11 las lámparas del bar
– *bar lamps*
12 la iluminación indirecta
– *indirect lighting*
13 la batería de proyectores *m*
– *colour* (Am. *color*) *organ (clavilux)*

14 la iluminación de la pista de baile *m*
– *dance floor lighting*
15 la caja del altavoz
– *speaker (loudspeaker)*
16 la pista de baile
– *dance floor*
17-18 la pareja
– *dancing couple*
17 la chica (la joven) que baila
– *dancer*
18 el chico (el joven) que baila
– *dancer*
19 el tocadiscos (*Amér.:* el pick-up)
– *record player*
20 el micrófono (*fam.:* el micro)
– *microphone*
21 el magnetófono
– *tape recorder*
22-23 el equipo de esterofonía *f* (la cadena hi-fi)
– *stereo system (stereo equipment)*
22 el tuner (el sintonizador)
– *tuner*
23 el amplificador
– *amplifier*
24 los discos
– *records (discs)*
25 el discjockey
– *disc jockey*

26 el pupitre de mezcla *f*
– *mixing console (mixing desk, mixer)*
27 la pandereta
– *tambourine*
28 la pared de cristal *m*
– *mirrored wall*
29 el revestimiento del techo
– *ceiling tiles*
30 el sistema de aireación *f*
– *ventilators*
31 los servicios
– *toilets (lavatories, WC)*
32 la bebida larga (la copa larga, el long drink)
– *long drink*
33 el cóctel
– *cocktail (*Am. *highball)*

1-33 el cabaret (el nightclub)
- *nightclub (night spot)*
1 el guardarropa
- *cloakroom (Am. checkroom)*
2 la señorita del guardarropa
- *cloakroom attendant (Am. checkroom attendant)*
3 la orquesta de baile *m*
- *band*
4 el clarinete
- *clarinet*
5 el clarinetista
- *clarinettist (Am. clarinetist)*
6 la trompeta
- *trumpet*
7 el trompetista
- *trumpeter*
8 la guitarra
- *guitar*
9 el guitarrista
- *guitarist (guitar player)*
10 la batería
- *drums*
11 el batería
- *drummer*
12 la caja del altavoz (el altavoz)
- *speaker (loudspeaker)*
13 el bar
- *bar*
14 la camarera del bar (*Col.:* la prendedera)
- *barmaid*

15 el mostrador del bar (la barra)
- *bar*
16 el taburete de bar *m*
- *bar stool*
17 el magnetófono
- *tape recorder*
18 el receptor (de radio *f*, el aparato de radio *f*, la radio)
- *receiver*
19 las bebidas alcohólicas
- *spirits*
20 el proyector de películas *f* estrechas para películas *f* pornográficas (películas *f* eróticas)
- *cine projector for porno films (sex films, blue movies)*
21 la caja de la pantalla con la pantalla
- *box containing screen*
22 la escena
- *stage*
23 la iluminación de la escena
- *stage lighting*
24 el reflector de escena
- *spotlight*
25 la iluminación de la bambalina
- *festoon lighting*
26 la bombilla de la bambalina
- *festoon lamp (lamp, light bulb)*
27-32 el striptease (el número del desnudo)
- *striptease act (striptease number)*

27 la artista de striptease *m*
- *striptease artist (stripper)*
28 la liga
- *suspender (Am. garter)*
29 el sostén (el sujetador)
- *brassière (bra)*
30 la estola de piel *f* (el cuello de piel *f*)
- *fur stole*
31 los guantes
- *gloves*
32 la media
- *stocking*
33 la animadora
- *hostess*

**1-33 la corrida de toros**
- *bullfight (corrida, corrida de toros)*
1 el quiebro
- *mock bullfight*
2 el novillero (el torero principiante)
- *novillero*
3 la imitación de toro (un carro en forma *f* de toro *m*)
- *mock bull (dummy bull)*
4 el banderillero principiante
- *novice banderillero (apprentice banderillero)*
5 la plaza de toros (la arena, el ruedo) [esquema]
- *bullring (plaza de toros) [diagram]*
6 la entrada principal
- *main entrance*
7 los palcos
- *boxes*
8 los tendidos (si son cubiertos, en la parte superior: las andanadas)
- *stands*
9 el ruedo (la arena)
- *arena (ring)*
10 la puerta de los toreros
- *bullfighters' entrance*
11 la puerta del toril (la puerta de los corrales)
- *torril door*
12 la puerta de salida *f* para los toros muertos
- *exit gate for killed bulls*
13 el desolladero
- *slaughterhouse*
14 el toril (el corral, el chiquero)
- *bull pens (corrals)*
15 el patio de los caballos
- *paddock*
16 el picador
- *lancer on horseback (picador)*
17 la pica (la vara, la garrocha)
- *lance (pike pole, javelin)*
18 el caballo encaparazonado
- *armoured (Am. armored) horse*
19 la coraza de hierro *m* de la pierna (la mona)
- *leg armour (Am. armor)*
20 el sombrero redondo del picador (el sombrero castoreño)
- *picador's round hat*
21 el banderillero, un torero, un peón
- *banderillero, a torero*
22 las banderillas
- *banderillas (barbed darts)*
23 la faja
- *shirtwaist*
24 el pase
- *bullfight*
25 el matador (el espada), un torero
- *matador (swordsman), a torero*
26 la coleta (la moña)
- *queue, a distinguishing mark of the matador*

27 la muleta (el trapo; *anál.*: la capa, el capote)
- *red cloak (capa)*
28 el toro de lidia *f* (el toro bravo)
- *fighting bull*
29 la montera
- *montera [hat made of tiny black silk chenille balls]*
30 la estocada
- *killing the bull (kill)*
31 el matador de corridas *f* benéficas [sin traje *m* de luces *f*]
- *matador in charity performances [without professional uniform]*
32 el estoque (la espada)
- *estoque (sword)*
33 la muleta (el trapo; *anál.*: la capa, el capote)
- *muleta*
**34 el rodeo**
- *rodeo*
35 el toro joven (el novillo)
- *young bull*
36 el vaquero
- *cowboy*
37 el sombrero del vaquero (el sombrero tejano)
- *stetson (stetson hat)*
38 el pañuelo de cuello *m*
- *scarf (necktie)*
39 el jinete de rodeo *m*
- *rodeo rider*
40 el lazo
- *lasso*

**1-2 notación ∫ medieval**
- *medieval (mediaeval) notes*
**1** la notación coral (la notación cuadrada)
- *plainsong notation (neumes, neums, pneumes, square notation)*
**2** la notación mensural
- *mensural notation*
**3-7 las notas**
- *musical note (note)*
**3** la cabeza (el punto, el neuma)
- *note head*
**4** la vírgula (el tallo, el vástago)
- *note stem (note tail)*
**5** el corchete
- *hook*
**6** la barra
- *stroke*
**7** el punto de alargamiento *m* (el puntillo)
- *dot indicating augmentation of note's value*
**8-11 las claves**
- *clefs*
**8** la clave de sol *m*
- *treble clef (G-clef, violin clef)*
**9** la clave de fa *m*
- *bass clef (F-clef)*
**10** la clave de do *m*, para viola *f*
- *alto clef (C-clef)*
**11** la clave de do *m*, para violencelo *m*
- *tenor clef*
**12-19 los valores de las notas**
- *note values*
**12** la breve (la cuadrada)
- *breve (brevis, Am. double-whole note)*
**13** la semibreve (la redonda)
- *semibreve (Am. whole note)*
**14** la mínima (la blanca)
- *minim (Am. half note)*
**15** la negra
- *crotchet (Am. quarter note)*
**16** la corchea
- *quaver (Am. eighth note)*
**17** la semicorchea
- *semiquaver (Am. sixteenth note)*
**18** la fusa
- *demisemiquaver (Am. thirty-second note)*
**19** la semifusa
- *hemidemisemiquaver (Am. sixty-fourth note)*
**20-27 los silencios** (las pausas)
- *rests*
**20** el silencio de cuadrada *f*
- *breve rest*
**21** el silencio de redonda *f*
- *semibreve rest (Am. whole rest)*
**22** el silencio de blanca *f*
- *minim rest (Am. half rest)*
**23** el silencio de negra *f*
- *crotchet rest (Am. quarter rest)*
**24** el silencio de corchea *f*
- *quaver rest (Am. eighth rest)*
**25** el silencio de semicorchea *f*
- *semiquaver rest (Am. sixteenth rest)*
**26** el silencio de fusa *f*
- *demisemiquaver rest (Am. thirty-second rest)*
**27** el silencio de semifusa *f*
- *hemidemisemiquaver rest (Am. sixty-fourth rest)*
**28-42 el compás** (el tiempo)
- *time (time signatures, measure, Am. meter)*

**28** el dos por ocho
- *two-eight time*
**29** el dos por cuatro
- *two-four time*
**30** el dos por dos
- *two-two time*
**31** el cuatro por ocho
- *four-eight time*
**32** el cuatro por cuatro
- *four-four time (common time)*
**33** el cuatro por dos
- *four-two time*
**34** el seis por ocho
- *six-eight time*
**35** el seis por cuatro
- *six-four time*
**36** el tres por ocho
- *three-eight time*
**37** el tres por cuatro
- *three-four time*
**38** el tres por dos
- *three-two time*
**39** el nueve por ocho
- *nine-eight time*
**40** el nueve por cuatro
- *nine-four time*
**41** el cinco por cuatro
- *five-four time*
**42** la barra de compás *m*
- *bar (bar line, measure line)*
**43-44 el pentagrama**
- *staff (stave)*
**43** la línea
- *line of the staff*
**44** el espacio (la línea y espacio *m*)
- *space*
**45-49 las escalas** (las gamas)
- *scales*
**45** la escala de do *m* mayor (la escala diatónica mayor); sonidos *m* fundamentales: do, re, mi, fa, sol, la, si, do
- *C major scale naturals: c, d, e, f, g, a, b, c*
**46** la escala de la *m* menor [natural]; notas fundamentales: la, si, do, re, mi, fa, sol, la
- *A minor scale [natural] naturals: a, b, c, d, e, f, g, a*
**47** la escala de la *m* menor [armónica]
- *A minor scale [harmonic]*
**48** la escala de la *m* menor [melódica] (la escala diatónica menor)
- *A minor scale [melodic]*
**49** la escala cromática
- *chromatic scale*
**50-54 las alteraciones** (los accidentales)
- *accidentals (inflections); also: key signatures*
**50-51 los signos de elevación *f***
- *signs indicating the raising of a note*
**50** el sostenido (la elevación de un semitono)
- *sharp [raising the note a semitone or half-step]*
**51** el doble sostenido (la elevación de dos semitonos *m*)
- *double sharp [raising the note a tone or full-step]*
**52-53 los signos que bajan la nota**
- *signs indicating the lowering of a note*
**52** el bemol (la bajada de un semitono)
- *flat [lowering the note a semitone or half-step]*

**53** el doble bemol (la bajada de dos semitonos *m*)
- *double flat [lowering the note a tone or full-step]*
**54** el becuadro
- *natural*
**55-68 las tonalidades** (tonalidades *m* mayores y sus relativas tonalidades *m* menores; con las mismas alteraciones)
- *keys [major keys and the related minor keys having the same signature]*
**55** do *m* mayor (la *m* menor)
- *C major (A minor)*
**56** sol *m* mayor (mi *m* menor)
- *G major (E minor)*
**57** re *m* mayor (si *m* menor)
- *D major (B minor)*
**58** la *m* mayor (fa *m* sostenido menor)
- *A major (F sharp minor)*
**59** mi *m* mayor (do *m* sostenido menor)
- *E major (C sharp minor)*
**60** si *m* mayor (sol *m* sostenido menor)
- *B major (G sharp minor)*
**61** fa *m* sostenido mayor (re *m* sostenido menor)
- *F sharp major (D sharp minor)*
**62** do *m* mayor (la *m* menor)
- *C major (A minor)*
**63** fa *m* mayor (re *m* menor)
- *F major (D minor)*
**64** si *m* bemol mayor (sol *m* menor)
- *B flat major (G minor)*
**65** mi *m* bemol mayor (do *m* menor)
- *E flat major (C minor)*
**66** la *m* bemol mayor (fa *m* menor)
- *A flat major (F minor)*
**67** re *m* bemol mayor (si *m* bemol menor)
- *D flat major (B flat minor)*
**68** sol *m* bemol mayor (mi *m* bemol menor)
- *G flat major (E flat minor)*

# 321 Notación musical II

## Musical Notation II

**1-5 el acorde**
- *chord*
**1-4** los acordes perfectos
(acordes *m* de quinta *f*, tríadas
*f*)
- *triad*
**1** el acorde perfecto mayor
- *major triad*
**2** el acorde perfecto menor
- *minor triad*
**3** el acorde de quinta *f*
disminuida
- *diminished triad*
**4** el acorde de quinta *f*
aumentada
- *augmented triad*
**5** el acorde de séptima *f*
- *chord of four notes, a chord of
the seventh (seventh chord,
dominant seventh chord)*
**6-13 los intervalos**
- *intervals*
**6** el unísono
- *unison (unison interval)*
**7** la segunda mayor
- *major second*
**8** la tercera mayor
- *major third*
**9** la cuarta
- *perfect fourth*
**10** la quinta
- *perfect fifth*
**11** la sexta mayor
- *major sixth*
**12** la séptima mayor
- *major seventh*
**13** la octava
- *perfect octave*
**14-22 los adornos**
- *ornaments (graces, grace notes)*
**14** la apoyatura larga
- *long appoggiatura*
**15** la apoyatura breve
- *acciaccatura (short
appoggiatura)*
**16** la apoyatura doble
- *slide*
**17** el trino sin mordente *m*
- *trill (shake) without turn*
**18** el trino con mordente *m*
- *trill (shake) with turn*
**19** el mordente superior (el
semimordente, el mordente
imperfecto)
- *upper mordent (inverted
mordent, pralltriller)*
**20** el mordente inferior
- *lower mordent (mordent)*
**21** el gruppetto
- *turn*
**22** el arpegio
- *arpeggio*
**23-26** otros signos *m* de notación *f*
- *other signs in musical notation*
**23** el tresillo, *por analogía:* el
dosillo (el bisillo), el cuatrillo,
el cinquillo (el quintillo), el
seisillo y el septillo

- *triplet;* corresponding
groupings: *duplet (couplet),
quadruplet, quintuplet, sextolet
(sextuplet), septolet (septuplet,
septimole)*
**24** la ligadura
- *tie (bind)*
**25** el calderón (la fermata), un
signo de duración *f*
- *pause (pause sign)*
**26** la doble barra *f* de repetición *f*
- *repeat mark*
**27-41 las indicaciones de
movimiento *m* (de velocidad *f*)**
- *expression marks (signs of
relative intensity)*
**27** el acento
- *marcato (marcando, markiert,
attack, strong accent)*
**28** presto (rápido)
- *presto (quick, fast)*
**29** portato
- *portato (lourer, mezzo staccato,
carried)*
**30** tenuto (manteniendo el
movimiento sin acelerar)
- *tenuto (held)*
**31** crescendo (aumentando)
- *crescendo (increasing gradually
in power)*
**32** decrescendo (disminuyendo)
- *decrescendo (diminuendo,
decreasing or diminishing
gradually in power)*
**33** legato (ligado)
- *legato (bound)*
**34** staccato (punteado)
- *staccato (detached)*
**35** piano (suave)
- *piano (soft)*
**36** pianissimo (muy suave)
- *pianissimo (very soft)*
**37** pianissimo piano (con la
máxima suavidad posible)
- *pianissimo piano (as soft as
possible)*
**38** forte (fuerte)
- *forte (loud)*
**39** fortíssimo (muy fuerte)
- *fortissimo (very loud)*
**40** forte fortíssimo (con la máxima
fuerza posible)
- *forte fortissimo (double
fortissimo, as loud as possible)*
**41** fortepiano (se ataca fuerte y se
continúa suave)
- *forte piano (loud and
immediately soft again)*
**42-50 la escala musical**
- *divisions of the compass*
**42** la subcontraoctava
- *subcontra octave (double contra
octave)*
**43** la contraoctava
- *contra octave*
**44** la primera octava
- *great octave*
**45** la segunda octava
- *small octave*

**46** la tercera octava
- *one-line octave*
**47** la cuarta octava
- *two-line octave*
**48** la quinta octava
- *three-line octave*
**49** la sexta octava
- *four-line octave*
**50** la séptima octava
- *five-line octave*

1  la lur, una trompeta de bronce *m*
- *lur, a bronze trumpet*
2  la flauta de Pan (la siringa)
- *panpipes (Pandean pipes, syrinx)*
3  la diaula, una flauta doble
- *aulos, a double shawm*
4  el aulos
- *aulos pipe*
5  la phorbeia (sujetador *m* de los labios)
- *phorbeia (peristomion, capistrum, mouth band)*
6  el cromorno
- *crumhorn (crummhorn, cromorne, krumbhorn, krummhorn)*
7  la flauta de pico *m* (la flauta dulce; *Perú:* la chaina; *Ec.:* el pijuano; *Chile:* la pivilca)
- *recorder (fipple flute)*
8  la cornamusa; *anál.:* la gaita, la musette
- *bagpipe;* sim.: *musette*
9  el saco del aire
- *bag*
10  el caramillo melódico
- *chanter (melody pipe)*
11  los bordones (para el acompañamiento)
- *drone (drone pipe)*
12  la cornete curvada
- *curved cornett (zink)*
13  la serpiente
- *serpent*
14  la chirimía; *más grande:* la bombarda (la dulzaina)
- *shawm (schalmeyes);* larger: *bombard (bombarde, pommer)*
15  la cítara; *anál. y más pequeña:* la lira
- *cythara (cithara);* sim. and smaller: *lyre*
16  el brazo de la caja
- *arm*
17  el puente
- *bridge*
18  la caja de resonancia *f*
- *sound box (resonating chamber, resonator)*
19  el plectro, una púa (*Chile:* la uñeta)
- *plectrum, a plucking device*
20  la pochette (el violín de bolsillo *m*, el violín de pequeño formato *m*)
- *kit (pochette), a miniature violin*
21  la cítara, un instrumento de cuerdas *f* punteadas; *anál.:* la pandora
- *cittern (cithern, cither, cister, citole), a plucked instrument;* sim.: *pandora (bandora, bandore)*
22  la rosa (la boca, la tarraja)
- *sound hole*
23  la viola, una viola de gamba *f; más grande:* el violón (el contrabajo; *Mé.:* el tololoche)

- *viol, e.g. descant viol, treble viol;* larger: *tenor viol, bass viol (viola da gamba, gamba)*
24  el arco de viola *f*
- *viol bow*
25  la zanfonía (la viella, la symphonia, la rotata, la chifonía, el organistrum)
- *hurdy-gurdy (vielle à roue, symphonia, armonie, organistrum)*
26  la rueda de fricción *f*
- *friction wheel*
27  la cubierta
- *wheel cover (wheel guard)*
28  el teclado
- *keyboard (keys)*
29  la caja de resonancia *f*
- *resonating body (resonator, sound box)*
30  las cuerdas melódicas
- *melody strings*
31  las cuerdas del bordón
- *drone strings (drones, bourdons)*
32  el cémbalo (el tímpano, el salterio, el dulcemele)
- *dulcimer*
33  el bastidor
- *rib (resonator wall)*
34  el macillo para el cémbalo de Valais
- *beater for the Valasian dulcimer*
35  el martillo para el cémbalo de Apenzelle
- *hammer (stick) for the Appenzell dulcimer*
36  el clavicordio; *clases:* el clavicordio ligado y el clavicordio independiente
- *clavichord;* kinds: *fretted or unfretted clavichord*
37  el mecanismo del clavicordio
- *clavichord mechanism*
38  la tecla
- *key (key lever)*
39  la palanca de balanza *f* (el soporte de la tecla)
- *balance rail*
40  la espiga guía
- *guiding blade*
41  la ranura guía
- *guiding slot*
42  el soporte (el apoyo)
- *resting rail*
43  la tangente (el martinete de latón *m*)
- *tangent*
44  la cuerda
- *string*
45  el clavicémbalo, un clavecín; *anál.:* la espineta (el virginal)
- *harpsichord (clavicembalo, cembalo), a wing-shaped stringed keyboard instrument;* sim.: *spinet (virginal)*
46  el teclado (manual) superior
- *upper keyboard (upper manual)*
47  el teclado (manual) inferior
- *lower keyboard (lower manual)*

48  el mecanismo del clavicémbalo
- *harpsichord mechanism*
49  la tecla
- *key (key lever)*
50  el saltador (el martinete)
- *jack*
51  la parrilla guía de los martinetes
- *slide (register)*
52  la lengüeta
- *tongue*
53  el plectro (el cañon de pluma *f*)
- *quill plectrum*
54  el apagador del sonido
- *damper*
55  la cuerda
- *string*
56  el órgano portátil (el órgano real); *más grande:* el órgano positivo
- *portative organ, a portable organ;* larger: *positive organ (positive)*
57  el tubo
- *pipe (flue pipe)*
58  el fuelle
- *bellows*

**1-62 los instrumentos de orquesta** *f*
- *orchestral instruments*
**1-27 los instrumentos de cuerda** *f*, los instrumentos de arco *m*
- *stringed instruments, bowed instruments*
1 el violín
- *violin*
2 el mástil (el mango) del violín
- *neck of the violin*
3 la caja de resonancia *f* (la caja del violín, el "barco")
- *resonating body (violin body, sound box of the violin)*
4 el costado
- *rib (side wall)*
5 el puente del violín
- *violin bridge*
6 la ranura en forma *f* de efe, una abertura acústica
- *F-hole, a sound hole*
7 el cordal (el ceja)
- *tailpiece*
8 el mentonero
- *chin rest*
9 las cuerdas (las cuerdas de violín *m*): la cuerda de sol, la cuerda de re, la cuerda de la, la cuerda de mi
- *strings (violin strings, fiddle strings): G-string, D-string, A-string, E-string*
10 la sordina
- *mute (sordino)*
11 la colofonia
- *resin (rosin, colophony)*
12 el arco de violín *m*
- *violin bow (bow)*
13 la nuez
- *nut (frog)*
14 la baqueta (la varilla; *Amér.*: el bolillo)
- *stick (bow stick)*
15 la mecha del arco de violín *m*, una mecha de cerdas *f* de caballo *m*
- *hair of the violin bow (horsehair)*
16 el violoncelo
- *violoncello (cello), a member of the da gamba violin family*
17 la voluta
- *scroll*
18 la clavija
- *tuning peg (peg)*
19 el clavijero
- *pegbox*
20 la ceja
- *nut*
21 el mástil (el mango)
- *fingerboard*
22 la púa (*Chile*: la uñeta)
- *spike (tailpin)*
23 el contrabajo (el violón; *Mé.*: el tololoche)
- *double bass (contrabass, violone, double bass viol, Am. bass)*
24 la tapa armónica
- *belly (top, sound- board)*
25 el costado
- *rib (side wall)*
26 el borde
- *purfling (inlay)*
27 la viola
- *viola*
**28-38 los instrumentos de viento-madera**
- *woodwind instruments (woodwinds)*

28 el fagote; *más grande:* el contrafagote
- *bassoon;* larger: *double bassoon (contrabassoon)*
29 la boquilla, con la lengüeta doble
- *tube with double reed*
30 el flautín (el piccolo)
- *piccolo (small flute, piccolo flute, flauto piccolo)*
31 la flauta mayor, una flauta travesera
- *flute (German flute), a cross flute (transverse flute, side-blown flute)*
32 la llave de la flauta
- *key*
33 el agujero
- *fingerhole*
34 el clarinete; *mayor:* el clarinete bajo (*Amér.*: la chirimía)
- *clarinet;* larger: *bass clarinet*
35 la llave
- *key (brille)*
36 la boquilla
- *mouthpiece*
37 el pabellón
- *bell*
38 el oboe; *variedades:* el oboe de amor *m*, los oboes tenor: el oboe de caccia, el corno inglés; el oboe barítono
- *oboe (hautboy); kinds: oboe d'amore; tenor oboes: oboe da caccia, cor anglais; heckelphone (baritone oboe)*
**39-48 los instrumentos de viento-metal**
- *brass instruments (brass)*
39 el cuerno tenor (el fiscorno), un cornetín
- *tenor horn*
40 el pistón (la válvula)
- *valve*
41 el corno de caza, una trompa de pistones *m*
- *French horn (horn, waldhorn), a valve horn*
42 el pabellón
- *bell*
43 la trompeta; *mayor:* trompeta baja; *más pequeña:* la corneta (de pistones *m*)
- *trumpet;* larger: *Bb cornet;* smaller: *cornet*
44 la tuba (el bombardón); *anál.:* el helicón, la tuba de contrabajo *m*
- *tuba (bombardon), a bass tuba; sim.: helicon (pellitone), contrabass tuba*
45 el pulsador
- *thumb hold*
46 el trombón de varas *f; variedades:* el trombón alto, el trombón tenor, el trombón bajo
- *trombone; kinds: alto trombone, tenor trombone, bass trombone*
47 la vara corredera
- *trombone slide (slide)*
48 el pabellón
- *bell*
**49-59 los instrumentos de percusión** *f*
- *percussion instruments*
49 el triángulo
- *triangle*
50 los platillos
- *cymbals*
**51-59 los instrumentos de membrana** *f*
- *membranophones*

51 el tambor pequeño (*Pan.*: el repicador; *Perú:* la tinya)
- *side drum (snare drum)*
52 la membrana (la piel, el parche)
- *drum head (head, upper head, batter head, vellum)*
53 el tornillo tensor
- *tensioning screw*
54 la baqueta (el palillo de tambor *m; Amér.*: el bolillo)
- *drumstick*
55 el tambor mayor (el bombo)
- *bass drum (Turkish drum)*
56 la baqueta (el mazo)
- *stick (padded stick)*
57 el timbal, un timbal de tornillos *m; anál.:* el timbal mecánico
- *kettledrum (timpano), a screw-tensioned drum; sim.: machine drum (mechanically tuned drum)*
58 la membrana (la piel del timbal)
- *kettledrum skin (kettledrum vellum)*
59 el tornillo tensor para afinar
- *tuning screw*
60 el arpa *f*, una arpa de pedales *m*
- *harp, a pedal harp*
61 las cuerdas
- *strings*
62 el pedal
- *pedal*

**1-46 instrumentos *m* de música *f* popular**
– *popular musical instruments (folk instruments)*
**1-31 instrumentos de cuerda *f***
– *stringed instruments*
**1** el laúd; *mayores:* la tiorba, el chitarrone
– *lute; larger: theorbo, chitarrone*
**2** la caja de resonancia *f*
– *resonating body (resonator)*
**3** la tabla armónica
– *soundboard (belly, table)*
**4** el cordal (la ceja inferior)
– *string fastener (string holder)*
**5** la rosa (la tarraja)
– *sound hole (rose)*
**6** la cuerda, una cuerda de tripa *f*
– *string, a gut (catgut) string*
**7** el cuello
– *neck*
**8** el mástil (el mango)
– *fingerboard*
**9** el traste
– *fret*
**10** el clavijero
– *head (pegbox), a bent-back pegbox; sim.: swan-head pegbox*
**11** la clavija
– *tuning peg (peg, lute pin)*
**12** la guitarra
– *guitar*
**13** el cordal
– *string holder*
**14** la cuerda, una cuerda de tripa *f* o de perlón *m*
– *string, a gut (catgut) or nylon string*
**15** la caja de resonancia *f*
– *resonating body (resonating chamber, resonator, sound box)*
**16** la mandolina (*Amér. Central, Chile y Perú:* la bandolina)
– *mandolin (mandoline)*
**17** el cubrecuerdas
– *sleeve protector (cuff protector)*
**18** el cuello
– *neck*
**19** el clavijero
– *pegdisc*
**20** el plectro (la púa; *Chile:* la uñeta)
– *plectrum*
**21** la cítara
– *zither (plucked zither)*
**22** la tablilla de afinar
– *pin block (wrest pin block, wrest plank)*
**23** la clavija de afinamiento *m*
– *tuning pin (wrest pin)*
**24** las cuerdas melódicas (las cuerdas de tocar)
– *melody strings (fretted strings, stopped strings)*
**25** las cuerdas de acompañamiento *m* (las cuerdas bajas, los cuerdas de bordón *m; Arg. y Urug.:* las bordonas)
– *accompaniment strings (bass strings, unfretted strings, open strings)*
**26** la encorvadura de la caja de resonancia *f*
– *semicircular projection of the resonating sound box (resonating body)*
**27** el plectro de sortija *f*
– *ring plectrum*
**28** la balalaica
– *balalaika*
**29** el banjo
– *banjo*
**30** la caja-tambor
– *tambourine-like body*
**31** la piel (la membrana)
– *parchment membrane*

**32** la ocarina, una flauta ovoide
– *ocarina, a globular flute*
**33** la embocadura (la boquilla)
– *mouthpiece*
**34** el agujero
– *fingerhole*
**35** la armónica de boca *f*
– *mouth organ (harmonica)*
**36** el acordeón; *anál.:* la concertina, el bandoneón
– *accordion; sim.: piano accordion, concertina, bandoneon*
**37** el fuelle
– *bellows*
**38** el cierre del fuelle
– *bellows strap*
**39** el teclado-piano melódico
– *melody side (keyboard side, melody keys)*
**40** el teclado
– *keyboard (keys)*
**41** el registro de tiple *m*
– *treble stop (treble coupler, treble register)*
**42** la tecla del registro
– *stop lever*
**43** los botones de los bajos (la parte del acompañamiento)
– *bass side (accompaniment side, bass studs, bass press-studs, bass buttons)*
**44** el registro de los bajos
– *bass stop (bass coupler, bass register)*
**45** la pandereta; *anál.:* el pandero
– *tambourine*
**46** las castañuelas (las castañetas)
– *castanets*
**47-78 instrumentos de jazz *m***
– *jazz band instruments (dance band instruments)*
**47-58 instrumentos de percusión *f***
– *percussion instruments*
**47-54 la batería de jazz *m***
– *drum kit (drum set, drums)*
**47** el bombo (el tambor gordo; *Pan.:* el pujador)
– *bass drum*
**48** la caja clara (el tambor)
– *small tom-tom*
**49** el tom-tom
– *large tom-tom*
**50** el doble platillo agudo
– *high-hat cymbals (choke cymbals, Charleston cymbals, cup cymbals)*
**51** el platillo grave
– *cymbal*
**52** el soporte del platillo
– *cymbal stand (cymbal holder)*
**53** la escobilla de jazz *m*, una escobilla de metal *m*
– *wire brush*
**54** el mecanismo del pedal
– *pedal mechanism*
**55** la conga
– *conga drum (conga)*
**56** el círculo tensor
– *tension hoop*
**57** los timbales
– *timbales*
**58** los bongoes
– *bongo drums (bongos)*
**59** las maracas (*Bol.:* los maracos); *anál.:* los sonajeros de rumba *f*
– *maracas; sim.: shakers*
**60** el guiro
– *guiro*
**61** el xilófono; *anál.:* la marimba, el balafo
– *xylophone; form.: straw fiddle; sim.: marimbaphone (steel marimba), tubaphone*
**62** la lámina de madera *f*
– *wooden slab*
**63** la caja de resonancia *f*
– *resonating chamber (sound box)*

**64** el mazo (el percusor)
– *beater*
**65** la trompeta de jazz *m*
– *jazz trumpet*
**66** el pistón (la válvula)
– *valve*
**67** el gancho de apoyo *m* del dedo
– *finger hook*
**68** la sordina
– *mute (sordino)*
**69** el saxófono
– *saxophone*
**70** el pabellón
– *bell*
**71** el tubo de embocadura *f*
– *crook*
**72** la boquilla
– *mouthpiece*
**73** la guitarra de jazz *m*
– *struck guitar, a jazz guitar*
**74** la escotadura (para facilitar la digitación)
– *hollow to facilitate fingering*
**75** el vibráfono
– *vibraphone* (Am. *vibraharp*)
**76** el bastidor metálico
– *metal frame*
**77** la lámina de metal *m*
– *metal bar*
**78** el tubo metálico
– *tubular metal resonator*

1 **el piano** (el piano recto, el piano
vertical), un instrumento de
teclado *m; forma pequeña:* el
pianino; *formas antecesoras:* el
pantaleón, el clavicordio; la
celesta que tiene lengüetas *f* en
lugar de cuerdas *f*
– **piano** *(pianoforte, upright piano,
upright, vertical piano, spinet piano,
console piano), a keyboard
instrument (keyed instrument);*
smaller form: *cottage piano
(pianino);* earlier forms: *pantaleon;
celesta, with steel bars instead of
strings*
**2-18** la mecánica del piano
– *piano action (piano mechanism)*
2 el cuadro de hierro *m*
– *iron frame*
3 el martillo; *en conjunto:* el
mecanismo de percusión *f*
– *hammer;* collectively: *striking
mechanism*
**4-5** el teclado (las teclas del piano)
– *keyboard (piano keys)*
4 la tecla blanca (la tecla de
marfil *m*)
– *white key (ivory key)*
5 la tecla negra (la tecla de
ébano *m*)
– *black key (ebony key)*
6 la caja del piano
– *piano case*
7 las cuerdas del piano
– *strings (piano strings)*
**8-9** los pedales del piano
– *piano pedals*
8 el pedal derecho (el pedal fuerte),
para reforzar la vibración
– *right pedal (sustaining pedal,
damper pedal;* loosely: *forte pedal,
loud pedal) for raising the dampers*
9 el pedal izquierdo (el pedal piano,
el pedal suave, el pedal dulce)
para amortiguar el sonido
– *left pedal (soft pedal;* loosely: *piano
pedal) for reducing the striking
distance of the hammers on the
strings*
10 las cuerdas de tiples *m* (las
cuerdas agudas)
– *treble strings*
11 el puente de las cuerdas tiples *m*
– *treble bridge (treble belly bridge)*
12 las cuerdas bajas (las cuerdas
graves, los bordones)
– *bass strings*
13 el puente de las cuerdas bajas
– *bass bridge (bass belly bridge)*
14 la clavija de sujeción *f*
– *hitch pin*
15 la barra soporte de los martillos
– *hammer rail*
16 el soporte del mecanismo
– *brace*
17 la clavija de afinamiento *m*
– *tuning pin (wrest pin, tuning peg)*
18 la tabla-clavijero
– *pin block (wrest pin block, wrest
plank)*
19 el metrónomo
– *metronome*
20 la llave de afinar
– *tuning hammer (tuning key, wrest)*
21 la cuña para afinar
– *tuning wedge*

**22-39** la mecánica de las teclas
– *key action (key mechanism)*
22 el travesaño del mecanismo
– *beam*
23 la palanca que acciona los
apagadores
– *damper-lifting lever*
24 la cabeza de macillo (el fieltro del
macillo)
– *felt-covered hammer head*
25 el mango del macillo
– *hammer shank*
26 el listón de apoyo *m* de los
macillos
– *hammer rail*
27 el apresador
– *check (back check)*
28 el fieltro del apresador
– *check felt (back check felt)*
29 el alambre del apresador
– *wire stem of the check (wire stem of
the back check)*
30 el cric (el gato)
– *sticker (hopper, hammer jack,
hammer lever)*
31 el contraapresador
– *button*
32 la palanca levadora
– *action lever*
33 el piloto
– *pilot*
34 el alambre del piloto
– *pilot wire*
35 el astil de la brida
– *tape wire*
36 la brida (una brida de cuero *m*)
– *tape*
37 el apagador
– *damper (damper block)*
38 el brazo del apagador
– *damper lifter*
39 el listón de apoyo *m* de los
apagadores
– *damper rest rail*
40 **el piano de cola** *f* (el piano de
concierto *m; más pequeño:* el
piano de media cola *f*; el piano de
cuarto de cola *f*; *otra forma:* el
piano cuadrado)
– **grand piano** *(horizontal piano,
grand, concert grand);* smaller:
*baby grand piano, boudoir piano;*
sim.: *square piano, table piano*
41 los pedales del piano de cola *f*; el
pedal derecho para reforzar la
vibración; el pedal izquierdo para
disminuir la resonancia (por
deslizamiento lateral del teclado;
es golpeada una sola cuerda "una
corda")
– *grand piano pedals; right pedal for
raising the dampers; left pedal for
softening the tone [shifting the
keyboard so that only one string is
struck 'una corda']*
42 el soporte del pedal
– *pedal bracket*
43 **el armonio** (el órgano)
– **harmonium** *(reed organ, melodium)*
44 el registro
– *draw stop (stop, stop knob)*
45 las rodilleras
– *knee lever (knee swell, swell)*
46 los pedales que accionan el fuelle
(los pedales neumáticos)
– *pedal (bellows pedal)*
47 la caja del armonio
– *harmonium case*
48 el teclado (manual)
– *harmonium keyboard (manual)*

**1-52 el órgano** (el órgano de
iglesia *f*)
– *organ;* here: *church organ*
**1-5** los cañones postizos (la tubería
postiza; la fachada de órgano *m*)
– *front view of organ (organ case)*
*[built according to classical*
*principles]*
**1-3** los tubos de la fachada del
órgano
– *display pipes (face pipes)*
**1** la caja principal
– *Hauptwerk (*approx. English
equivalent: *great organ)*
**2** la caja superior
– *Oberwerk (*approx. English
equivalent: *swell organ)*
**3** los tubos de pedal *m*
– *pedal pipes*
**4** la torre de pedal *m*
– *pedal tower*
**5** el positivo dorsal
– *Rückpositiv (*approx. English
equivalent: *choir organ)*
**6-16** la transmisión mecánica; *otros*
*sitemas:* la transmisión neumática,
la transmisión eléctrica
– *tracker action (mechanical action);*
other systems: *pneumatic action,*
*electric action*
**6** el registro
– *draw stop (stop, stop knob)*
**7** el registro de corredera *f*
– *slider (slide)*
**8** la tecla
– *key (key lever)*

**9** las varillas transmisoras
– *sticker*
**10** la válvula
– *pallet*
**11** el canal de viento *m* (el conducto
de aire *m*)
– *wind trunk*
**12-14** el secreto (el distribuidor de
aire *m*), un secreto de corredera *f;*
otros tipos: el cono resonante, la
membrana resonadora
– *wind chest, a slider wind chest;*
other types: *sliderless wind chest*
*(unit wind chest), spring chest,*
*kegellade chest (cone chest),*
*diaphragm chest*
**12** la cámara de aire *m*
– *wind chest (wind chest box)*
**13** el canal de la caja de resonancia *f*
– *groove*
**14** el canal de la caja superior
– *upper board groove*
**15** el soporte (el zócalo) de los tubos
– *upper board*
**16** el tubo de un registro
– *pipe of a particular stop*
**17-35** los tubos de órgano *m* (los
tubos acústicos)
– *organ pipes (pipes)*
**17-22** el tubo de lengüeta *f* de
metal *m*, un trombón de varas *f*
– *metal reed pipe;* set of pipes: *reed*
*stop, a posaune stop*
**17** el pie (la punta)
– *boot*

**18** la garganta
– *shallot*
**19** la lengüeta
– *tongue*
**20** la cabeza (el núcleo) de plomo *m*
– *block*
**21** el alambre afinador
– *tuning wire (tuning crook)*
**22** el pabellón
– *tube*
**23-30** el tubo abierto labial de
metal *m*, un salicional
– *open metal flue pipe, a salicional*
**23** el pie
– *foot*
**24** el paso del aire
– *flue pipe windway (flue pipe duct)*
**25** la boca
– *mouth (cutup)*
**26** al labio inferior
– *lower lip*
**27** el labio superior
– *upper lip*
**28** el obturador
– *languid*
**29** el cuerpo (el cañón) del tubo
– *body of the pipe (pipe)*
**30** la entalla, un dispositivo para
afinar
– *tuning flap (tuning tongue), a*
*tuning device*
**31-33** el tubo labial abierto de
madera *f*, un principal
– *open wooden flue pipe (open wood),*
*principal (diapason)*

**31** la cápsula (el secreto)
– *cap*
**32** el oído
– *ear*
**33** la entella de afinar, con
corredera *f*
– *tuning hole (tuning slot), with slide*
**34** el tubo labial tapado
– *stopped flue pipe*
**35** el sombrero metálico (el casquete
metálico)
– *stopper*
**36-52** la consola de un órgano de
transmisión *f* eléctrica
– *organ console (console) of an
electric action organ*
**36** el atril
– *music rest (music stand)*
**37** el indicador de posición *f* de los
rodillos
– *crescendo roller indicator*
**38** el voltímetro
– *voltmeter*
**39** la tecla de registro *m*
– *stop tab (rocker)*
**40** la tecla para juegos *m* libres
– *free combination stud (free
combination knob)*
**41** el anulador de los juegos de
lengüetería *f*, acoplamientos *m*,
etc.
– *cancel buttons for reeds, couplers
etc.*

**42** el manual I, para el positivo
dorsal (el órgano de coro *m*)
– *manual I, for the Rückpositiv (choir
organ)*
**43** el manual II, para la caja principal
– *manual II, for the Hauptwerk
(great organ)*
**44** el manual III, para la caja
superior
– *manual III, for the Oberwerk (swell
organ)*
**45** el manual IV, para el solo de
órgano *m*
– *manual IV, for the Schwellwerk
(solo organ)*
**46** los botones pulsadores y los
botones de combinación *f*, para el
registro manual, las
combinaciones libres o fijas y
combinaciones *f* mixtas
– *thumb pistons controlling the
manual stops (free or fixed
combinations) and buttons for
setting the combinations*
**47** los interruptores de aire *m* y de
corriente *f*
¬ *switches for current to blower and
action*
**48** el pistón a pedal *m*, para el
acoplamiento
– *toe piston, for the coupler*
**49** el rodillo de crescendo *m*
– *crescendo roller (general crescendo
roller)*

**50** el pedal de expresión *f*
– *balanced swell pedal*
**51** el pedal de notas *f* naturales
– *pedal key [natural]*
**52** el pedal de notas *f* alteradas
– *pedal key [sharp or flat]*
**53** el cable
– *cable (transmission cable)*

**1-61 seres** *m* **de fábula** *f* (animales *m* fabulosos), animales *m* y figuras *f* mitológicas
- *fabulous creatures (fabulous animals), mythical creatures*
**1** el dragón
- *dragon*
**2** el cuerpo de serpiente *f*
- *serpent's body*
**3** la garra
- *claws (claw)*
**4** el ala *f* de murciélago *m*
- *bat's wing*
**5** la boca de lengua *f* bífida
- *fork-tongued mouth*
**6** la lengua bífida
- *forked tongue*
**7** el unicornio (el monoceronte) [símbolo *m* de la virginidad]
- *unicorn [symbol of virginity]*
**8** el cuerno retorcido en espiral *f*
- *spirally twisted horn*
**9** el ave fénix
- *Phoenix*
**10** las llamas o cenizas *f* de la resurrección
- *flames or ashes of resurrection*
**11** el grifo
- *griffin (griffon, gryphon)*
**12** la cabeza de águila *f*
- *eagle's head*
**13** la garra de grifo *m*
- *griffin's claws*
**14** el cuerpo de león *m*
- *lion's body*
**15** el ala *f*
- *wing*
**16** la quimera, un monstruo
- *chimera (chimaera), a monster*
**17** la cabeza de león *m*
- *lion's head*
**18** la cabeza de cabra *f*
- *goat's head*
**19** el cuerpo de dragón *m* [y la cola de culebra *f*]
- *dragon's body*
**20** la esfinge, una figura simbólica
- *sphinx, a symbolic figure*
**21** la cabeza humana
- *human head*
**22** el cuerpo de león *m*
- *lion's body*
**23** la sirena, la sirena de cola *f* de pez *m* (la ondina, la náyade, la ninfa); *anál.:* la nereida, la oceánida (divinidades *f* marinas; diosas *f* del mar); *varón:* el tritón
- *mermaid (nix, nixie, water nixie, sea maid, sea maiden, naiad, water nymph, water elf, ocean nymph, sea nymph, river nymph);* sim.: *Nereids, Oceanids (sea divinities, sea deities, sea goddesses);* male: *nix (merman, seaman)*
**24** el cuerpo de mujer *f*
- *woman's trunk*
**25** la cola de pez *m* (la cola de delfín *m*)
- *fish's tail;* sim.: *dolphin's tail*
**26** Pegaso (el corcel de los poetas, el corcel de las musas, el caballo alado)
- *Pegasus (winged horse);* sim.: *hippogryph*
**27** el cuerpo de caballo *m*
- *horse's body*

**28** las alas
- *wings*
**29** el cancerbero (el perro del infierno)
- *Cerberus (hellhound)*
**30** el cuerpo de perro *m* con tres cabezas *f*
- *three-headed dog's body*
**31** la cola de serpiente *f*
- *serpent's tail*
**32** la hidra de Lerna
- *Lernaean (Lernean) Hydra*
**33** el cuerpo de serpiente *f* con nueve cabezas *f*
- *nine-headed serpent's body*
**34** el basilisco
- *basilisk (cockatrice) [in English legend usually with two legs]*
**35** la cabeza de gallo *m*
- *cock's head*
**36** el cuerpo de dragón *m*
- *dragon's body*
**37** el titán, un gigante
- *giant (titan)*
**38** la roca
- *rock*
**39** el pie de serpiente *f*
- *serpent's foot*
**40** el tritón, una divinadad del mar
- *triton, a merman*
**41** el cuerno de concha *f*
- *conch shell trumpet*
**42** el pie de caballo *m*
- *horse's hoof*
**43** la cola de pez *m*
- *fish's tail*
**44** el hipocampo (el caballo marino, el caballo de Neptuno)
- *hippocampus*
**45** el tronco de caballo *m*
- *horse's trunk*
**46** la cola de pez *m*
- *fish's tail*
**47** el toro marino, un monstruo marino
- *sea ox, a sea monster*
**48** el cuerpo de toro *m*
- *monster's body*
**49** la cola de pez *m*
- *fish's tail*
**50** el dragón de las siete cabezas de la revelación (la bestia del Apocalipsis)
- *seven-headed dragon of St. John's Revelation (Revelations, Apocalypse)*
**51** el ala *f*
- *wing*
**52** el centauro, un ser mitad hombre *m* y mitad caballo *m* (el hipocentauro)
- *centaur (hippocentaur), half man and half beast*
**53** el torso de hombre *m* con arco *m* y flecha *f*
- *man's body with bow and arrow*
**54** el cuerpo de caballo *m*
- *horse's body*
**55** la arpía, un espíritu del aire (un espíritu de la tempestad)
- *harpy, a winged monster*
**56** la cabeza de mujer *f*
- *woman's head*
**57** el cuerpo de ave *f*
- *bird's body*

**58** la sirena, mitad mujer *f* y mitad ave *f*, una divinidad infernal
- *siren, a daemon*
**59** el cuerpo de mujer *f*
- *woman's body*
**60** el ala *f*
- *wing*
**61** la garra de ave *f*
- *bird's claw*

**1-40** hallazgos prehistóricos
- *prehistoric finds*
**1-9 el período paleolítico y el período mesolítico**
- *Old Stone Age (Palaeolithic, Paleolithic, period) and Mesolithic period*
**1** el hacha *f* de sílex *m*, de pedernal *m*
- *hand axe (Am. ax) (fist hatchet), a stone tool*
**2** la punta de flecha *f* arrojadiza, de hueso *m*
- *head of throwing spear, made of bone*
**3** el arpón, de hueso *m*
- *bone harpoon*
**4** la punta
- *head*
**5** el dardo arrojadizo, de la cornamenta del reno
- *harpoon thrower, made of reindeer antler*
**6** el guijarro pintado
- *painted pebble*
**7** la cabeza de caballo *m* salvaje, una talla
- *head of a wild horse, a carving*
**8** el ídolo de la Edad de Piedra, una estatuilla de marfil *m*
- *Stone Age idol, an ivory statuette*
**9** el bisonte, una pintura rupestre [pintura *f* de las cavernas]
- *bison, a cave painting (rock painting) [cave art, cave painting]*
**10-20 el período neolítico**
- *New Stone Age (Neolithic period)*
**10** el ánfora *f* [cerámica *f* acordelada, cerámica *f* de cordel *m*]
- *amphora [corded ware]*
**11** la olla abombada [civilización *f* megalítica]
- *bowl [menhir group]*
**12** la botella de cuello *m* [cultura *f* de los vasos de embudo *m*]
- *collared flask [Funnel-Beaker culture]*
**13** la vasija adornada con espirales *f* [cerámica de cintas *f*]
- *vessel with spiral pattern [spiral design pottery]*
**14** el vaso campaniforme [cultura *f* de los vasos campaniformes]
- *bell beaker [beaker pottery]*
**15** el palafito, una vivienda lacustre
- *pile dwelling (lake dwelling, lacustrine dwelling)*
**16** el dolmen, una tumba megalítica; otras clases: el pasillo mortuorio, la galería mortuoria; *cubierto de tierra f, guijas f, piedras f:* el túmulo
- *dolmen (cromlech), a megalithic tomb (coll.: giant's tomb); other kinds: passage grave, gallery grave (long cist); when covered with earth: tumulus (barrow, mound)*
**17** el cofre sepulcral de piedra *f* con inhumación *f* en posición *f* encogida
- *stone cist, a contracted burial*
**18** el menhir (*anál.:* el Hinkelstein alemán, un monolito)
- *menhir (standing stone), a monolith*
**19** el hacha *f* en forma *f* de barco *m*, una hacha de combate *m* de piedra *f*
- *boat axe (Am. ax), a stone battle axe*
**20** la figurita humana de terracota *f* (un ídolo)
- *clay figurine, an idol*
**21-40 la Edad de Bronce y la Edad de Hierro;** *épocas:* el período de Hallstatt, el período de La Tène
- *Bronze Age and Iron Age;* epochs: *Hallstatt period, La Tène period*
**21** la punta de lanza *f* de bronce *m*
- *bronze spear head*
**22** el puñal de bronce *m* con empuñadura *f*
- *hafted bronze dagger*
**23** el hacha *f* de cubo *m*, una hacha de bronce *m* con el mango sujetado por medio de arandelas *f*
- *socketed axe (Am. ax) with haft fastened to rings, a bronze axe*
**24** el disco (el broche) del cinturón
- *girdle clasp*
**25** la gargantilla
- *necklace (lunula)*
**26** el collar de oro *m*
- *gold neck ring*
**27** la fíbula de arco *m* de violín *m*, una fíbula (imperdible *m*)
- *violin-bow fibula (safety pin)*
**28** la fíbula serpentiforme; otras clases: la fíbula de barca *f*; la fíbula de ballesta *f*
- *serpentine fibula;* other kinds: *boat fibula, arc fibula*
**29** la aguja de cabeza *f* esférica
- *bulb-head pin, a bronze pin*
**30** la fíbula de doble espiral *f*; *anál.:* la fíbula de discos *m*
- *two-piece spiral fibula;* sim.: *disc (disk) fibula*
**31** el cuchillo de bronce *m* con mango *m*
- *hafted bronze knife*
**32** la llave de hierro *m*
- *iron key*
**33** la reja de arado *m*
- *ploughshare (Am. plowshare)*
**34** la sítula de chapa *f* de bronce *m*, una ofrenda funeraria
- *sheet-bronze situla, a funerary vessel*
**35** el cántaro de asa *f* [cerámica *f* de incisiones *f* de muescas *f*]
- *pitcher [chip-carved pottery]*
**36** el carro para el culto en miniatura *f* (carro *m* para el culto)
- *miniature ritual cart (miniature ritual chariot)*
**37** la moneda celta de plata *f*
- *Celtic silver coin*
**38** la urna en forma *f* de cara *f*, una urna cineraria; *otras formas:* la urna en forma *f* de casa *f*; la urna abollonada
- *face urn, a cinerary urn;* other kinds: *domestic urn, embossed urn*
**39** la tumba-urna en una cámara hecha con piedras *f*
- *urn grave in stone chamber*
**40** la urna de cuello *m* cilíndrico
- *urn with cylindrical neck*

1 **el castillo** (el alcázar, la fortaleza)
- **knight's castle** *(castle)*
2 el patio del castillo
- *inner ward (inner bailey)*
3 el pozo
- *draw well*
4 la torre del homenaje (la torre principal)
- *keep (donjon)*
5 las mazmorras
- *dungeon*
6 la galería de almenas *f*
- *battlements (crenellation)*
7 la almena
- *merlon*
8 la plataforma de defensa *f*
- *tower platform*
9 el vigía
- *watchman*
10 los aposentos de las damas
- *ladies' apartments (bowers)*
11 la buharda (la lumbrera)
- *dormer window (dormer)*
12 la logia (el balcón)
- *balcony*
13 el almacén (la despensa)
- *storehouse (magazine)*
14 la torre de ángulo *m*
- *angle tower*
15 la muralla
- *curtain wall (curtains, enclosure wall)*
16 el bastión
- *bastion*
17 la torre del cuerpo de guardia *f*
- *angle tower*
18 la barbacana (la tronera, la saetera)
- *crenel (embrasure)*
19 la cortina
- *inner wall*
20 el adarve (el camino de ronda *f*)
- *battlemented parapet*
21 el parapeto
- *parapet (breastwork)*
22 la torre de entrada *f*
- *gatehouse*
23 el matacán [una abertura para dejar caer piedras *f*, pez *f*, aceite *m* y agua *f* hirviendo sobre los asaltantes]
- *machicolation (machicoulis)*
24 el rastrillo
- *portcullis*
25 el puente levadizo
- *drawbridge*
26 el contrafuerte
- *buttress*
27 las dependencias del servicio del castillo
- *offices and service rooms*
28 la garita de vigía *f*
- *turret*
29 la capilla del castillo
- *chapel*
30 la gran sala
- *great hall*
31 el palenque (la liza, la esplanada del castillo) [el campo de batalla *f* en los torneos]
- *outer ward (outer bailey)*
32 la barbacana
- *castle gate*
33 el foso de entrada *f*
- *moat (ditch)*
34 el camino de acceso *m*
- *approach*

35 la atalaya (la torre de vigía *f*)
- *watchtower (turret)*
36 la empalizada (la estacada)
- *palisade (pallisade, palisading)*
37 el foso
- *moat (ditch, fosse)*
38-65 **la armadura del caballero**
- **knight's armour** (Am. *armor)*
38 el arnés (la armadura)
- *suit of armour (Am. armor)*
39-42 el yelmo (la celada)
- *helmet*
39 la cimera (la campana)
- *skull*
40 la visera (la ventana)
- *visor (vizor)*
41 la babera
- *beaver*
42 la gola
- *throat piece*
43 la gorguera
- *gorget*
44 la espaldera
- *epaulière*
45 la hombrera
- *pallette (pauldron, besageur)*
46 el peto
- *breastplate (cuirass)*
47 el guardabrazo
- *brassard (rear brace and vambrace)*
48 el codal
- *cubitière (coudière, couter)*
49 la escarcela (el faldar)
- *tasse (tasset)*
50 el guantelete (la manopla)
- *gauntlet*
51 la cota de mallas *f*
- *habergeon (haubergeon)*
52 el quijote
- *cuisse (cuish, cuissard, cuissart)*
53 la rodillera
- *knee cap (knee piece, genouillère, poleyn)*
54 la greba
- *jambeau (greave)*
55 el escarpe
- *solleret (sabaton, sabbaton)*
56 la tarja (el escudo largo)
- *pavis (pavise, pavais)*
57 la rodela (el escudo redondo)
- *buckler (round shield)*
58 la bloca
- *boss (umbo)*
59 el capiello de fierro *m*
- *iron hat*
60 el morrión
- *morion*
61 la barbuta
- *light casque*
62 tipos de cotas *f* de malla *f* (de loriga *f*)
- *types of mail and armour (Am. armor)*
63 la malla de anillos *m* (la loriga de anillos *m*)
- *mail (chain mail, chain armour, Am. armor)*
64 la cota de escamas *f* (una malla clavada)
- *scale armour (Am. armor)*
65 la cota de placas *f* (una malla clavada)
- *plate armour (Am. armor)*
66 **la investidura de caballero**
- **accolade** *(dubbing, knighting)*
67 el señor feudal
- *liege lord, a knight*

68 el caballero novel
- *esquire*
69 el copero
- *cup bearer*
70 el trovador (el ministril, el juglar)
- *minstrel (minnesinger, troubadour)*
71 **el torneo (la justa)**
- *tournament (tourney, joust, just, tilt)*
72 el cruzado
- *crusader*
73 el templario
- *Knight Templar*
74 la gualdrapa
- *caparison (trappings)*
75 el heraldo (el rey de armas *f*)
- *herald (marshal at tournament)*
76 los pertrechos (los arneses, las armas) para el torneo
- *tilting armour (Am. armor)*
77 el yelmo de torneo *m* (de parada *f*)
- *tilting helmet (jousting helmet)*
78 el penacho (el airón)
- *panache (plume of feathers)*
79 la adarga de torneo *m* (de parada *f*)
- *tilting target (tilting shield)*
80 el ristre
- *lance rest*
81 la lanza de torneo *m*
- *tilting lance (lance)*
82 el guardamano de la lanza
- *vamplate*
83-88 la armadura del caballo (las bardas)
- *horse armour (Am. armor)*
83 la capizana
- *neck guard (neck piece)*
84 la testera
- *chamfron (chaffron, chafron, chamfrain, chanfron)*
85 la barda del pecho del caballo
- *poitrel*
86 la flanqueza
- *flanchard (flancard)*
87 la silla de torneo *m*
- *tournament saddle*
88 la barda de la grupa
- *rump piece (quarter piece)*

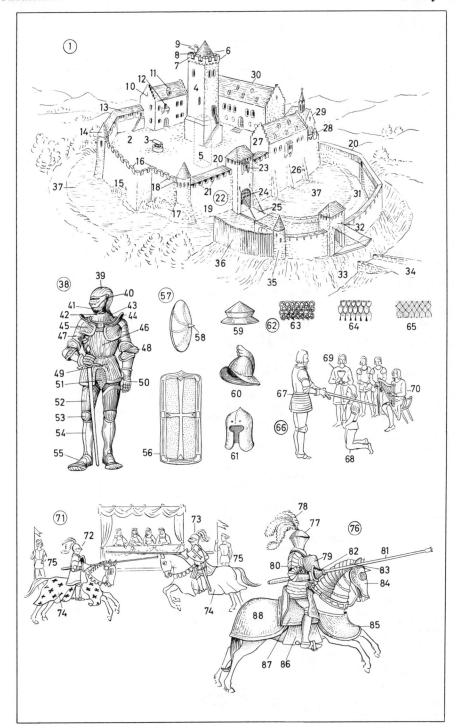

**1-30  la iglesia** (el templo)
**protestante (iglesia *f* evangélica)**
– *Protestant church*
1  el presbiterio
– *chancel*
2  el facistol con paramento *m*
– *lectern*
3  la alfombra del altar
– *altar carpet*
4  el altar (la mesa eucarística)
– *altar (communion table, Lord's table, holy table)*
5  las gradas del altar
– *altar steps*
6  el paño del altar
– *altar cloth*
7  el cirio del altar (*Mé.:* la veladora)
– *altar candle*
8  la píxide (la caja del pan ácimo)
– *pyx (pix)*
9  la patena
– *paten (patin, patine)*
10  el cáliz
– *chalice (communion cup)*
11  la Biblia (las Sagradas Escrituras)
– *Bible (Holy Bible, Scriptures, Holy Scripture)*
12  el crucifijo del altar
– *altar crucifix*
13  el cuadro del altar
– *altarpiece*
14  la vidriera
– *church window*
15  la pintura de vidrio *m* (la pintura sobre cristal *m*)
– *stained glass*
16  el candelabro de pared *f*
– *wall candelabrum*
17  la puerta de la sacristía
– *vestry door (sacristy door)*
18  la escalera del púlpito
– *pulpit steps*
19  el púlpito
– *pulpit*
20  el antipendio
– *antependium*
21  el sombrero del púlpito (el tornavoz)
– *canopy, a soundboard (sounding board)*
22  el predicador (el pastor) con las vestiduras sacerdotales (con el sobrepelliz)
– *clergyman, e.g. vicar, pastor, rector, in his robes (canonicals)*
23  la balaustrada del púlpito
– *pulpit balustrade*
24  el tablón indicador de los números de los himnos
– *hymn board showing hymn numbers*
25  la tribuna del templo (la galería)
– *gallery*
26  el sacristán
– *verger (sexton, sacristan)*

27  el pasillo central
– *aisle*
28  el banco de la iglesia; *en conjunto:* la sillería
– *pew;* collectively: *pews (seating)*
29  el fiel; *en conjunto:* la congregación de los fieles
– *churchgoer (worshipper);* collectively: *congregation*
30  el himnario (el libro de himnos *m*)
– *hymn book*
**31-62  la iglesia** (el templo) **católica**
– *Roman Catholic church*
31  las gradas del altar
– *altar steps*
32  el presbiterio (el coro)
– *presbytery (choir, chancel, sacrarium, sanctuary)*
33  el altar (el ara)
– *altar*
34  los cirios del altar
– *altar candles*
35  el crucifijo del altar
– *altar cross*
36  el paño del altar
– *altar cloth*
37  el ambón (atril *m* para la predicación)
– *lectern*
38  el misal
– *missal (mass book)*
39  el sacerdote (el cura)
– *priest*
40  el acólito (el monaguillo; *S. Dgo.:* el clérigo)
– *server*
41  los asientos para los sacerdotes [*asientos m unidos:* sillería *f;* separados, móviles:* no tiene un nombre particular]
– *sedilia*
42  el tabernáculo
– *tabernacle*
43  el soporte del tabernáculo
– *stele (stela)*
44  el cirio pascual (*Chile y Perú:* el velón)
– *paschal candle (Easter candle)*
45  el candelero del cirio pascual
– *paschal candlestick (Easter candlestick)*
46  la campanilla de la sacristía
– *sanctus bell*
47  la cruz de las procesiones
– *processional cross*
48  la decoración del altar
– *altar decoration*
49  la lámpara del Santísimo (la lámpara del sagrario) [una lámpara de aceite *m* siempre encendida]
– *sanctuary lamp*
50  el cuadro del altar, un cuadro de Cristo
– *altarpiece, a picture of Christ*
51  la imagen de la Virgen
– *Madonna (statue of the Virgin Mary)*

52  la mesa de los cirios votivos
– *pricket*
53  los cirios votivos
– *votive candles*
54  el cepillo de las limosnas (*Chile, Guat., Hond.:* la alcancía)
– *station of the Cross*
55  el cepillo (para limosnas *f*)
– *offertory box*
56  la estantería de las publicaciones
– *literature stand*
57  las publicaciones
– *literature, e.g. pamphlets, tracts*
58  el sacristán (*pop.:* rapavelas *m*)
– *verger (sexton, sacristan)*
59  la limosnera (la bolsa de las limosnas)
– *offertory bag*
60  la limosna
– *offering*
61  el fiel (el creyente)
– *Christian (man praying)*
62  el devocionario
– *prayer book*

1 la iglesia
– church
2 el campanario (anál.: la
espadaña, la torre de la iglesia)
– steeple
3 el gallo de la veleta
– weathercock
4 la veleta (la giralda, la
giraldilla)
– weather vane (wind vane)
5 el botón del chapitel
– spire ball
6 la aguja (el chapitel) de la torre
– church spire (spire)
7 el reloj de la torre
– church clock (tower clock)
8 la lumbrera del campanario
– belfry window
9 la campana eléctrica
– electrically operated bell
10 la cruz del caballete (de la
cumbrera)
– ridge cross
11 el tejado de la iglesia
– church roof
12 la capilla conmemorativa
(votiva)
– memorial chapel
13 la sacristía, un edificio anejo
– vestry (sacristy), an annexe
(annex)
14 la placa (la lápida)
conmemorativa, el epitafio
– memorial tablet (memorial plate,
wall memorial, wall stone)
15 la entrada lateral
– side entrance
16 el portal (la puerta) de la iglesia
– church door (main door, portal)
17 el feligrés
– churchgoer
18 el muro del cementerio (del
camposanto)
– graveyard wall (churchyard wall)
19 la puerta del cementerio (del
camposanto)
– graveyard gate (churchyard gate,
lichgate, lychgate)
20 la casa del párroco
– vicarage (parsonage, rectory)
21-41 el cementerio (camposanto
m)
– graveyard (churchyard, God's
acre, Am. burying ground)
21 la capilla mortuoria (el
depósito de cadáveres m)
– mortuary
22 el sepulturero (el enterrador;
Amér. Central y Perú: el
panteonero)
– grave digger
23 la tumba (el sepulcro)
– grave (tomb)
24 el montículo de la tumba
– grave mound
25 la cruz de la tumba
– cross
26 la lápida sepulcral
– gravestone (headstone,
tombstone)

27 la tumba familiar
– family grave (family tomb)
28 la capilla del cementerio
– graveyard chapel
29 la tumba de niño m
– child's grave
30 la tumba de urna f
– urn grave
31 la urna
– urn
32 la tumba de soldado m
– soldier's grave
33-41 el entierro (la inhumación,
el sepelio; Chile: la
sepultación)
– funeral (burial)
33 el acompañamiento (las
personas que asisten al
entierro)
– mourners
34 la fosa (la sepultura)
– grave
35 el ataúd (el féretro)
– coffin (Am. casket)
36 la pala
– spade
37 el clérigo
– clergyman
38 los dolientes
– the bereaved
39 el velo de viuda f, un velo de
luto m
– widow's veil, a mourning veil
40 los empleados de pompas f
fúnebres
– pallbearers
41 las parihuelas (las andas)
– bier
42-50 la procesión (la procesión
religiosa)
– procession (religious procession)
42 la cruz de la procesión, un
guión
– processional crucifix
43 el crucero (el cruciferario)
– cross bearer (crucifer)
44 el estandarte de la procesión,
un estandarte de la iglesia
– processional banner, a church
banner
45 el acólito (el monaguillo;
S. Dgo.: el clérigo)
– acolyte
46 el portador del palio
– canopy bearer
47 el sacerdote
– priest
48 la custodia con el Santísimo
– monstrance with the Blessed
Sacrament (consecrated Host)
49 el palio (si es de tela f de seda f:
baldaquín m, baldaquino m)
– canopy (baldachin, baldaquin)
50 las monjas (las religiosas)
– nuns
51 los participantes en la
procesión
– participants in the procession

52-58 el monasterio (el convento)
– monastery
52 el claustro
– cloister
53 el patio conventual
– monastery garden
54 el monje (el fraile), un
benedictino
– monk, a Benedictine monk
55 la cogulla
– habit (monk's habit)
56 la capilla (la capucha)
– cowl (hood)
57 la tonsura
– tonsure
58 el breviario
– breviary
59 la catacumba, un cementerio
subterráneo de los primeros
tiempos del cristianismo
– catacomb, an early Christian
underground burial place
60 el nicho sepulcral (el arcosolio)
– niche (tomb recess, arcosolium)
61 la losa (la lápida)
– stone slab

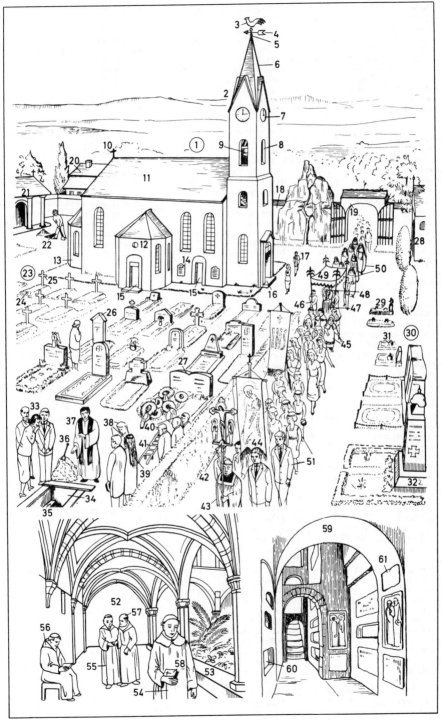

1 el bautizo cristiano (*el sacramento:* el bautismo)
- *Christian baptism (christening)*
2 el baptisterio
- *baptistery (baptistry)*
3 el clérigo (el pastor) protestante (clérigo *m* evangélico)
- *Protestant clergyman*
4 la ropa talar (el sobrepelliz)
- *robes (vestments, canonicals)*
5 el alzacuello
- *bands*
6 el cuello
- *collar*
7 el bautizado
- *child to be baptized (christened)*
8 la ropa de cristianar
- *christening robe (christening dress)*
9 el velo de cristianar
- *christening shawl*
10 la pila bautismal
- *font*
11 la taza de la pila bautismal
- *font basin*
12 el agua *f* bautismal (el agua *f* bendita)
- *baptismal water*
13 los padrinos
- *godparents*
14 el matrimonio canónico (la boda religiosa)
- *church wedding (wedding ceremony, marriage ceremony)*
15-16 los novios (los contrayentes)
- *bridal couple*
15 la novia
- *bride*
16 el novio
- *bridegroom (groom)*
17 el anillo de boda *f* (el anillo, la alianza; *Col.:* la argolla)
- *ring (wedding ring)*
18 el ramo de novia *f* (*Cuba y P. Rico:* la pucha)
- *bride's bouquet (bridal bouquet)*
19 la corona de novia *f* [en *España:* de azahar *m*]
- *bridal wreath*
20 el velo de novia *f*
- *veil (bridal veil)*
21 el ramito de mirto *m* [en *España:* un clavel o una gardenia]
- *[myrtle] buttonhole*
22 el clérigo (el sacerdote, el cura)
- *clergyman*
23 los testigos
- *witnesses [to the marriage]*
24 la dama de honor *m*
- *bridesmaid*
25 el reclinatorio
- *kneeler*
26 la comunión
- *Holy Communion*
27 los comulgantes
- *communicants*
28 la hostia (la sagrada forma, el pan eucarístico)
- *Host (wafer)*

29 el cáliz de la comunión (el cáliz del vino eucarístico)
- *communion cup*
30 el rosario
- *rosary*
31 la cuenta de los misterios (la cuenta de los padrenuestros, el diez; *Col.:* el pasador)
- *paternoster*
32 la avemaría (la cuenta del avemaría; *cada diez cuentas:* un misterio)
- *Ave Maria; set of 10: decade*
33 el crucifijo
- *crucifix*
34-54 objetos *m* litúrgicos (objetos *m* sagrados, objetos *m* de culto *m*)
- *liturgical vessels (ecclesiastical vessels)*
34 la custodia (el ostensorio)
- *monstrance*
35 la hostia (la hostia grande, el Santísimo)
- *Host (consecrated Host, Blessed Sacrament)*
36 el viril
- *lunula (lunule)*
37 la corona de rayos *m*
- *rays*
38 el incensario (el turíbulo) para incensaciones *f* litúrgicas
- *censer (thurible), for offering incense (for incensing)*
39 la cadenilla del incensario
- *thurible chain*
40 la tapa del braserillo del incensario
- *thurible cover*
41 el braserillo del incensario
- *thurible bowl*
42 la naveta del incienso
- *incense boat*
43 la cucharilla para coger el incienso
- *incense spoon*
44 las vinajeras
- *cruet set*
45 la vinajera del agua
- *water cruet*
46 la vinajera del vino
- *wine cruet*
47 el acetre
- *holy water basin*
48 el copón con las hostias pequeñas para la comunión de los fieles
- *ciborium containing the sacred wafers*
49 el cáliz
- *chalice*
50 la copa para la comunión de los fieles
- *dish for communion wafers*
51 la patena
- *paten (patin, patine)*
52 la campanilla del altar (la campanilla del Sanctus)
- *altar bells*

53 la píxide
- *pyx (pix)*
54 el hisopo
- *aspergillum*
55-72 formas *f* de cruces *f* cristianas
- *forms of Christian crosses*
55 la cruz latina (la cruz de la Pasión)
- *Latin cross (cross of the Passion)*
56 la cruz griega
- *Greek cross*
57 la cruz rusa
- *Russian cross*
58 la cruz de San Pedro
- *St. Peter's cross*
59 la cruz de San Antonio (la cruz de Tau; la cruz en T)
- *St. Anthony's cross (tau cross)*
60 la cruz de San Andrés (la cruz decusada, la cruz de Borgoña)
- *St. Andrew's cross (saltire cross)*
61 la cruz bifurcada (la cruz de infamia, la cruz de los ladrones del Calvario)
- *Y-cross*
62 la cruz de Lorena
- *cross of Lorraine*
63 la cruz egipcia (la cruz de asa *f*)
- *ansate cross*
64 la cruz patriarcal
- *patriarchal cross*
65 la cruz cardenalicia
- *cardinal's cross*
66 la cruz papal
- *Papal cross*
67 la cruz de Constantino, un monograma de Cristo
- *Constantinian cross, a monogram of Christ (CHR)*
68 la cruz recrucetada
- *crosslet*
69 la cruz anclada
- *cross moline*
70 la cruz potenzada
- *cross of Jerusalem*
71 la cruz trebolada (la cruz de San Lázaro, la cruz de Brabante)
- *cross botonnée (cross treflée)*
72 la cruz de Jerusalén (la cruz del Santo Sepulcro)
- *fivefold cross (quintuple cross)*

**1-18 arte egipcio**
- *Egyptian art*
1 la pirámide, una pirámide cuadrangular, una tumba real
- *pyramid, a royal tomb*
2 la cámara del rey
- *king's chamber*
3 la cámara de la reina
- *queen's chamber*
4 el canal de aireación *f*
- *air passage*
5 la cámara mortuoria
- *coffin chamber*
6 el complejo funerario (la pirámide con sus templos *m*)
- *pyramid site*
7 el templo funerario
- *funerary temple*
8 el templo del valle
- *valley temple*
9 el pilono (la portada)
- *pylon, a monumental gateway*
10 los obeliscos
- *obelisks*
11 la esfinge egipcia
- *Egyptian sphinx*
12 el disco solar alado
- *winged sun disc (sun disk)*
13 la columna lotiforme
- *lotus column*
14 el capitel en capullo *m* (el capitel cerrado)
- *knob-leaf capital (bud-shaped capital)*
15 la columna papiriforme
- *papyrus column*
16 el capitel campaniforme (el capitel abierto)
- *bell-shaped capital*
17 la columna de capitel *m* palmiforme
- *palm column*
18 el pilar hathórico
- *ornamented column*
**19-20 arte *m* babilónico**
- *Babylonian art*
19 el friso babilónico
- *Babylonian frieze*
20 el bajorrelieve de ladrillo *m* vidriado
- *glazed relief tile*
**21-28 arte *m* de los persas** [aqueménides]
- *art of the Persians*
21 la torre sepulcral (la torre mortuoria)
- *tower tomb*
22 la pirámide escalonada
- *stepped pyramid*
23 la columna persa aqueménide
- *double bull column*
24 el follaje invertido
- *projecting leaves*
25 el capitel palmiforme
- *palm capital*
26 la voluta
- *volute (scroll)*
27 el fuste estriado
- *shaft*
28 el capitel de toros *m* adosados por el dorso
- *double bull capital*
**29-36 arte *m* de los asirios**
- *art of the Assyrians*
29 el palacio de Sargón, una planta de un palacio
- *Sargon's Palace, palace buildings*

30 la muralla de la ciudad
- *city wall*
31 la muralla del palacio
- *castle wall*
32 la torre del templo (el zigurat), una pirámide escalonada
- *temple tower (ziggurat), a stepped (terraced) tower*
33 la escalinata
- *outside staircase*
34 la puerta principal
- *main portal*
35 la placa decorativa de la puerta
- *portal relief*
36 la figura de la puerta (un toro alado)
- *portal figure*
**37 arte *m* de Asia Menor**
- *art of Asia Minor*
38 la tumba excavada en la roca (un hipogeo)
- *rock tomb*

**1-48 arte griego**
- *Greek art*
**1-7** la Acrópolis
- *the Acropolis*
**1** el Partenón, un templo dórico
- *the Parthenon, a Doric temple*
**2** el peristilo (la galería de columnas *f*)
- *peristyle*
**3** el frontón (el frontispicio)
- *pediment*
**4** el estereóbato (el basamento)
- *crepidoma (stereobate)*
**5** la estatua
- *statue*
**6** la muralla del templo
- *temple wall*
**7** los propileos
- *propylaea*
**8** la columna dórica
- *Doric column*
**9** la columna jónica
- *Ionic column*
**10** la columna corintia
- *Corinthian column*
**11-14** la cornisa
- *cornice*
**11** la sima
- *cyma*
**12** el geison
- *corona*
**13** el mútulo
- *mutule*
**14** el dentículo
- *dentils*
**15** el triglifo
- *triglyph*
**16** la metopa, un adorno del friso
- *metope, a frieze decoration*
**17** el sofito (la cara interior del goterón, la régula)
- *regula*
**18** el arquitrabe (el epistilo)
- *epistyle (architrave)*
**19** la tenia (el cimacio)
- *cyma (cymatium, kymation)*
**20-25** el capitel
- *capital*
**20** el ábaco
- *abacus*
**21** el equino
- *echinus*
**22** el collarino
- *hypotrachelium (gorgerin)*
**23** la voluta [en el capitel corintio: el caulículo]
- *volute (scroll)*
**24** el cojinete
- *volute cushion*
**25** la corona de hojas *f*
- *acanthus*
**26** el fuste de la columna
- *column shaft*
**27** las estrías (la canaladura)
- *flutes (grooves, channels)*
**28-31** la basa
- *base*
**28** el toro (el bocel)
- *[upper] torus*
**29** la escocia (el troquilo)
- *trochilus (concave moulding, Am. molding)*
**30** el toro (el bocel) inferior
- *[lower] torus*
**31** el plinto
- *plinth*
**32** el estilóbato
- *stylobate*

**33** la estela
- *stele (stela)*
**34** la acrótera del frontispicio
- *acroterion (acroterium, acroter)*
**35** el hermes (el estípite con busto *m*)
- *herm (herma, hermes)*
**36** la cariátide; *masculino:* el atlante
- *caryatid; male: Atlas*
**37** el vaso griego
- *Greek vase*
**38-43** ornamentos *m* griegos
- *Greek ornamentation (Greek decoration, Greek decorative designs)*
**38** el cordón de perlas *f*, una cinta ornamental
- *bead-and-dart moulding (Am. molding), an ornamental band*
**39** la cinta de ondas *f*
- *running dog (Vitruvian scroll)*
**40** el adorno de hojas *f*
- *leaf ornament*
**41** las palmetas
- *palmette*
**42** la tenia (el filete, el listel) de ovas *f* (de ovos *m*, de óvolos *m*)
- *egg and dart (egg and tongue, egg and anchor) cyma*
**43** el meandro (la greca)
- *meander*
**44** el teatro griego (el anfiteatro griego)
- *Greek theatre (Am. theater)*
**45** la escena (el edificio de la escena)
- *scene*
**46** el proscenio
- *proscenium*
**47** la orquesta
- *orchestra*
**48** el altar de los sacrificios
- *thymele (altar)*
**49-52 arte *m* etrusco**
- *Etruscan art*
**49** el templo etrusco
- *Etruscan temple*
**50** el pórtico (el atrio)
- *portico*
**51** la cella (la sala principal)
- *cella*
**52** la viguería (las vigas)
- *entablature*
**53-60 arte *m* romano**
- *Roman art*
**53** el acueducto
- *aqueduct*
**54** el canal de agua *f*
- *conduit (water channel)*
**55** el edificio de planta *f* central
- *centrally-planned building (centralized building)*
**56** el pórtico
- *portico*
**57** el listel (el filete, la tenia)
- *reglet*
**58** la cúpula
- *cupola*
**59** el arco de triunfo *m* (el arco triunfal)
- *triumphal arch*
**60** el ático
- *attic*
**61-71 arte *m* paleocristiano**
- *Early Christian art*
**61** la basílica
- *basilica*
**62** la nave central
- *nave*

**63** la nave lateral
- *aisle*
**64** el ábside
- *apse*
**65** el campanario
- *campanile*
**66** el atrio
- *atrium*
**67** el pórtico de columnas *f* (la galería porticada)
- *colonnade*
**68** la fuente de las abluciones
- *fountain*
**69** el altar
- *altar*
**70** la claraboya lateral (el claristorio)
- *clerestory (clearstory)*
**71** el arco triunfal
- *triumphal arch*
**72-75 arte *m* bizantino**
- *Byzantine art*
**72-73** el sistema de cúpulas *f*
- *dome system*
**72** la cúpula central (la media esfera, la bóveda semiesférica)
- *main dome*
**73** la media cúpula (el cuarto de esfera *f*)
- *semidome*
**74** la pechina
- *pendentive*
**75** el ojo, una claraboya
- *eye, a lighting aperture*

**1-21 arte *m* románico**
- *Romanesque art*
**1-13** la iglesia románica, una catedral
- *Romanesque church, a cathedral*
**1** la nave central
- *nave*
**2** la nave lateral
- *aisle*
**3** el crucero (la nave transversal, el transepto)
- *transept*
**4** el coro (el presbiterio)
- *choir (chancel)*
**5** el ábside
- *apse*
**6** la torre del crucero (el cimborrio)
- *central tower (Am. center tower)*
**7** el tejado piramidal de la torre (el tejado a cuatro vertientes *f*, a cuatro aguas *f*)
- *pyramidal tower roof*
**8** la arcada
- *arcading*
**9** el friso de arquillos *m* ciegos (de arquillos *m* lombardos)
- *frieze of round arcading*
**10** la arcada ciega (la arcada mural)
- *blind arcade (blind arcading)*
**11** la lesena, una banda lombarda
- *lesene, a pilaster strip*
**12** el óculo
- *circular window*
**13** la portada lateral (la puerta del crucero)
- *side entrance*
**14-16** ornamentos *m* románicos
- *Romanesque ornamentation (Romanesque decoration, Romanesque decorative designs)*
**14** la moldura escaqueada (el ajedrezado)
- *chequered (Am. checkered) pattern (chequered design)*
**15** el adorno imbricado (el adorno en escamas *f*)
- *imbrication (imbricated design)*
**16** el adorno en zigzag *m* (el adorno dentado)
- *chevron design*
**17** el sistema románico de bóvedas *f*
- *Romanesque system of vaulting*
**18** el arco fajón (el arco perpiaño)
- *transverse arch*
**19** el formero
- *barrel vault (tunnel vault)*
**20** el pilar
- *pillar*
**21** el capitel cúbico (el capitel bloque *m*, el capitel cojín *m*)
- *cushion capital*
**22-41 arte *m* gótico**
- *Gothic art*
**22** la iglesia gótica [fachada *f* occidental], una catedral
- *Gothic church [westwork, west end, west façade], a cathedral*

**23** el rosetón
- *rose window*
**24** la portada de la iglesia, una puerta abocinada
- *church door (main door, portal), a recessed portal*
**25** la arquivolta
- *archivolt*
**26** el tímpano
- *tympanum*
**27-35** la arquitectura gótica (el sistema de construcción *f* gótico)
- *Gothic structural system*
**27-28** el sistema de soportes *m* exteriores
- *buttresses*
**27** el contrafuerte (el estribo)
- *buttress*
**28** el arbotante (el botarel)
- *flying buttress*
**29** el pináculo, un remate del contrafuerte
- *pinnacle*
**30** la gárgola
- *gargoyle*
**31-32** la bóveda de crucería *f* (la bóveda ojival, la bóveda de nervios *m*)
- *cross vault (groin vault)*
**31** las nervaduras (la crucería, los cruceros, los nervios, las costillas)
- *ribs (cross ribs)*
**32** la clave de bóveda *f*
- *boss (pendant)*
**33** el triforio (la galería interior de una iglesia por encima de la nave lateral)
- *triforium*
**34** el pilar fasciculado (el pilar en haz *m* de baquetones *m*)
- *clustered pier (compound pier)*
**35** la columna embebida (la columna entregada)
- *respond (engaged pillar)*
**36** el gablete
- *pediment*
**37** el florón
- *finial*
**38** el gancho
- *crocket*
**39-41** la ventana de tracería *f*, una ventana lanceolada
- *tracery window, a lancet window*
**39-40 la tracería**
- *tracery*
**39** el rosetón cuadrifolio
- *quatrefoil*
**40** el rosetón de cinco lóbulos *m* (el pentafolio)
- *cinquefoil*
**41** los montantes (los maineles, los parteluces)
- *mullions*
**42-54 arte *m* del Renacimiento**
- *Renaissance art*
**42** la iglesia renacentista
- *Renaissance church*

**43** el resalte, una parte saliente del edificio
- *projection, a projecting part of the building*
**44** el tambor
- *drum*
**45** la linterna
- *lantern*
**46** la pilastra (el pilar entregado)
- *pilaster (engaged pillar)*
**47** el palacio renacentista
- *Renaissance palace*
**48** la cornisa
- *cornice*
**49** la ventana con frontón *m* (la ventana de hastial *m*)
- *pedimental window*
**50** la ventana con frontón *m* curvo
- *pedimental window with round gable*
**51** el almohadillado (la obra rústica, una cadena almohadillada)
- *rustication (rustic work)*
**52** el listel (el filete, la cinta)
- *string course*
**53** el sarcófago (la tumba con figura *f* yacente)
- *sarcophagus*
**54** el festón (la guirnalda)
- *festoon (garland)*

**1-8 arte** *m* **barroco**
- *Baroque art*
1 la iglesia barroca
- *Baroque church*
2 el ojo de buey *m* (la lumbrera, la lucarna, el óculo)
- *bull's eye*
3 la linterna (el lucernario)
- *bulbous cupola*
4 la buharda
- *dormer window (dormer)*
5 el frontón rebajado (el frontón curvo)
- *curved gable*
6 las columnas geminadas
- *twin columns*
7 la tarja (la tarjeta, la cartela, el cartucho, el escusón)
- *cartouche*
8 la voluta
- *scrollwork*
**9-13 el arte rococó**
- *Rococo art*
9 la pared rococó
- *Rococo wall*
10 la corona, una mediacaña (una moldura cóncava)
- *coving, a hollow moulding (Am. molding)*
11 el marco ornamental
- *framing*
12 la sobrepuerta
- *ornamental moulding (Am. molding)*
13 la rocalla, un ornamento del rococó
- *rocaille, a Rococo ornament*
14 la mesa de estilo *m* Luis XVI
- *table in Louis Seize style (Louis Seize table)*
15 el edificio neoclásico (el edificio de estilo *m* neoclásico), una fachada (una entrada *f*)
- *neoclassical building (building in neoclassical style), a gateway*
16 la mesa de estilo *m* Imperio
- *Empire table (table in the Empire style)*
17 el sofá Biedermeier (el sofá de estilo *m* Biedermeier)
- *Biedermeier sofa (sofa in the Biedermeier style)*
18 el sillón de estilo *m* Art Nouveau
- *Art Nouveau easy chair (easy chair in the Art Nouveau style)*
**19-37 los arcos**
- *types of arch*
19 el arco (el arco mural)
- *arch*
20 la jamba
- *abutment*
21 la imposta
- *impost*
22 el salmer, una dovela
- *springer, a voussoir (wedge stone)*
23 la clave
- *keystone*

24 la cara frontal de la jamba
- *face*
25 el intradós
- *pier*
26 el extradós (el trasdós)
- *extrados*
27 el arco de medio punto *m*
- *round arch*
28 el arco rebajado (el arco escarzano)
- *segmental arch (basket handle)*
29 el arco elíptico
- *parabolic arch*
30 el arco de herradura *f* (el arco árabe)
- *horseshoe arch*
31 el arco ojival (el arco apuntado)
- *lancet arch*
32 el arco trebolado
- *trefoil arch*
33 el arco adintelado (el arco a nivel *m*)
- *shouldered arch*
34 el arco convexo (el arco en gola *f*)
- *convex arch*
35 el arco de cortina *f* (el arco festoneado)
- *tented arch*
36 el arco conopial (el arco aquillado)
- *ogee arch (keel arch)*
37 el arco Tudor
- *Tudor arch*
**38-50 bóvedas**
- *types of vault*
38 la bóveda de cañón *m* (la bóveda de medio cañón *m*)
- *barrel vault (tunnel vault)*
39 la corona
- *crown*
40 el riñón de la bóveda
- *side*
41 la bóveda claustral (la bóveda de rincón de claustro *m*, la bóveda de aljibe, la bóveda esquifada)
- *cloister vault (cloistered vault)*
42 la bóveda de arista *f*
- *groin vault (groined vault)*
43 la bóveda de crucería *f* (la bóveda nervada)
- *rib vault (ribbed vault)*
44 la bóveda estrellada
- *stellar vault*
45 la bóveda reticulada
- *net vault*
46 la bóveda en abanico *m*
- *fan vault*
47 la bóveda en artesa *f*
- *trough vault*
48 el faldón abombado
- *trough*
49 la bóveda de caveto *m* (la bóveda de esgucio *m*)
- *cavetto vault*
50 el caveto (el esgucio)
- *cavetto*

**1-6 arte** *m* **chino**
- *Chinese art*
1 la pagoda (pagoda *f* de varios pisos *m*), una torre templo *m*
- *pagoda (multi-storey, multistory, pagoda), a temple tower*
2 el tejado de gradas *f*
- *storey (story) roof (roof of storey)*
3 el pailu, una puerta de triunfo *m*
- *pailou (pailoo), a memorial archway*
4 el pasaje
- *archway*
5 el jarrón de porcelana *f*
- *porcelain vase*
6 la labor de esculpido *m* en laca *f*
- *incised lacquered work*
**7-11 arte** *m* **japonés**
- *Japanese art*
7 el templo
- *temple*
8 el campanil (la torre de las campanas)
- *bell tower*
9 la armazón de soporte *m*
- *supporting structure*
10 el Bodhisattva, un santo budista
- *bodhisattva (boddhisattva), a Buddhist saint*
11 el pórtico japonés (el torii)
- *torii, a gateway*
**12-18 arte** *m* **islámico**
- *Islamic art*
12 la mezquita
- *mosque*
13 el alminar (el minarete), una torre de oración *f*
- *minaret, a prayer tower*
14 el mihrab (el nicho de las plegarias)
- *mihrab*
15 el mimbar (el púlpito)
- *minbar (mimbar, pulpit)*
16 el mausoleo, una tumba
- *mausoleum, a tomb*
17 la bóveda de mocárabes *m* (de mucarnas *f*)
- *stalactite vault (stalactitic vault)*
18 el capitel árabe (un capitel nazarita)
- *Arabian capital*
**19-28 arte** *m* **indio**
- *Indian art*
19 el Siva danzante, un dios indio
- *dancing Siva (Shiva), an Indian god*
20 la estatua de Buda
- *statue of Buddha*
21 la estupa (la pagoda india), una construcción en bóveda *f*, un edificio sagrado budista
- *stupa (Indian pagoda), a mound (dome), a Buddhist shrine*
22 la sombrilla (el quitasol)
- *umbrella*
23 el vallado de piedra *f*
- *stone wall (Am. stone fence)*

24 la puerta de entrada *f*
- *gate*
25 las instalaciones del templo
- *temple buildings*
26 la sikhara (la torre del templo)
- *shikara (sikar, sikhara, temple tower)*
27 el interior de la chaitya
- *chaitya hall*
28 la chaitya, una estupa pequeña
- *chaitya, a small stupa*

**1-43 el estudio** (el taller)
- *studio*
**1** el ventanal del estudio (una lumbrera, un tragaluz)
- *studio skylight*
**2** el pintor, un artista
- *painter, an artist*
**3** el caballete de estudio *m*
- *studio easel*
**4** el boceto a tiza *f*, con el contorno de la figura
- *chalk sketch, with the composition (rough draft)*
**5** el lápiz de tiza *f*
- *crayon (piece of chalk)*
**6-19** utensilios *m* (materiales *m*) de pintura *f*
- *painting materials*
**6** el pincel plano
- *flat brush*
**7** el pincel de pelos *m*
- *camel hair brush*
**8** el pincel redondo
- *round brush*
**9** el pincel para la primera capa
- *priming brush*
**10** la caja de pinturas *f*
- *box of paints (paintbox)*
**11** el tubo de pintura *f* al óleo
- *tube of oil paint*
**12** el barniz
- *varnish*
**13** el aguarrás
- *thinner*

**14** el cuchillo paleta *f*
- *palette knife*
**15** la espátula para pintar
- *spatula*
**16** el carboncillo
- *charcoal pencil (charcoal, piece of charcoal)*
**17** el color para pintar al temple (a la aguada)
- *tempera (gouache)*
**18** la acuarela (el color al agua *f*)
- *watercolour (Am. watercolor)*
**19** el lápiz pastel
- *pastel crayon*
**20** el bastidor
- *wedged stretcher (canvas stretcher)*
**21** el lienzo (la tela)
- *canvas*
**22** el cartón preparado para la pintura, con la superficie de pintar
- *piece of hardboard, with painting surface*
**23** el tablero
- *wooden board*
**24** el tablero de fibras *f* (el tablero de madera *f* prensada, de conglomerado *m*)
- *fibreboard (Am. fiberboard)*
**25** la mesa de pintura *f*
- *painting table*
**26** el caballete plegable (portátil)
- *folding easel*
**27** la naturaleza muerta, un motivo
- *still life group, a motif*
**28** la paleta
- *palette*

**29** el soporte del pincel (el tarrito de la paleta)
- *palette dipper*
**30** la plataforma
- *platform*
**31** el maniquí
- *lay figure (mannequin, manikin)*
**32** la modelo de desnudos *m* (la modelo, el desnudo)
- *nude model (model, nude)*
**33** el ropaje
- *drapery*
**34** el caballete de dibujo *m*
- *drawing easel*
**35** el bloc (el cuaderno) de dibujo *m* (el bloque de apuntes *m*, de bocetos *m*)
- *sketch pad*
**36** el estudio al óleo
- *study in oils*
**37** el mosaico
- *mosaic (tessellation)*
**38** la figura del mosaico
- *mosaic figure*
**39** las teselas
- *tesserae*
**40** el fresco (la pintura mural)
- *fresco (mural)*
**41** el esgrafiado (la pintura con grafio *m*)
- *sgraffito*
**42** el enlucido
- *plaster*
**43** el boceto (el bosquejo, el esbozo)
- *cartoon*

**1-38 el taller**
- *studio*
**1** el escultor
- *sculptor*
**2** el compás de proporciones *f*
- *proportional dividers*
**3** el compás de espesor *m*
- *calliper (caliper)*
**4** el modelo de yeso *m*, un vaciado de yeso *m*
- *plaster model, a plaster cast*
**5** el bloque de piedra *f* (la piedra en bruto, sin labrar)
- *block of stone (stone block)*
**6** el modelador (el escultor en arcilla *f*)
- *modeller (Am. modeler)*
**7** la figura de arcilla *f*, un torso
- *clay figure, a torso*
**8** el rollo de arcilla *f*, una masa modelable
- *roll of clay, a modelling (Am. modeling) substance*
**9** la tarima para modelar
- *modelling (Am. modeling) stand*
**10** la espátula de modelar
- *wooden modelling (Am. modeling) tool*
**11** el alambre de modelar (el raspador de escultor *m*)
- *wire modelling (Am. modeling) tool*
**12** la espadilla
- *beating wood*

**13** el cincel dentado (el estique)
- *claw chisel (toothed chisel, tooth chisel)*
**14** el cincel plano (el formón)
- *flat chisel*
**15** el puntero
- *point (punch)*
**16** el martillo de cabeza *f* de hierro *m*
- *iron-headed hammer*
**17** la gubia
- *gouge (hollow chisel)*
**18** el cincel cuchara *f* (el cincel curvo)
- *spoon chisel*
**19** el escoplo en bisel *m*, un escoplo
- *wood chisel, a bevelled-edge chisel*
**20** la gubia triangular
- *V-shaped gouge*
**21** el mazo (el martillo de madera *f*)
- *mallet*
**22** la armazón (el esqueleto)
- *framework*
**23** la base (el tablero que sirve de base *f*)
- *baseboard*
**24** el soporte de la armazón (la barra de metal *m*)
- *armature support (metal rod)*
**25** la armadura
- *armature*
**26** la escultura de cera *f*
- *wax model*
**27** el bloque de madera *f*
- *block of wood*

**28** el escultor en madera *f* (el tallista)
- *wood carver (wood sculptor)*
**29** el saco de polvo *m* de yeso *m* (el yeso)
- *sack of gypsum powder (gypsum)*
**30** el cajón de arcilla *f*
- *clay box*
**31** la arcilla de modelar (la arcilla)
- *modelling (Am. modeling) clay*
**32** la estatua, una escultura
- *statue, a sculpture*
**33** el bajo relieve (el bajorrelieve)
- *low relief (bas-relief)*
**34** el tablero de modelar
- *modelling (Am. modeling) board*
**35** la armazón de alambre *m*, una alambrera
- *wire frame, wire netting*
**36** el medallón circular
- *circular medallion (tondo)*
**37** la máscara
- *mask*
**38** la placa conmemorativa
- *plaque*

**1-13 el grabado en madera** *f* (la xilografía), un procedimiento de grabado en relieve *m*
- *wood engraving (xylography), a relief printing method (a letterpress printing method)*
1 la plancha de madera *f* cortada contra la fibra para el grabado a tinta *f* sobre madera, un bloque de madera
- *end-grain block for wood engravings, a wooden block*
2 la plancha de madera *f* cortada en el sentido de la fibra para la talla en madera *f* (grabado *m* de relieve *m*), un molde de madera *f*
- *wooden plank for woodcutting, a relief image carrier*
3 el grabado en relieve *m* (las partes en relieve, reproducidas después por entintado *m*)
- *positive cut*
4 la talla (el vaciado) en el sentido de la fibra de la madera
- *plank cut*
5 el buril de contornear (el punzón)
- *burin (graver)*
6 la gubia redonda
- *U-shaped gouge*
7 el escoplo
- *scorper (scauper, scalper)*
8 la gubia
- *scoop*
9 el cincel de rincón *m* (el cincel de esquina *f*)
- *V-shaped gouge*
10 el cuchillo de contornear
- *contour knife*
11 la bruza
- *brush*
12 el rodillo de gelatina *f*
- *roller (brayer)*
13 el frotador (la muñeca)
- *pad (wiper)*
**14-24 el grabado en cobre *m*** (la calcografía, el grabado en talla *f* dulce), un procedimiento de huecograbado *m; clases:* el grabado al agua *f* fuerte, la mediatinta (grabado *m* al humo), el aguatinta, el grabado punteado
- *copperplate engraving (chalcography), an intaglio process;* kinds: *etching, mezzotint, aquatint, crayon engraving*
14 el martillo de moldear (la embutidera)
- *hammer*
15 el punzón
- *burin*
16 la punta seca para el grabado al agua *f* fuerte
- *etching needle (engraver)*
17 el bruñidor, con rascador *m*
- *scraper and burnisher*
18 la ruleta estriada para el grabado punteado (la moleta de graneado *m*)
- *roulette*
19 el graneador para el grabado al humo
- *rocking tool (rocker)*
20 el buril de cabeza *f* redonda, un buril de grabador *m*
- *round-headed graver, a graver (burin)*
21 la piedra de aceite *m*
- *oilstone*
22 el tampón entintador (la bola de entintar)
- *dabber (inking ball, ink ball)*
23 el rodillo entintador de cuero *m*
- *leather roller*
24 el tamiz de graneado *m*
- *sieve*
**25-26 la litografía** (el grabado en piedra *f*), un procedimiento de grabado de superficie *f* (planografía *f*)
- *lithography (stone lithography), a planographic printing method*

**25** la esponja para humedecer la piedra litográfica
– *sponge for moistening the lithographic stone*
**26** el lápiz (el jaboncillo) litográfico (el lápiz graso), un jaboncillo
– *lithographic crayons (greasy chalk)*
**27-64 el taller gráfico,** una imprenta
– *graphic art studio, a printing office (Am. printery)*
**27** la hoja volante
– *broadside (broadsheet, single sheet)*
**28** la impresión polícroma (la impresión en color *m*, la cromolitografía)
– *full-colour (Am. full-color) print (colour print, chromolithograph)*
**29** la minerva (la prensa de platina *f*), una prensa manual
– *platen press, a hand press*
**30** la rótula
– *toggle*
**31** la platina, una plataforma de la prensa
– *platen*
**32** la forma (el molde de imprenta *f*)
– *type forme* (Am. *form*)
**33** la manivela de alimentación *f*
– *feed mechanism*
**34** la barra de la prensa
– *bar (devil's tail)*
**35** el impresor
– *pressman*
**36** la prensa de plancha *f* de cobre *m*
– *copperplate press*
**37** la imposición de cartón *m*
– *tympan*
**38** el regulador de presión *f*
– *pressure regulator*
**39** el volante en estrella *f*
– *star wheel*

**40** el cilindro
– *cylinder*
**41** el tímpano (la mesa de impresión *f*)
– *bed*
**42** la mantilla de fieltro *m*
– *felt cloth*
**43** la prueba
– *proof (pull)*
**44** el grabador en cobre *m* (el calcógrafo)
– *copperplate engraver*
**45** el litógrafo, esmerilando la piedra
– *lithographer (litho artist), grinding the stone*
**46** el disco de esmerilar
– *grinding disc (disk)*
**47** el graneado
– *grain (granular texture)*
**48** la arena de cristal *m*
– *pulverized glass*
**49** la solución de goma *f*
– *rubber solution*
**50** las pinzas
– *tongs*
**51** la cubeta de agua *f* fuerte para el mordido del grabado al agua fuerte
– *etching bath for etching*
**52** la placa de zinc *m*
– *zinc plate*
**53** la placa pulimentada de cobre *m*
– *polished copperplate*
**54** el molde cuadriculado (el grabado de líneas *f* entrecruzadas)
– *cross hatch*
**55** la zona atacada por el ácido (la parte de la placa de cobre *m* puesta al desnudo por una punta seca y corroída por el ácido)
– *etching ground*

**56** la zona no grabada (cubierta por una capa protectora de barniz *m*)
– *non-printing area*
**57** la piedra litográfica
– *lithographic stone*
**58** las marcas de alineación *f* (las señales de ajuste *m*)
– *register marks*
**59** la superficie de impresión *f*
– *printing surface (printing image carrier)*
**60** la prensa litográfica
– *lithographic press*
**61** la palanca de impresión *f*
– *lever*
**62** el husillo de ajuste *m* del raspador
– *scraper adjustment*
**63** el raspador
– *scraper*
**64** la cama de piedra *f*
– *bed*

**1-20 escrituras _f_ de los diferentes pueblos**
- *scripts of various peoples*
1 jeroglíficos *m* del antiguo Egipto, una escritura pictográfica
- *ancient Egyptian hieroglyphics, a pictorial system of writing*
2 árabe
- *Arabic*
3 armenia
- *Armenian*
4 georgiana
- *Georgian*
5 china
- *Chinese*
6 japonesa
- *Japanese*
7 hebrea
- *Hebrew (Hebraic)*
8 escritura _f_ cuneiforme
- *cuneiform script*
9 devanagari *m* (la escritura del sánscrito)
- *Devanagari, script employed in Sanskrit*
10 siamesa
- *Siamese*
11 tamúlica
- *Tamil*
12 tibetana
- *Tibetan*
13 escritura _f_ sinaítica
- *Sinaitic script*
14 fenicia
- *Phoenician*
15 griega
- *Greek*
16 versal _f_ latina (mayúscula _f_ romana, capital _f_ romana)
- *Roman capitals*
17 unicial
- *uncial (uncials, uncial script)*
18 minúscula _f_ carolingia
- *Carolingian (Carlovingian, Caroline) minuscule*
19 runas _f_ (escritura _f_ rúnica)
- *runes*
20 rusa
- *Russian*
**21-26 escribanías antiguas**
- *ancient writing implements*
21 estilete *m* de acero *m* indio, un punzón para escribir sobre hojas _f_ de palmera _f_
- *Indian steel stylus for writing on palm leaves*
22 punzón *m* para la escritura del antiguo Egipto, una cañucela de junco *m*
- *ancient Egyptian reed pen*
23 pluma _f_ de caña _f_
- *writing cane*
24 pincel *m* de escribir
- *brush*
25 pluma _f_ romana de metal *m* (estilete *m*)
- *Roman metal pen (stylus)*
26 pluma _f_ de ganso *m*
- *quill (quill pen)*

**1-15 tipos *m* de letra *f*** (tipos *m* de caracteres *m*)
– **types** *(type faces)*
1 el tipo de letra *f* gótica
– *Gothic type (German black-letter type)*
2 la letra gótica (el tipo Schwabacher)
– *Schwabacher type (German black-letter type)*
3 la letra alemana
– *Fraktur (German black-letter type)*
4 la antigua renacentista (medieval)
– *Humanist (Mediaeval)*
5 la antigua preclasicista (antigua barroca)
– *Transitional*
6 la antigua clasicista
– *Didone*
7 la letra grotesca
– *Sanserif (Sanserif type, Grotesque)*
8 la egipcia
– *Egyptian*
9 el tipo de máquina *f* de escribir
– *typescript (typewriting)*
10 la letra inglesa
– *English hand (English handwriting, English writing)*
11 la letra alemana
– *German hand (German handwriting, German writing)*
12 la letra latina
– *Latin script*
13 la taquigrafía (la estenografía)
– *shorthand (shorthand writing, stenography)*
14 la escritura fonética (transcripción *f* fonética)
– *phonetics (phonetic transcription)*
15 el braille
– *Braille*
**16-29 signos *m* de puntuación *f***
– **punctuation marks** *(stops)*
16 el punto
– *full stop (period, full point)*
17 los dos puntos
– *colon*
18 la coma
– *comma*
19 el punto y coma
– *semicolon*
20 el signo de interrogación *f* [en español, para abrir: ?; para cerrar: ?]
– *question mark (interrogation point, interrogation mark)*
21 el signo de admiración [en español, para abrir: !; para cerrar: !]
– *exclamation mark (Am. exclamation point)*
22 el apóstrofo (la comilla de valor *m*)
– *apostrophe*
23 la raya
– *dash (em rule)*
24 los paréntesis
– *parentheses (round brackets)*
25 los corchetes
– *square brackets*
26 las comillas
– *double quotation marks (paired quotation marks, inverted commas)*
27 las comillas francesas
– *guillemet (French quotation mark)*
28 el guión
– *hyphen*
29 los puntos suspensivos
– *marks of omission (ellipsis)*

**30-35 acentos *m* y signos *m* diacríticos**
– **accents and diacritical marks** *(diacritics)*
30 el acento agudo [en español puede ir sobre cualquier vocal]
– *acute accent (acute)*
31 el acento grave [no existe en español]
– *grave accent (grave)*
32 el acento circunflejo [no existe en español]
– *circumflex accent (circumflex)*
33 la cedilla [debajo de la c]
– *cedilla [under c]*
34 la diéresis (la crema) [sobre la e]
– *diaeresis (Am. dieresis) [over e]*
35 la tilde [sobre la n], una eñe
– *tilde [over n]*
36 el signo de párrafo *m*
– *section mark*
**37-70 el periódico**, un diario nacional
– **newspaper,** *a national daily newspaper*
37 la página del periódico
– *newspaper page*
38 la primera página
– *front page*
39 la cabecera del periódico
– *newspaper heading*
40 la regla (el filete) de cabecera *f* con el pie de imprenta *f*
– *head rules and imprint*
41 el subtítulo
– *subheading*
42 la fecha de publicación *f*
– *date of publication*
43 el número de registro *m* postal del periódico
– *Post Office registration number*
44 el titular
– *headline*
45 la columna
– *column*
46 el título de la columna
– *column heading*
47 el filete de la columna
– *column rule*
48 el editorial (artículo *m* de fondo *m*)
– *leading article (leader, editorial)*
49 la referencia del artículo
– *reference to related article*
50 la noticia breve
– *brief news item*
51 la sección política
– *political section*
52 el titular de la página interior
– *page heading*
53 la caricatura
– *cartoon*
54 el reportaje del corresponsal
– *report by newspaper's own correspondent*
55 la sigla de la agencia de prensa *f*
– *news agency's sign*
56 el anuncio publicitario (la publicidad)
– *advertisement (coll. ad)*
57 la sección deportiva (los deportes)
– *sports section*
58 la foto de prensa *f*
– *press photo*
59 el pie de la foto
– *caption*
60 el reportaje deportivo
– *sports report*
61 la noticia deportiva
– *sports news item*

62 la sección de noticias *f* nacionales e internacionales
– *home and overseas news section*
63 las noticias diversas
– *news in brief (miscellaneous news)*
64 la programación de televisión *f*
– *television programmes (Am. programs)*
65 el parte meteorológico (el tiempo)
– *weather report*
66 el mapa meteorológico
– *weather chart (weather map)*
67 el folletín
– *arts section (feuilleton)*
68 la esquela mortuoria
– *death notice*
69 la sección de anuncios *m* [también: los anuncios por palabras *f*]
– *advertisements (classified advertising)*
70 el anuncio de empleo *m*, una oferta de empleo *m*
– *job advertisement, a vacancy (a situation offered)*

**𝔒𝔵𝔣𝔬𝔯𝔡** 1
**𝔒𝔵𝔣𝔬𝔯𝔡** 2
**𝔒𝔵𝔣𝔬𝔯𝔡** 3
**Oxford** 4

Oxford 5
Oxford 6
**Oxford** 7
Oxford 8

Oxford 9
*Oxford* 10
*Oxford* 11
*Oxford* 12

13
'ɔksfəd 14
15

• 16
: 17
, 18
; 19
? 20
! 21
' 22
— 23
() 24
[] 25
„ " 26

» « 27
- 28
... 29
é 30
è 31
ê 32
ç 33
ë 34
ñ 35
§ 36

37

69

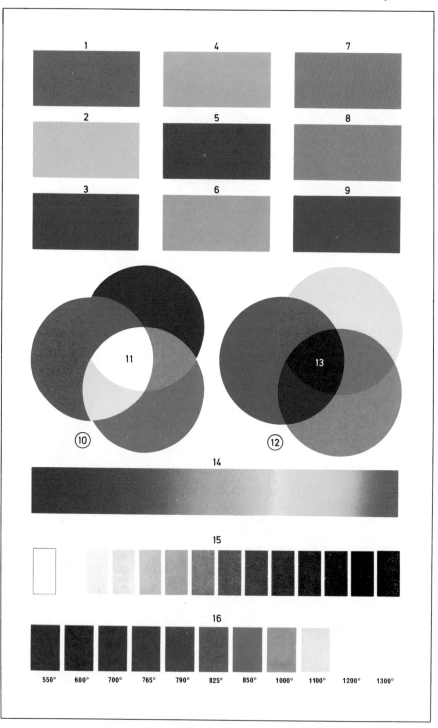

1 rojo
- *red*
2 amarillo
- *yellow*
3 azul (azul marino)
- *blue*
4 rosa
- *pink*
5 marrón
- *brown*
6 azul celeste
- *azure (sky blue)*
7 naranja
- *orange*
8 verde
- *green*
9 violeta (añil)
- *violet*
10 la mezcla aditiva de colores *m*
- *additive mixture of colours* (Am.
  *colors)*
11 blanco
- *white*
12 la mezcla sustractiva de
   colores *m*
- *subtractive mixture of colours*
  *(Am. colors)*
13 negro
- *black*
14 el espectro solar (los colores del
   arco iris)
- *solar spectrum (colours,* Am.
  *colors, of the rainbow)*
15 la escala de grises *m*
- *grey* (Am. *gray) scale*
16 los colores de la escala de
   incandescencia *f*
- *heat colours* (Am. *colors)*

① | I | II | III | IV | V | VI | VII | VIII | IX | X
② | 1 | 2 | 3 | 4 | 5 | 6 | 7 | 8 | 9 | 10

① | XX | XXX | XL | XLIX | IL | L | LX | LXX | LXXX | XC
② | 20 | 30 | 40 | 49 | | 50 | 60 | 70 | 80 | 90

① | XCIX | IC | C | CC | CCC | CD | D | DC | DCC | DCCC
② | 99 | | 100 | 200 | 300 | 400 | 500 | 600 | 700 | 800

① | CM | CMXC | M
② | 900 | 990 | 1000

③ 9 658    ④ 5 kg.    ⑤ 2    ⑥ 2.    ⑦ +5    ⑧ -5

**1-26 aritmética** *f*
– *arithmetic*
**1-22 el número**
– *numbers*
**1** las cifras romanas (los números romanos)
– *Roman numerals*
**2** las cifras arábigas (los números arábigos)
– *Arabic numerals*
**3** el número abstracto, un número de cuatro cifras *f* (de cuatro dígitos *m*, de cuatro guarismos *m*) [8: las unidades; 5: las decenas; 6: las centenas; 9: las unidades de millar *m*]
– *abstract number, a four-figure number [8: units; 5: tens; 6: hundreds; 9: thousands]*
**4** el número concreto
– *concrete number*
**5** el número cardinal
– *cardinal number (cardinal)*
**6** el número ordinal *[en español: 2º]*
– *ordinal number (ordinal)*
**7** el número positivo [con el signo positivo]
– *positive number [with plus sign]*

**8** el número negativo [con el signo negativo]
– *negative number [with minus sign]*
**9** símbolos *m* algebraicos
– *algebraic symbols*
**10** el número mixto [3: el número entero; ⅓ la fracción (el número fraccionario, el quebrado)]
– *mixed number [3: whole number (integer); ⅓: fraction]*
**11** números *m* pares
– *even numbers*
**12** números *m* impares
– *odd numbers*
**13** números *m* primos
– *prime numbers*
**14** el número complejo [3: la parte real; $2\sqrt{-1}$: la parte imaginaria]
– *complex number [3: real part; $2\sqrt{-1}$: imaginary part]*
**15-16** quebrados *m* comunes
– *vulgar fractions*
**15** la fracción propia (el quebrado propio) [2: el numerador; la raya de quebrado *m* (la línea horizontal, el signo de división *f*) 3: el denominador]
– *proper fraction [2: numerator; horizontal line; 3: denominator]*

**16** la fracción impropia (el quebrado impropio), *al mismo tiempo* la recíproca (fracción *f* inversa) de la 15
– *improper fraction, also the reciprocal of item 15*
**17** la fracción compuesta
– *compound fraction (complex fraction)*
**18** la fracción impropia [cuando al reducirla resulta un número entero]
– *improper fraction [when cancelled down produces a whole number]*
**19** fracciones *f* de diferente denominador *m* [35: el común denominador]
– *fractions of different denominations [35: common denominator]*
**20** la fracción decimal propia con la coma de decimales *m* y los lugares de los decimales [3: las décimas; 5: las centésimas; 7: las milésimas]
– *proper decimal fraction with decimal point [in German: comma] and decimal places [3: tenths; 5: hundredths; 7: thousandths]*

⑨ a, b, c ...    ⑩ $3\frac{1}{3}$    ⑪ 2, 4, 6, 8    ⑫ 1, 3, 5, 7

⑬ 3, 5, 7, 11    ⑭ $3 + 2\sqrt{-1}$    ⑮ $\frac{2}{3}$    ⑯ $\frac{3}{2}$

⑰ $\dfrac{\frac{5}{6}}{\frac{3}{4}}$    ⑱ $\frac{12}{4}$    ⑲ $\frac{4}{5} + \frac{2}{7} = \frac{38}{35}$    ⑳ 0,357

㉑ $0,6666.... = 0,\overline{6}$ ㉒    ㉓ $3 + 2 = 5$

㉔ $3 - 2 = 1$    ㉕ $3 \cdot 2 = 6$    ㉖ $6 : 2 = 3$

$\qquad\qquad\qquad\qquad 3 \times 2 = 6$

in Britain:

⑥ 2nd    ⑳ 0·357    ㉑ $0·6666... = 0·\overline{6}$ ㉒

㉖ $6 \div 2 = 3$

---

**21** la fracción decimal periódica infinita
– *recurring decimal*
**22** el período
– *recurring decimal*
**23-26 las operaciones fundamentales de aritmética** f
– *fundamental arithmetical operations*
**23** la adición (suma f); [3 y 2: los sumandos (términos m de la suma); + : el signo más (el signo de adición f); = : el signo de igualdad f; 5: la suma (el resultado)]
– *addition (adding) [3 and 2: the terms of the sum; + : plus sign; = : equals sign; 5: the sum]*
**24** la sustracción (resta f); [3: el minuendo; − : el signo menos (el signo de sustracción f); 2: el sustraendo; 1: el resto (la diferencia)]
– *subtraction (subtracting); [3: the minuend; - : minus sign; 2: the subtrahend; 1: the remainder (difference)]*

**25** la multiplicación; [3: el multiplicando; · o x: el signo de multiplicación f; 2: el multiplicador; 2 y 3: factores m; 6: el producto]
– *multiplication (multiplying); [3: the multiplicand; × (in German · ): multiplication sign; 2: the multiplier; 2 and 3: factors; 6: the product]*
**26** la división; [6: el dividendo; : = el signo de división f; 2: el divisor; 3: el cociente]
– *division (dividing); [6: the dividend; : (in German): division sign; 2: the divisor; 3: the quotient]*

---

① $3^2 = 9$     ② $\sqrt[3]{8} = 2$     ③ $\sqrt{4} = 2$

④ $3x + 2 = 12$

⑥

⑤ $4a + 6ab - 2ac = 2a(2+3b-c)$     $\log_{10} 3 = 0{\cdot}4771$

⑦ $$\frac{P[\pounds 1000] \times R[5\%] \times T[2\,years]}{100} = I\,[\pounds 100]$$

en España:

⑦ $$\frac{c\,[1000\ Pts.] \cdot r\,[5\%] \cdot t\,[2\,años]}{100} = i\,[100\ Pts.]$$

1-24 aritmética *f*
– *arithmetic*
1-10 operaciones *f* de aritmética *f* superior
– *advanced arithmetical operations*
1 la elevación a una potencia (la potenciación); [3 al cuadrado: la potencia; 3: la base; 2: el exponente (el índice); 9: el valor de la potencia]
– *raising to a power [three squared ($3^2$): the power; 3: the base; 2: the exponent (index); 9: value of the power]*
2 la extracción de raíces *f* (la radicación); [raíz *f* cúbica de 8: la raíz cúbica; 8: el radicando; 3: el índice de la raíz; $\sqrt{\ }$: el radical (el signo de extracción *f* de raíces *f*); 2: el valor de la raíz]
– *evolution (extracting a root); [cube-root of 8: cube root; 8: the radical; 3: the index (degree) of the root; $\sqrt{\ }$: radical sign; 2: value of the root]*
3 la raíz cuadrada
– *square root*
4-5 el álgebra *f*
– *algebra*

4 la ecuación de primer grado *m*; [3, 2: los coeficientes, x: la incógnita]
– *simple equation [3, 2: the coefficients; x: the unknown quantity]*
5 la ecuación idéntica (de identidad *f*) [a, b, c: los símbolos algebraicos]
– *identical equation; [a, b, c: algebraic symbols]*
6 el cálculo logarítmico (la logaritmación); [log: el símbolo de logaritmo *m*; lg: el símbolo del logaritmo decimal; 3: el número cuyo logaritmo *m* se busca; 10: la base; 0: la característica; 4771: la mantisa; 0,4771: el logaritmo]
– *logarithmic calculation (taking the logarithm, log); [log: logarithm sign; 3: number whose logarithm is required; 10: the base; 0: the characteristic; 4771: the mantissa; 0.4771: the logarithm]*
7 la fórmula de interés *m* simple; [c: el capital inicial; r: el rédito (el tanto por ciento *m*); t: el tiempo; i: el interés (la ganancia); % el signo del tanto por ciento m]

– *simple interest formula; [P: the principal; R: rate of interest; T: time; I: interest (profit); %: percentage sign]*
8-10 la regla de tres [≙: equivalente a]
– *rule of three (rule-of-three sum, simple proportion)*
8 el planteamiento de la ecuación con la incógnita x (con la cantidad desconocida)
– *statement with the unknown quantity x*
9 la ecuación (ecuación *f* determinada)
– *equation (conditional equation)*
10 la solución
– *solution*
11-14 matemáticas *f* superiores
– *higher mathematics*
11 la progresión aritmética con los términos 2, 4, 6, 8
– *arithmetical series with the elements 2, 4, 6, 8*
12 la progresión geométrica
– *geometrical series*

⑧ $\dfrac{2\ \text{years @ £ 50}}{4\ \text{years @ £ x}}$

⑪ $2 + 4 + 6 + 8 \dots$

⑨ $2 : 50 = 4 : x$

⑩ $x = £100$

⑫ $2 + 4 + 8 + 16 + 32 \dots$

⑬ $\dfrac{dy}{dx}$

⑭ $\int a x\, dx = a \int x\, dx = \dfrac{a x^2}{2} + C$

⑮ $\infty$     ⑯ $\equiv$     ⑰ $\approx$     ⑱ $\not\equiv$     ⑲ $>$

⑳ $<$     ㉑ $\parallel$     ㉒ $\sim$     ㉓ $\triangleleft$     ㉔ $\triangle$

en España:

⑧ $\dfrac{2\ \text{años} \cong 50\ \text{Pts.}}{4\ \text{años} \cong x\ \text{Pts.}}$

⑨ $2 : 50 = 4 : x$

⑩ $x = 100\ \text{Pts.}$

**13-14 el cálculo infinitesimal**
– *infinitesimal calculus*
**13** la derivada (el cociente diferencial, la derivación); [dx, dy: las diferenciales; d: el signo de diferencial]
– *derivative [dx, dy: the differentials; d: differential sign]*
**14** la integral (el cálculo integral, la integración) [x: la variable de integración; c: la constante de la integral; $\int$: el signo de la integral; dx: la diferencial]
– *integral (integration); [x: the variable; C: constant of integration; $\int$: the integral sign; dx: the differential]*
**15-24 signos *m* matemáticos**
– *mathematical symbols*
**15** infinito
– *infinity*
**16** idéntico (el signo de identidad *f*)
– *identically equal to [the sign of identity]*
**17** casi igual
– *approximately equal to*
**18** no idéntico (el signo de la no identidad)
– *unequal to*

**19** mayor que
– *greater than*
**20** menor que
– *less than*
**21-24 signos *m* geométricos**
– *geometrical symbols*
**21** paralelo (el signo de paralelismo *m*)
– *parallel [sign of parallelism]*
**22** semejante (el signo de la semejanza)
– *similar to [sign of similarity]*
**23** el signo de ángulo *m*
– *angle symbol*
**24** el signo de triángulo *m*
– *triangle symbol*

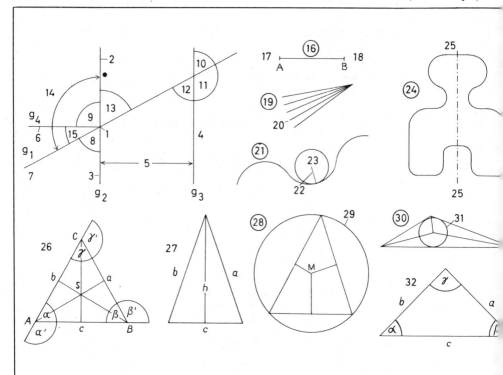

**1-58 geometría *f* plana** (geometría *f* elemental, geometría *f* euclidiana)
– *plane geometry (elementary geometry, Euclidian geometry)*
**1-23 punto *m*, línea *f*, ángulo *m***
– *point, line, angle*
**1** el punto [punto *m* de intersección *f* de $g_1$ y $g_2$], el vértice de 8
– *point [point of intersection of $g_1$ and $g_2$], the angular point of 8*
**2, 3** la línea recta $g_2$
– *straight line $g_2$*
**4** la paralela a $g_2$
– *the parallel to $g_2$*
**5** la distancia entre las líneas rectas $g_2$ y $g_3$
– *distance between the straight lines $g_2$ and $g_3$*
**6** la perpendicular $(g_4)$ a $g_2$
– *perpendicular $(g_4)$ on $g_2$*
**7, 3** los lados del ángulo 8
– *the arms of 8*
**8, 13** ángulos *m* opuestos por el vértice
– *vertically opposite angles*
**8** el ángulo
– *angle*
**9** el ángulo recto [90°]
– *right angle [90°]*
**10, 11, 12** el ángulo cóncavo
– *reflex angle*
**10** el ángulo agudo, *al mismo tiempo* ángulo *m* alterno con el 8
– *acute angle, also the alternate angle to 8*

**11** el ángulo obtuso
– *obtuse angle*
**12** el ángulo correspondiente al 8
– *corresponding angle to 8*
**13, 9, 15** el ángulo llano [180°]
– *straight angle [180°]*
**14** el ángulo adyacente; *en este caso:* el ángulo suplementario del 13
– *adjacent angle; here: supplementary angle to 13*
**15** el ángulo complementario del 8
– *complementary angle to 8*
**16** el segmento rectilíneo AB
– *straight line AB*
**17** el extremo A
– *end A*
**18** el extremo B
– *end B*
**19** el haz de rayos *m*
– *pencil of rays*
**20** el rayo
– *ray*
**21** la línea curva
– *curved line*
**22** un radio de curvatura *f*
– *radius of curvature*
**23** un centro de curvatura *f*
– *centre (Am. center) of curvature*
**24-58 las superficies planas**
– *plane surfaces*
**24** la figura semétrica
– *symmetrical figure*
**25** el eje de simetría *f*
– *axis of symmetry*
**26-32 triángulos *m***
– *plane triangles*

**26** el triángulo equilátero; [A, B, C: los vértices; a, b, c: los lados; α (alfa), β (beta), γ (gamma): los ángulos interiores; α', β', γ': los ángulos exteriores; S: el centro]
– *equilateral triangle; [A, B, C: the vertices; a, b, c: the sides; α (alpha), β (beta), γ (gamma): the interior angles; α', β γ': the exterior angles; S: the centre (Am. center)]*
**27** el triángulo isósceles; [a, b: los lados; c: la base; h: la perpendicular, una altura]
– *isosceles triangle [a, b: the sides (legs); c: the base; h: the perpendicular, an altitude]*
**28** el triángulo acutángulo con las mediatrices
– *acute-angled triangle with perpendicular bisectors of the sides*
**29** el círculo circunscrito
– *circumcircle (circumscribed circle)*
**30** el triángulo obtusángulo con las bisectrices
– *obtuse-angled triangle with bisectors of the angles*
**31** el círculo inscrito
– *inscribed circle*
**32** el triángulo rectángulo y las funciones trigonométricas de los ángulos; [a, b los catetos; c la hipotenusa; γ el ángulo recto; a:c = sen α (seno *m*); b:c = cos α (coseno *m*); a:b = tg α (tangente *f*); b:a = cotg α (cotangente *f*)]

- *right-angled triangle and the*
  *trigonometrical functions of angles;*
  *[a, b: the catheti; c: the hypotenuse;*
  *γ: the right angle;* $\frac{a}{c} = \sin \alpha$ *(sine);*
  $\frac{b}{c} = \cos \alpha$ *(cosine);* $\frac{a}{b} = \tan \alpha$
  *(tangent);* $\frac{b}{a} = \cot \alpha$ *(cotangent)*
- **33-39 cuadriláteros** *m*
- *quadrilaterals*
- **33-36 paralelogramos** *m*
- *parallelograms*
- **33** el cuadrado [d: una diagonal]
- *square [d: a diagonal]*
- **34** el rectángulo
- *rectangle*
- **35** el rombo
- *rhombus (rhomb, lozenge)*
- **36** el romboide
- *rhomboid*
- **37** el trapecio
- *trapezium*
- **38** el deltoide (cometa *f*)
- *deltoid (kite)*
- **39** el cuadrilátero irregular
- *irregular quadrilateral*
- **40** el polígono
- *polygon*
- **41** el polígono regular
- *regular polygon*
- **42 el círculo**
- *circle*
- **43** el centro
- *centre (Am. center)*
- **44** la circunferencia
- *circumference (periphery)*
- **45** el diámetro
- *diameter*

- **46** el semicírculo
- *semicircle*
- **47** el radio (r)
- *radius (r)*
- **48** la tangente
- *tangent*
- **49** el punto de contacto *m* (P)
- *point of contact (P)*
- **50** la secante
- *secant*
- **51** la cuerda AB
- *the chord AB*
- **52** el segmento circular
- *segment*
- **53** el arco de circunferencia *f*
- *arc*
- **54** el sector circular
- *sector*
- **55** el ángulo central
- *angle subtended by the arc at the*
  *centre (Am. center) (centre, Am.*
  *center, angle)*
- **56** el ángulo inscrito
- *circumferential angle*
- **57** la corona circular
- *ring (annulus)*
- **58** círculos *m* concéntricos
- *concentric circles*

1 el sistema de coordenadas $f$ ortogonales (rectangulares, cartesianas)
– *system of right-angled coordinates*
2-3 los ejes de coordenadas $f$
– *axes of coordinates (coordinate axes)*
2 el eje de abscisas $f$ (eje $m$ de las x)
– *axis of abscissae (x-axis)*
3 el eje de ordenadas $f$ (eje $m$ de las y)
– *axis of ordinates (y-axis)*
4 el origen de coordenadas $f$ (punto $m$ cero)
– *origin of ordinates*
5 el cuadrante [I–IV del $1°$ al $4°$ cuadrante]
– *quadrant [I - IV: 1st to 4th quadrant]*
6 la dirección positiva
– *positive direction*
7 la dirección negativa
– *negative direction*
8 los puntos [$P_1$ y $P_2$] en el sistema de coordenadas $f$; $x_1$ e $y_1$ [o $x_2$ e $y_2$ respectivamente]: sus coordenadas $f$
– *points [$P_1$ and $P_2$] in the system of coordinates; $x_1$ and $y_1$ [and $x_2$ and $y_2$ respectively] their coordinates*
9 el valor de la abscisa [$x_1$ o $x_2$ respectivamente] (las abscisas)
– *values of the abscissae [$x_1$ and $x_2$] (the abscissae)*
10 el valor de la ordenada [$y_1$ o $y_2$ respectivamente] (las ordenadas)
– *values of the ordinates [$y_1$ and $y_2$] (the ordinates)*
11-29 las secciones cónicas
– *conic sections*
11 las curvas en el sistema de coordenadas $f$
– *curves in the system of coordinates*
12 rectas $f$ [a: la pendiente de la recta; b: la intersección de la recta con la ordenada; c: la raíz de la recta]
– *plane curves [a: the gradient (slope) of the curve; b: the ordinates' intersection of the curve; c: the root of the curve]*
13 las curvas
– *inflected curves*
14 la parábola, una curva de segundo grado $m$
– *parabola, a curve of the second degree*
15 las ramas de la parábola
– *branches of the parabola*
16 el vértice de la parábola
– *vertex of the parabola*
17 el eje de la parábola
– *axis of the parabola*
18 una curva de tercer grado $m$
– *a curve of the third degree*
19 el máximo de la curva
– *maximum of the curve*
20 el mínimo de la curva
– *minimum of the curve*
21 el punto de inflexión $f$
– *point of inflexion (of inflection)*
22 la elipse
– *ellipse*
23 el eje mayor
– *transverse axis (major axis)*
24 el eje menor
– *conjugate axis (minor axis)*
25 los focos de la elipse [$F_1$ y $F_2$]
– *foci of the ellipse [$F_1$ and $F_2$]*
26 la hipérbola
– *hyperbola*
27 los focos [$F_1$ y $F_2$]
– *foci [$F_1$ and $F_2$]*
28 los vértices [$S_1$ y $S_2$]
– *vertices [$S_1$ and $S_2$]*
29 las asíntotas [a y b]
– *asymptotes [a and b]*
30-46 cuerpos $m$ geométricos
– *solids*
30 el cubo
– *cube*
31 el cuadrado, una cara
– *square, a plane (plane surface)*
32 la arista
– *edge*
33 el vértice
– *corner*
34 el prisma cuadrangular
– *quadratic prism*
35 la base
– *base*
36 el paralelepípedo rectangular
– *parallelepiped*
37 el prisma triangular
– *triangular prism*
38 el cilindro, un cilindro recto
– *cylinder, a right cylinder*
39 la base, una cara circular
– *base, a circular plane*
40 la superficie lateral
– *curved surface*
41 la esfera
– *sphere*
42 el elipsoide de revolución $f$
– *ellipsoid of revolution*
43 el cono
– *cone*
44 la altura del cono
– *height of the cone (cone height)*
45 el cono truncado
– *truncated cone (frustum of a cone)*
46 la pirámide cuadrangular
– *quadrilateral pyramid*

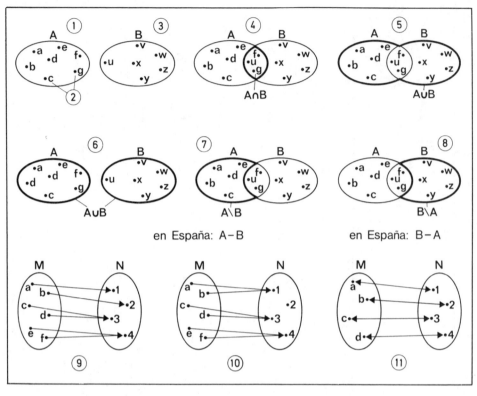

en España: A−B

en España: B−A

1 el conjunto A, el conjunto
{a, b, c, d, e, f, g}
- the set A, the set {a, b, c, d, e, f, g}
2 los elementos del conjunto A
- elements (members) of the set A
3 el conjunto B, el conjunto
{u, v, w, x, y, z}
- the set B, the set {u, v, w, x, y, z}
4 la intersección de los conjuntos
A y B, A ∩ B = {f, g, u}
- intersection of the sets A and B,
A ∩ B = {f, g, u}
5-6 la unión de los conjuntos A y
B, A ∪ B =
{a, b, c, d, e, f, g, u, v, w, x, y, z}
- union of the sets A and B, A ∪ B
= {a, b, c, d, e, f, g, u, v, w, x, y, z}
7 la diferencia de los conjuntos
A − B = {a, b, c, d, e}
- complement of the set B, B′ =
{a, b, c, d, e}
8 la diferencia de los conjuntos
B − A = {v, w, x, y, z}
- complement of the set A, A′ =
{v, w, x, y, z}
9-11 las aplicaciones
- mappings
9 la aplicación del conjunto M
sobre el conjunto N
- mapping of the set M onto the
set N

10 la aplicación del conjunto M en
el conjunto N
- mapping of the set M into the set
N
11 la aplicación biunívoca del
conjunto M en el conjunto N
- one-to-one mapping of the set M
onto the set N

**1-38 los aparatos de laboratorio** *m*
- *laboratory apparatus (laboratory equipment)*
1 el globo Scheidt
- *Scheidt globe*
2 el tubo en U
- *U-tube*
3 el embudo de separación *f*(el tubo de bromo *m*)
- *separating funnel*
4 el tapón octogonal
- *octagonal ground-glass stopper*
5 la llave
- *tap* (Am. *faucet*)
6 el refrigerador de serpentín *m*
- *coiled condenser*
7 la válvula de seguridad *f*
- *air lock*
8 el frasco lavador
- *wash-bottle*
9 el mortero
- *mortar*
10 la mano del mortero
- *pestle*
11 el filtro de vacío *m* (el filtro de Büchner)
- *filter funnel (Büchner funnel)*
12 el filtro (tamiz *m*)
- *filter (filter plate)*
13 la retorta
- *retort*
14 el baño María
- *water bath*
15 el trípode
- *tripod*

16 el indicador del nivel del agua *f*
- *water gauge* (Am. *gage*)
17 las arandelas
- *insertion rings*
18 el agitador
- *stirrer*
19 el medidor de alta y baja presión *f* (el manómetro)
- *manometer for measuring positive and negative pressures*
20 el manómetro (vacuómetro *m*) de espejo *m*, para medir presiones *f* pequeñas
- *mirror manometer for measuring small pressures*
21 el tubo de succión *f*
- *inlet*
22 la llave (la espita)
- *tap* (Am. *faucet*)
23 la escala de cursor *m*
- *sliding scale*
24 el bote de pesar
- *weighing bottle*
25 la balanza de análisis *m*
- *analytical balance*
26 la caja
- *case*
27 el panel anterior levadizo
- *sliding front panel*
28 el soporte de tres puntos *m* (el tornillo nivelador)
- *three-point support*
29 la columna de la balanza
- *column (balance column)*

30 el astil de la balanza
- *balance beam (beam)*
31 el carril de corredera *f*
- *rider bar*
32 el agarrador de corredera *f*
- *rider holder*
33 la corredera
- *rider*
34 el fiel
- *pointer*
35 la escala
- *scale*
36 el platillo
- *scale pan*
37 el inmovilizador
- *stop*
38 el botón de inmovilización *f*
- *stop knob*

# 350 Laboratorio de química II

**1-63 los aparatos de laboratorio** *m*
- *laboratory apparatus (laboratory equipment)*
1 el mechero Bunsen
- *Bunsen burner*
2 el tubo de entrada *f* del gas
- *gas inlet (gas inlet pipe)*
3 el regulador del aire
- *air regulator*
4 el mechero Teclu
- *Teclu burner*
5 el tubo de unión *f*
- *pipe union*
6 el regulador del gas
- *gas regulator*
7 el tubo
- *stem*
8 el regulador del aire
- *air regulator*
9 el soplete
- *bench torch*
10 el revestimiento
- *casing*
11 la entrada de oxígeno *m*
- *oxygen inlet*
12 la entrada de hidrógeno *m*
- *hydrogen inlet*
13 la boquilla del oxígeno
- *oxygen jet*
14 el trípode
- *tripod*
15 la anilla
- *ring (retort ring)*
16 el embudo
- *funnel*
17 el triángulo de arcilla *f*
- *pipe clay triangle*
18 la tela metálica
- *wire gauze*
19 la tela metálica con amianto *m*
- *wire gauze with asbestos centre (Am. center)*
20 el vaso de precipitados *m*
- *beaker*
21 la bureta, para medir líquidos *m*
- *burette (for measuring the volume of liquids)*
22 el soporte de la bureta
- *burette stand*
23 la abrazadera de la bureta
- *burette clamp*
24 la pipeta graduada
- *graduated pipette*
25 la pipeta ordinaria
- *pipette*
26 la probeta graduada
- *measuring cylinder (measuring glass)*
27 la probeta graduada con tapón *m*
- *measuring flask*
28 el matraz de mezclas *f*
- *volumetric flask*
29 la cápsula, de porcelana *f*
- *evaporating dish (evaporating basin), made of porcelain*
30 la abrazadera de tubos *m*
- *tube clamp (tube clip, pinchcock)*

31 el crisol de arcilla *f*, con tapadera *f*
- *clay crucible with lid*
32 las pinzas del crisol
- *crucible tongs*
33 la agarradera (la grapa)
- *clamp*
34 el tubo de ensayo *m*
- *test tube*
35 el soporte de los tubos de ensayo *m*
- *test tube rack*
36 el matraz de fondo *m* plano
- *flat-bottomed flask*
37 la boca esmerilada
- *ground glass neck*
38 el matraz redondo, de cuello *m* largo
- *long-necked round-bottomed flask*
39 el matraz cónico (el Erlenmeyer)
- *Erlenmeyer flask (conical flask)*
40 el frasco de filtración *f*
- *filter flask*
41 el filtro de papel *m* plegado
- *fluted filter*
42 la llave de un solo paso
- *one-way tap*
43 el tubo de cloruro *m* cálcico (el tubo de secado *m*)
- *calcium chloride tube*
44 el tapón con llave *f*
- *stopper with tap*
45 la probeta
- *cylinder*
46 el alambique (el aparato de destilación *f*)
- *distillation apparatus (distilling apparatus)*
47 el matraz de destilación *f*
- *distillation flask (distilling flask)*
48 el condensador (el refrigerante)
- *condenser*
49 la llave de retorno *m*, una llave de dos pasos *m*
- *return tap, a two-way tap*
50 el matraz de destilación *f*
- *distillation flask (distilling flask, Claisen flask)*
51 el desecador
- *desiccator*
52 la tapa con un tubo ajustado
- *lid with fitted tube*
53 la llave
- *tap*
54 la salvilla del desecador, de porcelana *f*
- *desiccator insert made of porcelain*
55 el matraz de tres bocas *f*
- *three-necked flask*
56 la pieza de conexión *f* (el tubo en Y)
- *connecting piece (Y-tube)*
57 el frasco de tres bocas *f*
- *three-necked bottle*
58 el frasco para limpiar gas *m*
- *gas-washing bottle*

59 el aparato para producir gas *m* (aparato *m* Kipp)
- *gas generator (Kipp's apparatus, Am. Kipp generator)*
60 el recipiente de rebosamiento *m*
- *overflow container*
61 el recipiente de la sustancia
- *container for the solid*
62 el recipiente del ácido
- *acid container*
63 la toma del gas
- *gas outlet*

**1-26** formas _f_ fundamentales de
los cristales y combinaciónes _f_
de cristales _m_ (estructura _f_ de
los cristales)
– **basic crystal forms and crystal
combinations** _[structure of
crystals]_
**1-17** el sistema regular de
cristalización _f_ (cúbico,
isométrico)
– **regular** _(cubic, tesseral,
isometric)_ **crystal system**
**1** el tetraedro (poliedro _m_ de
cuatro caras _f_, la tetraedrita)
[cobre _m_ gris]
– _tetrahedron (four-faced
polyhedron) [tetrahedrite,
fahlerz, fahl ore]_
**2** el hexaedro (cubo _m_,
poliedro _m_ de seis caras _f_), un
holoédrico [sal _f_ gema]
– _hexahedron (cube, six-faced
polyhedron), a holohedron [rock
salt]_
**3** el centro de simetría _f_ (el centro
del cristal)
– _centre_ (Am. _center) of symmetry
(crystal centre)_
**4** un eje de simetría _f_
– _axis of symmetry (rotation axis)_
**5** un plano de simetría _f_
– _plane of symmetry_
**6** el octaedro (poliedro _m_ de
ocho caras _f_) [oro _m_]
– _octahedron (eight-faced
polyhedron) [gold]_
**7** el dodecaedro romboidal (el
rombododecaedro) [granate _m_]
– _rhombic dodecahedron [garnet]_
**8** el dodecaedro pentagonal
[pirita _f_]
– _pentagonal dodecahedron
[pyrite, iron pyrites]_
**9** el pentágono (polígono _m_ de
cinco lados _m_)
– _pentagon (five-sided polygon)_
**10** el octaedro piramidado
[diamante _m_]
– _triakis-octahedron [diamond]_
**11** el icosaedro (poliedro _m_ de
veinte caras _f_), un poliedro
regular
– _icosahedron (twenty-faced
polyhedron), a regular
polyhedron_
**12** el icositetraedro (poliedro _m_ de
veinticuatro caras _f_) [leucita _f_]
– _icositetrahedron (twenty-four-
faced polyhedron) [leucite]_
**13** el hexaquioctaedro (poliedro _m_
de cuarenta y ocho caras _f_)
[diamante _m_]
– _hexakis-octahedron
(hexoctahedron, forty-eight-
faced polyhedron) [diamond]_
**14** el octaedro con cubo _m_ [galena
_f_]
– _octahedron with cube [galena]_

**15** un hexágono (polígono _m_ de
seis lados _m_)
– _hexagon (six-sided polygon)_
**16** el cubo con octaedro _m_
[espato _m_ flúor _m_]
– _cube with octahedron [fluorite,
fluorspar]_
**17** un octógono (polígono _m_ de
ocho lados _m_)
– _octagon (eight-sided polygon)_
**18-19** el sistema de cristalización _f_
tetragonal
– _tetragonal crystal system_
**18** la pirámide tetragonal
– _tetragonal dipyramid (tetragonal
bipyramid)_
**19** el protoprisma con
protopirámide _f_ [circón _m_]
– _protoprism with protopyramid
[zircon]_
**20-22** el sistema de cristalización _f_
hexagonal
– _hexagonal crystal system_
**20** el protoprisma con
protopirámide _f_ y
deutopirámide _f_ y base _f_
pinacoide [apatito _m_]
– _protoprism with protopyramid,
deutero-pyramid and basal
pinacoid [apatite]_
**21** el prisma hexagonal
– _hexagonal prism_
**22** el prisma hexagonal (el prisma
ditrigonal) con romboedro _m_
[calcita _f_ (espato _m_ de
Islandia)]
– _hexagonal (ditrigonal) biprism
with rhombohedron [calcite]_
**23** la pirámide ortorrómbica (el
sistema rómbico) [azufre _m_]
– _orthorhombic pyramid (rhombic
crystal system) [sulphur, Am.
sulfur]_
**24-25** el sistema de cristalización _f_
monoclínico (sistema _m_ oblicuo,
sistema _m_ monosimétrico)
– _monoclinic crystal system_
**24** el prisma monoclínico con
clinopinacoide _m_ y
hemipirámide _f_ (hemiedro _m_)
[yeso _m_]
– _monoclinic prism with
clinoprinacoid and hemipyramid
(hemihedron) [gypsum]_
**25** el ortopinacoide (cristal _m_
gemelo en cola _f_ de golondrina
_f_) [yeso _m_]
– _orthopinacoid (swallow-tail twin
crystal) [gypsum]_
**26** el pinacoide triclínico
(sistema _m_ triclínico) [sulfato _m_
de cobre _m_]
– _triclinic pinacoids (triclinic
crystal system) [copper sulphate,
Am. copper sulfate]_
**27-33** aparatos _m_ para medir
cristales _m_ (para la
cristalometría)
– **apparatus for measuring crystals**
_(for crystallometry)_

**27** el goniómetro de contacto _m_
– _contact goniometer_
**28** el goniómetro por reflexión _f_
– _reflecting goniometer_
**29** el cristal
– _crystal_
**30** el colimador
– _collimator_
**31** el telescopio de observación _f_
– _observation telescope_
**32** el círculo graduado
– _divided circle (graduated circle)_
**33** la lente, para leer el ángulo de
rotación _f_
– _lens for reading the angle of
rotation_

1 el poste totémico (el pilar totémico)
- *totem pole*
2 el totem, una representación ,esculpida y pintada, figurativa o simbólica
- *totem, a carved and painted pictorial or symbolic representation*
3 el indio de las praderas (*Amér.:* el indio de las sabanas)
- *plains Indian*
4 el mustang, un caballo de las estepas
- *mustang, a prairie horse*
5 el lazo, una larga cuerda arrojadiza con nudo *m* corredizo de fácil cierre *m*
- *lasso, a long throwing-rope with running noose*
6 la pipa de la paz
- *pipe of peace*
7 la tienda india (la tienda de los indios norteamericanos, el tipi)
- *wigwam (tepee, teepee)*
8 el poste de la tienda
- *tent pole*
9 la trampilla para el humo
- *smoke flap*
10 la mujer india norteamericana (la squaw)
- *squaw, an Indian woman*
11 el jefe indio
- *Indian chief*
12 el tocado, un adorno de plumas *f*
- *headdress, an ornamental feather headdress*
13 la pintura de guerra *f*
- *war paint*
14 el collar, de uñas *f* de oso *m*
- *necklace of bear claws*
15 el cuero cabelludo arrancado al enemigo, un trofeo
- *scalp, a trophy*
16 el hacha *f* de guerra *f* de los indios norteamericanos (el tomahawk)
- *tomahawk, a battle axe (Am. ax)*
17 las polainas (polainas *f* de cuero *m* de venado *m*)
- *leggings*
18 el mocasín, un zapato bajo (de cuero *m* y corteza *f* vegetal)
- *moccasin, a shoe of leather and bast*
19 la piragua de los indios de los bosques
- *canoe of the forest Indians*
20 el templo maya, una pirámide escalonada
- *Maya temple, a stepped pyramid*
21 la momia
- *mummy*
22 los quipos (la cuerda con nudos *m*, la escritura de nudos *m* de los incas)
- *quipa (knotted threads, knotted code of the Incas)*

23 el indio (el indio de Centro y Sudamérica); *en este caso:* el indio del altiplano
- *Indio (Indian of Central and South America);* here: *highland Indian*
24 el poncho, una manta con abertura *f* para el cuello, especie *f* de capote *m* sin mangas *f*
- *poncho, a blanket with a head opening used as an armless cloak-like wrap*
25 el indio de la selva tropical
- *Indian of the tropical forest*
26 la cerbatana (la bodoquera; *Bol.:* la pacuna)
- *blowpipe*
27 el carcaj
- *quiver*
28 la flecha
- *dart*
29 la punta de la flecha
- *dart point*
30 la cabeza reducida, un trofeo
- *shrunken head, a trophy*
31 las boleadoras, una arma arrojadiza y de captura *f*
- *bola (bolas), a throwing and entangling device*
32 la bola de piedra *f* o metal *m* forrada de cuero *m*
- *leather-covered stone or metal ball*
33 el palafito (una choza sobre pilares *m*)
- *pile dwelling*
34 el bailarín Duk-duk, un miembro de una sociedad secreta de hombres *m*
- *duk-duk dancer, a member of a duk-duk (men's secret society)*
35 la canoa con batanga *f* (con balancín *m*)
- *outrigger canoe (canoe with outrigger)*
36 la batanga (el balancín)
- *outrigger*
37 el aborigen (el indígena, el nativo) australiano
- *Australian aborigine*
38 el taparrabo de cabellos *m* humanos
- *loincloth of human hair*
39 el bumerang, una arma arrojadiza de madera *f*
- *boomerang, a wooden missile*
40 el lanzajabalinas con jabalinas *f*
- *throwing stick (spear thrower) with spears*

1 el esquimal
– Eskimo
2 el perro de trineo *m*, un perro
polar (un perro esquimal)
– sledge dog (sled dog), a husky
3 el trineo de perros *m*
– dog sledge (dog sled)
4 el iglú, una choza de nieve *f* en
forma *f* de cúpula *f*
– igloo, a dome-shaped snow hut
5 el bloque de nieve *f*
– block of snow
6 el túnel de entrada *f*
– entrance tunnel
7 la lámpara de aceite *m* de
pescado *m* (de ballena *f* o foca
*f*)
– blubber-oil lamp
8 la tablilla arrojadiza
– wooden missile
9 el espiche
– lance
10 el arpón de una sola punta
– harpoon
11 el saco de aire *m* (el flotador
del arpón)
– skin float
12 el kayak, una canoa ligera
individual
– kayak, a light one-man canoe
13 la armazón de madera *f* o
hueso *m* recubierta de piel *f*
– skin-covered wooden or bone
frame
14 el zagual (el canalete)
– paddle
15 el atalaje de reno *m*
– reindeer harness
16 el reno
– reindeer
17 el ostiaco
– Ostyak (Ostiak)
18 el trineo con respaldo *m* (el
trineo de viajeros *m*)
– passenger sledge
19 la yurta, una tienda vivienda *f*
de los nómadas de Asia *f*
Central y Occidental
– yurt (yurta), a dwelling tent of
the western and central Asiatic
nomads
20 la cubierta de fieltro *m*
– felt covering
21 la abertura para el humo
– smoke outlet
22 el kirghís
– Kirghiz
23 el gorro de piel *f* de oveja *f*
– sheepskin cap
24 el chamán
– shaman
25 el adorno de flecos *m*
– decorative fringe
26 el tambor de bastidor *m*
– frame drum
27 el tibetano
– Tibetan
28 la escopeta de horquilla *f*
– flintlock with bayonets

29 el molino de oraciones *f*
– prayer wheel
30 la bota de fieltro *m*
– felt boot
31 el barco vivienda (la casa
flotante, el sampán)
– houseboat (sampan)
32 el junco
– junk
33 la vela de estera *f*
– mat sail
34 la jinrikisha (la rikisha)
– rickshaw (ricksha)
35 el culí de la jinrikisha
– rickshaw coolie (cooly)
36 el lampión [un farolillo chino]
– Chinese lantern
37 el samurai
– samurai
38 la armadura enguatada
– padded armour (Am. armor)
39 la geisha
– geisha
40 el quimono
– kimono
41 el obi (faja *f* de seda *f*
japonesa)
– obi
42 el abanico
– fan
43 el culí
– coolie (cooly)
44 el cris, un puñal malayo
– kris (creese, crease), a Malayan
dagger
45 el encantador de serpientes *f*
– snake charmer
46 el turbante
– turban
47 la flauta
– flute
48 la serpiente danzante
– dancing snake

1 la caravana de camellos *m*
- *camel caravan*
2 el animal para montar
- *riding animal*
3 el animal de carga *f*
- *pack animal*
4 el oasis
- *oasis*
5 el palmeral
- *grove of palm trees*
6 el beduino
- *bedouin (beduin)*
7 el albornoz
- *burnous*
8 el guerrero masai
- *Masai warrior*
9 el peinado
- *headdress (hairdress)*
10 el escudo
- *shield*
11 el cuero de buey *m* pintado
- *painted ox hide*
12 la lanza de hoja *f* larga
- *long-bladed spear*
13 el negro
- *negro*
14 el tambor de danza *f* (el tam-tam)
- *dance drum*
15 el cuchillo arrojadizo
- *throwing knife*
16 la máscara de madera *f*
- *wooden mask*
17 la figura del antepasado
- *figure of an ancestor*
18 el tambor de señales *f*
- *slit gong*
19 el palillo (la baqueta; *C. Rica;* el bolillo) del tambor
- *drumstick*
20 la canoa, una embarcación hecha vaciando un tronco de árbol *m*
- *dugout, a boat hollowed out of a tree trunk*
21 la choza del negro
- *negro hut*
22 la negra
- *negress*
23 el disco labial
- *lip plug (labret)*
24 la piedra de moler
- *grinding stone*
25 la mujer herera
- *Herero woman*
26 la toca de cuero *m*
- *leather cap*
27 la calabaza (*Amér.:* el porongo) [calabaza *f* vinatera]
- *calabash (gourd)*
28 la choza en forma *f* de colmena *f*
- *beehive-shaped hut*
29 el bosquimano
- *bushman*
30 la estaquilla de la oreja
- *earplug*
31 el taparrabo
- *loincloth*

32 el arco
- *bow*
33 el quirri, una clava (cachiporra *f*) de cabeza *f* redonda y gruesa
- *knobkerry (knobkerrie), a club with round, knobbed end*
34 la mujer bosquimana obteniendo fuego *m* por taladramiento *m*
- *bushman woman making a fire by twirling a stick*
35 el abrigo contra el viento
- *windbreak*
36 el zulú en atuendo *m* de danza *f*
- *Zulu in dance costume*
37 el bastón de danza *f*
- *dancing stick*
38 el anillo de la pierna
- *bangle*
39 el cuerno de guerra *f* de marfil *m*
- *ivory war horn*
40 la cadena de amuletos *m* y dados *m*
- *string of amulets and bones*
41 el pigmeo
- *pigmy*
42 la chifla (el chifle, el silbato) mágico para conjurar los espíritus
- *magic pipe for exorcising evil spirits*
43 el fetiche
- *fetish*

1 mujer f griega
- *Greek woman*
2 el peplo
- *peplos*
3 hombre m griego
- *Greek*
4 el petaso (sombrero m tesalio)
- *petasus (Thessalonian hat)*
5 el chitón, una túnica interior de lino m
- *chiton, a linen gown worn as a basic garment*
6 el himatión, un manto de lana f
- *himation, woollen (Am. woolen) cloak*
7 mujer f romana
- *Roman woman*
8 el tupé de la frente
- *toupee wig (partial wig)*
9 la estola
- *stola*
10 la palla, un manto de color m
- *palla, a coloured (Am. colored) wrap*
11 hombre m romano
- *Roman*
12 la túnica
- *tunica (tunic)*
13 la toga
- *toga*
14 la orla de púrpura f
- *purple border (purple band)*
15 emperatriz f bizantina
- *Byzantine empress*

16 la diadema de perlas f
- *pearl diadem*
17 los pinjantes
- *jewels*
18 el manto de púrpura f
- *purple cloak*
19 el vestido
- *long tunic*
20 princesa f alemana [siglo m XIII]
- *German princess [13th cent.]*
21 la diadema
- *crown (diadem)*
22 el griñón (la impla)
- *chinband*
23 la campanilla
- *tassel*
24 la presilla del manto
- *cloak cord*
25 el vestido ceñido
- *girt-up gown (girt-up surcoat, girt-up tunic)*
26 el manto
- *cloak*
27 alemán m en indumentaria f española [alrededor de 1575]
- *German dressed in the Spanish style [ca. 1575]*
28 el birrete
- *wide-brimmed cap*
29 la capa corta (capa f a la española)
- *short cloak (Spanish cloak, short cape)*

30 el jubón enguatado
- *padded doublet (stuffed doublet, peasecod)*
31 las trusas (los gregüescos acolchados y acuchillados)
- *stuffed trunk-hose*
32 lansquenete m [alrededor de 1530]
- *lansquenet (German mercenary soldier) [ca. 1530]*
33 el jubón acuchillado
- *slashed doublet (paned doublet)*
34 los pantalones bombachos
- *Pluderhose (loose breeches, paned trunk-hose, slops)*
35 mujer f basiliense [alrededor de 1525]
- *woman of Basle [ca. 1525]*
36 el sobretodo
- *overgown (gown)*
37 la saya
- *undergown (petticoat)*
38 mujer f de Nuremberg [alrededor de 1500]
- *woman of Nuremberg [ca. 1500]*
39 la esclavina
- *shoulder cape*
40 hombre m borgoñón [siglo m XV]
- *Burgundian [15th cent.]*
41 el jubón corto
- *short doublet*
42 los zapatos de punta f (zapatos m a la polaca)
- *piked shoes (peaked shoes, copped shoes, crackowes, poulaines)*

**43** los chanclos (zuecos *m*, galochas *f*)
– *pattens (clogs)*
**44** joven *m* noble [alrededor de 1400]
– *young nobleman [ca. 1400]*
**45** el sayo corto
– *short, padded doublet (short, quilted doublet, jerkin)*
**46** la manga festoneada
– *dagged sleeves (petal-scalloped sleeves)*
**47** la calza
– *hose*
**48** patricia *f* de Augsburgo [alrededor de 1575]
– *Augsburg patrician lady [ca. 1575]*
**49** las mangas de bullones *m*
– *puffed sleeve*
**50** el sobretodo
– *overgown (gown), a sleeveless open gown*
**51** dama *f* francesa [alrededor de 1600]
– *French lady [ca. 1600]*
**52** la gorguera en muela *f* de molino *m*
– *millstone ruff (cartwheel ruff, ruff)*
**53** el talle encorsetado (la cintura de avispa *f*)
– *corseted waist (wasp waist)*
**54** caballero *m* [alrededor de 1650]
– *gentleman [ca. 1650]*
**55** el sombrero blando (flexible) sueco
– *wide-brimmed felt hat (cavalier hat)*

**56** el cuello de lino *m*
– *falling collar (wide-falling collar) of linen*
**57** el forro de tela *m* blanca
– *white lining*
**58** la bota alta (la bota con rodillera *f*)
– *jack boots (bucket-top boots)*
**59** dama *f* [alrededor de 1650]
– *lady [ca. 1650]*
**60** las mangas de bullones *m*
– *full puffed sleeves (puffed sleeves)*
**61** caballero *m* [alrededor de 1700]
– *gentleman [ca. 1700]*
**62** el sombrero de tres picos *m* (el tricornio)
– *three-cornered hat*
**63** el espadín
– *dress sword*
**64** dama *f* [alrededor de 1700]
– *lady [ca. 1700]*
**65** el tocado (la toca) de encajes *m*
– *lace fontange (high headdress of lace)*
**66** el manto de encajes *m*
– *lace-trimmed loose-hanging gown (loose-fitting housecoat, robe de chambre, negligée, contouche)*
**67** la orla recamada
– *band of embroidery*
**68** dama *f* [alrededor de 1880]
– *lady [ca. 1880]*
**69** el polisón (*Chile:* la potolina)
– *bustle*

**70** dama *f* [alrededor de 1858]
– *lady [ca. 1858]*
**71** la capota (la papalina)
– *poke bonnet*
**72** el miriñaque
– *crinoline*
**73** caballero *m* del período Biedermeier
– *gentleman of the Biedermeier period*
**74** el cuello alto (la marquesota; *fam.:* el foque)
– *high collar (choker collar)*
**75** el chaleco floreado
– *embroidered waistcoat (vest)*
**76** la levita
– *frock coat*
**77** la peluca de coleta *f*
– *pigtail wig*
**78** la cinta de la coleta (el lazo de la coleta)
– *ribbon (bow)*
**79** damas *f* en trajes *m* de corte *f* [alrededor de 1780]
– *ladies in court dress [ca. 1780]*
**80** la cola
– *train*
**81** el peinado rococó
– *upswept Rococo coiffure*
**82** el adorno del cabello
– *hair decoration*
**83** el tontillo (el guardainfante)
– *panniered overskirt*

1 el recinto (la instalación) al aire
 libre
– *outdoor enclosure*
2 la roca natural
– *rocks*
3 el foso de separación *f*, un foso
 lleno de agua *f*
– *moat*
4 el muro de protección *f*
– *enclosing wall*
5 los animales expuestos; *en este
 caso:* una manada de leones *m*
– *animals on show;* here: *a pride
 of lions*
6 el visitante del zoo
– *visitor to the zoo*
7 el cartel de advertencia *f*
– *notice*
8 la pajarera (el recinto para los
 pájaros)
– *aviary*
9 el recinto de los elefantes
– *elephant enclosure*
10 la casa de los animales (*por ej.:*
 la casa de las fieras, la casa de
 las jirafas, la casa de los
 elefantes, la casa de los monos)
– *animal house,* e.g. *carnivore
 house, giraffe house, elephant
 house, monkey house*
11 la jaula exterior (la jaula de
 verano *m*)
– *outside cage (summer quarters)*

12 el recinto de los reptiles
– *reptile enclosure*
13 el cocodrilo del Nilo
– *Nile crocodile*
14 el terrario-acuario
– *terrarium and aquarium*
15 la vitrina
– *glass case*
16 la entrada de aire *m* fresco
– *fresh-air inlet*
17 la salida de aire *m* (la
 ventilación)
– *ventilator*
18 la calefacción del fondo de la
 vitrina
– *underfloor heating*
19 el acuario
– *aquarium*
20 el cartel explicativo
– *information plate*
21 la flora de una zona climática
– *flora in artificially maintained
 climate*

**1-12 animales *m* unicelulares**
(protozoarios *m*, protozoos *m*,
infusorios *m*)
- *unicellular (one-celled, single-celled)*
  *animals (protozoans)*
1 la ameba, un rizópodo
- *amoeba, a rhizopod*
2 el núcleo de la célula
- *cell nucleus*
3 el protoplasma
- *protoplasm*
4 el seudópodo
- *pseudopod*
5 la vejiguilla excretora (la vacuola
  pulsátil), un orgánulo
- *excretory vacuole (contractile vacuole),*
  *an organelle*
6 la vejiguilla de alimentación *f* (la
  vacuola alimenticia)
- *food vacuole*
7 el actinomorfo, un heliozoario
- *Actinophrys, a heliozoan*
8 el radiolario; *en este caso:* el esqueleto
  silíceo
- *radiolarian; here: siliceous skeleton*
9 el animálculo zapatilla
  (paramecio *m*), un infusorio ciliado
- *slipper animalcule, a Paramecium*
  *(ciliate infusorian)*
10 el cilio
- *cilium*
11 el macronúcleo
- *macronucleus (meganucleus)*
12 el micronúcleo
- *micronucleus*
**13-39 animales *m* multicelulares**
(metazoarios *m*)
- *multicellular animals (metazoans)*
13 la esponja, un espongiario
- *bath sponge, a porifer (sponge)*

14 la medusa, un acalefo de disco *m*
  (medusa *f* de sombrilla *f*, aguamala *f*,
  un acalefo), un celentéreo
- *discomedusa, a medusa (jellyfish), a*
  *coelenterate*
15 la sombrilla
- *umbrella*
16 el tentáculo
- *tentacle*
17 el coral rojo, un coral (antozoario *m*,
  constructor de arrecifes *m*)
- *red coral (precious coral), a coral*
  *animal (anthozoon, reef-building*
  *animal)*
18 la rama de coral *m*
- *coral colony*
19 el pólipo coralígeno
- *coral polyp*
**20-26 gusanos *m* (vermes *m*)**
- *worms (Vermes)*
20 la sanguijuela, un anélido (gusano *m*
  de anillos *m*)
- *leech, an annelid*
21 la ventosa
- *sucker*
22 el espirógrafo, un gusano con
  filamentos *m*
- *Spirographis, a bristle worm*
23 el tubo
- *tube*
24 la lombriz de tierra *f*
- *earthworm*
25 el segmento
- *segment*
26 el clitelo [la zona de acoplamiento *m*]
- *clitellum [accessory reproductive*
  *organ]*
**27-36 moluscos *m***
- *molluscs (Am. mollusks)*

27 el caracol (el caracol de las viñas), un
  gasterópodo
- *edible snail, a snail*
28 el pie reptante
- *creeping foot*
29 la concha (la concha de caracol *m*)
- *shell (snail shell)*
30 el ojo peduncular
- *stalked eye*
31 los tentáculos (cuernos *m*)
- *tentacle (horn, feeler)*
32 la ostra
- *oyster*
33 la madreperla de río *m*
- *freshwater pearl mussel*
34 el nácar
- *mother-of-pearl (nacre)*
35 la perla
- *pearl*
36 la valva
- *mussel shell*
37 la jibia (la sepia), un cefalópodo
- *cuttlefish, a cephalopod*
**38-39 equinodermos *m***
- *echinoderms*
38 la estrella de mar *amb.* (la
  estrellamar)
- *starfish (sea star)*
39 el erizo de mar *amb.* (el equino)
- *sea urchin (sea hedgehog)*

# 358 Artrópodos                                    *Arthropods*

**1-2 crustáceos** *m*
- *crustaceans*
1 la dromia velluda (el cangrejo faquín), un cangrejo
- *mitten crab, a crab*
2 el asélido común (la cochinilla de agua *f*)
- *water slater*
**3-39, 48-56 insectos** *m*
- *insects*
3 la libélula (el caballito del diablo, el dragón volador), un odonato
- *water nymph (dragonfly), a homopteran (homopterous insect), a dragonfly*
4 el escorpión acuático (la nepa, la chinche acuática, el garapito), un hemiptero
- *water scorpion (water bug), a rhynchophore*
5 el sifón respiratorio
- *raptorial leg*
6 la efémera (la cachipolla, la efímera, la mosca de pesca *f*)
- *mayfly (dayfly, ephemerid)*
7 el ojo compuesto
- *compound eye*
8 la langosta migratoria (el saltamontes verde), un ortóptero
- *green grasshopper (green locust, meadow grasshopper), an orthopteron (orthopterous insect)*
9 la larva
- *larva (grub)*
10 el insecto adulto, el imago, un insecto perfecto
- *adult insect, an imago*
11 la pata saltadora
- *leaping hind leg*
12 la frigánea (el frígano, la mosca de primavera *f*, la polilla de agua *f*), un neuróptero
- *caddis fly (spring fly, water moth), a neuropteran*
13 el pulgón (la mosca verde), un piojo de las plantas
- *aphid (greenfly), a plant louse*
14 el pulgón áptero (la filoxera)
- *wingless aphid*
15 el pulgón alado
- *winged aphid*
**16-20 dípteros** *m*
- *dipterous insects (dipterans)*
16 el cénzalo (el mosquito; *Amér.:* el zancudo), un cínife
- *gnat (mosquito, midge), a culicid*
17 la trompa chupadora
- *proboscis (sucking organ)*
18 la mosca (azul) de la carne (la moscarda, el moscón, el moscardón)
- *bluebottle (blowfly), a fly*
19 la cresa
- *maggot (larva)*
20 la crisálida (la ninfa)
- *chrysalis (pupa)*
**21-23 himenópteros** *m*
- *Hymenoptera*
21-22 la hormiga
- *ant*
21 la hembra alada (la reina)
- *winged female*
22 la obrera
- *worker*
23 el abejorro (el abejón)
- *bumblebee (humblebee)*

**24-39 escarabajos** *m* (coleópteros *m*)
- *beetles (Coleoptera)*
24 el ciervo volante (el lucano ciervo, el escarabajo cornudo), un escarabeoideo
- *stag beetle, a lamellicorn beetle*
25 las mandíbulas (las tenazas)
- *mandibles*
26 los palpos maxilares
- *trophi*
27 la antena
- *antenna (feeler)*
28 la cabeza
- *head*
29-30 el tórax
- *thorax*
29 el protórax (el pronoto, el escudo del cuello, el escudo torácico)
- *thoracic shield (prothorax)*
30 el escutelo (el escudete)
- *scutellum*
31 los arcos dorsales de los segmentos
- *tergites*
32 el estigma (el orificio respiratorio)
- *stigma*
33 el ala *f* (el ala *f* posterior)
- *wing (hind wing)*
34 la nervadura del ala *f* (la vena del ala *f*)
- *nervure*
35 el punto por donde se pliega el ala *f*
- *point at which the wing folds*
36 el élitro
- *elytron (forewing)*
37 la mariquita (la vaca de San Antón), un coccinélido
- *ladybird (ladybug), a coccinellid*
38 el ergates carpintero, un cerambícido
- *Ergates faber, a longicorn beetle (longicorn)*
39 el escarabajo pelotero (el escarabajo del estiércol), un escarabeoideo
- *dung beetle, a lamellicorn beetle*
**40-47 arácnidos** *m*
- *arachnids*
40 el escorpión común (el alacrán)
- *Euscorpius flavicandus, a scorpion*
41 el pedipalpo prensil
- *cheliped with chelicer*
42 el palpo maxilar
- *maxillary antenna (maxillary feeler)*
43 el aguijón caudal (*Amér. Central:* el chuzo), una uña venenosa
- *tail sting*
**44-46 arañas** *f*
- *spiders*
44 la garrapata común (el ixodes, la garrapata de los perros), un ácaro
- *wood tick (dog tick)*
45 la araña de jardín *m* (la epeira, la araña de cruz *f*), una araña de telaraña *f* circular
- *cross spider (garden spider), an orb spinner*
46 la hilera
- *spinneret*
47 la telaraña
- *spider's web (web)*

**48-56 mariposas** *f* (lepidópteros *m*)
- *Lepidoptera (butterflies and moths)*
48 la mariposa de la seda (el bómbix del moral), un bombícido
- *mulberry-feeding moth (silk moth), a bombycid moth*
49 los huevos
- *eggs*
50 el gusano de la seda (la oruga)
- *silkworm*
51 el capullo
- *cocoon*
52 el macaón, una papiliónida (la cola de golondrina *f*)
- *swallowtail, a butterfly*
53 la antena
- *antenna (feeler)*
54 la mancha en forma *f* de ojo *m*
- *eyespot*
55 la esfinge del aligustre, una mariposa nocturna
- *privet hawkmoth, a hawkmoth (sphinx)*
56 la trompa
- *proboscis*

626

**1-3 aves *f* corredoras**
- *flightless birds*
1 el casuario de cresta, un casuario; *anál.:* el emú
- *cassowary;* sim.: *emu*
2 el avestruz; *anál.:* el ñandú, el avestruz de América (*Arg. y Bol.:* el suri; *Chile:* el tuyú)
- *ostrich*
3 la nidada de huevos *m* de avestruz *m* [12-14 huevos]
- *clutch of ostrich eggs [12 - 14 eggs]*
4 el pingüino imperial (el pájaro bobo, el pájaro niño; *Guat.:* el tolobojo), un pingüino (una palmípeda, nadadora, no voladora)
- *king penguin, a penguin, a flightless bird*
**5-10 palmípedas *f***
- *web-footed birds*
5 el pelícano común (el pelícano rosa, la platalea; *Amér.:* el alcatraz; *Pan.:* el cuaco; *Venez.:* el buchón, el tocotoco), una pelicánida
- *white pelican (wood stork, ibis, wood ibis, spoonbill, brent-goose,* Am. *brant-goose, brant), a pelican*
6 la pata palmípeda
- *webfoot (webbed foot)*
7 la membrana interdigital
- *web (palmations) of webbed foot (palmate foot)*
8 la mandíbula inferior, con la bolsa
- *lower mandible with gular pouch*
9 el alcatraz común (el onocrótalo, el pelícano americano), una súlida
- *northern gannet (gannet, solan goose), a gannet*
10 el cormorán moñudo (el cuervo marino, el corvejón; *Cuba:* la corúa), una falocrocorácida con las alas extendidas "posando"
- *green cormorant (shag), a cormorant displaying with spread wings*
**11-14 aves *f* de alas *f* largas** (aves marinas)
- *long-winged birds (seabirds)*
11 el charrancito, una golondrina de mar *amb.* (una esterna), zambulléndose en busca *f* de comida *f*
- *common sea swallow, a sea swallow (tern), diving for food*
12 el fulmar, un petrel (una ave de las tempestades; *anál.:* una pardela)
- *fulmar*
13 el arao común, una uría, un álcido
- *guillemot, an auk*

14 la gaviota reidora (la gaviota común, la gaviota de cabeza *f* negra), una gaviota
- *black-headed gull (mire crow), a gull*
**15-17 anserinos *m***
- *Anseres*
15 la serreta grande, un mergo
- *goosander (common merganser), a sawbill*
16 el cisne común (el cisne mudo, el cisne negro), un cisne
- *mute swan, a swan*
17 la protuberancia del pico
- *knob on the bill*
18 la garza real (la garza cenicienta), una ardeida, una ave zancuda
- *common heron, a heron*
**19-21 limícolas *m***
- *plovers*
19 la cigüeñuela (*Arg.:* el yabiru; *Venez.:* el soldado)
- *stilt (stilt bird, stilt plover)*
20 la foja (la focha, el fallaris, la gallareta), una fúlica, una rálida; *anál.:* el rascón, la polla
- *coot, a rail*
21 el avefría *f*
- *lapwing (green plover, peewit, pewit)*
22 la codorniz, una faisánida; *anál.:* la perdiz
- *quail, a gallinaceous bird*
23 la tórtola (*Mé.:* el mucuy), una paloma torcaz
- *turtle dove, a pigeon*
24 el vencejo (el arrejaco, el arrejaque); *anál.:* el avión, la salangana; una apodida
- *swift*
25 la abubilla común (la upupa), una tenuirrostra, una upúpida
- *hoopoe, a roller*
26 el penacho de plumas *f* eréctiles
- *erectile crest*
27 el pico picapinos (el pájaro carpintero, el picamaderos, el picaposte, el picarrelincho, el pico barreno, el pico carpintero), un pico, una pícida; *anál.:* el torcecuello (*Hond.:* el checo), el pito
- *spotted woodpecker, a woodpecker;* related: *wryneck*
28 la entrada del nido
- *entrance to the nest*
29 la cavidad nidal (el hueco de la empolladura)
- *nesting cavity*
30 el cuclillo (el cuco), una cucúlida; *anál.:* el críalo
- *cuckoo*

# 360  Aves II (Aves indígenas, pájaros)

**1, 3, 4, 5, 7, 9, 10** aves *f* canoras
- *songbirds*
**1** el jilguero (el sirguero, el
pintacilgo, el pintadillo, la
cardelina, el colorín, el
sietecolores), un fringílido
- *goldfinch, a finch*
**2** el abejaruco (el azulejo)
- *bee eater*
**3** el colirrojo de los jardines (el
colirrojo real), un túrdido
- *redstart (star finch), a thrush*
**4** el herrerillo común, un párido
- *bluetit, a tit (titmouse), a*
  *resident bird (non-migratory*
  *bird)*
**5** el camachuelo común, una ave
sedentaria
- *bullfinch*
**6** la carraca
- *common roller (roller)*
**7** la oropéndola (la lútea, el oriol,
el papafigo, el vireo, el virio),
una ave migratoria (una ave de
paso *m*)
- *golden oriole, a migratory bird*
**8** el martín pescador (el alción, el
guardarrío, el pájaro polilla;
*Perú:* el camaronero)
- *kingfisher*
**9** la lavandera blanca (la
aguzanieves, la aguanieves, el
andarríos, la apuranieves, la
nevatilla, la nevereta, la
pajarita de las nieves, la
pizpita), una lavandera
(pezpítalo *m*, caudatrémula *f*,
doradillo *m*, motacila *f*,
motalita *f*)
- *white wagtail, a wagtail*
**10** el pinzón vulgar (el pinchón)
- *chaffinch*

1-20 **aves** *f* **canoras**
- *songbirds*
1-3 **córvidos**
- *Corvidae (corvine birds, crows)*
1 el arrendajo común, un gárrulo
- *jay (nutcracker)*
2 la graja (el grajo, el cuervo merendero); *anál.:* la corneja (la chova), el cuervo, la grajilla
- *rook, a crow*
3 la urraca (la picaza, la marica, la cotorra, la gaya, la pega, la picaraza)
- *magpie*
4 el estornino pinto
- *starling (pastor, shepherd bird)*
5 el gorrión común (el pardal, el gurriato; *Mé.:* el burrión)
- *house sparrow*
6-8 **fringílidos** *m*
- *finches*
6-7 emberizas *f* (escribanos *m*)
- *buntings*
6 el escribano cerillo
- *yellowhammer (yellow bunting)*
7 el escribano hortelano
- *ortolan (ortolan bunting)*
8 el lúgano; *anál.:* el verderón (el verdecillo, el verdorol, el verdezuelo, el verdón)
- *siskin (aberdevine)*
9 el carbonero común
- *great titmouse (great tit, ox eye), a titmouse (tit)*

10 el reyezuelo sencillo; *anál.:* el reyezuelo listado; un régulo
- *golden-crested wren (goldcrest);*
  *sim.: firecrest, one of the Regulidae*
11 el trepador azul
- *nuthatch*
12 el chochín
- *wren*
13-17 **túrdidos** *m*
- *thrushes*
13 el mirlo común (la merla, la mirla)
- *blackbird*
14 el ruiseñor común (*poético:* la filomena, la filomela)
- *nightingale (poet.: philomel, philomela)*
15 el petirrojo
- *robin (redbreast, robin redbreast)*
16 el zorzal común, un tordo
- *song thrush (throstle, mavis)*
17 el ruiseñor alemán
- *thrush nightingale*
18-19 **alondras** *f*
- *larks*
18 la totovía (la tova)
- *woodlark*
19 la cogujada común (la cochevís, la copada, la golerita); *anál.:* la alondra (la calandria, la copetuda, la terrera)
- *crested lark (tufted lark)*
20 la golondrina común, una hirundínida
- *common swallow (barn swallow, chimney swallow), a swallow*

**1-13 aves *f* rapaces** (aves *f* de rapiña *f*) **diurnas**
– *diurnal birds of prey*
**1-4** falcónidas *f*
– *falcons*
**1** el esmerejón
– *merlin*
**2** el halcón común (el halcón peregrino)
– *peregrine falcon*
**3** los "calzones" (el plumaje del muslo)
– *leg feathers*
**4** el tarso
– *tarsus*
**5-9** águilas *f*
– *eagles*
**5** el pigargo
– *white-tailed sea eagle (white-tailed eagle, grey sea eagle, erne)*
**6** el pico corvo
– *hooked beak*
**7** la garra
– *claw (talon)*
**8** la cola
– *tail*
**9** el ratonero común
– *common buzzard*
**10-13** accípitres *m*
– *accipiters*
**10** el azor
– *goshawk*

**11** el milano rojo (el milano real)
– *common European kite (glede, kite)*
**12** el gavilán
– *sparrow hawk (spar-hawk)*
**13** el aguilucho lagunero
– *marsh harrier (moor buzzard, moor harrier, moor hawk)*
**14-19 aves *f* rapaces nocturnas** (estrígidas *f*)
– *owls (nocturnal birds of prey)*
**14** el búho chico; *más pequeño:* el autillo
– *long-eared owl (horned owl)*
**15** el búho real (*Perú:* el carancho)
– *eagle-owl (great horned owl)*
**16** el plumicornio (los mechones de plumas *f* en forma *f* de orejas *f*)
– *plumicorn (feathered ear, ear tuft, ear, horn)*
**17** la lechuza (*Arg. y Urug.:* el quitilipi)
– *barn owl (white owl, silver owl, yellow owl, church owl, screech owl)*
**18** el "velo" (el cerco facial de plumas *f*)
– *facial disc (disk)*
**19** el mochuelo común
– *little owl (sparrow owl)*

1 la cacatúa de cresta *f* amarilla,
un papagayo
- *sulphur-crested cockatoo, a*
*parrot*
2 el guacamayo (el ara)
- *blue-and-yellow macaw*
3 el ave del Paraíso azul
- *blue bird of paradise*
4 el colibrí sappho, un colibrí (el
pájaro mosca, el picaflor; *Arg.:*
el rundún; *Col.:* el rumbo; *Mé.*
*y. P. Rico:* el chupamirto)
- *sappho*
5 el cardenal (*Col.:* el titiribí)
- *cardinal (cardinal bird)*
6 el tucán (*Arg. y Venez.:* el
tucano), una ave trepadora
- *toucan (red-billed toucan), one of*
*the Piciformes*

**1-18 peces** *m*
- *fishes*
**1** el jaquetón (el tiburón azul), un
tiburón (lamia *f,* marrajo *m*),
un escualo
- *man-eater (blue shark, requin), a
shark*
**2** la nariz (el morro)
- *nose (snout)*
**3** las hendiduras branquiales
- *gill slit (gill cleft)*
**4** la carpa de laguna *f* (la carpa
de río *m*, la carpa de espejo *m*),
un ciprínido
- *carp, a mirror carp (carp)*
**5** el opérculo
- *gill cover (operculum)*
**6** la aleta dorsal
- *dorsal fin*
**7** la aleta pectoral
- *pectoral fin*
**8** la aleta ventral
- *pelvic fin (abdominal fin, ventral
fin)*
**9** la aleta anal
- *anal fin*
**10** la aleta caudal
- *caudal fin (tail fin)*
**11** la escama
- *scale*
**12** el siluro (*anál.: Venez.:* el
laulao)
- *catfish (sheatfish, sheathfish,
wels)*
**13** el barbillón
- *barbel*
**14** el arenque
- *herring*
**15** la trucha de río *m*, una trucha
- *brown trout (German brown
trout), a trout*
**16** el lucio común
- *pike (northern pike)*
**17** la anguila (*Amér.:* la anguilla)
- *freshwater eel (eel)*
**18** el caballito de mar *amb.* (el
hipocampo, el caballo marino)
- *sea horse (Hippocampus,
horsefish)*
**19** el penacho de branquias *f*
- *tufted gills*
**20-26 anfibios** *m* (batracios *m*)
- *Amphibia (amphibians)*
**20-22** urodelos *m* (anfibios *m* con
cola *f*)
- *salamanders*
**20** el tritón crestado, un tritón
(salamandra *f* acuática)
- *greater water newt (crested
newt), a water newt*
**21** la cresta dorsal
- *dorsal crest*
**22** la salamandra común, una
salamandra
- *fire salamander, a salamander*
**23-26** anuros *m* (anfibios *m* sin
cola *f*)
- *salientians (anurans,
batrachians)*

**23** el sapo común, un sapo
(escuerzo *m*)
- *European toad, a toad*
**24** la rana de San Antonio (la rana
de zarzal *m*, la rubeta, la rana
bermeja)
- *tree frog (tree toad)*
**25** el saco vocal
- *vocal sac (vocal pouch, croaking
sac)*
**26** el disco adhesivo (el cojinete
discoidal adhesivo)
- *adhesive disc (disk)*
**27-41 reptiles** *m*
- *reptiles*
**27, 30-37** saurios *m*
- *lizards*
**27** la lagartija (la regalterna, la
sargantana)
- *sand lizard*
**28** la tortuga de carey *m*
- *hawksbill turtle (hawksbill)*
**29** el caparazón (la concha, el
escudo, el espaldar)
- *carapace (shell)*
**30** el basilisco (*Amér.:* la iguana)
- *basilisk*
**31** el varano del desierto, un
varano; *más pequeño:* el lagarto
- *desert monitor, a monitor lizard
(monitor)*
**32** la iguana verde, una iguana
- *common iguana, an iguana*
**33** el camaleón, un camaleónido
- *chameleon, one of the
Chamaeleontidae (Rhiptoglossa)*
**34** la pata prensil
- *prehensile foot*
**35** la cola prensil
- *prehensile tail*
**36** la salamanquesa de pared *f,*
una salamanquesa
(salamandria *f*)
- *wall gecko, a gecko*
**37** el lución (*anál.:* la serpiente de
vidrio *m,* la serpiente
quebradiza, la serpiente ciega,
el lagarto de cristal *m*), un
ánguido, un lagarto ápodo
- *slowworm (blindworm), one of
the Anguidae*
**38-41 ofidios** m (serpientes *f;*
*Amér. Central:* los mazacotes)
- *snakes*
**38** la serpiente de collar *m* (la
serpiente acuática), una culebra
- *ringed snake (ring snake, water
snake, grass snake), a colubrid*
**39** los lunares (el collar)
- *collar*
**40-41** víboras *f*
- *vipers (adders)*
**40** la víbora común, una serpiente
venenosa
- *common viper, a poisonous
(venomous) snake*
**41** el áspid
- *asp (asp viper)*

**1-6  mariposas *f* diurnas**
(lepidópteros *m* diurnos)
– *butterflies*
**1** la vanesa atalanta, una
ninfálida
– *red admiral*
**2** el pavo real, una ninfálida
– *peacock butterfly*
**3** la aurora, una piérida
– *orange tip (orange tip butterfly)*
**4** la limonera, una piérida
– *brimstone (brimstone butterfly)*
**5** la antíope, una ninfálida
– *Camberwell beauty (mourning
cloak, mourning cloak butterfly)*
**6** la hormiguera de lunares *m,*
una licénida
– *blue (lycaenid butterfly,
lycaenid)*
**7-11  mariposas *f* nocturnas**
(lepidópteros *m* nocturnos)
– *moths (Heterocera)*
**7** la quelonia (la gitana)
– *garden tiger*
**8** la catocala nupcial
– *red underwing*
**9** la mariposa de calavera *f* (la
esfinge de calavera *f*), una
esfingida
– *death's-head moth (death's-head
hawkmoth), a hawkmoth
(sphinx)*
**10** la oruga
– *caterpillar*
**11** la crisálida (la ninfa)
– *chrysalis (pupa)*

1 el ornitorrinco, un monotrema
(un mamífero ovíparo)
- *platypus (duck-bill, duck-mole),*
*a monotreme (oviparous*
*mammal)*
2-3 **marsupiales** *m* (didelfos *m*)
- *marsupial mammals*
*(marsupials)*
2 la zarigüeya norteamericana
(*Mé.:* el tlacuache; *Arg.:* la
comadreja) un didelfo (un
marsupial)
- *New World opossum, a didelphid*
3 el canguro rojo gigante, un
canguro
- *red kangaroo (red flyer), a*
*kangaroo*
4-7 **insectívoros** *m*
- *insectivores (insect-eating*
*mammals)*
4 el topo
- *mole*
5 el erizo
- *hedgehog*
6 la púa
- *spine*
7 la musaraña doméstica (el
musgaño doméstico), una
musaraña
- *shrew (shrew mouse), one of the*
*Soricidae*
8 el armadillo (*Mé.:* el ayotoste;
*Arg., Bol. y Chile:* el tatú)
- *nine-banded armadillo (peba)*
9 el orejudo, un gimnorrino, un
mamífero volador (un
quiróptero, un murciélago)
(*Col.:* el chimbilá; *Amér.*
*Merid.:* el vampiro)
- *long-eared bat (flitter-mouse), a*
*flying mammal (chiropter,*
*chiropteran)*
10 el pangolín, un mamífero con
escamas *f*
- *pangolin (scaly ant-eater), a*
*scaly mammal*
11 el perezoso (*Arg. y Bol.:* el aí;
*Venez.:* el pereza; *Amér.*
*Central, Bol., Ec. y Venez.:* el
perico ligero; *Guayana:* el
unau)
- *two-toed sloth (unau)*
12-19 **roedores** *m*
- *rodents*
12 el conejillo de Indias (*Amér:* el
cobayo, la cobaya)
- *guinea pig (cavy)*
13 el puerco espín
- *porcupine*
14 el castor del Plata (*Arg. y Chile:*
el coipo, el coipú; *Arg. y Bol.:*
el quiyá)
- *beaver*
15 el jerbo
- *jerboa*
16 el hámster (la marmota de
Alemania, la rata del trigo)
- *hamster*

17 la rata de agua *f*, un arvícola
- *water vole*
18 la marmota
- *marmot*
19 la ardilla (*Costa Rica:* el tuche)
- *squirrel*
20 el elefante africano, un
proboscidio
- *African elephant, a proboscidean*
*(proboscidian)*
21 la trompa
- *trunk (proboscis)*
22 el colmillo
- *tusk*
23 el manatí (*Amér.:* el peje buey;
*Bol.:* el lamantín), un sirénido
- *manatee (manati, lamantin), a*
*sirenian*
24 el damán sudafricano, un
lamnungio
- *South African dassie (das,*
*coney, hyrax), a procaviid*
25-31 **ungulados** *m*
- *ungulates*
25-27 **perisodáctilos** *m*
(ungulados *m* de dedos *m*
impares)
- *odd-toed ungulates*
25 el rinoceronte africano, un
rinoceronte (un nasicornio)
- *African black rhino, a rhinoceros*
*(nasicorn)*
26 el tapir sudamericano (*Río de la*
*Plata, Bol. y Perú:* el anta *f*;
*Arg.:* la gran bestia, el
pinchaco; *Perú:* la sachavaca;
*Amér. Central, Bol. y Ec.:* el
tapiro)
- *Brazilian tapir, a tapir*
27 la cebra
- *zebra*
28-31 **artiodáctilos** *m*
(ungulados *m* de dedos *m*
pares)
- *even-toed ungulates*
28-30 **rumiantes** *m*
- *ruminants*
28 la llama (*Amér. Merid.:* la
oveja, el paco; *Ec.:* el llamingo,
la runallama); *anál.:* la alpaca
(*Amér. Merid.:* el paco)
- *llama*
29 el camello bactriano (el camello
de dos gibas *f*)
- *Bactrian camel (two-humped*
*camel)*
30 el guanaco (*Arg.:* el teque)
- *guanaco*
31 el hipopótamo
- *hippopotamus*

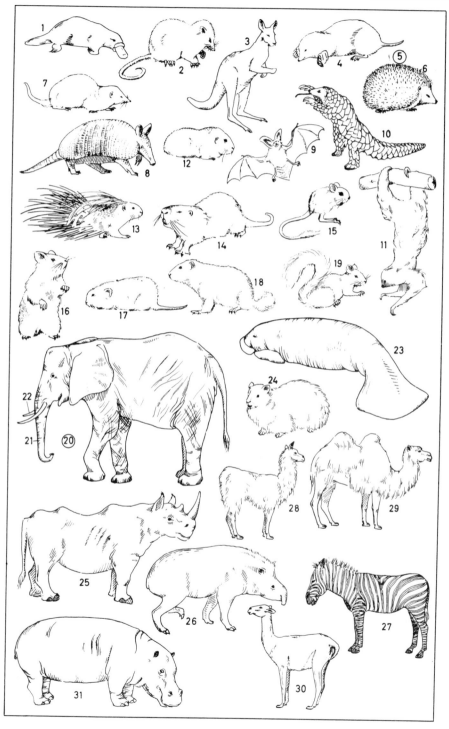

1-10 **ungulados** *m*, rumiantes *m*
- *ungulates, ruminants*
1 el alce (anta *f*)
- *elk (moose)*
2 el uapití
- *wapiti (Am. elk)*
3 la gamuza
- *chamois*
4 la jirafa
- *giraffe*
5 la cervicabra, un antílope
- *black buck, an antelope*
6 el muflón
- *mouflon (moufflon)*
7 el íbice (la cabra montés, el hirco)
- *ibex (rock goat, bouquetin, steinbock)*
8 el búfalo
- *water buffalo (Indian buffalo, water ox)*
9 el bisonte (*Mé.*: el búfalo)
- *bison*
10 el buey almizclero
- *musk ox*
11-22 **carnívoros** *m* (carniceros *m*)
- *carnivores (beasts of prey)*
11-13 **cánidos** *m*
- *Canidae*
11 el chacal (*Río de la Plata:* el aguará); *anál.:* el coyote
- *black-backed jackal (jackal)*
12 el zorro común (la zorra, la raposa, la vulpeja)
- *red fox*
13 el lobo
- *wolf*
14-17 **mustélidos** *m*
- *martens*
14 la garduña (la fuina)
- *stone marten (beach marten)*
15 la marta cibelina (la marta cebellina)
- *sable*
16 la comadreja (la mustela)
- *weasel*
17 la nutria marina, una nutria
- *sea otter, an otter*
18-22 **pinnípedos** *m*
- *seals (pinnipeds)*
18 el oso marino
- *fur seal (sea bear, ursine seal)*
19 la foca (el lobo marino, el becerro marino, el carnero marino, el vítulo marino)
- *common seal (sea calf, sea dog)*
20 la morsa
- *walrus (morse)*
21 el bigote
- *whiskers*
22 el colmillo
- *tusk*
23-29 **cetáceos** *m*
- *whales*
23 la marsopa (el puerco marino)
- *bottle-nosed dolphin (bottle-nose dolphin)*

24 el delfín común (el arroaz, el golfín, la tonina; *Hond., Mé. y Perú:* el bufeo)
- *common dolphin*
25 el cachalote
- *sperm whale (cachalot)*
26 las narices
- *blowhole (spout hole)*
27 la aleta dorsal
- *dorsal fin*
28 la aleta pectoral
- *flipper*
29 la aleta caudal
- *tail flukes (tail)*

**1-11 carnívoros** *m* (carniceros *m*)
- *carnivores (beasts of prey)*
**1** la hiena rayada, una hiena
- *striped hyena, a hyena*
**2-8 felinos** *m*
- *felines (cats)*
**2** el león
- *lion*
**3** la melena
- *mane (lion's mane)*
**4** la garra (la zarpa)
- *paw*
**5** el tigre
- *tiger*
**6** el leopardo (el pardal)
- *leopard*
**7** el guepardo (la onza)
- *cheetah (hunting leopard)*
**8** el lince (el lobo cerval)
- *lynx*
**9-11 úrsidos** *m*
- *bears*
**9** el mapache (el oso lavador,
   *Cuba:* el perro mudo)
- *raccoon (racoon,* Am. *coon)*
**10** el oso común (el oso pardo)
- *brown bear*
**11** el oso blanco (el oso polar)
- *polar bear (white bear)*
**12-16 primates** *m*
- *primates*
**12-13** monos *m*
- *monkeys*
**12** el macaco rheso
- *rhesus monkey (rhesus, rhesus
   macaque)*
**13** el babuino (el zambo)
- *baboon*
**14-16 antropoides** *m*
- *anthropoids (anthropoid apes,
   great apes)*
**14** el chimpancé
- *chimpanzee*
**15** el orangután (el jocó)
- *orang-utan (orang-outan)*
**16** el gorila
- *gorilla*

1 Gigantocypris agassizi (el ostrácodo gigante)
- *Gigantocypris agassizi*
2 Macropharynx longicaudatus (la anguila pelícano)
- *Macropharynx longicaudatus (pelican eel)*
3 Pentacrinus, un crinoideo (un lirio de mar *amb.*), un equinodermo
- *Pentacrinus (feather star), a sea lily, an echinoderm*
4 Thaumatolampas diadema (la lámpara maravillosa), una sepia [luminiscente]
- *Thaumatolampas diadema, a cuttlefish [luminescent]*
5 Atolla, una medusa abisal, un celentéreo
- *Atolla, a deep-sea medusa, a coelenterate*
6 Melanocetes, un pediculado [luminiscente]
- *Melanocetes, a pediculate [luminescent]*
7 Lophocalyx philippensis, una esponja silícea
- *Lophocalyx philippensis, a glass sponge*
8 Mopsea, un coral córneo [colonia *f*]
- *Mopsea, a sea fan [colony]*
9 Hydrallmania, un pólipo hidroide, un pólipo, un celentéreo [colonia *f*]
- *Hydrallmania, a hydroid polyp, a coelenterate [colony]*
10 Malacosteus indicus, un estomiátido [luminiscente]
- *Malacosteus indicus, a stomiatid [luminescent]*
11 Brisinga endecacnemos, un ofiuroideo, un equinodermo [luminiscente sólo cuando está excitado]
- *Brisinga endecacnemos, a sand star (brittle star), an echinoderm [luminescent only when stimulated]*
12 Pasiphaea, un camarón, un crustáceo
- *Pasiphaea, a shrimp, a crustacean*
13 Echiostoma, un estomiátido, un pez abisal [luminiscente]
- *Echiostoma, a stomiatid, a fish [luminescent]*
14 Umbellula encrinus, una pennatúlida, un celentéreo [colonia *f* luminiscente]
- *Umbellula encrinus, a sea pen (sea feather), a coelenterate [colony, luminescent]*
15 Polycheles, un crustáceo
- *Polycheles, a crustacean*
16 Lithodes, un crustáceo, un cangrejo
- *Lithodes, a crustacean, a crab*

17 Archaster, una estrella de mar *amb.* (una estrellamar, un asteroideo), un equinodermo
- *Archaster, a starfish (sea star), an echinoderm*
18 Oneirophanta, una holoturia, un equinodermo
- *Oneirophanta, a sea cucumber, an echinoderm*
19 Palaeopneustes niasicus, un erizo de mar *amb.*, un equinodermo
- *Palaeopneustes niasicus, a sea urchin (sea hedgehog), an echinoderm*
20 Chitonactis, una anémona de mar *amb.* (actinia *f*), un celentéreo
- *Chitonactis, a sea anemone (actinia), a coelenterate*

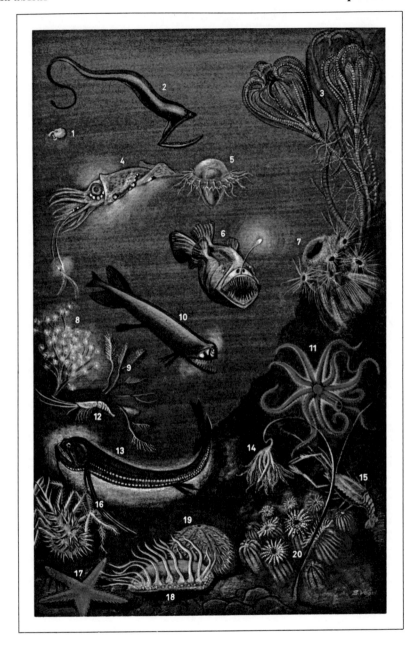

1 el árbol
– *tree*
2 el tronco
– *bole (tree trunk, trunk, stem)*
3 la copa (*Venez.:* el copo)
– *crown of tree (crown)*
4 la cima
– *top of tree (treetop)*
5 la rama
– *bough (limb, branch)*
6 el ramo
– *twig (branch)*
7 el tronco [corte transversal]
– *bole (tree trunk) [cross section]*
8 la corteza
– *bark (rind)*
9 el líber
– *phloem (bast sieve tissue, inner fibrous bark)*
10 el cambium
– *cambium (cambium ring)*
11 los radios medulares
– *medullary rays (vascular rays, pith rays)*
12 la albura (el alborno)
– *sapwood (sap, alburnum)*
13 el duramen (el corazón)
– *heartwood (duramen)*
14 la médula
– *pith*
15 **la planta**
– *plant*
16-18 la raíz
– *root*
16 la raíz principal
– *primary root*
17 la raíz secundaria
– *secondary root*
18 el pelo absorbente (el pelo radical)
– *root hair*
19-25 el tallo
– *shoot (sprout)*
19 la hoja
– *leaf*
20 el tallo
– *stalk*
21 el tallo secundario (la rama de primer orden *m*)
– *side shoot (offshoot)*
22 la yema terminal
– *terminal bud*
23 la flor
– *flower*
24 el botón floral (el capullo)
– *flower bud*
25 la axila foliar, con la yema axilar
– *leaf axil with axillary bud*
26 **la hoja**
– *leaf*
27 el peciolo
– *leaf stalk (petiole)*
28 el limbo (la lámina foliar)
– *leaf blade (blade, lamina)*
29 la nervadura de la hoja
– *venation (veins, nervures, ribs)*
30 el nervio medial
– *midrib (nerve)*
31-38 formas *f* de las hojas
– *leaf shapes*
31 linear (lineal)
– *linear*
32 lanceolada
– *lanceolate*
33 orbicular
– *orbicular (orbiculate)*
34 acicular
– *acerose (acerous, acerate, acicular, needle-shaped)*
35 acorazonada
– *cordate*
36 oval
– *ovate*
37 sagitada
– *sagittate*
38 arriñonada
– *reniform*

39-42 hojas *f* compuestas
– *compound leaves*
39 digitada (compuesta palmeada)
– *digitate (digitated, palmate, quinquefoliolate)*
40 compuesta pinnada (pinnatífida)
– *pinnatifid*
41 paripinnada
– *abruptly pinnate*
42 imparipinnada
– *odd-pinnate*
43-50 clases *f* de hojas *f* según el borde del limbo
– *leaf margin shapes*
43 entera
– *entire*
44 aserrada
– *serrate (serrulate, saw-toothed)*
45 denticulada
– *doubly toothed*
46 festoneada
– *crenate*
47 dentada
– *dentate*
48 lobulada
– *sinuate*
49 ciliada
– *ciliate (ciliated)*
50 el cilio
– *cilium*
51 **la flor**
– *flower*
52 el pedúnculo (el pedicelo, el pezón)
– *flower stalk (flower stem, scape)*
53 el receptáculo (el tálamo)
– *receptacle (floral axis, thalamus, torus)*
54 el ovario
– *ovary*
55 el estilo
– *style*
56 el estigma
– *stigma*
57 el estambre
– *stamen*
58 el sépalo
– *sepal*
59 el pétalo
– *petal*
60 ovario *m* y estambre *m* [corte]
– *ovary and stamen [section]*
61 la pared del ovario
– *ovary wall*
62 la cavidad del ovario
– *ovary cavity*
63 el óvulo
– *ovule*
64 el saco embrional
– *embryo sac*
65 el polen
– *pollen*
66 el tubo polínico
– *pollen tube*
67-77 inflorescencias *f*
– *inflorescences*
67 la espiga
– *spike (racemose spike)*
68 el racimo
– *raceme (simple raceme)*
69 la panícula
– *panicle*
70 la cima bípara (discasio *m*)
– *cyme*
71 el espádice
– *spadix (fleshy spike)*
72 la umbela
– *umbel (simple umbel)*
73 la cabezuela (el capítulo)
– *capitulum*
74 el capítulo convexo (la cabezuela discoide)
– *composite head (discoid flower head)*
75 el capítulo cóncavo (la cabezuela globulosa)
– *hollow flower head*

76 la cima unípara escorpioide
– *bostryx (helicoid cyme)*
77 la cima unípara helicoide (el ripidio)
– *cincinnus (scorpioid cyme, curled cyme)*
78-82 raíces *f*
– *roots*
78 las raíces adventicias
– *adventitious roots*
79 la raíz tuberosa
– *tuber (tuberous root, swollen taproot)*
80 las raíces aéreas (las raíces trepadoras, las raíces adventicias)
– *adventitious roots (aerial roots)*
81 las espinas de la raíz
– *root thorns*
82 las raíces respiratorias
– *pneumatophores*
83-85 el tallo de hierba *f*
– *blade of grass*
83 la vaina
– *leaf sheath*
84 la lígula
– *ligule (ligula)*
85 el limbo
– *leaf blade (lamina)*
86 la semilla
– *embryo (seed, germ)*
87 el cotiledón
– *cotyledon (seed leaf, seed lobe)*
88 la radícula
– *radicle*
89 el hipocótilo
– *hypocotyl*
90 la plúmula
– *plumule (leaf bud)*
91-102 frutos *m*
– *fruits*
91-96 frutos *m* deshicentes
– *dehiscent fruits*
91 el folículo
– *follicle*
92 la legumbre
– *legume (pod)*
93 la silicua
– *siliqua (pod)*
94 la cápsula loculicida
– *schizocarp*
95 el pixidio
– *pyxidium (circumscissile seed vessel)*
96 la cápsula foraminal (la cápsula poricida)
– *poricidal capsule (porose capsule)*
97-102 frutos *m* indehiscentes
– *indehiscent fruits*
97 la baya
– *berry*
98 la nuez
– *nut*
99 la drupa (la cereza)
– *drupe (stone fruit);* here: *cherry*
100 el fruto compuesto (el escaramujo)
– *aggregate fruit (compound fruit); here: rose hip*
101 la multidrupa (la frambuesa), un fruto compuesto
– *aggregate fruit (compound fruit);* here: *raspberry*
102 el pomo (la manzana)
– *pome;* here: *apple*

**1-73** árboles *m* de hoja *f* caduca
(árboles *m* caducifolios)
– *deciduous trees*
**1** el roble
– *oak (oak tree)*
**2** la rama florida
– *flowering branch*
**3** la rama con frutos *m*
– *fruiting branch*
**4** el fruto (la bellota)
– *fruit (acorn)*
**5** el cascabillo (la cúpula)
– *cupule (cup)*
**6** la flor femenina
– *female flower*
**7** la bráctea
– *bract*
**8** la inflorescencia masculina
– *male inflorescence*
**9** el abedul
– *birch (birch tree)*
**10** la rama con amentos *m*
(candelillas *f*), una rama
florida
– *branch with catkins, a flowering
branch*
**11** la rama con frutos *m*
– *fruiting branch*
**12** la sámara
– *scale (catkin scale)*
**13** la flor femenina
– *female flower*
**14** la flor masculina
– *male flower*
**15** el álamo; *anál.:* el chopo
– *poplar*
**16** la rama florida
– *flowering branch*
**17** la flor
– *flower*
**18** la rama con frutos *m*
– *fruiting branch*
**19** el fruto
– *fruit*
**20** la semilla
– *seed*
**21** la hoja del álamo temblón
– *leaf of the aspen (trembling
poplar)*
**22** la infrutescencia
– *infructescence*
**23** la hoja del álamo blanco
– *leaf of the white poplar (silver
poplar, silverleaf)*
**24** el sauce cabruno; *anál.:* el
salguero, la salguera, la sarga
– *sallow (goat willow)*
**25** la rama con los botones florales
(con los capullos)
– *branch with flower buds*
**26** el amento (la candelilla) con
detalle *m* de una flor
– *catkin with single flower*
**27** la rama con hojas *f* (*Chile:* el
quimpo)
– *branch with leaves*
**28** el fruto
– *fruit*

**29** la rama con hojas *f* de la
salguera blanca
– *osier branch with leaves*
**30** el aliso (el alno)
– *alder*
**31** la rama con frutos *m*
– *fruiting branch*
**32** la rama florida con los conos
(las piñas) del año anterior
– *branch with previous year's cone*
**33** el haya *f*
– *beech (beech tree)*
**34** la rama florida
– *flowering branch*
**35** el friz (la flor del haya *f*)
– *flower*
**36** la rama con frutos *m*
– *fruiting branch*
**37** el hayuco (el fruto del haya *f*)
– *beech nut*
**38** el fresno
– *ash (ash tree)*
**39** la rama florida
– *flowering branch*
**40** la flor
– *flower*
**41** la rama con frutos *m*
– *fruiting branch*
**42** el serbal (el serbo)
– *mountain ash (rowan,
quickbeam)*
**43** la inflorescencia
– *inflorescence*
**44** la infrutescencia
– *infructescence*
**45** el fruto (la serba) [corte
longitudinal]
– *fruit [longitudinal section]*
**46** el tilo (la tila, la teja)
– *lime (lime tree, linden, linden
tree)*
**47** la rama con frutos *m*
– *fruiting branch*
**48** la inflorescencia
– *inflorescence*
**49** el olmo (el negrillo)
– *elm (elm tree)*
**50** la rama con frutos *m*
– *fruiting branch*
**51** la rama florida
– *flowering branch*
**52** la flor
– *flower*
**53** el arce (el moscón, el sácere)
real (el arce platanoide)
– *maple (maple tree)*
**54** la rama florida
– *flowering branch*
**55** la flor
– *flower*
**56** la rama con frutos *m*
– *fruiting branch*
**57** el fruto en doble sámara *f*
(disámara *f*)
– *maple seed with wings (winged
maple seed)*
**58** el castaño de Indias
– *horse chestnut (horse chestnut
tree, chestnut, chestnut tree,
buckeye)*

**59** la rama con frutos *m* jóvenes
– *branch with young fruits*
**60** la castaña (la semilla del
castaño)
– *chestnut (horse chestnut)*
**61** el fruto maduro
– *mature (ripe) fruit*
**62** la flor [corte longitudinal]
– *flower [longitudinal section]*
**63** el carpe
– *hornbeam (yoke elm)*
**64** la rama con frutos *m*
– *fruiting branch*
**65** el fruto
– *seed*
**66** la rama florida
– *flowering branch*
**67** el plátano híbrido (*Amér.
Merid.:* el volador)
– *plane (plane tree)*
**68** la hoja
– *leaf*
**69** la infrutescencia y el fruto
– *infructescence and fruit*
**70** la robinia (la falsa acacia)
– *false acacia (locust tree)*
**71** la rama florida
– *flowering branch*
**72** parte *f* de la infrutescencia
– *part of the infructescence*
**73** la base del pecíolo con
estípulas *f*
– *base of the leaf stalk with
stipules*

# 372 Coníferas

1-71 coníferas *f* (árboles *m* de hojas *f* aciculares, árboles *m* de hoja *f* perenne)
– *coniferous trees (conifers)*
1 el abeto común (el abeto blanco, el pinabete)
– *silver fir (European silver fir, common silver fir)*
2 el cono (la piña, el estróbilo), un fruto
– *fir cone, a fruit cone*
3 el eje del cono
– *cone axis*
4 el cono femenino
– *female flower cone*
5 la escama de la bráctea
– *bract scale (bract)*
6 el cono masculino
– *male flower shoot*
7 el estambre
– *stamen*
8 la escama del cono
– *cone scale*
9 la semilla con ala *f*
– *seed with wing (winged seed)*
10 la semilla [corte longitudinal]
– *seed [longitudinal section]*
11 la aguja de abeto *m* (la hoja acicular)
– *fir needle (needle)*
12 la pícea (el abeto falso)
– *spruce (spruce fir)*
13 el cono (la piña) de la pícea
– *spruce cone*
14 la escama del cono
– *cone scale*
15 la semilla
– *seed*
16 el cono femenino
– *female flower cone*
17 el cono masculino (la inflorescencia masculina)
– *male inflorescence*
18 el estambre
– *stamen*
19 la aguja de la pícea (del abeto falso; la hoja acicular)
– *spruce needle*
20 el pino (el pino albar, el pino silvestre, el pino rojo)
– *pine (Scots pine)*
21 el pino enano (el pino de montaña *f*, el pino negro)
– *dwarf pine*
22 el cono femenino
– *female flower cone*
23 el haz de dos agujas *f* de un renuevo joven
– *short shoot with bundle of two leaves*
24 el cono masculino (las inflorescencias masculinas)
– *male inflorescences*
25 el vástago (el renuevo) anual
– *annual growth*
26 la piña del pino
– *pine cone*

27 la escama de la piña
– *cone scale*
28 la semilla
– *seed*
29 el cono del pino cembro, un fruto
– *fruit cone of the arolla pine (Swiss stone pine)*
30 el cono del pino de Weymouth (del pino blanco, del pino canadiense), un fruto
– *fruit cone of the Weymouth pine (white pine)*
31 el vástago joven [corte transversal]
– *short shoot [cross section]*
32 el alerce (el pino alerce, el lárice)
– *larch*
33 la rama florida
– *flowering branch*
34 la escama del cono femenino (la escama ovulífera)
– *scale of the female flower cone*
35 la antera
– *anther*
36 la rama con una piña de alerce *m*
– *branch with larch cones (fruit cones)*
37 la semilla
– *seed*
38 la escama de la piña
– *cone scale*
39 el árbol de la vida (la tuya)
– *arbor vitae (tree of life, thuja)*
40 la rama con frutos *m*
– *fruiting branch*
41 el cono, un fruto
– *fruit cone*
42 la escama
– *scale*
43 la rama con flores *f* masculinas y femeninas
– *branch with male and female flowers*
44 el brote (el vástago) masculino
– *male shoot*
45 la escama, con sacos *m* polínicos
– *scale with pollen sacs*
46 el brote (el vástago) femenino
– *female shoot*
47 el enebro (el junípero, la cada); *anál.:* la sabina
– *juniper (juniper tree)*
48 el brote (el vástago) femenino [corte longitudinal]
– *female shoot [longitudinal section]*
49 el brote (el vástago) masculino
– *male shoot*
50 la escama, con sacos *m* polínicos
– *scale with pollen sacs*
51 la rama con frutos *m*
– *fruiting branch*
52 la enebrina (la baya del junípero, del enebro)
– *juniper berry*

53 el fruto [corte transversal]
– *fruit [cross section]*
54 la semilla
– *seed*
55 el pino piñonero (el pino real, el pino manso, el pino donal)
– *stone pine*
56 el brote (el vástago) masculino
– *male shoot*
57 el cono con semillas *f* [corte longitudinal]
– *fruit cone with seeds [longitudinal section]*
58 el ciprés (*poético:* el ciprasio)
– *cypress*
59 la rama con frutos *m* (con piñuelas *f*)
– *fruiting branch*
60 la semilla
– *seed*
61 el tejo
– *yew (yew tree)*
62 el cono masculino y el cono femenino
– *male flower shoot and female flower cone*
63 la rama con frutos *m*
– *fruiting branch*
64 el fruto
– *fruit*
65 el cedro (*Perú:* el cibui)
– *cedar (cedar tree)*
66 la rama con frutos *m*
– *fruiting branch*
67 la escama del fruto
– *fruit scale*
68 el cono masculino y el cono femenino
– *male flower shoot and female flower cone*
69 la secoya (la secuoya)
– *mammoth tree (Wellingtonia, sequoia)*
70 la rama con frutos *m*
– *fruiting branch*
71 la semilla
– *seed*

1 la forsitia
 – *forsythia*
2 el ovario y el estambre
 – *ovary and stamen*
3 la hoja
 – *leaf*
4 el jazmín amarillo
 – *yellow-flowered jasmine (jasmin, jessamine)*
5 la flor [corte longitudinal] con estilo *m*, ovario *m* y estambre *m*
 – *flower [longitudinal section] with styles, ovaries, and stamens*
6 el aligustre común (la alheña, el ligustro)
 – *privet (common privet)*
7 la flor
 – *flower*
8 la infrutescencia
 – *infructescence*
9 la jeringuilla (la celinda)
 – *mock orange (sweet syringa)*
10 el viburno (la bola de nieve *f*, mundillo *m*, sauquillo *m*) común
 – *snowball (snowball bush, guelder rose)*
11 la flor
 – *flower*
12 los frutos
 – *fruits*
13 la adelfa (el baladre, el laurel rosa)
 – *oleander (rosebay, rose laurel)*
14 la flor [corte longitudinal]
 – *flower [longitudinal section]*
15 la magnolia roja
 – *red magnolia*
16 la hoja
 – *leaf*
17 el membrillo (el membrillero) japonés
 – *japonica (japanese quince)*
18 el fruto
 – *fruit*
19 el boj común
 – *common box (box, box tree)*
20 la flor femenina
 – *female flower*
21 la flor masculina
 – *male flower*
22 el fruto [corte longitudinal]
 – *fruit [longitudinal section]*
23 la weigelia
 – *weigela (weigelia)*
24 la yuca [parte *f* de la inflorescencia]
 – *yucca [part of the inflorescence]*
25 la hoja
 – *leaf*
26 el escaramujo (el agavanzo, la mosqueta silvestre, la zarzaperruna)
 – *dog rose (briar rose, wild briar)*
27 el fruto
 – *fruit*
28 la espirea del Japón (la kerria)
 – *kerria*

29 el fruto
 – *fruit*
30 el cornejo hembra (el cerezo silvestre)
 – *cornelian cherry*
31 la flor
 – *flower*
32 el fruto (la cereza silvestre)
 – *fruit (cornelian cherry)*
33 el mirto de Brabante (el arrayán brabántico; *Mé.:* el haya *f*)
 – *sweet gale (gale)*

1 el tulipero (el tulipanero)
común
- *tulip tree (tulip poplar, saddle tree, whitewood)*
2 los carpelos
- *carpels*
3 el estambre
- *stamen*
4 el fruto
- *fruit*
5 el hisopo
- *hyssop*
6 la flor [vista por delante]
- *flower [front view]*
7 la flor
- *flower*
8 el cáliz con fruto *m*
- *calyx with fruit*
9 el acebo (el agrifolio, el aquifolio)
- *holly*
10 la flor hermafrodita (la flor andrógina)
- *androgynous (hermaphroditic, hermaphrodite) flower*
11 la flor masculina
- *male flower*
12 el fruto con los huesos al descubierto
- *fruit with stones exposed*
13 la madreselva
- *honeysuckle (woodbine, woodbind)*
14 los botones florales (los capullos)
- *flower buds*
15 la flor [corte]
- *flower [cut open]*
16 la viña loca
- *Virginia creeper (American ivy, woodbine)*
17 la flor abierta
- *open flower*
18 la inflorescencia
- *infructescence*
19 el fruto [corte longitudinal]
- *fruit [longitudinal section]*
20 la retama de escobas *f* (la retama negra, el escobón)
- *broom*
21 la flor con los pétalos quitados
- *flower with the petals removed*
22 la vaina verde
- *immature (unripe) legume (pod)*
23 la espirea (la ulmaria)
- *spiraea*
24 la flor [corte longitudinal]
- *flower [longitudinal section]*
25 el fruto
- *fruit*
26 el carpelo
- *carpel*
27 el endrino
- *blackthorn (sloe)*
28 las hojas
- *leaves*
29 los frutos
- *fruits*

30 el espino (el espino albar, el espino blanco, el majuelo, la exiacanta, el níspero silvestre; *Amér.:* el espinillo)
- *single-pistilled hawthorn (thorn, may)*
31 el fruto
- *fruit*
32 el laburno (el cítiso de los Alpes, la lluvia de oro *m*, el ébano falso, el codeso, el borne, el piorno)
- *laburnum (golden chain, golden rain)*
33 el racimo de flores *f*
- *raceme*
34 los frutos
- *fruits*
35 el saúco negro (el sabuco, el canillero)
- *black elder (elder)*
36 las flores del saúco (una cima)
- *elder flowers*
37 las bayas del saúco
- *elderberries*

# 375 Flores de prados y linderos I

1 la saxífraga de hoja *f* redonda
(la saxífraga dorada)
- *rotundifoliate (rotundifolious)*
*saxifrage (rotundifoliate*
*breakstone)*
2 la hoja
- *leaf*
3 la flor
- *flower*
4 el fruto
- *fruit*
5 la anémona común (la
pulsatilla)
- *anemone (windflower)*
6 la flor [corte longitudinal]
- *flower [longitudinal section]*
7 el fruto
- *fruit*
8 el ranúnculo (la francesilla, la
marimoña)
- *buttercup (meadow buttercup,*
*butterflower, goldcup, king cup,*
*crowfoot)*
9 la hoja de la raíz
- *basal leaf*
10 el fruto
- *fruit*
11 el mastuerzo (la cardamina)
- *lady's smock (ladysmock, cuckoo*
*flower)*
12 la hoja basilar
- *basal leaf*
13 el fruto
- *fruit*
14 la campánula (la campanilla)
- *harebell (hairbell, bluebell)*
15 la hoja de la raíz
- *basal leaf*
16 la flor [corte longitudinal]
- *flower [longitudinal section]*
17 el fruto
- *fruit*
18 la hiedra terrestre
- *ground ivy (ale hoof)*
19 la flor [corte longitudinal]
- *flower [longitudinal section]*
20 la flor [vista desde arriba]
- *flower [front view]*
21 la uva de gato *m* (el racimillo,
la vermicularia)
- *stonecrop*
22 la verónica
- *speedwell*
23 la flor
- *flower*
24 el fruto
- *fruit*
25 la semilla
- *seed*
26 la hierba de la moneda
- *moneywort*
27 la cápsula dehiscente del fruto
- *dehisced fruit*
28 la semilla
- *seed*
29 la escabiosa menor
- *small scabious*
30 la hoja de la raíz
- *basal leaf*

31 la flor radiada (la lígula
radiada)
- *flower of outer series*
32 la florecilla del disco
- *disc (disk) floret (flower of inner*
*series)*
33 el periclino (el periforanto, la
periforiantia) con aristas *f*
- *involucral calyx with pappus*
*bristles*
34 el ovario con aristas *f*
- *ovary with pappus*
35 el fruto
- *fruit*
36 la celidonia menor
- *lesser celandine*
37 el fruto
- *fruit*
38 la axila de la hoja con
bulbillo *m*
- *leaf axil with bulbil*
39 la espiguilla (la hierba de
punta; *Chile:* el piojillo)
- *annual meadow grass*
40 la flor
- *flower*
41 la espiguilla [vista de costado]
- *spikelet [side view]*
42 la espiguilla [vista desde arriba]
- *spikelet [front view]*
43 la cariópside (fruto *m*
indehiscente)
- *caryopsis, an indehiscent fruit*
44 el manojo de hierba *f*
- *tuft of grass (clump of grass)*
45 la consuelda (el sínfito mayor)
- *comfrey*
46 la flor [corte longitudinal]
- *flower [longitudinal section]*
47 el fruto
- *fruit*

# 376 Flores de prados y linderos II

1 la margarita menor (*Arg.:* la
  coqueta; *Col.:* la pascua)
– *daisy (Am. English daisy)*
2 la flor
– *flower*
3 el fruto
– *fruit*
4 la margarita mayor
– *oxeye daisy (white oxeye daisy,*
  *marguerite)*
5 la flor
– *flower*
6 el fruto
– *fruit*
7 la astrancia
– *masterwort*
8 la vellorita; *anál.:* la primavera
– *cowslip*
9 el gordolobo (el verbasco)
– *great mullein (Aaron's rod,*
  *shepherd's club)*
10 la bistorta
– *bistort (snakeweed)*
11 la flor
– *flower*
12 la centaura negra
– *knapweed*
13 la malva común
– *common mallow*
14 el fruto
– *fruit*
15 la aquilea (la milenrama, la
  altarreina, la artemisa bastarda,
  la hierba meona, la milhojas;
  *Col.:* la viuda)
– *yarrow*
16 la hierba del carpintero
– *self-heal*
17 el cuernecillo
– *bird's foot trefoil (bird's foot*
  *clover)*
18 el equiseto (la cola de caballo
  *m*) [un retoño]
– *horsetail (equisetum) [a shoot]*
19 la flor (el cono)
– *flower, a strobile*
20 la cambronera (el arto)
– *campion (catchfly)*
21 la flor del cuclillo
– *ragged robin (cuckoo flower)*
22 la aristoloquia
– *birth-wort*
23 la flor
– *flower*
24 el geranio
– *crane's bill*
25 la achicoria común
– *wild chicory (witloof, succory,*
  *wild endive)*
26 la silene, una cariofilácea
– *common toadflax (butter-and-*
  *eggs)*
27 el zapatito de dama *f*
– *lady's slipper (Venus's slipper,*
  Am. *moccasin flower)*
28 el satirión, una orquídea
– *orchis (wild orchid), an orchid*

1 la nemorosa (la anémona de bosque *m*)
- *wood anemone (anemone, windflower)*
2 el lirio de los valles (la convalaria, el muguete)
- *lily of the valley*
3 el pie de gato *m; anál.:* la siempreviva (la perpetua)
- *cat's foot (milkwort);* sim.: *sandflower (everlasting)*
4 el martagón (la azucena silvestre, el lirio silvestre)
- *turk's cap (turk's cap lily)*
5 la barba de cabrón *m* (aruncus sylvestris)
- *goatsbeard (goat's beard)*
6 el ajo de oso *m*
- *ramson*
7 la pulmonaria
- *lungwort*
8 la fumaria
- *corydalis*
9 la hierba callera
- *orpine (livelong)*
10 la lauréola (el torvisco, el mezéreon, la adelfilla)
- *daphne*
11 la nometoques (la balsamina grande, la hierba de Santa Catalina; *Amér.:* la china, la chinarrosa)
- *touch-me-not*
12 el pampajarito, la pimienta de muros *m*
- *staghorn (stag horn moss, stag's horn, stag's horn moss, coral evergreen)*
13 la grasilla (la tiraña), una planta carnívora
- *butterwort, an insectivorous plant*
14 la drósera (la atrapamoscas)
- *sundew;* sim.: *Venus's flytrap*
15 la gayuba (la uvaduz)
- *bearberry*
16 el polipodio, un helecho; *anál.:* el aspidio, el culantrillo, la rueda de muros *m*
- *polypody (polypod), a fern;* sim.: *male fern, brake (bracken, eagle fern), royal fern (royal osmund, king's fern, ditch fern)*
17 el musgo capilar, un musgo
- *haircap moss (hair moss, golden maidenhair), a moss*
18 el erióforo, una ciperácea
- *cotton grass (cotton rush)*
19 el brezo (la brecina, la querihuela, el biércol, el urce); *anál.:* la carroncha (el brezo negro)
- *heather (heath, ling);* sim.: *bell heather (cross-leaved heather)*
20 el heliantemo, una jara
- *rock rose (sun rose)*
21 el ledo de los pantanos
- *marsh tea*
22 el cálamo aromático (el ácoro verdadero)
- *sweet flag (sweet calamus, sweet sedge)*
23 el arándano (el mirtilo, el ráspano, la anavia); *anál.:* el arándano rojo, el arándano negro
- *bilberry (whortleberry, huckleberry, blueberry);* sim.: *cowberry (red whortleberry), bog bilberry (bog whortleberry), crowberry (crakeberry)*

# 378 Plantas alpinas, acuáticas y de pantano

**1-13 plantas *f* alpinas**
- *alpine plants*
1 el rododendro
- *alpine rose (alpine rhododendron)*
2 la rama florida
- *flowering shoot*
3 la campanilla de los Alpes (la soldanella alpina)
- *alpine soldanella (soldanella)*
4 la corola desplegada
- *corolla opened out*
5 la cápsula de las semillas *f* con el estilo
- *seed vessel with the style*
6 la escobilla parda
- *alpine wormwood*
7 la inflorescencia
- *inflorescence*
8 la oreja de oso *m*
- *auricula*
9 el leontopodio (la flor de nieve *f*, la edelweiss)
- *edelweiss*
10 las formas de las flores
- *flower shapes*
11 el fruto con el vilano
- *fruit with pappus tuft*
12 el corte de una cabezuela
- *part of flower head (of capitulum)*
13 la genciana de primavera *f*
- *stemless alpine gentian*
**14-57 plantas *f* acuáticas y de pantano *m***
- *aquatic plants (water plants) and marsh plants*
14 el nenúfar (el lirio de agua *f*)
- *white water lily*
15 la hoja
- *leaf*
16 la flor
- *flower*
17 la Victoria regia (el lirio gigante del Amazonas)
- *Queen Victoria water lily (Victoria regia water lily, royal water lily, Amazon water lily)*
18 la hoja
- *leaf*
19 el envés de la hoja
- *underside of the leaf*
20 la flor
- *flower*
21 la anea, la espadaña
- *reed mace bulrush (cattail, cat's tail, cattail flag, club rush)*
22 la parte masculina del espádice
- *male part of the spadix*
23 la flor masculina
- *male flower*
24 la parte femenina
- *female part*
25 la flor femenina
- *female flower*
26 el nomeolvides
- *forget-me-not*
27 la rama en flor *f*
- *flowering shoot*

28 la flor [corte]
- *flower [section]*
29 la hidrocara (el mordisco de rana *f*)
- *frog's bit*
30 el berro amargo (el berro de fuente *f*)
- *watercress*
31 el tallo con flores *f* y frutos *m* jóvenes
- *stalk with flowers and immature (unripe) fruits*
32 la flor
- *flower*
33 la vaina con semillas *f*
- *siliqua (pod) with seeds*
34 dos semillas *f*
- *two seeds*
35 la lenteja de agua *f*
- *duckweed (duck's meat)*
36 la planta en flor *f*
- *plant in flower*
37 la flor
- *flower*
38 el fruto
- *fruit*
39 el junco florido
- *flowering rush*
40 la umbela
- *flower umbel*
41 las hojas
- *leaves*
42 el fruto
- *fruit*
43 el alga *f* verde
- *green alga*
44 la alisma (el llantén de agua *f*, el pan de ranas *f*)
- *water plantain*
45 la hoja
- *leaf*
46 la panícula (la inflorescencia)
- *panicle*
47 la flor
- *flower*
48 el golfo (el sargazo azucarado), una laminaria
- *honey wrack, a brown alga*
49 el talo
- *thallus (plant body, frond)*
50 el órgano de fijación *f*
- *holdfast*
51 la sagitaria
- *arrow head*
52 las formas de las hojas
- *leaf shapes*
53 la inflorescencia con flores *f* masculinas [arriba] y flores femeninas [abajo]
- *inflorescence with male flowers [above] and female flowers [below]*
54 la hierba marina (la zostera marina)
- *sea grass*
55 la inflorescencia
- *inflorescence*
56 la elodea
- *Canadian waterweed (Canadian pondweed)*
57 la flor
- *flower*

1  el acónito (el anapelo, el
   napelo); *anál.:* la uva lupina, el
   matalobos, el pardal, la verga
– *aconite (monkshood, wolfsbane,
   helmet flower)*
2  el digital (la dedalera, la
   gualdaperra, la viluria, la
   giloria)
– *foxglove (Digitalis)*
3  el cólquico (la quitameriendas,
   la flor de otoño *m; Bol., Col. y
   Perú:* el cólchico)
– *meadow saffron (naked lady,
   naked boys)*
4  la cicuta (el perejil lobuno;
   *Perú:* la montezanahoria)
– *hemlock (Conium)*
5  la hierba mora (el tomatillo del
   diablo, el solano negro; *Arg. y
   Par.:* el arachichú)
– *black nightshade (common
   nightshade, petty morel)*
6  el beleño negro
– *henbane*
7  la belladona
– *deadly nightshade (belladonna,
   banewort, dwale), a solanaceous
   herb*
8  el estramonio (la hierba
   hedionda, la higuera loca, la
   estramónica, la manzana
   espinosa; *Amér.:* el chamico;
   *Mé.:* el toloache; *Col.:* el
   gigantín)
– *thorn apple (stramonium,
   stramony, Am. jimson weed,
   jimpson weed, Jamestown weed,
   stinkweed)*
9  el aro (el alcatraz, el arón, el
   jaro, el jarillo, el jarrillo, la
   tragontina, el yaro; *Hond.:* el
   quiscamote; *Col.:* la rascadera)
– *cuckoo pint (lords-and-ladies,
   wild arum, wake-robin)*
10-13  hongos *m* venenosos (setas *f*
   venenosas)
– *poisonous fungi (poisonous
   mushrooms, toadstools)*
10  la amanita de las moscas (el
   agárico de las moscas, la falsa
   oronja, la matamoscas), un
   agárico
– *fly agaric (fly amanita, fly
   fungus), an agaric*
11  la oronja verde (la seta mortal)
– *amanita*
12  el boleto de Satanás (*Bol.,
   Chile, Ec. y Perú:* la callampa;
   *Col., Chile y Ec.:* la callamba)
– *Satan's mushroom*
13  el níscalo falso
– *woolly milk cap*

*Medicinal Plants*

1 la manzanilla (la camamila, la camomila; *Perú:* la sachamanzanilla)
– camomile (chamomile, wild camomile)
2 el árnica *f* (el tabaco de montaña *f*, el tabaco borde, la estornudadera)
– arnica
3 la menta (la hierbabuena, la hierba santa)
– peppermint
4 el ajenjo (el absintio)
– wormwood (absinth)
5 la valeriana (la hierba de los gatos; *Ec.:* la guasilla; *Perú:* el turpu)
– valerian (allheal)
6 el hinojo; *anál.:* el eneldo
– fennel
7 el espliego (la alhucema, la lavanda)
– lavender
8 el tusilago (la fárfara, la uña de caballo *m*, el pie de caballo *m*, la pata de asno *m*)
– coltsfoot
9 la atanasia (el tanaceto, la hierba lombriguera, la hierba de Santa María)
– tansy
10 la centáurea mayor
– centaury
11 el llantén menor (la lancéola, la quinquenervia)
– ribwort (ribwort plantain, ribgrass)
12 el malvavisco (la altea)
– marshmallow
13 el arraclán (la frángula)
– alder buckthorn (alder dogwood)
14 el ricino (la oherva, la querva, la higuera del infierno, la higuereta, la higuerilla, la palmacristi, el rezno; *Venez.:* el tártago)
– castor-oil plant (Palma Christi)
15 la adormidera
– opium poppy
16 el sen (la casia; *Col.:* la bajagua; *Cuba y S. Dgo.:* la guajaba; *Hond.:* el saragundí, el zambrano; *P. Rico:* la talantala); *las hojas secas:* las hojas de sen *m*
– senna (cassia); the dried leaflets: senna leaves
17 el quino (el árbol de la quina, el cascarillo)
– cinchona (chinchona)
18 el alcanforero
– camphor tree (camphor laurel)
19 el betel
– betel palm (areca, areca palm)
20 la nuez de betel *m* (la areca)
– betel nut (areca nut)

1 el champiñón silvestre (el hongo comestible)
– *meadow mushroom (field mushroom)*
2 el afieltramiento de hifas *f* (el micelio) con cuerpos *m* fructificados (hongos *m*)
– *mycelial threads (hyphae, mycelium) with fruiting bodies*
3 hongo *m* [corte longitudinal]
– *mushroom [longitudinal section]*
4 el sombrerete (el píleo) con laminillas *f* (hojuelas *f*)
– *cap (pileus) with gills*
5 la vola (el velum)
– *veil (velum)*
6 la laminilla [corte]
– *gill [section]*
7 el basidio [en la laminilla con basidioesporas *f*]
– *basidia [on the gill with basidiospores]*
8 las esporas germinales
– *germinating basidiospores (spores)*
9 la trufa (la criadilla de tierra *f*)
– *truffle*
10 el hongo [vista exterior]
– *truffle [external view]*
11 el hongo [corte]
– *truffle [section]*
12 interior *m* con la teca con esporas *f* [corte]
– *interior showing asci [section]*
13 dos tecas *f* con las esporas
– *two asci with the ascospores (spores)*
14 la cantarela
– *chanterelle (chantarelle)*
15 el rebozuelo (la cabrilla)
– *Chestnut Boletus*
16 el boleto comestible (la calabaza)
– *cep (cepe, squirrel's bread, Boletus edulis)*
17 la capa tuberosa
– *layer of tubes (hymenium)*
18 el tallo
– *stem (stipe)*
19 el bejín blando
– *puffball (Bovista nigrescens)*
20 el bejín plomizo
– *devil's tobacco pouch (common puffball)*
21 el boleto anillado
– *Brown Ring Boletus (Boletus luteus)*
22 el boleto áspero
– *Birch Boletus (Boletus scaber)*
23 el mízcalo (el níscalo)
– *Russula vesca*
24 el hidno imbricado
– *scaled prickle fungus*
25 la cabeza de fraile *m* (la platera)
– *slender funnel fungus*
26 la colmenilla redonda
– *morel (Morchella esculenta)*
27 la colmenilla cónica
– *morel (Morchella conica)*
28 la armilaria color *m* de miel *f*
– *honey fungus*
29 el tricoloma ecuestre (la seta de los caballeros)
– *saffron milk cap*
30 el apagador (la galamperna)
– *parasol mushroom*
31 la gamuza (la lengua de gato *m*)
– *hedgehog fungus (yellow prickle fungus)*
32 la ramaria apretada
– *yellow coral fungus (goatsbeard, goat's beard, coral Clavaria)*
33 la foliota cambiante
– *little cluster fungus*

1 el cafeto (el árbol del café)
- *coffee tree (coffee plant)*
2 la rama con frutos *m*
- *fruiting branch*
3 la rama florida
- *flowering branch*
4 la flor
- *flower*
5 el fruto con los dos granos [corte longitudinal]
- *fruit with two beans [longitudinal section]*
6 el grano de café *m; después de preparado:* el café
- *coffee bean;* when processed: *coffee*
7 el té
- *tea plant (tea tree)*
8 la rama florida
- *flowering branch*
9 la hoja del té: *después de preparada:* el té
- *tea leaf;* when processed: *tea*
10 el fruto
- *fruit*
11 el mate (la hierba mate, el té del Paraguay, el té de los jesuitas, la hierba del Paraguay)
- *maté shrub (maté, yerba maté, Paraguay tea)*
12 la rama florida con las flores hermafroditas
- *flowering branch with androgynous (hermaphroditic, hermaphrodite) flowers*
13 la flor masculina
- *male flower*
14 la flor hermafrodita
- *androgynous (hermaphroditic, hermaphrodite) flower*
15 el fruto
- *fruit*
16 el cacao (el teobroma)
- *cacao tree (cacao)*
17 la rama con flores *f* y frutos *m*
- *branch with flowers and fruits*
18 la flor [corte longitudinal]
- *flower [longitudinal section]*
19 el grano de cacao *m; después de preparado:* el cacao, el cacao en polvo *m*
- *cacao beans (cocoa beans);* when processed: *cocoa, cocoa powder*
20 la semilla [corte longitudinal]
- *seed [longitudinal section]*
21 el embrión
- *embryo*
22 el árbol de la canela (el canelo, el canelero)
- *cinnamon tree (cinnamon)*
23 la rama florida
- *flowering branch*
24 el fruto
- *fruit*

25 la corteza del canelo (la canela en rama *f*); *molida:* la canela en polvo *m*
- *cinnamon bark;* when crushed: *cinnamon*
26 el clavero (el árbol del clavo)
- *clove tree*
27 la rama florida
- *flowering branch*
28 la yema; *desecada:* el clavo
- *flower bud;* when dried: *clove*
29 la flor
- *flower*
30 la mirística
- *nutmeg tree*
31 la rama florida
- *flowering branch*
32 la flor femenina [corte longitudinal]
- *female flower [longitudinal section]*
33 el fruto maduro
- *mature (ripe) fruit*
34 la flor de mirística *f*, una semilla rodeada por el arilo (el macis)
- *nutmeg with mace, a seed with laciniate aril*
35 la semilla [corte transversal]; *seca:* la nuez moscada
- *seed [cross section];* when dried: *nutmeg*
36 el pimentero (el pimiento)
- *pepper plant*
37 la rama con frutos *m*
- *fruiting branch*
38 la inflorescencia
- *inflorescence*
39 el fruto [corte longitudinal] con el grano de pimienta *f* (la pimienta); *molida:* la pimienta molida, la pimienta en polvo *m*
- *fruit [longitudinal section] with seed, a peppercorn;* when ground: *pepper*
40 la planta de tabaco *m* de Virginia (*Chile:* de pitrén)
- *Virginia tobacco plant*
41 la rama florida
- *flowering shoot*
42 la flor
- *flower*
43 la hoja de tabaco *m; seca:* el tabaco
- *tobacco leaf;* when cured: *tobacco*
44 la cápsula de fruto maduro
- *mature (ripe) fruit capsule*
45 la semilla
- *seed*
46 la vainilla
- *vanilla plant*
47 la rama florida
- *flowering shoot*
48 la vaina de la vainilla; *curada:* el bastoncillo de vainilla
- *vanilla pod;* when cured: *stick of vanilla*

49 el pistachero (el alfóncigo)
- *pistachio tree*
50 la rama florida con las flores femeninas
- *flowering branch with female flowers*
51 la almendra del alfóncigo (el pistacho)
- *drupe;* here: *pistachio (pistachio nut)*
52 la caña de azúcar *m* (la caña dulce, la caña melar)
- *sugar cane*
53 la planta en flor *f*
- *plant (habit) in bloom*
54 la panícula (la inflorescencia)
- *panicle*
55 la flor
- *flower*

1 la colza (el nabo; *Col.:* la
  rabancá)
- *rape (cole, coleseed)*
2 la hoja basal
- *basal leaf*
3 la flor [corte longitudinal]
- *flower [longitudinal section]*
4 la silicua madura
- *mature (ripe) siliqua (pod)*
5 la semilla oleaginosa
- *oleiferous seed*
6 el lino
- *flax*
7 el tallo florido
- *peduncle (pedicel, flower stalk)*
8 la cápsula del fruto
- *seed vessel (boll)*
9 el cáñamo
- *hemp*
10 la planta femenina con frutos *m*
- *fruiting female (pistillate) plant*
11 la inflorescencia femenina
- *female inflorescence*
12 la flor
- *flower*
13 la inflorescencia masculina
- *male inflorescence*
14 el fruto
- *fruit*
15 la semilla
- *seed*
16 el algodonero (*Arg. y Par.:* el
  mandiyú; *Arg.:* el amandiyú)
- *cotton*
17 la flor
- *flower*
18 el fruto
- *fruit*
19 la borra (la pelusa del algodón,
  el algodón)
- *lint [cotton wool]*
20 la ceiba
- *silk-cotton tree (kapok tree,
  capoc tree, ceiba tree)*
21 el fruto
- *fruit*
22 la rama florida
- *flowering branch*
23 la semilla
- *seed*
24 la semilla [corte longitudinal]
- *seed [longitudinal section]*
25 el yute
- *jute*
26 la rama florida
- *flowering branch*
27 la flor
- *flower*
28 el fruto
- *fruit*
29 el olivo (la oliva, la olivera, el
  aceituno)
- *olive tree (olive)*
30 la rama florida
- *flowering branch*
31 la flor
- *flower*
32 la aceituna (la oliva)
- *fruit*

33 el árbol del caucho (la
  cauchera)
- *rubber tree (rubber plant)*
34 la rama con frutos *m*
- *fruiting branch*
35 el higo
- *fig*
36 la flor
- *flower*
37 el árbol de la gutapercha
- *gutta-percha tree*
38 la rama florida
- *flowering branch*
39 la flor
- *flower*
40 el fruto
- *fruit*
41 el cacahuete (el cacahuate, el
  cacahuey, el cacahué, el maní;
  *Arg. y Bol.:* el mandubí)
- *peanut (ground nut, monkey nut)*
42 la rama florida
- *flowering shoot*
43 la raíz con frutos *m*
- *root with fruits*
44 el fruto [corte longitudinal]
- *nut (kernel) [longitudinal
  section]*
45 el ajonjolí (la alegría, el
  sésamo)
- *sesame plant (simsim, benniseed)*
46 la rama con flores y frutas *f*
- *flowers and fruiting branch*
47 la flor [corte longitudinal]
- *flower [longitudinal section]*
48 el cocotero (el coco, la palma
  de coco *m*, la palma indiana)
- *coconut palm (coconut tree, coco
  palm, cocoa palm)*
49 la inflorescencia
- *inflorescence*
50 la flor femenina
- *female flower*
51 la flor masculina [corte
  longitudinal]
- *male flower [longitudinal
  section]*
52 el fruto [corte longitudinal]
- *fruit [longitudinal section]*
53 el coco
- *coconut (cokernut)*
54 la palmera de aceite *m*
- *oil palm*
55 el espádice masculino con la
  flor
- *male spadix*
56 la inflorescencia con el fruto
- *infructescence with fruit*
57 la semilla con los orificios
  germinativos
- *seed with micropyles (foramina)
  (foraminate seed)*
58 el sagú (*Venez.:* el guapo;
  *P. Rico:* la maranta; *P. Rico y
  S. Dgo.:* la yuquilla)
- *sago palm*
59 el fruto
- *fruit*

60 el bambú (*Amér.:* la caña
  brava; *Venez.:* el mavi; *Mé.:* el
  otate; *Cuba y Venez.:* el pito;
  *Col., Ec. y Venez.:* la guadua;
  *Bol. y Río de la Plata:* la
  tacuara; *Perú:* la zacuara)
- *bamboo stem (bamboo culm)*
61 la rama con hojas *f*
- *branch with leaves*
62 la espiga de flores *f*
- *spike*
63 el trozo de caña *f* con nudos *m*
- *part of bamboo stem with joints*
64 el papiro
- *papyrus plant (paper reed, paper
  rush)*
65 el copete de flores *f*
- *umbel*
66 la espiga de flores *f*
- *spike*

## 384 Frutos meridionales

1 la palmera datilera (la palma, la datilera)
- *date palm (date)*
2 la palmera con frutos *m*
- *fruiting palm*
3 la hoja de la palmera (la palma)
- *palm frond*
4 el espádice masculino
- *male spadix*
5 la flor masculina
- *male flower*
6 el espádice femenino
- *female spadix*
7 la flor femenina
- *female flower*
8 una rama con frutos *m*
- *stand of fruit*
9 el dátil
- *date*
10 el hueso del dátil (la semilla)
- *date kernel*
11 la higuera
- *fig*
12 la rama con frutas *f* compuestas
- *branch with pseudocarps*
13 el higo con flores *f* [corte longitudinal]
- *fig with flowers [longitudinal section]*
14 la flor femenina
- *female flower*
15 la flor masculina
- *male flower*
16 el granado
- *pomegranate*
17 la rama florida
- *flowering branch*
18 la flor [corte longitudinal, separada la corola]
- *flower [longitudinal section, corolla removed]*
19 el fruto (la granada)
- *fruit*
20 la semilla (el grano) [corte longitudinal]
- *seed [longitudinal section]*
21 la semilla [corte transversal]
- *seed [cross section]*
22 el embrión
- *embryo*
23 el limón; *anál.:* la mandarina, la naranja (*Antillas y Venez.:* la china), la toronja (el pomelo; *Filip.:* el luchán)
- *lemon;* sim.: *tangerine (mandarin), orange, grapefruit*
24 la rama florida
- *flowering branch*
25 la flor del naranjo (el azahar) [corte longitudinal]
- *orange flower [longitudinal section]*
26 el fruto
- *fruit*
27 la naranja [corte transversal]
- *orange [cross section]*

28 el banano (el plátano, el platanero; *P. Rico:* el comisario, el fotoco; *Antillas:* el guineo; *Par.:* la pacobá; *Pan.:* el patriota; *anál.: Amér. Central, Antillas, Col., Ec., Pan., Perú y Venez.:* el dominico; *Col., Cuba, Mé., Pan., Perú y P. Rico:* el morado)
- *banana plant (banana tree)*
29 la corona de hojas *f*
- *crown*
30 el seudotronco con las hojas envainadas
- *herbaceous stalk with overlapping leaf sheaths*
31 la florescencia con frutos *m* jóvenes
- *inflorescence with young fruits*
32 la infrutescencia
- *infructescence (bunch of fruit)*
33 la banana (el plátano) *[los nombres en América son variadísmos y coinciden con los del árbol]*
- *banana*
34 la flor de la banana
- *banana flower*
35 la hoja de banano *m* [esquema]
- *banana leaf [diagram]*
36 el almendro
- *almond*
37 la rama florida
- *flowering branch*
38 la rama con frutos *m*
- *fruiting branch*
39 el fruto (la almendra)
- *fruit*
40 la cáscara con la semilla [de la almendra]
- *drupe containing seed [almond]*
41 el algarrobo
- *carob*
42 la rama con flores *f* femeninas
- *branch with female flowers*
43 la flor femenina
- *female flower*
44 la flor masculina
- *male flower*
45 el fruto (la algarroba)
- *fruit*
46 la vaina-fruto [corte transversal]
- *siliqua (pod) [cross section]*
47 la semilla
- *seed*
48 el castaño
- *sweet chestnut (Spanish chestnut)*
49 la rama florida
- *flowering branch*
50 la inflorescencia femenina
- *female inflorescence*
51 la flor masculina
- *male flower*
52 la cúpula (el erizo) con las semillas (las castañas)
- *cupule, containing seeds*
53 la nuez del Brasil
- *Brazil nut*

54 la rama florida
- *flowering branch*
55 la hoja
- *leaf*
56 la flor [vista desde arriba]
- *flower [from above]*
57 la flor [corte longitudinal]
- *flower [longitudinal section]*
58 el fruto capsular abierto con las semillas
- *opened capsule, containing seeds*
59 la nuez del Brasil (la castaña del Marañón) [corte transversal]
- *Brazil nut [cross section]*
60 la nuez [corte longitudinal]
- *nut [longitudinal section]*
61 el ananás (la piña de América, la piña tropical)
- *pineapple plant (pineapple)*
62 la fruta compuesta (el seudocarpo) con la corona de hojas *f*
- *pseudocarp with crown of leaves*
63 la espiga de flores *f*
- *syncarp*
64 la flor del ananás
- *pineapple flower*
65 la flor [corte longitudinal]
- *flower [longitudinal section]*

# Für freundliche Unterstützung und Mitarbeit haben wir zu danken:

ADB GmbH, Bestwig; AEG-Telefunken, Abteilung Werbung, Wolfenbüttel; Agfa-Gevaert AG, Presse-Abteilung, Leverkusen; Eduard Ahlborn GmbH, Hildesheim; AID, Land- und Hauswirtschaftlicher Auswertungs- und Informationsdienst e. V., Bonn-Bad Godesberg; Arbeitsausschuß der Waldarbeitsschulen beim Kuratorium für Waldarbeit und Forsttechnik, Bad Segeberg; Arnold & Richter KG, München; Atema AB, Härnösand (Schweden); Audi NSU Auto-Union AG, Presseabteilung, Ingolstadt; Bêché & Grohs GmbH, Hückeswagen/Rhld.; Big Dutchman (Deutschland) GmbH, Bad Mergentheim und Calveslage über Vechta; Biologische Bundesanstalt für Land- und Forstwirtschaft, Braunschweig; Black & Decker, Idstein/Ts.; Braun AG, Frankfurt am Main; Bolex GmbH, Ismaning; Maschinenfabrik zum Bruderhaus GmbH, Reutlingen; Bund Deutscher Radfahrer e. V., Gießen; Bundesanstalt für Arbeit, Nürnberg; Bundesanstalt für Wasserbau, Karlsruhe; Bundesbahndirektion Karlsruhe, Presse- u. Informationsdienst, Karlsruhe; Bundesinnungsverband des Deutschen Schuhmacher-Handwerks, Düsseldorf; Bundeslotsenkammer, Hamburg; Bundesverband Bekleidungsindustrie e. V., Köln; Bundesverband der Deutschen Gas- und Wasserwirtschaft e. V., Frankfurt am Main; Bundesverband der Deutschen Zementindustrie e. V., Köln; Bundesverband Glasindustrie e. V., Düsseldorf; Bundesverband Metall, Essen-Kray und Berlin; Burkhardt + Weber KG, Reutlingen; Busatis-Werke KG, Remscheid; Claas GmbH, Harsewinkel; Copygraph GmbH, Hannover; Dr. Irmgard Correll, Mannheim; Daimler-Benz AG, Presse-Abteilung, Stuttgart; Dalex-Werke Niepenberg & Co. GmbH, Wissen; Elisabeth Daub, Mannheim; John Deere Vertrieb Deutschland, Mannheim; Deutsche Bank AG, Filiale Mannheim, Mannheim; Deutsche Gesellschaft für das Badewesen e. V., Essen; Deutsche Gesellschaft für Schädlingsbekämpfung mbH, Frankfurt am Main; Deutsche Gesellschaft zur Rettung Schiffbrüchiger, Bremen; Deutsche Milchwirtschaft, Molkerei- und Käserei-Zeitung (Verlag Th. Mann), Gelsenkirchen-Buer; Deutsche Eislauf-Union e. V., München; Deutscher Amateur-Box-Verband e. V., Essen; Deutscher Bob- und Schlittensportverband e. V., Berchtesgaden; Deutscher Eissport-Verband e. V., München; Deutsche Reiterliche Vereinigung e. V., Abteilung Sport, Warendorf; Deutscher Fechter-Bund e. V., Bonn; Deutscher Fußball-Bund, Frankfurt am Main; Deutscher Handball-Bund, Dortmund; Deutscher Hockey-Bund e. V., Köln; Deutscher Leichtathletik Verband, Darmstadt; Deutscher Motorsport Verband e. V., Frankfurt am Main; Deutscher Schwimm-Verband e. V., München; Deutscher Turner-Bund, Würzburg; Deutscher Verein von Gas- und Wasserfachmännern e. V., Eschborn; Deutscher Wetterdienst, Zentralamt, Offenbach; DIN Deutsches Institut für Normung e. V., Köln; Deutsches Institut für Normung e. V., Fachnormenausschuß Theatertechnik, Frankfurt am Main; Deutsche Versuchs- und Prüf-Anstalt für Jagd- und Sportwaffen e. V., Altenbeken-Buke; Friedrich Dick GmbH, Esslingen; Dr. Maria Dose, Mannheim; Dual Gebrüder Steidinger, St. Georgen/Schwarzwald; Durst AG, Bozen (Italien); Gebrüder Eberhard, Pflug- und Landmaschinenfabrik, Ulm; Gabriele Echtermann, Hemsbach; Dipl.-Ing. W. Ehret GmbH, Emmendingen-Kollmarsreute; Eichbaum-Brauereien AG, Worms/Mannheim; ER-WE-PA, Maschinenfabrik und Eisengießerei GmbH, Erkrath bei Düsseldorf; Escher Wyss GmbH, Ravensburg; Eumuco Aktiengesellschaft für Maschinenbau, Leverkusen; Euro-Photo GmbH, Willich; European Honda Motor Trading GmbH, Offenbach; Fachgemeinschaft Feuerwehrfahrzeuge und -geräte, Verein Deutscher Maschinenbau-Anstalten e. V., Frankfurt am Main; Fachnormenausschuß Maschinenbau im Deutschen Normenausschuß DNA, Frankfurt am Main; Fachnormenausschuß Schmiedetechnik in DIN Deutsches Institut für Normung e. V., Hagen; Fachverband des Deutschen Tapetenhandels e. V., Köln; Fachverband der Polstermöbelindustrie e. V., Herford; Fachverband Rundfunk und Fernsehen im Zentralverband der Elektrotechnischen Industrie e. V., Frankfurt am Main; Fahr AG Maschinenfabrik, Gottmadingen; Fendt & Co., Agrartechnik, Marktoberndorf; Fichtel & Sachs AG, Schweinfurt; Karl Fischer, Pforzheim; Heinrich Gerd Fladt, Ludwigshafen am Rhein; Forschungsanstalt für Weinbau, Gartenbau, Getränketechnologie und Landespflege, Geisenheim am Rhein; Förderungsgemeinschaft des Deutschen Bäckerhandwerks e. V., Bad Honnef; Forschungsinstitut der Zementindustrie, Düsseldorf; Johanna Förster, Mannheim; Stadtverwaltung Frankfurt am Main, Straßen- und Brückenbauamt, Frankfurt am Main; Freier Verband Deutscher Zahnärzte e. V., Bonn-Bad Godesberg; Fuji Photo Film (Europa) GmbH, Düsseldorf; Gesamtverband der Deutschen Maschen-Industrie e. V., Gesamtmasche, Stuttgart; Gesamtverband des Deutschen Steinkohlenbergbaus, Essen; Gesamtverband der Textilindustrie in der BRD, Gesamttextil, e. V., Frankfurt am Main; Geschwister-Scholl-Gesamtschule, Mannheim-Vogelstang; Eduardo Gomez, Mannheim; Gossen GmbH, Erlangen; Rainer Götz, Hemsbach; Grapha GmbH, Ostfildern; Ines Groh, Mannheim; Heinrich Groos, Geflügelzuchtbedarf, Bad Mergentheim; A. Gruse, Fabrik für Landmaschinen, Großberkel; Hafen Hamburg, Informationsbüro, Hamburg; Hagedorn Landmaschinen GmbH, Warendorf/Westf.; kino-hähnel GmbH, Erftstadt Liblar; Dr. Adolf Hanle, Mannheim; Hauptverband Deutscher Filmtheater e. V., Hamburg; Dr.-Ing. Rudolf Hell GmbH, Kiel; W. Helwig Söhne KG, Ziegenhain; Geflügelfarm Hipp, Mannheim; Gebrüder Holder, Maschinenfabrik, Metzingen; Horten Aktiengesellschaft, Düsseldorf; IBM Deutschland GmbH, Zentrale Bildstelle, Stuttgart; Innenministerium Baden-Württemberg, Pressestelle, Stuttgart; Industrieverband Gewebe, Frankfurt am Main; Industrievereinigung Chemiefaser e. V., Frankfurt am Main; Instrumentation Marketing Corporation, Burbank (Calif.); ITT Schaub-Lorenz Vertriebsgesellschaft mbH, Pforzheim; M. Jakoby KG, Maschinenfabrik, Hetzerath/Mosel; Jenoptik Jena GmbH, Jena (DDR); Brigitte Karnath, Wiesbaden; Wilhelm Kaßbaum, Hockenheim; Van Katwijk's Industrieën N. V., Staalkat Div., Aalten (Holland); Kernforschungszentrum Karlsruhe; Leo Keskari, Offenbach; Dr. Rolf Kiesewetter, Mannheim; Ev. Kindergarten, Hohensachsen; Klambt-Druck GmbH, Offset-Abteilung, Speyer; Maschinenfabrik Franz Klein, Salzkotten; Dr. Klaus-Friedrich Klein, Mannheim; Klimsch + Co., Frankfurt am Main; Kodak AG, Stuttgart; Alfons Kordecki, Eckernförde; Heinrich Kordecki, Mannheim; Krefelder Milchhof GmbH, Krefeld; Dr. Dieter Krickeberg, Musikinstrumenten-Museum, Berlin; Bernard Krone GmbH, Spelle; Pelz-Kunze, Mannheim; Kuratorium für Technik und Bauwesen in der Landwirtschaft, Darmstein-Kranichstein; Landesanstalt für Pflanzenschutz, Stuttgart; Landesinnungsverband des Schuhmacherhandwerks Baden-Württemberg, Stuttgart; Landespolizeidirektion Karlsruhe, Karlsruhe; Landwirtschaftskammer, Hannover; Metzgerei Lebold, Mannheim; Ernst Leitz Wetzlar GmbH, Wetzlar; Louis Leitz, Stuttgart; Christa Leverkinck, Mannheim; Franziska Liebisch, Mannheim; Linhof GmbH, München; Franz-Karl Frhr. von Linden, Mannheim; Loewe Opta GmbH, Kronach; Beate Lüdicke, Mannheim; MAN AG, Werk Augsburg, Augsburg; Mannheimer Verkehrs-Aktiengesellschaft (MVG), Mannheim; Milchzentrale Mannheim-Heidelberg AG, Mannheim; Ing. W. Möhlenkamp, Melle; Adolf Mohr Maschinenfabrik, Hofheim; Mörtl Schleppergerätebau KG, Gemünden/Main; Hans-Heinrich Müller, Mannheim; Müller Martini AG, Zofingen; Gebr. Nubert KG, Spezialeinrichtungen, Schwäbisch Gmünd; Nürnberger Hercules-Werke GmbH, Nürnberg; Olympia Werke AG, Wilhelmshaven; Ludwig Pani Lichttechnik und Projektion, Wien (Österreich); Ulrich Papin, Mannheim; Pfalzmilch Nord GmbH, Ludwigshafen/Albisheim; Adolf Pfeiffer GmbH, Ludwigshafen am Rhein; Philips Pressestelle, Hamburg; Carl Platz GmbH Maschinenfabrik, Frankenthal/Pfalz; Posttechnisches Zentralamt, Darmstadt; Rabe-Werk Heinrich Clausing, Bad Essen; Rahdener Maschinenfabrik August Kolbus, Rahden; Rank Strand Electric, Wolfenbüttel; Stephan Reinhardt, Worms; Nic. Reisinger, Graphische Maschinen, Frankfurt-Rödelheim; Rena Büromaschinenfabrik GmbH & Co., Deisenhofen bei München; Werner Ring, Speyer; Ritter Filmgeräte GmbH, Mannheim; Röber Saatreiniger KG, Minden; Rollei Werke, Braunschweig; Margarete Rossner, Mannheim; Roto-Werke GmbH, Königslutter; Ruhrkohle Aktiengesellschaft, Essen; Papierfabrik Salach GmbH, Salach/Württ.; Dr. Karl Schaifers, Heidelberg; Oberarzt Dr. med. Hans-Jost Schaumann, Städt. Krankenanstalten, Mannheim; Schlachthof, Mannheim; Dr. Schmitz + Apelt, Industrieofenbau GmbH, Wuppertal; Maschinenfabrik Schmotzer GmbH, Bad Windsheim; Mälzerei Schragmalz, Berghausen b. Speyer; Schutzgemeinschaft Deutscher Wald, Bonn; Siemens AG, Bereich Meß- und Prozeßtechnik, Bildund Tontechnik, Karlsruhe; Siemens AG, Dental-Depot, Mannheim; Siemens-Reiniger-Werke, Erlangen; Sinar AG Schaffhausen, Feuerthalen (Schweiz); Spitzenorganisation der Filmwirtschaft e. V., Wiesbaden; Stadtwerke–Verkehrsbetriebe, Mannheim; W. Steenbeck & Co., Hamburg; Streitkräfteamt, Dezernat Werbemittel, Bonn-Duisdorf; Bau- und Möbelschreinerei Fritz Ströbel, Mannheim; Gebrüder Sucker GmbH & Co. KG, Mönchengladbach; Gebrüder Sulzer AG, Winterthur (Schweiz); Dr. med. Alexander Tafel, Weinheim; Klaus Thome, Mannheim; Prof. Dr. med. Michael Trede, Städt. Krankenanstalten, Mannheim; Trepel AG, Wiesbaden; Verband der Deutschen Hochseefischerei e. V., Bremerhaven; Verband der Deutschen Schiffbauindustrie e. V., Hamburg; Verband der Korbwaren-, Korbmöbel- und Kinderwagenindustrie e. V., Coburg; Verband des Deutschen Drechslerhandwerks e. V., Nürnberg; Verband des Deutschen Faß- und Weinküfer-Handwerks, München; Verband Deutscher Papierfabriken e. V., Bonn; Verband Kommunaler Städtereinigungsbetriebe, Köln-Marienburg; Verband technischer Betriebe für Film und Fernsehen e. V., Berlin; Verein Deutscher Eisenhüttenleute, Düsseldorf; Verein Deutscher Zementwerke, Düsseldorf; Vereinigung Deutscher Elektrizitätswerke, VDEW, e. V., Frankfurt am Main; Verkehrsverein, Weinheim/Bergstr.; J. M. Voith GmbH, Heidenheim; Helmut Volland, Erlangen; Dr. med. Dieter Walter, Weinheim; W. E. G. Wirtschaftsverband Erdöl- und Erdgasgewinnung e. V., Hannover; Einrichtungshaus für die Gastronomie Jürgen Weiss & Co., Düsseldorf; Wella Aktiengesellschaft, Darmstadt; Optik-Welzer, Mannheim; Werbe & Graphik Team, Schriesheim; Wiegand Karlsruhe GmbH, Ettlingen; Dr. Klaus Wiemann, Gevelsburg; Wirtschaftsvereinigung Bergbau, Bonn; Wirtschaftsvereinigung Eisen- und Stahlindustrie, Düsseldorf; Wolf-Dietrich Wyrwas, Mannheim; Yashica Europe GmbH, Hamburg; Zechnersche Buchdruckerei, Speyer; Carl Zeiss, Oberkochen; Zentralverband der Deutschen Elektrohandwerke, ZVEH, Frankfurt am Main; Zentralverband der deutschen Seehafenbetriebe e. V., Hamburg; Zentralverband der elektrotechnischen Industrie e. V., Fachverband Phonotechnik, Hamburg; Zentralverband der Deutschen Bäckerhandwerks e. V., Bad Honnef; Zentralverband des Deutschen Friseurhandwerks, Köln; Zentralverband des Deutschen Handwerks ZDH, Pressestelle, Bonn; Zentralverband des Kürschnerhandwerks, Bad Homburg; Zentralverband für das Juwelier-, Gold- und Silberschmiedehandwerk der BRD, Ahlen; Zentralverband für Uhren, Schmuck und Zeitmeßtechnik, Bundesinnungsverband des Uhrmacherhandwerks, Königstein; Zentralverband Sanitär-, Heizungs- und Klimatechnik, Bonn; Erika Zöller, Edingen; Zündapp-Werke GmbH, München.

# Índice

Las cifras en negritas que siguen a las entradas corresponden a los números de los cuadros de ilustraciones, y las que están en redondas son las referentes a las ilustraciones de esos cuadros. Los homónimos de significación diferente, así como las palabras que figuran en varios cuadros, se distinguen a través de la indicación en cursiva de los dominios léxicos en que aparecen.

La siguiente lista contiene las abreviaturas que se han empleado para señalar los campos en que se utiliza la voz. No se especifican las abreviaturas que son fácilmente comprensibles.

alineador de dirección **195** 17
alisador **128** 11
alisadora **108** 42
alisio del Nordeste **9** 48
~ del Sudeste **9** 49
alisma **378** 44
aliso *Hierba* **61** 17
~ *Árbol* **371** 30
aliviadero **217** 60
alma **143** 4
almacén *Astron.* **5** 17
~ *Estación* **206** 53
~ *Puerto* **225** 7
~ *Caball.* **329** 13
almacenamiento de desechos atómicos en una mina de sal **154** 56
~ de desechos de actividad media en una mina de sal **154** 72
~ en toneles **93** 16
almacén con las matrices **174** 21
~ de clinker **160** 10
~ de diapositivas **176** 27
~ de flejes para la venta **148** 73
~ de las materias primas **160** 3
~ del cargador **255** 7
~ de los materiales **146** 6
~ de los tubos **146** 4
~ del retículo **177** 9
~ de mercancías **206** 7
~ de tránsito de mercancías a granel **225** 9
~ de ultramarinos **98** 1-87
~ de yeso **160** 13
~ para las tapas de cartón **184** 7
~ portacontenedores **225** 48
alma central del aspa **91** 2
almáciga **54** 2; **84** 6
alma de la pared **123** 45
~ del raíl **202** 3
almádena **158** 6
almajara **55** 16
almanaque de pared **22** 17; **245** 3; **248** 42
~ de propaganda **22** 10
almena **329** 7
almendra **59** 8; **384** 39
~ del alfóncigo **382** 51
almendrado **97** 37
almendras **45** 41
almendro **384** 36
alminar **337** 13
almohada **27** 27; **43** 12-13; **47** 4
almohadilla *Auxilio* **21** 13
~ *Textil* **168** 56
~ de alunizaje **6** 33
~ de cuero **108** 29
~ de freno **143** 100
~ de la base **292** 67
~ de la plataforma de elevación **195** 27
~ del freno **186** 16
~ de plumas **207** 68
~ de prensa **100** 16
~ de tinta **22** 30
almohadillado **335** 51
almohadilla flotadora para principiantes **282** 18
~ para clavar los alfileres **104** 20
~ para el oro **129** 50
almohadón del sofá **46** 17

almohaza **71** 54
almojaya **119** 49
~ del andamio **118** 27
almorta **69** 19
alno **371** 30
áloe **53** 13
alojamiento de la pila **115** 10
~ del filtro **112** 57
~ de los instrumentos **2** 5
~ del personal **270** 2
alondra **361** 18-19
alopecuro **69** 27
alpaca **366** 28
alpargata de cáñamo o esparto **122** 75
alpinismo **300** 1-57
alpinista **300** 5
Altair **3** 9
alta mar **227** 4
~ montaña **12** 39-47
~ presión **9** 5
altar **330** 4, 33; **334** 69
~ de los sacrificios **334** 48
altarreina **376** 15
altavoz **42** 10; **264** 12; **309** 34; **311** 46; **317** 15; **318** 12
~ de audición de prueba **238** 50
~ de caja **241** 14
~ de control **239** 9; **311** 13
~ de escucha **238** 15
~ del andén **205** 27
~ del estudio de resonancia **311** 32
~ de órdenes **238** 8, 52
~ de preescucha **238** 50
~ de sonidos agudos **241** 15
~ de sonidos graves **241** 17
~ de sonidos medios **241** 16
~ de sonorización **238** 37
~ estereofónico **241** 13-14
~ incorporado **249** 70
altea **380** 12
alteración **320** 50-54
alternador **190** 76
~ trifásico **153** 26
altímetro **230** 4
alto **286** 53
altocúmulo **8** 15
~ castellano **8** 16
~ floccus **8** 16
alto de la caña relleno **101** 20
altoestrato **8** 8
~ precipitante **8** 9
alto horno **147** 1
altoparlante del andén **205** 27
altozanero **205** 31
altramuz amarillo **69** 17
altura *Construc.* **123** 33
~ *Matem.* **346** 27
~ del cono **347** 44
~ del hombro **175** 45
~ del tipo **175** 44
alubia **57** 8
alud **304** 1
~ de de témpanos **304** 1
~ de nieve en polvo **304** 1
alumbrado **210** 46
~ de emergencia **312** 6
~ de escena **316** 14
~ de fondo **316** 15
~ del andén **205** 48
~ de seguridad **312** 6
~ horizontal **316** 15
~ superior **316** 13
alumbramiento de una fuente **269** 24-39

alumno **260** 3
~ de natación **282** 17
alunizaje **6**
alza *Caza* **87** 65
~ *FFAA* **255** 22, 36
~ *Dep.* **305** 56
alzacuello **332** 5
alzado de la locomotora **212** 51-67
alzaprima de activación de la hélice de paso variable **224** 19
alza telescópica **255** 28
ama de casa **39** 1
amandiyú **383** 16
amanita de las moscas **379** 10
amansador **307** 31
amantillo **219** 47
~ de la botavara **219** 48
~ del pico de la cangreja **219** 49
amapola **51** 30; **61** 2
amaranto **60** 21
amarilidácea **53** 8
amarillo **343** 2
amarre **75** 15-16
~ del cable oblicuo **215** 48
~ del cable portador **215** 43
~ del enrejado de alambre **78** 8
~ de seguridad **300** 10
amasadera **97** 59
~ del mortero **118** 39
amasadora **97** 55
ambón **330** 37
ambulancia **270** 19
~ blindada M **113** **255** 79
ameba **357** 1
amento **371** 10, 26
~ femenino **59** 38, 46
~ masculino **59** 39, 45
América **14** 12-13
~ del Norte **14** 12
~ del Sur **14** 13
americana **33** 2
ametralladora antiaérea **255** 63
~ MG 3 **255** 32
amianto *Bomberos* **270** 46
amianto *Quím.* **350** 19
amígdala **19** 23
aminorar la velocidad **286** 50
amoníaco **170** 24
amorcillo **272** 20
amortiguación **235** 53
~ del traqueteo **234** 13
amortiguador **191** 26; **192** 69, 76
~ de la espada **166** 65
~ del balanceo **214** 55
~ del retroceso **255** 34, 44
~ de muelle **214** 50
~ de oscilaciones **190** 26
~ electromagnético **11** 40
~ principal **6** 32
amperímetro **230** 18
~ de la calefacción **212** 18
~ de los motores de tracción **211** 26
ampliadora **116** 26
~ de color **116** 40
amplificación **310** 59
amplificador **241** 40; **312** 19; **317** 23
~ de imagen de rayos X **27** 16

~ del sonido magnético **311** 28
~ de registro **311** 11
~ de registro y de lectura del sonido magnético **311** 5
~ submarino **237** 57
ampolla de vidrio **127** 57
ampolleta **110** 31
amurada **221** 120; **222** 67
amura de la vela mayor **284** 37
análisis automático del ritmo del ECG sobre papel **25** 48
analizador del color **116** 36
~ del ECG de larga duración **25** 45
ananás **384** 61
anapelo **379** 1
anaquel **42** 3
~ de las bebidas **266** 59
~ de las botellas **267** 64
~ de las copas **267** 65
~ de los artículos **98** 14
~ de ropa blanca **43** 2
~ giratorio **39** 28
anavia **377** 23
anca **72** 32
ancla **223** 52; **258** 5; **259** 81; **286** 15-18
~ almirantazgo **286** 15
~ con cepo **222** 79; **286** 15
~ Danforth **286** 18
~ de patente **222** 78; **258** ; **286** 17
~ de piedra **224** 73
~ de proa **258** 39
~ de reja de arado **286** 16
anclaje **216** 13
~ del cable portante **214** 59
ancla ligera **286** 16-18
~ para embarcaciones pequeñas de recreo **286** 18
~ pesada **286** 15
~ sin cepo **222** 78; **286** 17
ancua **68** 31
anda **331** 41
andamiaje *Puente* **215** 62
~ *Cons. naval* **222** 18
~ de la grada **222** 19
andamio *Astron.* **5** 18
~ *Cons. naval* **228** 18
~ de caballete **118** 17
~ de escalera **118** 86-89
~ del pilón **214** 80
~ de trabajo **118** 17; **122** 34
~ hecho con tubos de acero **119** 46
andanada **319** 8
andarivel *Río* **216** 1
~ *Buque guerra* **259** 18
andarríos **360** 9
andén **205** 1
~ de la estación del valle **214** 51
~ número 1 **205** 14
Andrómeda **3** 24
andullo **107** 18
anea **378** 21
anélido **357** 20
anemómetro **10** 28
anémona común **375** 5
~ de bosque **377** 1
~ de mar **369** 20
anestesia del nervio **24** 53
anfibio **364** 20-26
~ con cola **364** 20-22

~ *Herr.* 137 5
atlante 334 36
atletismo 298
atmósfera 7
~ controlada 138 29
atolón 13 32
Atolla 369 5
átomo 1; 2
~ de carbono 242 63
~ de hidrógeno 1 1, 15; 242 62
~ de oxígeno 1 13; 242 65
~ de silicio 1 14
~ de sodio 1 8
~ Na 1 8
atornilladura 126 42
~ de ángulo 126 40
~ de ángulo con rosca interior 126 45
atrapamoscas 377 14
atril 326 36
~ para la predicación 330 37
atrio 334 50, 66
attitude 314 17
atuendo de danza 354 36
aubrietia 51 7
audiocassette 242 17
audiomecanógrafa 248 33
audiovisión 243
auditorio *Univ.* 262 2
~ *Elecc.* 263 8
~ *Cine* 310 14
aula 260 1-45; 262 2
aulos 322 4
áureo de Constantino el Grande 252 3
aurícula 20 24, 45
auricular *Anat.* 19 68
~ *Teléf.-telégr.* 237 7
~ *Electrón* 241 69
~ *Oficina* 245 15; 246 16
~ *Colegio* 261 38, 40
~ de casco *Electrón* 241 66
~ de casco *Oficina* 249 63
~ de casco *Rastro* 309 24
~ de casco sin hilo 242 30
~ de teléfono 246 16
~ en el pabellón de la oreja 248 35
Auriga 3 27
aurimelo 59 35
aurora 365 3
~ boreal 7 30
Australia 14 17
australiano 352 37
Austria 252 13
autillo 362 14
auto 191 1-56; 195 34
autobús 194; 194 17; 233 35
~ de dos pisos 194 36
~ pequeño en versión urbana 194 34
autocar 194 17
autoclave 170 12
autómata 273 36
automática 50 23
automático de seguridad 127 19
automotor, con adherencia forzada 214 1
~ de acumuladores 211 55
~ de los Ferrocarriles Federales Alemanes 209 1
~ de mantenimiento de catenarias 211 41
~ de plataforma regulable 211 41

~ de servicio local 208 13
~ de turbina de gas 209 1
~ Diesel 208 13; 209 1; 211 41
~ eléctrico rápido 211 60
~ experimental 209 23
~ ligero 208 13
automóvil 191 1-56; 192; 193; 195 34
~ de raíl 213 32
automovilista utilizando el surtidor de autoservicio 196 8
autopista 15 16
~ urbana 225 54
autorización de salto 288 52
autor y título de la obra 185 46
autosalvamento 21 33
autos de alquiler 233 33
autotipia 178 38
auxiliador 21 19
auxiliar del banquero 275 4
avalancha 304 1
ave 359-363
~ acuática 272 51-54
~ atraída 86 50
~ canora 360 1, 3, 4, 5, 7, 9, 10; 361 1-20
~ cívica de Atenas 252 2
~ corredora 359 1-3
~ de alas largas 359 11-14
~ de corral 73 19-36
~ de las tempestades 359 12
~ del Paraíso azul 363 3
~ de paso 360 7
~ de rapiña 362
~ de rapiña diurna 362 1-13
~ exótica 363
~ fénix 327 9
avefría 359 21
ave indígena 360
avellana 59 49
avellano 59 44-51
avemaría 332 32
ave marina 359 11-14
~ migratoria 360 7
avena 68 27
avenida 13 62
~ de fuentes 274 11
aventador para la limpieza con aire a presión 64 15
ave rapaz 362
~ rapaz diurna 362 1-13
~ rapaz nocturna 362 14-19
~ sedentaria 360 5
avestruz 359 2
~ de América 359 2
ave trepadora 363 6
~ zancuda 359 18
avicultura 74
avión 359-232
~ *Ave* 359 24
~ a motor 287 2
~ anfibio 232 8
~ a reacción 231 7-33
~ a reacción de adiestramiento 257 1-41
~ bimotor comercial y de viaje 231 3
~ biplaza acrobático y deportivo 288 18
~ birreactor comercial y de turismo 231 7
~ birreactor de gran capacidad para trayectos cortos y medios 231 17

~ birreactor de pasajeros para trayectos cortos y medios 231 11
~ cuadrirreactor para trayectos largos 231 13
~ de aeromodelismo 273 38
~ de ala alta 229 3
~ de ala baja 229 5
~ de ala baja con ala de pliegue 229 14
~ de ala pivotante 232 26
~ de ala semialzada 229 4
~ de combate polivalente 256 8
~ de despegue y aterrizaje verticales 232 26
~ de despegue y aterrizaje verticales cortos 232 26-32
~ de doble fuselaje 229 34
~ de gran capacidad para trayectos largos 231 14
~ de hélice 231 1-6
~ de pasajeros para trayectos cortos y medios 231 4
~ de pasajeros supersónico 231 15
~ de rotor pivotante 232 31
~ de transporte de alcance medio 256 14
~ de transporte y de enlace 256 24
~ en posición de carga 233 21
~ estratosférico 7 15
avioneta de viaje y de deporte 230 32-66
avión flotador 232 5
~ monomotor de viaje de ala alta 231 2
~ monomotor de viaje y de deporte de ala baja 231 1
~ movimientos principales 230 67-72
~ remolcador 287 2
~ tipos 231 1-33
~ trirreactor para trayectos medios 231 12
~ turbopropulsado 231 4
avío para la limpieza de las armas 87 61-64
avisador *Cocina* 39 21
~ *Reloj.* 109 35
~ luminoso *Central el.* 153 3
~ luminoso *FFCC* 212 15
avispa 82 35
~ de las agallas del roble 82 33
axiacanta 374 30
axila 16 26
~ de la hoja con bulbillo 375 38
~ foliar 370 25
ayotoste 366 8
ayudante *Univ.* 262 6
~ *Circo* 307 39
~ de bodega 79 12
~ de dirección 310 21, 46
~ del dentista 24 18
~ del director de escena 316 43
~ del hortelano 55 45, 46
~ del ingeniero de sonido 310 57
~ del micrófono 310 22
~ del operador 117 68; 310 42
~ del sonido 117 68

~ técnica del laboratorio 23 41
azada de arrastre 66 1
~ de desherbar 51 22
~ para el estiércol 66 8
~ para las patatas 66 6
azadón de patatas 66 24
~ de rozar 66 24
azafate de flores 266 29
azafrán 222 69
azahar 384 25
azalea 53 12
azor 362 10
azote de los frutales 80 16
azúcar 98 53-55
~ cristalizado 98 55
~ en polvo 98 54
~ en terrones 98 53
azucarero 44 32
azúcar refinado 98 55
azucena 60 12
~ silvestre 377 4
azud 91 42
azuela 120 73
azufre 351 23
azul 343 3
~ celeste 343 6
azulejo *Baño* 49 19
~ *Hierba* 61 1
~ *Ave* 360 2
~ de estufa 266 35
azul marino 343 3
azur 254 28

**B**

babera 329 41
babero 28 43
babilejo 118 56
babilla *Caballo* 72 33
~ *Matad.* 95 11, 36
babucha 101 25
babuino 368 13
baca 278 50
bacon 96 2
badil 137 2
bádminton 273 6; 293 43-44
baffle *Electrón* 241 13-14
~ *Rastro* 309 17
~ de tres altavoces 241 14
bahía 13 7
bailarín 314 28
bailarina 314 27
~ de ballet 314 26
bailarín Duk-duk 352 34
baile de disfraces 306 1-48
~ de máscaras 306 1-48
bajada de aguas 37 11
~ de dos semitonos 320 53
~ del agua 269 21
~ de un semitono 320 52
bajagua 380 16
bajante 122 29
baja presión 9 5
bajo 224 87, 91
~ a babor del canal de navegación principal 224 88
~ fuera del canal de navegación 224 97
~, límite del 15 9
bajorrelieve 339 33
~ de ladrillo vidriado 333 20

~ gimnástico 297 41
~ paraguas 205 12
bastón-taburete 86 10
bastos 276 42
basura comprimida y en descomposición 199 22
basura de las calles 268 22
basura reciente 199 17
basurero 199 10
bata 32 20, 35
~ blanca 33 56
~ de trabajo 106 2
batalla con bolas de nieve 304 14
batán de cilindros 168 1
~ doble 163 14
batanga Dep. inv. 302 46
~ Etnogr. 352 36
batayola 222 66
bate 292 62, 75
batea Parás. 83 17
~ Estación 206 21
~ FFCC 213 8
~ Hotel 267 50
~ Feria 308 52
~ con teleros 206 24
bateador 292 52, 74
~ intentando un batazo 292 63
~ suplente 292 58
batea impulsada a percha 283 1
~ para apósitos 26 22
~ rascadora fija 62 24
batelón 221 93
batería Agric. 65 53
~ Fotogr. 114 66
~ Autom. 191 50
~ FFCC 207 5, 25
~ FFAA 257 17
~ Cabar. 318 10
~ de acumuladores 259 83
~ de arranque 212 46
~ de botellas 141 1
~ de cinco tubos lanzatorpedos 259 36
~ de clarificación 92 51
~ de cocina 40 12-16
~ de horno de coque 144 7
~ de jazz 324 47-54
~ de lanzamiento de 4 misiles de corto recorrido 259 26
~ del horno de coque 156 8
~ de proyectores 317 13
~ de rodillos del cable tractor 214 60
~ de tintaje 249 51-52
~ mezcladora para el lavamanos 126 27
baticola 71 34
batida 86 34-39
batidor Leche 76 43
~ Caza 86 37
~ Cestero 136 36
batidora Cocina 39 22; 40 46
~ Cerv. 92 46
batidora-mezcladora 97 70
batiente 37 22, 23
batímetro 279 15
batín 32 35
batolito 11 29
batómetro 279 15
batracio 364 20-26
batuta 315 27
baúl 191 24; 193 17, 23
~ armario 267 29
bauprés 218 20
~ con botalón 219 1

bautismo 332 1
bautizado 332 7
bautizo cristiano 332 1
baya 58 9; 370 97
~ de la patata 68 43
~ del junípero 372 52
~ del saúco 374 37
bayadera 306 25
baya de tronco alto 52 11
~ no comestible 68 43
bayeta 50 55
bazo 20 12, 27
bebé 28 5
bebedero Avic. 74 6
~ Sider. 148 21
~ automático 74 16
bebida 99 71
~ alcohólica 98 56-59; 318 19
~ larga 317 32
becada 88 83
becerro marino 367 19
becuadro 320 54
beduino 354 6
begonia 53 10
~ de tubérculos 51 19
béisbol 292 40-69
bejín blando 381 19
~ plomizo 381 20
bejuco 136 32
beleño negro 379 6
belfo 70 26
~ inferior 72 10
~ superior 72 8
Bélgica 252 17
belladona 379 7
Bellatrix 3 13
bellota Juego 276 42
~ Árbol 371 4
bemol 320 52
benceno crudo 156 42
bencina ligera 145 39
~ pesada 145 40
benedictino 331 54
berbiquí de carrete 135 22
~ de vaivén 108 4
bergantín-goleta 220 14
bergantín redondo 220 17
berlina 186 1
~ inglesa 186 53
berma del dique 216 38
bermejo 88 51
bermudas 31 44
berro amargo 378 30
~ de fuente 378 30
berza 57 32
besito 97 14
beso de despedida 205 52
bestia del Apocalipsis 327 50
beta del aparejo 221 106
betel 380 19
Betelgeuse 3 13
betún 145 64
biberón 28 19
Biblia 330 11
biblioteca 223 25
~ de los libros de consulta 262 17
bibliotecaria 262 14
bibliotecario 262 19
biblioteca universitaria 262 11-25
biceps 18 37
~ crural 18 61
bici 187 1
bicicleta 187 1; 188
~ Natac. 282 39
~ de acumuladores 188 20
~ de carreras 290 15

~ de carreras por carretera 290 16
~ de carreras tras moto 290 15
~ de hombre 187 1
~ de niño 273 9
~ de paseo 187 1
~ eléctrica 188 20
~ plegable 188 1
bicornio 35 36
bicho 86 24
bidé 49 7
bidel 49 7
bidón de aceite adherente 84 35
~ de disolvente 129 16
~ de gasolina Silvic. 84 36
~ de gasolina Est. serv. 196 25
~ metálico 130 13
~ para el agua de lluvia 52 4
biela 187 41
~ 190 21
~ ajustable 166 52
~ con prensaestopa 210 33
~ de acoplamiento 210 11
~ oscilante de la rueda trasera 189 7
bielda para las patatas 66 5
biércol 377 19
bifurcación 224 89
bigornia 125 8
bigote Pein. 34 8
~ Mamíf. 367 21
~ de cepillo 34 19
~ estilo inglés 34 19
bigotera de bomba 151 59
bigudí 105 12
~ del tinte 105 4
bikini, parte inferior 280 27
~, parte superior 280 28
billar 277 1-19
billarda 90 25
billar de carambolas 277 7
~ de troneras 277 7
~ alemán 277 7
~ francés 277 7
~ inglés 277 7
billete Estación 204 36
~ Dinero 252 29-39
~ de 1 dólar 252 33
~ de 1 000 dracmas 252 39
~ de 1 libra esterlina 252 37
~ de 20 marcos alemanes 252 29
~ de admisión 315 11
~ de banco 252 29-39; 271 6
billetes 252
bimbalete 273 35
bimotor comercial y de viaje 231 3
binocular 23 6
binza 57 25
biombo 5 15
biplano 229 10
bípode 255 42
biquini 280 26
biriquí 135 22
birlocha Colegio 260 71
~ Parque 273 42
birlón 305 7, 13
birreactor comercial y de turismo 231 7
~ de gran capacidad para trayectos cortos y medios 231 17

~ de pasajeros para trayectos cortos y medios 231 11
birrete 355 28
bisagra acodada 140 50
~ de cruz 151 50
~ de la patilla 111 14
~ de ramal 140 51
biscote 97 50
bisectriz 346 30
bisel 143 62
biselado del clisé 178 44
bisel con muesca de encaje 121 90
~ de encaje, doble 121 91
bisillo 321 23
bisonte Prehist. 328 9
~ Mamíf. 367 9
bisoñé 34 2
bistorta 376 10
bisturí 26 43
bitoque Cocina 39 36
~ Baño 49 2
~ Font. 126 34
bituminadora 200 43
~ alquitranadora 200 46
bizantina 355 15
bizcocho 97 54; 99 21
~ de Saboya 97 33
~ enrollado 97 19
~ tostado blando 97 40
~ tostado para los niños 97 54
blanca Juego 276 4
~ Mús. 320 14
blanco Dep. 305 30-33, 66
~ Color 343 11
~ móvil 305 33
~ para el tiro con fusil a 50 m de distancia 305 30
~ para el tiro con fusil a 100 m de distancia 305 32
blanqueo 169 21
blanqueta 168 56
blanquillo 74 58
blanquín de gallina 74 58
blasón 254 1-36
blastodisco 74 65
blazer 33 54
blindaje Oficina 246 24
~ FFAA 255 81
~ aislante contra las radiaciones 259 70
~ de la cadena 255 85
~ del cañón 255 72, 90
~ interior magnético 240 20
bloca 329 58
bloc de dibujo 338 35
~ de taquigrafía 245 29; 248 32
bloque compacto de grabación y de reproducción magnéticas 238 55
~ de apuntes 338 35
~ de bocetos 338 35
~ de construcción 48 27
~ de formularios de inscripción 267 12
~ de galeras cubiertas 37 72-76
~ de inclinación 12 9
~ del motor Apar. hogar 50 82
~ del motor Motor 190 19
~ de madera 339 27; 340 1
~ de nieve 353 5
~ de piedra 339 5
~ de pisos 37 77-81

~ de roca **158** 8
~ de salida **298** 1
~ electrónico **112** 53
~ hueco de piedra pómez **119** 24
bloqueo **117** 62
~ de la caja **313** 33
~ del acelerador **85** 17
~ de tramos **203** 59
bloque para lijar **128** 13; **129** 26
~ para remachar **137** 16
blue jeans **31** 60; **33** 22
blusa **30** 9, 40
~ de chica **29** 58
~ de gala **30** 55
~ de peluquero **106** 2
~ de polo **30** 26
~ de trabajo **106** 2
~ de verano **31** 22
~ tirolesa **31** 29
blusón de muchacha **29** 48
bob **303** 19
bobby **264** 34
bob de dos **303** 19
bobina **163** 2
~ botella **167** 4
~ cónica de plegado cruzado **165** 8
bobina cruzada **164** 58; **165** 24
~ cruzada de plegado cruzado **165** 8
~ de alimentación **117** 31
~ de arrollado cruzado **170** 51
~ de arrollado cruzado lista para enviar **170** 52
~ de cinta magnética **244** 10
~ de cinta magnetofónica **241** 57
~ de hilo *Zapat.* **100** 29
~ de hilo *Modista* **103** 12
~ de hilo *Encuad.* **185** 18
~ de hilo para coser **104** 9
~ de la mechera **164** 23
~ de la película *RTV* **238** 6
~ de la película *Cine* **312** 32
~ de la película magnética **311** 2
~ de la película original **117** 79
~ del rollo de película **114** 20
~ de papel **181** 46
~ de papel no impreso **180** 2
~ de película **311** 24
~ de seda para coser **104** 10
bobinado **169** 25
bobinadora de cruzado **165** 1
bobina para enrollado automático **117** 80
~ para enrollar **148** 72
~ receptora **117** 32, 80
bobsleigh **303** 19-21
boca *Anat.* **16** 13; **19** 14-37
~ *Perro* **70** 3
~ *Caballo* **72** 9
~ *Caza* **88** 13
~ *Mús.* **322** 22; **326** 25
~ de aspiración **199** 43
~ de aspiración de aire **258** 57
~ de carga *Forja* **139** 49
~ de carga *Sider.* **147** 51
~ de carga *FFCC* **213** 19
~ de descarga **139** 2

~ de dragón **51** 32
~ de fuego **255** 58
~ de incendio **221** 4
~ de inyección del metal **178** 17
~ del cañón **305** 71
~ de lengua bífida **327** 5
~ del glaciar **12** 51
~ de riego de superficie **270** 35
~ de riego subterránea **270** 25
~ de salida **159** 13
bocadito **107** 3
bocado **71** 52
~ con la barbada **71** 13
~ de Adán **19** 13
boca esmerilada **350** 37
bocallave **140** 40
bocana **13** 1
boca sacaclavos **120** 75
bocateja **122** 5
bocel **334** 28
~ inferior **334** 30
boceto **338** 43
~ a tiza **338** 4
bocina *Bicicl.* **188** 53
~ *FFCC* **212** 70
~ *Remo* **283** 21
bocha **305** 21
~ estriada **305** 24
boda religiosa **332** 14
bodega **79** 1-22
~ *Cerv.* **93** 12
~ *Salvamento* **227** 26; **228** 27
~ *Avión* **231** 21
~ de fermentación **93** 7
~ del autobús **194** 18
~ de popa **223** 55
~ de proa **223** 75
bodeguero **79** 17
Bodhisattva **337** 10
bodollo **85** 11
bodoquera **352** 26
bogie **208** 4; **212** 2; **213** 13
~ con suspensión de muelles de acero y amortiguadores **207** 4
~ de impulsión **197** 9
~ portador **197** 10
boina **35** 27
boj común **373** 19
bola **187** 56
~ blanca **277** 11
~ blanca del tanto **277** 13
~ con agujeros para los dedos **305** 15
~ con que se juega **277** 11
~ de acero **143** 70
~ de agua **89** 47
~ de billar **277** 1
~ de confeti **306** 55
~ de croquet **292** 82
~ de entintar **340** 22
~ de lanzamiento estriada **305** 24
~ de la ruleta **275** 33
~ del cerrojo **87** 22
~ de marfil **277** 1
~ de materia plástica **277** 1
~ de nieve *Inv.* **304** 15
~ de nieve *Arb. ornam.* **373** 10
~ de piedra o metal forrada de cuero **352** 32
~ de plomo **89** 89
~ de tempestad **225** 35
~ en el cojinete **187** 68

~ para contar **47** 14
~ para grabar **108** 34
bolardo **217** 12
~ doble **217** 11
bola roja **277** 12
boleadora **352** 31
bolera **305** 14-20
bolero **35** 36
boleta de expedición **206** 30
boletería *Tranv.* **197** 8, 27
~ *Cine* **312** 2
boleto *Cine* **312** 3
~ *Teatro* **315** 11
~ anillado **381** 21
~ áspero **381** 22
~ comestible **381** 16
~ de Satanás **379** 12
boliche **305** 1-13, 23
bólido **290** 34-38
bolígrafo **47** 26
bolillo **323** 14, 54
~ del tambor **354** 19
bolín **305** 23
bolina *Barco* **218** 35
~ *Vela* **285** 10
bolita **47** 14
bolo **305** 12
~ de la calle anterior derecha **305** 4
~ de la calle anterior izquierda **305** 2
~ de la calle posterior derecha **305** 10
~ de la calle posterior izquierda **305** 9
~ de la esquina anterior **305** 1
~ de la esquina derecha **305** 8
~ de la esquina izquierda **305** 6
~ de la esquina posterior **305** 11
bolos **305** 1-13
Bolsa **251** 1-10
bolsa *Ave* **359** 8
~ antigua de turba **13** 22
~ cerrada herméticamente **76** 29
~ colectora de la correspondencia **236** 51
~ de agua **13** 16
~ de cadera **301** 28
~ de calco **129** 49
~ de control de la respiración **26** 25
~ de cuero flexible del objetivo **115** 105
~ de huevos **80** 2, 30
~ de la cámara **115** 103
~ de la compra **99** 3; **268** 19
~ de la miel **77** 18
~ de las limosnas **330** 59
~ del cartero **236** 54
~ del plegado **185** 10
~ de medias **99** 26
~ de papel **98** 48
~ de pastor **61** 9
~ de red **86** 27
Bolsa de valores y fondos públicos **251** 1-10
bolsa para abrigar los pies **28** 38
~ para las compras **98** 45
~ playera **280** 24
~ reciente de turba **13** 20
~ tabaquera **107** 43
bolsillo del abrigo **33** 61

~ delantero **260** 10
~ de las gafas de sol **6** 19
~ del pantalón **33** 47
~ del pecho **30** 23
~ de parche **29** 68; **30** 22; **31** 56; **33** 38
~ de pecho **33** 9, 46
~ exterior **33** 12
~ para el metro **33** 49
~ para la linterna **6** 24
~ para los lápices, los utensilios, etc. **6** 27
~ pegado **29** 68
~ sesgado **29** 63; **31** 4
bolso de chica **29** 56
~ de viaje **205** 10
bollo de Berlín **97** 29
~ de Navidad **97** 11
~ de nochebuena **97** 11
~ de pan **97** 14; **99** 12
bollón de la bandera **253** 8
bomba *Fibra* **170** 31
~ *Natac.* **282** 14
~ a motor **270** 8
~ a motor portátil **270** 52
~ aspirante con motor **269** 7
bomba centrífuga *Bodega* **79** 7
~ centrífuga *Abast. agua* **269** 44
~ centrífuga *Bomberos* **270** 8
~ de aceite **190** 42; **192** 16
~ de aceite del ventilador **211** 45
~ de agua **190** 61
~ de agua a presión **216** 60
~ de aire *Papel* **172** 40
~ de aire *Tipogr.* **181** 6, 35
~ de aire *Bicicl.* **187** 48
~ de alimentación de agua **210** 9
~ de alimentación de la caldera **152** 18
~ de bicicleta **187** 48
~ de calor **155** 22
~ de cimentación a alta presión **146** 34
~ de circulación **154** 43, 54
~ de circulación del aceite **152** 45
~ de circulación del aire **211** 12
~ de circulación primaria **154** 5
~ de circulación secundaria **154** 8
~ de cobalto **2** 28
~ de engrase automático **210** 42
~ de evacuación **67** 11, 23
~ de extracción del fango **145** 16
~ de gasolina **196** 1
~ de hélice **217** 47-52
~ de hidrógeno a alta presión **235** 41
~ de hilatura **169** 13
~ de inyección *Motor* **190** 65
~ de inyección *FFCC* **211** 48
~ de la cuajada **76** 39
~ del agua de alimentación **154** 13
~ de la leche cruda **76** 3
~ de la lejía **172** 33
~ de la lejía espesa **172** 34
~ de las aguas residuales **172** 63

~ de lectura del sonido 312
47
~ de león 327 17
~ del macillo 325 24
~ del malecón Geogr. 13 38
~ del malecón Río 216 20
~ del martillo 298 43
~ del objetivo 117 46-49
~ del raíl 202 2
~ del rotor 232 13
~ del timón 284 33
~ del tren 197 3
~ del ventilador 223 41
~ de mando 141 37
~ de moro 97 36
~ de mujer 327 56
~ de planchado 50 4
~ de plomo 326 20
~ de radiación 113 31
~ de radiografía con el tubo
de rayos X 27 18
~ de registro 311 25
~ de roblón 143 57
~ de rosca 187 75
~ de sincronización 243 34
~ de sonido 243 35
~ esférica 249 15
~ esférica de repuesto 249
28
~ guía de la maza 139 29
~ humana 327 21
~ inferior 121 73, 79
cabezal Mesa 45 55
~ Construc. 120 58
~ de estiraje 163 60
~ de grabación de
videocassettes 243 19
~ fijo 150 2
~ fijo con el cambio de
velocidades 149 2
~ móvil Torn. 135 7
~ móvil Mág.-herr. 149 29;
150 5
~ móvil Fotogr. 177 62
~ portabrocas 134 48
~ regulable 191 33
~ revólver 149 40
cabeza magnética de cuatro
pistas 312 51
~ mezcladora del color 116
43-45
~ motriz 209 2
~ motriz de turbina de gas
209 8
~ niveladora de cine 114 48
~ para cepillar la alfombra
50 79
~ para la peluca 105 39
~ para limpiar en seco la
alfombra 50 79
~ para sacudir la alfombra
50 79
~ reducida 352 30
~ sonora 312 47
~ superior 121 74, 80
~ supresora 311 25
~ unificadora del sonido y
de la imagen 117 102
~ vídeo 243 26, 36
~ y la parte del cuerpo
situada por encima de las
ingles en la esgrima de
sable 294 52
cabezuela 61 14; 370 73; 378
12
~ discoide 370 74
~ globulosa 370 75
cabina Autom. 194 2, 15
~ FFCC 214 20

~ alta 305 75
~ baja 305 76
~ Cassegrain 5 4
~ central de la toma del
sonido de la radio 238 1-6
~ con arco de seguridad 85
36
~ de combustible 234 62
~ de control 238 17
~ de control de la imagen
239 10
~ de control de las
imágenes 238 60-65
~ de control del sonido 238
27; 239 7
~ de gran capacidad 214 52
~ del conductor Agric. 64
36
~ del conductor Tranv. 197
25
~ del conductor Carret. 200
11
~ del conductor Puerto 226
52
~ del conductor de la grúa
119 35; 222 16
~ del locutor 238 18
~ del maquinista 209 6; 210
49; 211 19, 57; 213 2; 214
65
~ del maquinista de la
locomotora de vapor 210
39-63
~ del maquinista del
automotor 208 14
~ del maquinista de una
locomotora Diesel 212 5
~ del mecanismo de
elevación 217 71
~ de los pasajeros 231 22
~ del patrón 228 31
~ del piloto Avión 230 35
~ del piloto Policía 264 2
~ del piloto Remo 283 8
~ del piloto Dep. aéreo 288
10, 19
~ del torno 226 54
~ de mezcla del sonido 238
27
~ de mezcla de sonidos 238
17
~ de pilotaje Avión 230 35;
231 19
~ de pilotaje Astron. 235 16
~ de pilotaje de un
monomotor de viaje y de
turismo 230 1-31
~ de proyección Astron. 5
27
~ de proyección Cine 312
12
~ de radio 223 12
~ de toma de sonido 310 54
~ de un miembro de la
tripulación 228 32
~ de viajeros 214 52
~ electoral 263 23
~ inferior 234 49
~ para mirar los huevos al
trasluz 74 47
~ para viajeros 214 28
~ superior 234 45
~ telefónica 236 8; 237 1;
251 10; 268 56
~ telefónica del andén 205
57
~ telefónica pública 204 46
cabio 121 76
~ central 121 51

~ de hormigón 119 4
~ de la cresta 121 62
~ del caballete 121 43
~ de lima tesa 121 62
~ inferior 121 44; 122 40
~ lateral 121 39
cable Central el. 153 41
~ Fibra 169 28
~ Cons. hidr. 217 23
~ Barco a motor, esquí
acuát. 286 47
~ Esgr. 294 31
~ Mús. 326 53
~ auxiliar 214 47
~ Bowden 188 37
~ colgante 215 17
~ conductor de alta tensión
152 32
~ de acero 298 44
~ de alimentación 94 9
~ de alta tensión 152 33
~ de alta tensión, para
corriente trifásica 153 42
~ de apoyo 2 30
~ de arrastre Cons. hidr. 217
23
~ de arrastre Barco a motor,
esquí acuát. 286 47
~ de cámara 239 2
~ de conexión Soldadura
142 25
~ de conexión Electrón 241
71
~ de conexión con el
paciente 25 43
~ de conexión con la
impresora de papel 25 56
~ de conexión con la
unidad de control central
25 20
~ de conexión del sonido
117 8
~ de contacto 205 58
~ de control 271 53
~ de diagnosis 195 38
~ de diagnóstico 195 3
~ de enganche 215 47
~ de freno 259 16
~ de impulsos 117 72
~ de la balsa 216 2
~ de la corriente Cocina 39
~ de la corriente Jardín 56
32
~ de la grúa 222 13
~ del ancla 218 18
~ de las sondas de la red 90
14
~ del auricular 237 14
~ del electrodo del
estimulador cardíaco
temporal 25 25
~ del freno Tejido 166 61
~ del freno Moto 189 12
~ del micrófono 117 25;
239 14; 310 32
~ del sonido 311 41
~ del sonido piloto 313 29
~ del techo 211 5
~ de medida 116 38
~ de perforación 145 7
~ de remolque Río 216 24
~ de remolque Salvamento
227 8
~ de remolque Vuelo sin
motor 287 4
~ de retención 259 16
~ de sincronización 313 29
~ de soldar 142 19

~ de sonda de la
temperatura del aceite
195 40
~ de suministro de
corriente 198 14
~ de tracción FFCC 214 14,
26, 37, 45
~ de tracción Grandes alm.
271 52
~ de tracción Dep. inv. 301
63
~ de tres polos 127 44
~ disparador 114 38
~ eléctrico para
instalaciones técnicas 198
19
~ inferior 214 46
~ oblicuo 215 47
~ para cerrar la red 90 26
~ para el ajuste del ralentí
190 51
~ para medir la
temperatura del aceite
195 16
~ portador Construc. 119 37
~ portador Puente 215 16,
40
~ portante FFCC 214 27, 38,
44
~ portante y de tracción
214 21
~ sin fin 214 21
~ submarino 237 56
~ telefónico 198 15
~ termoplástico resistente a
la humedad 127 42
~ tractor 214 45
cabo Cestero 136 23
~ Cons. hidr. 217 23
~ Remo 283 12
~ de salvamento 228 3
Cabra 3 27; 4 62
cabra 73 14
Cabra de Mar 3 36; 4 62
cabra montés 367 7
~ naciente 254 32
cabrestante Fotogr. 117 34
~ Cons. hidr. 217 22
~ Buque guerra 258 23
~ Bomberos 270 56
~ de arrastre 217 22
~ del ancla 258 6; 259 82
cabria auxiliar de la grúa
147 61
cabrilla 381 15
cabrio 121 28, 36; 122 19
~ central 121 56
~ de copete 121 61
~ de la lima hoya 121 64
~ del copete 121 63
~ de quiebra 121 31
~ de unión 121 55, 61
cabriola Caballo 71 5
~ Ballet 314 21
cabriole 314 21
cabriolé 186 34
~ con pescante elevado por
detrás 186 29
~ sport 193 26
cabrio principal 121 55
cabrón 73 14
cabuchón 35 4
cabujón 36 78-81
~ octagonal 36 81
~ ovalado 36 80
~ redondo 36 78
cacahuate 383 41
cacahué 383 41
cacahuete 383 41

~ del guardabarrera **202** 43
~ del timón **223** 18; **224** 14-38
~ para pesar **206** 40
casia **380** 16
casi despejado **9** 21
~ igual **345** 17
casilla **236** 13
~ del guardavía **15** 24
~ de los cubiertos **266** 48
~ del tablero de ajedrez **276** 2
~ para anunciar el retraso del tren **205** 24
~ para anunciar la estación de destino **205** 22
~ para anunciar la hora de salida **205** 23
~ postal **236** 14
casillero de comida **207** 83
~ del correo **267** 2
~ de los discos **241** 48
~ de los huevos **74** 32
casimba *Geogr.* **12** 26
~ *Huerto* **52** 4
casino *Balneario* **274** 8
~ *Ruleta* **275** 1
Casiopea **3** 33
casquete **288** 38
~ de gas **12** 30
~ de la cabeza de imprimir **249** 30
~ de la hélice **230** 33
~ de ventilación **38** 52
~ giratorio del molino de viento **91** 30
~ metálico **326** 35
casquillo **149** 27
~ portabombillas **127** 60
cassette **241** 10
~ de audio **242** 17
~ de la cinta del sonido **117** 76
~ de película de luz diurna **311** 7
~ de película sonora de súper 8 **117** 29
~ de vídeo **242** 18
~ estereofónico **241** 33
~ para la luz de día **177** 50
castaña *Caballo* **72** 27
~ *Árbol* **371** 60
~ *Fruto merid.* **384** 52
~ del Marañón **384** 59
castañeta **324** 46
castaño **384** 48
~ de Indias **371** 58
castañuela **324** 46
castas de las abejas **77** 1, 4, 5
castillete armado **214** 77
~ con estructura de celosía **214** 31
~ de acero con estructura de celosía **214** 77
~ de extracción **144** 1
~ de perforación **146** 1-37
~ de tubos de acero **214** 78
~ soporte **214** 24
castillo *Mapa* **15** 96
~ *Barco* **218** 10
~ *Circo* **307** 28
~ *Caball.* **329** 1
~ de arena **280** 35
~ delantero **218** 19
~ de popa **218** 23; **258** 22
~ de popa con el puente de mando **221** 6
~ de proa **218** 19; **221** 13; **223** 48

~ de proa sumergible **258** 65; **259** 77
~ trasero **218** 23
castor del Plata **366** 14
Cástor y Pólux **3** 28
casuario **359** 1
~ de cresta **359** 1
casulla **30** 50
catacumba **331** 59
cata del vino **79** 16
catador de vino **79** 18
catafaro **187** 45
catalejo **111** 18
catálogo de las piezas de recambio **195** 32
~ de moda **104** 6
catamarán **284** 64
~ con motor fuera borda **286** 21
catapulta de lanzamiento doble **259** 14
catarata **11** 45
catavinos **79** 19
catcher **292** 54, 64
catchup **45** 43
cátedra **262** 4
catedral **335** 1-13, 22
catedrático de Universidad **262** 3
catenaria **197** 41
catéter **27** 30
~ en el envase estéril **26** 31
cateterización del corazón **27** 30
cateto **346** 32
catimbao **307** 23, 24
catocala nupcial **365** 8
cátodo **178** 6
~ de calentamiento rápido **240** 25
catrín **306** 33
cauchera **383** 33
caucho **383** 33
caudalímetro **76** 4
caudatrémula **360** 9
caulículo **334** 23
cauterio **24** 43
cava **79** 1-22
caveto **336** 50
cavidad de la rueda **195** 28
~ del ovario **370** 62
~ faríngea **19** 24
~ nasal **17** 53
~ nidal **359** 29
~ uterina **20** 80
cayado de la aorta **18** 10
cayana **39** 29; **40** 12
caza **86** 1-52, 38; **88**
~ a caballo **289** 41-49
~ acuática **86** 40
cazabombardero e interceptor **256** 1
~ F-104 G Starfighter **256** 29
caza con gerifaltes **86** 42-46
~ con halcones **86** 42-46
~ con hurón **86** 23
~ con papelillos **289** 41-49
~ con perro **86** 1-8
~ con reclamo **86** 47-52
~ con trampas **86** 19-27
~ de animales de presa con trampas **86** 19
~ de la liebre **86** 34-39
~ del jabalí **86** 31
~ del zorro **289** 41-49
~ de montería **88** 1-27
~ de patos **86** 40
~ de pluma **86** 41

~ de rastreo **289** 41-49
cazador *Caza* **86** 1
~ *Hípica* **289** 41
Cazador **3** 13
cazadora *Ropa* **29** 66; **30** 38; **31** 42; **33** 39
~ *Autom.* **194** 5
cazador de minas **258** 80
~ de pieles **306** 8
~ furtivo **86** 29
~ mayor **289** 45
caza en cotos **86** 1-8
~ en época de brama y celo **86** 9-12
~ mayor **88** 1-27
caz de salida **91** 44
~ de traída **91** 41
cazo **45** 14
cazoleta *Tabaco* **107** 36
~ *Bicicl.* **187** 59
~ *Esgr.* **294** 38, 43
cazo para medir la viscosidad **130** 32
cebada **68** 26
~ de las ratas **61** 28
~ en germinación **92** 23
~ perlada **98** 35
cebadera **218** 43
cebadilla **61** 28
cebellina **30** 60
cebo *Caza* **86** 21
~ *Pesca* **89** 65-76
~ de lombriz de tierra **89** 67
~ de ninfas **89** 66
~ de saltamontes **89** 68
cebolla **57** 24
cebolleta **57** 22
cebra **366** 27
cecina **96** 3
cedilla **342** 33
cedro **372** 65
cédula hipotecaria **251** 11-19
cefalópodo **357** 37
ceiba **383** 20
ceja *Anat.* **19** 38
~ *Mús.* **323** 7, 20
~ inferior **324** 4
celada *Heráld.* **254** 4, 7-9
~ *Caball.* **329** 39-42
~ de grilleta **254** 8
celadora **262** 14
celda **77** 26-30
~ con el huevo en su interior **77** 27
~ de incubación **77** 31
~ de obrera **77** 34
~ depósito de polen **77** 35
~ de zángano **77** 36
~ operculada llena de miel **77** 33
~ real **77** 37
~ tapada con la ninfa **77** 32
celentéreo **369** 5, 9, 14, 20; **357** 14
celesta **325** 1
celidonia menor **375** 36
celinda **373** 9
célula **357** 2
~ de medida **116** 55
~ fotoeléctrica **115** 37; **312** 49
~ solar **155** 34
cella **334** 51
cellisca **9** 35
cémbalo **322** 32
~ de Apenzelle **322** 35
~ de Valais **322** 34
cembro **372** 29

cementerio **15** 106; **331** 21-41
~ subterráneo de los primeros tiempos del cristianismo **331** 59
cemento *Anat.* **19** 29
~ *Construc.* **118** 43
cenador **52** 14
cenancle **68** 36
cenefa **223** 17
cenicero *Ester* **42** 29
~ *Sastre* **104** 5
~ *Central el.* **152** 8
~ *FFCC* **210** 6
~ *Oficina* **246** 33
~ del brazo del asiento **207** 46
~ esférico con soporte **266** 5
~ giratorio **208** 29
cénit **4** 11
ceniza de la resurrección **327** 10
cenizo **61** 25
censo electoral **263** 18
centaura negra **376** 12
centáurea **61** 1
~ mayor **380** 10
Centauro **3** 39
centauro **327** 52
Centaurus **3** 39
centavo **252** 19, 23, 33
centena **344** 3
centeno **68** 1
centésima **344** 20
centésimo **252** 20
céntimo **252** 15, 16, 22
central **237** 25
~ atómica **154** 19
~ de conexión **92** 25
~ de datos **248** 43
~ de la inercia **6** 43
~ de transmisión de datos **248** 43
~ eléctrica **144** 13; **152** 1-28; **153**
~ eólica **155** 42
~ hidráulica de bombeo **217** 39-46
centralita **237** 22
~ para supletorios **237** 17
~ telefónica interior **245** 13
central lechera **76** 1-48
~ maremotriz **155** 37
~ nuclear **154** 19
~ telefónica **237** 27-41
~ termoeléctrica **152** 1-28
centrifugación **169** 23
centrifuga de hilar **169** 17
~ de planchas **179** 1
~ depuradora **172** 22, 56
centrifugadora **23** 59
centrífuga pendular **168** 14
centro **346** 26, 43
centrocampista **291** 14
centro de cálculo **244**
~ de curvatura **346** 23
~ de la ciudad **268**
~ del blanco **288** 56
~ del canal **224** 98
~ del cristal **351** 3
~ del escudo **254** 17
~ del volante con protector antichoque **191** 57
~ de mecanizado **150** 41
~ de simetría **351** 3
~ para el ocio **281**
~ para el tiempo libre **281**
cénzalo **358** 16
cepa **78** 6

dos por cuatro 320 29
~ por dos 320 30
~ por ocho 320 28
~ puntos 342 17
dovela 336 22
dracma 252 39
Draco 3 32
draga *Puerto* 226 41
~ *Buque guerra* 258 87
~ con cadena de cangilones 216 56
~ de cangilones 226 41
~ de succión 216 59
~ flotante 216 56
dragaminas 258 84
Dragón *Astron.* 3 32
dragón *Ser fabul.* 327 1
~ *Vela* 284 57
~ de las siete cabezas de la revelación 327 50
~ marino 218 13-17
~ vikingo 218 13-17
~ volador 358 3
drenaje 145 32
~ de agua 144 46
~ del subsuelo 200 61
dríada 51 7
dribling 291 52
drive 293 83
driver 293 91
driza 253 2
~ de las banderas de señales 223 10
dromia velluda 358 1
drop 98 76
drósera 377 14
drupa *Fruta* 59 1-36
~ *Botán.* 370 99
~ dehiscente 59 41, 43
ducha *Salvamento* 228 30
~ *Aerop.* 233 46
~ *Natac.* 282 30
~ de mano *Baño* 49 41
~ de mano *Peluq.* 105 30; 106 13
~ de mano *Offset* 179 7
~ de tubo flexible 126 30
~ regulable 49 41
~ tibia 281 29
duela 130 9
dulce *Panad.* 97 17-47
~ *Comest.* 98 75-86
~ americano 97 39
~ cubierto de azúcar 97 43
~ de ciruelas 97 43
~ de molde cubierto con una capa de chocolate 97 34
~ de pisos 97 46
~ en trozos 97 43
~ espolvoreado con recortes de pasta 97°43
dulcemele 322 32
dulzaina 322 14
duna 13 39
~ en forma de media luna 13 40
~ movediza 13 39
duodeno 20 14, 43
duque de alba *Cons. naval* 222 35
~ de alba *Puerto* 225 12
duramen *Construc.* 120 84
~ *Botán.* 370 13
durmiente *Construc.* 120 49
~ *Estación* 205 60
~ de las bancadas 283 31

**E**

ébano falso 374 32
ebonita 300 45
écarté 314 15
eclipse lunar 4 29-35
~ solar 4 29-35
~ total 4 33
~ total de Sol 4 39, 41
eclíptica 3 2
eclisa *Construc.* 122 48
~ *FFCC* 202 12
eco 224 63
ecógrafo 224 24, 65
ecosonda 224 61-67
ecuación 345 9
~ con la incógnita x 345 8
~ de identidad 345 5
~ de primer grado 345 4
~ determinada 345 9
ecuador 14 1
~ celeste 3 3
echadora de cartas 308 36
Echiostoma 369 13
echona 56 8
Edad de Bronce 328 21-40
~ de Hierro 328 21-40
edelweiss 378 9
edificio anejo 331 13
~ colateral 62 14
~ contiguo 154 36
~ de administración *Cons. hidr.* 217 24
~ de administración *Aerop.* 233 16
~ de aduanas del puerto 225 6
~ de calderas 152 1-21
~ de la administración *Mina* 144 18
~ de la administración *Cons. naval* 222 1
~ de la administración *Cine* 310 4
~ de la escena 334 45
~ de la mina 144 4
~ del club 283 23
~ de los enseres de bomberos 233 8
~ del pozo 144 4
~ del reactor 154 20
~ de oficinas 225 53
~ de planta central 334 55
~ de recepción 205 13
~ neoclásico 336 15
~ público 15 54
~ sagrado budista 337 21
~ terminal de viajeros 233 15
editorial 342 48
edredón 43 8
educación preescolar 48 1-20
EEUU 253 18
efecto 251 11-19
~ de los terremotos 11 45-54
~ de una inundación 216 5
~ sonoro 310 30, 59
efémera 358 6
effacé 314 13
efímera 358 6
egipcia 342 8
eje *Peluq.* 106 36
~ *Construc.* 123 78
~ *Tornill* 143 18
~ *Estudio* 151 30
~ *Bicicl.* 187 61, 76

~ acoplado 210 36
~ ajustable 226 51
~ celeste 4 10
~ de abscisas 347 2
~ de coordenadas 347 2-3
~ de declinación 113 5, 17
~ de desbobinado 312 36
~ de fricción del bobinado 312 37
~ de giro 91 5
~ de la eclíptica 4 22
~ de la hélice *Barro* 223 65
~ de la hélice *Buque guerra* 259 59
~ del ánima 87 38
~ delantero 189 34
~ del anticlinal 12 17
~ de la parábola 347 17
~ de la suspensión 214 72
~ de las x 347 2
~ de las y 347 3
~ de la Tierra 4 22-28
~ del barco 285 5
~ del carrete 114 8
~ del cono 372 3
~ del molino 91 12
~ de los pedales 187 42
~ del pedal 187 81
~ del pistón 192 75
~ del sinclinal 12 19
~ de mando de la horquilla 192 41
~ de ordenadas 347 3
~ de ruedas provisto de motor 209 3
~ de simetría *Matem.* 346 25
~ de simetría *Cristal.* 351 4
~ fijo 65 33
~ horario *Astron.* 5 8
~ horario *Opt.* 113 18
~ hueco 312 49
~ instantáneo de rotación 4 25
~ longitudinal 230 72
~ mayor 347 23
~ medio de rotación 4 27
~ menor *Matem.* 347 24
~ motor *FFCC* 210 37
~, para el movimiento de las alas batidoras 163 24
~ „pedalier" 187 42
~ polar 113 18
~ portante 210 35
~ principal 166 50
ejercicio con los aparatos 296 48-60
~ de extinción, trepa, escalera salvamento 270 1-46
~ de los bomberos 270 1-46
~ del servicio de incendios 270 1-46
~ en los aparatos 297 15-32
~ gimnástico con aparatos 296, 297
~ gimnástico sin aparatos 295
ejército del aire 256, 257
~ de tierra 255
eje rígido 192 65-71
~ transversal 230 68
~ vertical 230 70
~ y soporte para impulsar el banco de anillas 164 42
ejote 57 8
elástico del calcetín 32 33
~ de punto 31 70
elaténido 80 37, 38

elección 263 16-30
~ de gafas 111 5
~ de montura 111 5
elecciones 263
electora 263 22
elector con derecho a voto 263 24
electricidad 235 55
electricista 127 1
~ *Cine* 310 37
~ *Teatro* 316 20
electrocardiógrafo *Med.* 23 28
~ *Hosp.* 25 27, 41
~ portátil 23 46
electrocardiograma 25 28
electroconmutador 168 58
electrodo *Hosp.* 25 35
~ *Matad.* 94 8
~ *Soldadura* 142 10
~ *Sider.* 147 52
~ central 2 3
~ de correa 23 30
~ del estimulador cardíaco temporal 25 25
~ de platino iridiado 24 44
~ de ventosa 23 29
~ introducido a través de la vena 25 38
~ para el tratamiento de un shock 25 26
~, salida del 25 34
electrofiltro *Coque* 156 20
~ *Cemen.* 160 7
~ *Papel* 172 39
electroimán 237 47
~ del vehículo inductivo 212 38
electrón 1 3, 17, 32
electrónica de entretenimiento 241
~ recreativa 241
electrón libre 1 25
electrotomo 22 38
electroválvula 139 23
elefante *Zoo* 356 9
~ africano 366 20
~ de tela 47 6
elemento *Estar* 42 1
~ *Oficina* 248 39
~ de ajuste 237 49
~ de central solar 155 28
~ de construcción intercambiable 273 56
~ de contacto 237 46
~ de control 259 69
~ de decoración 316 35
~ de ensamblaje 248 48
~ de entramado 215 24
~ de fijación 301 54-56
~ de imagen 243 60
~ del conjunto A 348 2
~ del diapasón 110 9
~ del plinton 296 16; 279 9
~ del radiador 38 77
~ de percepción 10 22
~ estructural del buque 222 44-61
~ impreso 178 39
~ lógico 242 68
~ oscilante 110 9
~ prefabricado 215 58
elementos dispuestos en forma de ángulo 248 39
elemento sensitivo 10 22
elevación a una potencia 345 1
~ con las piernas abiertas en las paralelas 296 49

~ de caderas y extensión de piernas 295 24
~ de dos semitonos 320 51
~ de las piernas en el pino sobre el suelo 296 52
~ del cuerpo 295 16, 17
~ del cuerpo con apoyo sobre las manos 295 18
~ de puntillas 295 5
~ de talones 295 5
~ de un semitono 320 50
elevador *Deut.* 24 48
~ *Caza* 87 18
~ de barcos 217 29-38
~ de cala 226 23
~ de cangilones 200 49; 201 21
~ de cebada 92 33
~ de espigas 64 2
~ de las hojas 64 90
~ de malta 92 35
~ de rosario 170 36
~, para transportar las matrices al distribuidor 174 22
elevón 235 33
el gorgojo 80 49
elimo arenario 15 7
elipse 347 22
elipsoide de revolución 347 42
élitro *Ins.* 81 8
~ *Plaga* 82 10
~ *Articul.* 358 36
elixir dentífrico 49 36
elodea 378 56
embalaje de yute 163 4
embaldosado del zócalo 123 21
embalse artificial 217 39
embarcación hecha vaciando un tronco de árbol 354 20
embarcadero *Mapa* 15 59
~ *Puerto* 225 30, 66
~ *Parque* 272 46
~ *Camping* 278 13
~ *Playa* 280 9
~ *Remo* 283 19
~ de los barcos de motor 216 7
embarque 233 12
emberiza 361 6-7
emblema 191 12
embocadura *Construc.* 122 30
~ *Mús.* 324 33
émbolo *Carp.* 133 47
~ *Teatro* 316 60
~ buzo 145 23
~ del motor Wankel 190 68
embotellado 93 22
embotellador circular semiautomático 79 9
embrague *Agric.* 65 39
~ *Autom.* 191 44, 96
~ *FFCC* 212 82
~ *Salvamento* 227 23
~ de disco en seco 190 78
~ de fricción de láminas 139 21
~ de impulsión 177 54
~ del ventilador 190 8
~ de toma de fuerza 65 40
~ hidráulico 65 37
~ monodisco 190 71
~ principal 65 39
embrión *Planta estim., trop.* 382 21

~ *Fruto merid.* 384 22
embudo *Fotogr.* 116 12
~ *Quím.* 350 16
~ de aspiración 217 51
~ de entrada de las mechas 164 15
~ de separación 349 3
~ guía de las mechas 164 15
embutidera 340 14
embutido *Carnic.* 96 6-11
~ *Comest.* 98 4
~ *Superm.* 99 54
embutidor de mano 96 49
~ de mesa 96 49
eminencia frontal 16 4
emisión radiofónica 238 16-26
emisor de sonido 224 61
empacadora de alta presión 63 35
~ de paja 63 35
empalizada *Huerto* 52 10
~ *Hípica* 289 8
~ *Caball.* 329 36
~ contra la nieve 304 6
empalme a presión 67 9
~ con la batería 115 75
~ de aire comprimido 213 20
~ de descarga 213 21
~ de la toma de fuerza 64 63
~ de tubo 67 5
empapelado 128 18-53
empapelador 128
empaquetadora automática de huevos 74 46
emparedado *Mesa* 45 39
~ *Restaur.* 266 54
emparrillado basculante 210 5
empaste 24 30
empavesado 221 85
empedrado de la acera 198 8
empeine 19 61
empella *Zapat.* 100 60
~ *Jue. pelota* 291 26
emperatriz bizantina 355 15
emplazamiento del almacén de material 144 17
~ de la madera cortada 157 32
~ de la tienda 278 42
~ del camping 278 1-59
~ del escritorio 46 21
empleada de banco *Banco* 250 5
~ de banco *Bolsa* 251 7
~ de la oficina de consignación 206 36
~ del despacho 204 9
~ del servicio al cliente 248 17
~ de oficina 248 7
~ de pompas fúnebres 331 40
~ de ventanilla 236 16
empolladura 359 29
empuje 234 21
~ de la aguja a través de la malla 167 63
~ del programa 177 71
~ hidráulico 139 9, 15
~ inferior 235 6
~ superior 235 5
empuñadura *Agric.* 65 2
~ *Orfebre* 108 5
~ *Fotogr.* 114 37; 117 61
~ *Carp.* 132 18

~ *Naveg.* 224 9
~ *Barco a motor, esquí acuát.* 286 48
~ *Dep.* 305 57
~ *Cine* 313 21
~ adicional 134 45
~ con distanciador 134 47
~ de batería 117 5
~ de corcho 89 50
~ de disparo 313 38
~ de la pila para el motor de la cámara 115 76
~ de la pistola 264 23
~ de pistola *FFAA* 255 38
~ de pistola *Bric.* 134 44
~ de revólver 134 44
~ enfundada 89 55
~ giratoria para la regulación del chorro 83 19
~ para abrir la puerta del hogar 210 63
~ para disparar 313 24
~ para el deslizamiento del carro 167 41
emú 359 1
enagua 32 14
enaguas 309 85
enano 308 22
encaje *Ropa* 31 32
~ *Labores* 102 30
~ *Moda* 355 65, 66
~ con lanzadera 102 19
~ de algodón 31 32
~ de bolillos 102 18
~ del pasador 143 66
~ del tope 166 44
encantador de serpientes 353 45
encapilladura 284 14
encargada del guardarropa 315 6
encargado de la planta 271 33
~ del departamento 271 60
~ del equipaje 205 30
~ del freno 303 21
~ del telar 316 7
~ del vestuario 315 38
encaro 86 34
encarretadora de cruzado 165 1
encendedor 191 88
~ de gas 107 30
~ de gasolina 107 27
~ del soplete 141 27
~ no recargable 107 30
encestador 292 35
encía 19 15
enciclopedia en varios volúmenes 42 18
encimera *Cocina* 39 11
~ *Apar. kogar* 50 31
encintado 198 7
encofrado 119 11, 13, 54
~ de hormigón 119 54-76
~ de la cornisa 122 42
~ de las jácenas 119 12
~ de puntales 119 73
~ de tablas horizontal 37 84
~ inferior de la jácena 119 12
~ lateral de la jácena 119 55
encolado 162 53
~ del lomo 183 14
encoladora de pliegue 185 28
encomienda 236 3

encorvadura de la caja de resonancia 324 26
encuadernación 183; 184; 185
~ a mano 183 1-35
~ del libro 185 40-42
~ en rústica 183 8, 32
~ térmica sin cosido 249 61
encuadernador 183 2
encuadernadora automática 249 61
~ sin costura 184 1
enchufe de bisagra de suelo 127 23
~ de la alargadera 127 12
~ de la lámpara para la luz transmitida 112 60
~ de pared 39 26
~ de superficie con caja de toma 127 25
~ de superficie tripolar 127 13
~ empotrable en el suelo con tapadera de bisagra 127 24
~ hembra 261 12
~ para el interruptor a pedal de la mecanógrafa 249 66
~ para el micrófono 249 69
~ para el teléfono 249 67
~ para los auriculares de casco 249 68
~ tripolar con interruptor 127 66
enderezador del plegado 181 53
endibia 57 39
endosante 250 27
endosatario 250 26
endoso 250 25
endrino 374 27
enebrina 372 52
enebro 372 47
eneldo 380 6
energía nuclear 154
~ solar 155 17-36
enfermera *Med.* 22 19
~ *Deut.* 24 18
~ radiógrafa 27 11
enfermería con camarote de operaciones y unidad de reanimación 228 21
enfermo 274 7
enfoque de la distancia 117 3
enfranque 100 68
enfriador de hidrógeno 153 27
enfurtido de los géneros de lana 168 1
enganchabobos 34 3
enganche 65 30
~ del remolque 278 55
~ de tres puntos 65 72
~ de vagones 208 16
~ rápido 65 86
engaste de la moneda 36 38
engomadora 185 31
engranaje *Reloj.* 110 11
~ *Tornill.* 143 82-96
~ *Sider.* 148 63
~ *Carret.* 201 11
~ cónico 91 25
~ de inversión de marcha 211 53
~ del molino de viento 91 11
~ diferencial 65 32

~ *Flor* 357 13
~ de baño 49 6
~ para humedecer la piedra litográfica 340 25
~ silícea 369 7
esponjilla humedecedora 247 31
espora 381 12, 13
~ germinal 381 8
espuela *Caballo* 71 50-51
~ *An. dom.* 73 27
~ clavada 71 50
~ de caballero 60 13
~ de correílla 71 51
~ de galán 53 4
~ fija 71 50
espuma *Baño* 49 3
~ *Cerv.* 93 31
~ de la cerveza 266 4
espumadera 96 43
espuma para la extinción de incendios 228 28
espumilla 265 5
esqueje 54 20
~ leñoso 54 25
esquela mortuoria 342 68
esqueleto *Anat.* 17 1-29
~ *Colegio* 261 14
~ *Esc.* 339 22
~ silíceo 357 8
esquema 260 34
~ de la carda 163 51
~ de la peinadora 163 63
~ de pistas de la grabación de videocassettes 243 28
~ funcional de la fábrica 76 9
esquí 301 1-72
~ acuático 280 16; 286 45-62
~ acuático, tipos 286 56-62
esquiadora 286 45
esquí compacto 301 1
~ de aterrizaje 256 21
~ de descenso 301 34
~ de figuras 286 56
~ de fondo 301 14
~ de salto 301 38
~ de saltos 286 62
~ de slalon 286 60
esquife 258 12, 45, 61; 259 35
esquimal 353 1
esquina 292 18
~ de la calle 198 12
esquinera *Estar.* 42 26
~ *Oficina* 246 34
esquiva lateral 299 29
estabilización del traqueteo 234 13
estabilizador *Fotogr.* 116 10
~ *FFAA* 256 31
~ *Dep.* 305 58
~ de cola 232 4, 7
~ de dirección 230 59; 231 6
~ de elevación 229 26, 27; 230 61
~ de O₂ 27 42
~ en T 287 10
~ horizontal 288 23
establecimiento de baños 281
establo 62 7
~ de las vacas lecheras 75 14
estaca 84 17
estacada 329 36
estaca de judías 52 28

~ de rama 54 25
estación *Mapa* 15 27
~ *Tranv.* 197 35
estacionamiento 233 3
estación central de mezcla 201 19
~ costera 237 53
~ de alzado 249 60
~ de autoservicio 196 1-29
~ de bombeo 146 22
~ de carga 206
~ de cinta magnética 242 32
~ de contenedores 206 54
~ de depuración 144 20
~ de destino 205 22
~ de enclavamiento 15 24
~ de ferrocarril *Mapa* 15 41
~ de ferrocarril *Estación* 204
~ del valle 214 39
~ de maniobras 206 42
~ de mercancías 206
~ de montaña 214 57
~ de ondas cortas 237 54
~ de servicio 196 1-29
~ eléctrica 310 8
~ espacial 235 65
~ meteorológica 9 7; 10 49
~ principal 224 40
~ secundaria 224 41
~ terrestre 237 51
estadística 248 36
~ de ventas 248 46
estado del cielo 9 20-24
~ del Vaticano 252 21
~ excitado 1 19
~ fundamental 1 18
Estados Unidos de América *Dinero* 252 33
~ Unidos de América *Bandera* 253 18
estalactita 13 80
estalagmita 13 81
estambre *Fruta* 58 45; 59 10
~ *Botán.* 370 57, 60
~ *Conif.* 372 7, 18
~ *Arb. ornam.* 373 2, 5; 374 3
estampación del tejido a la lionesa 168 59
estampa de banco 140 14
estampador textil 168 65
estampilla 236 15, 19, 20, 61
~ del médico 22 29
estancia 62
estanco 204 47
estandarte *Fotogr.* 177 11
~ *Bandera* 253 7-11
~ de caballería 253 13
~ de la iglesia 331 44
~ de la procesión 331 44
~ del Presidente de la República Federal Alemana 253 14
estanque *Mapa* 15 79
~ *Parque* 272 50
~ de agua 55 29
~ de cría 89 6
~ de hormigón para escenas acuáticas 310 11
~ del jardín 51 16
~ para carpas 89 6
~ para chapotear 37 44
~ para chapotear los niños 273 28
estante *Estar.* 42 3
~ *Comed.* 44 19
~ de botellas 317 4
~ de composición 174 9

~ de especias 47 29
~ de la cama-mueble 46 19
~ de las botellas 266 10
~ de las especias 39 31
~ de las medias 99 25
~ de las monturas 111 5
~ del material 100 36
~ de los libros 46 7
~ de los periódicos 265 8
~ de los tacos 277 19
~ de los vasos 266 9
~ de ropa blanca 43 2
~ de vasos 317 5
~ de vitrina 46 7
~ para las bandejas de los huevos 74 42
~ para libros 43 14
estantería *Apart.* 46 1
~ *Comest.* 98 14
~ *Superm.* 99 23
~ *Sastre* 104 8
~ *Grandes alm.* 271 27
~ colgante 248 40
~ de acero 262 12
~ de ficheros 262 22
~ de las bebidas 99 71
~ de las botellas 79 11
~ de las mercancías 47 36
~ de las publicaciones 330 56
~ de las revistas 262 15
~ de los archivadores 248 10
~ de los periódicos 262 16
~ de los vasos 274 16
~ de múltiples usos 248 28
~ de productos lecheros 99 43
~, para lingotes y blancos 174 8
~, para material de relleno 174 8
~ por elementos 42 1
~ por módulos 42 1
estaño fundido 162 17
~ para soldar 126 76
estapelia 53 15
estaquilla *Construc.* 123 11
~ *Camping* 278 24
~ de la oreja 354 30
~ de la tienda 278 24
estarcido 245 8, 9, 10
estatorreactor 232 33-50
estatua *Parque* 272 10
~ *Arte* 334 5
~ *Esc.* 339 32
~ de Buda 337 20
~ del puente 215 22
~ de piedra 272 2
estatuilla de marfil 328 8
estay 219 10
~ de foque 219 14
~ del mastelero de trinquete 219 11
~ de proa 284 15
~ de señales 223 11
~ mastelerillo de trinquete 219 12
~ mastelerillo sobrejuanete 219 13
este 4 14
estela *Barco* 223 58
~ *Arte* 334 33
~ de ionización 2 27
~ en la cámara de Wilson 2 27
estenografía 342 13
estera de cañizo 55 6
~ de paja 55 6

estéreo 84 16
estereóbato 334 4
estereomicroscopio de gran campo 112 40
campo 112 61
estereoplanígrafo 14 66
estereotopo 14 64
esterilizador *Cocina* 40 23
~ *Leche* 76 12
~ de aire caliente 22 71
~ de vapor 22 39
~ pequeño 26 35
esterilla de los pies 49 18
esterna 359 11
esternocleidomastoideo 18 34; 19 1
esternón *Anat.* 17 8
~ *Matad.* 95 27
estetoscopio 23 35
esteva 65 3
estiércol 63 15
estigma *Fruta* 58 41; 59 16
~ *Articul.* 358 32
~ *Botán.* 370 56
estigmómetro 115 55
estilete 341 25
~ de acero indio 341 21
estilo *Fruta* 58 42; 59 15
~ *Botán.* 370 55
~ *Arb. ornam.* 373 5
~ *Planta* 378 5
estilóbato 334 32
estilo delfín 282 35
~ de natación 282 33-39
estilográfica 260 14
estilo libre de relevos 282 24-32
~ mariposa 282 34
estilos y partes del tejado 121 1-26
estimulador cardíaco 25 31
~ cardíaco temporal 25 25
estimulante *Comest.* 98 65-68
~ *Superm.* 99 68-70
estípite con busto 334 35
estipula *Hortal.* 57 5
~ *Fruta* 58 48
~ *Árbol.* 371 73
estique 339 13
estirado 164 1
estiraje 170 46, 55
~ de la mechera 164 22
estocada 319 30
estola 355 9
estola de piel 318 30
estolón *Planta* 54 16
~ *Fruta* 58 20
estómago *Anat.* 20 13, 41-42
~ *Apic.* 77 16
estomiátido 369 10, 13
estopa de limpieza 87 63
estopor 223 51
estoque *Flor* 60 11
~ *Toros, rodeo* 319 32
estornino pinto 361 4
estornudadera 380 2
estramónica 379 8
estramonio 379 8
estratificación de las rocas sedimentarias 12 1
estrato 8 4
estratocúmulo 8 3
estrato de volcán 11 15
~ impermeable 12 28
estratosfera 7 8
estrecho de Gibraltar 14 24
~ de mar 14 24
estregadera 50 56

~ de baño *Baños* 281 8
~ de cascabeles 306 39
~ de esquí *Sombr.* 35 39
~ de esquí *Igl.* 301 10
~ de lana 35 26
~ del bufón 306 39
~ de papel 306 45
~ de piel 35 34
~ de piel de oveja 353 23
~ de piel de zorro con
solapas para las orejas 35
31
~ de punto 35 10
~ de tejido de moer 35 11
~ de visón 35 20
~ de zorro con la parte alta
de cuero 35 19
~ hecho con lana gruesa 35
9
gorrón *Tornill.* 143 63
~ *Autom.* 192 78
gota lisa 36 85
gotero 25 13
goterón 334 17
gozne 140 49
grabación 311 1-46
~ de sonido a doble pista
117 70
~ de videocassettes 243 28
~ estereofónica 310 30
~ magnética 238 55
~ vídeo en la superficie del
disco 243 58
grabado *Joya* 36 41
~ *Caza* 87 28
~ al agua fuerte 340 14-24
~ al humo 340 14-24
~ a tinta sobre madera 340
1
~ de líneas entrecruzadas
340 54
~ de relieve 340 2
~ de superficie 340 25-26
~ de trazo 178 42
~ en cobre 340 14-24
~ en madera 340 1-13
~ en piedra 340 25-26
grabado en relieve 340 1-13
~ en talla 340 14-24
~ punteado 340 14-24
grabadora de cassettes 117
73
~ de cintas 261 42
~ de programas
pedagógicos 261 42
~ de videocassettes 243 7
~ portátil de vídeo 243 4
grabador de punzones 175
32
~ en cobre 340 44
grada con dientes de tres
secciones 65 88
~ de andamiaje 222 19-21
~ de construcción 222 11-18
~ de grúa de cable 222
11-18
~ del altar 330 5, 31
~ de mano 55 21
~ de pórtico 222 11-18
~ para sentarse o tenderse
281 20
gradería de los espectadores
307 15
gradiente 12 37; 13 65
graduación 313 14
~ en centímetros y
milímetros 247 36
gráfica de las temperaturas 7
37

~ estadística 248 36
graja 361 2
grajilla 361 2
grajo 361 2
grama *Casa* 37 46
~ *Jardín* 51 33
~ *Hierba* 61 30
~ canina 61 30
~ de olor 61 30
~ de playa 61 30
~ en jopillos 69 25
gramil 120 69
gramínácea 69 27
gramínea 136 26
gramófono 309 31
granada *FFAA* 255 26
~ *Fruto merid.* 384 19
granado 384 16
gran angular 115 45
granate 351 7
gran bestia 366 26
Gran Bretaña *Dinero* 252 37
~ *Bretaña Bandera* 253 15
~ *Carro* 3 29
gran danés 70 14
Grande de España 306 26
grandes almacenes 268 41;
271
graneado 340 47
graneador para el grabado
al humo 340 19
granete 134 31
~ de marcar 140 64
granizada 9 36
granizal 9 36
granizo 9 36
granja 62
granjera 62 4
granjero 62 6
gran molinete 296 60
grano *Agric.* 68 13
~ *Fruto merid.* 384 20
~ de abatí 68 37
~ de arroz 68 30
~ de cacao 382 19
~ de café 382 6
~ deformado por un hongo
68 4
~ de maíz 68 37
~ de pimienta 382 39
~ germinado 68 14
~ verde para guisos 68 25
gran pie de rey 84 21
~ tambor 163 43
grapa *Construc.* 121 97
~ *Quím.* 350 33
~ de obra 119 58
~ de plástico 127 40
grapadora *Méd.* 22 25
~ *Oficina* 247 4
grasa de riñón de cerdo 95
45
~ vegetal 98 23
grasilla 377 13
grátil 284 42
grava 158 24
~ filtradora 269 10
gravilla 158 23
greba 329 54
greca 334 43
Grecia 252 39
gredal 15 88
green 293 82
gregüesco acolchado y
acuchillado 355 31
griega *Escrit.* 341 15
~ *Moda* 355 1
griego 355 3
grieta 13 50

~ del glaciar *Geogr.* 12 50
~ del glaciar *Alpin.* 300 23
grifería 126 26-37
~ mezcladora 106 14
grifo *Font.* 126 34
~ *Balneario* 274 17
~ *Ser. fabul.* 327 11
~ codillo 126 34
~ con trompa de agua 23 49
~ de agua *Cocina* 39 36
~ de agua *Font.* 126 34
~ de agua caliente 126 28
~ de agua fría 126 29
~ de agua fría y caliente 49
26
~ de carga y vaciado 38 65
~ de control 172 9
~ de desagüe 178 34
~ de doble cierre 126 35
~ de la cerveza 266 1
~ de la manguera 37 41
~ de lavabo 126 31
~ distribuidor de cerveza
317 8
~ giratorio 126 36
~ mezclador 39 36
~ mezclador 49 2
grifón 70 35
grifo para sacar la cerveza
93 14
grigallo 88 66
grillo doméstico 81 7
grímpola 284 48
griñón 355 22
gris 343 15
groschen 252 13
grosella 58 12
~ espinosa 58 1, 9
grosellero de racimo 58 10
~ negro 52 19
grosulariea 58 1-15
grotesca 342 7
grúa *Hab. niños* 47 39
~ *Buque guerra* 258 88
~ de a bordo 259 10
~ de brazo oscilante 222 34
~ de caballete 222 20
~ de cabeza de martillo 222
7
~ de carga 85 28, 44
~ de corredera 147 41
~ de la cámara 310 49
~ del arsenal 225 24
~ del dique 222 34
~ del puente 221 5, 61
~ de pórtico *Aserr.* 157 27
~ de pórtico *Estación* 206
55
~ de pórtico móvil 222 25
~ de puente rodante sobre
dos vías para la carga de
contenedores 225 46
~ de salvamento 270 48
~ de tenazas 148 47
~ de torre giratoria 119 31
~ de trípode 222 6
~ flotante 225 10; 266 48
~ giratoria 146 3
~ giratoria de brazo
oscilante 222 23
~ móvil 222 28
~ móvil de techo 222 20
~ para el horno de foso 148
47
~ -puente 222 25
gruesa 175 9
grueso 175 48
Grulla 3 42
grumete 221 112

grupa 72 31
grupo abierto de estrellas 3
26
~ de antenas dirigidas 234
64
~ de cazadores 289 41
~ de cohetes de control 234
63
~ de cola 287 10
~ de cola en T 256 31-32
~ de control 178 29
~ de empleados de servicio
250 4
~ de esparcimiento 62 22
~ de espejos 176 21
~ de estudios 310 10
~ de gente sentado en la
terraza del café 268 60
~ de jugadores *J. infancia*
48 20
~ de jugadores *Dep.* 305 25
~ de transporte con tornillo
sin fin mezclador 83 59
~ de turistas 272 28
~ Diesel 259 94
~ en carrera 289 51
~ fotoeléctrico de
producción del sonido
312 45
~ impulsor de bombeo 145
22
~ móvil de poleas 145 8
~ turboalternador a vapor
153 23-30
gruppetto 321 21
Grus 3 42
gruta 272 1
~, sistema de 13 76
guacamayo 363 2
guadaña 66 12
guadañeta 89 76
guadua 383 60
guagua *Autom.* 194 17
~ *Bebé* 28 5
guajaba 380 16
gualato 66 24
gualdaperra 379 2
gualdrapa 329 74
guampo 218 7
guanaco 366 30
guante *Ropa* 33 67
~ *Jue. pelota* 292 12
~ *Atlet.* 298 47
~ *Cabar.* 318 31
~ de béisbol 292 59-60
~ de boxeo 299 26
~ de catcher 292 60
~ de esgrima 294 12
~ de fielder 292 59
~ del portero 291 19
~ de sable 294 21
~ de soldador de cinco
dedos 142 32
~ de soldador de tres dedos
142 8
guantelete 329 50
guapo 383 58
guarapón 35 38
guarda *Agric.* 66 18
~ *Encuad.* 185 49
guardabarrera 202 42
guardabarros 186 6
~ delantero 187 13
~ trasero 187 43
guardabrazo 329 47
guarda-cabio 37 8
guardacadena cerrado
herméticamente 188 46
guarda de campo 63 13

lapicero 260 5
~ de presión 151 45
lápida 331 61
~ conmemorativa 331 14
~ sepulcral 331 26
lápiz *Hab. niños* 47 26
~ *Colegio* 260 5
~ de albañil 118 51
~ de borrar 151 41
~ de carpintero 120 77
~ de cera 48 11
~ de color *Hab. niños* 47 26
~ de color *J. infancia* 48 11
~ de maquillaje 315 46
~ de tiza 338 5
~ graso 340 26
~ litográfico 340 26
~ pastel 338 19
larguero *Casa* 38 16
~ *Avión* 230 45
~ FFAA 257 28
~ *Jue. pelota* 291 36
~ *Dep. inv.* 303 5
~ cajón 287 30
~ central del fuselaje 235 9
~ de la cama 43 5
~ inferior 215 10
~ lateral 235 3
~ oblicuo 287 33
~ principal 287 30
~ superior 215 9
lárice 372 32
laringe 20 2-3
larva *Fruta* 58 64
~ *Apic.* 77 29
~ *Paras.* 80 6, 19, 36, 41, 46
~ *Jus.* 81 20
~ *Plaga* 82 12, 25
~ *Articul.* 358 9
~ adulta 80 53
~ de agrótido 80 44
~ de elaténido 80 38
~ del abejorro sanjuanero
82 12
~ en la cámara larval 82 36
~ joven 80 54
láser 242 81
~ de enseñanza 242 81
lasioderma serricorne 81 25
lastra de ajuste 108 26
~ de medidas 108 25
lastre *Vela* 285 33
~ *Dep. aéreo* 288 65
lata con asa 129 8
~ con mango 129 7
~ de betún 50 39
~ de cerveza *Cerv.* 93 25
~ de cerveza *Superm.* 99 73
~ de conserva 99 91
~ del cebo 89 24
~ de los gusanos 89 24
~ de pintura 129 7-8
~ de zumo de frutas 99 75
lateral de descarga 213 25
~ derecho 291 13
~ izquierdo 291 13
látigo 307 53
latina 342 12
latitud 14 6
~ geográfica 14 6
latón 294 20
laúd 324 1
laulao 364 12
laurel rosa 373 13
laurente 173 46
lauréola 377 10
lavabo *Baño* 49 24
~ *Peluq.* 106 11

~ *Petról.* 146 29
~ FFCC 207 15, 40
~ Camping 278 6
~ del personal 207 26, 82
~ doble 267 32
~ para los cabellos 105 29
~ para los esputos 23 25
lavabos 207 72
lavadero 278 5
lavado 170 56
~ de las bobinas 170 48
~ de las botellas 93 18
~ por circulación 179 6
lavador *Baño* 49 24
~ *Caza* 87 61
~ *Papel* 173 49
lavadora 50 23
~ automática 50 23
lavador de ácido sulfhídrico
156 22
~ de amoníaco 156 23
~ de benceno 156 24
~ de gases 261 32
lavamanos *Deut.* 24 15
~ *Peluq.* 106 12
lava, meseta de 11 14
lavanda 380 7
lavandera 360 9
~ blanca 360 9
lavaplatos 39 33-36
lava, río de 11 18
lavatorio *Baño* 49 24
~ FFCC 207 15, 40
lavavajillas 39 40
laya *Jardín* 56 2
~ *Agric.* 66 22
~ semiautomática 56 12
lazareto 225 27
lazo *Ropa* 30 46
~ *Dep. inv.* 302 15
~ *Toros, rodeo* 319 40
~ *Etnogr.* 352 5
~ de la coleta *Pein.* 34 7
~ de la coleta *Moda* 355 78
~ de serpiente 302 16
~ de smoking 32 47; 33 11
lebrato 88 59
lebrón 88 59
lección 262 1
lector 262 3, 24
lectora de la cinta perforada
176 13
~ -perforadora de fichas
244 12
lector del sonido magnético
312 28
~ de microfilmes 237 36
~ de periódicos 265 24
lectura 175 28
~ de la cinta perforada 176
15
~ de los segundos 110 21
~ del sonido 312 46
~ digital con cifras
giratorias 110 20
~ para el viaje 205 18
leche 19 44
~ condensada 98 15
~ de larga duración 99 44
~ descremada 76 17
~ en lata 98 15
~ esterilizada 76 16
~ fresca 76 15
~ pasteurizada y
homogeneizada 99 44
lechera 309 89
lechocino 61 12
lecho de agujas 167 55
~ de arena 123 8

~ de cascajos 205 61
~ de hormigón 123 13
~ de impresión 180 78
~ de inundación 216 41
~ de la prensa 133 50
~ del río 13 68
~ de roca 13 70
lechón *An. dom.* 73 9
~ *Ganado* 75 42
lechoncillo 75 42
lechuga 57 36
~ silvestre 57 38
lechuguino 306 33
lechuza 362 17
ledo de los pantanos 377 21
legato 321 33
legumbre *Hortal.* 57 1-11
~ *Botán.* 370 92
~ en conserva 96 27
lencería 32 1-15
lengua *Anat.* 17 52; 19 25
~ *Caza* 88 2
~ bífida 327 6
~ de gato *Comest.* 98 84
~ de gato *Hongo* 381 31
lenguaje de los esquiadores
286 49-55
lengüeta *Zapat.* 100 65
~ *Calz.* 101 32
~ *Mús.* 322 52; 326 19
~ de la aguja 202 21
~ de la película 114 9
~ doble 323 29
~ enguatada 291 24
~ guía 248 4
lente 351 33
~ de aumento 113 38
~ de corrección 115 72
~ de Fresnel con anillo de
cristal esmerilado y
estigmómetro 115 64
~ del campo de la imagen
115 40
~ del condensador 113 32
~ del objetivo 113 36
~ de proyección con el
espejo inclinado 261 10
~ frontal 115 7
lenteja de agua 378 35
lente para imágenes lejanas
115 49
~ suplementaria 117 55
leñamen 120 85
Leo 3 17; 4 57
León 3 17; 4 57
león *Circo* 307 56
~ *Zoo* 356 5
~ *Mamíf.* 368 2
leontopodio 378 9
leopardo 368 6
leotardo 29 42; 32 12
~ sin pie 32 11
lepidóptero *Fruta* 58 62
~ *Parás.* 80 7
~ *Articul.* 358 48-56
~ *Lepidóp.* 365
~ diurno 365 1-6
~ nocturno 365 7-11
lepisma saccharina 81 14
lepta 252 39
lesena 335 11
letra 175 32-37, 38
~ A 253 22
~ aceptada 250 12
~ alemana 342 3, 11
~ capital 175 11
~ cursiva 175 7
~ de cambio 250 12
~ fina 175 8

~ G 253 23
~ girada 250 12
~ gótica 342 1, 2
~ grotesca 342 7
~ gruesa 175 9
~ inglesa 342 10
~ inicial 175 1
~ itálica 175 7
~ latina 342 12
~ mayúscula 175 11
~ minúscula 175 6
~ negra estrecha 175 10
~ negrita 175 3
~ seminegra 175 2
letras para designar los
escaques 276 6
~, tipos 342 1-15
letra supernegra 175 9
~ versal 175 11
~ versalita 175 14
letrero 118 47
~ con el precio especial 96
19
~ de la estación 205 28
leucita 351 12
leva 167 40
levade *Caballo* 71 4
~ *Circo* 307 30
leva de acoplamiento de las
agujas 167 57
~ de aguja 167 14
~ de ascenso de las agujas
167 59
~ de descenso de las agujas
167 58
levadura 97 53
levantador del acta 299 48
~ de pesos 299 2
levantamiento con arranque
299 1
~ con impulso 299 4
~ de pesos 299 1-5
levita 355 76
leyenda *Mapa* 14 27-29
~ *Ciudad* 268 4
lezna plana 109 8
libélula 358 3
liber 370 9
liberación de calor 1 55
~ del apretón 21 34
liberador del margen 249 6
líbero 291 11
Libra *Astron.* 3 19; 4 59
librado 250 21
librador 250 21
libra esterlina 252 37
librea 186 20, 21
librería *Univ.* 262 12
~ *Ciudad* 268 37
~ *de la estación* 204 26
librero 46 7
libreta 47 24
librillo de papel de fumar
107 17
libro *Estar* 42 4
~ *Apart.* 46 8
~ *Encuad.* 185 36
~ abierto 185 52
~ antiguo 309 55
~ cosido 185 22
~ de citas 22 11
~ de clase *Hab. niños* 47 25
~ de clase *Colegio* 260 23
~ de escena 316 44
~ de himnos 330 30
~ de lectura 260 16
~ de ortografía 260 17
~ de registro 267 8
~ de texto 261 28

montaje *Cine* 310 3; 311 42-46
~ de herradura 5 9
~ del hierro 119 54-76
~ de maquinaria agrícola 138
~ de películas 179 23
~ para los trabajos en los cables 214 80
montante *Apar. hogar* 50 36
~ *Agric.* 65 8
~ *Construc.* 118 86
~ *Cestero* 136 6
~ *Porja* 139 10
~ *Máq.-herr.* 150 10
~ *Avión* 229 11
~ *Arte* 335 41
~ con travesaños en cruz 37 35
~ de cilindros 148 57
~ de la mandriladora 150 31
~ de la máquina 139 19
~ del martillo pilón 139 16
~ vertical 65 67
~ vertical 65 5
montaña, alta 12 39-47
~ de bloques de fallas 12 4-11
~ de pliegues 12 12-20
~ plegada de fallas 12 20
~ rusa 308 39
~ secundaria 12 35
montañismo 300
~ 300 1-57
monte alto 84 4
~ bajo *Mapa* 15 15
~ bajo *Silvic.* 84 5
~ contorneado 13 12
montera 319 29
montería *Río* 216 15
~ *Remo* 283 9-15
~ *Hípica* 289 41-49
montero 86 1
montezanahoria 379 4
montgolfier 288 79
montgolfiera 288 79
montículo de la tumba 331 24
montón de arena 273 66
~ de bandejas 266 45
~ de los bloques 118 40
~ de loza 266 11
~ de nieve 304 24
~ de piedras sueltas 158 4
~ de rollizos 157 31
~ de rollizos seleccionados 157 31
~ de tierra 55 15
montura 111 10; 112 2
~ alemana 113 16
~ con columna de acodamiento 113 21
~ de carey 111 8
~ de herradura 113 25
~ de horquilla 113 24
~ de la lente frontal con fijación para filtros 115 6
~ de la mira 255 23, 37
~ de las gafas 111 10-14
~ de pasta 111 8
~ de prueba 111 3
~ de telescopio 113 16-25
~ en forma de horquilla 113 12
~ inglesa con soporte 113 23
~ inglesa de eje 113 22
~ metálica 111 7

monumento *Mapa* 15 92
~ *Parque* 272 10
monzón de verano 9 52
moña 319 26
moñito 88 78
moño *Pein.* 34 29
~ *Cabello* 72 2
Mopsea 369 8
moqueta *Vestib.* 41 18
~ *Dorm.* 43 23
~ del suelo 191 43
mora 58 29
morado 384 28
morcilla 99 56
morcillo 95 8
~ delantero 95 28
~ trasero 95 33
mordaza *Máq.-herr.* 149 35, 37
~ *Colegio* 260 47
~ del carril 202 12
~ de sujeción 149 36
~ inferior 163 65
~ para lucios 89 42
~ superior 163 66
mordazas de gas 140 68
~ para tubos 140 68
mordente 321 18
~ imperfecto 321 19
~ inferior 321 20
~ superior 321 19
mordido del grabado al agua fuerte 340 51
mordisco de rana 378 29
morena final 12 55
~ lateral 12 53
~ media 12 54
morón 13 42
morral 86 3
morrena final 12 55
~ lateral 12 53
~ media 12 54
morrión 329 60
morro 364 2
~ inferior 217 17
~ radar 231 18
~ superior 217 25
morsa 367 20
mortadela 96 7
mortero *Construc.* 123 27
~ *Quím.* 349 9
~ AM 50 de 120 mm 255 40
morueco 73 13
mosaico 338 37
~ de vidrio 260 69
mosca *Pein.* 34 17
~ *Pesca* 89 65
~ (azul) de la carne 358 18
~ de Hessen 80 40
~ del cerezo 80 18
~ del fruto del cerezo 80 18
~ del gusanillo del queso 81 15
~ del queso 81 15
~ del sueño 81 43
~ de pesca 358 6
~ de primavera 358 12
~ doméstica común 81 2
moscarda 358 18
moscardón 358 18
mosca taladradora 80 18
~ tsetsé 81 43
~ verde 358 13
moscón *Articul.* 358 18
~ *Árbol.* 371 53
mosqueta silvestre 373 26
mosquete 315 19
mosquetón 329 20, 46
mosquita doméstica 81 1

mosquito 358 16
~ de agalla 80 40
~ de Hessen 80 40
~ de la malaria 81 44
~ del paludismo 81 44
mostachón 97 37
mostaza 98 28
~ silvestre 61 18
mosto 93 1-5, 10
mostrador *Hab. niños* 47 28
~ *Café* 265 1
~ de entrega de los artículos 271 14
~ de información 250 9
~ del bar *Hotel* 267 54
~ del bar *Discont.* 317 9
~ del bar *Cabar.* 318 15
~ de venta 271 42, 61
~ frigorífico *Carnic.* 96 12
~ frigorífico *Comest.* 98 74
~ para los corredores 251 3
motacila 360 9
motalita 360 9
motera *Dorm.* 43 28
~ *Baño* 49 35
motivo 338 27
moto *Ciudad* 268 35
~ *Cicl., motor.* 290 24-28
motobomba *Parás.* 83 41
moto campera 189 16
motocicleta *Moto* 189 1
~ *Ciudad* 268 35
~ *Cicl., motor.* 290 24-28
~ con sidecar 189 53
~ de carreras 290 27
~ de gran cilindrada 189 31-58
~ todo terreno 189 16
motociclista 268 34
moto con sidecar 290 29
motocross 290 24-28
moto de carreras de línea aerodinámica 290 31
~ de carretera 189 31
~ de cuatro cilindros 189 49
~ del guía 290 12
~ grande 189 31
motón 221 105
motonave 223
moto pesada con carenado integral 189 43
motor *Aluniz.* 6 30
~ *Apar. hogar* 50 82
~ *Silvic.* 84 34
~ *Petról.* 145 12
~ *Sider* 148 64
~ *Tejido* 165 34
~ *Textil* 168 55
~ *Fotocomp.* 175 61
~ *Clisé* 178 24
~ *Abast. agua* 269 45
~ *Dep. aéreo* 288 35
motora *Playa* 280 13
~ *Remo* 283 2
~ *Barco a motor, esquí acuát.* 286 21-44
motor basculante 132 69
motor-cohete de separación delantera 235 60
~ de separación trasera 235 62
motor colector trifásico 164 35
~ de accionamiento 150 9
~ de arranque 190 44
~ de arranque eléctrico 212 30
~ de avance 177 43

~ de combustión interna 190
~ de corriente continua con velocidad regulable 150 9
~ de cuatro cilindros 230 34
~ de cuatro tiempos con cuatro cilindros refrigerados por aire 189 50
~ de dos cilindros con transmisión cardán 189 47
~ de dos tiempos *Jardín* 56 30
~ de dos tiempos *Dep.* 305 92
~ de dos tiempos refrigerado por aire 188 7
~ de explosión 190 2
~ de explosión de ocho cilindros en V con inyección de gasolina 190 1
~ de explosión monocilíndrico de dos tiempos 190 6
~ de impulsión *Avic.* 74 37
~ de impulsión *Modista* 103 9
~ de impulsión *Forja* 139 25
~ de impulsión *Clisé* 178 12, 28
~ de impulsión *Offset* 179 11
~ de impulsión *Cons. hidr.* 217 47
~ de la cámara desmontable 115 78
~ de la grúa 157 28
~ del ventilador 74 33
~ de metal precioso 237 42
~ de reserva 214 64
~ de sirga 216 29
~ de taladrar con broca de eje hueco 133 7
~ de tracción 211 6
~ de varios usos 109 13
~ Diesel *Motor* 190 4
~ Diesel *FFCC* 211 47; 212 25
~ Diesel *Barco* 223 73
~ Diesel auxiliar 209 19
~ Diesel con turbocompresor 212 51
~ Diesel de cinco cilindros en línea 190 3
~ Diesel de cuatro cilindros 65 44
~ Diesel de ocho cilindros 212 73
~ Diesel de seis cilindros 64 28
~ Diesel de tracción 209 4
~ Diesel o de gas natural 155 5
~ eléctrico *Casa* 38 59
~ eléctrico *Herr.* 138 2
~ eléctrico *Tejido* 166 18
~ eléctrico *Barco* 223 69
~ elevador 150 22
motoreta 188 56
motor fuera borda *Camping* 278 15
~ fuera borda *Remo* 283 7
~ fuera borda *Barco a motor, esquí acuát.* 286 21
~ fuera borda de carreras 286 23
~ hidráulico 64 65

navío de tres puentes **218** 51-60
náyade **327** 23
nectario peciolar **59** 18
negra *Juega* **276** 5
~ *Mús.* **320** 15
~ *Etnogr.* **354** 22
~ estrecha **175** 10
negrillo **371** 49
negrita **175** 3
negro *Ruleta* **275** 21
~ *Color* **343** 13
~ *Etnogr.* **354** 13
neguilla **61** 6
nematodo **80** 51
nemorosa **377** 1
nenúfar *Jardin* **51** 18
~ *Parque* **272** 56
~ *Planta* **378** 14
nepa **358** 4
Neptuno **4** 51
nereida **327** 23
nervado de refuerzo **200** 9
nervadura *Construc.* **123** 36
~ *Avión* **230** 46
~ *Arte* **335** 31
~ de la hoja **370** 29
~ del ala **358** 34
~ del radiador **126** 21
nervio *Anat.* **19** 33
~ *Arte* **335** 31
~ auditivo **17** 64
~ ciático mayor **18** 30
~ cubital **18** 29
~ de refuerzo **217** 78
~ femoral **18** 31
~ medial **370** 30
~ óptico *Anat.* **19** 51
~ óptico *Apic.* **77** 24
~ peroneo **18** 33
~ radical **18** 28
~ tibial **18** 32
~ torácico **18** 26
neuma **320** 3
neumático *Bicicl.* **187** 30
~ *Moto* **189** 26
~ *Autom.* **191** 15
~ *Parque* **273** 54
~ *Cicl., motor* **290** 19
~ de alta presión **187** 30
~ de camión **273** 19
~ de carreras **290** 19
~ de recambio **194** 4
~ de repuesto **290** 23
~ de una rueda direccional **64** 32
~ de una rueda motriz **64** 31
neumáticos **196** 27
neumático sin perfil **305** 86
~ todo terreno **194** 4
neuróptero **358** 12
neutrón **1** 30
~ absorbido **1** 53
~ de incidencia **1** 42
~ liberado **1** 39, 45, 52
~ que desintegra el núcleo atómico **1** 42
nevada *Meteor.* **9** 34
~ *Inv.* **304** 4
~ cubierta **8** 18
nevatilla **360** 9
nevazón **9** 34
névé **12** 48
nevera *Cocina* **39** 2
~ *Apart.* **46** 33
nevereta **360** 9
nevisca **9** 35
nicho **217** 70
~ bolardo **217** 10

~ de las plegarias **337** 14
~ sepulcral **331** 60
nidada de huevos de avestruz **359** 3
nido **359** 28
~ de abeja **171** 29
~ de invernación **80** 31
niebla **9** 31
~ alta **8** 4
nieve *Meteor.* **9** 34
~ *Inv.* **304** 24
~ *Etnogr.* **353** 5
~ amontonada **304** 5
~ fangosa **304** 30
~ fundida **304** 30
~ granulada **9** 35
nightclub **318** 1-33
nimboestrato **8** 10
ninfa *Apic.* **77** 30
~ *Parás.* **80** 25, 43
~ *Ins.* **81** 3, 21, 24
~ *Plaga* **82** 13, 21, 32
~ *Pesca* **89** 66
~ *Parque* **272** 2
~ *Ser fabul.* **327** 23
~ *Articul.* **358** 20
ninfálida **365** 1, 2, 5
niño del parvulario **48** 2
~ en edad preescolar **48** 33
~ gótico **306** 33
~ pequeño **28** 42
niqui **29** 47
níscalo **381** 23
~ falso **379** 13
níspero silvestre **374** 30
nivel *Mapa* **14** 48
~ *Font.* **126** 15
nivelación **14** 46
~ de bola **230** 12
niveladora **200** 19
~ del subsuelo **201** 1
nivelador compensador **112** 69
nivel cero **7** 6, 20
~ de agua *Font.* **126** 79
~ de agua *Bric.* **134** 29
~ de agua freática **269** 1
~ de aire **118** 55
~ de burbuja *Construc.* **118** 55
~ de burbuja *Font.* **126** 79
~ de burbuja *Bric.* **134** 29
~ de burbuja transversal **14** 61
~ de energía **1** 15
~ del agua *Puerto* **225** 37
~ del agua *Quím.* **349** 16
~ del agua del karst **13** 77
~ del agua subterránea **269** 42, 63
~ del combustible **234** 27
~ del mar *Geogr.* **11** 11
~ del mar *Petról.* **146** 39
~ enérgico del electrón **1** 27
noble **355** 44
nogal **59** 37-43
no idéntico **345** 12
nombre del barco **286** 7
~ del club **286** 8
~ del jugador **293** 36
nombres de estrellas **3** 9-48
nomenclatura **151** 32
nomeolvides **378** 26
nometoques **377** 11
nomparell **175** 23
nonio *Cerraj.* **140** 55
~ *Naveg.* **224** 5

~ de inclinación **14** 54
~ de rotación **14** 56
non plus ultra **175** 19
noray **217** 12
~ de doble cruz **217** 14
~ doble **217** 11
~ en forma de cruz **217** 13
noria gigante **308** 37
norte **4** 16
Noruega **252** 26
nota **320** 3-7, 12-19
~ a pie de página **185** 62
notación coral **320** 1
~ cuadrada **320** 1
~ medieval **320** 1-2
~ mensural **320** 2
~ musical **320**
~ musical **321**
nota marginal **185** 68
Noteamérica **14** 12
noticia breve **342** 50
~ deportiva **342** 61
~ diversa **342** 63
~ internacional **342** 62
~ nacional **342** 62
novia **332** 15
novillero **319** 2
novillo **319** 35
novio **332** 15-16, 16
nubarrón **7** 2
nube **8** 1-19
~ aborregada **8** 14, 15
~ baja **8** 1
~ baja y en capas **8** 3
~ de altura media **8** 8
~ de buen tiempo **8** 1
~ de cristales de hielo **8** 6
~ de cristales de hielo en forma de velo **8** 7
~ de formación vertical **8** 10
~ de forma lenticular **287** 19
~ de frente cálido **8** 5-12
~ de frente frío **8** 13-17
~ de lluvia **8** 10
~ en capas con precipitaciones en la parte superior **8** 9
~ enladrillada **8** 14
~ espesa y homogénea **8** 4
~ fluida **8** 1, 17
~ luminosa **7** 22
~ muy fluida **8** 2
nublado **9** 31
nublazón **9** 31
nubosidad **9** 20-24
nuboso **9** 23
nuca *Anat.* **16** 21
~ *Caballo* **72** 12
núcleo *Geogr.* **11** 5
~ *Central el.* **153** 17
~ antes de la fisión **1** 43
~ atómico **1** 2, 16, 29, 49
~ atómico nuevo **1** 51
~ atómico pesado **1** 35
~ de helio **1** 30-31
~ de la célula **357** 2
~ del reactor **259** 68
~ del tronco **120** 84
~ de plomo **326** 20
~ de plomo blando **87** 56
~ especial **301** 47
~ terrestre **11** 5
nudillo **19** 82
nudista **281** 16
nudo *Ropa* **31** 47
~ *Agric.* **68** 7
~ *Construc.* **122** 68

~ con ligamento de cabeza **171** 39
~ corredizo **300** 11
~ corredizo del descenso en rapel **300** 28
~ de la corbata **32** 42
~ de la malla **102** 23
~ del entramado **215** 37
nuégado **98** 81
nueva fuente de energía **155**
~ por cuatro **320** 40
~ por ocho **320** 39
nuez *Anat.* **19** 13
~ *Fruta* **59** 37-51, 41, 43
~ *Matad.* **95** 52
~ *Cerraj.* **140** 43
~ *Mús.* **323** 13
~ *Botán.* **370** 98
~ *Fruto merid.* **384** 60
~ de betel **380** 20
~ del Brasil **384** 53, 59
~ moscada **382** 35
numeración **85** 33
numerador **344** 15
número **344** 1-22
~ abstracto **344** 3
~ alto **275** 19
~ arábigo **344** 2
~ bajo **275** 22
~ cardinal **344** 5
~ cómico **307** 25
~ complejo **344** 14
~ concreto **344** 4
~ cuyo logaritmo se busca **345** 6
~ de andén **205** 4
~ de circo **307** 25
~ de copias **249** 35
~ de cuatro cifras **344** 3
~ de cuatro dígitos **344** 3
~ de cuatro guarismos **344** 3
~ de equilibrio **307** 44
~ de fabricación **187** 51
~ de folio del libro registro de acciones del banco **251** 14
~ de juegos **293** 38
~ de la bicicleta **187** 51
~ de la escena **310** 35
~ de lanzamiento **307** 43
~ de la página **185** 63
~ de la partida de la bala **163** 6
~ de la toma **310** 35
~ del desnudo **318** 27-32
~ del emplazamiento de la tienda **278** 42
~ del guardarropa **315** 7
~ de matrícula **286** 7
~ de orden **251** 13
~ de registro postal del periódico **342** 43
~ de reparación **195** 48
~ de salida *Hípica* **289** 33, 36
~ de salida *Cicl., motor.* **290** 28
~ de salida *Dep. inv.* **301** 37
~ de salida *Dep.* **305** 84
~ de serie **252** 36
~ de sets **293** 37
~ de velocidad **203** 37
~ entero **344** 10
~ fraccionario **344** 10
~ impar **344** 12
~ mixto **344** 10
~ negativo **344** 8
~ ordinal **344** 6

~ de cambio de velocidad de rotación de la broca de fresado 150 35
~ de cambio de velocidades 191 91
~ de cerrojo 203 55
~ de cierre 87 25
~ de cinco metros 282 8
~ de control 316 58
~ de desbloqueo de la varilla registradora 10 15
~ de diez metros 282 7
~ de elevación y descenso del cilindro 181 3
~ de embrague 188 32
~ de embrague de dos velocidades 188 12
~ de embrague y desembrague 166 8
~ de impresión 340 61
~ de introducción del papel 249 20
~ de la bomba 83 45
~ de la cisterna 49 17
~ del arenero 210 55
~ del embrague 189 28
~ del freno 187 66
~ del freno 166 62
~ del freno 56 38
~ del freno de mano 191 93
~ del gas 230 30
~ del mecanismo de avance 149 10
~ del pie 100 27
~ del silbato de vapor 210 51
~ del zoom Fotogr. 117 54
~ Cine 313 36
~ de mando Agric. 64 59
~ de mando Fotogr. 117 63
~ de mando Carret. 201 8
~ de mando FFAA 257 8
~ de mando Dep. aéreo 288 14
~ de mando de dirección 192 58
~ de mando del reductor 149 3
~ de mando para el accionamiento del alerón y del timón de profundidad 230 24
~ de maniobra 201 12
~ de maniobra para la marcha a la derecha o a la izquierda del husillo principal 149 11
~ de mano Carp. 132 55
~ Encuad. 183 31
~ Cine 313 11
~ de mezcla 230 31
~ de paro de la máquina 164 6, 32
~ de pedal 163 28
~ de potencia 257 9
~ de puesta en marcha 163 17
~ de rebobinado 114 6
~ de resorte para el disparador automático 115 15
~ de retorno 249 21
~ de señales 203 56
~ de servicio 126 19
~ de sujeción 132 67
~ de sujeción de la cinta 133 16
~ de tintaje de las placas de imprimir 249 50

~ de velocidad 65 35
~ de vía libre 203 58
~ flotante 65 43
~ levadora 325 32
~ liberadora del rodillo 249 24
~ oscilante 67 34
~ para cargar el arma 255 12
~ para descargar el volquete 214 35
~ para dirigir la cámara 240 29
~ para distribuir el aire caliente 191 87
~ para distribuir el aire frío 191 86
~ para el bloqueo del casquillo 149 28
~ para el mecanismo de viraje del husillo patrón 149 6
~ para el mecanismo inversor del sentido del avance 149 14
~ para el movimiento longitudinal y transversal 149 17
~ para el silbato 211 40
~ para graduar la ventilación 191 83
~ para la cabeza de afilado 157 46
~ para la tuerca partida del husillo principal 149 19
~ para los cambios de avance y de pasos de rosca 149 9
~ para parar 163 40
~ para regular el zoom 313 22
~ para regular la temperatura 191 84
~ para roscas normales y de paso empinado 149 4
~ que acciona los apagadores 325 23
~ registradora 10 7, 12, 21
~ reguladora 165 13
~ reguladora de alimentación 163 28
~ reguladora de la mezcla 288 16
~ selectora 192 47
~ selectora de la intesidad de la impresión 249 10
palancón 66 6
palangana Dent. 24 15
~ Rastro 309 65
palanganero 309 64
palangre 90 28
pala para el mantillo 55 14
~ para espárragos 45 77
~ para la nieve 304 23
~ para mover el fuego 137 2
~ para remover la tierra 56 2
~ quitanieves 304 9
palastro 140 36
palco Teatro 315 17, 18
~ Toros, rodeo 319 7
~ del circo 307 16
paleador 304 22
palendra 66 1
palenque 329 31
paleolítico 328 1-9
paleta Hortic. 55 36
~ Caza 88 9
~ Estación 206 32

~ Puerto 225 43
~ Pint., dib. 338 28
~ curva 91 38
~ de albañil 118 52
~ inferior del espéculo 23 14
~ móvil 315 36
~ para cortar el papel de la pared 128 41
~ para probar el café 98 72
~ plana 226 10
~ recta 91 40
paletilla Caballo 72 18
~ Matad. 95 30
~ con la mano 95 42
paleto 88 40
paletón 140 35
palillero 266 23
palillo de tambor Mús. 323 54
~ Etnogr. 354 19
palio 331 49
palma Caza 88 9
~ Fruto merid. 384 1, 3
palmacristi 380 14
palmada de sincronización 117 69
palma de coco 383 48
~ de la mano 19 71
~ indiana 383 48
palmer 149 62
palmera 97 30
~ con frutos 384 2
~ datilera 384 1
~ de aceite 383 54
palmeral 354 5
palmeta 334 41
~ de bufón 306 48
~ Verrier 52 1
palmilla 291 31
palmípeda 359 4, 5-10
palo Barco 219 1-9
~ Juego 276 38-45
~ Dep. inv. 302 39
~ alemán 276 42-45
~ de celosía 258 14
~ de goleta 220 15
~ de hockey 292 13
~ de la escoba 38 37
~ de la tienda 278 38
~ del cepillo 50 49
~ de mesana Barco 218 31; 219 8-9
~ de mesana 220 23, 24
~ de mimbre 136 15
~ de trinquete 218 42; 219 2-4
~ de una sola pieza 258 42; 259 6
paloma Ropa 32 25
~ An. dom. 73 33
paloma torcaz 359 23
palo mayor Barco 218 40; 219 5-7; 220 15, 22
~ mayor popel 220 30, 34
palometa 187 39
palomilla de arranque en frío 192 6
~ de gases 192 9
palomita 32 47; 33 11
palomo 73 33
palo trípode de celosía 258 41
palpo maxilar 358 26, 42
palto 31 35
palustre 118 52
palla 355 10
pamela 35 21
pampajarito 377 12

pámpana 78 4
pámpano 78 2
pan 97 2
~ ácimo 330 8
panadería 97 1-54
panadora 40 3
pan alargado 97 8
panal artificial 77 42
~ de miel 77 31-43
~ natural 77 60
panamá 35 16
pan blanco 97 9
~ blanco francés 97 12
pancarta de limitación de velocidad 203 19
~ electoral 263 13
pan casero 99 14
~ cateto Panad. 97 6
~ cateto Superm. 99 14
panceta 96 2
pancito 97 13
pan, clases 97 6-12
páncreas 20 44
pan de especias 97 51
~ de germen de trigo 97 48
~ de mezcla 97 8
~ de oro 183 5
~ de queso 99 40
~ de ranas 378 44
pandereta Discot. 317 27
~ Mús. 324 45
pandero Colegio 260 71
~ Parque 273 42
~ Mús. 324 45
pan de trigo y centeno 97 8
~ de Viena 97 9
pandora 322 21
pandorga Colegio 260 71
~ Parque 273 42
panecillo Mesa 45 21
~ Panad. 97 13, 13-16
~ Superm. 99 12
~ blanco 97 14
~ con adormidera 97 14
~ con comino 97 14
~ de canela 97 14
~ de centeno 97 16
~ de trigo 97 14
~ doble 97 15
~ salado 97 14
panel anterior levadizo 349 27
~, con los instrumentos de medición del control de ejecución 153 7
~ de anuncios 268 43
~ de conexión del micrófono 238 36
~ de conexión de los cables 239 3
~ de conjuntores 311 16
~ de control 177 60
~ de control del aire acondicionado 26 20
~ de control para los separadores 146 28
~ de enchufes para los módulos electrónicos 242 69
~ de exhibición 22 16
~ de interruptores 312 17
~ de la lumbrera 55 10
~ de la señal de aviso 203 24
~ de madera 266 37
~ de mando 311 17, 29
~ de mandos 177 36
~ de mando y de control 311 8

~ de manejo de la cámara 240 31
~ de registro con indicador del volumen respiratorio 26 28
~ divergente 90 13
~ giratorio de filtro coloreado 316 49
~ guía de ferrocarriles 204 16
~ indicador de las luces de navegación 224 29
~ indicador del nivel de la clase con indicadores individuales y contadores del total 242 3
~ lateral *Estar* 42 2
~ lateral *Apart.* 46 4
~ lateral *Granja* 62 25
~ lateral fijo 188 48
~ lateral reversible 260 35
~ luminoso 264 30
~ para el plano terminado 151 12
~ sinóptico 76 8
~ solar *Meteor.* 10 66
~ solar *Astron.* 234 53
~ triangular 203 13
pan empaquetado, clases 97 48-50
panera 45 20
pan eucarístico 332 28
panga *Barco* 221 78
~ *Salvamento* 228 17
~ *Remo* 283 9-16
pangolín 366 10
panícula *Agric.* 68 35
~ *Botán.* 370 69
~ *Planta* 378 46
pan inglés 97 10
~ integral 97 10, 48
~ moreno 97 6
~ negro de Westfalia 97 49
panó 71 44
panocha 68 36
panoja 68 36
pan redondo 97 6
~ redondo pequeño 97 7
pantaleón 325 1
pantalón 29 60; 33 3
~ bombacho *Ropa* 30 44
~ bombacho *Carnaval* 306 42
~ bombacho *Moda* 355 34
pantaloncillos 32 26
pantaloncito de jugar 29 21
pantalón con peto 29 40
~ corto *Ropa* 29 25; 33 25
~ corto *Jue. pelota* 291 57
~ corto de señora 31 39
~ de cinturilla en la rodilla 33 40
~ de cuero 29 32
~ de chica 29 49
~ de deporte 291 57
~ de escalada 300 7
~ de gimnasia 296 62
~ del chandal 33 29
~ del pijama 32 19
~ de media pierna 33 40
~ de piel 29 32
~ de salvamento 228 13
~ de trabillas 29 45
~ de verano 31 52
pantalones de montar blancos 289 5
pantalón largo de invierno 30 19

~ playero 280 22
~ vaquero 31 60; 33 22
pantalla *Astron.* 5 15
~ *Correo* 236 40
~ *Téc. ens.* 242 84
~ *Cine* 310 16; 312 11
~ *Cabar.* 318 21
~ absorbente 310 51
~ acústica *Electrón* 241 14
~ acústica *Rastro* 309 17
~ antideslumbrante 210 60
~ de ajuste 112 21
~ de enfoque 114 23
~ de la estufa 309 8
~ de la ventana 304 12
~ del videoteléfono 242 26
~ de plomo 259 70
~ de protección 157 59
~ de proyección *RTV* 238 32
~ de proyección *Colegio* 260 11
~ de proyección *Cine* 312 36
~ de radar 224 12
~ de vidrio de cristal 179 24
~ fluorescente de la imagen final 113 39
~ negra 310 51
~ para examinar la película 242 8
~ para impedir la vista del suelo 289 30
~ para mirar los huevos al trasluz 74 40
~ plegable protectora contra las llamaradas 259 15
~ protectora contra las llamaradas 259 27
~ terminal de datos 248 16
pantanero *Geogr.* 13 14-24
~ *Cons. hidr.* 217 57
pantano *Geogr.* 13 14-24
~ *Cons. hidr.* 217 57
~ alto 13 19
~ superficial 13 14
panteonero 331 22
panti 29 42
pantógrafo *Mapa* 14 65
~ *Fotocomp.* 175 58
~ *Tranv.* 197 2, 23
~ *Estación* 205 36
~ de toma de corriente 211 2
pantoque de proa 259 80
pantorrilla 16 53
pan trenzado 97 11
pantufla 101 25, 41
panul 57 27
pan, variedades 99 11
panza 95 39
~ de la red 90 30
pañal de un solo uso 28 22
~ de usar y tirar 28 22
paño 168 39
~ del altar 330 6, 36
~ de planchar 104 32
~ estéril 26 38
pañol *Barco* 223 57
~ *Salvamento* 227 26; 228 27
pañuelo de cuello *Ropa* 31 57; 32 40; 33 65
~ *Toros, rodeo* 319 38
~ del traje 33 10
papa 68 38, 40
papafigo 360 7
papagayo 363 1

papalina *Carnaval* 306 23
~ *Moda* 355 71
papaverácea 61 2
papel *Pesca* 89 22
~ *Estudio* 151 14
~ asfalto 153 48
~ bruto 173 29
~ de ampliación en color 116 51
~ de apresto 128 5
~ de cocina 40 1
~ de composición 174 34
~ de desecho fino 128 8
~ de envolver 98 46
~ de lija *Empapel.* 128 14
~ de lija *Pintor* 129 25
~ de lija *Bric.* 134 25
~ de lija *Torn.* 135 25
~ de protección 114 21
~ de registro 25 4; 27 29, 34, 40
papelera *Casa* 37 63
~ *Apart.* 46 25
~ *FFCC* 207 55
~ *Oficina* 248 45
~ *Ciudad* 268 5
~ *Parque* 272 43; 273 25
~ para los desperdicios 205 55
papelero 268 75
papeleta de voto 263 20
papel higiénico 49 11
~ indicador 128 16
~ metálico 153 44
~ moneda 252 29-39
~ para imprimir *Offset* 180 47
~ para imprimir *Tipogr.* 181 9
~ perforado 237 32
~ pintado 128 18
~ pintado del techo 128 53
papiliónida 358 52
papiro 383 64
paquete *Correo* 236 3
~ *Ciudad* 268 36
~ de algodón en rama 99 28
~ de bizcochos para perros 99 37
~ de cerveza 99 72
~ de cigarrillos 107 11
~ de cigarros 107 12
~ de doce cartones hecho con la hoja de plástico retractable 76 25
~ de especias 99 67
~ de huevos 99 50
~ de papel fotográfico 116 51
~ de pastas para sopas 99 65
~ de serrín para gatos 99 38
~ de tabaco 107 25
~ de tapones de algodón 99 30
~ de té 99 69
~ de un solo uso 93 28
~ de vendajes 21 4
~, pequeño 236 6
~ por expreso 204 2
~ postal 236 3
par *Construc.* 121 74, 80
~ *Ruleta* 275 20
para 252 28
parábola 347 14
parabrisas 191 21
~ abatible 255 97
~ del sidecar 189 58
~ panorámico 191 21

paracaídas *Meteor.* 10 57
~ *Dep. aéreo* 288 37
~ auxiliar *Astron.* 235 59
~ auxiliar *Dep. aéreo* 288 39
~ de frenado 257 24
~ del cable 287 7
~ de salvamento 235 60
paracaidismo 288 37-62
parachoques delantero con escudo de caucho 191 13
~ del sidecar 189 55
~ incorporado 193 33
parada *Mapa* 15 28
~ *Tranv.* 197 35
~ *Esgr.* 294 6
~ del tranvía 268 25
~ de taxis 268 63
~ en quinta 294 24
~ en sexta 294 8
~ en tercera 294 8
parafina 145 50, 60
paraguas *Vestib.* 41 15
~ *Estación* 205 12
~ plegable 41 12
paragüera 41 14
paragüero 41 14
paraíso 315 16
paralela 346 4
paralelas 296 2
~ asimétricas 297 3
paralelepípedo rectangular 347 36
paralelo *Mapa* 14 2
~ *Matem.* 345 21
paralelogramo 346 33-36
paramecio 357 9
paramento 330 2
páramo alto del pantano 13 19
~ bajo del pantano 13 14
paranza 86 9
parapeto *Puente* 215 70
~ *Caball.* 329 21
~ delantero 227 18
~ trasero 227 28
parar el motor 286 54
pararrayos *Casa* 38 30
~ estático *Avión* 230 51; 231 27
parásito 237 27
~ de la vid 80 20-27
~ del campo 80 37-55
~ del hombre 81 31-42
~ de los cereales 81 27
~ de los frutos 80 1-19
parásitos del jardín y del campo 80
parasol *Ciudad* 268 61
~ *Cine* 313 3, 39
pardal *Ave* 361 5
~ *Mamíf.* 368 6
~ *Planta ven.* 379 1
par de cilindros de sujeción 165 39
pardela 359 12
pared *Construc.* 120 29
~ *Tonel.* 130 23
~ *Jue. pelota* 291 69
~ central 215 68
~ cortada a pico 300 2
~ cortafuegos 121 9
~ de cristal *Casa* 37 16
~ de cristal *Discont.* 317 28
~ de hielo 300 14
~ de hormigón 123 1
~ de hormigón colado 119 7
~ de ladrillos *Construc.* 118 8

~ del dique **222** 32
~ del hogar **210** 61
~ del lavadero **118** 6
~ del maletero **191** 7
~ de los corrales **319** 11
~ de los toreros **319** 10
~ del parque **272** 31
~ del taller **120** 5
~ del toril **319** 11
~ del tramo final **217** 31
~ del tren de aterrizaje **231** 24
~ de pasajeros central **231** 25
~ de pasajeros trasera **231** 30
~ de persiana a corredera **245** 5
~ de quita y pon **118** 46
~ de salida para los toros muertos **319** 12
~ desmontable **118** 46
~ de tablas de madera **37** 34
~ de triunfo **337** 3
~ de vaivén **207** 18
~ doble **267** 27
~ doble plegable y giratoria **208** 7
~ elevadora **217** 31
~ en diagonal, doble **301** 68
~ exterior basculante **194** 35
~ giratoria de la pared lateral **213** 9
~ lateral corredera **194** 8
~ lateral pivotante **194** 12
~ levadiza *Forja* **139** 51
~ levadiza *Cons. hidr.* **217** 38
~ plegable **197** 14
~ plegable y giratoria **207** 39
~ posterior **193** 16, 20 **194** 11
~ principal *Vestíb.* **41** 25
~ principal *Arte* **333** 34
~, quinta **193** 16, 20
~ trasera *Autom.* **193** 3, 6
~ trasera *Puerto* **226** 18
~ vertical abierta **301** 67
~ vertical ciega **301** 66
~ vertical desplazada, doble **301** 70
puerto *Geogr.* **12** 47
~ *Puerto* **225**; **226**
~ de invierno **216** 14
~ de matrícula **286** 8
~ de protección **216** 14
~ franco **225** 2
~ pesquero **225** 56
~ petrolero *Petról.* **145** 74
~ petrolero *Puerto* **225** 61
puesto **86** 14-17
~ de agujas mecánico **203** 53
~ de carga a granel **226** 29
~ de claridad **226** 27
~ de control **316** 1
~ de control de maniobras **206** 44
~ de frutas **308** 53
~ de gasolina **196** 1-29
~ de información **237** 34
~ del comandante **235** 17
~ del conductor **64** 33
~ del fogonero **210** 39
~ del preparador **292** 56
~ de mando y navegación **224** 14

~ de manejo **177** 5
~ de máquinas **222** 33
~ de refrescos y bebidas **308** 3
~ de salchichas asadas **308** 32
~ de socorro *Estación* **204** 44
~ de socorro *Playa* **280** 46
~ de socorro *Feria* **308** 61
~ de tiro **305** 78
~ en alto **86** 14
puf **47** 8
púgil **299** 25
pugilato **299** 20-50
pujador **324** 47
pujamen **284** 40
pularda *Comest.* **98** 7
~ *Superm.* **99** 58
pulga del hombre **81** 42
pulgar **19** 64
pulgón *Plaga* **82** 39
~ *Articul.* **358** 13
~ alado **358** 15
~ áptero **358** 14
~ de la agalla del abeto **82** 38
~ lanígero **80** 32
pulidor **108** 51
pulidora **108** 42
pulimento **129** 28
~ del dibujo **129** 48
pulmón **18** 13; **20** 6-7
~ acuático **279** 19
pulmonaria **377** 7
pulmón derecho **20** 6
~, lóbulo superior **20** 7
pulpa **58** 24, 35, 58; **59** 6
~ dental **19** 32
pulpejo **19** 58, 75
pulpería **98** 1-87
púlpito *Igl.* **330** 19
~ *Arte* **337** 15
pulpo **278** 51
pulsador *FFCC* **203** 67
~ *Mús.* **323** 45
~ a presión **126** 37
~ automático **127** 20
~ de control **178** 15
~ de corte **100** 9
~ de la sección cassette **241** 3
~ del timbre para bajo voltaje **127** 2
~ eléctrico del hilo **166** 14
~ para el cambio de velocidad **134** 46
~ para la fecha y los segundos **110** 4
~ para la selección de las emisoras **309** 20
~ para las horas y los minutos **110** 3
~ y volante de control **168** 40
pulsatilla **375** 5
pulsera *Joya* **36** 3
~ *Reloj.* **110** 5
pulso **36** 3
pulverización de niebla **83** 8
~ de péndulo **83** 27
~ de superficie **83** 1
pulverizado **129** 28
pulverizador automático **181** 33
~ circular **83** 23
~ de discos **65** 82
~ de la ducha **49** 42
~ de mano **83** 24

~ de perfume *Dorm.* **43** 26
~ de perfume *Peluq.* **106** 21
~ de tinte **100** 35
~ de zapatos **50** 40
~ móvil **83** 38
~ para desinfectar la piel **22** 60
~ para el insecticida **56** 24
~ para humedecer la ropa **50** 13
~ portátil **83** 43
~ semitransportado **83** 47
pullman de ocho plazas **193** 1
punta *Agric.* **66** 4
~ *Caza* **88** 31
~ *Tornill.* **143** 23, 54
~ *Estudio* **151** 56
~ *Fotocomp.* **174** 17
~ *Bandera* **253** 10
~ *Heráld.* **254** 22-23
~ *Ballet* **314** 19
~ *Mús.* **326** 17
~ *Prehist.* **328** 4
~ con filete **143** 48
~ corrediza **151** 60
puntada al sesgo **171** 46
~ cruzada izquierda-derecha **171** 46
~ doble izquierda-derecha **171** 47
~ izquierda-derecha **171** 44
punta de contacto **149** 66
~ de corazón de las agujas **202** 24
~ de costillas **95** 16
~ de flecha arrojadiza **328** 2
~ de la espada **294** 27
~ de la flecha *Dep.* **305** 61
~ de la flecha *Etnogr.* **352** 29
~ delantera **300** 49
~ de lanza de bronce **328** 21
~ del anzuelo con púa **89** 80
~ del dedo **19** 79
~ del fuselaje **235** 20
~ del pisón **269** 61
~ de Paris *Construc.* **121** 95
~ de Paris *Tornill.* **143** 51
~ de penetración **269** 61
~ de vidrio **124** 24
~ esférica **143** 50
~ fija **135** 8
puntal *Agric.* **65** 8
~ *Construc.* **120** 27
~ *Puente* **215** 35
~ *Bomberos* **270** 12
~ *Gimn.* **295** 28
~ con muescas para la ventilación **55** 18
~ de arriostramiento **119** 14
~ de elevación **65** 29
~ de encabezamiento **119** 59
~ de la bodega **222** 61
~ delantero **303** 8
~ de la tienda **307** 13
~ del encofrado **119** 13
~ del extremo **119** 59
~ del toldo **221** 117
~ en diagonal **118** 25; **119** 51
~ longitudinal **230** 47, 57
~ para encofrados **119** 86
~ trasero **303** 9
punta metálica **166** 25
~ para cartón asfaltado **143** 55
~ rocosa **300** 9

~ seca para el grabado al agua fuerte **340** 16
punteado **321** 34
puntera **100** 58
~ de la bota **101** 16
~ reforzada **101** 40
puntería **86** 34
puntero **339** 15
puntilla **102** 18, 30
~ de tul **102** 15
~ para la piel **131** 22
puntillas (de) **295** 5
puntillo **320** 7
punto *Juego* **276** 32
~ *Mús.* **320** 3
~ *Escrit.* **342** 16
~ *Matem.* **346** 1, 1-23
~ cero **347** 4
~ ciego **19** 50
~ de adorno **102** 3
~ de alargamiento **320** 7
~ de arista **102** 9
~ de cadeneta **102** 2
~ de colcha **30** 17
~ de contacto **346** 49
~ de cordón **102** 8
~ de cruz **102** 5
~ de ejecución del penalty **291** 6
~ de encuentros **233** 11, 29
~ de escapulario **102** 9
~ de espiga **102** 7
~ de fantasía **102** 3
~ de festón **102** 6
~ de fijación a la popa para remolcar a un barco por la proa **221** 53
~ de inflexión **347** 21
~ de intersección **346** 1
~ de intersección de las cuerdas **118** 70
~ de lanzamiento **89** 34
~ del disparador **87** 11
~ de ligadura **171** 28
~ de ligamento de cabeza **171** 34
~ de ligamento de pie **171** 35
~ de mira *Caza* **87** 71
~ de mira *FFAA* **255** 3
~ de nudos **102** 13
~ de penalty **291** 6
~ de presión de las arterias **21** 14
~ de tallo **102** 4
~ de trama **178** 39
~ de tripa **171** 29
~ de zurcidura **102** 17
~ en el sistema de coordenadas **347** 8
~ equinoccial **3** 6-7
~ equinoccial de otoño **3** 7
~ equinoccial de primavera **3** 6
~ geodésico **15** 71
~ neutro **153** 22
~ por donde se pliega el ala **358** 35
puntos suspensivos **342** 29
punto tipográfico **175** 18
~ trigonométrico **14** 49; **15** 71
~ vernal **3** 6
~ y aparte **175** 15
~ y coma **342** 19
punzadora de la película **117** 95
punzón *Agric.* **65** 10, 68
~ *Orfebre* **108** 19, 31

retiración del amarillo **180** 6-7
~ del cyan **180** 8-9
~ del magenta **180** 10-11
~ del negro **180** 12-13
retocador **161** 19
~ efectuando un recubrimiento **182** 14
retoño **78** 3
~ enraizado **54** 17
retoque del rodillo **182** 12
retorta **349** 13
retraso del tren **205** 24
retrato **252** 31
retrete *Baño* **49** 12
~ *FFCC* **207** 16, 42; **211** 59
~ de la obra **118** 49
~ del personal **207** 82
retroceso **277** 4
retrocohete separado por etapas **234** 8, 37
retroproyector *Téc. ens.* **242** 6
~ *Colegio* **261** 8
retrovisor **189** 30
revelador **116** 10
~ de color **116** 10
~ de películas automático para las películas de scanner **177** 72
reventador **263** 15
reverberación **310** 59
reverso **252** 9
revés **293** 39
~ de la paletilla **95** 32
revestimiento *Dent.* **24** 32
~ *Vuelo sin motor* **287** 40
~ *Quím.* **350** 10
~ "acústico" de la pared **310** 15
~ aerodinámico del propulsor **234** 6
~ aislante de madera **10** 26
~ de aleación ligera enteramente reforzado **235** 11
~ de ataque móvil armado de fibras de carbono **235** 32
~ de chapa **188** 50
~ de cuero **291** 22
~ de espejos **267** 66
~ de la calzada **198** 5
~ de la pala **293** 47
~ de las paredes en madera **281** 19
~ del suelo **123** 41
~ del techo **317** 29
~ de material fluorescente **240** 19
~ de piedras **216** 55
~ exterior **122** 38
~ para el aislamiento del compartimiento de carga útil **235** 13
~ protector del frío **235** 15
revisión **237** 29
revisor **315** 10
revista **46** 20
~ de la sala de espera **22** 4
~ de moda **104** 4
~ de modas **271** 36
revistero **265** 8
revólver del objetivo **117** 46
~ de objetivos *Ópt.* **112** 11, 30
~ de objetivos *Cine* **313** 32
revoque, primera capa **123** 6
rey *Juego* **276** 8

~ *Dep.* **305** 7, 13
~ de armas **329** 75
reyezuelo listado **361** 10
~ sencillo **361** 10
rezno **380** 14
ría **289** 20
ribete *Ropa* **30** 13; **31** 7
~ *Cestero* **136** 17
~ de flores **30** 28
ribo **13** 4
ricino **380** 14
riego por aspersión **67**
riel de la cortina **44** 15
~ del parasol **313** 10
~ de regulación de la altura **49** 43
~ de tope **133** 11
~ guía *Punto* **167** 45
~ guía *Estación* **206** 38
~ transportador **133** 41
rienda *Caballo* **71** 33
~ *Coche* **186** 31
~ *Hípica* **289** 27
riendas **71** 33
rifle con depósito **87** 2
~ corto **86** 30
~ de caza de repetición automático **87** 2
~ de dos cañones superpuestos **87** 33
~ de repetición **87** 2
Rigel **3** 13
rikisha **353** 34
rincón de comer **44** 1-11
~ de la chimenea **267** 22
rinconera *Estar* **42** 26
~ *Tornill.* **143** 1
~ *Oficina* **246** 34
rincón neutral **299** 38
ring **299** 35
ringlera de heno segado **63** 23
rinoceronte **366** 25
~ africano **366** 25
riñonada **95** 7
riñón de la bóveda **336** 40
~ derecho **20** 28
~ : el caliz **20** 30
riñones **72** 30
riñón izquierdo **20** 30-31
~ : la pelvis **20** 31
río *Geogr.* **13** 61
~ *Mapa* **15** 76
~ *Río* **216** 31
~ *Parque* **272** 45
Río Celeste **3** 12
río de lava **11** 18
~ del cañón **13** 51
~ navegable **15** 45
riostra **118** 25; **119** 51; **120** 54; **121** 30
~ de alambre **119** 66
~ en forma de cruz **118** 88
río subterráneo **13** 83
ripidio **370** 77
ristre **329** 80
ristrel *Casa* **37** 9
~ *Construc.* **121** 31
rizador **105** 12
~ del tinte **105** 4
~ para el pelo **106** 26, 31
rizo *Pein.* **34** 3
~ *Barco* **219** 72
~ *Dep. aéreo* **288** 1
rizoma **58** 18
rizópodo **357** 1
robinia **371** 70
roble *Jardín* **51** 12
~ *Árbol* **371** 1

roblón *Tornill.* **143** 57-60
~ *Vela* **285** 52
roblonadura **143** 56
robot **273** 36
~ de cocina **40** 45
roca *Geogr.* **13** 25
~ *Alpin.* **300** 2
~ *Ser fabul.* **327** 38
~ calcárea **13** 71-83
~ de profundidad **11** 29
~ estratificada **13** 48
~ impermeable **12** 23
~ lunar **6** 15
rocalla *Geogr.* **13** 29
~ *Casa* **37** 40
~ *Jardín* **51** 6
~ *Arte* **336** 13
roca natural **356** 2
~ sedimentaria **12** 1; **13** 48
~ sólida **13** 70
rociadera *Hortic.* **55** 19
~ *Jardín* **56** 43
~ del césped **37** 43
roda *Barco* **218** 4; **221** 14, 83, 108
~ *Cons. naval* **222** 74
~ *Buque guerra* **258** 3
~ de bulbo **222** 74
rodaje **233** 2
~ en exteriores **310** 18
rodamiento **143** 69
~ de agujas **143** 75-76
~ de bolas **143** 69
roda recta **285** 40
~ vertical **285** 40
rodela **329** 57
rodeo **319** 34
rodete **34** 29
~ de pelo **34** 38
rodezno **91** 35
rodilla **16** 50
~ delantera **72** 22
rodillas (de) **295** 7
rodillera *Hípica* **289** 31
~ *Jue. pelota* **292** 9
~ *Dep. inv.* **303** 17
~ *Mús.* **325** 45
~ *Caball.* **329** 53
rodillo *Sider.* **148** 72
~ *Oficina* **249** 18
~ *Cicl., motor.* **290** 13
~ *Atlet.* **298** 17
~ aspirador del tamiz **173** 16
~ californiano **298** 16
~ con envoltura de muletón **50** 3
~ dador **181** 7
~ de apoyo del cable tractor **214** 49
~ de calandrar **173** 26
~ de cambio **312** 29
~ de caucho para comprimir el papel carbón **182** 8
~ de crescendo **326** 49
~ de discos de caucho **64** 82
~ de empapelador **128** 36
~ de entrada **64** 6
~ de excéntrica **166** 67
~ de frenada **138** 18
~ de gelatina **340** 12
~ de huecograbado copiado **182** 17
~ de impulsión **187** 73
~ de la calandria **173** 38
~ de la cinta **133** 18
~ del tren de poleas **214** 70
~ de piel de cordero **130** 31

~ de pintar **129** 11
~ de presión **243** 25
~ de recolección **64** 4
~ de secado **116** 49
~ de tintaje **249** 41
~ de transmisión **187** 9
~ de transporte **117** 34
~ distribuidor **249** 51
~ engomador **185** 33
~ entintador *Offset* **180** 21, 50, 60, 77
~ entintador *Tipogr.* **181** 18, 27
~ entintador *Oficina* **249** 52
~ entintador de cuero **340** 23
~ extendedor **181** 7
~ guía *Aserr.* **157** 5
~ guía *Textil* **168** 12
~ guía *Oficina* **249** 17
~ guía del cable **85** 39
~ guía del tejido **168** 5
~ guía para la viga niveladora **201** 4
~ huecograbado recubierto de papel carbón **182** 10
~ mojador **180** 23, 52, 61
~ para el papel pintado **128** 47
~ para empastar **184** 10
~ para granear **129** 13
~ para las junturas **128** 36
~ revelado **182** 13
~ tensor con brazo de extensión **133** 13
~ transportador **162** 11
~ transportador del papel **180** 4
rododendro **378** 1
rodón **132** 15
rodrigón *Huerto* **52** 31
~ *Vitic.* **78** 7
roedor **366** 12-19
rojo *Ruleta* **275** 24
~ *Juego* **276** 44
~ *Color* **343** 1
roldana **294** 29
~ de apoyo **270** 50
roleta **275** 1-33
rollito de nata **97** 17
rollizo *Construc.* **119** 13; **120** 2, 35
~ *Aserr.* **157** 30
rollo **157** 30
~ continuo de papel **173** 30, 45
~ de arcilla **339** 8
~ de cinta adhesiva **247** 29
~ de esparadrapo **26** 54
~ de hilo **89** 21
~ de la manguera **270** 54
~ de la película **312** 33
~ de madera **157** 30
~ de papel *Estudio* **151** 14
~ de papel *Oficina* **249** 33
~ de papel *Rastro* **309** 75
~ de papel acabado de extender **173** 35
~ de papel crepé **49** 11
~ de papel de desecho **128** 5
~ de película de 120 **114** 19
~ de plano **151** 10
~ de tela del batán **163** 47
romana **355** 7
romano **355** 11
rombo **346** 35
rombodecaedro **351** 7
romboedro **351** 22

~ del gas **156** 30
~ del hilo **170** 58
secador *Peluq.* **105** 33
~ *Fibra* **170** 38
secadora centrífuga vertical **179** 27
~ eléctrica **50** 28
~ múltiple para las fibras **169** 31
secador de cilindros **165** 53
~ de cilindros para el presecado **165** 50
~ de heno **63** 28
~ del pelo **106** 22
~ de películas **116** 23
~ eléctrico **105** 22
secante **346** 50
sección central del submarino **259** 55-74
~ cónica **347** 11-29
~ de anuncios **342** 69
~ de caja a mano **174** 1
~ de codificación **236** 35
~ de comer **44** 1-11
~ de cortinas **271** 66
~ de diagnóstico **195** 1-23
~ de la carne fresca **99** 51
~ de los productos de panadería y confitería **99** 9
~ del queso **99** 39
~ de mercería **271** 17
~ de noticias nacionales e internacionales **342** 62
~ deportiva **342** 57
~ de telas **271** 58
~ de transformación **23** 56
~ de verduras y frutas **99** 80
~ de vestidos de señora **271** 28
~ de videocodificación **236** 39
~ forestal **84** 2
~ política **342** 51
~ quirúrgica **26** 1-54
~ transversal de la bañera **281** 36
~ transversal de la popa **286** 34, 37, 41
~ transversal de la proa **286** 33, 36, 40
~ transversal normal de una carretera **200** 55
secoya **372** 69
secretaria de dirección **248** 31
~ del estudio **310** 39
~ del jefe **248** 31
~ del tren **209** 25, 27
secretario **263** 26
secreto **326** 31
~ **326** 12-14
~ de corredera **326** 12-14
sector circular **346** 54
secuoya **372** 69
sedal de algodón **90** 29
sedán de cuatro puertas **193** 4
~ de dos puertas **193** 25
segadora agavilladora **63** 19
~ -trilladora **63** 31
segmento **357** 25
~ circular **346** 52
~ de agujas **163** 70
~ de cuero **163** 69
~ dentado **249** 31
~ rectilíneo **346** 16
segunda base **292** 43
~ bordada **285** 20

~ docena **275** 26
~ etapa **234** 18
~ hilada **118** 68
~ mayor **321** 7
~ octava **321** 45
~ prensa húmeda **173** 20
segundo **299** 44
~ árbitro **293** 68
~ clasificador **172** 58
~ dedo **19** 53
~ de la cordada **300** 26
~ fieltro húmedo **173** 18
~ plato del sonido **117** 101
seguro **255** 14
seibó **266** 41
seibo **44** 20
seisillo **321** 23
seismo **11** 32-38
seis por cuatro **320** 35
~ por ocho **320** 34
seleccionador **168** 7
selección del formato del papel **249** 34
select **243** 42
selector **237** 42
~ de alcance **2** 4, 23
~ de banda alta y baja **114** 59
~ de entrada **238** 49
~ de entradas **241** 44
~ de escala **114** 59
~ de frecuencias **241** 9
~ de interlineado **249** 23
~ de la cinta **249** 11
~ de la velocidad de rotación **241** 29
~ de la zona de medida **112** 46
~ del modo de funcionamiento **117** 88
~ del tipo de medida **242** 74
~ de posición **50** 59
~ de programas *Apar. hogar* **50** 26
~ de programas *Audiovis.* **243** 39
~ de sensibilidad de la película **117** 18
~ de temperatura **50** 8
~ de toma de sonido **117** 13
~ de velocidades de la cinta **241** 62
~ VHF y UHF **240** 6
self-service **266** 45-78
sellado **236** 55-60
sello *Joya* **36** 40
~ *Correo* **236** 19, 20, 21, 61
~ de control **252** 35
~ de correos **236** 15
~ de impuestos **107** 26
~ de la letra **250** 24
~ del médico **22** 29
~ de recibo **236** 29
~ de sanidad **94** 24
~ de sobretasa **236** 58
~ postal **236** 61
semáforo *FFCC* **203** 1, 1-6
~ *Ciudad* **268** 52
~ eléctrico en posición de parada **203** 3
sembrador **63** 10
sembradora a chorrillo **63** 41; **65** 74
semejante **345** 22
sementera **63** 10-12
sementero **63** 11
sembreve **320** 13
semicírculo **346** 46
semiconserva **96** 25

semicopete **121** 16
semicorchea **320** 17
semicubierto **9** 22
semifusa **320** 19
semilla *Planta* **54** 3; **378** 5, 33, 34
~ *Hortal.* **57** 7
~ *Fruta* **58** 23, 37, 60; **59** 8
~ *Agric.* **63** 12; **68** 13, 15, 25
~ *Botán.* **370** 86
~ *Árbol* **371** 20
~ *Conif.* **372** 10, 15, 28, 37, 54, 60, 71
~ *Flor* **375** 25, 28
~ *Planta estim., trop.* **382** 20, 35, 45
~ *Planta ind.* **383** 15, 23, 24, 57
~ *Fruto merid.* **384** 10, 20, 21, 40, 47, 52, 58
~ con ala **372** 9
~ del castaño **371** 60
~ oleaginosa **383** 5
~ rodeada por el arilo **382** 34
semillero *Planta* **54** 2
~ *Silvic.* **84** 6
semimordente **321** 19
seminegra **175** 2
semirremolque **206** 59
sémola **98** 36
sen **380** 16
senda **15** 43
~ del jardín **51** 14
sendero cubierto de braba **272** 18
~ del huerto **52** 23
~ del parque **272** 38
senecio **61** 12
seno **346** 32
~ esfenoidal **17** 54
~ frontal **17** 55
sensor solar **10** 69
~ vertical del nivel del combustible **234** 27
sentido **16** 6
sentina de proa **259** 80
señal a cuadros indicando señales de parada **203** 30
~ de advertencia de "paso de peatones" **268** 29
~ de agujas **202** 19
~ de ajuste **340** 58
~ de alto **286** 53
~ de "autorización de salto" **203** 12
~ de aviso **203** 7-24
~ de aviso con indicación de velocidad **203** 18
~ de aviso con indicador de dirección **203** 20
~ de aviso con panel adicional para reducción de la distancia de frenado de más de 5 % **203** 12
~ de aviso de baliza a 100 m de distancia **203** 26
~ de aviso de baliza a 175 m de distancia **203** 27
~ de aviso de baliza a 250 m de distancia **203** 28
~ de aviso de baliza a menos de un 5 % de distancia de la vía de parada de la sección **203** 29
~ de aviso de balizas **203** 26-29

~ de aviso de parada próxima **203** 16
~ de aviso repetida **203** 17
~ de aviso sin brazo adicional en posición de parada próxima **203** 22
~ de aviso sin brazo adicional en posición de vía libre próxima **203** 23
~ de cambio con alumbrado eléctrico **202** 33
~ de cambio de vía *FFCC* **203** 45-52
~ de cambio de vía *Tranv.* **197** 38
~ de disminución de velocidad **203** 4
~ de disminución de velocidad próxima **203** 10
~ de indicación óptica **238** 30
~ de información del aeropuerto **233** 24-53
~ de la mano **268** 33
~ de la parada **268** 26
~ de limitación de señal velocidad **203** 36-44
~ de limitación de velocidad para una sección con limitación de velocidad permanente **203** 41
~ de llamada del práctico **253** 23
~ de "más deprisa" **286** 49
~ de parada para comunicación importante **253** 25
~ de "parar el motor" **286** 54
~ de partida **205** 47
~ de "prohibición de salto – aterrizar inmediatamente" **288** 54
~ de "prohibición de salto – reemprender el vuelo" **288** 53
~ de "ralentizar" **286** 50
~ de "regreso al embarcadero" **286** 55
~ de salida **253** 26
~ de sustitución **203** 6
~ de tempestad *Puerto* **225** 35
~ de tempestad *Playa* **280** 4
~ de tope **224** 78
~ de tráfico "parada de taxis" **268** 66
~ de un canal navegable **224** 84-102
~ de "velocidad en orden" **286** 51
~ de vía libre **203** 5
~ de vía libre próxima **203** 11
~ de viraje **286** 52
~ diurna **203** 36
~ eléctrica en posición de parada **203** 3
~ en aguas navegables **224** 68-83
~ en posición de parada **203** 1
~ en posición de parada próxima **203** 7
~ fija **185** 70
~ indicadora de las horas de baño **280** 5

~ de rinconera *Restaur.* 266 38
sofito *Construc.* 122 27
~ *Arte* 334 17
Sol 4 29, 36-41, 42
solana 37 70
solanácea 53 6
solano negro 379 5
solapa *Ropa* 31 23; 33 5
~ *Construc.* 122 100
~ de la sobrecubierta 185 38
~ del bolsillo 33 18
~ de seda 33 8
solario *Casa* 37 75
~ *Baños* 281 10
sol artificial 281 13
~ bemol mayor 320 68
soldadito de estaño 309 52
~ de plomo 309 52
soldado 359 19
soldador *Font.* 126 73
~ *Bric.* 134 19, 57
~ de gas propano 125 5
~ eléctrico *Elec.* 127 45
~ eléctrico *Soldadura* 142 2
~ instantáneo 134 58
~ tipo martillo 125 5
soldadura autógena 141
~ con gas inerte 142 33
~ eléctrica 142
~ por puntos 142 22
soldanella alpina 378 3
solera *Molino* 91 23
~ *Construc.* 118 58; 120 33
~ *Calle* 198 6
solería de ladrillos 123 7
solidificación de los hilos de poliamida 170 43
Soling 284 56
solitaria 81 35
sol mayor 320 56
~ menor 320 64
solo de órgano 326 45
solomillo 96 4
~ de cerdo 95 44
~ de vaca 95 24
sol sostenido menor 320 60
solsticio 3 8
~ de verano 3 8
solución 345 10
~ de goma 340 49
~ de sulfato de amonio 170 26
sombra 4 35
sombrajo 55 6
sombrerera 205 11
sombrerería 268 38
sombrerete *Bandera* 253 1
~ *Hongo* 381 4
~ de la chimenea 258 21, 59
~ del apoyo del cigüeñal 190 22
~ del convertidor 147 45
~ de zinc 122 102
sombrero 35 5
~ blando de fieltro 35 15
~ blando sueco 355 55
~ castoreño 319 20
~ con cinta de adorno 35 14
~ con encajes de adorno 35 7
~ con plumas 35 12
~ de artista 35 38
~ de caballero 35 22-40
~ de caza 86 5
~ de cazador 86 5
~ de copa 186 25
~ de copa alta 289 6

~ de copa hecho de tafetán de seda 35 36
~ de fibra de pita con cinta encordelada 35 13
~ de fieltro con borlas 35 24
~ de fieltro estilo ciudad 35 22
~ de hule 228 5
~ de jipijapa 35 16
~ de lana 29 57
~ del carpintero 120 13
~ de loden 35 23
~ del púlpito 330 21
~ del vaquero 319 37
~ de moer con plumas 35 6
~ de paja 35 35
~ de señora *Sombr.* 35 1-21
~ de señora *Vestíb.* 41 11
~ de sol 29 16
~ de tres picos 355 62
~ de verano de tela con bolsillito 35 37
~ de visón 35 18
~ flexible de alas anchas 35 38
~ florentino 35 21
~ metálico 326 35
~ playero 280 20
~ redondo del picador 319 20
~ tejano 319 37
~ tesalio 355 4
sombrilla *Ciudad* 268 61
~ *Parque* 272 58
~ *Arte* 337 22
~ *Invert.* 357 15
~ de jardín 37 48
sonajera 28 44
sonajero *Bebé* 28 44
~ *Carnaval* 306 40
~ de rumba 324 59
sonar de profundidad variable 259 40
sonda *Dent.* 24 46
~ *Pesca* 89 91
~ *Fotogr.* 114 63
~ *Naveg.* 224 58-67
~ sonda acanalada 26 41
~ acústica 224 61-67
~ de botón *Méd.* 22 53
~ de botón *Hosp.* 26 40
~ de la red 90 17
~ de llenado de combustible por gravedad 257 32
~ de mano 224 58
~ de medida *Fotogr.* 116 55
~ de medida *Astron.* 234 42
~ de temperatura 190 50
~ guía 23 21
sondaleza 224 60
~ para el reabastecimiento de combustible en vuelo 256 7
sondeo petrolífero 145 1-21
sonido de referencia 238 51
sopera *Comed.* 44 8
~ *Mesa* 45 15
soperte de fijación superior 192 73
soplado 162 28, 36
~ con la boca 162 38-47
~, primer 162 24
soplador 316 28
~ de vidrio 162 38
soplante *Energ. mod.* 155 14
~ *Papel* 172 4
~ *Avión* 232 34, 43
~ de aire primario 160 11

~ de la lámpara 179 22
~ del hogar de fuel-oil 199 35
~ del ventilador 165 4
~ móvil 165 2
soplete *Orfebre* 108 14
~ *Font.* 126 74
~ *Soldadura* 141 11, 28
~ *Quím.* 350 9
~ automático de mesa giratoria 148 39
~ de cilindro 108 16
~ de gas propano 125 5
~ de soldadura en atmósfera controlada 142 33
~ de soldar autógeno 130 14
~ equipado con boquilla de corte y carrito guía de la llama 141 19
soplón 316 28
soportal 274 9
soporte *Ópt.* 112 2
~ *Construc.* 121 83
~ *Font.* 126 6
~ *Fotocomp.* 175 50
~ *Offset* 179 20
~ *Mús.* 322 42
~ axial y radial 113 3
~ con los tubos inhaladores y el manómetro 26 29
~ de apoyo *Ópt.* 112 58
~ de apoyo *FFCC* 214 79
~ de cable metálico 155 44
~ de cañas 89 23
~ de columna 112 32
~ de datos 237 62-64
~ de declinación 113 6
~ de hombro *Fotogr.* 115 100
~ de hombro *Cine* 313 37
~ de la armazón 339 24
~ de la barra fija 296 9
~ de la bureta 350 22
~ de la herramienta de mano 135 5
~ de la lanza 64 62
~ de la mira 255 23, 37
~ de la motocicleta 189 21
~ de la palangana 309 67
~ del aparato de amplificación y de alimentación 238 3
~ de la plancha 178 35
~ de la quilla 235 7
~ del árbol 223 61
~ de las guías telefónicas 236 10
~ de la tecla 322 39
~ de la ventosa de centrado 111 22
~ del bastidor 133 43
~ del batán 166 53
~ del cable colgado 133 39
~ del cable portante 214 33, 58, 79
~ del canalón 122 32
~ del cojinete 177 61
~ del eje delantero 65 48
~ del enlucido 123 71
~ del enrejado paranieve 122 16
~ del esmerilador 163 41
~ del faro 187 6
~ del mecanismo 325 16
~ del micrófono 241 51
~ del momento de torsión 211 54

~ del motor 191 53
~ de los carriles guía 201 15
~ de los cuchillos 45 11
~ de los tubos 326 15
~ de los tubos capilares 23 42
~ de los tubos de ensayo *Papel* 173 8
~ de los tubos de ensayo *Quím.* 350 35
~ del pantógrafo 175 53
~ del pedal 325 42
~ del pie 298 2
~ del pincel 338 29
~ del platillo 324 52
~ del propulsor 234 21
~ del puente 177 13
~ del rollo 163 48
~ del sillín 187 24
~ del tabernáculo 330 43
~ del tubo flexible 27 47
~ de mesa de la cinta adhesiva 247 28
~ de pipetas para la fotometría 23 52
~ de proyección de las letras 111 46
~ de reja 235 12
~ de reproducción 115 92
~ de riego 62 28
~ de rodillo *Aserr.* 157 26
~ de rodillo *Autom.* 192 57
~ de tres puntos *Agric.* 64 45
~ de tres puntos *Quím.* 349 28
~ en forma de T 177 29
~ fijo 215 11
~ giratorio del bote 163 36
~ hidráulico 5 10
~ -motor 190 38
~ móvil *Hosp.* 27 22
~ móvil *Puente* 215 12
~ para brida 130 20
~ para el goteo intravenoso 26 9
~ para el papel 151 13
~ para la pierna 23 11
~ para las placas de rayos X 27 2
~ para las plumas de tinta china 151 37
~ para las telas 163 15
~ para la taladradora 134 54
~ para los dispositivos de infusión 25 11
~, para los resortes 167 38
~ para poner los pañales 28 4
~ para probarse los guantes 271 20
~ telescópico del tubo de rayos X 27 8
sorbete 35 36
sorda 88 83
sordina 323 10; 324 68
sortija 36 4
sortijero 108 27
sosa cáustica 169 3, 170 10
sosobre 220 32
sospechoso 264 32
sostén *Ropa* 32 1
~ *Cabar.* 318 29
~ de cuerpo 32 4
sostenido 320 50
sostén largo 32 4
sótano 37 1

tamiz *Papel* 173 14
~ *Quím.* 349 12
~ de graneado 340 24
~ de la paja 64 14
~ de la paja corta 64 17
~ giratorio 172 2
~ secador 173 23
tampón de tinta 22 30
~ entintador 340 22
tam-tam 354 14
tamúlica 341 11
tanaceto 380 9
tándem 186 50
tangana 278 19
tangente *Mús.* 322 43
~ *Matem.* 346 32, 48
tangona 216 16
tanque central del fuselaje 257 30
~ cisterna del mosto 78 16
~ de afinado de la nata 76 31
~ de agua *FFCC* 210 66
~ de agua *Aerop.* 233 22
~ de agua dulce 221 70; 223 79
~ de almacenamiento *Petról.* 145 72
~ de almacenamiento *Puerto* 225 72
~ de carburante para helicópteros 146 18
~ de combustible 221 80; 223 71
~ de forraje 221 73
~ de gasóleo 146 13
~ de gasolina 305 87
~ del ala 256 4
~ de la leche agria 76 42
~ de la leche cruda 76 5
~ de la leche descremada 76 17
~ de la leche esterilizada 76 16
~ de lastre de agua 223 78
~ del cuajo 76 48
~ de leche fresca 76 15
~ del estiércol 221 72
~ del fondo 222 38
~ del fuselaje 257 31
~ de materia plástica 79 4
~ de nata 76 19
~ de reserva para el agua salada 146 17
~ de suero 76 18
~ en el extremo del ala 256 30
~ esférico *Petról.* 145 73
~ esférico *Barco* 221 36
~ integrado en el ala 257 29
~ lateral 222 37
~ para disolver 172 37
~ para el agua potable 146 16
~ para el almacenamiento de cemento 146 15
tanques de oxígeno e hidrógeno 6 6
tanteador 293 71
tanto por ciento 345 7
tapa *Matad.* 95 13, 37
~ *Encuad.* 185 40
~ abovedada 38 48
~ armónica 323 24
~ con un tubo ajustado 350 52
~ de balancines 190 48
~ de cristal 269 56

~ de la cabeza de imprimir 249 30
~ de la cámara fotográfica 115 23
~ de la cazoleta 107 37
~ de la centrifuga 168 18
~ de la escotilla 222 65
~ de la pantalla de enfoque 114 23
~ del baño 178 37
~ del batán 166 6
~ del braserillo del incensario 332 40
~ del conmutador 211 18
~ del escotillón 316 33
~ del motor 191 8
~ del motor trasero 195 50
~ del registro 38 46
~ del retrete con una cubierta de felpa 49 14
~ de proyección 243 47
tapadera *Cocina* 40 13
~ *Orfebre* 108 9
~ *Electrón* 241 32
~ *Quím.* 350 31
~ de la caldera 92 45
~ del agujero de entrada 130 19
~ de la pipa 107 37
tapa de rosca 83 40
~ deslizante 179 2
~ de vacío 177 35
tapado 30 61
tapadora 76 27
tapa especial para el registro de los datos de toma de vistas 115 67
tapafuegos 255 18
tapa guardapolvo 187 57, 82
tapajuntas 123 64
tápalo 31 71
tapanca 71 7-11
tapa roscada 115 11
taparrabo 354 31
~ de cabellos humanos 352 38
tapa transparente 249 27
tapegua 86 20
tapete de juego 275 9
~ de la mesa 46 35
~ del juego de la ruleta 275 17
~ de piel 108 21
~ verde 275 17
~ verde 275 9
tapicería 134 59
tapioca 98 39
tapiro 366 26
tapir sudamericano 366 26
tapizado de un sillón 134 59
tapón *Riego* 67 36
~ *Quím.* 350 27
~ "bueno" 149 57
~ con llave 350 44
~ de aceptación 149 57
~ de la botella 93 27
~ del tubo 260 52
~ de rechazo 149 58
~ de vaciado del aceite 190 24
~ "malo" 149 58
~ octogonal 349 4
taquigrafía 342 13
taquilla 134 10
~ de apuestas 289 34
~ del cine 312 2
~ de venta de billetes 204 35
taquillero 204 39

tarima 78 20
~ para modelar 339 9
tarja *Caball.* 329 56
~ *Arte* 336 7
tarjeta 336 7
~ amarilla 291 63
~ de elector 263 19
~ de expulsión 291 63
~ de mesa 45 13
~ roja 291 63
tarjetero 249 19
tarlatana 185 20
tarraja 322 22; 324 5
tarraza 72 31
tarrito de la paleta 338 29
tarro de crema 99 27
~ de cuajada 76 45
~ de especia 39 32
~ de miel 77 63
tarso *Anat.* 17 26
~ *Ave* 362 4
tarta *Panad.* 97 22-24
~ *Superm.* 99 15
~ *Café* 265 4
~ de cerezas 97 22
~ de cerezas de la Selva Negra 97 24
~ de crema 97 24
~ de crema de mantequilla 97 24
~ de fresas 97 22
~ de frutas *Panad.* 97 22
~ de frutas *Superm.* 99 20
~ de grosellas 97 22
~ de melocotón 97 22
~ de nata 97 22
~ de queso 97 23
~ de ruibarbo 97 22
tártago 380 14
tartita 97 20
tas 125 23
~ de banco 140 14
tatetí 276 23-25
tatú 366 8
tatuaje 306 44
Tauro 4 54
tauromaquia 319
Taurus 3 25
taxi 268 64
taxis 233 32
tayacán 63 10
taza 24 15
~ de café *Comed.* 44 29
~ de café *Café* 265 19
~ de la pila bautismal 332 11
~ del retrete 49 13
~ inferior de la fuente 272 24
~ para niño 28 27
~ superior de la fuente 272 23
té *Superm.* 99 69
~ *Font.* 126 44
~ *Planta estim., trop.* 382 7, 9
teatro 315; 316
~ al aire libre 272 67
~ griego 334 44
teca con esporas 381 13
~ con esporas 381 12
teckel 70 39
~ de pelo corto 70 39
tecla 322 38, 49; 326 8
~ blanca 325 4
~ de anulación del tabulador 249 8
~ de cálculo del porcentaje 247 23

~ de cifra 247 18
~ de coma 247 19
~ de control 243 13, 48
~ de conversación 242 24
~ de ébano 325 5
~ de función 247 17
~ de interlineado 249 4
~ de la escucha de prueba 238 46
~ de la memoria 247 22
~ de la sección cassette 241 3
~ de las mayúsculas 249 3
~ del piano 325 4-5
~ del registro 324 42
~ del tabulador 249 7
~ de llamada 246 15
~ de mando 117 98
~ de manejo 246 19
~ de marcha adelante 249 73
~ de marcha atrás 249 73
~ de marfil 325 4
~ de margen 249 6
~ de número *Grandes alm.* 271 3
~ de número *Rastro* 309 76
~ de operación aritmética 247 21
~ de parada *Audiovis.* 243 43
~ de parada *Oficina* 249 73
~ de π para el cálculo de las longitudes de las circunferencias 247 24
~ de preescucha 238 46
~ de programa rápido 195 12
~ de puesta en marcha 243 41
~ de registro 326 39
~ de repetición de escena 243 42
~ de resultado 247 20
~ de selección de emisoras 241 4
~ de selección de emisoras de frecuencia modulada 241 38
~ de selección del canal 243 17
teclado *Fotocomp.* 174 32, 37; 176 2
~ *Correo* 236 44
~ *Teléf.-telégr.* 237 70
~ *Oficina* 249 2-6
~ *Mús.* 322 28; 324 40; 325 4-5, 48
~ de codificación 242 11
~ de la máquina de escribir 245 27
~ de mandos 261 45
~ de pulsadores 246 14
~ de pulsadores para las comunicaciones interiores 245 14
~ de selección del programa de análisis del ECG 25 50
~ (manual) inferior 322 47
~ (manual) superior 322 46
~ para introducir los datos en la computadora 238 13
~ para la instalación telefónica de servicio 238 14
~ -piano melódico 324 39
~ selector 242 25
tecla fijamayúsculas 249 5

~ de color **240** 36
~ de cortes ópticos **112** 38
~ de crema **99** 33
~ de desagüe **122** 29
~ de desagüe del agua filtrada **269** 12
~ de desagüe del agua sobrante **269** 20, 33
~ de drenaje **26** 47
~ de drenaje de cemento **200** 62
~ de embarque **226** 34
~ de embocadura **324** 71
~ de empalme **67** 28
~ de ensayo **350** 34
~ de entrada **122** 30
~ de entrada del gas **350** 2
~ de escape *Autom.* **191** 51
~ de escape *FFCC* **210** 25
~ de escape cuatro en uno **189** 51
~ de escape de gas con silencioso **209** 12
~ de escape de las turbinas **146** 5
~ de escape de los generadores **146** 2
~ de escape elevado *Bicicl.* **188** 15
~ de escape elevado *Moto* **189** 15
~ de extracción del fango **145** 13
~ de eyección **64** 37
~ de flash **176** 26
~ de hierro fundido **37** 14
~ de imágenes **240** 3
~ de inhalación **26** 2
~ de inyección **83** 35
~ de inyección de agua **281** 40
~ de inyección de aire *Sider.* **147** 68
~ de inyección de aire *Baños* **281** 41
~ de la bajada de aguas **37** 13; **38** 10
~ de la calefacción **55** 8
~ de la estufa **309** 5
~ de la fachada del órgano **326** 1-3
~ del agua *Hortic.* **55** 30
~ del agua *Avic.* **74** 7
~ del agua *Central el.* **152** 7
~ del aire **75** 28
~ de la leche **75** 27
~ de la pipa **107** 38
~ del chorro **83** 22
~ de lengüeta de metal **326** 17-22
~ del escobén *Cons. naval* **222** 76
~ del escobén *Buque guerra* **258** 54
~ del gas *Parás.* **83** 14, 35
~ del gas *Soldadura* **141** 9
~ del humo **210** 8
~ del microscopio **113** 31-39
~ del objetivo **115** 3
~ del oxígeno **141** 10
~ del pozo **12** 25
~ del producto de decoloración **105** 3
~ del recalentador **210** 17
~ del telescopio **113** 8
~ de luz fluorescente **271** 23
~ de luz relámpago **176** 26
~ de llegada **65** 77

~ de medida **196** 14
~ de neón **271** 23
~ de órgano **326** 17-35
~ de pasta dentífrica **99** 31
~ de pedal **326** 3
~ de pegamento **260** 51
~ de perforación **145** 6
~ de pintura al óleo **338** 11
~ de Pitot **256** 11; **257** 1
~ de poliéster **67** 26
~ de pomada **22** 47
~ de presión **217** 50
~ de prolongación **50** 70
~ de pulsación **75** 29
~ de rayos catódicos **242** 40
~ de rayos X **27** 7, 18
~ de reacción **192** 65
~ de rellenar **96** 50
~ de resina sintética **130** 26
~ de retorno **38** 79
~ de salida del gas del tragante **147** 13
~ de secado **350** 43
~ de soporte **64** 51
~ de soporte de las púas **64** 53
~ de succión *Meteor.* **10** 37
~ de succión *Apar. hogar* **50** 75
~ de succión *Teatro* **316** 52
~ de succión *Quím.* **349** 21
~ de televisión **240** 3
~ de terracota **269** 35
~ de unión **350** 5
~ de un registro **326** 16
~ de vaciado **126** 17
~ de vacío **75** 29
~ de vidriero **162** 39
~ digestivo **77** 15-19
~ elevador **145** 24
~ emulsionante **192** 10
~ en U **349** 2
~ envolvente **269** 64
~ en Y **350** 56
~ extractor del aire **133** 40
~ flexible *Hosp.* **27** 47
~ flexible *Bomberos* **270** 30
~ flexible de la máquina pulmonar **279** 20
~ flexible de vacío **74** 50
~ fluorescente *Baño* **49** 32
~ fluorescente *Elec.* **127** 61
~ giratorio **172** 10
~ horizontal **119** 48
~ indicador de la sintonización **309** 18
~ inferior del cuadro **187** 17
~ labial abierto de madera **326** 31-33
~ labial tapado **326** 34
~ lanzatorpedos **258** 78; **259** 79
~ lanzatorpedos de defensa antisubmarina **258** 33; **259** 36
~ metálico **324** 78
~ monocular **111** 18
~ oscilante con surtidores **67** 1
~ para echar la arena **210** 19
~ para el goteo intravenoso **25** 13
~ para el refrigerante **149** 25
~ para la diseminación de cebo envenenado **83** 31
~ para la fijación del pie **23** 10

~ perpendicular a la pared **119** 49
~ polínico **370** 66
~ pulverizador **172** 72
~ quitalimaduras **140** 17
~ respiratorio *Hosp.* **27** 37
~ respiratorio *Surf, Buceo* **279** 11
~ respiratorio *Playa* **280** 39
~ sifón **10** 43
~ snorkel **259** 72, 90
~ soporte del sillín **187** 18
~ superior del cuadro **187** 16
~ telescópico **65** 77
~ transformador **27** 19
~ transporte de la mantequilla **76** 34
~ vertical *Papel* **173** 12
~ vertical *Astron.* **234** 25
~ vertical *Bomberos* **270** 26
~ vertical de revestimiento **145** 18
tubuladura de ensacado **83** 55
~ de inflado **196** 21
~ del aire de escape **142** 16
~ de propulsión **67** 19
tucán **363** 6
tucano **363** 6
tuco **19** 28-37
tucucho **308** 13
tuche **366** 19
tuerca *Bicicl.* **187** 53
~ *Gimn.* **297** 32
~ corona **143** 24
~ de ajuste **143** 35
~ de inclinación **14** 55
~ del pie **115** 30
~ de orejas **143** 42
~ de palometa **187** 39
~ de rotación **14** 57
~ de seguridad **187** 64
~ hexagonal **143** 18
~ hexagonal con entalladuras **143** 24, 77
~ redonda con agujero **143** 35
tulipanero **374** 1
tulipero **374** 1
tumba *Silvic.* **84** 4-14
~ *Igl.* **331** 23
~ *Arte* **337** 16
~ con figura yacente **335** 53
~ de niño **331** 29
~ de soldado **331** 32
~ de urna **331** 30
~ excavada en la roca **333** 38
~ familiar **331** 27
~ megalítica **328** 16
~ real **333** 1
~ -urna **328** 39
tumbo **53** 2
tumbona *Casa* **37** 47
~ *Jardín* **51** 2
~ *Balneario* **274** 13
~ *Camping* **278** 59
~ *Baños* **281** 5
túmulo **328** 16
tundra **9** 57
túnel *Mapa* **15** 70
~ *FFCC* **214** 6
~ de acceso al andén **204** 23
~ de entrada **353** 6
~ de entrada a la terminal de equipajes **233** 6
~ de esclusas **235** 71

~ de espera de los artistas **307** 12
~ de la jaula de fieras **307** 51
~ del árbol de la hélice **223** 66
~ del metro **198** 29
~ de los cables **152** 20
~ de plástico **55** 40
~ por debajo del puerto **225** 55
tuner **317** 22
túnica *Ropa* **30** 29; **31** 61
~ *Moda* **355** 12
~ interior de lino **355** 5
tupé de la frente **355** 8
tupia *Río* **216** 49
~ *Cons. hidr.* **217** 57-64
turba **55** 31
~ de aliso **13** 18
~ de juncos y cañas **13** 17
~ del pantano **13** 17
~ de musgo **13** 20, 22
turbante **353** 46
turbina *Riego* **67** 20
~ *Energ. nucl.* **154** 33
~ *Avión* **232** 40, 47
~ de alta o baja presión **259** 62
~ de alta presión **232** 53
~ de baja presión **232** 54
~ de gas **209** 9
~ de gas auxiliar **231** 33
~ del mecanismo propulsor **232** 17
~ de vapor *Central el.* **153** 23-30
~ de vapor *Energ. nucl.* **154** 14, 46, 52
~ de vapor con alternador **152** 23
~ motor soplante **232** 38
~ reversible **155** 39
turboalternador **259** 58
~ a vapor **153** 23-30
turbogrupo con silencioso **209** 24
turbohélice **256** 16
turbopropulsor *Avión* **231** 5; **232** 30, 51
~ *FFAA* **256** 16
turborreactor *Avión* **232** 17, 24, 33-50
~ *FFAA* **257** 15
~ con el mecanismo propulsor **231** 26
turbosoplador refrigerador de la película **312** 34
túrdido **360** 3; **361** 13-17
tureca **86** 43
turíbulo para incensaciones litúrgicas **332** 38
turismo *Autom.* **191** 1-56
~ *Taller* **195** 34
~ de cuatro puertas **193** 4
~ de dos puertas **193** 25
~ de tres puertas **193** 18
turno **308** 44
turpu **380** 5
Turquía **253** 19
turrón de nueces **98** 81
turrumote **11** 32-38
tusa **72** 14
tusilago **380** 8
tutú **314** 29
tuya **372** 39
tuyú **359** 2

# Index

## Ordering
In this index the entries are ordered as follows:
1. Entries consisting of single words, e.g.: 'hair'.
2. Entries consisting of noun + adjective. Within this category the adjectives are entered alphabetically, e.g. 'hair, bobbed' is followed by 'hair, closely-cropped'.
Where adjective and noun are regarded as elements of a single lexical item, they are not inverted, e.g.: 'blue spruce', not 'spruce, blue'.
3. Entries consisting of other phrases, e.g. 'hair curler', 'ham on the bone', are alphabetized as headwords.
Where a whole phrase makes the meaning or use of a headword highly specific, the whole phrase is entered alphabetically. For example 'ham on the bone' follows 'hammock'.

## References
The numbers in bold type refer to the sections in which the word may be found, and those in normal type refer to the items named in the pictures. Homonyms, and in some cases uses of the same word in different fields, are distinguished by section headings (in italics), some of which are abbreviated, to help to identify at a glance the field required. In most cases the full form referred to by the abbreviations will be obvious. Those which are not are explained in the following list:

| | | | |
|---|---|---|---|
| *Agr.* | Agriculture/Agricultural | *Hydr. Eng.* | Hydraulic Engineering |
| *Alp. Plants* | Alpine Plants | *Impl.* | Implements |
| *Art. Studio* | Artist's Studio | *Inf. Tech.* | Information Technology |
| *Bldg.* | Building | *Intern. Combust. Eng.* | Internal Combustion Engine |
| *Carp.* | Carpenter | *Moon L.* | Moon Landing |
| *Cement Wks.* | Cement Works | *Music Not.* | Musical Notation |
| *Cost.* | Costumes | *Overh. Irrign.* | Overhead Irrigation |
| *Cyc.* | Cycle | *Platem.* | Platemaking |
| *Decid.* | Deciduous | *Plant Propagn.* | Propagation of Plants |
| *D.I.Y.* | Do-it-yourself | *Rm.* | Room |
| *Dom. Anim.* | Domestic Animals | *Sp.* | Sports |
| *Equest.* | Equestrian Sport | *Text.* | Textile[s] |
| *Gdn.* | Garden | *Veg.* | Vegetable[s] |

## A

Aaron's rod 376 9
abacus 309 77
abacus *Art* 334 20
abattoir 94
abdomen *Man* 16 35-37, 36
abdomen *Bees* 77 10-19
abdomen *Forest Pests* 82 9
abdomen, lower ~ 16 37
abdomen, upper ~ 16 35
abductor hallucis 18 49
abductor of the hallux 18 49
aberdevine 361 8
aborigine, Australian ~ 352 37
abrasion platform 13 31
abrasive wheel combination 111 28, 35
abscissa 347 9
abseiling 300 28-30
abseil piton 300 39
abseil sling 300 28
absinth 380 4
absorber attachment 27 44
absorption dynamometer 143 97-107
absorption muffler 190 16
absorption silencer 190 16
abutment *Bridges* 215 27, 29, 45
abutment *Art* 336 20
abutment pier 215 29
acanthus 334 25
acceleration lane 15 16
acceleration rocket 234 22, 48
accelerator 191 46
accelerator lock 85 17
accelerator pedal 191 46, 94
accelerometer 230 10
accent, acute ~ 342 30

accent, circumflex ~ 342 32
accent, grave ~ 342 31
accent, strong ~ 321 27
accents 342 30-35
acceptance 250 12, 23
access balcony 37 72-76
access flap 6 21, 25
accessories 115 43-105
accessory shoe 114 4; 115 20
accessory shop 196 24
access ramp 199 15
acciaccatura 321 15
accipiters 362 10-13
accolade 329 66
accommodation 146 33
accommodation bureau 204 28
accommodation ladder 221 98
accomodation module 146 33
accompaniment side 324 43
accompaniment string 324 25
accordion 324 36
account, private ~ 250 4
accounting machine 236 26
accumulator 309 41
accumulator *Theatre* 316 55
accumulator railcar 211 55
accuracy jump 288 55
acerate 370 34
acerose 370 34
acerous 370 34
acetylene connection 141 31
acetylene control 141 32
acetylene cylinder 141 2, 22
achene 58 23
achievement 254 1-6
achievement, marital ~ 254 10-13
achievement of arms 254 1-6
Achilles' tendon 18 48
acicular 370 34

acid container 350 62
Ackermann steering system 85 31, 37
acolyte 331 45
aconite 379 1
acorn 371 4
acorns 276 42
acrobat 307 47
Acropolis 334 1-7
acroter 334 34
acroterion 334 34
acroterium 334 34
acting area light 316 16
acting area spotlight 316 16
actinia 369 20
Actinophrys 357 7
action 326 6-16
action lever 325 32
activated blade attachment 84 33
actor 316 37
actress 316 38
actuating transistor 195 19
acuity projector 111 47
acute 342 30
ad 342 56
Adam's apple 19 13
adapter 112 55
adapter, four-socket ~ 127 8
adapter, four-way ~ 127 8
adapter ring 115 82
adapter unit 242 34
adders 364 40-41
adding 344 23
adding and subtracting machine 309 74
adding mechanism 271 9
addition 344 23
address 236 42
address display 236 41
addressing machine, transfer-type ~ 245 7

address label 236 4
address system, ship's ~ 224 30
A-deck 223 28-30
adhesion railcar 214 1
adhesive, hot ~ 249 61
adhesive binder *Bookbind.* 184 1
adhesive binder *Office* 249 61
adhesive tape dispenser 247 27
adhesive tape dispenser, roller-type ~ 247 28
adhesive tape holder 247 28
adjusting cone 187 58
adjusting equipment 148 61-65
adjusting knob 116 54
adjusting nut 143 35
adjusting screw *Bldg. Site* 119 79
adjusting screw *Mach. Parts etc.* 143 107
adjusting screw *Inf. Tech.* 242 78
adjusting spindle 226 51
adjusting washer 187 55
adjustment, circular ~ 14 62
adjustment, coarse ~ 112 4
adjustment, fine ~ *Optic. Instr.* 112 5
adjustment, fine ~ *Photog.* 116 33
adjustment, fine ~ *Joiner* 133 36
adjustment, fine ~ *Drawing Off.* 151 66
adjustment knob 11 41
administration area 5 17
administration building *Coal* 144 18
administration building

anchor, stocked ~ 222 79; 286
15
anchor, stockless ~ 222 78;
258 5; 286 17
anchorage 216 13
anchor cable 218 18; 222 77;
223 50; 227 12
anchor capstan 258 6
anchor hawser 218 18
anchor rib 287 32
anchor rope 218 18
anchors 286 15-18
anchor winch 259 82
ancillary brake valve 211
23
Andromeda 3 24
anemometer 10 28
anemone 375 5; 377 1
aneroid barometer 10 4
aneroid box 10 6
aneroid capsule 10 6
angiographic examination
table 27 26
angiography room 27 12
angle *Mach. Parts etc.* 143 1
angle *Maths.* 346 1-23; 346
8-13, 8, 55
angle, acute ~ 346 10
angle, adjacent ~ 346 14
angle, alternate ~ 346 10
angle, circumferential ~ 346
56
angle, exterior ~ 346 26
angle, interior ~ 346 26
angle, obtuse ~ 346 11
angle, straight ~ 346 13,9-15
angle brace 118 25; 119 63;
121 57
angle deck 259 12
angle iron 143 1
angle of departure 87 75
angle of descent 87 78
angle of dip 12 3
angle of elevation 87 76
angle of rotation 351 33
angle of the mouth 16 14; 19
19
angle shears 125 2
angle symbol 345 23
angle tie 118 25; 121 57
angle tongs 137 37
angle tower 329 14, 17
angling 89 20-94
angling fence 133 19
Angora cat 73 17
Angoumois grain moth 81 29
Angoumois grain moth
caterpillar 81 30
Angoumois moth 81 29
Anguidae 364 37
animal, bovine ~ 73 1
animal, cloven-hoofed ~ 73 9
animal, horned ~ 73 1
animal, inflatable ~ 280 33
animal, rubber ~ 280 33
animal, toy ~ 46 13; 47 6
animal, wild ~ 307 56
animal enclosure 272 49
animal house 356 10
animals, domestic ~ 73 18-36
animals, fabulous ~ 327 1-61
animals, multicellular ~ 357
13-39
animals, one-celled ~ 357
1-12
animals, single-celled ~ 357
1-12
animals, unicellular ~ 357
1-12
ankle guard 291 33
ankle sock, children's ~ 29 30
annealing lehr 162 18
annelid 357 20

annexe 331 13
annuity 251 11-19
annulus 346 57
Annunciation lily 60 12
anode, copper ~ 178 5
anode rod 178 5
anorak *Child. Clothes* 29 62
anorak *Mountain.* 300 6
anorak hood 300 19
Anseres 359 15-17
ant 358 21-22
Antarctica 14 18
Antarctic Circumpolar Drift
14 44
Antarctic Continent 14 18
Antarctic Ocean 14 22
antelope 367 5
antenna *Meteorol. Instr.* 10
59, 68
antenna *Forest Pests* 82 3
antenna *Air Force* 256 17
antenna *Warships* 258 16, 46;
259 7, 47, 89
antenna *Airsports* 288 20,
88
antenna *Articulates* 358 27,
53
antenna, maxillary ~ 358 42
antenna, trichotomous ~ 81 5
antenna down-lead 223 4
antenna lead-in 223 4
antenna mast 259 6
antependium 330 20
anther 372 35
anthozoan 357 17
anthropoid apes 368 14-16
anthropoids 368 14-16
anti-aircraft gun 258 73
anti-aircraft gun, automatic
~ 259 34
anti-aircraft machine gun
255 63
anti-aircraft missile launcher
258 32; 259 5, 20
anti-aircraft rocket launcher
258 32; 259 5, 20
anticline 12 16, 27
anticlinorium 12 20
anticollision light 230 64
anticyclone 9 6
antifriction bearing 143 69
anti-frost layer 198 1; 200 60
antimacassar 207 48
anti-mist windscreen 189 46
anti-mist windshield 189 46
anti-radiation screen 154 74
anti-rolling system 224 26
antirrhinum 51 32
anti set-off apparatus 181 10
anti set-off spray 181 10
anti-skate control 241 25
anti-skid brake switch 211 33
anti-slosh baffle 234 13
anti-submarine missile
launcher 258 30, 50
anti-submarine rocket
launcher 258 30, 50
anti-submarine torpedo tube
258 33
anti-syphon trap *Bathrm. etc.*
49 27
anti-syphon trap *Plumb. etc.*
126 26
anti-tank rocket launcher
255 25
anti-tank tank 255 88
anti-torque rotor 232 14
anti-vortex system 234 11
antler, palmate ~ 88 40
antler, royal ~ 88 8
antler, surroyal ~ 88 9
antlers 88 5-11, 29-31
anurans 364 23-26

anus 20 62
anvil *Plumb.* 125 22
anvil *Blacksm.* 137 11, 11-16;
138 33
anvil *Forging* 139 17, 31, 40
anvil *Office* 247 5
anvil, clockmaker's ~ 109 7
aorta 18 10; 20 54
aorta, abdominal ~ 18 16
Apache girl 306 9
apartment 37 64-68, 69-71;
46
apartment, ladies' ~ 329 10
apartment building 37 72-76
apartment building, high-rise
~ 37 82
apartment building,
multistory ~ 37 77-81
apartment house 37 72-76
apartment house, high-rise ~
37 82
apartment house, multistory
~ 37 77-81
apatite 351 20
aperture 115 62, 63
aperture control, automatic ~
117 20
aperture control ring 115 5;
117 4
aperture ring 115 5; 117 4
aperture scale 115 56
aperture setting 117 4
aperture-setting control 114
34
aperture-setting ring 115 5;
117 4
aperture-stop slide 112 16
apex *Hunt.* 87 77
apex *Airsports* 288 47
aphid 80 32; 358 13
aphid, winged ~ 82 39; 358 15
aphid, wingless ~ 358 14
apiarist 77 57
apiary 77 56
apiculture 77
à pointe 314 19
Apollo booster 234 1, 2
Apollo service module 234 56
Apollo space capsule 6 9
Apollo spacecraft 6 1
apostrophe 342 22
apparatus, auxiliary ~ 296
12-21; 297 7-14
apparatus exercises 297 15-32
apparatus gymnastics 296;
297
appendix 20 18
appendix, vermiform ~ 20 18
Appenzell dulcimer 322 35
apple 58 56; 99 86; 370 102
apple blossom 58 54
appleblossom weevil 80 10
apple core 58 59
apple pip 58 60
apple skin 58 57
apple stalk 58 61
apple tree 58 51, 52
appliance room 270 1
appliqué 29 20
appoggiatura 321 14, 15
appointments book 22 11
appointments diary 246 8
approach 203 34
approach sign 203 26, 27, 28,
29
approach signs 203 26-29
apricot 59 35
apricot blossom 59 34
apricot branch, flowering ~
59 33
apricot flower 59 34
apricot leaf 59 36
apricot tree 59 33-36

apron *Mach. Tools* 149 16
apron *Electrotyp. etc.* 178 9
apron *Airport* 233 3
apron *Theatre* 316 25
apron, butcher's ~ 96 39
apron, composition ~ 164 16
apron, frilled ~ 31 33
apron, leather ~ *Arc Weld.*
142 11
apron, leather ~ *Cotton Spin.*
164 16
apron taxiway 233 4
apse 334 64; 335 5
aquafer 12 22; 269 2, 38
aqualung 279 19
aquarium 356 14, 19
Aquarius 4 63
aquatint 340 14-24
aqueduct 334 53
aquifer 12 22; 269 2, 38
Aquila 3 9
aquilegia 60 10
arabesque *Free Exerc.* 295 30
arabesque *Ballet* 314 18
arachnids 358 40-47
araucaria 53 16
arbor 272 17
arbor vitae 372 39
arbour 272 17
arc *Films* 312 42
arc *Maths.* 346 53, 55
arc, graduated ~ 224 2
arcade, blind ~ 335 10
arcading 335 8
arcading, blind ~ 335 10
arcading, round ~ 335 9
arc fibula 328 28
arch *Bldg. Site* 119 6
arch *Bridges* 215 20
arch *Free Exerc.* 295 34
arch *Theatre* 316 11
arch *Art* 336 19
arch, convex ~ 336 34
arch, longitudinal ~ 19 61
arch, parabolic ~ 336 29
arch, reinforced concrete ~
215 50
arch, round ~ 336 27
arch, segmental ~ 336 28
arch, shouldered ~ 336 33
arch, superciliary ~ 16 5
arch, tented ~ 336 35
arch, transverse ~ 335 18
arch, trellis ~ 52 12
arch, triumphal ~ 334 59, 71
arch, trussed ~ 215 25
arch, Tudor ~ 336 37
arch, types of ~ 336 19-37
Archaster 369 17
arch board file 247 40
arch bridge, spandrel-braced
~ 215 28
arch bridge, stone ~ 215 19
arched front support 295 24
Archer *Astron.* 3 37; 4 61
archer *Sports* 305 53
archery 305 52-66
archimedes drill 108 4
architrave 334 18
archivolt 335 25
arch span 215 26
arch unit 247 41
archway 337 4
archway, memorial ~ 337 3
arcing horn 152 47; 153 61
arcosolium 331 60
Arctic Ocean 14 21
arc welder 142 2
arc welding, gas-shielded ~
142 33
arc welding helmet 142 3, 39
area, epicentral ~ 11 38
area spraying 83 1

# areca

# E 4

bridge, covered ~ 215 32
bridge, cross-section of ~ 215 1
bridge, dental ~ 24 26
bridge, flat ~ 215 52
bridge, iron ~ 15 56
bridge, reinforced concrete ~ 215 49
bridge, rope ~ 215 15
bridge, solid ~ 215 19
bridge, stone ~ 15 50
bridge bearing 215 55
bridge deck 223 12-18
bridge over railway 15 40
bridge ring 89 58
bridges 215
bridge strut 215 30
bridge superstructure 258 14
bridge support 222 12
bridge under railway 15 42
bridle 71 7-13
bridle path 12 46
briefcase 41 17
briefs 32 26
brig 220 17
brigantine 220 14
brightness control 240 33
brille 323 35
brilliant 175 21
brilliant cut 36 44
brimstone butterfly 365 4
brine channel 274 3
brine pipe 274 4
briolette, faceted ~ 36 86
Brisinga endecacnemos 369 11
brisket, hind ~ 95 25
brisket, middle ~ 95 26
brisket of beef 95 23
bristle 88 52
bristles Hairst. etc. 34 23
bristles Household 50 47
bristletail 81 14
bristle worm 357 22
broach 109 8
broaching tap 93 14
broach roof 121 22
broach roof, conical ~ 121 24
B road 15 36
broad axe 120 70
broad bean Veg. 57 8
broad bean Fodder Plants 69 15
broadcasting 238; 239; 240
broadcasting centre 238 16-26
broadcasting station 15 33
broadsheet 340 27
broadside 340 27
broadside fire 218 59
broadtail Ladies' Wear 30 60
broadtail Furrier 131 21
brochure 250 7
broderie anglaise 102 11
broiler 98 6; 308 33
broiler chicken 74 12
broiler rearing 74 11-17
broken thread detector roller 164 4
broken thread stop motion 165 19
broker, commercial ~ 251 5
broker, inside ~ 251 4
broker, outside ~ 251 5
bronchus 20 5
Bronze Age 328 21-40
brooch, ivory ~ 36 30
brooch, modern-style ~ 36 19
brooch, pearl ~ 36 7
brood bud bulblet 54 27, 29
brood cell 77 31
brood chamber 77 46
brooder 74 3

brook 13 8; 15 80
broom 38 36; 50 46; 62 5; 199 6; 268 21; 272 67
broom Shrubs etc. 374 20
broom, circular ~ 199 40
broom, cylinder ~ 199 42
broom, inverted ~ 224 99
broom, upward-pointing ~ 224 100
broom handle 38 37; 50 49
broom head 50 48
broomstick 38 37; 50 49
brougham 186 3
brow antler 88 6
browband 71 9
brown 343 5
brown ale 93 26
brown bear 368 10
brown leaf-eating weevil 80 49
Brown Ring Boletus 381 21
brown-tail moth 80 28
brown trout 364 15
brow point 88 6
brow snag 88 6
brow tine 88 6
brush Roof & Boilerr. 38 32
brush Household 50 42, 53
brush Bees 77 7
brush Forestry 84 5
brush Game 88 47
brush School 260 59
brush Graphic Art 340 11
brush Script 341 24
brush, camel hair ~ 338 7
brush, dry ~ 128 49
brush, flat ~ Painter 129 17
brush, flat ~ Art. Studio 338 6
brush, rotating ~ 168 46
brush, round ~ 338 8
brush, stiff-bristle ~ 105 16
brush, wire ~ Gas Weld. 141 26
brush, wire ~ Arc Weld. 142 18
brush, wire ~ Music. Instr. 324 53
brush head 50 79
brush head, detachable ~ 49 30
brushwood Map 15 15
brushwood Forestry 84 5
brushwood Spa 274 2
Brussels lace 102 18
Brussels sprout 57 30
bubble bath 49 3
bubble chamber 1 58
bubble float, oval ~ 89 47
buccaneer 306 43
Büchner funnel 349 11
buck Dom. Anim. 73 18
buck Game 88 28, 40, 59
buck Gymn. 296 17
buck, young ~ 88 39
bucket Household 50 54
bucket Mills 91 36
bucket Bldg. Site 118 82
bucket Road Constr. 200 5
bucket chain 226 42
bucket dredger 226 41
bucket elevator 200 49; 201 21
bucket elevator chain 216 57
bucket ladder 226 43
bucket pump 269 7
bucket seat Car 193 11
bucket seat Sports 305 90
bucket teeth 200 6
bucket-top boot 355 58
buckeye 371 58
buckle 101 52
buckle and knife folder 185 8
buckle and knife folding machine 185 8

buckle fold 185 11
buckler 329 57
bucksaw 120 61
bud 54 23, 26; 58 27; 59 22; 60 16; 61 3
bud, axillary ~ 370 25
bud, terminal ~ 370 22
bud cutting 54 22
Buddha 337 20
budding 54 30
budding knife 54 31
buffalo 367 8
buffalo horn 254 34
buffer Station 206 51
buffer Railw. 213 7
buffer Army 255 27, 44, 52
buffer recuperator 255 52
buffer ring 255 44
buffer storage 242 33
buffet 207 78-79
buffet car, quick-service ~ 207 73
buffet compartment 207 78-79
buffing machine 108 46
buffing wheel 100 10
buffoon 306 38, 69
bug 81 39
buggy 193 12
buggy, American ~ 186 49
buggy, English ~ 186 48
bugle 309 54
building, centralized ~ 334 55
building, centrally-planned ~ 334 55
building, model ~ 48 28
building, neoclassical ~ 336 15
building, public ~ 15 54
building berth 222 11-18
building berths 222 11-26
building block 28 41; 48 27
building board, lightweight ~ 123 58
building brick Infant Care etc. 28 41
building brick Kindergart. 48 27
building glazier 124 8
building site 118; 119
building slips 222 11-26
building timber 120 10, 83-96
built piece 315 32
built unit 315 32
bulb, glass ~ 127 57
bulb, old ~ 54 28
bulb-head pin 328 29
bulbil 54 27, 29; 375 38
bulk cargo 221 11
bulk cargo handling 226 29
bulk carrier Ship 221 9
bulk carrier Docks 225 67; 226 30
bulk goods 221 11
bulkhead, protective ~ 305 91
bulk material 200 12
bulk transporter barge 226 35
Bull Astron. 3 25; 4 54
bull Dom. Anim. 73 1
bull Heraldry 254 15
bull, mock ~ 319 3
bull, young ~ 319 35
bulldog 70 1
bulldozer 199 16; 200 28
bulldozer blade 200 29
bulldozer for dumping and compacting 199 18
bullfight 319 1-33, 24
bullfight, mock ~ 319 1
bullfighting 319
bullfinch 360 5

bull pen 319 14
bullring 319 5
bull's eye 336 2
bull's-eye glass 124 6
bull terrier 70 16
bulrush 136 27
bulwark 221 120; 222 67
bumblebee 358 23
bumper Tram 197 12
bumper Station 206 51
bumper, front ~ 191 13
bumper, integral ~ 193 33
bumper car 308 62, 63
bumper steel 166 44
bumper steel stop rod 166 45
bump rubber 192 82
bun 34 29
bun, plaited ~ 97 41
bunches 34 30
bunch of fruit 384 32
bunch of grapes 78 5; 99 89
bunch pink 60 6
bungalow 278 7
bunghole 130 7
bunk, folding ~ 259 84
bunk, rear ~ 85 49
bunk-bed 47 1
bunker 293 81
bunkering boat 225 13
Bunsen burner 173 5; 350 1
Bunter downthrow 154 61
bunting 253 3, 11
buntings 361 6-7
bunt line 218 36; 219 71
buoy 90 2; 216 12; 224 71; 285 17, 18; 286 31
buoy, conical ~ 224 76
buoy, green ~ 224 84
buoy, port hand ~ 224 95
buoy, starboard hand ~ 224 96
buoyancy tube 286 27
buoy rope 90 3
bur 24 37
burden chain 139 44
burette 350 21
burette clamp 350 23
burette stand 350 22
burgee 253 22; 284 48
Burgundian 355 40
burial 331 33-41
burial place, underground ~ 331 59
burin 175 33; 340 5, 15, 20
burner Power Plant 152 6
burner Glass Prod. 162 6
burner, gas ~ 139 3, 48
burner platform 288 80
burner ventilator 92 17
burning-in oven 179 32
burnisher Goldsm. etc. 108 51
burnisher Watchm. 109 17
burnishing 109 17
burnous 354 7
burr 88 5, 29
burrow Soft Fruit 58 63
burrow Hunt. 86 26
burying ground 331 21-41
bus 194 17
bus, double-deck ~ 194 36
bus, double-decker ~ 194 36
bus, electrical system ~ 235 55
busbar 152 29
buses Lorries etc. 194
'buses' Airport 233 35
bush, rubber ~ 192 67
bushing 162 50
bushing chain, double ~ 190 49
bushing tip 162 51
bushman 354 29
bushman woman 354 34
business and passenger aircraft 231 3, 7

compressed-air supply 213 20
compressed-air system 138 1
compressed-air tank Blacksm. 138 4
compressed-air tank Power Plant 153 51
compressed-air vessel 269 17, 50
compressed-gas container 234 32
compressed-helium bottle 234 14
compressed-helium tank 234 43, 50
compression bandage 21 17
compression plate 2 25
compressor Painter 129 33
compressor Blacksm. 138 3
compressor Oil, Petr. 145 45
compressor Energy Sources 155 4
compressor Ship 223 51
compressor Office 247 43
compressor, high-pressure ~ 232 36
compressor, low-pressure ~ 232 35
computer 23 53; 177 70; 195 1
computer cable 195 3, 38
computer centre 244
computer data 238 13
computer harness 195 3, 38
computer socket, main ~ 195 2, 39
computer test, automatic ~ 195 33
computing scale 98 12
concave 64 11
concave ridge 302 22
concentrator 172 24, 42, 44, 48, 62
concert grand 325 40
concertina 324 36
conch shell trumpet 327 41
concrete, heavy ~ 119 72
concrete, rammed ~ 118 1
concrete, tamped ~ 118 1
concrete aggregate 118 36; 119 26
concrete bucket 119 38
concrete mixer 47 40; 118 33; 119 29; 201 23
concrete-mixing plant 201 19
concrete pump hopper 201 24
concreter 119 9
concrete road construction 201 1-24
concrete scraper 200 13
concrete spreader 201 5
concrete spreader box 201 6
concrete tamper 119 83
concrete test cube 119 84
concrete-vibrating compactor 201 10
concrete vibrator 119 88
condensate 172 17
condenser Brew. 92 6
condenser Optic. Instr. 112 8; 113 32
condenser Oil, Petr. 145 44
condenser Nucl. Energy 154 17, 35
condenser Energy Sources 155 8
condenser Synth. Fibres 170 5
condenser Paperm. 172 30
condenser Warships 259 64
condenser Chem. 350 48
condenser, coiled ~ 349 6
condenser, universal ~ 112 66
condensing locomotive 210 69
condensing tender 210 69

condition report 195 7
conductor Power Plant 153 34, 43
conductor Spa 274 21
conductor Theatre 315 26
conductor, copper ~ 127 43
conductor, electrostatic ~ 230 51; 231 27
conductor, high-voltage ~ 152 33
conduit 334 54
cone Phys. Geog. 11 24
cone Mach. Parts etc. 143 67
cone Synth. Fibres 169 27
cone Bicycle 187 58
cone Maths. 347 43
cone Decid. Trees 371 32
cone, cross-wound ~ 165 8, 24
cone, pyrometric ~ 161 6
cone, truncated ~ 347 45
cone axis 372 3
cone breaker 172 82
cone chest 326 12-14
cone creel 165 9
cone drum box 163 30
cone height 347 44
cone nozzle 83 23
cone refiner 172 27, 60, 73, 83
cone scale 372 8, 14, 27, 38
cone-winding frame 165 1
cone-winding machine 169 26
coney 366 24
confectionery 97 17-47; 98 75-86
confectionery unit 97 67-70
conference circuit 242 22
conference connection 242 22
conference grouping 246 31-36
conference hook-up 242 22
conference table 246 31
confetti 306 62
configuration, angular ~ 248 39
confluence 224 90
conga drum 324 55
congregation 330 29
conifers 372 1-71
Conium 379 4
connecting corridor 208 11
connecting door, sliding ~ 207 19
connecting element 248 48
connecting hose 208 16, 21
connecting lead 25 20, 56
connecting piece 350 56
connecting rod Agr. 63 20
connecting rod Intern. Combust. Eng. 190 21
connecting rod Railw. 210 11
connecting-rod bearing 192 25
connecting seal, rubber ~ 207 8; 208 12
connecting shaft 63 20
connecting system, automatic ~ 237 25
connection, internal ~ 245 14
connection, pneumatically sprung ~ 194 45
connection, rubber ~ 194 45
connection of modules 242 70
connection rebar 119 10, 71
connector Moon L. 6 28
connector Weaving 166 52
connector, thermoplastic ~ 127 29
connector fitting 287 31
consignment, general ~ 206 4
consignment, mixed ~ 206 4
consignment note 206 30
console Joiner 133 24

console Serv. Stat. 196 29
console School 261 37
console Music. Instr. 326 36-52
console operator 244 3
console piano 325 1
console typewriter 244 4
consolidating beam 201 2
constant of integration 345 14
constellations 3 9-48
construction, close-seamed ~ 285 54
construction, wooden ~ 260 72
construction of circuit 242 72
construction set 48 22
construction site 118; 119
construction unit, precast ~ 215 58
construction vehicle 255 75
consulting room 23 1
contact, auxiliary ~ 153 57
contact, magnetic ~ 242 71
contact arc 237 43
contact arm 237 44
contact arm tag 237 46
contact breaker 242 49
contact field 237 45
contact goniometer 351 27
contact maker 127 38-39
contact sleeve, metal ~ 166 31
contact spring 127 28
contact wire maintenance vehicle 211 41, 44-54
contact wire voltage indicator 211 28
container 206 57; 221 22; 226 3, 6
container Chem. 350 61
container, plastic ~ 83 25
container, railroad-owned ~ 206 19
container, railway-owned ~ 206 19
container, shielded ~ 154 82
container berth 225 48; 226 1
container car 206 58
container carrier truck 225 47
container for vegetables 96 51
container platform 194 27
container ship 221 89; 225 45
container station 206 54
container terminal 225 48; 226 1
container wagon 206 58
containment, steel ~ 154 21
continents 14 12-18
continuity girl 310 39
continuity tester 127 55
continuous feed grate 199 34
continuous filament process 162 48
continuous reheating furnace 148 69
continuous rolling mill train 148 66-75
contouche 355 66
contour 15 62
contour, submarine ~ 15 11
contour knife 340 10
contrabass 323 23
contrabassoon 323 28
contrabass tuba 323 44
contracted burial 328 17
contractile vacuole 357 5
contra octave 321 43
contrast control 240 32; 249 36
contrast medium injector 27
control, digital ~ 242 35
control, manual ~ 115 52
control, sliding ~ 311 18

control and monitoring panel 311 8
control arm 240 29; 313 11
control board 153 1
control box Moon L. 6 23
control box Mach. Tools 150 36
control box Offset Platem. 179 33
control button Hosp. 25 30
control button Cine Film 117 98
control button Text. Finish. 168 40
control button Navig. 224 32
control button Audiovis. 243 13
control button Office 246 19
control button School 261 45
control cable 271 53
control column 230 24; 257 8; 288 14
control console Power Plant 153 1-6
control console Photomech. Reprod. 177 5
control console Films 311 12
control console Theatre 316 2
control desk Hosp. 27 10
control desk Brew. 93 1
control desk Iron & Steel 147 66
control desk Power Plant 153 1-6
control desk Nucl. Energy 154 80
control desk Offset Print. 180 16
control desk Photograv. 182 28
control desk Films 311 12
control desk, driver's ~ 212 32
control desk, engineer's ~ 212 32
control device 26 7
control frame 287 46
control gear 164 38
control grip Pest Contr. 83 19
control grip Photog. 115 76
control handle, cranked ~ 168 52
control knob Hosp. 25 49; 27 41
control knob Electrotyp. etc. 178 15
controller 197 27
controller, rear ~ 197 8
controller handwheel 211 20; 212 12
control lever Agr. Mach. 64 59
control lever Pest Contr. 83 21
control lever Cine Film 117 63
control lever Cotton Spin. 163 28
control lever Road Constr. 201 8, 12
control lever Navig. 224 19
control lever Broadcast. 240 29
control lever Films 313 11
control lever Theatre 316 58
control line model 288 89
control linkage 190 30
control loudspeaker 311 13
control mechanism 181 26
control module 238 45; 240 11
control panel Hosp. 26 20; 27 10
control panel Roof & Boilerr. 38 67
control panel Dairy. 76 11
control panel Brew. 93 1, 20

# crocket

## Z